Digital Forensics Processing

Digital Forensics Processing and Procedures

Meeting the Requirements of ISO 17020, ISO 17025, ISO 27001 and Best Practice Requirements

David Watson

Andrew Jones

Frank Thornton, Technical Editor

ELSEVIER

AMSTERDAM • BOSTON • HEIDELBERG • LONDON
NEW YORK • OXFORD • PARIS • SAN DIEGO
SAN FRANCISCO • SINGAPORE • SYDNEY • TOKYO

Syngress is an Imprint of Elsevier

SYNGRESS

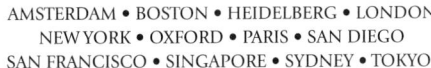

Acquiring Editor: *Chris Katsaropoulos*
Editorial Project Manager: *Heather Scherer*
Project Manager: *Priya Kumaraguruparan*
Designer: *Russell Purdy*

Syngress is an imprint of Elsevier
225 Wyman Street, Waltham, MA 02451, USA

Library of Congress Cataloging-in-Publication Data
Watson, David (David Lilburn)
Digital forensics processing and procedures : meeting the requirements of ISO 17020, ISO 17025, ISO 27001 and best practice requirements / David Watson, Andrew Jones.
pages cm
Includes bibliographical references and index.
1. Computer crimes–Investigation. 2. Evidence preservation–Standards. 3. Forensic sciences–Standards. 4. Computer science. I. Title.
HV8079.C65W38 2013
363.250285–dc23

2013021249

British Library Cataloguing-in-Publication Data
A catalogue record for this book is available from the British Library.

ISBN: 978-1-59749-742-8

Printed in the United States of America
13 14 15 10 9 8 7 6 5 4 3 2 1

Contents

About the Authors

David Lilburn Watson heads up Forensic Computing Ltd., a specialist digital forensic recovery and investigation company. He is responsible for the coordination and efficient delivery of the digital forensic evidence recovery services and digital investigations, and provides support for a broad range of investigative, information security and risk consulting assignments. He holds the following certifications and degrees:

- Certificate in Governance of Enterprise IT Systems (CGEIT);
- Certificate of Cloud Security Knowledge (CSSK);
- Certified Computer Crime Investigator (CCCI);
- Certified Computer Forensics Technician—Advanced (CCFT);
- Certified Fraud Examiner (CFE);
- Certified Identity Risk Manager (CIRM);
- Certified in Risk and Information System Control (CRISC);
- Certified Information Forensics Investigator (CIFI);
- Certified Information Security Manager (CISM);
- Certified Information System Security Professional (CISSP);
- Certified Information Systems Auditor (CISA);
- Certified Management Consultant (CMC);
- Certified Software Manager (CSM);
- Chartered Fellow (BCS—UK);
- Chartered IT Professional (BCS—UK);
- MSc—Distributed Computer Networks (University of Greenwich);
- MSc—IT Security (University of Westminster)—Distinction;
- MSc—Fraud Risk Management (Nottingham Trent University)—Distinction.

David has also led Forensic Computing Ltd. to ISO 27001, ISO 9001, and BS 25999 (now ISO 22301) certification. Forensic Computing Ltd. complies with ISO 17020 and ISO 17025 but has not sought accreditation. This makes Forensic Computing Ltd. one of the very few consultancies to hold such important credentials in the field of digital forensic services.

Among other achievements, David was the HTCIA Chapter President in the UK and a member of the Metropolitan Police Computer Crime Unit—Expert Advisors Panel.

Andy Jones served for 25 years in the British Army's Intelligence Corps. After this he became a manager and a researcher and analyst in the area of information warfare and computer crime at a defense research establishment. In 2002, he left the defense environment to take up a post as a principal lecturer at the University of Glamorgan in the subjects of network security and computer crime and as a researcher on the threats to information systems and computer forensics. At the university, he developed and managed a well-equipped Computer Forensics Laboratory and took the lead on a large number of computer investigations and data recovery tasks. He holds a PhD in the area of threats to information systems. In January 2005, he joined the Security Research Centre at BT where he became a chief researcher and the head of information security research. From BT he went on sabbatical to Khalifa University in the UAE to establish a post graduate programme in Information Security and computer crime and to create a research capability. Andy holds posts as a visiting professor at Edith Cowan University in Perth, Australia, and the University of South Australia in Adelaide.

Technical Editor Bio

Frank Thornton runs his own technology consulting firm, Blackthorn Information Security, which specializes in digital forensics, network penetration testing, and e-discovery. He holds certifications as a Certified Computer Examiner for the International Association of Forensic Computer Examiners, and as an AccessData Certified Examiner.

Frank's past experiences have been in the fields of Law Enforcement, Forensics, and Computer Sciences. As a detective and forensics expert, he has investigated over one hundred homicides and thousands of other crime scenes.

Combining both professional interests, he was a member of the workgroup to establish ANSI Standard "ANSI/NIST-CSL 1-1993 Data Format for the Interchange of Fingerprint Information."

Frank has been the author, co-author, contributor, or technical editor for 12 books covering police procedures, digital forensic processes, and information security.

Acknowledgments

The writing of this book has been an epic endeavor that went far beyond what was originally conceived. A large number of people have either knowingly or unknowingly helped, and provided knowledge, inspiration, support, coffee, and sympathy at the right time.

To this end, we would particularly like to thank the following individuals who have helped us in achieving our goal:

> Prof. Craig Valli, Frank Thornton, Clive Blake, Matthew Pemble, Phil Swinburne, Bill Millar, Paul Wright, and Steve Anson.

We would also like to thank the project team and the publishing professionals at Elsevier—Heather Scherer, Chris Katsaropoulos, and Priya Kumaraguruparan for their patience and support during the rather lengthy process.

In addition, we would like to acknowledge our wives and partners, Kath Jones and Pat Sims, for their ongoing tolerance, and editorial and inspirational support when the writing (and sometimes the authors) became difficult.

David would like to thank J. M. M., who was never sure he would make it and M. J. W. R., who said, "He will do well" (Summer 1975)—it just took some time.

Finally, we would like to thank all of you that have taken the trouble to use this book. We hope that the information that we have provided contributes to the smooth running of your laboratories.

Preface

Anyone who has been involved in working in or managing a digital forensic laboratory will be aware of the large number of processes and procedures that are essential for the efficient and safe running of the laboratory. If the laboratory also aspires to achieve an accreditation from one of the accreditation bodies such as American Society of Crime Laboratory Directors/Laboratory Crediting Board (ASCLD/LAB) or the International Standards Organization (ISO), then additional processes and procedures will have to be implemented and followed.

This book has been written as a follow-on from the book *Building a Digital Forensic Laboratory*, which, as the name suggests, was aimed at providing guidance for creating and managing the Forensic Laboratory. When that book was written, the aim was to guide the user through the issues that needed to be addressed when a laboratory was created and on the issues of managing it. This book is written to provide the reader with guidance on the policies and procedures that need to be adopted in order to run the Forensic Laboratory in a professional manner and also to allow the Forensic Laboratory to be conformant with the standards that apply to the Forensic Laboratory. The book has not been designed to address the legal issues of any specific jurisdiction, but instead to provide advice and guidance on good practice in the broader aspects of management of a digital forensic laboratory.

As part of this book, a large number of templates and checklists have been included to provide a "one-stop shop" for the reader. These in themselves have been produced as the result of best practice and an understanding of the requirements from running a number of different forensic laboratories (collectively referred to as the "Forensic Laboratory"). The scope of the policies and procedures that are covered in this book go into a great deal of detail in some areas where it is considered necessary and in other areas less so.

This book is divided into three logical areas: policies and procedures for setting up the Forensic Laboratory, policies and procedures that will be required during the normal running of the Forensic Laboratory, and the policies and procedures that are required for gaining and maintaining accreditation and accredited certification.

As the requirements for the running of the Forensic Laboratory develop, the policies and procedures will inevitably change. In order to address this problem, the following Web site has been created and will contain the most up-to-date material: http://www.forensic-computing.ltd.uk.

Chapter 1

Introduction

Table of Contents

1.1 INTRODUCTION

1.1.1 What is Digital Forensics?

Digital forensics is a highly specialized and fast-growing field of forensic science relating to the recovery of evidence from digital storage media. Digital forensics applies traditional forensics processes and procedures to this new evidential source.

It can also be referred to as computer forensics, but technically speaking, the term only relates to recovery of evidence from a computer, and not the whole range of digital storage devices that may store digital data to be used as evidence. Computer forensics is also often referred to as cyber forensics.

In this book, as in the case of Forensic Laboratory, the term digital forensics is used.

Digital forensics can be used in civil and criminal cases or any other area of dispute. Each has its own set of handling requirements relevant to the jurisdiction in which the case is being investigated.

Typically, digital forensics involves the recovery of data from digital storage media that may have been lost, hidden, or otherwise concealed or after an incident that has affected the operation of an information processing system. This could be an accidental or deliberate act, carried out by an employee or outsider, or after a malware attack of any type.

No matter what the specific details of the case, the overview of processing a digital forensic case by the Forensic Laboratory follows the same series of processes, interpreted for the jurisdiction according to case requirements. The processes are as follows:

- preserving the evidence;
- identifying the evidence;
- extracting the evidence;
- documenting the evidence recovered and how it was recovered;
- interpreting the evidence;
- presenting the evidence (either to the client or a court).

Inspection of numerous sources gives differing definitions of "Digital (or Computer) Forensics," depending on the organization and its jurisdiction. They all contain some or all of the elements mentioned above (explicitly defined or implied). The Forensic Laboratory uses the following definition:

The use of scientifically derived, proved, and repeatable methods for:

- preserving the evidence;
- identifying the evidence;
- extracting the evidence;
- documenting the evidence recovered and how it was recovered;
- interpreting the evidence;
- presenting the evidence.

to reconstruct relevant events relating to a given case.

The same processes and techniques are used for any digital media, whether it is a hard disk drive, a SIM card from a mobile phone, digital music players, digital image recording devices, or any other digital media.

Details of handling different types of cases are given in Chapter 9. A list of typical types of cases where the Forensic Laboratory has been involved is given in Appendix 1.

1.1.2 The Need for Digital Forensics

The world population was estimated as on June 30, 2012 to be 7,017,846,922 and the number of Internet users at the same time to be 2,405,518,378, some 34.3% of the population. This is an increase of 566.4% since December 31, 2000.[a]

As the world increasingly embraces information processing systems and the Internet, there are more data being held on digital media. At the same time, an individual country's Gross Domestic Product (GDPs) is being boosted by an increasing Internet-based component. The current percentage of the Internet economy in the GDP was calculated for the G20 by Boston[b] and also produced an estimate for 2016 was also produced. This is reproduced below.

Country	% of GDP 2012	Estimated % of GDP 2016	% Increase
United Kingdom	8.3	12.4	4.1
South Korea	7.3	8.0	0.7
China	5.5	6.9	1.4
Japan	4.7	5.6	0.9
United States	4.7	5.4	0.7
India	4.1	5.6	1.5
G 20	4.1	5.3	1.2
EU 27	3.8	5.7	1.9
Australia	3.3	3.7	0.4
Germany	3.0	4.0	1.0
Canada	3.0	3.6	0.6
France	2.9	3.4	0.5
Mexico	2.5	4.2	1.7
Saudi Arabia	2.2	3.8	1.6
Brazil	2.2	2.4	0.2
Italy	2.1	3.5	1.4
Argentina	2.0	3.3	1.3
Russia	1.9	2.8	0.9
South Africa	1.9	2.5	0.6
Turkey	1.7	2.3	0.6
Indonesia	1.3	1.5	0.2

Continued

At the same time as the Internet economy has been growing, the size of local digital storage for personal computers has grown as can be seen in Appendix 2. IBM likes to think that they produced the first personal computer (the "PC" or Model 5150) on August 12, 1981; there were a number of personal computers in operation for years prior to this, including Tandy TRS, Apple, Nascom, Commodore PET, Texas Instruments, Atari, variety of CP/M machines, as well as those running proprietary operating systems. A random view of digital storage growth is given in Appendix 2.

While this table shows disks available for personal computer users, those available to corporate users or those with mainframes can have considerably larger capacities. Details of disk size nomenclature are given in Appendix 3.

The amount of growth of digital information worldwide is reported in real time on http://uk.emc.com/leadership/programs/digital-universe.htm.

At the same time, information processing systems of all types are being used to perpetrate or assist in criminal acts or civil disputes as well as just holding evidence relating to the matter. This rapidly changing technology has spawned a completely new range of crimes such as hacking (unauthorized access to a computer system or unauthorized modification to or disclosure of information contained in it) or distributed denial of service attacks. It can be argued that there are no new crimes just variations of old ones, but that legislation needs to be amended to handle new types of execution of offenses.[c] Whatever the outcome of this argument, more and more information processing devices are used in the commission of criminal acts or are assisting in their execution. There are no hard and fast statistics for the total number of crimes committed where an information processing device is involved, but there are many "guesstimates." All show increasing use. At the same time, corporate use of information processing devices and digital storage is increasing rapidly.

a. From Internet World Stats http://www.internetworldstats.com/stats.htm.

b. The $4.2 Trillion Opportunity, The Boston Consulting Group, March 2012.

c. A Decade of Financial Crime on the Internet (1992-2002) New Technology—New Crimes?, David Lilburn Watson, MSc Dissertation, University of Westminster, 2004.

Given the rapid expansion of both information processing systems and stored data on digital media, it is not difficult to see that Digital Forensics, with its ability to search through vast quantities of data in a thorough, efficient, and repeatable manner, in any language, is essential. This allows material to be recovered from digital media and presented as evidence that may not otherwise be recoverable and presentable in a court.

At this stage, the needs of the corporate world and that of law enforcement (LE) differ on a number of levels:

- LE works under more restrictive regulations that their counterparts in the corporate world.
- The burden of proof is typically more stringent in criminal cases than in civil cases.
- Each is governed by the "good practices" defined by their various governing bodies, and these often differ (e.g., LE relates to the criminal process in the jurisdiction and corporates are more focused on implementation of information security and security incident management).

Corporates are often loathe to involve LE in any incident for a variety of reasons, but legislation now exists in some jurisdictions to report any security incident that discloses personal information or that makes nominated individuals personally liable for breaches or other information security failures. In cases such as this, Digital Forensics may be called on not only to determine how the breach occurred but also to determine the effectiveness of the risk treatment (typically controls) in place to minimize the risk of unauthorized access or disclosure.

1.1.3 The Purpose of This Book

This book has been produced to provide as close as possible to a one stop shop for a set of procedures that meet industry good practice and international standards for handling Digital Evidence through its complete lifecycle. The procedures encompass the needs of groups from "First Responders," forensic laboratories, individual employee, and management whether they are LE, other government, or civilian. The procedures are distilled from international standards, government procedures, corporate practices and procedures, police and LE procedures, and generally accepted good practice. The procedures are jurisdiction independent and will need to be reviewed for specific jurisdictions.

If Digital Evidence can be handled properly from the start of its lifecycle for an investigation using standard operating procedures based on good practice to meet relevant standards, then there will be consistent handling throughout the industry and the many cases that fail on account of evidence contamination at the outset, or at some point during its processing, will be avoided.

Anyone who has been involved in working in, or managing, a digital forensic laboratory will be aware of the large number of processes and procedures that are essential for the efficient and safe running of the laboratory. If the laboratory also aspires to achieve a accreditation from one of the accreditation bodies such as American Society of Crime Laboratory Directors/Laboratory Crediting Board or the International Standards Organization (ISO), then additional processes and procedures will have to be implemented and followed.

This book has been written as a follow-on from the book "Building a Digital Forensic Laboratory," which as the name suggests was aimed at providing guidance for creating and managing a digital forensic laboratory. When that book was written, the aim was to guide the user through the issues that needed to be addressed when a laboratory was created and to give guidance on the issues of managing it. This book is written to provide the reader with guidance on the policies and procedures that need to be adopted and maintained in order to run the laboratory in an efficient and professional manner and also to allow the laboratory to be compliant with the numerous standards that apply to a digital forensic laboratory. The book has not been designed to address the legal issues of any specific region, but instead to provide advice and guidance on good practice in the broader aspects of laboratory management.

1.1.4 Book Structure

As part of this book, a large number of templates and check lists have been included to provide a "one stop shop" for the reader. These, in themselves, have been produced as the result of good practice and an understanding of the requirements imposed by various standards. The policies and procedures that are covered in this book are covered in a great deal of detail in some areas where it is considered necessary and in other areas where it is not, less so.

This book is divided into three logical areas: policies and procedures for setting up the Forensics Laboratory, policies and procedures that will be required during the normal running the Forensics Laboratory, and the policies that are required for gaining and maintaining accreditation and/or certification.

As the requirements for the running of the Forensic Laboratory develop, the policies and procedures will inevitably need to change to meet new requirements. In order to address this problem, the Website[d] has been created and will contain the most up to date material available.

1.1.5 Who Should Read This Book?

The anticipated audience for this book is anyone that is involved in the teaching, conduct, or management of any

d. Website at www.forensic-computing.ltd.uk

aspect of the Digital Forensics lifecycle. This will include the following:

- **academics**: who are educating the next generation of practitioners and managers;
- **practitioners**: who are conducting investigations;
- **managers**: of forensic laboratories and facilities.

For the academics, it is important not only that they teach the tools and techniques that the Forensic Analyst and Investigator will need to be able to carry out investigations but also the principles, rules of evidence, and appropriate standards to ensure that the evidence that their students will recover is acceptable in the courts and has been collected, preserved, and analyzed in a scientifically sound manner.

For the Forensic Analyst and Investigator, it is intended to be an aide memoire of the procedures and standards that they need to follow and also a repository of the forms that they will need in their everyday jobs. Some of these they will use everyday and be very familiar with, others they will only use occasionally or rarely. For the Forensic Laboratory Manager, this book will cover all of the standards and procedures for all aspects of an investigation or a Forensic Laboratory.

Anyone who is, or wants to become, a Forensic Analyst can benefit from this book. It will also assist Forensic Laboratory Managers who wish to submit to, and pass, relevant ISO standards certification or accreditation, as appropriate.

It contains cross references from relevant ISO standards to this book and the procedures in it that can be amended to suit working practices in the jurisdiction while still meeting the relevant ISO requirements.

1.1.6 The Need for Procedures in Digital Forensics

In order to understand the need for procedures in Digital Forensics, we must first be clear on what we mean by Digital Forensics. Digital Forensics was defined at the Digital Forensic Research Workshop in 2001 as "The use of scientifically derived and proven methods toward the preservation, collection, validation, identification, analysis, interpretation, documentation and presentation of digital evidence derived from digital sources for the purpose of facilitating or furthering the reconstruction of events found to be criminal, or helping to anticipate unauthorized actions shown to be disruptive to planned operations."[e,f]

e. Digital Forensic Research Workshop (DFRWS) 2001, DFRWS Technical Report, DTR—T001-01 Final, A Road Map for Digital Forensic Research http://www.dfrws.org/2001/dfrws-rm-final.pdf.

f. As can be seen, this only relates to criminal or "unauthorized actions shown to be disruptive to planned operations." The definition used by the Forensic Laboratory in Section 1.1 overcomes this hurdle.

The use of scientifically derived and proven methods means that there is a requirement for a high level of consistency and repeatability. This is commonly represented as meaning that any other skilled practitioner should, given the data available, be able to reproduce the results obtained. In the United States, two cases have defined the acceptability of evidence for courts.

The first was a federal case, Frye v. United States in 1923, a federal case that was decided by the District of Columbia (DC) Circuit. In Frye, the DC Circuit considered the admissibility of testimony based on the systolic blood pressure test, a precursor of the modern polygraph. The court stated that any novel scientific technique "must be sufficiently established to have gained general acceptance in the particular field in which it belongs." The court found that in this case, the systolic blood test had "not yet gained such standing and scientific recognition among physiological and psychological authorities." As a result of this, under the Frye standard, it is not sufficient that a qualified individual expert, or even a group of experts, testify that a particular technique is valid. Under the Frye standard, scientific evidence will only be allowed into the courtroom if it is generally accepted within the relevant scientific community. Frye imposes the burden that the technique must be "generally" accepted by the relevant scientific community.

The second case was that of Daubert v. Merrell Dow in 1993. In this case, the U.S. Supreme Court rejected the Frye test with regard to the admissibility of scientific evidence. Instead of the "general acceptance" in the scientific community standard stipulated in Frye, under Daubert the new test required an independent judicial assessment of reliability. Under the Daubert ruling, to be admissible in a court in the United States, evidence must be both relevant and reliable. The reliability of scientific evidence, which includes the output from a digital forensics tool, is determined by the Judge (as opposed to a jury) in a pretrial "Daubert hearing." The responsibility of a judge in a Daubert hearing is to determine whether the underlying methodology and techniques that have been used to isolate the evidence are sound, and whether as a result, the evidence is reliable. The Daubert process identifies four general categories that are used as guidelines when a procedure is assessed:

- **testing**: Can and has the procedure been tested?
- **error rate**: Is there a known error rate for this procedure?
- **publication**: Has the procedure been published and subject to peer review?
- **acceptance**: Is the procedure generally accepted in the relevant scientific community?

As a result of this, the "Daubert Test" replaced the "Frye Standard" with regard to the admissibility of scientific evidence. Prior to this, under the "Frye Standard," the courts placed responsibility of determining acceptable procedures within the scientific community through the use of peer-reviewed journals. The shortcoming of this approach was that not every area of science, and particularly the "newer" areas, has peer-reviewed journals digital (or computer) forensics, with its short history and rapidly changing environment, clearly falls into this category. The adoption of the Daubert Test provides the opportunity for additional methods to be used to test the quality of evidence.

In ensuring that potential evidence in the field of Digital Forensics is handled in a manner that complies with the legal and regulatory requirements and will be in a condition that allows it to be presented in a court of law, it is important to know what to do and what not to do. What should or should not be done will vary from incident to incident, the approach taken by an individual or group and the laws in effect in the relevant jurisdiction(s). If it is left to decisions by individual organizations or people, the outcome will inevitably be a range of interpretations of the requirements and the situations. This does not align with the standards required for repeatability and consistency for scientific processes. In order to reduce the potential for this happening, the industry has adopted good practices, processes, and procedures. In addition to this, there have been numerous standards introduced for forensic laboratories, including accreditation, as well as a range of certifications for individual Forensic Analysts. This is covered in detail in Chapter 19 and Chapter 6, Appendix 27 respectively.

In addition to the obvious benefits across the whole community of developing a consistent approach to all aspects of the Digital Forensic process, there are also significant potential business advantages of gaining certification or accreditation, whether for the individual to demonstrate a level of skill or for a forensic laboratory to demonstrate that they have achieved a level of competency and compliance with a range of industry and international standards. For LE agencies, compliance with standards gives an external validation that the processes and procedures being used are appropriate and of a suitable quality and, if the procedures have been followed, will make challenges to them in the court more difficult. In commercial organizations, compliance with and maintenance of standards gives a quality mark that gives confidence to potential clients.

There are a number of good practices and standards that have been developed to ensure that both within a region and also globally, the way in which the processes of Digital Forensics are conducted are in a manner that is acceptable to the relevant court. The applicable standards cover a far wider spectrum than just the area of Digital Forensics and encompass health and safety, quality, and security.

When we talk of good practices and standards, there is a presumption that there will only be one that applies to a particular aspect of a process. Unfortunately, this is rarely true, so while we can be compliant with a standard, it does not mean that it can be assumed that other organizations or laboratories that are also "compliant" will be adhering to the same standard. It is also likely that at any given time there will be a number of standards that the Forensic Laboratory will be expected to meet. For example, in the Forensic Laboratory just a few of the standards that are relevant include the following:

- **ISO 9000**—Quality Management systems series;
- **ISO 14000**—Environmental Management systems series;
- **OHSAS 18000**—Occupational Health and Safety series;
- **ISO 27000**—Information technology—Security techniques—Information security management systems series;
- **ISO 31000**—Risk management—Principles and guidelines series;
- **ISO 17025**—General requirements for the competence of testing and calibration laboratories.

In addition to this, there are a range of relevant good practice guides that include the following:

- **ACPO**—Good Practice for Computer-based Electronic Evidence;
- **US-DOJ**—Electronic Crime Scene Investigation, A guide for first responders;
- **US-DOJ**—Searching and seizing computers and obtaining electronic evidence in criminal investigations;
- **IOCE**—Guidelines for best practice in the forensic examination of digital technology;
- **RFC 3227**—Guidelines for evidence collection and archiving;
- **G8**—Digital Evidence Principles;
- **CTOSE**—Cyber Tools On-Line Search for Evidence.

The scope of the procedures that are covered in this book has been made as wide as is reasonably possible. The intention of this book is to aid the reader in the whole spectrum of policies and procedures that they will need to be aware of when they are operating in the Digital Forensics arena.

1.1.7 Problems with Electronic Evidence

All stages of the process of electronic evidence are potentially prone to problems. These result from a number of causes:

- the first is of the rapid developments that are continuing to take place in technology which cause the need for the development of new tools, techniques, and procedures and the need for them to be validated and tested;
- the second is the fact that Digital Evidence cannot be seen with the naked eye and as a result is difficult for a nontechnologist to conceive;

- the third is that the general public and a large proportion of the judiciary do not understand the technologies, the way in which electronic evidence is recovered, or the relevance of the evidence;
- the fourth is that laws take a long time to bring into effect and by their nature need to be relatively generic, which means that the technology has moved on by the time they are in use.

To give some ideas of the problems faced, a 2010 survey[g] of 5000 lawyers across Europe, the Middle East and Africa that was carried out by the security firm Symantec, found that more than half of those surveyed (51%) admitted to having had problems identifying and recovering e-discovery evidence in the previous 3 months. In addition, 98% of them said that "Digital Evidence" identified during e-discovery had been vital to the success of legal matters in which they had been involved in the past 2 years. Sixty percent of the lawyers admitted to having encountered problems with the amount of information that had to be searched and nearly the same number felt that improvements to search technology used to identify, preserve, and process electronically stored information were needed in order to improve the situation.

In some ways, Digital Evidence is the same as any other evidence. In many ways, it is no different from a gun that is seized in a murder case or a knife that is seized in a domestic dispute case. For evidence to be admissible in a Court of Law, it must have been legally obtained. In a Civil Case, the organization's policies and procedures must have been followed fully and with care. If the organization has an incident response plan, then this should be followed. It is always prudent to ensure that in all cases, whether criminal or civil, the relevant laws related to search and seizure are followed as what is initially thought to be a civil case may, as evidence is recovered, become a criminal matter. In either type of case, the evidence must have been:

- **legally obtained**—the evidence must have been collected in accordance with the scope and instructions of the search warrant or in accordance with the incident response plan. For Digital Evidence to be admissible, it must conform to current laws, which will depend on the legal system in force in the jurisdiction, and which may be a problem if it has been collected in another jurisdiction. It must also be the evidence which the trial judge finds useful and which cannot be objected to on the basis that it is irrelevant, immaterial, or violates the rules against hearsay and other objections. If it does not, in reality you may as well not have spent the effort in collecting it, as it will be of no value;
- **relevant**—"relevant evidence" means evidence having any tendency to make the existence of any fact that is of consequence to the determination of the action more probably or less probably than it would be without evidence. The question of relevance is thus different from whether evidence is *sufficient* to prove a point;[h]
- **complete**—to satisfy the concept of completeness, the story that the material purports to tell must be complete. Consideration must also be given to other stories that the material may tell that might have a bearing on the case. In other words, the evidence that is collected must not only include evidence that can prove the suspect's actions (inculpatory) but also evidence that could prove their innocence (exculpatory);
- **reliable**—the evidence must remain unchanged from its original. Following accepted procedures and best practices will help in ensuring that fragile and potentially volatile Digital Evidence does not get modified in any way or deleted. Ensuring that the chain of custody is maintained will help to ensure that evidence remains reliable;
- **authentic**—for Digital Evidence to be authentic, it must explicitly link the data to physical person and must be self-sustained. This is one of the fundamental problems of Digital Forensics. The Forensic Analyst or Investigator can often associate the evidence to a specific computer or device, but the problem is then to associate the user with that device. To achieve this, it may be possible to use supporting evidence from access control systems, audit logs, or other supporting or collateral evidence, such as CCTV;
- **accurate**—for Digital Evidence to be accurate it should "be free from any reasonable doubt about the quality of procedures used to collect the material, analyze the material if that is appropriate and necessary and finally to introduce it into court—and produced by someone who can explain what has been done. In the case of exhibits which themselves contain statements—a letter or other document, for example—'accuracy' must also encompass accuracy of content; and that normally requires the documents originator to make a Witness Statement and be available for cross examination;"[i]
- **believable**—a jury and/or a judge in a criminal case or the corporate managers and auditors in a civil case need to be able to understand and be convinced by the evidence.

The term "chain of custody" refers to the process used by computer forensics specialists to preserve the scene of a

g. Survey Reveals Poor Availability of Digital Evidence Brings Legal Process to a Halt Across EMEA http://www.symantec.com/en/uk/about/news/release/article.jsp?prid=20100907_01.

h. Lorraine v. Markel American Insurance Co, 241 F.R.D. 534 (D.Md. May 4, 2007).

i. Sommer P., Intrusion Detection Systems as Evidence, RAID 98 Conference, 1998.

crime. This can include the collection and preservation of data stored on computers, storage devices, or even the computer logs on the hard drive of a network server. Each step in the process has to be carefully documented so that, if the case is taken to court, it can be shown that the electronic records were not altered during the investigation process.

Maintaining the chain of custody is a fundamental requirement for all investigations, whether the evidence is physical or logical. A definition of the chain of custody from a legal dictionary[j] states that, "A proper chain of custody requires three types of testimony:

- that a piece of evidence is what it purports to be (for example, a litigant's blood sample).
- of continuous possession by each individual who has had possession of the evidence from the time it is seized until the time it is presented in court.
- and by each person who has had possession that the particular piece of evidence remained in substantially the same condition from the moment one person took possession until the moment that person released the evidence into the custody of another (for example, testimony that the evidence was stored in a secure location where no one but the person in charge of custody had access to it)."

Proving the chain of custody is necessary to "lay a foundation" for the evidence in question, by showing the absence of alteration, substitution, or change of condition. Specifically, foundation testimony for tangible evidence requires that exhibits be identified as being in substantially the same condition as they were at the time the evidence was seized, and that the exhibit has remained in that condition through an unbroken chain of custody. For example, suppose that in a prosecution for possession of illegal narcotics, Police Sergeant A recovers drugs from the defendant; X gives police officer B the drugs; B then gives the drugs to police scientist C, who conducts an analysis of the drugs; C gives the drugs to Detective D, who brings the drugs to court. The testimony of A, B, C, and D constitutes a "chain of custody" for the drugs, and the prosecution would need to offer testimony by each person in the chain to establish both the condition and identification of the evidence, unless the defendant stipulated as to the chain of custody in order to save time.[k]

An example of a failure in the chain of custody is found in the case from the Philippines against the "Alabang Boys,"[l] who were arrested in 2008 for the alleged possession and sale of 60 "ecstasy" tablets. The court noted that during the trial, Philippine Drug Enforcement Agency (PDEA) Forensic Chemist Rona Mae Aguillon had testified receiving six plastic sachets of ecstasy tablets—each sachet containing 10 tablets—for laboratory analysis around 12:15 p.m. of September 20, or the day after the arrests. And that it had taken about 16 hours to complete the examination of the tablets. But the court also noted that while the tablets were supposedly being examined by the chemist, the former chief of the PDEA, Dionisio Santiago held a press conference in the afternoon of the same day and showed the media the tablets he said were taken from the "Alabang Boys." Justice Secretary Leila de Lima stated that "That (breach) in the chain of custody of evidence became a fatal flaw," citing the prosecution's failure to prove guilt beyond reasonable doubt.

Another example of a failure to handle Digital Evidence correctly is that of the CD Universe case, in which three companies, Network Associates, Kroll O'Gara, and Infowar.com, failed to establish a proper chain of custody.[m] This case related to "Maxim" (or "Maxus" depending on which report you read), claimed to be a 19-year-old Russian male, who broke into the computers of Internet retailer CD Universe and stole 300,000 credit cards. While the investigation was ongoing, an FBI source commented that "The chain of custody was not established properly," and that this had virtually eliminated the possibility of a prosecution.

In contrast to a written document, because Digital Evidence cannot be seen with the naked eye, it has to be presented with an accurate interpretation, which identifies its significance in the context of where it was found. The hard disk of a computer will contain raw binary data which may be encoded in a simple binary form or as binary-coded decimal or as hexadecimal data. Even dates and times can be encoded in a number of ways including both the "big endian" and "little endian" approach. If there is doubt on the interpretation of a piece of evidence, it can often be supported with other evidence such as the Internet history, logs files, link files, and a range of other information sources.

Having said earlier in this chapter that there are many similarities between physical and Digital Evidence, there are also many potential differences from other types of evidence because Digital Evidence:

- can be changed during the process of evidence collection;
- can be duplicated exactly. This means that it is possible to examine a copy and avoid the risk of damaging or altering the original;
- can be easily altered without trace;
- can change from moment to moment both while within a computer and while being transmitted;
- is not human readable, and cannot always be "read" or "touched." It may need to be printed out;

j. Lehman J., Phelps S., West's encyclopedia of American law: Volume 2.
k. http://legal-dictionary.thefreedictionary.com/chain+of+custody.
l. http://newsinfo.inquirer.net/48423/2-%E2%80%98alabang-boys%E2%80%99-acquitted.
m. http://www.zdnet.com/news/cd-universe-evidence-compromised/96132.

- is relatively difficult to destroy and can be recovered even if it has been "deleted." When an attempt is made to destroy digital evidence, it is common for copies of that evidence to remain stored in other locations of which the user is unaware;
- may be created by a computer (and not the user) as well as recorded on it;
- may be encrypted;
- may be stored on a number of computers and devices in more than one jurisdiction.

There are any numbers of issues that may cause problems in each stage of the process. Through every step of the process, it is crucial to develop and to maintain the chain of custody. It is vitally important to accurately record and document everything that is done and every tool and process and procedure that is used. This ensures that the process is repeatable. Unfortunately, this can be a tedious and difficult task and is probably the single biggest cause of failure in court for cases involving digital evidence. Looking at each of the phases of the digital evidence process, a few examples of issues in each of the phases of the process are detailed in the next section.

In the collection phase, the data must have been searched and seized in a manner consistent with the law. The acquisition processes and the procedures that were used must be adequate and the relevant rules of evidence have been followed. The tools and techniques that are used must also be acceptable. Care must be taken to stay within the scope of the search warrant or Court Order. The chain of custody process and documentation must be initiated and adequate. Care must also be taken with the packing and the transportation of the evidence. For example, did the equipment need to be shielded from radio emissions and were steps taken to ensure that batteries did not become exhausted? Once the material has arrived at the Forensic Laboratory, has it been documented and stored in an appropriate manner?

The search and seizure of digital evidence is the first process that is often disputed. If it can be shown that this step was not completed properly, the evidence may not be admitted. If the search and seizure was not legal or the methodology that was used during the search and seizure was not an accepted practice, then the evidence obtained may be rejected. While there is a long history of the precedent for the search and seizure of physical evidence, the relative short history of digital devices and the rapid development of hardware and software has meant that in the area of digital evidence, there are few precedents that apply. To date there are few standards that apply to search and seizure and, as highlighted above, the guidelines and recommendations differ between LE entities depending on the jurisdiction.

An example of evidence being rejected as a result of a failure in this phase can be found in a case reported in 2009 in the Ann Arbour News. In this case, child pornography charges against William Calladine were dismissed when Washtenaw County Circuit Court Judge Archie Brown ruled that evidence had been improperly obtained. The police had seized the material from a box that was sent to the Greyhound Bus Station in downtown Ann Arbor in February 2008. A member of the Ann Arbor Police had testified that the Station Manager called police after receiving an anonymous tip from a man who said pornography was within the box. A computer and other digital media were in a box that Calladine had carried with him on a Greyhound bus en route home after his truck broke down in Arizona. Calladine had sent his daughter Kimberly to pick up the box because he was out of town and she had signed a consent form to search the items once Hansen, a member of the Ann Arbor Police, had explained the allegations. William Calladine later gave police multiple passwords to access the computer's files where the images were ultimately found. Judge Archie Brown ruled that Calladine's daughter had no more legal authority to turn over the property than anyone else even though he asked her to reclaim the items.

Another case in which evidence was thrown out was reported in the Arizona Daily Star[n] in 2010. This case related to the Triano killing and Digital Evidence was excluded after Pima County Superior Court Judge Christopher Browning ruled that "The Court specifically finds that the primary motivation underlying the search of the defendant's computer was largely, if not exclusively, related to a desire to obtain information related to the Triano investigation." Most of the evidence the agents found pertained to Triano's death. The Defense Attorneys had argued that when Federal Agents obtained a search warrant to go through the computer, they told the Judge they were searching for evidence of financial crimes and said nothing about Triano's homicide. The Judge found that evidence found in Young's laptop computer should be kept from Jurors because Investigators found it under false pretenses.

When transporting the evidence back to the secure evidence store in the Forensic Laboratory, there are a number of precautions that must be taken. Good practice in the preparation of a computer or other type of electronic device for transport includes:

- making sure that the evidence is not exposed to any magnetic sources such as police radios;
- creating and maintaining the chain of custody;
- ensuring that the electronic evidence is kept in the possession of one of the Investigators at all times and

n. Smith K., Evidence thrown out in Triano killing, http://azstarnet.com/news/local/crime/evidence-thrown-out-in-triano-killing-case/article_822b3f9b-e858-5a0c-929e-943eb6690e42.html, February 10, 2010.

making sure that they do not stop anywhere on the way back to the Forensic Laboratory from the crime scene;
- ensuring that the computers or cell phones that have been seized are not used;
- placing tape over all the drive slots and other openings of computers;
- the evidence tag should be created and the manufacturer, make, model, and serial number of the equipment should be recorded;
- the Evidence Custodian must log each piece of evidence in an evidence log.

In the preservation phase, the evidence that is found must be preserved in a state that is as close as possible to its original state. Any changes that are made to the state of the evidence during this phase must be documented and justified. All procedures that are used in the examination should be auditable, that is, a suitably qualified independent expert appointed by the other side of a case should be able to track all the investigations carried out by the prosecution's experts and produce the same results.

Full details of handling of different types of physical evidence and their transportation to the Forensic Laboratory are given in Chapter 8.

In the analysis phase, once the potential evidence has been collected and preserved, it must then be analyzed to extract the relevant information and recreate the chain of events. Care must be taken to ensuring that the tools that are used are appropriate and that any results obtained can be reproduced. It is also essential that all of the relevant evidence is obtained, including exculpatory evidence. Problems that can occur in the analysis phase include dealing with the volume of data that may be involved. It is not uncommon for a desktop computer to contain between 1 and 2 Tb of storage and for servers to contain from tens of terabytes to petabytes of storage. Sifting through this can be extremely time consuming, but there is a duty to find all of the evidence relevant to a case. Increasingly, there are tools available to assist the Forensic Analyst, but the use of these can create its own set of problems such as can the results that have been obtained be replicated using other tools or techniques? Have the tools been tested and validated?

Full details of case processing for different types of physical evidence in the Forensic Laboratory are given in Chapter 9.

In the presentation phase, it is essential to ensure that the method of presentation is appropriate for the audience for which it will be used. Communicating the meaning of the evidence is essential, otherwise it has no value. The presentation must be clear and also represent all of the facts. The problems in this phase of the process are all about communication of the findings but not every Forensic Analyst or Investigator is highly skilled in this area. When presenting Digital Evidence to a tribunal, a jury, or a judge, it has to be presented in a form that can be understood and which is convincing. This may entail significant additional effort to creating the evidence in a form such as a slide show, PowerPoint presentation, or an animation to represent a timeline of events that is outside the normal skills of the Forensic Analyst or Investigator.

Another issue that has to be considered in every stage of the process is that of spoliation, which is "the destruction or significant alteration of evidence or the failure to preserve the property for another's use as evidence in pending or reasonably foreseeable litigation."[o] In law, the spoliation of evidence can be either as the result of an intentional act or through negligence and may be caused by the withholding, hiding, altering, or destroying of evidence relevant to a legal proceeding.

There are two possible consequences that will result from spoliation:

- in jurisdictions where the intentional act is criminal by statute, it may result in fines and/or imprisonment.
- in jurisdictions where relevant case law precedent has been established, proceedings possibly altered by spoliation may be interpreted under a *spoliation inference*.

This means it may be considered that a negative evidentiary inference can be drawn from the destruction of a document or other object that is relevant to ongoing or reasonably foreseeable civil or criminal proceedings. There are many examples of the spoliation of Digital Evidence. For example, it may simply be electronically deleted or the media that the information had been stored on can be physically destroyed. Another example is that the digital information may also have its attributes, such as the date, modified which could mean that evidence has been created after the event or modified after the event. It is also possible that the metadata[p] may have been modified.

One of the most significant spoliation decisions from the electronic information arena is the opinions that came from the *Zubulake v. UBS Warburg*[q] case, in which sanctions

o. West v. Goodyear Tire & Rubber Co., 67 F.3d 776, 779 (2d Cir.1998).

p. Metadata describes other data. It provides information about a certain item's content. For example, an image may include metadata that describes how large the picture is, the color depth, the image resolution, when the image was created, and other data. A text document's metadata may contain information about how long the document is, who the author is, when the document was written, and a short summary of the document. Web pages often include metadata in the form of meta tags. Description and keywords meta tags are commonly used to describe the Web page's content. Most search engines use this data when adding pages to their search index. (from http://www.techterms.com/definition/metadata).

q. Zubulake v. UBS Warburg, LLC, 229 F.R.D. 422 (S.D.N.Y. 2004) ("Zubulake V"), http://www.ediscoverylaw.com/2004/12/articles/case-summaries/zubulake-v-court-grants-adverse-inference-instruction-and-outlines-counsels-role-in-locating-preserving-and-producing-relevant-evidence/.

were sought for a failure to preserve electronic evidence. In the *Zubulake v. UBS Warburg* case, the court first imposed sanctions of redepositions for failure to preserve all relevant backup tapes, and then, in a follow-on decision, imposed the sanction of adverse inference instruction to be given for willful destruction (deletion) of relevant email.

1.1.8 The Principles of Electronic Evidence

In Digital Forensics, there are a number of underpinning principles that have been generally accepted throughout the community. One of the most widely used explanations of these principles can be found in the UK Association of Chief Officers (ACPO) Good Practice Guide for Computer-Based Electronic Evidence. The guide defines four principles[r] that have been widely accepted as the basic principles for the handling of electronic evidence:

- **principle 1**: No action taken by LE agencies or their agents should change data held on a computer or storage media which may subsequently be relied upon in court;
- **principle 2**: In circumstances where a person finds it necessary to access original data held on a computer or on storage media, that person must be competent to do so and be able to give evidence explaining the relevance and the implications of their actions;
- **principle 3**: An audit trail or other record of all processes applied to computer-based electronic evidence should be created and preserved. An independent third party should be able to examine those processes and achieve the same result;
- **principle 4**: The person in charge of the investigation (the Case Officer) has overall responsibility for ensuring that the law and these principles are adhered to.

While these principles provide an excellent base from which to start, there are some limitations. The principles apply primarily to investigations that have a single source of evidence and network, cloud-based evidence, or real-time investigations may cause problems. Consideration should also be given to whether or not Locard's Exchange Principle[s] applies.

Locard's exchange principle is the underlying principle for all forensic science and when applied to a crime scene, says that the perpetrator(s) of the crime will both bring something into the scene and take away something from the scene when they leave. Kirk[t] interprets Locard's exchange principle as: "Wherever he steps, whatever he touches, whatever he leaves, even unconsciously, will serve as a silent witness against him. Not only his fingerprints or his footprints, but his hair, the fibres from his clothes, the glass he breaks, the tool mark he leaves, the paint he scratches, the blood or semen he deposits or collects. All of these and more, bear mute witness against him. This is evidence that does not forget. It is not confused by the excitement of the moment. It is not absent because human witnesses are. It is factual evidence. Physical evidence cannot be wrong, it cannot perjure itself, and it cannot be wholly absent. Only human failure to find it, study and understand it, can diminish its value."

While this interpretation applies to potential physical traces, the same principle equally applies to the digital world. In the following chapters, the procedures that are needed to support all phases of an investigation and also the wider management of an efficient digital forensics laboratory are given in more depth.

1.1.9 Nomenclature Used in This Book

A standard set of naming for task roles has been used in this book, and are the ones used in the Forensic Laboratory, and this is as follows:

- **Case**—any investigation carried out by the Forensic Laboratory that uses the processes and disciplines of Digital Forensics;
- **Employee**—a person employed by an organization, either as a member of staff, a consultant, contractor, or any other third party under contract to the organization;
- **First Responder**—a person who is first on the scene after an incident or the first Forensic Laboratory Forensic Analyst on the scene of an incident;
- **Forensic Analyst**—person responsible for performing forensic work on a case in the Forensic Laboratory;
- **Forensic Team**—the Forensic Analysts deployed on a given case;
- **Incident Manager**—the person managing an incident irrespective of what organization they are from;
- **Information processing system**—any system capable of processing digital information. This covers computers of all types (e.g., desktops, laptops, and servers as well as PDAs, smart phones, and other computer-related peripherals). However, this definition can also include nontypical devices that may contain a computer chip and these can include, but are not limited to:
  - a car's engine management system;
  - a fridge, freezer, microwave, or similar;
  - a shop till;
  - any system with an embedded chip.
- **Laboratory Manager**—the person in charge of the Forensic Laboratory;

r. ACPO Good Practice Guide for Computer-Based Electronic Evidence—http://www.7safe.com/electronic_evidence/ACPO_guidelines_computer_evidence.pdf.

s. Dr. Edmond Locard of Lyon, France, formulated the basic principle of forensic science: "Every contact leaves a trace."

t. Kirk, P., L. Crime investigation: physical evidence and the police laboratory, 1953, Interscience Publishers, Inc.: New York.

- **Lead Forensic Analyst**—the person who is in charge of a team of Forensic Analysts. Where there is only one Forensic Analyst in the Forensic Team, he or she is the Lead Forensic Analyst for the case;
- **Officer in the Case – also known as the Case Officer**—the lead investigator in a case, typically a Police Officer or similar;
- **Third party**—an entity (organization or person) that is not directly involved in the legal interactions between the involved parties, but may affect it or be influenced by it.

There are times when a person may have more than one role (e.g., a single Forensic Analyst going out on site to deal with a search and seizure and being appointed the Lead (and only) Forensic Analyst for the case would be the Forensic Team, First Responder, Lead Forensic Analyst, Forensic Analyst, and may be the Laboratory Manager as well).

These, and other definitions relating to Digital Forensics, are given in the Glossary.

APPENDIX 1 - SOME TYPES OF CASES INVOLVING DIGITAL FORENSICS

Some types of cases that the Forensic Laboratory has dealt with include the following:

CRIMINAL CASES

- abduction;
- auction fraud;
- burglary;
- cyber stalking;
- deliberate circumvention of information processing security system measures;
- denial of service attacks;
- drugs;
- electronic vandalism;
- forgery;
- fraud achieved by the manipulation of computer records;
- identity theft (and subsequent exploitation of the theft of identity);
- industrial espionage (which could include unauthorized access or theft of equipment);
- information warfare;
- intellectual property theft, including software piracy;
- murder;
- pedophilia (creating it and distributing it);
- phishing (and its variants);
- rape;
- release of malware of any kind (e.g., a virus, Trojan horse, worm, etc.);
- sexual crimes;
- spamming (if it is illegal in the jurisdiction);
- terrorism;
- theft;
- unauthorized access to information (often called hacking);
- unauthorized modification of data or software.

CIVIL CASES

- allegations of breaches of duty of care;
- asset recovery;
- breach of contract;
- copyright issues;
- defamation;
- employee disputes;
- questioned documents;
- theft of corporate resources for private gain;
- to avoid charges of breach of contract;
- to meet requirements of discovery in civil claims;
- tort;
- to support a variety of civil claims;
- unauthorized access by employees.

> **Note**
> In some cases, cases may be pursued through the civil and criminal courts, either simultaneously or consecutively, depending on the legislation and practices within the jurisdiction. Examples may include, but are not limited to, copyright issues, defamation, unauthorized access.

APPENDIX 2 - GROWTH OF HARD DISK DRIVES FOR PERSONAL COMPUTERS

Year	Capacity	Details
Pre 1981	Various	Floppy disks or cassette tapes
1981	360 Kb	IBM PC—one or two 5¼″ floppy drives
1983	10 Mb	IBM XT
1984	20/1.2 Mb	IBM AT 6 MHz hard disk and floppy disk. They also had a 360 Kb floppy disk drive
1986	30 Mb	IBM AT 8 MHz
1986	720 Kb	IBM Convertible—3½″ floppy disks
1987	20/1.44 Mb	IBM PS/2—PS/2s also had the capability to utilize 2.88 Mb floppy disks
1989	30 Mb	IBM PS/2
1991	60-130 Mb	Available range of hard disk drives, but not all fitted to a PC as standard
1996	1.6-6.4 Gb	Available range of hard disk drives, but not all fitted to a PC as standard

Continued

Year	Capacity	Details
1998	3.2-16.8 Gb	Available range of hard disk drives, but not all fitted to a PC as standard
2003	20-80 Gb	Available range of hard disk drives, but not all fitted to a PC as standard
2005	200-500 Gb	Available range of hard disk drives, but not all fitted to a PC as standard
2006	750 Gb	First 750 Gb drive available
2007	1 Tb	First 1 Tb drive available
2008	1.5 Tb	First 1.5 Tb drive available
2009	2 Tb	First 2 Tb drive available
2010	3 Tb	First 3 Tb drive available
2011	4 Tb	First 4 Tb drive available

APPENDIX 3 - DISK DRIVE SIZE NOMENCLATURE

Name	Approximate Size[a]
Kilobyte (Kb)	1000 bytes
Megabyte (Mb)	1,000,000 bytes
Gigabyte (Gb)	1,000,000,000 bytes
Terabyte (Tb)	1,000,000,000,000 bytes
Petabyte (Pb)	1,000,000,000,000,000 bytes
Exabyte (Eb)	1,000,000,000,000,000,000 bytes
Zettabyte (Zb)	1,000,000,000,000,000,000,000 bytes
Yottabyte (Yb)	1,000,000,000,000,000,000,000,000 bytes
Brontobyte (Bb)	1,000,000,000,000,000,000,000,000,000 bytes

[a]Actually a kilobyte is 1024 bytes.

Note 1

A typed page of A4 requires between 2 and 5 Kb for storage, a low-resolution photograph is about 100 Kb.

Note 2

In 2007, the amount of data created, captured, or replicated was 281 Eb[u] and was estimated as 1.8 Zb in 2011.

u. The Diverse and Exploding Digital Universe, IDC, 2007.

Chapter 2

Forensic Laboratory Accommodation

Table of Contents

2.1 THE BUILDING

2.1.1 General

In general terms, it is unlikely that many forensic laboratories will have the luxury of being able to be built from the "ground up." More likely, it will be housed in an existing building and this will be tailored to the ideal requirements of the Forensic Laboratory.

In most cases, some sort of business case is necessary, even if an existing building is to be converted to a forensic laboratory and a varying degree of conversion is needed to make it an efficient Forensic Laboratory.

This chapter makes the assumption that the Forensic Laboratory is being built from scratch with all current good practice included and it is being built as a data center with additional workspace for all necessary office or laboratory purposes.

2.1.2 Business Case

It is worth starting with the business case that is needed to develop to justify the expenditure (which may be considerable) and to establish the requirements for the type of accommodation and the square footage that is needed for the Forensic Laboratory. Experience shows that there are a number of factors that must be considered when designing the layout of a Forensic Laboratory. The first of these is that, however, the modest or comprehensive requirements are for the Forensic Laboratory, they will inevitably be too small. The factors that affect the size and design of the laboratory include the following:

- estimation of the space needed for each work area;
- the role of the laboratory and the range of tasks that it will undertake;
- size reduction during the costing and management approval process;

- underestimating the space required for evidence and consumable storage.

In law enforcement or government, it is often thought that this is not relevant, but for the most part this is a mistake. Although it may be not a full business case that has to be developed, it is almost certain that there will have to be some sort of justification and plan, with costs, for the creation or the development of the Forensic Laboratory. In reality, whatever it is called, it is the outline justification and costing for the development of a Forensic Laboratory.

Developing a business case will always be a subjective affair, and there is considerable advice and examples of good practice available to assist in this task. Additionally, there may be accepted and documented ways of preparing a business case within an organization. As with any document that senior management is to review and absorb to achieve a successful outcome, there should be an executive summary at the front explaining briefly, what the document is about and giving them the "elevator pitch" level of information that they are required to approve.

A business case outline that was successfully used within an organization for the establishment of the Forensic Laboratory is given in Appendix 1.

There are two main options when selecting the building in which the Forensic Laboratory will be located. The options are to either take over space in an existing building or to have a new build Forensic Laboratory. There are advantages and disadvantages to both options.

A new building has the advantage that it will be built to the Forensic Laboratory's specifications and should have a low maintenance bill for the first few years of operation. It will also be possible to have the latest technology built into the infrastructure. Some of the disadvantages of a new building are the time to get it through the design and approval and then build phases and the cost.

When taking over space in an existing building, some of the advantages are that much of the infrastructure that is required may already be in place and that the time scale is likely to be much shorter. The disadvantages include the fact that the space will have to be adapted and may not meet all of the organization's requirements.

The ultimate choice for the location of the Forensic Laboratory may well be decided by a higher authority or dictated by the requirements for it to be in a specific area.

Issues that should be considered, and that are often overlooked, include that of vehicular access and parking, good communication and transport links, and proximity to the area where the Forensic Laboratory will operate. If any of these are missing, while the building being considered may be ideal for siting the Forensic Laboratory, it will not be as effective as it could have been and the Forensic Laboratory employees will have pressures put upon them that they do not need.

The location of the Forensic Laboratory will be dictated by a number of factors, some of which are within the organization's control and some of them will not. The location may be dictated by the need to be close to other parts of the organization or to be central to an area of operations. The cost of real estate in different areas may also have some influence. In reality, if the location is not fixed because it is going to be sited in a building that is already in use by the organization, it is usual to end up with a trade-off between some or all of the other influences.

Within a building, careful consideration must be given to the exact location of the Forensic Laboratory. There are plenty of arguments from a security perspective for it to be located in the cellar (no windows, control of access, thick walls, and a host of other factors), but this must be balanced against the fact that electricity and water do not mix well and the fact that water flows downhill. This may seem a bit obvious, but this is just one of the many considerations and compromises that will have to be made.

The size of the Forensic Laboratory will be determined, in part, by the scope of the services that have been defined in the business case and the predicted volume of throughput. Other factors that will affect the size of the Forensic Laboratory are issues such as health and safety regulations. One issue that is often underestimated when planning the Forensic Laboratory is the space that will be required for the storage of evidence. Remember that secure storage will be needed not only for cases in progress (or to be processed) but also for past cases. The length of time that evidence must be retained will vary from jurisdiction to jurisdiction but may be as long as for 75 years (currently in Australia and being considered in the UK).

2.1.3 Standards

Depending on the jurisdiction, there are a number of standards that are applicable to creating the Forensic Laboratory; these include the following:

- ISO—generally amended as required and have a 5-10 years update cycle;
- TIA—reviewed, amended, or rescinded on a 5-year cycle;
- IEEE—remain current until a change is needed;
- local/national standards—vary.

The most important thing for anyone setting up the Forensic Laboratory is to ensure that the relevant standards are checked for the jurisdiction and that all current revisions are considered.

2.2 PROTECTING AGAINST EXTERNAL AND ENVIRONMENTAL THREATS

When deciding on the location of the Forensic Laboratory, consideration must be given to minimizing the risk from external environmental threats. This section lists necessary conditions for the operations of the Forensic Laboratory to be protected against external and environmental threats.

1. When choosing a building where the Forensic Laboratory operates, the following must be considered:
   - risk from fire;
   - risk from flood;
   - risk from civil unrest;
   - risk from other facilities in the locality;
   - risks from any other relevant manmade or natural sources.
2. Determination of recovery times based on risk profiles, including business continuity planning.
3. When storing any hazardous material on site, they must be securely and safely stored, preferably away from the main Forensic Laboratory area.
4. Appropriate fire detection and water detection systems must be put in place, preferably connected to a centralized annunciator panel at a manned site.
5. The installed burglar alarm is connected to a centralized manned station.
6. Appropriate fire quenching materials must be made available with Forensic Laboratory employees trained in their use and an appropriate number of Fire Wardens present.
7. Where appropriate polythene sheeting or similar should be held to protect the Forensics Laboratory's assets from any water spillage from above.
8. Consideration should be given to complete environmental monitoring, if thought to be appropriate.
9. The Forensic Laboratory backup systems and media store must be at a secure location that cannot be affected by any disaster affecting the main laboratory area.
10. The ongoing requirement for "green computing" and environmental control in the management of forensics cases.

2.3 UTILITIES AND SERVICES

When setting up the Forensic Laboratory, whether in a new build site or in a conversion to an existing building, it will be necessary to have a number of utilities and services supplied and operational.

> **Note**
>
> It is assumed that all utilities supplied to the Forensic Laboratory are under the control of the utility companies, and the Forensic Laboratory is dependent on these and has no control over their supply.

2.3.1 Signage

There is always a trade-off between the school of thought that requires that there is no external signage to advise the function of the building and having signs to guide visitors to the Forensic Laboratory (directional signs) and then when they arrive there, information signs. The directional signs are pretty much optional and if present, they will need to comply with the organizational scheme, if appropriate. If, when operating the Forensic Laboratory, there is a need determined not to advertise its presence, then appropriate "dummy" signage to provide a passable explanation of what the space is being used for is required (people get curious when they see people entering and leaving an area that has no advertised reason to exist).

The information signs will serve a number of functions and they may be on the outside the Forensic Laboratory or within the "airlock." These signs are intended to advise who can enter the relevant parts of the Forensic Laboratory (do they have the requisite clearances and the need to enter?) and if they are allowed to enter, under what conditions (escorted, equipment that they are not allowed to bring in), and the first line health and safety notices (fire escape, hazardous materials, etc.).

Once inside, signs may be needed for the different areas or zones of the Forensic Laboratory, emergency exits, health and safety and hazardous materials, access limitation, and a range of other purposes.

2.3.2 Power and Cabling

The Forensic Laboratory will be a high-tech facility and will therefore have above average requirements for power supply to keep equipment operational and within operational tolerances defined by the manufacturer.

When determining the power requirements for the Forensic Laboratory, the following must be considered:

- lighting;
- air conditioning;
- building infrastructure requirements;
- forensic and information-processing equipment;
- other equipment that may be present, such as photocopiers, kettles, water coolers, and fridges.

While considering power requirements, it is essential to consider future growth and ensure that there is sufficient capacity to accommodate future demands.

Forensic and information-processing equipment falls into two specific categories:

- LAN/WAN infrastructure;
- Forensic Analysts work space.

The LAN/WAN infrastructure may be a dedicated and purpose-built server room or in a secure room used as a server and comms room. If a dedicated server room is to be used, design standards exist from a variety of standards bodies. These include, but are not limited to,

- ANSI/TIA 942 Telecommunications Infrastructure Standard for Data Centers (plus the Addenda);
- ANSI/BICSI—002 Data Center Design and Implementation Best Practices;

- CENELEC EN 50173-5—Information Technology—Generic Cabling Systems—Part 5 Data Centers;
- ISO/IEC 24764—Information Technology—Generic Cabling systems for Data Centers;
- AS 2834—Computer Accommodation.

The LAN/WAN infrastructure will depend on operational requirements. In the Forensic Laboratory, there are two separate and distinct LANs, one for business operations and one for forensic examinations support. Each is physically and logically separated. Both LANs will need careful planning and provision of appropriate power and cabling requirements, which are typically different.

The Forensic Analyst's workspace will be totally different to that of a "standard corporate" environment. In the corporate environment, the user will typically have a PC, two monitors, and maybe one or two peripherals attached (e.g., a local scanner or printer). The Forensic Laboratory workspace for Forensic Analysts may have a number of different cases running at any one time and a variety of different technology running at any one time. Additionally, the Forensic Analyst's equipment is usually in an "always on" state as it is often performing overnight operations (e.g., searches or indexing). The workspace will also require numerous electrical outlets for all possible equipment that may be in use, as opposed to those required in the "normal" business environment. Even taking a simple operation of cloning, a disk will require five electrical sockets:

- forensic workstation;
- monitor;
- power to disk to be cloned;
- write blocker;
- power to target disk.

And the Forensic Analyst may be running numerous operations simultaneously.

Sockets should be ergonomically sited, as no Forensic Analyst likes to be crawling under their desk every time they want to power up or power down some electrical equipment!

A backup power system, typically dual routing from different suppliers, and/or a generator should be considered.

An uninterruptible power supply (UPS) must be installed to protect all relevant information-processing equipment that is able to take the load of that equipment, perform a graceful close down if required, and seamlessly integrate with the generator (if installed). Significant losses of processed data can occur due to power failures or power surges. All relevant equipment must be subject to UPS, and this must be regularly tested and maintained. Details of required maintenance and testing are given in Chapter 7, Section 7.5.4.

If backup power cannot be arranged, a secure alternate location for undertaking forensic processing must be considered.

All power and telecommunications cabling used by the Forensic Laboratory must be safeguarded from interception or damage to minimize security risks, and protect against loss of data.

While the Forensic Laboratory may not implement ANSI/TIA 942 Telecommunications Infrastructure Standard for Data Centers (plus the Addenda), a checklist for implementation of a Tier 4 data center is given in http://www.ctrls.in/wp-content/themes/twentyten/downloads/Tier_IV_Specs.pdf.

In addition to main power, the risks of static electricity and electromagnetic interference must be considered. Static electricity countered by the use of antistatic equipment on an individual basis is covered by the requirements of personal protective equipment in Chapter 17, Section 17.6.3.

2.3.3 Heating, Ventilation, and Air Conditioning

All equipment has a manufacturer's recommended operating temperature and humidity range. It is essential that the operation of equipment is within this range. Careful consideration of the local environment (e.g., location, elevation, and building construction) is essential as these may materially affect requirements for heating, ventilation, and air conditioning (HVAC).

Forensic Laboratory employees also will want to work in comfortable working temperature and humidity ranges, and in some jurisdictions, working environments are mandated by law.

The HVAC system must have adequate capacity for all of the current and foreseeable future requirements. It will need to be an effective system that is reliable and has a high level of availability.

A backup plan or spare or redundant capacity for the HVAC systems must be considered. This may include the use of portable HVAC units.

It may be necessary to install shielding in the ducting to ensure that the system is not acting as an antenna into and out of the Forensic Laboratory. It may also be necessary to consider grilles in the ducts to prevent unauthorized access.

2.3.4 Fire Detection and Quenching

With the range of equipment that will be in use in the Forensic Laboratory, effective fire detection and quenching systems are essential. If the accommodation is located in a larger building, the fire detection system should be tied into the building management system. The fire detection system should cover all rooms, as well as any ceiling voids and subfloor plenum gaps.

Fire detection is usually controlled by standards, regulations, and legislative requirements in most jurisdictions.

In whatever environment the Forensic Laboratory is located, the alarm system must be connected to a manned control point and should have a centralized annunciator panel.

Fire classes are not universally used and vary from location to location. The most common ones are given below:

American	European	Australian/ Asian	Fuel/heat source
Class A	Class A	Class A	Ordinary combustibles
Class B	Class B	Class B	Flammable liquids
	Class C	Class C	Flammable gasses
Class C	Class F/D	Class E	Electrical equipment
Class D	Class D	Class D	Combustible metals
Class K	Class F	Class F	Cooking oil or fat

The most likely fire classes encountered in the Forensic Laboratory will be:

- ordinary combustibles;
- electrical equipment.

Detection systems fall mainly into three different types:

- smoke detectors;
- heat detectors;
- flame detectors.

Careful consideration of the correct types of detection devices must be undertaken by a competent authority, often in conjunction with the local fire service. As well as automatic detection devices, there shall be a range of manual alarms installed.

The main types of fire quenching systems are:

- wet pipe;
- dry pipe;
- inert gas;
- foam;
- dry chemical.

As can be seen, there are a range of fire quenching devices and again, careful consideration of the correct types of quenching devices must be undertaken by a competent authority, often in conjunction with the local fire service. In addition to the automated quenching systems, there are always a range of hand-held quenching devices available for the different classes of fire identified above.

2.3.5 Close Circuit Television and Burglar Alarms

Issues that need to be considered with close circuit television (CCTV) and alarm systems include the resolution and placement of the cameras. The resolution and the placement should be such that individuals can be identified, but a decision will need to be made as to whether the cameras are capable of capturing the contents of any monitors that they overlook (is it a requirement to be able to see what was on the screen at any time or are there other security systems in place that will identify what activity was taking place?).

Consideration should also be given to whether it is a requirement to have continuous monitoring or whether the cameras should be motion activated. Another issue should be whether there is a requirement for low-light cameras. The output from the cameras will probably be saved to a digital store within the Forensic Laboratory (assuming that the Forensic Laboratory has a modern digital system rather than a tape storage system). The volume of data that will need to be stored will depend on the period that the data need to be stored and this should be taken into consideration. In a number of jurisdictions, there are legislative requirements for the retention periods for CCTV tapes.

CCTV shall be used to cover all entry and exit points in the Forensic Laboratory (inside and out), as well as access to and egress from any restricted area.

Off-site storage options should be investigated.

2.3.6 Communications

Communications for the Forensic Laboratory primarily will consist of the telephone system and internet access. The type of phone system to be used will depend on the numbers of employees in the Forensic Laboratory but will typically have the following minimum functionality:

- automatic call back;
- busy extension diversion;
- call hold;
- call transfer;
- conference calling;
- group pickup;
- save and use number dialed;
- system short code dialing;
- voice mail functionality.

In addition to the landline capability, a number of corporate cell phones shall be used. These all must have the capability of remote wiping in case of loss. They shall be used for Forensic Laboratory business purposes and may include additional functionality in addition to standard telephony. Security requirements for these devices are given in Chapter 12, Section 12.3.9 and 12.3.10.

Internet access will be dependent on the local internet service providers (ISPs). In general terms, the bigger the internet pipe available, the better. Each ISP local to the Forensic Laboratory will have broadly similar services. It may also be sensible to have the ISP host the Forensic

Laboratory Web site so long as there is no confidential or customer information located on it.

2.3.7 Water

Water services are required for building management services as well as the supply of a potable drinking source and sewage purposes. In some locations, main water should not be used for drinking purposes so that a bottled supply or water coolers must be used.

Water pipes should not be located above the server room if possible. Water detection and portable pumps may be required depending on specific circumstances.

2.4 PHYSICAL SECURITY

2.4.1 General

As part of the selection of a location for the Forensic Laboratory, physical security must be an underpinning consideration in the selection of the location and design of the Forensic Laboratory. Physical security should be designed in layers to meet the requirements for the Forensic Laboratory and its working practices.

Depending on the type of building in which the Forensic Laboratory is housed, this may start with the area outside the Forensic Laboratory and include the following:

- fences or walls;
- barriers;
- alarms;
- sensors;
- CCTV systems;
- guard forces.

Inside the building, there should be:

- access control systems;
- security doors;
- alarms;
- sensors;
- CCTV systems;
- guard forces.

Within the laboratory itself, there should be:

- physical and logical access control systems;
- security doors;
- alarms;
- sensors;
- CCTV systems;
- encryption of data.

The issue here that is often missed is that if all of the separate security measures are not integrated and used as a single system, then they will not be optimally effective and there may be gaps or overlaps in the security systems. For example, if the guard force cannot respond in time to an incident that is captured on the CCTV, then there is little point in having them. If the CCTV cameras do not cover all of the access points and any potential weaknesses in the perimeter defenses, then again there is little point in spending money on them. The bad guys will spend time identifying the flaws in the systems.

Physical security of the Forensic Laboratory premises is the first step in the process of securing the Forensic Laboratory's information-processing systems. It is essential that appropriate physical security is in place for all the Forensic Laboratory premises. The Forensic Laboratory physical security policy is given in Appendix 2.

2.4.2 Building Infrastructure

Both at the external interface to the rest of the building and within the laboratory, any walls will have to be of an appropriate thickness and to the full height (all the way to the fixed ceiling and into subfloor plenum spaces).

Doors will have to be a specification that protects against both physical assault and fire.

If there are windows, they will have to be secured not only from break-ins but also from being opened. It is desirable to avoid things being blown or thrown out of an open window, as well as the possibility of someone monitoring from outside (even with a telescope).

Air conditioning vents will need to be secured with grills through the ducting that are fixed to the walls where they enter and leave the area.

If the services that are being offered require it, then the installation of a Faraday Cage or room will need to be planned with all of the commensurate issues that this will cause. In addition, the space that is allocated for evidence and other equipment storage must meet both health and safety and security requirements as well as being placed in a location that makes it as convenient as possible for the anticipated level of traffic.

2.4.3 Access Control

When implementing an access control system in the Forensic Laboratory, it should, if possible and practical, be integrated into the building or organizational access control system. This helps in providing defence in depth (layers of security). Integration will also make any post-incident access violation investigation easier, as the logs can be centrally accessed. This does not mean that there will not be a local log of accesses and egresses to and from the Forensic Laboratory.

The access control system must also be comprehensive, effective, managed, and regularly tested. The choice of type of access control system will depend on:

- budget;
- contractual requirements;

- existing installations;
- relevant standards and good practice;
- the highest security or sensitivity level of the material being processed.

The system should be as state-of-the-art as possible, while a tested and proven system with a low false alarm and failure rate. There will always be a trade-off between these two sets of requirements, and, at the end, it will be a decision based on a risk assessment. Whatever system is implemented, it must be practical and meet the Forensic Laboratory's needs. Perhaps a good example of what may not suit the Forensic Laboratory is the use of the Security interlock systems. This is essentially a revolving tube system, just large enough for a person, which is fine for controlling people in and out of the environment, but makes the movement of equipment very difficult.

To maintain a secure infrastructure in the Forensic Laboratory, the layered physical security implementation will cover the following:

- access to the Forensic Laboratory building;
- access to the Forensic Laboratory forensics processing areas;
- access to the server room;
- access by visitors;
- deliveries to, and collections from, the Forensic Laboratory.

Procedures for access controls are given in Chapter 12, Section 12.4.2 and 12.4.3.

Failure to control access to the Forensic Laboratory, or any part of it by appropriately authorized employees or visitors, could leave the Forensic Laboratory open to challenge over maintaining the "chain of custody."

2.4.4 On-Site Secure Evidence Storage

Secure evidence storage is dedicated storage space for the sole purpose of securely storing evidence relating to any forensic cases that the Forensic Laboratory may process or has processed. The secure evidence storage facility is the physical embodiment of the chain of custody, supported by robust procedures for management of evidence. Evidential storage must be the most secure area of storage in the Forensic Laboratory and the most rigorously controlled area with full CCTV and alarm coverage. All access to it must be regularly reviewed and restricted to the minimum possible number of employees.

The secure evidence storage facility must be constructed so that it can defeat any forced or otherwise unauthorized entry as well as being resistant to any environmental threats.

Depending on requirements, the secure evidence storage may require physical protection such as electronic magnetic shielding. All access and egress to and from the secure evidence store must be logged and have an available audit trail.

Within the Forensic Laboratory, a single evidence custodian (with an alternate) has been appointed.

2.4.5 Clean Room

The first question that must be answered is

Is a clean room needed?

They are expensive to set up and also to maintain. If the services that the Forensic Laboratory was to offer included the disassembly of disks, then a clean room facility may be needed. However, depending on the number of disks to be disassembled, it may be that a positive pressure table or compartment will be sufficient.

The final decision will depend on the expected role of the Forensic Laboratory and also the anticipated level of use. No provision has been made for a clean room in the layout suggested in Section 2.5 as the Forensic Laboratory does not have one, or expect to need one. A clean room can be included if needed. There are a number of standards relating to the implementation of clean rooms and these include the following:

- BS 5295 Cleanroom Standards;
- ISO 14644, Cleanrooms and controlled environments;
- US Federal Standard 209E—Airborne Particulate Cleanliness Classes in Cleanrooms and Clean Zones.

2.4.6 Fire Safes

In addition to the evidence storage space requirements, there will always be the requirement for protecting some material in the event of a fire. This may require the installation of fire safes within the Forensic Laboratory or alternatively, access to a fire safe in another location or part of the organization. In the planning phase, consideration should be given to the size required and the location of the safe as well as the quality of fire resistance required. One thing that is often overlooked is the floor loading required for a fire safe, and on account of this they are usually on the ground floor if of any significant size.

The most common standards for these are those operated by the Underwriters' Laboratory which has a number of different classes for protection of the safe's contents.

2.4.7 Secure Off-Site Storage

All IT operations require a secure off-site to store backup media and other operational necessities to be used in case of a disaster at the main processing site.

All media storing Forensic Laboratory information must be stored in accordance with the manufacturer's recommendations. Details of this are included in Chapter 12, Section 12.3.12.

The Forensic Laboratory uses an off-site storage service provider, rather than having its own remote site. If considering a dedicated and owned secure off-site location, then the following should be considered:

- ease of access to the storage facility;
- the distance from the Forensic Laboratory;
- logistics of storing and recovering off-site material;
- security;
- cost.

2.5 LAYOUT OF THE FORENSIC LABORATORY

There are a number of issues that need to be considered when setting up the internal layout of the Forensic Laboratory. If the square footage of floor that was required in the initial plans is achieved, then some of the issues detailed below may not be relevant. Unfortunately, this is not often the case and the premises that are acquired for the Forensic Laboratory will usually be a compromise in one way or another. The main issues to be considered when designing the Forensic Laboratory include the following.

2.5.1 Separation of Space for Specific Roles and Tasks

This will be influenced by the scope of the tasks that the Forensic Laboratory will undertake. The wider the range of tasks that the Forensic Laboratory will undertake, the more effort and consideration will need to go into working out how to organize the available space so that each task can be carried out in an appropriate environment and in a sensible ergonomic order.

The main issue is that a number of separated areas need to be in a specific order from the entrance. From the entrance door, an "air lock" should be implemented so that people entering the laboratory can enter the environment and seal the outer door before they are allowed to move on into the working parts of the Forensic Laboratory. In this space, anyone entering the Forensic Laboratory can be properly identified and authorized prior to entry. This area will also be used to manage any visitors and employees as well as for storage of any electronic equipment (phones, radios, laptops) that is not allowed in the laboratory.

The Forensic Laboratory has a secure-viewing area in an isolated room where visitors can view cases without being given access to the working areas of the Forensic Laboratory (e.g., other experts, Lawyers, Clients, etc.). Controlled access to this area is also needed from the working areas of the Forensic Laboratory.

Once in the working space of the Forensic Laboratory, then the available space needs to be divided into a number of functional areas. These may include the following:

- analysis and report writing area;
- bathrooms;
- coffee area;
- equipment storage;
- hard disk imaging area;
- mobile device imaging area (Faraday Room);
- office space;
- research area;
- secure evidence storage area;
- server room;
- unpacking and disassembly area.

A possible layout for the Forensic Laboratory is given below:

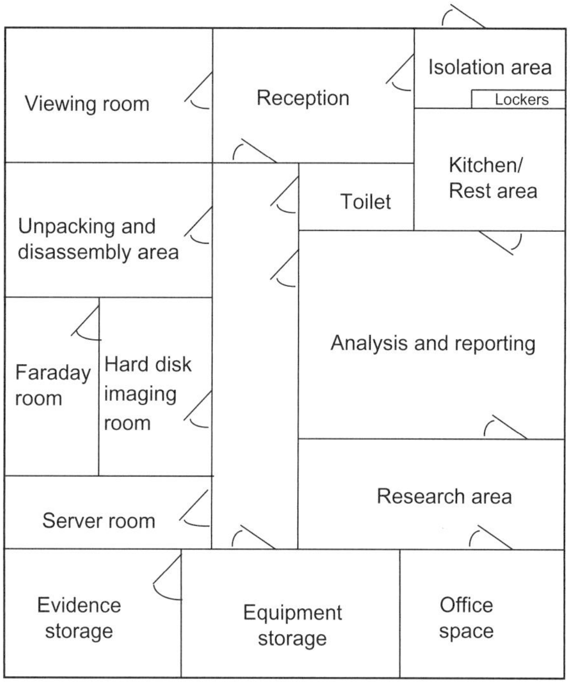

The need to segregate duties and operations in the same area is another area often overlooked, and there will inevitably be a number of investigations taking place in the Forensic Laboratory at any one time and these may be of differing sensitivities. It may be worth organizing the space so that each of the workstations has a degree of privacy, so that the work being undertaken on one workstation cannot be seen from the others. It may also be worth considering, in the design of the laboratory, creating an environment that clearly separates out the areas by role.

Security requirements for equipment siting are given in Chapter 7, Section 7.3.4.

2.5.2 Ergonomics

An often overlooked area of the design of the Forensic Laboratory is the ergonomics of processing a case. Ergonomics are an important consideration when designing the Forensic Laboratory. Ergonomics is defined by the freedictionary as:

"Design factors, as for the workplace, intended to maximize productivity by minimizing operator fatigue and discomfort."[1]

In terms of the Forensic Laboratory, this relates to the arrangement of the work areas to enable the work to "flow" through the Forensic Laboratory. For example, the disassembly area will be at one end of the laboratory, and next to it would be the disk imaging area, then the analysis area, etc. While it may seem trivial and is often not achievable, it should be considered and implemented wherever possible. It makes sense and will save on movement back and forward within the Forensic Laboratory.

2.5.3 Personal Workspace

Each Forensic Analyst will require a significant work area to enable them to carry out all of the tasks that they are expected to perform. Their workspace is in effect a personalized miniature laboratory completely equipped to allow them to perform all their assigned forensic tasks as well as perform necessary business functions. This will require two separate information-processing systems, the forensic workstation and the business system necessary for day-to-day non-forensic operations.

There will be the need for a number of common area operations, rather than replicating all forensic operations for all Forensic Analysts. The scope of shared resources will vary depending on the tasks that the Forensic Laboratory undertake but would include business as well as forensic equipment such as:

- dedicated media copiers;
- dedicated media production equipment;
- disk duplication equipment;
- printers;
- scanners.

2.5.4 Size Estimating

When estimating the square footage needed, a good rule of thumb is to double the size of the original estimate. There is nothing worse that discovering a year after moving into a new premises and finding that it has run out of space and that a move to a larger building is needed.

2.5.5 Infrastructure Rooms

Depending on how the Forensic Laboratory is set up (dedicated or part of a shared building), there will be the need for a number of dedicated areas, that may, or may not be dedicated to the Forensic Laboratory, and may be in the building containing the Forensic Laboratory, these include the following:

- battery room;
- electrical power rooms;
- HVAC control room;
- switch room;
- UPS room.

1. Design factors, as for the workplace, intended to maximize productivity by minimizing operator fatigue and discomfort—http://www.thefreedictionary.com/ergonomics.

APPENDIX 1 - SAMPLE OUTLINE FOR A BUSINESS CASE

An executive summary

1. An outline of the business proposal
   - The nature of the of the digital forensic service offering
   - The scope of the digital forensic service
   - Business strategy for the parent organization vis-à-vis digital forensics
2. Product, customers, markets, channels, brand and pricing for digital forensics
   - The need for a digital forensics service
   - Customers
   - Markets
   - Channels
   - Pricing
3. Competitive strength of the digital forensic service
   - Competitor analysis
   - Differentiators
   - Unique selling points (USPs)
4. Key business issues for the parent organization vis-à-vis digital forensics
5. Summary of compelling business proposition for the parent Organization
6. Organization of the digital forensic Service
   - Key staff for the digital forensic service
   - Interfaces and dependencies
   - Resources
   - Location and facilities
   - Intellectual Capital
   - Intellectual property for the digital forensic service
   - Know-how of the digital forensic service
   - Financial approach
   - Anticipated revenues and costs for the digital forensic service
7. Formation costs for the Digital Forensic Laboratory
   - Legal and Regulatory issues affecting the digital forensic service
   - Benefits to the parent organization
   - Financial
   - Nonfinancial

8. Risks and critical success factors (CSFs) for the digital forensic service
9. Set-up phase
10. Product liability
11. Market development
12. Management and service delivery
    Financial
    Legal
13. Exit Plan for the parent organization
    Responsibilities for exit management
    Distribution of assets and liabilities

APPENDIX 2 - FORENSIC LABORATORY PHYSICAL SECURITY POLICY

The Forensic Laboratory physical security policy is reproduced below:

INTRODUCTION

Physical security of Forensic Laboratory premises is the first step in the process of securing the Forensic Laboratory's information-processing systems. It is essential that appropriate physical security is in placc for all Forensic Laboratory premises.

PURPOSE

This policy provides rules for anyone wanting to access to Forensic Laboratory premises.

Effective implementation of this policy will minimize unauthorized access to Forensic Laboratory and provides more effective auditing of physical access controls.

DEFINITIONS

Employee: An individual employed by Forensic Laboratory.
Visitor: An individual, not an employee, who visits Forensic Laboratory premises for any reason.
Host: A Forensic Laboratory employee who sponsors a Visitor.
Escort: A Forensic Laboratory employee who accompanies a Visitor during their time on Forensic Laboratory premises.

SCOPE

This policy applies to all Forensic Laboratory premises, including the Server Room and DR site.

AUDIENCE

This policy applies to all Forensic Laboratory employees.

POLICY STATEMENTS

Access cards shall be granted to Forensic Laboratory employees according to their rights.

Access cards must not be shared between Forensic Laboratory employees.

Forensic Laboratory employees are not permitted in Forensic Laboratory premises outside the time permitted by their access cards.

Forensic Laboratory employees with personal offices must lock them when not in use.

All Forensic Laboratory employees must wear their access cards in a visible manner when on Forensic Laboratory premises.

Forensic Laboratory employees who forget their access cards must obtain a visitor badge for the day.

Forensic Laboratory employees who lose their access cards must report the loss to the Information Security Manager immediately on discovering their loss.

Access to the Server Room and DR site shall be restricted to named Forensic Laboratory employees and service engineers with a justified "need to access," and authorized by the IT Manager or his nominated alternate.

Emergency "out of hours" access for Forensic Laboratory employees will only be granted as an exception and subject to next day review by the employee's Line Manager

All visitors must be authorized in advance of their visit and authenticated on arrival.

All visitors must be accompanied at all times by their Escort till they leave Forensic Laboratory premises.

All visitors must clearly display their visitor badges while on site at all times.

All access to Forensic Laboratory premises shall be logged and regularly reviewed.

RESPONSIBILITIES

The following responsibilities are defined in this policy:

- **Host**: to ensure that a visitor is preauthorized for their visit.
- **Escort**: to accompany a visitor at all times and ensure that he/she sign out and leave Forensic Laboratory premises.
- **IT Manager (or alternate)**: to authorize access to the Server Room or DR site.
- **Employees**: to comply with this policy and report any breaches of it to the Information Security Manager.

- **Information Security Manager**: to manage the access control system, review access, and take action on being advised of any breach of this policy.

ENFORCEMENT, MONITORING, AND BREACHES

All Forensic Laboratory employees are responsible for monitoring and enforcing this policy.

Breaches of this policy by Forensic Laboratory employees will be dealt with under the Disciplinary rules. Visitors breaching this policy will have appropriate action taken.

OWNERSHIP

This policy is owned by the Information Security Manager.

REVIEW AND MAINTENANCE

The policy shall be effective from the date of approval and shall be reviewed at least annually, after any significant breach or on influencing change.

APPROVAL

This policy has been approved by the Forensic Laboratory management.

Chapter 3

Setting up the Forensic Laboratory

Table of Contents

3.1 SETTING UP THE FORENSIC LABORATORY

This chapter is the summary of many small elements, each of which gives guidance on areas that will need to be considered from the planning stage onward. All of the elements discussed below will need to be addressed both for good management and for preparation for accreditation and certification for the Forensic Laboratory.

When initially setting up the Forensic Laboratory, there are a number of issues that will need to be considered. Many of these have been touched on in the previous chapters, and some are expanded here, others have dedicated chapters later in the book. Once the business case (or the equivalent if in government or law enforcement) has been developed, a range of issues will need to be addressed and these must be documented to describe the fundamental basis on which the Forensic Laboratory is being established and on which it will be run. The first issue that should be clearly documented is that of the Forensic Laboratory's Terms of Reference (ToR). There will also normally be a ToR for the project to develop and deliver to the Forensic Laboratory, but the concepts that are given below hold good for both cases.

3.1.1 Forensic Laboratory Terms of Reference

The ToR is the document that serves as the basis of the relationship between the owning organization of the Forensic Laboratory and the team responsible for carrying out the work. It describes the purpose and structure of the Forensic Laboratory and shows how the scope of the Forensic Laboratory will be defined and verified. It will also provide the yardstick against which the success of the Forensic Laboratory will be measured. It provides a documented basis for future decisions and for a common understanding of the scope among the stakeholders.

The ToR sets out a clear path for the operation of the Forensic Laboratory by stating what needs to be achieved, by whom and when. It identifies the set of deliverables that satisfy the requirements and the scope and any constraints should be set out in this document. The ToR for the operation of the Forensic Laboratory should be created during the earliest stages of the project for the establishment of the Forensic Laboratory immediately after the business case has been approved. Once the ToR has been approved, there is a clear definition of the scope of the Forensic Laboratory.

The ToR will also identify the success factors, risks, and boundaries. The ToR needs to be written in some detail and should include the following:

- vision;
- scope and objectives;
- deliverables;
- boundaries, risks, and limitations;
- roles, responsibilities, authority, accountability, and reporting requirements;
- stakeholders;
- the regulatory framework;
- resources available;
- work breakdown structure and schedule;
- success factors;
- intervention strategies.

A description of the ToR is given in Appendix 1.

Once the ToR has been developed, a range of other elements that outline how the Forensic Laboratory is structured and how it will operate need to be developed.

3.1.2 The Status of the Forensic Laboratory

There should be clear statement of the status of the Forensics Laboratory. This should define the ownership, the services that it will offer, the structure of the laboratory, the standards that it will work to, and the expected customers. This should be prepared in some detail as it will be the foundation for future decisions.

3.1.3 The Forensic Laboratory Principles

The Forensic Laboratory shall be run in accordance with the following laboratory principles:

3.1.3.1 Responsibilities

The Forensic Laboratory relies upon the Laboratory Manager to develop and maintain an efficient, high-quality forensic laboratory.

The Laboratory Manager holds a unique role in the balance of scientific principles, requirements of the Criminal Justice System, and the effects on the lives of individuals that may be subject of an investigation that relies on digital forensic evidence. The decisions and judgments that are made in the Forensic Laboratory must fairly represent all interests with which they have been entrusted.

Users of the Forensic Laboratory services must be able to rely on the reputation of the Forensic Laboratory, the abilities of their Forensic Analysts, and the standards of the profession.

3.1.3.2 Integrity

The Forensic Team must be honest and truthful with their peers, supervisors, and subordinates. They must also be trustworthy and honest when representing the Forensic Laboratory to outside organizations.

3.1.3.3 Quality

The Forensic Team is responsible for implementing quality assurance procedures which effectively monitor and verify the quality of the work product of their laboratories.

The Forensic Laboratory complies with the requirements of ISO 9001 and ISO 17025.

3.1.3.4 Efficiency

The Forensic Team should ensure that the Forensic Laboratory's products and services are provided in a manner which maximizes organizational efficiency and ensures an economical expenditure of resources and personnel.

3.1.3.5 Productivity

The Laboratory Manager should establish reasonable goals for the production of forensic casework in a timely fashion. Highest priority should be given to cases which have a potentially productive outcome and which could, if successfully concluded, have an effective impact on the enforcement or adjudication process.

3.1.3.6 Meet Organizational Expectations

The Laboratory Manager must implement and enforce the relevant organizational policies and procedures and should establish additional internal procedures designed to meet the ever-changing needs of forensic case processing.

3.1.3.7 Health and Safety

The Laboratory Manager shall be responsible for planning and maintaining systems that reasonably assure safety in the Laboratory as well as when the Forensics Team are in the field. Such systems should include mechanisms for input by the Forensic Team, maintenance of records of injuries, and routine safety inspections as defined by existing Health and Safety procedures.

The Forensic Laboratory complies with the requirements of OHSAS 18001.

3.1.3.8 Information Security

The Laboratory Manager shall be responsible for planning and maintaining the security of the Forensic Laboratory. Security measures should include control of access both during and after normal business hours.

The Forensic Laboratory complies with the requirements of ISO 27001.

3.1.3.9 Management Information Systems

The Laboratory Manager shall be responsible for developing management information systems. These systems should provide information in a timely manner regarding current and past work carried out by the Forensic Laboratory.

3.1.3.10 Qualifications

The Laboratory Manager must hire employees of sufficient academic qualifications or experience to provide them with the fundamental scientific principles for work in the Forensic Laboratory and must be assured that they are honest, forthright, and ethical in their personal and professional life.

3.1.3.11 Training

The Laboratory Manager shall provide training in the principles and the details of forensic science as it applies to the Forensic Laboratory requirements.

Training must include handling and preserving the integrity of physical evidence. Before analysis and casework are performed, specific training for the processes and procedures as well as for the specific tools to be utilized must be undertaken. A full training program for all Forensic Analysts and Investigators must be developed.

3.1.3.12 Maintaining Employee Competency

The Laboratory Manager must monitor the skills and proficiency of the Forensic Analysts on a continuing basis as well as on an annual basis as required by Human Resources procedures. The Forensic Laboratory has an ongoing program of training, awareness, and competency.

3.1.3.13 Employee Development

The Laboratory Manager must foster the development of the Forensic Analysts and Investigators for greater job responsibility by supporting internal and external training, providing sufficient library resources to permit the Forensic Analysts and Investigators to keep abreast of changing and emerging trends in forensic science, and encouraging them to do so. The Forensic Laboratory has an ongoing program of training, awareness, and competency.

3.1.3.14 Environment

The Laboratory Manager must ensure that a safe and functional work environment is provided with adequate space to support all the work activities required by the Forensic Laboratory. Facilities must be adequate so that evidence under the control of the Forensic Laboratory is protected from contamination, tampering, or theft.

3.1.3.15 Supervision

The Laboratory Manager must provide the Forensic Analysts and Investigators with adequate supervisory review to ensure the quality of their work product. The Laboratory Manager must be held accountable for the performance of the Forensic Analysts and Investigators and the enforcement of clear and enforceable processes and procedures.

The Forensic Analysts and Investigators should be held to realistic performance goals which take into account reasonable workload standards.

The Laboratory Manager must ensure that the Forensic Analysts and Investigators are not unduly pressured to perform substandard work through case load pressure or unnecessary outside influence. The Forensic Laboratory shall have in place a performance evaluation process.

3.1.3.16 Conflicts of Interest

The Laboratory Manager, the Forensic Analysts, and the Investigators must avoid any activity, interest, or association that interferes or appears to interfere with their independent exercise of professional judgment.

The Forensic Laboratory Conflict of Interest Policy is given in Appendix 3.

3.1.3.17 Legal Compliance

The Laboratory Manager shall establish and publish, with appropriate training, operational procedures in order to meet good procedural, legislative, and good practice requirements.

3.1.3.18 Accountability

The Laboratory Manager and the Lead Forensic Analyst must be accountable for their decisions and actions.

These decisions and actions should be supported by appropriate documentation and be open to legitimate scrutiny.

3.1.3.19 Disclosure and Discovery

The Forensic Laboratory records must be open for reasonable access when legitimate requests are made by Officers of the Court or other legitimate requesters.

Specific requirements are necessary for the release of unlawful material.

3.1.3.20 Work Quality

The Laboratory Manager must establish a quality assurance program.

The Forensic Analysts and Investigators must accept responsibility for evidence integrity and security; validated, reliable methods; and casework documentation and reporting.

The Forensic Laboratory complies with the requirements of ISO 9001 and ISO 17025.

3.1.3.21 Accreditation and Certification

The Laboratory Manager shall achieve and maintain whichever certifications and accreditation that the Top Management deem necessary.

3.1.3.22 Membership of Appropriate Organizations

The Laboratory Manager shall ensure that the Forensic Team joins appropriate professional organizations and that they are encouraged to obtain the highest professional membership grade possible.

3.1.3.23 Obtain Appropriate Personal Certifications

The Laboratory Manager shall ensure that the Forensic Team achieves appropriate certifications of both generic and tool-specific types to demonstrate their skill levels.

3.1.4 Laboratory Service Level Agreements

A Service Level Agreement (SLA) is a part of a service contract where the level of service that will be provided by the digital forensics laboratory is formally defined. The SLA is sometimes used to refer to the contracted delivery time for the services offered by the Forensic Laboratory (usually called the "Turn Round Time") or the quality of the work. The SLA should be considered from the start of the planning and development process to ensure that the Forensic Laboratory will be structured to the appropriate level. Service providers normally include SLAs within the terms of their contracts with customers to define the level of service that is being provided in plain language using easily understood terms. Any metrics included in a SLA must be measurable and should be tested on a regular basis. The SLA will also normally outline the remedial action and any penalties that will take effect if the delivered service falls below the defined standard. The SLA forms an essential element of the legal contract between the Forensic Laboratory and the customer. The actual structure of the SLA will be dependent on the services offered by the Forensic Laboratory, but the general structure of the agreement is as follows:

- contract;
- amendments;
- service description;
- service availability;
- reliability;
- customer support;
- service performance;
- change management procedures;
- security;
- service reviews;
- glossary;
- amendment sheet.

If the Forensic Laboratory takes services from either an external supplier (e.g., Internet Access or utility supplier) or from the owning organization (e.g., human resources or logistics), then suitable SLAs will need to be agreed with the service provider.

3.1.5 Impartiality and Independence

In order to obtain and retain accreditation to ISO 17025 (general requirements for the competence of testing and calibration laboratories), there is a requirement for the Forensic Laboratory to be able to show evidence that its work and results are "free from undue influence or pressure from customers or other interested parties" and that "laboratories working within larger organizations where influence could be applied (such as police laboratories), are free from such influence and are producing objective and valid results."[a]

3.1.6 Codes of Practice and Conduct

In the United Kingdom, the Forensic Regulator has produced Codes of Practice and Conduct for forensic science

a. UK House of Commons, Publications on Science and Technology, http://www.publications.parliament.uk/pa/cm201012/cmselect/cmsctech/855/85506.htm#n129.

providers and practitioners in the Criminal Justice System. These Codes of Practice and Conduct were the first stage in the development of a single quality standards framework for forensic science for use in the Criminal Justice System to replace the *ad hoc* approach to standards that had been used in the past. These Codes of Practice and Conduct were built on the internationally recognized good practice of ISO 17025 as the preferred standard for forensic science laboratories.

An appendix to these Codes of Practice and Conduct provides guidance to deal with the specific requirements for the providers of forensic science services at scenes of incidents based on ISO 17020 (general criteria for the operation of various types of bodies performing inspection). This standard for inspection bodies is gradually being adopted across Europe as the most appropriate standard for crime scene investigations.

The requirements that are described in the Codes of Practice and Conduct and the associated appendices are targeted at three levels:

- the organization: to outline what is required of it, particularly from the management, with regard to quality assurance and compliance. Most forensic services are supplied by people working in organizations and the organizational culture with regard to quality is a major factor. Accountability for quality rests with the management, and each organization is required to nominate a senior manager as the "accountable person";
- the practitioner: to outline the professional standards to which they are expected to perform; and
- the scientific methodology: to ensure that the methodology is robust and will reliably produce, and continue to produce, valid results.

These Codes of Practice and Conduct were developed so that they can be applied to all organizations and practitioners whose primary role is the provision of forensic services into the Criminal Justice System in England and Wales. While these Codes of Practice and Conduct were designed for the UK community, they are based on sound principles and international standards, are a good guideline and a basis for codes of practice for other regions, and have been adopted by the Forensic Laboratory.

3.1.7 Quality Standards

Quality standards in forensic science are essential to ensure that the highest possible standards are maintained by the Forensic Laboratory as a supplier of forensic services. This should include resourcing, training, equipment, processes, and integrity benchmarks such as accreditation. Unless these standards are maintained, there is an increased possibility that those guilty of crimes may not be brought to justice or that those who are innocent may be convicted. Quality standards in forensic science are best attained through accreditation to the international standard ISO 17025, which builds on the older ISO 9001 standard. However, on its own, ISO 17025 will not guarantee quality, as it does not cover areas like setting of the Forensic Laboratory strategy for a case, or the interpretation of the results, or the presentation of the evidence in the Court. A cross reference between ISO 9001 and ISO 17025 is given in Appendix 2. This clearly shows a close correlation, but ISO 17025 has more technical competences in it than ISO 9001.

3.1.8 Objectivity

A professional Forensic Analyst or Investigator, when providing any service, must determine whether there are any threats to compliance with the fundamental principle of objectivity. These threats will normally result from the Forensic Analyst, Investigator (or the Forensic Laboratory itself) having interests in, or a relationship with any member of the Client organization. An example of a familiarity threat to objectivity could be created from a family or close personal or business relationship. Independence of thought is necessary to enable the professional Analyst or Investigator to express a conclusion, without bias, conflict of interest, or undue influence from others.

The existence of threats to objectivity when providing any professional service will depend upon the specific circumstances of the engagement and the nature of the work. A professional Forensic Analyst or Investigator must evaluate the significance of any threats and, when necessary, ensure that suitable measures are taken to eliminate threats or reduce them to an acceptable level. Examples of the types of measures that may be considered include the following:

- advising the management of the Forensic Laboratory of the potential threat;
- the Forensic Analyst or Investigator removing themselves from the case;
- the Forensic Laboratory having in place suitable peer review and supervisory procedures;
- terminating the relationship that gives rise to the threat.

If the measures that have been put in place to eliminate or reduce threats to an acceptable level are not effective, the Forensic Laboratory management must either decline or terminate the contract with the customer. The Forensic Laboratory Conflict of Interest Policy is given in Appendix 3.

3.1.9 Management Requirements

There are many ways in which management requirements can be expressed. The Forensic Laboratory has implemented an Integrated Management System (IMS) based on the Publicly Available Specification 99 (PAS 99). Full details of the IMS are given in Chapter 4.

This has allowed the Forensic Laboratory to implement the following ISO standards:

- ISO 15489—Information and documentation—Records management;
- ISO 17020—Conformity assessment—Requirements for the operation of various types of bodies performing inspection;
- ISO 17025—General requirements for the competence of testing and calibration laboratories;
- ISO 22301—Societal security—Business continuity management systems;
- ISO 27001—Information technology—Security techniques—Information security management systems—Requirements;
- ISO 9001—Quality management systems—Requirements;
- OHSAS 18001—Occupational Health and Safety Management Systems;
- In-house digital forensic procedures.

3.1.10 Forensic Laboratory Policies

In order to assure the integrity of their results, the Forensic Laboratory must have appropriate policies in place. The implementation of these policies will be in the form of practices and procedures that define how the Forensic Laboratory will operate to meet the relevant good practice and forensic science and quality standards. The constant developments in technology mean that there is an ongoing need to update the policies in order to meet changing laws and regulations in order to prevent unfairness and wrongful conviction. The Forensic Laboratory policies must ensure the integrity of any results produced.

The main purpose of policies within the Forensic Laboratory is to assure the integrity of results and to prevent miscarriages of justice. There are many examples of mistakes within laboratories. One example is the analysis of the data in the Casey Anthony trial in July 2011, when the number of times that she had accessed the internet to search for the word "Chloroform" was initially reported as 84 times but was later found to be only one time.[b,c] Another example is the CD Universe case where the evidence was compromised because the chain of custody was not properly established.[d] Policies are also necessary to ensure that the employees within the Forensic Laboratory receive and are able to maintain a suitable level of training and certification, and they should also address funding levels and the policy on investigation of allegations of misconduct or negligence. The policies should also contain sections on the code of ethics and the relevant standards and regulations.

b. Forensic Data Recovery, Digital Evidence Discrepancies—Casey Anthony Trial, July 11, 2011, http://wordpress.bladeforensics.com/?p=357.

c. The State v. Casey Anthony: Analysis of Evidence from the Case, July 18, 2011, http://statevcasey.wordpress.com/tag/digital-forensics/.

d. CD Universe evidence compromised, http://www.zdnet.com/news/cd-universe-evidence-compromised/96132.

3.1.11 Documentation Requirements

The relevant standards implemented within the Forensic Laboratory will dictate much of the required documentation for everyday operations. Documented procedures are included in the relevant chapters in this book.

3.1.12 Competence, Awareness, and Training

All management standards have requirements for competence, awareness, and training. All Forensic Laboratory employees must also be aware of client requirements and the relevance of their activities. They should understand how their actions contribute to achieving the Forensic Laboratory's Quality Policy and objectives. This is normally achieved by awareness training, performance reviews, and employee participation in internal audit processes. Top Management should define the necessary skills, experience, and training required for each role and identify the records of education, training, skills, and experience that need to be maintained. The Forensic Laboratory Quality Policy is given in Appendix 4.

3.1.13 Planning

There are a number of actions that need to be taken throughout the planning process. These include the following:

3.1.13.1 Risk Assessment and Management

A fundamental element of the planning process is the Risk Assessment. The objective of the Risk Assessment is to discover and document the current risks and threats to the business and to identify and implement measures to mitigate or reduce the risks that carry the highest probability of occurring or the highest impact. This Risk Assessment document should give guidance on how to conduct the Risk Assessment and also how to evaluate and analyze the information that is collected. It should also contain guidance for the organization on how to implement strategies to manage the potential risks.

Risk Management in the Forensic Laboratory is covered in Chapter 5.

3.1.13.2 Business Impact Analysis

The Risk Assessment is only one part of an overall Business Assessment. The Business Assessment is divided into two parts, the Risk Assessment and a Business Impact Analysis (BIA). The Risk Assessment is intended to measure the present risks and vulnerabilities to the business's environment, while the BIA evaluates the probable losses that could occur as a result of an incident. To maximize the value of a Risk Assessment, a BIA should also be completed. A BIA is an essential element of an organization's business continuity plan. The BIA should include an assessment of any vulnerabilities and plans for the development of strategies to minimize risk. The BIA describes the potential risks to the organization studied and should identify the interdependencies between the different parts of the organization and which are the critical elements. For example, the Forensic Laboratory may be able to continue to operate more or less normally if the plumbing system failed but would not be able to function if the network failed.

As part of a business continuity plan, the BIA should identify the probable costs associated with failures, such as loss of cash flow, cost of facility repair, cost of equipment replacement, overtime payments to address the backlog of work, loss of profits, etc. A BIA report should quantify the importance of the individual elements of the Forensic Laboratory and suggest appropriate levels of funding for measures to protect them. Potential failures should be assessed in terms of the financial cost and the impact on legal compliance, quality assurance, and safety. Business Continuity is covered in Chapter 13.

3.1.13.3 Legal and Regulatory Considerations

The investigation of crimes involving digital media and the examination of that digital media in most countries are covered by both national and international legislation. In criminal investigations, national laws normally restrict how much information can be seized and under what circumstances it can be seized. For example, in the United Kingdom, the seizure of evidence by law enforcement officers is governed by the Police and Criminal Evidence Act (1984) and the Regulation of Investigatory Powers Act (2000) (RIPA). The Computer Misuse Act (1990) provides legislation regarding unauthorized access to computer material, and this can affect the Investigator as well as the criminal and is a particular concern for civil investigators who have more limitations on what they are allowed to do than law enforcement officers.

In the United States, one of the pieces of legislation that the investigator must be aware of is the rights of the individual under the Fourth Amendment, which limits the ability of government agents to search for and seize evidence without a warrant. The Fourth Amendment states:

"The right of the people to be secure in their persons, houses, papers, and effects, against unreasonable searches and seizures, shall not be violated, and no Warrants shall issue, but upon probable cause, supported by Oath or affirmation, and particularly describing the place to be searched, and the persons or things to be seized."

According to OLE,[e] the Supreme Court stated that a "seizure of property occurs when there is some meaningful interference with an individual's possessory interests in that property," *United States v. Jacobsen*, 466 U.S. 109, 113 (1984), and the Court has also characterized the interception of intangible communications as a seizure. *See Berger v. New York*, 388 U.S. 41, 59–60 (1967). Furthermore, the Court has held that a "search occurs when an expectation of privacy that society is prepared to consider reasonable is infringed." *Jacobsen*, 466 U.S. at 113.

OLE goes on to state that "A search is constitutional if it does not violate a person's 'reasonable' or 'legitimate' expectation of privacy. *Katz v. United States*, 389 U.S. 347, 361 (1967) (Harlan, J., concurring)."

Another piece of legislation in the United States is the Patriot Act, which provides law enforcement agents with an increased ability to use surveillance tools such as roving wiretaps. The Patriot Act introduced important changes that have increased the prosecutorial power in fighting computer crimes. The Patriot Act references the Computer Fraud and Abuse Act (18 U.S.C. § 1030) with both procedural and substantive changes. There were also changes to make it easier for law enforcement to investigate computer crimes.

Also relevant piece of legislation in the United States is with regard to border searches. According to the Supreme Court, routine searches at the border do not require a warrant, probable cause, or even reasonable suspicion that the search may uncover contraband or evidence.

Similar to the UK's RIPA, since 1968, in the United States, the Wiretap Statute (Title III), 18 U.S.C. §§ 2510–2522 has been the statutory framework used to control the real-time electronic surveillance of communications. When law enforcement officers want to place a wiretap on a suspect's phone or monitor a hacker breaking into a computer system, they have to do so in compliance with the requirements of Title III. The statute prohibits the use of electronic, mechanical, or other devices to intercept a private wire, an oral, or electronic communication between two parties unless one of a number of statutory exceptions applies. Title III basically prohibits eavesdropping (subject to certain exceptions and interstate requirements) by anyone, everywhere in the United States.

---

e. Hagen E., Searching and Seizing Computers and Obtaining Electronic Evidence in Criminal Investigations Computer Crime and Intellectual Property Section Criminal Division Published by Office of Legal Education, Executive Office for United States Attorneys.

In the United States, the Electronic Communications Privacy Act (ECPA) places limitations on the ability of Investigators to intercept and access potential evidence. In Europe, Article 5 of the European Convention on Human Rights gives similar privacy limitations to the ECPA and limits the processing and sharing of personal data both within the EU and with other countries outside the EU.

The Convention on Cybercrime (ETS No. 185), also known as the Budapest Convention on Cybercrime, is an international treaty that was created to try to address the harmonization of national laws relating to computer crime and Internet crimes in order to improve the investigative techniques and increase cooperation between nations. The Convention was adopted by the Committee of Ministers of the Council of Europe on November 8, 2001 and was opened for signature in Budapest, later that month. The convention entered into force on July 1, 2004 and by the end of 2010, 30 states had signed, ratified, and acceded to the convention. These included Canada, Japan, the United States, and the Republic of South Africa. A further 16 countries have also signed the convention but not yet ratified it. The Convention is the only binding international instrument dealing with cybercrime.

The "International Organization on Computer Evidence" is an organization that was established in 1999 and has been working to establish compatible international standards for the seizure of evidence to guarantee the ability to use digital evidence collected by one state in the Courts of another state.

In civil investigations, the relevant laws of many countries restrict the actions that the Investigator can undertake in an examination. Regulations that are in place with regard to network monitoring and the accessing of personal communications or data stored in the network exist in many countries, and the rights of an individual to privacy is still an area which is still subject to decisions in the Courts.

This is intended only to highlight the range of laws and regulations that the Investigator will need to be aware of and that the Forensics Laboratory will need to ensure that have been taken into account when developing the guidelines for operational processes and procedures.

3.1.14 Insurance

The Forensic Laboratory must regularly review its insurance coverage to ensure that it is appropriate for the types of insurance required in the jurisdiction and at a level commensurate with the business undertaken, specific contractual requirements, and the number of employees.

3.1.15 Contingency Planning

This is activity that is undertaken to ensure that suitable and immediate steps can be taken by management and staff in the event of an emergency. The main objectives of contingency planning are to ensure the containment of the incident and to limit any damage or injury or loss and to ensure the continuity of the key operations of the organization. The contingency plan identifies the immediate actions that should be taken and also the longer-term measures for responding to incidents. The process of developing the contingency plan involves the identification of critical resources and functions and the establishment of a recovery plan that is based on the length of time that the enterprise can operate without specific functions. The plan will be a "living document" and will need to be continuously updated to keep pace with changes in regulations, the environment, and the work taking place within the Forensic Laboratory. The contingency plan will need to be documented in straightforward terms and tested at regular intervals to ensure that it is effective and that all of the parties involved understand their roles and responsibilities. Contingency plans are part of business continuity planning. Business Continuity is covered in Chapter 13.

3.1.16 Roles and Responsibilities

The roles of all Forensic Laboratory employees must be defined together with the responsibilities that are related to that role. Specific job roles are given in the relevant chapters relating to the implemented management systems.

3.1.17 Business Objectives

It is common for business objectives to be set in financial terms; however, not all objectives have to be expressed in these terms. Ideally objectives should adhere to the SMART acronym, which describes five characteristics:

- S—Specific;
- M—Measurable;
- A—Achievable;
- R—Realistic;
- T—Time Bound.

Objectives could include the following:

- desired throughput and profit levels;
- amount of income generated;
- value of the business or dividends paid to shareholders;
- quality of customer service;
- innovation.

3.1.18 Laboratory Accreditation and Certification

Accreditation is something that the Forensic Laboratory will normally aspire to achieve at the earliest opportunity. The most widely recognized accreditation is ISO17025. Once accreditation has been achieved, the activities of the Forensic Laboratory will be monitored on a periodic basis by the relevant accreditation body. Once it has been achieved, the Forensic Laboratory must comply with specific criteria relating to the laboratory's management and operations, personnel, and physical plant in order to maintain its accreditation. The criteria and standards address the areas of laboratory administrative practices, procedures, training, evidence handling, quality control, analysis protocols, testimony, proficiency testing, personnel qualifications, space allocation, security, and a number of other topics. The issue of laboratory accreditation and certification is dealt with in much greater detail in Chapter 19.

3.1.19 Policies

The Forensic Laboratory has developed policies that contain clear statements covering all of the major forensic issues, including subcontracting; contacting law enforcement; carrying out monitoring; and conducting regular reviews of forensic policies, guidelines, and procedures. At the top level, the Forensic Laboratory's policies must only allow authorized personnel to carry out their tasks which may include monitoring systems and networks and performing investigations. The Forensic Laboratory may also need a separate policy to cover incident handlers and other forensic roles. There is a requirement for the policies to be reviewed and updated at frequent intervals because of changes in technology or changes to laws and regulations, as well as to take account of new court rulings. The Forensic Laboratory case handling policies must also be consistent with other policies, including policies related to privacy.

3.1.20 Guidelines and Procedures

The Forensic Laboratory has developed and maintains guidelines and procedures for carrying out all tasks relating to processing forensic cases and management systems. These shall be based on the parent organizations policies (if there is a parent organization), consistent with them and all applicable laws. The Forensic Laboratory's forensic guidelines shall include general guidelines for investigations and shall also include step-by-step procedures for performing the routine tasks, such as the imaging of a hard disk or the capturing of volatile data from live systems.

The reason for developing these guidelines and procedures is that they will help to ensure that there is consistency in the way in which material is processed. This will lead to good practices and a consistent approach to tasks within the Forensic Laboratory and will ensure that the cases are all processed to the same standard whether it is anticipated that they will go to the Court or not. It will also ensure that evidence collected, for example, for a case that starts off as an internal disciplinary action into computer misuse, can be used if it discovered that there was a more serious crime that may lead to a prosecution. By using guidelines and policies to ensure consistency, the integrity of any data that is used or results that are created can be demonstrated. The guidelines and procedures will support the admissibility of any evidence produced in the laboratory into legal proceedings.

If tasks are outsourced to external third parties, the way in which the Forensic Laboratory engages with the third party and the way in which they are engaged and the material that is provided to them and recovered from them shall be described in the guidelines and policies. Normally, when a third party carries out work in behalf of the Forensic Laboratory, the contract with the third party will require that they adhere to the Forensic Laboratory's handling and processing standards.

The process of outsourcing is covered in Chapter 14.

Once the guidelines and procedures have been developed, it is important that they are regularly reviewed and maintained so that they remain accurate and represent the current laws, technology, and good practice. The frequency with which they are reviewed and updated will be determined by Top Management and should be regular but may also be influenced by changes in the relevant laws or technologies.

APPENDIX 1 - THE FORENSIC LABORATORY TOR

THE VISION

A short statement, normally of one or two paragraphs, which explains the mandate given to the team and defines the reason for the Forensic Laboratory's creation and its purpose.

SCOPE AND OBJECTIVES

It is essential to define the scope of the work that is to be conducted by the Forensic Laboratory. The ToR should specify the work to be undertaken and the types of deliverables from this work. It should also give timescales for the production of deliverables.

DELIVERABLES

The deliverables of the Forensic Laboratory should be defined. This should not only include the outcome of the investigations but also the internal deliverables such as accounts, audits, and test results and reports.

BOUNDARIES, RISKS, AND LIMITATIONS

This section describes where the process/system/operation of the Forensic Laboratory starts and ends. A statement of the authority delegated to the Forensic Laboratory to implement change and any powers given to it should be included. It is in this section that the systems, policies, procedures, relevant legislation, etc., should be mentioned. The risks should also be detailed.

ROLES, RESPONSIBILITIES, AUTHORITY, ACCOUNTABILITY, AND REPORTING REQUIREMENTS

The Forensic Laboratory policy should clearly define the roles and responsibilities of all people working within the Forensic Laboratory. It shall detail the roles, responsibilities, and functions of each employee and clearly define the authority that is associated with each of the roles. It should also define the accountability associated with each of the roles and the reporting requirements for each role and task. It shall include the actions to be performed during both routine work activities and an incident. The policy shall clearly indicate who is responsible for, and authorized to contact which internal teams and external organizations and under what circumstances.

STAKEHOLDERS

It is important to identify the main stakeholders and their interests, roles, and responsibilities. The stakeholders will include the representatives of the owning organization, Forensic Laboratory employees, Clients and may extend to other parties who have an interest in the efficient running of the Forensic Laboratory.

REGULATORY FRAMEWORK

The legal, institutional, and contractual framework for the operation of the Forensic Laboratory needs to be stated. This should include regulations of regional bodies such as the European Union, Federal (National), State (Provincial), or Municipal Governments, and any legislation or policies and practices that pertain to parent corporations, partnerships, etc.

RESOURCES

The resources identified should include real estate, employees, equipment, and support services. The elements that need to be considered will include the following:

- administrative support;
- available budget;
- employees;
- materials and supplies;
- other supporting functions (e.g., security);
- resources available and how they are to be accessed;
- information processing equipment (business and forensic);
- training requirements and how this will be provided.

WORK BREAKDOWN STRUCTURE AND SCHEDULE

The work breakdown structure is a list of tasks that require action. When the individual tasks are considered together with relevant dependencies and timelines are introduced, then the schedule is created. The work that is to be undertaken by the Forensic Laboratory is broken down into smaller and smaller tasks that eventually become the work breakdown structure. Additional details of task durations and dependencies will be required to aid in the building of the schedule.

SUCCESS FACTORS

Success Factors (SFs), also sometimes referred to as Critical Success Factors, are the measure of those factors or activities required for ensuring the success of the Forensic Laboratory. They are used to identify a small number of key factors that the Forensic Laboratory will need to focus on to be successful. SFs are important as they are things that are capable of being measured and because of this they get done more often than things that are not measured. Each SF should be measurable and associated with a target goal. Primary measures that should be included are aspects such as success levels for areas such as the number of jobs processed in the month and number of hours spent on each task. SFs should be identified for any of the aspects of the business that are identified as vital for defined targets to be reached and maintained. SFs are normally identified in such areas as laboratory processes, staff and organization skills, tools, techniques, and technologies. SFs will inevitably change over time as the business undertaken by the laboratory changes.

INTERVENTION STRATEGIES

These should cover the contingency plans for any emergency and should define what constitutes an emergency.

APPENDIX 2 - CROSS REFERENCE BETWEEN ISO 9001 AND ISO 17025

ISO 9001	ISO 17025
Clause 1	Clause 1
Clause 2	Clause 2
Clause 3	Clause 3
4.1	4.1, 4.1.1, 4.1.2, 4.1.3, 4.1.4, 4.1.5, 4.2, 4.2.1, 4.2.2, 4.2.3, 4.2.4
4.2 1	4.2.2, 4.2.3, 4.3.1
4.2.2	4.2.2, 4.2.3, 4.2.4
4.2.3	4.3
4.2.4	4.3.1, 4.12
5.1	4.2.2, 4.2.3
5.1 a)	4.1.2, 4.1.6
5.1 b)	4.2.2
5.1 c)	4.2.2
5.1 d)	4.15
5.1 e)	4.1.5
5.2	4.4.1
5.3	4.2.2
5.3 a)	4.2.2
5.3 b)	4.2.3
5.3 c)	4.2.2
5.3 d)	4.2.2
5.3 e)	4.2.2
5.4.1	4.2.2 c)
5.4.2	4.2.1
5.4.2 a)	4.2.1
5.4.2 b)	4.2.1
5.5.1	4.1.5 a), 4.1.5 f), 4.1.5 h)
5.5.2	4.1.5 i)
5.5.2 a)	4.1.5 i)
5.5.2 b)	4.11.1
5.5.2 c)	4.2.4
5.5.3	4.1.6
5.6.1	4.15
5.6.2	4.15
5.6.3	4.15
6.1 a)	4.10
6.1 b)	4.4.1, 4.7, 5.4.2, 5.4.3, 5.4.4, 5.10.1

Continued

ISO 9001	ISO 17025
6.2.1	5.2.1
6.2.2 a)	5.2.2, 5.5.3
6.2.2 b)	5.2.1, 5.2.2
6.2.2 c)	5.2.2
6.2.2 d)	4.1.5 k)
6.2.2 e)	5.2.5
6.3.1 a)	4.1.3, 4.12.1.2, 4.12.1.3, 5.3
6.3.1 b)	4.12.1.4, 5.4.7.2, 5.5, 5.6
6.3.1 c)	4.6, 5.5.6, 5.6.3.4, 5.8, 5.10
6.4	5.3.1, 5.3.2, 5.3.3, 5.3.4, 5.3.5
7.1	5.1
7.1 a)	4.2.2
7.1 b)	4.1.5 a), 4.2.1, 4.2.3
7.1 c)	5.4, 5.9
7.1 d)	4.1, 5.4, 5.9
7.2.1	4.4.1, 4.4.2, 4.4.3, 4.4.4, 4.4.5, 5.4, 5.9, 5.10
7.2.2	4.4.1, 4.4.2, 4.4.3, 4.4.4, 4.4.5, 5.4, 5.9, 5.10
7.2.3	4.4.2, 4.4.4, 4.5, 4.7, 4.8
7.3	5, 5.4, 5.9
7.4.1	4.6.1, 4.6.2, 4.6.4
7.4.2	4.6.3
7.4.3	4.6.2
7.5.1	5.1, 5.2, 5.4, 5.5, 5.6, 5.7, 5.8, 5.9
7.5.2	5.2.5, 5.4.2, 5.4.5
7.5.3	5.8.2
7.5.4	4.1.5 c), 5.8
7.5.5	4.6.1, 4.12, 5.8, 5.10
7.6	5.4, 5.5
8.1	4.10, 5.4, 5.9
8.2.1	4.10
8.2.2	4.11.5, 4.14
8.2.3	4.11.5, 4.14, 5.9
8.2.4	4.5, 4.6, 4.9, 5.5.2, 5.5.9, 5.8, 5.8.3, 5.8.4, 5.9
8.3	4.9
8.4	4.10, 5.9
8.5.1	4.10, 4.12
8.5.2	4.11, 4.12
8.5.3	4.9, 4.11, 4.12

APPENDIX 3 - CONFLICT OF INTEREST POLICY

This policy describes the Forensic Laboratory Conflict of Interest Policy for all work undertaken, including digital forensics, general management consultancy, and regulatory work.

There is no right or wrong approach to handling potential conflicts of interest. Ultimately, the issue is about the application of common sense within a legislative, regulatory, contractual, or ethical framework. The key principles to any effective policy are as follows:

- *Define a conflict of interest in relation to the Forensic Laboratory:* Would there have to be some personal financial or other interest for a Forensic Laboratory employee for a conflict of interest to be considered, or would historical connection to the beneficiary of a decision be sufficient to trigger the procedures;
- *Consider the future likelihood of such conflicts:* Is the conflict of interest likely to be exceptional in which case the employee's membership of the decision-making body is unproblematic, or would it be so frequent that it might be best to consider alternative membership of the council;
- *Agree the method of declaring an interest:* This may be a written declaration completed annually before undertaking a task (project, case, etc.) or may be prior to a meeting, etc.;
- *Agree the method of addressing the conflict:* Again, there are numerous ways of addressing a conflict of interest. The employee in question might absent themselves completely from all consideration or they may participate in the discussion but not the decision. Each case will be decided on the factors involved;

It is the Forensic Laboratory's policy to have an open, transparent, fair, objective, customer-focused, yet accountable process for any possible conflict of interest. The Forensic Laboratory owes contractual duties, as well as a duty of care, to all of its Clients, and this must be observed and complied with, as well as be seen to be observed and complied with;

The aim of this policy is to protect the Forensic Laboratory and all employees from the appearance of an impropriety;

At the start of any the Forensic Laboratory case or assignment, the employees involved must consider the scope of the assignment and consider if they have now, in the past, or in the foreseeable future, any possible conflicts of interest relating to the assignment. These may arise from such issues as:

- personal, or familial involvement, with someone who is involved in the management of the contract of the assignment;
- personal, or familial involvement, with someone who is the subject of a forensic case or assignment;
- a breach of the code of ethics of any professional organization of the organization that any employee on the case or assignment may belong to or be bound by;
- the offer (or acceptance) of any inducement; hospitality; or gift that may impair, limit the extent, rigor, or objectivity in the performance of the assignment, case, or project;
- having a financial interest in the outcome of the case or assignment;
- impaired decisions or actions that may not be in the best interest of the Forensic Laboratory's Client or the Court;
- a perception that the Forensic Laboratory or its employees are acting improperly because of a perceived conflict of interest.

Where a possible conflict is identified after the start of any assignment, it must be brought to the attention of the Laboratory Manager, who has accountability and responsibility for Compliance and Governance, as soon as is practicably possible, and within 24 hours at the maximum. As soon as the conflict is identified, the employee should excuse themselves from any decision taking until the conflict has been resolved. In some cases, it will be necessary for the employee to excuse themselves from any work on the case or assignment. This is specifically the case for forensic work and may be applicable in other assignments, as identified.

In some cases, a "Declaration of Interest Form" will be required to be executed before each assignment, and in other cases, an annual (or regular) declaration will be required.

Where a conflict is declared to the Laboratory Manager, they will take such action as they see fit to both declare and resolve the conflict. This may (and probably will) involve communication with the other parties in the case or assignment. All discussions and decisions shall be regarded as records and be retained and secured appropriately.

All possible or actual conflicts of interest shall be investigated thoroughly, quickly, impartially, and all relevant parties shall be advised of the outcome.

A review of all conflicts and possible conflicts is undertaken at Management Reviews.

This policy is issued and maintained by the Laboratory Manager, who also provides advice and guidance on its implementation and ensures compliance.

All the Forensic Laboratory employees shall comply with this policy.

APPENDIX 4 - QUALITY POLICY

The Forensic Laboratory is committed to good quality practice. The objective for all employees is to perform their activities in accordance with the Forensic Laboratory standards to ensure that all the products and services provided meet those standards and meet or preferably exceed the Client's expectations.

Management strives to underline this approach in all their day-to-day activities.

Quality at the Forensic Laboratory is measured by Key Performance Indicators (designated as Quality Objectives) which Top Management review and set each year to ensure that the Forensic Laboratory and its employees attain quality standards, and to ensure continuous improvement of the defined Quality Objectives.

Quality is the responsibility of all employees. Each employee shall ensure that they are familiar with those aspects of the Forensic Laboratory's policies and procedures that relate to their day-to-day work and understand how their contribution affects the Forensic Laboratory's products and services.

The Key Performance Indicators which define the Forensic Laboratory Quality Objectives are set out in Planning within the Business in Chapter 6, Section 6.2.2.1.

The scope of the Quality System implemented at the Forensic Laboratory is the whole of the digital forensics operations undertaken.

It is the Forensic Laboratory's policy to:

- only purchase from approved suppliers, who shall be regularly audited, this includes all outsourcing partners (Chapter 14);
- handle all Client feedback, including complaints, in an effective and efficient manner and use them as input to continuously improve the Forensic Laboratory's products and services (Chapter 6, Section 6.14);
- ensure that all agreed Client requirements are met;
- implement a process of continuous improvement (Chapter 4, Section 4.8 and Appendix 14);
- ensure that all employee training needs are identified at a Training Needs Analysis as part of the employee's annual appraisal process or as required (Chapter 4, Section 4.6.2 and Chapter 18, Section 18.2.2).

Where a Client requests that the Forensic Laboratory conform to their own Quality System, the Forensic Laboratory shall apply this system as described in Chapter 6.

This policy is issued and maintained by the Quality Manager who also provides advice and guidance on its implementation and ensures compliance.

All the Forensic Laboratory employees shall comply with this policy.

Chapter 4

The Forensic Laboratory Integrated Management System

Table of Contents

4.1 INTRODUCTION

In order to cohesively and consistently manage processes and procedures across the organization, the Forensic Laboratory has implemented an Integrated Management System (IMS) based on PAS 99. PAS 99 is the world's first IMS requirements specification based on the six common requirements of ISO Guide 72, which is a standard for writing management system standards. This approach gives one holistic approach to manage all processes and procedures within the Forensic Laboratory in a single cohesive system and ensures continuous improvement, while eliminating duplication and increasing efficiently.

The common requirements in ISO Guide 72 are:

- policy;
- planning;
- implementation and operation;
- performance assessment;
- improvement;
- Management Review.

This process is effectively the J. Edwards Deming or PDCA cycle, and the mapping of ISO Guide 72 to PAS 99 is given in Appendix 1.

While PAS 99 was originally developed to integrate ISO type Management Systems such as

- ISO 9001—Quality Management Systems—Requirements;
- ISO 14001—Environmental Management Systems;
- OHSAS 18001—Occupational Health and Safety Management Systems;
- ISO 27001—Information Technology—Security Techniques—Information Security Management Systems—Requirements;
- ISO 22000—Food Safety Management Systems—Requirements for any organization in the food chain Food Safety;
- ISO 20000 Information Technology—Service Management.

The Forensic Laboratory has adopted and adapted it to include:

- ISO 15489—Information and Documentation—Records Management;
- ISO 17020—Conformity Assessment—Requirements for the operation of various types of bodies performing inspection;
- ISO 17025—General requirements for the competence of testing and calibration laboratories;
- ISO 22301—Societal Security—Business Continuity Management Systems (BCMSs);
- ISO 27001—Information Technology—Security Techniques—Information Security Management Systems—Requirements;
- ISO 9001 Quality Management Systems—Requirements;
- OHSAS 18001 Occupational Health and Safety Management Systems;
- In-house digital forensic procedures.

All are managed through the same IMS.

PAS 99 (Section **4.3.1**) ensures that the whole process is business-risk based, so that there is a common framework within the Forensic Laboratory to identify, evaluate, and treat business risks of any type. Risk Management is covered in detail in Chapter 5.

A glossary of terms relating to PAS 99 is given in Appendix 2.

4.2 BENEFITS

The Forensic Laboratory has found the following benefits in adopting the single IMS to manage all of its processes and procedures:

- *reduced costs*—by avoiding duplication in internal audits, document control, training, and administration, adopting future management systems will be much more effective;
- *time savings*—by having only one Management Review and integrated internal audits;
- *a holistic approach to managing business risks*—by ensuring that all consequences of any action are taken into account, including how they affect each other and their associated risks, across all systems managed by the IMS;
- *reduced duplication and bureaucracy*—having one set of core processes ensures that the requirements of the specific standards are coordinated, workloads streamlined, and disparate systems avoided;
- *less conflict between systems and departments*—by avoiding separate "empires" or "silos" for the requirements of different system and defining responsibilities clearly from the outset within the IMS;
- *improved communication, both internal and external*—by having one set of objectives, a team approach culture can thrive and improve communication. Using one communication channel for all systems consistently ensures that all employees are made aware of updated changes for all systems, as required;
- *enhanced business focus*—by having one IMS linked to the Forensic Laboratory's strategic objectives, the IMS contributes to the overall continual improvement process within the Forensic Laboratory;
- *improved staff morale and motivation*—by involving and linking roles and responsibilities to objectives, it makes change and new initiatives easier to implement and makes the Forensic Laboratory more dynamic, efficient, and able to adopt change;
- *optimized internal and external audits*—by minimizing the number of audits required by undertaking integrated audits and maximizing the number of people involved.

4.3 THE FORENSIC LABORATORY IMS

There are an increasing number of standards, national and international, that follow the W. Edwards Deming (or Plan, Do, Check, Act Cycle). Historically, these have been standalone systems and this has led to:

- duplication of effort;
- conflict between management systems;
- increased bureaucracy;
- multiple audits of systems.

The Forensic Laboratory has adopted the approach outlined in PAS 99 and has created an IMS for all of its business processes that are either legislative requirements, standards requirements, good practice requirements, or internal process requirements. This allows one single view of the operation of the Forensic Laboratory to be seen by Top Management and so:

- provides improved business focus;
- provides a more holistic approach to Risk Management;
- reduces conflict between management systems;
- reduces bureaucracy;
- reduces duplication of effort;
- provides a streamlined audit and Management Review process;
- has a common continuous improvement process;
- provides management oversight.

The mapping of the requirements of PAS 99 and how they are met in this book is given in Appendix 3.

4.3.1 General Requirements

The Forensic Laboratory has implemented this process for all of the management systems standards that are implemented within the company. These follow the well-established seven step process as below:

4.3.1.1 Overview

If the Forensic Laboratory is not continually improving the way that it provides services and products to its Clients, it is losing competitive advantage. The Forensic Laboratory's core values require it, its work environment needs it, and its Clients demand it. PDCA is the Forensic Laboratory's methodology for conducting all process improvement projects. Regardless of position or role in the Forensic Laboratory, if the PDCA method is followed, whether in a project team or for a complete management system, it has been found that the opportunity of success is greatly increased. The PDCA method is made up of seven simple steps (or questions):

4.3.1.2 Plan

1. *Goal Statement*—What is to be achieved? In clear terms, define the purpose and goal of the project or management system. Usually, this is to increase a desirable effect or decrease an undesirable one. The Goal Statement sets the scope and alignment for the rest of the project or management system's actions. The Forensic Laboratory Goal Statement is given in Appendix 4.
2. *Cause Analysis*—What are the significant causes keeping the Forensic Laboratory from achieving the Goal Statement, and how are the significant causes defined? Causes are usually a brainstormed list, but their significance (impact) is validated with data.
3. *Baseline Measure*—What is the baseline measure(s) of the Goal Statement? The Forensic Laboratory Baseline Measures are given in Appendix 5.
4. *Solution Development*—What are the proposed fixes (changes in processes) that, when properly implemented, will make a dramatic impact toward achieving the Goal Statement?
5. *Implementation Planning*—What are the detailed plans that will successfully implement the proposed solution into the work environment? These plans address the people, process, technology, and equipment/facility changes needed to transition from the current way to the proposed way.

4.3.1.3 Do

Implement the solution that was planned. If possible, implement the solution in a proof of concept or pilot (manageable) fashion before rolling it out in its entirety. During implementation, adjustments are made to refine the proposed solution to match reality.

4.3.1.4 Check

6. *Measure of Improvement*—What is the measured improvement of the Goal Statement?

4.3.1.5 Act

7. *How will the solution be sustained over time?* What are the Forensic Laboratory's plans to measure and adjust the solution in order to keep its gains from degrading over time?

The PDCA model is implemented in the Forensic Laboratory for all management systems and business processes.

4.3.2 Goals

The Forensic Laboratory's Goals are to:

- create a high-performance customer-facing organization;
- enhance the operational value from our existing portfolio;
- expand our portfolio profitably;
- be known as a digital forensic center of excellence.

4.4 THE FORENSIC LABORATORY POLICIES

The Forensic Laboratory has a number of policies that are integral to the Forensic Laboratory's business processes.

4.4.1 Policies

4.4.1.1 Legislative

There is the need for a number of policies that are specific to the legislation in the jurisdiction. These can cover issues such as:

- disability;
- discrimination;
- equal opportunities;
- conflict of interest (Chapter 3, Appendix 3);
- undue influence (Appendix 8);
- data privacy; etc.

4.4.1.2 ISO High-Level Policy Documents

The following high-level policy documents based on ISO Standards are implemented in the Forensic Laboratory:

- Quality Management Policy (ISO 9001) (Chapter 3, Appendix 4);
- Environmental Management Policy (ISO 14001) (Appendix 6);
- Health and Safety Policy (OHSAS 18001) (Appendix 7);
- Business Continuity Policy (ISO 22301) (Appendix 9);
- Information Security Policy (ISO 27001) (Appendix 10).

Note

The relevant standards follow the policy name above.

4.4.1.3 ISO Detailed Policy Documents

The following high-level policy documents based on ISO Standards are implemented in the Forensic Laboratory:

- Access Control Policy (ISO 27001) (Appendix 11);
- Change or Termination of Employment Policy (ISO 27001) (Appendix 12);
- Clear Desk and Clear Screen Policy (ISO 27001 and ISO 20000) (Appendix 13);
- Continuous Improvement Policy (all standards) (Appendix 14);
- Cryptographic Control Policy (ISO 27001) (Appendix 15);
- Document Retention Policy (all standards) (Appendix 16);
- Financial Management Policy (ISO 20000) (Appendix 17);
- Mobile Devices Policy (ISO 27001) (Appendix 18);
- Network Services Policy (ISO 27001) (Appendix 19);
- Personnel Screening Policy (ISO 27001) (Appendix 20);
- Relationship Management Policy (ISO 20000) (Appendix 21);
- Release Management Policy (ISO 20000) (Appendix 22);
- Service Management Policy (ISO 20000) (Appendix 23);
- Service Reporting Policy (ISO 20000) (Appendix 24);
- Third-Party Access Control Policy (ISO 27001) (Appendix 25).

4.4.1.4 Forensic Laboratory-Specific Policy Documents

The following Forensic Laboratory-specific policy documents are implemented in the Forensic Laboratory:

- Acceptable Use Policy (Appendix 26);
- Conflict of Interest Policy (Chapter 3, Appendix 3).

4.4.2 Policy Review

The Forensic Laboratory performs reviews of their management system and other business policies to:

- assess the continuing suitability, adequacy, and effectiveness of the policy;
- identify and manage improvements to the policy.

Reviews of the management system policies must take place regularly (ideally at least once a year) and are the responsibility of the relevant Management System Owner. Reviews of the management system policies may take place in parallel with the Management Review of the management system or as the subject of a separate review process as needed (Figure 4.1).

1. The relevant Management System Owner identifies areas of the management system policy that require a possible review or update, based on, but not limited to;
    - issues arising from the annual review of the management system (including feedback from independent audits of the system);
    - any feedback from Forensic Laboratory employees concerning the effectiveness of the management policy;
    - the Forensic Laboratory management issues concerning the policy;
    - compliance with the relevant standard;
    - changes to the Forensic Laboratory systems and infrastructure that have been or are about to be implemented;
    - changes to risks arising from changes to the Forensic Laboratory, its technology, and its products and services, and which may impact on management system objectives;
    - incidents and faults;
    - service problems;
    - risks arising from changes to the organization, technology or business processes;
    - emerging threats and vulnerabilities;
    - emerging legislation and regulation changes;
    - emerging trends in Client's requirements;
    - the continuing effectiveness of the current policy.
2. The Management System Owner raises the policy issues with the relevant management committee as defined in Section 4.4.3.
3. The relevant management committee discusses the issues and the possible requirements for the further development of the policy—if necessary, other Forensic Laboratory employees may be appointed/delegated to investigate and report back to the relevant management committee.
4. If necessary, the relevant management committee recommends updates to the management system policy, in which case changes are drafted by an agreed member of the relevant management committee (usually appointed by the Chairman of that management committee).
5. Draft changes to the policy are circulated to all members of the relevant management committee.
6. Proposed changes to the policy are formally discussed by the relevant management committee. Changes that are accepted are formally approved.
7. The policy is updated in accordance with the Forensic Laboratory procedures for writing and updating documents as defined in Section 4.6.3.4.
8. Changes to the policy are publicized to the relevant employees, along with any changes to documented procedures or work instructions.
9. If necessary, an updated management system handbook is circulated to all employees.

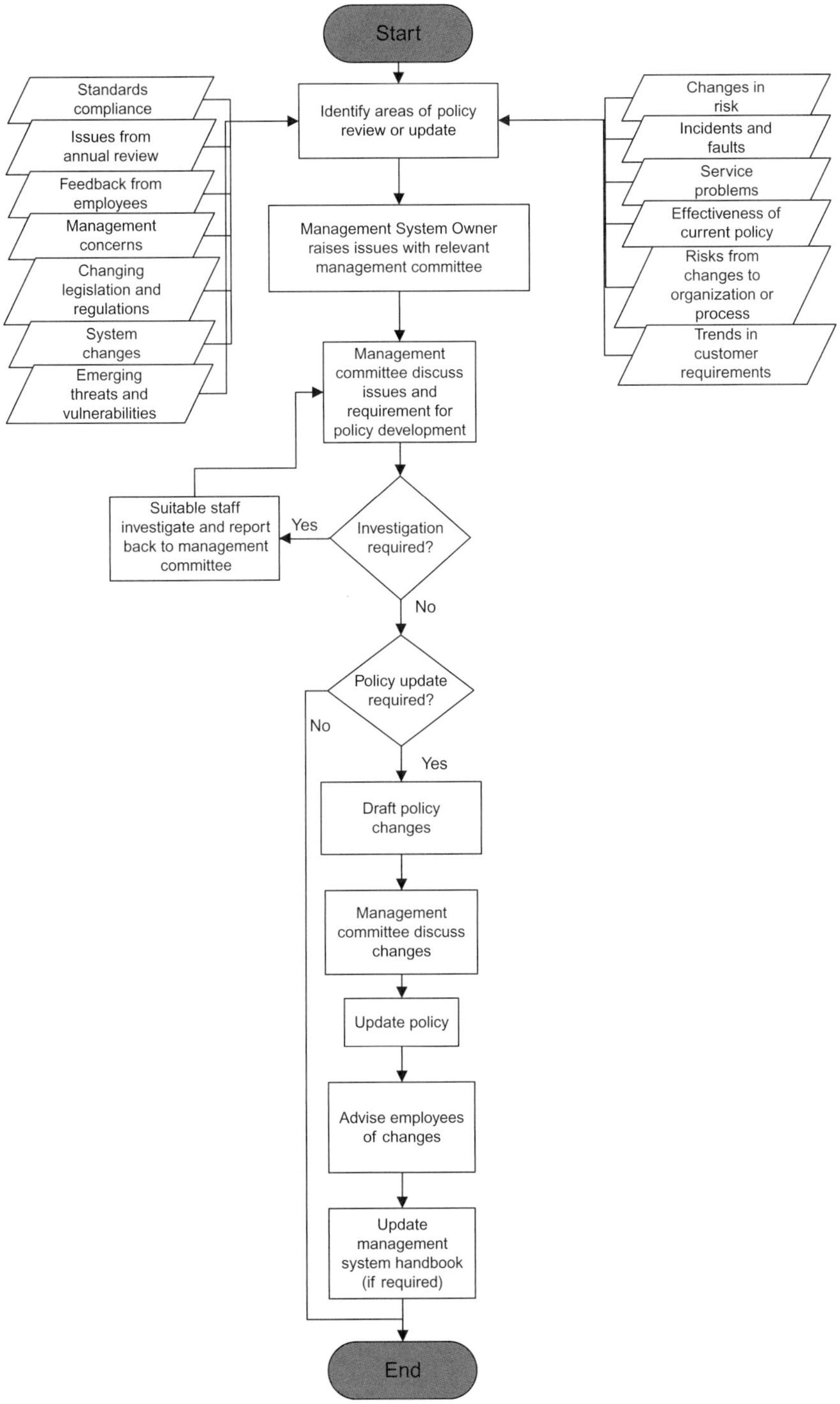

FIGURE 4.1 Policy review. (For color version of this figure, the reader is referred to the online version of this chapter.)

4.4.3 Management Committees

The following management committees, with associated Terms of Reference, exist in the Forensic Laboratory.

- Audit Committee (Appendix 27);
- Business Continuity Committee (Appendix 28);
- Environment Committee (Appendix 29);
- Health and Safety Committee (Appendix 30);
- Information Security Committee (Appendix 31);
- Quality Committee (Appendix 32);
- Risk Committee (Appendix 33);
- Service Delivery Committee (Appendix 34).

Each Terms of Reference is under regular review.

4.5 PLANNING

The Forensic Laboratory is committed to planning its management systems and business processes to ensure that they are appropriate and effective. It achieves this by adopting the following:

4.5.1 Identification and Evaluation of Aspects, Impacts, and Risks

The Forensic Laboratory Top Management is committed to a process of continuous improvement to its management systems and business processes. The Forensic Laboratory evidences this by:

- defining various policies to support the management systems as defined in Section 4.4.1;
- defining the scope of the management systems as defined in Chapter 5, Appendix 11;
- business processes have been identified as part of the ISO 9001 process for those processes that affect quality of outputs (i.e., deliverables) to all Clients (internal and external) as defined in Chapter 6;
- making available resources to implement, operate, and monitor the implemented management systems and business processes as defined in Section 4.6.2.1;
- ensuring that employees who implement, operate, and monitor the management systems and business processes are competent as defined in Section 4.6.2.2;
- identifying, evaluating, and treating business risk by managing a corporate risk register. The Forensic Laboratory risk assessment and risk treatment process is covered in detail in Chapter 5;
- identifying relevant legislation that can affect the management systems and business processes implemented as defined in Section 4.5.2 of this chapter and Chapter 12, Section 12.3.13.1;
- maintaining fault logs and fault reporting and actioning processes as defined in Chapter 7, Section 7.4.10.6;
- maintaining problem logs and problem reporting and actioning processes as defined in Chapter 7, Section 7.4.2;
- maintaining incident logs and incident reporting and actioning processes as defined in Chapter 7, Section 7.4.1;
- performing business impact analyses as defined in Chapter 13, Appendix 4.

4.5.2 Identification of Legal, Regulatory, and Other Requirements

Identification of legal, regulatory, and other requirements that may affect the relevant management systems is part of the remit of the various oversight committees. This is also part of the Management Review process. The agenda of the Forensic Laboratory is given in Section 4.9 and Appendix 36.

Owners of business processes and projects are responsible for ensuring that legislative, regulatory, contractual, and other requirements are considered as part of the normal business processes for managing their risks through the corporate risk register or providing them as stakeholder input to the Management Review process.

4.5.3 Contingency Planning

Not all of the management systems require a contingency planning process, but ISO 9001 (S8.3) refers to "product recall," ISO 27001 has a major clause relating to business continuity (S14). ISO 22301 is a standard that exclusively addresses business continuity, and it is this standard on which the Forensic Laboratory has based their contingency planning. Early notice of the possible invocation of contingency plans is provided through:

- training and awareness of the Forensic Laboratory employees and any third parties working for them;
- fault reporting and management of the fault log;
- problem reporting and management of the problem log;
- incident reporting and management of the incident log.

A Business Continuity Manager has been appointed in the Forensic Laboratory and his specific job description is given in Chapter 13, Appendix 3. All relevant employees are trained in contingency issues and records of this training are maintained by the Forensic Laboratory Human Resources Department.

The risk of needing to invoke the contingency plans is reduced through the risk management process and the application of appropriate controls to lessen the likelihood of occurrence and so the need to invoke the plan(s).

Business continuity is fully covered in Chapter 13.

4.5.4 Objectives

The Forensic Laboratory sets a variety of business objectives in various business processes and within this IMS. Where possible, metrics have been set and these are measurable.

ISO 14001 defines "targets" as well as objectives. Targets are what the Forensic Laboratory intends to achieve but that is not critical to the Forensic Laboratory's future. If these targets are not met, then it may be necessary to review the objectives that define the targets.

Each of the management systems implemented is responsible for meeting these objectives. These are measured and reviewed through:

- internal audits;
- external audits;
- self-assessment;
- test and exercises;

- the Management Review;
- the continuous improvement process.

4.5.5 Organizational Structures, Roles, Responsibilities, and Authorities

The organization chart for the Forensic Laboratory is specific to the Forensic Laboratory alone, and every forensic laboratory will work in a slightly different manner.

Roles, responsibilities, and authorities are given in relevant job descriptions. A number of those relevant to this IMS are given in Chapter 18, Section 18.1.5. These are under constant review by the Human Resources Department.

4.6 IMPLEMENTATION AND OPERATION

Each management system and business process has differing requirements but there are a number of common ones, defined below. Where there are specific requirements for a management system or business process, they are defined in the relevant section of the IMS, and so also this book.

4.6.1 Operational Control

Operational control varies between each of the different requirements, processes, and management systems, and is covered in the procedures for each management standard and business process individually.

4.6.2 Management of Resources

4.6.2.1 Provision of Resources

The Forensic Laboratory shall ensure that it provides appropriate resources (employees, technology, services, etc.) for each management system and business process to:

- identify the legal requirements for the relevant management systems and business processes implemented in the Forensic Laboratory;
- address the legal requirements for the relevant management systems and business processes implemented in the Forensic Laboratory;
- meet the contractual requirements for the relevant management systems and business processes implemented in the Forensic Laboratory;
- implement the relevant management systems and business processes implemented in the Forensic Laboratory;
- operate the relevant management systems and business processes implemented in the Forensic Laboratory;
- monitor the relevant management systems and business processes implemented in the Forensic Laboratory;
- review the relevant management systems and business processes implemented in the Forensic Laboratory;
- maintain the relevant management systems and business processes implemented in the Forensic Laboratory;
- implement appropriate controls to manage the relevant management systems and business processes implemented in the Forensic Laboratory;
- continually improve the effectiveness of the relevant management systems and business processes implemented in the Forensic Laboratory by ensuring that internal audits, external audits, self-assessments, exercises, tests, and Management Reviews are carried out to ensure continued suitability, adequacy, and effectiveness of the relevant management systems and business processes;
- enhance Client satisfaction by meeting, and where possible exceeding, Client requirements;
- manage the relevant management systems and business processes in place in the Forensic Laboratory.

The Forensic Laboratory Top Management is committed to supporting this IMS and its supported processes and procedures.

4.6.2.2 Competence, Training, and Awareness

The Forensic Laboratory is committed to ensuring that all employees receive appropriate training for the tasks that they are required to perform.

All the Forensic Laboratory employees shall be suitably trained and competent to provide the services that the Forensic Laboratory and its Clients require, based on:

- education;
- skills;
- training;
- experience;
- their own levels of requirement;
- their own levels of ability.

There are corporate development programs for all employees and some specific training requirements, these are classed as

- general HR training;
- project-specific training;
- management system-specific training.

Records of training and competence are held by the Human Resources Department.

Initially, all training is discussed between the employees and their Line Manager. This will agree initial personal development standards for the year, and these are, when agreed, submitted to the Human Resources Department for action. Ongoing discussion throughout the year between employees and their Line Managers may identify further training or development needs and objectives.

The Forensic Laboratory ensures that there is equal opportunity for all employees to have access to appropriate training and personal development to meet their personal objectives.

All the Forensic Laboratory employees will have annual appraisals as defined in Chapter 18, Section 18.2.4 to monitor their performance and provide an avenue for dialog between the employees and their Line Managers and permit constructive feedback leading to continuous improvement of the employee's skill and competence.

Employees who show exceptional competence or excellence shall be recognized for their effort by the Forensic Laboratory Top Management. This shall be in an appropriate manner as decided by the Top Management.

4.6.2.2.1 General Human Resources Training

Through the Human Resources Department, the Forensic Laboratory shall:

- determine necessary competences for all employees in association with the relevant Line Managers;
- produce job descriptions for all posts;
- identify, through training needs analysis, the training requirements for all employees working for the Forensic Laboratory as defined in Chapter 18, Section 18.2.2;
- provide training or take other actions to enable staff (e.g., hiring suitably competent resources) to achieve and maintain these competences;
- encourage all employees to take vocational training;
- evaluate effectiveness of training;
- ensure that all employees understand the relevance and importance of conforming with the requirements of the relevant business processes and management systems in the Forensic Laboratory;
- ensure that all employees understand the relevance and importance of their contribution to the Forensic Laboratory's success;
- ensure that all employees understand the benefits to the Forensic Laboratory of their personal performance in conforming with the requirements of the relevant business processes and management systems in the Forensic Laboratory;
- ensure that employees understand the potential consequences (actual or potential) that could occur in the Forensic Laboratory if they do not conform to the requirements of the relevant business processes and management systems in the Forensic Laboratory;
- ensure that all employees understand the emergency procedures and contingency plans in place, should they be needed, for supporting the relevant business processes and management systems in the Forensic Laboratory;
- book employees on external training course;
- arrange in-house training courses;
- maintain records of all training undertaken by all Forensic Laboratory employees;
- ensure that those employees appointed to manage the relevant business processes and management systems have appropriate skills, competence, and experience;
- training needs and competencies shall be regularly reviewed by the Human Resources Department.

4.6.2.2.2 Project Training

At the planning stage of a new project, Forensic Laboratory employees may require specific training to enable them to effectively contribute on being assigned to the project.

An employee identifies training that he/she would like to receive and seeks approval from his/her Line Manager to attend a course.

If training is required, the Human Resources Department arranges suitable in-house training or contacts external training organizations to assess and then book a place on a training course.

4.6.2.2.3 Management System-Specific Training

Each individual management system has its own requirements for training and each is covered within the requirements for the specific management system.

4.6.2.3 Training Records

All the Forensic Laboratory employees have their CVs (resumes) held by the Human Resources Department.

The Forensic Laboratory encourages all of its employees to maintain Continual Professional Development or Continuous Professional Education logs for their relevant professional organizations. The records of these are held by the individual employee and the Human Resources Department.

Specific requirements are given under each management system or business process as appropriate.

4.6.2.4 Infrastructure

The Forensic Laboratory shall determine, provide, and maintain the work infrastructure to ensure that it is suitable for all the Forensic Laboratory employees to achieve the requirements of the business processes and management standards implemented in the Forensic Laboratory. Infrastructure includes:

- buildings, offices, and workspace equipment;
- technology;
- finance;
- competent employees;
- services.

4.6.2.5 Environment

The Forensic Laboratory shall determine and manage the work environment to ensure that it is suitable for all the

Forensic Laboratory employees to achieve the requirements of the business processes and management standards implemented in the Forensic Laboratory.

4.6.3 Documentation Requirements

Note 1

Documentation may be created and maintained in Word and Microsoft Office documents in stand-alone format or may be deposited in a Wiki or in SharePoint. This section has been written for a manual system, rather than for a Wiki or SharePoint.

Note 2

If SharePoint is used, this automatically provides workflow capabilities, and audit trail, automated document review reporting, controlled access. A SharePoint implementation will require changes to this section based on SharePoint's implementation.

The Forensic Laboratory maintains strict control over its documentation, as is shown below:

4.6.3.1 *General*

The Forensic Laboratory IMS comprises:

- management system policies for each management standard implemented in the Forensic Laboratory as defined in Chapter 3, Appendices 3 and 4, as well as various appendices in this chapter;
- manuals, where appropriate, to support the relevant management systems and business processes implemented in the Forensic Laboratory;
- documented procedures to support the relevant management systems and business processes implemented in the Forensic Laboratory;
- documented procedures to support the effective and efficient planning, implementation, operation, and management to support the relevant management systems and business processes implemented in the Forensic Laboratory;
- records required by the relevant management systems and business processes implemented in the Forensic Laboratory to provide proof of the effective and efficient operation of the IMS.

Documented procedures are crucial to the day-to-day operations in the Forensic Laboratory as they:

- act as a repository of information to assist with legislative and regulatory, as well as compliance, with the Forensic Laboratory's own internal objectives;
- formally document and accurately reflect the current processes and practices implemented in the Forensic Laboratory;
- present all the documentation in a consistent and usable style and therefore make documents easier to maintain;
- extract knowledge from key and experienced employees;
- act as a training tool for new employees and provide a first point of reference for problem solving;
- help employees identify roles and responsibilities, and help reduce misunderstanding;
- improve the quality of service.

4.6.3.2 *System Documentation*

For all the Forensic Laboratory management systems and business processes, the following are defined, where relevant:

- management system policies;
- a scope statement for the management systems;
- justifications for the exclusion and, where appropriate, inclusion of clauses or controls from the relevant management system;
- documented procedures for the various Forensic Laboratory systems;
- manuals, where appropriate, for management systems;
- records generated by the relevant management systems and business processes.

Documentation will typically comprise a number of different document types that reflect their use. These include the following document types:

- policies;
- procedures;
- manuals;
- technical documents;
- forms;
- Terms of Reference;
- records required by the relevant standard, management system or business process;
- plans;
- service level agreements (SLAs); etc.

These documents are all controlled within the Forensic Laboratory and are subject to change control.

All other document types are uncontrolled.

All documents are in HTML or Microsoft Office format.

4.6.3.3 *Control of Documents*

When drafting, editing, and issuing of all documentation that is generated by the Forensic Laboratory, Forensic Laboratory employees must comply with the following responsibilities.

4.6.3.3.1 Roles and Responsibilities

For those employees involved in the production of documentation, the following responsibilities are defined.

4.6.3.3.1.1 Document Owner Responsibilities The Document Owner is the relevant management system or business process owner who has management responsibility for all of their management system and management system documentation within the Forensic Laboratory, and is responsible for:

- appointing a Document Author as required;
- investigation and planning of a document where required;
- monitoring the research for a document;
- managing the writing/updating a document;
- circulating documents for review;
- approving the document after final review;
- issuing a "live" version of the document.

> **Note**
>
> A Document Owner may write/update a document for which they have management responsibility or delegate the writing to a Document Author.

4.6.3.3.1.2 Document Author Responsibilities A Document Author is any Forensic Laboratory employee who has the responsibility to research and write or update a document, and is responsible for:

- investigation and planning of a document;
- researching a document;
- writing/updating a document;
- reporting to the Document Owner on the progress of the work on a document;
- issuing draft revisions of a document for review;
- checking comments from the reviewers in conjunction with the Document Owner;
- implementing comments made by reviewers for a document;
- archiving all previous versions of a document through the Document Registrar.

4.6.3.3.1.3 Reviewer Responsibilities The Document Reviewer(s) is/are the employee(s) who is/are appointed by the Document Owner to review a document, using specific knowledge, and is/are responsible for:

- reviewing the document content using their specific knowledge;
- making comments/suggestions as appropriate for the document;
- returning comments and/or edits to the Document Owner.

4.6.3.3.1.4 Quality Assurance Manager Responsibilities The Quality Assurance Manager should be a "sign off" for documents produced in the Forensic Laboratory as part of the workflow for document review and updating, or may audit documents produced as part of standard internal audits to ensure that:

- the document has been properly reviewed by the Reviewer(s) appointed by the Document Owner;
- the requirements of Document Style Checklist have been met, as defined in Appendix 37;
- metadata entered into all documents are appropriate and that a full version history is maintained, as defined in Appendix 38;
- other tasks as the Quality Assurance Manager determines are appropriate, dependent on the document being reviewed.

4.6.3.3.1.5 Site Owners Responsibilities

> **Note**
>
> This relates to any location where the IMS may be stored. This could be in a Wiki, SharePoint, or a set of directories used for the IMS.

A Site Owner is any Forensic Laboratory employee who is responsible for the management of all or part of the IMS, his/her responsibilities include:

- copy, move, or delete files;
- create new libraries, lists, subsites, etc.;
- ensure that current documents are the only ones available to authorized Forensic Laboratory employees;
- ensure that records are available, as required;
- ensuring that obsolete documents are archived;
- give appropriate access to the site for all Forensic Laboratory employees;
- make sure all "INTERNAL USE ONLY" documents are available to all authorized employees;
- optionally appoint a Custodian to undertake regular site maintenance on their behalf;
- regularly review access rights to their site;
- the overall structure and content of their site.

4.6.3.3.1.6 Document Registrar Responsibilities The Document Registrar is the Forensic Laboratory employee who has the responsibility for issuing and tracking documents. They are independent from the Document Owner and Document Author, and are responsible for:

- maintaining the Document Register;
- controlling documents within the Forensic Laboratory during the writing and approval process;
- generating PDF versions of issued documents for publication, as applicable;

- withdrawing and marking up obsolete documents;
- regularly auditing the Document Register.

4.6.3.4 Writing and Updating Documents

When a Document Owner (or delegated Document Author) writes a new document or updates an existing document, a standard process is followed in the Forensic Laboratory. This ensures that there is a standard methodology for the whole document life cycle for all documents in the Forensic Laboratory. The process involves (Figure 4.2):

4.6.3.4.1 Generating a Request

The tasks that are performed to request a document are:

1. An employee identifies a need for a new document or an update to an existing document. Typically, this may happen when:
   - an employee is working and discovers errors or lack of information within an existing document;
   - an employee suggests an improvement to a document;
   - the management system or business process changes and implementation necessitates an update to a document;
   - an audit highlights an area that is not adequately covered by a documented procedure;
   - legislation affects the Forensic Laboratory's working practices;

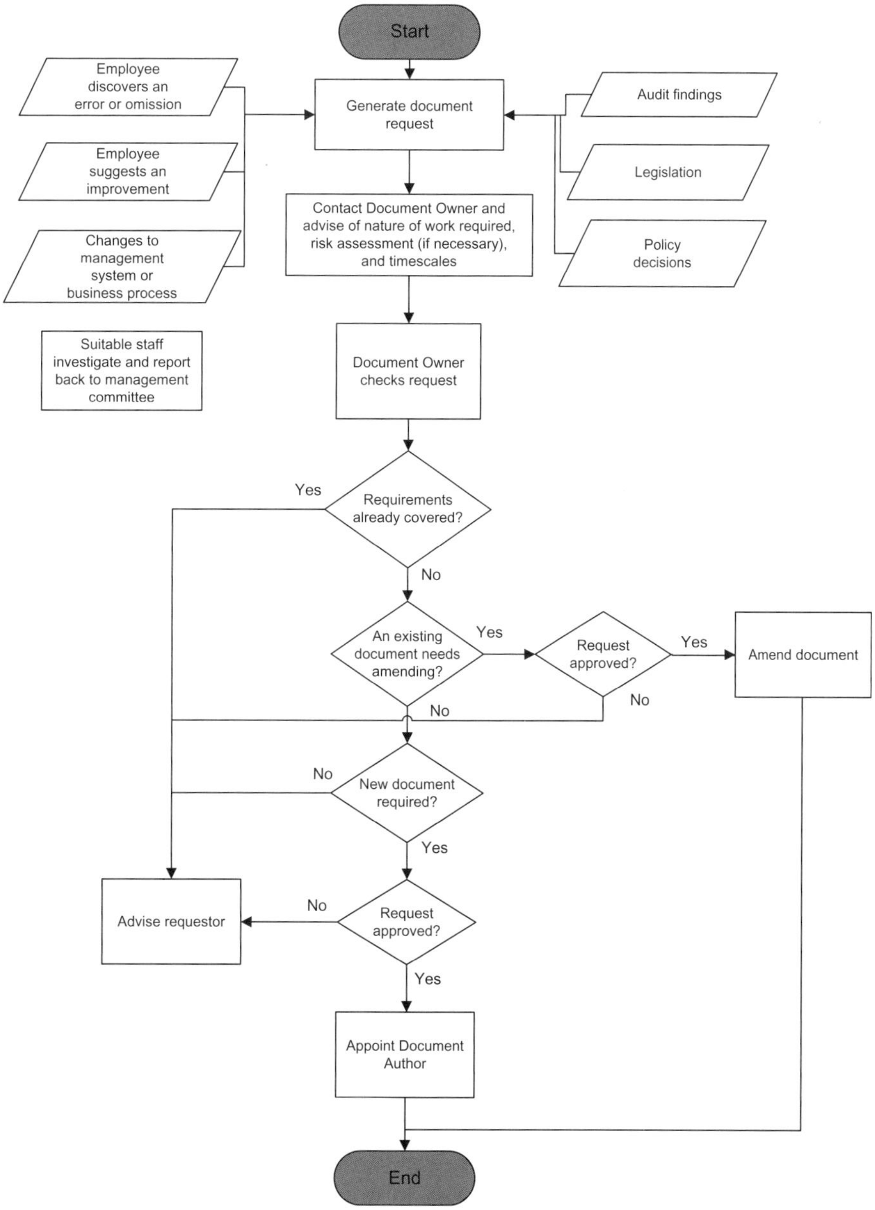

FIGURE 4.2 Generating a request. (For color version of this figure, the reader is referred to the online version of this chapter.)

- policy decisions by the Forensic Laboratory require a change in management system operations or business processes.

2. The employee contacts the Document Owner and advises them of the following:
   - the nature of work that requires documenting;
   - a risk assessment, if required;
   - estimated writing and issuing timescales for the document.
3. The Document Owner checks the request and determines whether:
   - the requirements are already covered in other documents;
   - an existing document should be amended to reflect the additional requirements;
   - a completely new document is required.
4. The Document Owner does either of the following:
   - if a request is approved—appoints a Document Author to write or update the document;
   - if a request is not approved—informs the Requestor and takes no further action.

Note

Where a Document Owner does not exist (i.e., a new document is required), the person performing the role of Document Owner is the relevant management system or business process Owner.

If the document is controlled, it is subject to change control and all changes to the document shall be approved by the Forensic Laboratory document change management process before final approval and issue.

4.6.3.4.2 Researching and Writing/Updating a Document

The Document Author researches the document requirements as follows (Figure 4.3).

1. Plan changes to the document by considering the following:
   - assess the requirements for the area to be documented;
   - assess existing work methods;
   - scope the amount of work involved;
   - decide timescales;
   - arrange information-gathering meetings where required.
2. Gather the information required to write or amend the document as required, issues to consider are:
   - decide what is covered by the document in terms of scope—what to include and what to exclude;
   - produce a simple list of the main steps in the document from a normal start point to a normal end point, making sure that any monitoring tasks are covered, if appropriate;
   - for each step identified in the document, decide:
     - why the step is performed?
     - what is an input to the step?
     - what happens during the step?
     - what is an output from the step?
     - who performs tasks during the step?
     - what evidence exists that the step has been performed?
   - identify any areas where reviews/sign offs are performed and note the:
     - review method;
     - feedback and update loops;
     - authorization required;
     - documentary evidence of the review.
   - identify other employees or external organizations that have input to the document;
   - identify the risk areas in the work;
   - compile a set of documents, forms, checklists, and reports that provide more information. Remember to highlight the areas that are relevant.
3. Create a new document or obtain the current version from the Document Registrar.
4. Write or update the draft document as required by:
   - creating/modifying text and graphics, as required;
   - creating/modifying process flowcharts, as required;
   - formatting the document, as required.
5. Every day, the document name shall be updated according to the file-naming convention, as defined in Appendix 39. This allows the reversion to any previous version of a document.
6. Review the document and check it for:
   - content;
   - style and structure;
   - spelling and grammar;
   - layout.
7. Trial the document in a real situation, then review and refine the text and rewrite it as required.
8. Generate an Acrobat PDF file of the document for circulation and formal review, if appropriate.

4.6.3.4.3 Reviewing a Document and Implementing Edits

All draft documents produced by a Document Author are thoroughly reviewed and edited. The Document Owner ensures that reviews are properly conducted as follows (Figure 4.4):

1. The Document Author passes the draft document to Document Owner;

Note

In this case, the Document Owner will be the employee who owns the business process to which the document relates.

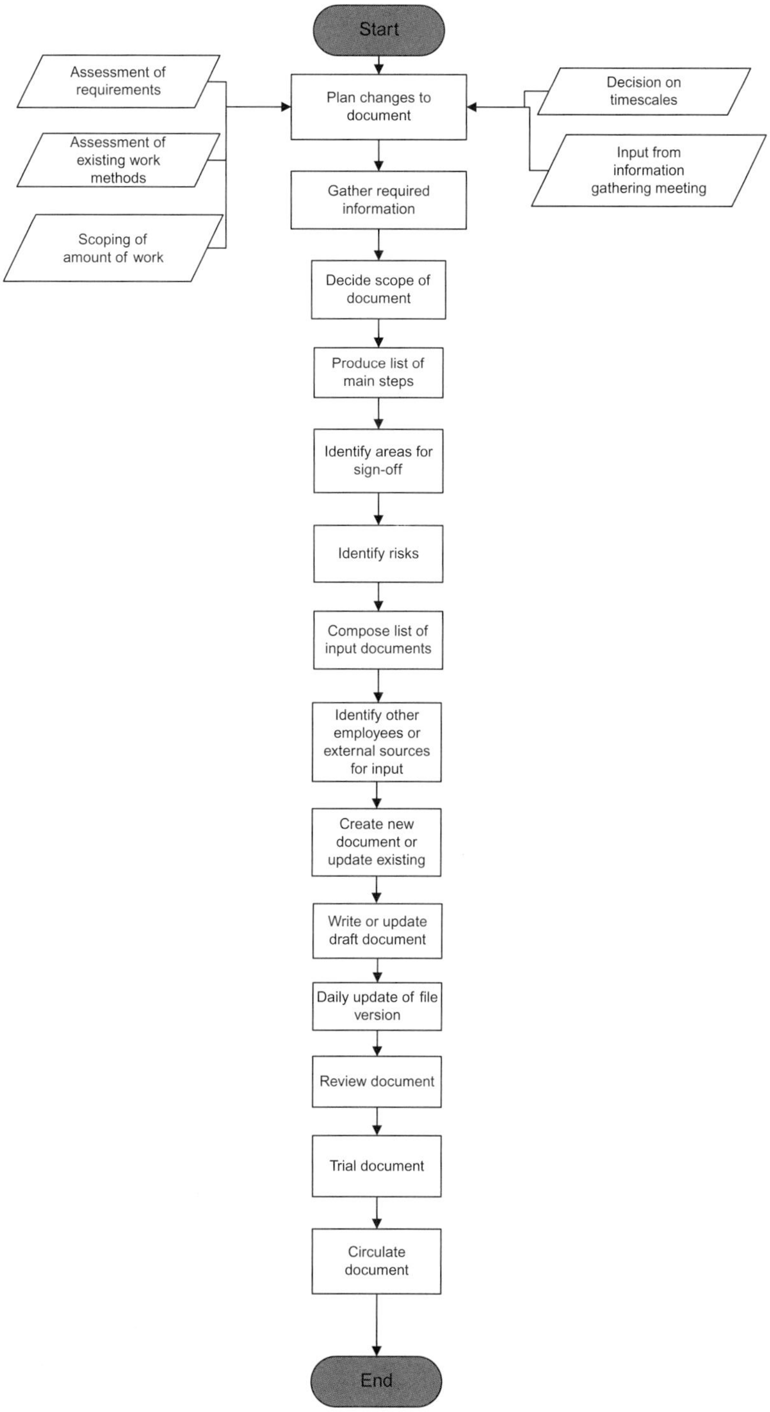

FIGURE 4.3 Reviewing a document and implementing edits. (For color version of this figure, the reader is referred to the online version of this chapter.)

2. The Document Owner circulates copies of the draft document to the relevant employees for review, using the relevant document review process ensuring that the following is stated:
   - that this is a draft of the document by ensuring that is suitably watermarked. Watermarks in use in the Forensic Laboratory are defined in Appendix 40;
   - that the document must be printed and all edits required must be written on the printed copy;
   - a date by when all comments must be received.
3. The Document Owner collates all returned edits. These are:
   - evaluated;
   - agreed by the Document Owner for inclusion in the document.

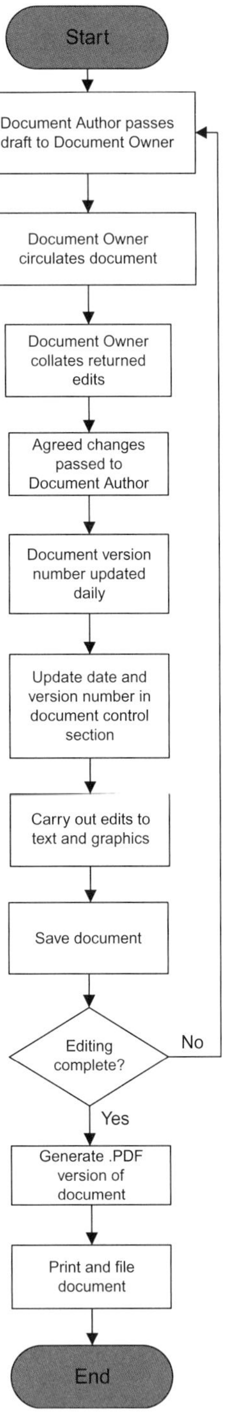

FIGURE 4.4 Researching and writing/updating a document. (For color version of this figure, the reader is referred to the online version of this chapter.)

4. The Document Owner passes the agreed changes to the Document Author.
5. Every day, the document name shall be updated according to the file-naming standards defined in Appendix 39. This allows the reversion to any previous version of a document.
6. Update the date and version information in the document control section.
7. Perform the required edits to the text and graphics.
8. Save the document.
9. Repeat steps 1-8 until no further comments on the document are received.
10. Generate an Acrobat PDF file of the document for circulation and final review, if appropriate.
11. File the marked-up printed copies of the reviewed document.

Note 1

Where a Document Owner does not exist (i.e., a new document is required), the person performing the role of Document Owner is the relevant management system or business process Owner.

Note 2

Typically, no longer than a week (5 working days) should be allowed for return of review comments.

Note 3

A document review form can be used or comments be written on the original document. A content list for a document review form is given in Appendix 41.

4.6.3.4.4 Reviewing a Proposal or Work Product and Implementing Edits

All draft proposals and work products produced by a Document Author are thoroughly reviewed and edited. The Document Owner ensures that reviews are properly conducted as follows (Figure 4.5):

1. The Document Author passes the draft proposal or work product to the Document Owner;

Note

In this case, the Document Owner will be the person in charge of the relationship with the Client.

2. The Document Owner circulates copies of the draft document using the draft review process to the relevant employees for review, ensuring that the following is stated:
   - that this is a draft of the document by ensuring that is suitably watermarked. Watermarks in use in the Forensic Laboratory are defined in Appendix 40;
   - that the document must be printed and all edits required must be written on the printed copy;
   - a date by when all comments must be received.

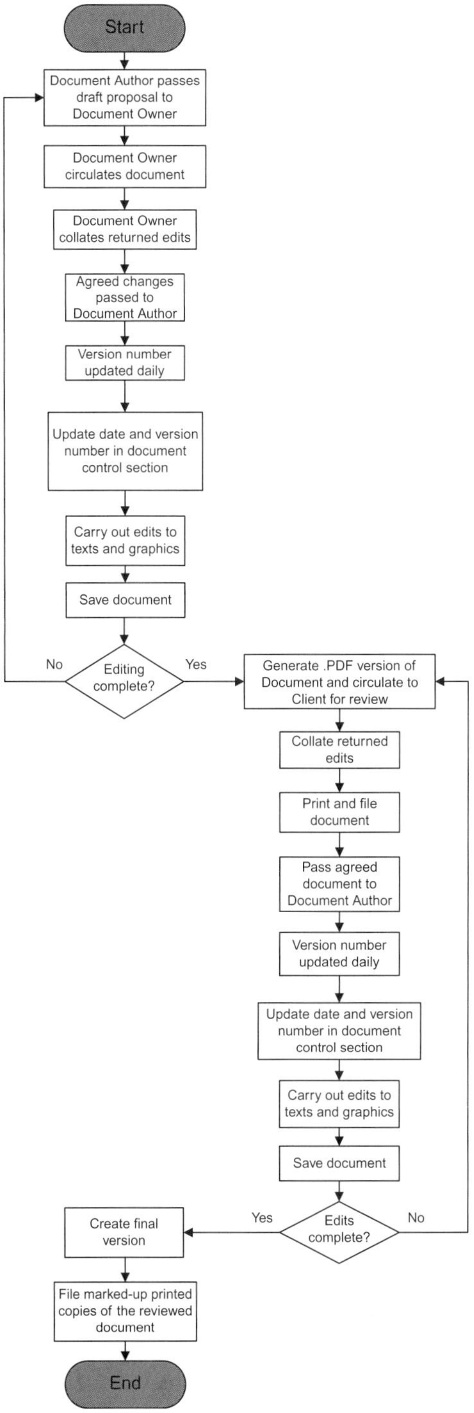

FIGURE 4.5 Reviewing a proposal or work product and implementing edits. (For color version of this figure, the reader is referred to the online version of this chapter.)

3. The Document Owner collates all returned edits. These are:
   - evaluated;
   - discussed with the Reviewer, if appropriate;
   - agreed by the Document Owner for inclusion in the document.
4. The Document Owner passes the agreed changes to the Document Author.
5. Every day, the document name shall be updated according to the file-naming standards defined in Appendix 39. This allows the reversion to any previous version of a document.
6. Update the date and version information in the document control section.
7. Perform the required edits to the text and graphics.
8. Save the document.
9. Repeat steps 1-8 until no further internal comments on the document are received.
10. Generate an Acrobat PDF file of the document for circulation to the Client for review.
11. The Document Owner circulates copies of the draft document with the draft review comments to the (proposed) Client for review, ensuring that the following is stated:
    - that this is a draft of the document by ensuring that is suitably watermarked. Watermarks in use in the Forensic Laboratory are defined in Appendix 40;
    - that the document must be printed and all edits required must be written on the printed copy;
    - a date by when all comments must be received.
12. The Document Owner collates all returned edits. These are:
    - evaluated;
    - discussed with the Client, if appropriate;
    - agreed by the Document Owner for inclusion in the document.
13. The Document Owner passes the agreed changes to the Document Author.
14. Every day, the document name shall be updated according to the file-naming standards defined in Appendix 39. This allows the reversion to any previous version of a document.
15. Update the date and version information in the document control section.
16. Perform the required edits to the text and graphics.
17. Save the document.
18. Steps 11-17 are repeated, then a final version of the document is produced in PDF format for formal release to the Client.
19. File the marked-up printed copies of the reviewed document.

Note 1

Typically, no longer than a week (5 working days) should be allowed for return of review comments.

4.6.3.4.5 Issuing a Document

Note

When a new document is issued, and where practical, the new text should be identified in the new document. Typically, this is done with vertical markings in the margin. If the changes are significant, consideration of addition training for those changes affect should be given.

Once a document has passed through the edit process, it can be issued for use within the Forensic Laboratory, the Document Author performs the following tasks:

4.6.3.4.5.1 Word Documents

1. Open the Word document and save the file as the first/next release version according to the file-naming standards defined in Appendix 39.
2. Generate an Acrobat PDF file of the document, if appropriate.
3. Send all versions of the Word documents to the Document Registrar for archive purposes.
4. E-mail the PDF to the Document Registrar for publishing.
5. The Document Registrar should e-mail all relevant Forensic Laboratory employees indicating that a new document exists. The e-mail should invite comment from all employees.

4.6.3.4.5.2 HTML Documents

1. Open the HTML document and save the file as the first/next release version according to the Forensic Laboratory file-naming standards.
2. Send all versions of the HTML documents to the Document Registrar for archive purposes.
3. E-mail the HTML document(s) to the Document Registrar for publishing.
4. The Document Registrar should e-mail all the Forensic Laboratory employees indicating that a new document exists. The e-mail should invite comment from all staff.

4.6.3.4.6 Reviewing Management System or Business Process Documents

Each year all management system or business process documents including policies are reviewed to ensure that the details stated within the documentation are current and effective.

This review is performed by the relevant management system or business process Owner and senior management of the Forensic Laboratory as part of a management system review. Details of this management system or business process review are contained in the Management Review, as defined in Chapter 4, Section 4.9.

In general, the review of management system or business process documentation covers:

- operational changes that have occurred within the relevant management system or business process during the year;
- effect of these changes on each relevant management system or business process document to determine whether changes are required.

If changes are required, the document is updated using the procedure described above. If no changes are required, the existing document remains current. Records of the Management Review are retained.

4.6.4 Control of Records

The Forensic Laboratory shall record and maintain records to provide evidence of conformity and the effective operation of their management systems and business processes.

The Forensic Laboratory shall ensure that these remain:

- legible;
- readily identifiable;
- retrievable.

The Forensic Laboratory has procedures in place to:

- identify;
- store;
- protect;
- retrieve;
- set retention times;
- dispose of;

records.

4.6.5 Communication

The Forensic Laboratory has put in place procedures and processes to ensure that effective internal, and where appropriate external, distribution of communication of the contents of the management systems and business processes takes place. These take the form of:

- the in-house IMS as a repository of procedures and records;
- e-mail for alerting the Forensic Laboratory employees of updates to this intranet system;
- competence, training, and awareness programs;
- feedback to stakeholders from internal audits;
- feedback to stakeholders from external audits;
- feedback to stakeholders from self-assessments;
- feedback to stakeholders from exercises and other tests;
- feedback to stakeholders from Management Reviews;
- relevant committees for the management systems installed in the Forensic Laboratory, as defined in Section 4.4.3.

4.7 PERFORMANCE ASSESSMENT

To ensure that the Forensic Laboratory is able to continuously improve its management systems and all associated procedures, it is necessary to monitor and measure how well the applicable requirements from those systems are being met. This is carried out using the following processes:

4.7.1 Monitoring and Measurement

The Forensic Laboratory shall carry out monitoring and measurement of its management systems and other internal processes to determine the extent to which their requirements are met. This shall be carried out using a mix of the following:

- examination of fault logs;
- examination of incident reports;
- examination of problem reports;
- exercise feedback;
- external audits;
- internal audits;
- Management Reviews;
- penetration testing;
- self-assessments;
- such other processes as Top Management sees fit;
- trend analysis.

The scope, frequency, aims, and objectives of these tests shall be defined and be agreed with the Audit Committee. Records of these monitoring and measurement processes shall be maintained with associated Corrective Action Requests (CARs) and/or Preventive Action Requests (PARs).

The results of these tests and any associated CARs and/or PARs shall be communicated to relevant stakeholders, as appropriate.

Where an incident results in the invocation of the business continuity plan a Post Incident Review (PIR) shall take place.

4.7.2 Evaluation of Compliance

The results of the monitoring and measurement processes above shall be used to evaluate the level of compliance that the Forensic Laboratory has for the aims and objectives of its management systems, other governing processes, and legislative requirements.

A formal report of these evaluations shall be maintained and presented, with their supporting records, to the relevant oversight committee.

At a high level, metrics are quantifiable measurements of some aspect of a management system. For a management system, there are some identifiable attributes that collectively characterize the level of compliance of the management system. This is a quantitative measure of how much of that attribute the management system and can be built from lower-level physical measures that are the outcome of monitoring and measurement.

Typically, the following types of metrics are being identified and studied:

- Process Metrics—Specific metrics that could serve as quantitative or qualitative evidence of the level of maturity for a particular management system that could serve as a binary indication of the presence or absence of a mature process;
- Management System Metrics—A measurable attribute of the result of a capability maturity process that could serve as evidence of its effectiveness. A metric may be objective or subjective, and quantitative or qualitative.

The first type of metric provides information about the processes themselves. The second type of metric provides information on the results of those processes and what they can tell the stakeholders about how effective use of the processes has been in achieving an acceptable outcome. These metrics categories tailor their own metrics program to measure their progress against defined objectives.

There are a number of Capability Maturity Models (CMMs) that can be used to evaluate compliance levels that are recognized worldwide These include:

- CMM for quality;
- CMM for health and safety;
- CMM for services;
- CMM for IT services;
- CMM for business continuity;
- CMM for System Security Engineering (this has since become ISO/IEC 21827:2008);
- CMM for information security;
- Building in Security Maturity Model;
- CMM for people;
- CMM for portfolio, program, and project management;
- CMM for service integration.

4.7.3 Internal Auditing

4.7.3.1 Overview

Note 1

The performing of internal audits is applicable to all the Forensic Laboratory systems, this includes:

- internal processes;
- legislative processes;
- management systems;
- regulatory systems;
- forensic case processing;
- other systems or processes as required.

Note 2

Non-Compliance refers to breach of a legislative or Regulatory requirement. Non-conformance refers to a breach of internal procedures. Unless specifically indicated otherwise, non-conformance is used throughout this book.

The Forensic Laboratory undertakes regular audits of their management systems to:

- determine whether activities covered by the management systems are performing as expected;
- review controls, procedures, processes, and the management systems policies;
- review the level of risk based on changes to the Forensic Laboratory's organization, technology, business objectives and processes, and identified threats;
- review the scope of the management systems;
- identify improvements to management systems processes.

The key points about an internal audit are:

- they involve a systematic approach;
- they are carried out, where possible, by independent Auditors who ideally have received relevant training;
- they are conducted in accordance with a documented audit procedure;
- their outcome is a documented audit report.

All audits and tests within the Forensic Laboratory are carried out according to a defined schedule, called the *IMS Calendar*, unless circumstances require an audit or test to be carried out that is not on the schedule (e.g., postincident, non-conformity identified, Client requirement, etc.). While every forensic laboratory will undertake audits and tests according to their own requirements, the outline of the types of tests and audits undertaken are given in Appendix 42. The *IMS Calendar* ensures that a rolling series of tests and audits are carried out throughout the year and that all relevant areas of operation in the Forensic laboratory are covered at least annually or as required by Top Management.

4.7.3.2 Audit Responsibilities

4.7.3.2.1 Owners

The Management System or business process Owner to be audited is responsible for the following aspects of internal audits:

- arranging audits and Management Reviews of their management systems or business processes;
- ensuring that the audits and Management Reviews of the management systems or business processes are performed;
- providing the resources needed by the Auditor to ensure that the audit is conducted effectively;
- cooperating with the Auditor when an audit is performed to ensure that the audit is conducted effectively;
- recording recommended improvements to the relevant management system or business process;
- identifying, with the Auditor and other relevant stakeholders, and agreeing improvements to the relevant management system or business process;
- ensuring ongoing compliance with the relevant management standard(s);
- generating, processing, and tracking CARs and PARs to implement recommended improvements to the relevant system;
- verifying that remedial action (corrective or preventive) has been performed within the agreed timescales;
- reviewing the relevant management system policies on an annual basis or after influencing change.

4.7.3.2.2 Auditors

The Auditor is responsible for the following aspects of relevant system audits:

- defining the requirements of an audit;
- planning an audit;
- reviewing documentation for the area of operation being audited;
- auditing the area of operation;
- reporting critical non-compliance during the audit to the Auditee immediately;
- reporting non-compliance during the audit to the Auditee;
- recording recommended improvements to the management system or business process;
- reporting the audit results to the Auditee and the Forensic Laboratory Top Management;
- verifying the effectiveness of remedial actions within a timescales agreed with the Auditee;
- collating and filing all audit documentation;
- updating the audit list following the audit;
- being suitably qualified and competent to perform the audit.

4.7.3.2.3 Auditees

The Auditee is responsible for the following aspects of relevant system audits:

- liaising with the Auditor to arrange for an audit of their area of operation;
- providing all resources needed by the Auditor to ensure that the audit is conducted effectively;
- cooperating with the Auditor when an audit is performed to ensure that the audit is conducted effectively;
- providing evidential material and other records when asked by the Auditor;
- determining and initiating remedial action based on the findings in the audit report.

> **Note**
>
> The term Auditee also refers to the individual being audited.

4.7.3.3 Auditing Management System(s)

> **Note**
>
> The performing of internal audits is applicable to all the Forensic Laboratory systems, this includes:
> - internal processes;
> - legislative processes;
> - management systems;
> - regulatory systems;
> - other systems or business processes as required.

The Forensic Laboratory undertakes regular audits of their management systems to:

- determine whether activities covered by the management system are performing as expected;
- review controls, procedures, processes, and the management systems policies;
- review the level of risk based on changes to the Forensic Laboratory organization, technology, business objectives and processes, and identified threats;
- review the scope of the management systems;
- identify improvements to management systems processes.

4.7.3.4 Audit Planning Charts

To assist in the audit planning process, the Forensic Laboratory uses audit planning charts to effectively plan an annual cycle of audits to ensure that all controls are audited at least once through the audit year.

An audit planning chart is typically a list of requirements of a management system or business process and assigning an Auditee to be audited on that specific part of the management system or business process.

4.7.3.5 Audit Non-Compliance Definitions

A non-compliance must be recorded whenever the Auditor discovers that the documented procedures are inadequate to prevent breaches of the system requirements or they are adequate but are not being followed correctly.

4.7.3.5.1 Major Non-Compliance

4.7.3.5.1.1 Definition A failure to implement or comply to one or more of the applicable control requirements such that it raises significant doubts as to the adequacy of measures to comply with the requirements of the audit and/or represents an unacceptable risk as would be perceived by the relevant stakeholders.

4.7.3.5.1.2 Examples These occur in the following circumstances:

- ongoing and systematic breaches of the requirements have been found.

4.7.3.5.2 Minor Non-Compliance

4.7.3.5.2.1 Definition An isolated situation in which some aspect of an applicable control requirement has not been fulfilled such that it raises some doubts as to the adequacy of measures to comply with the requirements of the audit and/or represents a minor risk as would be perceived by the stakeholders.

4.7.3.5.2.2 Examples These occur in the following circumstances:

- one-off breaches of the requirements have been found to be usually caused by human error.

It should be noted, however, that a number of minor non-compliances in the same area can be symptomatic of a system breakdown and could therefore be compounded into a major non-compliance.

4.7.3.5.3 Observation

In situations where the Auditor considers that potential non-compliant situations may arise or where a possible improvement can be identified, an observation may be issued. Organizations are free to identify corrective and preventive actions to observations as they wish, but Auditors should take note of previous observations raised when performing their audits and look for signs of improvement.

4.7.3.6 Planning an Internal Audit

The first stage in performing an internal audit is to plan the audit.

Initial considerations that are considered as input to the audit planning stage include:

- CARs and PARs that have been implemented in the system being audited;
- previous audits performed on the system;
- system changes that have been, or are about to be implemented;
- occurrence of security breaches/incidents;
- risks arising from changes to the Forensic Laboratory's organization and its technology and business processes;
- ensuring that all areas of the system are audited at least once in any "audit year";

- any outstanding issues from previous system Management Reviews.

To plan an audit, the appointed internal Auditor performs the following tasks:

1. Checks the Audit Schedule and determines which area within the Forensic Laboratory requires an audit. Typically, an audit schedule is agreed that shows the proposed:
   - BCP exercises;
   - external audits;
   - internal audits;
   - Management Reviews;
   - other evaluations of management systems and business processes;
   - penetration tests;
   - self-assessment tests.

   Planned for the year. Usually, this is agreed at the Management Review.
2. Reviews the relevant documentation for the area to be audited. This may include some of the following documents:
   - *policies*—copies of the policies relevant to the scope of the audit;
   - *codes of practice*—any industry or sector-specific codes of practice that regulate how the Forensic Laboratory operates within the scope of the audit;
   - *guidelines*—in-house guidance or training materials that the Forensic Laboratory has produced to increase employee awareness for the scope of the audit;
   - *procedures*—in-house procedures that provide detailed step-by-step instructions to employees on how to deal with the specific requirements of the systems within the scope of the audit.
   - the ISO 19011 standard on auditing.
3. Plans for the audit:
   - define the objectives and scope;
   - identify the employees (Auditees) who have responsibilities within the area of operation;
   - identify a suitable date and time for the audit, based on the Audit Schedule;
   - identify the time and duration of each major audit activity;
   - liaise with the Audit Committee, as appropriate;
   - liaise with the relevant management system committee, as appropriate;
   - confirm timescales for the delivery of the audit report.
4. Completes the Audit Plan and issues it to the Auditees. The Auditee can comment on the proposed audit, if necessary. An Audit Plan Letter is given in Appendix 43.
5. Confirms the arrangements with the Auditee to conduct the audit using the Audit Plan Letter.
6. Reviews and amends the standard Audit Work Programmes for use during the audit, as required. The Audit Work Programmes are used to assist in the evaluation of compliance and are merely the requirements of a management system standard or business process turned into a list of questions and requirements for records to support any audit finding.

   When preparing a checklist, there is the need to:
   - collect objective evidence about the status of the system within the scope of the audit so that an informed judgement can be made about its adequacy and effectiveness;
   - take samples from the selected area and check for implementation and effectiveness of the system in order to arrive at that informed judgement;
   - ensure that where the system is thoroughly documented, the Audit Work Programme questions may be quite specific, but in the absence of documentation, questions may need to be of a broader nature;
   - consider "what to look at" and "what to look for" when preparing Audit Work Programmes questions;
   - ensure the audit sample is representative—first focus on the main function of the area;
   - not neglect more peripheral activities completely as these may not be quite as well controlled and hence are more likely to be the cause of non-compliance.

     It is also a good idea to examine what happens when systems are under pressure rather than functioning as normal, for example, what happens:
     - when a lot of employees are off sick or on holiday?
     - at the end of the month or the financial year?
     - when the computer system breaks down?
     - when work levels are abnormally high?

4.7.3.7 Conducting an Internal Audit

The second stage of an audit is to conduct the audit itself to determine whether an area of operation within the Forensic Laboratory complies with the requirements of the audit for the scope.

When conducting an audit, it is essential to:

- remain within the audit scope;
- exercise objectivity;
- collect and analyze evidence that is relevant and sufficient to draw conclusions regarding the scope of the audit;
- remain alert for indications of areas that may require further examination;
- question thoroughly all employees involved in the area of operation.

To conduct an audit, the appointed internal Auditor performs the following tasks (Figure 4.6):

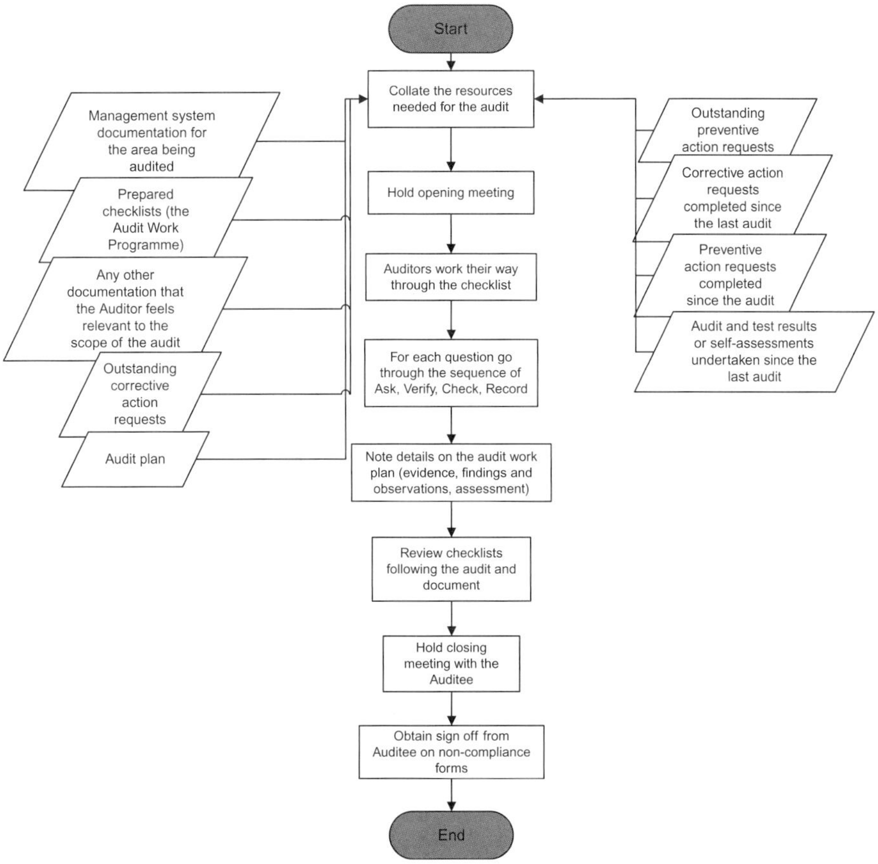

FIGURE 4.6 Conducting an internal audit. (For color version of this figure, the reader is referred to the online version of this chapter.)

1. Collates all the resources that are needed to perform the audit, including:
   - copy of the management system documentation for the area being audited;
   - Audit Plan;
   - prepared checklists (the Audit Work Programme);
   - outstanding CARs;
   - outstanding PARs;
   - CARs completed since the last audit;
   - PARs completed since the audit;
   - any audits, test results, or self-assessments undertaken since the last audit;
   - audit reporting forms, and example of an audit reporting form is given in Appendix 44;
   - corrective and preventive action request forms (an example is given in Appendix 45);
   - any other documentation that the Auditor feels relevant to the scope of the audit.
2. Holds an opening meeting with the Auditee in the area to be audited. An opening meeting agenda is given in Appendix 46. At the meeting, outline the following:
   - inform employees of the purpose of the audit;
   - confirm which functions will be involved in the audit;
   - confirm which employees within the area will be involved in the audit;
   - confirm the schedule for the Auditor which employees will be involved at each stage, i.e., supply a copy of the Audit Plan;
   - confirm the time and location of the closing meeting and establish who will be present;
   - confirm the format of written/oral feedback that will be presented at the closing meeting, i.e., the audit report with associated non-compliance forms;
   - discuss the arrangements for any potential follow-up audits to confirm that any required corrective and/or preventive action has been taken.
3. Works his/her way through the checklists, remembering to concentrate on the processes and the procedures that form the scope of the audit.
4. Works through the following sequence for each question on the checklist:
   - *Ask:* Ask the question to establish the facts;
   - *Verify:* Listen to the Auditee's answer and verify where necessary the understanding of the actual situation;
   - *Check:* Confirm that what the Auditee says corresponds with what the system being audited actually

says should occur. Also check that any associated records and logs are correct and up-to-date;
- *Record:* Write down the audit findings.

It is important that the Auditor is prepared to change the order of questions from those drawn up in the checklists. This is to encourage the flow of information from the Auditee and so obtain the required information faster.

5. Note details on the Audit Work Plan as follows:
   - *Evidence (Documents) Examined:* Record details of the evidence presented in answer to the question. In the case of documents, reference numbers that uniquely identify them should be recorded such as procedure reference, etc. Where possible borrow a copy of the evidence if a full audit report is to be written so that full details can be recorded;
   - *Findings and Observations:* Record the assessment of how well the evidence presented demonstrates compliance with the requirements of the system being audited and its documented policies and procedures;
   - *Assessment:* Grade the answer for each requirement:
     - Pass: The evidence demonstrates full compliance;
     - Major: The evidence demonstrates a Major non-compliance;
     - Minor: The evidence demonstrates a Minor non-compliance;
     - Observation: No non-compliance was found but an observation about potential problems and how improvements could be made has been made.

   Audit Marking definitions are given in Section 4.7.3.5.
6. Reviews checklists following the audit and document.
7. Holds a closing meeting with the Auditee. A closing meeting agenda is given in Appendix 47. At the meeting, outline the following.
8. Obtains sign off from the Auditee on the non-compliance forms.

4.7.3.8 Preparing the Audit Report

1. The Auditor produces an audit report using the audit report template that documents the findings and observations of the audit. An example audit report template is given in Appendix 48. The report must reflect accurately the content of the audit and include as a minimum:
   - objectives and scope of the audit;
   - an objective assessment of whether the area of operation is conformant with the relevant management system standard;
   - an objective assessment of the effectiveness of the area of operation;
   - an objective assessment of the system's ability to achieve its stated objectives;
   - recommendations for improvements to the management system based on objective assessments of policy and operation, and the ability of the management system or business process to achieve its objectives;
   - recommendations on how improvements are to be implemented;
   - timeframe for completion of actions in the CARs and/or PARs;
   - responsibility for performing those actions.
2. The Auditor prints, dates, and signs the report. The report is then sent to the Auditee for action and a copy sent to the Audit Committee and the Chairman of the relevant management standard committee.

4.7.3.9 Completing the Audit

1. At the end of the audit, the Auditor collates all documentation that formed the audit including (Figure 4.7):
   - their own working notes;
   - their Audit Plan;
   - their audit report;
   - their Audit Work Programme;
   - supporting records.
2. All relevant documentation is scanned by the Auditor and then stored in the internal audit virtual folder.
3. The paper documentation is shredded and then disposed.
4. If there are corrective or preventive actions, the Auditor sets a deadline/follow-up date with the Auditee for corrective actions to have been completed. Corrective action is performed as follows:
   - all non-conformities and their causes are identified from the audit report;
   - feedback from any Management Reviews should also be considered (where relevant) for purposes of taking preventive action;
   - for operational non-conformities, corrective action is proposed by the Auditee and discussed and agreed with the Auditor;
   - all agreed action is documented in the relevant audit report;
   - the Auditee updates the management systems in accordance with the agreed action.

   If there are no corrective actions (or when all further action from an audit is complete), the Auditor informs the Owner of the system that was the scope of the internal audit that the audit is complete.

4.8 CONTINUOUS IMPROVEMENT

The Forensic Laboratory is committed to a program of continuous improvement of their management systems and business processes. This process covers all of the management systems and business processes implemented in the Forensic Laboratory and the continuous improvement policy, as defined in Appendix 14, has been approved by Top Management.

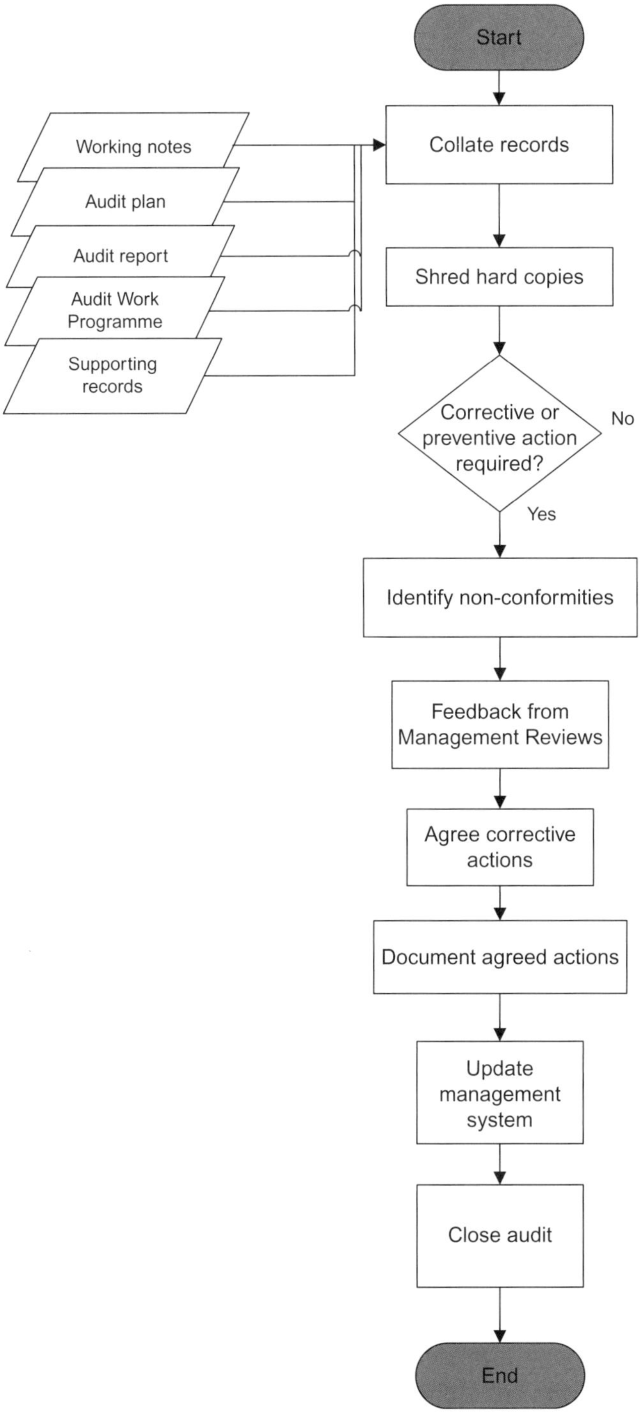

FIGURE 4.7 Completing the audit. (For color version of this figure, the reader is referred to the online version of this chapter.)

Top Management ensures that there are regular audits and Management Reviews of the management systems and business processes with a view to continuous improvement, and focus on:

- how the services supported by the management systems and their supporting activities are performing (in particular, whether any activities are not performing as expected);
- the effectiveness of system controls, policies, and procedures;
- the level of risk to the Forensic Laboratory based on changes to technology, business objectives and processes, and potential threats;
- the scope of the management systems, and whether it requires changing;
- potential improvements to management systems processes.

4.8.1 Handling of Non-Conformities

Where non-conformities have been identified either from:

- *External Audit Finding*—Any discrepancy in the management system found and reported by External Auditors;
- *Incident*—any incident identified and reported that affects the expected outcome of the management system and may lead to Corrective or Preventive Action;
- *Internal Audit Finding*—Any discrepancy in the management system found and reported by Internal Auditors;
- *Management Review Finding*—Any discrepancy in the management system found and reported by a Management Review of the management system;
- *Preventive Action*—The processing of ideas or suggestions for process and product improvement within the management systems;
- *System Accreditation Service Audit Finding*—Any discrepancy in the management system found and reported during the Accreditation Audit cycle by the relevant Accreditation Service;
- *System Certification Body Audit Finding*—Any discrepancy in the management system found and reported during the Certification Audit cycle by the relevant Certification Body;

They shall be reviewed to determine action to be taken, based on the root cause of the non-conformities occurring. While there may be any number of root causes for non-conformity, the most common that the Forensic Laboratory has discovered are defined in Appendix 49. Often the root cause is not obvious and therefore a careful analysis of all possible causes is required.

The review shall be in the form of a formal response to the audit report or incident.

Preventive action shall be raised as a Preventive Action Request.

In some cases, the response to the audit report will suffice, but if action is needed, it shall be raised as a Corrective Acton Request and communicated to all relevant stakeholders as appropriate.

In the Forensic Laboratory, a Corrective Action and Preventive Action (CAPA) database system is used although a paper-based system could be used and an example of the information required is given in Appendix 45.

4.8.2 Planning and Implementing Corrective Actions

Corrective action stems from either an audit non-conformity or an incident leading to the identification of a weakness or fault that requires corrective action.

The Forensic Laboratory also uses trend analysis for identification of persistent non-conformance or incidents or faults.

If an immediate corrective action is required to protect the Forensic Laboratory from suffering a serious security breach or failure of a service, this should be treated as an emergency change for implementation. The relevant Management System Owner can determine the appropriate implementation actions as required in conjunction with specialist Forensic Laboratory employees. Following the implementation, all supporting documentation and approvals must be obtained.

Depending on the nature and severity of the non-conformance, the employee identifying the non-conformity should do one the following:

- report it using the normal incident management process as defined in Chapter 7, Section 7.4.1;
- report it to their Line Manager;
- report it to the relevant Management System Owner;
- report it to Top Management.

Depending on the nature and severity of the non-conformance, it will be discussed at the next relevant management system meeting. In exceptional circumstances, an emergency meeting can be, and may be, called. It is essential to:

- determine the root cause of the non-conformity, examples of common root causes are given in Appendix 49;
- evaluate the corrective action needed to be taken to ensure that triage is carried out and that the non-conformity does not recur.

The non-conformance will be actioned and tracked. The resulting action may be:

- a change in policy or working practices that will then be documented and publicized. Changes to documented procedures or work instructions resulting from corrective and preventive action are performed as described in the Forensic Laboratory document control procedures in Section 4.6.3;
- to reinforce the application and observation of an existing policy or practice;
- to post advice through e-mail or on the corporate intranet;
- to make operational changes to the infrastructure;
- to consider, but reject, any change.

4.8.3 Determining Preventive Action

Corrective action is the result of something going wrong (e.g., an incident or accident). Preventive action seeks to identify potential issues before they become faults, failures, incidents, or accidents. The implementation of preventive action that often costs less than corrective action and is typically easier to implement.

Preventive action is usually more difficult to identify, but the Forensic Laboratory regularly assess its services and infrastructure to help identify trends:

- ongoing employee awareness is essential so that all employees are encouraged to spot things that appear wrong or "not quite right" and they are encouraged to report them through the normal fault or incident reporting process—or where warranted to the relevant Management System Owner or the Forensic Laboratory Director. The Forensic Laboratory has a "no blame culture";
- the Forensic Laboratory analyzes trends to see if there are specific incidents that occur more frequently than others;
- the Forensic Laboratory maintains a corporate risk register as do specific projects. These, with the results from the Business Impact Analysis (BIA), shall be used to determine high-level risks that should be addressed and so controls are defined to treat these risks.

When a potential preventive action is identified, it is assessed and processed as a corrective action, where the Auditee is the relevant owner for the operational area.

4.8.4 Corrective and Preventive Action Requests

Once a corrective or preventive action has been identified, it must be recorded, have appropriate resources assigned to it, be managed to a satisfactory conclusion, and be monitored by management during the time between the identification and closure of the corrective or preventive action. All CAPAs must be subject to Post Implementation Review (PIR), with the results reported to the relevant Management System Owner or other process owner as required.

4.8.5 Corrective and Preventive Action Ownership

Corrective or preventive action must be owned by the relevant management system manager, as below:

- ISO 9001—Quality Manager;
- OHSAS 18001—Health and Safety Manager;
- ISO 20000—Service Delivery Manager;
- ISO 22301—Business Continuity Manager;
- ISO 27001—Information Security Manager;
- ISO 15489—Records Manager.

Job descriptions given for each role are given in Chapter 18, Section 18.1.5.

4.8.6 Corrective and Preventive Action Oversight

Oversight of the relevant CARs and PARs shall be performed by:

- ISO 9001—Quality Committee;
- ISO 14001—Environment Committee;
- OHSAS 18001—Health and Safety Committee;
- ISO 20000—Service Delivery Committee;
- ISO 22301—Business Continuity Committee;
- ISO 27001—Information Security Committee.

In addition, there are the following committees:

- Audit Committee;
- Risk Committee.

Terms of Reference are given in the appendices in this chapter for each committee above.

4.9 MANAGEMENT REVIEWS

4.9.1 General

Reviews of the management systems must take place at least once a year (and more often if required—such as on influencing change or after a major incident) to ensure the continued suitability, adequacy, and effectiveness of the relevant management systems. The provision of details for the Management Review is the responsibility of the relevant Management System Owner.

While the provision of the details of the review of the management system remains the responsibility of the relevant Management System Owner, the review shall be carried out by the Forensic Laboratory Top Management with such employees as they see fit to include.

- the review shall include assessing opportunities for improvement and the need for changes to the management systems, including their supporting policies, policy objectives, and procedures.
- the results (i.e., records) of the reviews shall be clearly documented and records shall be maintained of the meeting in the form of minutes and CARs.

4.9.2 Review Input

The input to a Management Review shall include, where appropriate:

- any changes that could affect the management systems, including regulatory and legal issues;
- approvals needed (operate, residual risk acceptance, SoA, etc.);
- customer (or any other stakeholders) feedback;
- financial effects of management system-related activities;
- management systems performance and effectiveness;
- marketplace evaluation and strategies;
- other opportunities for improvement not covered by the above;
- performance and status of suppliers and strategic partners;
- recommendations for improvement to the management systems;
- results of management systems audits, management systems reviews, penetration tests, benchmarking, other audits or self-assessments of the management systems;
- results of reviews of the management system policies;
- review of all external third-party documents in IMS to ensure they are up-to-date;
- review of KPIs and annual review of business;
- security issues, faults, and incidents reported of note;
- status and follow-up of Management Review action items;
- status and results of management systems objectives and management system improvement activities;
- status of preventive and corrective actions;
- techniques, products, or procedures, which could be used in the organization to improve the management systems;
- vulnerabilities or threats not adequately addressed in the previous risk assessment.

These inputs comprise the agenda of the Management Review.

4.9.3 Review Output

The output from the Management Review shall include any decisions and actions related to the following, where appropriate.

- amended resource needs;
- continuous improvement of the effectiveness of the management systems;
- corrective actions identified;
- financial or budgetary requirements;
- formally agreed minutes of the Management Review by the stakeholders;
- improve Client deliverability;
- improvement to how the effectiveness of controls is being measured;
- modification of procedures and controls that effect the management systems, as necessary, to respond to

internal or external events that may impact on the management systems, including changes to:
  - business processes affected by changes in technology;
  - business requirements and objectives;
  - contractual obligations;
  - increased resilience requirements from the business and/or Clients;
  - levels of risk and/or criteria for accepting risks;
  - management system requirements;
  - regulatory or legal requirements;
  - supporting policies.
- revised performance objectives;
- update of the BIA, risk assessment, and risk treatment plan for the relevant management systems;
- updated approvals (risk acceptance, approval to operate, update of SoA, etc.);
- updated management system policies, if appropriate;
- variation of the scope of the management system.

Typically, actions will be articulated in the form of CARs and shall be managed to completion through the relevant Line Managers and Management System Owners.

Reviews of the management system must take place at least once a year (and ideally more often as required) and are the responsibility of the relevant Management System Owner.

4.9.4 Agendas

The agenda for the Management Review is based on the required inputs from each relevant standard. The Forensic Laboratory agenda is given in Appendix 36.

This agenda may be used for a Management Review of a single management system or for a review of multiple management systems. Where used for a single management system, the details related only to that management system are considered. Where used for multiple management systems, the details related to the management systems being reviewed are considered.

APPENDIX 1 - MAPPING ISO GUIDE 72 REQUIREMENTS TO PAS 99

This section contains the mapping of PAS 99 to ISO Guide 72.

ISO Guide 72 Requirement	PAS 99 Section	PAS 99 Control
	4.1	General Requirements
Policy	4.2	Management System Policy
Planning (Plan)	4.3	Planning
Implementation and operation (Do)	4.4	Implementation and operation
Performance assessment (Check)	4.5	Performance assessment
Improvement (Act)	4.6	Improvement
Management Review (Act)	4.7	Management Review

APPENDIX 2 - PAS 99 GLOSSARY

Term	Definition
Aspect	Characteristic of an activity, product, or service that has or can have an impact
Contingency planning	Consideration of the potentially serious incidents that could affect the operations of the organization and for the formulation of a plan(s) to prevent or mitigate the effects and to enable the organization to operate as normally as possible
Document	Information and its supporting medium **Note 1** The medium can be paper, magnetic, electronic, or optical computer disc, photograph or master sample, or a combination thereof. **Note 2** A set of documents, for example, specifications or records, is frequently called "documentation."
Impact	Effect on the organization's policy commitments and objectives, its interested parties, the organization itself, and/or on the environment **Note** An effect can be positive or negative.
Interested Party	Person or group concerned with or affected by the activities, products, and/or services of an organization **Note 1** This could include customers, owners, regulators, non-governmental organizations, people in an organization, suppliers, bankers, unions, partners, or society.

Continued

Term	Definition
	Note 2 A group can comprise an organization, a part thereof, or more than one organization.
Management System	System(s) to establish policy and objectives and to achieve those objectives **Note** A management system comprises the elements of policy planning, implementation and operation, performance assessment, improvement, and Management Review.
Procedure	Specified way to carry out an activity or a process **Note** Procedures can be documented or not.
Process	Set of interrelated or interacting activities that transforms inputs into outputs **Note** Processes may be classified in a number of different ways. A distinction is sometimes made between operational processes that are directly concerned with the planned outputs of the organization, and management processes that provide the framework that enables the operational processes to take place.
Risk	Likelihood of an event occurring that will have an impact on objectives **Note 1** Risk is normally determined in terms of combination of the likelihood of an event and its consequences. **Note 2** An event may be the occurrence of an aspect with the associated impact as its consequence.

APPENDIX 3 - PAS 99 MAPPING TO IMS PROCEDURES

This section contains the mapping of PAS 99 to the procedures developed to implement the standard.

PAS 99 Section	Control	Procedure(s)
4	Common management system requirements	This chapter, Section 4.3
4.1	General requirements	This chapter, Section 4.3
4.2	Management System Policy	This chapter, Section 4.4.1 and various policies from the Forensic Laboratory are given throughout this book
4.3	Planning	This chapter, Section 4.5
4.3.1	Identification and evaluation of aspects, impacts, and risks	This chapter, Section 4.5.1
4.3.2	Identification of legal and other requirements	This chapter, Section 4.5.2
4.3.3	Contingency planning	This chapter, Section 4.5.3
4.3.4	Objectives	This chapter, Section 4.5.4
4.3.5	Organizational structure, roles, responsibilities, and authorities	This chapter, Section 4.5.5 Chapter 18, Section 18.1.5
4.4	Implementation and operation	This chapter, Section 4.6
4.4.1	Operational control	This chapter, Section 4.6.1
4.4.2	Management of resources	This chapter, Section 4.6.2
4.4.3	Documentation requirements	This chapter, Section 4.6.3
4.4.4	Communication	This chapter, Section 4.6.5
4.5	Performance assessment	This chapter, Section 4.7
4.5.1	Monitoring and measurements	This chapter, Section 4.7.1
4.5.2	Evaluation of compliance	This chapter, Section 4.7.2
4.5.3	Internal audit	This chapter, Section 4.7.3

Continued

PAS 99 Section	Control	Procedure(s)
4.6	Improvement	This chapter, Section 4.8
4.6.1	General	This chapter, Section 4.8
4.6.2	Corrective, preventive, and improvement action	This chapter, Section 4.8
4.7	Management Review	This chapter, Section 4.9
4.7.1	General	This chapter, Section 4.9.1
4.7.2	Input	This chapter, Section 4.9.2
4.7.3	Output	This chapter, Section 4.9.3

APPENDIX 4 - THE FORENSIC LABORATORY GOAL STATEMENT

The Forensic Laboratory's Goal Statement is to:

- create a high-performance customer-facing organization;
- enhance the operational value from our existing portfolio;
- expand our portfolio profitably;
- be known as a digital forensic center of excellence.

APPENDIX 5 - THE FORENSIC LABORATORY BASELINE MEASURES

The Forensic Laboratory's Baseline Measures to support the Goal Statement are:

- minimize complaints;
- achieve or exceed SLAs, specifically TRTs;
- achieve an average of over 4 for all customer feedback;
- attend major conferences with speakers;
- publish in learned journals/magazines;
- increase repeat business from existing Clients;
- increase new business;
- minimize any incidents.

Note

The Forensic Laboratory has figures for these measures as KPIs, but these are not repeated here as this must be a business-based decision for any other laboratory. Additionally, a laboratory may chose to add or remove baseline measures from this list according to its business requirements.

APPENDIX 6 - ENVIRONMENT POLICY

All Forensic Laboratory employees are committed to the care of the environment and the prevention of pollution.

The Forensic Laboratory ensures that all its activities are carried out in conformance with the relevant environmental legislation.

The Forensic Laboratory seeks to:

- create as little waste as possible and disposing of waste responsibly;
- recycle waste, where possible;
- use recycled materials where recycling alternatives are available;
- encourage the use of electronic media to lessen the amount of paper used;
- ensure the energy-efficiency of the equipment used;
- switch off equipment when not in use, where possible;
- encourage employees to make use of public transport, where possible;
- where practical, to use fair-traded products;
- use low-energy lighting where possible, with dimmers and timers where appropriate;
- ensure a "No Smoking" office;
- train employees to understand their environmental responsibilities and encourage new ideas on improving our environmental performance.

An essential feature of the environmental management system is a commitment to improving environmental performance. This is achieved by setting annual environmental improvement objectives and targets that are regularly monitored and reviewed. The objectives and targets are publicized throughout the Forensic Laboratory organization and all employees are committed to their achievement.

In order to ensure the achievement of the above commitments, the organization has implemented an environmental management system that satisfies the requirements of ISO 14001.

This policy and the obligations and responsibilities required by the environmental management system have been communicated to all employees.

The policy is available to the public on request.

This policy is issued and maintained by the Environment Manager, who also provides advice and guidance on its implementation and ensures compliance.

All Forensic Laboratory employees shall comply with this policy.

APPENDIX 7 - HEALTH AND SAFETY POLICY

It is the Forensic Laboratory's intention to provide a safe and healthy working environment in accordance with the relevant Health and Safety legislation and other requirements to which the Forensic Laboratory subscribes.

The responsibility for health, safety, and welfare within the Forensic Laboratory is placed with Top Management. At the heart of this commitment to health and safety are the seven core safety principles that all Forensic Laboratory's employees are required to embrace and which will facilitate this commitment to continual improvement of health and safety performance. These are:

1. all injuries can be prevented;
2. employee involvement is essential;
3. management is responsible for preventing injuries;
4. working safely and contributing to safety improvements is a condition of employment;
5. all operating exposures can be safeguarded;
6. training employees to work safely is essential;
7. prevention of personal injury is good business sense.

Top Management, through the various business streams and line management, will ensure that all employees on the Forensic Laboratory's premises fulfill these commitments by:

- pursuing the deployment of the Forensic Laboratory's safety strategy and the goal of zero injuries;
- ensuring that arrangements and resources exist to support this policy;
- effective management of health and safety;
- recognizing the risks inherent in a consultancy and service management organization;
- conducting and maintaining risk assessments and safe systems of work;
- working toward meeting the requirements of OHSAS 18001, the Health and Safety Management specification;
- ensuring that they meet all legislative and regulatory requirements relating to Health and Safety;
- setting, reviewing, and agreeing to Health and Safety Objectives at the Management Review;
- ensuring that management sets an example for all employees in the areas of Health and Safety;
- ensuring that there are appropriate financial, technical, and human resources present to implement, manage, and continuously improve the Forensic Laboratory's Health and Safety Management System;
- ensuring that all relevant Health and Safety issues are taken into consideration when influencing changes are made to business processes;
- providing advice, training, and support for all Forensic Laboratory's employees to maintain a safe and healthy workplace;
- ensuring that any preventive and corrective actions required by the performance assessments process are fully implemented on time to reduce risk to an acceptable level;
- ensuring that documented risk assessments are maintained and that a risk register of all hazards and controls is maintained;
- ensuring that any identified hazards and their controls are communicated to all relevant Forensic Laboratory's employees;
- ensuring that a regular schedule of internal audits for Health and Safety are undertaken;
- undertaking Management Reviews of the Forensic Laboratory's Health and Safety processes in accordance with the requirements of OHSAS 18001;
- maintaining OHSAS 18001 certification, as appropriate.

The Forensic Laboratory shall continue to invest in Health and Safety improvements on a progressive basis, setting objectives and targets in our annual Health and Safety programs.

The Forensic Laboratory will seek to engage and involve all employees in creating and maintaining a safe working environment.

This policy is issued, reviewed, and maintained by the Health and Safety Manager, who also provides advice and guidance on its implementation and ensures compliance.

All Forensic Laboratory employees shall comply with this policy.

APPENDIX 8 - UNDUE INFLUENCE POLICY

The Forensic Laboratory recognises that trust and confidence in the propriety of its activities is essential to its continuing success and growth. In order to foster the trust and confidence that Clients, suppliers, employees, and the community in general have in the Forensic Laboratory and its products and services, it is essential that the Forensic Laboratory and its employees, behave, and are seen to behave, appropriately and honestly at all times.

This policy has been implemented to:

- protect the Forensic Laboratory's reputation;
- protect employees from accusations of impropriety;
- ensure that all Clients and suppliers are dealt with on an equal basis;
- support the Conflict of Interest Policy.

Employees are advised that, notwithstanding anything contained herein, where there is any doubt over the permissibility or propriety of accepting a gift or hospitality offer they should decline the offer.

GIFTS

Nothing should be accepted which would bring the Forensic Laboratory into disrepute.

With the exception of gifts of low value and which are mere tokens (such as promotional pens, calendars, stationary) or similar, and always excluding money, Forensic Laboratory employees are not permitted to accept any gifts from Clients, suppliers, other third parties involved with the Forensic Laboratory or those seeking to be become involved.

The Forensic Laboratory recognises that there may be exceptional instances when refusing a gift will cause significant offence or embarrassment. In such instances, the gift may be accepted and any items of high value will be donated to a charity of the Forensic Laboratory's choosing. Where practicable, any employee minded to accept such a gift should first seek approval from Top Management. If it is not practicable to gain prior approval, the accepting employee should inform Top Management as soon as possible after receiving the gift.

The Forensic Laboratory requires that an accurate record must be kept of all gift offers made to any employee in the "Hospitality and Gifts Register" (the Register). Any employee who is offered a gift which is not merely a token shall record, as soon as is reasonable practicable:

- a description of the gift offered;
- an estimation of the value of the gift offered;
- whether it was rejected or accepted;
- if accepted, why it was accepted;
- whether prior approval was obtained, and if so, from whom;
- if appropriate, to which charity it was donated.

CORPORATE HOSPITALITY

Corporate Hospitality, for the purposes of this policy, is any form of accommodation, entertainment, or other hospitality provided for a Forensic Laboratory employee by a third party and which is extended to the employee solely or significantly due to their position in the Forensic Laboratory.

For the purposes of this policy and for the sake of clarity, the following are not normally considered Corporate Hospitality and will not require any approval prior to acceptance:

- normal working lunches or refreshments provided during a business visit;
- hospitality extended to employees attending a Forensic Laboratory approved seminar, conference, or other external event, provided that such hospitality is extended to all who are in attendance;
- benefits derived from frequent traveller schemes, awarded during travel paid for by the Forensic Laboratory;
- free seminars, talks, or workshops, provided that they are free to all in attendance and are not provided solely for Forensic Laboratory employees.

All employees are required to obtain Line Management approval before accepting any form of Corporate Hospitality which is offered to them. Approval must be sought from Top Management for hospitality offered is values above the equivalent of USD 100 in any local currency.

An accurate record must be kept of all Corporate Hospitality offered to any Forensic Laboratory employee, whether accepted or not, in the Register. Details that shall be recorded include:

- description of the hospitality offered;
- an estimation of the likely value of the hospitality;
- whether it was rejected or accepted;
- if accepted, why it was accepted;
- from whom prior approval was obtained.

HOSPITALITY AND GIFTS REGISTER

The Register shall be held by Legal Counsel.

All offers of gifts or hospitality must be recorded on a Register Entry Form, available from Legal Counsel.

The Register Entry Form must be signed by the employee and countersigned by the relevant Manager before being returned to the Legal Counsel for being included in the Register.

The Register Entry Form must be completed as soon as is reasonably practicable and be filed with the Legal Counsel within 5 working days of the offer of the gift or hospitality.

BREACHES OF THIS POLICY

A breach of this policy and shall result in appropriate disciplinary action being taken against the employee.

This policy is issued and maintained by Legal Counsel, who also provides advice and guidance on its implementation and ensures compliance.

All Forensic Laboratory employees shall comply with this policy.

APPENDIX 9 - BUSINESS CONTINUITY POLICY

The business success of the Forensic Laboratory is reliant upon the preservation of its critical business activities to ensure that products and services are delivered to Forensic Laboratory employees and externally to Clients.

The Forensic Laboratory sets out the framework for how the Forensic Laboratory responds to business disruptions in its critical business activities, how the Forensic Laboratory manages the continuation of these activities, and how the Forensic Laboratory manages its subsequent restoration.

The scope of business continuity at the Forensic Laboratory is to provide resilience for its critical business activities through the implementation of controls that minimize the impact of a disruption on its business products, services, employees, and infrastructure located in all Forensic Laboratory offices.

It is Forensic Laboratory policy to:

- regard business continuity as a key organizational activity and maintain a comprehensive business continuity program to implement and manage this;

- identify the critical business activities in the Forensic Laboratory through BIA on the events that could cause significant business disruption;
- implement an appropriate business continuity strategy that meets the needs of the Forensic Laboratory;
- develop and implement plans to manage business disruptions that cover the Forensic Laboratory's information systems, business premises, and staff;
- regularly test business continuity plans to ensure that they:
  - maintain or rapidly recover critical activities;
  - maintain the availability of key resources to support critical activities;
  - prevent or limit the disruption to employees and Clients.
- define the responsibilities of all employees involved in business continuity activities and provide training to ensure that these responsibilities can be carried out successfully;
- provide training to raise employee awareness of business continuity;
- regularly review the Forensic Laboratory business continuity activities, policies, plans, tests, and responsibilities to ensure that the business continuity strategy remains appropriate to the Forensic Laboratory's needs.

This policy, and the subordinate policies, processes, and procedures to this document, provides a clear statement of our commitment to ensure that critical Forensic Laboratory business activities can be maintained during a disruption. This policy is subordinate to the Forensic Laboratory Information Security Policy, which also gives further guidance on risk management and information assurance.

The Forensic Laboratory has implemented ISO 22301 to manage its business continuity operations and this is managed by this IMS.

The Business Continuity Management System (BCMS) provides the framework for the implementation of this policy within the Forensic Laboratory and is supported by a comprehensive set of processes and procedures. This system is regularly reviewed to ensure it remains effective and that all critical business activities are covered.

This policy is issued and maintained by the Business Continuity Manager, who also provides advice and guidance on its implementation and ensures compliance.

All Forensic Laboratory employees shall comply with this policy.

APPENDIX 10 - INFORMATION SECURITY POLICY

The Forensic Laboratory owes its success, and its excellent reputation, to its high-quality and professional products and services.

The Forensic Laboratory's ability to maintain this reputation, and the levels of service to their Clients, depends on the highest standards of professionalism and integrity. It is paramount that these standards include the way in which the Forensic Laboratory uses and protects information and information systems. Any loss of confidence in the Forensic Laboratory's ability to provide these services could cause the business to suffer. New technology exposes the Forensic Laboratory to new and potentially greater risks because much greater reliance is placed on automated systems, and because of the extensive use of networked computers. The Forensic Laboratory wants to reap the benefits of the new technology but will not take unacceptable risks to do so.

It is the Forensic Laboratory's policy to secure information and systems in a manner that meets or exceeds accepted good practice. The Forensic Laboratory will ensure the continuity of their business operations and manage business damage by the implementation of controls to minimize the impact of security incidents.

It is Forensic Laboratory policy to ensure that:

- all Client data are appropriately protected and are not divulged to any third party without authorization;
- the premises are protected by suitable physical security and environmental controls, and where appropriate, access is restricted to authorized staff;
- confidentiality and integrity of all information is maintained;
- information is accessible to all employees and third parties according to business need and is protected against unauthorized access;
- access to Forensic Laboratory data and personal data is appropriately controlled;
- contractual, regulatory, and legislative requirements are met;
- a business continuity plan is devised, tested, and maintained;
- all in-house systems development is appropriately controlled and tested before live implementation;
- all employees are provided with training in information security awareness and individual responsibilities defined;
- all employees are aware of their responsibility to adhere to the policy and ensure that all breaches of information security, actual or suspected, are reported to the Information Security Manager, and where appropriate investigated by the Information Security Committee.

This policy provides a clear statement of the Forensic Laboratory's commitment to protect all information assets from threats internal and external, intentional or accidental.

An Information Security Management System (ISMS) provides the framework for the implementation of this policy within the Forensic Laboratory and is supported by a comprehensive set of procedures. This system is regularly reviewed via a risk management process to ensure that all identified risks are covered.

This policy is issued and maintained by the Information Security Manager, who also provides advice and guidance on its implementation and ensures compliance.

All Forensic Laboratory employees shall comply with this policy.

APPENDIX 11 - ACCESS CONTROL POLICY

This policy defines the principles, standards, guidelines, and responsibilities related to accessing Forensic Laboratory information-processing systems. This policy is intended to support information security by preventing unauthorized access to information and information processing systems.

New technologies and more automation are increasing opportunities for data sharing, meaning that the Forensic Laboratory must seek a balance between the need to protect information resources and allow greater access to information and information processing systems. Several factors affect how the Forensic Laboratory controls access to its information and information processing systems, networks, and data—this includes some calculation of risk and consequences of unauthorized access.

The primary objectives of the Access Control Policy are to:

- communicate the need for access control;
- establish specific requirements for protecting against unauthorized access;
- create an infrastructure that will foster data sharing without sacrificing security of information and information processing systems.

Access control protects information by managing access to all entry and exit points, both logical and physical. Adequate perimeter security and logical security measures must protect against unauthorized access to sensitive information on Forensic Laboratory information-processing systems. These measures ensure that only authorized users have access to specific information and information processing systems.

- Forensic Laboratory security administration activity regarding access control violations or incidents should be reported via the standard incident management process;
- applications used in the Forensic Laboratory incorporate controls for managing access to selected information and functions;
- Forensic Laboratory systems shall authenticate functions that are consistent with the level of confidentiality or sensitivity of the information they contain and process. Identification is unique for each user of the system, and the system provides a method to accurately identify the user through a directory system, passwords, smart tokens, smart cards, or other means;

Note

Some system accounts are generic (therefore shared). These accounts are authorized, regularly reviewed, and records are kept.

- the authorities to read, write, modify, update, or delete information from automated files or databases are established by the Owner(s) of the information. Individuals may be granted a specific combination of authorities. Individuals shall not to be given any authority beyond their needs. Access rules or profiles are established in a manner that restricts users from performing incompatible functions or functions beyond their responsibility and enforces a separation of duties;
- Forensic Laboratory computer operations that support sensitive information operate in accordance with procedures approved by the information Owner(s) and assure that:
  - information cannot be modified or destroyed except in accordance with procedures;
  - operating programs prohibit unauthorized access or changes to, or destruction of, records;
  - operating programs are used to detect and store all unauthorized attempts to penetrate the system;
  - special requirements, all contractual and legal obligations are all met.
- access to the Forensic Laboratory network is subject to the security policies and procedures of the network;
- passwords should be confidential and at least 10 alphanumeric characters long. Passwords are not a single dictionary word, repeating character strings, or identifying information that is linked to the user;
- strong passwords are automatically forced on the user by the operating system, so there is no account expiration requiring a password change. The Forensic Laboratory took the view that it is better to have one strong password to remember than to keep changing them. Given that there are so few staff and the level of physical security, the Top Management have accepted this risk;
- for forensic workstations, all access is controlled by biometric fingerprint scanners for additional security;
- employees with broad access to data in sensitive positions will be required to undergo additional security screening as a condition of employment;
- security is required not only for software and information but also for physical security of equipment, which include at least the following:
  - restrict physical access to information and information processing systems where continued operation is essential or where sensitive or confidential data are stored online;
  - restrict access to computer facilities to employees who need such access to perform assigned work duties;

  - restrict access to software documentation and data storage to employees who need such access to perform assigned work duties.
- the Forensic Laboratory will revoke access to the network to ensure the security, integrity, and availability of the network to other users;
- all Forensic Laboratory users must be aware of workstation security:
  - sensitive or confidential information shall not be on the workstation hard drive for security and business reasons. Most workstations pose a risk of unauthorized access because the drives are accessible;
  - reasonable efforts should be made to safeguard individual workstations to protect against unauthorized access to the workstation, network, or data;
  - passwords for workstation logon should not be built into the logon script for auto-sign on;
  - mobile device users must follow the Forensic Laboratory guidelines to protect against the theft, destruction, or loss of equipment and information;
  - users shall sign off when the system will be left inactive or unattended;
  - a Clear Desk and Clear Screen Policy operates throughout the Forensic Laboratory.

This policy is issued and maintained by the Information Security Manager, who also provides advice and guidance on its implementation and ensures compliance.

All Forensic Laboratory employees shall comply with this policy.

APPENDIX 12 - CHANGE OR TERMINATION POLICY

The Forensic Laboratory pursues an active policy of promoting awareness of information security to ensure that security issues are addressed when all employees terminate or change employment.

Consideration of security during termination and change of employment helps reinforce the Forensic Laboratory's commitment to information security by ensuring that all employees are properly managed, that all relevant issues concerning information security are properly addressed, and that issues concerning the removal of all employee's access rights are fully resolved.

The Forensic Laboratory policies and procedures for termination and changes to employment are controlled and maintained by the Human Resources Department.

The Forensic Laboratory policy for managing security during termination and change of employment is:

- all employment termination and changes (permanent, temporary, and third party) must be managed in accordance with the Human Resources policies and procedures for managing termination and changes to employment;
- Forensic Laboratory Managers must work in accordance with the Human Resources policy and procedures when terminating employment as defined in the Human Resources Leavers Checklist for Line Managers—it is the responsibility of the relevant Line Manager to ensure they comply with requisite policy and procedures;
- all security considerations outlined in the Human Resources Leavers Checklist for Line Managers—both information and physical—must be addressed and resolved when an employee leaves the Forensic Laboratory or changes employment within the Forensic Laboratory;
- termination or changes to employment roles with specific information security tasks or activities must be managed appropriately by either the relevant Business Manager and/or Human Resources personnel;
- all employees must return any Forensic Laboratory assets that are in their possession on termination or change of employment;
- all access rights to information and information-processing facilities (both physical and virtual) must be removed on termination or change of employment;
- removal of access rights to Forensic Laboratory information-processing and network facilities must be performed in accordance with the Forensic Laboratory procedures for managing user accounts;
- removal and review of access privileges to Forensic Laboratory information-processing facilities must be performed in accordance with the Forensic Laboratory procedures for managing system access.

This policy is issued and maintained by the Information Security Manager and the Human Resources Manager, who also provide advice and guidance on its implementation and ensures compliance.

All Forensic Laboratory employees shall comply with this policy.

APPENDIX 13 - CLEAR DESK AND CLEAR SCREEN POLICY

CLEAR DESK POLICY

The Forensic Laboratory operates a Clear Desk Policy that is designed to reduce risks by unauthorized access, loss, and damage to classified paper and storage media.

The following is the Clear Desk Policy operated by the Forensic Laboratory:

- all Forensic Laboratory employees must maintain a clear desk for classified information when leaving their work area for a significant period of time (including lunch breaks, and at the end of each working day) or be locked away at the least;
- all classified information must be properly archived into secure file cabinets, closets, or storage rooms after use;

- classified information that is not to be used or archived must be shredded;
- all printed documents (print outputs, faxes, photocopies) must be collected and then used, shredded, or archived;
- printers, faxes, and photocopiers must be checked regularly (at least every day after business hours) for print outs that are not collected (the items should be secured until the proper owners of the documents are available);
- all information on whiteboards, work boards, etc., must be wiped after use.

CLEAR SCREEN POLICY

The Forensic Laboratory operates a Clear Screen Policy that is designed to reduce risks by unauthorized access, loss, and damage to information held in Forensic Laboratory information-processing systems.

The following is the Clear Screen Policy operated by the Forensic Laboratory:

- no system that is available via a workstation must be accessible if the workstation is left temporarily unattended;
- workstations that are left temporarily unattended (up to 60 min for desktop or portable devices and 30 min for Servers) must have access temporarily blocked using either:
  - a manual, password-protected keyboard lock facility initiated by a user before leaving their workstation or
  - an automatic, password-protected screen saver that is activated after 60 min of workstation inactivity.
- personnel must not stick attachments to workstation screens (particularly sensitive information such as customer data or passwords).

This policy is issued and maintained by the Information Security Manager, who also provides advice and guidance on its implementation and ensures compliance.

All Forensic Laboratory employees shall comply with this policy.

APPENDIX 14 - CONTINUOUS IMPROVEMENT POLICY

The Forensic Laboratory is committed to operating efficiently and effectively in order to meet the needs of its Clients. Continuous improvement in all activities is vital for the Forensic Laboratory's continued success.

The Forensic Laboratory undertakes ongoing quality control and evaluation of all its services to ensure maintenance of standards appropriate to the expectations of its Clients.

Continuous improvement within the Forensic Laboratory is based on adherence to the following principles:

- a commitment by all employees to continuous improvement of services and their management;
- input and involvement of all employees in identifying and implementing improvements to services and their management;
- systematic use of qualitative and quantitative feedback as the basis for identifying and prioritizing improvement opportunities.

Continuous improvement is carried out through:

- monitoring and review of Forensic Laboratory processes and procedures;
- professional development of employees;
- monitoring and implementation of standards;
- Client satisfaction surveys;
- responding to unsolicited feedback on the Forensic Laboratory's products and services.
- *ad hoc* continuous improvement working parties;
- internal and external audits;
- Management Reviews on services and operations.

All suggested improvements are assessed, authorized, and implemented via the Service Improvement Plan (SIP).

Implemented Preventive and Corrective actions shall be subject to a PIR to ensure that the implemented measures meet the required outcome.

All improvement activities are monitored on an ongoing basis.

This policy is issued and maintained by the Quality Manager, in association with other Management System Owners, who also provides advice and guidance on its implementation and ensures compliance.

All Forensic Laboratory employees shall comply with this policy.

APPENDIX 15 - CRYPTOGRAPHIC CONTROL POLICY

Cryptographic controls are implemented by the Forensic Laboratory to provide additional safeguards against the compromise of data transmitted across the public network infrastructure as follows:

- the Information Security Manager is the authority responsible for the management of all cryptographic controls within the Forensic Laboratory;
- all cryptographic keys used are secret keys;
- the same cryptographic keys are used on all equipment;
- cryptographic keys are stored as part of an equipment's configuration and are backed up;
- the use of cryptographic keys is reviewed yearly and are changed on an "as needed" basis;
- the management of cryptographic keys is restricted to the Information Security Manager and the Network Manager.

This policy is issued and maintained by the Information Security Manager, who also provides advice and guidance on its implementation and ensures compliance.

All Forensic Laboratory employees shall comply with this policy.

APPENDIX 16 - DOCUMENT RETENTION POLICY

Note

Different jurisdictions will have differing document retention requirements. Below are some areas to consider for document retention without values being inserted.

To prevent unauthorized or accidental disclosure of the information, it is important to protect its security and confidentiality during storage, transportation, handling, and destruction.

All employees have a responsibility to consider safety and security when handling information in the course of their work. Consideration is given to the nature of the information involved (how sensitive is it?) and the format in which it is held.

The Forensic Laboratory has procedures appropriate to the information held and processed by them, and ensures that all employees are aware of those procedures. In addition, a record of disposal may be required to be maintained by legislation or regulation.

"Forensic Laboratory records" mean any data recorded in any form, including (but not limited to):

- paper files;
- computer files;
- audio tapes;
- video tapes;
- film and microfiche;
- any other data maintained by Forensic Laboratory employees in the course of their employment.

The controls in place in the Forensic Laboratory are:

- no record is destroyed without authorization by the Information Security Manager or a business stream manager (if there is any doubt about the need for authorization in a specific case, employees must consult their Line Managers);
- when records are disposed of, on-site or off-, methods are used to prohibit future use or reconstruction;
- paper records containing personal information should be shredded, not simply thrown out with other rubbish or general records;
- special care is taken with electronic records, which can be reconstructed from deleted information;
- similarly, erasing or reformatting computer disks or personal computers with hard drives that once contained personal information is not enough. Software tools are used that remove all data from the medium so that it cannot be reconstructed. Floppy disks are physically destroyed;
- a disposal record is maintained indicating what records have been destroyed, when, by whom, and using what method of destruction;
- records that have been kept or archived are also being tracked. The record may consist of a simple list on paper or be part of an electronic records management system;
- all disposition is controlled by relevant legislative, regulatory, or contractual terms and good practice.

Record types, retention periods, and approved destruction methods are as follows:

BUSINESS AND REGULATORY

Record Type	Retention Period	Destruction Methods
Vital business records		
Important business records		
Useful business records		
Non-essential business records		

Specific regulatory or legislative requirements for document retention may override the above baseline standards are as follows:

Type of data	Retention Period	Reason
Personnel files		
Pension records		
Application forms		
Redundancy		
Tax		
Maternity pay		
Sick pay		
Wages and salaries		
Accident books		
Occupational health records		
Occupational health records where health is a reason for terminating work		
Disciplinary records		
Appointment and appraisal records		

CONTRACTS AND CONTRACTORS

Type of Data	Retention Period	Reasons
Contract documents and specifications		
Tender returns (non-appointed contractors and suppliers)		
Management and amendments to contracts (variation orders/AI's and the like)		
Tenancy agreements		
Indemnity documents		
Authority to access notices and permits to work		

PROPERTY AND LAND

Type of Data	Retention Period	Reasons
Title deeds		
Lease documentation		
Management of acquisition process—land or leases		
Management of all other buildings and estate—plans, reports, surveys, maintenance documents, etc.		
Statutory consents		
Property valuations		

PREMISES OPERATIONS AND MAINTENANCE INSPECTIONS

Type of Data	Retention Period	Reasons
Main equipment inspection records/ Insurance inspections (lifts, boilers/ pressure vessels, etc.)		
Minor equipment		
Process of monitoring that processes are safe		
Maintenance manuals		
Health and Safety files		
General building maintenance records		
Process for ensuring safe systems of work		
Process to assess the level of risk—general		
Recorded images from CCTV		

WASTE MANAGEMENT

Type of Data	Retention Period	Reasons
Process for arranging the collection/transport of controlled waste		
Process for arranging the collection/transport of normal commercial waste		
Waste transfer notes—special waste		
Waste transfer notes—normal waste		

ASSETS

Type of Data	Retention Period	Reasons
Asset register—small equipment		

TRAINING RECORDS

Type of Data	Retention Period	Reasons
Training records		

This policy is issued and maintained by the Information Security Manager in association with various Forensic Laboratory employees and external legal counsel, who also provides advice and guidance on its implementation and ensures compliance.

All Forensic Laboratory employees shall comply with this policy.

APPENDIX 17 - FINANCIAL MANAGEMENT POLICY

This policy describes the financial practices used within the Forensic Laboratory to manage budgets.

It is the policy of the Forensic Laboratory to:

- agree budgets based upon the products and services that the Forensic Laboratory provides to its Clients;
- maintain effective financial management programs and systems;
- conduct a continuous program of monitoring to improve financial operations and systems and to identify more efficient methods of operations regarding budgeting, accounting, financial reporting, and auditing;
- be responsive to management needs at the various levels of the Forensic Laboratory;
- be responsive to the financial reporting and other requirements of the Forensic Laboratory's Top Management.

Budget holders shall ensure that:

- initial budget planning for their operational area is performed;
- their operational area budgets are monitored at least each month;
- the correct allocation of budgets from their operational area is performed.

This policy is issued and maintained by the Finance Manager, who also provides advice and guidance on its implementation and ensures compliance. All Forensic Laboratory budget holders are directly responsible for implementing and complying with this policy.

APPENDIX 18 - MOBILE DEVICES POLICY

With the increase of mobile devices, comes the increased risk to the safety and security of the hardware used and more importantly the information held on it. Information held, whether it be the Forensic Laboratory's own data or that belonging to someone else for which the Forensic Laboratory is responsible shall be protected against unauthorized access modification, erasure, and disclosure.

This policy describes the Mobile Devices Policy for the Forensic Laboratory.

USERS

- must accept the conditions of use contained within this policy;
- must not attach unauthorized equipment to the Forensic Laboratory computer network;
- must not share passwords with anyone. Passwords must not to be written down and attached to mobile devices;
- only those who have specific authorization from the Forensic Laboratory can connect to the Forensic Laboratory network using a mobile device;
- must not connect any mobile device that is not under the direct supervision of the IT department. Where Forensic Laboratory users, third parties working for the Forensic Laboratory, or visitors require a connection, they must seek approval from the IT Department prior to connection;
- shall be responsible for "their" mobile devices that are connected to the network infrastructure and for ensuring that they are in good working condition;
- must ensure the physical protection of "their" mobile devices (including risks from theft and leaving equipment unattended);
- must ensure that no business-critical data is stored locally on "their" mobile device;
- must not allow "their" mobile devices to act as a server of any kind;
- must exercise particular care when using mobile devices in public places to:
  - avoid unauthorized access to the Forensic Laboratory network;
  - avoid disclosure of information stored locally on a mobile device;
  - avoid overlooking by unauthorized persons.

THE FORENSIC LABORATORY

- shall develop, maintain, and update the Mobile Devices Policy and security standards;
- shall resolve mobile communication problems;
- shall authorize mobile connections to the network following an approved request from the relevant Line Manager;
- shall monitor performance and security, as required;
- shall monitor the development of new mobile device technology and security and evaluate and implement where necessary;
- shall safeguard the security of Forensic Laboratory information and information-processing resources;
- shall ensure that system administrators and users understand the security implications and performance limitations of mobile device technology.

USB DEVICES

USB devices, including memory sticks, shall not be connected to any networked desktop or laptop computer if:

- the device has not been authorized for use by the user's Line Manager;
- the device has not been registered with the IT Department.

PROTECTION OF DATA

To protect data from unauthorized use or access, the following apply:

- mobile devices must only be used by Forensic Laboratory employees for legitimate business purposes;
- mobile devices may not be used by or loaned to anyone else;
- the registered Owner is responsible for all data held on any mobile devices, including ensuring that data is fully backed up;
- password protect (when necessary) any personal data that is kept on a mobile devices.

Warning

The use of password protection on documents is at the user's own risk. If the password is forgotten, the document may not be able to be accessed.

GENERAL INFORMATION

- the Forensic Laboratory has overall responsibility for the Forensic Laboratory IT infrastructure and is responsible for the deployment, management, and support of all mobile devices;
- business proposals that may require a resource of mobile devices must be discussed with relevant Forensic Laboratory employees (e.g., IT Manager, Information Security Manager, etc.);
- the Forensic Laboratory shall not accept responsibility or liability for any damage or loss of data to any device or machine while in transit or connected to the network;
- traffic on the IT network may be monitored by the Forensic Laboratory to secure effective operation and for other lawful purposes.

The Forensic Laboratory may suspend access to the network via a mobile device for any user found in breach of this or any Forensic Laboratory security policy.

Failure to comply is in breach of this policy and shall be considered a serious disciplinary offence.

This policy is issued and maintained by the Information Security Manager in association with the Human Resources Manager, who also provide advice and guidance on its implementation and ensure compliance.

All Forensic Laboratory employees shall comply with this policy.

APPENDIX 19 - NETWORK SERVICE POLICY

This policy defines the principles, standards, guidelines, and responsibilities related to connections to the Forensic Laboratory network system. This policy is intended to support information security by reducing the opportunity for unauthorized access to information and information processing systems on the Forensic Laboratory network.

The primary objectives of the networked services policy are that:

- users are provided with direct access to the services that they have been specifically authorized to use;
- users can only access the network and network services that they are allowed to access;
- users are authorized to access networks and networked services via their job role and function;
- controls and procedures protect access to network connections and network services.

The following guidelines apply:

- devices are only connected to the Forensic Laboratory network from approved connection points;
- only approved devices can be connected to the Forensic Laboratory network;
- all devices connected to the network comply with the Forensic Laboratory naming conventions and IP address schemes;
- the Network Manager takes appropriate steps to protect the Forensic Laboratory network if a network device, computer, or server exhibits characteristics that could be regarded as a threat to the Forensic Laboratory network, this includes:
  - a device that imposes an exceptional load on a service;
  - a device that exhibits a pattern of malicious network traffic associated with scanning or attacking others;
  - a device that exhibits behavior consistent with host compromise;
  - a device that exhibits behavior consistent with illegal activity.
- all devices that connect to the Forensic Laboratory network must meet the prevailing security standards as defined by the Information Security Manager and the IT Manager, including:
  - installation of antivirus software and updated definition files on all computers;
  - installation of security patches on the system as soon as practical.
- addition protection for systems with sensitive and personal data that complies with relevant legislation;
- the Network Manager is responsible for reliable network services and must give approval to any individual or department that may want to run its own particular service to ensure that this service does not interfere with the functioning of centrally provided services. This includes:
  - IP address assignment (i.e., Dynamic Host Configuration Protocol servers), Domain Name System, or other management services for networking;

    - e-mail services should not be provided by any other departments, unless warranted by exceptional circumstances, must first be reviewed and approved to ensure that they are secure and that they interface properly with other services;
    - provision of authorized user accounts to access network services;
    - the Network Manager and the Information Security Manager reserves the right to restrict certain types of traffic coming into and across the Forensic Laboratory network.

This policy is issued and maintained by the Information Security Manager in association with the Network Manager, who also provide advice and guidance on its implementation and ensure compliance. All Forensic Laboratory employees are directly responsible for implementing and complying with this policy.

All Forensic Laboratory employees shall comply with this policy.

APPENDIX 20 - PERSONNEL SCREENING POLICY

This policy describes the Personnel Screening Policy for the Forensic Laboratory.

SCREENING EMPLOYEES AT RECRUITMENT STAGE

Successful job applicant screening and verification is a routine policy in the Forensic Laboratory that helps to minimize risks from theft, fraud, and misuse of facilities. All job applicants at the Forensic Laboratory are subject to screening and verification checks, particularly new recruits who may require access to sensitive data.

The Forensic Laboratory screening policy for applicants of permanent employment is:

- all potential permanent employees must be screened in accordance with the Forensic Laboratory policy for screening job applicants as outlined in this policy;
- responsibility for performing screening checks lies with the Human Resources Manager and the Information Security Manager;
- any failures or issues that arise as a consequence of a screening check and which may affect information security must be reported by the Human Resources Manager to the Information Security Manager;
- verification checks must be performed on all applicants for permanent employment as follows:
    - employees applications, CV details, experience, and qualifications must be matched against a job description to verify the potential suitability of the applicant;
    - interviews must be conducted on an individual basis to verify suitability. Formal offers of employment may only be made to an individual subject to the following checks being made by the Human Resources Manager;
    - character and professional references must be confirmed by obtaining two employer references;
    - academic and professional qualifications must be confirmed by requesting original printed copies (certified copies will suffice if originals are not available) of the most relevant qualifications;
    - an applicant's identity must be verified via a passport or a driving license;
    - the right to work in the jurisdiction must be checked.
- a criminal record check shall be performed (if available) on all new employees immediately after an individual commences employment (the check is initiated and monitored by the Human Resources Manager). Credit checks may be performed by, and at the discretion of, the Human Resources Manager under the following circumstances:
    - during application for employment by individual who may have access to sensitive data or financial information periodically, for senior management, and/or employees with access to financial data.

TEMPORARY AND CONTRACT STAFF

All screening of temporary and contract staff must be performed by the preferred recruitment agency in accordance with these screening requirements:

- character and professional references must be obtained via a minimum of two employer references;
    - where relevant, academic and professional qualifications must be confirmed;
    - an applicant's identity must be verified via a passport or a driving license;
    - the Human Resources Manager is responsible for notifying the agency of the Forensic Laboratory's screening requirements for temporary or contract staff.
- the Human Resources Manager must confirm with the recruitment agency that employee screening has been completed and verify the results.

If the recruitment agency does not perform these tasks, the Human Resources Manager shall arrange for them to be carried out in-house.

This policy is issued and maintained by the Human Resources Manager, who also provides advice and guidance on its implementation and ensures compliance.

All Forensic Laboratory employees shall comply with this policy.

APPENDIX 21 - RELATIONSHIP MANAGEMENT POLICY

The Forensic Laboratory policy for relationship management is to:

- enable the Forensic Laboratory to provide better products and services to its Clients;
- enable the Forensic Laboratory to better serve Clients through the introduction of reliable processes and procedures for interacting with both Clients and suppliers;
- improve the quality of service provided by the Forensic Laboratory;
- simplify customer-related and supplier-related processes, and enhance relationships;
- provide a mechanism for identifying potential problems with the Forensic Laboratory products and services on a proactive basis;
- provide a means of registering and resolving formal customer complaints;
- provide a mechanism for identifying and correcting products and services deficiencies;
- allow the Forensic Laboratory to better understand their Client's requirements, so that they can identify how Clients define quality and thus design a products and services strategy that is tailored to their needs;
- involve Client and supplier relationship management in all aspects of product and service level management at the Forensic Laboratory.

This policy is issued and maintained by the Quality Manager, who also provides advice and guidance on its implementation and ensures compliance.

All Forensic Laboratory employees shall comply with this policy.

APPENDIX 22 - RELEASE MANAGEMENT POLICY

Release Management is the process of planning, building, testing, deploying hardware/software, and the version control and storage of software. Its purpose is to ensure that a consistent method of deployment is followed. It reduces the likelihood of incidents as a result of rollouts and ensures that only tested and accepted versions of hardware and software are installed at any time.

To ensure that all releases are performed to a consistent standard and in a timely manner, the Forensic Laboratory has implemented a release policy to govern releases at a high level. Additional release management documentation in the service management system provides further guidance on planning and implementing releases.

It is the policy of the Forensic Laboratory to:

- ensure that all types of release, major, minor, and emergency, including hardware and software, are performed in a controlled manner;
- ensure that all releases are performed at the time agreed with business Clients to minimize service disruption but in line with the Forensic Laboratory operational situation;
- ensure that releases can only be performed following full approval through the change management system;
- ensure that all releases planned and documented by the Release Manager in conjunction with business Clients (where appropriate) are uniquely identified and contain full descriptions of what is contained in the release;
- ensure that a release can only be approved for implementation by the Release Manager after all planning and implementation activities are agreed within the Forensic Laboratory and business Clients (where appropriate);
- ensure that, where appropriate, several releases can be grouped into a single release or reduced number of releases to minimize service disruption;
- ensure that the processes and procedures for building, testing, and distributing releases are fully documented and agreed;
- ensure that the success of a release is verified and confirmed by the Release Manager and Forensic Laboratory employees and is accepted by business Clients.

This release policy is revised or extended when the Forensic Laboratory IT infrastructure is changed.

This policy is issued and maintained by the Release Manager in association with other relevant Forensic Laboratory Managers, who also provide advice and guidance on its implementation and ensures compliance.

All Forensic Laboratory employees shall comply with this policy.

APPENDIX 23 - SERVICE MANAGEMENT POLICY

The provision of a secure, stable and well-managed IT infrastructure has a critical role in ensuring that the products and services provided to its Clients meet the demands placed upon it by the business. The Forensic Laboratory is committed to ensuring that these services are properly designed, implemented, and managed.

It is Forensic Laboratory policy to:

- ensure that a full-service management system is planned and implemented so that the Forensic Laboratory can meet their Client's requirements;
- design all services in consultation with Forensic Laboratory's business Clients and ensure that the appropriate product and service operations objectives are agreed;

- perform continuous improvement activities to ensure that all services are monitored and improved where necessary and that the Forensic Laboratory meets, and exceeds, Client's expectations;
- provide the appropriate resources to ensure that the products and services required by the Forensic Laboratory's Clients are maintained at the correct level to meet their business needs;
- ensure that all Forensic Laboratory employees are aware of their responsibility to adhere to this policy and ensure that high-quality products and are maintained for the Forensic Laboratory's Clients.

The Service Manager is the person responsible for the coordination and management of services within the Forensic Laboratory.

All Forensic Laboratory Managers are directly responsible for implementing the policy within their operational area and for its adherence.

A service management system provides the framework for the implementation of this policy within the Forensic Laboratory and is supported by a comprehensive set of policies and procedures. This system is regularly reviewed to ensure that it remains valid.

This policy is issued and maintained by the Service Level Manager, who also provides advice and guidance on its implementation and ensures compliance.

All Forensic Laboratory employees shall comply with this policy.

APPENDIX 24 - SERVICE REPORTING POLICY

Timely and accurate reporting is the key to supporting and improving service management. Reporting enables Forensic Laboratory management and business Clients to assess the state of services being provided, and provides a sound basis for decision making.

It is the policy of the Forensic Laboratory to:

- agree all reporting requirements during service management planning with a business Client or supplier;
- document all reporting requirements in SLAs including report types, frequency, and responsibilities for production;
- provide timely and accurate service reports for internal management and business Clients;
- provide reporting that covers all measurable aspects of products and services that details both current and historical analysis;
- use appropriate reporting tools to ensure that the information within reports is comprehensive, accurate, and has clear presentation;
- use service reporting as an input into the service review and Service Improvement Plan (SIP).

All Forensic Laboratory Managers are responsible for producing reports in their operational areas.

This policy is issued and maintained by the Service Level Manager, who also provides advice and guidance on its implementation and ensures compliance.

All Forensic Laboratory employees shall comply with this policy.

APPENDIX 25 - THIRD-PARTY ACCESS CONTROL POLICY

This policy describes the requirements for third-party access control within the Forensic Laboratory:

- unescorted access to server or networking equipment will only be granted to Forensic Laboratory employees who require routine physical access to this equipment in order to perform their primary job functions and who are on the access list (all others will be classified as "Third Party");
- the access list for authorized, unescorted persons shall be held by the IT Manager;
- exceptions can be made, when warranted, but only by Top Management and the Network Manager;
- all others will require an Escort anytime access is required;
- the individual providing Escort must remain with the individual requiring escort until their access requirement is finished;
- former Forensic Laboratory employees are not permitted access to server or networking equipment whether with, or without, an Escort;
- server and networking equipment must remain secured at all times. Only those individuals with unescorted access rights will be authorized to access it;
- all requests for unescorted access rights must be made in writing to the IT Manager;
- the relevant Department Manager must submit all requests.

This policy is issued and maintained by the Information Security Manager in association with the IT Manager, who also provides advice and guidance on its implementation and ensures compliance.

All Forensic Laboratory employees shall comply with this policy.

APPENDIX 26 - ACCEPTABLE USE POLICY

GENERAL

The Forensic Laboratory encourages the use of electronic communications to share information and knowledge in support of their goals and to conduct their business. To this end, the Forensic Laboratory supports and provides interactive electronic communications services and facilities such as:

- telephones;
- voicemail;
- teleconferencing;
- video teleconferencing;
- electronic mail;
- bulletin boards;
- list servers;
- newsgroups;
- intranets;
- extranets;
- electronic publishing services such as the Worldwide Web; and
- electronic broadcasting services such as Web radio and Webcasting.

These communications services rely on underlying voice, video, and data networks delivered over both physical and wireless infrastructures. Digital technologies are unifying these communication functions and services, blurring traditional boundaries. This policy recognizes this convergence and establishes an overall policy framework for electronic communications.

This policy clarifies the applicability of relevant legislation within the jurisdiction and other Forensic Laboratory policies relating to electronic communications. It also establishes new policy and procedures where existing policies do not specifically address issues particular to the use of electronic communications. Where there are no such particular issues, this policy defers to other Forensic Laboratory policies.

An integrated policy cannot anticipate all the new issues that might arise in electronic communications. One purpose of this policy is to provide a framework within which these new issues can be resolved and that recognizes the intertwining legal, corporate, and individual interests involved.

All Forensic Laboratory information-processing resources are provided to support the Forensic Laboratory's business and administrative activities. The data held on the network forms part of its critical assets and are subject to possible security breaches that may compromise confidential information and expose the Forensic Laboratory to losses and other legal risks.

These Forensic Laboratory guidelines and policies change from time to time; therefore, users are encouraged to refer to online versions of this and other Forensic Laboratory policies in the IMS.

Any infringement of this policy may be subject to penalties under civil or criminal law, and such law may be invoked by the Forensic Laboratory. Any infringement of this policy by employees shall also constitute a disciplinary offence and may be treated as such regardless of legal proceedings.

This policy is regularly reviewed by the Information Security Manager who also provides advice on its implementation and ensures compliance.

PURPOSE

This policy has been established to:

- provide guidelines for the conditions of acceptance and the appropriate use of the Forensic Laboratory's information-processing resources;
- provide mechanisms for responding to external complaints about actual or perceived abuses originating from the Forensic Laboratory's information-processing resources;
- protect the privacy and integrity of data stored on the Forensic Laboratory's information-processing resources;
- mitigate the risks and losses from security threats to information and information processing resources such as virus attacks and compromises of the Forensic Laboratory's information and information processing resources;
- reduce interruptions and ensure a high availability of an efficient network essential for sustaining the Forensic Laboratory's business;
- encourage users to understand their own responsibility for protecting the Forensic Laboratory's information and information processing resources.

APPLICABILITY

This policy applies to:

- users using either personal or Forensic Laboratory provided equipment connected locally or remotely to the Forensic Laboratory's information-processing resources;

> **Note**
>
> Throughout this policy, the word "user" will be used collectively to refer to all such individuals or groups.

- all equipment connected (locally or remotely) to the Forensic Laboratory's information-processing resources;
- information-processing resources owned by and/or administered by the Forensic Laboratory;
- connections made to external networks through the Forensic Laboratory's information-processing resources;
- all external entities that have an executed contractual agreement with the Forensic Laboratory for use of the Forensic Laboratory's information-processing resources.

The Forensic Laboratory's information-processing resources are to only be used for business purposes in serving the Forensic Laboratory's interests and its users in the course of normal operations.

Any information-processing equipment or electronic communications address, site, number, account, or other identifier associated with the Forensic Laboratory or assigned by the Forensic Laboratory to users, remains the property of the Forensic Laboratory.

The Forensic Laboratory's information-processing records relating to their business are considered Forensic Laboratory records whether or not the Forensic Laboratory owns the information-processing resources, systems, or services used to create, send, forward, reply to, transmit, store, hold, copy, download, display, view, read, print, or otherwise record them.

All of the Forensic Laboratory's information-processing resources have nominated Owners and Custodians.

This policy is owned by the Information Security Manager.

RESPONSIBILITIES

Holders of user accounts or Owners of information-processing resources connected to the Forensic Laboratory's information-processing resources are responsible for the actions associated with their user account or information-processing resources.

Users must ensure that they use all reasonable means to protect their equipment and their account details and passwords.

Engaging in any activities referred to in the Section Unacceptable Use is prohibited and shall result in disciplinary action being taken.

Users shall assist IT and the Information Security Manager with investigations into suspected information security incidents.

ACCEPTABLE USE

The Forensic Laboratory's information-processing resources are provided to support the Forensic Laboratory's business mission, its users, and Clients. The use of these facilities constitutes acceptance of this policy and is subject to the following limitations, necessary for the reliable operation of the information processing resources:

- users shall comply with all applicable legislation within the jurisdiction;
- the Forensic Laboratory's information-processing resources shall be used for the purpose for which they are intended;
- users shall respect the rights, privacy, and property of others;
- users shall adhere to the confidentiality rules governing the use of passwords and accounts and details of which must not be shared;
- passwords shall not be disclosed to anyone even if the recipient is a member of the IT Department. Temporary passwords provided by the IT Department to users must be changed immediately following a successful login;

> **Note**
>
> It is noted that some passwords may, no matter what the sensitivity of the system, have to be shared and be known by IT employees, no preventive action is taken, however, wherever possible, users shall input their own passwords.

- The Forensic Laboratory's information-processing resources shall only be used for work that complies with this policy and the requirements of the IMS;
- where the Forensic Laboratory's information-processing resources are used to access other networks, any abuses against that network will be regarded as an unacceptable use of the Forensic Laboratory's information-processing resources and a breach of this policy and shall result in disciplinary action being taken.

PERSONAL USE

The Forensic Laboratory's information-processing resources may be used for incidental personal purposes provided that:

- the purposes are of a private nature not for financial gain and do not contravene any other Forensic Laboratory policies;
- such use does not cause noticeable or unavoidable cost to the Forensic Laboratory;
- such use does not inappropriately interfere with official business of the Forensic Laboratory;
- such use does not degrade the provision of products and services to Clients;
- such use does not include any actions defined in the Section Unacceptable Use.

UNACCEPTABLE USE

The Forensic Laboratory's information processing resources must not be provided to users or third parties where such information processing resources do not support the mission of the Forensic Laboratory or are not in the commercial interests of the Forensic Laboratory.

Any misuse of the Forensic Laboratory's information-processing resources shall result in disciplinary action being taken and may include legal action.

The Forensic Laboratory's information-processing resources may not be used for the following activities:

- the creation, dissemination, storage, and display of obscene or pornographic material;
- the creation, dissemination, storage, and display of indecent images of children;
- the creation, dissemination, storage, and display of hate literature;
- the creation, dissemination, storage, and display of defamatory materials or materials likely to cause offence to others;
- the creation, dissemination, storage, and display of any data that is illegal;
- the downloading, storage, and disseminating of copyrighted materials including software and all forms of electronic data without the permission of the holder of the copyright or under the terms of the licenses held by the Forensic Laboratory;
- initiating spam e-mails and sending them or forwarding other types of spam e-mail, included, but not limited to, chain letters, etc.;
- any activities that do not conform to the legislation in the relevant jurisdiction and other Forensic Laboratory policies and procedures regarding the protection of intellectual property and data. Specific emphasis is placed on the downloading and copying of both music and video files through the Internet using peer-to-peer file-sharing utilities;
- the deliberate interference with, or attempting to gain unauthorised access to user accounts and data including viewing, modifying, destroying, or corrupting the data belonging to other users;
- use of a username and password belonging to another user;
- attempts to crack, capture passwords, or decode encrypted data;
- any other use that may bring the name of the Forensic Laboratory into disrepute or expose the Forensic Laboratory to the risk of civil or criminal action;
- intentional creation, execution, forwarding, or introduction of any viruses, worms, Trojans, or software code designed to damage, self-replicate, or hinder the performance of the Forensic Laboratory network;
- deliberate actions that might reduce the effectiveness of any antivirus or other information security management precautions installed by authorized Forensic Laboratory employees;
- attempts to penetrate information security measures (hacking) whether or not this results in a corruption or loss of data;
- purposefully scanning internal or external machines in an attempt to discover or exploit known computer software or network vulnerabilities, except for those employees who are authorized to perform this as part of their job;
- engaging in commercial activities that are not under the auspices of the Forensic Laboratory. Third-party employees must declare all other commercial activities at engagement time or during their employment to ensure that they are not in conflict with the Forensic Laboratory's objectives;
- intentionally using computing resources (CPU, time, disk space, bandwidth) in such a way that it causes excessive strain on the computer systems or disrupts, denies, or create problems for other authorized Forensic Laboratory users;
- connecting any device to Forensic Laboratory's information-processing resources without authorization.

E-MAIL POLICY

The Forensic Laboratory provides electronic mail services (e-mail) to support the business and administrative objectives of the Forensic Laboratory for use by authorized users.

E-mail is a critical means of communication and many official Forensic Laboratory communications are transmitted between employees, and to Clients, using e-mail.

This policy applies to authorized users and has been established to provide guidelines for the acceptable use of the e-mail service.

E-mail between computers connected to the Forensic Laboratory's information-processing resources and the Internet must be relayed via the Forensic Laboratory e-mail gateway.

The Forensic Laboratory mail server will not accept mail to external addresses sent from an address, which is itself, external to the Forensic Laboratory.

The Forensic Laboratory mail server will accept mail sent from a computer, which has not been properly registered with an authorized network address.

All e-mail communication from the Forensic Laboratory shall contain any legally required disclaimers and other required information, as well the full contact details of the sender.

All official Forensic Laboratory e-mail communication to Forensic Laboratory employees will be delivered to their Forensic Laboratory account and should not be automatically forwarded to external e-mail accounts.

Forensic Laboratory employees may redirect e-mail from their official Forensic Laboratory account to an external ISP. This is done at the employee's risk and does not absolve the user of any responsibility for the official e-mail account and neither would the Forensic Laboratory be responsible for the e-mail servers of the external ISP.

Users of the Forensic Laboratory's information-processing resources shall not give the impression that they are representing, giving opinions, or otherwise making statements on behalf of the Forensic Laboratory unless appropriately authorized (explicitly or implicitly) to do so. While it is permissible to indicate one's affiliation with the Forensic Laboratory, unless it is clear from the context that the author is not representing the Forensic Laboratory an explicit disclaimer must be included.

Users of the Forensic Laboratory's information-processing resources facilities may only send unsolicited mass communications in support of the Forensic Laboratory's business.

In general, the Forensic Laboratory cannot, and does not wish to, be the arbiter of the contents of electronic communications. Neither can the Forensic Laboratory, in general, protect users from receiving electronic communications they might find offensive.

Users of the Forensic Laboratory's information-processing resources are strongly encouraged to use the same personal and professional courtesies and considerations in e-mails as they would in other forms of communication.

Mobile devices may only be connected to the Forensic Laboratory's information-processing resources subject to the Forensic Laboratory rules for connection.

Users who wish to directly connect their own personal information-processing equipment to the Forensic Laboratory information-processing resources are only allowed to connect via designated official physical network ports or wireless access points and subject to complying with the Forensic Laboratory rules for connection.

LOSS AND DAMAGE

Save as set out below, the Forensic Laboratory accepts no liability to users (whether in contract, tort (including negligence), breach of statutory duty, restitution, or otherwise) for:

- any loss or damage incurred by a user as a result of personal use of the Forensic Laboratory's information-processing resources. Users should not rely on personal use of the Forensic Laboratory's information-processing resources for communications that might be sensitive with regard to timing, financial effect, privacy, or confidentiality;
- the malfunctioning of any Forensic Laboratory information-processing resources, or for the loss of any data or software, or the failure of any security or privacy mechanism, whether caused by any defect in the Forensic Laboratory's information-processing resources or by any act or neglect by the Forensic Laboratory;
- the acts or omissions of other providers of telecommunications services or for faults in or failures of their networks and equipment;
- any injury, death, damage, or direct, indirect, or consequential loss (all three of which terms include, without limitation, pure economic loss, loss of profits, loss of business, loss of data, loss of opportunity, depletion of goodwill and like loss) howsoever caused arising out of, or in connection with, the use of the Forensic Laboratory's information-processing resources.

The Forensic Laboratory does not exclude its liability under this, or any other policy to users for:

- personal injury or death resulting from the Forensic Laboratory's negligence;
- for any matter which it would be illegal for the Forensic Laboratory to exclude or to attempt to exclude its liability; or
- for fraudulent misrepresentation.

Users agree not to cause any form of damage to the Forensic Laboratory information-processing resources or to any accommodation associated with them. Should such damage arise, the Forensic Laboratory shall be entitled to recover from such user, by way of indemnity, any and all losses, costs, damages, and/or expenses that the Forensic Laboratory incurs or suffers as a result of such damage.

DELETION OF DATA

Users should be aware that data deleted from local disks by the users may still be accessible in some cases, via certain system tools.

Newsgroup articles, contributions to online bulletin boards, non-Forensic Laboratory-owned mailing lists, and e-mails once sent are stored on machines outside the jurisdiction of the Forensic Laboratory, and in these cases, withdrawal or deletion of these messages or e-mails may not be possible.

BACKUP SERVICES

The Forensic Laboratory information-processing resources are backed up to protect system reliability and integrity, and to prevent potential loss of data.

The backup process results in the copying of information on the Forensic Laboratory's information-processing resources onto storage media that might be retained for periods of time and in locations unknown to the originator or recipient of the information.

The practice and frequency of backups and the retention of backup copies vary from system to system and are detailed in the Forensic Laboratory backup procedures.

Data can sometimes be susceptible to corruption due to hardware or software failure and users are encouraged to keep regular backups of their data on the server. The IT Department would make reasonable attempts to recover data; if the backup becomes corrupted, however, it might not be possible to provide this in all situations.

SOFTWARE AND HARDWARE AUDITING

The Forensic Laboratory has an obligation to ensure that only legal software is used on Forensic Laboratory information-processing resources and to support this appropriate technology shall be used to audit Forensic Laboratory-owned software on Forensic Laboratory-owned equipment without employee permission.

Note

While the Forensic Laboratory has control over their own employees and information-processing resources, they cannot necessarily control third-party employees and information-processing resources to the same level. This may mean that these employees have non-Forensic Laboratory software on their systems. This shall be excluded from any audits.

Top Management shall be notified of any illegal or unlicensed software discovered as part of the audit process.

REMOVAL OF EQUIPMENT

No Forensic Laboratory information-processing resources may be borrowed, removed, or moved from a designated location, without the explicit permission of the IT Manager or Owner, as appropriate.

For permission to be granted, the necessary forms detailing the purpose of the removal of the equipment and the equipment details must be filled by the applicant and countersigned by the appropriate Line Manager, IT Manager, or Owner as mentioned above.

TELEPHONE SYSTEMS

In some jurisdictions, the Law protects the privacy of telephone conversations. Without Court approval, it is illegal to record or monitor audio or visual telephone conversations without advising the participants that the call is being monitored or recorded.

Monitoring and recording of telecommunications by employers for the purpose of evaluating customer service, measuring workload, or other business reasons is permitted by law but requires that participants be informed that the call is being monitored or recorded.

The use of the Forensic Laboratory telephone equipment creates transaction records (which include the number called and the time and length of the call) that are reviewed by Forensic Laboratory management as part of routine accounting procedures.

Employees who use Forensic Laboratory telephones for personal or other purposes should be aware that Line Managers have access to records of all calls made from Forensic Laboratory telephones assigned to their use and that such records may be used for administrative purposes.

ACCESS BY THIRD PARTIES

Third parties with access to Forensic Laboratory information-processing resources who have executed contractual agreements with the Forensic Laboratory may access appropriate resources and must comply with the Forensic Laboratory's guidelines and policies.

All requests from third parties that have responsibilities for accessing Forensic Laboratory information-processing resources shall submit a request via the Service Desk and include the following:

- date;
- name of individual requesting access;
- organization;
- address and telephone number of person requesting access;
- name of the Forensic Laboratory systems contact;
- resources required;
- IP address of internal machine to be accessed;
- IP address of external company;
- port number and service required;
- operating system;
- application software required;
- length of time for which access is required (maximum 12 months).

The Information Security Manager shall review and determine the level of risk associated with each request. Additional security controls may be required prior to access being granted. The Service Desk will notify the Requester with the account and access information, if access is granted.

Third parties may access Forensic Laboratory information-processing resources to gain access to their home site; however, they must obey and sign any published rules for their use.

The employer of external contractors or companies shall be held jointly liable for any actions on their part or that of their employees, agents, or subcontractors that violate the Forensic Laboratory's Acceptable Use Policy.

Any external visitors or conferences that have been authorized to use Forensic Laboratory information-processing resources are bound by the Forensic Laboratory's procedures and their employees are liable for the actions of the attendees.

INVESTIGATION OF INFORMATION SECURITY INCIDENTS

The Forensic Laboratory has an obligation to protect the confidentiality, integrity, and availability of the Forensic Laboratory information-processing resources by ensuring that the relevant resources are available and accessible.

To meet this obligation, the Information Security Manager shall monitor and respond to network breaches as they occur.

The Forensic Laboratory recognizes the principles of freedom of speech and privacy of personal information hold important implications for the use of electronic communications. The Forensic Laboratory affords privacy protections to e-mail communications comparable to those it traditionally affords paper mail and telephone conversations. This policy reflects these firmly held principles within the context of Forensic Laboratory's legal and other obligations.

The Forensic Laboratory policy prohibits its employees from seeking out, using, or disclosing personal information without authorization, and requires them to take necessary precautions to protect the confidentiality of personal information encountered in the performance of their duties or otherwise. This prohibition applies to e-mail.

Incidents and information security breaches shall be advised to the Information Security Manager either directly or via the Service Desk via internal or external complaints, the intrusion detection system, or discovered in the normal course of business.

The actions taken after a violation of this policy or any supporting Forensic Laboratory procedures will be dependent on the particular circumstances.

The Information Security Manager shall do the following:

- determine the impact of the alleged violation and take, without notice, any necessary action if Forensic Laboratory information, information processing resources, products and services are adversely affected to prevent immediate and further damage to the Forensic Laboratory network. Such actions may include:
  - suspension of an account;
  - disconnection of systems or disable network ports;
  - termination of running processes and programs;
  - any other actions deemed necessary to protect and/or restore network services.
- gather evidence and provide information as required to comply with any internal investigation. In some cases, the users may not be notified first or it may be required by law to provide the information without notifying the user;
- determine if the Forensic Laboratory is legally obliged to report the alleged incident to the relevant Police authorities;
- investigate and address the complaint. Such investigation may involve examining systems and network activity logs and transaction logs. Contents of e-mails and other files will not be examined as part of a routine examination except in the following circumstances without the holder being notified:
  - a court order requires that the content be examined and disclosed;
  - the Information Security Manager is instructed in writing either by Top Management as part of an internal investigation.

The Information Security Manager and other relevant Forensic Laboratory Managers shall conduct an internal investigation relating to systems performance or problems, which require that user files must be examined to identify a cause. In this case, guidance must be sought from Top Management prior to the work being undertaken. During such investigations, if any illegal activity is discovered, then the investigation shall be referred immediately to the Information Security Manager.

If the violation does not prevent other users from accessing information processing resources or result in a disciplinary procedure being instigated, the Information Security Manager shall notify the IT Manager of the activities causing the violation. The matter will, however, result in disciplinary action if the user refuses to comply.

Network access may be terminated immediately if the violation has been caused by a third party with a contractual agreement with the Forensic Laboratory while the violation is investigated.

Users should be aware that, during the performance of their duties, employees who operate and support the Forensic Laboratory information-processing resources need, from time to time, to monitor transmissions or observe certain transactional information to ensure proper functioning of the Forensic Laboratory's information-processing resources. On these and other occasions, they might inadvertently observe the contents of e-mails.

Except as provided elsewhere in this policy or by law, they are not permitted to hear, see, or read the contents intentionally; observe transactional information where not germane to the foregoing purpose; or disclose or otherwise use what they have seen, heard, or read. Disciplinary action will be taken against any employees observed intentionally gaining access to user data that has no relevance to the investigation.

One exception to the foregoing paragraph is the need for systems personnel to inspect the contents of electronic communications and transactional records when redirecting or disposing of otherwise undeliverable e-mail or other electronic communications.

Such unavoidable inspection of e-mail or other electronic communications is limited to the least invasive level of inspection required to perform such duties. This exception does not exempt employees from the prohibition against disclosure of personal and confidential information, except insofar as such disclosure equates with good faith attempts to route the otherwise undeliverable e-mail or other electronic communication to its intended recipients.

Rerouted e-mail and other electronic communications normally should be accompanied by notification to the recipient that the e-mail or other electronic communication has been inspected for such purposes.

Except as provided above, employees shall not intentionally search e-mail, other electronic communications records, or transactional information for violations of law or policy but shall report violations discovered inadvertently in the course of their duties.

REPORTING INFORMATION SECURITY INCIDENTS

All users of the Forensic Laboratory's information and information processing resources are required to note and report any observed or suspected information security incident, and security weaknesses in or threats to those systems and services.

> **Note**
> This also applies to any physical security incidents.

SOME RELEVANT LEGISLATION AND REGULATION

The use of Forensic Laboratory information-processing resources and resources is subject, but not limited, to the applicable legislation within the jurisdiction. Legal Counsel shall provide advice and guidance.

APPENDIX 27 - AUDIT COMMITTEE

TITLE

The title of this committee shall be:

"The Forensic Laboratory Audit Committee"

CONSTITUTION

The Forensic Laboratory Audit Committee (the "Committee") is constituted as a Committee of the Management Board, with a remit to oversee and coordinate all audit and Management Review activities in Forensic Laboratory.

The Committee's Terms of Reference may be amended at any time by the Management Board.

AUTHORITY

The Committee is authorized by the Management Board to review or investigate any activity within its Terms of Reference.

The Committee is authorized by the Management Board to require of the executive such additional information to support audit and Management Review activities and/or corrective or preventive action as it deems appropriate.

MEMBERSHIP

The Committee shall be appointed by the Management Board from among Forensic Laboratory employees, as appropriate, and shall consist of not less than three members.

The Chairman of the Committee shall be the Forensic Laboratory Audit Manager.

Appointments to the Committee shall be for a period of 1 year and reviewed at the annual Management Board meeting.

Nominations for the Committee shall be submitted to the Management Board by the Forensic Laboratory Audit Manager.

The Forensic Laboratory Audit Manager shall appoint the Secretary to the Committee.

AGENDA AND MINUTES

Agendas shall be distributed to all members of the Committee at least 5 working days before the meeting. Any relevant attachments shall be attached to the agenda (typically, this may include relevant audit reports, exercise tests or other similar reports, etc.) as agreed by the Chairman of the Committee.

Minutes of the meeting shall be distributed within 10 working days of the meeting.

ATTENDANCE AT MEETINGS

The quorum necessary for the transaction of the business of the Committee shall be a simple majority of the Committee members.

Meetings that are inquorate cannot pass formal resolutions but can undertake business and make recommendation for consideration at the next meeting.

Other Management Board members may attend meetings of the Committee, as Observers.

At the request of the Committee, any Forensic Laboratory employee shall attend meetings.

FREQUENCY OF MEETINGS

Meetings shall be held at least once a quarter or more if required.

Additional meetings may be called by the Management Board, or the Chairman of the Management Board acting for the Management Board, or by the Chairman of the Committee.

RESPONSIBILITIES

The Audit Committee has a number of responsibilities:

Financial Reporting

The Committee shall monitor the integrity of the Forensic Laboratory financial statements, including its annual and interim reports, preliminary results, announcements, and any other formal announcement relating to its financial performance, reviewing significant financial reporting issues and judgments that they contain. The Committee shall also review summary financial statements, significant financial returns to regulators and any financial information contained in certain other documents, such as announcements of a price sensitive nature.

The Committee shall review and challenge where necessary:

- the consistency of, and any changes to, accounting policies both on a year basis and across Forensic Laboratory;
- the methods used to account for significant or unusual transactions where different approaches are possible;
- whether Forensic Laboratory has followed appropriate accounting standards and made appropriate estimates and judgements, taking into account the views of the external Auditor;
- the clarity of disclosure in Forensic Laboratory's financial reports and the context in which statements are made;
- all material information presented with the financial statements, such as the operating and financial review and the corporate governance statement;
- The Committee shall review the annual financial statements of the pension funds where not reviewed by the Management Board as a whole, if appropriate.

Internal Controls and Management Systems

The Committee shall:

- keep under review the effectiveness of Forensic Laboratory's internal controls, risk management systems, and management systems in association with the Risk Committee and each of the management system committees;
- review and approve the statements to be included in the Annual Report concerning internal controls, risk management, and management systems (unless this is done by the Management Board as a whole).

Whistle Blowing and the Code of Conduct

The Committee shall review the Forensic Laboratory's arrangements for its employees to raise concerns, in confidence, about possible wrongdoing in financial reporting or other matters through a Whistle Blowing Policy as defined in Appendix 35. The Committee shall ensure that these arrangements allow proportionate and independent investigation of such matters and appropriate follow-up action. It shall also review Forensic Laboratory's arrangements for ensuring its employees are made aware of what is expected of their behavior and business conduct.

Internal Audit

The Committee shall:

- monitor and review the effectiveness of Forensic Laboratory's internal audit function in the context of Forensic Laboratory's overall risk management system;
- approve the appointment and removal of the Internal Audit Manager;
- consider and approve the remit of the internal audit function and ensure it has adequate resources and appropriate access to information to enable it to perform its function effectively and in accordance with the relevant professional standards. The Committee shall also ensure the function has adequate standing and is free from management or other restrictions;
- review and assess the annual IMS Calendar and Management Review plan;
- review promptly all reports on the Forensic Laboratory from the internal Auditors;
- review and monitor Top Management's responsiveness to the findings and recommendations of the internal Auditors;
- meet the Internal Audit Manager at least once a year, without management being present, to discuss their remit and any issues arising from the internal audits carried out. In addition, the Internal Audit Manager shall be given the right of direct access to the Chairman of the Management Board and to the Committee.

External Audit

The Committee shall:

- consider and make recommendations to the Management Board, to be put to shareholders for approval, in relation to the appointment, reappointment, and removal of Forensic Laboratory's external Auditor. The Committee shall oversee the selection process for new Auditors, and if an Auditor resigns, the Committee shall investigate the issues leading to this and decide whether any action is required;
- oversee the relationship with the external Auditor including (but not limited to):
  - approval of their remuneration, whether fees for audit or non-audit services and that the level of fees is appropriate to enable an adequate audit to be conducted;
  - approval of their terms of engagement, including any engagement letter issued at the start of each audit, the audit criteria and the scope of the audit;

    - assessing annually their independence and objectivity taking to account relevant professional and regulatory requirements and the relationship with the Auditor as a whole, including the provision of any nonaudit services;
    - satisfying itself that there are no relationships (such as family, employment, investment, financial, or business), that may give rise to a conflict of interest, between the Auditor and Forensic Laboratory (other than in the ordinary course of business);
    - agreeing with the Management Board a policy on the employment of former employees of Forensic Laboratory's Auditor, then monitoring the implementation of this policy;
    - monitoring the Auditor's compliance with relevant ethical and professional guidance on the rotation of audit partners;
    - assessing annually their qualifications, expertise, and resources, and the effectiveness of the audit process that shall include a report from the external Auditor on their own internal quality procedures.
- meet regularly with the external Auditor, including once at the planning stage before the audit and once after the audit at the reporting stage. The Committee shall meet the external Auditor at least once a year, without management being present, to discuss their remit and any issues arising from the audit;
- review and approve the IMS Calendar and ensure that it is consistent with the scope of the audit engagement;
- review the findings of the audit with the external Auditor. This shall include, but not be limited to, the following:
    - a discussion of any major issues that arose during the audit;
    - any accounting and audit judgements;
    - levels of errors identified during the audit.
- review any representation letter(s) requested by the external Auditor before they are signed by Top Management;
- review the management letter and Top Management's response to the Auditor's findings and recommendations;
- develop and implement a policy on the supply of non-audit services by the external Auditor, taking into account any relevant ethical guidance on the matter.

Other

- be responsible for coordination of the internal and external Auditors;
- oversee any investigation of activities that are within its Terms of Reference and act as a "Court of the last resort";
- at least once a year, review its own performance, constitution, and Terms of Reference to ensure it is operating at maximum effectiveness and recommend any changes it considers necessary to the Management Board for approval;
- review the effectiveness of the internal audit, external audit, Management Review, and other testing processes;
- approve the text of the section of the Forensic Laboratory annual review dealing with corporate governance issues and the Committee.

Reporting Procedures

The minutes of the Committee shall normally be considered at the Management Board meeting following the Committee meeting.

Where this proves to be impractical, the minutes shall be circulated to all members of the Management Board as soon as possible.

Review of Terms of Reference

These Terms of Reference shall be reviewed on an annual basis by the Committee with input from all stakeholders.

APPENDIX 28 - BUSINESS CONTINUITY COMMITTEE

TITLE

The title of this committee shall be:

"The Forensic Laboratory Business Continuity Committee".

CONSTITUTION

The Forensic Laboratory Business Continuity Committee (the "Committee") is constituted as a Committee of the Management Board, with a remit to oversee the continuity of products and services within the Forensic Laboratory both to internal and external Clients.

The Committee's Terms of Reference may be amended at any time by the Management Board.

AUTHORITY

The Committee is authorized by the Management Board to review or investigate any activity within its Terms of Reference.

The Committee is authorized by the Management Board to require of the executive such additional business continuity audits, tests, or Management Reviews and/or corrective or preventive action as it deems appropriate.

MEMBERSHIP

The Committee shall be appointed by the Management Board from among Forensic Laboratory employees, as appropriate and shall consist of not less than three members.

The Chairman of the Committee shall be the Forensic Laboratory Business Continuity Manager.

Appointments to the Committee shall be for a period of 1 year and reviewed at the annual Management Board meeting.

Nominations for the Committee shall be submitted to the Management Board by the Forensic Laboratory Business Continuity Manager.

The Forensic Laboratory Business Continuity Manager shall appoint the Secretary to the Committee.

AGENDA AND MINUTES

Agendas shall be distributed to all members of the Committee at least 5 working days before the meeting. Any relevant attachments shall be attached to the agenda (typically, this may include audit reports, incident reports, exercise test results, etc.) as agreed by the Chairman of the Committee.

Minutes of the meeting shall be distributed within 10 working days of the meeting.

ATTENDANCE AT MEETINGS

The quorum necessary for the transaction of the business of the Committee shall be a simple majority of the Committee members.

Meetings that are inquorate cannot pass formal resolutions but can undertake business and make recommendation for consideration at the next meeting.

Other Management Board members may attend meetings of the Committee.

At the request of the Committee, any members of senior management shall attend meetings.

Any Independent Assessors may also be invited to attend.

FREQUENCY OF MEETINGS

Meetings shall be held at least twice a year or more if required.

Additional meetings may be called by the Management Board, or the Chairman of the Management Board acting for the Management Board, or by the Chairman of the Committee.

RESPONSIBILITIES

To keep under review Forensic Laboratory's business continuity procedures and systems, ensuring that they meet the Forensic Laboratory's requirements and reflect good practice.

To receive, and consider, on a regular basis reports about, where relevant:

- updates of legislation, regulation, or good practice that may affect the management systems;
- results of management systems audits and reviews;
- results of performance reviews;
- results of audits of key suppliers, outsourcing partners, and other associated third parties;
- feedback from interested parties (including any complaints about the products and services supplied by the Forensic Laboratory);
- techniques, products, or procedures that could be used in the Forensic Laboratory to improve the management system's performance and effectiveness;
- status of preventive and corrective actions;
- vulnerabilities or threats not adequately addressed in the previous risk assessments (where appropriate);
- review of the level of risk present and the risk appetite;
- results from effectiveness measurements and any business continuity testing carried out;
- incidents or other non-conformances;
- follow-up actions from previous Management Reviews;
- any changes that could affect the management systems;
- feedback from awareness and similar training;
- feedback from any Line Manager affected by the management system;
- feedback from the Management System Owner, including adequacy of resources (financial, personnel, material);
- lessons learned from any incidents, testing, or similar events;
- lessons learned from similar organizations;
- recommendations for improvement.

To receive and consider six-monthly reports from the Independent Assessor, where an Independent Assessor is appointed.

In conjunction with the Audit Committee, to commission and/or review internal audit reports, results of other tests and exercises pertaining to business continuity matters within the Forensic Laboratory, and the management responses to the recommendations.

To approve the text of the section of the Forensic Laboratory annual review dealing with business continuity matters and the Committee.

REPORTING PROCEDURES

The minutes of the Committee shall normally be considered at the Management Board meeting following the Committee meeting.

Where this proves to be impractical, the minutes shall be circulated to all members of the Management Board as soon as possible.

REVIEW OF TERMS OF REFERENCE

These Terms of Reference shall be reviewed on an annual basis by the Committee with input from all stakeholders.

APPENDIX 29 - ENVIRONMENT COMMITTEE

TITLE

The title of this committee shall be:

"The Forensic Laboratory Environment Committee".

CONSTITUTION

The Forensic Laboratory Environment Committee (the "Committee") is constituted as a Committee of the Management Board, with a remit to oversee the environmental protection activities within the Forensic Laboratory.

The Committee's Terms of Reference may be amended at any time by the Management Board.

AUTHORITY

The Committee is authorized by the Management Board to review or investigate any activity within its Terms of Reference.

The Committee is authorized by the Management Board to require of the executive such additional environmental audits or Management Reviews and/or corrective or preventive action as it deems appropriate.

MEMBERSHIP

The Committee shall be appointed by the Management Board from among Forensic Laboratory employees, as appropriate, and shall consist of not less than three members.

The Chairman of the Committee shall be the Forensic Laboratory Environment Manager.

Appointments to the Committee shall be for a period of 1 year and reviewed at the annual Management Board meeting.

Nominations for the Committee shall be submitted to the Management Board by the Forensic Laboratory Environment Manager.

The Forensic Laboratory Environment Manager shall appoint the Secretary to the Committee.

AGENDA AND MINUTES

Agendas shall be distributed to all members of the Committee at least 5 working days before the meeting. Any relevant attachments shall be attached to the agenda (typically, this may include audit reports, incident reports, etc.) as agreed by the Chairman of the Committee.

Minutes of the meeting shall be distributed within 10 working days of the meeting.

ATTENDANCE AT MEETINGS

The quorum necessary for the transaction of the business of the Committee shall be a simple majority of the Committee members.

Meetings that are inquorate cannot pass formal resolutions but can undertake business and make recommendation for consideration at the next meeting.

Other Management Board members may attend meetings of the Committee, as observers.

At the request of the Committee, any Forensic Laboratory employee shall attend meetings.

Any Independent Assessors may also be invited to attend.

FREQUENCY OF MEETINGS

Meetings shall be held at least twice a year or more if required.

Additional meetings may be called by the Management Board, or the Chairman of the Management Board acting for the Management Board, or by the Chairman of the Committee.

RESPONSIBILITIES

To keep under review Forensic Laboratory's environmental protection procedures and systems, ensuring that they meet the Forensic Laboratory's requirements and reflect good practice.

To receive, and consider, on a regular basis reports about, where relevant:

- updates of legislation, regulation, or good practice that may affect the management systems;
- results of management systems audits and reviews;
- results of performance reviews;
- results of audits of key suppliers, outsourcing partners, and other associated third parties;
- feedback from interested parties (including any complaints about the Forensic Laboratory products and services);
- techniques, products, or procedures that could be used in the Forensic Laboratory to improve the management systems performance and effectiveness;
- status of preventive and corrective actions;
- vulnerabilities or threats not adequately addressed in the previous risk assessments (where appropriate);
- review of the level of risk present and the risk appetite;
- results from effectiveness measurements and any testing carried out;
- incidents or other non-conformances;
- follow-up actions from previous Management Reviews;
- any changes that could affect the management systems;
- feedback from awareness and similar training;
- feedback from any Line Manager affected by the management system;
- feedback from the Management System Owner, including adequacy of resources (financial, personnel, material);
- lessons learned from any incidents, testing, or similar events;

- lessons learned from similar organizations;
- recommendations for improvement.

To receive and consider six-monthly reports from the Independent Assessor, where an Independent Assessor is appointed.

In conjunction with the Audit Committee, to commission and/or review internal audit reports, results of other tests and exercises pertaining to environmental protection within the Forensic Laboratory, and the Top Management responses to the recommendations.

To approve the text of the section of the Forensic Laboratory annual review dealing with environmental protection matters and the Committee.

REPORTING PROCEDURES

The minutes of the Committee shall normally be considered at the Management Board meeting following the Committee meeting.

Where this proves to be impractical, the minutes shall be circulated to all members of the Management Board as soon as possible.

REVIEW OF TERMS OF REFERENCE

These Terms of Reference shall be reviewed on an annual basis by the Committee with input from all stakeholders.

APPENDIX 30 - HEALTH AND SAFETY COMMITTEE

TITLE

The title of this committee shall be:

"The Forensic Laboratory Health and Safety Committee".

CONSTITUTION

The Forensic Laboratory Health and Safety Committee (the "Committee") is constituted as a Committee of the Management Board, with a remit to oversee the Health and Safety activities within the Forensic Laboratory.

The Committee's Terms of Reference may be amended at any time by the Management Board.

AUTHORITY

The Committee is authorized by the Management Board to review or investigate any activity within its Terms of Reference.

The Committee is authorized by the Management Board to require of the executive such additional health and safety audits or Management Reviews and/or corrective or preventive action as it deems appropriate.

MEMBERSHIP

The Committee shall be appointed by the Management Board from among the Forensic Laboratory employees, as appropriate and shall consist of not less than three members.

The Chairman of the Committee shall be the Forensic Laboratory Health and Safety Manager.

Appointments to the Committee shall be for a period of 1 year and reviewed at the annual Management Board meeting.

Nominations for the Committee shall be submitted to the Management Board by the Forensic Laboratory Health and Safety Manager.

The Forensic Laboratory Health and Safety Manager shall appoint the Secretary to the Committee.

AGENDA AND MINUTES

Agendas shall be distributed to all members of the Committee at least 5 working days before the meeting. Any relevant attachments shall be attached to the agenda (typically, this may include audit reports, incident reports, "near misses," etc.) as agreed by the Chairman of the Committee.

Minutes of the meeting shall be distributed within 10 working days of the meeting.

ATTENDANCE AT MEETINGS

The quorum necessary for the transaction of the business of the Committee shall be a simple majority of the Committee members.

Meetings that are inquorate cannot pass formal resolutions but can undertake business and make recommendation for consideration at the next meeting.

Other Management Board members may attend meetings of the Committee, as observers.

At the request of the Committee, any Forensic Laboratory employee shall attend meetings.

Any Independent Assessors may also be invited to attend.

FREQUENCY OF MEETINGS

Meetings shall be held at least twice a year or more if required.

Additional meetings may be called by the Management Board, or the Chairman of the Management Board acting for the Management Board, or by the Chairman of the Committee.

RESPONSIBILITIES

To keep under review Forensic Laboratory's Health and Safety procedures and systems, ensuring that they meet the Forensic Laboratory's requirements and reflect good practice.

To act as a focus for joint participation between employer and safety representatives.

To receive, and consider, on a regular basis reports about, where relevant:

- updates of legislation, regulation, or good practice that may affect the management systems;
- results of management systems audits and reviews;
- results of performance reviews;
- results of audits of key suppliers, outsourcing partners, and other associated third parties;
- feedback from interested parties (including any complaints about the Forensic Laboratory products and services);
- techniques, products, or procedures that could be used in the organization to improve the management systems performance and effectiveness;
- status of preventive and corrective actions;
- vulnerabilities or threats not adequately addressed in the previous Health and Safety risk assessments (where appropriate);
- review of the level of risk present and the risk appetite;
- results from effectiveness measurements and any testing carried out;
- incidents or other non-conformances;
- follow-up actions from previous Management Reviews;
- any changes that could affect the management systems;
- feedback from awareness and similar training;
- feedback from any Line Manager affected by the management system;
- feedback from the Management System Owner, including adequacy of resources (financial, personnel, material);
- lessons learned from any incidents, near misses, testing, or similar events;
- lessons learned from similar organizations;
- recommendations for improvement.

To receive and consider six-monthly reports from the Independent Assessor, where an Independent Assessor is appointed.

In conjunction with the Audit Committee, to commission and/or review internal audit reports, results of other tests and exercises pertaining to Health and Safety matters within the Forensic Laboratory, and the Top Management responses to the recommendations.

To approve the text of the section of the Forensic Laboratory annual review dealing with Health and Safety matters and the Committee.

REPORTING PROCEDURES

The minutes of the Committee shall normally be considered at the Management Board meeting following the Committee meeting.

Where this proves to be impractical, the minutes shall be circulated to all members of the Management Board as soon as possible.

REVIEW OF TERMS OF REFERENCE

These Terms of Reference shall be reviewed on an annual basis by the Committee with input from all stakeholders.

APPENDIX 31 - INFORMATION SECURITY COMMITTEE

TITLE

The title of this committee shall be:

"The Forensic Laboratory Information Security Committee".

CONSTITUTION

The Forensic Laboratory Information Security Committee (the "Committee") is constituted as a Committee of the Management Board, with a remit to oversee the information security activities within the Forensic Laboratory both to internal and external Clients.

The Committee's Terms of Reference may be amended at any time by the Management Board.

AUTHORITY

The Committee is authorized by the Management Board to review or investigate any activity within its Terms of Reference.

The Committee is authorized by the Management Board to require of the executive such additional information security audits, tests, or Management Reviews and/or corrective or preventive action as it deems appropriate.

MEMBERSHIP

The Committee shall be appointed by the Management Board from among Forensic Laboratory employees, as appropriate and shall consist of not less than three members.

The Chairman of the Committee shall be the Forensic Laboratory Information Security Manager.

Appointments to the Committee shall be for a period of 1 year and reviewed at the annual Management Board meeting.

Nominations for the Committee shall be submitted to the Management Board by the Forensic Laboratory Information Security Manager.

The Forensic Laboratory Information Security Manager shall appoint the Secretary to the Committee.

AGENDA AND MINUTES

Agendas shall be distributed to all members of the Committee at least 5 working days before the meeting. Any relevant attachments shall be attached to the agenda (typically, this may include audit reports, incident reports, penetration tests, the risk register, exercise test results, etc.) as agreed by the Chairman of the Committee.

Minutes of the meeting shall be distributed within 10 working days of the meeting.

ATTENDANCE AT MEETINGS

The quorum necessary for the transaction of the business of the Committee shall be a simple majority of the Committee members.

Meetings that are inquorate cannot pass formal resolutions but can undertake business and make recommendation for consideration at the next meeting.

Other Management Board members may attend meetings of the Committee, as observers.

At the request of the Committee, any Forensic Laboratory employee shall attend meetings.

Any Independent Assessors may also be invited to attend.

FREQUENCY OF MEETINGS

Meetings shall be held at least twice a year or more if required.

Additional meetings may be called by the Management Board, or the Chairman of the Management Board acting for the Management Board, or by the Chairman of the Committee.

RESPONSIBILITIES

To keep under review Forensic Laboratory's information security procedures and systems, ensuring that they meet the Forensic Laboratory's requirements and reflect good practice.

To receive, and consider, on a regular basis reports about, where relevant:

- updates of legislation, regulation, or good practice that may affect the management systems;
- results of management systems audits and reviews;
- results of performance reviews;
- results of audits of key suppliers, outsourcing partners, and other associated third parties;
- feedback from interested parties (including any complaints about the Forensic Laboratory products and services);
- techniques, products, or procedures, which could be used in the Forensic Laboratory to improve the management systems performance and effectiveness;
- status of preventive and corrective actions;
- vulnerabilities or threats not adequately addressed in the previous risk assessments (where appropriate);
- review of the level of risk present and the risk appetite;
- results from effectiveness measurements and any testing carried out;
- incidents or other non-conformances;
- follow-up actions from previous Management Reviews;
- any changes that could affect the management systems;
- feedback from awareness and similar training;
- feedback from any Line Manager affected by the management system;
- feedback from the Management System Owner, including adequacy of resources (financial, personnel, material);
- lessons learned from any incidents, testing, or similar events;
- lessons learned from similar organizations;
- recommendations for improvement.

To receive and consider six-monthly reports from the Independent Assessor, where an Independent Assessor is appointed.

In conjunction with the Audit Committee, to commission and/or review internal audit reports, results of other tests and exercises pertaining to information security matters within the Forensic Laboratory, and the Top Management responses to the recommendations.

To approve the text of the section of the Forensic Laboratory annual review dealing with information security matters and the Committee.

REPORTING PROCEDURES

The minutes of the Committee shall normally be considered at the Management Board meeting following the Committee meeting.

Where this proves to be impractical, the minutes shall be circulated to all members of the Management Board as soon as possible.

REVIEW OF TERMS OF REFERENCE

These Terms of Reference shall be reviewed on an annual basis by the Committee with input from all stakeholders.

APPENDIX 32 - QUALITY COMMITTEE

TITLE

The title of this committee shall be:

"The Forensic Laboratory Quality Committee".

CONSTITUTION

The Forensic Laboratory Quality Committee (the "Committee") is constituted as a Committee of the Management Board, with a remit to oversee the quality assurance activities within the Forensic Laboratory.

The Committee's Terms of Reference may be amended at any time by the Management Board.

AUTHORITY

The Committee is authorized by the Management Board to review or investigate any activity within its Terms of Reference.

The Committee is authorized by the Management Board to require of the executive such additional quality assurance audits or Management Reviews and/or corrective or preventive action as it deems appropriate.

MEMBERSHIP

The Committee shall be appointed by the Management Board from among Forensic Laboratory employees, as appropriate, and shall consist of not less than three members.

The Chairman of the Committee shall be the Forensic Laboratory Quality Manager.

Appointments to the Committee shall be for a period of 1 year and reviewed at the annual Management Board meeting.

Nominations for the Committee shall be submitted to the Management Board by the Forensic Laboratory Quality Manager.

The Forensic Laboratory Quality Manager shall appoint the Secretary to the Committee.

AGENDA AND MINUTES

Agendas shall be distributed to all members of the Committee at least 5 working days before the meeting. Any relevant attachments shall be attached to the agenda (typically, this may include audit reports, incident reports, quality reporting against quality objectives, etc.) as agreed by the Chairman of the Committee.

Minutes of the meeting shall be distributed within 10 working days of the meeting.

ATTENDANCE AT MEETINGS

The quorum necessary for the transaction of the business of the Committee shall be a simple majority of the Committee members.

Meetings that are inquorate cannot pass formal resolutions but can undertake business and make recommendation for consideration at the next meeting.

Other Management Board members may attend meetings of the Committee, as observers.

At the request of the Committee, any Forensic Laboratory employee shall attend meetings.

Any Independent Assessors may also be invited to attend.

FREQUENCY OF MEETINGS

Meetings shall be held at least twice a year or more if required.

Additional meetings may be called by the Management Board, or the Chairman of the Management Board acting for the Management Board, or by the Chairman of the Committee.

RESPONSIBILITIES

To keep under review Forensic Laboratory's quality assurance procedures and systems, ensuring that they meet the Forensic Laboratory's requirements and reflect good practice.

To receive, and consider, on a regular basis reports about, where relevant:

- updates of legislation, regulation, or good practice that may affect the management systems;
- results of management systems audits and reviews;
- results of performance reviews;
- results of audits of key suppliers, outsourcing partners, and other associated third parties;
- feedback from interested parties (including any complaints about the Forensic Laboratory products and services);
- techniques, products, or procedures, which could be used in the Forensic Laboratory to improve the management systems performance and effectiveness;
- status of preventive and corrective actions;
- review of the level of risk present and the risk appetite;
- results from effectiveness measurements and any testing carried out;
- incidents or other non-conformances;
- follow-up actions from previous Management Reviews;
- any changes that could affect the management systems;
- feedback from awareness and similar training;
- feedback from any Line Manager affected by the management system;
- feedback from the Management System Owner, including adequacy of resources (financial, personnel, material);
- lessons learned from any incidents, testing, or similar events;
- lessons learned from similar organizations;
- recommendations for improvement.

To receive and consider six-monthly reports from the Independent Assessor, where an Independent Assessor is appointed.

In conjunction with the Audit Committee, to commission and/or review internal audit reports, results of other tests and exercises pertaining to quality within the Forensic Laboratory, and the management responses to the recommendations.

To approve the text of the section of the Forensic Laboratory annual review dealing with quality matters and the Committee.

REPORTING PROCEDURES

The minutes of the Committee shall normally be considered at the Management Board meeting following the Committee meeting.

Where this proves to be impractical, the minutes shall be circulated to all members of the Management Board as soon as possible.

REVIEW OF TERMS OF REFERENCE

These Terms of Reference shall be reviewed on an annual basis by the Committee with input from all stakeholders.

APPENDIX 33 - RISK COMMITTEE

TITLE

The title of this committee shall be:

"The Forensic Laboratory Risk Committee".

CONSTITUTION

The Forensic Laboratory Risk Committee (the "Committee") is constituted as a Committee of the Management Board, with a remit to oversee and coordinate risk management activities to identify, evaluate, and manage all of the key business and technical risks in the Forensic Laboratory.

The Committee's Terms of Reference may be amended at any time by the Management Board.

AUTHORITY

The Committee is authorized by the Management Board to review or investigate any activity within its Terms of Reference.

The Committee is authorized by the Management Board to require of the executive such additional information to support risk management activities and/or corrective or preventive action as it deems appropriate.

MEMBERSHIP

The Committee shall be appointed by the Management Board from among Forensic Laboratory employees, as appropriate and shall consist of not less than three members.

The Chairman of the Committee shall be the Forensic Laboratory Risk Manager.

Appointments to the Committee shall be for a period of 1 year and reviewed at the annual Management Board meeting.

Nominations for the Committee shall be submitted to the Management Board by the Forensic Laboratory Risk Manager.

The Forensic Laboratory Risk Manager shall appoint the Secretary to the Committee.

AGENDA AND MINUTES

Agendas shall be distributed to all members of the Committee at least 5 working days before the meeting. Any relevant attachments shall be attached to the agenda (typically, this may include updated risk registers, incident report, risk reports, etc.) as agreed by the Chairman of the Committee.

Minutes of the meeting shall be distributed within 10 working days of the meeting.

ATTENDANCE AT MEETINGS

The quorum necessary for the transaction of the business of the Committee shall be a simple majority of the Committee members.

Meetings that are inquorate cannot pass formal resolutions but can undertake business and make recommendation for consideration at the next meeting.

Other Management Board members may attend meetings of the Committee, as observers.

At the request of the Committee, any Forensic Laboratory employee shall attend meetings.

FREQUENCY OF MEETINGS

Meetings shall be held at least once a quarter or more if required.

Additional meetings may be called by the Management Board, or the Chairman of the Management Board acting for the Management Board, or by the Chairman of the Committee.

RESPONSIBILITIES

The committee focuses on the risk management process with the following responsibilities:

- approve methodologies and processes for risk management in the Forensic Laboratory, e.g., risk assessment, information classification;
- identify significant threat changes and exposure of information and information-processing facilities to threats;
- raise the level of management awareness and accountability for the business risks faced by the Forensic Laboratory;
- develop risk management as part of the culture of Forensic Laboratory;
- provide a mechanism for risk management issues to be discussed and disseminated to all areas of the Forensic Laboratory;
- coordinate activities to obtain a more effective risk management process from existing resources;
- prioritize and accelerate those risk management strategies that are critical to the achievement of corporate objectives;
- assess the adequacy and coordinate the implementation of information security controls;
- manage and oversee the management of the risk registers within the Forensic Laboratory.

In conjunction with the Audit Committee, to commission and/or review internal audit reports, results of other tests and exercises pertaining to risk-related issues within the Forensic Laboratory, and the management responses to the recommendations.

To approve the text of the section of the Forensic Laboratory annual review dealing with risk management issues and the Committee.

REPORTING PROCEDURES

The minutes of the Committee shall normally be considered at the Management Board meeting following the Committee meeting.

Where this proves to be impractical, the minutes shall be circulated to all members of the Management Board as soon as possible.

REVIEW OF TERMS OF REFERENCE

These Terms of Reference shall be reviewed on an annual basis by the Committee with input from all stakeholders.

APPENDIX 34 - SERVICE DELIVERY COMMITTEE

TITLE

The title of this committee shall be:

"The Forensic Laboratory Service Delivery Committee".

CONSTITUTION

The Forensic Laboratory Service Delivery Committee (the "Committee") is constituted as a Committee of the Management Board, with a remit to oversee the service delivery within the Forensic Laboratory both to internal and external Clients.

The Committee's Terms of Reference may be amended at any time by the Management Board.

AUTHORITY

The Committee is authorized by the Management Board to review or investigate any activity within its Terms of Reference.

The Committee is authorized by the Management Board to require of the executive such additional service delivery audits or Management Reviews and/or corrective or preventive action as it deems appropriate.

MEMBERSHIP

The Committee shall be appointed by the Management Board from among Forensic Laboratory employees, as appropriate and shall consist of not less than three members.

The Chairman of the Committee shall be the Forensic Laboratory Service Delivery Manager.

Appointments to the Committee shall be for a period of 1 year and reviewed at the annual Management Board meeting.

Nominations for the Committee shall be submitted to the Management Board by the Forensic Laboratory Service Delivery Manager.

The Forensic Laboratory Service Delivery Manager shall appoint the Secretary to the Committee.

AGENDA AND MINUTES

Agendas shall be distributed to all members of the Committee at least 5 working days before the meeting. Any relevant attachments shall be attached to the agenda (typically, this may include audit reports, incident reports, etc.) as agreed by the Chairman of the Committee.

Minutes of the meeting shall be distributed within 10 working days of the meeting.

ATTENDANCE AT MEETINGS

The quorum necessary for the transaction of the business of the Committee shall be a simple majority of the Committee members.

Meetings that are inquorate cannot pass formal resolutions but can undertake business and make recommendation for consideration at the next meeting.

Other Management Board members may attend at meetings of the Committee., as observers.

At the request of the Committee, any Forensic Laboratory employee shall attend meetings.

Any Independent Assessors may also be invited to attend.

FREQUENCY OF MEETINGS

Meetings shall be held at least twice a year or more if required.

Additional meetings may be called by the Management Board, or the Chairman of the Management Board acting for the Management Board, or by the Chairman of the Committee.

RESPONSIBILITIES

To keep under review Forensic Laboratory's service delivery procedures and systems, ensuring that they meet the Forensic Laboratory's requirements and reflect good practice.

To receive, and consider, on a regular basis reports about, where relevant:

- updates of legislation, regulation, or good practice that may affect the management systems;
- results of management systems audits and reviews;
- results of performance reviews;
- results of audits of key suppliers, outsourcing partners, and other associated third parties;
- feedback from interested parties (including any complaints about the Forensic Laboratory products and services);
- techniques, products, or procedures that could be used in the Forensic Laboratory to improve the management systems performance and effectiveness;
- status of preventive and corrective actions;
- vulnerabilities or threats not adequately addressed in the previous risk assessments (where appropriate);
- review of the level of risk present and the risk appetite;
- results from effectiveness measurements and any testing carried out;
- incidents or other non-conformances;
- follow-up actions from previous Management Reviews;
- any changes that could affect the management systems;

- feedback from awareness and similar training;
- feedback from any Line Manager affected by the management system;
- feedback from the Management System Owner, including adequacy of resources (financial, personnel, material);
- lessons learned from any incidents, testing, or similar events;
- lessons learned from similar organizations;
- recommendations for improvement.

To receive and consider six-monthly reports from the Independent Assessor, where an Independent Assessor is appointed.

In conjunction with the Audit Committee, to commission and/or review internal audit reports, results of other tests and exercises pertaining to service delivery matters within the Forensic Laboratory, and the management responses to the recommendations.

To approve the text of the section of the Forensic Laboratory annual review dealing with service delivery matters and the Committee.

REPORTING PROCEDURES

The minutes of the Committee shall normally be considered at the Management Board meeting following the Committee meeting.

Where this proves to be impractical, the minutes shall be circulated to all members of the Management Board as soon as possible.

REVIEW OF TERMS OF REFERENCE

These Terms of Reference shall be reviewed on an annual basis by the Committee with input from all stakeholders.

APPENDIX 35 - WHISTLE BLOWING POLICY

Internal whistle blowing encourages and enables employees to raise serious concerns within the Forensic Laboratory rather than overlooking a problem or "blowing the whistle" outside.

Employees are often the first to realize that there is something seriously wrong with the Forensic Laboratory. However, they may not express their concerns as they feel that speaking up would be disloyal to their colleagues or to the Forensic Laboratory.

The Forensic Laboratory is committed to the highest possible standards of openness, probity, and accountability. In line with that commitment, employees, who have serious concerns about any aspect of the Forensic Laboratory's work are encouraged to come forward and voice those concerns.

This policy has been developed to:

- encourage employees to feel confident in raising concerns and to question and act upon concerns about any aspect of the Forensic Laboratory's business;
- provide avenues for raising concerns in confidence and receive feedback on any action taken;
- ensure that any concerns are acknowledged and how to pursue them if the whistleblower is not satisfied with the actions taken by the Forensic Laboratory's Top Management;
- reassure employees that they will be protected from possible reprisals or victimization if they have a reasonable belief that the disclosure has been made in good faith.

The types of concern that can be raised include, but are not limited to:

- actions that are unprofessional, inappropriate, or conflict with a general understanding of what is right and wrong;
- conduct that is an offence or a breach of legislation or regulation within the jurisdiction;
- damage to the environment;
- disclosures related to miscarriages of justice;
- failure to comply with a legal obligation in the jurisdiction;
- Health and Safety risks, including risks to the public as well as other employees;
- other unethical conduct;
- possible fraud and corruption;
- sexual, physical, or other abuse of other employees;
- the unauthorized use of corporate funds;
- undeclared conflicts of interest.

The Forensic Laboratory recognizes that the decision to report a concern can be a difficult one for an employee to make. If the concerns raised are true, they should have nothing to fear because, by raising these concerns, the employee is doing their duty to both the Forensic Laboratory and to any Client to whom the Forensic Laboratory provides a product or service.

The Forensic Laboratory will not tolerate any harassment or victimization (including informal pressures) and will take appropriate action to protect any employee who raises a concern in good faith.

All concerns will be treated in confidence and every effort will be made not to reveal the employee's identity, but it must be recognized that the employee may need to come forward as a witness.

Prior to raising a concern, the employee must:

- disclose the information in good faith;
- believe it to be substantially true;
- not act maliciously or make false allegations;
- not seek any personal gain.

As a first step, any employee with a concern should normally raise the concern with immediate Line Manager or their superior. This may depend, however, on the seriousness and sensitivity of the issues involved and who is suspected of the malpractice.

This policy is issued and maintained by the Legal Counsel in association with various Forensic Laboratory employees and external legal counsel, who also provides advice and guidance on its implementation and ensures compliance.

All Forensic Laboratory employees shall comply with this policy.

APPENDIX 36 - MANAGEMENT REVIEW AGENDA

There is no defined Management Review agenda for ISO 15489. Those management systems with Management Review inputs mandated by the relevant standards are shown below, where implemented in the Forensic Laboratory:

Item No	Description	ISO 9001[a]	ISO 14001	ISO 22301	ISO 27001	OHSAS 18001
1	Apologies for absence			✓		
2	Approval of previous minutes			✓		
3	Matters arising			✓		
4	Results of reviews of the management system policies	5.3 e)		9.3 d)	7.2 g)	
5	Status and results of management systems objectives and management system improvement activities	5.4.1	4.6 d)	9.3 d)	7.2 c)	4.6 e)
6	Results of management systems audits, management systems reviews, other audits, or self-assessments of the management systems	5.6.2 a)	4.6 a)	9.3 c), 9.3 d)	7.2 a)	4.6 a)
7	Customer (or any other stakeholders) feedback	5.6.2 b)	4.6 b)		7.2 b)	4.6 c)
8	Performance and status of suppliers and strategic partners	5.6.2 c)		9.3 d)		
9	Review of quality objectives versus business objectives and their appropriateness	5.6.2 c) and 5.3 c)				
10	Status of preventive and corrective actions	5.6.2 d)	4.6 e)	9.3 c), 9.3 d)	7.2 d)	
11	Status and follow-up of Management Review action items	5.6.2 e)	4.6 f)	9.3 a)	4.6 g)	7.2 g)
12	Any changes that could affect the management systems, including regulatory and legal issues	5.6.2 f)	4.6 g)	9.3 d)	4.6 h)	7.2 h)
13	Recommendations for improvement to the management systems	5.6.2.g)		9.3 d)		7.2 c) 7.2.i)
14	Vulnerabilities or threats not adequately addressed in the previous risk assessment			9.3 d)		7.2 e)
15	Results from effectiveness measurements			9.3 d)		7.2 f)
16	Security issues and incidents raised since the last Management Review meeting					✓
17	Approvals and authorities needed				4.2.1 i) and j)	✓
18	Environmental performance of the organization		4.6 c)			
19	Results of participation and consultation					4.6 b)
20	The OH&S performance of the organization					4.6 d)
21	Status of incident investigations, corrective actions, and preventive actions			9.3 d)		4.6 f)
	Changes in internal and external issues relevant to the BCMS			9.3 b)		
22	Other opportunities for improvement not covered by the above			✓		
23	Any other business			✓		
24	Date, place, and time of next meeting			✓		

[a]ISO 17025 has the same requirements for a Management Review as ISO 9001, but uses different standards numbering system, which is not reproduced above. ISO 17025 does not mandate inputs and outputs, as is the case in some other management standards. ISO 17025 requires that the Management Review "shall take account of" the items listed under ISO 9001 above.

Requirement	Completed on (dd/mm/yyyy)	Completed by (sign)[a]
Requirements of Forensic Laboratory document and Record Control procedures shall be met		
References to other documents shall not refer to a version but the document title		
No names shall be referred to—only job titles, apart from the Document Author in the document control section for reports and procedures. All Owners and Reviewers shall be referred to by job role		
The correct and current Forensic Laboratory template shall be used for the document		
All document control metadata shall be entered as required by the template on document creation		
Tables of content shall be regenerated using <f9> (Function Key F9) or Insert I Reference I Index and Tables		
The copyright notice shall always be present and appropriate. It shall never be removed		
All documents shall be written in second or third person (i.e., it is permissible to use "you must . . . ," "The user should . . . ," etc). Addressing style (i.e., second or third person use) should be consistent throughout a document and not mixed However, gender should not be used (i.e., "he" and "she," etc.		
All tables and figures shall have appropriate captions underneath them. A list of figures shall be produced after the table of contents		
Where acronyms are used they shall be defined in full on first use, followed by the acronym. The acronym should then be used in the text. A glossary shall be inserted at the end of the document as an Appendix		
Tense use shall be consistent throughout and always in the present tense		
"Shall" and "must" are to be used for mandatory requirements, "should" is to be used for expected results		
Short sentences shall be used		
Wordiness shall be avoided		
Jargon shall be avoided		
Visio and other diagrams shall be embedded in the text so that they can be edited in the document (Insert I Object I Create From File)		
Footnote and endnote use should be kept to a minimum		
Formatting shall be correct and consistent		
Spell checking shall be undertaken using word (<f7>—Function Key F7) as well as a visual check		
All documents shall be peer reviewed prior to release		

[a] *While this is a checklist for document production, the auditing and signing process is optional. It helps to prove that the document has gone through the processes on the checklist.*

APPENDIX 37 - DOCUMENT CONTROL CHECKLIST

DIGITAL FORENSICS PROCEDURES

The following checklist must be filled in for all documents produced in the Forensic Laboratory and should be retained for audit.

APPENDIX 38 - DOCUMENT METADATA

> **Note**
>
> The metadata below is that used in the Forensic Laboratory, other laboratories will use their own internal standards for metadata.

Document metadata is entered on the first page of any report produced by the Forensic Laboratory.

HEADER

The header is as below

CLASSIFICATION

Forensic Laboratory Logo	Subject

Classification

This is the classification of the report, as defined by the Forensic Laboratory's classification process.

- alignment center;
- font Arial 14, bold;

- paragraph spacing before 12 pt;
- paragraph spacing after 12 pt;
- tabs 1 inch, left;

Logo

The Forensic Laboratory Logo.

Subject

This is the Subject from Word Properties.

- alignment right;
- font Arial 7;
- paragraph spacing before 3 pt;
- paragraph spacing after 3 pt;
- tabs 1 in., left.

Note

The box surround is not visible.

DOCUMENT DETAILS TABLE

The document details table is as below:

		Title	
		Subject	
Synopsis	:	Synopsis	
Authors	:	Author(s)	
Keywords	:	Keywords	
Issue	:	Issue	
Release Date	:	Date of Release	
File Name	:	File name	
Status	:	Status	
Deliverability	:	Original	File
	:	Copy 1	Recipient 1
	:	Copy 2	Recipient 2
Page Count	:	number of pages	
Signed	:		
Proposal Wording if appropriate			

Title

This is the Title from Word Properties.

Subject

This is the Subject from Word Properties.

The Title and Subject are both:

- alignment center;
- font Arial 16, bold;
- paragraph spacing before 12 pt;
- paragraph spacing after 12 pt;
- tabs 1 in., left.

Note

All of the following are:

- alignment left;
- font Arial 12, normal;
- paragraph spacing before 6 pt;
- paragraph spacing after 6 pt;
- tabs 1 in., left.

Synopsis

A synopsis of the document in two or three paragraphs.

Author(s)

Name of author(s) from Word Properties.

Keywords

Keywords from Word Properties.

Issue

The version number of the document.

Release Date

The date the document was released to the recipient.

File Name

The name of the file from Word Properties.

Status

The status of the document (Draft or Issued).

Deliverability

To whom the document is issued. Typically, original is to file and copies are numbered.

Page Count

Number of pages in document from Word Properties.

Signature

Signature of the Document Owner.

Proposal Wording

Where the document is a proposal, the following text shall be added.

This proposal contains information that is commercially confidential to Client. It is supplied to Client on the understanding that it will not be communicated to any third party, either in whole or in part, and that it will be used solely in connection with the evaluation of the commercial bid contained herein.

FOOTER

The footer is as below

© 20xx The Forensic Laboratory	Copy *x* of *y*	Page *x* of *y* Issue
	CLASSIFICATION	

Copyright

This is standard text

- alignment left;
- font Arial 7;
- paragraph spacing before 3 pt;
- paragraph spacing after 3 pt;
- tabs 1 in., left.

Copy Number

This is in the form "Copy *x* of *y*."

- alignment center;
- font Arial 7;
- paragraph spacing before 3 pt;
- paragraph spacing after 3 pt;
- tabs 1 in., left.

Note

This is an optional field, depending on the classification of the document.

Page Number

This is in the form "Page *x* of *y*" and is from Word Properties.

- alignment right;
- font Arial 7;
- paragraph spacing before 3 pt;
- paragraph spacing after 3 pt;
- tabs 1 in., left.

Classification

This is the classification of the report, as defined by the Forensic Laboratory's classification process.

- alignment center;
- font Arial 14, bold;
- paragraph spacing before 12 pt;
- paragraph spacing after 12 pt;
- tabs 1 in., left.

Note

The box surround is not visible.

SECOND AND SUBSEQUENT PAGES

The second and subsequent pages only contain the header and footer as defined above.

APPENDIX 39 - FILE-NAMING STANDARDS

DOCUMENTS AND RECORDS

Files are all named as follows:

<date><name><version><author's initials>.<extension>

The date is inserted in "yymmdd" order so that the most recent version can always be "sorted" to the top of the directory listing.

DRAFT DOCUMENTS

Draft documents are those documents that have not been formally issued. These documents are still in production and undergo several review phases before they are issued.

Documents typically pass through a number of draft stages, typically three, which are identified by the version numbers 0.1, 0.2, etc.

Version	Description
0.1	First draft of a document. It includes the Document Author's edit pass of the document. The version number can increment to 0.11, 0.12, 0.13, etc., until the Document Author is sure that the document is ready for an internal review
0.2	Second draft of a document. It includes the implemented edits from the Reviewer(s). The version number can increment to 0.21, 0.22, 0.23, etc., until the Document Author is sure that the document is ready to be issued for a final internal or external review
0.3	Third draft of a document. It includes the implemented edits from the internal or external review. The version number can increment to 0.31, 0.32, 0.33, etc., until the Document Author is sure that the document is ready to be issued for release

As illustrated within each main draft stage, version numbers can increment (for example, to 0.21 and 0.22) if the document progresses without moving on to the next stage. This allows for the fact that editing is an iterative process and enables an employee to identify different versions of a document when it is at any one draft stage.

For example:

130101 Proposal V0.1 DLW.doc

Indicating that the file was created on January 1, 2013, it is a Client proposal first draft (v0.1), was created or updated by DLW, and is a Word document.

File names are to be made as meaningful as possible and kept as short as practical.

Every day that the document is worked on, the date will be updated and if appropriate, the author's initials and version. Where the document is worked on or reviewed by the same person, a number of times in the day after it has been worked on or reviewed by someone else, the day's data shall be suffixed by an "a," "b," "c," etc., as required.

For example:

130101a Proposal V0.1 DLW.doc

Indicating that the file was created on January 1, 2013, this is the second time that DLW has worked on this document after someone else has worked on it during January 1, 2013, it is a Client proposal first draft (v0.1), was created or updated by DLW, and is a Word document.

Files of different types such as flowcharts, presentations, spreadsheets, etc., follow the same principles and always begin at document number V0.1 with appropriate file extensions.

ISSUED DOCUMENTS

Issued documents are those documents that have passed through the draft review process internally. These documents are no longer in production and are issued for use (i.e., are live).

The first issued version of a document is version 1.0.

For example:

130111 Proposal V1.0 DLW.doc

Indicating that the file was created on January 11, 2013, it is a client proposal released (v1.0), was updated by DLW, and is a Word document.

The second issued version of the document is version 2.0.

For example:

130111 Proposal V2.0 DLW.doc

Indicating that the file was created on January 11, 2013, it is the second version of the client proposal released (v2.0), was updated by DLW, and is a Word document.

If only a small change is required to an issued document, the Document Author should consider an intermediate increment for the document number. For example, if only one paragraph is changed in the proposal above, the updated issued version could be:

130111 Proposal V1.1 DLW.doc

Indicating that the file was created on January 11, 2013, it is an updated client proposal released (v1.1), was updated by DLW, and is a Word document.

All documents must be retained for an indefinite period from the date of issue, but they may be archived.

THE IMS

> **Note**
>
> All documents must conform to this standard apart from those that form part of the IMS (apart from records). The logic for this is that the manual maintenance of links between a large number of files that comprise the IMS means that where the system is updated, there would be disproportionate effort in checking the linkages. Therefore, FrontPage files and forms used in the IMS will be named as below:
>
> **<name>.<extension>**

The version number of all documents is that set at the change control page.

APPENDIX 40 - WATERMARKS IN USE IN THE FORENSIC LABORATORY

The following watermarks are in use:

- Draft—for Comment;
- Issued;
- Not Authorized for Release;
- Uncontrolled Copy when Printed.

These are applied in Word using Format | Background | Printed Watermarks.

> **Note**
>
> "Uncontrolled Copy when Printed" is used for all copies of procedures printed from the IMS and is used to ensure that the integrity of the document control system is enforced. However, occasionally IMS-documented procedures may be released outside the Forensic Laboratory, and it is essential that they are marked with this watermark.

APPENDIX 41 - DOCUMENT REVIEW FORM

The following is used in the Forensic Laboratory:

Please review the attached document(s) and then sign and return this form together with one fully marked-up copy of the document(s).

- project, Client, business process, or management system name;
- client name;
- document name;
- version;
- Document Author name;
- Reviewer name;
- date sent;
- return by date;
- comments.

Please mark up all edits on the attached printed document. Write any overall comments in this space.

- reviewed by:
- signature;
- position;
- date.

Please note that our continuing ISO 9000 quality system compliance relies upon this form being returned.

APPENDIX 42 - IMS CALENDAR

The IMS calendar contains details of the following types of audits and tests to be carried out during the year on a month by month basis:

- first party (internal) audits—case processing;
- first party (internal) audits—management systems;
- second party (supplier) audits;
- third-party (Certification Body) audits;
- third-party audit response;
- access reviews (physical access);
- account rights and access reviews (logical access);
- business continuity (BCP) tests;
- calibration tests;
- CAPA audits and PIR reviews;
- clear screen and clear desk inspections;
- contract reviews;
- external penetration testing;
- firewall audits;
- internal penetration and vulnerability tests for the network;
- maintenance audits;
- Management Reviews;
- management system committee meetings;
- perimeter scans for open ports;
- physical asset audits;
- post implementation audits for new equipment or processes;
- produce metrics for management system objectives;
- refresher training for all employees;
- regular management system refresher training;
- UPS testing;
- vulnerability testing for servers;
- workstation scans.

Note 1

All audits and test results are regarded as records within the Forensic Laboratory and filed in the ERMS. Where relevant, CAPAs are raised and followed through to conclusion.

Note 2

Audits of management system may be structured according to the relevant management standard or be process based, following a process through from start to finish for representative samples to determine that relevant procedures have been followed. Forensic case processing always follows this approach for sample cases to be audited.

APPENDIX 43 - AUDIT PLAN LETTER

Note

The details of the audit need to be filled in as appropriate where DEFINE is shown in the text below.

This document is a plan for the internal audit of the Forensic Laboratory DEFINE.

OBJECTIVES OF THE AUDIT

The objectives of this audit are to:

- determine the conformity or non-conformity of the area within the DEFINE;
- determine the effectiveness of the process;
- fulfill the requirements of the Forensic Laboratory DEFINE regarding the regular auditing of procedures;
- fulfill the requirements of the relevant legislation, standard, or business process for the on-going auditing of the Forensic Laboratory DEFINE;
- ensure that the Forensic Laboratory's DEFINE is continuously monitored, managed, and improved.

SCOPE OF THE AUDIT

This audit covers all activities within the area.

The basis of the audit will be the procedure and associated files within the DEFINE.

The Auditor is NAME.

The Owner of DEFINE (the Auditee) is NAME.

AUDIT SCHEDULE

The audit will take place at the Forensic Laboratory office at NAME on the DD/MM/YYYY.

AUDIT REPORT

An audit report is to be produced following the audit, to be issued on DD/MM/YYYY.

APPENDIX 44 - AUDIT REPORTING FORM

- department;
- reference;
- area;
- audit date;
- details of the non-conformance;
- non-compliance category (major, minor, or observation);
- Auditee function;
- Auditee name;
- Auditee signature;
- Audit date;
- Auditor name;
- follow-up date.

APPENDIX 45 - CAR/PAR FORM

- CAR/PAR number;
- requestor name;
- date;
- business area;
- contact;
- phone;
- e-mail;
- issue requiring corrective or preventive action;
- source (e.g., Management Review, internal audit, external audit, self-assessment test, etc.);
- source reference (detail the actual origin—i.e., audit document reference, etc.);
- standard (e.g., ISO 9001, ISO 14001, OHSAS 18001, ISO 20000, ISO 22301, ISO 27001, other—define);
- action type (corrective/preventive);
- Audit Marking (major non-conformance/minor non-conformance/observation);
- what is the non-conformity/observation/issue to be addressed;
- details of where is the evidence of this to be found (document reference, system, or procedure);
- what is the impact of this on the Forensic Laboratory;
- action to be taken (what—e.g., Change *xyz* document, Change Procedure "Procedure name," etc.);
- where is the Action to be taken (define location);
- action owner (name);
- date for completion;
- action owner (signature);
- agreed CAR or PAR coordinator (name);
- date agreed;
- agreed CAR or PAR coordinator (signature);
- CAR or PAR Action is approved/rejected;
- what further is required and by whom (if CAR or PAR is rejected);
- CAR or PAR action agreed (name);
- date agreed;
- CAR or PAR action agreed (signature);
- CAR or PAR action referred to (name);
- date;
- CAR or PAR PIR carried out by (name);
- date;
- what further is required and by whom (if appropriate);
- CAR or PAR action referred to (name);
- date;
- CAR or PAR PIR agreed (signature);
- date.

APPENDIX 46 - OPENING MEETING AGENDA

- introduce auditing staff;
- Auditee introduces their staff;
- confirm the statement of confidentiality and ensure that the Auditee is aware of the security procedures for retaining the Auditee's sensitive information and how this will be cared for during the audit, if appropriate;
- enquire if there are any secure facilities that can be used during the audit for securing sensitive information when the Auditor(s) is/are off site;
- confirm the standard against which the audit will be performed is <Define Standard(s)>;
- confirm the Statement of Applicability is up-to-date, if appropriate;
- confirm the scope of the audit;
- explain how the audit will proceed;
- describe method of non-conformance reporting;
- provide definitions of non-conformance (major and minor);
- explain how corrective actions relating to non-conformities should be undertaken;
- confirm the Audit Plan (interviews and dates/times);
- identify any problems (staff absences, etc.);
- obtain any documentation that was not submitted in advance and requested (for whatever reason);
- ensure that other employees are aware of the visit (where necessary);
- ensure management approval is in place for asking sensitive questions, viewing sensitive documents, or accessing sensitive areas;
- confirm that "Guides" are available to assist Auditors;
- confirm availability of office services (desk, etc.—as agreed);
- confirm start and finish times and lunch arrangements;

- answer any questions from Auditee;
- thank them all for their assistance;
- final plan for audit—last minute issues;
- start the Audit.

APPENDIX 47 - CLOSING MEETING AGENDA

- the Auditor thanks the Auditee for their hospitality, assistance, and cooperation;
- reconfirm confidentiality undertaking, if appropriate;
- reconfirm the standard against which the audit was performed;
- reconfirm the scope of the Audit;
- inform Auditee of the overall outcome of the Audit;
- provide definitions of non-conformance (major and minor)—if required;
- summarize any non-conformities and observations—if required;
- invite the Auditee to comment on the non-conformities observations—if required;
- explain the required corrective actions and invite the Auditee to comment them—if required;
- obtain Auditee signature on all reports;
- inform the Auditee of the requirement to maintain the systems and advise the Forensic Laboratory of any changes to the system that may affect the Forensic Laboratory management system, if appropriate;
- return any paperwork to the Auditee that is not to be taken off site as part of the Audit file;
- thank the Auditee again, pack up, and leave.

APPENDIX 48 - AUDIT REPORT TEMPLATE

- executive summary;
- introduction;
- audit objective;
- major non-conformances;
- minor non-conformances;
- observations;
- opportunities for improvement and other tasks;
- follow-up;
- 1 audit overview;
- 1.1 introduction;
- 1.2 audit objectives;
- 1.3 audit scope;
- 1.4 audit criteria;
- 1.5 audit logistics;
- 1.6 approach;
- 1.7 purpose;
- 1.8 distribution;
- 2 summary of findings;
- 2.1 major non-conformances;
- 2.2 minor non-conformances;
- 2.3 observations;
- 2.4 opportunities for improvement and other tasks;
- Appendix A—Auditees;
- Appendix B—Audit Team;
- Appendix C—Distribution list;
- Appendix D—Audit Markings;
- Document control.

APPENDIX 49 - ROOT CAUSES FOR NON-CONFORMITY

- an isolated incident;
- Client requirements changed without advising the Forensic Laboratory;
- component failure (e.g., media);
- defined procedure is not complete;
- defined procedure not followed;
- deliberate act;
- equipment failure;
- lack of training;
- no defined procedure;
- no one accepts responsibility;
- operator error;
- process changed, but procedure not updated;
- records that should be kept are not being kept;
- supplier failure;
- tool failure.

Chapter 5

Risk Management

Table of Contents

5.1 A SHORT HISTORY OF RISK MANAGEMENT

Risk management has been used by man since the dawn of time on a personal basis. Typically, it was used then for personal survival: Is it safe to walk through the jungle? Is it safe to attack this animal for food? This was individual responsibility and accountability.

One of the greatest moves from individual responsibility and accountability was when Chancellor Otto von Bismarck started the "social insurance" schemes in Germany in 1881. This signaled a move from individual responsibility and accountability to corporate and governmental. This spread throughout much of the world over the next 50 years.

The 1920s saw British Petroleum setting up the Tanker Insurance Company which was a "captive," emphasizing internal financing of risk. Historically, insurance had always, where it existed, been to a third party. The 1920s also saw Frank Knight publish *Risk, Uncertainty, and Profit*, separating risk from uncertainty. John Maynard Keynes published *A Treatise on Probability*, where he emphasized the importance of relative perception and judgment when determining probabilities of events.

The 1950s saw Life Insurance companies determining mortality rates for smokers and how they could affect premiums. In 1956, Dr. Wayne Snider of the University of Pennsylvania suggested that the "professional insurance manager should be a risk manager."

1965 saw Ralph Nader published *Unsafe at any Speed*—unmasking the faults in the Corvair. This heralded the birth of the consumer movement and turned *caveat emptor* to *caveat vendor*.

1980 saw the birth of the Society for Risk Analysis in the United States, and in 1986, the Institute for Risk Management was formed in London.

In 1992, the Cadbury Committee in the United Kingdom suggested that organizational governing boards are responsible for setting risk management policy, assuring that the Forensic Laboratory understands the risk it faces and accepting oversight for the risk management process. This was later followed by other countries following this lead and there were successor committees set up in the United Kingdom (Greenbury 1995, Hempel 1998, Turnbull 1999 and a review of Turnbull in 2004).

In 1993, the title *Chief Risk Officer* was used in GE Capital.

1995 saw the fall of Barings, precipitated by Nick Leeson. The failures leading up to this reignited interest in risk management. 1995 also saw the development of the first risk management standard—AS/NZS 4360. Since then there have been many risk-based initiatives and the risk management culture is becoming firmly embedded in corporate culture.

The current information risk management standards exist:

- 2002—SP 800-30—Risk Management Chapter for Information Technology Systems—Recommendations of the National Institute of Standards and Technology;
- 2004—AS/NZS 4360:2004 Risk Management;
- 2005—ISO 27001:2005 Information technology—Security techniques—information security management systems (ISMSs)—Requirements;
- 2006—BS 7799 Part 3: 2006 Guidelines for information security risk management;
- 2008—ISO 27005: 2008 Information technology—Security techniques—information security risk management;
- 2008—BS 31100—Code of Practice for Risk Management;
- 2008—ISO 31000—Risk Management—Guidelines on principles and implementation of risk management.

In addition to these standards, there are a number of well-established risk management methodologies that can be used to manage information security risk. These include the following:

- A&K analysis (the Netherlands);
- CRAMM (CCTA Risk Analysis and Management Method (United Kingdom);
- EBIOS (France);
- MARION (France);
- MEHARI (France);
- OCTAVE (the United States);
- Österreichisches IT-Sicherheitshandbuch (Austria).

Even if it has deeper foundations, risk management, as it is practiced today, is essentially a post-1960s phenomenon rather than relying on purchasing third-party insurance policies.

While the Forensic Laboratory holds appropriate insurance for its areas of operations and to meet the legislative requirements in it jurisdiction of operations, it also uses risk management for managing both its business and its information security risk treatment. This chapter focuses on information security risk and not business opportunity risk, though the same processes can be used for both.

5.2 AN INFORMATION SECURITY RISK MANAGEMENT FRAMEWORK

5.2.1 Some Definitions

- a *Resource* is defined as a physical asset or an element or component of an information system, manual, or computerized. It could be the process itself, a part of the process, data, hardware or software, data files, paper files, transaction profiles, terminals, terminal input/output, disk/tape volumes, user IDs, and programs;

> **Note**
>
> Reference is made to resources rather than assets as specified in ISO 27001. This is because the term asset has an implied Finance Department meaning. All assets are resources, but all resources are not treated as assets in the traditional view. This terminology overcomes this implied limitation.

- an *Owner* is the person who has responsibility for a predetermined set of resources and who is therefore accountable for the integrity, availability, confidentiality, auditability, and accountability of the resources. An Owner is also accountable for the consequences of the actions of users of these resources;
- a *Custodian* may be appointed by the Owner to undertake day-to-day tasks and decision making on the data, on their behalf;
- a *Resource Owner* is the Owner of a Resource.

5.2.2 Overview

The loss of confidentiality, integrity, availability, accountability, auditability, authenticity, and reliability of the Forensic Laboratory's information and related products and services can have a severe, if not catastrophic, impact. The Forensic Laboratory needs to secure information and information-processing systems that it owns or has in its custody.

The provision of effective, unobtrusive, and affordable information security has always been a major organizational challenge. This is becoming increasingly critical with the increase in system connectivity, information and information processing systems, the amount of information and data being processed, and the distributed nature of the processing. Too often, the provision of appropriate security measures is secondary to the provision of functionality and is often a "bolt on" afterthought.

Protecting information-processing assets is an essential organizational goal and can be achieved by:

- establishing and implementing a comprehensive and systematic program for information security risk management within, and appropriate to, the Forensic Laboratory;
- recognizing that management of information security risk is an integral part of the risk management process.

A generic comprehensive and systematic framework for such a program is shown below and it can be applied to all, or any part of the Forensic Laboratory.

It must be remembered that risk management is not a "fire and forget" process; it is a process of continuous improvement and the Forensic Laboratory's risk profile changes as its business processes, or the environment in which it operates, change.

BS 31100, ISO 27001, ISO 27005, and ISO 31000, along with other management standards, recommend or mandate a Plan-Do-Check-Act (PDCA) process as shown below:

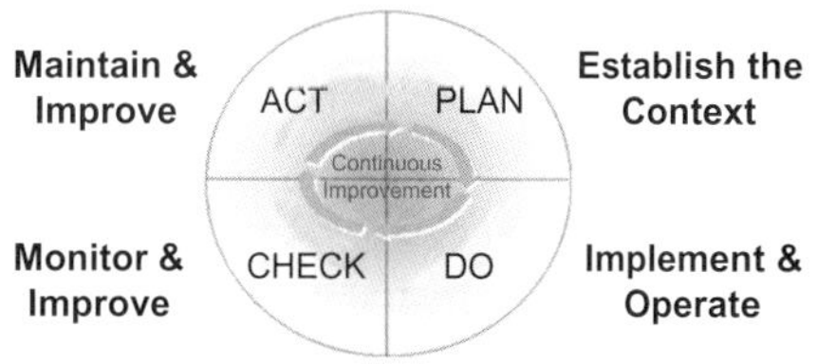

- *Plan*—establish the context, develop risk treatment plan, define risk acceptance criteria, etc.;
- *Do*—implement the risk treatment plan;
- *Check*—assess and where possible measure compliance, reporting results to Management for review;
- *Act*—take corrective action for continuous improvement.

This has been implemented in the Forensic Laboratory, as shown below:

Information Security Management System Framework

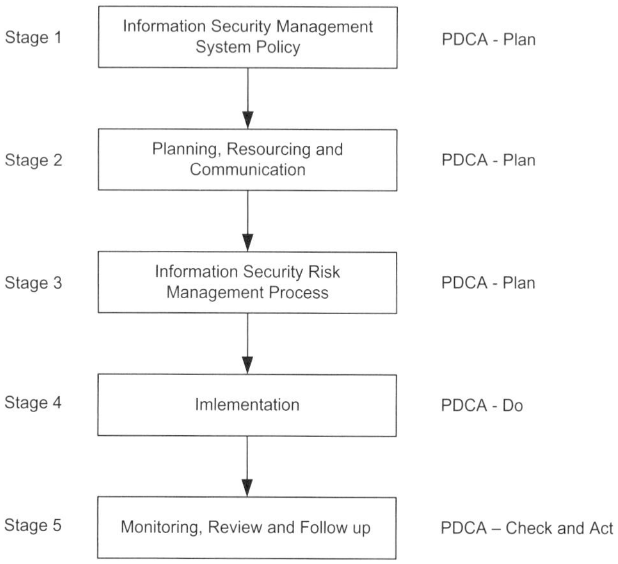

Each of the stages in the diagram is described briefly below, and in depth later in this chapter. The relevant part of the PDCA process is identified on the right of the diagram above for reference:

- *Stage 1*—the starting point for implementing appropriate information security based on risk management is to define the scope or context of the ISMS. Once this process has been completed an information security policy appropriate for the scope, or context, is developed based on the scope or context defined. The Forensic Laboratory Information Security Policy is given in Chapter 4, Appendix 10;
- *Stage 2*—to effectively implement the information security policy, roles and responsibilities shall be identified and adequate resources allocated. It is also essential that there is effective communication with all internal and external stakeholders, as appropriate, at each stage of the risk management process and concerning the process as a whole. A communication and consultation plan should be developed. A template for a communication plan is given in Appendix 1;
- *Stage 3*—the assets within the scope or context identified must be considered in terms of risks that they face and impacts to the Forensic Laboratory should the risks occur. Controls to treat the likelihood or impact of the risk must be identified and agreed with the Resource Owners and the residual risk must be agreed with the Resource Owners. The outcome of this step is an information security plan and the Statement of Applicability (SoA). The residual risk is formally accepted by the Resource Owner. A template for a security plan is given in Appendix 2;
- *Stage 4*—the information security plan is implemented with an appropriate security awareness and training program;
- *Stage 5*—to ensure that implemented controls work effectively, monitoring and reviewing of their effectiveness must be undertaken. This will include follow-up activities for continuous improvement.

5.2.3 Critical Success Factors

The successful implementation of information security within the Forensic Laboratory will depend on a number of factors, such as:

- a clear understanding of the security requirements and risks facing the Forensic Laboratory or assets within the scope or context;
- an approach to implementing information security that is consistent with the Forensic Laboratory's culture;
- appropriate communication of comprehensive guidance on the information security policy, standards, and procedures to all employees and third parties with access to the Forensic Laboratory's information or information processing systems;
- appropriate training, awareness, and education;
- effective selling and marketing of information to all employees and third parties with access to the Forensic Laboratory's information or information processing systems;
- establishing an effective information security incident management process as defined in Chapter 7, Section 7.4.1;
- implementing an appropriate process for measuring the effectiveness of the implemented controls for treating the risks within the scope or context as defined in this Chapter, Section 5.5.4.1;
- knowledge of all relevant regulatory and legislative requirements as defined in all implemented management standards in the Forensic Laboratory, specifically in Chapter 4, Section 4.5.2, Chapter 12, Section 12.3.13.1 and evaluated at the management reviews. The management review agenda is given in Chapter 4, Appendix 36;
- security policy, objectives, and activities being based on business objectives;
- visible and demonstrable support and commitment from Top Management as defined in all implemented management standards in the Forensic Laboratory.

5.2.4 Information Security Risk Components

5.2.4.1 *The Components*

There are a number of component parts to the information security risk process. Each is briefly described below:

- *assets*—something of value to a person or organization and therefore has to be protected. Examples of asset types are given in Appendix 3.
- *asset values*—assets have values to a person or organization. These values can be expressed in financial terms as defined in Appendix 4 or they can be expressed in terms of the potential business impacts of undesirable events affecting loss of confidentiality, integrity, and/or availability. Potential impacts include financial losses, loss of revenue, market share or image. Examples of impacts and consequences are given in Appendix 5;
- *business risks*—modeling risk with the "business" in the Forensic Laboratory means that risks have to be considered in business terms and then converted to information-processing terms. Some common business risks are given in Appendix 6;
- *project risks*—Forensic cases can be viewed as projects, though some are mini-projects. Every project has risks associated with it, and some common project risks are given in Appendix 7;
- *security controls*—these are the processes, procedures, tools, or mechanisms that are used to reduce the vulnerabilities of, or the impact of, an undesirable event to, an asset. ISO 27001, CobIT, and NIST 800-53 have details of controls that may be used to treat any risks identified;
- *security requirements*—there are three main sources of information security requirements, and these are:
  - legal, statutory, and contractual requirements with which the Forensic Laboratory has to comply;
  - policies, principles, objectives, and requirements to support its business operations that the Forensic Laboratory undertakes;
  - unique security risks which could result in significant losses if they occur.
- *security risk*—a security risk is the potential that a given threat will exploit a vulnerability to cause loss or damage to an asset or group of assets, and directly or indirectly affect the Forensic Laboratory. The security risk level is determined from the combination of the asset values, levels of threats to, and associated vulnerabilities of an asset and their impact values;
- *threats*—a threat is something that could cause a risk to happen. They can come from the natural environment or from human action (accidental or deliberate). Some examples of security threats are given in Appendix 8;
- *vulnerabilities*—a flaw or weakness in a system that could be exploited by one or more threats. A vulnerability that cannot be exploited by a threat is not harmful to the asset. Some examples of security vulnerabilities are given in Appendix 9.

5.2.4.2 *Relationship Between the Components*

The relationship between the components was clearly described in BS 7799 and is shown below:

Note
This diagram is not in ISO 27001, BS 7799's successor.

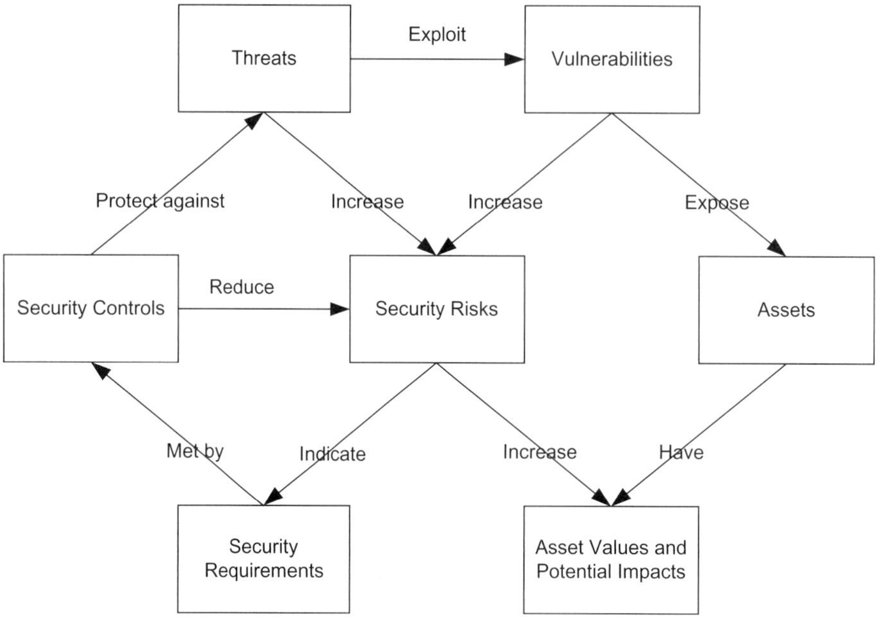

5.3 FRAMEWORK STAGE 1—ISMS POLICY

5.3.1 Overview

As part of the risk management process, the Forensic Laboratory will have a risk management policy. This policy will include the objectives for, and management commitment to, information security risk management. It will be aligned with Forensic Laboratory goals and objectives. The Forensic Laboratory risk management policy is given in Appendix 10.

Top Management should set a clear direction and demonstrate their support for and commitment to the ISMS by issuing a formally agreed and documented ISMS policy across the Forensic Laboratory. The policy has been approved by Top Management and is reproduced in Chapter 4, Appendix 10.

However, before a policy can be prepared, the scope or context of the ISMS has to be defined. It may be the entire organization but could be a single site or a particular system or service. The Forensic Laboratory's scope statement is given in Appendix 11.

The ISMS policy serves as the foundation of the ISMS program and the basis for adopting specific procedures and technical controls. It is the first step in establishing a security culture that strives to make everyone in the Forensic Laboratory aware of the need for information security and the role they personally have to play.

5.3.2 Establish the Context and Scope

This process occurs within the framework of the Forensic Laboratory's strategic, organizational, and risk management context. This must be established to define the basic parameters within which risks must be managed and to provide guidance for decisions within more detailed risk management studies. This sets the context and scope for the rest of the risk management process and defines the boundaries for the ISMS policy.

5.3.2.1 External Context

This involves defining the Forensic Laboratory and its relationship to its environment, identifying the strengths, weaknesses, opportunities, and threats. The context can include the financial, operational, competitive, political, social, client, cultural, and legal aspects of the Forensic Laboratory's functions. Identify both internal and external stakeholders, consider their perceptions, and establish communication strategies with these parties. This step is focused on the environment in which the Forensic Laboratory operates.

5.3.2.2 Internal Context

Before the process can be undertaken, it is necessary to understand the Forensic Laboratory and its capabilities, as well as its goals and objectives and the strategies to achieve them. Areas to be considered include:

- any projects and their relationship to the Forensic Laboratory;
- costs of activities, both direct and indirect;
- intangibles (reputation, goodwill, etc.);
- legal context;
- laboratory behavior;
- laboratory capability;

- laboratory missions and goals;
- revenue, entitlements and budgets;
- the criticality of operations;
- the structure of the Forensic Laboratory.

5.3.2.3 *Establish the Scope*

Setting the scope and boundaries of an application or the part of the Forensic Laboratory that has assets to be protected involves defining the:

- assets in the scope;
- extent of the risk management activities to be carried out in the defined area;
- extent of the risk management project in time and location;
- Forensic Laboratory roles, and responsibilities for supporting risk management and information security management in the defined scope;
- physical location, its boundaries, the project or activity, and establishing their goals and objectives;
- relationships across the boundaries of the defined scope area;
- technology is use in the defined area.

ISO 27001 recommended defining the scope as a minimum using the following four headings:

- assets;
- location;
- organization;
- technology.

The Forensic Laboratory's scope statement is given in Appendix 11.

5.3.2.4 *Risk Evaluation Criteria*

The Forensic Laboratory must determine its risk appetite against which the risks are to be evaluated. Decisions concerning risk acceptability and risk treatment may be based on operational, technical, financial, legal, social, or other criteria. These will depend on the Forensic Laboratory's policies, goals and objectives, and the interests of stakeholders.

The risk criteria will assist in determining a tolerable level of risk for management and aspects and activities that are critical to the outputs, functions, and activities of the Forensic Laboratory.

Defining risk criteria will assist in:

- identifying the more important risks;
- preparing appropriate treatments and/or counter measures;
- providing a benchmark against which the success of the action plan can be measured.

Sample criticality ratings are given in Appendix 12.

5.3.3 ISMS Policy Content and Format

A well written and appropriate ISMS policy is the cornerstone of, and the first regular step in, implementing appropriate information security and good corporate governance in any organization. It informs and gives directions to employee that has access to the Forensic Laboratory's information or information-processing facilities of information security requirements.

The ISMS policy provides executive direction and support for the Forensic Laboratory in establishing and maintaining appropriate information security. Policies vary widely in their scope, detail, and content, but they all establish the overall management intention and outcomes.

Typically, a policy document is short and high level. In the laboratory, these are typically one or two pages long.

Within its scope, an effective ISMS policy must be:

- achievable with clearly defined responsibilities for all Forensic Laboratory employees;
- enforceable both procedurally and technically, and with sanctions when breaches occur;
- implementable through processes, procedures, technical controls, or other methods;
- support legislative, regulatory, and other business requirements.

There are no defined rules for the format or content of an ISMS policy. However, a structure of the policy using four main headings may be useful.

The Forensic Laboratory Information Security Policy is given in Chapter 4, Appendix 10.

5.3.3.1 *Statement of Executive Intent*

This is a short statement in the Information Security Policy setting the scene for the Forensic Laboratory and the required executive outcomes. It shall include:

- a definition of information security, its overall objectives, and scope within the Forensic Laboratory;
- emphasis on why information and information-processing facilities need to be protected.

5.3.3.2 *Responsibilities and Accountabilities*

This should cover the responsibilities and accountabilities of individual employees and any third parties having access to the Forensic Laboratory's information or information-processing facilities. This must be explicit and enforceable and should focus on the proper and authorized use of information and information-processing facilities. Typically, it will refer to detailed requirements found in the contract of employment (or service provision for third parties), the employee handbook and job descriptions. A variety of job descriptions are given in Chapter 18, Section 18.1.5 that relate specifically to the IMS.

5.3.3.3 General Direction

A number of areas are covered in the policy and these include:

- auditing and monitoring and review requirements;
- business continuity planning;
- information handling;
- security incident management;
- security requirements derived from legal and regulatory sources;
- security training and awareness;
- the method of risk assessment and criteria for the acceptability of risks.

Inspection of the Forensic Laboratory's information security policy in Chapter 4, Appendix 10, shows that all of these elements are present.

5.3.3.4 Policy Review and Ownership

All IMS policies must be owned and regularly reviewed.

Typically, the owner of the Information Security Policy is the Information Security Manager and his delegated authority comes from the Forensic Laboratory's Top Management who endorses all IMS policies.

Policies should be reviewed on at least an annual basis unless any influencing changes affect this regular review. This is defined in all of the policies in the Appendices in Chapters 3 and 4.

5.3.4 Information Security Policy Communication

Once the Information Security Policy has been developed and endorsed by the Top Management, it must be distributed, understood, implemented, and maintained by appropriate means to all employees and any third parties that have access to Forensic Laboratory information or information-processing systems. This can include:

- ensuring that as revisions occur the training, awareness, and contractual measures are updated as defined in Chapter 4, Section 4.6.2.2;
- including the Information Security Policy as part of the contract for all third-party service providers;
- including the Information Security Policy, or at least a reference to compliance with it and all other Forensic Laboratory policies and procedures as part of the contract of employment for employees;
- including the Information Security Policy as part of the induction and ongoing awareness training, where records are kept of all attendees and all members of the Forensic Laboratory must attend, as defined in Chapter 4, Section 4.6.2.2 and 4.6.2.3;
- making employees sign two copies of the Information Security Policy and the Human Resources Department and the employee each retain a copy.

The Forensic Laboratory will have to choose how they achieve this requirement, but the five listed above are the most common. Further guidance is given in Chapter 4, Section 4.6.5.

5.4 FRAMEWORK STAGE 2: PLANNING, RESOURCING, AND COMMUNICATION

5.4.1 Management Commitment

According to the ISMS International User Group, one of the key factors for successful information security in any organization is the:

- "visible and demonstrable support and commitment from all levels of management starting with the Chief Executive Officer or equivalent";

Top Management direction on, and commitment to, information security does seriously influence the whole culture of the Forensic Laboratory. Demonstrable and visible Top Management commitment ensures that information security is taken seriously at the top levels of the Forensic Laboratory and so presents this message at the lower levels.

Top Management's commitment to information security can be demonstrated by ensuring that:

- an ISMS is established, implemented, and maintained in accordance with internal requirements and relevant international standards as appropriate;
- appropriate resources are allocated to information security as defined in Chapter 4, Section 4.6.2;
- there is a process of evaluating the performance of the ISMS in place and that the results of the evaluation are reported to management for review and are used as a basis for continuous improvement as defined in Chapter 4, Section 4.8, with the ISMS metrics used defined in Appendix 22;
- this is reflected in the ISMS policy.

5.4.2 Planning

Information security planning is the product of the ISMS scope, the ISMS policy, and information security risk management processes. Some of the outputs of the planning process may affect the policy and scope and vice versa. This may lead to iteration between planning and policy as organizational and resourcing issues are resolved. It may also be that the development of the Statement of Applicability (SoA) also requires further iterative work.

Any new information-processing system, changes in existing information processing system, or take on of work that may affect existing information-processing systems must ensure that information security requirements, based on risk management, are addressed throughout the project from the initiation to the post implementation review (PIR).

After developing the draft Information Security Policy, preparations for the subsequent stages in the framework must be made. This will include:

- defining IMS and ISMS responsibilities. Specific ones are defined in job descriptions in Chapter 18, Section 18.1.5;
- defining physical security responsibilities based on the Forensic Laboratory's Physical Security Policy, defined in Chapter 2, Appendix 2;
- determining and implementing interactions between IT and information security;
- establishing an effective risk management structure;
- establishing an effective IMS and ISMS management structure.

There may be other plans to consider, and these will depend on the specific requirements of the Forensic Laboratory, but those above are probably the minimum set for any organization.

5.4.3 Responsibility and Authority

It is essential that the responsibilities, authorities, and interactions of the employees who manage the IMS and the ISMS are defined and documented. This is specifically important where cross-departmental boundary actions have to be taken, such as:

- any problem areas of the Forensic Laboratory for the management of risk;
- areas of the Forensic Laboratory where information security risks need to be managed;
- areas that may need further treatment of risks until the level of risk becomes acceptable according to the agreed risk appetite;
- areas that will need appropriate cross-functional business continuity plans developed, documented, and tested;
- areas where incident management processes may affect the different departments in Forensic Laboratory;
- areas where risk treatment solutions may have to be recommended, initiated, installed, maintained, and monitored;
- internal and external communication channels to all levels of Forensic Laboratory employees and relevant third-party suppliers.

5.4.3.1 Cross-Functional Fora

In the Forensic Laboratory, a number of committees to oversee all aspects of the IMS, including risk management, are defined with their terms of reference in Chapter 4, Section 4.4.3.

5.4.3.2 Information Security Manager

The Forensic Laboratory will probably appoint a full time Information Security Manager (ISM), however, depending on the size of the organization, this may be designated as a part time role. The ISM may have a functional reporting path to any department but must have a "dotted line" responsibility to the Top Management, if needed.

The ISM directs, coordinates, plans, and organizes information security activities throughout the Forensic Laboratory. The ISM acts as the focal point for all communications related to information security, both with employees and any relevant third parties, including Clients and suppliers. The ISM works with a wide variety of employees from different departments, bringing them together to implement controls that reflect workable compromises as well as proactive responses to current and future information security risks.

The ISM is responsible for defining and implementing the controls needed to protect both Forensic Laboratory information and information that has been entrusted to the Forensic Laboratory by any third parties. The position involves overall Forensic Laboratory responsibility for information security regardless of the form that the information takes (paper, blueprint, CD-ROM, audio tape, embedded in products or processes, etc.), the information handling technology employed (servers, desktops, laptops, fax machines, telephones, local area networks, file cabinets, etc.), or the people involved (contractors, consultants, employees, vendors, outsourcing firms, etc.).

Threats to information and information systems addressed by the ISM and other Forensic Laboratory employees include, but are not limited to:

- information unavailability;
- information corruption;
- unauthorized information destruction;
- unauthorized information modification;
- unauthorized information usage;
- unauthorized information disclosure.

These threats to information and information systems include consideration of physical security matters only if a certain level of physical security is necessary to achieve a certain level of information security (e.g., as is necessary to prevent theft of portable computers).

A job description for the Forensic Laboratory's ISM is given in Chapter 12, Appendix 4.

5.4.3.3 Information Security Management Team

The responsibility for the security of the Forensic Laboratory's information and information-processing systems will ultimately rest with Top Management, supported by the ISM. The ISM may be supported in this task by an Information Security Management Team, whose size will depend on the size of the Forensic Laboratory and its identified needs.

Where it exists, the Information Security Management Team undertakes the following:

- assist in developing, implementing, and monitoring information security matters, including risk management;
- assist the Human Resources Department in the areas of information security and investigations, including training and awareness;
- manage and monitor information security incidents;
- operational management and monitoring of control systems;
- perform internal audits of information security controls;
- provision of advice on information security matters to the Forensic Laboratory, its projects, and trading partners, as appropriate;
- undertake business continuity management responsibilities.

This is not an exhaustive list but is possibly the minimum set of requirements for an Information Security Management Team tasking. Where the Information Security management team does not exist, these functions are performed by the ISM.

5.4.3.4 Resource Owners

Resource Ownership conveys authority and responsibility for:

- assigning Custodian(s);
- authorizing access to "their" resources, as appropriate;
- classifying their resources and reviewing control and classification decisions;
- communicating control and protection requirements to suppliers of products and services and users;
- ensuring that backup data are available in the event of any destruction or other outage that may affect the availability or integrity of "their" information;
- ensuring that information asset security and application system controls are in place;
- judging the resource's value and importance to the Forensic Laboratory, in association with the ISM;
- participating in the risk assessment, risk management, and risk treatment process;
- reviewing service delivery against service level agreements (SLAs);
- taking action where service delivery does not meet the contractual SLA;
- the implementation of adequate physical and logical security controls for their resources.

For practical purposes, the day-to-day responsibility for implementing the security measures and monitoring them shall be delegated to the Custodian.

Resource Owners and Custodians will be registered in the asset register and the service catalog with details of the resources that they manage.

Note

Even if a Custodian is appointed, the Resource Owner retains personal accountability and responsibility for the resource(s) that they "own."

5.4.3.5 Custodians

A Custodian may be appointed by the Resource Owner to undertake day-to-day tasks and decision making on the data, on behalf of the Resource Owner.

The Custodian is usually a member of the IT Department.

Custodian responsibilities include:

- complying with the requirements set by the Resource Owner;
- ensuring the confidentiality and availability of the Resource Owner's information and information processing systems on a continuing process;
- monitoring, with the System Administrators, any access violations;
- reporting all violations to the ISM.

5.4.3.6 Information Users

The success of security, in practice, depends on the performance of the users. An information user is an individual user, who has permission from the Resource Owner to access and use the Resource Owner's information, information processing systems or other resources. An information user may well be a Resource Owner of his/her own information, or someone else's.

Information user responsibilities include:

- being responsible and accountable for all access to information processing systems made by their user identity;
- bringing security exposures, misuse, or non-conformance situations to management and the ISM in a timely manner;
- complying with all security controls designated by the Resource Owner, the ISM, or Forensic Laboratory Top Management;
- complying with information asset security and application system controls as specified by the Resource

Owner and Top Management and any relevant third party service supplier;

- effectively using control facilities and capabilities;
- ensuring that their system, information, and application passwords meet specified requirements;
- ensuring that their passwords are not shared and are properly protected;
- not disclosing any information to anyone without the consent of the Resource Owner, or their Line Manager;
- using Forensic Laboratory information and information processing systems only when authorized by the Resource Owner and only for approved purposes.

5.4.4 Resourcing

Resourcing requirements within the Forensic Laboratory will depend on the implementation, management, and monitoring requirements for information security within the Forensic Laboratory and the size and complexity of the organization.

Top Management must make available the appropriate resources to implement, manage, and maintain the ISMS program. These resources must have appropriate skills and a planned training agenda to ensure that their skills are maintained and match the Forensic Laboratory's requirements as defined in Chapter 4, Section 4.6.2.

A simple Information Security Management Team structure showing its place in the Forensic Laboratory is shown below:

5.4.5 Communications and Consultation

5.4.5.1 Communications

Throughout the process of designing, implementing, maintaining, monitoring, and improving the information security within the Forensic Laboratory, it is essential that there is communication with the target audience.

There is no "one size fits all," but the messages to be sent must be tailored for the specific intended audience.

A communication plan should be developed at the earliest stages of the process, therefore ensuring that both internal and external stakeholders are aware of the issues relating to both the risk itself and the process to manage it.

Appropriate communication seeks to:

- ensure that all participants are aware of their roles and responsibilities;
- ensure that the varied views of stakeholders are considered;
- improve understanding of risk and the risk management process.

Security Communication is generally defined as an interactive process of exchange of information and opinion, involving multiple messages about the nature of risk and risk management. Inappropriate communication can lead to a breakdown in trust by stakeholders or poor information security implementation.

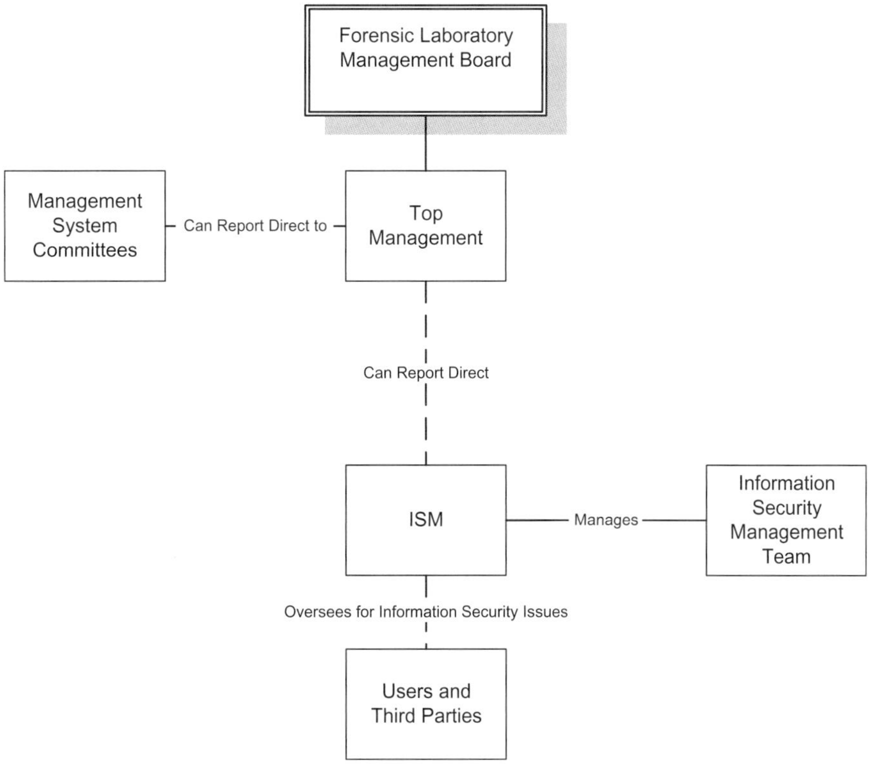

These requirements are in addition to the requirements defined in Chapter 4, Section 4.6.5 and Appendix 1.

5.4.5.2 Consultation

Consultation is a process of informed communication between stakeholders and the Forensic Laboratory on an issue prior to the making of a decision or a determination. It can be characterized as:

- a process not an outcome;
- focuses on inputs to decision making, not necessarily joint decision making;
- impacts on a decision through influence not power.

Note

More detailed guidance on Communication and Consultation for risk management is given in Section 5.5.

5.5 FRAMEWORK STAGE 3: INFORMATION SECURITY RISK MANAGEMENT PROCESS

5.5.1 Overview

Information security risk management is the systematic application of management policies, procedures, and practices to the task of establishing the context, identifying, analyzing, evaluating, treating, monitoring, and communicating information security risks.

Information Security Management can be successfully implemented with an effective information security risk management process. There are a number of national and international standards that specify risk approaches, and the Forensic Laboratory is able to choose which it wishes to adopt, though ISO 27001 is the preferred standard and the Forensic Laboratory will want to be Certified to this standard. A list of some of these is given in Section 5.1.

An ISMS is a documented system that describes the information assets to be protected, the Forensic Laboratory's approach to risk management, the control objectives and controls, and the degree of assurance required. The ISMS can be applied to a specific system, components of a system, or the Forensic Laboratory as a whole.

5.5.2 Benefits to the Organization of Risk Management

As with all processes, the Forensic Laboratory has to see some benefits from expending effort on implementing, managing, and monitoring them with associated resource costs.

For risk management, the benefits include:

- a move from reactive to proactive management;
- awareness for the need to identify, quantify, and treat risk;
- compliance with relevant legal and regulatory requirements;
- confident decision making based on a rigorous risk management process;
- effective allocation and use of resources in the risk management process;
- enhanced safety and security;
- improved financial reporting;
- improved identification of threats and opportunities;
- improved incident management and prevention;
- improved operation effectiveness and efficiency;
- improved stakeholder confidence and trust;
- loss reduction.

5.5.3 Principles for Managing Risks

ISO 31000 gives a number of principles for the management of risk, and the Forensic Laboratory must adhere to these principles, which are:

- risk management should be an integral part of decision making;
- risk management should be based on best available information;
- risk management should be capable of continuous improvement and enhancement;
- risk management should be dynamic, iterative, and responsive to change in the Forensic Laboratory;
- risk management should be integrated into all Forensic Laboratory processes;
- risk management should be structured and systematic;
- risk management should be tailored to the Forensic Laboratory's needs;
- risk management should be transparent and inclusive;
- risk management should create value in one or more areas in the Forensic Laboratory;
- risk management should explicitly address uncertainty;
- risk management should take into account human factors.

5.5.4 A Generic Approach to Risk Management

Note

The Forensic Laboratory has based their approach to risk on ISO 31000 and ISO 27001.

A generic model is given below based on good practice and combining common areas from well-known standards. The Forensic Laboratory will need to determine what steps can be combined or omitted. Each of the steps below is dealt within the subsequent sections of this chapter.

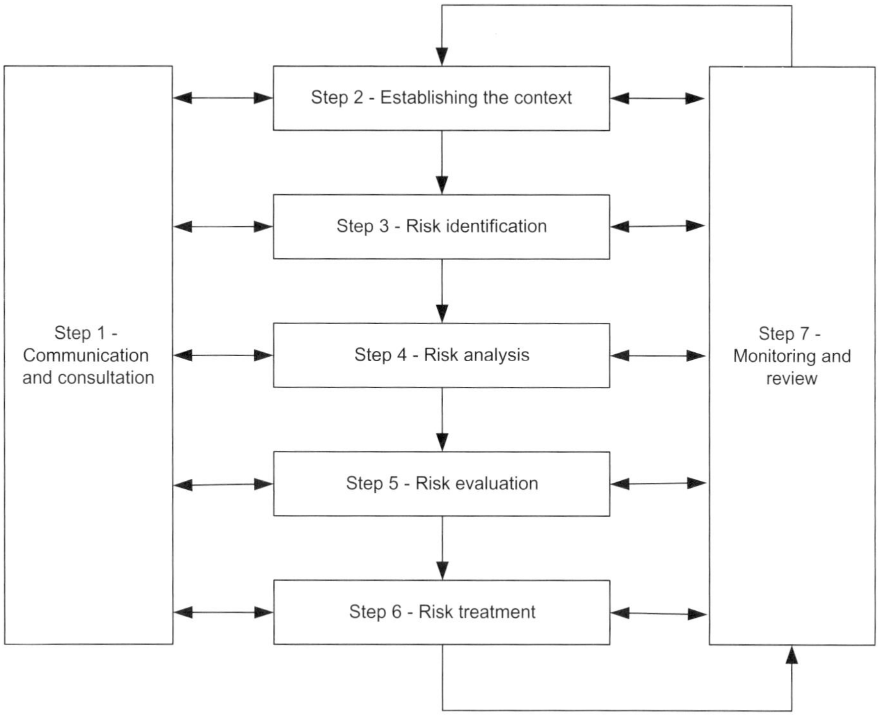

- *step 1*: Communication and consultation—with internal and external stakeholders as appropriate at each stage of the risk management process and concerning the process as a whole. A communication and consultation plan should be developed early in the process. A template for a communication plan is given in Appendix 1;
- *step 2*: Establishing the context—this involves the establishment of the strategic, organizational, and risk management context in which the rest of the process will take place. Risk evaluation criteria against which risk will be evaluated shall be established and agreed. The risk analysis process must be defined; The resources and assets within the scope also must be identified so that the risks to them can be analyzed and managed;
- *step 3*: Risk identification—identifying the risks that are relevant to the assets and resources identified in the last step. This will seek to determine what can happen and how it can happen. Some common types of risks that may be considered are given in Appendices 6 and 7;
- *step 4*: Risk analysis—determine the existing controls and analyze risks in terms of consequence and likelihood in the context of those controls. The analysis should consider the range of potential consequences and how likely those consequences are to occur. Consequence and likelihood may be combined to produce an estimated level of risk. A consequences table is given in Appendix 5 and the likelihood table is given in Appendix 13;
- *step 5*: Evaluate the risk—compare the estimated levels of risk against the preestablished criteria. This enables risks to be ranked so as to identify management priorities. If the levels of risk established are low, then risks may fall into an acceptable category and treatment may not be required. The Forensic Laboratory's risk appetite is defined in Appendix 14;
- *step 6*: Treat the risk—accept and monitor the low-priority risks. For those above the tolerable level of risk set by the risk appetite, develop and implement a specific risk treatment and management plan which includes consideration of funding. ISO 27001 requires the use of the controls in Annex A, and those not included must have their reasons for exclusion defined. However, there is nothing to say that other controls cannot be used. Appendix 15 gives details of controls defined in NIST 800-53 and CobIT;
- *step 7*: Monitor and review—the performance of the risk management system and changes which might affect it.

Each of the steps is defined below:

5.5.5 Step 1: Communication and Consultation

> **Note**
>
> This section is specifically aimed at communication and consultation relating to risk management. It is in addition to Chapter 4, Section 4.6.5 and this chapter, Section 5.4.5.

5.5.5.1 Overview

At each step of the risk management process, it is important to consider communication and consultation with stakeholders. A communication plan should be developed at the earliest stages of the process, therefore ensuring that both internal and external stakeholders are aware of the issues relating to both the risk itself and the process to manage it. A template for a Forensic Laboratory communication plan is given in Appendix 1.

5.5.5.2 Defining Communication and Consultation

"Risk communication" is generally defined as an interactive process of exchange of information and opinion, involving multiple messages about the nature of risk and risk management.[a] Inappropriate communication can lead to a breakdown in trust by stakeholders or poor risk management.

Consultation is a process of informed communication between stakeholders and the Forensic Laboratory on an issue prior to the making of a decision or a determination about risk management.

5.5.5.3 The Importance of Communication and Consultation

Communication and consultation are an intrinsic part of the process that should be considered at each step of risk management and a most important aspect of "establishing the context." The identification of stakeholders and interested parties will assist in the consideration of their needs and views.

Good communication is essential in the development of a risk culture within the Forensic Laboratory. Communication about the risks faced by the Forensic Laboratory will establish a positive attitude toward risk management.

Involving others is an essential and crucial ingredient of an effective approach to risk management.

Other benefits include:

- *adding value to the Forensic Laboratory*: the sharing of information and perspectives on risk will help to create coherence within the Forensic Laboratory. It will identify crucial areas of joint achievement and strategies for the Forensic Laboratory and any involved stakeholder;
- *integrating multiple perspectives*: those involved within the Forensic Laboratory and relevant stakeholders will make judgments about risk based on their perceptions. These perceptions can be varied by a number of factors such as values, beliefs, assumptions, experiences, needs, and concerns. It is important to document these perceptions of identified risks and the understanding of the reasons for them:
  - perceptions also vary between technical experts and other stakeholders. It is essential to effectively communicate the level of risk of informed decisions are to be made and implemented;
  - decisions about acceptability of risk are often based on a range of factors including:
    - the degree of personal control that can be exercised;
    - the potential for an event to result in catastrophic consequences;
    - the distribution of the risks and benefits among those affected;
    - the degree to which exposure is voluntary;
    - the degree of familiarity with, or understanding of, the activity.
  - there is less understanding of risks where the respondent has little control over them.
- *making risk management explicit and relevant*: risk is considered implicitly in the Forensic Laboratory's decision making and thinking. By discussing each step with other relevant stakeholders, it becomes a conscious and formal discipline and provides a mechanism to help ensure that past lessons are taken into account.

a. National Research Council, 1989. Improving risk communication.

5.5.5.4 Developing Trust

Communication between the Forensic Laboratory and its stakeholders allows it to develop an association with its "community of interest" and to establish relationships based on trust.

5.5.5.5 Developing a Process of Risk Communication and Consultation

5.5.5.5.1 Stakeholder Identification

Stakeholders are those who may affect, be affected by, or perceive themselves to be affected by the Forensic Laboratory or the risk management process. These may be internal or external to the Forensic Laboratory.

It is important to identify stakeholders and to realize that the Forensic Laboratory does not pick the stakeholders they choose themselves. If a stakeholder is initially overlooked, it is possible that they will be identified later but the benefits of early consultation will be missed.

Note

As well as stakeholders in the Forensic Laboratory, there can also be 'interested parties' as defined in the Glossary.

5.5.5.5.2 The Risk Communication and Consultation Plan

The extent of risk communication and consultation will depend on the situation and this varies from situation to situation. For example, risk management in the course of local and operational decision making entails a less formal communication process than strategic risk management at the level of the Forensic Laboratory overall.

The essential elements of a risk communication and consultation plan include:

- the risk communication and consultation plan will be influenced by what it is trying to achieve. Typically, it sets out to:
  - build awareness and understanding about risk within the Forensic Laboratory's area of operations;
  - learn about perceived risk from stakeholders;
  - influence the target audience;
  - obtain a better understanding of the context, the criteria, the risks faced, or the effectiveness of the risk treatment;
  - achieve an attitude or behavior shift;
  - a combination of the above.
- the communication methods to be used (this may vary throughout the risk management cycle);
- the objectives of the communication;
- the participants who need to be included (i.e., the stakeholders, risk experts, and the communications team with others as the situation requires);
- the perspectives of all participants that need to be taken into consideration.

5.5.6 Step 2: Define the Approach to Risk Assessment

The scope and the parameters of the IMS and ISMS must be clearly defined at the beginning of the process, building on the work in the previous step. This sets the framework for the rest of the process within which risks must be managed and provides guidance for making decisions. A definition of the boundaries avoids unnecessary work and improves the quality of risk management within the Forensic Laboratory.

This step aims to clarify the following:

- the information and resources that need to be protected;
- the information security requirements of the Forensic Laboratory;
- the issues that need to be considered in assessing information security risks;
- the parts of the Forensic Laboratory that rely on the accuracy, integrity, or availability of information for essential decisions.

The key components in the scoping of the IMS and ISMS for risk management are:

- define the information assets;
- define the risk activity structure;
- develop risk evaluation criteria;
- establish the Forensic Laboratory context;
- establish the risk management context;
- establish the strategic context.

5.5.6.1 Establish the Strategic Context

Any decisions regarding the management of information security risk need to be consistent with the Forensic Laboratory's environment.

This component is focused on the environment in which the Forensic Laboratory operates. The Forensic Laboratory should determine the crucial elements that might support or impair its ability to manage its information security risks. The Information Security Policy created at Stage 1 in Section 5.2.2 is one of the inputs at this stage.

The Forensic Laboratory should understand the following:

- its internal and external stakeholders and other interested parties, taking into account their objectives and perceptions;
- its strengths, weaknesses, opportunities, and threats (SWOT analysis);
- the financial, operational, competitive, political (public perceptions/image), social, Client, cultural, and legal aspects of the Forensic Laboratory's functions.

There should be a close inter-relationship between information security risk management and the Forensic Laboratory's strategic business objectives.

5.5.6.2 Establish the Organizational Context

This component requires an understanding of the Forensic Laboratory, its organization, its capabilities, goals, objectives, and the strategies that are in place to achieve them. This will help to define the criteria to determine whether a risk is acceptable or not and form the basis of controls and risk treatment options. The general nature of the Forensic Laboratory's information assets in broad terms of their tangible and intangible value is a part of the organizational context.

Failure to achieve the objectives of the Forensic Laboratory, specific business activity, or project being considered may be partially due to poorly managed information security risks.

5.5.6.3 Establish the Risk Management Context

This component determines the scope and depth of the review of information security risks. This involves:

- defining the information security risk management review project and establishing its goals and objectives. This could be a review for the whole Forensic Laboratory, a specific site, a specific department, or a specific case or project. The assets within the scope of the review will need to be identified;
- defining the resources required to conduct the information security risk management review. The review could be conducted by internal employees or external contractors. The scope of the review will determine the need for employee input both for the review team and their respondents. The respondents chosen must be those best able to answer the relevant questions and also be available. The tools to be used must also be made available for the review;
- defining the timeframe and locations to be covered by the information security risk management review project, the time allocated to the review must be defined and understood, so the review team can work toward this goal. Depending on the scope of the review, the locations where the review will take place can be determined.

5.5.6.4 Develop Risk Evaluation Criteria

In order to assess the risks, impacts, consequences, and the selection of controls, the quantitative and / or qualitative criteria to be used should be defined. The Forensic Laboratory risk appetite must be considered as part of this process; this is defined in Appendix 14.

The development of the detailed risk criteria will be influenced by a number of factors such as:

- expectations of stakeholders, other interested parties and specifically Clients;
- legal and regulatory requirements;
- the Forensic Laboratory's policies, goals, and objectives.

It is essential that appropriate risk criteria be determined at the outset of the risk assessment and be continually reviewed throughout the risk assessment process. Risk criteria may be further developed and refined to ensure that risk criteria remain current and appropriate.

Decisions concerning risk acceptability and the subsequent risk treatment may be based on the operational, technical, financial, legal, social, humanitarian, or other criteria.

When defining risk criteria, factors to be considered should include, but not be limited to:

- how likelihood will be defined (Appendix 13);
- how the level of risk is to be determined (Appendices 5 and 13);
- nature and types of consequences that may occur and how they will be measured (this will, typically, not just be based on financial loss) (Appendix 5);
- the level where the risk becomes acceptable (Appendix 14);
- the timeframe of the likelihood or consequence (Appendix 13);
- what level of risk may require treatment (Appendix 14).

When considering consequence, this will typically consider the following areas:

- availability breach;
- confidentiality breach;
- integrity breach;
- regulatory or legislative breach;
- reputational and employees morale loss.

Each of which is considered in the consequences table in Appendix 5.

5.5.6.5 Define the Information Assets

An asset is something which the Forensic Laboratory finds useful or valuable and therefore requires protection. In the identification of assets, information should be considered in the wider context than just the IT system(s) within the Forensic Laboratory and its associated hardware and software. Hence, it may be appropriate to structure the risk activity based on the type of assets.

All assets within the risk management context must be identified and recorded to an appropriate level of detail. Any assets to be excluded from the context, for whatever reason, may need to be assigned to another review to ensure that they are not forgotten or overlooked and that all major assets are accounted for.

The Asset Inventory should include the following information:

- asset identification number;
- asset description;
- asset classification (if appropriate);
- asset Custodian (if appropriate);
- asset location;
- Resource Owner;
- asset type;
- date the asset was last audited.

A high level list of example assets is given in Appendix 3.

5.5.6.6 Information Classification and Labeling

To provide a consistent basis for determining the level of protection required, information (whether electronic, paper, or on any other media) is labeled in accordance with security classification based on the criteria established by the Forensic Laboratory.

Classifications will vary between forensic laboratories, different governments have different classification schemes for all government-classified information, and commercial enterprises will also vary.

The Forensic Laboratory's information classification system is given in Appendix 16. Associated with the classifications will be a minimum level of security to be applied to the classified asset, these are defined in Chapter 12, Section 12.3.14.6.

5.5.6.7 Outputs

This step should produce the following deliverables:

- information and resources required for the information security risk management review;
- risk evaluation criteria;
- the asset listing for those assets within the scope and context of the information security risk management review;
- the scope and structure of the information security risk management review;
- the strategic and organizational context of the Forensic Laboratory that is the subject of the information security risk management review.

All the above information could be included in a project plan, which should be endorsed by Top Management and / or the relevant Risk Owner(s).

5.5.7 Step 3: Undertake a Risk Assessment

There are a number of different tools and methodologies for undertaking a risk assessment. These range from a paper-based, checklist-based approach to a fully functional integrated software tool. Different digital forensics laboratories will adopt different tools and methodologies depending on their own unique requirements. A list of some relevant standards and methodologies are given in Section 5.1.

Whatever standard, tool, or methodology is chosen, all broadly follow the same framework approach. Specialized risk management tools can be used for a detailed or specialized risk assessment in addition to a general one for the Forensic Laboratory, if needed. Whatever approach is chosen, it should be used consistently so that a comparison for "risk on risk" evaluations can be undertaken.

The output from the process is then captured in the Forensic Laboratory business risk register where it can be managed. The business risk register structure for the Forensic Laboratory is given in Appendix 17.

5.5.7.1 Risk Identification

Risk identification seeks to identify, classify, and list all the risks, vulnerabilities, or threats that may affect information assets identified in Section 5.5.6.5. This should produce a comprehensive list of risks that may enhance, prevent, degrade, or delay the achievement of the Forensic Laboratory's objectives.

It is essential that a well-structured systematic approach is used to ensure a comprehensive identification of risks. This identification should include all risks whether they can be controlled by the Forensic Laboratory or not. Potential risks not identified at this stage will be excluded from further analysis, until they are indentified and included.

It is not uncommon that certain risks, vulnerabilities, or threats may affect more than one of the aspects of information security (integrity, confidentiality, availability, accountability, auditability, authenticity, and reliability). The Forensic Laboratory should be aware that risks, vulnerabilities, and threats are continually changing.

The focus is on the nature and source of the risk, such as:

- how could it happen?
- what could happen or go wrong?
- who or what can be harmed?
- why can it happen?

The sources of risk should be evaluated from the perspective of all stakeholders and other interested parties, whether internal or external.

In identifying risks, it is also important to consider the risks associated with not pursuing an opportunity and remembering that risk also encompasses opportunities.

5.5.7.2 Risk Analysis

Risk analysis will separate the minor acceptable risks from the major risks and provides data for the evaluation and treatment of risks within the Forensic Laboratory. It involves the determination of the consequences arising from an undesirable event and the likelihood of the risk occurring. The level of risk is determined by the combination of asset values, likelihood, and consequence assessments in the context of the existing risk treatment.

In determining the existing risk treatment present, various methods may be used including audit, inspection of records, or self-assessment processes for the relevant employees. If a control does exist, it does not mean that it is being used effectively or efficiently. This must also be assessed and objective evidence that it is being used effectively and efficiently must be sought.

The risk analysis may be qualitative or quantitative, and some details of the difference between the two methods are given in Appendix 18. The decision whether to use qualitative or quantitative risk management is an individual choice based on circumstance. The Forensic Laboratory has found it easier to use qualitative risk.

- the asset valuation used in the Forensic Laboratory is given in Appendix 4;

- examples of some generic risks used in the Forensic Laboratory are given in Appendices 6 and 7;
- examples of some common threats used in the Forensic Laboratory are given in Appendix 8;
- examples of some common vulnerabilities used in the Forensic Laboratory are given in Appendix 9;
- the consequences of risks crystallizing used in the Forensic Laboratory are given in Appendix 5;
- the likelihood of a risk crystallizing used by the Forensic Laboratory is a 5 level one, though a 10 level one can be used if more granularity is needed, is given in Appendix 13;
- the risk evaluation process used in the Forensic Laboratory and its risk appetite are given in Appendix 14.

Each of the tables above can be adjusted to suit differing requirements, but it is essential to maintain consistency.

There are a number of published sources that can assist in assessing consequences and likelihoods of risks; these include:

- benchmarks and statistics;
- expert and specialist judgments;
- historical records;
- industry practice and experience;
- past recorded experience;
- research and studies.

5.5.7.3 Recommended Approach

Risk analysis can be both time consuming and resource hungry. The optimum method for conducting a risk analysis is to perform an initial high-level risk analysis of the Forensic Laboratory's assets to identify risks that are common and for which there is an established set of baseline controls to treat them and, at the same time, identify risks that need more investigation.

These are typically risks that are potentially serious and a detailed risk analysis is undertaken. This approach has the advantage of treating the majority of risks quickly with a baseline approach and allows time for the detailed risk analysis focusing on the potentially serious risks.

5.5.7.3.1 High-level risk analysis

This high-level risk analysis considers the business values of the Forensic Laboratory's information processing systems and the information it handles, and the risks from a business point of view. The following should be considered in determining which risks require further analysis:

- the business objectives of the information processing system;
- the level of importance of the information-processing system and its information to the Forensic Laboratory;
- the value of the Forensic Laboratory's investment to the information-processing system;
- the value to the Forensic Laboratory of the information produced by the information-processing system.

However, if the business objectives of its information processing systems are essential to the Forensic Laboratory's business objectives, the system replacement costs are high, or if the values of the assets are at high risk, then a detailed risk analysis is required. Any one of these conditions may be enough to justify conducting a detailed risk analysis.

The "rule of thumb" for high level and detailed information security risk assessment is that:

- if a lack of information security can result in significant harm or damage to the Forensic Laboratory, its business processes, or its assets, then a detailed risk analysis is required to identify suitable risk treatment options;
- otherwise, a baseline approach to risk treatment is appropriate.

5.5.7.3.2 Inter-dependencies

There may well be information-processing systems that are interdependent. In this case, a seemingly insignificant system that feeds critical data to another information-processing system may well affect the risk analysis results.

These inter-dependencies must be examined and where necessary detailed explanations given for the risk analysis results.

5.5.7.3.3 Detailed risk analysis

For assets that require a detailed risk analysis, this involves an asset valuation, a threat, and vulnerability assessment, similar to the high-level risk analysis described in Section 5.5.7.3.1. In this case, however, a more detailed or granular approach may be needed; this could include specialized tools.

5.5.7.4 Risk Evaluation

Once the assets, their values, the vulnerabilities and threats that may exploit them, their likelihood, and consequences have been identified and assessed, the risks can be prioritized.

At this point, the risk is "gross," in that it has not had any existing controls factored into the gross score to produce the "net" risk values. As has been said earlier, the effective or efficient use of risk treatment should be evaluated and factored in to reduce the gross risk score appropriately.

This process will produce a list of risks that can be sorted into a prioritized listing in the Corporate Risk Register so that it is possible to determine the risks that are acceptable and those that are not. This will also:

- assist the Forensic Laboratory's Top Management in deciding the allocation of resources to support risk treatment;
- assist Risk Owners to prioritize risk treatment;
- give an overview of the general level and pattern of risk in the Forensic Laboratory;
- identify the higher risk items.

Some reasons for accepting a risk include:

- the level of risk is so low that risk treatment is not appropriate;
- the risk is controlled outside the Forensic Laboratory (but the Forensic Laboratory could choose to avoid the risk);
- the total cost of the risk treatment (implementation and management) exceeds the benefits.

5.5.7.5 Outputs

This step should produce the following deliverables:

- a list of assets and their values relative to integrity, confidentiality, availability, accountability, auditability, authenticity, and reliability, and replacement costs;
- a list of assets and their asset values mapped to the threats and vulnerabilities and the likelihood and the consequences of the threat occurring;
- a list of assets for which a baseline approach is appropriate;
- a list of assets for which further analysis is required and the results of that detailed risk analysis.
- a prioritized list of risks for determining risk treatment.

5.5.8 Step 4: Manage the Risk

5.5.8.1 Managing the Risk

The Forensic Laboratory must manage risks and safeguard its operations to effectively protect its information processing systems, its own information, or information entrusted to it by any Clients or other third parties. Part of this is understanding how to treat the risks to those assets appropriately and realizing that risk can never be eliminated but can be reduced to an acceptable level.

Risk treatment options include:

- reduce the consequences—by implementing controls to reduce the threats and vulnerabilities or by modifying the assets at risk in some way;
- reduce the likelihood of the risk occurring—by implementing controls to treat the threats and vulnerabilities;
- retain the risk;
- risk avoidance—by deciding not to go ahead with an activity likely to generate risk;
- risk transfer—by arranging for another party to bear part or all of the risk, for example, insurers;
- sharing the risk with another party or parties.

These options may be used on their own or in association with one or more other options.

When selecting appropriate risk treatment options, the following should be borne in mind:

- the current risk treatment in place;
- the effectiveness of the treatment in managing risks, if implemented and operated correctly;
- the fit of the proposed treatment with the current implemented treatments and architecture;
- the identity of the Risk Owner;
- the resources needed for implementation and management (i.e., employees, funds, equipment);
- the risk treatment needed to reduce risk to an acceptable level.

5.5.8.2 Outputs

This step should produce the following deliverables:

- a list of knowingly accepted risks. These may well be affected by the treatment options addressing other risks. Additionally, the accepted residual risks must be approved by the Risk Owner;
- a list of treatment options for the unacceptable risks identified.

5.5.9 Step 5: Select Controls

Having identified risk treatment options for the risks identified and had them approved by the Risk Owner, it is necessary to identify suitable controls to reduce the risks to an acceptable level in line with the Forensic Laboratory risk appetite. It is usual that these are selected with a Cost-Benefit Analysis.

Existing and planned controls should have been taken into account already for the risk evaluation process. These may be considered at this stage for application to other risks than they were implemented or planned for. It must be emphasized that unnecessary duplication of controls should be avoided. It is also possible that an existing or planned control may no longer be justified and may need to be removed, replaced by a more suitable control, or remain implemented due to cost reasons.

When considering controls to be selected, experience dictates that the function of the control should be identified. Typical functions of controls are:

- *detection*: identify the occurrence of an undesired event;
- *deterrence*: avoid or prevent the occurrence of an undesired event;

- *protection*: protect assets from the occurrence or consequences of undesired events;
- *recovery*: restore the assets to their correct state following the occurrence of an undesired event;
- *response*: react to or counter the occurrence of an undesired event.

Many protective controls can serve multiple functions. It is usually more cost effective to select protective controls that can serve multiple functions. A well-designed security regime provides "defence in depth" by using controls that provide a mixture of these functions.

Using the clauses in ISO 27001, these types of controls can be deployed in the following areas:

- security policy;
- organization of information security;
- asset management;
- human resources security;
- physical and environmental security;
- communications and operations management;
- access control;
- information systems acquisition, development, and maintenance;
- information security incident management;
- business continuity management;
- compliance.

5.5.9.1 Risk Appetite

Once controls have been selected, the remaining risk must be evaluated to ensure that they are either within the Forensic Laboratory's risk appetite or, if not, additional controls are selected until they are. If this is not possible, the Risk Owner must knowingly accept the risk.

The Forensic Laboratory's risk appetite is defined in Appendix 14.

5.5.9.2 Baseline Approach

A baseline approach to risk treatment requires the establishment of a minimum set of controls to safeguard the Forensic Laboratory's assets against the most common threats. These baseline controls are compared with existing or planned controls for the scope or context being considered; this is typically done by use of a gap analysis exercise. Those that are not in place are implemented, if applicable.

The risk of the baseline approach is that there may be unidentified assets, threats, or vulnerabilities that are missed by the baseline approach or gap analysis that may seriously prejudice the Forensic Laboratory's assets in the event of an undesired event. To overcome this, the Forensic Laboratory can set its own baseline of controls to be implemented.

Note

ISO 27001 certification requires that the risk management process is carried out and the baseline approach is not used. However, this does not preclude using a baseline approach combined with a detailed risk management process for assets that fall outside the baseline.

There are a number of sources that can be used for the selection of baseline controls: these include:

- ISO 27001;
- NIST 800-xx series provides a number of different documents that can provide baselines[b];
- CobIT.[c]

ISO 27001 is the only international standard and it has been mapped against control functionality defined in Section 5.5.9, Appendix 19 and against security concerns in Appendix 20.

5.5.9.3 Factors Influencing Control Selection

There are a number of factors that influence the selection of controls by the Forensic Laboratory, and these include:

- compatibility with existing controls;
- compatibility with existing security architecture;
- cost of control to manage over time;
- cost of control to purchase;
- ease of use of the control;
- external mandatory requirements (legislative, governmental, or contractual);
- in house skill to support control;
- proximity of control to asset requiring protection;
- user transparency;
- where using assured products, the assurance level.

5.5.9.4 Some Constraints Affecting Control Selection

There are a number of constraints that can affect the selection of controls; some common ones include:

- *budget*: there will often be financial constraints on the amount of security which can be implemented. The Forensic Laboratory may have many conflicting demands on the limited financial resources available. For example, funds may not be available to fully implement a proposed control and the Risk Owner is prepared

b. International Standards are chargeable whilst the NIST 800-xx series are free downloads from www.nist.gov.

c. CobIT is free to members of ISACA, but otherwise chargeable.

to accept a partial implementation and carry the residual risk until such time as additional funds become available;

- culture: sociological constraints on the implementation of requirements may be specific to a jurisdiction, a business sector, or a location. Control measures will be ineffective if they are not accepted by all employees and / or Clients;
- *environment*: environmental factors may influence the selection of controls, such as space availability, climate conditions, and surrounding natural and urban geography;
- *legal*: privacy laws may well affect the choice of controls. Legislation that is not computer or privacy specific may also affect the implementation of controls (e.g., fire regulations, health, and safety legislation, etc.);
- *skills*: there may not be sufficient skill available in the Forensic Laboratory to implement or manage the selected controls;
- *technology*: some measures are technically infeasible due to the incompatibility of hardware and software. Often, the retrospective implementation of controls to an existing information system is often hindered by technical constraints;
- *time*: there may be problems with fully implementing the required controls within the lifetime remaining for the project or within a time period that is acceptable to the Risk Owner. Some controls may need to wait for budgetary relaxation, and others for a suitable opportunity to arise in a wider improvement plan, for example, a building upgrade which permits more secure runs to be implemented at a lower cost than if that were the only task to be completed;
- *others*: there may be reasons for nonimplementation other than those listed above.

5.5.9.5 Outputs

This step should produce the following deliverables:

- the information security plan based on the outputs of the risk review.

While no two plans are ever the same, the template used by the Forensic Laboratory is given in Appendix 2.

5.5.10 Step 6: Prepare Statement of Applicability

The SoA documents the control objectives and controls for each risk where treatment is considered necessary as well as the mandatory controls defined in Sections 4–8 of the standard.

The decision to select (or reject) particular controls within ISO 27001 must be recorded and explained. In some cases, this explanation can be very brief, but in other cases, where the choice is complex or has a significant impact on risks more detail will be necessary.

The risk treatment process may also indicate that controls not found in ISO 27001 are included. These must also be documented in the SoA.

The SoA should be signed off Top Management at the management review. The Forensic Laboratory's Management Review agenda is given in Chapter 4, Appendix 36.

An SoA template is given in Appendix 21.

5.5.11 Step 7: Management Approval

The final step in the planning phase is to obtain management approval for the residual risks and for a program to develop, operate the ISMS, and implement a risk treatment plan. Budgetary cycles may require that an initial risk treatment plan is developed and costed at this step.

Approval is granted at the Management Review to operate the ISMS and accept residual risks, though the Risk Owner can accept residual risks and implement a risk treatment plan at any time through the Risk Management Committee.

The management review agenda is given in Chapter 4, Appendix 36.

5.5.12 Records and Documentation

Documenting each step of the information risk management process and maintaining records (i.e., proof of having performed a task) is imperative for the following reasons:

- it demonstrates that the process has been carried out correctly;
- it facilitates continuing monitoring and review;
- it facilitates sharing information and communication;
- it provides an accountability mechanism;
- it provides an audit trail;
- it provides evidence of decisions and processes made.

The level of documentation required will depend on the Forensic Laboratory's requirements. The Forensic Laboratory document and record control procedures are given in Chapter 4, Sections 4.6.3 and 4.6.4.

5.6 FRAMEWORK STAGE 4: IMPLEMENTATION AND OPERATIONAL PROCEDURES

5.6.1 Implementation of the Risk Treatment Plan

The risk treatment plan is produced from the deliverables created during the planning phases of the risk management process defined earlier. The correct implementation of security controls relies on a well-structured and documented risk treatment plan. When the risk treatment plan is completed, the Risk Owner's approval should be obtained for the implementation of the security controls for their risks and/or assets. Top Management approval may also be required for all risks as their implementation will have resource and financial implications.

The main elements of the risk treatment plan are:

- information security training;
- performance measures;
- proposed actions, priorities, or time plans;
- reporting and monitoring requirements;
- resource requirements;
- roles and responsibilities of all parties involved in the proposed actions.

Day-to-day management of IMS and ISMS operations and resources will also be required.

5.6.2 Implementation of Controls

While the Risk Owner will be accountable and responsible for the protection of his/her assets at risk, it may not be them that are responsible for the actual implementation of the agreed security controls. Usually, the Custodian is responsible for the implementation of the risk treatment plan. They must ensure that the priorities and the schedule(s) outlined in the risk treatment plan are followed and the plan is fully implemented.

Much of the risk treatment plan and supporting documentation, specifically risk information, can be very sensitive and must be protected against unauthorized disclosure.

5.6.3 Training

In addition to the Forensic Laboratory information security awareness and training program, which should apply to all employees and third parties with access to Forensic Laboratory information and information-processing facilities, specialist training is required for those with specific risk management responsibilities. These may include those who:

- are Risk Owners or Custodians;
- perform risk management;
- undertake audits and security reviews;
- will develop and implement risk treatment.

5.7 FRAMEWORK STAGE 5: FOLLOW-UP PROCEDURES

5.7.1 Follow-Up

Implemented controls can only work effectively if they are used correctly, properly managed, and monitored, and any changes or breaches are detected and dealt with appropriately and in a timely manner.

Over time, there is the real possibility that performance of the information security plan and risk treatment plan will deteriorate if there is no follow-up or monitoring.

The management of information security is an ongoing process that continues after the implementation of the information security plan. All aspects of it should be audited on a regular basis and at least annually.

Follow-up includes:

- compliance checking;
- configuration management;
- incident management;
- maintenance;
- monitoring.

5.7.1.1 Compliance Checking

Compliance checking is the process of review and analysis of the implemented controls to check whether the implemented controls, and their output, meet the security requirements documented in the information security plan and risk treatment plan. Compliance checks are sometimes called internal or external audits, technical testing, management reviews, or ongoing checking, and they are used to check the conformance of:

- existing information-processing systems if changes to the implemented controls have been made, to see which adjustments are necessary to maintain the required security level;
- existing information-processing systems if there are influencing changes that may affect the risk profile;
- existing information-processing systems on a regular basis to ensure they are still meeting their documented objectives;
- new information-processing systems as part of their implementation and after they have been implemented as part of their PIR.

The controls protecting the information-processing systems may be checked by:

- conducting a planned series of internal or external audits or reviews (Chapter 4, Section 4.7.3 for internal audits and Chapter 12, Section 12.3.1.5 for external audits);
- conducting periodic planned inspections and tests (Chapter 12, Section 12.3.13.2.2.2 and Chapter 13, Section 13.6.2 for BCP tests);
- conducting periodic planned management reviews (Chapter 4, Section 4.9);
- conducting periodic unplanned inspections and tests;
- conducting spot checks;
- monitoring operational performance against actual incidents occurring;
- reviewing the continuous improvement process (Chapter 4, Section 4.8);

- technical testing on an ongoing basis (Chapter 12, Section 12.3.13.2.2.3).

Compliance checking should be based on the agreed controls from the risk analysis results for the scope or context as well as security-operating procedures which the Top Management has approved. The objectives are to ascertain whether controls are implemented and used correctly and are fit for purpose.

5.7.1.2 Configuration Management

Information systems and the environment in which they operate are constantly changing. Changes can result in new risks, threats, and vulnerabilities.

Changes to information systems may include:

- new locations where the Forensic Laboratory operates (buildings or countries);
- new or updated connections or interconnectivity;
- new or updated equipment;
- new or updated features;
- new or updated procedures;
- new or updated software (application or operating system);
- new users which may include groups outside the Forensic Laboratory.

When a change to an information-processing system occurs or is planned, it should be managed within the configuration management process as defined in Chapter 7, Section 7.4.5. It is important to determine what impact the change will have on the security of the existing information-processing systems. For major changes that involve the purchase of new hardware, software, or services, an updated risk assessment may be required to determine additional controls needed to treat the risks identified. Minor changes may not require any additional risk assessments. Whether a risk assessment is required or not is a management decision made by the Risk Owner.

5.7.1.3 Information Security Incident Handling

No information security system works perfectly all the time and information security incidents do occur. ISO 27001 and 27002 have a clause dedicated to information security incidents (Clause 13). This refers to a complete ISO standard on incident handling, which is based on ISO/IEC TR 18044, Information technology—Security techniques—information security incident management.

It is essential for the Forensic Laboratory that employees and third parties with access to their information-processing systems, to know what to report and where to report it in the case of an information security incident. The Forensic Laboratory should have the capability to analyze the incidents reported, take appropriate action if needed, and collect forensic evidence if required.

The purpose of the information security incident analysis is to:

- assist in the prevention of incidents;
- improve risk analysis and management reviews;
- learn from their experiences;
- raise the level of awareness of information security-related issues;
- understand the main areas of risk that the Forensic Laboratory faces.

Security incident management is fully covered in Chapter 7, Section 7.4.1.

5.7.1.4 Maintenance

Most equipment and controls will require maintenance and administrative support to ensure that they continue to function correctly and meet evolving business needs. The cost of maintenance and administration of the controls should have been considered when selecting the relevant equipment and controls. This is because costs can vary greatly from one control to another.

Maintenance activities include:

- addressing identified vulnerabilities;
- checking of log files;
- installing new versions of software;
- modifying configuration and parameters to reflect changes and additions;
- replacing obsolete or ineffective hardware and controls;
- undertaking regular preventive maintenance.

Modifications may require changes to documentation, which must be under formal document change control and configuration management.

Maintenance of IT equipment is fully covered in Chapter 7, Section 7.5.1.

5.7.1.5 Monitoring

It is essential, once controls are implemented, to monitor and measure the effectiveness of the controls implemented. While traditional auditing and management reviews check that the controls are in place and operate according to the documented requirements, it is difficult to determine the effectiveness of the controls. This requires the implementation of Information Security Metrics.

Like business objectives, they should be SMART, as defined in Chapter 3, Section 3.1.17.

Information Security Metrics are an effective and valuable tool for security managers to discern the effectiveness of various components of their security programs. Metrics can also help identify levels of risk in not taking a given action and so provide guidance in prioritization of preventive or corrective actions. If the results of security metrics are published within the Forensic Laboratory, this can be used in awareness training. Given the feedback from metrics, security managers can now start to justify return on investment and answer Top Management's questions, such as:

- is the Forensic Laboratory getting value for money?
- is the Forensic Laboratory more secure today than it was before?
- is the Forensic Laboratory secure enough?
- how does the Forensic Laboratory compare to others in the same industry sector?
- where are the Forensic Laboratory's major problems so can be addressed.

There are few standards for security metrics; however, the following exist:

- ISO 27004—Information technology—Security techniques—Information Security Management—Measurement;
- SP 800-55—Performance Measurement Guide for Information Security.

To implement a security metrics plan, the top level steps are:

- create an corrective or preventive action plan and implement it;
- decide which security metrics are important and so the ones to generate;
- define the security metrics program goal(s) and objectives;
- determine the security metrics reporting process, media, and audience;
- develop strategies for generating the security metrics;
- establish a continuous improvement process;
- establish benchmarks and targets.

The Forensic Laboratory has developed its own security metrics reporting process, based on ISO 27001, and this is given in Appendix 22.

Other areas of this book include monitoring, including:

- Chapter 4, Section 4.7.1;
- Chapter 5, Section 5.7.1.5;
- Chapter 6, Section 6.13;
- Chapter 7, Section 7.4.6.3;
- Chapter 7, Section 7.4.7.3;
- Chapter 7, Section 7.7.1.8;
- Chapter 9, Section 9.5.5;
- Chapter 9, Section 9.5.8;
- Chapter 12, Section 12.6.7;
- Chapter 14, Section 14.2.1.2;
- Chapter 14, Section 14.8.2.2;
- Chapter 16, Section 16.2;
- Chapter 17, Section 17.4.1;
- Chapter 18, Section 18.2.3.

APPENDIX 1 - SAMPLE COMMUNICATION PLAN

No two communications plans are the same, but a Forensic Laboratory template for one is given below:

- capture all current thoughts from stakeholders about communications for this initiative, e.g. ideas, concerns, options, barriers;
- determine the best possible outcomes for this initiative;
- how might these targets be met?
- what are the most acceptable outcomes?
- what is the timetable?
- what monitoring and evaluation system is going to be used for the communications?
- what sorts of messages are to be conveyed?
- who are the internal "targets" of the information security message and what particular issues are there that might motivate or worry them?
- who are the key external "targets" for each of these objectives?

APPENDIX 2 - SAMPLE INFORMATION SECURITY PLAN

There is no single template for an information security plan, but the Forensic Laboratory template below gives a high-level approach:

DESCRIBE THE ASSET

For each asset within the scope or context:

- name and details of all Resource Owners;
- description and purpose of the information asset;
- describe the information flow for the information asset from input to output;
- who are the users of the information asset?
- what hardware, software, and communication equipment is needed for the asset?
- what interrelationships are there between this information asset and other information assets?

INFORMATION SECURITY REQUIREMENTS

The information security requirements will be defined in terms of the aspects of information. For each of the clauses, it should categorize the requirement. The level of requirements should be defined by the Forensic Laboratory, but typically they are:

- very high;
- high;
- medium or moderate;
- low;
- very low.

In addition to the risk level, any security drivers such as legislative, regulatory, contractual or other relevant requirements that may affect the assets should be defined.

RISK ASSESSMENT METHODOLOGY

The risk assessment methodology shall be defined. This is a requirement of ISO 27001 (S4.2.1.c).

REVIEW OF SECURITY CONTROLS

Have any independent security reviews or tests recently been conducted on the information asset and if so, list them with their results.

THREATS AND VULNERABILITIES

Summarize the threats and vulnerabilities identified and the consequences and impacts arising from these.

VALUE OF ASSETS

The value of the assets within the scope should be identified. This may be the whole asset or its components. Briefly summarize the value of the asset or the component of the asset, if applicable, and the basis for the valuation.

LEVEL OF PROTECTION REQUIRED

The level of protection required for the asset should be defined.

ACCEPTABLE LEVEL OF RISK

The criteria for the acceptance of the residual risk should be defined. This will include a high-level matrix of the controls mapped to the threats identified.

The controls implemented or planned for the information asset will be defined for the scope or context.

ORGANIZATIONAL AND MANAGEMENT CONTROLS

ISO 27001 and ISO 27002 provided guidance in this area; it has eleven clauses:

- Security policy;
- Organization of Information Security;
- Asset management;
- Human resources security;
- Physical and environmental security;
- Communications and operations management;
- Access control;
- Information systems acquisition, development and maintenance;
- Information security incident management;
- Business continuity management;
- Compliance.

These are a good basis the implementation of management controls.

APPENDIX 3 - ASSET TYPE EXAMPLES

For example, asset types (in no particular order) can be any of the following:

- application and operating system software;
- buildings and structures;
- communications equipment;
- electronic information and data;
- firmware;
- hard copy documents;
- hardware;
- image and reputation;
- information;
- knowledge (usually either in people or documented);
- office equipment;
- paper documents;
- people, whether employees or external contractors;
- physical equipment;
- services supplied by third parties;
- employee's morale.

APPENDIX 4 - ASSET VALUES

Note
The values used by the Forensic Laboratory are given below:

Value	Description	Interpretation
5	Very high	Value to the Forensic Laboratory of over £1,000,000
4	High	Value to the Forensic Laboratory of between £500,000 and £1,000,000
3	Medium	Value to the Forensic Laboratory of between £250,000 and £500,000
2	Low	Value to the Forensic Laboratory of between £50,000 and £250,000
1	Very low	Value to the Forensic Laboratory of less than £50,000

In this case, the asset value for information is the highest value that it could be—values could be calculated by a number of ways, such as:

- cost to create;
- cost to recreate (if possible);
- value to a competitor;
- cost of loss sales due to information being unavailable.

APPENDIX 5 - CONSEQUENCES TABLE

		Confidentiality		Integrity		Availability	
Value	Type of effect; severity	Disclosure of information	Personal Privacy Infringement	Corruption of data	Published outside the organization	Disruption to Activities (£)	Non Availability of systems
1	Very low	Unauthorized disclosure of one or two records	Unauthorized disclosure of one or two sets of personal details	Very small corruption, easily recoverable	No	Up to 50 k	Less than half a day
2	Low	Unauthorized disclosure of a few records	Unauthorized disclosure of a few sets of personal details	Small corruption, easily recoverable	No	50 k-250 k	Less than a day
3	Medium	Unauthorized disclosure of many records	Unauthorized disclosure of many sets of personal details	Medium-sized corruption, can be recovered, large effort	Yes	250 k-500 k	Between a day and 2 days
4	High	Unauthorized disclosure of a large number of records	Large number of personal details revealed and/or compromised	Major corruption, may be recovered, very considerable effort	Yes	500 k-1 m	Between 2 days and a week
5	Very high	Unauthorized disclosure of a very large number of records	All personal details revealed and/or compromised	Major corruption, may be recovered, major effort	Yes	Above 1 m	More than a week

APPENDIX 6 - SOME COMMON BUSINESS RISKS

- a delay in one task causes cascading delays in dependent tasks;
- accidental disclosure of data;
- acquisition of required employees takes longer than expected;
- actions taken by all in a timely manner;
- additional requirements are added;
- backup failures (i.e., failure to recover from backup tapes);
- budget cuts;
- budgeting failures due to unclear priorities;
- cannot build a product of the size specified in the time allocated;
- capacity of information-processing systems;
- cash flow inwards;
- Client finds products and services to be unsatisfactory;
- Client introduces new requirements after agreed upon requirements' specification is complete;
- client review/decision cycles are slower than expected;
- communication failure between departments;
- components developed separately cannot be integrated easily;
- conflicts between team members;
- conflicts between team objectives;
- contractor delivers components of unacceptably low quality, and time must be added to improve quality;
- contractor does not deliver components when promised;
- contractor does not provide the level of domain expertise needed;
- contractor does not provide the level of technical expertise needed;
- corrupted data (held);
- corrupted data (received);
- critical dependency on third parties;
- critical dependency on a technology that is new or still under development;
- critical dependency on key suppliers;
- critical employee loss;
- data conversion activities are underestimated or are ignored;
- database failure;
- design fails to address major issues;
- design requires unnecessary and unproductive implementation overhead;

- developers unfamiliar with development tools;
- development environment structure, policies, and procedures are not clearly defined;
- development in an unfamiliar or unproved hardware environment;
- development in an unfamiliar or unproved software environment;
- development of extra software functions that are not required extends the schedule;
- development of flawed software functions requires redesign and implementation;
- development of flawed user interface results in redesign and implementation;
- disaster recovery failure to recover in time;
- effort is greater than estimated (per line of code, function point, module, case, etc.);
- employee's assignments do not match their strengths;
- employees need extra time to learn unfamiliar hardware environment;
- employees need extra time to learn unfamiliar tools or operating systems;
- employees with critical skills needed for the project cannot be found;
- excessive schedule pressure;
- facilities are available but inadequate (e.g., no phones, network wiring, furniture, office supplies, etc.);
- facilities are crowded, noisy, or disruptive;
- facilities are not available on time;
- failure of disaster recovery site to mirror the production site;
- failure of utilities supplying the Forensic Laboratory office;
- failure to comply with legislative and regulatory requirements;
- failure to consistently use documented processes;
- failure to detect and respond to security incidents in a timely manner;
- failure to enhance contracts as contract life progresses;
- failure to follow processes/procedures;
- failure to have and communicate long-term plans (strategic planning);
- failure to have and use a capacity plan;
- failure to manage contracts properly;
- failure to meet customer needs;
- failure to meet disaster recovery SLA;
- failure to meet financial objectives;
- failure to monitor contract performance;
- failure to monitor, measure, and manage systems for SLA reporting automatically;
- failure to process cases in a timely manner;
- failure to provide clear operational budgets;
- failure to respond to business changes in operational delivery;
- failure to test business continuity plans, as appropriate;
- failure to test changes properly;
- failures leading to reputation loss;
- flawed design;
- fraudulent manipulation of data (external sources);
- fraudulent manipulation of data (internal employees);
- having the wrong contract in place;
- human error;
- impact of planned outages;
- impact of unplanned outages;
- improper infrastructure, design, and implementation of solutions;
- improper management of SLAs (suppliers);
- inability of the information-processing systems to scale to customer needs;
- inaccurate progress tracking;
- inaccurate status reporting;
- inappropriate change and configuration management;
- inappropriate incident and problem management;
- inappropriate privileges on information-processing systems according to job function;
- inappropriate TRTs;
- incomplete data (held);
- incomplete data (received);
- inconsistent data (held);
- inconsistent data (received);
- inconsistent management direction;
- inefficient team structure reduces productivity;
- information-processing system/infrastructure failure;
- infrastructure is not resilient;
- key employees are available only part time;
- key software or hardware components become unavailable, unsupported, or are unexpectedly scheduled for withdrawal of support;
- lack of appropriate business continuity planning;
- lack of continuous innovation;
- lack of information classification and so protection;
- lack of needed specialization (includes technical and domain knowledge) increases defects and rework;
- lack of office space and facilities;
- lack of spares on site;
- lack of specific technical expertise;
- lack of tools for managing and monitoring operational systems;
- lack of tools to manage and monitor information-processing systems and business processes;
- layoffs and cutbacks reduce the Forensic Team's capacity;
- long decision-making process;
- loss of customers;
- management review/decision cycle is slower than expected;
- marketing objectives not clear;
- meeting product's size or speed constraints requires more time than expected, including time for redesign and reimplementation;

- multiple stakeholders outside the normal department chain of command;
- necessary functionality cannot be implemented using the selected methods and tools;
- new development personnel are added late in the project, and additional training and communications overhead reduces existing team members' effectiveness;
- non-technical third-party tasks take longer than expected (control agency approvals, procurement, equipment purchase, legal reviews, etc.);
- payment failures to suppliers;
- poor external vendor support;
- poor planning;
- poor quality administrative support;
- poor quality assurance;
- poor quality software delivered;
- premises and facilities failures (space, parking, etc.);
- pressure of work on the Forensic Team;
- pricing wrong;
- problem team members are not removed from the forensic team;
- procurement failures;
- re-estimation in response to schedule slips does not occur, is overly optimistic or ignores project history;
- requirement to operate under multiple operating systems takes longer to satisfy than expected;
- requirements are poorly defined, and further definition expands the scope of the case or assignment;
- requirements have been base lined but continue to change;
- schedule is optimistic, "best case," rather than realistic, "expected case";
- schedule savings from productivity enhancing tools are overestimated;
- SLA failure;
- supplier failure;
- system availability;
- task pre-requisites (e.g., training, completion of other cases, or tasks) cannot be completed on time;
- too little formality (lack of adherence to policies and procedures);
- too much formality (bureaucratic adherence to policies and procedures);
- tools are not in place by the desired time;
- tools do not provide the planned productivity;
- tools do not work as expected developers need time to create workarounds or to switch to new tools;
- unacceptable performance;
- unplanned turnover of key employees;
- upstream quality assurance activities are limited or cut short;
- use of unfamiliar methodology;
- weak risk management fails to detect major risks;
- wrong technology in place.

APPENDIX 7 - SOME COMMON PROJECT RISKS

Forensic cases can be regarded as projects and may suffer from some of the project risks below:

- a contingency plan has not been identified for the appropriate risks;
- adequate competent employees have not been identified and allocated to the project or case;
- all external interfaces are not under the Forensic Laboratory's control;
- all key players have not lived up to their accountabilities and responsibilities and this has not been addressed;
- all known management and technical risks have not been assessed and there are few mitigation strategies in place for all identified risks;
- all the contingency plans have not been documented and do not include anticipated cost and effort;
- an adequate business case analysis has not been performed;
- budget may not cover project or case;
- business case is not based on the full cost of the project or case;
- changes in scope are not being managed;
- clearly defined, documented, and understood responsibilities, accountabilities, and authorities do not exist for each of the major players in this project or case;
- costs are not allocated in accordance with work breakdown structures;
- each risk has not been assigned a loss (impact) if risk occurs;
- each risk has not been assigned a probability of occurrence;
- failure to get interviews scheduled;
- failure to review drafts and return without prejudicing timetable;
- for any risk exceeding defined trigger values, the appropriate level of management has not approved the implementation of the contingency plan;
- for each risk rated high, no specific risk mitigation has been documented;
- for each risk to be mitigated, an effort and/or cost has not been estimated for the mitigation action plan;
- hidden agenda;
- in the event of serious problems, decisive actions are often not taken;
- inadequate employees allocated to the scheduled tasks at the scheduled time;
- independent review of this project or project plan been not conducted;
- lack of documentary proof available;
- lack of employee training;
- lack of power and authority of Project Manager or Lead Forensic Analyst;

- management not fully and demonstrably committed;
- mandated to interview wrong people;
- necessary information not always available to support decisive action;
- no clear escalation path documented;
- no formal mechanisms and tools in place to monitor the project or case schedule and costs;
- Project Manager and Sponsor cannot list the current top project or case risks;
- project or case specifications are not precisely defined;
- project or case specifications have changed significantly; these changes have not been well documented and approved by the appropriate stakeholders;
- relevant risks have not been rated;
- resource conflicts;
- status / progress meetings do not occur regularly;
- the Client commitment level is passive and hard to engage;
- the Client demonstrates a poor understanding of the requirements;
- the project or case is not on time or budget;
- the project or case justification is not based on a Return on Investment with an attractive projected return;
- the risks have not been ranked in order of exposure and agreed to by the Forensic Team;
- the technology being used is not validated and employees do not have sufficient experience or knowledge in using it;
- there is dependence on facilities not under control of the employees on this project or case;
- there was no formal process used to break down the work and estimate task duration.

APPENDIX 8 - SECURITY THREAT EXAMPLES

Some of the most common security threats are:

- abduction;
- accidental disclosure of sensitive material via waste;
- acts of omission;
- acts of war;
- adverse media coverage;
- air conditioning failure;
- alcohol abuse;
- angry or hostile clients;
- animals;
- armed hold-up;
- assault—mental;
- assault—verbal;
- blackmail;
- bomb threats;
- break and enter to the office;
- bribery;
- building structural collapse;
- chemical / biological hazards;
- civil unrest;
- commercial espionage;
- communication problems;
- communication system exploitation;
- communications interception;
- communications services failure (phones or computers);
- communications system or cabling damage;
- competitors;
- compromise;
- computer malfunction;
- contamination;
- corrupt employees;
- criminal acts by employees;
- criminal acts by partners or suppliers;
- currency fluctuations;
- cyclone;
- deliberate disclosure of data by employees;
- demonstrations;
- denial of services;
- design error;
- deterioration of storage media;
- disaffected groups;
- disgruntled Clients;
- disgruntled employees;
- drought;
- drug abuse;
- dust or similar;
- earthquake;
- eavesdropping (electronic or physical);
- embezzlement;
- employee death from industrial accident or disease;
- employee pilfering / theft;
- employee sabotage;
- employee shortage;
- environmental contamination;
- errors and omissions;
- espionage;
- extortion;
- extreme of temperature / humidity;
- fire;
- flood;
- foreign intelligence services activity;
- fraud—external;
- fraud—internal
- hacking of computer system;
- hardware failure;
- health and safety issues to employees or Clients;
- hostage situations;
- hurricane;
- illegal import / export of software;
- illegal use of software;
- incompetent employees;

- incompetent management;
- industrial accidents;
- industrial action;
- industrial espionage;
- injury to employees or Clients through accidents;
- internal security problems;
- issue-motivated groups;
- kidnapping;
- lightning;
- litigation by Clients or suppliers;
- loss of data and records;
- loss of key employees;
- loss of physical and infrastructure support;
- maintenance error;
- major price undercutting by competitors;
- malicious code;
- malicious hacking, for example, through masquerading;
- malicious rumor mongering by competitors;
- maverick acts;
- misrouting or rerouting of messages;
- misuse of resources;
- money laundering;
- network failure;
- nonpaying Clients;
- operations error (of any type);
- organized crime—any sort;
- phreaking (breaking into phone/comms systems);
- political upheaval;
- politically motivated violence;
- pollution;
- power loss/failure/cutoff;
- religious objections;
- repudiation (service/transaction/receipt/delivery);
- sabotage;
- siege;
- sit-ins;
- smuggling;
- software failure;
- spamming (multi/large messages to e-mail);
- sting operations;
- structural faults;
- subornment;
- substandard quality control;
- subversion;
- terrorist act;
- theft.

APPENDIX 9 - COMMON SECURITY VULNERABILITIES

There are a number of vulnerabilities that can be exploited by threats. These are some of the vulnerabilities that have been identified—there are many others. Each vulnerability at should be considered in relation to the threat that may exploit it.

A number of headings are given and some vulnerabilities are given for each.

Some common security vulnerabilities are:

COMMUNICATIONS

- ease of access to communications cabinets and equipment;
- inadequate network management;
- lack of identification and authentication of sender and receiver;
- lack of proof of sending or receiving a message;
- poor cable jointing;
- transfer of passwords in clear;
- unprotected communication lines;
- unprotected public network connections;
- unprotected sensitive traffic.

DOCUMENTS

- inappropriate disposal;
- inappropriate storage;
- uncontrolled copying.

ENVIRONMENT AND INFRASTRUCTURE

- building in location which is a terrorist target;
- inappropriate access control to buildings, rooms;
- lack of evacuation procedures;
- lack of physical protection of the building, doors, and windows;
- location in an area susceptible to flood;
- poor building design—unable to absorb shock;
- uncertainty of utility supply.

GENERALLY APPLYING VULNERABILITIES

- inadequate service maintenance response;
- inappropriate or no business continuity plan;
- single points of failure.

HARDWARE

- ineffective configuration or change control;
- insufficient maintenance/faulty installation;
- lack of maintenance or upgrades;
- lack of replacement or upgrade of storage media;
- susceptibility to environment;
- susceptibility to temperature variations;
- susceptibility to voltage variations.

HUMAN RESOURCES

- absence or shortage of competent employees;
- inadequate recruitment procedures;
- incorrect use of software and hardware;
- insufficient security training;
- lack of monitoring mechanisms;
- lack of security awareness;
- susceptibility of employees to environmental contamination;
- unsupervised work by employees.

SOFTWARE AND SYSTEM MANAGEMENT

- complicated user interface;
- failure to have appropriate system and data backups;
- failure to log off when leaving the workstation;
- inadequate audit trail;
- inadequate work instruction;
- inappropriate identification and authentication mechanisms;
- ineffective configuration or change control;
- insufficient software testing;
- poor or incomplete documentation;
- poor password management;
- uncontrolled downloading and using unauthorized software;
- unprotected password tables;
- well-known flaws in the software;
- wrong allocation of access rights.

This is not an exhaustive list.

APPENDIX 10 - RISK MANAGEMENT POLICY

Risk management is about managing threats and opportunities to the Forensic Laboratory.

By managing risk effectively, the Forensic Laboratory is in a stronger position to meet its business objectives. By managing opportunities well, the Forensic Laboratory is in a better position to provide improved products and services and offer better value for money.

In this policy and its supporting management framework, risk is defined as something happening that may have an impact on the achievement of the Forensic Laboratory's objectives. When management of the risks that the Forensic Laboratory faces goes well, it often remains unnoticed. When it fails, however, the consequences can be significant and high profile. Effective risk management is needed to prevent such failures and capitalize on successes.

This policy is supported by a complete risk management framework, and this supports the Forensic Laboratory business plan. There are a number of specific requirements for different legislation, regulations, management systems, and business processes. These specific requirements will be addressed in the correct part of the Forensic Laboratory's Integrated Management System, but the central core of risk management in the Forensic Laboratory is this risk management policy and its supporting management framework.

This risk management framework describes the processes that the Forensic Laboratory has put in place and link together to identify, assess, treat, review, and report on the identified risks and their status. This policy and its supporting risk management framework shall be used for the management of risk across the whole of the Forensic Laboratory.

Overall, the goals of the Forensic Laboratory risk management policy and its supporting framework are to have procedures in place to:

- clearly identify risk exposures;
- ensure conscious and properly evaluated risk decisions;
- fully document major threats and opportunities;
- identify a risk management and treatment process that fits into the Forensic Laboratory culture;
- implement cost-effective actions to reduce risks;
- integrate risk management into the Forensic Laboratory's culture;
- manage risk in accordance with good practice.

This policy is issued and maintained by the Information Security Manager, who also provides advice and guidance on its implementation and ensure compliance.

All Forensic Laboratory employees shall comply with this policy.

APPENDIX 11 - THE IMS AND ISMS SCOPE DOCUMENT

The Forensic Laboratory's IMS and ISMS Scope Statement is given below:

GENERAL

The IMS covers the following standards:

- ISO 15489—Information and documentation—Records management
- ISO 17020—Conformity assessment—Requirements for the operation of various types of bodies performing inspection
- ISO 17025—General requirements for the competence of testing and calibration laboratories
- ISO 22301—Societal security—Business continuity management systems;
- ISO 27001—Information technology—Security techniques—ISMS—Requirements
- ISO 9001 Quality management systems—Requirements

- OHSAS 18001 Occupational Health and Safety Management Systems

It also includes:

- In-house digital forensic procedures;
- In-house management procedures as required.

The IMS is based on PAS 99—Specification of common management system requirements as a framework for integration.

The IMS is common for all of the standards and the specific requirements for each standard are given below:

ISO 27001 is the only standard that defines the components of a scope statement and this is the one used as the basis for the IMS. It requires this to be defined in terms of:

- organization;
- location;
- assets;
- technology;
- exclusions (ISO 9001);
- scope statement.

OVERVIEW OF THE FORENSIC LABORATORY

The overview of the Forensic Laboratory and its products and services is given here.

ORGANIZATION

The organization of the Forensic Laboratory is given here, with an organogram to show how the component parts all fit together. It also may have a link to the relevant job descriptions in the IMS.

All Forensic Laboratory employees have a duty to:

- safeguard Forensic Laboratory information, information-processing systems, and other assets in their care;
- comply with the Forensic Laboratory management system policies and supporting procedures;
- comply with the Forensic Laboratory business process procedures;
- report any suspected or actual incidents as soon as possible to the their line management.

LOCATION

The location of the Forensic Laboratory is given here. If there is more than one, those within the scope of certification and accreditation are given here.

ASSETS

The assets that come under the scrutiny of the IMS for the Forensic Laboratory are as follows.

- *information*: Details of all databases are held in the Asset Register. All case-processing files are held in the Client virtual files in the ERMS on the corporate business or forensic network;
- *software*: Details of all software are held in the Asset Register;
- *hardware*: Details of all hardware are held in the Asset Register;
- *people*: All Forensic Laboratory employees;
- *services*: All services to the Forensic Laboratory office(s) and includes, but is not limited to, gas, water, electricity, telephone, internet, local and national government services and suppliers;
- *image and reputation*: the Forensic Laboratory's image and reputation is a huge asset. Any mishandling of information that compromises this asset will have a major effect on company business.

TECHNOLOGY

Hardware

Computers

Define business and forensic hardware in place.

Network Equipment

Define network equipment in place.

Servers

Define servers in place.

Printers

Define printers in place.

Other Peripherals

Define other peripherals in place.

Operating Systems

Desktop

Define operating systems in place on workstations and mobile devices.

Server

Define operating systems in place on servers.

Network Operating System

Define network operating systems in place.

Desktop Applications

Define desktop applications (i.e., Non Forensic tools) in place.

Diagrams

The Forensic Laboratory uses physical layout diagrams and network diagrams to support the scope statement.

EXCLUSIONS (ISO 9001)

The following exclusions apply in the Forensic Laboratory for ISO 9001 certification as they are inappropriate for the reasons below:

ISO 9001 clause	Reason for Exclusion
7.4—Purchasing	General purchasing such as hardware, software, stationery, etc. are not included in the system as this is not an element of the core business provided by the Forensic Laboratory. The contracting of services from associates is covered in this system
7.6—Control of monitoring and measuring devices	No monitoring or measuring devices are used in the Forensic Laboratory

SCOPE STATEMENT

The agreed scope statement for the management system standards that are included in this IMS is:

The provision of forensic case processing and forensic consultancy services.

APPENDIX 12 - CRITICALITY RATINGS

The criticality rating of an asset or function is determined from an analysis of the *consequences* of its loss, compromise, or destruction.

- *Vital*: Loss or compromise will result in the possible abandonment or long-term cessation of the Forensic Laboratory's business capability and/or functions;
- *Major*: Loss or compromise will necessitate a major change in the Forensic Laboratory's practices and activities and will have a major impact on the Forensic Laboratory's operation and/or reputation;
- *Significant*: Loss or compromise will have a significant affect on the Forensic Laboratory's practices, activities, and financial position;
- *Low*: Loss or compromise will be covered by usual business practices;
- *Unknown*: Insufficient data are available for evaluation.

APPENDIX 13 - LIKELIHOOD OF OCCURRENCE

Below is a 5-level likelihood table, alternates, such as a 3-level or 10-level table can be used.

FIVE-LEVEL LIKELIHOOD TABLE

Value	Description	Interpretation
1	Very Low	Infrequently (Yearly or less frequently)
2	Low	Occasionally (Two or three times a year)
3	Medium	Sometimes (Monthly)
4	High	Frequently (Weekly)
5	Very High	Frequently (Daily)

TEN-LEVEL LIKELIHOOD TABLE

Value	Description	Interpretation
1	Negligible	Once every 1000 years or less
2	Extremely unlikely	Once every 200 years
3	Very unlikely	Once every 50 years
4	Unlikely	Once every 20 years
5	Feasible	Once every 5 years
6	Probable	Annually
7	Very probable	Quarterly
8	Expected	Monthly
9	Confidently expected	Weekly
10	Certain	Daily

Very approximately each one is four times more likely than the previous one, which covers the range "once in 1000 years" to "daily" in a range of 1-10.

APPENDIX 14 - RISK APPETITE

The Forensic Laboratory has established levels of risk that it is prepared to accept and those that must be treated. Using its five levels of likelihood for its five levels of severity of impact if the risk crystallizes gives a 5 × 5 matrix as shown below:

		Likelihood				
		1 (Very Low)	2 (Low)	3 (Medium)	4 (High)	5 (Very High)
Severity of Impact	1 (Very Low)	1	2	4	7	11
	2 (Low)	3	5	8	12	16
	3 (Medium)	6	9	13	17	20
	4 (High)	10	14	18	21	23
	5 (Very High)	15	19	22	24	25

This gives a risk level of between 1 and 25.

Note

The values are representative of the levels and no more.

The risk level is banded as:

Exposure level	Risk Level
1 – 5	Very Low
6 – 10	Low
11 – 15	Medium
16 – 20	High
20 – 25	Very High

Where the risk levels are defined as:

- *very low risk* is a condition where risk is identified as having minimal effects on the identified Forensic Laboratory assets; the probability of occurrence is sufficiently low to cause only minimal concern. These risks must be reviewed on an annual basis;
- *low risk* is a condition where risk is identified as having minor effects on identified the Forensic Laboratory assets; the probability of occurrence is sufficiently low to cause only minor concern. These risks must be reviewed on a six monthly basis;
- *medium risk* is a condition where risk is identified as one that could possibly affect the identified Forensic Laboratory assets. The probability of occurrence is high enough to require close control of all contributing factors. These risks must be reviewed on a 3 monthly basis;
- *high risk* is the condition where risk is identified as having a high probability of occurrence and the consequence would affect the identified Forensic Laboratory assets. The probability of occurrence is high enough to require close control of all contributing factors, the establishment of risk actions, and an acceptable fallback position. These risks must be reviewed on a monthly basis;
- *very high risk* is the condition where risk is identified as having a very high probability of occurrence and the consequence would affect the identified Forensic Laboratory assets. The probability of occurrence is so high as to require very close control of all contributing factors, the establishment of risk actions, and an acceptable fall-back position. These risks must be reviewed on a two weekly basis, or more frequently is appropriate.

Note 1

The target level is to reduce all risks to the green (very low or low) level.

Note 2

Where this cannot be achieved by application of appropriate risk treatment, the risk must be knowingly accepted by the Risk Owner (who typically is the Resource or Asset Owner).

Note 3

Risks must be reviewed as defined above, unless an incident occurs involving them or there is some other influencing change, in which case they must be reviewed more frequently.

APPENDIX 15 - SECURITY CONTROLS FROM COBIT AND NIST 800-53

Note

A number of the controls below, in fact the majority of them, are mappable to those in ISO 27001, but there are a number of them that are not and these may be considered for risk treatment.

COBIT CONTROLS

Planning and Organization

PO 1	*Define a strategic IT plan*
PO 1.1	IT as part of the organization's long- and short-range plan
PO 1.2	IT long-range plan
PO 1.3	IT long-range planning-approach and structure
PO 1.4	IT long-range plan changes
PO 1.5	Short-range planning for the IT function

Continued

PO 1.6	Communication of IT plans
PO 1.7	Monitoring and evaluating of IT plans
PO 1.8	Assessment of existing systems
PO 2	*Define the information architecture*
PO 2.1	Information architecture model
PO 2.2	Corporate data dictionary and data syntax rules
PO 2.3	Data classification scheme
PO 2.4	Security levels
PO 3	*Determine technological direction*
PO 3.1	Technological infrastructure planning
PO 3.2	Monitor future trends and regulations
PO 3.3	Technological infrastructure contingency
PO 3.4	Hardware and software acquisition plans
PO 3.5	Technology standards
PO 4	*Define the IT organization and relationships*
PO 4.1	IT planning or steering committee
PO 4.2	Organizational placement of the IT function
PO 4.3	Review of organizational achievements
PO 4.4	Roles and responsibilities
PO 4.5	Responsibility for quality assurance
PO 4.6	Responsibility for logical and physical security
PO 4.7	Ownership and Custodianship
PO 4.8	Data and system ownership
PO 4.9	Supervision
PO 4.10	Segregation of duties
PO 4.11	IT staffing
PO 4.12	Job or position descriptions for IT staff
PO 4.13	Key IT personnel
PO 4.14	Contracted staff policies and procedures
PO 4.15	Relationships
PO 5	*Manage the IT investment*
PO 5.1	Annual IT operating budget
PO 5.2	Cost and benefit monitoring
PO 5.3	Cost and benefit justification
PO 6	*Communicate management aims and direction*
PO 6.1	Positive information control environment
PO 6.10	Management's responsibility for policies
PO 6.11	Communication of organization policies
PO 6.2	Policy implementation resources
PO 6.3	Maintenance of policies

Continued

PO 6.4	Compliance with policies, procedures, and standards
PO 6.5	Quality commitment
PO 6.6	Security and internal control framework policy
PO 6.7	Intellectual property rights
PO 6.8	Issue-specific policies
PO 6.9	Communication of IT security awareness
PO 7	*Manage human resources*
PO 7.1	Personnel recruitment and promotion
PO 7.2	Personnel qualifications
PO 7.3	Roles and responsibilities
PO 7.4	Personnel training
PO 7.5	Cross-training or staff backup
PO 7.6	Personnel clearance procedures
PO 7.7	Employee job performance evaluation
PO 7.8	Job change and termination
PO 8	*Ensure compliance with external requirements*
PO 8.1	External requirements review
PO 8.2	Practices and procedures for complying with external requirements
PO 8.3	Safety and ergonomic compliance
PO 8.4	Privacy, intellectual property, and data flow
PO 8.5	Electronic commerce
PO 8.6	Compliance with insurance contracts
PO 9	*Assess risks*
PO 9.1	Business risk assessment
PO 9.2	Risk assessment approach
PO 9.3	Risk identification
PO 9.4	Risk measurement
PO 9.5	Risk action plan
PO 9.6	Risk acceptance
PO 9.7	Safeguard selection
PO 9.8	Risk assessment commitment
PO 10	*Manage projects*
PO 10.1	Project management framework
PO 10.10	User department participation in project initiation
PO 10.11	Project team membership and responsibilities
PO 10.12	Project definition
PO 10.13	Project approval
PO 10.2	Project phase approval
PO 10.3	Project master plan

Continued

PO 10.4	System quality assurance plan
PO 10.5	Planning of assurance methods
PO 10.6	Formal project risk management
PO 10.7	Test plan
PO 10.8	Training plan
PO 10.9	Postimplementation review plan
PO 11	*Manage quality*
PO 11.1	General quality plan
PO 11.2	Quality assurance approach
PO 11.3	Quality assurance planning
PO 11.4	Quality assurance review of adherence to IT standards and procedures
PO 11.5	System development life cycle methodology
PO 11.6	System development life cycle methodology for major changes to existing technology
PO 11.7	Updating of the system development life cycle methodology
PO 11.8	Coordination and communication
PO 11.9	Acquisition and maintenance framework for the technology infrastructure
PO 11.10	Third-party implementer relationships
PO 11.11	Program documentation standards
PO 11.12	Program testing standards
PO 11.13	System testing standards
PO 11.14	Parallel/pilot testing
PO 11.15	System testing documentation
PO 11.16	Quality assurance evaluation of adherence to development standards
PO 11.17	Quality assurance review of the achievement of IT objectives
PO 11.18	Quality metrics
PO 11.19	Reports of quality assurance reviews

Acquisition and Implementation

AI 1	*Identify automated solutions*
AI 1.1	Definition of information requirements
AI 1.2	Formulation of alternative courses of action
AI 1.3	Formulation of acquisition strategy
AI 1.4	Third-party service requirements
AI 1.5	Technological feasibility study
AI 1.6	Economic feasibility study
AI 1.7	Information architecture
AI 1.8	Risk analysis report
AI 1.9	Cost-effective security controls
AI 1.10	Audit trails design
AI 1.11	Ergonomics
AI 1.12	Selection of system software
AI 1.13	Procurement control
AI 1.14	Software product acquisition
AI 1.15	Third-party software maintenance
AI 1.16	Contract application programming
AI 1.17	Acceptance of facilities
AI 1.18	Acceptance of technology
AI 2	*Acquire and maintain application software*
AI 2.1	Design methods
AI 2.2	Major changes to existing systems
AI 2.3	Design approval
AI 2.4	File requirements definition and documentation
AI 2.5	Program specifications
AI 2.6	Source data collection design
AI 2.7	Input requirements definition and documentation
AI 2.8	Definition of interfaces
AI 2.9	User-machine interface
AI 2.10	Processing requirements definition and documentation
AI 2.11	Output requirements definition and documentation
AI 2.12	Controllability
AI 2.13	Availability as a key design factor
AI 2.14	IT integrity provisions in application program software
AI 2.15	Application software testing
AI 2.16	User reference and support materials
AI 2.17	Reassessment of system design
AI 3	*Acquire and maintain technology infrastructure*
AI 3.1	Assessment of new hardware and software
AI 3.2	Preventative maintenance for hardware
AI 3.3	System software security
AI 3.4	System software installation
AI 3.5	System software maintenance
AI 3.6	System software change controls
AI 3.7	Use and monitoring of system utilities
AI 4	*Develop and maintain procedures*
AI 4.1	Operational requirements and service levels

Continued

AI 4.2	User procedures manual
AI 4.3	Operations manual
AI 4.4	Training materials
AI 5	*Install and accredit systems*
AI 5.1	Training
AI 5.2	Application software performance sizing
AI 5.3	Implementation plan
AI 5.4	System conversion
AI 5.5	Data conversion
AI 5.6	Testing strategies and plans
AI 5.7	Testing of changes
AI 5.8	Parallel/pilot testing criteria and performance
AI 5.9	Final acceptance test
AI 5.10	Security testing and accreditation
AI 5.11	Operational test
AI 5.12	Promotion to production
AI 5.13	Evaluation of meeting user requirements
AI 5.14	Management's postimplementation review
AI 6	*Manage changes*
AI 6.1	Change request initiation and control
AI 6.2	Impact assessment
AI 6.3	Control of changes
AI 6.4	Emergency changes
AI 6.5	Documentation and procedures
AI 6.6	Authorized maintenance
AI 6.7	Software release policy
AI 6.8	Distribution of software

Delivery and Support

DS 1	*Define and manage service levels*
DS 1.1	Service level agreement framework
DS 1.2	Aspects of service level agreements
DS 1.3	Performance procedures
DS 1.4	Monitoring and reporting
DS 1.5	Review of service level agreements and contracts
DS 1.6	Chargeable items
DS 1.7	Service improvement program
DS 2	*Manage third-party services*
DS 2.1	Supplier interfaces
DS 2.2	Owner relationships
DS 2.3	Third-party contracts
DS 2.4	Third-party qualifications
DS 2.5	Outsourcing contracts
DS 2.6	Continuity of services
DS 2.7	Security relationships
DS 2.8	Monitoring
DS 3	*Manage performance and capacity*
DS 3.1	Availability and performance requirements
DS 3.2	Availability plan
DS 3.3	Monitoring and reporting
DS 3.4	Modeling tools
DS 3.5	Proactive performance management
DS 3.6	Workload forecasting
DS 3.7	Capacity management of resources
DS 3.8	Resources availability
DS 3.9	Resources schedule
DS 4	*Ensure continuous service*
DS 4.1	IT continuity framework
DS 4.2	IT continuity plan strategy and philosophy
DS 4.3	IT continuity plan contents
DS 4.4	Minimizing IT continuity requirements
DS 4.5	Maintaining the IT continuity plan
DS 4.6	Testing the IT continuity plan
DS 4.7	IT continuity plan training
DS 4.8	IT continuity plan distribution
DS 4.9	User department alternative processing backup procedures
DS 4.10	Critical IT resources
DS 4.11	Backup site and hardware
DS 4.12	Off-site backup storage
DS 4.13	Wrap-up procedures
DS 5	*Ensure systems security*
DS 5.1	Manage security measures
DS 5.2	Identification, authentication, and access
DS 5.3	Security of online access to data
DS 5.4	User account management
DS 5.5	Management review of user accounts
DS 5.6	User control of user accounts
DS 5.7	Security surveillance

Continued

DS 5.8	Data classification
DS 5.9	Central identification and access rights management
DS 5.10	Violation and security activity reports
DS 5.11	Incident handling
DS 5.12	Reaccreditation
DS 5.13	Counterparty trust
DS 5.14	Transaction authorization
DS 5.15	Nonrepudiation
DS 5.16	Trusted path
DS 5.17	Protection of security functions
DS 5.18	Cryptographic key management
DS 5.19	Malicious software prevention, detection, and correction
DS 5.20	Firewall architectures and connections with public networks
DS 5.21	Protection of electronic value
DS 6	*Identify and allocate costs*
DS 6.1	Chargeable items
DS 6.2	Costing procedures
DS 6.3	User billing and chargeback procedures
DS 7	*Educate and train users*
DS 7.1	Identification of training needs
DS 7.2	Training organization
DS 7.3	Security principles and awareness training
DS 8	*Assist and advise customers*
DS 8.1	Help desk
DS 8.2	Registration of customer queries
DS 8.3	Customer query escalation
DS 8.4	Monitoring of clearance
DS 8.5	Trend analysis and reporting
DS 9	*Manage the configuration*
DS 9.1	Configuration recording
DS 9.2	Configuration baseline
DS 9.3	Status accounting
DS 9.4	Configuration control
DS 9.5	Unauthorized software
DS 9.6	Software storage
DS 9.7	Configuration management procedures
DS 9.8	Software accountability
DS 10	*Manage problems and incidents*

Continued

DS 10.1	Problem management system
DS 10.2	Problem escalation
DS 10.3	Problem tracking and audit trail
DS 10.4	Emergency and temporary access authorizations
DS 10.5	Emergency processing priorities
DS 11	*Manage data*
DS 11.1	Data preparation procedures
DS 11.2	Source document authorization procedures
DS 11.3	Source document data collection
DS 11.4	Source document error handling
DS 11.5	Source document retention
DS 11.6	Data input authorization procedures
DS 11.7	Accuracy, completeness, and authorization checks
DS 11.8	Data input error handling
DS 11.9	Data-processing integrity
DS 11.10	Data-processing validation and editing
DS 11.11	Data-processing error handling
DS 11.12	Output handling and retention
DS 11.13	Output distribution
DS 11.14	Output balancing and reconciliation
DS 11.15	Output review and error handling
DS 11.16	Security provision for output reports
DS 11.17	Protection of sensitive information during transmission and transport
DS 11.18	Protection of disposed sensitive information
DS 11.19	Storage management
DS 11.20	Retention periods and storage terms
DS 11.21	Media library management system
DS 11.22	Media library management responsibilities
DS 11.23	Backup and restoration
DS 11.24	Backup jobs
DS 11.25	Backup storage
DS 11.26	Archiving
DS 11.27	Protection of sensitive messages
DS 11.28	Authentication and integrity
DS 11.29	Electronic transaction integrity
DS 11.30	Continued integrity of stored data
DS 12	*Manage facilities*
DS 12.1	Physical security
DS 12.2	Low profile of the IT site

Continued

DS 12.3	Visitor escort
DS 12.4	Personnel health and safety
DS 12.5	Protection against environmental factors
DS 12.6	Uninterruptible power supply
DS 13	*Manage operations*
DS 13.1	Processing operations procedures and instructions manual
DS 13.2	Start-up process and other operations documentation
DS 13.3	Job scheduling
DS 13.4	Departures from standard job schedules
DS 13.5	Processing continuity
DS 13.6	Operations logs
DS 13.7	Safeguard special forms and output devices
DS 13.8	Remote operations

Monitoring

M 1	*Monitor the processes*
M 1.1	Collecting monitoring data
M 1.2	Assessing performance
M 1.3	Assessing customer satisfaction
M 1.4	Management reporting
M 2	*Assess internal control adequacy*
M 2.1	Internal control monitoring
M 2.2	Timely operation of internal controls
M 2.3	Internal control level reporting
M 2.4	Operational security and internal control assurance
M 3	*Obtain independent assurance*
M 3.1	Independent security and internal control certification/accreditation of IT services
M 3.2	Independent security and internal control certification/accreditation of third-party service providers
M 3.3	Independent effectiveness evaluation of IT services
M 3.4	Independent effectiveness evaluation of third-party service providers
M 3.5	Independent assurance of compliance with laws and regulatory requirements and contractual commitments
M 3.6	Independent assurance of compliance with laws and regulatory requirements and contractual commitments by third-party service providers
M 3.7	Competence of independent assurance function
M 3.8	Proactive audit involvement
M 4	*Provide for independent audit*

Continued

M 4.1	Audit charter
M 4.2	Independence
M 4.3	Professional ethics and standards
M 4.4	Competence
M 4.5	Planning
M 4.6	Performance of audit work
M 4.7	Reporting
M 4.8	Follow-up activities

NIST SP 800-53

AC	*Access control*
AC-1	Access control policies and procedures
AC-2	Account management
AC-3	Access enforcement
AC-4	Information flow enforcement
AC-5	Segregation of duties
AC-6	Least privilege
AC-7	Unsuccessful login attempts
AC-8	System use notification
AC-9	Previous login notification
AC-10	Concurrent session control
AC-11	Session lock
AC-12	Session termination
AC-13	Supervision and review—access control
AC-14	Permitted actions without identification or authentication
AC-15	Automated marking
AC-16	Automated labeling
AC-17	Remote access
AC-17	Remote access
AC-18	Wireless access restrictions
AC-19	Access control for portable and mobile devices
AC-20	Use of external information systems
AT	*Awareness and training*
AT-1	Security awareness and training policy and procedures
AT-2	Security awareness
AT-3	Security training
AT-4	Security training records
AT-5	Contacts with security groups and associations
AU	*Audit and accountability*

Continued

AU-1	Audit and accountability policy and procedures
AU-2	Auditable events
AU-3	Content of audit records
AU-4	Audit storage capacity
AU-5	Response to audit processing failures
AU-6	Audit monitoring, analysis, and reporting
AU-7	Audit reduction and report generation
AU-8	Time stamps
AU-9	Protection of audit information
AU-10	Nonrepudiation
AU-11	Audit record retention
CA	*Certification, accreditation, and security assessments*
CA-1	Certification, accreditation, and security assessment policies and procedures
CA-2	Security assessments
CA-3	Information system connections
CA-4	Security certification
CA-5	Plan of actions and milestones
CA-6	Security accreditation
CA-7	Continuous monitoring
CM	*Configuration management*
CM-1	Configuration management policy and procedures
CM-2	Baseline configuration
CM-3	Configuration change control
CM-4	Monitoring configuration changes
CM-5	Access restrictions for change
CM-6	Configuration settings
CM-7	Least functionality
CM-8	Information system component inventory
CP	*Contingency planning*
CP-1	Contingency planning policy and procedures
CP-2	Contingency plan
CP-3	Contingency training
CP-4	Contingency planning testing and exercises
CP-5	Contingency plan update
CP-6	Alternate storage site
CP-7	Alternate processing site
CP-8	Telecommunications services
CP-9	Information system backup

Continued

CP-10	Information system recovery and reconstitution
IA	*Identification and authentication*
IA-1	Identification and authentication policy and procedures
IA-2	User identification and authentication
IA-3	Device identification and authentication
IA-4	Identifier management
IA-5	Authenticator management
IA-6	Authenticator feedback
IA-7	Cryptographic module authentication
IR	*Incident response*
IR-1	Incident response policy and procedures
IR-2	Incident response training
IR-3	Incident response testing and exercises
IR-4	Incident handling
IR-5	Incident monitoring
IR-6	Incident reporting
IR-7	Incident response assistance
MA	*Maintenance*
MA-1	System maintenance policy and procedures
MA-2	Controlled maintenance
MA-3	Maintenance tools
MA-4	Remote maintenance
MA-5	Maintenance personnel
MA-6	Timely maintenance
MP	*Media protection*
MP-1	Media protection policy and procedures
MP-2	Media access
MP-3	Media labeling
MP-4	Media storage
MP-5	Media transport
MP-6	Media sanitization
MP-7	Media destruction and disposal
PE	*Physical and environmental protection*
PE-1	Physical and environmental protection policy and procedures
PE-2	Physical access authorizations
PE-3	Physical access control
PE-4	Access control for transmission medium
PE-5	Access control for display medium

Continued

PE-6	Monitoring physical access
PE-7	Visitor control
PE-8	Access records
PE-9	Power equipment and power cabling
PE-10	Emergency shutoff
PE-11	Emergency power
PE-12	Emergency lighting
PE-14	Temperature and humidity controls
PE-15	Water damage protection
PE-16	Delivery and removal
PE-17	Alternate work site
PE-18	Location of information system components
PE-19	Information leakage
PL	*Planning*
PL-1	Security planning policy and procedures
PL-2	System security plan
PL-3	System security plan update
PL-4	Rules of behavior
PL-5	Privacy impact assessment
PL-6	Security-related system activity
PS	*Personnel security*
PS-1	Personnel policy and procedures
PS-2	Personnel policy and procedures
PS-3	Personnel screening
PS-4	Personnel termination
PS-5	Personnel transfer
PS-6	Access agreements
PS-7	Third-party personnel security
PS-8	Personnel sanctions
RA	*Risk assessment*
RA-1	Risk assessment policy and procedures
RA-2	Security categorization
RA-3	Risk assessment
RA-4	Risk assessment update
RA-5	Vulnerability scanning
SA	*System and services acquisition*
SA-1	System and services policy and procedures
SA-2	Allocation of resources
SA-3	Lifecycle support

Continued

SA-4	Acquisitions
SA-5	Information system documentation
SA-6	Software usage restrictions
SA-7	User-installed software
SA-8	Security engineering principles
SA-9	External information system services
SA-10	Developer configuration management
SA-11	Developer security testing
SC	*System and communication protection*
SC-1	System and communications protection policy and procedures
SC-2	Application partitioning
SC-3	Security function isolation
SC-4	Information remanence
SC-5	Denial of service protection
SC-6	Resource priority
SC-7	Boundary protection
SC-8	Transmission integrity
SC-9	Transmission confidentiality
SC-10	Network disconnect
SC-11	Trusted path
SC-12	Cryptographic key establishment and management
SC-13	Use of cryptography
SC-14	Public access protections
SC-15	Collaborative computing
SC-16	Transmission of security parameters
SC-17	PKI certificates
SC-18	Mobile code
SC-19	VoIP
SC-20	Secure name/address resolution service (authoritative source)
SC-21	Secure name/address resolution service (recursive or caching resolver)
SC-22	Architecture and provisioning for name/address resolution service
SC-23	Session authenticity
SI	*System and information integrity*
SI-1	System and information integrity policy and procedures
SI-2	Flaw remediation
SI-3	Malicious code protection

Continued

SI-4	Information system monitoring tools and techniques
SI-5	Security alerts and advisories
SI-6	Security functionality verification
SI-7	Software and information integrity
SI-8	Spam protection
SI-9	Information input restrictions
SI-10	Information accuracy, completeness, validity, and authenticity
SI-11	Error handling
SI-12	Information output handling and retention

APPENDIX 16 - INFORMATION CLASSIFICATION

Information held or created by the Forensic Laboratory must be evaluated against the following criteria and classified accordingly:

PUBLIC

"Public" information is information that can be disclosed to anyone without violating an individual's right to privacy or prejudice the Forensic Laboratory in any way, including financial loss, embarrassment, or jeopardizing the security of any assets.

INTERNAL USE ONLY

"Internal Use Only" information is information that, due to technical or business sensitivity, is limited to Forensic Laboratory employees and relevant third-party suppliers. It is intended for use only within the Forensic Laboratory. Unauthorized disclosure, compromise, or destruction should not have a significant impact on the Forensic Laboratory or its employees.

CONFIDENTIAL

"Confidential" information is information that the Forensic Laboratory and its employees have a legal, regulatory, or social obligation to protect. It is intended for use solely within defined groups in the Forensic Laboratory. Unauthorized disclosure, compromise, or destruction would adversely impact the Forensic Laboratory or its employees.

STRICTLY CONFIDENTIAL

"Strictly confidential" information, the highest level of classification in the Forensic Laboratory, is information whose unauthorized disclosure, compromise, or destruction could result in severe damage, provide significant advantage to a competitor, or incur serious financial impact to the Forensic Laboratory or its employees. It is intended solely for named individuals within the Forensic Laboratory and is limited to those with an explicit, predetermined "need to know."

APPENDIX 17 - THE CORPORATE RISK REGISTER

The contents of the Forensic Laboratory risk register are shown below:

- risk number;
- risk;
- business process;
- value;
- probability;
- impact;
- gross exposure;
- gross risk level;
- consequence
- gross total risk;
- mitigation (treatment);
- Risk Owner;
- residual probability;
- residual exposure;
- residual risk level;
- residual total risk;
- last reviewed;
- date for next review;
- days overdue.

APPENDIX 18 - COMPARISON BETWEEN QUALITATIVE AND QUANTITATIVE METHODS

Both qualitative and quantitative approaches to security risk management have their advantages and disadvantages. Certain situations may adopt the quantitative approach, and others will find the qualitative approach much more to their liking. The following table summarizes some of the benefits and drawbacks of each approach:

In years past, the quantitative approaches seemed to dominate security risk management and this is still prevalent in some countries. This has changed recently as more and more practitioners have admitted that strictly following quantitative risk management processes typically results in difficult, long-running projects that see few tangible benefits. This has led to the favoring of qualitative risk assessment.

	Quantitative	Qualitative
Benefits	Risks are prioritized by financial impact; assets are prioritized by financial values Results facilitate management of risk by return on security investment Results can be expressed in management-specific terminology (e.g., monetary values and probability expressed as a specific percentage) Accuracy tends to increase over time as the organization builds historic record of data while gaining experience	Enables visibility and understanding of risk ranking Easier to reach consensus Not necessary to quantify threat frequency Not necessary to determine exact financial values of assets Easier to involve people who are not experts on security or computers
Drawbacks	Impact values assigned to risks are based on subjective opinions of participants Process to reach credible results and consensus is very time consuming Calculations can be complex and time consuming Results are presented in monetary terms only, and they may be difficult for nontechnical people to interpret Process requires expertise, so participants cannot be easily coached through it	Insufficient differentiation between important risks Difficult to justify investing in control implementation because there is no basis for a cost-benefit analysis Results are dependent upon the quality of the risk management team that is created

APPENDIX 19 - MAPPING CONTROL FUNCTIONS TO ISO 27001

ISO 27001 Section	Control	Protect	Deter	Detect	Respond	Recover
A.5.1.1	Information security policy document	√				
A.5.1.2	Review of the information security policy	√				
A.6.1.1	Management commitment to information security	√	√			
A.6.1.2	Information security coordination	√	√			
A.6.1.3	Allocation of information security responsibilities	√				
A.6.1.4	Authorization process for information-processing facilities	√	√			
A.6.1.5	Confidentiality agreements	√	√			
A.6.1.6	Contact with authorities	√	√	√	√	
A.6.1.7	Contact with special interest groups	√	√			
A.6.1.8	Independent review of information security	√	√	√	√	
A.6.2.1	Identification of risks-related external parties	√	√			
A.6.2.2	Addressing security when dealing with customers	√	√			
A.6.2.3	Addressing security in third-party agreements	√	√			
A.7.1.1	Inventory of assets	√	√			
A.7.1.2	Ownership of assets	√	√			
A.7.1.3	Acceptable use of assets	√	√			
A.7.2.1	Classification guidelines	√				
A.7.2.2	Information labeling and handling	√	√	√		
A.8.1.1	Roles and responsibilities	√	√			

Continued

ISO 27001 Section	Control	Protect	Deter	Detect	Respond	Recover
A.8.1.2	Screening	√	√	√		
A.8.1.3	Terms and conditions of employment	√	√			
A.8.2.1	Management responsibilities	√	√	√		
A.8.2.2	Information security awareness, education, and training	√	√			
A.8.2.3	Disciplinary process		√			
A.8.3.1	Termination responsibilities	√	√			
A.8.3.2	Return of assets	√	√	√		
A.8.3.3	Removal of access rights	√	√	√		
A.9.1.1	Physical security perimeter	√	√			
A.9.1.2	Physical entry controls	√	√	√		
A.9.1.3	Securing offices, rooms, and facilities	√	√	√		
A.9.1.4	Protecting against external and environmental threats	√		√		√
A.9.1.5	Working in secure areas	√	√			
A.9.1.6	Public access, delivery, and loading areas	√	√			
A.9.2.1	Equipment siting and protection	√	√	√		
A.9.2.2	Supporting utilities	√			√	√
A.9.2.3	Cabling security	√				
A.9.2.4	Equipment maintenance	√		√		
A.9.2.5	Security of equipment off premises	√				
A.9.2.6	Secure disposal or reuse of equipment	√	√			
A.9.2.7	Removal of property	√	√	√		
A.10.1.1	Documented operating procedures	√			√	√
A.10.1.2	Change management	√	√			
A.10.1.3	Segregation of duties	√	√			
A.10.1.4	Separation of development, test, and operational facilities	√	√			
A.10.2.1	Service delivery	√				
A.10.2.2	Monitoring and review of third-party services	√				
A.10.2.3	Managing changes to third-party services	√	√			
A.10.3.1	Capacity management	√				
A.10.3.2	System acceptance	√		√		
A.10.4.1	Controls against malicious code	√	√	√	√	√
A.10.4.2	Controls against mobile code	√	√	√	√	√
A.10.5.1	Information backup	√				√
A.10.6.1	Network controls	√	√	√	√	
A.10.6.2	Security of network services	√				
A.10.7.1	Management of removable media	√				√
A.10.7.2	Disposal of media	√				

Continued

ISO 27001 Section	Control	Protect	Deter	Detect	Respond	Recover
A.10.7.3	Information handling procedures	√	√	√		
A.10.7.4	Security of system documentation	√				√
A.10.8.1	Information exchange policies and procedures	√				
A.10.8.2	Exchange agreements	√				
A.10.8.3	Physical media in transit	√				
A.10.8.4	Electronic messaging	√	√			
A.10.8.5	Business information systems	√	√			
A.10.9.1	Electronic commerce	√	√			
A.10.9.2	Online transactions	√	√	√		
A.10.9.3	Publicly available information	√				
A.10.10.1	Audit logging	√	√	√		
A.10.10.2	Monitoring system use	√	√	√		
A.10.10.3	Protection of log information	√	√	√		
A.10.10.4	Administrator and operator logs	√	√	√		
A.10.10.5	Fault logging	√			√	
A.10.10.6	Clock synchronization	√				
A.11.1.1	Access control policy	√	√			
A.11.2.1	User registration	√	√			
A.11.2.2.	Privilege management	√	√	√		
A.11.2.3	User password management	√	√			
A.11.2.4	Review of user access rights	√	√	√		
A.11.3.1	Password use	√	√			
A.11.3.2	Unattended user equipment	√	√			
A.11.3.3	Clear desk and clear screen policy	√	√			
A.11.4.1	Policy on use of networked services	√	√			
A.11.4.2	User authentication for external connections	√	√	√		
A.11.4.3	Equipment identification in networks	√	√	√		
A.11.4.4	Remote diagnostic and configuration port protection	√	√			
A.11.4.5	Segregation in networks	√	√			
A.11.4.6	Network connection control	√	√			
A.11.4.7	Network routing control	√	√			
A.11.5.1	Secure log-on procedures	√	√			
A.11.5.2	User identification and authentication	√	√			
A.11.5.3	Password management system	√	√			
A.11.5.4	Use of system utilities	√				
A.11.5.5	Session time-out	√	√			
A.11.5.6	Limitation of connection time	√	√			

Continued

ISO 27001 Section	Control	Protect	Deter	Detect	Respond	Recover
A.11.6.1	Information access restriction	√	√			
A.11.6.2	Sensitive system isolation	√	√			
A.11.7.1	Mobile computing and communications	√				
A.11.7.2	Teleworking	√				
A.12.1.1	Security requirements analysis and specification	√	√			
A.12.2.1	Input data validation	√				
A.12.2.2	Control of internal processing	√				
A.12.2.3	Message integrity	√	√	√		
A.12.2.4	Output data validation	√				
A.12.3.1	Policy on the use of cryptographic control	√	√	√		
A.12.3.2	Key management	√	√	√		
A.12.4.1	Control of operational software	√	√			
A.12.4.2	Protection of system test data	√	√			
A.12.4.3	Access control to program source code	√	√			
A.12.5.1	Change control procedures	√	√			
A.12.5.2	Technical review of applications after operating system changes	√	√	√		
A.12.5.3	Restrictions on changes to software packages	√		√		
A.12.5.4	Information leakage	√				
A.12.5.5	Outsourced software development	√	√			
A.12.6.1	Control of technical vulnerabilities	√	√	√		
A.13.1.1	Reporting information security events		√		√	√
A.13.1.2	Reporting security weaknesses		√		√	√
A.13.2.1	Responsibilities and procedures		√		√	√
A.13.2.2	Learning from information security incidents	√	√	√		
A.13.2.3	Collection of evidence	√	√		√	
A.14.1.1	Including information security in the business continuity management process	√	√	√	√	√
A.141.1.2	Business continuity and risk assessment	√	√	√	√	√
A.14.1.3	Developing and implementing continuity plans including information security	√	√	√	√	√
A.14.1.4	Business continuity planning framework	√	√	√	√	√
A.14.1.5	Testing, maintaining, and reassessing business continuity plans	√	√	√	√	√
A.15.1.1	Identification of applicable legislation	√				
A.15.1.2	Intellectual property rights (IPR)					
A.15.1.3	Protection of organizational records	√				
A.15.1.4	Data protection and privacy of personal information	√				
A.15.1.5	Prevention of misuse of information-processing facilities	√	√			

Continued

ISO 27001 Section	Control	Protect	Deter	Detect	Respond	Recover
A.15.1.6	Regulation of cryptographic controls	√				
A.15.2.1	Compliance with security policies and standards		√	√		
A.15.2.2	Technical compliance checking		√	√		
A.15.3.1	Information systems audit controls		√	√		
A.15.3.2	Protection of information systems audit tools	√		√		

Note

These are the Forensic Laboratory's opinion.

APPENDIX 20 - MAPPING SECURITY CONCERNS TO ISO 27001

ISO 27001 section	Control	Confidentiality	Integrity	Availability	Accountability	Authenticity	Reliability
A.5.1.1	Information security policy document	√	√	√	√		
A.5.1.2	Review of the information security policy	√	√	√	√		
A.6.1.1	Management commitment to information security	√	√	√	√	√	√
A.6.1.2	Information security coordination	√	√	√	√	√	√
A.6.1.3	Allocation of information security responsibilities	√	√	√	√		
A.6.1.4	Authorization process for information-processing facilities				√	√	
A.6.1.5	Confidentiality agreements	√			√		
A.6.1.6	Contact with authorities						
A.6.1.7	Contact with special interest groups						
A.6.1.8	Independent review of information security				√		

Continued

ISO 27001 section	Control	Confidentiality	Integrity	Availability	Accountability	Authenticity	Reliability
A.6.2.1	Identification of risks-related external parties	√	√	√	√	√	
A.6.2.2	Addressing security when dealing with customers	√	√	√	√	√	
A.6.2.3	Addressing security in third-party agreements	√	√	√	√		
A.7.1.1	Inventory of assets	√	√	√	√		
A.7.1.2	Ownership of assets	√	√	√	√		
A.7.1.3	Acceptable use of assets	√			√		
A.7.2.1	Classification guidelines	√			√		
A.7.2.2	Information labeling and handling	√	√		√	√	
A.8.1.1	Roles and responsibilities	√	√	√	√		
A.8.1.2	Screening	√	√	√	√		
A.8.1.3	Terms and conditions of employment	√	√	√	√		
A.8.2.1	Management responsibilities	√	√	√	√		
A.8.2.2	Information security awareness, education, and training	√	√	√	√		
A.8.2.3	Disciplinary process	√	√	√	√		
A.8.3.1	Termination responsibilities	√	√	√			
A.8.3.2	Return of assets	√		√	√		
A.8.3.3	Removal of access rights	√			√		
A.9.1.1	Physical security perimeter	√	√	√			
A.9.1.2	Physical entry controls	√	√	√		√	
A.9.1.3	Securing offices, rooms, and facilities	√	√	√			
A.9.1.4	Protecting against external and environmental threats	√	√	√			
A.9.1.5	Working in secure areas	√	√	√			

Continued

ISO 27001 section	Control	Confidentiality	Integrity	Availability	Accountability	Authenticity	Reliability
A.9.1.6	Public access, delivery, and loading areas	√	√	√			
A.9.2.1	Equipment siting and protection	√		√			√
A.9.2.2	Supporting utilities			√			√
A.9.2.3	Cabling security	√	√	√			√
A.9.2.4	Equipment maintenance		√	√			√
A.9.2.5	Security of equipment off premises	√	√	√			
A.9.2.6	Secure disposal or reuse of equipment	√	√	√			
A.9.2.7	Removal of property						
A.10.1.1	Documented operating procedures		√		√		
A.10.1.2	Change management		√		√		√
A.10.1.3	Segregation of duties		√		√		
A.10.1.4	Separation of development, test, and operational facilities		√		√		
A.10.2.1	Service delivery		√	√	√		√
A.10.2.2	Monitoring and review of third-party services		√			√	√
A.10.2.3	Managing changes to third-party services		√		√	√	√
A.10.3.1	Capacity management			√			√
A.10.3.2	System acceptance				√	√	√
A.10.4.1	Controls against malicious code	√	√	√			
A.10.4.2	Controls against mobile code	√	√	√			
A.10.5.1	Information backup		√	√			√
A.10.6.1	Network controls			√			√
A.10.6.2	Security of network services			√			√
A.10.7.1	Management of removable media	√					

Continued

ISO 27001 section	Control	Confidentiality	Integrity	Availability	Accountability	Authenticity	Reliability
A.10.7.2	Disposal of media	√					
A.10.7.3	Information handling procedures	√	√				
A.10.7.4	Security of system documentation	√					
A.10.8.1	Information exchange policies and procedures	√			√		
A.10.8.2	Exchange agreements	√			√		
A.10.8.3	Physical media in transit	√	√	√			√
A.10.8.4	Electronic messaging	√	√				
A.10.8.5	Business information systems	√		√			
A.10.9.1	Electronic commerce	√	√				
A.10.9.2	Online transactions	√	√				
A.10.9.3	Publicly available information	√	√	√			
A.10.10.1	Audit logging		√		√		√
A.10.10.2	Monitoring system use	√	√	√	√		√
A.10.10.3	Protection of log information	√			√		
A.10.10.4	Administrator and operator logs			√	√		
A.10.10.5	Fault logging			√	√		
A.10.10.6	Clock synchronization		√				
A.11.1.1	Access control policy	√	√		√	√	
A.11.2.1	User registration	√	√		√	√	
A.11.2.2.	Privilege management	√	√		√	√	
A.11.2.3	User password management	√	√		√	√	
A.11.2.4	Review of user access rights		√		√	√	
A.11.3.1	Password use	√	√		√	√	
A.11.3.2	Unattended user equipment	√			√		
A.11.3.3	Clear desk and clear screen policy	√			√		

Continued

ISO 27001 section	Control	Confidentiality	Integrity	Availability	Accountability	Authenticity	Reliability
A.11.4.1	Policy on use of networked services			√			√
A.11.4.2	User authentication for external connections	√	√		√	√	
A.11.4.3	Equipment identification in networks	√	√		√	√	
A.11.4.4	Remote diagnostic and configuration port protection	√			√		
A.11.4.5	Segregation in networks	√	√		√		
A.11.4.6	Network connection control		√		√		
A.11.4.7	Network routing control		√		√		
A.11.5.1	Secure log-on procedures	√	√		√	√	
A.11.5.2	User identification and authentication	√	√		√	√	
A.11.5.3	Password management system	√	√		√	√	
A.11.5.4	Use of system utilities	√	√			√	
A.11.5.5	Session time-out	√	√	√			
A.11.5.6	Limitation of connection time	√	√	√			
A.11.6.1	Information access restriction	√			√		
A.11.6.2	Sensitive system isolation	√			√		
A.11.7.1	Mobile computing and communications	√			√		
A.11.7.2	Teleworking	√			√		
A.12.1.1	Security requirements analysis and specification	√	√				
A.12.2.1	Input data validation	√	√				√
A.12.2.2	Control of internal processing	√	√				√
A.12.2.3	Message integrity	√	√			√	
A.12.2.4	Output data validation	√	√				√

Continued

ISO 27001 section	Control	Confidentiality	Integrity	Availability	Accountability	Authenticity	Reliability
A.12.3.1	Policy on the use of cryptographic control	√	√			√	
A.12.3.2	Key management	√	√			√	
A.12.4.1	Control of operational software					√	
A.12.4.2	Protection of system test data	√					
A.12.4.3	Access control to program source code	√	√		√		
A.12.5.1	Change control procedures		√		√		
A.12.5.2	Technical review of applications after operating system changes		√		√	√	√
A.12.5.3	Restrictions on changes to software packages		√				√
A.12.5.4	Information leakage	√			√		
A.12.5.5	Outsourced software development	√	√	√	√		√
A.12.6.1	Control of technical vulnerabilities	√	√	√			√
A.13.1.1	Reporting information security events	√	√	√			
A.13.1.2	Reporting security weaknesses	√	√	√			
A.13.2.1	Responsibilities and procedures	√	√	√	√		
A.13.2.2	Learning from information security incidents	√	√	√	√		
A.13.2.3	Collection of evidence		√		√	√	
A.14.1.1	Including information security in the business continuity management process			√			√
A.14.1.2	Business continuity and risk assessment			√			√

Continued

ISO 27001 section	Control	Confidentiality	Integrity	Availability	Accountability	Authenticity	Reliability
A.14.1.3	Developing and implementing continuity plans including information security			√			√
A.14.1.4	Business continuity planning framework			√			√
A.14.1.5	Testing, maintaining, and reassessing business continuity plans			√			√
A.15.1.1	Identification of applicable legislation	√	√	√			
A.15.1.2	Intellectual property rights (IPR)	√					
A.15.1.3	Protection of organizational records		√	√	√	√	
A.15.1.4	Data protection and privacy of personal information	√	√				
A.15.1.5	Prevention of misuse of information processing facilities		√	√			√
A.15.1.6	Regulation of cryptographic controls	√	√			√	
A.15.2.1	Compliance with security policies and standards		√		√		
A.15.2.2	Technical compliance checking		√		√		√
A.15.3.1	Information systems audit controls		√				√
A.15.3.2	Protection of information systems audit tools		√				√

Note

These are the Forensic Laboratory's opinion.

APPENDIX 21 - SOA TEMPLATE

The ISMS is split into two specific parts, the mandatory management part from ISO 27001 Sections 4–8 and the controls derived from the risk assessment from ISO 27001 Annex A.

It may also have a third part where controls not listed in ISO 27001 Annex A are indicated by the risk treatment process.

Below is the template in use in the Forensic Laboratory.

Note

This only shows a few entries to demonstrate how both parts are implemented in the Forensic Laboratory.

MANDATORY SOA

Control section	Management components	
4.1	General requirements	
	The organization shall develop, implement, maintain, and continually improve a documented ISMS within the context of the organization's overall business activities and risk. For the purpose of this standard, the process used is based on the PDCA model	
4.2	Establishing and managing the ISMS	
	Requirement	Interpretation
4.2.1	Establish the ISMS	
4.2.1. a)	Define the scope of the ISMS in terms of the characteristics of the business, the organization, its location, assets, and technology	The scope statement is reviewed prior to audits by the Information Security Manager to ensure that it remains appropriate The scope statement is defined in "the Forensic Laboratory scope statement"

ANNEX A

This SoA assumes that a risk management tool was used as well as a business risk workshop, to define which of the controls in Annex A are indicated, as currently performed in the Forensic Laboratory.

ISO 27001 clause	Control	Include	Exclude	RA tool	Workshop	Notes
A.5.1.1	Information security policy document	√		√		Policy to be approved by Top Management and appropriately published to all employees and third parties with access to Forensic Laboratory information and informational-processing systems
A.5.1.2	Review of the information security policy	√		√		

CONTROLS NOT IN ANNEX A

Control	Include	Exclude	RA tool	Workshop	Notes
All employees should be forced to take their annual holiday entitlement	√		√		Redundancy and resilience have been built in wherever possible

APPENDIX 22 - THE FORENSIC LABORATORY'S SECURITY METRICS REPORT

The table below shows metrics for the reporting period to support the agreed Security Objectives, which are defined in Chapter 12, Appendix 5. All of the metrics below support objectives 1 and 4, so this is not shown in the right hand column

ISO 27001 control	Control	Metric	Description	How calculated	Responsible for collection (owner)[a]	Target	Score	Cross reference to Security Objective(s)
4.2.1 d	Identify the risks	Number of risk register reviews per month	Number of risk register reviews per month	Count of risk register review meetings		1		3, 4, 6, 7, 8, 10, 12, 13
4.2.1 e	Assess and evaluate risks	% of risks in the Forensic Laboratory by category	Numbers of risks in the risk register in each of the high and medium risk categories	From risk register		VH=0 H=0 M=<20		3, 6, 7
4.2.1 f	Identify and evaluate risk treatment options	% of risks accepted	Number of identified risks that are knowingly accepted without treatment	The number of accepted risks that have not been treated as a percentage of all risks identified. As in the current risk register		VH=0 H=0 M=<5%		3, 6, 7
4.2.1 h	Management approval for residual risks	Last time residual risk was accepted	Last date of residual risk acceptance	From Management Review minutes or form		<= 365 days		3, 6, 7
4.2.1 j	Statement of applicability	% of controls in Annex A implemented	Number of controls in Annex A that are implemented in the Forensic Laboratory	The number of controls in the SoA as a percentage of those in Annex A		>=90%		2, 3, 5, 6, 7, 8, 9, 10, 11, 12, 13, 14, 15
4.2.2	Implement and operate the ISMS	% of controls that are operating correctly in SoA	Number of controls included in the SoA that are operating correctly (i.e., no audit failings or metric failings)	The number of controls in the SoA working correctly as a percentage of those implemented		>=95%		2, 3, 5, 6, 7, 8, 9, 10, 11, 12, 13, 14, 15
4.2.2	Implement and operate the ISMS	% of metrics calculated for Information Security Committee and Management Review meetings	The number of agreed metrics that the Information Security Manager calculates in time for the Information Security Committee or Management Review	Number of metrics calculated and presented as percentage of all agreed metrics to be produced		100%		2, 3, 5, 6, 7, 8, 9, 10, 11, 12, 13, 14, 15
4.3.2	Control of documents	% of documents that meet the document control requirements	Number documents examined that meet the Forensic Laboratory document control procedures and standards	The number of documents examined that meet document control procedures and standards as a percentage of those examined during audits or document reviews within the scope		>=95%		4

Continued

ISO 27001 control	Control	Metric	Description	How calculated	Responsible for collection (owner)	Target	Score	Cross reference to Security Objective(s)
5.2.1	Resource management — provision of resources	% of budget assigned to information security	The percentage of the Forensic Laboratory's budget assigned to information security	Percentage of IT budget assigned		3%		3, 7, 10, 15
5.2.1	Resource management — provision of resources	Full-time support for maintaining ISO 27001 certification	Number of full-time equivalent employees that are dedicated to maintaining ISO 27001 certification	Head count of dedicated information security professionals employed		2		1, 2, 3, 5, 6, 7, 8, 9, 10, 11, 12, 13, 14, 15
5.2.2	Resource management — training, awareness, and competence	% of new employees undergoing induction training within 31 days of joining the Forensic Laboratory	Number of new employees, and third parties working for the Forensic Laboratory, that have undergone induction training within 31 days of joining that have stated in the reporting period	Number new employees, and third parties working for the Forensic Laboratory, that have undergone induction training within 31 days of joining that have started in the reporting period as a percentage of new starters		>=95%		3, 5
5.2.2	Resource management — training, awareness, and competence	% of new employees undergoing information security training	Number of new employees, and third parties working for the Forensic Laboratory, that have undergone information security training that have stated in the reporting period	Number of new employees, and third parties working for the Forensic Laboratory, that have undergone information security training that have started in the reporting period as a percentage of new starters		>=95%		3, 5
5.2.2	Resource management — training, awareness, and competence	% of new all employees undergoing information security refresher training	Number of employees, and third parties working for the Forensic Laboratory, that have undergone refresher information security training that have stated in the reporting period	Number of new employees, and third parties working for the Forensic Laboratory, that have undergone information security refresher training as a percentage of all employees and third parties working for the Forensic Laboratory		>=20%		3, 5

Continued

ISO 27001 control	Control	Metric	Description	How calculated	Responsible for collection (owner)	Target	Score	Cross reference to Security Objective(s)
6	Internal ISMS audits	% of audits completed on time	Number of audits completed on time in the Forensic Laboratory measured against those planned	The number of audits completed on time as a percentage of those planned		>=95%		3, 5, 6, 7, 8, 9, 10, 11, 12, 13, 14, 15
7.2	Review input	Number of mandatory inputs not covered at Management Review	The number of mandatory agenda items that were not covered at the last Management Review	Inspection of minutes		0%		3, 5, 6, 7, 8, 9, 10, 11, 12, 13, 14, 15
7.3	Review output	% of actions completed	Number of actions raised at the Management Review that have been converted into CAPAs	The number of actions from Management Reviews that have been raised as CAPAs as a percentage of all Management Review actions.		>=95%		3, 5, 6, 7, 8, 9, 10, 11, 12, 13, 14, 15
8.2	Corrective action	% of corrective actions completed on time (including PIRs)	Number of corrective actions completed on time in the Forensic Laboratory measured against all corrective actions opened in the time period	The number of corrective actions completed on time as a percentage of those opened in the quarter		>=95%		3, 5, 6, 7, 8, 9, 10, 11, 12, 13, 14, 15
8.3	Preventative action	% of preventive actions completed on time (including PIRS)	Number of preventive actions completed on time in the Forensic Laboratory measured against all preventive actions opened in the time period	The number of preventive actions completed on time as a percentage of those opened in the quarter		>=95%		3, 5, 6, 7, 8, 9, 10, 11, 12, 13, 14, 15
A.5.1.2	Review of the information security policy	Last time information policy document was reviewed	Last date of information security policy review	From Management Review minutes or policy		<= 365 days		5
A.6.1.2	Information security coordination	% of Management Reviews held on time	The number of Management Reviews, with total agendas covered, on time	Difference between date of actual meeting as a percentage of planned meetings		100%		3

Continued

ISO 27001 control	Control	Metric	Description	How calculated	Responsible for collection (owner)	Target	Score	Cross reference to Security Objective(s)
A.6.1.3	Allocation of information security responsibilities	% of JDs with security responsibilities defined	All JDs should have all security responsibilities defined	Numbers of JDs with security responsibilities defined in them as a percentage of all the Forensic Laboratory JDs		100%		5
A.6.1.8	Independent review of information security	Number of third-party audits in last year	Number of third-party audits in last year	Number of third-party audits in last year		>2		2
A.6.2.1	Identification of risks-related external parties	% of external parties risk assessments	The number of external parties having risk assessments performed on them prior to granting access to the Forensic Laboratory information or information-processing facilities	The number of external parties having risk assessments performed on them prior to granting access to the Forensic Laboratory information or information-processing facilities as a percentage of all external parties having such access		100%		4, 5, 7
A.6.2.1	Identification of risks related external parties	% of external parties risk assessments updated	The number of external parties having risk assessments performed on them since they were originally granting access to the Forensic Laboratory information or information-processing facilities within the period	The number of external parties having risk assessments performed on them since they were originally granted access to the Forensic Laboratory information or information-processing facilities as a percentage of all external parties having such access		25%		5, 7
A.7.1.2	Ownership of assets	% of Asset Owners who understand responsibilities	The percentage of Asset Owners who both understand their responsibilities and implement them	The number of Asset Owners understanding and implementing duties as a percentage of all Asset Owners.		>=95%		3, 5, 6
A.7.1.2	Ownership of assets	% of assets without owners	The percentage of assets without Asset Owners	The number of assets without owners as a percentage of all assets		<=5%		3, 5, 6

Continued

ISO 27001 control	Control	Metric	Description	How calculated	Responsible for collection (owner)	Target	Score	Cross reference to Security Objective(s)
A.7.2.1	Classification guidelines	% of assets that are unclassified	The percentage of assets that have not been classified	The number of assets that are unclassified as a percentage of all assets		<=5%		5, 6, 13
A.7.2.2	Information labeling and handling	% of assets that do not have an asset tag	The percentage of assets in the Forensic Laboratory that do not have an asset tag — that should have them. Note — not every assets will have a tag (e.g., keyboards, screens, etc.)	Number of untagged assets as a percentage of all assets		<1%		5, 6
A.8.1.1	Roles and responsibilities	% of JDs with security responsibilities defined	All JDs should have all security responsibilities defined	Numbers of JDs with security responsibilities defined in them as a percentage of all the Forensic Laboratory JDs		100%		5
A.8.1.2	Screening	% of relevant new entrants fully screened prior to employment	The number of employees, and third parties employed by the Forensic Laboratory, who have been security screened prior to being employed who are subject to screening, for whatever reason	Numbers of new entrants screened as a percentage of all new entrants who are designated as subject to screening		100%		5
A.8.1.2	Screening	% of relevant new entrants subject to criminal record or financial screening not screened	The number of employees, and third parties employed by the Forensic Laboratory, who have not been criminal record or financial screened prior to being employed who are subject to criminal record or financial screening, for whatever reason	Numbers of new entrants not criminal record or financial screened as a percentage of all new entrants who are designated as subject criminal record or financial screening		0%		5

Continued

ISO 27001 control	Control	Metric	Description	How calculated	Responsible for collection (owner)	Target	Score	Cross reference to Security Objective(s)
A.8.2.1	Management responsibilities	% of JDs with security responsibilities defined	All JDs should have all security responsibilities defined	Numbers of JDs with security responsibilities defined in them as a percentage of all the Forensic Laboratory JDs		100%		5
A.8.2.2	Information security awareness, education, and training	% of new employees undergoing information security training	Number of new employees, and third parties working for the Forensic Laboratory, that have undergone information security training that have stated in the reporting period	Number of new employees, and third parties working for the Forensic Laboratory, that have undergone information security training that have started in the reporting period as a percentage of new starters		>=95%		5
A.8.2.2	Information security awareness, education, and training	% of new all employees undergoing information security refresher training	Number of employees, and third parties working for the Forensic Laboratory, that have undergone refresher information security training that have started in the reporting period	Number of new employees, and third parties working for the Forensic Laboratory, that have undergone information security refresher training as a percentage of all employees and third parties working for the Forensic Laboratory		>=20%		5
A.8.3.3	Removal of access rights	% of users whose access rights are removed late	The number of leavers that have not had their access rights removed in a timely manner	Number of leavers who have not had access rights removed as a percentage of leavers. This is the kick off process from HR for automated process		<=5%		11
A.9.1.2	Physical entry controls	% of unauthorized access attempts	The number of unauthorized access attempts made using access cards	Number of unauthorized access attempts made using access cards as a percentage of all access attempts		<=1%		8

Continued

ISO 27001 control	Control	Metric	Description	How calculated	Responsible for collection (owner)	Target	Score	Cross reference to Security Objective(s)
A.9.1.2	Physical entry controls	% of staff complying with ID Card Policy	% of staff wearing their ID cards visibly inside the office	Bi-monthly sampling		>90%		8
A.9.1.2	Physical entry controls	Number of cardholders signing in as visitors	% of cardholders forgetting ID cards	Number signing in as visitors as % of cardholders		<1%		
A.9.1.2	Physical entry controls	Tailgaters	Number of tailgating incidents per month	Number of alarms set off		0		
A.9.1.2	Physical entry controls	Alarms set	Alarms set off where someone has tried to access a location they are not authorized to access	Number of alarms set off		0		
A.9.1.5	Working in secure areas	% of unauthorized access attempts	The number of unauthorized access attempts made using access cards	Number of unauthorized access attempts made using access cards as a percentage of all access attempts		<=0.1%		8
A.9.2.2	Supporting utilities	Number of times UPS tested	The number of times the UPS has been tested for taking the load within the reporting period	Number of times UPS tested per month		>=1		9, 10
A.9.2.3	Cabling security	% of cables unlabeled or undocumented	The number of cables in the server room or in patch panels that are not labeled and/or documented	The number of cables in the server room or in patch panels that are not labeled and/or documented as a percentage of all cables examined		<5%		6, 9, 10
A.9.2.4	Equipment maintenance	% of equipment in warranty (servers)	The amount of the Forensic Laboratory equipment that is in warranty	The amount of the Forensic Laboratory equipment that is in warranty		100%		9, 10
A.9.2.4	Equipment maintenance	% of equipment in warranty (network equipment)	The amount of the Forensic Laboratory equipment that is in warranty	The amount of the Forensic Laboratory equipment that is in warranty		100%		9, 10

Continued

ISO 27001 control	Control	Metric	Description	How calculated	Responsible for collection (owner)	Target	Score	Cross reference to Security Objective(s)
A.9.2.4	Equipment maintenance	% of equipment with maintenance contracts (servers)	The amount of the Forensic Laboratory equipment that is subject to regular maintenance	The number of assets maintained as a percentage of the number of assets to be maintained		100%		9, 10
A.9.2.4	Equipment maintenance	% of equipment with maintenance contracts (network equipment)	The amount of the Forensic Laboratory equipment that is subject to regular maintenance	The number of assets maintained as a percentage of the number of assets to be maintained		100%		9, 10
A.9.2.5	Security of equipment off premises	Number of equipment losses	The number of items that are lost that can store/ process data, whether encrypted or not	Service desk log of losses		0		6, 7
A.10.1.1	Documented operating procedures	% of current documented operating procedures	Number of documented operating procedures that have been reviewed in the past year	The number of up to date documents (i.e., reviewed in the past year) as a percentage of those examined during audits or document reviews		>=95%		3
A.10.1.2	Change management	% of failed changes	Number of change requests that have to be abandoned, fail, or need to be backed out	The number of change requests that failed as a percentage of all change attempted in the period		<=5%		9, 10, 12
A.10.2.1	Service delivery	% of service delivery failures	Number of times the Forensic Laboratory delivers services that fail their delivery date, quality objectives, or other SLA	Number of times the Forensic Laboratory services are delivered that fail their delivery date, quality objectives, or other SLA as percentage of all services delivered to clients		0		9, 10
A.10.2.1	Service delivery	Cost of service delivery failures	Cost of the Forensic Laboratory service delivery failures against SLAS or other contractual measures	Penalties from financial view plus estimated of reputational loss		0		9, 10

Continued

ISO 27001 control	Control	Metric	Description	How calculated	Responsible for collection (owner)	Target	Score	Cross reference to Security Objective(s)
A.10.2.2	Monitoring and review of third-party services	% of service delivery failures	Number of times that third-party suppliers fail their SLAS For key suppliers, this should be reported individually by supplier	Number of times that third-party suppliers fail their SLA as a percentage of all services delivered to the Forensic Laboratory		0		5, 10
A.10.3.1	Capacity management	Date of last capacity plan	Date since the capacity plan was last updated It is noted that capacity is monitored in real time — but the plan allows for future planning	Days since last formal review		<= 90 days		10
A.10.4.1	Controls against malicious code	Number of security incidents caused by malware	The number of information security incidents that have been caused by malware of some sort or another	From service desk logs		0		10, 13
A.10.5.1	Information backup	% of backup failures	Number of times a backup job has failed on first attempt	Number of times a backup job has failed as percentage of all backups undertaken		<5%		10, 13, 14
A.10.5.1	Information backup	% of failed restores	Number of times a restoration job has failed on first attempt	Number of times a restore job has failed as percentage of all restores undertaken		<5%		10, 13, 14
A.10.7.3	Information handling procedures	% of laptops encrypted (IT)	The percentage of encrypted as a percentage of all laptops	Amount of laptops encrypted as a percentage of all laptops		100%		6
A.10.7.3	Information handling procedures	% of laptops encrypted (Forensic Laboratory-wide)	The percentage of encrypted as a percentage of all laptops	Amount of laptops encrypted as a percentage of all laptops		100%		6
A.10.10.1	Audit logging	% of systems where full logging is enabled	Number of systems where full event log and event log correlation are carried out	The number of systems where full event log and event log correlation are carried out as a percentage of all systems in the Forensic Laboratory		100%		6, 10

Continued

ISO 27001 control	Control	Metric	Description	How calculated	Responsible for collection (owner)	Target	Score	Cross reference to Security Objective(s)
A.11.1.1	Access control policy	% of owners defining requirements	The number of system owners who have accepted their responsibilities and discharged them	Number of system owners fulfilling their obligations measured against all system owners		>=95%		6, 11
A.11.2.2.	Privilege management	Number of users with more than one accountable ID	The number of users who have more than one system account that they can use	Number of users with more than one accountable ID		0		6, 11
A.11.2.2.	Privilege management	Number of users with use of Administrator or root access directly	The number of users who have access to privileged accounts with no accountability	Number of users with unaccountable access to top level accounts		0		6, 11
A.11.2.2.	Privilege management	Number of users with use of local Administrator rights	The number of users who have local administrative rights to their own hardware	Number of users with local administration rights as a percentage of all users		<=1%		6, 11
A.11.2.4	Review of user access rights	Date of last full access review	Date of last full access rights review for all user accounts	Date		<=90 days		6, 11
A.11.2.4	Review of user access rights to the server room	Date of last full access review to server room	Date of last full access rights review to server room	Date		<=90 days		6, 11
A.11.3.1	Password use	% of users who do not meet password policy	The number of users who do not meet the Forensic Laboratory Password Policy (weak passwords)	Inspection and percentage of failures against compliers		0%		6, 11
A.11.3.2	Unattended user equipment	% of users without mandated clear screen policy implemented	The number of users who have not implemented the clear screen policy	Inspection and percentage of failures against compliers		0		6, 11
A.11.3.3	Clear desk and clear screen policy	% of users without mandated clear screen policy implemented	The number of users who have not implemented the clear desk policy	Inspection and percentage of failures against compliers		0		6, 11

Continued

ISO 27001 control	Control	Metric	Description	How calculated	Responsible for collection (owner)	Target	Score	Cross reference to Security Objective(s)
A.11.7.1	Mobile computing and communications	% of mobile users trained	The percentage of mobile users who have received teleworking security training	The number of mobile users receiving training as a percentage of all teleworkers		100%		5, 6
A.11.7.1	Mobile computing and communications	% of laptops and other mobile devices encrypted	The percentage of laptop and other mobile device users who have encrypted devices	The number of encrypted devices as a percentage of all relevant devices		100%		5, 6
A.11.7.2	Teleworking	% of teleworkers trained	The percentage of teleworkers who have received teleworking security training	The number of teleworkers receiving training as a percentage of all teleworkers		100%		5, 6
A.12.1.1	Security requirements analysis and specification	Number of specifications or requirements that do not specify appropriate information security requirements	The number of specifications or requirements that do not specify appropriate information security requirements	The number of specifications or requirements that do not specify appropriate information security requirements as a percentage of requirements of specifications examined		0		7, 12
A.12.6.1	Control of technical vulnerabilities	Number of systems with "Critical" severity vulnerabilities	The number of servers or other patchable systems that have "Critical" severity vulnerabilities determined by Nessus vulnerability scans.	Count of critical vulnerabilities as determined by Nessus scan.		0		6, 10, 13
A.12.6.1	Control of technical vulnerabilities	Number of systems with "High" severity vulnerabilities	The number of servers or other patchable systems that have "High" severity vulnerabilities determined by Nessus Vulnerability scans	Count of servers with "High" severity vulnerabilities as determined by Nessus scan		0		6, 10, 13

Continued

ISO 27001 control	Control	Metric	Description	How calculated	Responsible for collection (owner)	Target	Score	Cross reference to Security Objective(s)
A.13.1.1	Reporting information security events	Number of security incidents reported to the service desk	Number of security incidents reported to the service desk	From Service Desk Records		0		13, 14
A.13.1.1	Reporting information security events	Number of security incidents not resolved in time	Number of security incidents reported to the service desk that were not resolved according to SLAS or other times set for resolution	From service desk records		0		13, 14
A.13.1.1	Reporting information security events	Number of security incidents resulting in invocation of BCP	Number of security incidents resulting in invocation of BCP	From service desk records		0		13, 14
A.13.2.2	Learning from information security incidents	Costs of security incidents	All security incidents shall be costed for both direct costs and indirect costs	Costs		0		5, 13, 14
A.14.1.2	Business continuity and risk assessment	% of risk assessments undertaken for BCPs	The number of BCP risk assessments for BCPs to ensure that the risks are updated	The number of risk assessments redone in the period as a percentage of BCPs in place		>=20%		6, 14
A.14.1.3	Developing and implementing continuity plans including information security	% of business functions with a BCP	The percentage of the Forensic Laboratory business functions with a BCP	Percentage of business units with a BCP as a percentage of all identified business units		100%		6, 14
A.14.1.5	Testing, maintaining, and reassessing business continuity plans	% of BCPs updated	The number of BCPs updated in the period	The number of BCPs updated in the period as a percentage of BCPs in place		>=20%		6, 14
A.14.1.5	Testing, maintaining, and reassessing business continuity plans	% of BCPs tested	The number of BCPs tested in the period	The number of BCPs tested in the period as a percentage of BCPs in place		>=20%		6, 14

[a] *Where the person responsible for collection is also the owner, only one name is given. If someone other than the owner collects the results, then their name is given with the Owner in (brackets).*

APPENDIX 23 - MAPPING ISO 31000 AND ISO 27001 TO IMS PROCEDURES

ISO 31000 section	Control	Procedure(s)	ISO 27001 section
3	Principles	Section 5.3	
4	Framework	Section 5.2	
4.1	General		
4.2	Mandate and commitment	Chapter 4, Section 4.3 Section 5.4.1	5.1
4.3	Design of framework for managing risk	Sections 5.5.2–5.5.7	4.2.1 c)
4.3.1	Understanding of the organization and its context	Sections 5.3.2, 5.6.1–5.6.3, and Appendix 11	4.2.1 a)
4.3.2	Establishing risk management policy	Appendix 10	
4.3.3	Accountability	Section 5.3.3.2 and 5.4.3 Chapter 12, Section 12.2.1	5
4.3.4	Integration into organizational processes	The IMS and the IMS as a whole	
4.3.5	Resources	Chapter 4, Section 4.6.3 Sections 4.3 and 4.4	5.2
4.3.6	Establishing internal communication and reporting mechanisms	Section 5.3.4 and 5.5	5.2.2
4.3.7	Establishing external communication and reporting mechanisms	Sections 5.3.4 and 5.5	5.2.2
4.4	Implementing risk management	Sections 5.3–5.7	4.2.1 d)-g)
4.4.1	Implementing the framework for managing risk	Section 5.6	4.2.1 d)-g)
4.4.2	Implementing the risk management process	Section 5.5	4.2.1 d)-g)
4.5	Monitoring and review of the framework	Section 5.6	6
4.6	Continual improvement of the framework	Chapter 4, Section 4.8	8
5	Process		
5.1	General		
5.2	Communication and consultation	Sections 5.3.4 and 5.4.5	5.2.2
5.3	Establishing the context	Sections 5.3.2, 5.6.1–5.6.3	4.2.1 a)
5.3.1	General		
5.3.2	Establishing the external context	Section 5.5.6.1 and Appendix 11	4.2.1 a)
5.3.3	Establishing the internal context	Section 5.5.6.2 and Appendix 11	4.2.1 a)
5.3.4	Establishing the context of the risk management process	Section 5.5.6.3	4.2.1 d)-g)
5.3.5	Defining risk criteria	Section 5.5.6.4	4.2.1 d)-g)
5.4	Risk assessment	Section 5.7	4.2.1 d)-g)
5.4.1	General		
5.4.2	Risk identification	Section 5.5.7.1	4.2.1 d)
5.4.3	Risk analysis	Section 5.5.7.2	4.2.1 e)
5.4.4	Risk evaluation	Section 5.5.7.4	4.2.1 e)
5.5	Risk treatment	Sections 5.5.9 and 5.6	4.2.1 f) and g)

Continued

ISO 31000 section	Control	Procedure(s)	ISO 27001 section
5.5.1	General		
5.5.2	Selection of risk treatment options	Sections 5.5.9 and 5.6	4.2.1 f) and g)
5.5.3	Preparing and implementing risk treatment plans	Section 5.6.1	4.2.2 a) and 4.2.2 b)
5.6	Monitoring and review	Chapter 4, Sections 4.7, 4.8, and 4.9 Sections 5.7 and 5.7.1.5 specifically	6, 7 and 8
5.7	Recording the risk management process	Chapter 4, Section 4.6.4 Section 5.5.12	4.3.3

Chapter 6

Quality in the Forensic Laboratory

Table of Contents

6.1 QUALITY AND GOOD LABORATORY PRACTICE

Every forensic laboratory, in every discipline, throughout the world should strive to achieve good practice and meet, or preferably exceed, their Client's expectations by producing a quality product or service.

To achieve this, a number of organizations have produced good guidance documentation (guidance, standards, or procedures) for advising a forensic laboratory how to achieve this. A number of these are general in their nature and some are sector specific. Some of the general ones are applicable to all forensic laboratories, and these include:

- ISO 9000—Quality Management Systems series;
- ISO 17025—General requirements for the competence of testing and calibration laboratories.

Others are specifically defined for digital forensic laboratories, and some of these include:

- Scientific Working Group on Digital Evidence (SWGDE), Quality Assurance and Standard Operating Procedures Manual, Version 3, 2012;
- NIST Handbook 150, National Voluntary Laboratory Accreditation program, Procedures and General Requirements, 2006;
- European Network of Forensic Science Institutes (ENFSI) Guidelines for Best Practice in the Forensic Examination of Digital Technology, Version 6, 2009;
- UK Forensic Science Regulator (FSR), Codes of Practice and Conduct for forensic science providers and practitioners in the Criminal Justice System, Version 1, December 2011.[a]

As can be imagined, there is a large degree of overlap between these documents.

This chapter concentrates on the requirements of ISO 9001 Certification as achieved by the Forensic Laboratory and the requirements for ISO 17025 accreditation. The mapping of ISO 17025 requirements to the procedures in the Forensic Laboratory IMS is given in Appendix 1, with the mapping of ISO 17025 requirements to the procedures in the Forensic Laboratory IMS given in Appendix 2.

The specific requirements of SWGDE, NIST, ENFSI, and the FSR relating to quality processes in the Forensic Laboratory have been mapped to the Forensic Laboratory's IMS procedures in Appendices 3, 4, 5, and 6, respectively.

6.2 MANAGEMENT REQUIREMENTS FOR OPERATING THE FORENSIC LABORATORY

Having physically set up the Forensic Laboratory as defined in Chapters 2 and 3, it is necessary to implement number of management processes. Some of these relate to quality processes, some to gaining and maintaining Accreditation and Certification, and others to everyday operation of the Forensic Laboratory. This is not meant to be a primer on running a business but to identify some issues relevant to the Forensic Laboratory.

6.2.1 Forensic Laboratory Organization

6.2.1.1 Legal Status

The Forensic Laboratory will be set up according to its own requirements and in line with the legal requirements of the jurisdiction(s) in which it operates. This will ensure that it is a "legal person" within the jurisdiction(s) of operations and can be legally responsible for its actions.

The Forensic Laboratory is an independent forensic laboratory processing digital evidence to resolve Client's evidential requirements on a commercial basis.

6.2.1.2 Ownership

The ownership of the Forensic Laboratory shall be clearly defined and made public, if required, for the jurisdiction(s) where it operates. The shareholder details are recorded in the relevant business register.

If the Forensic Laboratory is part of a larger organization, then this should be clearly stated and the whole organizational structure be clearly documented. This will include the organizational structure of the Forensic Laboratory, its position in the parent organization's structure, and all relationships between other parts of the organization, including operations, support, and management.

Where the Forensic Laboratory is part of a larger organization that performs activities other than digital forensic services, the clear delineations of roles and responsibilities must be clearly defined so that any potential conflicts of interest may be identified and addressed at the earliest possible opportunity. No employee of any other part of the organization should be able to exert any undue influence on the Forensic Laboratory, its employees, or Clients.

6.2.1.3 Organization

While the actual Forensic Laboratory organization chart is not reproduced (see comment in Chapter 4, Section 4.5.5), a generic forensic laboratory organizational chart is shown below (Figure 6.1):

Details of the Management System Committees are given in Chapter 4, Section 4.4.3 and their Terms of Reference in Chapter 4, Appendices 27-34.

6.2.1.4 Job Descriptions

Within the Forensic Laboratory, all jobs have defined general job descriptions as defined by the Human Resources Department in Chapter 18, Section 18.1.5.

Top Management shall appoint a Quality Manager who has appropriate authority and responsibility to carry out their duties and to ensure that the Forensic Laboratory's quality system is implemented, monitored, and continuously improved.

The Quality Manager's job description is given in Appendix 7. There are a number of specialist roles that have detailed job descriptions relevant to the IMS (e.g., Health and Safety, Information Security, Service Delivery, Change Management, etc.), and these are given in the relevant chapters in the rest of the book.

a. While this has been published, the guidance is generic and the "Digital Data Recovery" standards to be available in October 2015. However, the generic requirements exist.

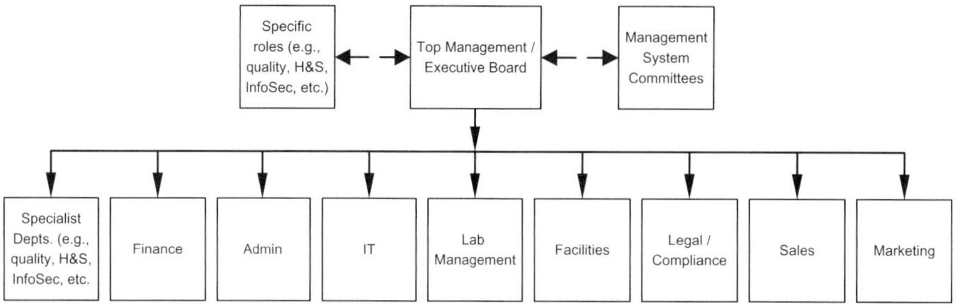

FIGURE 6.1 Generic Forensic Laboratory Organization.

Note

Depending on the size of the forensic laboratory, full-time appointees to these specialized roles may not be possible in a small- to medium-sized laboratory. In this case, it may be necessary to have a single employee undertake a number of roles, so long as segregation of duties can be maintained as far as possible, as defined in Chapter 12, Section 12.3.5 and 12.3.6. In a large laboratory, deputies for these roles should be appointed.

6.2.1.5 Authorities and Responsibilities

It is the Forensic Laboratory's duty to meet all legislative, regulatory, and other relevant requirements. "Other relevant requirements" include requirements of such organizations as Certification Bodies, Accreditation Bodies, professional bodies, etc.

Specific authorities, responsibilities, reporting procedures, and taskings for all employees are contained in their job descriptions. Those that are relevant to the IMS are given in this book, while generic job descriptions are the remit of the Human Resources Department and relevant Line Managers.

6.2.1.6 Impartiality and Independence

Impartiality and independence have been mentioned in Chapter 3, Section 3.1.5; however, if the Forensic Laboratory is part of a larger organization, it may have problems demonstrating this to any third party. To demonstrate this and that its employees are free from any undue commercial, financial, and other influences which might affect their technical judgment, the Conflict of Interest Policy has been introduced, as defined in Section 3.1.3.16 and Appendix 3 of Chapter 3.

While the Conflict of Interest Policy primarily applies to individuals, Top Management must ensure that the Forensic Laboratory does not undertake any work that may endanger the Client and public trust in its perceived impartiality, independence, and integrity in relation to its provision of digital forensic services.

6.2.1.7 Finances

The Forensic Laboratory must ensure that its accounting and financial procedures meet the requirements of the jurisdiction. Appropriate reporting and public disclosure must be implemented.

6.2.1.8 Insurance

The provision of appropriate insurance cover has been covered in Chapter 3, Section 3.14.

6.2.1.9 Accreditation and Certification

Accreditation for the Forensic Laboratory is covered in Chapter 3, Section 3.18, and the relevant chapters in the book specific to the relevant accreditations and certifications that the Forensic Laboratory wishes to achieve.

Mappings between the requirements of the relevant standards to the procedures in the IMS are also given in the relevant chapters in the book. This will assist any forensic laboratory to choose those that are relevant to their business model and implement the relevant procedures. The structure of the book is such that each Accreditation and Certification will stand on its own in a chapter but may require procedures from other chapters (or management systems) where there is an overlap (e.g., Chapter 4, which has many procedures common to all management standards).

6.2.2 Operations

6.2.2.1 Business Planning Within the Forensic Laboratory

The main planning tool is the Forensic Laboratory's business plan, and the template that the Forensic Laboratory uses for all business plans is given in Appendix 8.

Reviews of the plan are performed on a regular basis by Top Management, generally as follows:

- a monthly review of the business, financial and case processing metrics, and key performance indicators (KPIs) to check whether the business is performing in line with

expectations. The business KPIs are given in Appendix 9, the Quality KPIs are integrated with the Information Security ones and are given in Chapter 5, Appendix 22, and case processing KPIs are given in Chapter 16, Section 16.2.2;
- a yearly review of the entire business plan to assess the state of the Forensic Laboratory and to plan for the next financial year—this involves reviewing the services, market, financial forecasts, and resources and then generating a new or revised plan. This is typically carried out as part of the Management Review.

6.2.2.2 *Managing the Forensic Laboratory*

The Forensic Laboratory operates in an effective and efficient manner by following the processes and procedures embedded in the IMS and ensuring that all employees are aware of their responsibilities and the opportunities available. Employee meetings within departments occur on a regular and frequent basis to discuss, as applicable to each department, the following types of matters:

- development of the business—financial performance, Client news, new business, etc.;
- cases—progress on cases, problems encountered, timescales, changes to requirements, new possibilities, meetings arranged, etc.;
- design developments—new ways of working to improve the levels of service to Clients including new methodologies and tools, new or revised standards, training opportunities, technological developments in the field, etc.

Formal meetings all have agendas and are minuted, and their minutes kept as records in the IMS as defined in Chapter 4, Section 4.6.4.

Some information exchange also occurs on an informal basis through informal meetings, telephone conversations, and e-mail between individuals and is not always formally documented.

At the end of each case, a formal audit is performed on the case that covers the business and technical aspects of the case and the training and development aspects of the employees involved in the project. Any gaps or areas where improvements could be obtained, such as a change in a procedure, additional employee training, additional tools, or any other relevant matter, are assessed and appropriate action is taken. This is defined in Chapter 4, Section 4.7, and the results are fed into the continuous improvement process defined in Chapter 4, Section 4.8.

6.2.2.3 *Service to Clients*

The Forensic Laboratory's raison d'être is to provide digital forensic products and services to its Clients in line with the requirements of its Accreditation(s), Certification(s), and in-house procedures defined in the IMS. It is the Forensic Laboratory's responsibility to ensure that *all* products and services supplied to the Client satisfy legislative, regulatory, Accreditation Body, Certification Body, as well as in-house requirements. Meeting legal Client requirements is a primary goal for the Forensic Laboratory.

6.2.2.4 *Management System (The IMS)*

The IMS covers all activities carried out by the Forensic Laboratory, wherever they may be performed (the office, Client site, scene of crime, or other locations, as appropriate). The IMS is a "one stop shop" for all policies, processes, procedures, work instructions, forms, and checklists used in the Forensic Laboratory. Regular training and updating of all employees on its contents are undertaken and records of this training is maintained as formal records, as defined in Chapter 18, Section 18.2.1.8.

6.2.2.5 *Applicability of the IMS*

The IMS shall apply to all employees for all tasks performed by the Forensic Laboratory in the provision of products and services to their Clients.

6.2.2.6 *Confidentiality of Information*

The Forensic Laboratory shall ensure the confidentiality of all information entrusted to it (either its own information or information trusted to it by a Client or other third party) for the duration it is under the Forensic Laboratory's control. Details of how confidentiality of case files is maintained are given in Section 6.11 and use the processes defined in Chapter 12.

6.3 ISO 9001 FOR THE FORENSIC LABORATORY

6.3.1 Goal

The goal of the Forensic Laboratory is to be known and recognized as a reputable forensic laboratory that is highly regarded for the quality of its products, services, and employee skills by a stable and varied set of Clients. The Forensic Laboratory's goal statement is given in Chapter 4, Appendix 4.

To achieve this, the Forensic Laboratory shall achieve ISO 9001 certification by an Accredited Certification Body.

6.3.2 Quality Policy

The Forensic Laboratory quality policy is given in Chapter 3, Appendix 4. It has been endorsed by Top Management, as have all other management system policies defined in Chapter 4, Section 4.4.1.

6.3.3 Quality Policy Statements

The Forensic Laboratory's Top Management endorses the following quality statements:

- the Forensic Laboratory is committed to good quality working practice in all tasks relating to its products and services for delivery to its Clients;
- all Forensic Laboratory employees must always perform their activities in accordance with policies, procedures, and standards documented in the IMS and to ensure that all the products and services that the Forensic Laboratory meets, and exceed, Client expectations;
- all Forensic Laboratory case processing must meet the requirements of the IMS, be scientifically sound, repeatable, and provide the Client with reliable results;
- all Forensic Laboratory employees shall undergo appropriate training to ensure that they are competent to perform their tasks, as appropriate;
- the Forensic Laboratory commits to meet the requirements of the relevant Accreditation Bodies, Certification Bodies, and other relevant professional organizations;
- quality in the Forensic Laboratory shall be measured by "KPIs" (designated as Quality Objectives) which Forensic Laboratory management review and set each year to ensure that all employees attain quality standards, and to ensure continuous improvement of the Forensic Laboratory's quality and other objectives. The Forensic Laboratory "KPIs" are defined in Section 6.2.2.1;
- all Forensic Laboratory employees shall ensure that they are familiar with those aspects of the Forensic Laboratory's policies and procedures in the IMS that relate to their day-to-day work;
- the Forensic Laboratory is committed to a process of continuous improvement in all of its products and services as defined in Chapter 4, Section 4.8;
- quality is the responsibility of all Forensic Laboratory employees.

6.3.4 Scope of the Quality Management System

The Quality Management System (QMS) is a part of the IMS and they share a common scope which is defined in Chapter 5, Appendix 11. This also includes the scope statement for all of the management standards that are Certified or Accredited.

6.3.5 Using a Client's QMS

The Forensic Laboratory may occasionally be required to use and conform to a Client's QMS and procedures as a condition of performing work for that Client.

The Forensic Laboratory's QMS may not match the Client's QMS, in a number of areas. In the event that a situation such as this arises, the Forensic Laboratory shall attempt to conform to as much as possible to their own QMS within the constraints imposed upon them by the Client's QMS, as appropriate.

Ideally, at the proposal stage of work with a Client, the Forensic Laboratory Client Account Manager shall ascertain whether the Forensic Laboratory's QMS is acceptable to the Client.

If the Client decides not to accept the Forensic Laboratory's QMS and requires that the Forensic Laboratory conforms to its QMS, the Client Account Manager must document and agree to the differences between the Forensic Laboratory's and the Client's QMS and confirm to the Client the following items, in writing:

- those aspects of the Forensic Laboratory QMS that will be followed;
- those aspects of the Client QMS that will be followed;
- areas where no provision is identified or agreed. This may be subject to later agreement and updated documentation.

The Forensic Laboratory will then proceed with the case using the identified "hybrid" QMS.

Top Management may also consider excluding the case from the Forensic Laboratory's QMS.

6.3.6 Benefits to the Forensic Laboratory of ISO 9001 Certification

Some of the benefits that the Forensic Laboratory has determined include:

- allowing the Forensic Laboratory to bid for tenders, contracts, quotations, and proposals, where they may have been precluded by not having Certification;
- communicating a positive message about commitment to quality to employees and Clients;
- constantly monitoring quality of products and services;
- defining quality responsibilities throughout the whole of the Forensic Laboratory;
- enhancing image and reputation of the Forensic Laboratory's products and services;
- having an independent audit by an Accredited Certification Body demonstrates commitment to quality pro cesses and continuous improvement;
- having well-defined and documented procedures improves the consistency of products and services delivered to Clients;
- identifying non-conforming products and services early in the production cycle and continuously improving production processes to address failures;
- improving efficiency;
- improving employee attitudes to "right, first time, every time";
- improving focus on Client needs;

- international acceptability;
- lessening reliance on key individuals by having processes all documented as well as facilitating new employee take on;
- moving the Forensic Laboratory from being in "detection mode" to "prevention mode";
- providing a basis for adding new management systems to the IMS as the QMS models the business processes and is the ideal start point;
- providing a competitive edge for marketing by demonstrable Certification to ISO 9001;
- providing consistent training for all employees;
- providing continuous assessment and improvement;
- providing Top Management with an efficient management process and improved business oversight;
- proving marketing opportunities;
- reducing costs;
- reducing waste and rework, as Client requirements are confirmed and there is continuous Client communication in place.

6.4 THE FORENSIC LABORATORY'S QMS

The Forensic Laboratory must establish, document, implement, and maintain a QMS as part of its IMS. This QMS, like the other management systems in the IMS, shares a common set of procedures for a number of requirements, as covered in Chapter 4.

The Forensic Laboratory must:

- identify the business processes to be included in the QMS;
- identify the sequence and interaction of these processes;
- determine criteria and methods needed to ensure that the operation and control of these processes is, and remains, effective;
- document appropriate policies and procedures to ensure that all products and services are delivered to meet, and exceed Client expectations and all external drivers;
- ensure that management responsibilities to establish, document, implement, and maintain the QMS exist and are effective, as defined in Section 6.5;
- ensure the availability of resources and information necessary for the operation and monitoring of these processes. Management of resources is covered in Chapter 4, Section 4.6.2;
- undertake regular audits of the QMS as defined in Chapter 4, Section 4.7.3;
- undertake Management Reviews on a regular basis as defined in Chapter 4, Section 4.9;
- implement actions necessary for continuous improvement of these processes, as defined in Chapter 4, Section 4.8.

Note 1

Where the Forensic Laboratory outsources services to third party, the Forensic Laboratory must ensure that the outsourcing supplier complies with the requirements of the IMS and that it maintains control over the provision of these products and services as defined in Chapters 14 and 16.

Note 2

The Forensic Laboratory developed its original Quality Plan in 2003 for the original requirements for a QMS. The QMS was the first management standard to be implemented and since then, the IMS has grown, but this plan is still appropriate and demonstrates the original requirements. The outline for the plan is given in Appendix 10.

6.5 RESPONSIBILITIES IN THE QMS

There are a number of specific responsibilities within the Forensic Laboratory QMS for Forensic Laboratory Top Management and all employees, these include:

The Forensic Laboratory is committed to ensuring that all of their products and services are of a suitable quality for both internal and external Clients and that:

- this requirement has been communicated to all employees as defined in Chapter 4, Section 4.6.5 and forms part of the induction process for all new employees. The induction checklist is given in Appendix 11;
- the Forensic Laboratory has developed and implemented a Quality Policy which is also included in the induction process as defined in Chapter 3, Appendix 4;
- regular Management Reviews are carried out for the QMS as part of the IMS Management Review process, as defined in Chapter 4, Section 4.9;
- the Forensic Laboratory has ensured that appropriate resources are available for the efficient and effective operation and management of this IMS and specifically the QMS, as defined in Section 6.5 and Chapter 4, Section 4.6.2;
- the Forensic Laboratory has ensured that a Quality Manager has been appointed and trained and whose job description is defined in Appendix 7;
- the Forensic Laboratory ensures that up-to-date QMS procedures are present for all processes covered by the IMS;
- regular audits are undertaken as part of the continuous improvement process for this IMS as defined in Chapter 4, Section 4.7.3 and specifically for case processing in Section 6.13.3.

The Forensic Laboratory products and services are always Client focused whether they are internal or external to the Forensic Laboratory. To ensure that this is the case, the following processes are implemented in the Forensic Laboratory:

- the Client requirements are carefully collated and documented as part of the sales cycle as defined in Section 6.6;
- these requirements are captured in the Forensic Laboratory proposal to the Client. The table of contents of a standard Forensic Laboratory proposal are given in Appendix 13;
- when the proposal has been internally reviewed, it is reviewed with the Client to ensure that it meets their requirements and where necessary, it is amended and approved prior to formal release to the Client by the Forensic Laboratory.

Note 1

In some cases, just a quotation is required for a job (typically, this is where a contractual business relationship already exists between the Client and the Forensic Laboratory and the Client requires a quotation for a single case). The table of contents of a standard Forensic Laboratory quotation for processing a case is given in Appendix 15.

Note 2

The standard Forensic Laboratory Terms and Conditions are given in Appendix 16.

The Forensic Laboratory shall develop and implement a quality management policy, as defined in Chapter 3, Appendix 4 that is appropriate to its business that:

- has been endorsed by Top Management;
- the supporting QMS is continuously monitored and improved as part of the IMS performance assessment as defined in Section 6.13 and Chapter 4, Section 4.7, as well as the continuous improvement process defined in Chapter 4, Section 4.8;
- provides a framework to establish and review the Forensic Laboratory KPIs (quality objectives). Details of the Forensic Laboratory KPIs are given in Appendix 9;
- is communicated to all employees as part of their induction process, the checklist for which is given in Appendix 11;
- is regularly reviewed during the Management Review process for continued suitability within the Forensic Laboratory as defined in Chapter 4, Section 4.9 and Chapter 4, Appendix 36.

The Forensic Laboratory will plan and define its QMS so that it is appropriate to the way that Top Management operates the Forensic Laboratory, this includes:

- ensuring all changes to the IMS and specifically the QMS are subject to the Forensic Laboratory Change Management System as defined in Chapter 7, Section 7.4.1;
- ensuring all changes to the IMS and specifically the QMS are communicated appropriately to all employees as described in Chapter 4, Section 4.6.5.

The Forensic Laboratory must define responsibilities within the organization and these will be documented in:

- the IMS scope statement (at a high level) (Chapter 5, Appendix 11);
- defined job descriptions for all employees (Chapter 18, Section 18.1.5);
- the appointment of a Quality Manager with defined responsibilities and authority (Appendix 7);
- the ongoing internal audit process (Chapter 4, Section 4.7.3, and specifically Section 6.13.3, for auditing case processing);
- the Management Review process (Chapter 4, Section 4.9);
- the continuous improvement process (Chapter 4, Section 4.8);
- the internal communication process (Chapter 4, Section 4.6.5).

The Forensic Laboratory has provided appropriate resources to implement, operate, manage, and monitor their QMS. This is evidenced by:

- managing the resources available in the optimal manner to support the QMS as defined in Chapter 4, Section 4.6.2;
- appointing employees to specific roles and documenting these in their job descriptions as defined in Chapter 18, Section 18.1.5;
- regularly auditing the QMS as defined in Chapter 4, Section 4.7.3 and specifically Section 6.13.3 for auditing case processing;
- undertaking regular Management Reviews of the QMS as defined in Chapter 4, Section 4.9;
- enhances Client satisfaction by ensuring that proposals, products, and services meet, and hopefully exceed, the Client's expectation;
- obtains, where appropriate and possible, feedback on work performed for Clients using the case feedback process defined in Chapter 9, Section 9.6.9;
- takes action on any Client complaints to ensure continuous improvement as defined in Sections 6.14.

6.6 MANAGING SALES

The sales cycle is essential to the Forensic Laboratory and is the start of the "Client Engagement" process. This covers two specific situations:

- new business;
- repeat business.

In the Forensic Laboratory, new business is where a new Client is taken on for forensic case work and requires the "full treatment" including marketing material and a formal proposal as defined in Appendix 13. While basic details about the Forensic Laboratory are supplied to a prospective Client either as part of a marketing campaign or with a proposal, a Client may request additional details. The details are given in Section 6.2.1, assuming they contain no confidential information that should be supplied to the Client, as well as any references to support the quality of the products and services they provide that are relevant to the prospective Client.

Repeat business is where an existing Client is already under a blanket contract and requires one or more additional cases processed.

6.6.1 Handling a Sales Enquiry

A contact from an existing or potential new Client is received from the following source (Figure 6.2):

- telephone;
- post;
- e-mail;
- face to face at a conference or similar.

All contact from existing Clients is handled by the Forensic Laboratory Account Manager who currently services their needs.

Prospective new Clients are handled by a Forensic Laboratory Account Manager with the appropriate skill set or experience. This contact establishes the Client's:

- name;
- job title;
- company name;
- telephone number;
- e-mail address;
- initial work requirements;
- timescales.

Initial work requirements are only ever accepted as required outcomes rather than a series of prescribed set of tasks that may not agree with the Forensic Laboratory's in-house procedures, methodologies, or approach. Some issues to consider when taking on a case for a new or existing Client are given in Appendix 14.

Whenever a query from a potential Client is received by the Forensic Laboratory, the objective is to secure a meeting

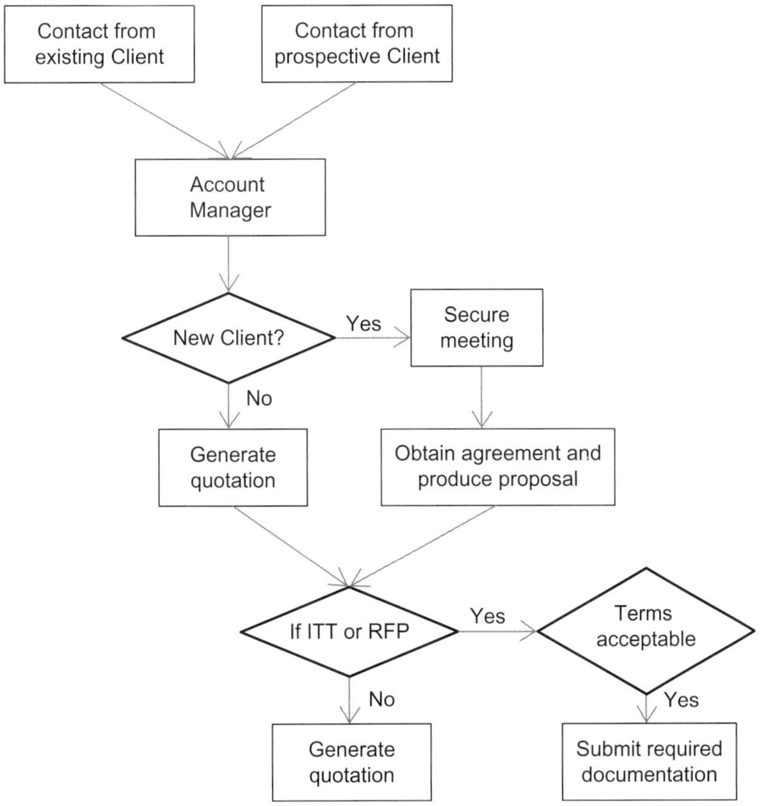

FIGURE 6.2 Handling a sales enquiry.

where the proposed work is discussed and the result of the meeting is to obtain go-ahead for the presentation of a proposal.

Where an existing Client requires additional work and is subject to an existing contract, a quotation is usually given to the Client for their consideration, as defined in Appendix 15.

The Forensic Laboratory may well be invited to bid on a contract (e.g., an invitation to tender, request for proposal, or similar). In these situations, the Forensic Laboratory must make a decision whether it wants to proceed according to the terms set. If it does, then it shall submit the relevant documentation required.

6.6.2 A New Client

6.6.2.1 Attending an Initial Meeting for a New Client

The relevant Forensic Laboratory Account Manager, with other Forensic Laboratory employees, as appropriate, attend an initial meeting with the potential Client.

At the meeting, the Forensic Laboratory work methods are described, the skills that the Forensic Laboratory can bring to the Client are outlined, and the conclusion of the meeting is to determine how to proceed with the proposed work. Agreement will be reached on the next step and when contact will be made between the parties again.

The Account Manager writes to the potential Client within five working days of the meeting, summarizing the discussions and highlighting the actions they should now take and the next steps that were agreed at the meeting.

6.6.2.2 Setting up a Client Virtual File

Where a meeting with a potential Client is to be attended, records of this must be retained. These will be stored in the Client's virtual file, which is set up at this point. Assuming the proposed work goes ahead, the Client's virtual file contains all documentation relating to the Client's relationship with the Forensic Laboratory. If the proposed work does not proceed, then the Client virtual file is filed with other "Failed Proposals," in case of later need. To set up a Client's virtual file (Figure 6.3):

1. The Account Manager creates a folder on the relevant area of the server in the Electronic Records Management System (ERMS). This will contain all documentation relating to the Client. There are four different areas for Client matters in the ERMS; these are defined in Appendix 17.
2. The Account Manager follows up as required until notification of the Client's decision is received.
3. If a positive response is received from the Client, the Account Manager moves the Client's virtual file into the "current" area.

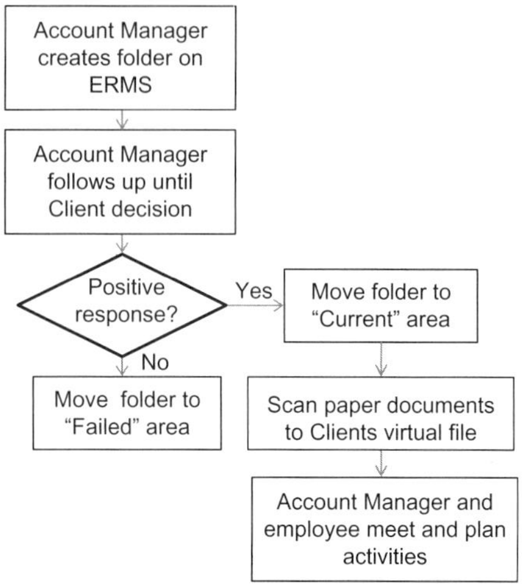

FIGURE 6.3 Setting up a Client virtual file.

4. Any paper correspondence and notes made are then scanned into the Client virtual file. The paper documents are shredded and then disposed of appropriately.
5. The Account Manager and any other relevant Forensic Laboratory employees meet to discuss the project and plan the production of a proposal to scope the work.
6. On many occasions, an order for work will initially be a verbal request that is followed later by written confirmation.
7. If a negative response is received from the prospective Client, the Account Manager moves the Client's virtual file to the "failed" area and calls a meeting with the relevant Forensic Laboratory employees to determine the reasons for the negative response and how to improve the sales process from the lessons learned. Any outcomes from this meeting are formally recorded as records and filed in the Client's virtual file. Any paper correspondence and notes made are then scanned into the Client virtual file. The paper documents are shredded and then disposed of appropriately.

6.6.2.3 The Proposal Creation Life Cycle

A proposal is typically produced for requested work for a new Client. The proposal is a thorough scoping exercise which typically includes a detailed fixed-price cost based upon an agreed set of deliverables required, although "time and materials" based cases may be undertaken.

Note 1

There are circumstances when a proposal is not produced for a Client, for example, a letter may be produced that details costs that is subsequently used as the basis for a project or a quotation for a case is requested.

Note 2

Within the Forensic Laboratory, all documents, including proposals, follow the document control process in Chapter 4, Section 4.6.3.3. In the case of the production of a proposal, the Account Manager is the Document Owner, may be the Document Author, or may appoint one.

The responsibilities for producing the proposal lie with the Client's Account Manager. The proposal production process is shown below.

6.6.2.3.1 Planning for the Information Gathering Meeting

Ideally, a clarification or information gathering meeting between the prospective Client and the Forensic Laboratory takes place. This will be attended by the Account Manager and such other employees, as appropriate.

An internal information gathering meeting is the first stage in this process. It is therefore important that the Document Author checks all information about the Client before the meeting so that pertinent questions can be asked. The steps for gathering information for the meeting are:

- gather all relevant information from the original sales meeting and other meetings with the Client;
- research past cases with similar content or structure, and review the methods used and work produced for these;
- if appropriate, prepare a list of questions for the information gathering meeting;
- collect items to take to the information gathering meeting, such as samples, brochures, case studies, white papers, etc.

Note

As early as possible (at least two working days) before an information gathering meeting, the Account Manager and the Forensic Laboratory Manager should discuss and agree the objective of the meeting and any additional issues.

6.6.2.3.2 Attending an Information Gathering Meeting

The Account Manager attends the information gathering meeting with any other appropriate employees. Every meeting is different, but there are always the following stages:

- introduction session with the Client staff;
- confirmation of the plans and objectives of the meeting;
- information gathering session that typically includes:
  - interviewing Client staff;
  - reading Client documents;
  - presentations from Client staff;
  - shadowing Client staff.
- closing session with the Client staff.

During the information gathering, it is essential that the Account Manager:

- projects a professional image;
- demonstrates that the Forensic Laboratory has the relevant expertise—discuss examples of past work;
- obtains a walk-through of the case—from which the work is scoped;
- understands the case and requirements fully—so that accurate time and cost estimates can be produced;
- covers all relevant topics—referring to their question list;
- takes full notes—to help when writing the proposal.

Note

When discussing past Clients, ensure that the existing confidentiality agreements in force are not breached.

The Account Manager should arrange a date for when the proposal is reviewed with the Client. This is typically 1-2 weeks after the submission of the proposal.

6.6.2.3.3 Writing the First Draft of the Proposal

Unless they are the same person, the Document Author and the Account Manager meet to discuss the proposed content of the proposal following the information gathering meeting. At this meeting, they must ensure they agree on the:

- deliverables to be produced;
- sections to include in the proposal;
- approach for the case;
- timescales for the case (the Turn Round Time required).

To save time, the Document Author normally bases a proposal on a previous one. To do this, the Document Author selects a previous proposal on which the current one can be based. The Document Author may need to look through all Client virtual files in the ERMS to find a similar proposal. The Document Author should select one that is fairly recent (within a year) that reflects any new developments in work practice, including any lessons learned if a proposal from the "Failed" area is chosen.

The Document Author makes a copy of a proposal from the relevant Client virtual file or creates a new one using the Forensic Laboratory proposal template. The usual tool for writing a proposal is Microsoft Word. The new proposal is saved into the new Client virtual file. If the Document Author uses an existing proposal on which to base the new one, then all references to the original recipient of the proposal must be removed. Just using the "search and replace" function in a word processor is not enough to perform this task. They must perform this task manually and remove all references to the original recipient of any type that exist. It is for this reason that it is preferred that the proposal template is used rather than editing an existing one, but time pressures do not always allow this. They should check for references in:

- all the text;
- document properties;
- headers and footers;
- information on any sample screen shots;
- metadata in the document;
- text on diagrams;
- text on flowcharts.

The Document Author writes the proposal and:

- pays close attention to their notes from the information gathering meeting;
- is not tempted to include text from the copied proposal if it is not absolutely relevant;
- is not afraid to vary the proposal headings in the template, given in Appendix 13, if necessary—the proposal must be adapted to address the Client's concerns and requirements;
- estimates the time and cost of the case. Costs are calculated according to the number of days required per deliverable, as well as materials required based upon past experience. To assist in this, a case costing spreadsheet is used as defined in Appendix 18. These may be confirmed by the Forensic Laboratory Manager;
- follows the Forensic Laboratory document control requirements defined in Chapter 4, Section 4.6.3 and the proposal template given in Appendix 13.

6.6.2.3.4 Internally Reviewing the Proposal

1. The Forensic Laboratory Manager reviews the proposal and provides comment on the changes as required. Particular attention must be made to the project costs. All comments are stored in the Client virtual file in the ERMS (Figure 6.4).
2. The Document Author checks all comments received and judges which comments to implement. The Document Author consults the Account Manager and/or Laboratory Manager when in doubt as to the validity of comments and asks for explanations of these comments.
3. The Document Author amends the proposal in accordance with the Writing and Updating Documents procedures in Chapter 4, Section 4.6.3.4.
4. The Account Manager double-checks the proposal to ensure that edits have been implemented correctly and that no new errors have been introduced. This is the version to be issued to the Client for review.
5. If a hard copy is required, then the Document Author prints two copies of the proposal:
   - one for the Client;
   - one for the Forensic Laboratory.
6. If a soft copy is to be sent to the Client, then it should be converted to "secured" PDF format and sent by e-mail with a receipt request.

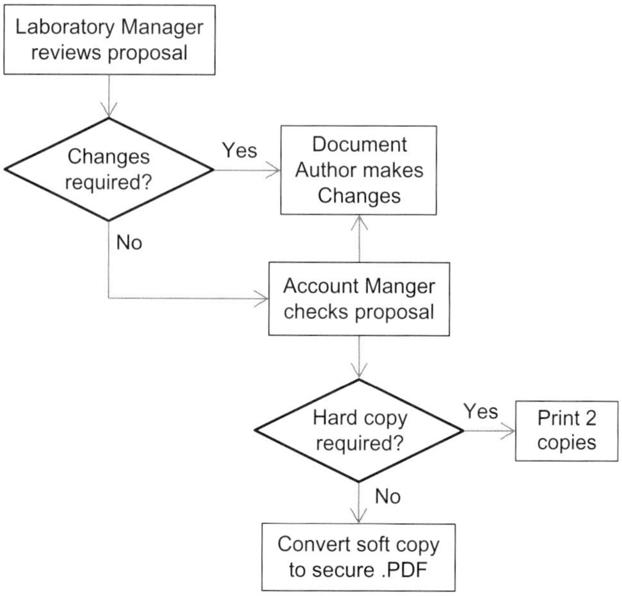

FIGURE 6.4 Internally reviewing the Proposal.

7. Depending on the information classification of the proposal, as defined in Chapter 5, Appendix 16, appropriate means of protection of the proposal shall be applied according to the controls defined in Chapter 12, Section 12.3.14.

> **Note**
>
> Extra copies can, of course, be produced if necessary. The Client can circulate their copy of the proposal if additional people need to see it at the Client site, but the Forensic Laboratory has no control over this process.

6.6.2.3.5 Issuing the Proposal

The Document Author writes to the Client enclosing the proposal. The normal delivery method is post, but if time is short and it is essential that the proposal arrives on the following day, it can be sent by courier, be faxed, or e-mailed.

The method of transmission must also ensure that data handling procedures for the classification for the proposal are met, as defined in Chapter 12, Section 12.3.14.

6.6.2.4 The Proposal Review Life Cycle

> **Note**
>
> For simplicity, the Forensic Laboratory "team" attending the review have been referred to as the "Document Author" irrespective of who actually attends.

Once a proposal has been produced and sent to a Client, the Document Author liaises with the Client to discuss it and to arrange a review of the proposal.

It is not always required to hold a formal review meeting with a Client to discuss a proposal. Sometimes, a telephone call or an e-mail can suffice, particularly when the work required is straightforward. In all cases, however, the proposal is discussed with the Client.

The responsibilities for planning and holding a plan review with a Client lie with the Account Manager. It may well be that the Forensic Laboratory Manager or another employee attends the review process with the Document Author.

6.6.2.4.1 Planning the Review

The Document Author's major objectives of the review are to agree with the Client regarding the:

- deliverables covered in the proposal;
- production schedule for the deliverables;
- costs, including a payment schedule;
- start date for the case.

The Document Author must ask the Client to confirm any order in writing and send a purchase order for the case. It is vital that the Document Author conducts successful plan reviews since the meeting agrees production details for the subsequent case.

6.6.2.4.2 Reviewing the Proposal with the Client

The Client reviews their copy of the proposal sent by the Document Author. This may be a meeting, or can be telephone or e-mail based.

The Document Author answers any Client questions on the proposal and resolves any issues that remain. Any negotiations on cost and content of the work usually take place at this stage. The Document Author must take full notes to ensure that an updated proposal can be produced after the meeting that contains all the necessary information and reflects the Client's view. The notes are added to the Client virtual file in the ERMS.

The proposal is updated as required.

6.6.2.4.3 Approving the Case

If the Client is proceeding with the case, the Document Author must arrange the following:

- confirmation from the Client of the case going ahead, preferably with a purchase order or at least with a letter of intent;
- a case start date when the work can begin;
- the signing of the contract;
- updated proposal, if required.

Under no circumstances can work on the case be started until a signed contract is received from the Client by the Forensic Laboratory. This is to ensure that Professional Indemnity insurance applies to all work performed.

6.6.2.4.4 Following up the Review

The Document Author must confirm in writing to the Client the outcome of the review:

- if the project is going ahead as planned—confirm the start date, costs, and what the Client can expect to happen next;
- if the project is not going ahead—confirm the outcome of the meeting and arrange any follow-up meetings as necessary, including moving the virtual client file to "Failed Proposals";
- if the project is not going ahead, the Document Author (and any other stakeholders) must hold a debrief to determine the cause of the failure to proceed and promulgate any lessons learned for future sales;
- if there is another way forward—confirm the tasks required on both sides, arrange any follow-up meetings;
- if there are many changes to a plan, the Document Author updates the proposal and the Account Manager checks that the proposal has been updated as required. The review processes have been used, note must be taken of any influencing changes to the proposal.

When signed off by the Client, unless there are further changes to the case, the proposal is the Terms of Reference for the project.

The Document Author sends version V1.0 of the plan, if required, to the Client with a covering letter.

The Document Author files all documentation relating to the proposal in the Client virtual file in the ERMS.

The next stage in the project lifecycle is for work to begin on the project.

6.6.3 An Existing Client

Where the Client is already an existing one, the same process is followed as above, if an existing contract does not exit.

If it exists, the quotation route is followed, with a new quotation supplied under the existing contract as defined in Appendix 15.

Part of the above process will be carried out by the Account Manager, as appropriate.

6.7 PRODUCT AND SERVICE REALIZATION

Note

ISO 9001 refers to "product realization" as its generic term for deliverables of any sort so the standard can be adopted and adapted universally. This term has been used throughout the book as it is the term used in the standard. Should the Forensic Laboratory undertake any digital services other than case processing, the term "product realization" will still be relevant.

Within ISO 9001, the process of product realization is producing the Forensic Laboratory's products and services for their Clients, (i.e., the results of the case processing carried out by the Forensic Laboratory).

The Forensic Laboratory products and services are usually documents of one type or another and the type of document varies depending on the Client requirements. Due to the varied nature of the cases that the Forensic Laboratory undertake, it is not possible to provide exact procedures for the whole product or service realization process; in some cases, these are only guidelines that need to be interpreted in the context of the specific case. That having been said, there are a number of procedures that can be followed and guidelines interpreted to ensure that product and service realization is effective.

6.7.1 Planning of Product Realization

The Forensic Laboratory's product realization process is the process needed to identify, create, and supply the required product or service (usually a case) to a Client. This is made up of the following processes (Figure 6.5):

- identification of the products and services required by the Forensic Laboratory's Clients during the sales process;
- agreeing the deliverables with the Client in an agreed proposal as defined in Sections 6.6.2.3 and 6.6.2.4;
- confirming the terms and conditions of delivery in a contract for the product or services to be provided as defined in Appendix 16;
- ensuring that the Account Manager and other resources are available to deliver the product or service to the Client, as required;
- ensuring that the relevant Document Authors are aware of the standards for producing documents for delivery to the Client, as defined in Section 6.6.2.3 and Chapter 4, Section 4.6.3.

Typically, all of the Forensic Laboratory cases are split into a number of phases and their inputs, tasks, and outputs defined.

The Forensic Laboratory will then use standard project planning methods to ensure that delivery of the product or service meets the Client's requirements. This typically uses Microsoft Project as a project management tool.

At this stage, the quality assurance and communication process will be agreed in the proposal to the Client by the Quality Manager.

The Forensic Laboratory will keep records of all changes requested to any product or service delivered in the Client virtual file in the ERMS. These must be agreed between the parties in writing.

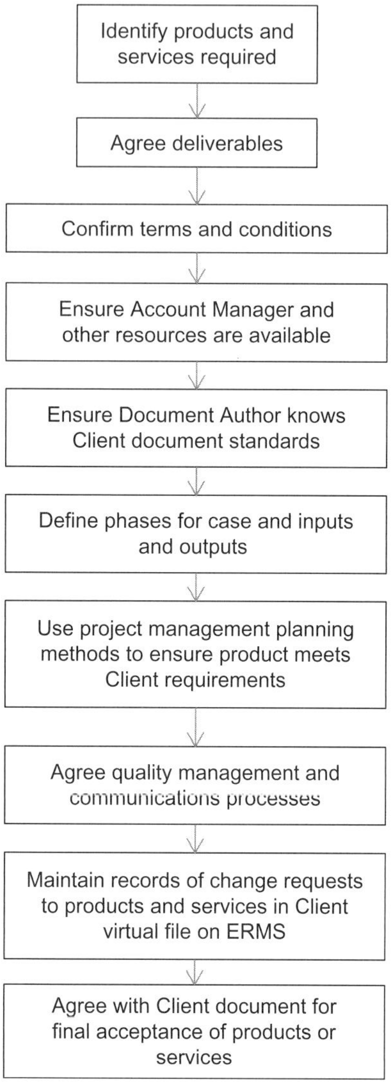

FIGURE 6.5 Planning of product realization.

The Forensic Laboratory will also agree with the Client, as part of the proposal, the documentation for final acceptance of the product or service defined in the proposal. Typically, this is a signed copy of the contract, quotation, or other similar and acceptable document.

6.7.2 Client-Related Processes

The Forensic Laboratory has a number of Client-related processes to ensure that product realization is achieved. These include:

- the production of proposals for internal review, as defined in Section 6.6.2.3.4;
- the Client review of the draft proposal to permits any feedback for amending the proposal to ensure that the proposal meets the Client's requirements, as defined in Section 6.6.2.4;

- knowledge of applicable legislation or regulation applicable to the product or service to be supplied either based on the Client's stated requirements or the Forensic Laboratory's knowledge and experience of similar projects as defined in Chapter 12, Section 12.3.13.1;
- the Forensic Laboratory ensuring that it has resources available to meet the requirements of the Client, as defined in Chapter 4, Section 4.6.2;
- the Forensic Laboratory ensuring that the resources are suitably skilled with appropriate training and competence, as defined in Chapter 4, Section 4.6.2.2;
- ensuring that all documentation (marked-up proposals and draft reviews) are maintained in the Client's virtual file folder in the ERMS, as defined in Chapter 15;
- ensuring that any changes to the requirements are documented and included in the proposal as part of the internal or Client review process, as defined in Sections 6.6.2.3 and 6.6.2.4;
- where changes occur after the project has started to ensure that any changes are catered for in the proposal and/or contract;
- communication with the Client at all relevant stages of the case;
- handling of complaints, as defined in Chapter 14, Section 14.6.14;
- formal sign-off of deliverables, if applicable;
- feedback from the Client, as defined in Chapter 9, Section 9.6.9.

6.7.3 Design and Development

The Forensic Laboratory provides one off solutions to all of its Clients, as each case is different. Each of these is subject to an individual proposal, or where a proposal is already present, a quotation or purchase order for additional cases to be processed. The Forensic Laboratory:

- determines the Client need and articulates it in a proposal, as defined in Section 6.6.2.3;
- reviews the proposal internally prior to submission to the Client, as defined in Section 6.6.2.3.4;
- reviews the proposal with the Client to ensure that the proposal is correct, making amendments where appropriate, as defined in Section 6.6.2.4.2;
- arranges for suitable resources to be available to ensure that the client requirements are met, as defined in Chapter 4, Section 4.6.2;
- must have knowledge of applicable legislation or regulation applicable to the product or service to be supplied either based on the Client's stated requirements or the Forensic Laboratory's knowledge and experience of similar projects;
- ensures that each iteration of the proposal is archived, with documented annotations of changes required.

At the point of product or service planning, changes to documentation, products, or services are not subject to the Forensic Laboratory Change Management Process.

6.7.4 Purchasing

The Forensic Laboratory has excluded general purchases from the scope of their QMS and the IMS generally.

General purchases for Commercial off the Shelf (COTS) items are from suppliers approved by the Finance Department, who maintain a list of approved suppliers.

The use of consumables in the Forensic Laboratory is controlled for their life cycle in forensic case processing, where appropriate (e.g., hard disks and other media used for case processing but not paper and stationery).

All products received in the Forensic Laboratory are checked for appropriateness and that they are fit for purpose, according to the asset management procedures, as defined in Chapter 12, Section 12.3.14. Records of all deliveries and inspection of incoming material shall be retained.

Annual reviews of suppliers are carried out. Key suppliers are subject to second party audits, others may be subject to formal second party audits or informal reviews, as defined in Chapter 14, Section 14.5.1.4. The measure of their acceptance is their continued use.

On occasion, the Forensic Laboratory employs third parties on contract when it has no other skills or the capacity to fulfill a Client's requirements. All deliverables from these third parties are reviewed as if they were from Forensic Laboratory employees. Where there is a shortfall, they either undergo the appraisal process or have their contracts terminated. Managing outsourcing suppliers is defined in Chapter 14, Section 14.8.

6.7.5 Product and Service Provision

The Forensic Laboratory ensures that product and Service Delivery (typically a case report or statement) for a Client is maintained by:

- use of a virtual file for each Client, as defined in Section 6.6.2.2 and Appendix 17;
- the collection or delivery of exhibits to be processed to produce the required case report or statement; as defined in Chapter 9, Section 9.6;
- ensuring that the appropriate resources are available to the Forensic Laboratory Manager to produce the required deliverables, as defined in Chapter 4, Section 4.6.2;
- work is carried out by the Forensic Laboratory for their Clients according to:
  - the agreed contract;
  - the agreed proposal that defines the deliverables;

- good practice for the delivery of the case report or statement as understood by the Forensic Laboratory;
- the relevant legislation or regulation that affects the delivery of the document;
- any changes to the requirements based on feedback or other reasons from the Client.
- once a draft deliverable has been created, it is reviewed internally, as defined in Section 6.8.1;
- when considered suitable for release, the deliverable is issued to the Client, as defined in Section 6.8.3;
- the deliverable is reviewed by the Client, as defined in Section 6.8.4;
- the Document Author meets with the Client to discuss any proposed edits, as defined in Section 6.8.5;
- the document is edited accordingly and reviewed again internally, as defined in Section 6.8.1;
- the document is released again to the Client, as defined in Section 6.8.3;
- this process continues until the final draft is issued to the Client as the deliverable;
- if this document is the final deliverable for the Client, the project is signed off as defined in Section 6.9;
- the case and all matters relating to the case is archived when the case is concluded according to the Forensic Laboratory's retention schedule, as defined in Chapter 4, Appendix 16, and Section 6.10. This may involve archiving just a specific case or the whole Client virtual file if there is no other case processing required for the Client;
- if there are any complaints, these are resolved using the Forensic Laboratory complaint procedure, as defined in Section 6.14;
- during the whole case lifecycle, the Forensic Laboratory ensures that all Client information is handled according to its classification, as defined in Chapter 5, Appendix 16, and Section 6.11, so that Client confidentiality is maintained.

6.8 REVIEWING DELIVERABLES

All deliverables produced by the Forensic Laboratory for a Client are thoroughly reviewed and edited at several stages in the project lifecycle, as can be seen from the previous chapter. This ensures that any deliverable that is sent to a Client for their review has:

- conformed to the Forensic Laboratory's document standards (Sections 6.6.2.3, 6.6.2.4, and 6.8) and Chapter 4, Section 4.6.2;
- conformed to the Forensic Laboratory's quality assurance process;
- conformed to the deliverables identified by the project proposal and/or quotation (Section 6.6.2.3);
- been reviewed internally and externally and has achieved the required level of quality to be sent to a Client (Section 6.8).

Typical deliverables include an interim report, a final report, and any other documentation that the Client may require during the case processing.

The responsibilities for reviewing documents lie with the Document Author, the relevant Account Manager, and Client.

The process for reviewing deliverables is as follows:

6.8.1 Reviewing the Document Internally

1. The Document Author performs final checks on the document including:
   - spell-checking the document;
   - regenerating any contents list;
   - checking fonts and layouts;
   - checking formatting;
   - ensuring that the document meets the requirements set by the Client;
   - setting the correct version number.
2. The Document Author prints a copy of the document for review and completes a *Draft Review Form*, as defined in Appendix 19, with the correct details, and attaches it to the printed copy of the document and sends it to the Account Manager. Typically, no more than one elapsed week should be allowed for the return of comments.
3. The Account Manager reviews the document and provides comment on the changes as required. The Account Manager:
   - checks for consistency and ambiguities;
   - checks for structure and layout;
   - checks that the content complies with the Client's requirements.
4. The Account Manager writes all comments on the printed document, then signs the *Draft Review form* and returns the document and the *Draft Review Form* to the Document Author.
5. The Document Author checks all comments received and judges which comments to implement. The Author consults the Account Manager when in doubt as to the validity of comments and asks for explanations on their comments.

Note

The document may well be sent to more than the Account Manager for review, the reviewers will be determined by the Account Manager and the Laboratory Manager.

6.8.2 Implementing Edits Internally

The Document Author implements comments received on the document as follows:

1. Scans the marked up document for storage in the Client virtual file. The Draft Review Form is disposed of by shredding.
2. Renames the original file according to the document control procedure.
3. Updates the version information in the document.
4. Performs the required edits.
5. Saves the document.
6. Performs final checks on the document including:
   - spell-checking the document;
   - regenerating any contents list;
   - checking fonts and layouts;
   - checking formatting;
   - setting the correct version number.
7. Prints a copy of the document for final check by the Account Manager together with a *Draft Review Form* with the correct details and attaches it to the printed copy of the document and sends it to the Account Manager. Typically, no more than one elapsed week should be allowed for the return of comments.
8. The Account Manager performs a final edit on the document and then returns it to the Document Author.
9. The Document Author repeats steps above until the document is agreed as ready to release to the Client.
10. Records of all reviews undertaken, including the date, reviewer, and any relevant feedback shall be added to the Draft Review Form and stored in the Client virtual file in the ERMS.
11. The document is now ready for issue to the Client.
12. If a soft copy is to be sent to the Client, then it should be converted to "secured" PDF format and sent by e-mail with a receipt request.
13. Depending on the information classification of the deliverable, as defined in Chapter 5, Appendix 16, and Section 6.11, appropriate means of protection of the proposal shall be applied as defined in Chapter 12, Section 12.3.14.

> **Note**
>
> Extra copies can, of course, be produced if necessary. The Client can circulate their copy of the deliverable if additional people need to see it at the Client site.

6.8.3 Issuing the Document

The Document Author writes to the Client enclosing the deliverable. The normal delivery method is post, but if time is short and it is essential that the deliverable arrives on the following day, it can be sent by courier, be faxed, or e-mailed.

The method of transmission must also ensure that data handling procedures for the classification for the proposal are met as defined in Chapter 12, Sections 12.3.12 and 12.3.14.

6.8.4 Reviewing the Document with the Client

Once a document has been produced and sent to a Client, the Document Author liaises with the Client to discuss the document.

It is not always required to hold a formal review meeting with a Client to discuss a document. Sometimes a telephone call or an e-mail can suffice, particularly when the work required is straightforward. In all cases, however, the document is always discussed with the Client.

The responsibilities for planning and holding a document review with a Client lie with the Document Author assisted by the relevant Account Manager. It may well be that the Account Manager or another employee attends the review process with the Document Author.

> **Note**
>
> For simplicity, the Forensic Laboratory "team" attending the review have been referred to as the "Document Author" irrespective of who actually attends.

The Document Author's major objectives of the review are to ensure that there are no changes to the deliverables or, if there are, they are discovered early enough that they can be addressed without wasting time and effort.

The Client reviews their copy of the document(s) sent by the Document Author. This may be a meeting, or can be telephone or e-mail based. Where there have been amendments to the Client's original instructions, these shall have been recorded in the Client's virtual case file and reviewed at this point.

The Document Author answers any Client questions on the document and resolves any issues that remain. The Document Author must take full notes to ensure that an updated document can be produced after the meeting that contains all the necessary information and reflects the Client's view.

The document is edited as required, as defined in Section 6.8.2.

6.8.5 Following up the Review

The Document Author must return the updated document to the Client within the agreed timescale. If no timescale is agreed, then this should be within five working days.

The Document Author issues the updated version of the document to the Client as defined in Section 6.8.2.

The Document Author files all documentation relating to the update in the Client virtual file in the ERMS.

Note

The review process may occur more than once, if required.

6.9 SIGNING OFF A CASE

Once all work on a case has been completed, the Client checks the work and then signs it off as completed. The sign-off process also provides an opportunity for the Account Manager and the Client to review the case to ensure that the Forensic Laboratory has met, or preferably exceeded, Client expectations. The sign-off form is given in Appendix 20.

The Account Manager is responsible for ensuring that the Client signs off a case, though in practice this may be performed by the Forensic Analyst undertaking the Client's case.

1. The Account Manager sends the sign-off form to the Client;
2. The Account Manager telephones or e-mails the Client and arranges a sign-off meeting;
3. The Account Manager and any other relevant Forensic Laboratory employees attend the sign-off meeting at the appointed time, chair the meeting and:
   - provide an overview of the case;
   - work through the deliverables produced for the Client and request
   - confirmation that each has been completed to their satisfaction;
   - any lessons learned for continuous improvement.
4. The Account Manager receives the signed sign-off form;
5. The Account Manager files all correspondence and meeting minutes in the Client's virtual case file in the ERMS.

6.10 ARCHIVING A CASE

After all work on a case has been completed and the Client has signed off the case, all case material can be considered for archiving according to the Document Retention Schedule as defined in Chapter 4, Appendix 16.

1. The Account Manager is responsible for ensuring the case is archived.
2. The Account Manager archives a case by moving the entire case folder from the "current" area to the "finished" in the ERMS. The Account Manager may have to create a new Client folder within the "finished" area if the case is the first one completed for a Client.
3. All data on the Forensic Laboratory servers are backed up according to the current Forensic Laboratory backup procedures defined in Chapter 7, Section 7.7.4.

6.11 MAINTAINING CLIENT CONFIDENTIALITY

During work on a case, authorized Forensic Laboratory employees may be issued with a great deal of information about a case. Much of this information is confidential.

1. The Forensic Laboratory undertakes to keep this information confidential by:
   - signing confidentiality agreements with Client, if requested;
   - safeguarding all material issued by a Client to the Forensic Laboratory whether in paper or electronic form;
   - returning material to a Client, if requested or contractually agreed;
   - securely disposing of Client material when no longer required by appropriate secure disposal methods according to the type of media and its classification, as defined in Chapter 5, Appendix 16.

Top Management is responsible for ensuring that Client confidentiality is maintained, though in practice it may be Account Manager that undertakes all tasks relating to confidentiality of Client information.

6.12 TECHNICAL REQUIREMENTS FOR THE FORENSIC LABORATORY

6.12.1 General

While ISO 9001 concentrates on management requirements for quality, ISO 17025 has management requirements as well as technical requirements. Much of the management requirement defined in ISO 17025 duplicates the requirements in ISO 9001. International Laboratory Accreditation Cooperation G19—Guidelines for Forensic Laboratories clarifies the application of ISO 17025 in a forensic laboratory context. The cross-referencing between ISO 9001 and ISO 17025 is given in Chapter 3, Appendix 2.

Accreditation to ISO 17025 by an Accreditation Body demonstrates that it not only operates a QMS, but they are "technically competent and are able to generate technically valid results" and it "specifies the requirements for the competence to carry out tests and/or calibrations including sampling."

There are a number of factors that can affect the correctness and reliability of results for case processing performed by the Forensic Laboratory. These can vary but include such issues as:

- accuracy of documented procedures;
- all employees following documented procedures in the IMS;
- employee training and awareness;
- ensuring continual improvement;
- environmental and accommodation conditions in the laboratory;
- hardware, software, and tools in use;
- traceability, auditing, and sampling.

Some of these are covered by ISO 9001 and others by ISO 17025. Those not covered above in ISO 9001 are covered below as part of ISO 17025 quality procedures.

6.12.2 Benefits of ISO 17025

In addition to the benefits of ISO 9001, the benefits of ISO 17025 Accreditation include:

- allowing for the comparable quality of evidence produced in cross-border cases;
- provides demonstrable proof of a competent workforce for performing tasks within the Forensic Laboratory;
- demonstration of continuing technical competence;
- demonstration of impartiality.

6.12.3 The Laboratory Manager

The Laboratory Manager is in charge of the technical management of forensic case processing in the Forensic Laboratory. This role is distinctly different from that of the Quality Manager, even though the Laboratory Manger has a duty of care to ensure that all technical forensic case processing meets the quality requirements set by the Quality Manager. The Laboratory Manager is responsible for all first response, case processing, and evidence presentation within the Forensic Laboratory and their job description is given in Appendix 24.

6.12.4 Key Questions ISO 17025 Answers

For any specific case that has been processed by the Forensic Laboratory, from initial contact to evidence presentation, the Forensic Laboratory can show:

- the case processing, from initial contact to evidence presentation, was performed by a competent and properly qualified Forensic Analyst who has been trained in the tools and methodologies that they used in processing the case and had access to all necessary information necessary for processing the case;
- the methods and tools used to process a case were technically sound and appropriate to the Client's requirements;
- all tools, hardware, and software used in processing the case were properly maintained and licensed during their use on the case;
- the case was thoroughly reviewed prior to delivery and met the Client's requirements;
- that any non-conformity identified during case processing was addressed in a timely manner that it was effective;
- that documented procedures exist for all aspects of case processing;
- that records exist in the Client virtual case file in the ERMS to support this.

6.12.5 Technical Qualifications

In addition to the management system training defined in Chapter 4, Sections 4.6.2.2, ISO 17025 requires that all Forensic Laboratory employees shall be competent and have records to support this competence. Job descriptions shall be reviewed every year to ensure that they remain current as part of the employee's annual appraisal process as defined in Chapter 18, Section 18.2.4.

For each role within the Forensic Laboratory, a job description is defined, typically by the Human Resources Department; details of specific job descriptions relating to the management of implemented management systems and case processing are given in Appendices 7 and 24 and Appendices in Chapter 18. The job description for a Forensic Analyst is given in Appendix 25. This job description is a generic one for any employee performing forensic case processing and includes all levels of Forensic Analysts.

All training requirements for forensic processing employees shall be agreed with the Laboratory Manager, and where appropriate, the Quality Manager. This will start with induction training when the employee first joins the Forensic Laboratory. Management system training and refresher training will carry on for the duration that the employee remains with the Forensic Laboratory. While new entrants to the Forensic Laboratory may have considerable experience, it is required that they are trained in the methods and tools used by the Forensic Laboratory. This is not a reflection on their competence, but a requirement that they know, understand, and use the Forensic Laboratory's processes and procedures.

All new employees shall undergo induction training when starting to work for the Forensic Laboratory; this includes any employees of outsourcing partners who work for the Forensic Laboratory. Ongoing refresher training, for all employees, is mandatory for all employees.

An example of the requirements of the training for Forensic Analysts for their initial training process is given in Appendix 26, though it is expected that most inductees will have completed part of the training prior to employment. The requirement of undertaking a Training Needs

Analysis as part of annual appraisals is given in Chapter 18, Section 18.2.2. After this level of training, any further training will depend on specialisms sought, case file processing, or other relevant matters. However, it must be noted that the identification of training needs will be focused on the needs of the Forensic Laboratory, rather than those of the individual employee, as this is what the Forensic Laboratory is being Accredited against—and not the individual Forensic Analyst.

All employees shall have records of all training undertaken during their employment with the Forensic Laboratory filed with their personnel files. This must include feedback on all training, internal and external, that the employee undertakes. Training records provide evidence that an employee is competent to perform a task and can be used to provide an audit trail to prove this. Copies of all certifications and qualifications gained during employment should be held on the employee's personnel file.

When an employee claims a new competence, the Laboratory Manager should be satisfied that the employee is technically competent to carry out case processing using the new competence. Typically, this is carried out using reference material (e.g., a reference case with known outcomes).

Employee competence must be regularly reviewed and reassessed, as required. Identification for the need for reassessment may also come from a Client or as the result of presentation of evidence produced to Court or Tribunal, where the Forensic Analyst's findings are successfully challenged. In this case, the Forensic Laboratory manager should take action as appropriate, which may include withdrawing authorization to use specific tools or methodologies within the Forensic Laboratory.

Individual Forensic Analysts should be encouraged to obtain specialized certifications relevant to forensic case processing, in addition to those given in Appendix 26, and a list of some of the better known individual certifications are given in Appendix 27. Many of these require the certification holder to undergo reassessment on an annual basis and the submission of supporting statements, copies of qualifications, and evidence of Continuing Professional Development/Education.

In addition to retaining a comprehensive digital forensic library of relevant manuals, books, and journals (hard copy or online subscriptions), the Forensic Laboratory shall maintain documentation relating to the digital forensic qualifications and their exams as referred to, but not limited to, those defined in Appendix 27.

6.12.6 Accommodation and Environmental Conditions

The general requirements for accommodation and environment are given in Chapters 2 and 3. General security requirements for the accommodation and environment are given in Chapter 12. This section is related to the requirements for accommodation and environment for testing, calibration, and forensic case processing. In general terms, the Forensic Laboratory shall ensure that the accommodation and environment used for forensic case processing do not impact the correct performance of any test, calibration, or case processing.

6.12.6.1 Accommodation

Access levels and authorizations to areas in the Forensic Laboratory are defined in Chapter 4, Appendix 11. The levels of access control used within the Forensic Laboratory are based on confidentiality of cases being processed, the "need to know" principle, the "need to access principle," the need to protect the integrity of forensic case processing, and the requirements for segregation of duties (Chapter 12, Sections 12.3.5 and 12.3.6).

It is essential that areas where segregation of duties or tasks is required have appropriate access control (e.g., restricted access to the secure evidence store to ensure continuity of evidence). Physical security for the Forensic Laboratory is defined in Chapter 12, Section 12.4.

6.12.6.2 Environment

Within the Forensic Laboratory, there is the specific need to protect against environmental conditions that may affect the processing of forensic cases. A number of these have been covered in previous chapters and include:

- electrical power fluctuations;
- electromagnetic disturbances;
- the Forensic Laboratory shall ensure that all Forensic Analysts have appropriate ergonomic conditions in their workspace to perform their case processing duties. This shall include, but not be limited to furniture settings, lighting, and computer equipment positioning. In some jurisdictions, the ergonomic settings of a workspace are legislative requirements (e.g., The Health and Safety (Display Screen Equipment) Regulations 1992, for the EU);
- temperature and humidity controls to ensure that evidence (typically digital media) remains within manufacturer's recommended limits.

Typically, the first and third items are subject to automatic monitoring and reporting to a central annunciator panel or control workstation. These are always recorded either on paper (that must be regularly changed and stored as records) or retained as computer files, retained according to the retention schedule defined in Chapter 4, Appendix 16. The second one is dependent on Forensic Analysts ensuring that they follow the procedures laid down for evidence handling defined in Chapter 8, Section 8.6.9.

6.12.6.3 Health and Safety

While ISO 17025 does not explicitly define Health and Safety requirements, the Forensic Laboratory has implemented the requirements of OHSAS 18001, as defined in Chapter 17.

6.12.6.4 Off-Site Issues

Where the Forensic Laboratory is performing case processing outside the Forensic Laboratory (e.g., on a Client site or a crime scene), all Forensic Analysts must ensure that the procedures used in the Forensic Laboratory are used off site. This includes both first response, as defined in Chapter 8, and outsourcing, as defined in Chapter 14, Section 14.8.

6.12.6.5 Other Issues

While other types of forensic laboratories may have other specific requirements (e.g., control of chemicals or equipment used in testing non-digital samples), the Forensic Laboratory does not have these direct requirements, though they may be secondary (e.g., further testing by different forensic laboratories of evidence under the Forensic Laboratory's control).

6.12.7 Test Methods and Validation

During the proposal stage of negotiations, as defined in Sections 6.6.2.3 and 6.6.2.4, the Client will define their outcomes. It is the Forensic Laboratory's responsibility to ensure that these needs are met. If a specific process or methodology that is required by the Client is required, then the Forensic Laboratory must ensure that the methods or process required is internationally acceptable, either by reference to standards or recognized benchmarking (e.g., NIST Computer Forensic Tool Testing Program). In general terms, case processing software is provided by the developer as "fit for purpose" in relation to forensic case processing. Usage among the digital forensic fraternity will rapidly discover where this is not the case, and it is usual that this is made public in relevant journals or on the Internet.

In many cases, the use of digital forensic tools has been accepted in a court and having results that are repeatable by any other competent Forensic Analyst provides this evidence. These are defined as standard methods for digital forensic case processing, as they follow the processes defined in the tool's instruction manual, accepted validated processes, or relevant standards, and the Forensic Laboratory uses these wherever possible. In general terms, the Forensic Laboratory does not need to use non-standard methods in case processing as it does not develop its own case processing tools, preferring to rely on tried and tested methods. Before going live in the Forensic Laboratory, all new tools must go through the Forensic Laboratory Change Management Process, as defined in Chapter 7, Section 7.4.1. Part of this process is testing expected output using the Forensic Laboratory reference case and/or dual tool verification, where the "other" tool has already been validated. Should a nonstandard method be required by the Client or proposed by the Forensic Laboratory for processing the Client's case, this shall be covered in the proposal or quotation, as appropriate.

The handling and transport of items to be tested in the Forensic Laboratory is covered in Chapter 8, Section 8.7. Typically, instruction manuals for forensic hardware and software tools in the Forensic Laboratory are accepted as "definitive use" documents. However, a "watching brief" must be kept on their use in relevant cases to ensure that their use is not discredited in any way. Any variations from the Client's outcome requirements, including tool and methodology usage, must be both agreed with the Client and documented. Should a tool, method, or process required to be used by the Client be deemed as inappropriate by the Forensic Laboratory, for any valid reason, then the Client shall be advised, and the Forensic Laboratory takes appropriate steps. The records of this will be added to the Client's virtual file in the ERMS.

Where the Forensic Laboratory develops its own internal methodologies and processes for forensic case processing, they shall be only developed and used by competent employees. Before use for processing any Client cases, any such methods shall be validated by appropriate method within the Forensic Laboratory. The process for validating, and revalidating a tool where appropriate, is given in Chapter 7, Section 7.5.5. Assuming they are successful, all relevant documentation shall be updated and relevant employees trained to use the new process. All records of training shall be updated to show competence of the employees using the new method or procedure.

In most cases, the Forensic Laboratory will use existing tools and technologies (e.g., basic forensic case processing tools such as Encase, FTK, and Paraben) that are accepted by the Courts, have detailed procedural manuals and provide training in their use and additional certification of competence (some of these certifications are defined in Appendix 27). The maintenance of the hardware on which they operate is covered in Chapter 7, Section 7.5.

Where output from any forensic tools is produced in a report or statement for a Client, the origin of that data must be defined. This will include the tool name, version number, and any other relevant details so that the tests can be reproduced by any other competent Forensic Analyst.

For general office software (e.g., COTS products, such as Microsoft Office), these are regarded by the Forensic Laboratory as validated products, even given the alarming level of security and other patches being released.

ISO 17025 requires that the Forensic Laboratory shall "have instructions on the use and operation of all relevant equipment, and on the handling and preparation of items for testing and/or calibration, or both, where the absence of such instructions could jeopardize the results of tests and/or calibrations." This is not really appropriate for the Forensic Laboratory as it does not test the same type of samples continuously. Each case is different, but the competence of the Forensic Analysts, the use of the case processing forms as used in Chapter 9, and the manuals for tool usage are seen as meeting this requirement.

Validation of methods of case processing is not really practical after each change of the Forensic Analysts workstation, given the number of patches that are required for the operating system. However, where a new tool is installed or a new version of an existing tool is installed, the known reference case is run and the output compared to ensure that the same results are achieved, as from the previous version of the tool, for existing tools, and from a similar outcome from a different tool for new tools. One problem that is introduced here is that there is an assumption that the original output is correct that is used as a baseline measure. This is also the case where new technology is to be examined. As forensic case evidence is almost always contested, another competent Forensic Analyst working for the "other side" will have to run their own tests, and discrepancies between the findings will be investigated and resolved. This may require the updating of procedures used in the Forensic Laboratory.

For this reason, the Forensic Laboratory undertakes dual tool verification of results, as required. The decision for performing dual tool verification rests with the Laboratory Manager.

6.12.8 Equipment

The Forensic Laboratory contains all equipment (hardware, software, procedures, and infrastructure) needed to satisfy Client requirements for digital forensic case processing. If a need for additional equipment is needed, it can be purchased using the process defined in Chapter 12, Section 12.3.14.2. Where external resources are required, they shall be managed in accordance with the requirements in Chapter 14. Annual second party audits of all suppliers shall be undertaken in accordance with the requirements defined in Chapter 4, Section 4.7.3.

All equipment (assets) purchased by the Forensic Laboratory that are above the "de minimus" level (i.e., fixed assets) are recorded in the asset register maintained by the Finance Department. The asset purchasing process is defined in Chapter 12, Section 12.3.14. All IT assets, including any equipment for forensic case processing, are recorded in the IT Service Desk system; however, this excludes consumables. The contents of the IT asset register in the Service Desk system are given in Chapter 12, Appendix 7. This covers hardware as well as software in use and contains the whole life history of the equipment from its introduction into the Forensic Laboratory to its eventual disposal and records all Forensic Laboratory employees that have "owned" it, as defined in Chapter 12, Section 12.3.14.

After receipt and checking for completeness and correctness of any equipment, it shall only be commissioned into service in the Forensic Laboratory through the Change Management Process defined in Chapter 7, Section 7.4.1. Where this includes equipment used for case processing, the known reference case is used to ensure that expected results are produced. This does not happen for business-related or infrastructure equipment. The results of the running of the reference case are retained as records for the equipment in question and associated with the equipment record in the IT Service Desk. All equipment in the Forensic Laboratory is given its own unique asset tag that is securely affixed to it and is readily visible. This asset tag remains with the equipment for its "life" in the Forensic Laboratory. ISO 17025 mandates that records of all equipment in use shall be held and gives a recommendation for a minimum set of data to be retained. This is reproduced in Appendix 28 with locations for the procedures implemented or locations where the records are stored, to meet these requirements.

Where forensic case processing is carried out off site by Forensic Laboratory Forensic Analysts, all equipment shall be transported to and from the remote site securely, according to the procedures in Chapter 8, Section 8.7.

Where any case processing is outsourced to any third party, these procedures and the requirements of the rest of the Forensic Laboratory's IMS must be met and regular second party audits shall confirm this as defined in Chapter 4, Section 4.7.3 and Chapter 4, Appendix 42.

A random sample of all equipment used in the Forensic Laboratory shall be undertaken. This shall occur on introduction into the Forensic Laboratory and after any significant or influencing changes (e.g., new software upgrades, hardware replacements, etc.).

6.12.9 Measurement Traceability

There are rarely national metrology laboratories that can be used by a forensic laboratory that holds the standards for all measurements in case processing or any traceability to the International System of Units. The Forensic Laboratory uses its own reference case as there is no currently recognized certified reference material (CRM) available. Use of recognized forensic tool providers with the ability to have results challenged in a Court, Tribunal, or similar, provides assurance of the methods in use. Additionally, the Forensic Laboratory ensures that all of its Forensic Analysts are technically competent on the tools that they use in forensic case processing. This includes relevant training courses from the manufacturer and obtaining and maintaining relevant individual certifications, where possible.

Records of this testing are maintained in the Forensic Laboratory's ERMS to provide an audit trail of measurement and testing. In addition to this, forensic acquisition tools usually provide evidence of successful acquisition by use of hashing techniques. Actual output is performed, as required by the Forensic Laboratory, by use of dual tool verification. This ensures that the same result is achieved by two different forensic case processing tools from the same source evidence. This is specifically used in the Forensic Laboratory where there is very little relevant evidence for the Client.

6.12.10 Administration of Forensic Case Work and Sampling

Before starting any forensic case processing in the Forensic Laboratory, the proposal and contract review process defined in Sections 6.6.2 and 6.6.3 must have been completed, in addition to ensuring that the Forensic Laboratory has appropriate resources in place to process the case.

The Laboratory Manager shall oversee all cases from the initial receipt of an exhibit to be processed (whether delivered by the Client, collected by the Forensic Laboratory from the Client, or seized as part of a first response). On receipt, or recovery, it shall be recorded as an exhibit. The Laboratory Manager shall appoint the relevant Forensic Team to process the Client's forensic case, but only if the relevant preconditions have been met.

On receipt of an exhibit, the exhibit shall be inspected and securely stored in the secure evidence store as defined in Chapter 9, Section 9.6.1. If it is to be rejected for any reason, then the procedure in Chapter 9, Section 9.6.1 shall be followed, including the advising of the Client. On receipt to the Forensic Laboratory, all exhibits shall be uniquely identified using the Forensic Laboratory's exhibit naming procedures. This may well be in addition to other naming conventions used for the exhibit.

When all relevant details are present, the Laboratory Manager shall allocate the case to the relevant Forensic Analyst*, based on the case requirements and the Forensic Analyst's competence and workload. This is usually in the form of the documented requirements from the Client or those defined by the Account Manager after consultation with the Client as part of the contract negotiations as defined in Sections 6.6.2 and 6.6.3. After the forensic case has been processed, the deliverable (typically a report, statement, or deposition) shall be produced. This shall contain all relevant document control information, as defined in Chapter 9, Sections 9.13, 9.15, and 9.16. All reports must go through the deliverable review process defined in Section 6.8, prior to final delivery to the Client. This ensures that the deliverable is meeting internal standards as well as the original Client expectations.

Post case processing retention and disposal of case material is covered in Chapter 9, Section 9.18.

All documents relating to a specific case shall be recorded in the Client's virtual case file in the ERMS.

6.12.11 Assuring Technical Quality of Products and Services

The majority of the Forensic Laboratory's products and services are reports or statements relating to forensic case processing. Much of the quality process is covered by the requirements of ISO 9001; however, this does not cover technical quality of the results.

There is no available CRM for forensic case processing, and the Forensic Laboratory has its own reference case that is used whenever a hardware or software upgrade is performed as part of its change control process as defined in Chapter 7, Section 7.4.1. The details of the reference case test results are outlined in Appendix 29; however, more reference results can be added as required for new tools and methods. However, as discussed above, this is based on the assumption that the original reference material results are correct.

The principles used in ISO Guide 35, Reference materials—General and statistical principles for certification contain much advice that was used for the production of in-house reference case material. Due to the sensitivity of forensic cases processed and the need to maintain Client confidentiality, as defined in Section 6.11, it is not really possible to undertake inter-laboratory proficiency or comparison exercises apart from those derived results that are actually challenged in a Court of competent jurisdiction. The Forensic Laboratory uses dual tool validation wherever there is any doubt as to the veracity of results produces.

Should any results produced by the Forensic Laboratory be challenged and be proved to be incorrect, they are treated through the non-conforming product route as defined in Chapter 6, Section 6.13.2. This may come from a challenge from the Client themselves via their feedback as defined in Appendix 20 or from a public challenge in a Court or Tribunal. This ensures that the root cause is determined and appropriate corrective action is undertaken. This may include advising other Clients of possible non-conforming products and product (i.e., case reports or statement) recall. The results of any challenge or negative feedback are treated as records and stored in the relevant Client's virtual case file. The corrective action undertaken is recorded in the CAPA database.

* More than one Forensic Analyst may be assigned to a specific case.

While almost all digital forensic case processing will follow the steps provided in the relevant tool's instruction manual, there may be occasions where an in-house method is required. In this case, all steps undertaken will be recorded in the Forensic Case Work Log, as given in Chapter 9, Appendix 9. This allows for both traceability of actions and providing for repeatability by another competent Forensic Analyst. Any deviations from established practice or development of in-house methods shall be formally authorized by the Laboratory Manager, and records of this maintained in the Client's virtual file. This may also require an update to the forensic reference case results. Where a non-standard method is to be used or developed, it is prudent, and mandatory in the Forensic Laboratory, to involve the Client in the process and obtain their consent. Again, records of meetings with the Client, actions arising from them, and formal consent shall be stored in the Client's virtual case file.

6.12.12 Case Processing Reports

ISO 17025 is quite specific about what information must be present in a report, which must also include the Client's requirements, as defined in Sections 6.6.2.4 and 6.8.4. The requirements defined by ISO 17025 are given in Appendix 30. While ISO 17025 allows the relaxation of these requirements with agreement of the Client, they must be readily available in the Forensic Laboratory, and so the Forensic Laboratory standard report format includes them, as defined in Appendix 31.

While the Forensic Laboratory issues reports based on recoverable facts and these should be repeatable by any other competent Forensic Analyst, Clients often require an opinion or interpretation to be made based on recovered digital forensic evidence. In these cases, the Forensic Laboratory must be able to show that these opinions and interpretations are made based on sound judgment by competent Forensic Laboratory Forensic Analysts who have the relevant qualifications and experience to back their competence. In all cases, opinions or interpretations shall be endorsed by the Laboratory Manager as part of the document review process, as defined in Chapter 4, Section 4.6.3.4. Forensic Laboratory employee training, awareness, and competence are covered in Chapter 4, Sections 4.6.2.2 and 4.6.2.3.

All reports and statements (i.e., deliverables for a Client) must go through the review process defined in Section 6.8, prior to relapse to the Client. Where appropriate, changes shall be made to meet Client requirements or where results are challenged. All versions of any deliverables shall be retained within the ERMS for the relevant Client virtual file. Records of reviews and authorization for release shall be retained, whether in the SharePoint ERMS or in paper records which are scanned and added to the Client virtual file in the ERMS.

All authorized deliverables for a Client are to be issued in the Adobe Portable Document Format (PDF) that is secured. These shall be protected against unauthorized modification and, where the classification requires it, be numbered copies issued on an individual recipient basis. This shall be based on the classification of the report as defined in Chapter 5, Section 5.5.6.6, and be agreed by the Client as part of the proposal, as defined in Section 6.11.

All records of issue and receipt of any Client deliverables shall be retained and added to the Client virtual file in the ERMS, whether it is issue by e-mail, post, or hand-to-hand issue, along with the agreed recipient.

Where any amendment of a Client deliverable is required, the process defined in Section 6.8 must be followed and all copies of previous versions of the deliverable retained in the Client's virtual case file, allowing reversion to any previous version of the deliverable.

6.13 MEASUREMENT, ANALYSIS, AND IMPROVEMENT

The Forensic Laboratory must ensure that there are appropriate measurement, analysis, and improvement processes in place for all of its products and services. Measurement of the suitability of the Forensic Laboratory products and services is the only way to determine if the Forensic Laboratory is "getting it right." The analysis of feedback provides inputs to the improvement process to ensure that the Forensic Laboratory gets it right, first time, every time.

The Forensic Laboratory should plan and implement monitoring, measurement, analysis, and continuous improvement processes that are appropriate for its products and services (primarily case processing reports and expert testimony).

To achieve this, the Forensic Laboratory employs the following processes:

6.13.1 Monitoring and Measurement

The Forensic Laboratory determines that its documents meet Client's requirements throughout the whole document life cycle. At all stages, feedback is obtained from the Client to ensure that the deliverable(s) meet their expectations, as defined in Sections 6.6 and 6.8.

6.13.2 Control of Non-conforming Product

The Forensic Laboratory must aim to ensure that there are no non-conforming products delivered to a Client. It is the objective of the management system to ensure that this is so. As the Client is involved in the complete case processing life cycle, it is likely that this will be the case.

Where appropriate, the Client shall be advised of any non-conformance discovered and this may require the recall of material delivered to the Client. This will require the repeating of the deliverables as defined in Section 6.8.

6.13.3 Case Processing Audits

Audits covering all aspects of forensic case processing (e.g., casework, research, training, etc.) should be conducted at least once a year by the Quality Manager or the Laboratory Manager, whichever is appropriate. All internal audits shall be conducted in line with the requirements of Chapter 4, Section 4.7.3.

Where Client case files are reviewed in audits, they should be chosen randomly taking into account any sensitive issues related to the case. This will include, but not be limited to its profile, any negative feedback received, work of a specific Forensic Analyst where there is any question about their competence, etc.

Records of each audit shall be kept and stored in the ERMS. Where non-conformance are identified, they shall be tracked through to completion in the Forensic Laboratory CAPA database.

6.13.4 Analysis of Data

The Forensic Laboratory must ensure that its IMS (and the QMS that forms part of it) is suitable and effective for its purposes. This process takes input from a variety of sources and uses it to continuously improve its products and services to its Clients.

6.13.5 Improvement

The Forensic Laboratory strives to continuously improve its delivery of products and services to its internal and external Clients. To do this, it employs the following processes:

- quality management policy (Chapter 3, Appendix 4);
- reviewing deliverables (Section 6.8);
- client complaints (Section 6.14);
- handling non-conformities (Section 6.13.2);
- internal audit (Chapter 4, Section 4.7.3);
- case processing sign-off (Section 6.9);
- management review (Chapter 4, Section 4.9);
- continuous improvement (Chapter 4, Section 4.8).

6.14 MANAGING CLIENT COMPLAINTS

The Forensic Laboratory's complaints policy is to ensure all complaints relating to the quality of results or the level of service provided by the Forensic Laboratory to their Clients are fully investigated and reported promptly. The Forensic Laboratory must learn lessons learned from any complaints made and ensure that corrective action addresses them.

The Forensic Laboratory may receive, process, and resolve formal complaints that may be made by internal or external Clients concerning any aspect of a product or service that is provided to the business by the Forensic Laboratory.

The Forensic Laboratory defines a complaint as a written or verbal expression of dissatisfaction by a Client about the Forensic Laboratory, its products or services that requires investigation, response, and closure.

A complaint may be raised at any point in the relationship between the Forensic Laboratory and its Clients and not just at the sign-off and feedback form at the end of a case.

Managing complaints effectively in the Forensic Laboratory is one way of continuously improving the products and services that the Forensic Laboratory provides to its Clients.

A Client only needs to know three things about a complaint:

- where to complain;
- how to complain;
- to feel confidant that the complaint is being handled effectively and efficiently.

Top Management have committed to make the complaints management process highly visible and accessible to all Clients; this includes those that may have any disabilities. Complaints can be made using the following methods:

- e-mail;
- face to face;
- fax;
- letter;
- phone;
- sign-off and feedback forms;
- Web site.

As a complaint may be made to any Forensic Laboratory employee, the complaint handling process is covered as part of the employee's induction training.

The information that is required for recording a complaint is given in Appendix 21.

6.14.1 Responsibilities for Managing Client Complaints

There are a number of responsibilities in the client complaint process; these are as defined below.

6.14.1.1 Laboratory Manager

The Laboratory Manager is the person with overall responsibility for the complaint management process and for ensuring that complaints received from internal and external Clients about the Forensic Laboratory products and services are resolved promptly and to the Client's satisfaction. For external Clients, this will be via the relevant Client Account Manager, and for internal complaints, via the relevant Line Manager, where it is a case processing issue.

Responsibilities include:

- monitoring the progress of formal complaints;
- assisting with complaint investigation and resolution if required;
- acting as a contact point between the Forensic Laboratory and the Client for complaints relating to the Forensic Laboratory products and services, unless this has been devolved to the relevant Client Account Manager;
- collating reports of complaints, their progress, and their resolution as necessary to relevant stakeholders; these will include the Client and any relevant mandatory reporting bodies (e.g., Regulators, the relevant Accreditation Body);

> **Note**
> Should a complaint be critical, it may be escalated directly to Top Management.

6.14.1.2 Service Desk

The Service Desk is responsible for recording and tracking of any complaints from Clients concerning any of the Forensic Laboratory supplied products and services.

Responsibilities of the Service Desk are:

- recording and tracking all complaints in the Service Desk system in accordance with the Forensic Laboratory procedures for incident management;
- escalating a complaint to the appropriate person for investigation and resolution;
- closing a formal complaint in the Service Desk system on advice from the relevant Account Manager, Line Manager, or Laboratory Manager;
- maintaining the complaint process.

6.14.1.3 Client Complaint Process

> **Note**
> Within the Forensic Laboratory, the incident reporting process is used for recording complaints. Complaints are regarded as a type of incident.

The process by which the Forensic Laboratory manages a complaint from a Client about products and services provided to them is:

1. The Forensic Laboratory receives a complaint about an aspect of a business service they provide. Sources of complaints may include:
   - by any of the methods defined in Chapter 14;
   - directly from a Client via the Service Desk;

> **Note**
> Any complaints about the Forensic Laboratory services which are received informally at Top Management level must be referred to the Service Desk so that they can initiate the formal complaint process.

2. The Service Desk initiates the complaint process by logging the complaint in the Service Desk system.
3. When a complaint is registered by the Service Desk:
   - the complaint is registered in accordance with these procedures;
   - the complaint is always assigned a high-priority response;
   - the person registering the complaint is notified in accordance with the procedure for managing incidents, as defined in Chapter 7, Section 7.4.1;
   - the Laboratory Manager is automatically notified of the complaint registration and details (the Laboratory Manager may choose to notify the Top Management and other relevant stakeholders or employees if the complaint is of a serious nature).
4. The Service Desk sends the details of the complaint to the appropriate Forensic Laboratory employee for action. For external Clients, this is usually the relevant Account Manager and for internal Clients, the relevant Line Manager.
5. The employee who has been delegated to deal with the complaint receives the complaint. If necessary, they contact the Client to:
   - obtain further information as required;
   - confirm the issues that are to be investigated.
6. Any additional information is recorded and allows the tracking of the complaint through its whole lifecycle from initial receipt through to final resolution.
7. The complaint is acknowledged by the Forensic Laboratory and the complainant formally advised accordingly.
8. When a complaint has been received, it should be assessed as soon as practically possible to see if it requires immediate action, is a known problem, impact on the Forensic Laboratory's reputation and other relevant factors.
9. The complaint is investigated and guidance taken on the actions that are required to resolve it to the Client's satisfaction.
10. Corrective actions are determined and agreed to resolve the complaint.

11. The relevant Account Manager, Line Manager, or the Laboratory Manager, as appropriate, contacts the Client to outline and confirm the proposed resolution action.
12. The Forensic Laboratory performs the resolution action.

Note

Any changes to product and service provision or the IT infrastructure must be performed in accordance with the Forensic Laboratory Change Management procedures, as defined in Chapter 7, Section 7.4.3.

13. The relevant Account Manager, Line Manager, or the Laboratory Manager, as appropriate, contacts the Client to confirm the resolution action has been performed.
14. Details are logged in the Service Desk system in accordance with the standard Forensic Laboratory procedures for recording and managing incidents, as defined in Chapter 7, Section 7.4.1, and the Laboratory Manager is notified.
15. The relevant Account Manager, Line Manager, or the Laboratory Manager, as appropriate, contacts the Client to confirm their satisfaction with the resolution (the Forensic Laboratory contacts 100% of external Clients who register complaints to confirm their satisfaction with the resolution).
16. If the Client is satisfied with the resolution, the complaint is closed in the Service Desk system and the Laboratory Manager is notified.
17. If the Client is not satisfied with the resolution, the complaint is escalated in accordance with the standard Forensic Laboratory procedure for managing and escalating incidents, as defined in Chapter 7, Section 7.4.1, and the Laboratory Manager is notified. Depending on the Client and the complaint, Top Management may also be advised.

APPENDIX 1 - MAPPING ISO 9001 TO IMS PROCEDURES

ISO 9001 Section	Control	Procedure(s)
4	Quality Management System	Chapter 4
4.1	General requirements	Chapter 4, Sections 4.6, 4.6.3, 4.6.4, 4.7.3, and 4.8 Chapter 5, Appendix 11 This chapter
4.2	Documentation requirements	Chapter 4, Sections 4.6.3 and 4.6.4 Chapter 5, Appendix 11
5	Management responsibility	Chapter 4, Section 4.6.2
5.1	Management commitment	Chapter 3, Appendix 4 Chapter 4, Sections 4.2.2.1, 4.4, 4.6.2, 4.7.3, and 4.9 This chapter, Appendix 7
5.2	Customer focus	This chapter, Section 6.6 Chapter 16
5.3	Quality policy	Chapter 3, Appendix 4 Chapter 4, Sections 4.2, 4.7, and 4.9
5.4	Planning	This chapter, Sections 6.2.2.1 and 6.7
5.4.1	Quality Objectives	Chapter 4, Sections 4.7 and 4.9
5.4.2	Quality Management System planning	Chapter 4, Sections 4.7 and 4.9
5.5	Responsibility, authority, and communication	Chapter 4, Sections 4.7 and 4.9
5.5.1	Responsibility and authority	Chapter 5, Appendix 11 This chapter, Appendix 7 Chapter 18, Section 18.3.3
5.5.2	Management representative	This chapter, Appendix 7
5.5.3	Internal communication	Chapter 4, Sections 4.6.2 and 4.6.5, Chapter 4, Appendix 39
5.6	Management review	Chapter 4, Section 4.9
5.6.1	General	Chapter 4, Section 4.9

Continued

ISO 9001 Section	Control	Procedure(s)
5.6.2	Review input	Chapter 4, Section 4.9
5.6.3	Review output	Chapter 4, Section 4.9
6	Resource management	Chapter 4, Section 4.6.2
6.1	Provision of resources	Chapter 4, Sections 4.6.2, 4.7, and 4.9 Chapter 5, Appendix 11 This chapter, Section 6.14 Chapter 18, Section 18.6.2
6.2	Human Resources	Chapter 5, Appendix 11 Chapter 18
6.2.1	General	Chapter 18, Section 18.2.4
6.2.2	Competence, skill, and training	Chapter 4, Section 4.6.6.2
6.3	Infrastructure	Chapter 5, Appendix 11
6.4	Work environment	Chapter 2 Chapter 3 Chapter 5, Appendix 11
7	Product realization	This chapter, Section 6.7 Chapter 9
7.1	Planning of product realization	This chapter, Sections 6.6, 6.7.1, and 6.8
7.2	Customer-related processes	This chapter, Sections 6.6, 6.7.2, and 6.14
7.3	Design and development	This chapter, Sections 6.6, 6.6.2, and 6.7.3
7.4	Purchasing	Not applicable for general processes or equipment Chapter 5, Appendix 11 This chapter, Section 6.7.4
7.4.1	Purchasing process	This chapter, Sections 6.7.4 and 6.14 Chapter 12, Section 12.3.14.
7.4.2	Purchasing information	This chapter, Section 6.7.4 Chapter 12, Section 12.3.14.
7.4.3	Verification of purchased product	This chapter, Sections 6.14 and 6.7.4 Chapter 12, Section 12.3.14.
7.5	Production and service provision	This chapter, Section 6.7.5 Chapter 8 Chapter 9
7.5.1	Control of production and service provision	Chapter 4, Section 4.6.2.2 This chapter, Sections 6.2.2, 6.6.2.3.1, 6.6.2.3.2, 6.8, 6.9, and 6.10 Chapter 7, Section 7.7.4.
7.5.2	Validation of processes for production and service provision	This chapter, Sections 6.8 and 6.9
7.5.3	Identification and traceability	Chapter 4, Sections 4.6.3 and 4.6.4 This chapter, Section 6.8
7.5.4	Customer property	This chapter, Section 6.11
7.5.5	Preservation of product	This chapter, Sections 6.8 and 6.10 Chapter 7, Section 7.7.4.
7.6	Control of monitoring and measuring devices	Not applicable
8	Measurement, analysis, and improvement	This chapter, Section 6.13

Continued

ISO 9001 Section	Control	Procedure(s)
8.1	General	This chapter, Section 6.13
8.2	Monitoring and measurement	Chapter 4, Section 4.6.4 and 4.7.3 This chapter, Sections 6.2.2, 6.8, and 6.9
8.2.1	Customer satisfaction	Chapter 4, Section 4.9 This chapter, Section 6.8
8.2.2	Internal audit	Chapter 4, Section 4.7.3
8.2.3	Monitoring and measurement of processes	Chapter 4, Section 4.9 This chapter, Sections 6.8 and 6.9
8.2.4	Monitoring and measurement of product	Chapter 4, Section 4.9 This chapter, Sections 6.8 and 6.9
8.3	Control of non-conforming product	Chapter 4, Sections 4.6.3, 4.6.4, and 4.7.3 This chapter, Sections 6.8 and 6.14
8.4	Analysis of data	Chapter 4, Section 4.7.3 This chapter, Sections 6.8, 6.9, and 6.14
8.5	Improvement	Chapter 3, Section 3.4 Chapter 4, Sections 4.7.3, 4.8, and 4.9 This chapter, Sections 6.8, 6.9, 6.13.2, and 6.14
8.5.1	Continual improvement	Chapter 4, Sections 4.7.3, 4.8, and 4.9 This chapter, Sections 6.8, 6.9, 6.13.2, and 6.14
8.5.2	Corrective action	Chapter 4, Sections 4.8 and 4.9
8.5.3	Preventive action	Chapter 4, Sections 4.8 and 4.9

There are two exclusions identified:

- *7.4 Purchasing*—general purchasing such as hardware, software, stationery, etc., are not included in the system as this is not an element of the core business provided by the Forensic Laboratory. The contracting of services from associates is covered in this system.
- *7.6 Control of monitoring and measuring devices*—no monitoring or measuring devices are used for any core business provided by the Forensic Laboratory.

These are defined in the Forensic Laboratory's Scope Statement given in Chapter 5, Appendix 11.

APPENDIX 2 - MAPPING ISO 17025 TO IMS PROCEDURES

ISO 17025 Section	Control	Procedure(s)
4	Management requirements	This chapter, Section 6.2
4.1	Organization	This chapter, Section 6.2.1
4.1.1	Organization	This chapter, Sections 6.2.1.1 and 6.2.1.2
4.1.2	Organization	This chapter, Sections 6.2.2.3 and 6.2.2.4
4.1.3	Organization	This chapter, Section 6.2.2.4
4.1.4	Organization	This chapter, Sections 6.2.1.5 and 6.2.1.6 Chapter 3, Appendix 3
4.1.5	Organization	Chapter 3, Appendix 3 Chapter 4, Sections 4.6.2 and 4.6.2.2.1, Appendix 35 This chapter, Sections 6.2.1.6, 6.2.2.6, 6.11, and 6.2.1.3, Appendix 24 Chapter 18, Sections 18.2.2 and 18.2.5

Continued

ISO 17025 Section	Control	Procedure(s)
4.1.6	Organization	Chapter 4, Sections 4.6.5 and 4.4 This chapter, Sections 6.6.2.3, 6.6.2.4, and 6.8
4.2	Management system	Chapter 4
4.2.1	Management system	Chapter 4
4.2.2	Management system	Chapter 4, Sections 4.6.2.2 and 4.8; Chapter 3, Appendix 4 This chapter, Appendix 9
4.2.3	Management system	Chapter 4, Sections 4.4 and 4.6.2
4.2.4	Management system	Chapter 4, Sections 4.6.2.2 and 4.6.5
4.2.5	Management system	Chapter 4
4.2.6	Management system	This chapter, Appendices 7 and 24
4.2.7	Management system	Chapter 4, Section 4.6.3
4.3	Document control	Chapter 4, Section 4.6.3
4.3.1	General	Chapter 4, Section 4.6.3
4.3.2	Document approval and issue	Chapter 4, Sections 4.6.3.2 and 4.6.4.3.5
4.3.3	Document changes	Chapter 4, Section 4.6.3.3
4.4	Review of requests, tenders, and contracts	This chapter, Section 6.6
4.4.1	Review of requests, tenders, and contracts	This chapter, Sections 6.1, 6.6.2.3, and 6.6.2.4, Appendix 14
4.4.2	Review of requests, tenders, and contracts	This chapter, Sections 6.6.2.3.4 and 6.6.2.4
4.4.3	Review of requests, tenders, and contracts	This chapter, Sections 6.6.2.3, and 6.6.2.4, Appendix 14 Chapter 14
4.4.4	Review of requests, tenders, and contracts	This chapter, Section 6.6.2.4
4.4.5	Review of requests, tenders, and contracts	This chapter, Section 6.6.2.4
4.5	Subcontracting of tests and calibrations	Chapter 14
4.6	Purchasing services and supplies	This chapter, Section 6.7.4 Chapter 12, Section 12.3.14.2
4.7	Service to the customer	This chapter, Sections 6.6, 6.7, 6.8, and 6.11
4.7.1	Service to the customer	This chapter, Sections 6.6.2.3, 6.6.2.4, 6.7, 6.8, 6.9, and 6.11, Appendix 20
4.7.1	Service to the customer	This chapter, Section 6.9, Appendix 20
4.8	Complaints	This chapter, Section 6.14
4.9	Control of non-conforming testing and/or calibration work	This chapter, Section 6.13.2
4.9.1	Control of non-conforming testing and/or calibration work	Chapter 4, Sections 4.8.1 and 4.9 This chapter, Sections 6.8 and 6.14
4.9.2	Control of non-conforming testing and/or calibration work	Chapter 4, Section 4.8
4.10	Improvement	Chapter 4, Section 4.8
4.11	Corrective action	Chapter 4, Section 4.8
4.11.1	General	Chapter 4, Section 4.8, Appendix 14
4.11.2	Cause analysis	Chapter 4, Section 4.8.1, Appendix 48
4.11.3	Selection and implementation of corrective actions	Chapter 4, Sections 4.6.3.4 and 4.8.2 Chapter 7, Section 7.1

Continued

ISO 17025 Section	Control	Procedure(s)
4.11.4	Monitoring of corrective actions	Chapter 7, Section 7.4.3
4.11.5	Additional audits	Chapter 4, Section 4.7.3, Appendix 42
4.12	Preventive action	Chapter 4, Sections 4.8.3, 4.8.5, and 4.8.6
4.13	Control of records	Chapter 4, Section 4.6.4
4.13.1	General	Chapter 4, Section 4.6.4 Chapter 5, Appendix 16 This chapter, Section 6.11 Chapter 12, Section 12.3.14.9
4.13.2	Technical records	Chapter 9, Appendix 27
4.14	Internal audits	Chapter 4, Sections 4.7.3 and 4.8 Chapter 7, Section 7.4.3
4.15	Management Reviews	Chapter 4, Section 4.9, Appendix 36
5	Technical requirements	This chapter, Section 6.12
5.1	General	This chapter, Section 6.12
5.2	Personnel	This chapter, Section 6.12.5
5.3	Accommodation and environmental conditions	This chapter, Section 6.12.6
5.4	Test and calibration methods and method validation	This chapter, Section 6.12.7
5.4.1	General	This chapter, Section 6.12.7
5.4.2	Selection of methods	This chapter, Section 6.12.7
5.4.3	Laboratory-developed methods	This chapter, Section 6.12.7
5.4.4	Non-standard methods	This chapter, Section 6.12.7
5.4.5	Validation of methods	This chapter, Section 6.12.7
5.4.6	Estimation of uncertainty of measurement	This chapter, Section 6.12.7
5.4.7	Control of data	This chapter, Section 6.12.7
5.5	Equipment	This chapter, Section 6.12.8
5.6	Measurement traceability	This chapter, Section 6.12.9
5.6.1	General	This chapter, Section 6.12.9
5.6.2	Specific requirements	This chapter, Section 6.12.9
5.6.3	Reference standards and reference materials	This chapter, Section 6.12.9
5.7	Sampling	This chapter, Section 6.12.10
5.8	Handling of test and calibration items	This chapter, Section 6.12.10
5.9	Assuring the quality of test and calibration results	This chapter, Section 6.12.11
5.10	Reporting the results	This chapter, Section 6.12.12
5.10.1	General	This chapter, Section 6.12.10
5.10.2	Test reports and calibration certificates	This chapter, Section 6.12.10
5.10.3	Test reports	This chapter, Section 6.12.10, Appendix 31
5.10.4	Calibration certificates	Not applicable
5.10.5	Opinions and interpretations	This chapter, Section 6.12.10
5.10.6	Testing and calibration results obtained from subcontractors	This chapter, Section 6.12.10 Chapter 14

Continued

ISO 17025 Section	Control	Procedure(s)
5.10.7	Electronic transmission of results	Chapter 5, Appendix 16 Chapter 12, Section 12.3.7.2
5.10.8	Format of reports and certificates	This chapter, Section 6.12.12
5.10.9	Amendments to test reports and calibration certificates	This chapter, Sections 6.8 and 6.12.12

APPENDIX 3 - MAPPING SWGDE QUALITY REQUIREMENTS TO IMS PROCEDURES

SWGDE Section	Control	Procedure(s)
4	Management requirements	This chapter, Section 6.2
4.1	Organization	This chapter, Section 6.2
4.1.1	Legal entity	This chapter, Sections 6.2 and 6.2.1.1
4.1.2	Responsibilities to provide Customer Service	This chapter, Section 6.2.2.3
4.1.3	Scope of Quality System	Chapter 5, Appendix 11
4.1.4	Potential Conflicts of Interest	Chapter 3, Appendix 3
4.1.5	Organization	This chapter, Sections 6.2.1.3 and 6.11, Appendices 7 and 24 Chapter 18, Sections 18.1.5 and 18.1.2 Chapter 4 Chapter 3, Appendix 3.4
4.1.6	Top Management Communication	Chapter 4, Section 4.6.5 Chapter 4
4.1.7	Health and Safety Manager	This chapter, Section 6.12.6.3 Chapter 17 Chapter 18, Section 18.1.5
4.1.8	Key Management	This chapter, Section 6.2.1.3
4.2	Quality System	Chapter 4 Chapter 3, Appendix 4
4.2.1	Documenting the Quality System	Chapter 4
4.2.2	Quality Policy Statement	Chapter 3, Appendix 4
4.2.3	Continually Improving Effectiveness	Chapter 4, Section 4.8, Appendix 14
4.2.4	Meeting Customer Requirements	This chapter, Sections 6.2.2.3, 6.6, 6.7, and 6.8
4.2.5	Documentation Structure	Chapter 4 Chapter 4, Section 4.6.3
4.2.6	Roles and Responsibilities	This chapter, Appendices 7 and Appendix 24 Chapter 18, Section 18.1.5
4.2.7	Integrity of the Quality System	This chapter, Section 6.4
4.3	Document Control	
4.3.1	Document Control Procedures	Chapter 4, Section 4.6.3
4.3.2	Document approval and issue procedures	Chapter 4, Sections 4.6.3 and 4.6.4
4.3.3	Document change procedures	Chapter 4, Sections 4.6.3 and 4.6.4
4.4	Reviews of Requests, Tenders, and Contracts	Chapter 4, Section 4.6.3.3 This chapter, Section 6.3.4 Chapter 14, Sections 14.5.1.4 and 14.8.2.3

Continued

SWGDE Section	Control	Procedure(s)
4.4.1	Request Review Procedures	Chapter 4, Sections 4.6.3.3 and 4.6.3.4
4.4.2	Records	The Client virtual case file
4.4.3	Review of subcontracted work	Chapter 14, Sections 14.5.1.3 and 14.8.2.2
4.4.4	Notifying Customer of deviations from the Request	Chapter 4, Section 4.8
4.4.5	Amendments to the Request	Chapter 4, Section 4.6.3.4.4
4.5	Subcontracting examinations	Chapter 14, Section 14.9.1
4.6	Purchasing Services and Supplies	This chapter, Section 6.7.4 Chapter 12, Section 12.3.14.2 Chapter 14, Sections 14.5, 14.6, 14.7, and 14.8
4.6.1	Service and supply procurement procedure	Chapter 14, Sections 14.5, 14.6, 14.7 and 14.8
4.6.2	Procedure for inspecting supplies and consumable materials	Chapter 14, Sections 14.5.1.3 and 14.8.2.2
4.6.3	Purchasing documents	Chapter 14, Section 14.5.1.3
4.6.4	Procedure for evaluating suppliers of critical supplies and services	Chapter 4, Section 4.7.3 Chapter 14, Sections 14.5.1.3 and 14.8.2.2.
4.7	Service to the Customer	Chapter 4, Section 4.6.3.4.4 This chapter, Sections 6.6 and 6.8
4.7.1	Clarifying customer's request	This chapter, Section 6.6.2.4.2 and 6.6
4.7.2	Customer feedback	This chapter, Section 6.9, Appendix 20
4.8	Complaints	This chapter, Section 6.14, Appendices 20, 21, 22, and 23
4.8.1	Policy for tracking and resolving complaints	This chapter, Section 6.14
4.8.2	Policy for complaints from laboratory employees	This chapter, Section 6.14
4.9	Control of non-conforming work	This chapter, Section 6.13.2
4.9.1	Policy for actions when non-conforming work or procedures are identified	Chapter 4, Section 4.8.1 This chapter, Section 6.13.2
4.9.2	Possibility of recurrence or doubt of compliance	Chapter 4, Section 4.8.2 and 4.8.3, Appendix 49
4.10	Improvement	Chapter 4, Section 4.8, Appendix 14
4.11	Procedure for corrective action	Chapter 4, Sections 4.8.1, 4.8.2, and 4.8.4
4.11.1	Authority for corrective action	Chapter 4, Sections 4.8.5 and 4.8.6
4.11.2	Root cause determination	Chapter 4, Section 4.8.1, Appendix 49
4.11.3	Corrective action steps	Chapter 4, Sections 4.8.1, 4.8.2, and 4.8.4
4.11.4	Monitoring and verifying corrective actions	Chapter 4, Section 4.8.6
4.11.5	Additional audits	Chapter 4, Section 4.7.3 This chapter, Section 6.13.3
4.12	Preventive action	Chapter 4, Section 4.8.3
4.12.1	Identifying improvement opportunities	Chapter 4, Section 4.8.3
4.12.2	Actions and controls for preventive actions	Chapter 4, Sections 4.8.4, 4.8.5, and 4.8.6
4.13	Control of records	Chapter 4, Section 4.6.4
4.13.1	General	Chapter 4, Section 4.6.2.3, Appendix 16
4.13.2	Technical records (case record)	This chapter, Section 6.12

Continued

SWGDE Section	Control	Procedure(s)
4.14	Internal audits	Chapter 4, Section 4.7.3 This chapter, Section 6.13.3
4.14.1	Procedure for internal audits	Chapter 4, Section 4.7.3
4.14.2	Timely corrective actions in response to audit findings	Chapter 4, Section 4.8
4.14.3	Procedure for documenting the audit results	Chapter 4, Section 4.7.3.8, Appendix 47
4.14.4	Verifying implementation and effectiveness of corrective actions	Chapter 4, Section 4.8
4.14.5	Annual accreditation audit report	Chapter 19, Section 19.2.1.21
4.15	Management Reviews	Chapter 4, Section 4.9, Appendix 36
4.15.1	Procedure for annual management quality system review	Chapter 4, Section 4.9, Appendix 36
4.15.2	Review findings	Chapter 4, Section 4.9, Appendix 36
5.	Technical requirements	This chapter, Section 6.12
5.1	General	This chapter, Section 6.12.1
5.2	Personnel	Chapter 18
5.2.1	Competence of Personnel	Chapter 18, Section 18.1.6
5.2.2	Education, training, and skills	Chapter 4, Section 4.6.2.2 This chapter, Appendix 27 Chapter 18, Section 18.2
5.2.3	Employees and contractors	Chapter 14, Section 14.9.
5.2.4	Job descriptions	This chapter, Appendices 7, 24, and 25 Chapter 18, Section 18.1.5
5.2.5	Training records and authorizations	Chapter 4, Section 4.6.2.3 Chapter 18, Section 18.2.1.8
5.2.6	Technical Personnel qualifications	Chapter 4, Section 4.6.2.3 This chapter, Section 6.12.5, Appendix 27 Chapter 18, Section 18.2.1.8
5.2.7	Forensic library	This chapter, Section 6.12.5
5.3	Accommodation and environmental conditions	Chapter 2 Chapter 3 This chapter, Section 6.12.6 Chapter 7, Section 7.3
5.3.1	Laboratory facilities	This chapter, Section 6.12.6.1
5.3.2	Environmental conditions	This chapter, Section 6.12.6
5.3.3	Separation between activity areas	Chapter 2 Chapter 3 Chapter 12, Sections 12.3.5 and 12.3.6
5.3.4	Access	Chapter 2 Chapter 3 Chapter 12, Section 12.4.4
5.3.5	Good housekeeping	Chapter 4
5.3.6	Health and safety program	Chapter 4, Appendix 7 Chapter 17
5.4	Forensic methods and method validation	This chapter, Sections 6.6 and 6.12.7 Chapter 12

Continued

SWGDE Section	Control	Procedure(s)
5.4.1	General	This chapter, Section 6.12.7
5.4.2	Selection of methods	This chapter, Section 6.12.7
5.4.3	Laboratory-developed methods	This chapter, Section 6.12.7
5.4.4	Non-standard methods	This chapter, Section 6.12.7
5.4.5	Validation of methods	This chapter, Section 6.12.7
5.4.6	Estimation of uncertainty of measurement	This chapter, Section 6.12.7
5.4.7	Control of data	This chapter, Section 6.12.7
5.5	Equipment	This chapter, Section 6.12.8
5.5.1	Laboratory equipment	This chapter, Section 6.12.8 Chapter 7, Section 7.4.5
5.5.2	Performance verification and calibration	This chapter, Section 6.12.7
5.5.3	Operators and instructions	This chapter, Section 6.12.5
5.5.4	Unique identification	This chapter, Section 6.12.8
5.5.5	Equipment records	This chapter, Section 6.12.8 Chapter 12, Section 12.3.14.2.1.3
5.5.6	Handling and maintenance of measuring equipment	This chapter, Section 6.12.8 Chapter 7, Section 7.5.4
5.5.7	Defective equipment	This chapter, Section 6.12.8
5.5.8	Calibration labels	Not applicable
5.5.9	Critical equipment that leaves laboratory control	Chapter 12, Section 12.3.10
5.5.10	Performance verification and calibration procedure	This chapter, Section 6.12.7 Chapter 7, Section 7.5.5
5.6	Measurement traceability	This chapter, Section 6.12.9
5.6.1	Calibrating equipment	Not applicable
5.7	Sampling	This chapter, Section 6.12.10
5.8	Handling evidence	Chapter 8, Section 8.7.1 Chapter 9, Section 9.1.5
5.8.1	Evidence procedures	Chapter 8, Section 8.7.1 Chapter 9, Section 9.1.5
5.8.2	Identification system	Chapter 8, Section 8.7.1 Chapter 9, Section 9.1.5
5.8.3	Evidence abnormalities	Chapter 8, Section 8.7.1 Chapter 9, Section 9.1.5
5.8.4	Avoiding deterioration, loss or damage	Chapter 8, Section 8.7.1 Chapter 9, Section 9.1.5
5.9	Assuring quality of examinations	This chapter, Section 6.12.11
5.9.1	Monitoring validity of examinations	This chapter, Section 6.12.11
5.9.2	Quality control data analysis	This chapter, Section 6.12.11
5.9.3	Proficiency testing	This chapter, Section 6.12.11
5.9.4	Technical review of results	Chapter 6, Section 6.8
5.9.5	Administrative review of results	This chapter, Section 6.8.4
5.9.6	Monitoring testimony	Chapter 11, Appendix 8

Continued

SWGDE Section	Control	Procedure(s)
5.9.7	Retaining records of testimony monitoring	Chapter 11, Section 11.6.7.2
5.10	Reporting examination results	This chapter, Sections 6.8 and 6.12.12, Appendix 31
5.10.1	General	This chapter, Section 6.8
5.10.2	Examination reports	This chapter, Sections 6.8.4 and 6.12.12, Appendix 31
5.10.3	Examination reports and deviations from standard procedures	This chapter, Sections 6.8.4 and 6.12.12, Appendix 31
5.10.4	Calibration certificates	Not applicable
5.10.5	Opinions and interpretations	This chapter, Section 6.12.12
5.10.6	Examination results obtained from subcontractors	This chapter, Section 6.12.12 Chapter 14, Sections 14.5.1.3 and 14.8.2.2
5.10.7	Electronic transmission of results	This chapter, Section 6.12.12 Chapter 12, Sections 12.3.7.2 and 12.3.14.9
5.10.8	Format of reports	This chapter, Appendix 31
5.10.9	Amendments to examination reports	This chapter, Section 6.8
Appendix A	Forms	Various throughout the Forensic Laboratory's Integrated Management System but specifically in this chapter and in Chapters 8 and 9
Appendix B1	Request for examination	This chapter, Sections 6.6 and 6.8 Chapter 8, Section 8.1.1
Appendix B2	Case assignment	Chapter 9, Section 9.7.2
Appendix B3	Security	Chapter 12
Appendix B4	Tool test and validation	Chapter 7, Section 7.5.5
Appendix B5	Shipping evidence	Chapter 8, Section 8.7
Appendix B6	Inventorying and identifying evidence	Chapter 8, Section 8.6.11
Appendix B7	Internal proficiency tests	Chapter 18, Section 18.2.6

APPENDIX 4 - MAPPING NIST-150 QUALITY REQUIREMENTS TO IMS PROCEDURES

NIST-150 Section	Control	Procedure(s)
4	Management requirements for accreditation	
4.1	Organization	This chapter, Section 6.2.1
4.2	Management system	Chapter 4
4.3	Document control	Chapter 4, Section 4.6.3
4.4	Review of requests, tenders, and contracts	This chapter, Section 6.6, Appendix 14
4.5	Subcontracting of tests and calibrations	Chapter 14
4.6	Purchasing services and supplies	This chapter, Section 6.7.4 Chapter 12, Section 12.3.14.2 Chapter 14, Sections 14.5, 14.6, 14.7, 14.8, and 14.9
4.7	Service to the customer	This chapter, Sections 6.2.2.3, 6.6, 6.7, and 6.8
4.8	Complaints	This chapter, Section 6.14

Continued

NIST-150 Section	Control	Procedure(s)
4.9	Control of non-conforming testing and/or calibration work	Chapter 4, Section 4.8.1 This chapter, Section 6.13.2
4.10	Improvement	Chapter 4, Section 4.8
4.11	Corrective action	Chapter 4, Sections 4.8.2, 4.8.4, 4.8.5, and 4.8.6
4.12	Preventive action	Chapter 4, Section 4.8.3
4.13	Control of records	Chapter 4, Section 4.6.4
4.14	Internal audits	Chapter 4, Section 4.7.3
4.15	Management Reviews	Chapter 4, Section 4.9
5	Technical requirements for accreditation	This chapter, Section 6.12
5.1	General	This chapter, Section 6.12.1
5.2	Personnel	This chapter, Sections 6.12.3 and 6.12.5 Chapter 18
5.3	Accommodation and environmental conditions	Chapter 2 Chapter 3 This chapter, Section 6.12.6 Chapter 12
5.4	Test and calibration methods and method validation	This chapter, Section 6.12.7
5.5	Equipment	This chapter, Section 6.12.8
5.6	Measurement traceability	This chapter, Section 6.12.9
5.7	Sampling	This chapter, Section 6.12.10
5.8	Handling of test and calibration items	Chapter 7, Section 7.5.5
5.9	Assuring the quality of test and calibration results	This chapter, Section 6.12.11
5.10	Reporting the results	This chapter, Section 6.12.12, Appendix 31

APPENDIX 5 - MAPPING ENFSI QUALITY REQUIREMENTS TO IMS PROCEDURES

ENFSI Section	Control	Procedure(s)
3	Quality Assurance	This chapter
3.3	Personnel	Chapter 4, Section 4.6.2.2 This chapter, Appendices 7, 24, and 25
3.4	Competence requirements	Chapter 4, Section 4.6.2.2 This chapter, Appendix 27 Chapter 18, Section 18.2.5
3.5	Proficiency tests	Chapter 18, Section 18.2.6
3.6	Documentation	Chapter 4, Section 4.6.3 This chapter, Sections 6.6, 6.8, and 6.12.12
3.7	Equipment	This chapter, Section 6.12.8 Chapter 2 Chapter 3 Chapter 7
3.8	Validation	This chapter, Section 6.12.7 Chapter 7, Section 7.5.5

Continued

ENFSI Section	Control	Procedure(s)
3.9	Digital software/hardware	This chapter, Section 6.12.8 Chapter 7
3.10	Accommodation	This chapter, Section 6.12.6
3.11	Audit	Chapter 4, Section 7.3 This chapter, Section 6.13.3
4	Establishing the customer requirement	This chapter, Section 6.6
5	Case assessment	Chapter 9, Section 9.7.2
6	Prioritization and sequence of examinations	Chapter 9, Section 9.1.5
7	General principles applying to the recovery of digital evidence	Chapter 9, Section 9.1.5
8	Practices applicable to digital evidence examinations	Chapter 9, Section 9.1.5
9	Location and recovery of digital evidence at the scene	Chapter 8, Section 8.6
9.1		Does not have a heading but refers to ACPO Guidance
9.2	Anticontamination procedures	Chapter 8, Sections 8.5.4, 8.6.2, 8.6.11.17.5, and 8.7.2
9.3	Searching the Scene	Chapter 8, Section 8.6.5
9.4	Collecting the Evidence	Chapter 8, Section 8.6.9
9.5	Packaging, labeling, and documentation	Chapter 8, Section 8.7
10	Laboratory examinations	
10.1	Does not have a heading but refers precautions before examination	Chapter 8, Section 8.6.9
10.2	Does not have a heading but refers to integrity of packaging and evidential refusal	Chapter 8
10.3	Does not have a heading but refers to minimizing risks from electronic discharge	Chapter 8, Sections 8.6.14 and 8.7.2
10.4	Does not have a heading but refers to written procedures	The IMS
10.5	Analysis Protocols	The IMS and Chapters 8, 9 and 10
10.6	Case Records	This chapter, Section 6.12.12 Chapter 9, Sections 9.13 and 9.15
11	Evaluation and interpretation	Chapter 9, Section 9.10
12	Presentation of written evidence	This chapter, Section 6.12.12
13	Case file review	Chapter 4, Section 4.8 This chapter, Sections 6.8 and 6.13
13.1	Does not have a heading but refers to technical and administrative reviews	This chapter, Sections 6.8 and 6.13
13.2	Technical review	This chapter, Sections 6.8 and 6.13
13.3	Administrative review	This chapter, Sections 6.8 and 6.13
14	Presentation of oral evidence	Chapter 11, Section 11.6
15	Health and Safety	This chapter, Section 6.12.6.3 Chapter 17
16	Complaints procedure	This chapter, Section 6.14

APPENDIX 6 - MAPPING FSR QUALITY REQUIREMENTS TO IMS PROCEDURES

FSR Section	Control	Procedure(s)
5	Management requirements	This chapter, Section 6.2.1.4, Appendices 7, 24, and 25
6	Business continuity	Chapter 3, Section 3.1.15 Chapter 13
7	Independence, impartiality, and integrity	Chapter 3, Section 3.1.3.16 Chapter 3, Appendix 3
8	Confidentiality	This chapter, Sections 6.2.2.6 and 6.11 Chapter 12, Section 12.3.3.3 Chapter 5, Appendix 16
9	Document control	Chapter 4, Section 4.6.3
10	Review of requests, tenders, and contracts	This chapter, Section 6.6, Appendix 14
11	Subcontracting	Chapter 14
12	Packaging and general chemicals and materials	This chapter, Section 6.7.4
13	Complaints	This chapter, Section 6.14
14	Control of non-conforming testing	Chapter 4, Section 4.8.1 This chapter, Section 6.13.2
15	Control of records	Chapter 4, Section 6.4, Appendix 16 Chapter 12, Sections 12.3.13 and 12.3.14
15.1	General	Chapter 4, Section 4.6.4 Chapter 5, Appendix 16 This chapter, Section 6.11 Chapter 12, Section 12.3.14
15.2	Technical records	Chapter 8, Section 8.6.15 Chapter 9
15.3	Checking and review	This chapter, Sections 6.8 and 6.13.2, Appendix 19
16	Internal audits	Chapter 4, Section 4.7.3, Appendix 42 This chapter, Section 6.13.3 Chapter 7, Section 7.4.3
17	Technical requirements	This chapter, Section 6.12
17.1	Personnel	Chapter 18, Sections 18.1.3 and 18.1.4
17.2	Code of Conduct	There are a number of codes of conduct—examples are from the relevant individual certifications Chapter 4
17.3	Training	Chapter 4, Sections 4.6.2.2 and 4.6.2.3 Chapter 18, Section 18.2.1
18	Competence	Chapter 4, Section 4.6.2.2 This chapter, Appendix 27 Chapter 18, Section 18.2.5
19	Accommodation and environmental conditions	Chapter 2 Chapter 3 This chapter, Section 6.12.6 Chapter 12, Section 12.3.8 Chapter 12, Section 12.3.14.10 Chapter 12, Section 12.4 Chapter 12, Section 12.3.10.14

Continued

FSR Section	Control	Procedure(s)
19.4[a]	Contamination avoidance, monitoring, and detection	Chapter 5 Chapter 8, Sections 8.2 and 8.3 Chapter 8, Section 8.7 Chapter 12, Sections 12.4.4 and 12.6
20.	Test methods and method validation	This chapter, Section 6.12.7 Chapter 7, Section 7.5.5
20.1	Selection of methods	This chapter, Sections 6.6.2.3, 6.6.2.4, and 6.12.7, Appendix 14
20.2	Validation of methods	This chapter, Section 6.12.7 Chapter 7, Section 7.5.5
20.3	Determining the end-user's requirements and specification	This chapter, Sections 6.6 and 6.8, Appendices 13 and 15 Chapter 12, Section 12.9.6
20.4	Risk assessment of the method	Chapter 5 Chapter 7, Section 7.5.5
20.5	Review of the end-user's requirements and specification	This chapter, Sections 6.6 and 6.8
20.6	The acceptance criteria	This chapter, Sections 6.6 and 6.8
20.7	The validation plan	This chapter, Section 6.12.7
20.8	Validation of measurement-based methods	Not applicable to the Forensic Laboratory
20.9	Validation of interpretive methods	This chapter, Section 6.12.7 Chapter 7, Section 7.5.5
20.10	Verification of the validation of adopted methods	This chapter, Section 6.12.7 Chapter 7, Section 7.5.5
20.11	Minor changes in methods	This chapter, Section 6.12.7 Chapter 7, Section 7.4.3
20.12	Validation outcomes	This chapter, Section 6.12.7 Chapter 7, Section 7.5.5
20.13	Assessment of acceptance criteria compliance	This chapter, Section 6.12.7 Chapter 7, Section 7.5.5
20.14	Validation report	This chapter, Section 6.12.7 Chapter 7, Section 7.5.5
20.15	A statement of validation completion	This chapter, Section 6.12.7 Chapter 7, Section 7.5.5
20.15[b]	Validation library	This chapter, Section 6.12.7 Chapter 7, Section 7.5.5
20.16	Implementation plan and any constraints	This chapter, Section 6.12.7 Chapter 7, Section 7.4.3 Chapter 7, Section 7.5.5
20.17	Estimation of uncertainty of measurement	This chapter, Section 6.12.7 Chapter 7, Section 7.5.5
20.18	Control of data	This chapter, Section 6.12.7 Chapter 12
20.18.1	General	This chapter, Section 6.12.7 Chapter 12
20.18.2	Electronic information capture, storage, transfer, retrieval, and disposal	Chapter 12

Continued

FSR Section	Control	Procedure(s)
20.18.3	Electronic Information Security	Chapter 12
20.18.4	Databases	Not applicable in the Forensic Laboratory
21	Equipment	This chapter, Section 6.12.8 Chapter 7, Section 7.4.3 Chapter 7, Section 7.5.5
21.1	Computers and automated equipment	This chapter, Section 6.12.8 Chapter 7, Section 7.4.3 Chapter 7, Section 7.5.5 Chapter 7, Section 7.1 Chapter 12, Section 12.3.14 Chapter 12, Section 12.3.13.1.2
22	Measurement traceability	This chapter, Section 6.12.9 Chapter 7, Section 7.5.5
22.1	Reference standards and reference materials	This chapter, Section 6.12.9 Chapter 7, Section 7.5.5
22.1.1	Intermediate checks	This chapter, Section 6.12.9 Chapter 7, Section 7.5.5
23	Handling of test items	This chapter, Section 6.12.9
23.1	Receipt of cases and exhibits at the laboratory	Chapter 9, Section 9.6
23.2	Case assessment and prioritization	Chapter 9, Section 9.7
23.3	Exhibit handling, protection, and storage	Chapter 8, Sections 8.6.9, 8.6.10, 8.6.11, 8.6.13, 8.6.14, and 8.6.15 Chapter 9, Section 9.7 Chapter 12, Section 12.3.14
23.4	Exhibit return and disposal	Chapter 9, Sections 9.6 and 9.20 Chapter 12, Section 12.3.14.10
24	Assuring the quality of test results	This chapter, Sections 6.8 and 6.13
24.1	Inter-laboratory comparisons (proficiency tests and collaborative exercises)	Not applicable
25	Reporting the results	This chapter, Section 6.12.12 Chapter 12, Sections 12.3.12, 12.3.14.8, and 12.3.14.9
25.1	General	Chapter 4, Appendix 16 This chapter, Section 6.12.12 Chapter 18, Sections 18.2.5 and 18.2.6
25.2	Reports and statements to the CJS	This chapter, Section 6.12.12, Appendix 31
25.2.3[c]	Report types	This chapter, Sections 6.6, 6.8 and 6.12.12, Appendix 31 Chapter 9, Sections 9.13 and 9.15
25.3	Retention, recording, revelation, and prosecution disclosure	Specific to Legislation in England and Wales only
25.4	Defence examinations	Specific to Legislation in England and Wales only
25.5	Opinions and interpretations	This chapter, Section 6.12.12 Chapter 9, Section 9.16

[a] *There is no 19.1, 19.2, or 19.3 in the CoP.*
[b] *There are two 20.15 references in the CoP.*
[c] *There is no 25.2.1 or 25.2.2 in the CoP.*

APPENDIX 7 - QUALITY MANAGER, JOB DESCRIPTION

OBJECTIVE AND ROLE

The Quality Manager is responsible for establishing and monitoring adherence to ISO 9001 and other quality standards in the Forensic Laboratory. Quality includes both the qualitative and quantitative measures. This includes complying with all mandated requirements including maintaining ISO 9001 certification and any other relevant quality certifications and accreditations.

PROBLEMS AND CHALLENGES

The primary challenge for the Quality Manager is establishing a good working relationship with the Forensic Laboratory employees that encourage cooperation and teamwork instead of conflict and avoidance. The Quality Manager needs to work on all the Forensic Laboratory employees to ensure that quality is built into all Forensic Laboratory products and services to all Clients from the beginning.

PRINCIPAL ACCOUNTABILITIES

The Quality Manager:

- promotes quality achievement and performance improvement throughout the Forensic Laboratory;
- sets Quality Assurance compliance objectives and ensures that targets are achieved;
- maintains awareness of the business context and company profitability, including budgetary control issues;
- assesses the Forensic Laboratory's product and service specifications and their suppliers, comparing them with Client requirements;
- works with purchasing employees to establish quality requirements from external suppliers;
- ensures compliance with relevant international and national standards and legislation; this also specifically includes the requirements for ISO 17025;
- considers the application of environmental and Health and Safety standards;
- agrees standards and establishes clearly defined quality methods for the Forensic Laboratory's employees to apply to their products and service offerings to their Clients;
- defines quality procedures in conjunction with relevant Forensic Laboratory business units;
- sets up and maintains controls and documentation procedures in the IMS;
- identifies relevant quality-related training needs and delivers relevant training;
- collates and analyzes performance data and charts against defined quality parameters;
- ensures quality tests and procedures are properly understood, carried out, and evaluated and that product modifications are investigated, if necessary;
- supervises technical staff in carrying out quality tests and checks;
- writes relevant technical and management systems reports;
- brings together employees of different disciplines within the Forensic Laboratory to plan, formulate, and agree comprehensive quality procedures;
- persuades reluctant employees to change their way of working to incorporate quality methods;
- liaises with Clients' auditors and ensures the execution of corrective action and compliance with Clients' specifications;
- establishes standards of service, in association with relevant Forensic Laboratory departments for all of the Forensic Laboratory's Clients;
- prepares clear explanatory quality documents;
- monitors performance by gathering relevant quality data and producing statistical reports;
- maintains ISO 9001 certification, any other relevant quality certifications and accreditations;
- ensures that the Forensic Laboratory's quality systems are continuously improved;
- ensures that all corrective actions are completed in a timely manner;
- develops plans for migration of quality management policies and procedures to support the Forensic Laboratory's future directions;
- develops the Forensic Laboratory's long-range quality management strategy;
- participates in international, national, and local SIG presentations, and publishes management-approved articles describing the Forensic Laboratory's quality management initiatives and how they relate to the business;
- develops and manages effective working relationships with all appropriate internal and external stakeholders;
- maintains external links to other forensic laboratories to gain competitive assessments and share information, where appropriate;
- identifies the emerging technologies to be assimilated, integrated, and introduced within the Forensic Laboratory, which could significantly impact the Forensic Laboratory's product and service offering SLAs;
- interfaces with external industrial and academic organizations in order to maintain state-of-the-art knowledge in emerging quality management issues and to enhance the Forensic Laboratory's image as a first-class solution provider utilizing the latest thinking in this field;
- adheres to all established Forensic Laboratory policies, standards, and procedures;

- performs all responsibilities in accordance with, or in excess of, the requirements of the Forensic Laboratory Integrated Management System.

AUTHORITY

The Quality Manager has the authority to:

- monitor product and service offerings for adherence to the Forensic Laboratory's quality standards;
- monitor the Forensic Laboratory's internal processes and procedures for adherence to the Forensic Laboratory's quality standards;
- monitor Service Level Agreements and their associated metrics;
- take appropriate action to ensure that quality is maintained and continuously improved throughout the Forensic Laboratory and for all of its product and service offerings.

CONTACTS

Internal

Contacts within the Forensic Laboratory are throughout the whole organization.

External

Those external to the Forensic Laboratory will be with appropriate Special Interest Groups (SIGs), other Quality professionals, and organizations such as the Chartered Quality Institute, the Institute of Quality Assurance, etc.

REPORTS TO

The Quality Manager reports to:

- Top Management.

APPENDIX 8 - BUSINESS PLAN TEMPLATE

EXECUTIVE SUMMARY

- the Forensic Laboratory business, an overview;
- the market for Forensic Laboratory products and services;
- the business potential;
- forecast profit.

DESCRIPTION OF THE FORENSIC LABORATORY'S BUSINESS

- a brief description of the business;
- history of the Forensic Laboratory and its ownership;
- legal status;
- location of provision of products and services;
- a description of the Forensic Laboratory's products and services;
- unique selling points;
- competitor analysis—by size, location, market share, ownership, pricing structure, services offered;
- a description of the Forensic Laboratory's proposed new products and services;
- intangible assets and how assets are protected;
- current size and expected growth of the market;
- analysis of the Forensic Laboratory's market by segments;
- identification of new markets segments;
- existing and potential Clients;
- routes to market;
- management team.

SITUATIONAL AUDIT (CURRENT SITUATION)

This is based on metrics from the business, including sales and marketing information and allows the Forensic Laboratory to:

- identify competitive advantages;
- identify the Forensic Laboratory's strengths, weaknesses, opportunities, and threats;
- prioritize new opportunities to pursue (from the risk register—Chapter 5, Appendix 17);
- provide accurate details for business planning and strategy development.

AIMS AND OBJECTIVES (TARGET SITUATION)

- overview of a "5-year plan";
- SMART[b] objectives—quantitative goals.

STRATEGY AND TACTICS (HOW TO GET THERE)

- the strategic approach to achieving the objectives;
- the tactics refer to the details of the strategy.

Note

The details will be contained in subordinate departmental plans.

b. SMART has been defined in Chapter 3, Section 3.1.17.

MARKETING PLAN

- brand development;
- customer service strategy;
- market research;
- pricing strategy;
- segmentation and targeting of Clients;
- unique selling points.

The marketing plan seeks to answer the following questions:

- how is the digital forensics market segmented?
- what are the Forensic Laboratory's competitive advantages?
- what is special about the Forensic Laboratory's products and services?
- what is the Forensic Laboratory's marketing strategy?
- what is the size and growth rate of the digital forensics market?
- who are the Forensic Laboratory's competitors?
- who are the Forensic Laboratory's customers?

OPERATIONS PLAN

- capacity—current and potential with current employees;
- implementation plans—with departmental breakdowns, accountabilities, budgets, and target delivery dates;
- IT strategy;
- key suppliers and alternates;
- purchasing arrangements;
- quality control plans;
- research and development.

MANAGEMENT, STAFFING, AND ORGANIZATION

- corporate governance requirements;
- key employees;
- organizational chart (current and proposed);
- recruitment strategy;
- remuneration (salaries and bonuses);
- senior management details;
- staffing requirements;
- training.

FINANCIAL PLAN

- details of any financing required (internal or external);
- financial ratios required;
- forecast balance sheet;
- forecast cash flow;
- forecast profit and loss;
- forecast sales.

Note 1

Any assumptions made for any forecast must be included.

Note 2

Forecasts should be a month-by-month basis for a minimum of 3 years.

APPENDIX 9 - BUSINESS KPIs

The following business KPIs are used in the Forensic Laboratory:

- *financial governance compliance*—ensuring that financial returns are made on time and are correct;
- *legislative governance*—ensuring that all relevant legislative requirements are met in the jurisdiction of operations;
- *profit levels*—the current profit levels are checked against forecasts on a monthly basis;
- *repeat business*—50% of Clients place one repeat order (where possible since some Clients require only a single piece of work) which is checked against the accounts system;
- *accreditation and certification*—successful gaining and maintaining of any relevant organizational accreditations and certifications;
- *audits (internal and external)*—passing all audits with no non-conformance. If a non-conformance is raised, it is cleared in the agreed time.

Note

There are other metrics and KPIs embedded within the management systems standards in the IMS, but these are not reproduced here.

APPENDIX 10 - QUALITY PLAN CONTENTS

Below is the table of contents of the Forensic Laboratory's quality plan to meet the requirements of ISO 9001. ISO 9001 was, and should be, the first management system implemented in the Forensic Laboratory as it maps the business processes, and all other management systems can flow from that. It is recommended that it is implemented with PAS 99 so that it is possible to implement other management standards and processes in any order, as they are needed.

- table of contents;
- introduction;
- Forensic Laboratory overview;
- quality system scope;
- quality system structure;
- quality manual structure;
- document retention;

- ISO 9001 mapping;
- quality manual format;
- auditing;
- proposed development and certification timescales;
- initial list of required quality procedures;
- document control.

APPENDIX 11 - INDUCTION CHECKLIST CONTENTS

All Forensic Laboratory employees go through the Human Resources Department induction process and the checklist for this includes:

PRIOR TO EMPLOYEE STARTING

- confirm start date and time;
- confirm reporting location and any special requirements;
- book welcome meeting with Line Manager and others, as appropriate;
- submit new user form to IT Department to set up access to information processing systems, as appropriate and authorized;
- advise relevant Forensic Laboratory employees or inductees start details.

ON THE FIRST DAY

Company and Role Details

Introduction to the Forensic Laboratory

These are details of the Forensic Laboratory and its processes and procedures given to the inductee by the Human Resources Department. The inductee signs to confirm that they have received them.

- who and what are the Forensic Laboratory staff;
- values;
- products and services;
- meeting internal and external expectations;
- business planning and development;
- Clients and partners;
- finance;
- communications.

Role Details

These are details of the inductee's role and responsibilities in the Forensic Laboratory given to the inductee by the Human Resources Department. The inductee signs to confirm that they have received them.

- introduction to Line Manager, mentor, and colleagues;
- management structure as applicable to employee;
- responsibility and accountability;
- key goals and targets;
- training and development;
- facilities.

General

- issue temporary ID card if permanent one not available;
- identify location of toilets and refreshment facilities;
- explain first aid procedures and identify first aiders;
- explain emergency evacuation procedures, identify emergency exit and fire wardens;
- if disabled, identify "emergency buddy";
- explain telephone system;
- explain building security and out of hours working procedures;
- explain car parking facilities;
- explain procedures for reporting sickness;
- explain on-site Health and Safety procedures, including accident and "near miss" reporting;
- explain pay and expense claim process;
- explain or demonstrate any other relevant issues to the employee.

INFORMATION CAPTURE

Ensure that the following information is already captured by the Forensic Laboratory, verify it or capture it on the first day the employee starts work:

Personal Details

- full name;
- title;
- date of birth;
- marital status;
- home address;
- home telephone number;
- mobile telephone number;
- personal e-mail address;
- social security (or equivalent) number.

Work Details

- start date;
- probation period;
- department;
- Line Manager;
- position;
- term (permanent, contract, etc.);
- status (full time, part time, etc.);
- salary;
- grade.

Bank Details

- bank name;
- branch name;
- branch address;
- account number;
- account name;
- branch code;
- IBAN;
- BIC.

Next of Kin Details

- full name;
- relationship;
- address;
- home telephone number;
- work telephone number;
- e-mail address.

Comments

- e.g., special needs (e.g., disability);
- e.g., languages;
- e.g., training requirements.

Employee Number and Identity

- employee number issued;
- employee photo identity badge issued (will require photo)—unless already issued;
- printed name;
- signature;
- date.

DOCUMENTATION

Received

All documents must be signed for by the inductee and any relevant comments added:

- signed contract;
- tax documents;
- evidence of right to work in the country;
- signed Information Security policy;
- induction feedback form (Appendix 12);
- qualifications.

Issued

All documents and items issued must be signed for by the inductee and any relevant comments added:

- Forensic Laboratory policies, as applicable to the employee (specify);
- employee handbook;
- keys/access codes (specify);
- other (specify).

TRAINING

General Training

This is details of any initial training given to the inductee by the Human Resources Department or others; the date is recorded and the inductee's signature is recorded against each of the training programs attended.

- induction;
- others—define.

Management System Training

This is details of all relevant management system training given to the inductee by the Management System Owner(s).

- understanding the management system;
- objectives;
- policies and procedures;
- employee responsibilities;
- metrics;
- using the management system.

Note 1

Responsibilities for completing the induction process are given in Chapter 18, Section 18.1.7.

Note 2

For all of the items on the checklist, the date they were performed and the signature of the person managing the induction will be required. In some cases, countersignature by the inductee will be required to signify that the action has taken place.

APPENDIX 12 - INDUCTION FEEDBACK

The inductee's feedback on the induction process is sought after induction training has finished. This is a confidential process and seeks to answer the following questions:

- does the inductee understand their responsibilities?
- does the inductee understand how they fit into the Forensic Laboratory?
- does the inductee understand how their input affects the Forensic Laboratory's products and services?
- does the inductee understand the opportunities available?
- were documents easy to understand and relevant?

- was there anything missed from the induction process?
- any other issues that could improve the induction experience?
- the answers are used for continuous improvement of the induction process.

APPENDIX 13 - STANDARD PROPOSAL TEMPLATE

Below is the standard proposal template for the Forensic Laboratory; it is amended according to Client requirements, as needed. It gives details about:

- the Forensic Laboratory;
- the Forensic Laboratory organization;
- the benefits to the Client of using the Forensic Laboratory;
- the Terms of Reference;
- general;
- scope;
- detailed deliverables statements;
- proposed methodology;
- general approach;
- phase life cycle;
- quality assurance;
- assumptions;
- risks;
- terms and conditions;
- CVs/resumes of employees working for the Client;
- document control.

Note

Within the Forensic Laboratory, the proposal forms part of the contract.

APPENDIX 14 - ISSUES TO CONSIDER FOR CASE PROCESSING

While the Forensic Laboratory is usually happy to accept most requests for case processing, there are a number of evaluation criteria and points to agree that must be considered prior to final acceptance of a case. These include, in no particular order, but not be limited to:

- are there the required skills in-house (or via trusted partner) to deliver the case on time?
- are there any special requirements or precautions to be taken to preserve the evidence?
- are there jurisdictional issues?
- do any conflicts of interest exist?
- does the Client want to use a method or process that is out of date, unacceptable to the Forensic Laboratory, or discredited in some other way?
- does the Forensic Laboratory have capacity to deliver to Client TRT?
- does the Forensic Laboratory want, or need, to use a non-standard method—if so, the Client must be advised and must approve this as part of the proposal;
- how is transfer of the evidence from the Forensic Laboratory to be effected (collection by Client, delivery to Client, or delivery to a third party)?
- how is transfer of the evidence to the Forensic Laboratory to be effected (on-site acquisition, collection from Client, or delivery by Client)?
- how will the case be assessed, and what is the strategy for production of the required deliverables?
- if an expert witness needed—is one available?
- is it legally permissible?
- is their required price (where stated) feasible?
- is there adequate security for classification/sensitivity of the case?
- is there anything about the case that could bring the Forensic Laboratory into disrepute or affect its reputation negatively?
- retention and disposal requirements?
- the financial status of Client (regarding past payments);
- what exactly is the required deliverable(s)?
- what is the reporting format type required?
- what items are to be examined and are there any risks related to them that must be considered?
- what will be the sequence of the examination process—is this a Client requirement or will it follow the Forensic Laboratory's standard methods?
- will taking on the specific Client cause a key risk?

Note

If any of the issues above, or any other relevant issues, are raised for a specific case, these must be raised with the Client and resolved prior to proceeding with the case.

APPENDIX 15 - STANDARD QUOTATION CONTENTS

Quotations may vary on Client requirements, but the standard contents include:

- instructing Client details;
- Client reference;
- hardware to be processed;
- outcomes required;
- specific methodologies to be used, if appropriate;
- report type required;
- any other deliverables required;
- Turn Round Time required;
- delivery and collection details;

- what is to be done with the original material supplied by the Client at the end of the case;
- price.

APPENDIX 16 - STANDARD TERMS AND CONDITIONS

The standard terms and conditions for any forensic laboratory will depend on the jurisdiction, but the one used by the Forensic Laboratory contains the basic requirements, and is reproduced below:

- hourly rate for forensic case processing;
- hourly rate for traveling;
- travel class (planes and trains);
- hourly rate for attending courts/tribunals whether evidence is given or not;
- miscellaneous expenses charging;
- tax on fees;
- terms of payment;
- penalties for late payment;
- requirement for full-written instructions;
- communication for case processing;
- acceptance of only written instructions by authorized representatives;
- use of best ability to assist Client;
- legislation for agreement;
- dispute resolution.

APPENDIX 17 - ERMS CLIENT AREAS

Within the ERMS, the area relating to Client matters is separated into four distinct areas. These relate to the status of the Client (or prospective Client) in their relationship life cycle with the Forensic Laboratory. The four areas are:

- *prospects*—where the virtual file is initially opened and will contain all correspondence relating to the prospective Client until the "stop/go" decision relating to the proposed work is received;
- *current*—where the virtual file is moved if there is a positive outcome from the initial meeting and the proposed work proceeds. All case processing files will be stored in this directory along with any other matters relating to the Client. The virtual file stays in this area until the Client terminates their relationship with the Forensic Laboratory;
- *failed*—where the virtual file is moved if the initial proposal is rejected by the Client. If there is a further possibility of working with the Client, the virtual file is moved back to the prospects area;
- *finished*—where the virtual file is moved for archive purposes when the relationship with the Client is finished. Should the Client restart their relationship with the Client, the virtual file is returned to the "current" area.

Note

Virtual files are retained in the "Failed" and "Finished" areas for a set period of time until they are considered for archive or disposal according to the document retention policy in force in the Forensic Laboratory, as defined in Chapter 4, Appendix 16.

APPENDIX 18 - COST ESTIMATION SPREADSHEET

The cost per item of the items below should be evaluated and also the hourly rate for Forensic Laboratory employee's time spent on a case and an estimate for the hours to be spent. The spreadsheet includes the following:

CASE START UP

- cost of collection (driver hourly rate);
- booking in exhibit and checking it;
- photographing and describing it;
- examination, labeling, and writing up;
- performing backups to disk/tape;
- case admin—virtual and paper file setup, etc.

CASE PROCESSING

- backup to disk (original evidence);
- backup to tape (original evidence);
- working disk(s);
- disk for backup images;
- disk for backup case;
- caddies to hold hard disks;
- performing case processing;
- report production (paper);
- report (binder);
- report (dividers);
- report (packaging);
- CDs;
- CD verify;
- DVDs;
- DVD verify;
- cost of delivery (driver hourly rate).

Note

Some of these are hard costs (e.g., the cost of consumables), while others will depend on time estimations (e.g., case processing or collection/delivery). Therefore, if a fixed price is to be offered, it is essential that estimates are accurate.

MAINTAINING CASES AFTER PROCESSING HAS FINISHED

- disks;
- tapes;
- overheads for storage.

Note

The length of time, and possibly the conditions under which storage must take place, may well be dictated by Legislation or Regulation in the jurisdiction.

APPENDIX 19 - DRAFT REVIEW FORM

While a draft review form may be used, it is preferable to use the SharePoint system to manage document control and other reviews. Where a draft review form is used, it should contain the following:

- project name;
- Client name;
- document name(s);
- version(s);
- author name;
- reviewer name;
- date sent;
- return by date;
- comments;
- reviewed by;
- signature;
- position;
- date.

APPENDIX 20 - CLIENT SIGN-OFF AND FEEDBACK FORM

CASE DETAILS

- Forensic Laboratory Case No;
- Forensic Laboratory Case Name;
- Client details.

FEEDBACK

The Forensic Laboratory requires feedback on the following aspects of how they handled this case:

- communication;
- speed of delivering results;
- quality of results;
- timeliness of delivery;
- quality of deliverables;
- understandability of the deliverables;
- meeting requirements (as defined).

The above are all marked as follows:

1. Very poor;
2. Poor;
3. Good;
4. Very good;
5. Excellent.

CASE RESULT

What was the result of the case/investigation that this recovered evidence was used to support (Did the recovered evidence play a pivotal role)?

SIGN-OFF

- confirmation of sign-off of the case;
- signed;
- date;
- name.

APPENDIX 21 - INFORMATION REQUIRED FOR REGISTERING A COMPLAINT

- complaint number;
- date of complaint;
- time of complaint;
- name of complainant;
- complainant's details;
- details of complaint;
- action taken, from initial action chronologically recorded till closure;
- was the complaint justified?
- root cause identified as;
- date closed;
- time closed;
- closed by.

APPENDIX 22 - COMPLAINT RESOLUTION TIMESCALES

Action	Target Time
Complaint received	Start to investigate immediately
Refer to Line Manager/Client Account Manager/Laboratory Manager	2 h
Enter complaint into Service Desk System	When advised
Attempt to resolve	Within 24 h
Acknowledge complaint	Within 1 working day

Continued

Action	Target Time
Find resolution	Within 5 working days
Present report on complaint to Top Management, if applicable	Within 10 working days
Present complaints summary report	Management Review agenda item

APPENDIX 23 - COMPLAINT METRICS

The Forensic Laboratory uses the following metrics for complaint reporting:

- complaints received;
- complaints resolved at source;
- complaints incorrectly prioritized;
- complaints incorrectly categorized;
- complaints not acknowledged within target time;
- repeat complaints;
- complaints not justified;
- complaints not resolved within target time;
- complaint reports not presented to management within target time.

APPENDIX 24 - LABORATORY MANAGER, JOB DESCRIPTION

OBJECTIVE AND ROLE

The Laboratory Manager is responsible for establishing and monitoring adherence to ISO 9001 and ISO 17025 from a technical requirements viewpoint in the Forensic Laboratory. This includes complying with all mandated requirements including maintaining ISO 17025 Accreditation and assisting the Quality Manager in maintaining ISO 9001 Certification.

PROBLEMS AND CHALLENGES

The primary challenge for the Laboratory Manager is to ensure that the Forensic Laboratory is staffed by competent employees who can produce consistent case processing results that meet Client's requirements. As digital forensic technology is a rapid changing area, it is essential that the Laboratory Manager keeps up-to-date with all relevant developments in this area. Depending on the number of cases being processed at any one time, the ability to manage resources to meet Client requirements can be problematic. Often, cases are required to be processed in a rush and the Laboratory manger must ensure that this is achieved, but without sacrificing quality of deliverables to the Client.

PRINCIPAL ACCOUNTABILITIES

The Laboratory Manager:

- promotes quality achievement and technical performance improvement throughout the Forensic Laboratory;
- sets technical competence and case processing objectives and ensures that targets are achieved;
- maintains awareness of the business context and company profitability, including budgetary control issues;
- assesses the Forensic Laboratory's product and service specifications and their suppliers, comparing them with Client requirements;
- ensures compliance with relevant international and national standards and legislation; this also specifically includes the requirements for ISO 17025 and ISO 9001;
- defines technical quality procedures for case processing in the Forensic Laboratory;
- sets up and maintains technical documentation procedures in the IMS;
- identifies relevant competence training needs and delivers relevant training;
- collates and analyzes case performance data and charts against defined performance parameters;
- ensures validation, tests, and procedures are properly understood, carried out, and evaluated;
- supervises all laboratory employees in carrying out all aspects of case processing, including first response and evidential recovery from Client sites or crime scenes;
- manages multiple concurrent cases;
- writes relevant technical and management systems reports;
- establishes standards of service for case processing and seeks to continuously improve them;
- administers and/or conducts tests and examinations, evaluating test results and making recommendations based on those results;
- manages the process of evidence presentation for the Forensic Laboratory's cases to Clients or the relevant Court or Tribunal;
- prepares clear explanatory technical documents;

- monitors performance by gathering relevant case processing and producing statistical reports;
- maintains ISO 17025 accreditation and assists the Quality Manager in maintaining ISO 9001 certification relating to case processing;
- ensures that all corrective actions are completed in a timely manner;
- develops plans for technical delivery to support the Forensic Laboratory's future directions;
- develops the Forensic Laboratory's long-range case processing management strategy;
- participates in international, national, and local SIG presentations, and publishes management-approved articles describing the Forensic Laboratory's case processing capabilities;
- develops and manages effective working relationships with all appropriate internal and external stakeholders;
- ensures that all Forensic Analysts have access to counseling, if required, after handling disturbing case;
- maintains external links to other forensic laboratories to gain competitive assessments and share information, where appropriate;
- identifies the emerging technologies to be assimilated, integrated, and introduced within the Forensic Laboratory, which could significantly impact the Forensic Laboratory's product and service offering SLAs;
- interfaces with external industrial and academic organizations in order to maintain state-of-the-art knowledge in emerging case processing issues and to enhance the Forensic Laboratory's image as a first-class solution provider utilizing the latest thinking in this field;
- adheres to all established Forensic Laboratory policies, standards, and procedures;
- performs all responsibilities in accordance with, or in excess of, the requirements of the Forensic Laboratory Integrated Management System.

AUTHORITY

The Laboratory Manager has the authority to:

- monitor product and service offerings for adherence to the Forensic Laboratory's technical and quality standards;
- monitor Service Level Agreements and Turn Round Times and their associated metrics;
- take appropriate action to ensure that Client deliverability for forensic case processing is maintained and continuously improved.

CONTACTS

Internal

Contacts within the Forensic Laboratory are throughout the whole organization.

External

Those external to the Forensic Laboratory will be with appropriate SIGs, other technical case processing for a, such as the High Tech Crime Association (HTCIA), International Association of Computer Investigative Specialists (IACIS), Association of Digital Forensics, Security, and Law (ADFSL), etc.

REPORTS TO

The Forensic Analyst reports to the Laboratory Manager:

- adheres to all established Forensic Laboratory policies, standards, and procedures;
- performs all responsibilities in accordance with, or in excess of, the requirements of the Forensic Laboratory Integrated Management System.

APPENDIX 25 - FORENSIC ANALYST, JOB DESCRIPTION

Note

This job description relates to all those involved in forensic case processing and refers to both Forensic Case Analysts and their Supervisors. The only difference is that the Supervisors will have supervisory experience that the Analysts will not have, marked with an "*" below.

OBJECTIVE AND ROLE

The Forensic Analyst is responsible for all stages of forensic case processing. This can start with first response for on-site evidence collection through to presentation of evidence to the Client, a Court, or Tribunal. The exact tasks will depend on the requirements of the case and the Forensic Analyst's competence.

PROBLEMS AND CHALLENGES

The primary challenges for the Forensic Analyst is the rate of change of the technology and the varying technologies that they may be called upon to examine. It is essential that the Forensic Analyst keeps up-to-date with all relevant developments in this area. Depending on the number of cases being processed at any one time, another challenge will be the ability of the Forensic Laboratory to process cases to meet Client requirements without sacrificing quality of deliverables.

PRINCIPAL ACCOUNTABILITIES

The Forensic Analyst:

- conducts forensic examinations on a range of information processing systems;
- physically disassembles hardware and examines it;
- uses software tools to analyze recovered evidence;
- makes forensic images of media, where appropriate;
- maintains the chain of custody of any evidence under their control;
- attends incident or crime scenes to recover evidence, as required;
- examines digital and optical media to recover evidence;
- records all actions taken on forensic case they are processing and producing reports and statements relating to the case;
- gives oral evidence, as required;
- researches and develops new methodologies of case processing;
- consults with external agencies and Clients, as required;
- analyzes and interprets evidence;
- collects, labels, transports, and secures evidence from incident or crime scenes and/or during processing;
- knows relevant legislation relating to case processing in the jurisdiction;
- understands computer hardware, standard software, and network processing, relevant to cases that they are processing;
- prioritizes cases processing to meet Client Turn Round Times;
- performs forensic case processing to a high degree of accuracy;
- ensures compliance with relevant international and national standards and legislation, this also specifically includes the requirements for ISO 17025 and ISO 9001;
- manages multiple concurrent cases;
- prepares clear explanatory technical documents;
- *manages employees that report to them to achieve the Forensic Laboratory's case processing requirements;
- participates in international, national, and local SIG presentations, and publishes management-approved articles describing the Forensic Laboratory's case processing capabilities;
- develops and manages effective working relationships with all appropriate internal and external stakeholders;
- identifies the emerging technologies which could be assimilated, integrated, and introduced within the Forensic Laboratory;
- interfaces with external industrial and academic organizations in order to maintain state-of-the-art knowledge in emerging case processing issues and to enhance the Forensic Laboratory's image as a first-class solution provider utilizing the latest thinking in this field;
- adheres to all established Forensic Laboratory policies, standards, and procedures;
- performs all responsibilities in accordance with, or in excess of, the requirements of the Forensic Laboratory Integrated Management System.

AUTHORITY

The Forensic Analyst has the authority to:

- undertake case processing as required within the Forensic Laboratory.

CONTACTS

Internal

Contacts within the Forensic Laboratory are throughout the whole organization.

External

Those external to the Forensic Laboratory will be with appropriate SIGs other technical case processing for a, such as the HTCIA, IACIS, ADFSL, etc.

REPORTS TO

The Forensic Analyst reports to the Laboratory Manager.

APPENDIX 26 - TRAINING AGENDA

The following chart is a recommended approach to the technical requirements for the Forensic Laboratory[c]

> **Note**
>
> The Forensic Laboratory's main case processing tools are Encase and FTK, so much of the details below are only relevant to them.

c. This is taken from ACPO guidance—but appears universally applicable.

DIGITAL EVIDENCE RECOVERY STAFF

Months 1-6	Months 6-12	Months 12-24	Months 24-36
Understanding equipment in the Forensics Laboratory	Forensic computing foundation course	Introduction to Linux forensics course	Forensic Internet course
Hardware qualification such as A+	Introductory training on secondary forensic tool	Intermediate Internet forensics course	Intermediate Linux forensics course
Core data recovery and analysis skills	Other specialized training as required depending on case work	Network foundation course	Advanced training on Forensic Laboratory primary forensic tool
Introductory training on Forensic Laboratory primary forensic tool		Intermediate training on Forensic Laboratory primary forensic tool	Intermediate and/or advanced court, evidence requirements and report writing skills course
		Introduction to court, evidence requirements, and report writing skills course	Other specialized training as required depending on case work
		Other specialized training as required depending on case work	

NETWORK INVESTIGATORS

Months 1-6	Months 6-12	Months 12-24	Months 24-36
Core network investigator skills	Hands on Linux training	Advanced network investigation	Covert Internet investigation course
Researching, identifying, and tracing the electronic suspect	Introductory and/or intermediate training on the Forensic Laboratory primary forensic tool (cross-training)	Consider product-specific certification courses, e.g., Cisco CCNA, etc. (depending on environment)	Consider further product-specific certification courses, e.g., Cisco CCNA, etc. (depending on environment)
Open source intelligence research	Other specialized training as required depending on case work	Network intrusion, hacking, or penetration testing courses (leading to certification?)	Advanced training on the Forensic Laboratory primary forensic tool (cross-training)
Introductory training on the Forensic Laboratory primary forensic tool		Introduction to court, evidence requirements, and report writing skills course	Intermediate and/or advanced court, evidence requirements, and report writing skills course
		Other specialized training as required depending on case work	Other specialized training as required depending on case work

APPENDIX 27 - SOME INDIVIDUAL FORENSIC CERTIFICATIONS

Some current certifications that may be considered by the Forensic Laboratory for their employees or the employees themselves are listed below:

Post Nominals	Certification	Specifically Forensic
A+	CompTIA A+ certification	
ACE	AccessData Certified Examiner	Yes

Continued

Post Nominals	Certification	Specifically Forensic
CCCI	Certified Computer Crime Investigator	Yes
CCFT	Certified Computer Forensic Technician	Yes
CCFE	Certified Forensic Computer Examiner (only for law enforcement)	Yes
CCE	Certified Computer Examiner	Yes
CDFE	Certified Digital Forensics Examiner	Yes
CDFS	Certified Digital Forensics Examiner	Yes
CEDS	Certified E-Discovery Specialist	Yes
CFE	Certified Fraud Examiner	
CFIP	Certified Forensic Investigation Practitioner	Yes
CHFI	Computer Hacking Forensic Investigator	Yes
CIFI	Certified Information Forensics Investigator	Yes
CISM	Certified Information System Manager	
CISSP	Certified Information System Security Professional	
CMFS	Certified Mac Forensics Specialist	Yes
CMI	Certified MalWare Investigator	
CSFA	CyberSecurity Forensic Analyst	Yes
EnCE	EnCase® Certified Examiner	Yes
EnCEP	Encase Certified e-Discovery Practitioner	Yes
GCFA	GIAC Certified Forensics Analyst	Yes
GCFE	GIAC Certified Forensics Examiner	Yes
SSCP	System Security Certified Practitioner	

Note

Some of these are only available to Law Enforcement or have other specific requirements associated with them that may preclude some individuals from applying for them.

APPENDIX 28 - MINIMUM EQUIPMENT RECORDS REQUIRED BY ISO 17025

ISO 17025, Section 5.5.5 mandates the following minimum records for all equipment:

- the identity of the item of equipment and its software (Chapter 12, Appendix 7);
- the manufacturer's name, type identification, and serial number or other unique identification (Chapter 12, Appendix 7);
- checks that equipment complies with the specification (Chapter 12, Appendix 7);
- the current location, where appropriate (Chapter 12, Appendix 7);
- the manufacturer's instructions, if available, or reference to their location (in the IMS);
- dates, results, and copies of reports and certificates of all calibrations, adjustments, acceptance criteria (Chapter 12, Appendix 7);
- the due date of next calibration (Chapter 4, Appendix 42);
- the maintenance plan, where appropriate, and maintenance carried out to date (Chapter 4, Appendix 42 and Chapter 12, Appendix 7);
- any damage, malfunction, modification, or repair to the equipment (Chapter 12, Appendix 7).

APPENDIX 29 - REFERENCE CASE TESTS

The Forensic Laboratory reference case tests include the following standard tests and results:

- acquisition testing (usually by hashing);
- documents and settings (Windows);
- extracted files by document type;
- Favorites (Windows);
- hash analysis of defined files;
- Internet history;

- link parser;
- Recent (Windows);
- recovered files;
- searches by keyword;
- signature analysis;
- unique e-mail addresses.

Note 1

These are standard tests and any others can be added according to the Client's (or the Forensic Laboratory's) requirements. They should be regression tested to ensure that they are robust.

Note 2

Dual tool verification is also used.

APPENDIX 30 - ISO 17025 REPORTING REQUIREMENTS

ISO 17025 requires the following:

a. a title (e.g., "Test Report" or "Calibration Certificate");
b. the name and address of the Forensic Laboratory, and the location where the tests and/or calibrations were carried out, if different from the address of the laboratory;
c. unique identification of the test report or calibration certificate (such as the serial number), and on each page an identification in order to ensure that the page is recognized as a part of the test report or calibration certificate, and a clear identification of the end of the test report or calibration certificate;
d. the name and address of the customer;
e. identification of the method used;
f. a description of, the condition of, and unambiguous identification of the item(s) tested or calibrated;
g. the date of receipt of the test or calibration item(s) where this is critical to the validity and application of the results and the date(s) of performance of the test or calibration;
h. reference to the sampling plan and procedures used by the laboratory or other bodies where these are relevant to the validity or application of the results;
i. the test or calibration results with, where appropriate, the units of measurement;
j. the name(s), function(s), and signature(s) or equivalent identification of person(s) authorizing the test report or calibration certificate;
k. where relevant, a statement to the effect that the results relate only to the items tested or calibrated.

Note

Hard copies of test reports and calibration certificates should also include the page number and total number of pages.

APPENDIX 31 - STANDARD FORENSIC LABORATORY REPORT

The report format below is used for a Windows forensic case processing report and is the most commonly used template. Other operating systems or devices will have variations of this, as appropriate to the Client's instructions, and the content of the case. In the right hand column is a cross-reference back to Appendix 30 to show how this meets the requirements defined in ISO 17025.

Report Contents	ISO 17025 5.10.2	ISO 17025 5.10.3.1	ISO 17025 5.10.3.2
Front page			
Title of Report—defining the evidence examined, usually the Client's reference number (assuming it exists)	a)		
Client Details	d)		
Forensic Laboratory details	b)		
Protective Marking—front page classification of report as defined in Chapter 4, Appendix 38 and Chapter 5, Appendix 16			
Every Page			
Title of Report in header—typically using the unique exhibit number(s) processed	c)		
Copyright notice in footer			
Pagination in footer (page *x* of *y*) to show the report is complete	Note 1		
Version details in footer, according to the Forensic Laboratory's document control defined in Chapter 4, Section 4.6.3			
Protective Marking—front page classification of report as defined in Chapter 4, Appendix 38 and Chapter 5, Appendix 16			
Document Control Page			
Review History—part of the Forensic Laboratory's document control system, showing the history of the document and its updates	j)		a)
Issue Status—draft or issued			
Table of Contents			
Table of Contents			
Body of Report			

Continued

Report Contents	ISO 17025 5.10.2	ISO 17025 5.10.3.1	ISO 17025 5.10.3.2
Client instructions		b)	
Receipt and identification of exhibits to be processed, including photographs as appropriate clearly showing identification of each exhibit. If part of a first response operation, the location where they were each recovered. This will also include all movements of the exhibit(s) as recorded in the Forensic Laboratory Exhibit log, as defined in Chapter 8, Appendix 7 and the Exhibit Movement Forms, as defined in Chapter 8, Appendix 17.	g)		c) e)
Initial physical examination of exhibit(s)	f)		a) b)
Action summary	e)		a)
Detailed findings matched to the Client's requirements. This includes tools used, version numbers of software, screenshots of results, if appropriate, and details of methods used from the Examination record, as defined in Chapter 9, Section 9,10 and Appendix 9. The report structure is: • acquisition details including hash verification; • file integrity; • PC details; • hard disk details; • BIOS details; • Registry information; • files identified and found; • Profiles; • Desktop; • Favorites; • Links; • Media; • Recent; • My Documents; • E-mail addresses; • Internet history; • FTK view of evidence (dual tool verification); • recovered files; • HTML carver; • answers to specific questions raised by the Client; • text search results.	e) h) i)	a) d) e)	a) d) f)
Appendices			
The appendices will vary depending on the specifics of a case but would typically include: • malware reports from more than one tool—to counter the Trojan Defence; • EnCase case summary; • recovered files, where relevant • recovered e-mail, where relevant; • search hits; • additional tasks; • instructions for using the case report (held on a DVD and how to access the DVD); • details of the Forensic Analyst's qualifications.	j) k)		

Continued

Chapter 7

IT Infrastructure

Table of Contents

7.1 HARDWARE

Within the Forensic Laboratory, there are different types of hardware used for different processes. These include:

- dedicated forensic hardware;
- desktop business workstations;
- desktop forensic workstations;
- mobile business devices;
- mobile forensic workstations;
- peripherals;
- servers.

The choice of hardware will be driven by a number of factors, including:

- budget;
- equipment available and maintainable in the region where the Forensic Laboratory operates;
- local and regional preferences;
- past experience of the Forensic Analysts selecting the hardware;
- size of the Forensic Laboratory;
- tools that the Forensic Analysts have been trained on;
- type of work that is expected to be undertaken.

The rule of thumb for forensic case processing hardware is that one buys the fastest workstations with the most memory that you can afford.

7.1.1 Accommodation

All Forensic Laboratory hardware, and all assets, must be appropriately protected against unauthorized access and loss. The first layer of security in the Forensic Laboratory is the building security, as defined in Chapter 12, Section 12.4. Within the Forensic Laboratory itself, there are areas segregated according to business role, with strict access control enforced between different operating areas. The business servers are stored in the server room where access is restricted to authorized members of the IT Department. The general business area houses the relevant desktop, laptop, mobile devices, and peripherals that relate to non-forensic case processing.

The forensic case processing network is secured within the Forensic Laboratory itself, as can be seen from the diagram in Chapter 2, Section 2.5.1. This shall contain all components of the forensic case processing network, including all cabling, network devices, and infrastructure. The Forensic Analysts will have their own "personal" workspace for case processing, as defined in Chapter 2, Section 2.5.3. Peripherals and specialized hardware and tools for forensic case processing are located in the Forensic Laboratory, so access is restricted to only the Forensic Analysts. The Forensic Analysts will also require some access to the business network; however, all forensic case processing is carried out on the forensic network. These two networks shall be physically, not logically, separated.

7.1.2 Servers

Business servers are commercially purchased and their specification depends on the Forensic Laboratory capacity plan, as defined in Section 7.4.6.

7.1.3 Desktop Workstations

Desktop workstations are also commercially purchased and their specification depends on Forensic Laboratory capacity plan and the specific requirements of the department where they are used. The Forensic Laboratory decided that it would use thin client technology to support its security model. While this is known as a possible single point of failure, by building a resilient business network, the risk of this was reduced to an acceptable level. Local departmental variations include dual screen requirements and some specialized local peripherals.

7.1.4 Mobile Devices

Mobile devices are becoming more prevalent and the Forensic Laboratory uses mobile devices where the requirement is identified and the business case justifies it. There are many different types of mobile devices available and mobile device security is defined in Chapter 12, Section 12.3.9 and Section 12.3.10.

The Forensic Laboratory does not subscribe to the fashion for bring your own device (BYOD) for security and support reasons.

7.1.5 Business Peripherals

The Forensic Laboratory uses centralized departmental peripherals where possible, although some departments have specialized local processing needs. Centralized peripherals used include the following functionality:

- printing;
- scanning;
- photocopying;
- faxing.

These are known as multifunction peripherals or all-in-one devices. Access to their functionality is restricted by use of the Forensic Laboratory's access control card, allowing monitoring of use, security of use, and correct departmental chargeback.

7.1.6 Forensic Servers

The Forensic Laboratory server farm must be capable of storing huge amounts of data and processing it for the Forensic Analysts. Given that a home user can currently buy disks with multiple terabytes of storage, the Forensic Laboratory must ensure it has the capacity to store (or archive) this amount of data according to its record retention requirements, as given in Chapter 4, Appendix 16 or specific Client SLAs.

The Forensic Laboratory has implemented a local Storage Area Network (SAN) that is expandable based on Client and forensic case processing needs.

The Forensic Laboratory has made the conscious decision that it would not use cloud computing as it considered the following risks and decided to retain control in-house. This is not a complete list of risks as they will depend on specifics of case processing and jurisdictional issues:

- data location—this may breach contractual agreements without the Forensic Laboratory being aware of it;
- having the right to audit a cloud supplier to ensure that the Forensic Laboratory's requirements are met;
- how backups are managed to meet legislative, regulatory, and Forensic Laboratory requirements, and how these are regularly tested;
- how the cloud supplier can guarantee service continuity;
- how the cloud supplier screens its employees;
- how the cloud supplier undertakes a forensic investigation in the cloud;
- the ability to prove compliance to a third party;
- the eventual responsibility in case of breach;
- the possibility of unequal contracting parties;
- who else can access the Forensic Laboratory's information (and so Client data).

7.1.7 Desktop Forensic Workstations

There are a number of suppliers who can supply "off the shelf" forensic workstations. A list of some of these is given in Appendix 1.

The Forensic Laboratory builds and validates its own forensic workstations, as defined in Section 7.5.5.

While technology is changing all the time, the following are the base set of requirements for a forensic case processing workstation in the Forensic Laboratory:

- fastest processor(s) available—typically quad processors currently;
- maximum RAM;
- maximum disk capacity—typically now SATA drives;
- hot swappable disk drives;
- best video card available;
- sound card and speakers;
- at least two 21″+ monitors;
- support for a variety of 32 and 64 bit operating systems;
- modular PCI ports;
- modular Firewire ports;
- DVD burner.

The Forensic Laboratory will probably not buy COTS workstations for use in forensic case processing, preferring instead to build their own. This gives flexibility and will help the Forensic Analysts to understand the hardware that they use, and that they will encounter in forensic case processing, instead of just "using a box." In many forensic cases, the hardware makeup of a forensic workstation is reconfigured and with in-house-built forensic workstations, this is usually easier to perform than some COTS products.

At the end of the day, it is up to a Forensic Laboratory to decide what hardware and tools they want to use to meet the Client's requirements, though these will be agreed by the Client.

7.1.8 Mobile Forensic Workstations

Mobile forensic workstations in the Forensic Laboratory must have all the capabilities required for forensic case processing outside the Forensic Laboratory offices (i.e., on-site and first response situations) as the desktop equivalents, where possible.

A list of some of these is given in Appendix 2.

Some of the requirements for desktop workstations given in Section 7.1.7 are relevant to mobile forensic workstation, but some are evidently not (e.g., multiple 21″+ monitors). In addition to these requirements, a portable forensic workstation should also include, but not be limited to, the following functionality:

- ability to bypass hard disk passwords;
- compact and transportable—preferably able to fit on an aircraft as "carry on" luggage;
- disk imaging capability;
- easy to use;
- hot swappable capability;
- multiple hard disk-type connectivity;
- multiple interfaces;
- preview capability for on-site working;
- safe and robust casing;
- technical support available in case of need while on site;
- theoretical unlimited capacity—a modular disk capability (this could also include tape capacity);
- write blocking built-in.

7.1.9 Building Forensic Workstations

As has been said above, the Forensic Laboratory prefers to have its Forensic Analysts build their own workstations from a variety of components as needed for a specific case. Some of the reasons for this decision taken by the Forensic Laboratory included:

- ability to build a workstation to specific requirements for a case, which is often not possible from COTS products;
- ability to choose best of breed components;
- ability to explain the operation of a workstation by a Forensic Analyst, if offering expert testimony;
- ability to upgrade a component as required, rather than need to replace the whole workstation;
- building and retaining in-house knowledge of hardware and components;
- cost considerations.

Having made the decision to build in-house forensic workstations, a standard build was developed for all workstations, but this can be amended as required by a Forensic Analyst for processing a specific case. Technology and components are constantly changing, so there is no point in defining the specific builds used in the Forensic Laboratory in detail, as it would be soon out of date. The types of components used for building a forensic workstation are given in Appendix 3, but with no model or manufacturer detail.

7.1.10 Dedicated Forensic Hardware

There are a number of dedicated forensic hardware devices that the Forensic Laboratory uses, these include, but are not limited to:

- Cellebrite UFEDs;
- dedicated malware "sheep dip" workstation;
- dedicated stand-alone imaging workstations;
- degausser;
- forensic workstation on a USB stick;
- multiple disk copiers;

- stand-alone Internet access workstation;
- various adapters;
- various cables;
- XRY hardware.

7.1.11 Forensic Peripherals

The Forensic Laboratory uses the same peripherals as the rest of the business, as defined in Section 7.1.5, but they are located within the secure laboratory environment. Some Forensic Analysts will have specialized peripherals attached to their workstations, and these will vary on the requirements of specific cases.

7.2 SOFTWARE

As with hardware, the choice of software will be driven by many of the same factors that apply to the hardware, including:

- budget;
- certification, training, and experience that the Forensic Analysts have obtained;
- experience of the Forensic Analysts selecting the software;
- hardware in use in the Forensic Laboratory;
- local and regional preferences;
- size of the Forensic Laboratory;
- software and its support available in the region;
- type of work that is expected to be undertaken.

7.2.1 Operating Systems

The operating system that is selected may be dependent on the hardware that has been selected, the software that is required for the tasks within the Forensic Laboratory, or the equipment that was selected. For example, if the Forensic Laboratory is using Apple Mac hardware, then it is likely that the operating system in use is an Apple operating system.

It must be remembered that the selection of the hardware, operating system, and tools is not sequential (i.e., firstly selecting the hardware then the operating system, then the tools). It may be that the tools that are to be used will dictate the operating system and that this will dictate the type of hardware.

Within the Forensic Laboratory, the following operating systems are in use:

- BSD;
- Helix;
- Knoppix;
- Linux;
- OSX;
- Slackware;
- Ubuntu;
- Windows (various).

7.2.2 Desktop Applications

On the business network, the Forensic Analysts have access to the following:

- Adobe products;
- e-mail;
- malware detection;
- Microsoft office applications;
- other applications that may be necessary;
- the Forensic Laboratory ERMS—but for non-case processing files;
- the Internet.

Any software to be added must be supportable by the IT Department, be legally licensed, as defined in Chapter 12, Section 12.3.13.1.2, and be installed only by the IT Department after being submitted to, and approved by, the Change Advisory Board (CAB), as defined in Section 7.4.3.5.

7.2.3 COTS Forensic Tools

There are many COTS forensic tools available. It is not possible to provide an up to date list as the range of tools is so volatile, however a list of the current tools is given in Appendix 4.

7.2.4 VM Ware

The concept of a Virtual Machine (VM) is that of a virtual computer running inside a physical computer. One host computer may be capable of running multiple VMs at the same time and VMs have been created to run on most of the major operating systems. The benefit of VMs is that they allow the Forensic Laboratory to run forensic tools in a controlled environment (allowing states to be saved and restored at will) or to recreate a replica of a suspect's "computer" in a virtual environment. The Forensic Laboratory uses VMs wherever possible.

7.2.5 Open Source Tools

There are a number of open-source forensic case processing tools available, and often forensic laboratories use them for pure economic reasons. The issue that has to be considered with open-source software is whether or not they are producing scientifically sound tools and that the results are consistent and repeatable.

The Forensic Laboratory has made the decision not to use open-source tools for forensic case processing.

If this were to change, and the Forensic Laboratory must ensure that the source of the tool is carefully selected (a trusted source), the tool package should then be verified (normally by checking the MD5 hash of the file) to ensure that it has not been tampered with and that it undergoes full validation, as defined in Section 7.5.5.

7.2.6 Updates

Operating system software, business tools, and forensic case processing tools will have updates released that will add new functionality as well as to fix flaws (bugs) and vulnerabilities. The process used in the Forensic Laboratory for controlling technical vulnerabilities is covered in Section 7.6.2.

Updates are only released into the live environment after full testing, as defined in Chapter 12, Section 12.8.3 and then formal approval by the CAB as part of the Forensic Laboratory's Change Management Process, as defined in Section 7.4.3.

7.2.7 Upgrades

A software upgrade is when a newer version of software, whether a forensic tool, an application, or operating system that is being used in the Forensic Laboratory is brought into use. The reasons for upgrading the software may be that it has more features, is more efficient, or that the provider will no longer be willing to support the existing version. It will be necessary from time to time to upgrade software in the Forensic Laboratory.

Release of upgrades is handled in the same manner as updates, as defined in Section 7.2.6.

7.3 INFRASTRUCTURE

The Forensic Laboratory network infrastructure is in two separate parts, the business infrastructure and the physically separated forensic case processing infrastructure.

The forensic case processing network is a totally closed network in that it has no external links permitted.

The business network is also a closed network but with access to the Internet, but this is strictly controlled by using firewalls.

The Forensic Laboratory does not permit wireless access to any of its resources.

Security of the network connections within the Forensic Laboratory is covered in Chapter 7, Section 7.7.

7.3.1 Equipment

The network infrastructure for both the business and the case processing networks comprise the following components:

- cabling;
- firewalls;
- routers;
- servers;
- switches;
- the SAN.

The networks are built and maintained by the IT Department, as required, in the Forensic Laboratory.

7.3.2 Securing of Cabling

Cabling is used to connect all IT equipment within the Forensic Laboratory. The Forensic Laboratory has made the conscious decision not to permit wireless connections on account of the material it processes and the possible risks of wireless networking. The policy for securing IT cabling in the Forensic Laboratory is given in Appendix 5.

7.3.2.1 Procedure for Siting and Protecting IT Cabling

When installing new or upgraded IT cabling, all possible steps must be taken to protect it from physical risks, to protect information from security threats, and to minimize possible risks from environmental hazards. The following steps are undertaken:

1. A need is identified for installation of new IT cabling or replacement or repair of existing cabling.
2. The IT Manager, the Information Security Manager, and the Laboratory Manager (if appropriate) perform an assessment to:
   - consider the requirements of the Forensic Laboratory with regard to installation of the cabling;
   - consider all physical and environmental issues;
   - consider all security issues regarding the physical location of cabling within the Forensic Laboratory premises;
   - consider all security issues regarding the information carried on cabling and its classification;
   - determine where the cabling is best routed, and where any associated equipment is best sited;
   - during this assessment the IT Manager, the Information Security Manager, and the Laboratory Manager (if appropriate) may:
     - consult other Forensic Laboratory employees as required (for example, IT, or non-IT employees, or Managers who may be using or sited near to the new cabling and associated equipment);
     - consider all issues outlined in the Forensic Laboratory Policy for Securing IT Cabling, as defined in Appendix 5;
     - consider isolation of the equipment (to allow the Forensic Laboratory IT to reduce the general level of protection that is required) if required and defined in Section 7.3.3;
     - consider the impact of a disaster in nearby premises.
3. The IT Manager, in association with the Information Security Manager and the Laboratory Manager

(if appropriate), makes a decision as to where the new cabling and any associated equipment is to be sited.
4. The IT Manager communicates with all interested parties as needed to:
   - outline the decision regarding the routing of the new cabling and the siting of any associated equipment;
   - outline the reasons for the decision;
   - invite further comments (if required).
5. Any issues that arise at this stage must be agreed and confirmed before the new cabling is installed.
6. The cabling is installed in accordance with the agreed conditions.
7. The IT Manager, the Information Security Manager, and the Laboratory Manager (if appropriate) perform a review to:
   - ensure that the new cabling has been routed in accordance with the agreed conditions;
   - ensure that the new cabling has been afforded the best possible protection from all potential security threats;
   - address any issues that may have become evident after installation.
8. In the event that changes are required, the IT Manager e-mails the relevant stakeholders to outline proposed changes, and the changes are implemented in accordance with standard Forensic Laboratory IT change management procedures, as defined in Section 7.4.3.

Note

In the United States, much of this is dictated by the National Fire Protection Association publication #70: National Electrical Code, which is the benchmark for safe electrical design, installation, and inspection to protect people and property from electrical hazards. Other jurisdictions may have similar requirements, and these must be followed as applicable.

7.3.3 Isolating Sensitive Systems

In the event that the Forensic Laboratory manages or uses a system that contains sensitive or confidential information where a Client requires a dedicated computing environment that is physically and logically segregated from other systems holding less critical information, the following guidelines should be followed for a dedicated computing environment:

- apply operating system and applications hardening procedures where possible;
- logical segregation via VLANs;
- physical segregation via separate rooms, dedicated servers, or computers;
- use of physical access control mechanisms;
- use of strong authentication methods;
- when a sensitive application is to run in a shared environment, employ strict resource, file, or object share or permission controls.

7.3.4 Siting and Protecting IT Equipment

IT equipment within the Forensic Laboratory has specific needs in addition to the baseline physical security implemented within the Forensic Laboratory as a whole. All information processing equipment and information under the control of the Forensic Laboratory IT Department must be carefully sited to physically protect that information processing equipment or information from security threats, and to minimize potential risks from environmental hazards. The Forensic Laboratory policy for siting and protecting IT equipment is given in Appendix 6.

7.3.4.1 Procedure for Siting and Protecting IT Equipment

The Forensic Laboratory should have the following procedures in place to determine how new information processing equipment is to be installed in order to physically protect it from security threats and to minimize possible risks from environmental hazards.

1. A need is identified for installation of a new item of IT equipment.
2. The IT Manager, in association with the Information Security Manager and the Laboratory Manager (if appropriate), performs a risk assessment to:
   - consider all usage requirements;
   - consider all security issues regarding the equipment's usage and location within the Forensic Laboratory premises;
   - determine where the equipment is best sited;
   - during this assessment the IT Manager, in association with the Information Security Manager and the Laboratory Manager (if appropriate):
     - consults other employees as required (for example, members of the IT Department, other business users, and/or Managers who may be using or sited near to the new equipment);
     - considers all issues outlined in the Forensic Laboratory Policy for Siting and Protecting IT Equipment, as defined in Appendix 6.
   - additional items that may warrant consideration for particular items of equipment that may require special protection are:
     - isolation of the equipment (to allow the Forensic Laboratory to reduce the general level of protection that is required);
     - the impact of a disaster in nearby premises.

3. The IT Manager, in association with the Information Security Manager and the Laboratory Manager (if appropriate), makes a decision as to where the new equipment is to be sited to afford it the best protection within the Forensic Laboratory.
4. The IT Manager e-mails all interested parties as needed to:
   - outline the decision regarding the siting of the new equipment;
   - outline the reasons for the decision/proposed location;
   - invite further comments (if required).
5. Any issues that arise at this stage must be agreed and confirmed before the new equipment is installed.
6. The new equipment is installed in accordance with the agreed conditions after being approved by the CAB, as part of the Forensic Laboratory Change Management Process, as defined in Section 7.4.3.
7. The IT Manager performs a review to:
   - ensure that the new equipment has been sited in accordance with the agreed conditions;
   - ensure that the new equipment cabling has been afforded the best possible protection from all potential security threats;
   - address any issues that may have become evident after installation.

7.3.5 Securing Supporting Utilities

The IT Manager controls the security of information processing equipment and information in terms of supporting utilities in order to minimize loss and damage to the business.

Special controls are implemented to safeguard supporting utilities for information processing equipment and information processing facilities:

- a generator or other alternate power supplies for the Forensic Laboratory is available and is maintained and regularly tested;
- all of the utilities are monitored to determine if thresholds are breached at which point alarms are sounded. This includes:
  - water detection;
  - power failure or variation;
  - UPS battery life and stability;
  - air conditioning;
  - humidity;
  - heat;
  - smoke.
- all servers are dual power sourced from different supplies;
- a UPS for the Forensic Laboratory is available on all critical servers, telephone switches, and other critical infrastructure, and is regularly tested;
- basic safeguards are used, i.e., health and safety best practice;
- CAT 5 or Cat 6 cabling and mains electrical cabling must be separated and not use the same ducting;
- emergency power-off switches are available near the exit doors of the Server Rooms;
- fire detection and fire quenching is appropriate and in place, as defined in Chapter 2, Section 2.3.4;
- the air conditioning has sufficient redundancy to allow for a single failure and have enough power to keep the area at the appropriate temperature;
- the water supply is stable and adequate for fire suppression purposes.

All of the above are monitored using a centralized building management system and alerts raised and sent to the appropriate managers. The Facilities Manager is always alerted for all breaches.

Note

All other utilities in the building are normally under the control of the utility companies and the Forensic Laboratory will be dependent on these and have no control over their supply.

7.4 PROCESS MANAGEMENT

A number of these processes meet the requirements of ISO 20000-1, Information technology—Service management—Part 1: Service management system, requirements and where they do, they are mapped to ISO 20000-1 in Appendix 7.

Note

A Client may be an internal Forensic Laboratory employee or an external Client to whom the Forensic Laboratory supplies products or services.

7.4.1 Incident Management

The primary goal of incident management is to restore normal service operations as quickly as possible and to minimize the adverse impact on business operations within the Forensic Laboratory, thus ensuring that the best possible levels of service quality and availability are maintained for all Clients.

An incident is:

- any event that which is not part of the standard operation of a service and that causes, or may cause, an interruption to, or a reduction in, the quality of that service.

> **Note**
> Incidents may be IT related or a business (non-IT) related incident.

Examples of an incident include, but are not limited to:

- a business service is not available;
- an application bug is preventing work being carried out;
- a system is down;
- a printer is not printing;
- a service request;
- a request for a change (all changes at the IT Department are performed in accordance with the Forensic Laboratory Change Management Process, as defined in Section 7.4.3);
- an information security incident, as defined in Section 7.4.1;
- any disruption to service provision to internal Forensic Laboratory Clients;
- any disruption to service provision to external Forensic Laboratory Clients.

Incidents are related to problems. In terms of Incident Management, a "problem" is an unknown underlying cause of one or more incidents (not the difficulty that a Client is experiencing).

7.4.1.1 Role of the Service Desk

The Service Desk is central to the Forensic Laboratory's provision of an effective incident management service, and the following should be in place:

- the Forensic Laboratory Service Desk is operational 24/7 (either by e-mail or phone);
- the Forensic Laboratory Service Desk is the first point of contact for all Client-related problems and queries regarding the Forensic Laboratory services;
- calls registered by the Forensic Laboratory Service Desk are typically categorized as:
  - a Client request for a service or information;
  - a Client reporting a difficulty with IT hardware, software, or a service (incident).
- all requests and incidents to the Forensic Laboratory Service Desk must be registered in the Service Desk system;
- the Forensic Laboratory Service Desk provides first-line support to attempt solutions for all incidents;
- incidents are escalated from the Service Desk to second line and third line IT Support as necessary (for example, to PC Support, Technical Support, Management System Manager(s), etc.);
- critical incidents that require additional support because of their critical nature generally follow the normal incident management process but with additional investigation, communication, and reporting, as defined in Section 7.4.1.5;
- incidents are only closed when a resolution is provided and to the satisfaction of the Client.

7.4.1.2 Classification of Incidents and Resolution Times

The Forensic Laboratory must endeavor to restore normal business service and operations or provide a workaround solution to all incidents and service requests according to their classification. Incident classifications, and target resolution times for each incident classification, are defined for Clients in their specific SLAs for individual products and services where required.

7.4.1.3 Incident Management Responsibilities

Within the incident management process, there are a number of defined roles, these are:

- Service Desk;
- Service Desk Manager (SDM) (see Appendix 8);
- Management System Manager(s);
- IT Support;
- other specialist employees;
- employees;
- Clients.

7.4.1.3.1 Service Desk

The Service Desk is the body that acts as a first point of contact for the Forensic Laboratory's Clients that use the products and services that they provide, and they provide first-line IT Support to resolve all incidents and service requests. The responsibilities of the Service Desk include:

- receiving calls, categorizing incidents, and service requests;
- first-line Client liaison;
- recording and tracking all incidents and service requests;
- making an initial assessment of an incident or service request, and attempting to resolve it or referring them to second or third line IT Support;
- monitoring incidents and service requests and escalating them when necessary;
- confirming an incident or service request resolution, and confirming Client satisfaction with a resolution (this task is normally the responsibility of the SDM but may be designated to other Service Desk employees, as necessary);
- closing incidents and service requests that have been satisfactorily resolved (as required by the SDM).

7.4.1.3.2 Service Desk Manager

The SDM has managerial responsibility for the Service Desk and its employees. The responsibilities of this role with respect to incident management include:

- managing the work of the Service Desk (incident and service request recording, classification, and first-line IT Support);
- acting as a contact point between the IT Department, the relevant business streams, and Clients for management-level activity relating to incidents and service requests;
- monitoring incidents and their appropriate escalation to other specialist Forensic Laboratory employees, as appropriate;
- liaising with third party and relevant third parties;
- confirming 25% of resolved incidents, and confirming customer satisfaction (this task may be designated to other Service Desk employees as necessary);
- closing incidents and service requests that have been confirmed as satisfactorily resolved (this task may be designated to other Service Desk employees);
- managing critical incidents through to resolution in association with other IT management;
- generating statistics and reports on incident management for input to Clients and the Management Review, as defined in Chapter 4, Section 4.9.

> **Note**
>
> In the Forensic Laboratory, the SDM acts as the Incident Manager (IM) for all incidents.

The Forensic Laboratory's Service Desk and IM's job description is given in Appendices 8 and 9, respectively.

7.4.1.3.3 Management System Manager(s)

The relevant Management System Manager has managerial responsibility for managing the resolution of incidents and disruptions to their management systems or disruptions to the services that they provide, and for reviewing the incidents or disruptions, identifying trends and recommending continuous improvement to "their" management systems. The responsibilities of this role include:

- recording and categorizing incidents and disruptions;
- liaising with Forensic Laboratory management and specialist employees on incidents and disruptions;
- determining initial investigations;
- assigning specialist employees for incident or disruption resolution;
- communicating with Forensic Laboratory employees during incident resolution;
- communicating with Clients during incident resolution;
- monitoring investigation and resolution activities;
- approving incident resolution;
- invoking a BCP response, if appropriate;
- reviewing incidents and disruptions to identify trends;
- creating CAPAs, as appropriate.

7.4.1.3.4 IT Department

As well as managing day-to-day IT operations, the Forensic Laboratory IT Department mainly provides second or third line IT Support to resolve incidents and service requests, for example, PC support or technical support. Responsibilities of the IT Department include:

- documenting resolutions and workarounds for resolved incidents and service requests in the Service Desk system;
- escalating incidents to third-party organizations where required, additional reporting to relevant business units may be required;
- incident investigation and diagnosis (including resolution where possible);
- providing second and third line IT Support for incidents and service requests that cannot be resolved on receipt or initial investigation by the Service Desk.

7.4.1.3.5 Other Specialist Employees

Forensic Laboratory specialist employees are responsible for the following:

- conducting response and recovery actions as directed by the Business Continuity Manager (BCM) and management, according to the BCP response procedures, if applicable;
- determining resolution actions;
- implementing, or assisting to implement, resolution activities;
- investigating incidents and disruptions to determine a diagnosis.

7.4.1.3.6 Employees

Forensic Laboratory employees are responsible for the following:

- identifying incidents and weaknesses in the Forensic Laboratory Management Systems;
- reporting incidents and weaknesses to the Service Desk and the relevant Management System Manager;
- reporting service disruptions (either internally or from Clients) to the Service Desk and the relevant Management System Manager;
- responding to incidents or disruptions as directed by the relevant Management System Manager or the IM.

7.4.1.3.7 Clients

Clients are the internal or external users of products and services supplied and supported by the Forensic Laboratory. Their responsibilities include:

- agreeing SLAs and TRTs with the Forensic Laboratory for their services;
- reporting incidents in a timely manner to the Service Desk;
- requesting services via the Service Desk;
- assisting the Service Desk or other Forensic Laboratory employees in closing their incidents;
- confirming closure of their incidents.

7.4.1.4 Incident Management Procedures

7.4.1.4.1 Receiving and Categorizing an Incident

A Forensic Laboratory Client contacts the Service Desk to report an incident, or to place a service request. Contact may be made via:

- a telephone call to the Service Desk;
- a fax to the Service Desk;
- an e-mail to the Service Desk;
- a self-service request into the Service Desk system;
- a visit to the Service Desk in person.

The Service Desk receives and processes the incident or service request as follows (Figure 7.1):

1. The Service Desk use the Service Desk system to locate and confirm the Client's details, as recorded in the system. These details must include:
   - caller's name;
   - job role;
   - Client name;
   - Client location;
   - Client cost center;
   - Client contact details.

> **Note 1**
>
> The caller, and therefore the Client, may be an internal or external Client.

2. The Service Desk creates a Service Desk Request (SDR) in the Service Desk system (the Client details are automatically transferred into the new SDR).
3. The incident or service request details are recorded, and the SDR is automatically assigned a status of Open.
   Details of incident status levels are given in Appendix 10.
4. The Service Desk agrees a Priority level for the SDR with the Client based on the following:
   - priority—the effect that the incident or the service request has on the businesses capability to function normally;
   - impact—the number of Clients affected by the incident/service request.

> **Note 2**
>
> Priority levels and Impact are defined in the individual Client's SLA or TRT.

Details of incident priority levels are given in Appendix 11.

If the Priority of the incident is 1, the Service Desk must contact the IM immediately and a decision is made on the immediate measures to begin response actions in accordance with the procedure for Managing Critical Incidents, as defined in Section 7.4.1.5.

5. The Service Desk completes and saves the details of the incident or service request. An SDR number is automatically generated and the status of the SDR is changed to "Current" in the Service Desk system.
6. The Service Desk attempts to provide a solution to the request or the incident, if possible (they may already know a resolution, or may search the Service Desk system to try and find a matching incident and a solution).
7. If the Service Desk resolves the incident:
   - all action taken is recorded in the SDR;
   - the action is confirmed with the Client;
   - the SDR status is changed to Resolved;
   - the incident is now closed as described in Section 7.4.1.4.4.
8. If the Service Desk cannot resolve the incident, or if the incident is a service request that needs to be performed by some other Forensic Laboratory employee, the Service Desk assigns the incident to second or third line Support (this may be a technical expert, a Forensic Analyst, or a Management System Manager).
9. To do this, the Service Desk:
   - informs the Client that the incident or service request must be assigned to second or third line IT Support for resolution;
   - informs the Client that second or third line IT Support will contact them for either information or to agree a resolution or workaround;
   - assign the SDR to second or third line IT Support, as appropriate;
   - the incident is now progressed as described in Section 7.4.1.4.2.

> **Note**
>
> The Service Desk may also telephone the second or third line IT Support to inform them that a new incident has been assigned to them.

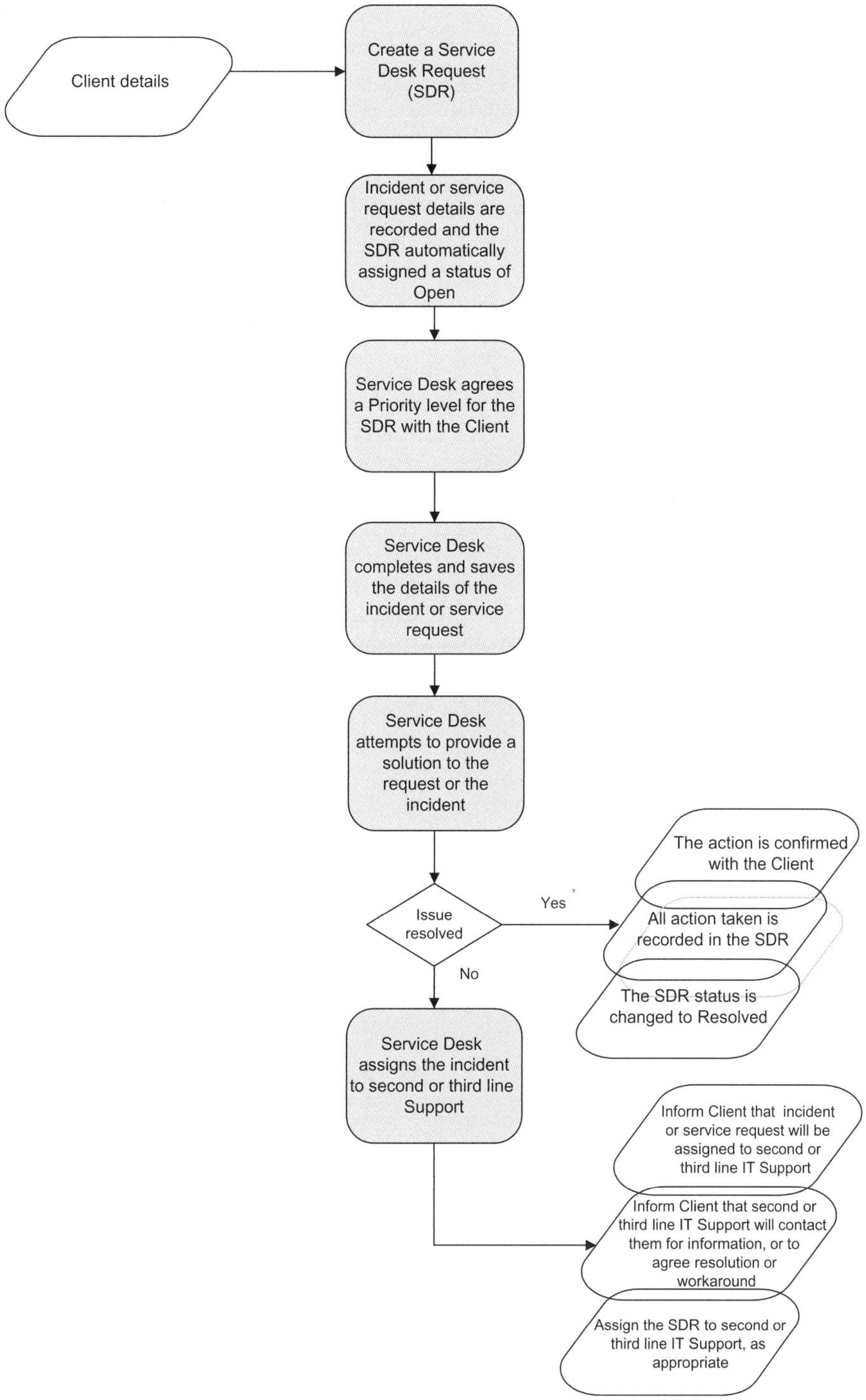

FIGURE 7.1 Receiving and categorizing an incident. (For color version of this figure, the reader is referred to the online version of this chapter.)

7.4.1.4.2 Investigating an Incident

If an incident or service request that is received and logged cannot be resolved at the Service Desk, it is assigned to second or third line IT Support. An incident investigation is then performed as follows:

1. The second or third level IT Support opens the SDR in the relevant queue in the Service Desk system (new incidents that have been assigned to them may also be confirmed verbally by the Service Desk).
2. The second or third level IT Support checks the SDR details displayed for the incident and determines whether further information is required from the Client.
3. If additional information is required, the assigned second or third level IT Support contacts the Client and obtains the required information. All actions performed

by the second or third line IT Support must be recorded in the SDR log in the Service Desk system.

4. If the incident has been assigned to the wrong person, the second or third line IT Support reassigns the incident to the appropriate person using the Service Desk system.
5. The second or third line IT Support investigates the incident to identify all possible means of resolving it, both procedural and technical, this includes:
   - determining possible solutions or workarounds;
   - examining courses of actions that require further investigation;
   - testing possible solutions or workarounds before implementing the most suitable one.
6. If a solution cannot be obtained, second line IT Support may reassign the incident to third IT Support as necessary.
7. Where a resolution is not possible internally, Support will assign the incident to the appropriate third party for resolution as follows:
   - contact the SDM and brief them on the progress on the incident;
   - contact the required third party for resolution using the appropriate method;
   - monitor the third party, and coordinate any resolution activity;
   - record all activity in the SDR log.
8. The third party should deliver a fix or a workaround to the incident within an agreed timescale. If a fix or a workaround is not delivered within the agreed timescale, the incident is escalated to the SDM.

Note

All evidence collected during investigation work must be handled in accordance with the procedures for evidence collection, as defined in Section 7.4.1.7, in case of later need, to ensure that the evidence is not contaminated.

7.4.1.4.3 Resolving an Incident

1. When an incident or service request has been investigated and a solution or workaround has been discovered, the resolution is applied as follows:
   - second or third line IT Support performs the required resolution, and tests that the resolution works correctly;
   - second or third line IT Support contacts the Client to discuss the resolution and to confirm that the resolution is satisfactory.
2. In the event that a solution to an incident cannot be provided, IT Support discusses possible courses of action with the IM and other Managers as required. These include:
   - reassigning the incident to a different IT Support person for further investigation and attempted resolution;
   - suspending the incident, if IT Support is certain that a solution cannot currently be provided or is outside the scope of IT Support, examples are:
     - delaying investigation of an incident with the agreement of the Client (for example, to resume investigation in 24 hours, 7 days, etc.)—in which case, the Service Desk auto wake-up function should be used to automatically notify Service Desk and/or IT Support when investigation is to be resumed;
     - known errors such as a bug fix for application software;
     - seeking the involvement of a third-party supplier.
   - closing the incident with the agreement of the Client;
   - IT Support enters full and comprehensive information about the solution to the incident into the Service Desk system;
   - IT Support changes the status of the incident to "Resolved."
3. This reassigns the SDR to the call closure queue in the Service Desk system for closure by the SDM.

7.4.1.4.4 Closing an Incident

1. Incidents and service requests are closed by the Service Desk in the following circumstances only:
   - a solution or workaround has been provided;
   - the Client agrees that a solution is not required—that is the incident is not important;
   - all required information about an incident has been entered into the Service Desk system;
   - all required information for changed configuration items (CIs) relating to an incident has been entered into the Configuration Management Database (CMDB), as defined in Section 7.4.5.
2. If the resolution to an incident involves a change to the IT infrastructure, a request or incident cannot be closed until the change has been formally approved and signed off through the Forensic Laboratory Change Management process, as defined in Section 7.4.3.
3. It is Service Desk policy to perform a quality control check on 25% of all SDRs that are recorded in the Service Desk system. The Client feedback form for the Service Desk is defined in Appendix 12. Normally, this check is performed by the SDM (but may be delegated to other Service Desk staff) to:
   - confirm that an incident has been resolved;
   - confirm that a Client is satisfied with the resolution;
   - allow the SDR to be closed.

Warning

Incidents can only be closed by the SDM after confirmation by the Client. Service Desk employees cannot close incidents.

4. The Service Desk accesses the SDR in the Service Desk system call closure queue and:
   - reviews the progress of the incident or service request since the SDR was first logged;
   - confirms that IT Support has fully documented the incident or request solution;
   - confirms that IT Support has resolved all actions generated during the resolution process.
5. For a random sample of 25% of SDRs with a status of "Resolved," the SDM (or some other designated person) contacts the Client to:
   - confirm that a solution or a workaround has been implemented;
   - confirm that the incident or the request is successfully resolved;
   - confirm that the Client is satisfied with the resolution or workaround;
   - confirm that the SDR can be closed in the Service Desk system.
6. If the Client is not satisfied with the solution or workaround that has been provided, the Service Desk:
   - obtains further details from the Client about the continuing issues or problem;
   - informs that Client that the incident will be reassigned for further investigation;
   - reassigns the incident to second or third line IT Support as necessary (the SDR status is changed to "Reopened");
   - updates the SDR details in the Service Desk system.
7. If the resolution of the incident is not satisfactory and third-party supplier has been used, the SDM must contact the third party and request a different solution or workaround. As a minimum requirement, a new fix or workaround must be received and successfully implemented.
8. The SDM closes the incident or service request in the Service Desk system.

7.4.1.5 Critical Incident Management

A business-critical incident in the Forensic Laboratory is one that causes serious disruption to the Forensic Laboratory's business, either for internal Clients or external Clients. These incidents are those incidents that need greater management input that for normal incidents to ensure that a resolution is provided as soon as possible (Figure 7.2).

To manage a critical incident, the Forensic Laboratory performs the following:

1. The Service Desk logs a critical incident and contacts the IM immediately.

> **Note**
>
> A critical incident may also be raised during the analysis, investigation, or resolution phase of a normal incident. In this case, the incident is already logged in the Service Desk system, and the incident category and priority requires modification before processing.

2. The IM escalates the incident to the Top Management to alert relevant key Client management to the critical incident so they can initiate the response.
3. Top Management may involve other Forensic Laboratory employees, as appropriate, including the Management System Manager(s).
4. The IM and IT Support initiate and manage the response to the critical incident through to successful resolution. All actions performed during the incident investigation and resolution must be recorded in the Service Desk system.
5. The IM initiates immediate actions to start the resolution process. These actions vary depending upon the incident.
6. During the resolution process the IM must:
   - determine whether to initiate standby solutions;
   - keep affected business Clients informed of progress throughout the incident resolution process on a regular basis (e.g., telephone, e-mail, discussion, etc.);
   - obtain business stream agreement, as needed, to any actions affecting service levels;
   - document all actions in the Service Desk system;
   - keep the Service Desk system updated with details of significant events in the resolution process as they occur;
   - keep all stakeholders informed of progress as required.
7. The IM and IT Support gather information to assist in resolving the incident and:
   - confirm the true cause by testing, fixing, and checking results—this may require third-party assistance;
   - identify possible causes of the incident—in many cases, this may be obvious and this step in the process may be minimal, but in all cases, it is essential that the root cause of the incident is identified before any actions are taken. Standard root causes are given in Chapter 4, Appendix 49. These are not the only root causes possible and others will be defined as needed;
   - plan Forensic Laboratory employee involvement—who does what, and when, where and how.
8. IT Support develops a solution to the incident and then implements it.
9. If the resolution to the incident involves a change to the IT infrastructure, the change can be fast-tracked through the Forensic Laboratory Change Management Process for immediate resolution.

FIGURE 7.2 Critical incident management.

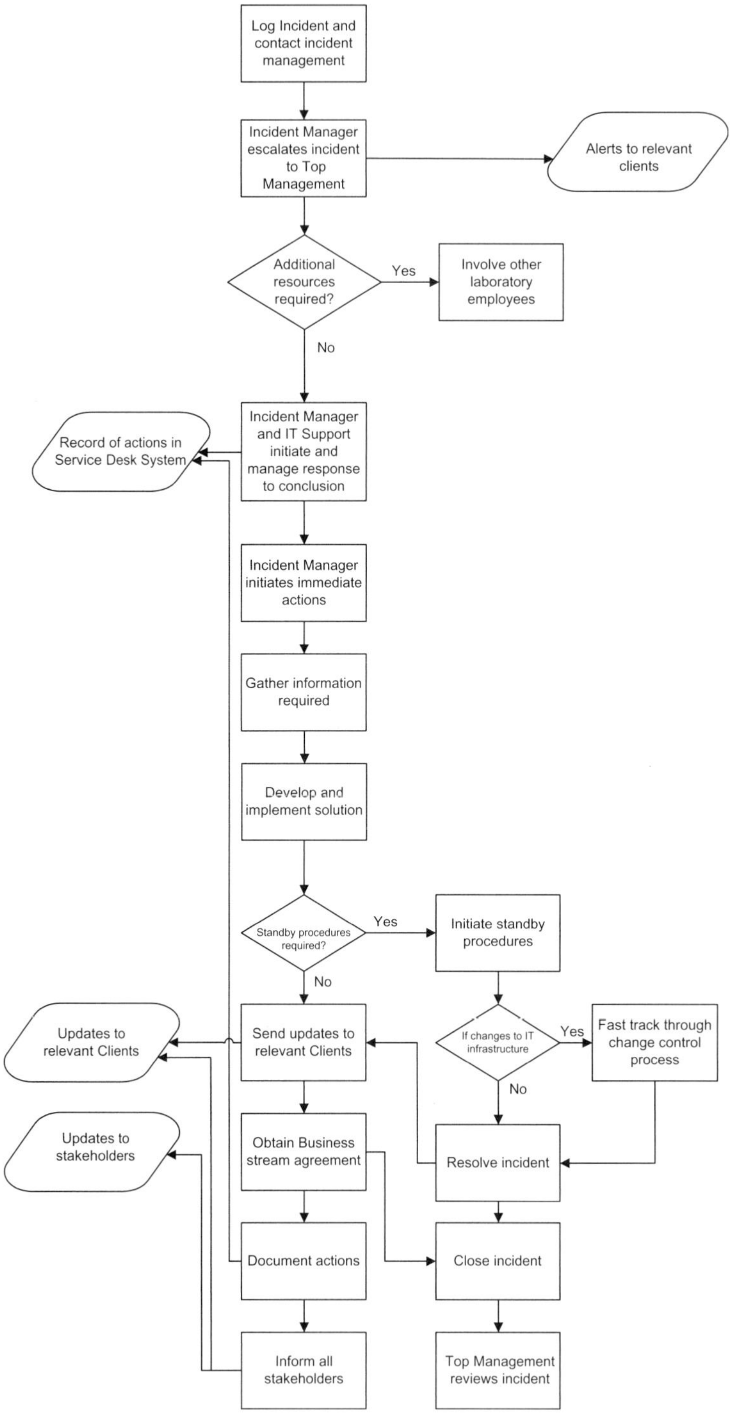

10. The IM contacts the Account Managers of the business Clients who are affected to agree that the incident has been resolved, and the agreed level of service has been restored.
11. The IM closes the incident in accordance with the closure procedure, as defined in Section 7.4.1.4.4.
12. Forensic Laboratory Top Management review the incident with a view to future provision and improvement of services.

Note

Any infrastructure or service improvement changes that arise from the review must be implemented in accordance with the relevant the Forensic Laboratory processes, including change management, as defined in Section 7.4.3.

7.4.1.6 Reviewing Incidents

As part of the incident management improvement process, the Forensic Laboratory regularly reviews incidents, weaknesses, and disruptions to:

- evaluate and continually improve the Forensic Laboratory incident management responses and processes;
- improve the Forensic Laboratory systems, products, and services in order to minimize disruption to the business;
- learn and identify trends;
- review business-critical incidents.

Management System Managers perform monitoring and trend analysis as part of their ongoing role to review causes and outcomes of security incidents and incidents that cause service disruptions.

> **Note**
>
> Business-critical incidents classed as "Priority 1" (or "Critical") are always reviewed by the Top Management immediately following their successful resolution.

The Forensic Laboratory incident management review process is as follows:

1. Incidents are always reviewed at the Management Review meeting, unless a critical incident requires a specific meeting to discuss it. The relevant Management System Manager is also present at the meeting and optionally the Forensic Laboratory employees involved in specific incident investigation or resolution activities (as required).
2. Incidents are discussed at the meeting with a view to identifying improvements to the Forensic Laboratory infrastructure, management systems, service offerings to Clients, and the incident management system itself. Inputs to the discussion may include:
   - future projects;
   - outcomes from business continuity response and recovery;
   - outcomes from incident investigation and resolution (including outcomes from a business-critical incident);
   - outcomes from previous incident management reviews and improvement activities;
   - planned upgrades or changes to the Forensic Laboratory information systems, processes, or services;
   - reports from the Forensic Laboratory employees relating to incidents, weaknesses, or disruptions reported to the Service Desk;
   - trend analysis by the relevant Management System Manager(s).
3. The Management System Manager provides recommendations on possible actions for agreement by the Forensic Laboratory Top Management. This may include:
   - changes and improvements to the Forensic Laboratory systems and infrastructure;
   - changes and improvements to the Forensic Laboratory operating practices;
   - changes to BCPs.

> **Note**
>
> Outcomes and agreed actions are documented in the meeting minutes and are raised as CAPAs.

4. The relevant Management System Manager oversees the agreed actions for:
   - changes to Incident Management Plans and Business Continuity Plans (BCPs) are developed and updated in accordance with the Forensic Laboratory procedures for developing and implementing a BCM response, as defined in Chapter 13;
   - changes to the infrastructure are conducted in accordance with the Forensic Laboratory Change Management Process, as defined in Section 4.6.3;
   - changes to working practices that impact on documented procedures are developed and updated in accordance with the Forensic Laboratory procedures for document control, as defined in Chapter 4, Section 4.6.3.

7.4.1.7 Evidence Collection

Where evidence needs to be collected, either for internal disciplinary proceedings or for a case, the first responder procedures must be followed, as defined in Chapter 8.

7.4.2 Problem Management

The process whereby the Forensic Laboratory responds to and resolves the underlying causes of incidents is called problem management.

The primary goals of problem management in the Forensic Laboratory are to:

- determine the root cause of incidents;
- identify incident trends;
- minimize the effect on the business of incidents and problems caused by errors in the infrastructure, the products or services supplied by the Forensic Laboratory to its Clients;
- prevent the recurrence of incidents related to problems;
- proactively prevent the occurrence of incidents and problems, and to reduce their severity.

A problem is the unknown underlying cause of one or more incidents (or one or more *potential* incidents). Examples of problems in the Forensic Laboratory include:

- a problem interpreting evidence in a forensic case due to software issues or incompatibilities between the image and the available tools;
- a problem with imaging a case;
- a server capacity issue that causes degraded performance of a service;
- a software bug;
- an intermittent hardware fault.

A "known error" is a problem for which a root cause has been diagnosed and for which a solution or workaround (temporary or permanent) can be provided.

The Forensic Laboratory Service Desk acts as the repository for all information concerning problems and known errors including the tool for recording, monitoring, and closing of all problems and known errors. The Service Desk system records the following information:

- all problems and known errors;
- classification of problems;
- details of known error solutions, fixes, and workarounds;
- results of problem investigation, diagnosis, and resolution.

The Service Desk is critical to the Forensic Laboratory's provision of an effective problem management process:

- all problems identified are registered by the Service Desk and classified appropriately;
- problems are escalated by the Service Desk for investigation, diagnosis, and resolution;
- problems are only closed in the Service Desk after a resolution has been implemented and all associated incidents are closed;
- the Service Desk is the first point of contact for all problems.

7.4.2.1 Responsibilities

7.4.2.1.1 Problem Manager

The Problem Manager (PM) is the member of the Forensic Laboratory IT Department who has managerial responsibility for the problem management process. Responsibilities include:

- allocating resources for problem support efforts;
- ensuring the effectiveness of the problem management process and for successful diagnosis of problems, and resolution of known errors;
- generating statistics and reports on problem management for review;
- managing problem support or third parties acting on their behalf;
- monitoring all problem and known error activity, and their appropriate escalation to other employees, or third parties acting on their behalf;
- reviewing, developing, and maintaining the problem management process.

The Forensic Laboratory's PMs job description is given in Appendix 13.

7.4.2.1.2 Service Desk

The Service Desk is the body that acts as a first point of contact for all Clients that use the Forensic Laboratory products and services. The responsibilities of the Service Desk with regard to problem management include:

- recording and classifying problems;
- first-line Client liaison;
- monitoring and tracking all problems through the Service Desk system;
- escalating problems as necessary;
- closing problems and associated incidents.

7.4.2.1.3 IT Department

The IT Department provides support for investigation, diagnosis, and resolution of problems and known errors. Responsibilities of IT Support with respect to problem management include:

- identifying problems (by analyzing incident information, for example);
- investigating problems, according to impact, through to resolution or error identification;
- implementing solutions to known errors (where possible);
- escalating problems or known errors to third-party organizations for diagnosis and/or resolution as required;
- documenting resolutions and workarounds for known problems and known errors in the Service Desk system (and advising other Forensic Laboratory employees of such).

The procedure that the Forensic Laboratory follows to manage a problem involves these key stages:

- recording and classifying a problem;
- investigating and diagnosing a problem;
- resolving a problem;
- closing a problem.

> **Note**
>
> The process for processing problems through the Service Desk is very similar to the process for recording, monitoring, and progressing incidents.

7.4.2.2 Recording and Classifying a Problem

1. A problem is identified, typically by:
   - an analysis of incidents received at the Service Desk;
   - routine monitoring of systems across the network;

- information provided by a third party;
- activity by management or IT Support.

2. The problem is recorded in the Service Desk system in accordance with the procedure for recording an incident, as defined in Section 7.4.1.4.1. During this stage, the Service Desk:
   - receives details about a problem;
   - enters the details;
   - agrees a Priority level with the Client;
   - relates the problem to other incidents and/or problems recorded in the Service Desk system.
3. If the problem is a known error, the Service Desk informs the Client that a permanent or temporary solution is available. Possible courses of action are:
   - if a solution or workaround is easily performed by the customer, the Service Desk provides the details and then changes the status of the problem in the Service Desk system to "Resolved." This reassigns the problem report to the call closure queue in the Service Desk system for closure by the Service Desk;
   - if a solution needs to be implemented by IT Support, the Service Desk assigns the problem to IT Support and the problem is now progressed to resolution;
   - if a solution needs to be implemented via the Change Management Process, the Service Desk assigns the problem to the PM for progression through the Change Management Process.
4. If the problem is not a known error, the Service Desk assigns the problem to IT Support for investigation and diagnosis. To do this, the Service Desk:
   - informs the Client that the problem request must be assigned to another Forensic Laboratory employee for further investigation;
   - assigns the problem to the relevant Forensic Laboratory employee.
5. The problem is now progressed.

7.4.2.3 *Investigating and Diagnosing a Problem*

If a problem is logged by the Service Desk that is not a known error, it is assigned to IT Support and investigation and diagnosis is then performed as follows:

1. IT Support investigates the problem to identify all possible causes, this includes:
   - determining possible causes;
   - examining courses of action;
   - testing solutions.
2. If a solution cannot be obtained, IT Support may reassign the incident to further IT Support employees, or third parties acting on their behalf, as necessary.
3. If a diagnosis cannot be made internally, IT Support may assign the problem to the appropriate third party for diagnosis and development of a solution as follows:
   - contact the PM and brief them on the progress;
   - contact the appropriate third party for problem diagnosis using the appropriate method;
   - monitor the third party, and coordinate any solution activity;
   - record all activity in the Service Desk system.
4. The third party should deliver a fix or a workaround to the problem within an agreed timescale. If a fix or a workaround is not delivered within the agreed timescale, the issue is escalated to the PM.
5. IT Support implements a fix or a workaround (permanent or temporary), this includes:
   - determining possible solutions or workarounds;
   - testing solutions/workarounds to establish the most suitable.
6. All activity is recorded in the Service Desk system, and the PM is kept informed of progress.
7. In the event that a fix or workaround cannot be provided, IT Support discusses possible courses of action with the PM (and other Forensic Laboratory Managers as required). Options may include:
   - further investigation;
   - suspending the problem;
   - seeking the involvement of a different third-party supplier.
8. A problem for which a fix or workaround is successfully developed (or made available by a third party) is reclassified as a known error, and full details of the error and resolution are recorded in the Service Desk system.

7.4.2.4 *Resolving a Problem*

1. When a problem has been diagnosed and a solution or workaround has been discovered, a resolution is applied as follows:
   - where a solution or fix can be implemented without the need for a formal change:
     - IT Support performs the required resolution and tests that the resolution works correctly;
     - IT Support contacts the Client to discuss the resolution and to confirm that the resolution is satisfactory;
     - IT Support records the activity in the Service Desk system so that the problem and any associated incidents can be closed.
2. Where a solution to a known error can only be implemented via change management, the resolution is progressed in accordance with the Change Management procedures, as defined in Section 7.4.3. The PM is usually responsible for progressing all known errors through Change Management (though this task may be delegated as necessary).

7.4.2.5 Closing a Problem

When a problem has been resolved, it can be closed. The process is:

1. The Service Desk closes all related incidents, in accordance with the incident closure procedure, as defined in Section 7.4.1.4.4.
2. The Service Desk closes the problem, in accordance with the standard incident closure procedures, as defined in Section 7.4.1.4.4.

7.4.2.6 Reviewing Problems

As part of the problem management improvement process, the Forensic Laboratory regularly reviews problems to:

- determine actions for improvement in problem management;
- determine if problem management activities are performing as expected;
- review outstanding or resolved problems and known errors.
  1. The PM identifies areas of the problem management system that require review based upon:
     - occurrences of problems, known errors, and incidents;
     - effectiveness of problem resolution;
     - planned changes to the organization, technology, and business processes;
     - inputs from Forensic Laboratory Management and Clients.
  2. The PM plans the review and:
     - defines the objectives and scope of the review;
     - identifies the inputs to the review, which typically include reports and statistics from the Service Desk system on incidents, problems, and known errors;
     - identifies a suitable date and time for the review.
  3. The PM prepares a brief outline review plan describing the above details. The plan is issued to all relevant employees, and third parties working on their behalf, involved in the review (they may comment on the plan and suitable arrangements are then made to conduct the review).
  4. The PM, and any other relevant stakeholders, reviews the problem management system and discusses:
     - availability of information to Incident Management;
     - how problem management activities are performing (in particular, whether any activities are not performing as expected);
     - outstanding problems and known errors;
     - the effectiveness of problem resolutions;
     - the effectiveness of the problem management process.
  5. Improvements may be identified, and where possible agreed. These may include possible changes for inclusion in the Service Improvement Plan (SIP). The standard contents of a Forensic Laboratory SIP are given in Appendix 14.
  6. The PM e-mails all relevant stakeholders, with the results of the review and any agreed follow-up actions. Follow-up actions are then implemented, as appropriate.

7.4.3 Change Management

Controlling changes to the Forensic Laboratory IT infrastructure is crucial for the provision of products and services to all Clients. The purpose of change management is to ensure that:

- change processes are properly planned and managed;
- communication channels are in place to inform the Forensic Laboratory management and all stakeholders of changes, the effect on the provision of products and services, and the progress of change implementation (where appropriate);
- resources to implement a change are identified and made available;
- risks associated with a change are identified and minimized;
- standard methods and procedures allow efficient and prompt handling of all changes to the IT Infrastructure (or services for Clients dependent on the IT Infrastructure);
- the impact of any changes made on the whole IT infrastructure is considered;
- the impact on the Forensic Laboratory business of implementing a change is minimized.

7.4.3.1 General

Change management enables operational systems (hardware, software, documented procedures, and the products and services that they deliver) within the Forensic Laboratory to be modified in a planned, controlled, and methodical manner. The purpose of change management is not to block or hinder changes, but to ensure the effective communications between all relevant stakeholders and minimize the risk of failure while increasing the chances of successful implementation for improved products and services.

Change management is applied to the provision of new elements, and changes to existing elements within the processes, infrastructure, systems, computers, and applications that affect the products and services provided by the Forensic Laboratory to its internal and external Clients.

7.4.3.2 Types of Change

Changes are typically to the IT infrastructure but can include other parts of operational processes such as documentation, products, or services provided to internal and external Clients. The Forensic Laboratory defines three types of change:

- *standard*—a change that is predefined, and proved as reliable, which is not processed through the normal Change Management Process but which is instead logged and processed by the relevant department, typically the IT Department. Standard changes have no downtime. This includes some documentation changes;
- *normal*—a change that is processed through the normal Change Management Process. This includes critical documentation changes;
- *emergency*—a change that is implemented and then processed retrospectively through the Change Management Process.

The categories of change within the Forensic Laboratory and the service levels that apply are defined in Appendix 15.

7.4.3.3 Change Status

During the Change Management Process, a change may be assigned a status that is updated at each stage of the life cycle. A timeline for submitting a change is as follows:

- day 1—the final time by which a change can be submitted for review at the weekly CAB meeting;
- day 0—the CAB meeting to approve a change;
- day 5—implementation of change.

7.4.3.4 Change Management Responsibilities

Note

If the forensic laboratory is a small organization, some of the roles within the Change Management Process may be undertaken by one person; however, the process of maintaining segregation of duties should be strictly enforced so that no one personal can control the whole Change Management Process, wherever possible.

Within the Change Management Process, there are a number of defined roles, these are discussed below:

7.4.3.4.1 Change Manager

The Change Manager (CM) controls the Change Management Process within the Forensic Laboratory. The Deputy CM is the person who acts as the CM in the event of their absence.

Responsibilities of the CM include:

- assessing and approving business-critical, non-complex, or minimal impact changes according to risk exposure;
- establishing and maintaining a schedule of planned and proposed changes, including changes that require IT action, (e.g., updating the infrastructure);
- informing Clients of changes, the effect of these changes, and the progress of change implementation (where appropriate);
- liaising with Requestors to ensure requests are fully documented and that all necessary agreements are in place before a CAB meeting takes place;
- organizing and leading CAB meetings;
- recording and filing all change requests submitted;
- reviewing submitted changes and establishing their category (emergency, normal, or standard);
- supporting the review of the Change Management Process through feedback from Requestors to ensure that the process remains effective.

The CM may need to involve the Forensic Laboratory Top Management in some changes, for example, emergency changes, which have a serious impact on service delivery.

The Forensic Laboratory's CM's job description is given in Appendix 16.

7.4.3.4.2 Requestor

A Requestor is a person who owns a change in the Change Management Process, and whose responsibilities may include:

- attending CAB meetings, as required, to support a submitted change;
- consulting all teams involved in, or affected by, a change and have agreed to the proposed approach, including resource demands, and have confirmed this in writing or e-mail;
- fully testing a change;
- leading the change process for a particular RfC from inception to completion;
- leading the implementation of a change;
- performing an initial evaluation of a change covering risk assessment and impact analysis;
- sufficient and accurate documentation is produced to successfully implement a change;
- testing implementation and back-out plans.

Note 1

The Requestor may originate from a business stream or the IT Department.

Note 2

The information needed for an RfC may change between different types of change, but the standard requirements for an RfC are given in Appendix 17.

7.4.3.4.3 Change Advisory Board

The CAB is the body that approves or rejects a change request.

The CAB is not a technical discussion forum, but is formed from stakeholders that will be affected by the proposed change who meet to ensure that the appropriate management processes have been fully addressed in planning the change. The responsibilities of the CAB include:

- approving or rejecting a change;
- assessing a change based upon a submitted request;
- assessing a change based upon risk to the business at crucial production periods;
- conducting reviews of changes that have failed;
- providing a forum for shared learning gained from particular changes and the change process overall;
- requesting further information regarding a change to assist in making a decision.

Within the Forensic Laboratory, CAB meetings should occur as required, but as the Forensic Laboratory grows, this may need to change to a regular weekly or monthly meeting. The Requestor, or their representative, must be present at these meetings to ensure that the requested change is discussed. If the Requestor or their representative is not present, the change can be automatically rejected. These meetings are intended to:

- discuss any changes taking place during the coming period;
- prepare for upcoming changes;
- review changes that have been implemented during the period.

CAB meetings are primarily used to identify all proposed changes that will impact upon live services. All issues concerning a change must be documented using the RfC process and discussed in these meetings.

7.4.3.4.4 The IT Department

The IT Department is assigned responsibility for assisting with or implementing a change, and whose responsibilities may include:

- assessing change requirements based upon a submitted request via an RfC;
- logging details in the CMDB of any new assets installed when a standard change is performed;
- logging details of standard change requests;
- maintaining a store of completed RfCs;
- marking changes that have been performed as "Complete" in the change management system.

7.4.3.5 Managing a Standard Change

The procedure for requesting and implementing a standard category change is (Figure 7.3):

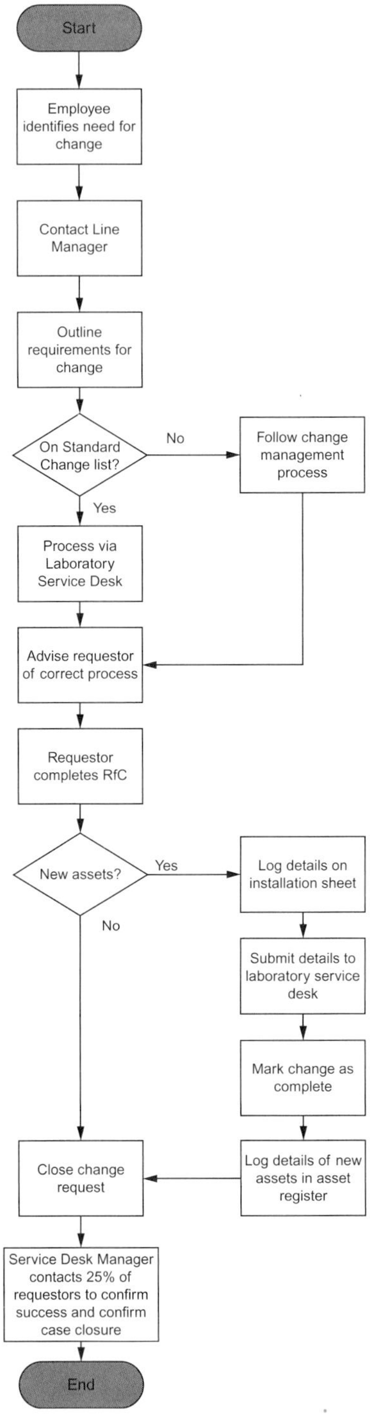

FIGURE 7.3 Managing a standard change. (For color version of this figure, the reader is referred to the online version of this chapter.)

1. A Forensic Laboratory employee identifies a need for a change.
2. They contact their Line Manager to informally discuss the change. The Line Manager is designated the Requestor.
3. The Requestor contacts the Forensic Laboratory Service Desk and outlines the requirements of the change.

4. The Forensic Laboratory Service Desk:
   - checks whether the requested change is on the Standard Change list, if so, the process continues via the Forensic Laboratory Service Desk. If the change is not listed the Normal Change Management Process is followed, as defined in Section 7.4.3.6;
   - advises the Requestor of the appropriate procedure required to progress the change.
5. The Requestor completes the RfC process; the following information must be included:
   - service requested—the services affected by the change;
   - originator information—Requestor name, business stream, contact details, and authorization;
   - application access requests—the application required;
   - user information for access requests—information about the users affected by the change.

     The following information may additionally need to be provided depending on the type of change:
   - purchased items—details of PCs/laptops, printers, other hardware, and software;
   - software installation details—including PCs, users affected, location, intended use;
   - software transfer information—if moving products between PCs;
   - equipment loan information—if loaning PCs and/or printers;
   - equipment relocation details—details of assets being moved, current location, and intended destination.

Note

All relevant sections of the RfC process must be completed.

   - the Requestor submits the completed RfC to the CM;
   - the CM logs details of the change in the change system using the information provided on the RfC;
   - the CM assigns the change for implementation after being authorized by the CAB;
   - the change is performed by IT Support;
   - IT Support obtains sign-off from the Requestor on an Installation Sheet to confirm that the change has been successfully implemented.
6. If any new assets have been installed as part of the change, details of these are logged on the Installation Sheet. IT Support submits the Installation Sheet to the Service Desk, who:
   - mark the change as complete in the Service Desk system;
   - log details of any new assets in the CMDB and update the asset register, if appropriate, as defined in Section 7.4.5 and Chapter 12, Section 12.3.14, respectively.
7. The Service Desk closes the change request in accordance with standard call logging procedures.
8. In line with standard call closure procedures, the SDM contacts a sample of 25% of users who request standard changes to confirm that:
   - the change has been successfully performed;
   - the RfC can be closed.

7.4.3.6 Managing a Normal Change

The procedure for requesting and implementing a normal change to the IT Department IT systems and services is (Figure 7.4):

1. A Forensic Laboratory employee identifies a need for a change.
2. They contact their manager to informally discuss the change. The Manager is designated the Requestor.
3. The Requestor contacts the Forensic Laboratory Service Desk and outlines the requirements of the change.
4. The Forensic Laboratory Service Desk:
   - checks whether the requested change is on the Standard Change list. If so the Standard Change Management Process is followed. If the change is not listed, the Normal Change process continues;
   - advises the Requestor of the appropriate procedure required to progress the change.
5. The Requestor completes the RfC process, the following information must be included, together with an initial impact assessment:
   - Requestor's name, business stream, and contact details;
   - IT applications or services, which are involved in the change;
   - business case for implementing the changes—the reasons for the change, and all associated costs including equipment and staff time as relevant;
   - business impact—including the date by which the change needs to be implemented;
   - signature for budgetary authorization for all associated costs.
6. The Requestor submits the RfC (together with any relevant supporting documentation) to the CM.
7. The CM allocates the change to a relevant member(s) of the IT Department to:
   - investigate the technicalities of preparing and implementing the change;
   - complete the technical sections of the RfC process;
   - submit the RfC and all associated documentation to the CM.
8. The IT Department, in conjunction with the Requestor and any other relevant IT or business staff, prepares details about the change for formal submission. These

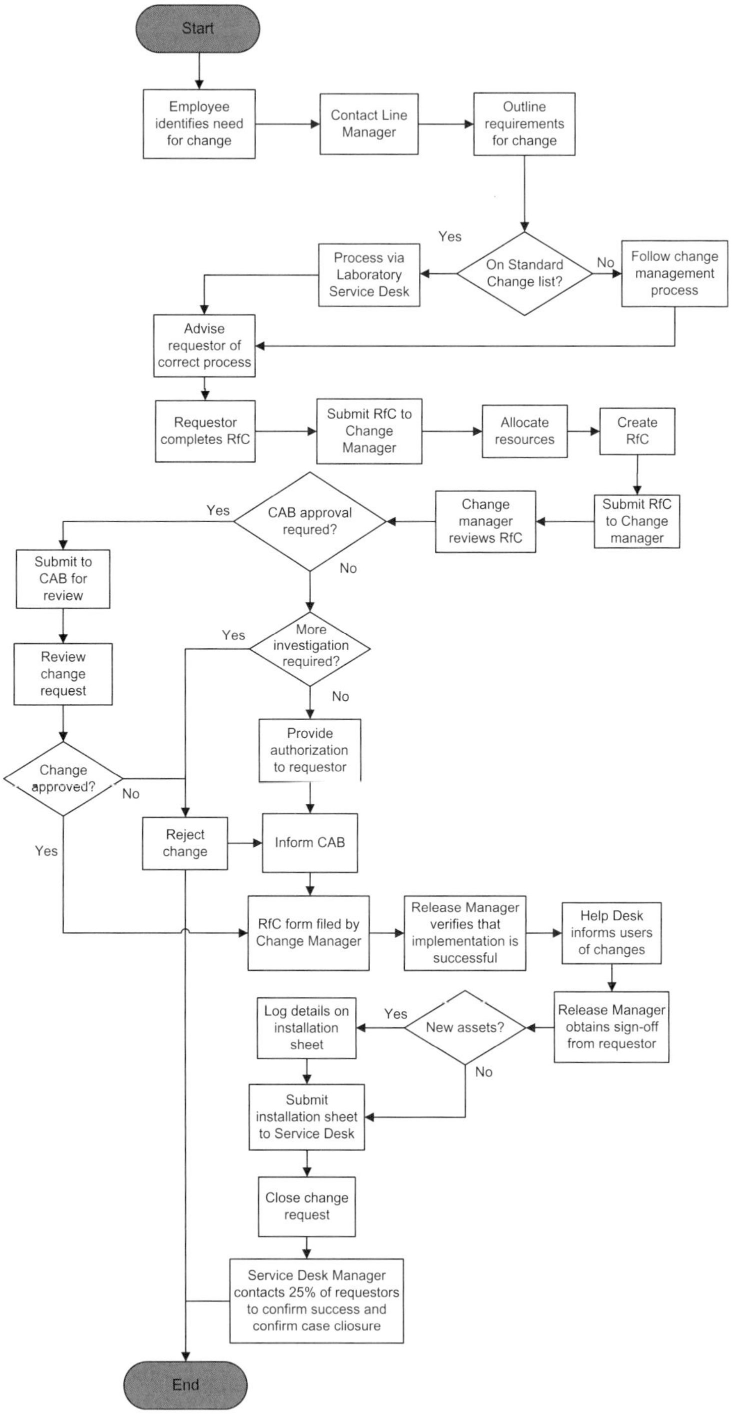

FIGURE 7.4 Managing a normal case. (For color version of this figure, the reader is referred to the online version of this chapter.)

details are documented in the technical sections of the RfC Form and usually include:

- environments—the environments in which the change is to be implemented (UAT, Staging, Production, Products, Services, etc.);
- implementation plan—a description about how the change will be implemented including timescales and schedule, system downtime, and resource deployment and risk analysis;
- test pack—a set of documents that describe how the change has been tested to ensure that it has been implemented successfully (this test pack may cover a test plan, details of test results expected and/or achieved, and test sign-off as appropriate);

- back-out plan—a description and procedure describing how the change can be reversed if a problem occurs during implementation.

> **Note**
>
> Individual Forensic Laboratory employees may be tasked with investigating particular aspects of a change to enable a full report to be included with the formal change submission.

9. The Requestor and the IT Department submit the RfC Form and all associated documentation to the CM.
10. The change must be submitted in accordance with the user notification requirements associated with a standard change type (5 working days).
11. The CM reviews the RfC Form and associated documentation and determines whether the change can be approved without being submitted to the CAB. Typically, the following changes may be approved without being discussed in advance by the CAB:
    - changes that are not complex (of a non-routine nature);
    - changes that have a minimal impact upon users and systems.
12. If the CM assesses the change as one that can be approved without consultation by the CAB, authorization is provided to the Requestor. The CAB is informed of the approval. The Requestor is accountable for the success of the change and for reporting its closure to the CM.
13. If the CM assesses the change as one that requires discussion in the CAB, it is formally submitted for review.
14. If the CM decides that the change requires further investigation work, the change is rejected at this time.
15. The CAB meets at the regular time. During the meeting, the submitted change is assessed to ensure:
    - full consultation/communication with users has occurred either on an informal basis or through formal committee meetings, as appropriate depending on the impact of the change;
    - risks and impact have been fully addressed;
    - full consultation within the IT Department and the business has occurred;
    - appropriate scheduling is considered;
    - an effective back-out plan is available.

> **Note**
>
> If a change is particularly complicated, or additional factors need to be considered, the CM may request further details about a change, or may talk to the Requestor to clarify areas of concern, before a decision on the change can be made.

16. The CAB approves or rejects the change;
    - if the change is approved:
        - the status of the change is amended to "Approved";
        - the CM authorizes the change using the Approvals section of the RfC Form;
        - the change can be implemented at the scheduled time.
    - if the change is rejected:
        - the status of the change is amended to "Rejected";
        - the CM details the rejection using the Rejection Summary section of the RfC Form;
        - no further work is performed on the change.
17. The RfC Form and any associated documentation is filed by the CM.

> **Note 1**
>
> If the change is rejected in its current form but is still required, the CAB may opt to convert the change status to "Pending" until further clarification and investigation work is performed. The change must be resubmitted to the CAB.

> **Note 2**
>
> In cases where CAB is unable to agree, the CM should escalate to the IT Manager.

> **Note 3**
>
> If a Pending change is not resubmitted within five working days, the change is automatically rejected and all work on the change is stopped. The Release Team performs the change. During the implementation of the change, it is important that all stakeholders involved in supporting applications and services prior to any change are informed on progress, so any failed changes can be managed.

> **Note 4**
>
> It is important that all Forensic Laboratory employees involved carefully monitor the change as it is implemented so that any perceived risk is immediately brought to the attention of the Release Manager (RM), the Requestor, and the CM.

18. The RM checks whether the implementation has been performed successfully against the success criteria agreed:
    - if the implementation has been successfully performed, the Requestor:
        - reports the successful outcome to the CM (and other relevant employees as needed);
        - obtains sign-off from the Requestor;
        - ensures that all relevant documentation is updated to reflect the impact of the change.
    - if the implementation has not been successfully performed, the Release Team initiates the back-out

plan to return the systems to their previous state. The CM is informed of the failure, whether the back-out plan was successful, and any follow-up actions that are required.

19. In addition, if IT services to users are affected, the Service Desk must also be informed so that users can be kept fully up-to-date. The status of the change is amended to "Failed." The Requestor assesses the reasons for the failure and after investigation, resubmits the change to the CAB and reports back the reasons for the failure.
20. The RM obtains sign-off from the Requestor on an Installation Sheet to confirm that the change has been successfully implemented.
21. If any new assets have been installed as part of the change, details of these are logged on the Installation Sheet.
22. The RM submits the Installation Sheet to the Service Desk, who:
    - marks the change as complete in the Service Desk system;
    - logs details of any new assets in the CMDB and updates the asset register, if appropriate, as defined in Section 7.4.5 and Chapter 12, Section 12.3.14, respectively.
23. The Service Desk closes the change request in accordance with standard call logging procedures.
24. In line with standard call closure procedures, the SDM contacts a sample of 25% of users who request standard changes to confirm that:
    - the change has been successfully performed;
    - the change request can be closed.

7.4.3.7 Managing an Emergency Change

Emergency changes are those designated as top priority, which need to be implemented immediately to prevent or rectify a serious service failure within the Forensic Laboratory. The Forensic Laboratory Emergency Change policy is given in Appendix 18.

7.4.3.7.1 Managing an Emergency Change

The procedure for implementing an emergency change to the Forensic Laboratory information processing systems and services is (Figure 7.5):

1. A Forensic Laboratory employee identifies a need for an emergency change, for example:
    - prevention or fix of business-critical system failure;
    - elimination or fix of a major security breach;
    - for reasons of health and safety.
2. The Forensic Laboratory employee contacts their Line Manager to inform them of the need for the change. The Manager is designated the Requestor.

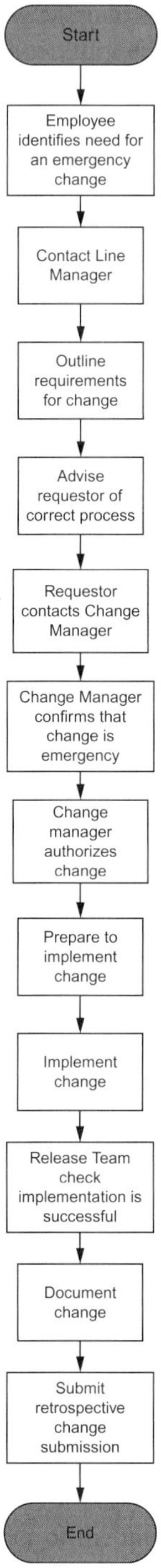

FIGURE 7.5 Managing an emergency change. (For color version of this figure, the reader is referred to the online version of this chapter.)

3. The Requestor contacts the Forensic Laboratory Service Desk and outlines the need for the change.
4. The Service Desk advises the Requestor of the appropriate procedure required to progress the change.

5. The Requestor contacts the CM (or a nominated deputy in the CM's absence) to notify them of the circumstances of the emergency change request.
6. The CM:
   - confirms that the change is an emergency;
   - authorizes the change;
   - allocates the change to a relevant member of the IT Department for implementation.

> **Note**
>
> If the CM decides that the change is not an emergency, the change is passed back to the Forensic Laboratory Service Desk for processing as a standard change.

7. The IT Department Team, in conjunction with the Requestor and any other relevant Forensic Laboratory employees, prepares to implement the change:
   - individual Forensic Laboratory employees are tasked with investigating particular aspects of change implementation as required;
   - the change is implemented;
   - during the implementation of the change, it is important that Forensic Laboratory employees involved in supporting applications and services prior to any change are informed on progress, so that any problems can be managed.

> **Note**
>
> It is important that all Forensic Laboratory employees involved carefully monitor the change as it is implemented so that any perceived risk is immediately brought to the attention of the RM, the Requestor, and the CM.

8. The Release Team performing the change checks whether the implementation has been performed successfully:
   - if the implementation has been successfully performed:
     - the RM reports the successful outcome to the CM and the Requestor (and other relevant staff as needed);
     - the RM obtains sign-off from the Requestor.
   - if the implementation has not been successfully performed, the RM continues until the change is performed successfully.
9. The change is fully documented via an RfC Form and any other supporting documentation, which is then processed retrospectively through the standard Change Management Process, via the CM and the CAB, before the change is closed.
10. The Requestor and the RM are responsible for progressing the retrospective change submission.

7.4.3.8 Managing Changes to Third Party Services

There will be occasions when there are changes required to third-party services supplied to the Forensic Laboratory. These may be on account of, but not limited to:

- addressing weaknesses or addressing security incidents;
- change of vendor or vendor takeover/merge;
- changes needed to reflect the Forensic Laboratory's changing needs;
- changes of medium that the services are being delivered by;
- changes to physical locations where services are being delivered;
- improving and upgrading existing services;
- maintaining existing services;
- provision of new services or features for existing services;
- use of new technologies.

Where changes are to be made to the services supplied to the Forensic Laboratory by a third party, they shall all go through the Forensic Laboratory Change Management Process as defined in Section 7.4.3.

Any unauthorized changes to services supplied by the third party shall be dealt with under the terms of the contract between the Forensic Laboratory and the third party.

7.4.3.9 Managing Changes to Forensic Workstations

All forensic workstations are connected to the dedicated forensic network, which is primarily used to provide information storage and printing facilities.

Where appropriate, Forensic Analysts have a separate workstation that is on the main business network.

A number of stand-alone workstations also exist in the Forensic Laboratory for Forensic Analysts, these are all for dedicated processes (e.g., forensic imaging, malware testing, multiple media copying devices, stand-alone Internet access, etc.).

Forensic workstations are frequently rebuilt, upgraded for a specific case, or have specific hardware added to them.

Changes to these forensic workstations do not need to go through any change control process, the Forensic Analysts are all presumed to be competent to make changes to their workstations as required. If the change is considered a risk, a stand-alone workstation is used.

7.4.3.10 Outsource Providers

Where backend services are outsourced, the outsource provider will undertake these actions. Any outsource providers shall be audited as second party suppliers to ensure that they have appropriate processes and procedures in place using the Forensic Laboratory Audit process, as defined in Chapter 4, Section 4.7.3. The provision of outsourcing providers is covered in detail in Chapter 14, Section 14.8.

7.4.4 Release Management

Release Management is the process of planning, building, testing, deploying hardware/software, and the version control and storage of software. Its purpose is to ensure that a consistent method of deployment is followed. It reduces the likelihood of incidents as a result of rollouts and ensures that only tested and accepted versions of hardware and software are installed at any time.

To ensure that all releases are performed to a consistent standard and in a timely manner, the Forensic Laboratory has implemented a release policy to govern releases at a high level, as defined in Appendix 19.

There are typically three types of release:

- *major software releases and hardware upgrades*—normally containing large areas of new functionality, some of which may make intervening fixes to problems redundant. A major upgrade or release usually supersedes all preceding minor upgrades, releases, and emergency fixes;
- *minor software releases and hardware upgrades*—normally containing small enhancements and fixes, some of which may have already been issued as emergency fixes. A minor upgrade or release usually supersedes all preceding emergency fixes;
- *emergency software and hardware fixes*—normally containing the corrections to a small number of known problems.

Release Management is proactive technical support focused on the planning and preparation of new services. Some of the benefits are:

- the opportunity to plan expenditure and resource requirements in advance;
- a structured approach to rolling out all new software or hardware, which is efficient and effective;
- changes to software are "bundled" together for one release, which minimizes the impact of changes on users;
- testing before rollout, which minimizes incidents affecting users and requires less reactive support;
- an opportunity for users to accept functionality of software before it is fully implemented;
- training in advance of rollout, which means that users do not experience system downtime while learning new features;
- version control and central storage of software, ensuring that correct versions are installed at all times, which minimizes incidents and the need for reinstallation.

The Release Management process works by providing a consistent framework for defining and creating new products and services, and ensuring that the correct versions of tested and approved software are implemented on a day-to-day basis (that is, after initial rollout).

Release Management links with the Change Management Process to enable implementation and to the Configuration Management process to maintain configuration records, as defined in Sections 7.4.3 and 7.4.5, respectively.

7.4.4.1 Roles and Responsibilities

The following responsibilities are defined in the Forensic Laboratory Release Management system.

7.4.4.1.1 Release Manager

The RM is the person who controls the Release Management process within the Forensic Laboratory. The RM's job description is given in Appendix 20. The Deputy RM is the person who acts as the RM in the event of their absence.

Responsibilities of the RM include:

- ensuring that the Release Management process is followed within the Forensic Laboratory;
- developing release policies, plans, and operational procedures;
- ordering hardware and software for use in a release;
- providing a management interface to the change management and configuration management processes;
- supervising a release and managing the Release Team;
- leading a review of the release process and managing the implementation of changes if required.

7.4.4.1.2 Release Team

The Release Team are members of the IT Department responsible for building and implementing a release.

Responsibilities of the Release Team include:

- assembling all hardware and software required for a release;
- creating a release build;
- testing the stability of a build and resolving any issues relating to the release;
- testing the impact of new services on existing components of the build and resolving any issues relating to the release;
- creating build procedures for all new hardware and software installation;
- testing the functionality of new hardware and software from the user perspective and determining whether the product does what it was intended to do;
- preparing a suitable build environment for testing;
- implementing a release using the agreed installation procedure;
- reviewing of the release process and managing the implementation of changes, if required.

7.4.4.1.3 Users

Users are either Forensic Laboratory employees or third-party employees with authorized access to the Forensic Laboratory's information or information processing resources. Who are responsible for testing and approving a release.

Responsibilities of users include:

- agreeing test criteria with the Release Team;
- performing full testing on a release build;
- signing off a release.

7.4.4.2 Managing a Release

All releases in the Forensic Laboratory are managed by the RM and implemented by the Release Team (Figure 7.6).

To manage a release:

1. The RM is informed about a potential release from one of the following sources:
   - the CM via an approved or potential change;
   - the Helpdesk via a user request.
2. The RM performs initial checks on the requirements for the release and may need to develop a policy for the release. A release policy should reflect the overall Forensic Laboratory release policy but can include specific details for the release in hand. The policy developed can include the following:
   - release naming and numbering conventions;
   - identification of business-critical times to avoid for the implementations;
   - expected deliverables for the release;
   - the policy on the production and degree of testing of back-out plans;
   - descriptions of the release control process (e.g., review meetings, progress assessments, escalation, impact analysis, etc.).
3. The RM discusses the details of the release with the relevant members of the IT Department and then draws up a release plan. The content of the plan can vary depending upon the type of release.

Note

A release plan is not mandatory but for anything more than a small release, it is recommended that a plan is produced.

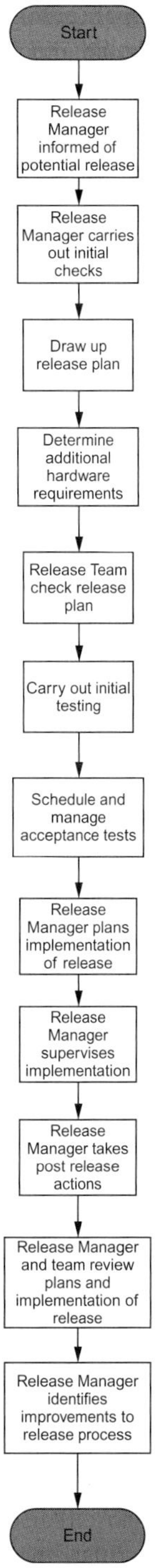

FIGURE 7.6 Managing a release. (For color version of this figure, the reader is referred to the online version of this chapter.)

A typical plan can include:

- resources required for the release including IT Department and other employees, hardware, and software;
- detailed quotes and negotiating with suppliers for new hardware, software, or installation services;
- acceptance criteria for the IT Department and users;
- roles and responsibilities of all Forensic Laboratory employees and any third-party employees involved in the release;
- procedures for building and implementing the release;
- details about tools to support the release of hardware and software into the live environment, e.g.,

- software distribution;
- training of IT Department employees and users before and after the release;
- outline release schedules;
- template documents to assist with the planning of the releases;
- the build and test environments for the release are available;
- the correct release mechanisms within IT are in place;
- back-out plans for reversing the release.

4. The RM, in conjunction with relevant members of the IT Department, determines the additional hardware requirements for the release and places an order by following the IT purchasing procedures, as defined in Chapter 6, Section 6.7.4 and Chapter 12, Section 12.3.14.2.
5. The RM, in conjunction with relevant members of the IT Department, determines the additional software requirements for the release and places an order.

Note

If bespoke software development is required, additional work must be performed to prepare system design documents and put the development work out to tender, if required.

- building and configuring hardware;
- developing, installing, and configuring software;
- developing installation packages;
- producing a test plan;
- developing test criteria in conjunction with users.

6. The Release Team checks the release plan and obtains all the relevant hardware and software and builds the release according to the requirements. The build process varies but typically includes:
   - building and configuring hardware;
   - developing, installing, and configuring software;
   - developing installation packages;
   - producing a test plan;
   - developing test criteria in conjunction with users.
7. The Release Team performs initial testing on the release and confirms that the release is performing as expected. For areas not performing as expected, the build is reviewed and corrected, as appropriate.
8. The Release Team schedules and manages a full IT and user acceptance test of the release. The testing must be performed in a controlled test environment that matches the existing live infrastructure as closely as possible so that known configurations of both software and hardware can be easily reinstated. The testing covers:
   - installation procedures and the functional integrity;
   - system hardware and software together with network infrastructure;
   - updated IT support procedures;
   - back-out procedures.

   The RM must obtain sign-off of each activity within the test.

   If the testing is not successful, the Release Team investigates the failed items and performs another build and then repeats the test, until it is successful.

   If the testing is successful, the RM signs off the test. The release implementation is planned and scheduled.

Note

All unsuccessful releases should be tracked and reported through Change Management as failed changes. Failed releases and their impact on operations should be monitored.

9. The RM plans the implementation of the release ensuring that the following is considered and produced where necessary:
   - producing an implementation timetable that outlines all actions, resources, and staff assigned;
   - listing all CIs to install and decommission;
   - producing release notes where appropriate;
   - planning communications between all involved parties including regular formal updates from the Service Desk to users;
   - acquiring the hardware and software for the implementation including procedures for secure storage prior to rollout and asset tagging during deployment;
   - scheduling meetings for managing the release and all those involved in it or affected by it;
   - listing all training and support documentation that is required to support the release.

   The release is now ready for implementation.
10. The RM supervises the Release Team during the implementation.
11. The Release Team performs the required implementation actions. If the implementation has been successfully performed, the RM:
    - reports the successful outcome to all parties including the CM and affected users (via the Service Desk).

    If the implementation has not been successfully performed, the RM initiates the back-out plan for the Release Team to return the systems to their previous state. The CM is informed of the failure, whether the back-out plan was successful, and any follow-up actions that are required.

    In addition, if IT services to users are affected, the Service Desk must also be informed so that users can be kept fully up-to-date. The RM assesses the reasons for the failure and after investigation resubmits the release to the CAB, and reports back the reasons for the failure.

12. The RM follows up the successful implementation and:
    - collates all CI information and passes this to the Configuration Manager (CfM) to enable an update of the CMDB;
    - stores all decommissioned CIs prior to recycling or disposal;
    - storing all software in the Definitive Software Library (DSL);
    - ensures that all relevant systems and operations documentation is updated to reflect the impact of the release;
    - confirms the release details with the Service Manager to enable an SLA update if required;
    - confirms the release details with the BCM to enable an update of the BCP if required.
13. The RM and Release Team meet to review the planning and implementation of the release, and discuss:
    - the effectiveness of the release process including all planning, build, testing, and implementation activities;
    - communications and relationship links between all parties involved in the release including the business and users;
    - possible improvements to the release process.
14. The RM identifies improvements to the release process and implements them.

7.4.5 Configuration Management

Configuration management is a major component of successful service delivery. Without effective configuration management, the integrity of assets and the ability to report on the status and configuration of the assets are jeopardized.

Configuration management establishes a consistent method for formally identifying and controlling CIs. It is an integral function in delivering IT services because it facilitates the protection of project assets and communicates changes that have been made to them. Configuration management, effectively planned and executed, protects assets and contributes to production of high-quality Forensic Laboratory products and services, with the avoidance of rework. The configuration management system is designed to:

- accounts for all the IT assets and configurations;
- provides accurate information on configurations and their documentation to support all the other Service Management processes;
- provides a sound basis for Incident Management, Problem Management, Change Management, and Release Management;
- verifies the configuration records against the infrastructure and corrects any exceptions.

In addition, information security asset classification is applied to elements of configuration management to ensure that assets and data are suitably protected.

In the Forensic Laboratory, the Configuration Management Plan serves as the core-planning tool describing the overall planning efforts for implementing and executing configuration management throughout the organization, and on a project basis if needed. The template used by the Forensic Laboratory is given in Appendix 21. It provides visibility and control of assets including hardware, software, user interfaces, project documentation, and system documentation. Configuration management facilitates orderly management of information about, and changes to, developmental baseline assets that need to be controlled.

Configuration management consists of four basic functions as follows:

- *identification*—identifying and specifying all components that go to make up the Forensic Laboratory infrastructure (including assets such as software, desktop systems, servers);
- *control*—agreeing and baselining CIs and then making changes only with the agreement of appropriate authorities (this includes controlling product releases);
- *status accounting*—the recording and reporting of all current and historical data concerned with each CI;
- *verification*—reviewing and auditing to ensure that there is conformity between all CIs and the authorized configuration record.

Configuration management within the Forensic Laboratory is defined as follows:

- *configuration*—the complete technical description required to build, test, accept, install, operate, maintain, and support a system (it includes all documentation relating to the system as well as the system itself);
- *configuration item*—a component of a configuration that has a defined function and is designated for configuration management. CIs may vary widely in complexity, size, and type from a complete system including all hardware, software, and documentation to a single module or a minor hardware component. A complete system is a top-level CI that can be broken down into components that are themselves CIs and so on;
- *CMDB*—a repository that holds details of CIs. It can include CI name, description, owner, serial and license numbers, file reference, purpose, location, author, version number, etc.

The configuration management process is closely aligned with the change and release processes, as defined in Sections 7.4.3 and 7.4.4, respectively. Change and Release Management are tasked with providing component change information to configuration management, which then records the information in the CMDB. The Forensic

Laboratory Configuration Management Policy is given in Appendix 22.

Configuration management in the Forensic Laboratory is monitored and maintained by the CfM. The CfM ensures that:

- all assets both physical and electronic are identified and classified and the appropriate controls applied;
- all CIs are identified and baselined;
- changes to CIs are only performed with the agreement of appropriate authorities via the correct processes (including change management and Release Management);
- regular reporting is performed on current and historical data for CIs;
- regular reviews and audits are performed to ensure that there is conformity between all CIs and the authorized configuration record;
- all members of the IT Department are aware of configuration management and follow the implemented configuration management system using the guidance and procedures provided.

The full job description for the CfM is given in Appendix 23.

7.4.5.1 Configuration Management and Information Security

To ensure that assets (both physical and electronic) are suitably protected, the Forensic Laboratory applies a classification of the asset according to its sensitivity and value in a uniform manner across the Forensic Laboratory, as defined in Chapter 5, Appendix 16 and Chapter 12, Section 12.3.14.6. This enables risks to be managed so that CIs and information is protected in a consistent and cost effective way.

These classifications are applied to all classified assets including paper, films, recordings, magnetic or paper tapes, disks/diskettes, and microfilm. Data held in other forms such as shorthand notebooks are also classified. This classification process also includes data from any third party that has been entrusted to the Forensic Laboratory, in the course of normal business dealings.

The Forensic Laboratory classifies information into four categories as follows:

- information assets;
- software assets;
- physical assets;
- services.

7.4.5.1.1 Information Assets

These include, but are not limited to:

- *Forensic Laboratory information*—this information has been collected, classified, organized, and stored in various forms;
- *databases*—information about Clients, employees, production, sales, marketing, finances. This information is critical for the business. Its confidentiality, integrity, and availability are of utmost importance;
- *data files*—transactional data giving up-to-date information about each event;
- *operational and support procedures*—these have been developed over the years and provide detailed instructions on how the Forensic Laboratory performs various activities;
- *archived information*—old information that may be required to be maintained by law or Client contracts;
- *case processing files*—Client deliverables;
- *IT Service Continuity plans, fallback arrangements*—these are developed to overcome any disaster and maintain the continuity of business.

7.4.5.1.2 Software Assets

These include, but are not limited to:

- *application software*—application software implements business rules of the organization. Creation of application software is a time-consuming task. Integrity of application software is very important. Any flaw in the application software could impact the business adversely, especially using forensic tools for processing Client's cases;
- *system software*—packaged software programs like operating systems, DBMS, development tools and utilities, software packages, office productivity suites, etc. Most of the software under this category are available off the shelf, unless the software is obsolete or non-standard.

All software is stored in the DSL.

7.4.5.1.3 Physical Assets

These include, but are not limited to:

- *computer equipment*—mainframe computers, servers, desktops, and mobile computing devices;
- *communication equipment*—modems, routers, PABXs, and fax machines;
- *specialized equipment*—CCTV, specialized forensic case processing hardware/tools;
- *storage media*—magnetic tapes, disks, CDs, and DATs;
- *technical equipment*—power supplies, air conditioners;
- *furniture and fixtures.*

7.4.5.1.4 Services

These include, but are not limited to:

- *computing services*—provided by the Forensic Laboratory (or managed services for which negotiated contracts are in place);

- *communication services*—like voice communication, data communication, value added services, wide area network, etc.;
- *environmental conditioning services*—heating, lighting, air conditioning, power.

7.4.5.2 Roles and Responsibilities

7.4.5.2.1 Resource Owner

The duties of a Resource Owner are defined in Chapter 5, Section 5.4.3.4.

7.4.5.2.2 Custodian

The duties of a Custodian are defined in Chapter 5, Section 5.4.3.5.

7.4.5.2.3 Configuration Manager

The CfM is responsible for the configuration process and to act as sponsor for all configuration issues within the Forensic Laboratory. The responsibilities of this role include:

- producing and maintaining a Configuration Management Plan, as defined in Appendix 21;
- liaising with other Forensic Laboratory Resource Owners and Line Managers to implement consistent change management, configuration management, and Release Management across the Forensic Laboratory;
- identifying, managing, and controlling CIs;
- ensuring consistency of the CMDB and DSL so that the authorized state of the Forensic Laboratory infrastructure is properly reflected;
- maintaining control of hardware, technical standards, and all documents;
- providing supporting services (such as registration and checking) of releases delivered by third parties;
- producing regular reports on the configuration database and all CI status;
- promoting the awareness of configuration management processes and procedures appropriate to their work;
- managing the configuration audit process and monitor exceptions and implement corrective actions;
- providing advice on configuration management issues to the Forensic Laboratory.

7.4.5.2.4 Configuration Librarian

The Configuration Librarian is responsible maintaining the configuration database. The responsibilities include:

- storing, retrieving, and maintaining CIs in the database;
- maintaining an audit trail of changes to a CI (revision history);
- deleting CIs as directed by the CfM;
- producing regular reports on the configuration database and all CI status;

7.4.5.3 Producing a Configuration Management Plan

To ensure that a configuration management system is implemented and maintained successfully within the Forensic Laboratory on an organizational and project level, the CfM produces a Configuration Management Plan, as defined in Appendix 21.

This plan describes the actions for assuring that the configuration management has adequate control over all items necessary for creating or supporting the deliverables.

The Configuration Management Plan is developed in coordination with, and be accessible by, all affected Forensic Laboratory employees and any relevant Clients. All schedule and work plan activities and roles and responsibilities required for execution of this plan is integrated into any project or organizational plan.

1. The CfM meets with other relevant Forensic Laboratory Managers to discuss configuration management. This discussion covers:
   - the scope of configuration management within the Forensic Laboratory and how it is defined;
   - roles and responsibilities of all parties.

   This meeting is minuted, and the minutes form a basis for the requirements of configuration management within the Forensic Laboratory. These are stored in the Forensic Laboratory ERMS as records of the meeting.
2. The CfM produces a draft Configuration Management Plan. This plan reflects the requirements of the Forensic Laboratory and contains the information defined in Appendix 21 and any other relevant information for the release.
3. The CfM circulates the plan to all relevant Forensic Laboratory Managers, affected Clients, and third parties for comment.
4. The Forensic Laboratory Managers, affected Clients, and relevant third parties review the plan and ensure that all items raised are satisfactory from the Forensic Laboratory perspective. All comments are passed back to the CfM.
5. The CfM reviews and then implements the comments, as appropriate.
6. Once the plan has been accepted, configuration management implementation is undertaken.

7.4.5.4 Implementing Configuration Management

Once the Configuration Management Plan has been agreed, the next stage is to implement the provisions of the plan within the Forensic Laboratory.

1. The CfM arranges for a meeting with all relevant Forensic Laboratory Managers, affected Clients, and relevant third parties and requests that they review the Configuration Management Plan and prepare further details for input to the meeting.
2. The CfM, relevant Forensic Laboratory Managers, affected Clients, and relevant third parties meet to discuss the implementation of the plan.
   The following details must be confirmed during the discussion:
   - the allocation of funds and budgets for each aspect of the plan;
   - the allocation of roles and responsibilities for overall implementation and each aspect of the plan;
   - provision for documenting and maintaining the policies, plans, procedures, and definitions for each process or set of processes;
   - the management of the teams including the Service Desk and operations;
   - the process for reporting progress against the plans.

   The outcome of the meeting (or meetings, if required) can be series of implementation documents or resource plans to implement service management. These are stored in the ERMS.
3. The CfM implements the plan according to the service management plan, regularly reporting to the IT Manager on the progress of the implementation.
4. The IT Manager reports regularly on the progress of implementation and then confirms that configuration management is now successfully running.

The maintenance and auditing of configuration management can now be performed.

7.4.5.5 Maintaining Configuration Items

The CfM and the IT Department ensure that the CMDB is regularly updated and this includes:

- adding a new CI;
- changing a CI;
- deleting a CI.

7.4.5.5.1 Adding a New Configuration Item

1. The CfM receives details of a new CI.
2. The CfM checks the details of the item and confirms that all the relevant information is available. If information is missing, the CfM contacts the provider and requests the outstanding details.
3. The CfM passes the details to Configuration Librarian to enter into the configuration database.
4. The Configuration Librarian creates a new record in the CMDB and enters the relevant details. A check is performed to ensure that all required information has been entered.

> **Note**
> It is important that all items are entered correctly using the appropriate CI categories and codes.

At the end of each month, the CfM produces a report that details all new CIs added to the CMDB.

7.4.5.5.2 Changing a Configuration Item

1. The CfM receives details of a change to a CI, for example:
   - a change, e.g., a replacement hardware item is installed;
   - a configuration move;
   - as a result of a configuration audit.
2. The CfM checks the details of the item and confirms that all the relevant information is available. If information is missing, the CfM contacts the provider and requests the outstanding details.
3. The CfM passes the details to Configuration Librarian to update the existing item in the CMDB.
4. The Configuration Librarian opens the existing item record in the CMDB and updates it with changed details. A check is performed to ensure that all required information has been entered.

> **Note**
> It is important that all items are entered correctly using the appropriate CI categories and codes.

At the end of each month, the CfM produces a report that details all CIs that have changed in the CMDB.

7.4.5.5.3 Deleting a Configuration Item

1. The CfM receives details of a CI that is no longer needed. Typically, this is when an item is disposed of.
2. The CfM checks the details of the item and confirms that it can be deleted from the CMDB.
3. The CfM passes the details to Configuration Librarian to delete the CI.
4. The Configuration Librarian opens the existing item record in the configuration database and deletes it. A check is performed to ensure that all associated CI information is also deleted or retained as appropriate.

At the end of each month, the CfM produces a report that details all CIs that have been deleted from the CMDB.

7.4.5.6 Maintaining the Definitive Libraries

All information processing equipment purchased by the Forensic Laboratory is recorded in the CMDB. The information recorded for hardware and software are given in Appendix 24.

7.4.5.7 Auditing Configuration Items

The CfM undertakes a program of configuration audits to:

- ensure that the configuration management system remains effective;
- ensure that the baseline is correctly identified and properly versioned;
- ensure that the baseline is complete (i.e., it contains the proper versions of the proper CIs);
- determine whether operational activities are performing as expected;
- determine actions that need to be taken to resolve CI breaches.

All audits are performed by the CfM or his nominee.

1. The CfM schedules an area of the configuration system to audit based upon:
   - any outstanding issues from a previous audit;
   - configuration changes that have been or are about to be implemented;
   - occurrence of errors in the configuration database;
   - a regular audit as recorded in the IMS calendar of audits.
2. The CfM appoints an Auditor to perform the review on the identified area of the management system. The Auditor must not have any management responsibility for the area being audited.
3. The CfM produces a report of all CIs for the area being audited and passes this to the Auditor.
4. The Auditor performs a floor check on all CIs and notes whether the correct CIs are present. This includes all items that make up the baseline.
5. The Auditor collates the results of the audit and produces an configuration audit report that details configuration defects that require correction.
6. The CfM tasks the Configuration Librarian to apply corrections to CIs in the CMDB that were identified in the report.
7. The CfM circulates a copy of the report to the IT Manager for reference.

7.4.5.8 Producing Configuration Reports

The CfM regularly produces reports on the items in the CMDB. Typical reports produced are:

- CIs detailed status report;
- CIs change history;
- released items report;
- product baseline status report;
- results of audits.

7.4.6 Capacity Management

The Forensic Laboratory IT Department must ensure that information systems meet anticipated capacity requirements through proper capacity planning and management. This covers:

7.4.6.1 Roles and Responsibilities

7.4.6.1.1 Capacity Manager

The Forensic Laboratory Capacity Manager (CaM) is responsible for the following aspects of capacity planning and management:

- creating the yearly capacity plan in coordination with relevant internal and external Clients;
- ensuring that the Forensic Laboratory capacity plan is up-to-date.

> **Note**
> The Forensic Laboratory CaM Job Description is given in Appendix 25.

7.4.6.1.2 IT Manager

The Forensic Laboratory IT Manager is responsible for the following aspects of capacity planning and management:

- conducting a monthly system capacity review in coordination with the CaM and other relevant stakeholders;
- providing trending and analysis information relating to capacity, as required;
- reviewing any incidents raised at the Service Desk that relate to capacity issues;
- determining anticipated capacity requirements for all new systems to be implemented in the Forensic Laboratory;
- reporting these new capacity requirements to the CaM;
- updating the Forensic Laboratory IT Department capacity plan with the CaM;
- authorizing changes to information systems for enhanced capacity purposes.

7.4.6.2 Scope of Capacity Planning

Capacity planning at the Forensic Laboratory includes, but is not limited to, the following:

- Data Center requirements (e.g., temperature, space);
- electrical requirements;
- e-mail capacity;
- human resources requirements;
- network and security systems capacity (e.g., ports, processors, memory);
- network internal and external link bandwidth;
- servers capacity (e.g., CPU, memory, storage);
- software licenses;
- storage space requirements.

7.4.6.3 Monitoring System Capacity

System capacity is monitored through the use of utilization reports that document the use of information processing capability within the Forensic Laboratory.

Software specific monitors are used to capture utilization measurements for processors, channels, and secondary storage media such as disk and tape drives.

Depending on the operating system, resource utilization for multiuser computing environments should not reach 75% with allowances for utilization that occasionally reach 100% and may, at times, fall below 70%. Trends provided by utilization reports should be used by the CaM and the IT Manager to predict where more or less processing resources are required.

If utilization is routinely above the 95% level, the IT Manager may consider:

- reviewing user and application patterns to free up space;
- upgrading computer hardware and/or investigating where savings can be made by eliminating non-essential processing or moving less critical processing to less demanding periods (such as during the night).

If the utilization is routinely below 75%, there is a need to determine whether hardware exceeds processing requirements.

7.4.6.4 Reviewing System Capacity

As part of the overall IT planning process, the Forensic Laboratory CaM reviews existing system capacity on an annual basis. The findings of the review are documented in a plan to ensure that cost-justifiable capacity always exists to:

- process the agreed workloads;
- provide the required performance quality and quantity.

The template for the Forensic Laboratory Capacity Plan is given in Appendix 26.

The system capacity review procedure is as follows:

1. At least once a year the CaM convenes a meeting to review system capacity, this should include:
   - the IT Manager;
   - the Information Security Manager;
   - other relevant stakeholders.
2. System capacity is discussed with a view to the Forensic Laboratory IT Department being able to provide capacity for processing anticipated workloads. Inputs to the discussion include:
   - results of capacity monitoring activity;
   - trend analysis;
   - reports regarding system capacity;
   - planned upgrades or changes to information systems;
   - business-based capacity planning requirements based on sales information projected and actual;
   - future projects.
3. The meeting agrees any action required.
4. The CaM documents the agreed actions with recommendations for processing agreed workloads.

Note

Changes to the IT infrastructure are conducted in accordance with the Forensic Laboratory Change Management procedures, as defined in Section 7.4.3.

7.4.7 Service Management

The Forensic Laboratory ensures that service management is implemented across the whole organization by following a defined process. This process covers:

- planning for service management through reviews and discussions with Forensic Laboratory Clients (internal and external);
- implementing service management through action plans;
- monitoring service management through audits and Client contact, as defined in Chapter 4, Section 4.7.3 and Chapter 6, Sections 6.6 and 6.8;
- improving service management via a policy of continuous service improvement using feedback, improvement plans, and service actions. The Forensic Laboratory continuous improvement policy is given in Chapter 4, Appendix 14. The Client feedback forms are given in Chapter 6, Appendix 20.

7.4.7.1 Planning for Service Management

To ensure that service management is implemented effectively within the Forensic Laboratory, the relevant Management System Owner(s) define and produce service management plans. These plans cover all the required aspects of implementing services by management within the Forensic Laboratory.

1. Relevant Forensic Laboratory and the relevant Account Managers meet to discuss service management requirements. This discussion covers:
   - the scope of service management within the Forensic Laboratory and how it is defined, for example, by location and service;
   - the services that the Forensic Laboratory or their Clients require;
   - the services that the Forensic Laboratory can provide;
   - roles and responsibilities of all parties.

Note

This meeting is minuted, and the minutes form a basis for the requirements of service management within the Forensic Laboratory and are stored in the ERMS.

2. Relevant Forensic Laboratory Managers meet to review the meeting held with Business Managers and prepare a draft service management plan. This plan reflects the requirements of the business and also the capability of the Forensic Laboratory to provide the required services.
   The IT Manager leads the meeting and takes responsibility for producing a draft service management plan. The plan contains the following information:
   - the scope of service management within the business based upon the agreed outline with relevant Account Managers and internal Forensic Laboratory Managers;
   - the objectives that are to be achieved by implementing service management;
   - an outline of the resources and facilities necessary to meet the defined objectives;
   - an outline of management roles and responsibilities for implementing service management, including the management of third-party suppliers;
   - the interfaces between service management processes and the manner in which processes are to be coordinated;
   - the approach taken in identifying, assessing, and managing risks so that the defined objectives are achieved;
   - a resource schedule showing when financial resources, employee (and any third-party suppliers) skills, and equipment resources are available;
   - the approach to changing the plan and the services defined by the plan;
   - the approach to continuing quality control through interim audits.

   The service management plan should include provisions to cater for service management process and service changes triggered by events such as:
   - service improvement;
   - service changes;
   - infrastructure standardization;
   - changes to legislation;
   - regulatory changes.
3. The IT Manager drafts the plan and then circulates it to all relevant Forensic Laboratory Managers for comment.
4. Several elements of the plan can be delegated to the relevant Forensic Laboratory Managers for production and return to the IT Manager, for example, roles and responsibilities or resource requirements within particular area of operation. If processes already exist for sections of the plan, for example, an auditing or risk identification and management process, this can be referenced.
5. Forensic Laboratory Managers review the service management plan and ensure that all items raised are satisfactory from the Forensic Laboratory perspective. All comments are passed back to the IT Manager.
6. The IT Manager reviews and then implements the comments as appropriate.
7. The plan is then circulated again to the relevant Forensic Laboratory Managers as a final draft. At this stage, the IT Manager only requires confirmation from all parties that the plan is suitable and acceptable.
8. The IT Manager forwards the plan to the relevant Account Manager and arranges a meeting with them to review it.
9. The IT Manager and relevant Account Manager(s) meet to discuss the plan.

If additional or detailed information is required, relevant Forensic Laboratory or third-party employees present this at the meeting to prepare further information for input to the plan.

The goal at this stage is to obtain management approval for the approach of service management within the Forensic Laboratory's business streams.

1. Top and business management confirm that the plan is acceptable.
2. The next stage is to implement the plan within the Forensic Laboratory.

7.4.7.2 Implementing Service Management

Once a service management plan has been agreed, the next stage is to implement the provisions of the plan within the Forensic Laboratory.

1. The IT Manager arranges for a meeting with all relevant Forensic Laboratory Managers and requests that they review the service management plan and prepare further details for input to the meeting.
2. The IT Manager and other relevant Managers meet to discuss the implementation of the plan.
   The following details must be confirmed during the discussion:
   - provision for documenting and maintaining the policies, plans, procedures, and definitions for each process or set of processes;
   - the allocation of funds and budgets for each aspect of the plan;
   - the allocation of roles and responsibilities for overall implementation and each aspect of the plan;
   - the coordination of service management processes as they are implemented;
   - the identification and management of risks to the services defined in the plan;
   - the identification of the managing teams for the services, for example, recruiting and developing appropriate Forensic Laboratory employees or relevant third-party employees;
   - the management of facilities and budget;

- the management of the teams including the Service Desk and operations;
- the process for reporting progress against the plans.

The outcome of the meeting (or meetings, if required) can be series of implementation documents or resource plans to implement service management.
3. The Managers for the operational areas implement service management according to the service management plan. They report regularly to the IT Manager on the progress of the implementation.
4. The IT Manager reviews the progress of implementation and then confirms to Top Management and the relevant business Managers that service management is now successfully running.
5. The planning, implementation, and review of services can now be performed within the framework of service management. Service management must be reviewed at least each year.

7.4.7.3 Monitoring and Reviewing Service Management

The monitoring and reviewing of service management is performed regularly.

A formal review is performed at least each year and when a significant change is required to the service management system. The review determines whether service management:

- conforms with the service management plan;
- conforms to the relevant parts of ISO 20000;
- is effectively implemented and maintained.

Procedures for performance measurement, including internal audits on the management system, are defined in Chapter 4, Section 4.7.

7.4.8 Managing Service Improvement

The Forensic Laboratory has a program of service improvement to improve the Client satisfaction levels via the continuous improvement of the products and services it provides. The Forensic Laboratory's continuous improvement policy is defined in Chapter 4, Appendix 14 and the procedures for this in Chapter 4, Section 4.8.

7.4.8.1 Planning and Implementing Service Improvements

Once service management is implemented and being measured, opportunities arise for improvements. The Forensic Laboratory ensures that these improvements are planned and controlled to achieve effective change.

1. On a regular basis, relevant Forensic Laboratory Managers collect performance information on the delivery of products and services to Clients (internal and external). This information comes from a variety of sources:
   - management meetings;
   - account management meetings;
   - Client meetings;
   - incident follow-up calls for customer satisfaction;
   - system management metrics;
   - case feedback analysis.
2. The relevant Managers meet to assess the collected information at the monthly service management meeting. The discussion includes:
   - trends in service provision;
   - assessment on whether the figures meet the agreed baseline or other targets (e.g., Turn Round Times);
   - identification of products, services, and areas of the business that require improvement.
3. The relevant Managers draft an improvement plan for their respective service area. The plan covers the resources, communications, and documentation needed to implement the required improvements.

   New targets for improvements in quality, costs, and resource utilization should be included, in addition to details on the predicted improvement measures, to assess the effectiveness of the change.

> **Note**
> If the plans require input from the business streams, the relevant Managers arrange for this input via meetings, etc.

4. The plan is circulated to the relevant Managers, including Top Management, for comment.
5. The Managers meet to discuss the various improvement plans. Relevant inputs about improvements from all service management processes should be considered. Any relevant comments and feedback are incorporated into the plan.
6. The Managers prepare for the implementation of the service improvement in their service area, including:
   - communicating the service improvements to all affected employees and relevant third parties;
   - revising all affected service management policies, plans, and procedures.
7. The relevant Managers implement the service improvement in their service areas.

> **Note**
> All improvements affecting a service should be processed through the change management system, as defined in Section 7.4.3.

Initial additional measuring and reporting is undertaken by the relevant Managers to ensure that the improvements are achieving their intended objectives. Comparisons must be made against the baseline and predicted improvements to assess the effectiveness of the change.

7.4.9 Service Reporting

Timely and accurate reporting is key to supporting and improving service management. Reporting enables the Forensic Laboratory management and all Clients to assess the state of products and services being provided, and provides a sound basis for decision making. The Forensic Laboratory service management and reporting policy is given in Appendix 27.

All Forensic Laboratory Managers are responsible for producing reports in their operational area. The Service Level Manager (SLM) is responsible for service reporting for the whole of the Forensic Laboratory and their job description is given in Appendix 28.

7.4.9.1 Producing Service Reports

Service reports are produced by Forensic Laboratory Managers on a regular basis as specified in service level agreements (SLAs).

1. For the reporting period, the SLM collates information about a service for inclusion in a report.
2. The SLM uses various reporting tools to generate report information as agreed.
3. Reports are reviewed at the relevant oversight committees, as defined in Chapter 4, Section 4.4.3, or other business streams, as appropriate.
4. Where needed, corrective action is taken, as defined in Chapter 4, Section 4.8.

7.4.10 Managing Logs

All activities on information and information processing facilities within the Forensic Laboratory are logged and the logs for audit trails of actions undertaken with individual accountability as all user IDs are uniquely assigned to an individual (apart from service accounts), as defined in Chapter 12, Section 12.6.

The Forensic Laboratory has implemented a log consolidation tool to permit reporting across multiple audit logs to a central point so that log management is simplified.

7.4.10.1 Roles and Responsibilities

7.4.10.1.1 Information Security Manager

The Information Security Manager is responsible for:

- investigation into suspicious activity identified by the log reports;
- performing the risk assessment to identify the type and level of audit logging and monitoring that might be required for each individual information asset;
- undertaking regular reporting from logs.

7.4.10.1.2 Asset Owners

Asset Owners are responsible for:

- identifying and agreeing with the Information Security Manager on logging and monitoring capabilities of the assets they own and for having them configured to meet the requirements of the risk assessment. Detailed requirements of owners are given in Chapter 12, Section 12.3.14.7.

7.4.10.1.3 IT Department

The IT Department is responsible for:

- configuring the information systems to meet the requirements of this procedure.

7.4.10.2 Audit, Operator, and Administrator Logging Guidelines

- the Forensic Laboratory maintains a list of all systems for which user activity audit logging is configured, together with the audit log requirements;
- this list is reviewed at least annually by the Information Security Manager, the SLM, relevant Account Managers, and the relevant System Owners. However, some logs are reviewed on a more frequent basis for the risk committee, as defined by the risk exposure identified to the Forensic Laboratory.

> **Note**
>
> The list of systems with their audit log requirements and the audit log reports are classified as "confidential information" and must be handled in line with the Forensic Laboratory's requirements for handling confidential information, as defined in Chapter 12, Section 12.3.14.9.

- system administrators are prohibited from erasing or deactivating logs of their own activities;
- all logs must be archived and available for later independent audit according to the Forensic Laboratory Retention Schedule, as defined in Chapter 4, Appendix 16.
- operator and administrator activity that must be recorded in each log event must include:
  - date and time of operator activity;
  - name of operator or administrator;
  - description of activity;
  - error handling details or resolution.

7.4.10.3 Checking Operator and Administrator Logs Procedure

The process by which the Forensic Laboratory checks operator and administrator logs is as follows:

1. The logs are monitored 24/7 in the Forensic Laboratory by the Information Security Manager.
2. The Information Security Manager regularly checks the operator and administrator logs for completeness, ensuring that the relevant information is being recorded:
   - date and time of operator activity;
   - name of operator or administrator;
   - description of activity;
   - error handling details or resolution.
3. If some information is missing:
   - the Service Desk creates a new incident in the Service Desk system and assigns the incident to the relevant IT Department member and marks it as an information security incident, as defined in Section 7.4.1;
   - after the relevant IT Department member completes their investigation, the incident is updated in the Service Desk system;
   - the Service Desk closes the incident.

7.4.10.4 Reviewing Event Logs

Event logging is reviewed on an ongoing basis using the event log consolidation software.

Reviews are organized by the Information Security Manager with System Owners and the process is as follows:

1. The Information Security Manager receives regular reports of suspicious activity from the event log correlation software.
2. On a planned basis, according to the IMS Calendar, specific reports are run and investigated. These include:
   - administration level access;
   - access to sensitive systems;
   - access to case files.
3. At the review session, the following are discussed:
   - outcomes and outstanding actions from the previous review;
   - types of events that are logged and methods by which logging needs to be changed;
   - additional needs for tools for automated event logging and event log correlation;
   - risk factors (e.g., the value of information, the extent of the network, past experience of infiltration, etc.);
   - trends that may indicate potential security risks;
   - security of the logging facility from potential tampering;
   - further action required (which is agreed by all attending the review). These are to be raised as CAPAs, as appropriate.
4. The Information Security Manager documents the findings of the review, the CAPAs raised and responsibilities for clearing them.

7.4.10.5 Protection of Log Information

The general guideline by which the Forensic Laboratory protects logs is as follows:

- Administrators are prohibited from disabling logging activity; disabling audit logs or tampering with audit log information will be subject to disciplinary action;
- controls must be implemented to ensure that the log files are protected against:
  - alterations to the message types that are recorded;
  - log files being edited or deleted;
  - storage capacity of log files being exceeded.
- log files that are required to be retained for legislative or contractual reasons shall be written to archive and retained as required.

7.4.10.6 Managing Fault Logs

The Forensic Laboratory IT Department manages fault logging to record faults and ensures that appropriate corrective and preventive action is performed.

7.4.10.6.1 Guidelines for Fault Logging

The following guidelines are in place for fault logging with the Forensic Laboratory information processing and communication systems:

- the Forensic Laboratory IT Department must log all reports of errors or problems with information processing or communication systems;
- all error or problem logs must be recorded in the Service Desk system in accordance with the IT procedures for managing incidents and managing problems, as defined in Sections 7.4.1 and 7.4.2, respectively.

Fault logs must include details of the following; however, this is a minimum part of the required input to the Service Desk System:

- name of person reporting fault;
- date/time of fault;
- description of error/problem/fault;
- description of initial Service Desk response;
- description of problem resolution (if known) or action taken;
- date/time of resolution.

7.4.10.6.2 Resolving Faults

All faults that are logged by the Forensic Laboratory IT Department in the Service Desk system must be resolved in accordance with the IT procedures for managing incidents and managing problems, as defined in Sections 7.4.1 and 7.4.2, respectively.

7.4.10.6.3 Reviewing Faults

All faults that are logged by the Forensic Laboratory IT Department must be reviewed on a regular basis to ensure resolution. At the Service Desk:

- open incidents or problems must remain open until satisfactorily resolved;
- all fault logs are stored in the Service Desk ticketing system;
- the SDM reviews fault progress on a daily basis, taking action, as appropriate.

7.4.10.6.4 Checking Fault Logs

The general process by which the Forensic Laboratory manages fault logs is as follows:

1. The SDM checks the logs from all monitoring systems. This includes all automatic network monitoring logs.
2. The SDM checks the logs for completeness, ensuring that the relevant information is being recorded, such as user, date, time, etc.
3. If there are any issues found in the fault logs, the SDM passes details to the relevant Forensic Laboratory or third-party employee for investigation and completion:
   - the Service Desk creates a new incident in the Service Desk ticketing system and assigns the incident, as appropriate;
   - the incident is updated in the Service Desk ticketing system;
   - resolution of the incident is undertaken in accordance with the processes for incident management, as defined in Section 7.4.1.

7.5 HARDWARE MANAGEMENT

7.5.1 Maintaining IT Equipment

All equipment, including IT equipment must be maintained according to the manufacturer's specifications in order to meet their requirements and minimize loss and damage in case of equipment failure.

All information processing equipment owned or used by the Forensic Laboratory is subject to these policies and procedures. Proper maintenance of IT equipment is essential to ensure continued availability and integrity, and the policy for maintaining and servicing IT equipment is given in Appendix 30.

7.5.1.1 Maintaining and Servicing IT Equipment

When Forensic Laboratory equipment must be serviced or maintained, the following procedures must be followed to enable continued availability and integrity (Figure 7.7):

1. A need for IT equipment maintenance or servicing is identified, for example:
   - a member of the IT Department identifies a need for equipment service or maintenance as part of the IT Department's routine servicing and maintenance schedule;
   - a member of the IT Department identifies a need for equipment maintenance or servicing as a consequence of an incident investigation;
   - an Engineer arranges a visit as part of service maintenance contract;
   - a call to the Service Desk reports a fault.
2. If the need for equipment maintenance is identified via a call to the Service Desk, the request is logged in the Service Desk system and the call is assigned to IT Support Specialist in accordance with the procedure for Managing Incidents, as defined in Section 7.4.1.
3. A member of IT Support (either the person who identified the need for equipment maintenance or the person who is assigned to an incident by the Service Desk) assesses the requirements for the equipment service. The options are:
   - on-site maintenance/service by the IT Department—in which case, the maintenance activity may be performed either at the location of the equipment or at some other location within the Forensic Laboratory premises (for example, a designated equipment build/maintenance room);
   - on-site maintenance/service by a service engineer from an approved and authorized third party (either a routine visit as part of an agreed maintenance contract or an arranged visit initiated at the request of the Forensic Laboratory IT Department);
   - off-site maintenance/service by an approved and authorized third party.
4. If the service operation involves internal maintenance/service within IT:
   - the member of IT who is performing the maintenance/service plans the activity as required (plans may not be considered necessary for routine servicing of equipment, for example, cleaning of printers). Planning activities may include:
     - scheduling of the maintenance activity, if required;
     - informing the Forensic Laboratory business users of a temporary reduction in, or loss of, service, if appropriate;
     - ordering of parts in accordance with the appropriate Forensic Laboratory procedure, as defined in Chapter 12, Section 12.3.14.2 and relevant Finance Department procedures in force;
     - arranging for equipment to be transferred to a designated build/maintenance area if it cannot be serviced at its permanent location;
     - involving other IT Department members, as required.

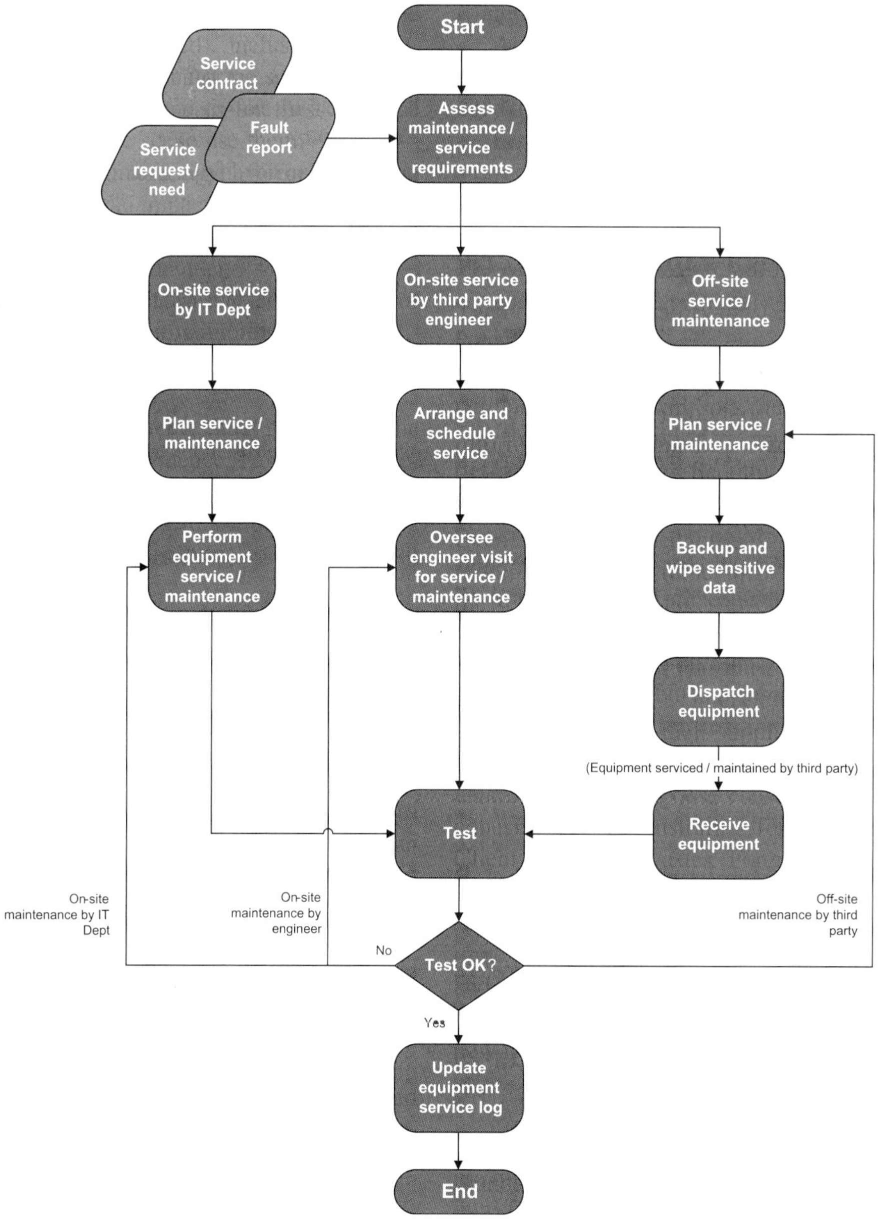

FIGURE 7.7 Maintaining and servicing IT equipment. (For color version of this figure, the reader is referred to the online version of this chapter.)

- at the scheduled time, the member of the IT Department performs the necessary equipment maintenance and servicing;
- the member of the IT Department who performs the maintenance activity tests the equipment to confirm:
  - the necessary servicing has been performed correctly;
  - the equipment is fully operational.
- the member of the IT Department who performs the maintenance activity completes any other activities as required, for example:
  - transfer equipment back to its permanent location (and then confirm through testing that the equipment is operating correctly);
  - inform the Forensic Laboratory business users of a resumption of a service.

5. If the service or maintenance operation involves on-site maintenance/service by a service engineer:
   - the member of the IT Department who is responsible for the equipment maintenance contacts an approved and authorized third party to arrange and schedule a visit from a service engineer. If relevant, the member of the IT Department informs the Forensic Laboratory business users that the maintenance will cause a temporary reduction or loss in service;
   - the service engineer performs the necessary equipment maintenance at the arranged time.

> **Note**
>
> If required, the member of the IT Department must ensure that they first obtain the necessary authorization from the IT Manager.

6. The visit by the engineer must be hosted by the member of the IT Department who is responsible for the equipment maintenance and in accordance with the Forensic Laboratory procedure for hosting visitors and service engineers, as defined in Chapter 12, Section 12.4.2.
   - the member of the IT Department who is responsible for the equipment maintenance ensures that the equipment is tested to confirm that the servicing activity has been performed and that the equipment is fully operational. Testing may be performed by either the service engineer (in the presence of the member of the IT Department) or the member of the IT Department.

> **Note**
>
> Equipment must be tested to the satisfaction of the Forensic Laboratory IT Department before the engineer leaves the Forensic Laboratory premises.

7. If the service or maintenance operation involves off-site maintenance/servicing:
   - the member of the IT Department who is responsible for the maintenance/service plans the activity, as required. This may include:
     - seeking authorization from the IT Manager, or the Laboratory Manager, if appropriate, for the off-site maintenance;
     - contacting an approved and authorized third party to arrange and schedule maintenance of the equipment;
     - informing relevant Forensic Laboratory business users of a planned temporary reduction or loss in service (if relevant);
     - scheduling a swap-in of equipment to offset a service loss (or arranging some other service), if appropriate;
     - assessing risks to the security of any of the Forensic Laboratory or Client information held on the equipment.
   - if the equipment holds sensitive the Forensic Laboratory or Client information, the member of IT responsible for the equipment servicing performs the following (as required) immediately prior to sending the equipment off-site:
     - back up any critical information held on the equipment;
     - securely wiping any sensitive information from the equipment.
     - the equipment is sent off-site for maintenance/servicing and in accordance with the Forensic Laboratory procedures for securing IT equipment off-premises, as defined in Chapter 12, Section 12.3.10;
   - the member of the IT Department who arranges the equipment maintenance updates the service log for the equipment. Details recorded are:
     - date and time of log entry;
     - reasons for maintenance;
     - maintenance/service activity details (including information securely wiped, date restored, etc.).
   - the equipment is returned and received in accordance with the Forensic Laboratory IT procedures for isolating deliveries from operational areas, as defined in Chapter 12, Section 12.4.3;
   - the member of the IT Department who is responsible for the equipment maintenance ensures that the equipment is tested to confirm that the necessary servicing activity has been performed and that the equipment is fully operational. If necessary, testing may be performed in a development or test environment;
   - the member of the IT Department who performs the maintenance activity completes any other activities as required, for example:
     - restoration of information;
     - transfers equipment back to its permanent location (and then confirm, through testing, that the equipment is operating correctly);
     - informs the Forensic Laboratory business users of a resumption of a service.
8. The member of IT who performs or arranges the equipment maintenance updates the service log for the equipment item. Information recorded in a service log always includes:
   - date and time of log entry;
   - maintenance/service activity details (including any parts replaced, information wiped, date restored, etc.);
   - details of persons who performed the maintenance or service activity (including any necessary management authorizations where required);
   - additionally, a service log may include:
     - date of next scheduled maintenance or servicing;
     - details of faults (actual and suspected);
     - fault prevention and correction actions.
9. If the maintenance activity has been initiated via a call to the Service Desk, the call is closed by the member of IT in accordance with the Forensic Laboratory IT procedure for managing incidents, as defined in Section 7.4.1.

7.5.2 Managing Voice Communications

As well as ensuring that appropriate security is applied to information processing systems, the Forensic Laboratory must also ensure that all voice communications are secured against the same threats of unauthorized access, disclosure, modification, or deletion.

7.5.2.1 Guidelines for Voice Communications

It is essential that all Forensic Laboratory employees, and third parties working for the Forensic Laboratory, are conscious of disclosing business confidential or strictly confidential information during conversations with the other Forensic Laboratory employees or third parties working for the Forensic Laboratory. When there is a business need to discuss the Forensic Laboratory information:

- Forensic Laboratory employees or third parties working for the Forensic Laboratory shall not discuss Forensic Laboratory business information in public places;
- Forensic Laboratory employees or third parties working for the Forensic Laboratory shall not leave Forensic Laboratory business information (particularly confidential or strictly confidential information) in voicemails or on answer phones.

If maintenance of the corporate telephone system is fully outsourced, this must be monitored by the IT Department as follows:

1. The service provider must maintain records of key voice facilities, e.g., PBX configurations and settings, and an inventory of telephones and associated wiring and cables.
2. Changes to the configuration settings for the Forensic Laboratory voice communications must only be performed by authorized third-party service provider personnel and must be approved by the IT Manager and processes through the Forensic laboratory Change Management Process, as defined in Section 7.4.3.
3. The performance of voice communications services is monitored by the IT Manager to ensure capacity is sufficient to meet target levels of service.
4. The IT Manager should ensure that the service provider has taken specific resilience measures to provide continuity of service to the Forensic Laboratory users.
5. Invoices for telecommunications services must be reviewed to identify errors, misuse, or fraud.

7.5.2.2 Reviewing Voice Communications Security

The process by which the Forensic Laboratory reviews voice communications security is as follows:

1. The IT Manager receives details about changes to the voice communications systems from the supplier or from internal Managers.
2. The IT Manager assesses the requirements from a security perspective, taking particular notice of changes in configuration settings and access by third-party suppliers.
3. The IT Manager sends an e-mail outlining his findings to the Information Security Manager, together with any recommendations, as appropriate.
4. The Information Security Manager checks the findings and determines whether the voice communications requirements can be approved. Additional discussions are held by the Information Security Manager and any other relevant stakeholders to clarify any of the findings or recommendations.
5. The Information Security Manager confirms the decisions as follows:
   - if approved, the Information Security Manager sends an e-mail to the IT Manager confirming that the request can be implemented (subject to any changes to the configuration, etc., that are recommended).

Note

The request is not granted on a permanent basis. A review of the request must be scheduled by the Information Security Manager and the IT Manager within 12 months to ensure that the request remains valid.

   - if rejected, the Information Security Manager sends an e-mail to the IT Manager outlining the reasons for rejection.
6. The IT Manager implements the change to the voice communications system.
7. At the appointed time according to the review schedule, the voice communications system is assessed again to check whether it remains valid using the above procedure.

7.5.2.3 Voice Recording System

If it is allowed within the jurisdiction and the Forensic Laboratory implements a voice recording system to record all external calls between the Forensic Laboratory and its Clients, this system must be effectively managed to protect the exchange of information and insure the quality of the Forensic Laboratory services.

7.5.2.4 Voice Recording System Guidelines

- all calls relating to forensic case files shall be associated with the relevant case in the ERMS and retained for the duration that the virtual case file is retained.
- all other recorded calls should be available and retrievable for a minimum of 3 months.

7.5.2.5 Procedures for Retrieving Calls

Where a call is to be retrieved either for a forensic case by an authorized Forensic Laboratory employee or an authorized third party working for the Forensic Laboratory, or for any other call.

1. An authorized Forensic Laboratory Line Manager sends a request to the IT Manager and the Information Security Manager to retrieve a call. The request should include:
   - time of call;
   - telephone extension;
   - justification;
   - authorization.
2. The IT Manager logs on to the voice recording system or the ERMS, as appropriate, copies the file, and sends it to the requester.
3. If the call contains disclosure of confidential or strictly confidential information or it shows misbehavior from a Forensic Laboratory employee toward a customer, the employee becomes subject to disciplinary actions, as given in the AUP in Chapter 4, Appendix 26.

7.5.3 Managing the Video Surveillance System

If it is allowed within the jurisdiction, the Forensic Laboratory may decide to implement a closed-circuit television (CCTV) system to monitor its entrances and secure areas. These cameras can operate continuously and be linked to a recording system.

The Forensic Laboratory should implement a policy supported by a number of guidelines and procedures for managing the CCTV system along with the video recording system to protect the Forensic Laboratory information and provide legally admissible evidence in incident investigations when needed.

> **Note**
>
> Some jurisdictions may require warning or other signage to alert people that they are under video surveillance.

7.5.3.1 Roles and Responsibilities

7.5.3.1.1 Information Security Manager

The Information Security Manager is responsible for:

- ownership of the CCTV system and video recording;
- annual review and maintenance of both systems;
- detecting any abnormal behavior through the regular review of the CCTV records;
- retrieving video recordings of approved requests.

7.5.3.1.2 IT Department

The IT Department is responsible for:

- the regular CCTV and video recording systems maintenance;
- act as the technical support for the systems.

7.5.3.2 Video Surveillance System Guidelines

- all video monitoring activities should be available and retrievable for a minimum of 3 months, where permissible within the jurisdiction.
- the video surveillance system is part of the physical security controls and is subject to the physical security audits, as defined in Chapter 4, Section 4.7.3 and Chapter 12, Section 12.4.6.

7.5.3.3 Procedures for Retrieving Video Recordings

Where a video recording is to be retrieved by an authorized Forensic Laboratory employee or an authorized third-party working for the Forensic Laboratory.

1. An authorized Forensic Laboratory Line Manager sends a request to the IT Manager and the Information Security Manager to retrieve a video recording. The request should include:
   - time and day of recording;
   - location of recording (camera);
   - justification;
   - authorization.
2. The Information Security Manager logs on to the video recording system and arranges to show it to the Requestor.
3. If authorized and appropriate, a copy is provided to the Requestor.

> **Note**
>
> Care must be taken to comply with all relevant privacy legislation within the jurisdiction.

7.5.4 Equipment Maintenance

Proper maintenance of information processing equipment is essential to ensure its continued availability and integrity. The following guidelines are in place for information processing equipment at the Forensic Laboratory:

- information processing equipment can only be maintained by either an appropriately trained member of the IT Department or by an authorized and competent service engineer;
- information processing equipment maintenance must only be performed in accordance with the manufacturer's recommended service intervals and specifications;
- all information processing equipment faults must be recorded by the Service Desk as an incident, as defined in Sections 7.4.1 and 7.4.10.6;

- all information processing equipment maintenance by service engineers or other third parties must be undertaken in accordance with the procedures for hosting visits by third parties, as defined in Chapter 12, Section 12.4.2;
- a record of all information processing equipment maintenance is maintained which records:
  - all information processing equipment maintenance performed by the Forensic Laboratory (including corrective and preventative action);
  - all information processing equipment maintenance performed by service engineers and third parties;
  - information processing equipment which needs to be sent off-site for maintenance is subject to the following controls:
    - equipment may only be sent for off-site maintenance to an approved and authorized third party;
    - the IT Manager is responsible for coordinating all off-site maintenance;
    - where possible all information processing equipment that is sent off-site for repair is wiped or media holding information is removed;
    - all off-site maintenance must be recorded.

7.5.5 Tool Validation

7.5.5.1 Requirements

With the rapid growth of digital forensics, the validation of operations of the technology and software associated with conducting digital forensic examinations is increasingly important.

According to the National Institute of Standards and Technology (NIST), results of tests must be both *repeatable* and *reproducible* for them to be considered admissible as electronic evidence. NIST defines these terms as follows:

- *repeatability* refers to obtaining the same results when using the same method on identical test items in the same laboratory by the same operator using the same equipment within short intervals of time.
- *reproducibility* refers to obtaining the same results being obtained when using the same method on identical test items in different laboratories with different operators utilizing different equipment.

Clause 5.5.2 of ISO 17025 requires that:

"Equipment and its software used for testing, calibration and sampling shall be capable of achieving the accuracy required and shall comply with specifications relevant to the tests and/or calibrations concerned. Calibration programs shall be established for key quantities or values of the instruments where these properties have a significant effect on the results. Before being placed into service, equipment (including that used for sampling) shall be calibrated or checked to establish that it meets the laboratory's specification requirements and complies with the relevant standard specifications. It shall be checked and/or calibrated before use."

In addition to this, a result of the *Daubert v. Merrell Dow Pharmaceuticals Inc.* ruling in the United States was the definition by the courts of scientific methodology as:

"the process of formulating hypotheses and then conducting experiments to prove or falsify the hypothesis."

The Daubert Standard allows for new and novel tests to be admitted into Court as long as they meet a number of criteria. The criteria listed below were identified to as being necessary to determine the reliability of a particular scientific technique:

- has the method in question undergone empirical testing?
- has the method been subjected to peer review?
- does the method have a known or potential error rate?
- do standards exist for the control of the technique's operation?
- has the method received general acceptance in the relevant scientific community?

While the Daubert Standard is not a legal requirement in all jurisdictions, the Forensic Laboratory has adopted its criteria for all forensic case processing.

7.5.5.2 Benefits of Independent Validation and Testing

The benefits to the Forensic Laboratory of independent testing and validation include:

- using a tested tool means that the Forensic Laboratory can be assured of its capabilities;
- limitations of the tool are known;
- Clients can be advised if their required tool is not "fit for purpose" based on objective evidence;
- when validating tools in the Forensic Laboratory, the tools capabilities are known, much of the validation will then just be conformation that they perform as expected on Forensic Laboratory forensic workstations;
- independent testing and validation by a recognized body, such as NIST, is usually accepted without question in a Court or Tribunal. The currently tested tools list is maintained by NIST in the Computer Forensics Tool Testing (CFTT) program at http://www.cftt.nist.gov/tool_catalog/index.php. The current tool testing handbook, available from the site, is dated 02/01/2012.

Tools tested by NIST fall under the following categories:

- disk imaging;
- forensic media preparation;
- write block (software);
- write block (hardware);
- mobile devices.

7.5.5.3 Tool Testing and Validation in the Forensic Laboratory

Within the Forensic Laboratory, the forensic network is segregated into the three traditional domains that should be present in all properly run IT Departments, namely:

- development;
- production;
- test.

How these are created, managed, and used are defined in Chapter 7, Section 7.7.

The Forensic Laboratory mandates that tools must be tested and validated prior to them being used for any case processing activities where their results support the evidence and findings presented to the Client. While independent testing, such as NIST's CFTT program, gives generally accepted results, there are three major drawbacks to just accepting these tests "carte blanche" in the eyes of the Forensic Laboratory and this represents an unacceptable risk. The reasons for this are:

- many of the tests undertaken are for non-current versions of the software (e.g., the most recent version of EnCase tested was 6.5 (from the current tool testing handbook, available from the site, is dated 02/01/2012), whereas the current version released and implemented is v7.05);
- many of the tools used by the Forensic Laboratory have never been tested or validated by the CFTT program;
- the amount of time taken for independent testing and validation may not fit in with the Client's or the Forensic Laboratory's requirements;
- the tests performed were not undertaken in the specific environment that the Forensic Laboratory uses (e.g., different hardware or operating system versions).

Therefore, the Forensic Laboratory always undertakes its own validation and testing. This is performed by the Forensic Analyst on a Clients' case and the results reviewed by the Laboratory Manager and approved if the tests are successful. This allows the Laboratory Manager and the Forensic Analyst to testify to having authorized the tool's use after testing and validation that they personally had carried out the testing and validation, respectively, and that spoliation of the evidence did not occur.

The Forensic Laboratory undertakes testing and validation to demonstrate and provide documented proof that tools and methods used in processing a forensic case preserved the integrity of the evidence delivered for forensic case processing.

7.5.5.4 Roles and Responsibilities

7.5.5.4.1 Laboratory Manager

The Laboratory Manager:

- agrees the testing and validation process proposed by the Forensic Analyst or defines it themselves;
- authorizes the Forensic Analyst to undertake the relevant testing and validation;
- reviews the results of the testing and validation;
- authorizes the use of the tool or method for the case;
- ensures that records of the test and its results are stored securely in the Client virtual case file in the ERMS;
- advises the Client, if appropriate.

7.5.5.4.2 Forensic Analyst

The Forensic Analyst:

- defines the testing and validation process needed for the forensic case, and alternatively, the Laboratory Manager may direct a specific test to be undertaken;
- undertakes the agreed testing and validation;
- produces the results and documents them for review by the Laboratory Manager;
- assuming they are acceptable, uses the tested and validated tool and or method;
- if they are not acceptable, identifies an alternative and advises the Laboratory Manager, which must be tested and validated as above;
- uses the authorized tool and/or method for processing the case.

7.5.5.5 Planning for Validation and Testing

The method, tool, and Client requirements will determine the actual tests to be undertaken for validation of the tool or method. The Forensic Laboratory has a standard test case that is used for all testing.

The Forensic Laboratory's approach for forensic tool testing and validation consists of a number of well-defined stages:

- identify the method or tool to be tested;
- identify the requirements for the test;
- develop test assertions based on the requirements;
- amend the standard test case to cater for these requirements, if necessary;
- develop test method and any supporting procedures;
- undertake test(s);
- produce test results;
- review results with Laboratory Manager;
- file results in the Client virtual file in the ERMS.

The test method documentation required for any non-standard test is defined by ISO 17025, Clause 5.4.4, reproduced in Appendix 31. These 16 items form the basis for all non-standard method testing and validation in the Forensic Laboratory.

Most of the testing required has been built into the standard test case and this is the standard used. If the requirements of the test to be undertaken are not met by the existing standard test case, then additional evidence is added to it to ensure that the test can be carried out. Any additions to the standard test case are approved by the Laboratory Manager and formally authorized, with records kept of the additional evidence and expected tested test results. The new case is then hashed and the hash recorded with the new standard test case in the Forensic Laboratory ERMS. The standard tests used in the Forensic Laboratory are given in Appendix 32. While this is the base set of tests, not all may be required for the testing of a specific tool.

Its use is then formally authorized for use by the Laboratory Manager and a record of the authorization is added to the ERMS.

There are other tool validation tests available, such as:

http://dftt.sourceforge.net;

http://www.cfreds.nist.gov/.

7.5.5.6 Testing and Validating Procedure

Within the Forensic Laboratory, the following procedure is performed for all testing and validation (Figure 7.8):

1. A "clean" disk is prepared by securely wiping it and validating the deletion.
2. A copy of the current standard test case, authorized by the Laboratory Manager, is copied to the "clean disk."
3. The case is hashed to ensure that it is not corrupted in any way prior to use and records of the "correct" state of the standard test case are used.
4. Perform the relevant tests on the standard test case.
5. Create a forensic image of the case.
6. Ensure that the image is correct by hashing it.
7. Analyze the image with the tool or method being tested and ensure that that the results meet expected outcome. If they do not, then the Laboratory Manager must take appropriate action.
8. Results of the test or validation must be created, the Forensic Laboratory test report template is given in Appendix 33.
9. The Laboratory Manager must approve the test, expected outcomes, and results.
10. The results of the test or validation are stored in the ERMS.

Note 1

In processing cases and as part of the validation process, dual tool verification is often used.

Note 2

While the above is the practical testing procedure, the requirements of ISO 17025, Clause 5.4.4, given in Appendix 31 are also met.

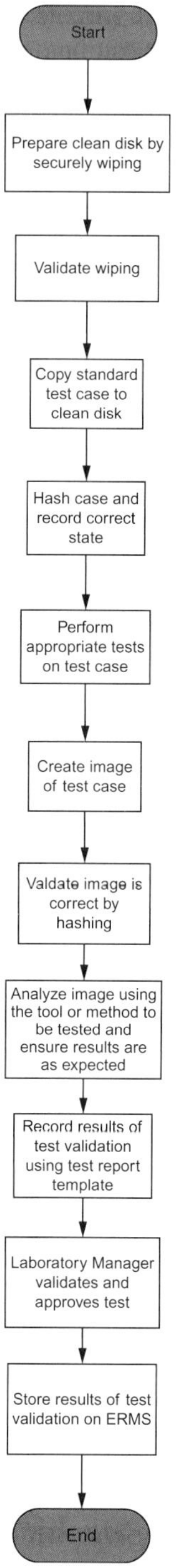

FIGURE 7.8 Test and validation procedure. (For color version of this figure, the reader is referred to the online version of this chapter.)

7.5.5.7 Review, Retesting, and Revalidating

The ongoing testing, and retesting, of methods and tools provides an audit trail of testing and validation that the tools and methods in use are repeatable and reproducible, with a documented audit trail in the ERMS.

When installing a test bed for testing and validation, all installed software should be hashed and tested against the known file filter to ensure that the installed software is of known provenance. On an ongoing basis, a file integrity checker should be used to ensure the integrity of the test bed.

This process should also be used for all forensic workstations and is regarded as good practice.

7.6 SOFTWARE MANAGEMENT

7.6.1 Controlling Malicious Software

Malicious software (Malware) is the generic term used to describe any software that may affect the Forensic Laboratory's information or information processing resources by disrupting operations, corrupting information, or allowing unauthorized access to it. All Forensic Laboratory and Client information and information processing systems must be protected against all malware.

Malware includes:

- adware;
- backdoors;
- computer viruses;
- root kits;
- spyware;
- Trojan Horses;
- worms;
- other malicious programs.

7.6.1.1 An Overview of Malicious Software Control

Since new and mutant viruses are appearing with increasing frequency, malware software and identification files must be frequently updated to counter attacks, and these procedures must be regularly reviewed to ensure that the Forensic Laboratory processes are suitable for containing and removing viruses.

The malware protection system implemented at the Forensic Laboratory is as follows:

- all workstations, servers, and gateways are protected against known viruses;
- anti-malware software is installed on servers, network workstations, stand-alone computers, laptops, and mobile devices, where available;
- on mail servers, malware software is configured to scan for viruses on inbound and outbound e-mails;
- anti-malware software is installed on the Forensic Laboratory gateways and is configured to scan for viruses on inbound and outbound files and e-mails;
- anti-spam and Internet site blacklisting is performed;
- blocking rules are applied on all incoming files to filter unwanted content;
- checks for updated virus identification files are automatically performed each hour and downloaded and distributed to all relevant information processing devices;
- mobile computing devices are automatically updated following a virus identification file distribution when a connection is made to the Forensic Laboratory network(s), where possible;
- anti-malware software updates are done automatically via the Internet;
- anti-malware software patches are implemented via automatic updates to the implemented anti-malware software;
- real-time scanning on disks is performed regularly on e-mail and file servers and on workstations;
- the Forensic Laboratory gateways are setup to:
  - automatically stop executable, batch and script files and offensive material where it can be identified;
  - check that Web requests are valid;
  - check the origination of an e-mail to reduce spoofing;
  - check for spam e-mails.
- anti-malware notification services, such as CERTs and vendor notifications are subscribed to and checked when received by the Information Security Manager and the IT Manager.

Note 1

All Forensic Laboratory employees have a training session on malware and how to deal with it during their security induction.

Note 2

Exceptions to the application of anti-malware software needs to be made for certain software tools as many of the tools that are used for things like breaking passwords are considered "malware" by many anti-malware products. This must be carried out on stand-alone dedicated forensic workstations.

E-mail malware and content validation checks are performed at the following points:

- all gateways;
- all servers;
- all workstations;
- e-mail incoming;
- e-mail outgoing;
- where possible, all mobile devices.

Internet access malware scanning and address validation checks are performed at the following points:

- content returned;
- Web site access request against blacklist;
- Web site access request for validity.

7.6.1.2 Roles and Responsibilities

7.6.1.2.1 Service Desk

The Service Desk acts as a first point of contact for users with malware problems. The responsibilities of this role include receiving calls and first-line user liaison for virus information.

7.6.1.2.2 IT Department

The IT Department acts as second line support for malware control. The responsibilities of this role include:

- checking that anti-malware update files are successfully downloaded and propagated to the Forensic Laboratory systems;
- maintaining Web site blacklist and spam listings;
- manually downloading and updating anti-malware software, if required;
- responding to malware incidents.

7.6.1.2.3 IT Manager

The IT Manager is the central authority for malware control. The responsibilities of this role include:

- ensuring that adequate malware controls are in place;
- managing response to malware incidents, as defined in Section 7.4.1.

7.6.1.3 Maintaining Malware Protection

The Forensic Laboratory anti-malware is automatically updated hourly. Regular manual checks are performed by the IT Department Team.

7.6.1.4 Handling a Malware Outbreak

If a malware outbreak is received at the Forensic Laboratory, the following occurs:

1. The Service Desk is advised of an incident by e-mail or telephone alerts.
2. The Service Desk raises an incident at the Service Desk, as defined in Section 7.4.1.
3. The IT Manager and the Information Security Manager organizes a short review meeting with the IT Department to determine how the malware entered the Forensic Laboratory systems and decide response actions. These actions may include:
   - obtaining updated anti-malware files;
   - scanning systems to detect and remove the malware;
   - checking the automatic update system;
   - reviewing current anti-malware procedures;
   - e-mailing all relevant Forensic Laboratory users to inform them about the malware incident;
   - invoking the relevant BCP in the event of a serious outbreak, as defined in Chapter 13.
4. The IT Manager e-mails all relevant members of the IT Department summarizing the review meeting and confirming the actions required.
5. The relevant members of the IT Department implement the required actions.
6. The relevant members of the IT Department review the outbreak with the IT Manager and the Information Security Manager. Any changes that can be applied to the IT infrastructure to avoid similar malware outbreaks are initiated in accordance with the Change Management Process, as defined in Section 7.4.3.
7. The incident is closed at the Service Desk, as defined in Section 7.4.1.4.4.

7.6.1.5 Processing Bounced E-mails

E-mails and file requests that meet the criteria as a malware or a spam attack are automatically "bounced" into a quarantine area. This area is checked by the IT Department on a regular basis or when required.

In general, the criteria for bouncing e-mails is to ensure that as much material as possible is allowed onto the Forensic Laboratory network without additional work being placed on the IT Department to deal with trivial e-mails.

There are occasions when a user is expecting material via an e-mail that has been bounced. The user may contact the IT Department and request that a bounced e-mail is released. The IT Department opens the quarantine area and checks the items. If the item does not contain malware or is not spam, it is released to the user. If an item is malware or spam it is deleted.

At regular intervals, and at least each month, a review is performed of the bounced material to review the types of e-mails being bounced. If the review determines that a certain type of previously blacklisted e-mail is acceptable, then it is removed from the malware/spam listings.

7.6.1.6 Maintaining Blacklists and Graylists

All incoming e-mails, and internal Web site requests, are checked against rules within the SMTP Gateway Server. If the file or request breaks these rules, the file is blocked and the request is denied. A log of these is retained within gateway logs.

The IT Department adds in additional Forensic Laboratory specific blacklist items, such as e-mail subjects containing links to graphics files or inappropriate wordings.

The IT Department creates and maintains and views blocking rules and blacklists and graylists via the SMTP Console.

7.6.1.7 Information Leakage

Information leakage may occur and opportunities for this must be prevented in the Forensic Laboratory. Typically, this occurs through malicious software such as "Trojan Horses" or through "covert channels."

The Forensic Laboratory must ensure that, as a minimum, the following are implemented to reduce the chances of information leakage:

- scanning of outbound media and communications for hidden information;
- monitoring of personnel and system activities logs can be obtained from proxy servers upon request;
- monitoring resource usage in computer systems;
- using tools to reduce the likelihood of Trojan Horse infections;
- use of key features and benefits of the Forensic Laboratory firewalls, for example, the blocking of unnecessary outgoing ports on a physical firewall;
- comprehensive high-availability solution for sub-second failover between interfaces or devices;
- full mesh configurations to allow for redundant physical paths in the network, thereby providing maximum resilience;
- virtual system support to allow partitioning into multiple security domains, each with a unique set of administrators, policies, VPNs, and address books;
- interface flexibility for varying network-connectivity requirements and future growth requirements;
- virtual router support to map internal, private, or overlapped IP addresses to a new IP address, providing an alternate route to the final destination and concealing it from public view;
- customizable security zones to increase interface density without additional hardware expenditures, lower policy-creation costs, contain unauthorized users and attacks, and simplify management of firewall/VPNs;
- transparent mode to allow the device to function as a Layer 2 IP security bridge, providing firewall, VPN, and DoS protections, with minimal change to the existing network;
- management through central management consoles;
- policy-based management to allow centralized, end-to-end life cycle management.

7.6.2 Control of Technical Vulnerabilities

Technical vulnerability management should be implemented in an effective, systematic, and repeatable way with measurement taken to confirm its effectiveness. These considerations include operating systems and any applications in use.

7.6.2.1 Roles and Responsibilities

7.6.2.1.1 IT Department

The IT Department is responsible for:

- monitoring vulnerabilities and vendors' releases of patches and fixes and installing operational software updates, patches, and fixes on the operational systems.

7.6.2.1.2 Information Security Manager

The Information Security Manager is responsible for vulnerability risk assessments.

7.6.2.2 Evaluation of Assets at Risk

The following guidelines are in place for evaluation of assets at risk within the Forensic Laboratory:

- all assets are recorded in the IT Asset Register with details of owners;
- software details in the IT asset register will include:
  - vendor;
  - version number.
- assets will be continuously reviewed by the Asset Owner to ensure that they are maintained at the correct technical level.

7.6.2.3 Vulnerability Management Process

The Forensic Laboratory must ensure that the following processes are in place to address technical vulnerabilities:

- vulnerability monitoring from such sources as vendors, CERTs, etc.;
- coordination of responsibilities within the IT Department and the business for patching;
- a timeline for reacting to vulnerability notifications;
- a suitable risk assessment process to determine risks and countermeasures, as defined in Chapter 5;
- required controls are implemented through the Forensic Laboratory change management procedure, as defined in Section 7.4.3;
- vulnerability control decisions are tracked (and can be audited) through either the change management procedure or the incident management procedure;
- the patch testing and evaluation process must be followed;
- the Information Security Committee receives reports on vulnerability management, including information about the number of identified vulnerabilities, what additional controls are in place, what outstanding issues there are, and updates on previous issues.

7.6.3 Implementing Software Patches and Updates

The update of software includes responses to specific security alerts that the Forensic Laboratory has received from software vendors or other reputable sources. This includes:

- firmware;
- operating systems;
- applications.

7.6.3.1 An Overview of Software Patches and Updates

The software patch and update system implemented at the Forensic Laboratory is as follows:

- updates and patches are implemented manually on servers;
- if a patch is available, the risks associated with installing the patch should be assessed (the risks posed by the vulnerability should be compared with the risk of installing the patch);
- updates and patches should be automatically implemented on networked workstations and laptops;
- updates and patches are implemented manually on all stand-alone workstations;
- automatic scanning is used to scan all information processing devices for building the patch list regularly (Figure 7.9).

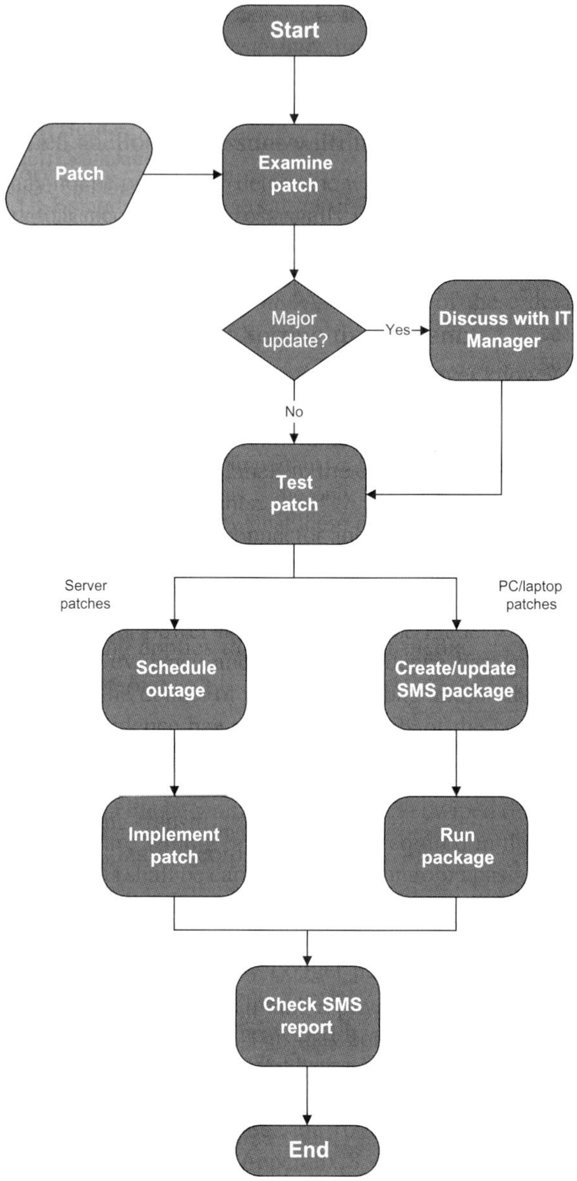

FIGURE 7.9 An overview of software patches and updates.

7.6.3.2 Roles and Responsibilities

7.6.3.2.1 IT Department

The IT Department is the primary instigator of software updates and patches. The responsibilities of this role include:

- checking vendor sites for updates on a regular basis;
- implementing patches and updates on servers;
- generating update packages for servers, workstations, and other mobile devices;
- checking reports to confirm implementation;
- liaising with the IT Manager for updates and patches on critical servers;
- determining update implementation schedules.

7.6.3.2.2 IT Manager

The IT Manager is the central authority for updates and patches. The responsibilities of this role include:

- ensuring that adequate patch and update controls are in place;
- liaising with Service Delivery Manager about changes to critical servers or changes that have a major impact on services.

7.6.3.3 Implementing Patches and Updates on Servers

Most servers in the Forensic Laboratory are of a standard configuration, and therefore, patches required for one will also be needed for several others.

Updates and patches implemented on servers shall be managed via the Change Management Process, as defined in Section 7.4.3.

1. The IT Department identifies the patch required for a server. This is via a range of sources that include the vendor alerts, security alerts, software upgrade programs, etc.
2. The IT Department checks the details of the patch available and evaluates it. If it is determined that the patch has a minor impact on the server or the services provided by it, the IT Department can schedule the update. If it is determined that the patch has a major impact on the server or the services provided by it, the IT Department discusses the installation of the patch with the IT Manager and confirms appropriate actions in an e-mail.

> **Note**
>
> In all circumstances for both minor and major patches, no critical server has a patch or update installed without the patch or update first being installed on a non-critical server.

3. The IT Department tests the patch on a suitable test machine in the Forensic Laboratory IT Department.
4. The IT Department schedules an outage of the relevant server via the Service Desk. Scheduled outages should ideally take place at time of low user activity such as at weekends or overnight.
5. The IT Department logs on to the relevant server and then updates the server software by:
   - downloading and manually running the relevant patch(es);
   - inserting a CD received from the software vendor and installing the update using the installation program;
   - manually running an update to select the patch(es) required and install them;
   - running the previously downloaded patch.
6. Once the patch is installed, the IT Department logs off the server and then logs back in and checks the event log to ensure that the update or patch has been successfully installed.
7. The IT Department views the next scheduled scan report as a second check that the patch or update has been installed.

7.6.3.4 *Implementing Patches and Updates on Workstations, PCs, and Laptops*

Most workstations, PCs, and laptops at the Forensic Laboratory are of a standard configuration, apart from those that are used as forensic workstations, and therefore, patches required for one will also be needed for others.

Updates and patches implemented on workstations may need to be performed and shall be managed via the Change Management Process, as defined in Section 7.4.3.

1. The IT Department identifies the patch required for a workstation, PC, or laptop. This is via a range of sources that include the vendor alerts, security alerts, software upgrade programs, etc.
2. The IT Department checks the details of the patch available and evaluates it. If it is determined that the patch has a minor impact on the services provided to users, the IT Department can schedule the update. If it is determined that the patch has a major impact on the services provided to users, the IT Department discusses this with the IT Manager and confirms appropriate actions in an e-mail.
3. The IT Department tests the patch on a suitable test machine in the Forensic Laboratory IT Department.
4. The IT Department creates a new installation package (or updates an existing package) and sets it to run once a week, or more frequently if required.
5. The IT Department views the next scheduled scan report and checks the machines the patch has been installed on. A regular check is performed each week until all machines have the patch installed.

7.7 NETWORK MANAGEMENT

7.7.1 Managing Network Security

The Forensic Laboratory Network Services Policy is given in Chapter 4, Appendix 19.

7.7.1.1 *Guidelines for Network Management*

Information security at the Forensic Laboratory is highly dependent on network operations and management functions, and therefore, specific measures are taken to ensure security is not compromised by network failures or information security breaches of the network.

For security purposes, network management arrangements include, where possible, the following:

- establish SLAs with users and third-party service providers and develop connection rules, as defined in Chapter 7, Section 7.7.3;
- segregate the duties within the IT Department of those who are running the network from those developing/designing the network, as defined in Chapter 12, Section 12.3.5;
- reduce dependence on key individuals by automating key tasks, ensuring complete and accurate documentation of operational procedures, and arranging alternative cover for key positions;
- closely control activities of network administrators, by supervision and logging of activity, as defined in Chapter 7, Section 7.4.10.2 and Section 7.10.4.3;
- fully screen applicants for positions that involve running the network, as defined in Chapter 18, Section 18.1.3;
- use awareness and training programs to ensure that all employees are aware of the existence and importance of information and network security controls, as defined in Chapter 12, Section 12.3.2;
- all network administrators should be equipped with the necessary know-how and skills to run the network under normal and peak conditions, as defined in Chapter 4, Section 4.6.2.2;
- all network administrators should be competent to deal with error, exception, and emergency conditions and required to report faults and other disruptive events.

7.7.1.2 Network Design

The design of the Forensic Laboratory network is based on sound design principles so that it:

- has security functionality built-in;
- is designed to be compatible with other networks;
- can cope with foreseeable developments in the Forensic Laboratory's use of information technology, including capacity planning, as defined in Section 7.4.6.

These are the principles upon which the Forensic Laboratory IT bases the network design:

- coherent technical standards are used to support consistent naming conventions, and to comply with legislative, regulatory, contractual, and industry requirements;
- proper capacity planning ensures growth and interconnection with other networks is possible if needed (based upon known and projected bandwidth requirements) and to ensure that the network technologies selected can cope with the existing volume of traffic and are capable of accommodating growth and changing requirements, as defined in Section 7.4.6;
- a combination of static and dynamic routing methods are used to ensure easier administration and build resistance to the introduction of routing errors;
- the physical topography should attempt to avoid areas that are prone to disruption (e.g., areas where building work is likely to take place);
- guidelines on the depth of burial and the physical protection requirements of cables (e.g., armored conduit) should be clearly documented in the design;
- where possible, key devices perform only one major function and all other services and functions that are not required are disabled or removed according to the defined hardened builds;
- distinct sub-networks should be used, protected by rule-based traffic filtering;
- common servers should be centralized to enable better management of network traffic;
- switched networks should be used where possible (as opposed to slower shared networks);
- the number of entry points into the network should be limited, and each entry point should serve a valid business purpose;
- strong authentication mechanisms must be used, where appropriate or required;
- network management reports and audit trails must be maintained.

7.7.1.3 Network Resilience

Communications facilities and devices are critical to the continuity of network services, and specific measures must be taken to:

- reduce single points of failure by:
  - automatic rerouting of communications should critical nodes or links fail;
  - rerouting in the event of a network failure or changes in the network topology;
  - all critical network devices can be reached via more than one path, use of network traffic load balancing, and redundancy of key devices;
  - duplicate devices are provided where necessary.
- reduce the risk of malfunction of critical communications equipment, software, links, and services by:
  - giving high priority to reliability, compatibility, and capacity in the acquisition process;
  - using only proven products, keeping them up-to-date, and in good working order;
  - ensuring that key network components can be replaced quickly or that spares are held on site;
  - using modern protocols that can be updated quickly and withstand high capacity to ensure that the network is supported by a robust and reliable set of hardware and software;
  - maintaining network system devices according to vendor standards.

To maximize network resilience at the Forensic Laboratory:

- minimizes single points of failure by:
  - automatic rerouting of communications should critical nodes or links fail;
  - rerouting in the event of a network failure or changes in the network topology;
  - all critical network devices can be reached via more than one path, use of network traffic load balancing, and redundancy of key devices;
  - duplicate devices are provided where necessary.
- risks of malfunctions with critical communication equipment, software, and links are minimized by:
  - giving high priority to reliability, compatibility, and capacity in the acquisition process;
  - using only proven products, keeping them up-to-date, and in good working order;
  - ensuring that key network components can be replaced quickly or that spares are held on site;
  - using modern protocols that can be updated quickly and withstand high capacity to ensure that the network is supported by a robust and reliable set of hardware and software;
  - maintaining network system devices according to vendor standards.

7.7.1.4 Network Documentation

The Forensic Laboratory maintains accurate, up-to-date, documentation to support network operations, which is consistent with security requirements. Accurate documentation (in paper or electronic form) is maintained for the configuration of the network (internal and external), including all nodes and connections, communications equipment, software, links and services (including up-to-date inventories and labeling of equipment), and in-house cabling (including identification of cable runs and labeling of cables). The documentation is readily accessible to authorized personnel, subject to supervisory review, and checked periodically to ensure that no unauthorized changes have been made.

The Forensic Laboratory network documentation covers:

- network hardware and software manuals, and operating procedures covering, network devices, test equipment, network management software, and network monitoring software;
- recovery and continuity plans, specifying the requirements for holding network documentation in secure off-site locations networking roles and responsibilities;
- descriptions of the network (network topology diagrams);
- circuits;
- devices;
- cabling.

7.7.1.5 Traffic Management and Control

All important network devices must be properly configured and network-filtering methods applied across all of the Forensic Laboratory's internal and external networked services. This ensures that networks are protected against undesirable network traffic and prevents unauthorized users gaining access.

All internal and external network connections must be compliant with the Forensic Laboratory access control policy, as given in Chapter 4, Appendix 11, the procedures for controlling network access as defined in Section 7.7.2, and the procedures for controlling remote access as defined in Section 7.7.3. Elements of the network that may be accessed, and the authorization procedure for gaining access, are determined on the rules and rights of users or groups of users, which is driven by business requirements.

Access to the Forensic Laboratory network is controlled via the use of enforced paths, user or node authentication, segregation of networks and network connections, routing and filtering controls.

The minimum acceptable authentication requirements for all users wishing to access information resources via the Forensic Laboratory network is by means of an unique User ID and password, while access to the forensic network is by fingerprint biometric authentication.

The Forensic Laboratory's internal network addressing scheme must not be visible to external connections to keep hackers or other unauthorized external parties from easily gaining information about the structure of the Forensic Laboratory network, and its information processing systems.

7.7.1.6 Device Configuration

All important Forensic Laboratory network devices (network servers, routers, front-end processors, bridges, switches, firewalls, and IDS/IPS) must be properly configured to:

- comply with a standard technical build where undesirable and inessential services are always disabled;
- ensure they function as required and do not compromise the security of the network;
- highlight overload or exception conditions, where possible.

The following guidelines have been adopted at the Forensic Laboratory:

- all changes to the network must go through the Forensic Laboratory Change Management Process, as defined in Section 7.4.3;
- all network devices log events in a form suitable for review via the event log correlation software, as defined in Section 7.4.10;
- all network devices must be tested after the build to ensure the device is working correctly;
- build and configuration settings must be documented;
- log events are reviewed regularly and appropriate action taken where anomalies are found, as defined in Section 7.4.10.4;
- logging alerts the network administrators to changes;
- measures must be taken to prevent unauthorized or incorrect updates to network devices;
- network devices are built to a standard hardened build, where possible;
- network services on systems must be disabled, unless a specific business reason for the service is needed;
- new patches and bug fixes must be thoroughly tested before being applied, as defined in Section 7.6.3;
- passwords (and privileges) are set up on all network devices (e.g., firewalls, routers, IDS, etc.) for all means of connection that are required (e.g., directly, via the network, via dial-up link, or via console connection);
- passwords are changed on a periodic basis where this is practical (for example, it is not always practical to change some hard-coded password on legacy systems) or are strong passwords as defined in Chapter 12, Section 12.6.

7.7.1.7 Traffic Filtering

The Forensic Laboratory employs traffic filtering to ensure unauthorized or undesirable network traffic is not allowed to gain access to specified parts of the network.

Network-filtering devices are configured to filter specific types of traffic, to block, or otherwise restrict particular types or sources of traffic.

Filtering of traffic should be based on pre-defined, documented, and signed-off rules or tables based on the principle of "least access" (that which is not expressly permitted is denied). These rules and tables are developed by the Information Security Manager with the network administrators and are subject to operational review by the IT Manager and relevant Resource Owners.

Network-filtering devices (i.e., firewalls) are implemented to ensure that they cannot be bypassed, are fully resilient, and can only be accessed from designated workstations or network addresses. Any failure or vulnerabilities identified must be raised as an incident at the Service Desk, as defined in Section 7.4.1.

While filtering devices are typically used to detect inbound attacks upon the network, measures should be taken to detect and prevent outbound attacks upon external networks. This will prevent Forensic Laboratory employees or third parties working for the Forensic Laboratory using the internal network as a launch pad to attack the networks of other organizations. If the source of attacks upon an external organization can be clearly identified, it may be possible for the victim to seek legal redress. That is the organization from which the attack originated may be regarded as liable for the malicious act.

Protection against outbound attacks can be achieved by ensuring connection to the Internet occurs via a proxy server or with the appropriate placement of intrusion detection sensors combined with proper logging and monitoring of outbound traffic. This minimizes the risk of legal action against the Forensic Laboratory.

7.7.1.8 Monitoring the Network

Network monitoring is performed by the Forensic Laboratory network administrators to assess the performance of the network, reduce the likelihood of network overload, and detect potential or actual malicious intrusions:

- routine monitoring includes current and projected volumes of network traffic, utilization of network facilities, and identification of any potential bottlenecks or overloads;
- firewall activity is monitored via separate system logs.

7.7.1.9 Reviewing and Assessing Network Security

The procedures for reviewing and assessing network access and security are as follows:

1. The Forensic Laboratory network administrators are responsible for managing network security and reviewing the network security. They also receive authorized requests from network users to change aspects of the network security system via the Service Desk.
2. The network administrators assess the requirements (or the existing setup for a review) and takes particular notice of:
   - network design—determine whether the requirements have security built-in;
   - network resilience—determine whether the requirements reduce single points of failure and/or reduce the risk of malfunction of critical communications equipment, software, links, and services;
   - network documentation—determine the changes needed in network documentation to ensure it is current;
   - traffic management and control—determine whether the requirements affect network traffic to ensure that the network is protected against undesirable network traffic and prevent unauthorized users gaining access;
   - device configuration—determine whether the requirements affect network device configuration (network servers, routers, front-end processors, bridges, switches, firewalls, and IDS/IPS);
   - traffic filtering—determine whether the requirements affect network-filtering method;
   - monitoring the network—determine whether the requirements affect the performance of the network, reduce the likelihood of network overload, and to detect potential or actual malicious intrusions.
3. The network administrators send an e-mail outlining their findings to the IT Manager and the Information Security Manager, together with any recommendations as appropriate.
4. The IT Manager checks the findings and determines whether the requirements can be approved. Additional discussions are held with the Information Security Manager and network administrators to clarify any of the findings or recommendations.
5. The IT Manager confirms the decisions as follows:
   - if approved, the IT Manager sends an e-mail to the network administrators and the Information Security Manager confirming that the request can be implemented (subject to any changes to the configuration, etc., that are recommended).

Note

The request is not granted on a permanent basis. A review of the request must be scheduled by the Network Administration Team Leader within 12 months to ensure that the request remains valid.

6. If rejected, the IT Manager sends an e-mail to the Network Administration Team Leader and the Information Security Manager outlining the reasons for rejection.
7. The network administrators implement the changes to the network as required.
8. At the appointed time, according to the review schedule, the network is assessed again to check whether it remains valid using the above procedures.

7.7.2 Controlling Network Access

Network access control is essential to implement in the Forensic Laboratory and is implemented using a variety of controls, as below:

7.7.2.1 Segregation in Networks

The Forensic Laboratory divides its network into distinct groups to provide additional security. The following controls are in place:

- Active Directory is utilized to create domain divisions and can be used to manage issues such as password limits and logon retries via the Active Directory's Group Policy Object;
- domains serve as containers for security policies and administrative assignments.

7.7.2.2 Network Connection Control

The Forensic Laboratory ensures that unauthorized or undesirable network traffic is not allowed to gain access to any part of the network.

The types of controls that should be in place are:

- filtering of traffic is based on predefined rules and tables based on the principle of "least access" (that which is not expressly permitted is denied). These rules and tables are developed and maintained by the Forensic Laboratory IT Department;
- internal connection to the Internet occurs via a proxy server to protect against outbound attacks;
- network-filtering devices (i.e., firewalls) are implemented to ensure they cannot be bypassed;
- network-filtering devices are configured to filter specific types of traffic (e.g., IP address, ports, etc.) block or otherwise restrict particular types or sources of traffic, such as those that can be used to execute "denial of service" attacks and limit the use of communications that are prone to abuse;
- network-filtering devices limit information about the network (and its hosts) being divulged;
- network traffic is routed through an effective filtering device, such as intelligent routers, application proxies, or firewalls prior to being allowed access to the network.

7.7.2.3 Network Routing Control

Network routing controls ensure that computer connections and information flows do not breach the access control policy of the Forensic Laboratory.

The following controls apply:

- access rules are added as business needs arise;
- access rules are reviewed regularly;
- all routers connected to the network are operated and managed by the Forensic Laboratory IT Department;
- no local user accounts are configured on routers;
- router passwords are kept in a secure encrypted form on all routers. The router has the "enable password" set to the current production password;
- standardized Simple Network Management Protocol (SNMP) community strings are used on routers and switches and they are not the defaults of "public" and "private."

7.7.2.4 Reviewing and Assessing Network Access Controls

The procedures for reviewing and assessing network access control are as follows:

1. The network administrators are responsible for managing access to review the security aspects or receive requests from IT users to change aspects of network access.
2. The network administrators assess the requirements (or the existing setup for a review) from a security perspective, taking particular notice of:
   - segregation in networks—determine whether the network or the new requirements have sufficient segregation to provide additional security;
   - network connection control—determine whether the network or new requirements ensure that unauthorized or undesirable network traffic is not allowed to gain access;
   - network routing control—determine that existing or new computer connections and information flows do not breach the access control policy.
3. The network administrators sends an e-mail outlining their findings to the IT Manager and the Information Security Manager, together with any recommendations as appropriate.
4. The IT Manager checks the findings and determines whether the requirements can be approved. Additional discussions are held with the Information Security Manager and the network administrators to clarify any of the findings or recommendations.
5. The IT Manager confirms the decisions as follows:
   - if approved, the IT Manager sends an e-mail to the Network Administration Team Leader and the Information Security Manager confirming that the request

can be implemented (subject to any changes to the configuration, etc., that are recommended).

Note

The request is not granted on a permanent basis. A review of the request must be scheduled by the Network Administration Team and the Information Security Manager within 12 months to ensure that the request remains valid.

- if rejected, the IT Manager sends an e-mail to the Network Administration Team Leader and the Information Security Manager outlining the reasons for rejection.

6. The Network Administration Team implements the changes to the environments as required.
7. At the appointed time according to the review schedule, the network access controls are assessed again to check whether it remains valid using the above procedure.

7.7.3 Remote Connections

The Forensic Laboratory's network must be protected from any remote host, untrusted host, and remote network. These standards are designed to minimize the potential exposure to the Forensic Laboratory from damage.

This applies to remote access connections used to do work on behalf of the Forensic Laboratory, including but not limited to, reading or sending e-mail and viewing intranet Web resources. The remote access implementations that are covered by this document include, but are not limited to, dial-in modems, DSL, VPN, SSH, and cable modems, etc.

7.7.3.1 Guidelines for Remote Connections

The guidelines that apply are:

- access to diagnostic ports is restricted and controlled by the Forensic Laboratory IT Department;
- all hosts that are connected to the Forensic Laboratory internal networks via remote access technologies must use the most up-to-date anti-malware software, as defined in Section 7.6.1;
- at no time should any Forensic Laboratory employee provide his or her login or e-mail password to anyone—business, IT Department, or family;
- remote access must be approved and managed by the IT Manager and the Information Security Manager;
- secure remote access is strictly controlled and is enforced via strong authentication;
- where possible, the Forensic Laboratory uses secure methods for remote access, i.e., SSH in place of Telnet, secure Web servers, SCP in place of FTP.

7.7.3.2 Managing Remote Connections

The procedures for managing remote connection access are as follows:

1. A request for a remote connection is received from a user at the Service Desk. The user must complete the service access request form and be approved by the user's Line Manager before it can be processed further.
2. If it is not authorized by the Line Manager, then the Service Desk returns it.
3. The Service Desk assigns the request to the relevant member of the IT Department for processing.
4. The IT Manager and the Information Security Manager assess the requirements (or the existing connection for a review) and take particular notice of:
   - the Forensic Laboratory remote connection standards that apply;
   - the actual business need for the connection;
   - security implications of using the connection;
   - period for which the connection is required.
5. Additional discussions are held with the IT Manager, the Information Security Manager, and the Requestor to clarify any of the findings or recommendations.
6. The IT Manager confirms the decisions as follows:
   - if approved, the IT Manager sends an e-mail to the Requestor and the Information Security Manager confirming that the request can be implemented (subject to any changes to the configuration etc. that are recommended).

Note

The request is not granted on a permanent basis. A review of the request must be scheduled by the Information Security Manager with the IT Manager for the end of the requested period or within 12 months to ensure that the request remains valid.

7. If rejected, the IT Manager sends an e-mail to the Requestor and the Information Security Manager outlining the reasons for rejection. This e-mail is passed on to the user.
8. The IT Department implements the new connection and tests it before enabling user access. The Service Desk is informed that the connection is ready.
9. The Service Desk e-mails the user and the Requestor and confirms that the connection is available.
10. At the appointed time according to the review schedule, the connection is assessed again to check whether it remains valid using the above procedure.

7.7.3.3 Managing Third Party Remote Access

There are a number of third parties that may have legitimate access to the Forensic Laboratory information and information processing facilities. It is essential that these connections are properly managed and do not allow unauthorized access.

Specific third-party support groups may also be given remote access to secure systems.

- access rights are restricted via the login account;
- all access must be by a named individual using an account to the network, i.e., there shall be no sharing of user IDs by a third party. This shall be a contractual requirement;
- access tokens shall be used, or other strong authentication methods, as appropriate, shall be used to provide secure authentication;
- all remote access is from specific telephone lines that are authenticated via call line ID, if appropriate;
- requests for remote access are initiated by business Line Managers for a specific and justified need.

7.7.3.3.1 Roles and Responsibilities

7.7.3.3.1.1 Service Desk The Service Desk acts as first-line IT Support for remote access user group maintenance. The responsibilities of this role include:

- establishing accounts for remote access;
- periodically monitoring remote access;
- revoking remote access.

7.7.3.3.1.2 IT Manager The IT Manager is the central authority for managing remote access. The responsibilities of this role include:

- ensuring that adequate remote access controls are in place;
- performing risk assessments, in association with the Information Security Manager;
- reviewing remote access rights for third parties.

7.7.3.3.1.3 Information Security Manager The Information Security Manager is the central authority for approving remote access. The responsibilities of this role include:

- ensuring that adequate remote access controls are in place;
- performing second party audits on suppliers who have remote access, as defined in Chapter 4, Section 4.7.3;
- performing risk assessments, in association with the IT Manager;
- reviewing remote access rights for third parties.

7.7.3.4 Granting Remote Access

The procedures for granting remote access are as follows:

1. A Forensic Laboratory Line Manager sends a request for remote access to the Service Desk, with the details filled in the Account Management Form.
2. The Service Desk checks the request to ensure that all the required details are available including the expiry date of the needed access, logs it in the Forensic Laboratory Service Desk system, and then contacts the IT Manager.
3. The IT Manager and the Information Security Manager assess the requirements of the remote access and grant or refuse access. If appropriate, a risk assessment is performed—this is normally based on the extent of remote access required and the sensitivity of information accessible to the third party.
4. The IT Manager confirms the decision to the Service Desk. Any additional details, such as the risk assessment, are also recorded.
5. The Service Desk logs the decision in Service Desk system and e-mails the Requestor. If access is granted, the IT Department implements the relevant access process. If appropriate, the change must be processed through the Forensic Laboratory Change Management Process.

> **Warning**
>
> Contracts and Confidentiality Agreements must be in place before remote access is enabled.

6. The Service Desk adds the new remote access to the third-party remote access list.

7.7.3.5 Reviewing and Revoking Remote Access

The procedures for reviewing and revoking remote access are as follows:

1. Every 3 months, or at any time when required for operational reasons, the IT Manager and the Information Security Manager check the third-party remote access list and determine whether access is still required (e.g., a third-party support contract has expired, or employee with remote access leaves, the remote access must be revoked).
2. The IT Manager e-mails the Service Desk and confirms those remote access accounts that are no longer required.
3. The Service Desk logs the details in Service Desk system and then blocks access to secure systems for the user. The user is removed from the third-party remote access list.
4. The removal is confirmed to the original Requestor.

7.7.4 Managing Backups

The Forensic Laboratory IT Department is responsible of ensuring that servers are properly backed up and the information is safeguarded.

7.7.4.1 An Overview of Backups

All information in the Forensic Laboratory must be stored on relevant dedicated servers, whether this is in the ERMS or other dedicated information repositories. In the case of laptops, data are stored locally until it can be uploaded to the relevant server as a manual process.

Servers are all backed up as below:

- backup media shall be cycled off-site to a location remote from the Forensic Laboratory office to ensure that any event that affects the Forensic Laboratory office will not also affect the remote location;
- closed forensic cases and business data are considered for archival according to the *Document Retention Policy*, as defined in Chapter 4, Appendix 16;
- daily backups of all Forensic Laboratory work directories overnight on every weekday and on the weekend;
- redirection of users' home directories and the use of online synchronization should be implemented as this ensures that the users' files are on the appropriate server(s), and will be backed up automatically when the server is backed up;
- the backup types are all full backups;
- where possible, laptops and other mobile devices can use local cached file copies and be automatically synchronized when attached to the local network;
- where possible, no business-critical data shall be stored on local hard drives, as these will not be backed up by the centralized Forensic Laboratory backup system. Those using laptops or other non-office based information processing resources shall ensure that all of their information is uploaded to the Forensic Laboratory centralized information processing resources so that it can be included in the overnight backup process. However, to overcome the possibility of this process failing, technology is used to back up all local drives on laptops to a third party where they are securely stored in an encrypted format.

7.7.4.2 Roles and Responsibilities

7.7.4.2.1 IT Manager

The IT Manager is the central authority for backups. The responsibilities of this role include:

- analyzing the failure of overnight backup jobs and implementing appropriate resolution actions;
- authorizing the secure destruction of damaged backup media, as defined in Chapter 12, Section 12.3.14.10;
- checking the completion of overnight backup jobs;
- ensuring that adequate server access controls are in place;
- liaising with the Forensic Laboratory Information Owners and Custodians about backup requirements;
- restoring files from backup media (when required).

7.7.4.2.2 Information Owners

The Information Owner (or their Custodian) has ownership responsibility for backups, as defined in Chapter 12, Section 12.4.14.7. The responsibilities of this role include:

- determining the value of their business information;
- determining in conjunction with the IT Manager the backup requirements;
- reviewing the backup processes for continued business need;
- requesting changes to the backup process as required.

7.7.4.3 Checking Daily Backups

Each workday morning, the IT Manager (or their nominated deputy) checks the overnight backups to see whether any backup jobs have failed or have not fully completed.

Causes for any job to fail are determined and logged as an incident in the Service Desk, as defined in Section 7.4.1.

Any jobs that have to be rerun are run; otherwise, the IT Manager may decide to abandon the backup for the day.

The daily backup checklist is updated and signed off by the IT Manager (or their nominated deputy) and filed, where appropriate. Where records are retained on the server, the full details of the manual process are not required. The Forensic Laboratory *Overnight Backup Checklist* is given in the Appendix 34.

7.7.4.4 Performing Restores from a Backup

The procedures for restoring files from a backup are as follows:

1. A Forensic Laboratory employee contacts the Service Desk and requests a restore.
2. The Service Desk discusses the request with the user and determines the date on which the data were last available.
3. The Service Desk assigns the restore job to a member of the IT Department.
4. The relevant backup media is recovered and mounted.
5. The relevant files are recovered and the employee advised.
6. The backup media is returned to store and the job closed.

7.7.4.5 Disposing of Damaged Backup Media

During the backup process, backup media are occasionally damaged and cannot be used again. Any damaged backup media shall be securely destroyed by the Information Security Manager, as defined in Chapter 12, Section 12.3.14.10.

7.7.4.6 Tape Cleaning and Retensioning

Tape cleaning and retensioning is carried out according to the manufacturers' instructions. A record of this is held on the Forensic Laboratory *Overnight Backup Checklist* as defined in Appendix 34.

7.7.5 Synchronizing System Clocks

Using synchronized clocks is essential for assisting with system problem diagnosis and resolution and also helps with reliable event logging, automatic software updates, and other security-related activities. If clocks are not synchronized and accurate, security investigations will be hampered, and the evidence uncovered may be unreliable, and therefore unusable as the reason for disciplinary action or prosecution.

The Forensic Laboratory uses the NTP protocol with a time source, obtained from the NASA or the U.S. Navy NTP servers and distributed via a specified server. The following controls are in place:

- a periodic resynchronization is performed to correct system clock drifts from NASA NTP Server;
- all clocks on the Forensic Laboratory servers and workstations are automatically set to UTC standard time;
- clocks are reset following a system crash, a power outage, an operating system upgrade, or some other event that might affect the clock.

The procedures for checking system clocks are as follows:

1. The IT Department checks (or sets) the system clock as follows:
2. When installing a new server, the system clock is set to the correct time.
3. On a system failure that affects a server, a check is performed to reset the clock to the correct time if required.
4. The IT Department e-mails details of any synchronization failures, and the corrective action taken, to the IT Manager. If there is a failure, it is raised as an incident in the Service Desk, as defined in Section 7.4.1.
5. The Information Security Manager reviews system clocks as part of the internal audits, as defined in the IMS calendar.

APPENDIX 1 - SOME FORENSIC WORKSTATION PROVIDERS

Dedicated forensic workstation providers can assist in the processing of digital forensic cases and some are listed here. The providers change, so it is essential that correct workstations are provided, and have support available and also longevity. These include, but are not limited to:

Platform	Notes
DIBS	A complete forensic platform with a variety of capabilities http://www.dibsforensics.com/
Forensic Tower	A complete forensic platform with a variety of capabilities http://www.forensiccomputers.com/workstations/lab-workstations/forensic-tower.html
FRED	A complete forensic platform with a variety of capabilities http://www.digitalintelligence.com/forensicsystems.php
ImageMASSter	A complete forensic platform with a variety of capabilities http://www.ics-iq.com/

Note

The Forensic Laboratory does not endorse any product and does not use the platforms above; it prefers to build its own and validate them.

APPENDIX 2 - SOME MOBILE FORENSIC WORKSTATION PROVIDERS

Dedicated forensic mobile workstation providers can assist in the processing of digital forensic cases, and some are listed here. The providers change, so it is essential that correct workstations are provided, have support available and also longevity. These include, but are not limited to:

Platform	Notes
DIBS	A complete mobile forensic platform with a variety of capabilities http://www.dibsforensics.com/
Forensic Mobile Workstation I—Triple Screen	A complete mobile forensic platform with a variety of capabilities http://www.forensiccomputers.com/workstations/mobile-workstations/forensic-mobile-workstation-i.html
FREDDIE	A complete mobile forensic platform with a variety of capabilities http://www.digitalintelligence.com/forensicsystems.php
LogiCube	The Talon Enhanced features the ability to capture from one source drive to one destination drive or one source drive to two destination

Continued

Platform	Notes
	drives. SATA or IDE Source drive and SATA destination support is built-in. IDE destination drives require an IDE to SATA adapter http://www.logicube.com/shop/talon-enhanced/
NextComputing	A complete mobile forensic platform with a variety of capabilities http://www.nextcomputing.com/images/datasheets/digital-forensics.pdf
Vogon Mobile Forensic Workstation	A complete mobile forensic platform with a variety of capabilities http://www.vogon-investigation.com/mobile-station.htm
True Traveler	A complete mobile forensic platform with a variety of capabilities http://integrate.cdac.in/index.aspx?id=cs_cf_True%20Traveller
Forensic Air-Lite VII i7 Laptop	A complete mobile forensic platform with a variety of capabilities http://www.forensiccomputers.com/workstations/mobile-workstations/forensic-mobile-workstation-i.html

Note

The Forensic Laboratory does not endorse any product and does not use the platforms above.

APPENDIX 3 - STANDARD BUILD FOR A FORENSIC WORKSTATION

The typical components that go into a Forensic Laboratory's forensic workstation include, but are not limited to:

- CD and DVD writer;
- floppy drive;
- hot swappable SATA hard drives;
- IDE/Firewire/SCSI/Raid controllers;
- keyboard and pointing device;
- memory card reader;
- monitors;
- motherboard;
- multiple multicore processors;
- network interface;
- power supply;
- quad head graphics card;
- sound card;
- speakers;
- tower case with multiple bays;
- UPS;
- various other disk drive types (e.g., jazz, zip, etc.);
- various other tape drives (e.g., QIC, DAT, DLT, AIT, LTO, etc.);
- write blocker.

APPENDIX 4 - SOME CASE PROCESSING TOOLS

There are a variety of case processing tools available in the marketplace. This list is growing on a daily basis, so it is pointless listing the current ones as this will soon be out of date.

Different categories of forensic case processing software is used in the Forensic Laboratory and this includes:

- data recovery and investigation;
- forensic tools for Windows;
- image and document readers;
- laboratory tools – non forensic;
- Linux/Unix investigation;
- mobile device investigation;
- network investigation;
- password cracking;
- phone investigation.

APPENDIX 5 - POLICY FOR SECURING IT CABLING

All power and telecommunications cabling used in the Forensic Laboratory must be safeguarded from interception or damage to minimize security risks, and protect against loss of information and information processing facilities. The following standard controls are implemented to secure IT cabling:

- all IT cabling is CAT 5 or Cat 6 certified;
- all wiring cabinets are physically secured, and access is only provided to authorized IT Department employees, where necessary, or possible. They are defined as secure areas within the Forensic Laboratory;
- cabling is routed through secure ducting;
- cabling that passes through public areas is secured to as great a degree as is possible (e.g., fiber or secure ducting). Passing through public areas should be avoided if at all possible;
- fiber cabling is used, when possible;
- network elements are sited to maximize access protection, where necessary or possible;
- no CAT 5 or Cat 6 cabling is greater than 100 m in length;

- power cabling is physically segregated from communications cabling;
- underground ducting is used where possible.

For sensitive or critical systems, further controls to consider include:

- consideration of TEMPEST shielding;
- initiation of technical sweeps and physical inspections for unauthorized devices being attached to the cables;
- use of alternative routings and/or transmission media providing appropriate security;
- use of electromagnetic shielding to protect the cables.

APPENDIX 6 - POLICY FOR SITING AND PROTECTING IT EQUIPMENT

The following rules govern the physical positioning of IT equipment and information at the Forensic Laboratory:

- IT computing equipment must always be placed in an environmentally controlled location;
- IT computing resources and equipment must always be stored in secure locations with restricted access to authorized Forensic Laboratory employees and visitors only. Hosting visitors and engineers is defined in Chapter 12, Section 12.4.2;
- printers or faxes that are used for handling sensitive information must always be stored in a secure location.

Physical positioning of IT equipment in the Forensic Laboratory is determined by many factors; however, the Forensic Laboratory IT Department shall always follow these guidelines when determining the location of equipment and information:

- always minimize potential damage from electrical or electromagnetic interference;
- equipment and information is always sited so that unnecessary access to work area is minimized;
- equipment siting is always located to minimize risks of theft or misuse;
- potential security risks from Forensic Laboratory employees and visitors are always considered in ensuring that those with no "need to access" have no access rights to information or information processing facilities;
- when considering risks from fire, flooding, humidity, and other potential environmental hazards, and site equipment/information to minimize those risks, consider implementing environmental monitoring devices, where appropriate.

APPENDIX 7 - ISO 20000-1 MAPPING

ISO 20000-1 Section	Control	Procedure(s)
3	Quality management system	Chapter 6
3.1	Management responsibility	Chapter 4, Sections 4.4.3 and 4.6.2
3.2	Documentation requirements	Chapter 4, Section 4.6.3
3.3	Competence, awareness, and training	Chapter 4, Section 4.6.2.2
4	Planning and implementing service management	Chapter 4, Appendix 23 This chapter, Section 7.4 Chapter 12 Chapter 13
4.1	Plan service management (Plan)	Chapter 4, Section 4.3.1.2 This chapter, Section 7.4
4.2	Implement service management and provide the services (Do)	Chapter 4, Section 4.3.1.3 This chapter, Section 7.4
4.3	Monitoring, measuring and reviewing (Check)	Chapter 4, Section 4.3.1.4 This chapter, Section 7.4
4.4	Continual improvement (Act)	Chapter 4, Sections 4.3.1.5 and 4.8 This chapter, Section 7.4
4.4.1	Policy	Chapter 4, Appendix 14
4.4.2	Management of improvements	Chapter 4, Section 4.8
4.4.3	Activities	Chapter 4, Section 4.8
5	Planning and implementing new or changed services	This chapter, Section 7.4.7
6	Service delivery process	This chapter, Section 7.4.7
6.1	Service level management	This chapter, Section 7.4.7
6.2	Service reporting	This chapter, Section 7.4.9

Continued

ISO 20000-1 Section	Control	Procedure(s)
6.3	Service continuity and availability management	Chapter 13
6.4	Budgeting and accounting for IT services	Not covered
6.5	Capacity management	This chapter, Section 7.4.6
6.6	Information security management	Chapter 12
7	Relationship processes	
7.1	General	
7.2	Business relationship management	Chapter 6, Sections 6.6, 6.8, and 6.14
7.3	Supplier management	Chapter 4, Section 6.7.3 This chapter, Section 7.4.3.10 Chapter 14
8	Resolution processes	This chapter, Section 7.4
8.1	Background	This chapter, Section 7.4
8.2	Incident management	This chapter, Section 7.4.1
8.3	Problem management	This chapter, Section 7.4.2
9	Control processes	
9.1	Configuration management	This chapter, Section 7.4.5
9.2	Change management	This chapter, Section 7.4.3
10	Release process	
10.1	Release Management process	This chapter, Section 7.4.4

APPENDIX 8 - SERVICE DESK MANAGER, JOB DESCRIPTION

OBJECTIVE AND ROLE

The role of the SDM is to provide service support for all users of IT technology within the Forensic Laboratory and for Clients. This scope of responsibility is to capture, log, and provide immediate first-level support to all users and coordinate all other issues relating to products and services within the Forensic Laboratory. Regular reporting of all calls (incidents, problems, complaints, service requests, and service level reporting) is produced from the Service Desk to assist the Forensic Laboratory in the continuous improvement process. Liaison internally with second-level support and external third-level support is undertaken.

PROBLEMS AND CHALLENGES

The SDM faces the challenge of meeting Client demand and service levels with limited resources in a rapidly changing environment. As new systems and applications are implemented, the SDM must ensure that the Service Desk is properly trained to handle all calls.

The SDM must be able to communicate effectively with all levels of employees within the Forensic Laboratory, third parties working for them or third-party vendors.

PRINCIPAL ACCOUNTABILITIES

The SDM:

- identifies and initiates resolutions to all Client service issues and concerns associated with all IT applications, computer equipment, hardware, software, and service requests to the Client's satisfaction;
- plans and coordinates the training for installation and implementation of desktops, Client servers, hardware, and software according to the Forensic Laboratory IT Department standards and procedures;
- assists HR in analyzing the training needs of users, developing user curricula, providing quality individual and group training programs designed to ensure maximum utilization of IT within the Forensic Laboratory;
- maintains software and hardware versions, maintenance levels, registration and inventory to provide upgrades as necessary, and ensure appropriate security levels are maintained;
- maintains current technical expertise in the rapidly changing technology and utilizes state-of-the-art techniques when implementing any IT-related solutions;
- prepares daily, weekly, monthly, and quarterly status reports quantitatively reporting results of relevant Service Desk activities;
- recognizes and identifies potential areas where existing policies and procedures require change, or where new ones need to be developed, especially regarding future business expansion;
- fulfills business requirements in terms of providing work coverage and administrative notification at all times;

- trains, supervises, assigns projects to, evaluates, and is responsible for hiring/termination of Service Desk staff to maintain optimum performance of the Service Desk;
- interfaces with external industrial and academic organizations in order to maintain state-of-the-art knowledge in emerging service management issues and to enhance the Forensic Laboratory's image as a first-class solution provider utilizing the latest thinking in this field;
- adheres to established Forensic Laboratory policies, standards, and procedures;
- performs all responsibilities in accordance with, or in excess of, the requirements of the Forensic Laboratory Integrated Management System.

AUTHORITY

The SDM has the authority to:

- resolve problems with all Forensic Laboratory products and services;
- resolve issues with all Client-related issues reported to the Service Desk;
- plan and coordinate implementation of all internal IT hardware, software, and infrastructure;
- carry out relevant training for internal Forensic Laboratory users on relevant IT issues;
- assist HR in identifying training needs and possible solutions;
- work with all Forensic Laboratory users and with external vendors;
- identify potential service-level problems before they occur and implement solutions;
- schedule and prioritize work to accommodate business requirements and Client needs while minimizing impact on current projects and service delivery.

CONTACTS

Internal

Contacts within the Forensic Laboratory are with those in the operational areas that directly affect service delivery. This will include a variety of Forensic Laboratory employees, and any third parties working for the Forensic Laboratory, as well as Clients.

External

Those external to the Forensic Laboratory will be with suppliers of hardware, software, and other relevant services that the Service Desk supports.

REPORTS TO

The SDM reports to the IT Manager.

APPENDIX 9 - INCIDENT MANAGER, JOB DESCRIPTION

OBJECTIVE AND ROLE

The IM is responsible for ensuring that normal service in the Forensic Laboratory is restored as soon as possible, after an incident that affects the provision of product(s) and service(s).

Failure to provide appropriate services is defined as failing to meet an agreed SLA between the Forensic Laboratory and their Clients.

The role is closely integrated with the BCM and the SDM.

PROBLEMS AND CHALLENGES

Incident management is an absolutely critical function of the Forensic Laboratory's everyday business operations. For this responsibility, there is no substitute for advanced planning.

The IM faces the challenge of developing ever-current response plans to a volatile set of possible incidents that may affect service delivery. These can be internal to the Forensic Laboratory, the Client, or a third-party supplier.

PRINCIPAL ACCOUNTABILITIES

The IM:

- establishes procedures and priorities for the business continuity process;
- responds to all reported incidents;
- logs, categorizes, and prioritizes incidents;
- provides initial incident support;
- responds and records, as appropriate, based on the incident, including the invocation of BCPs;
- undertakes incident investigation and diagnosis;
- implements incident resolution or recovery using workarounds;
- closes incidents after confirmation from affected Clients;
- provides input to the BCP for major incident handling;
- evaluates incidents to see if they may occur or are problems to be referred to the PM;
- ensures adherence to the relevant SLAs, even during incidents;
- produces regular incident management reports as required to different levels of management within the Forensic Laboratory;
- provides input to the SIP;
- ensures that all incident management procedures are documented and maintained;

- performs risk assessments and implements risk management to reduce risk to an acceptable level to reduce the likelihood of service interruptions, where practical and cost justifiable;
- assesses changes submitted to the CAB for impact on the service provisions;
- attends the CAB, as appropriate;
- defines direction of in-house technical training seminars to improve overall employee awareness, response time, and ability to look into the Forensic Laboratory's future business continuity and business recovery requirements;
- participates in international, national, and local SIG presentations, and publishes articles describing the Forensic Laboratory's activities and assessments of incident management and business recovery and how they relate to the business;
- develops and manages effective working relationships with all appropriate internal and external stakeholders;
- maintains external links to other companies in the industry to gain competitive assessments and share information, where appropriate;
- identifies the emerging information technologies to be assimilated, integrated, and introduced within the Forensic Laboratory, which could significantly impact the Forensic Laboratory's incident management and business recovery ability;
- interfaces with external industrial and academic organizations in order to maintain state-of-the-art knowledge in emerging incident management and business recovery issues and to enhance the Forensic Laboratory's image as a first-class solution provider utilizing the latest thinking in this field;
- adheres to established Forensic Laboratory policies, standards, and procedures;
- performs all responsibilities in accordance with, or in excess of, the requirements of the Forensic Laboratory Integrated Management System.

AUTHORITY

The IM has the authority to:

- attend the CAB and comment on proposed changes;
- develop, maintain, and implement, if necessary, the incident response procedures and processes in the Forensic Laboratory;
- provide improvements to the SIP.

CONTACTS

Internal

This position requires contact with all levels of Forensic Laboratory employees to determine business recovery and deal with incidents.

External

Externally, the IM will maintain contacts with suppliers and vendors, as required. Additionally, contact will be maintained with the Forensic Laboratory's Clients to determine their requirements as well as the Forensic Laboratory's insurers to ensure that insurance coverage is appropriate.

REPORTS TO

The IM reports to the IT Manager and Top Management, as required.

APPENDIX 10 - INCIDENT STATUS LEVELS

The Forensic Laboratory uses the following status levels for incidents:

Status	Description
Opened	When no action has been taken on an incident (usually when the incident has been logged)
In Progress	Move into this status when actively working on the incident (if started working on another incident, then this status remains current)
Pending	Move into this status when working on the ticket but not actively working on (e.g., request for a meeting room setup/desk move/started a virus scan on a machine and have moved onto another ticket)
Contact Made	Move into this status when attempts to contact the user via phone and by leaving a incident comment explaining attempted contact have been made for further information (In the Forensic Laboratory, if the user does not respond within 3 days the ticket will automatically close.)
Response Made	This is a system-generated status. When an incident is in contact made and the user responds via e-mail, the system will move the status into contact made
Need More Info	Move into this status when the user has not provided enough information in the request. This should always be followed up by a call and a comment in the ticket stating a call has been made requesting more information.
Awaiting Third Party	Move into this status when the incident is escalated to a third party and the Forensic Laboratory are awaiting further communication

Continued

Status	Description
Ordered Awaiting Delivery	Move into this status once the product is received and the job number for implementation is available
Reopened	This is a system-generated status. When an incident is closed and the user e-mails back about the incident, it will reopen a closed incident and this is moved to this status
Escalated	This is a system-generated status. When an incident has passed the required time agreed to act on an incident, the system moves this into this status and e-mails an escalation e-mail
Resolved	Move to this status when the Service Desk think that they have resolved the issue, but still need Client approval to close the incident
Closed	Move to this status when the incident is closed and the Client confirms satisfaction with the resolution. In theory, the Client should update this and not the Service Desk

APPENDIX 11 - INCIDENT PRIORITY LEVELS

The Forensic Laboratory endeavors to correct, restore normal business service and operations, or provide a workaround solution, to all incidents and service requests according to their classification. Incident classifications, and target resolution times for each incident classification, are defined for Clients in their specific SLAs for individual services where required, but standard Forensic Laboratory ones are given below:

Priority	Category	Status	Resources Affected	Example	Target Response Time	Target Resolution Time
1	Critical	Business-critical failure (critical incident)	All or most Clients, business severely disrupted	Failure of central IT systems and services	Immediate	1 h
2	High	Serious incident	Most (or a high proportion) of Clients affected to a fairly serious degree or a smaller number of important Clients severely affected	ADSL line failure, failure of service from third-party supplier, service performance severely degraded	10 min	4 h
3	Medium	Moderate incident	Most slightly affected, or a fewer number of Clients are more seriously affected, but business operational	New users, new equipment, new minor changes to offices, upgrades to equipment and software, telecoms installations, moves, additions, and changes	1 h	8 h
4	Low	Low-level incident	Minimal impact on the Client's day-to-day business		1 day	24 h

APPENDIX 12 - SERVICE DESK FEEDBACK FORM

The following details are on the feedback form to evaluate the Service Desk's performance:

- overall service received from the Service Desk;
- initial information received on contacting the Service Desk;
- desk side service received (if applicable);
- accuracy and completeness of technical information (if applicable);
- product knowledge relating to the call (if applicable);
- courtesy and professionalism;
- availability of resources to complete service request;
- timeliness of closure.

The above are all marked as follows:

0—not applicable;
1—extremely dissatisfied;
2—dissatisfied;
3—neither dissatisfied nor satisfied;
4—satisfied;
5—extremely satisfied.

This provides quantitative feedback while there is a text box to allow for any recommendations for improvement that provides for qualitative feedback.

APPENDIX 13 - PROBLEM MANAGER, JOB DESCRIPTION

OBJECTIVE AND ROLE

To minimize the adverse effects of incidents and problems on the Forensic Laboratory and its internal and external Clients caused by errors within the IT infrastructure, and prevent the recurrence of incidents related to those errors.

PROBLEMS AND CHALLENGES

The PM is challenged by having to identify problems from incident and fault reports and then take action to resolve them and prevent their reoccurrence.

PRINCIPAL ACCOUNTABILITIES

The PM:

- develops, maintains, and reviews efficiency and effectiveness of the Problem and Error Control processes;
- reviews effectiveness and efficiency of proactive problem management activities;
- manages all problems in the Forensic Laboratory;
- prevents incidents from happening, where possible;
- minimizes the effect of incidents that do occur;
- determines root causes for incidents and uses this as input to the problem solving process;
- maintains information about known errors and workarounds;
- provides workarounds, where available, to the IM while developing final solutions for known errors;
- maintains, in association with the Service Desk, trending information for the early identification of problems;
- logs, categorizes, and prioritizes problems;
- provides initial problem support;
- investigates and diagnoses problems;
- closes problems;
- maintains the known error database (KEDB);
- ensures adherence to the relevant SLAs;
- produces management information;
- allocates resources for problem resolution from within the Forensic Laboratory or externally, as required;
- raises Requests for Change (RfCs) where appropriate;
- assesses changes submitted to the CAB for impact on the service provisions;
- attends the CAB, as appropriate;
- assists in handling major incidents, if required;
- prevents problems from recurring, where possible;
- develops plans for migration of problem management policies and procedures to support the Forensic Laboratory's future directions;
- develops the Forensic Laboratory's long-range problem management strategy;
- participates in international, national, and local SIG presentations, and publishes articles describing the Forensic Laboratory's problem management initiatives and how they relate to the business;
- develops and manages effective working relationships with all appropriate internal and external stakeholders;
- maintains external links to other companies in the industry to gain competitive assessments and share information, where appropriate;
- identifies the emerging information technologies to be assimilated, integrated, and introduced within the Forensic Laboratory, which could significantly impact the Forensic Laboratory's service offering SLAs;
- interfaces with external industrial and academic organizations in order to maintain state-of-the-art knowledge in emerging problem management issues and to enhance the Forensic Laboratory's image as a first-class solution provider utilizing the latest thinking in this field;
- adheres to established Forensic Laboratory policies, standards, and procedures;
- performs all responsibilities in accordance with, or in excess of, the requirements of the Forensic Laboratory Integrated Management System.

AUTHORITY

The PM has the authority to:

- be the central focus for all problem management issues;
- utilize appropriate resources to assist in problem resolution;
- monitor all operational processes for trend analysis for incidents and problems;
- establish and make decisions about management reporting methods and outputs.

CONTACTS

Internal

Contacts within the Forensic Laboratory are throughout the whole business who have reported faults or issues that turn out to be problems. Close cooperation with the IM, the Service Desk, and the Information Security Manager will be routine, and contact with other managers will be as required.

External

Those external to the Forensic Laboratory will be with appropriate Special Interest Groups (SIGs), other PMs, external vendors, and service providers.

REPORTS TO

The PM reports to the IT Manager.

APPENDIX 14 - CONTENTS OF THE FORENSIC LABORATORY SIP

While an SIP in the Forensic Laboratory can relate to internal initiatives (e.g., optimize resource usage) or Client driven ones (e.g., reviewing SLAs that are no longer achievable), the Forensic Laboratory uses the following template as the basis of all SIPs. It is amended as required based on the specific SIP being implemented.

- process or service to be improved;
- process or service Owner;
- SIP Owner (who may or may not be the process or service Owner);
- management approval;
- SIP priority—agreed by Top Management;
- description of the SIP;
- source of the requirement being defined (e.g., internal review, internal audit, Client feedback, etc.);
- business case, including:
  - expected outcome of the initiative;
  - cost estimate;
  - desired result of the SIP (e.g., a specific decrease in cost for providing a service to Clients, a new service for Clients, etc.).
- implementation schedule, and for each milestone:
  - description of the deliverable to be completed;
  - key deliverables;
  - owner of each milestone;
  - target delivery date.
- monitoring and reporting;
- training requirements.

Note

SIPs are typically IT Infrastructure Library (ITIL) based, but the Forensic Laboratory uses them as part of its continuous improvement process in the Plan, Do, Check, Act (PDCA) (W. Edwards Deming) cycle.

APPENDIX 15 - CHANGE CATEGORIES

The following change categories are in use in the Forensic Laboratory with their notification times:

Category	Description	Minimum notification time to Clients
Emergency	A top priority change that needs to be implemented immediately to prevent or rectify a serious service failure within the Forensic Laboratory.	Immediately
Normal	A change that could cause an impact on services to users, multiple areas, or business groups. Typical examples are software upgrades, changes to critical applications, infrastructure upgrades, router moves, new service provision.	5 working days
Standard	A change that potentially has minimal affect on users. Typical examples include user moves, printer additions, documentation.	None

APPENDIX 16 - CHANGE MANAGER, JOB DESCRIPTION

OBJECTIVE AND ROLE

The CM is responsible for managing the quality of the Forensic Laboratory's production environment by implementing and overseeing a change management system for promoting products and services from the test environment to the production environment. This will result in high-quality systems, thus providing internal and external Clients with quality products and services.

The CM will also define "standard changes."

PROBLEMS AND CHALLENGES

The challenges facing the CM involve facilitating a "zero defect" environment for all production and operational systems within the Forensic Laboratory. This involves managing the review of new or modified products and services, keeping abreast of the continuous flow of changes within the volatile Forensic Laboratory development environment, controlling access to source and object code, and overseeing the airtight methodology for running and documenting non-standard or one-time jobs.

PRINCIPAL ACCOUNTABILITIES

The CM:

- manages the change control system and procedures for the movement of systems and documents into the production environment;
- maintains or develops change management procedures as needed;

- receives, logs, and allocates priorities to all RfCs, and rejects impractical RfCs;
- ensures that all RfCs have been fully completed as required by the Change Management Process and its supporting forms;
- categorizes received RfCs;
- defines and manages duties of CAB;
- tables all RfCs for CAB meetings where appropriate;
- issues agenda and issues all RfCs to CAB members in advance of CAB meetings to allow prior consideration;
- decides who will attend meetings depending on nature of the RfC;
- convenes CAB or emergency CAB (ECAB) meetings for urgent RfCs;
- chairs all CAB and ECAB meetings;
- authorizes accepted changes;
- produces and distributes via the Forensic Laboratory Service Desk, a Forward Schedule of Changes;
- coordinates all change building, testing, and implementations;
- owns and maintains all change logs;
- manages all actions to correct problems and feedback to SIP;
- reviews all changes to ensure compliance to objectives, appropriately referring all failures and back outs;
- reviews all RfCs awaiting consideration and action;
- analyzes change records to determine trends and apparent problems, and feedback to appropriate parties;
- closes RfCs;
- produces regular and accurate management reports on changes to the operational the Forensic Laboratory systems;
- assures the integrity of all Code Management System libraries. This involves overseeing a system of organization for these libraries;
- maintains training and awareness throughout the Forensic Laboratory and third parties acting on their behalf, on the importance and impact of maintaining stringent controls;
- manages the Post Implementation Review (PIR) process;
- participates in international, national, and local SIG presentations, and publishes articles describing the Forensic Laboratory's change management system and how it relates to the business;
- develops and manages effective working relationships with all appropriate internal and external stakeholders;
- maintains external links to other companies in the industry to gain competitive assessments and share information, where appropriate;
- identifies the emerging information technologies to be assimilated, integrated, and introduced within the Forensic Laboratory, which could significantly impact the Forensic Laboratory's Change Management Processes;
- interfaces with external industrial and academic organizations in order to maintain state-of-the-art knowledge in emerging change management issues and to enhance the Forensic Laboratory's image as a first-class solution provider utilizing the latest thinking in this field;
- adheres to the established Forensic Laboratory policies, standards, and procedures;
- performs all responsibilities in accordance with, or in excess of, the requirements of the Forensic Laboratory Integrated Management System.

AUTHORITY

The CM has the authority to:

- determine the categorization of changes submitted via the RfC process;
- ensure that the appropriate level of authorization is present for reach RfC submitted;
- establish and make decisions about the change control process;
- establish the CAB;
- make changes to the change control process as required;
- manage the CAB process with the ability to co-opt required the Forensic Laboratory employees for CAB meetings.

CONTACTS

Internal Contacts

This position requires contact with business and IT support personnel within the Forensic Laboratory. Within the Forensic Laboratory, contacts will be made with Project Teams and their Project Managers and the IT Department.

External Contacts

The primary external contacts are with contract service providers, Clients, vendors, and industry peers. Contact with information technology product and service companies is also made on a periodic basis.

REPORTS TO

The CM reports to:

- the IT Manager.

APPENDIX 17 - STANDARD REQUIREMENTS OF A REQUEST FOR CHANGE

The following are the standard template for requirements for an RfC in the Forensic Laboratory:

- change name;
- date created;
- date required;
- change owner name;
- change owner contact details;
- description of change;
- reason for change;
- location of change;
- change type;
- whom the change will affect and to what level;
- products and services affected by the change;
- duration of the change;
- duration of impact to users of affected products and services;
- support resources required;
- change category;
- change window;
- impact to users of the Forensic Laboratory's products and services;
- impact if the change is not carried out;
- risk assessment;
- change status;
- reason for rejection, if appropriate;
- details of the configuration of the change;
- communications plan;
- period of notification prior to the change;
- testing results and test packs;
- UAT sign-off by the business, if appropriate;
- back-out plan;
- prerequisites and dependencies;
- change review decision;
- change progress and actions;
- change outcome;
- reason for failure, if appropriate;
- results of PIR;
- approvals;
- closure date.

APPENDIX 18 - EMERGENCY CHANGE POLICY

The IT Department must operate a strict policy for emergency changes. The policy is:

- no standard change (of any priority) can be implemented via the emergency change process;
- only changes that prevent or rectify a serious service failure within the business can be classed as an emergency;
- only changes designated as "Emergency" by the CM can be implemented immediately;
- all Clients (internal and external) that may be affected must be informed about downtime, when practical, during an emergency change;
- all emergency changes are fully documented and then processed retrospectively through the standard Change Management Process.

APPENDIX 19 - RELEASE MANAGEMENT POLICY

It is the Forensic Laboratory's Release Management policy to:

- ensure that all types of release, major, minor, and emergency, including hardware and software, are performed in a controlled manner;
- ensure that all releases are performed at the time agreed with Clients to minimize service disruption but in line with the Forensic Laboratory's operational situation;
- ensure that releases can only be performed following full approval through the change management system;
- ensure that all releases are planned and documented by the RM, in conjunction with external Clients where appropriate, are uniquely identified and contain full descriptions of what is contained in the release;
- ensure that a release can only be approved for implementation by the RM after all planning and implementation activities are agreed within the Forensic Laboratory and Clients, where appropriate;
- ensure that, where appropriate, several releases can be grouped into a single or reduced number of releases to minimize service disruption;
- ensure that the processes and procedures for building, testing, and distributing releases is fully documented and agreed;
- ensure that the success of a release is verified and confirmed by the RM and is accepted by the Forensic Laboratory's Clients.

The RM is responsible for Release Management within the Forensic Laboratory and ensures that all release policies and procedures are maintained, implemented, and followed by relevant Forensic Laboratory employees.

APPENDIX 20 - RELEASE MANAGER, JOB DESCRIPTION

OBJECTIVE AND ROLE

The RM's role is to plan and oversee the successful rollout of all software, hardware, and changes into the Forensic Laboratory production environment. This will include:

- planning the test environment;
- planning the actual releases;
- testing the release packages;
- testing the deployment environment;
- managing the release and deployment;
- PIRs.

PROBLEMS AND CHALLENGES

The RM is challenged with ensuring that only approved releases are promoted to the production environment.

PRINCIPAL ACCOUNTABILITIES

The RM:

- designs and implements an effective Release Policy;
- plans and manages all software and hardware rollouts;
- manages extensive testing of planned releases to predefined acceptance criteria, including:
  - scope of release;
  - effectiveness of release with third-party suppliers;
  - planning rollback models;
  - planning building of tests;
  - planning pilot test phases in test environment;
  - service operation test;
  - service operation readiness test;
  - implementing the pilot;
  - verification of implemented deployment.
- signs off releases that pass acceptance testing for release implementation.
- ensures accurate audits performed prior to and following implementation of changes to CIs.
- builds, maintains, and manages the DSL and Definitive Hardware Library (DHL).
- designs, verifies, and tests appropriate Release Back-Out Plan (RBOP).
- identifies appropriate resources required to support the RBOP;
- plans the release and delivery;
- manages the resources needed for the release, testing, and deployment;
- creates the release packages;
- manages the deployment team;
- develops plans for migration of Release Management policies and procedures to support the Forensic Laboratory's future directions;
- transfers and deployment of the release;
- removes of old, obsolete, or superfluous deployments;
- ensures that users can actually use the deployed service as required/expected;
- develops the Forensic Laboratory's long-range Release Management strategy;
- makes recommendations to the SIP;
- participates in international, national, and local SIG presentations, and publishes articles describing the Forensic Laboratory's Release Management initiatives and how they relate to the business;
- develops and manages effective working relationships with all appropriate internal and external stakeholders;
- maintains external links to other companies in the industry to gain competitive assessments and share information, where appropriate;
- identifies the emerging information technologies to be assimilated, integrated, and introduced within the Forensic Laboratory, which could significantly impact its service offering SLAs;
- interfaces with external industrial and academic organizations in order to maintain state-of-the-art knowledge in emerging Release Management issues and to enhance the Forensic Laboratory's image as a first-class solution provider utilizing the latest thinking in this field;
- adheres to established Forensic Laboratory policies, standards, and procedures;
- performs all responsibilities in accordance with, or in excess of, the requirements of the Forensic Laboratory's Integrated Management System.

AUTHORITY

The RM has the authority to:

- be the central focus for all Release Management issues;
- define the planning and timing of all releases and deployments;
- control all releases into, and changes to, the Forensic Laboratory production environment;
- define tools, processes, and procedures for release and deployment;
- manage all resources for testing and deploying the release;
- establish and make decisions about management reporting methods and outputs.

CONTACTS

Internal

Contacts within the Forensic Laboratory are with personnel in the operational areas that directly affect configuration management. This will specifically include the CfM and the CM, but may include a variety of the Forensic Laboratory's employees.

External

Those external to the Forensic Laboratory are those for Clients, and their relevant staff, who determine systems requirements delivered by the Forensic Laboratory.

REPORTS TO

The RM reports to the IT Manager.

APPENDIX 21 - CONFIGURATION MANAGEMENT PLAN CONTENTS

The following is the basic plan template used in the Forensic Laboratory, but it can be amended as required, depending on the specific requirements of a release.

- plan approval;
- introduction;
  - scope;
  - purpose;
  - system overview;
  - roles and responsibilities;
  - points of contact;
  - resource requirements.
- configuration control;
  - CAB;
  - CIs;
  - baseline identification;
  - CMDB;
  - the various configuration libraries and their maintenance.
- change control;
- configuration status accounting;
- configuration auditing;
- configuration management libraries;
- release management;
- tools;
- training;
- references;
- acronyms and key terms.

APPENDIX 22 - CONFIGURATION MANAGEMENT POLICY

Configuration management is a set of techniques and procedures that provide the mechanism to manage CIs in the Forensic Laboratory by:

- controlling the versions of CIs in use, and maintaining information on their status, ownership, and relationships;
- managing CIs by ensuring changes are made only with the agreement of appropriate authorities;
- auditing the record of CIs to ensure it is accurate and relevant;
- ensuring there is one configuration management process;
- representing the actual known state of the IT environment in the CMDB;
- ensuring each CIs has an Owner responsible for ensuring CIs data are complete, accurate, and current;
- ensuring changes to the CMDB are authorized and implemented by authorized members of the IT Department;
- maintaining configuration records in a timely manner;
- regularly undertaking exception reporting and formal CMDB audits.

Configuration management provides the assurance of product and service integrity and allows for coherent set of information on Forensic Laboratory CIs to be held and maintained.

This policy applies to all operational Forensic Laboratory systems.

APPENDIX 23 - CONFIGURATION MANAGER, JOB DESCRIPTION

OBJECTIVE AND ROLE

The CfM is responsible for ensuring that the CMDB is maintained for all CIs through the Forensic Laboratory Change Management Process.

PROBLEMS AND CHALLENGES

The CfM is challenged with having to maintain the CMDB with all CIs for all internal and external operations and Clients.

PRINCIPAL ACCOUNTABILITIES

The CfM:

- produces and maintains Configuration Management Plan;
- populates and manages the CMDB;
- identifies, manages, and controls CIs;
- ensures consistency and accuracy of the CMDB so that the authorized state of the Forensic Laboratory IT Infrastructure is properly reflected;
- implements consistent Change Management, Configuration Management, and Release Management across the Forensic Laboratory;
- maintains control of hardware, technical standards, and all documents;
- provides supporting services (such as registration and checking) of releases delivered by third parties;
- produces regular reports on CMDB and all CI status;
- makes recommendations to the SIP;
- ensures that the Configuration Management System (CMS) is aware of, and capable of coping with, future workloads and growth;
- ensures that all members of the IT Department are aware of and familiar with the Configuration Management system process and procedures appropriate to their work;
- defines status accounting requirements to support all Service Management processes;
- aids with audit process, monitors exceptions, and implements corrective actions;
- investigates problems caused by poor control and recommends remedial action;

- provides advice where release components should be located on infrastructure;
- advises internal and external projects on what to include in the Configuration Management System and Release Plans to ensures successful transfer to final service;
- develops plans for migration of configuration management policies and procedures to support the Forensic Laboratory's future directions;
- develops the Forensic Laboratory's long-range configuration management strategy;
- defines direction of in-house technical training seminars to improve overall employee awareness, response time, and ability to look into the Forensic Laboratory's future configuration management requirements;
- participates in international, national, and local SIG presentations, and publishes articles describing the Forensic Laboratory's configuration management activities and how they relate to the business;
- develops and manages effective working relationships with all appropriate internal and external stakeholders;
- maintains external links to other companies in the industry to gain competitive assessments and share information, where appropriate;
- identifies the emerging information technologies to be assimilated, integrated, and introduced within the Forensic Laboratory, which could significantly impact the Forensic Laboratory's configuration demands;
- interfaces with external industrial and academic organizations in order to maintain state-of-the-art knowledge in emerging configuration management and to enhance the Forensic Laboratory's image as a first-class solution provider utilizing the latest thinking in this field;
- adheres to established the Forensic Laboratory's policies, standards, and procedures;
- performs all responsibilities in accordance with, or in excess of, the requirements of the Forensic Laboratory Integrated Management System.

AUTHORITY

The CfM:

- is the central focus for all configuration management issues;
- defines the requirements for the CMDB and the capacity management system;
- establishes and makes decisions about management reporting methods and outputs.

CONTACTS

Internal Contacts

This position requires contact with business and IT support personnel within the Forensic Laboratory. This will specifically include the RM and the CM, but may include a variety of Forensic Laboratory employees.

External Contacts

The primary external contacts are with Clients, contract service providers, Clients, vendors, and industry peers. Contact with information technology product and service companies is also made on a periodic basis.

REPORTS TO

The CfM reports to the IT Manager.

APPENDIX 24 - INFORMATION STORED IN THE DSL AND DHL

DEFINITIVE HARDWARE LIBRARY

- *site*—where the equipment is installed;
- *business stream*—business stream which owns the equipment;
- *group*—the group within the business stream;
- *name*—name of the owner of the equipment;
- *asset number*—asset number of the equipment;
- *item type*—what the equipment is, i.e., workstation, server, printer, etc.;
- *make/model*—make and model of the equipment;
- *processor*—for workstations and servers, this fields records the processor type and speed;
- *RAM*—for workstations, servers and some printers, this shows the amount of memory installed;
- *hard disks*—for workstations, servers and some printers, this shows the size of the hard disk drives installed;
- *monitor type*—for workstations and servers, this shows the type of monitor the system has;
- *monitor serial number*—serial number of the screen associated with the workstation or server;
- *operating system*—operating system of the workstation or server;
- *serial number*—serial number of the device;
- *MAC address*—MAC address of the device;
- *mobile number*—for cell phones, his field records the mobile phone number of the unit;
- *purchase date*—date on the purchase order against which the goods were ordered;
- *purchase order*—the purchase order number for purchasing the device;
- *install date*—date when the unit was installed for the users;
- *last healthcheck*—the date of the last health check carried out on the device;
- *outside supplier*—the supplier supporting the equipment in the event of a hardware failure;

- *Service Desk ticket*—the ticket against which the device were installed (this will be the change request ticket number for installation);
- *modified by*—the user ID of the last person to update the current record;
- *modified date*—the date when the record was last updated;
- *comments*—a free text field to record any additional information as required;
- *software profile*—a subtable, shown only for workstations and servers, detailing which items of software are installed;
- *audit trail*—of all changes made to the record.

DEFINITIVE SOFTWARE LIBRARY

- *supplier name*—the name of the supplier from whom the software was purchased;
- *order date*—the date recorded on the purchase order against which the software was purchased;
- *software ID*—the ID number associated with the software in question;
- *software description*—name of the software;
- *purchased copies*—number of licenses purchased on this particular order;
- *additional details*—free text field to record any additional information about the software;
- *purchase order number*—the number of the purchase order against which the software was purchased;
- *Service Desk reference*—the Service Desk ticket number used to request the purchase;
- *business stream*—the business stream that purchased the software;
- *site*—site from where the purchase request originated;
- *license reference number*—not always applicable, but if there is a reference number for the software it is recorded here;
- *license key*—if the software has a license key, it is recorded here;
- *license date*—date when the license was received;
- *modified by*—the user ID of the last person to update the current record;
- *modified date*—the date when the record was last updated;
- *comments*—a free text field to record any additional information as required;
- *audit trail*—of all changes made to the record.

APPENDIX 25 - CAPACITY MANAGER, JOB DESCRIPTION

OBJECTIVE AND ROLE

The CaM is responsible for initiating the capacity planning process and developing capacity planning for the technical and operational functions of IT in the future within the Forensic Laboratory in a cost effective manner.

The CaM is also responsible for long-range capacity planning to provide the highest level of Client service possible in the future and for developing and maintaining a management reporting system. This will include the prediction of future demands from Clients in association with the Sales Team and other Forensic Laboratory. These future demands are the input to capacity planning.

PROBLEMS AND CHALLENGES

The CaM is challenged with having the vision to plan for future IT capacity needs, determine future requirements from Clients, as well as developing a comprehensive and useful management reporting system, according to budgetary criteria.

PRINCIPAL ACCOUNTABILITIES

The CaM:

- determines future business needs for capacity;
- provides capacity planning services to the relevant Forensic Laboratory employees, including the Sales Team and the IT Department. This includes performance related issues, if appropriate;
- produces the Capacity Plan, reflecting current and future capacity needs for the Forensic Laboratory to service its Clients;
- ensures cost-justified capacity exists to process the agreed workloads;
- provides the required performance quality and quantity agreed in the SLAs;
- assists in fault and problem resolution, where appropriate and relevant;
- assesses changes submitted to the CAB for impact on the demand and capacity requirements and the need to revise the Capacity Plan, if appropriate;
- attends the CAB, as appropriate;
- recommends proactive measures to improve performance, where relevant and cost effective;
- determines the needs for upgrades to systems to maintain or improve capacity requirements;
- provides long-range planning for operational areas;
- serves as a "futurist" within the Forensic Laboratory for demand and capacity issues;
- develops, implements, and updates the Forensic Laboratory Capacity Management System;
- monitors the IT services used, the products and services provided, checking performance levels experienced as agreed in the SLAs, recommending corrective action where deviations exist by feedback to the Service Level Manager (SLM);

- works to insure quality Client service levels through capacity planning functions;
- works closely with the BCM to ensure that the BCPs are updated appropriately;
- assists in developing and maintaining SLAs with the Forensic Laboratory's Clients;
- ensures that capacity is used to its optimum, and where under utilization exists suggest methods of spreading workloads;
- manages the inputs and outputs of the system through performance, workload, resources, demands, modeling;
- ensures maximum utilization of all CIs;
- develops plans for migration of capacity planning policies and procedures to support the Forensic Laboratory's future directions;
- develops the Forensic Laboratory's long-range capacity management strategy;
- defines direction of in-house technical training seminars to improve overall employee awareness, response time, and ability to look into the Forensic Laboratory's future demand and capacity requirements;
- participates in international, national, and local SIG presentations, and publishes articles describing the Forensic Laboratory's capacity planning and management activities and how they relate to the business;
- develops and manages effective working relationships with all appropriate internal and external stakeholders;
- maintains external links to other companies in the industry to gain competitive assessments and share information, where appropriate;
- identifies the emerging information technologies to be assimilated, integrated, and introduced within the Forensic Laboratory, which could significantly impact the Forensic Laboratory's capacity demands;
- Interfaces with external industrial and academic organizations in order to maintain state-of-the-art knowledge in emerging capacity planning and management and to enhance the Forensic Laboratory's image as a first-class solution provider utilizing the latest thinking in this field;
- adheres to established Forensic Laboratory policies, standards, and procedures;
- performs all responsibilities in accordance with, or in excess of, the requirements of the Forensic Laboratory Integrated Management System.

AUTHORITY

The CaM has the authority to:

- develop long-term demand requirements for the Forensic Laboratory's Clients;
- develop long-range budget estimation and capacity estimates;
- establish and make decisions about management reporting methods and outputs.

CONTACTS

Internal Contacts

This position requires contact with all stakeholders, including owners and the IT Department. Within the Forensic Laboratory, contacts will be made with Account Managers, project teams and their Project Managers, the Sales Team, and the IT Department.

External Contacts

The primary external contacts are with Clients, contract service providers, vendors, and industry peers. Contact with information technology product and service companies is also made on a periodic basis.

REPORTS TO

The CaM reports to the IT Manager.

APPENDIX 26 - CAPACITY MANAGEMENT PLAN

The Forensic Laboratory's capacity plan template is given below.

> **Note**
>
> All capacity requirements are dependent on Client requirements, so the Forensic Laboratory monitors capacity in real time, while updating their plans.

The Capacity Plan contains the following:

- current requirements;
- projected, as known now, requirements;
- future desires.

These cover, but are not limited to:

- ability to meet TRTs;
- capability requirements in Forensic Analysts;
- capacity (storage requirements);
- processing requirements for a Forensic Laboratory case processing tools;
- other requirements as required.

APPENDIX 27 - SERVICE MANAGEMENT POLICY

It is the Forensic Laboratory's policy to:

- ensure that a full service management system is planned and implemented so that Client requirements are met, if not exceeded;
- design all services, in consultation with Clients, and ensure that the appropriate service operations objectives are agreed;
- perform continuous improvement activities to ensure that all products and services are monitored and improved where necessary and that Client requirements are met, if not exceeded;
- provide the appropriate resources to ensure that the products and services required by Clients are maintained at the correct level to meet their business needs;
- ensure that all Forensic Laboratory employees are aware of their responsibility to adhere to this policy and ensure that high-quality services are maintained for all Forensic Laboratory Clients.

The SLM is the person responsible for the coordination and management of products and services within the Forensic Laboratory.

This policy is issued and maintained within the Forensic Laboratory by the Service Manager. All Forensic Laboratory Managers are directly responsible for implementing the policy within their operational area and for its adherence by their employees.

A service management system provides the framework for the implementation of this policy within the Forensic Laboratory and is supported by a comprehensive set of policies and procedures. This system is regularly reviewed to ensure that it remains valid.

This policy has been approved by the Top Management.

APPENDIX 28 - SERVICE LEVEL MANAGER, JOB DESCRIPTION

OBJECTIVE AND ROLE

The role of the SLM is to define, agree, record, and manage levels of service offered to all Clients and ensure that the mandated service levels as defined in the SLAs are met for both new and existing products and services. The SLM will not only have to define the services in financial value terms to the Forensic Laboratory but also define them in terms of differentiation—i.e., why Clients should have the Forensic Laboratory as a provider of choice.

PROBLEMS AND CHALLENGES

The SLM is challenged with ensuring that the services offered to the Client meets or exceeds the SLA while managing the internal resources to meet the SLAs. This will involve a delicate balancing act between resources and deliverables. The ability to define the offered services in financial terms may cause variety as it is often viewed differently by different Clients. The production of differentiation information will vary between Clients.

PRINCIPAL ACCOUNTABILITIES

The SLM:

- evaluates service offerings for value definitions;
- analyzes existing services for cost cutting options;
- creates business value while managing the service risk;
- defines the services in the Service catalogue in terms of value to the Forensic Laboratory;
- formulates, agrees, and maintains appropriate Service Level Management structure to include:
  - the SLA structure;
  - all Operation Level Agreements (OLAs);
  - Underpinning Contracts (UCs);
  - Accommodating the SIP within the Service Level Management process.
- negotiates, agrees, and maintains SLAs, OLAs, and UCs;
- negotiates and agrees with Clients and the Forensic Laboratory as a service provider, the SLAs for new and developing products and services;
- analyzes and reviews service performance against SLAs, OLAs, and UCs;
- measures service delivery against SLAs;
- produces regular reports on performance against SLAs, OLAs, and UCs to internal and external Clients and relevant third parties;
- develops a service measurement and reporting model;
- organizes and maintains regular Service Level reviews with internal and external Clients and relevant third parties to cover:
  - outstanding actions from previous reviews;
  - current performance;
  - Service Level targets.
- agrees appropriate action to maintain/improve service levels;
- initiates actions to maintain and improve Service Levels;
- conducts the Annual Review of the entire Forensic Laboratory service offering to internal and external Clients;
- agrees and coordinates temporary amendments to SLAs;
- makes recommendations to the SIP;
- assists in developing the Forensic Laboratory's long-range service strategy;
- participates in international, national, and local SIG presentations, and publishes articles describing the Forensic Laboratory's service management initiatives and how they relate to the business;

- develops and manages effective working relationships with all appropriate internal and external stakeholders;
- maintains external links to other companies in the industry to gain competitive assessments and share information, where appropriate;
- identifies the emerging information technologies to be assimilated, integrated, and introduced within the Forensic Laboratory, which could significantly impact the Forensic Laboratory's product and service offerings;
- interfaces with external industrial and academic organizations in order to maintain state-of-the-art knowledge in emerging service management issues and to enhance the Forensic Laboratory's image as a first-class solution provider utilizing the latest thinking in this field;
- adheres to established Forensic Laboratory policies, standards, and procedures;
- performs all responsibilities in accordance with, or in excess of, the requirements of the Forensic Laboratory Integrated Management System.

AUTHORITY

The SLM has the authority to:

- define the level of products and services provided, as authorized by Top Management;
- design tools and technology required to produce the SLAs;
- design SLA models with predefined activities. Any changes to these activities must be transitioned;
- identify potential service level problems before they occur and implement solutions;
- evaluate operating advantages and cost benefits of proposed and existing SLAs;
- arrange for systems reviews against SLAs and evaluate the results;
- schedule and prioritize work to accommodate internal and external Client needs while minimizing impact on current projects;
- monitor and report on product and service offering and compare them with the SLA. Where appropriate, make changes to the product and service offering to improve them for the Client.

CONTACTS

Internal

Contacts within the Forensic Laboratory are with employees in the operational areas that directly affect service delivery. This will include a variety of Forensic Laboratory employees.

Close cooperation with the Service Desk, Sales Team, Project Managers, and other Managers will be as required.

External

Those external to the Forensic Laboratory will be with appropriate SIGs, Clients, external vendors, and service providers.

REPORTS TO

The SLM reports to Top Management.

APPENDIX 29 - SERVICE REPORTING POLICY

It is the policy of the Forensic Laboratory to:

- agree all reporting requirements during service management planning with all Clients, internal and external;
- document all reporting requirements in SLAs including report types, frequency, and responsibilities for production;
- provide timely and accurate service reports for internal and external Clients;
- provide reporting that covers all measurable aspects of a product or service that details both current and historical analysis;
- use appropriate reporting tools to ensure that the information within reports is comprehensive, accurate, and has clear presentation;
- use service reporting as an input into the service review and the Forensic Laboratory's continuous improvement process.

APPENDIX 30 - POLICY FOR MAINTAINING AND SERVICING IT EQUIPMENT

It is the policy of the Forensic Laboratory to:

- IT equipment can only be maintained by either an appropriate member of the IT Department, or by an appropriate service engineer or third party;
- IT equipment maintenance must only be performed in accordance with the manufacturer's recommended service intervals and specifications;
- all IT equipment faults must be recorded by the Service Desk as an incident;
- all IT equipment maintenance by service engineers or other third parties must be undertaken in accordance with the guidelines for hosting visits to the Forensic Laboratory;

- a record of all IT equipment maintenance is maintained which records:
  - all IT equipment maintenance performed by the Forensic Laboratory IT Department (including corrective and preventive action);
  - all IT equipment maintenance performed by service engineers and third parties.
- IT equipment that needs to be sent off-site for maintenance is subject to the following controls:
  - equipment may only be sent for off-site maintenance to an approved and authorized third party;
  - the Forensic Laboratory IT Department is responsible for coordinating all off-site maintenance;
  - all off-site maintenance must be recorded.

Note 1

Where possible all equipment that is sent off-site for repair is securely wiped or the media removed. If this is not possible and the equipment contains any classified data, there are only two options:

- ensure maintenance is carried out on site;
- dispose of the equipment securely.

Note 2

The option chosen must be agreed by the Information Security Manager and the Owner of the information on the equipment, based on a risk assessment.

APPENDIX 31 - ISO 17025 TOOL TEST METHOD DOCUMENTATION

a. appropriate identification.
b. scope.
c. description of the type of item to be tested or calibrated.
d. parameters or quantities and ranges to be determined.
e. apparatus and equipment, including technical performance requirements.
f. reference standards and reference materials required.
g. environmental conditions required and any stabilization period needed.
h. description of the procedure, including:
  - affixing of identification marks, handling, transporting, storing and preparation of items;
  - checks to be made before the work is started;
  - checks that the equipment is working properly and, where required, calibration and adjustment of the equipment before each use;
  - the method of recording the observations and results;
  - any safety measures to be observed.

i. criteria and/or requirements for approval/rejection.
j. data to be recorded and method of analysis and presentation.
k. the uncertainty or the procedure for estimating uncertainty.

APPENDIX 32 - STANDARD FORENSIC TOOL TESTS

The following are the basic tests undertaken for a new forensic tool, an upgrade to an existing tool, or a new operating environment:

- acquisition hashing;
- recovery of deleted files;
- recovery of deleted folders;
- recovery of deleted partitions;
- text searches;
- Internet history searches;
- detection of bad file names from signature analysis;
- identification of "known files";
- image recovery;
- e-mail address recovery;
- specific artifact recovery;
- other tests as appropriate to either the specific case or tool.

APPENDIX 33 - FORENSIC TOOL TEST REPORT TEMPLATE

The standard template used in the Forensic Laboratory for testing non-standard methods is:

- title defining product tested;
- unique test identifier;
- test environment, including hardware and software;
- details of the product vendor;
- unambiguous identification of the product tested including version, patches, etc.;
- test criteria;
- details of standard test case relevant to this test;
- test results;
- details of the Forensic Analyst performing testing, including qualifications;
- where appropriate and needed, opinions and interpretations;
- any other pertinent matters relevant to the test;
- details of Laboratory Manager reviewing the results and authorizing the product use;
- signatures of the Forensic Analyst and Laboratory Manager, with dates.

In addition to this, the requirements for document control, as defined in Chapter 4, Section 4.6.3, are met along with the report's classification, as defined in Chapter 5, Appendix 16.

APPENDIX 34 - OVERNIGHT BACKUP CHECKLIST

For each server, a backup checklist is maintained on a paper in the server room. This ensures that the member of the IT Department who checks the backups actually signs the checklist to show the task has been performed. The checklist contains the following information:

- day of week;
- date;
- tape ID;
- success?
- tape cleaned?
- tape retensioned?
- tape replaced?
- comments;
- signature;
- name;
- incident number if a failure occurs.

Each checklist for a server is for a month, and when completed, they are scanned and added to the ERMS as records of the backup process.

Chapter 8

Incident Response

Table of Contents

8.1 GENERAL

Note 1

While many books refer to the scene to be investigated as a "crime scene" or a "locus of a crime," the Forensic Laboratory refers to the scenes as an "incident scene" as it is not always certain that a crime has been committed.

Note 2

This chapter only deals with the actual seizure of evidence from an incident scene and its transportation to the Forensic Laboratory; actual processing of the evidence, rather than the incident scene, is covered in Chapter 9.

8.1.1 Overview

The Forensic Laboratory may be asked to act as a First Responder in the following situations:

- as part of a planned seizure operation for a Client;
- as an advisor "after the event";
- as an attendee in any relevant role at a crime scene.

Only those members of the Forensic Laboratory who are competent and have received the relevant First Responder training shall attend as a First Responder. Other members of the team may comprise qualified Forensic Technicians or Analysts.

ISO 17020—General criteria for the operation of various types of bodies performing inspection are applied to crime scene investigation. Depending on the actual services the Forensic Laboratory supplies, it may be an "A," "B," or a type "C" inspection body. The mapping of the Forensic Laboratory Procedures to ISO 17020 is given in Appendix 1. Additional guidance for the implementation of ISO 17020 in the Forensic Laboratory was obtained from EA 5/03—Guidance for the implementation of ISO 17020 in the field of crime scene investigation IAF /ILAC-A4: 2004 Guidance on the application of ISO/IEC 17020.

The work of the Forensic Response team attending an incident where First Response is required is, among other things, to:

- plan the initial response for attending the scene based on facts available (Plan);
- assess the scene, on arrival (Do);
- revise and update as appropriate, the examination and seizure strategy (Check and Act);
- examine the scene and collect evidence using the relevant Forensic Laboratory recovery procedures for exhibit identification and seizure, as required (Do);
- remove evidence from the scene securely, if appropriate (Do);
- document all findings both contemporaneously and as part of the final report, if requested (Do);
- review the results and rework if appropriate (Check and Act).

8.1.2 Legislative Considerations

All incident scenes are unique, and the judgment of the Forensic Laboratory First Response Team Leader, any legislative requirements, and other relevant issues should all be considered in any First Response attendance. Where appropriate, these generic procedures should be amended to ensure compliance with the requirements of the relevant jurisdiction.

There may be any number of legislative considerations that apply to the collection of electronic evidence for the specific jurisdiction.

These may dictate actions to be undertaken, orders of actions, or additional requirements. The First Response Team Leader must understand the generic Forensic Laboratory procedures and be able to adapt them for the incorporation of local requirements for the jurisdiction as the situation dictates.

As part of the planning process for the seizure or attending a possible crime scene, the First Response Team Leader must ensure that the requirements have been identified, that all members of the First Response Team are aware of the requirements that this places on them for every aspect of the First Response process, and that these requirements are met.

The First Response Briefing should cover the specific requirements, and a sample First Response Briefing Agenda is given in Appendix 2.

The Forensic Laboratory First Response Team must use caution when seizing any electronic or digital evidence, as improper seizure may not only prejudice any legal proceedings but also be illegal.

Before collecting any electronic or digital evidence, the Forensic Laboratory First Response Team Leader must ensure that Legal authority exists for seizure of evidence. No one wants to have the doctrine of "fruits of the poison tree" applied to any evidence that they seize as all subsequent information derived from illegally seized physical evidence is inadmissible in a court of law and cannot be used to support the findings in any case.

8.1.3 Work Standards

There may be forensic First Response or evidence collection work standards that are mandated for the collection of electronic evidence for the specific jurisdiction. When dealing with electronic or digital evidence, the basic principles that the Forensic Laboratory adhere to include, but are not limited to, are:

- the process of identifying, collecting, securing, and transporting electronic or digital evidence should not change the original evidence, and this should be provable;
- in specific circumstances where the First Response Team members need to access original data, rather than a forensically produced image, they should be both competent to perform the actions and be able to give evidence explaining the relevance and the implications of their actions;
- electronic or digital evidence should only be seized or examined by competent Forensic Laboratory employees;
- an audit trail of any actions relating to the search for, seizure of, transportation of and booking in of electronic or digital evidence shall be supported by a contemporaneous audit trail. The audit trail must be fully documented, securely preserved, and available for later examination;
- any independent third party should be able to examine the source evidence, the processes and procedures involved, and if competent, produce the same results;
- the instructing Client (Law Enforcement or Corporate) who is in charge of the forensic case has ultimate responsibility to ensure compliance with all relevant legislation, regulation, and accepted working practices within the jurisdiction and be personally accountable for compliance.

Note

It must be remembered that the Health and Safety of the Forensic Laboratory First Response Team and any others must remain the primary responsibility and concern of the First Response Team Leader.

8.1.4 Health and Safety Issues

Compliance with Health and Safety legislation is essential in all of the work carried out by the Forensic Laboratory First Response Team during all stages of the First Response process.

As part of the planning process for the seizure or attending a possible crime scene, the Forensic Laboratory First Response Team Leader must ensure that the relevant Health and Safety requirements have been identified, that all members of the First Response Team are aware of the requirements that this places on them for every aspect of the First Response process, and that these requirements are met.

Details of generic Health and Safety requirements are given in Chapter 17. However, specific requirements for the Forensic Laboratory First Response Team include:

- a Health and Safety briefing must be held prior to the Forensic Laboratory Forensic Team departing to the incident scene. The briefing may indicate the need for Personal Protective Equipment (PPE) to be used by the Forensic Laboratory Forensic Team on-site;

- where appropriate, a Health and Safety Risk Assessment shall be carried out on-site by the Forensic Laboratory Forensic Team Leader or other competent authority;
- all Forensic Laboratory Forensic Teams shall wear protective latex gloves for all searching and seizing operations on-site. This is to both protect the Forensic Laboratory employees and preserve any fingerprints that may be required to be recovered at a later date;
- gloves should be used only once and then disposed of in appropriate containers or returned to the Forensic Laboratory for disposal;
- care must be taken in handling computer hardware and it is the responsibility of the Forensic Laboratory First Response Team Leader to ensure that any member of the Forensic Laboratory First Response Team who may lift heavy equipment has been given appropriate "manual handling" training, as defined in Chapter 17, Section 17.2.6.1.8;
- additionally, all grab bags shall contain a full medical first aid kit for minor injuries such as cuts from sharp edges on equipment, etc.;
- any such injuries shall be recorded in the Forensic Laboratory accident book in accordance with the Forensic Laboratory Health and Safety policy and supporting procedures.

8.1.5 Competence

The Forensic Laboratory First Response Team must all be competent to perform their tasks. No one at the incident scene shall attempt to explore the contents of evidence, or recover information from an information processing or storage device, with the exception of recording what is on-screen or in the location of the evidence to be seized unless they are competent to perform the tasks.

The successful seizure of evidence at the scene is the "making or breaking" of any forensic case. No matter how rigorous the Forensic Laboratory's investigation of recovered evidence is after seizure, it is worthless if the seizure itself was flawed or inappropriately carried out. In many cases, where the First Response Team attend, they will be under the guidance of a third party (usually Law Enforcement) and will have to operate under their rules, but they provide specialist experience in the seizure and recovery of digital evidence and information processing equipment.

It is essential that the Forensic Laboratory has competent employees that can staff the First Response Team and that this can be demonstrated as required.

8.1.6 Consent

There are times that the suspect is present and that their consent is required and also the consent is given.

In cases such as this, appropriate forms for the jurisdiction shall be used and these must be carried in the Forensic Grab Bag. Sample contents of the Forensic Laboratory's Forensic Grab Bag are given in Appendix 3.

This must be used and distributed according to the requirements of the legislation in force in the jurisdiction.

8.2 EVIDENCE

Evidence at the incident scene can take many forms and may be readily visible or may require later analysis to recover it. The value of physical evidence in any case is to:

- be the deciding factor is determining guilt or innocence;
- corroborate other evidence discovered;
- establish the key elements in a case;
- exonerating those under suspicion, where appropriate;
- identification of the person or persons responsible;
- link together a chain of circumstantial evidence;
- test the statements of assertions of others in the case, e.g., witnesses or suspects;
- verifying that an event occurred.

In digital forensic cases, the evidence may be easy to find or steps may have been taken to try to hide or delete it.

The best evidence rule states that the best evidence is the original exhibit, rather than a copy. However, with hashing techniques, it is possible that no more, or no less, is present at the time of acquisition and that the copy made is as good as the original exhibit.

There is rarely a second chance to obtain evidence at the scene, so it is essential that the incident scene is properly and methodically processed. The First Response Team can fail to do this for a number of reasons, and of these include:

- external pressure to reach a certain conclusion;
- external pressure to reach results;
- lack of seizure of potential physical evidence at the scene;
- poor communication in the First Response Team;
- poor instructions from the Client or at briefing time;
- potential evidence destroyed at the scene by accident;
- potential evidence destroyed at the scene by carelessness or sloppy work practices;
- potential evidence destroyed at the scene on purpose;
- preconceived ideas;
- premature conclusions;
- time constraints;
- volatility of evidence.

It is therefore essential that First Response is carried out in a slow, methodical, and thorough manner.

RFC 3227—Evidence Collecting and Archiving states that evidence needs to be:

- *admissible*: it must conform to certain legal rules before it can be put before a court;

- *authentic*: it must be possible to positively tie evidentiary material to the incident;
- *complete*: it must tell the whole story and not just a particular perspective;
- *reliable*: there must be nothing about how the evidence was collected and subsequently handled that casts doubt about its authenticity and veracity;
- *believable*: it must be readily believable and understandable by a court.

Physical evidence should be handled as little as possible to avoid any possible contamination.

8.3 INCIDENT RESPONSE AS A PROCESS

Incident scene investigation must be carried out as a process and it is generally accepted that there are seven stages of processing a scene, and these are:

- assessment;
- control;
- examination;
- interpretation;
- recording;
- collection;
- case management.

While these are the ideal steps, this may not be what actually happens in fact, as First Responders may be local management not trained in crime scene processing.

The objectives of processing an incident scene are:

- safety of those at the scene, specifically Forensic Laboratory employees;
- preservation and recovery of evidence and intelligence;
- minimization of contamination;
- maximizing the potential to detect and solve crime;
- maximizing the potential to apprehend offenders and exonerate the innocent;
- meet the Client's other legal requirements, as agreed and if possible.

8.4 INITIAL CONTACT

Depending on the exact scenario of the deployment of the First Response Team, the method of first contact and how the case develops cannot be predicted.

As soon as a New Case to be processed is identified, a "New Case" form is filled in containing the initial data captured from the Client. All cases must start with this initial data capture, and the information required for this is given in Appendix 4. While reference is to paper forms in the book, these are all duplicated in the Forensic Laboratory's Case Management System, MARS.

Where the incident is a planned seizure, more information may be available as opposed to the Forensic Laboratory First Response Team being invited to attend an existing incident.

The procedures for starting a New Case in the Forensic Laboratory are given in Figure 8.1.

1. A request is made to the Forensic Laboratory for a First Response presence by phone, fax, e-mail, personal attendance, etc., to the Service Desk.
2. The Service Desk create a New Case in MARS and fill in as much as they know of the details on the New Case form;
3. The Laboratory Manager is advised of the request and assigns Forensic Analyst(s) to the First Response Team, as appropriate, based on the case requirements and the competencies of the Forensic Analysts.
4. The First Response Team Leader will need to be in possession of some information about the incident, typically this will include:
   - description of the incident;
   - instructing Client's details;
   - name of the on-site Incident Manager running the incident, if applicable;
   - case name/title for the incident;
   - location of the incident;
   - what jurisdiction the case and/or seizure is to be performed under;
   - details of what is to be seized (make, model, location, ID, etc.);
   - other work to be performed at the scene (e.g., full search, evidence required, etc.);
   - whether the search and seizure is to be overt or covert and whether local management are to know;
   - whether local Law Enforcement agencies are involved, and if so which ones.
5. If the Forensic Laboratory First Response Team is invited to an incident that has already happened, then it may be that someone local to the incident has secured the scene, stopped anyone contaminating the scene, even pulled the power to the relevant computer(s), and made basic notes of their findings. Typically, the Forensic Laboratory First Response Team will be invited to provide assistance in some, or all, of the following areas:
   - (further) securing the scene;
   - identifying the required evidence;
   - determining the jurisdiction and ensuring that the work is carried out in accordance with the requirements of the jurisdiction;
   - preserving the required evidence according to the Forensic Laboratory's First Responder procedures, as amended for the jurisdiction;
   - documenting the scene;
   - maybe undertaking an initial interview with the suspect;

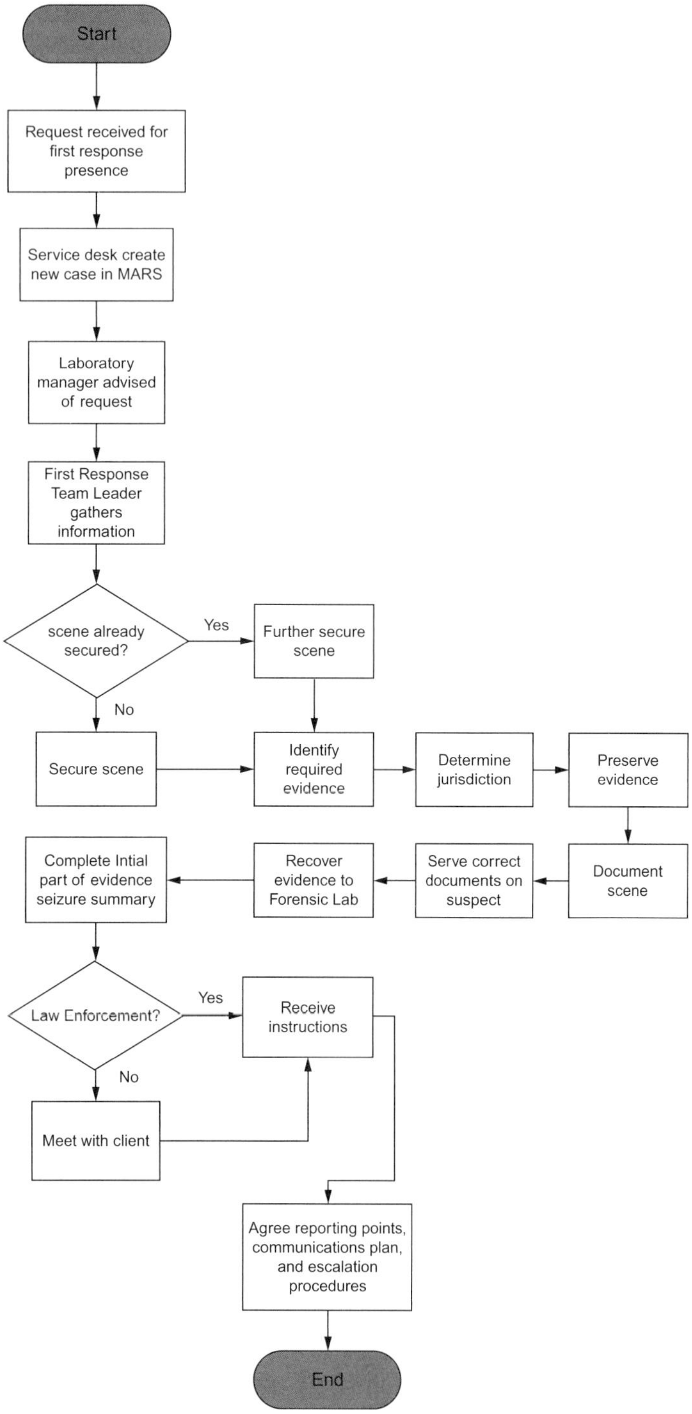

FIGURE 8.1 Starting a New Case. (For color version of this figure, the reader is referred to the online version of this chapter.)

- ensuring that the correct paperwork has been served on the suspect;
- recovering the evidence to the Forensic Laboratory for investigation or performing recovery work on-site.

6. Once the initial information has been captured requiring the Forensic Laboratory First Response Team to attend the site, the initial part of the evidence seizure summary is filled in for the case. The details for the Seizure Summary Log are given in Appendix 5.
7. Where the Client is Law Enforcement, the legislation within the jurisdiction is usually well known and specific instructions for the jurisdiction can be expected to be received from the Client to allow a proposal to

be prepared in accordance with the requirements of Chapter 6, Section 6.6.

8. Where the Client is a corporate and the matter relates to an internal issue (which may become a tribunal or become the subject of a court case), the Forensic Laboratory always requires the Client to contact their own Legal Counsel and Human Resources Department, where appropriate) for advice and guidance and revert. This may take the form of written instructions or requests for meeting or a mixture of both. Issues to be discussed include, but are not limited to:
   - employee privacy issues;
   - employee use of Client assets;
   - employee conduct at work;
   - relevant Client policies and procedures relating to the incident;
   - other issues relating to the incident as identified.

   The outcome of any meetings and any written instructions shall be used to finalize the proposal and are all filed in the Client's virtual case file in the ERMS as records for the case.
9. Reporting points, a communications plan, and escalation procedures should be agreed between the Client and the Forensic Laboratory.

8.5 TYPES OF FIRST RESPONSE

Note

Under no circumstances should anyone, with the exception of competent and trained First Responders or the Forensic Laboratory First Response Team, make any attempts to recover information from any information processing system. It must be remembered that the information present within the storage media is potential evidence and should be treated accordingly. Any attempts to retrieve evidence by unqualified individuals could either compromise the integrity of the evidence or result in recovered evidence being inadmissible in legal or in administrative proceedings.

First Response to an incident may involve three different groups of people, and each will have differing skills and need to carry out differing tasks based on the circumstance of the incident.

The three groups are:

- Client System Administrators;
- Client Management;
- The Forensic Laboratory First Response Team.

Each is dealt with in turn below.

8.5.1 First Response for System Administrators

The role of a System Administrator is vital in ensuring all aspects of network security and maintenance, but this individual also plays the most important role in the event a computer is used in, or is subject to, a security incident. The System Administrator will most likely be the primary point of contact for individuals wishing to make a report of computer use violations after the incident has been reported to the Service Desk. In addition, a System Administrator may come across a violation during the normal course of their duties.

The actions taken by the System Administrator after the discovery of a potential computer violation will play a vital role in the investigation, forensic evaluation of the computer system, and potential prosecution or administrative actions.

From a forensic standpoint, the ideal situation is to isolate the computer from additional use or tampering. However, many of the systems that may be compromised are of critical importance to the business, and isolation of the system may not be possible or feasible.

A suspected computer violation will result in difficult decisions in weighing the loss of potential evidence to the inability to utilize a computer system tied to the network. It is essential that Top Management in the victim's organization is in a position to make decisions knowingly about the immediate actions to be taken and the implications of any action undertaken.

After the System Administrator either is alerted to a possible incident or becomes aware of it through his/her own observations, it is essential that the Systems Administrator takes appropriate action.

This could include doing nothing until full instructions are received from Top Management unless immediate actions are needed to minimize the effect of the breach or incident. If any actions are taken, then the System Administrator must make full and contemporaneous notes of all actions undertaken for later records and possible action.

Depending on the actual incident, some or all of the following actions should be undertaken.

- call in the in-house First Response Team, if there is one;
- record what is on-screen and what is happening;
- try to take copies of any system logs onto clean media;
- if the computer is switched on and the screen display is on:
  - make records of what happened from initial discovery of incident;
  - seek Top Management direction, especially if there is an ongoing attack or the business may be prejudiced prior to powering any systems down;

- seek Top Management approval to get competent and qualified help, if it is not available in-house;
- ensure that the area surrounding the information processing systems that are linked to the incident are kept secured and that no unauthorized, or unneeded, person has access to them;
- keep a watching brief until qualified assistance arrives, recording anything that happens that is relevant to the incident.

The Systems Administrator should wait for the arrival of qualified First Responders or direction from Top Management.

8.5.2 First Response by Client Management

Typically, this will be the case where one of the Client's Management or some other non-forensic expert will be on-site with the suspect or victim and/or their information processing system and they need to secure the scene.

Once initial perimeter security has been established, the scene should not be left unattended or unsecured for any reason until the processing of the scene by the competent internal First Responder Team or the Forensic Laboratory First Response Team is completed. Instructions should be provided to any individuals securing the scene concerning access. Only individuals with a direct need for access relating to the incident will be allowed to enter the incident scene and the numbers of individuals involved in working in the incident scene should be kept at a minimum. Detailed contemporaneous notes should be maintained regarding how perimeter and scene security was established to include the identification of all security and other personnel involved.

Detailed notes should be maintained during all aspects of the scene processing. This not only includes the usual:

- who;
- what;
- when;
- what,
- why;
- how.[a]

but also the overall observations of the scene.

Notes and/or photographs/videos should record exactly what the scene looked like upon arrival. This would include items of furniture within the scene and their locations, the condition of the room (clean, dirty, etc.), locations of any information processing equipment, disks, tapes, etc., along with the locations and descriptions of any potential evidence.

a. These are Kipling's six "friends"!

During initial observations, a determination should be made concerning the possibility that potential evidence is at immediate risk of destruction (i.e., disk format or upload of information in progress). This may require an immediate decision to disconnect the power supply. All factors, such as the potential loss of data, need to be taken into consideration when making this decision, but it must be made quickly and in association with the local management and the relevant competent First Response Team.

When dealing with PCs and mobile processing devices, this can include, but not be limited to the following tasks:

- not letting the suspect or anyone else touch the computer;
- photographing (if possible) or drawing a sketch map of the computer and/or media and how it is connected;
- recording what is on-screen if the computer is switched on and the screen display is on;
- if the screen appears blank—press the 'down arrow' key to see if there is a screen saver and if so continue as below—if the screen restores, record what is on the screen as above;
- if the computer is switched on, pull the power by removing the power lead from the equipment—*not at the wall end*;
- if the computer is switched off on arrival—then leave it switched off;
- if the system is a server—wait until qualified help arrives;
- remove batteries from portable PCs then pull power if they are switched on;
- with PDAs ensure that the cradle and chargers are taken and that the PDA is kept charged until it is examined by a competent Forensic Laboratory First Responder—this may require charging, i.e., connecting it to the mains;
- record whether the computer is connected to a telephone/modem or network;
- check for wireless connectivity.

The Client Management should then wait for qualified assistance to arrive without undertaking any other actions.

While the above are the ideal situations, this rarely happens and the level of information available at an incident scene can vary greatly.

8.5.3 Forensic Laboratory First Responder Team

While the Client's management may be the first attendees at an incident, it may also be their First Response Team (if they have one) or the Forensic Laboratory First Response Team. The procedures below are for the Forensic Laboratory First Response Team but will also be applicable to any in-house First Response Team.

Once the target information processing system, office, or location for seizure has been identified, it is necessary to determine whether the seizure will be overt or covert. This may depend on a number of factors such as nature of the incident or position of the suspect or victim in the Client's organization.

The procedures below will be relevant to either type of seizure, but covert seizures are typically carried out during the "quiet hours." This may have some impacts on office services such as removal of waste paper bins—this must be addressed at this stage.

At this point, it will also be possible to identify what hardware is to be seized, where it is located, and possibly what ancillary equipment may need to be seized. It may well be that the local management have already seized this equipment as a precaution.

Given this, the Forensic Laboratory First Responder Team should be able to plan what resources and equipment will be needed to affect the required seizure. Contact with the local management or other investigative teams at this point are essential for other local knowledge as required.

On arrival at the incident scene, the Forensic Laboratory First Response Team, depending on their tasking, will undertake some or all of the following tasks (Figure 8.2).

1. Start to fill in a Site Summary Form, given in Appendix 6.
2. Receive the handover briefing from the Client team when they arrive and take over the scene to:
   - obtain assistance as required from any Client or third party employees;
   - obtain transfer of control of notes or other information relating to the incident scene.

Note

Much of this will depend on the actual incident, but circumstances will dictate the actions to be taken.

3. Undertake an initial assessment to include:
   - assess Health and Safety risks and take adequate safety precondition;
   - ascertain any new information regarding the incident scene and confirm the information already held;
4. Establish and preserve incident scene boundaries to:
   - establish incident scene boundaries by identifying the focal point(s) of the incident scene and extending outward;
   - set up physical barrier(s), using appropriate means (e.g., locking doors, tape, or similar);
   - control the flow of personnel and animals, if appropriate, entering and exiting the scene and document all people entering and exiting the scene; maintain integrity of the scene;

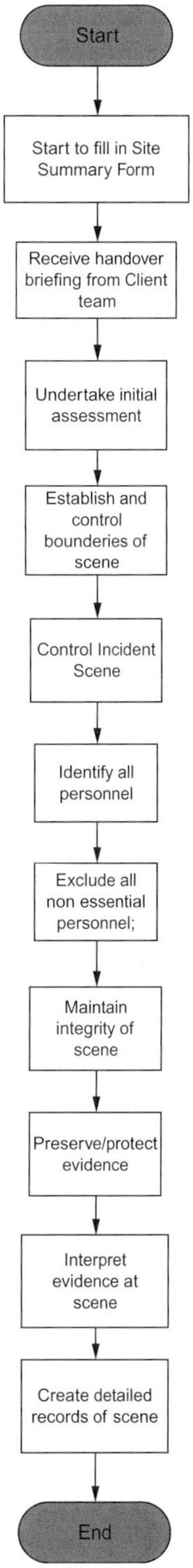

FIGURE 8.2 Initial tasks on arrival. (For color version of this figure, the reader is referred to the online version of this chapter.)

   - preserve/protect evidence at the scene;
   - document the original location of the suspect/victim(s) or objects at the scene that were observed being moved;
   - follow jurisdictional laws related to search and seizure, if known. If they are not known, then do not attempt any search or seizure;

5. Control the incident scene and all persons at the scene to:
   - restrict movement of persons at the scene;
   - define and access and exit path for the scene and ensure all attending the scene use them;
   - prevent persons from altering physical or logical evidence;
   - prevent persons from destroying physical or logical evidence;
   - continue to maintain safety at the scene;
   - restrict areas of movement within the scene;
   - continue to control the scene by maintaining a Client Management presence;
6. Identify all persons at the scene.

> **Note**
>
> Identify means to obtain verifiable personal information.

   - Identify victims/suspects (keep them secure and separate);
   - Identify witnesses (keep them secure and separate where possible);
   - Instruct the witnesses not to discuss the incident if they cannot be separated, as this may distort each other's impressions by suggestion;
   - Identify bystanders and others not intimately related to the incident (remove from the scene);
   - identify suspects/victims/family members/friends (keep them under control while showing compassion) if appropriate;
   - identify medical and assisting personnel, if appropriate.
7. Exclude unauthorized/non-essential personnel from the incident scene, including:
   - other Client staff, or third parties acting on their behalf, who are not involved in the incident;
   - other non-essential personnel (e.g., any persons not performing investigative or safety functions at the scene).
8. Maintain integrity of the scene by:
   - ensuring that an appropriate communication plan is in place and that all communications are through authorized channels.
9. Preserve/protect evidence at the scene.
   - Protect evidence from environmental elements, if possible;
   - Identify and apply an appropriate search pattern;
   - Accurately record the scene as it is being processed;
   - Locate all relevant evidence relating to the incident;
   - Make appropriate arrangements for evidence collection;
   - Obtain advice and assistance from other specialists, including the Client's employees or other Forensic Laboratory employees, as required.
10. Interpret the evidence at the incident.
   - Establish possible significance of the evidence;
   - Establish the possible sequence of events, if appropriate;
   - Document all actions.
11. Make detailed records of the incident scene.

8.5.4 Planning the Next Steps

While the Forensic Laboratory may be able to obtain some information regarding the incident, it is not usually possible to plan the actions to be taken, with the exception of site security or site takeover, without detailed investigation. Even with an agreed proposal in place, this will define required outcomes rather than detailed work plans. Once the scene has been taken over, or initial response secures the scene, the First Response Team Leader must plan, in detail, the next steps. This may require detailed examination of the scene as well as interviews with a number of the Client's employees or their suppliers.

The time spent in planning at this stage is essential as an unstructured "wild goose chase" without any detailed and cohesive plan is frustrating for all concerned, wastes the Client's money, wastes Forensic Laboratory resources, and does not present a professional approach to the processing of the scene. At this stage, it is also possible to determine whether the Client's required outcomes are realistic and achievable, and any final amendments to the resourcing, costing, and proposal can be made based on the new information determined from the scene. The following should be performed by the First Response Team Leader:

Develop a detailed forensic plan for undertaking the scene processing. While it is accepted that all incidents are different, the Forensic Laboratory has a defined procedure for processing the incident scene, as shown earlier.

A checklist for the process is given in Appendix 20.

1. Revise the proposal and agree with the Client, including the Forensic Plan.
2. Identify and additional resources, whether internal to the Forensic Laboratory, the Client or third parties and ensure their availability.
3. Collect the evidence relating to the incident in a manner that precludes contamination and ensures integrity of the evidence. This will include ensuring that sanitized media is used for on-site evidence collection by competent employees, electrostatic and other protection measures are in place to prevent contamination, including write blockers.
4. Ensure that only those items covered by the Search Warrant, consent, or other authority to seize are examined.

5. Review the collected evidence for any anomalies or fresh leads that may indicate the requirement for other evidence to be seized, so long as it is within the terms of the Legal authority in step 5 above. If other evidence is authorized for collection, then steps 2–4 above should be repeated until all relevant evidence has been collected.
6. Depending on circumstances, time constraints may affect this process, but shortcuts must not be undertaken.
7. Ensure the Chain of Custody is in place for all exhibits and that appropriate security is in place, until they are securely logged in the Secure Property Store at the Forensic Laboratory.

In addition to the above, any of the following may be of interest to the First Response Team and should, where possible, be collected for later evaluation:

- handwritten notes, loose magnetic storage media;
- tapes and CD-ROMs;
- any "personal organizers," mobile phones, or other mobile devices;
- desk/personal calendars and/or address books;
- any potential passwords and Web site/IP addresses written on scraps of paper within the crime scene area;
- the contents of waste paper bins.

In addition, the First Responder should:

- locate and secure any backup storage media relating to the incident. In some instances, files that are deleted from the hard drive will be present within the backup on the backup storage media;
- contact the relevant communications support point or communications supplier and attempt to obtain a printout of phone numbers dialed from the incident scene and also the mobile phone details for the users located in the incident scene;
- possibly conduct interviews of individuals with access to the system or network, if appropriate;
- determine the type and information security classification of the work normally performed on the suspect/victim's computer or computer system. If classified information may have been breached, the impact of this must be evaluated. If personal data are involved, there may legislative requirements for reporting the breach to either a Regulator or the individuals whose personal information has been compromised. Contractual requirements may also require the organization to advise their Clients of any possible incidents or breaches affecting their information;
- determine the identity of all individuals that have both physical and logical access to the information processing system involved;
- determine if the information processing system is part of a network and the type of network system involved, as well as the furthest reach that any possible attacker may have exploited and caused damage.

The First Responder shall fill in, to the best of his or her ability, all of the other details found on the Site Summary Form, given in Appendix 6, covering the details above including topology, operating systems as well as other occupancy of the crime scene, and details of any personal effects found there.

This form shall be countersigned by the victim/suspect (or if this is refused or not possible, the fact annotated on the form).

8.6 THE INCIDENT SCENE

Any location could be the scene of an incident, and the Forensic Laboratory always regards every incident as a possible crime scene and process it accordingly so that the same procedures are used whether the case ends up in Court or not. This allows rigorous procedures to be applied at the start of a case, rather than having to "back track."

The primary scene is the location where the incident was reported and is being investigated by the First Response Team. This investigation may in turn lead to a secondary scene (e.g., an employee's work place is the primary scene and their home becomes the second scene). Both may need investigation and evidence seizure.

8.6.1 Forensic Laboratory First Response Team Taking Over an Incident Scene

When the First Response Team arrives at a scene that has been secured by the local management, they will address or perform the following:

1. The manner in which the information processing equipment and storage media is secured after a suspected computer incident is reported will be dependent on the facilities available and the information processing system involved. In some instances, it may be impractical to seize the computer as in the case of a large mainframe or a networked mail server, but it may be more appropriate to seize the backup media or to make a backup at the time of the event and perform remote forensics or perform real-time forensics on-site. However, the forensic examination of backup media means that there are typically only files available and there is no access to such information areas as defined in "Other Data Areas" in Appendix 8. It also precludes any volatile information that may have been present on the original evidence.
2. In many instances, systems are backed up on a daily basis. If the victim or the individual suspected in a

security incident attempts to delete files from the primary storage device (e.g., a hard drive), these files could still remain on the backup storage media.

3. The ideal situation would call for the System Administrator to merely ensure no destructive programs are in operation, secure the scene and have security personnel trained in the seizure of computer systems respond to process the workstation. Sadly, there are few situations that are ideal, and advice on less than ideal situations is given below:
   - in addition to these immediate actions and taking control of the incident site, the Forensic Laboratory First Response Team should liaise with the local management and undertake a full handover from the local management team to the Forensic Laboratory First Responder Team. This will include a full briefing and transfer of all notes and documentation relating to the incident;
   - some items may have already been seized by the local management in the victim/suspect's area and already have been documented;
   - once the handover has been completed, the local management team should be stood down unless specialized local information is needed.

8.6.2 Physical Security of the Scene

When the First Response Team takes over an incident scene, they will immediately reassess the security of the scene. It is essential in any incident scene processing to be able to prove that the scene was secured, that security was maintained and documented while the First Response Team was on-site, and that the Chain of Custody was maintained. The objective of securing the incident scene is to:

- prevent evidence being destroyed or contaminated;
- control release of information and ensure that proper communication channels are maintained;
- ensure that the Chain of Custody is maintained and documented for each item of evidence handled and recovered;
- ensure that the minimum number of people is present at the scene. The more people present, the greater the likelihood of evidence contamination and it may also inhibit the processing of the scene;
- ensure that all relevant evidence for the case has been recovered, recorded, and securely transported to the Forensic Laboratory for further examination.

Physical security at the scene can be provided by:

- physically locking or sealing rooms;
- posting guards;
- use of barrier tape or rope.

8.6.3 Health and Safety at the Scene

The safety of all Forensic Laboratory employees, and anyone else present, is the primary responsibility of the Incident Manager or the First Response Team Leader. The issue of Health and Safety at the Forensic Laboratory is covered in Chapter 17; however, there are some incident scene concerns that are raised here. The First Response Team Leader must be aware of the safety and well being of the team; this includes appropriate use of PPE as well as fatigue or other stress issues. Breaks and refreshments may need to be considered. Typical PPE that is used at digital crime scenes includes protection for:

- eyes;
- hands—also to preclude the First Responder leaving their own fingerprints and contaminating the scene;
- feet;
- antistatic—also to prevent contamination of the evidence;
- other PPE may be indicated, depending on the specifics of the incident scene.

Secure areas need to be defined and protected (e.g., for temporary storage of exhibits prior to transportation) and areas where refreshments can be taken, if on site for a prolonged period. Health and Safety issues must be covered at the initial briefing, as given in Appendix 2.

In addition to the physical Health and Safety of the First Response Team, it is often possible that the risks encountered are mental rather than physical (e.g., dealing with child abuse). Details for assessment for psychological risks are given in Chapter 17, Section 17.2.6.2.13.

8.6.4 The Chain of Custody

1. If more than one PC is to be seized, consideration must be given to the appointing of an Evidence Custodian who can hold all seized evidence in a secure area prior to being removed for transportation to the Forensic Laboratory.
2. If a single item is to be seized, then the Forensic Analyst can be his/her own Evidence Custodian and hand-carry the evidence back to the Forensic Laboratory where it will be signed into the Secure Property Store.
3. The "Chain of Custody" refers to a written account of individuals who had sole physical custody of a piece of evidence from the time it was seized until the end of the case.
4. By becoming a "link" in the "Chain of Custody" and taking possession for a piece of evidence, an individual has the responsibility to secure it in a manner that can later stand legal scrutiny in case later claims are raised that the evidence was tampered with.

5. A piece of evidence is only as good as the Chain of Custody accompanying it. An item could be seized that has great evidentiary value, but unless the manner it was secured and accounted for can be articulated, it may be worthless in legal or administrative proceedings.
6. An individual who assumes physical possession of a piece of evidence is responsible for the security of it. Evidence should be secured in a manner where only the individual who has signed for it can gain access to it, though it is noted that this is not always possible.
7. The use of a property store in the Forensic Laboratory with a single Evidence Custodian able to access the exhibits is the preferred manner of handling exhibits.
8. Signing for evidence and becoming a "link" in the Chain of Custody is not to be taken lightly by any Forensic Laboratory employee, who must ensure that they can fulfill their duties in the Chain of Custody before committing to becoming the link.

8.6.5 Searches and Recovery

No matter where or why the Forensic Laboratory are involved, a search of the scene of the alleged incident is required, whether it is for the victim or the suspect. While each case requires separate and different handling, many of the common issues are below:

Once the First Response Team has arrived at the scene and unloaded their equipment, they will move to the scene of the incident.

The isolation of a computer system (workstation, standalone, or network server) or other forms of media that can contain digital evidence so evidence will not be lost is of utmost importance.

Some of these may have already been seized by the local Manager in the suspect's area and documented them already.

The manner in which the computer equipment and storage media is secured after a suspected computer incident is reported will be dependent on the facilities available and the computer system involved. In some instances, it may be impractical to seize the computer as in the case of a large mainframe or a networked mail server, but it may be more appropriate to seize the backup media or to make a backup at the time of the event, perform remote forensics or perform real-time forensics on-site.

A search may have been done by the local management. This initial search and seizure conducted within an information processing-related scene is much like any traditional crime scene. The area of primary importance should be the location and identification of any fragile or volatile evidence that could be altered or lost if not immediately collected.

In many instances, systems are backed up on a daily basis. If the individual suspected in a security incident attempts to delete files from the primary storage device (hard drive), these files could still remain on the backup storage media.

A formal handover of the scene from the local Manager who has maintained the security of the scene to the First Response Team Leader shall take place and this must be fully documented.

Photocopies of the actions undertaken and the notes that the local Manager made should be provided to the Case Officer—the originals should be retained by the local Manager in case a formal statement is needed—based on the notes.

Note

A search may have been done by the local management.

8.6.6 Photographing the Scene

The old adage of incident scene processing, "you cannot take too many pictures" is also true when processing a scene where computer evidence is involved. Photographing a scene should be the first step taken by the Forensic Team on arrival. This will accurately depict the condition of the scene prior to any evidence collection or disruption that will occur during processing (unless a local management search or seizure has been carried out).

The order photographs are taken should be carried out in a manner that will not corrupt the scene. The ideal situation is to first take several photographs that will establish the location of the scene (i.e., building, office number, etc.), followed by an entry photograph (what is seen as one enters the room), followed by a series of "360°" photographs.

"360°" photographs are simply overlapping photographs depicting the entire crime scene. The key to remember in crime scene photography is to go from the overall scene down to the smallest piece of evidence. This all should be completed prior to any evidence collection taking place or the scene being disturbed in any manner. At this point, there should be no attempt to search the contents of desks or any other containers within the scene (unless a local management search or seizure has been carried out). The initial set of photographs should depict exactly the condition of the scene as the Forensic Team found it.

If the target computer(s) is/are operational on arrival, photographs should be taken of the monitor screen depicting what is currently displayed.

In the event, a "screen saver" is being utilized, press the "down arrow" key to redisplay the open file or the password-protected login screen.

Other than touching that one key, DO NOT make any other keystrokes and DO NOT turn the computer off unless a self-destruct program is running.

Photographs should also be taken of the immediate work area involved in the incident to include information processing equipment, handwritten notes, diaries, digital media, and other information processing equipment (e.g., printers, external drives, etc.). Photographs should also be taken of the rear of the information processing equipment (where appropriate) to accurately display how the cables are connected. If this cannot be done *in situ*, then all cables must be labeled and the information processing equipment reconnected back at the Forensic Laboratory to be photographed.

Even if equipment is not to be seized and it is present at the incident scene, it should be photographed.

In the past, detailed photo logs were used by the Forensic Laboratory, but the advent of digital cameras and Exif metadata has obviated this need as the details of the photographer to be recorded in the seizure log is given in Appendix 7. The photographs are all added to the Client's virtual case file held in the ERMS from the series of pictures taken; the photograph's metadata can be extracted and added to the case file.

8.6.7 Sketching the Scene

An incident scene sketch should be prepared, which details the overall scene. This should include the locations of items within the incident area. Again, the rule of thumb for incident scene sketching is to go from the overall scene to the smallest piece of evidence. This may require several sketches to accurately depict the scene. An overall sketch could be completed, followed by a sketch of the (for example) top of a desk detailing where items of evidence are present, followed by a projection sketch of the rear of the information processing equipment detailing where different cables are plugged in.

Measurements showing the location of all evidence seized should be taken, and the measurements are always taken from at least two non-movable items, such as windows, doors, walls, etc.

In the event that the incident scene is information processing equipment within a large office area or in an office where more than one individual has access, consideration should be given to the preparation of a sketch detailing the location of the scene in relation to other offices or information processing equipment in the vicinity of the incident scene.

This should support the photographs taken or be instead of them if photographs are not possible.

Even if equipment is not to be seized and is present at the incident scene, it should be located on the sketches. This should include network access points.

Depending on the quality of the sketch, the Laboratory Manager may decide (or the First Response Team Leader may suggest) that a computer-aided diagram (CAD) be produced based on the sketch(es). The advantage with CAD-produced images is that they can be much clearer and understandable by the intended audience and also, depending on the CAD software, different perspectives can be produced from the initial plan.

In addition, the Client should be asked for any:

- cabling plans;
- floor plans;
- network diagrams.

that relate to the incident scene. It should be determined that these are not only up-to-date, but accurate.

8.6.8 Initial Interviews

It may be that the First Response Team wants answers from a suspect, if present. It may be that the First Response Team assists at the interview or supply questions for the interviewer to ask.

> **Note**
> The First Response Team should not undertake interviews on their own unless qualified to interview and in the presence of a witness.

1. If the suspect is present at the search and seizure time, the Incident Manager or the First Response Team Leader may consider asking some questions of the suspect, but these must comply with the relevant Human Resources or legislative guidelines for the jurisdiction.
2. At initial interviews, the suspect often has little time to concoct any alibis, etc., and often when asked questions they answer truthfully to questions like "what are the passwords for the account," etc. Typical questions could include:
   - are there any keys?—some computer cases have physical key locks;
   - What are the user IDs and passwords for the computer?
   - What e-mail addresses are in use and what are the user IDs and passwords for them?

This is not a complete list—circumstances will dictate.

8.6.9 Evidence Collection

As the Forensic Team complete their search of the incident area, there will be a number of items that may be regarded as evidence that need to be seized.

The scene should be searched in a circular motion with the concept of the computer being at the center of the circle.

Items of evidence, as located, should be photographed, identified, and documented within notes and then collected. While the Forensic Laboratory may use the circular (or spiral) approach to searching an incident scene, the other options are using the:

- "strip";
- "grid";
- "quadrant";
- "zone"

approaches. All of these are valid, and it is really up to the First Response Team Leader to define the optimum approach, based on the specifics of the scene. All searching must be methodically and diligently carried out following whichever search pattern is appropriate to the incident scene.

Evidence should be identified, recorded, seized, bagged, and tagged on-site with no attempts to determine contents or status. This may be different for some devices such as PDAs that need to maintain charge or systems that show evidence that is volatile and that the evidence will be lost if the device is powered off.

As items that need to be evaluated as evidence must be collected, care must be taken to note their position at the time of processing and to ensure they are not altered from their original state. Under no circumstances, should any investigative personnel tamper with any items that might be used as evidence.

This deals primarily with any information processing equipment or storage media (disks, tapes, etc.) that are identified during processing. They should be collected in the state that they are found in, with no attempts to determine contents or status—unless an on-site preview or processing is required.

When processing a scene where information processing equipment is suspected to have played a part in a security incident or criminal act, the natural instinct is to seize the relevant information processing equipment as the first item of evidence.

In reality, due to the time involved and the number of items involved in seizing any information processing equipment, this should be one of the last items removed from the scene.

Entries within the seizure log should contain a description of the item (to include model and serial number if the item is a piece of hardware), the evidence log number and the locations from where it was seized. The contents of the Forensic Laboratory seizure log for each item seized are given in Appendix 7.

8.6.10 Exhibit Numbering

All evidence collected should be marked as exhibits, so it can be easily identified at a later date. All exhibits and possible exhibits (i.e., anything removed from an incident scene in this case) must be properly seized, labeled, transported, and handled for evidence recovery purposes. The Forensic Laboratory may use something like the following naming convention for all evidence seized or created during forensic evidence processing:

$$aaa/ddmmyyyy/nnnn$$

where:

- aaa are the initials of the Forensic Laboratory First Response Team member (or other person) seizing the equipment;
- dd/mm/yyyy is the date of the seizure;
- nnnn is the sequential number of the exhibits seized by aaa—starting with 001 and going to nnnn.

The labels must be affixed as appropriate to all equipment that is being seized, typically on dedicated evidence bags.

Note 1

There may be other types of evidence obtainable from seized or examined evidence that can corroborate digital forensic evidence recovered (e.g., fingerprints, DNA, etc.).

Note 2

All devices on a network will have network identification information to allow them to be addressed on the network.

Note 3

All information processing equipment, and many component parts (e.g., "cards" inserted into the information processing devices) have serial numbers that can often be traced from the location that they were seized back to the manufacturer and possibly all intervening stages in the purchasing cycle.

Note 4

All software and manuals relating to any equipment seized should also be seized.

8.6.11 What to Take?

In a word, everything! Every case is different and needs to be viewed on its merits. It may well be that the items seized are limited by a Search Warrant of other issues (e.g., business imperatives for maintaining operations). In an ideal world, everything that may relate to the incident should be seized and examined, as there are usually no second chances for seizure.

Note

While the Forensic Laboratory is competent in recovery and processing of digital forensic evidence, they are not experts in all forensic fields. There may well be other latent evidence present at the scene that should be preserved. The First Response Team must ensure that they do not compromise non-digital evidence and this may involve other experts or Law Enforcement.

Each different item to be seized is handled differently and guidance for this is given below:

8.6.11.1 Mainframes, Minis, and Servers

8.6.11.1.1 Description

The main processing device used on a system by multiple users, typically through a network.

8.6.11.1.2 Primary Use

Mainframes, minis, and servers are typically used for processing data and providing file and print services. These manage all file management processes, e-mail use, and I/O services for all of the users on the system to ensure that there are no conflicts and to ensure that all users have appropriate access to these services. The file and print service engine is the main workhorse of all networks.

Any computer, including a laptop, can be configured as a server.

8.6.11.1.3 Potential Evidence Obtainable

1. There are a number of areas on a computer where evidence may be found, some of these are given in Appendix 8.
2. Different types of evidence will be needed for different case types, and some of these are given in Appendix 9.

8.6.11.1.4 Possible Issues with the Evidence

1. Because of their size, it is unlikely that a mainframe or minicomputer can be seized.
2. Additionally, all of these devices are usually critical to operations and business reasons may preclude them from being removed for investigative purposes.
3. There are few forensic tools that are capable of interrogating mainframes and mini computers.
4. In some cases, the physical amount of data that has to be processed will preclude in-depth investigation.

8.6.11.1.5 Process of Seizing the Evidence

Note

The most likely of these devices that may be seized is the server. This may hold multiple terabytes or even petabytes of data, and if it is to be imaged, then a suitably sized system to contain this volume of data must be available. If a server is to be seized, the following steps should be undertaken:

- photograph the server in place, including all components;
- using adhesive labels, label each of the server's connections (ports);
- using adhesive labels, label each of the cables connected to the server with numbers or letters corresponding to the server connection they were attached to;
- seal the power plug connector and "power on" switch on the device with tape so that inadvertent powering up does not happen and a conscious decision to remove the "do not power up" label has to be made;
- seal any disk drives or removable media bays with tape to ensure that nothing can fall out or be inserted without removing the tape. If there is any removable media in the drives, it should be recorded on the seizure form, as given in Appendix 7;
- depending if the device is powered on or off and is to be seized or not follow the "On/Off Rules" given in Appendix 10;
- assuming it is to be seized and the "On/Off Rules" have been followed, disconnect all the cables from the server;
- mark as evidence and place items in evidence bags and seal. Record the details of the evidence bag and on the front of the evidence bag record the details of the contents;
- pack in original packaging, if possible. If not possible, ensure that the server is protected from accidental damage during transit;
- update seizure records.

8.6.11.2 Desktop Computers

8.6.11.2.1 Description

A device for processing data for a user.

8.6.11.2.2 Primary Use

These are primary devices for a user to interact with a network or other devices on the network. In other cases, they may be stand-alone devices just connected to local peripherals (e.g., scanner, printer, etc.).

8.6.11.2.3 Potential Evidence Obtainable

1. There are a number of areas on a computer where evidence may be found, and some of these are given in Appendix 8.
2. Different types of evidence will be needed for different case types, and some of these are given in Appendix 9.

8.6.11.2.4 Possible Issues with the Evidence

1. Some desktops may be critical to operations and business reasons may preclude them from being removed for investigative purposes.
2. In some cases, the amount of data that has to be processed will preclude an on-site investigation.
3. There are a number of different operating systems that may be encountered, and this may also cause problems for on-site investigation, in cases where there are no appropriate tools in the Forensic Laboratory First Response Kit.
4. Some hardware (e.g., Apple equipment) may need to have all equipment related to the desktop computer seized to ensure proper operation (e.g., integral screens, keyboards, and mice). Therefore, it is essential that the hardware is understood and that all relevant hardware for proper in-depth investigation.

8.6.11.2.5 Process of Seizing the Evidence

- Photograph the computer in place, including all components;
- using adhesive labels, label each of the computer connections (ports);
- using adhesive labels, label each of the cables connected to the computer with numbers or letters corresponding to the computer connection they were attached to;
- disconnect all the cables from the computer;
- seal the power plug connector and "power on" switch on the device with tape so that inadvertent powering up does not happen and a conscious decision to remove the "do not power up" label has to be made;
- seal any disk drives or removable media bays with tape to ensure that nothing can fall out or be inserted without removing the tape. If there is any removable media in the drives, it should be recorded on the seizure form, as given in Appendix 7;
- mark as evidence and place in evidence bag and seal. Record the details of the evidence bag and on the front of the evidence bag record the details of the contents;
- pack in original packaging, if possible. If not possible, ensure that the computer is protected from accidental damage during transit;
- update seizure records.

8.6.11.3 Laptop Computers and Tablet Computers

8.6.11.3.1 Description

A device for processing data for a user, really a mobile desktop computer.

8.6.11.3.2 Primary Use

The same as a desktop, but that can be transported and used outside the office.

8.6.11.3.3 Potential Evidence Obtainable

The same as a desktop.

8.6.11.3.4 Possible Issues with the Evidence

1. Similar issues relate to laptops as to desktops.
2. However, the use of hibernation files and ensuring that the battery is disconnected to ensure that there is not accidental power up occurring.

> **Note**
>
> Some laptops may be powered up by opening the lid. Beware of laptops in hibernation mode and deal with them accordingly.

8.6.11.3.5 Process of Seizing the Evidence

- photograph the computer in place, including all components;
- using adhesive labels, label each of the computer connections (ports);
- using adhesive labels, label each of the cables connected to the computer with numbers or letters corresponding to the computer connection they were attached to;
- disconnect all the cables from the computer;
- seal the power plug connector and "power on" switch on the device with tape so that inadvertent powering up does not happen and a conscious decision to remove the "do not power up" label has to be made;
- seal any disk drives or removable media bays with tape to ensure that nothing can fall out or be inserted without removing the tape. If there is any removable media in the drives, it should be recorded on the seizure form, as given in Appendix 7;
- remove the battery and store with the laptop and any charger recovered;
- mark as evidence and place in evidence bag and seal. Record the details of the evidence bag and on the front of the evidence bag record the details of the contents;
- pack in original packaging, if possible. If not possible, ensure that the computer is protected from accidental damage during transit;
- update seizure records.

8.6.11.4 Monitors

8.6.11.4.1 Description

The typical interface between the user and a computer displays the output from an information processing system. There are a variety of different types of monitor and some of them are essential to have present for an information processing system to work properly as they are integral to the system.

8.6.11.4.2 Primary Use

The main interface between an information processing device and the user.

8.6.11.4.3 Potential Evidence Obtainable

If the computer is turned on, the monitor will show what is happening at the time on a computer. This may show the output from a running system or may require a new process to be run to show what is happening on the information processing device to which it is connected. Information from the screen can be:

- "screen shotted";
- photographed;
- documented.

To show what was on-screen at the time. Ideally, a screen shot is best with contemporaneous notes.

8.6.11.4.4 Possible Issues with the Evidence

If the whole system is not seized, then it may not work properly as some peripherals are essential for the operation of the information processing system.

8.6.11.4.5 Process of Seizing the Evidence

- if the computer is switched on and operational, photograph the screen (avoid using videotape to record data present on the monitor as a video will usually be of poor quality due to the refresh rate of the monitor), also beware of flash photography as this can affect the image quality;
- disconnect the power source;
- mark the connection from the monitor to the computer for facilitating reconnection;
- mark as evidence and place in evidence bag and seal. Record the details of the evidence bag and on the front of the evidence bag record the details of the contents;
- pack in original packaging, if possible. If not possible, ensure that the monitor is protected from accidental damage during transit;
- update seizure records;
- seize other connected peripherals as defined in this section.

8.6.11.5 Keyboards

8.6.11.5.1 Description

The typical input device for most desktop and laptop computers. Keyboards can be separate devices or integral to the information processing device (e.g., a laptop).

8.6.11.5.2 Primary Use

The main user input device for communications between an information processing device and the user. However, as time goes by, other devices are being used for providing input from the user.

8.6.11.5.3 Potential Evidence Obtainable

There is usually little forensic evidence that can be recovered from a keyboard itself, but it can be used to corroborate other evidence identified (e.g., an integral fingerprint scanner can provide evidence of biometric authentication to use an information processing device).

In some cases, a dedicated keyboard may be required to actually operate the information processing device, hence the requirement to seize a complete information processing system if at all possible.

8.6.11.5.4 Possible Issues with the Evidence

There are few, if any, issues with evidence obtainable from a keyboard.

8.6.11.5.5 Process of Seizing the Evidence

> **Note**
>
> In many cases, keyboards do not need to be seized as they are a standard issue item, however, with specialized keyboards they should be seized (e.g., Apple or those with specialized functionality or non-standard keys). In case of doubt, seize anyway.

- if the keyboard has removable cables, attach hand-numbered adhesive labels to the cables and their associated connecting points;
- if any other devices are attached to the keyboard or if the keyboard is attached to another device, label all connecting points and cables;
- mark as evidence and place in evidence bag and seal. Record the details of the evidence bag and on the front of the evidence bag record the details of the contents;
- pack in original packaging, if possible. If not possible, ensure that the keyboard is protected from accidental damage during transit;
- update seizure records.

8.6.11.6 *Pointing Devices (Mouse, Light pen, etc.)*

8.6.11.6.1 Description

There are a variety of other types of input devices that a user can use to provide input to an information processing device. While the standard input devices are still a keyboard and mouse, other input devices can be used. These can be used by "normal users," some are used in dedicated and specialized information processing devices.

The main user input device for communications between an information processing device and the user. However, as time goes by, other devices are used for providing input from the user.

8.6.11.6.2 Potential Evidence Obtainable

There is usually little forensic evidence that can be recovered from a pointing device itself.

In some cases, a dedicated pointing device may be required to actually operate the information processing device, hence the requirement to seize a complete information processing system if at all possible.

8.6.11.6.3 Possible Issues with the Evidence

There are few, if any, issues with evidence obtainable from a pointing device.

8.6.11.6.4 Process of Seizing the Evidence

- if the pointing device has removable cables, attach hand-numbered adhesive labels to the cables and their associated connecting points;
- mark as evidence and place in evidence bag and seal. Record the details of the evidence bag and on the front of the evidence bag record the details of the contents;
- pack in original packaging, if possible. If not possible, ensure that the pointing device is protected from accidental damage during transit;
- update seizure records.

8.6.11.7 *External Drives*

8.6.11.7.1 Description

An external drive is usually a sealed container holding one or more hard disks that are used to boost storage, either for a desktop computer, a laptop, or a server. At the time of writing, there are drives available that can contain many Terabytes of data.

Additionally, there are a number of technologies that provide external disk storage. These include:

- *NAS* (Network Attached Storage) systems;
- *RAID* (Redundant Array of Inexpensive Disks) systems—there are a variety of different levels of RAID systems that may be encountered in any seizure or investigation process;
- *JBOD* (Just a Bunch of Disks) systems.

8.6.11.7.2 Primary Use

The only use of external drives is for storage of information in any form.

8.6.11.7.3 Potential Evidence Obtainable

Any evidence may be recovered from these devices.

8.6.11.7.4 Possible Issues with the Evidence

1. Some external drive systems may be critical to operations and business reasons, and this may preclude them from being removed for investigative purposes.
2. In some cases, the physical amount of data that has to be processed will preclude an on-site investigation.
3. There are a number of different operating systems that may be encountered, and this may also cause problems for an on-site investigation, in case there are no appropriate tools in the Forensic Laboratory First Response Kit.

8.6.11.7.5 Process of Seizing the Evidence

> **Note**
>
> A variety of different external drives may be encountered. These can include USB drives, hard disk drives of any size or type, CD and DVD drives, removable drives, as well as tape drives or any type or others may all be encountered. Each drive (except hard disk or solid-state drives) will have media associated with it. This may be in the drive, close to it, or stored in some remote location. Media for all such devices should be seized along with any relevant software and manuals relating to their operation.

- if the external drive has removable cables, attach hand-numbered adhesive labels to the cables and their associated connecting points;
- seal the power plug connector on the device with tape so that inadvertent powering up does not happen and a conscious decision to remove the "do not power up" label has to be made;
- there are a number of different types of external drives. If the external drive uses removable media, the media should be removed (if possible) prior to packaging the drive for shipping;
- mark as evidence and place in evidence bag and seal. Record the details of the evidence bag and on the front of the evidence bag record the details of the contents;
- any media that was removed from the device should be marked as evidence, placed in a static-free container, and notes generated indicating that it was removed from the external drive;

- pack in original packaging, if possible. If not possible, ensure that the external drive is protected from accidental damage during transit;
- update seizure records.

8.6.11.8 Printers

8.6.11.8.1 Description

A method for printing hard copy images. Types can include:

- inkjet;
- laser;
- thermal;
- impact.

All are connected to a computer system either through a cable or a wireless connection, typically:

- serial cables;
- parallel cables;
- USB connectors;
- Firewire connectors;
- Infra-red ports or wireless connections.

8.6.11.8.2 Primary Use

The primary use of a printer is to print documents of any type (text, images, etc.) from a computer system to hard copy media, which typically could be:

- paper;
- transparencies.

8.6.11.8.3 Potential Evidence Obtainable

1. In some cases, it may be possible to identify the specific printer that produced a hard copy document (e.g., by marks on the output). Therefore, printers may need to be seized.
2. There can often be printer output of note, in the printer output tray, beside it or in a bin close by—all of these areas should be searched.
3. Some printers contain a memory buffer, allowing them to receive and store multiple page documents while they are spooling their print prior to actually printing it. Often printer artifacts can be found on a hard disk on the computer that was linked to the computer.
4. Some printers may also contain a hard drive.
5. Printers may maintain usage logs, time and date information, and, if attached to a network, they may store network identity information.
6. Some printers may display unique characteristics that may allow for positive identification of a specific printer (e.g., printing a serial number or other unique watermarking device as well as intrinsic or extrinsic signatures that can uniquely identify a printer).
7. Some printers may use ribbons from which it is possible to recover details of documents printed.
8. In more modern printers, it is often a requirement that the user logs into the printer to receive their printout, and so this is recorded in the printer log.

8.6.11.8.4 Possible Issues with the Evidence

It may not be possible to determine who has printed out hard copy to a specific printer, especially if it is a network printer.

In some cases, it is possible to identify when a printer was installed on a computer.

8.6.11.8.5 Process of Seizing the Evidence

- allow the printer to finish printing, you never know what it will reveal;
- if the printer has removable cables, attach hand-numbered adhesive labels to the cables and their associated connecting points;
- seal the power plug connector and "power on" switch on the device with tape so that inadvertent powering up does not happen and a conscious decision to remove the "do not power up" label has to be made;
- mark as evidence and place in evidence bag and seal. Record the details of the evidence bag and on the front of the evidence bag record the details of the contents;
- pack in original packaging, if possible. If not possible, ensure that the printer is protected from accidental damage during transit;
- update seizure records.

8.6.11.9 Scanners

8.6.11.9.1 Description

An optical device that can take a physical image and convert it into a digital form. This may comprise copies of hard copy documents or biometric images used for access control purposes.

8.6.11.9.2 Primary Use

Scanners provide a method of:

1. Converting hard copy (e.g., documents) into a digital form that can be made into a searchable database or provide space saving for documents being scanned and then disposed of after scanning verification. Images created by a scanner can also be manipulated by a specialized software and transmitted to other users over an internal network or over the Internet.
2. Providing a trial template for checking against a reference template in biometric terms to authenticate a person using the service that the biometric authorization provides access to.

8.6.11.9.3 Potential Evidence Obtainable

1. Often there are hard copy documents that are either on the scanner or in its vicinity, that have either been scanned or are waiting to be scanned into the computer.

In addition, there are the scanned images themselves. These could be any type of document.

2. Scanners can be used in a variety of crimes, including but not limited to:
   - paedophilia;
   - identity theft;
   - counterfeiting;
   - forgery;
   - IPR theft.
3. The biometric scanner provides identification and authentication information relating to the person (typically) using the scanner, the level of access they have and when they presented these credentials, and gained access to the services.

In addition to the above, evidence can be gained from the device itself, be it from fingerprints or DNA or from its dates of installation, and possibly installer, on a computer system.

Depending on the scanner, it may be possible to link an image to a specific scanner where there are imperfections or scratches on the glass or in the scanning device itself. In addition to this, intrinsic and extrinsic signatures can uniquely identify a scanner.

In some cases, it is possible to identify when a scanner was installed on a computer.

8.6.11.9.4 Possible Issues with the Evidence

Biometric scanners may be hard wired into the infrastructure and it may not be possible to seize them, especially in building access control systems. However, it should be possible to produce a variety of access control reports from their records.

8.6.11.9.5 Process of Seizing the Evidence

- if the scanner is removable and has removable cables, attach hand-numbered adhesive labels to the cables and their associated connecting points. This can include scanners used for creating soft copy images from hard copy ones as well as authentication scanners;
- seal the power plug connector and "power on" switch on the device with tape so that inadvertent powering up does not happen and a conscious decision to remove the "do not power up" label has to be made;
- some scanners are extremely fragile and care must be exercised when handling them. If the owner's manual for the scanner is available, determine the proper way to prepare the scanner for shipping. Mark as evidence and place in evidence bag and seal, Record the details of the evidence bag and on the front of the evidence bag record the details of the contents;
- pack in original packaging, if possible. If not possible, ensure that the scanner is protected from accidental damage during transit;
- update seizure records.

8.6.11.10 Fax Machines

8.6.11.10.1 Description

A device that can send an electronic copy of a document from one phone number to any other phone number in the world that has a corresponding fax machine to receive the transmission. The fax machine may be stand-alone device or be a part of a computer.

8.6.11.10.2 Primary Use

Transmitting electronic images of hard copy documents from one location to another.

8.6.11.10.3 Potential Evidence Obtainable

1. Often, there are hard copy documents that are either on the fax scanner or in its vicinity, that have been sent to a recipient;
2. Phone numbers that have been stored in the fax machine indicating possible recipients of faxes;
3. The send/receive fax log indicating details of the source and destination of faxes linked to the fax machine. Additionally, phone records can be sought to collaborate the fax log;
4. Most fax machines have a facility for storing received faxes prior to them being printed, as well as storage prior to transmission. Some fax machines can allow preprogramming of printing or transmitting of faxes. In some fax machines, many hundreds of pages can be stored and forensically recovered;
5. Usually, fax machines have a speed dial facility that is used to store frequently used numbers for fax destinations;
6. Typically, a fax will have a header set indicating ownership (or origin of the fax) details. This can contain owner name, address, contact details, or any other details the owner wishes to enter;
7. In some cases, especially if a computer is used, images of the faxes sent or received can be stored in the fax system itself;
8. In more modern fax machines, it is often a requirement that the user logs into the fax machine to send or receive a fax, and so this is recorded in the fax log.

In addition to the above, evidence can be gained from the device itself, be it from fingerprints or DNA or from its dates of installation, and possibly installer, on a computer system.

8.6.11.10.4 Possible Issues with the Evidence

1. Often, with fax machines in an open office, there is no accountability for action with "open" faxes and so it may not be possible to identify the sender or intended recipient of a specific fax.

2. Fax machines usually have their own clocks and this may not be correct, so the variation between the "real" time and the time on the fax machine must be calculated and be factored into any investigations.
3. It is not possible to determine whether the date and time of the clock has been changed (and possibly changed back) and by whom.
4. Powering off a switched-on fax may lose any volatile data present.

8.6.11.10.5 Process of Seizing the Evidence

- if the fax is a stand-alone fax machine and has removable cables, attach hand-numbered adhesive labels to the cables and their associated connecting points;
- seal the power plug connector and "power on" switch on the device with tape so that inadvertent powering up does not happen and a conscious decision to remove the "do not power up" label has to be made;
- if the fax is integral to a computer, handle as per computers above;
- record the phone number that the fax machine is connected to;
- if the owner's manual for the scanner is available, determine the proper way to prepare the scanner for shipping. Mark as evidence and place in evidence bag and seal, if possible, Record the details of the evidence bag and on the front of the evidence bag record the details of the contents;
- pack in original packaging, if possible. If not possible, ensure that the fax is protected from accidental damage during transit;
- update seizure records.

8.6.11.11 Copiers

8.6.11.11.1 Description

A copier is usually a device that is used to copy paper documents and produce one or more hard copies of the original document. While the primary output of a copier is paper, but a variety of hard copy media can be used.

8.6.11.11.2 Primary Use

Their primary use is making hard copies of original documents.

8.6.11.11.3 Potential Evidence Obtainable

1. Often, there are hard copy documents that are either on the copier or in any waste bins located close by.
2. In more modern copiers, it is often a requirement that the user logs into the copier to make copies, and so this information is recorded in the copier log.
3. In some cases, especially if a hard disk is used in the copier, images of copies made may be stored and so be recoverable.

8.6.11.11.4 Possible Issues with the Evidence

1. With copiers in an open office and no logging facility, it may not be possible to determine who has made a specific copy or when it was made.
2. On account of their criticality of business operations, it may not be possible to seize a copier.

8.6.11.11.5 Process of Seizing the Evidence

- if the copier is a stand-alone device and has removable cables, attach hand-numbered adhesive labels to the cables and their associated connecting points;
- seal the power plug connector and "power on" switch on the device with tape so that inadvertent powering up does not happen and a conscious decision to remove the "do not power up" label has to be made;
- if the owner's manual for the copier is available, determine the proper way to prepare the copier for shipping. Mark as evidence and place in evidence bag and seal, if possible, Record the details of the evidence bag and on the front of the evidence bag record the details of the contents;
- pack in original packaging, if possible. If not possible, ensure that the copier is protected from accidental damage during transit;
- update seizure records.

8.6.11.12 Multifunction Devices

8.6.11.12.1 Description

Multifunction devices are typically printers, scanners, and copiers all combined into one device.

8.6.11.12.2 Primary Use

Their primary use is a combination of the uses of the three individual devices and often used to save space or reduce costs.

8.6.11.12.3 Potential Evidence Obtainable

The evidence available from a multifunction device is the same as the evidence from each of the individual devices.

8.6.11.12.4 Possible Issues with the Evidence

The issues with evidence for a multifunction device will be the same as the combined issues with the individual devices.

8.6.11.12.5 Process of Seizing the Evidence

The seizure process for a multifunction device is the same as the process for all of the individual devices, where appropriate.

8.6.11.13 Access Control Devices

8.6.11.13.1 Description

There are a number of devices that can be used in the access control process, in addition to biometric scanners. These include, but are not limited to:

- smart cards;
- dongles.

8.6.11.13.2 Primary Use

Smart cards are small handheld devices that contain a microprocessor that can contain an encryption key or authentication information (password), digital certificate, or other information used for authentication purposes. Smart cards also can be used for storing a monetary value (e.g., a digital wallet), or any other electronic files. They often resemble a credit card.

A dongle is a small device that plugs into a computer port that contains types of information similar to information on a smart card that is used for authorizing access to specific items of hardware or software.

8.6.11.13.3 Potential Evidence Obtainable

1. Where a smart card is used for storing access credentials, these can be recoverable from the card. Likewise, any encryption keys can be recovered to allow access to any documents that have been encrypted using the keys.
2. Where a smart card is used for authentication and access management, it will give details of the access rights relating to the user that the card is assigned to. Some cards may also store access log details.
3. Where a smart card is used only for storage, the files stored on it will be available for investigation,
4. Where a dongle has been used, it may show what the user has been able to access and allow the Forensic Analysts to have access to the same resources as the user who has been assigned the dongle.
5. Often, there will be a smart card reader or device for writing data to it, with connecting cables, in the vicinity of any smart cards found. Additionally, there may be software, manuals, and other associated materials related to a smart card. These shall also be seized.

8.6.11.13.4 Possible Issues with the Evidence

1. Smart cards and dongles are small devices and may not always be available at the information processing device. Typically, they are retained by the user and they may be overlooked in the seizure process if they are not immediately identified.
2. Data held on a smart card or dongle may be encrypted and must be decrypted before use.

8.6.11.13.5 Process of Seizing the Evidence

- a smart card or dongle must be identified, and its use and contents are determined. The user should be asked, at the time of seizure for any relevant passwords and what the device is used for. If this is not done at the time of seizure, the opportunity of determining these details may be lost forever. All details should be documented and enclosed in the evidence bag with the smart card or dongle;
- take the smart card or dongle and mark as evidence and place in evidence bag and seal, if possible, Record the details of the evidence bag and on the front of the evidence bag record the details of the contents;
- pack in original packaging, if possible. If not possible, ensure that the smart card or dongle is protected from accidental damage during transit;
- update seizure records.

8.6.11.14 Photographic Recording Devices

8.6.11.14.1 Description

There are two main types of photographic recording devices that will be encountered in everyday seizure:

- still image capture devices (e.g., cameras or mobile devices);
- moving image capture devices (e.g., videos or still cameras or other devices with the ability to capture moving images).

The difference between the two types of device is blurring with increased functionality and storage space. Additionally, there are devices other than cameras that can capture both still and moving images, and the differentiation between device types is also blurring.

In addition to the standard still or video cameras, there are a number of specialized image recording devices that may be encountered. These include, but are not limited to:

- web cameras, capturing images to an image processing device;
- closed-circuit TV cameras, capturing images to an image processing device;
- video conferencing systems, capturing images to an image processing device;
- other specialized image-capturing devices—which will vary according to a range of different requirements.

8.6.11.14.2 Primary Use

The primary use of a camera or video recorder is the capture of still or video images. Whether the device is a digital one or the one that uses the older type of traditional film or tape is irrelevant for seizure purposes, but will be significant in the investigation process.

Once captured, an image can be stored, modified, or transmitted to others.

8.6.11.14.3 Potential Evidence Obtainable

Depending on the type of image capturing device to be seized, there may be a range of evidence available, and this will depend on the device and circumstance. This will include, but not be limited to the following:

1. In the case of traditional film and storage cartridges from still or video cameras, the film is in a cartridge and may be available. However, it may need to be developed and printed (or converted to digital images), for further processing. The Chain of Custody and maintaining the integrity of the evidence in these cases is essential.
2. From any type of image recording equipment, the actual image(s) themselves should be recovered. Where captured, sound may also be present.
3. With images recorded by a digital process, there is usually metadata associated with them. However, this will depend on the operator having set the correct parameters. Some of the possible metadata associated with images is given in Appendix 11.

8.6.11.14.4 Possible Issues with the Evidence

1. With traditional image recording devices that use physical film, it may not be possible to determine the date and time that an image was created or any of the other metadata that may be recoverable from a digital image recording device.
2. Where a digital recording device is seized, the metadata to be input to the device may be wrong or never have been entered. This may seriously impact the credibility of the evidence produced from such devices.
3. Digital devices, after being stored for a period of time, may lose their battery charge. In cases such as this, it may not be possible to determine the time difference between "local" time at the point of seizure and the time recorded in the device.
4. A digital device can have its clock reset during the sequence of images stored on it thus possibly "confusing the evidence trail." It is essential that all images recovered are "time lined" to identify any such anomalies.

8.6.11.14.5 Process of Seizing the Evidence

- few, if any, standard image recording devices have password-protected access to them; however, the user should be asked, at the time of seizure for any relevant passwords and what the device is used for. If this is not done at the time of seizure, the opportunity of determining these details may be lost forever. All details should be documented and enclosed in the evidence bag with the smart card or dongle;
- take the image recording device and mark as evidence and place in an evidence bag and seal, if possible. Record the details of the evidence bag and on the front of the evidence bag record the details of the contents;
- pack in original packaging, if possible. If not possible, ensure that the image recording device is protected from accidental damage during transit;
- update seizure records.

8.6.11.15 Closed-Circuit Television

8.6.11.15.1 Description

Closed-Circuit Television (CCTV) is often in place in a Client location that is the incident scene. The CCTV system should record all activity carried out in the area(s) that the CCTV system covers.

8.6.11.15.2 Primary Use

The primary use of a CCTV system is the recording of actions taken that are covered by the CCTV camera.

Once captured, the CCTV image can be an image that can be stored and made available to those investigating an incident.

8.6.11.15.3 Potential Evidence Obtainable

The evident obtained from a CCTV system will cover all actions taken where the CCTV camera(s) is pointing.

8.6.11.15.4 Possible Issues with the Evidence

1. The time and date of the CCTV cameras may be incorrectly set.
2. The CCTV camera may not include evidence required and may include evidence that is neither required nor helpful for the case.

8.6.11.15.5 Process of Seizing the Evidence

Different requirements will be present in different jurisdictions, and these must be met; however, the following guidelines may be used:

- all details of the CCTV system (including all cameras) shall be recorded;
- photographs of their location shall be taken and their location recorded on the sketch of the incident scene;
- record the system settings as are current on the system, including differences in time and date settings;
- determine the cameras for which images are required and the time period. Then request them;

- preferably copy the CCTV images to write only media (e.g., CD/DVD) for later analysis or seize the original equipment with all of the backups (though this is usually impossible);
- the copy made should be at the same resolution as the original, rather than applying compression algorithms to it;
- if a proprietary format is used, a copy of the software needed to view it should be acquired;
- check the image to see that it is a match for the original, though this should be carried out on some equipment other than the original recording equipment;
- ensure that the CCTV equipment is working properly after the seizure;
- take the image and mark as evidence and place in an evidence bag and seal, if possible. Record the details of the evidence bag and on the front of the evidence bag record the details of the contents;
- pack in original packaging, if possible. If not possible, ensure that the image is protected from accidental damage during transit;
- update seizure records.

8.6.11.16 Removable Media

8.6.11.16.1 Description

Removable media is a term used to describe any media that is easily and habitually removed from an information processing device that stores information in any form. Typical forms of information that can be stored on removable media are:

- computer programs;
- text files;
- digital images;
- multimedia files;
- spreadsheets;
- presentations;
- databases;
- output from specific programs.

Typical media types used for removable storage include, but are not limited to:

- floppy disks;
- high-capacity removable drives (e.g., Jazz and Zip drives);
- CDs and DVDs;
- tape and cartridge storage;
- USB devices (e.g., thumb drives or memory sticks).

The unique thing about removable media is that the information written to the removable media is not "lost" or deleted when the power to them is removed.

Additionally, it is usually possible to recover deleted information from removable media after it has been "deleted."

As technology changes, there will be newer and different types of removable media that can hold information in different formats.

8.6.11.16.2 Primary Use

The primary use of removable media is to store data. Typically, this is for backup or information exchange purposes.

8.6.11.16.3 Potential Evidence Obtainable

The types of evidence that can be recovered from removable media will be similar to, if not the same as, that which can be recovered from any type of information processing device, as it is almost always created by an information processing device.

8.6.11.16.4 Possible Issues with the Evidence

1. Removable media are usually small devices and may not always be available in the information processing device or in their vicinity. Typically, they are retained by the user or are stored off-site, and they may be overlooked in the seizure process if they are not immediately identified and recovered.
2. Data held on a removable device may be encrypted and must be decrypted before use.
3. There are a large number of possible removable devices, and it is essential that Forensic Analysts keep up-to-date with this fast changing area of information storage.
4. On account of the fact that removable devices are, by their very nature, removable, there can be issues in determining who has written information to a removable device and more importantly (in some cases) who has accessed or copied that information.

8.6.11.16.5 Process of Seizing the Evidence

Note 1

Removable media require special attention during the evidence collection phase. The media can be found in a variety of locations at a incident scene or remote from it (e.g., remote or off-site backup storage). It is important to note the location and other pertinent information about the collection of removable media. If removable media are stored in the case, box, or other storage container, it is recommended that the media remain in the storage container when it is collected.

Note 2

Some removable media (e.g., diskettes and backup tapes) are covered with a fragile magnetic media. If they are packed loosely and allowed to strike each other repeatedly during transit, the media could be damaged. Ensure that they are packed in a suitable manner to reduce this possibility.

To protect this type of media, the following procedures must be undertaken:

- *5¼″ inch disks*—write protect 5¼″ disks by placing tape over the notch. Mark with initials, time, date on corners using a permanent marker or Dymo label;
- *3½″ disks*—write protect 3½″ disks by placing the write protect tab in the open position. Mark with initials, date on corners using a permanent marker or Dymo label;
- *reel-to-reel tape*—write protect reel-to-reel tapes by pulling the small plastic write enable ring off (located on back of tape around the hub). Write initials, time, and date on first 10–13 ft (leader) of tape using a permanent marker or Dymo label;
- *cassette tape*—write protect cassette tapes by removing the record tab. Mark with time, date, and initials on plastic surface of tape case using a permanent marker or Dymo label;
- *disk cartridges*—write protect disk cartridges (removable hard drives) by placing tape over notch. Mark with time, date, and initials with a permanent marker or Dymo label;
- *cartridge tapes*—write protect cartridge tapes by turning the dial until arrow is aligned with "safe" mark or white dot is facing out. Mark initials, time, and date on plastic surface or cartridge case using a permanent marker or Dymo label;
- *ribbon containers*—mark initials, time, and date on ribbon containers, do not mark on the ribbon itself, using a permanent marker or Dymo label. Remember, printer ribbons, like typewriter ribbons, may contain the last document typed;
- *USB drives*—mark initials, time and date on the case, using a permanent marker or Dymo label. Apply any write protection devices present on the media, if present;
- *other media*—secure according to the manufacturer's guidance and mark initials, time and date on plastic surface or cartridge case using a permanent marker or Dymo label.

Once marked, the media should be placed, where possible in an antistatic bag, and then placed in an evidence bag and sealed as normal.

- Pack in original packaging, if possible. If not possible, ensure that the removable media is protected from accidental damage during transit;
- update seizure records.

8.6.11.17 Network Management Devices

8.6.11.17.1 Description

While individual users can use dedicated devices for their own use, many First Response situations encountered by the Forensic Laboratory First Response Team will encounter networked systems, where a number of users will use shared devices.

These will have a number of network management devices that may need to be investigated as part of a First Response capability and this could include, but not be limited to, the following types of devices:

- Network Interface Cards (NICs);
- routers;
- bridges;
- hubs;
- switches;
- firewalls;
- wireless connection devices;
- hard wired cables.

8.6.11.17.2 Primary Use

The primary use of network management devices is to facilitate the sharing of resources and exchange of information across a network by connecting them.

8.6.11.17.3 Potential Evidence Obtainable

Note

The types of evidence that network devices can contain will depend on the actual device itself; however, some types of evidence that may be recovered include the following:

1. The device itself, and the functionality it provides.
2. The configuration tables, where appropriate.
3. The address of the device, this is typically a Media Access Control (MAC) address. The address may also be referred to as an Ethernet Hardware Address, hardware address, or physical address. Device may have more than one NIC and each one will have its own MAC.
4. A network node may have multiple NICs and will then have one unique MAC address per NIC.

8.6.11.17.4 Possible Issues with the Evidence

1. Data traveling across a network is volatile and is lost after transmission of if the power is lost.
2. Interpreting core dumps or other output from network devices required specialized tools for the specific device in a number of cases, or there may not be tools that can easily perform analysis of output from network devices.
3. Volatile information may not contain the evidence needed for the case.
4. Where volatile evidence is seized, especially where it is a covert investigation or where there are tight time constraints, the Forensic Laboratory First Response Team may not have the right tools for undertaking the evidence capture.

8.6.11.17.5 Process of Seizing the Evidence

> **Note**
> There are two different types of evidence seizures for network devices; these are for the volatile information as it is passing through the device and for "burned in" information.

- Volatile information will have to be seized in real time using appropriate tools. Typically, this will be written to forensically "clean media";
- devices where the evidence is obtained must be photographed and all of their device information (make, model, serial number, etc.) must be recorded;
- where the device is located on the network (both logically and physically) must be located. This may be recorded by the Forensic Analyst or using the Client's own network diagram(s);
- seal the power plug connector and "power on" switch on the device with tape so that inadvertent powering up does not happen and a conscious decision to remove the "do not power up" label has to be made;
- the media on which the evidence is located must be treated as an exhibit and be marked as evidence and placed in an evidence bag and sealed. Record the details of the evidence bag and on the front of the evidence bag record the details of the contents;
- ensure that the media is protected against any possible contamination by electric or magnetic fields;
- where a physical network device is to be seized, take the device and mark it as evidence, and place it in an evidence bag and seal, if possible. Record the details of the evidence bag and on the front of the evidence bag record the details of the contents;
- pack in original packaging, if possible. If not possible, ensure that the smart card or dongle is protected from accidental damage during transit;
- update seizure records.

8.6.11.18 Cabling

8.6.11.18.1 Description

Cables are typically copper, coaxial, or fiber optic cables of a variety of colors, sizes, thicknesses with differing connectors depending on the devices that they are connected to.

8.6.11.18.2 Primary Use

The primary use of cables is to connect two devices together; this may be for a stand-alone computer or may be a network.

8.6.11.18.3 Potential Evidence Obtainable

1. The evidence obtainable will be the cables themselves and the ability to reconnect devices whether on a stand-alone computer or a network, to investigate how the devices work and interact.

8.6.11.18.4 Possible Issues with the Evidence

1. Cables are inert devices that only transfer information between devices or, in the case of power cables, electricity to the device. Given that there are few possible evidential issues with cables.

8.6.11.18.5 Process of Seizing the Evidence

- where cables are seized as part of another exhibit, they will be seized as part of the device. This is the majority of cases;
- where cabling is seized on its own, record its location (photographs, diagrams and/or evidence logs), and its purpose;
- take the cable(s) and mark as evidence and place in evidence bag and seal, if possible. Record the details of the evidence bag and on the front of the evidence bag record the details of the contents;
- update seizure records.

8.6.11.19 Telephones

8.6.11.19.1 Description

Telephones come in four generic types, each with their own issues for evidential recovery, these are:

- cell (or mobile phones)—a wireless handset on its own that draws its power from its own integral battery that is charged when connected to a charging source (computer or electrical outlet);
- smart phones—typically, a smart phone is a cellular phone with the ability to run applications and have internet access;
- cordless—a handset that usually resides in a remote base station that draws its power from an internal battery that is permanently charging when the handset is located in its base station;
- landline—that is permanently connected to the telephone system and the power for the telephone is taken directly from the telephone system itself.

Telephones come in a variety of colors and shapes. Depending on the country, different phone connections are used for landline systems. A list of countries with different phone connections is given in Appendix 12.

8.6.11.19.2 Primary Use

The primary use of a telephone is to have multiway communication between two or more communicants. Communication can be over the following media:

- dedicated land lines;
- radio transmission;
- cellular transmission.

Transmissions may use a combination of the above.

> **Note**
> Some telephone have integral message taking capability (e.g., answer phone or voicemail).

8.6.11.19.3 Potential Evidence Obtainable

Depending on the telephone type, make and model, a range of evidence may be recoverable from any telephone seized. Possible recovered evidence may include:

- browser bookmarks;
- browser URLs (Uniform Resource Locator) visited;
- caller ID for incoming calls;
- chat logs;
- contact list;
- cookies and passwords for site access;
- databases;
- e-mail addresses for e-mails sent or received;
- e-mails sent and received;
- map locations;
- messages, if a voicemail service is used;
- numbers called or calling the phone;
- numbers stored for speed dial;
- phone book, giving names, addresses, and phone numbers;
- photographs and other images;
- SMS (Short Message Service) messages sent and received;
- social networking information (e.g., FaceBook, Twitter, MySpace, etc.);
- stored files in folders;
- task list;
- the calendar;
- the carrier the phone uses;
- the device number;
- the image on the start-up screen;
- the IMEI (International Mobile Station Equipment Identity)
- the make and mode of the phone;
- the phone's serial number;
- the SIM (Subscriber Identity Module);
- the software and version for installed applications;
- user dictionary of words added for spell checking purposes;
- user entered data, such as the user's name;
- voice mail;
- voicemail or other messages left on the phone;
- Web sites visited.

8.6.11.19.4 Possible Issues with the Evidence

- depending on the phone type, it is possible to remotely manipulate the phone, including deleting all information on it. Care must be taken to ensure that the remote access service cannot connect to the phone;
- as mobile phone batteries have a finite life, evidence may be lost if the batteries fail. This is why all chargers must also be seized to overcome the issue of loss of battery power;
- consideration should be given to charging the device on a regular basis or immediate investigation at the Forensic Laboratory;
- the use of Faraday Cages and other shielding device must be considered; however, phone jamming devices may be illegal within the jurisdiction;
- care must be taken if the phone is to be switched off as this may activate the password lockout feature;
- where a phone is password protected, unless the Forensic Laboratory First Response Team have the password, incorrect password entry may erase all of the information on the phone;
- in some cases, there may not be the appropriate tools in the First Responder kit, so seizure must be undertaken;
- while there are few issues with corporately owned phones, those that are privately owned may cause legal issues for search and seizure. Ideally, this issue should be resolved prior to attending the site.

8.6.11.19.5 Process of Seizing the Evidence

> **Note**
> There is usually little point in seizing land lines that are hard wired in an office and the impracticality of this usually precludes it. It is usual that the phones that are seized are cellular, or smart.

- PIN numbers should be sought if possible and recorded in the search documentation. It may be that these are written down on loose paper or often in the back of a diary;
- where a cellular or smart phone is seized, all associated manuals and charging equipment should be seized;
- in some cases, on-site imaging may need to be undertaken, especially if the phone has no charger, to ensure that the battery remains in operation. If on-site imaging

is undertaken, then the phone should be packed after imaging has been undertaken;
- pack in original packaging, if possible. If not possible, ensure that the phone is protected from accidental damage during transit;
- update seizure records.

8.6.11.20 Pagers

8.6.11.20.1 Description

A pager is a handheld, portable electronic device that can contain volatile evidence (telephone numbers, voice mail, e-mail messages). Early pagers only produced a sound, but more modern ones can send and receive messages and e-mail. Cell Phones, smart phones, and PDAs can all be used as paging devices.

8.6.11.20.2 Primary Use

The primary use of a pager is to send and receive electronic messages, which can be numeric (phone numbers, etc.) and alphanumeric (text, often including e-mail).

8.6.11.20.3 Potential Evidence Obtainable

- text messages;
- e-mail messages;
- voice messages;
- phone numbers.

8.6.11.20.4 Possible Issues with the Evidence

- as pagers are battery powered, volatile memory may be lost when the battery power is lost.

8.6.11.20.5 Process of Seizing the Evidence

- where a pager is seized, all associated manuals and charging equipment should be seized;
- pack in original packaging, if possible. If not possible, ensure that the phone is protected from accidental damage during transit;
- update seizure records.

8.6.11.21 PDAs

8.6.11.21.1 Description

A Personal Digital Assistant (PDA) is a small device that can include computing, telephone/fax, paging, networking, and other features. It is typically used as a personal organizer. A handheld computer approaches the full functionality of a laptop or desktop computer system.

Some PDAs do not contain disk drives, but may contain PC card slots that can hold a modem, hard drive, or other device. They usually include the ability to synchronize their data with other computer systems.

There are four rules for PDA seizure:

1. Keep the device powered;
2. Seize all cables and accessories (i.e., power charger and cradles);
3. Be aware that the data are constantly changing;
4. Keep current with PDA technology to understand them.

The most important for the First Responder is "PDA Rule 1," as when the switch off or lose power they can be password protected and this will kick in or there may be encryption set.

8.6.11.21.2 Primary Use

PDAs and other handheld devices are used as mobile computing devices with some or all of the functionality of a desktop or laptop computer, depending on the device.

8.6.11.21.3 Potential Evidence Obtainable

Typically, the evidence that can be recovered from a PDA is the same as that recoverable from a computer.

8.6.11.21.4 Possible Issues with the Evidence

- as PDAs are battery powered, volatile memory may be lost when the battery power is lost. Therefore, it is essential that all manuals, chargers, and cabling is seized.

8.6.11.21.5 Process of Seizing the Evidence

1. When seizing a PDA, ensure that the cradle and chargers are taken and that the PDA is kept charged until it is examined by a Forensic PDA expert—this may require charging, i.e., connecting it to the mains.
2. It may also be necessary to ensure that the PDA does not allow encryption to be activated, as it can happen in "doze mode" in Palm OS.
3. There is sometimes the need to ensure that there is permanent input to the screen or keyboard until the PDA has been acquired—this may take some time.
4. When seizing a PDA:
   - photograph the PDA and ancillary (connected) equipment;
   - photograph or sketch the connectors in the back of the computer and individually label them;
   - consideration may be given to switching off a PDA to save battery power, but this will lose data. This is a decision that must be made by the Incident Manager or the Laboratory Manager;
   - ensure that all power leads, transformers, the cradle, and any other ancillary parts of the PDA are seized;
   - follow each of the leads that was connected to the PDA and identify what it was connected to, label the "other end of the cable (now the cable should be labeled with the same number at both ends)";

- place the PDA in an evidence bag with the power plug left outside so that the PDA can be kept on charge. Seal the bag. Insert the exhibit number;
- pack in original packaging, if possible. If not possible, ensure that the phone is protected from accidental damage during transit;
- update seizure records.

Note 1

It is essential that the charge in the PDA is not lost or that the PDA enters encrypted mode or loses data as this could prejudice recovery of any evidence. The batteries must be regularly checked to ensure that there is no loss of evidence until the data on it have been acquired.

Note 2

As it is necessary to power up (if not already powered up) a PDA to perform any recovery, the Forensic Analyst will necessarily be in breach of the principle of not changing evidence. As this is the case, it is essential that a competent person carries out this task and a full audit trail is maintained.

8.6.11.22 Global Positioning Systems

8.6.11.22.1 Description

A Global Positioning System (GPS) is a device that allows a user to navigate between locations using radio signals to indicate current position and directions to the planned destination.

8.6.11.22.2 Primary Use

The primary use of a GPS is navigation between the current location and the planned destination.

8.6.11.22.3 Potential Evidence Obtainable

- favorite destinations;
- home location;
- previous journeys undertaken;
- previous routes;
- travel logs;
- way points.

8.6.11.22.4 Possible Issues with the Evidence

Note

Smart phones often have GPS capability.

- As GPS devices are battery powered, volatile memory may be lost when the battery power is lost. Therefore, it is essential that all manuals, chargers, and cabling are seized.

8.6.11.22.5 Process of Seizing the Evidence

- where a dedicated GPS device is seized, all associated manuals and charging equipment should be seized;
- seal the power plug connector and "power on" switch on the device with tape so that inadvertent powering up does not happen and a conscious decision to remove the "do not power up" label has to be made;
- pack in original packaging, if possible. If not possible, ensure that the GPS device is protected from accidental damage during transit;
- update seizure records.

8.6.11.23 Audio Devices

8.6.11.23.1 Description

Audio devices come in a variety of forms, by the three most common are:

- a *media player* is typically a device that can store and play audio files in a variety of different recording formats. Usually, this relates to music or video files, but can be any recorded audit file. Because this is digital storage, other types of files and programs may be stored on these devices.
- a *dictating machine* is used to store a message for later transcription to a document or as a memo. Typically, it is a portable device and used by an individual user.
- an *answering machine* is usually in a telephone and is dedicated to taking messages specifically for the phone to which it is attached.

Note 1

There are a number of different devices that have the ability to record or play audio files.

Note 2

Older audio devices used physical media to record data, typically reel-to-reel tape, cassettes, or cartridges.

8.6.11.23.2 Primary Use

Recording devices are used for recording and/or playing audio and video files. They can be dedicated or general purpose devices.

8.6.11.23.3 Potential Evidence Obtainable

- the contents of the audio file or the media containing the recording;
- time and date of the recording;
- with files created by a computer, a variety of metadata can be recovered;
- answering machines can also store call subscriber information, as well as caller information.

8.6.11.23.4 Possible Issues with the Evidence

This will depend on the device.

8.6.11.23.5 Process of Seizing the Evidence

- where an audio device is seized, all associated manuals and charging equipment should be seized;
- seal the power plug connector on the device with tape so that inadvertent powering up does not happen and a conscious decision to remove the "do not power up" label has to be made;
- pack in original packaging, if possible. If not possible, ensure that the audio device is protected from accidental damage during transit;
- update seizure records.

8.6.11.24 Other Devices

8.6.11.24.1 Description

There are a variety of other devices that may be encountered by the Forensic Laboratory First Response Team. It is impossible to provide a comprehensive list of devices that may be encountered, as there are so many possibilities.

8.6.11.24.2 Primary Use

This will depend on the device.

8.6.11.24.3 Potential Evidence Obtainable

This will depend on the device.

8.6.11.24.4 Possible Issues with the Evidence

This will depend on the device.

8.6.11.24.5 Process of Seizing the Evidence

It is not possible to provide hard and fast procedures for handling other devices that may be encountered, but the advice given above should be used as a basis for handling any other device.

8.6.11.25 Seizing Paperwork

8.6.11.25.1 Description

There are a variety of different types of paperwork that may be considered for seizure. This can include handwritten notes, manuals, and books as well as diaries, printer output, and the contents of waste paper baskets.

8.6.11.25.2 Primary Use

This will depend on the paperwork seized.

8.6.11.25.3 Potential Evidence Obtainable

This will depend on the paperwork seized.

8.6.11.25.4 Possible Issues with the Evidence

This will depend on the paperwork seized.

8.6.11.25.5 Process of Seizing the Evidence

1. The search team should concentrate on the recovery of the following types of evidence:
   - passwords or IP addresses written on paper (check in the drawers, back of diaries, under blotters, etc.);
   - address books;
   - diaries;
   - items of interest in the bins;
   - computer keys;
   - manuals for hardware or software seized.
2. Where found and thought to be relevant and deserving of later evaluation, these items should also be "tagged and bagged" as follows:
   - photograph the items being seized *in situ*;
   - place the items in an evidence bag and seal. Insert the exhibit number;
   - update seizure records.

8.6.12 Interviews

Where appropriate, the suspect or the victim may be present at the site and may be available for interview. Interviews should only be undertaken by competent interviewers, and this may not be a member of the Forensic Laboratory First Response Team, but a member of Law Enforcement.

While the information to be determined at interview will depend on the specifics of the case, the standard list of questions that are used a basis for interviews are given in Appendix 13.

8.6.13 Evidence Bags

Appropriate evidence bags should be used for the different types and sizes of evidence.

It is essential that all parts of an exhibit are included in the sealed evidence bag (e.g., power supplies for portables or mobile phones), unless they need to be accessible (e.g., to maintain charge for batteries).

8.6.14 Faraday Bags and Boxes

For battery-powered devices that use wireless communications, such as Cell Phones, PDAs, etc., it may be necessary to isolate them from the networks or from wireless signals to ensure that the evidence is not changed by incoming calls that take place once the device has been seized. This is normally achieved by the use of Faraday bags or boxes that isolate the device from the radio frequency environment.

8.6.15 Seizure Records

Scanned copies of all records shall be added to the Client's virtual case file held in the ERMS, as defined in Chapter 15.

8.6.15.1 Personal Notebooks

1. All Forensic Analysts shall keep personal notebooks recording actions taken on any given incident response case. These are preferred for off-site working as they have a better audit trail with numbered pages than the traditional case work forms used for laboratory work.
2. These notes shall be contemporaneous.
3. The following rules apply to all forensic notebooks:
   - should be pocket sized with all pages numbered so as to refute claims of evidence tampering;
   - pocket books to be issued on an individual basis;
   - once filled, pocket books shall be securely stored by the Laboratory Manager;
   - blank parts of pages should have a line through them and initialed;
   - no pages shall be ripped out or otherwise removed from the notebook.
4. When filling in a notebook, the following should be on all pages:
   - case no;
   - date;
   - time;
   - actions;
   - initialed by the notebook holder—countersigned if appropriate.
5. All notebooks shall be audited on a regular basis by the Laboratory Manager.

Note

When a Forensic Analyst leaves the Forensic Laboratory, their pocket books shall be handed over to the Laboratory Manager, who shall securely store them.

8.6.15.2 Evidence Bag Contents List

The panel on the front of evidence bags must be filled in with at least the following details:

- date and time of seizure;
- seized by;
- exhibit number;
- where seized from;
- details of the contents of the evidence bag.

8.6.15.3 Seizure Records

1. The First Responder Seizure Record Forms for each item seized must be filled in and the First Responder Seizure Summary Form updated as the search/seizure progresses, as given in Appendix 7 and Section 8.5, respectively.
2. All details required on the form are to be filled in and the form signed and dated by the Forensic Analyst completing the form.

8.6.15.4 Witness Signatures

Depending on the legislation in the jurisdiction, a signature (or two) may or may not be required to certify collection of evidence.

1. Typically, where one is required this is the Forensic Analyst or Law Enforcement Officer performing the seizure.
2. Where two are required, guidance should be sought to determine who the second signature should be. Whoever it is will need to understand what they are doing and may be called upon to provide a witness statement or attend court.

8.6.15.5 Evidence Bags and Tags

Depending on circumstances, either preprinted evidence bags or evidence tags to be affixed to the exhibit shall be used. The type used will depend on the physical make up of the exhibit, availability of correct size of bags, local custom within the jurisdiction or the Client's own standards (e.g., a Law Enforcement Agency).

Whichever is used, the minimum information that shall be recorded on either the bag is given in Appendix 14.

8.6.16 Forensic Previewing

There are occasions when forensic previewing of evidence should be undertaken to determine whether the device contains evidence relevant to the case. Previewing can identify, but is not limited to:

- examinations that may require experience outside the Forensic Laboratory's competence;
- exhibits requiring prioritized investigation (depending on the case parameters);
- investigation strategy where more detailed investigation is needed;
- media likely to contain evidence.

To do this:

1. This shall be performed if the Laboratory Manager or the Incident Manager requires and authorizes it.
2. Typically, previewing is used to determine if there are grounds for seizing a particular system.
   - a portable acquisition write blocking device or portable PC with suitable write blocker shall be used and the preview function of EnCase or similar tools used with no image made.
   - the Laboratory Manager or the Incident Manager shall be advised of any results as soon as possible.
   - if previewing is to be undertaken, then the Forensic Preview Form is used. This has been designed in the Forensic Laboratory to be used with Encase as this is one of the tools of choice. The form is given in Appendix 15. Should another tool be used, then the form may need to be amended

8.6.17 On-Site Imaging

On-site imaging is carried out in specific situations:

- if Client's management require a copy;
- if the First Response Team Leader believes that there are insufficient grounds for seizing a particular system but that there are grounds for obtaining a copy;
- if the First Response Team Leader believes that there are grounds for seizing a system but that this would result in unacceptable loss or hardship to the suspect where the computer or evidence is located.

Normal Forensic Laboratory Procedures for imaging procedures shall be followed—but on-site rather than in the Forensic Laboratory's premises. The process for imaging is defined in Chapter 9, Section 9.9.

8.6.17.1 Performing Imaging on-Site with Dedicated Hardware

1. Imaging can be performed on-site using dedicated forensic acquisition hardware so long as it is used by trained and qualified Forensic Analysts. It is essential that the acquired image has its hash values checked against the original to ensure that the two images are identical;
2. Once the image is captured in this way, it is essential that appropriate backups of it are made and that they also have matching hashes.

8.6.17.2 Performing Imaging on-Site with a Traveling Laboratory

1. It is possible to use a portable PC with a copy of forensic imaging software to capture the required images from a suspect machine if required. The process to be followed is the same as that which is carried out in the Forensic Laboratory but on-site with a portable PC. It is essential that, if this is to be carried out, appropriate equipment is carried in the Grab Bag, as defined in Appendix 3.
2. The specification for the Forensic Laboratory traveling PC is given in Appendix 16.

8.6.18 Direct Data Access and Live Acquisition

This shall be considered in the same circumstances as "on-site imaging" but with the additional difficulty that even shutting the system concerned down for a short period may result in unacceptable loss or hardship or that traditional "pulling the plug" was not an appropriate approach to securing relevant evidence.

8.6.18.1 The Need for Live Acquisition

The need for live acquisition is being driven by rapid changes in technology and the computing environment, including:

- applications can be installed from external media and then virtualized into RAM, leaving no trace on a hard disk;
- data in RAM are lost when the device is rebooted, powered off, or when an open session or shell is closed;
- dedicated software can be used to "scrub" a disk and delete the audit trail and history of actions on closedown;
- hidden areas of a hard disk are often used, that are not visible to the standard operating system;
- malware that is fully RAM resident and may have no trace on a hard disk;
- root kits are designed to remain "hidden" to the operating system so trusted tools are required;
- software, and specifically web browsers, have evidence eradication processes that delete the audit trail or history when the browser is closed;
- some parts of a suspect computer at the incident scene may have "booby trapped" software that may trigger Trojans, time bombs, or other destructive programs;
- web-based e-mail does not leave trace evidence on a hard disk, as with traditional e-mail clients like Microsoft Outlook or Mozilla.

8.6.18.2 The Order of Volatility

Live forensic acquisition provides for digital evidence collection in the order that acknowledges the volatility of the evidence and collects it in the order of volatility to maximize the preservation of evidence. The order of volatility within a computer and supporting storage media can range from nano-seconds cache memory) to tens of years (CDs, DVDs, paper output).

The order of volatility (OOV) is:

- CPU, memory cache, and the registers;
- routing tables;
- ARP cache;
- process state and processes running;
- kernel modules and statistics;
- main memory (RAM);
- temporary system files;
- swap files;
- network configuration and connections;
- system settings;
- command history;
- open files, clipboard data, logged on users;
- the file system.

Appropriate tools must be used for live capture and details of these are given in Chapter 7, Appendix 4.

8.6.18.3 Procedure for Live Capture

The process for live capture is similar to that of remote acquisition as defined in Section 8.5.3 of this chapter with the following differences (Figure 8.3).

1. The Laboratory Manager, the Incident Manager, the First Response Team Leader, and the relevant Business Manager shall be informed of the potential consequences of obtaining evidence in this manner and authorize the process in writing.
2. The acquisition is either done on-site or remotely from the Forensic Laboratory.
3. Network traffic dumps should be taken, as this can reveal important information about the machine to be processed, especially if it is accessed remotely or across a network. This information can influence the next steps.
4. Evidence should be collected according to the order of volatility (OOV), starting with the most volatile evidence and then capturing other evidence as required by the specifics of the case.
5. A dedicated hardware capture device or the Forensic Analyst's portable Forensic Laboratory must be used for this.
6. Evidence may then be processed as normal in the Forensic Laboratory, in which case, the process in Section 8.5.3 is followed.
7. If the evidence is to remain on-site, then this process is followed without the physical seizure.

Live capture shall only be attempted when the conditions listed in the relevant forensic guidance for the jurisdiction can clearly be shown to have been complied with, particularly with reference to the competence of the Forensic Analyst concerned.

In addition, with the use of malware software detection, the ability to deny the "Trojan Horse Defence" must be considered.

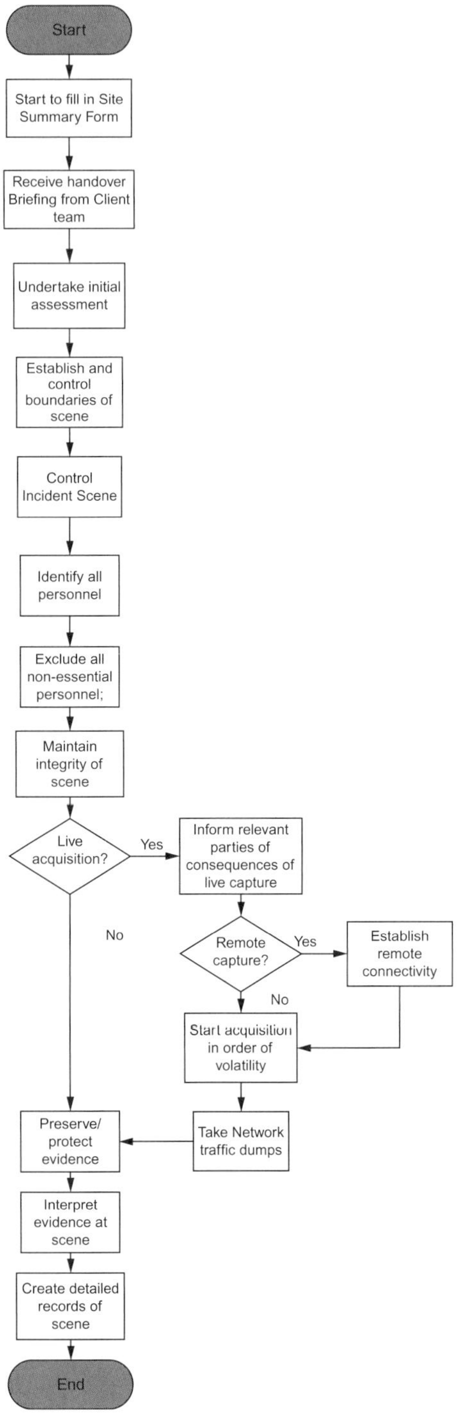

FIGURE 8.3 Live forensics. (For color version of this figure, the reader is referred to the online version of this chapter.)

> **Note**
>
> Live capture in an intrusion detection situation may alert the intruder while either monitoring the system or acquiring evidence.

8.6.19 Secondary Search of Scene

Once all evidence has been collected, it is recommended that an additional search be conducted of the scene. In the event that additional evidence is located during this second search, it should be noted, photographed, and collected.

It is recommended that all paperwork relating to the scene is reviewed and at least two people perform the search, if possible, to ensure completeness and that the chances of anything being overlooked are minimized.

8.6.20 Release of Scene

1. Prior to release of the scene, the secondary or final search has been carried out, it is recommended that photographs of the scene are made showing its final condition.
2. The First Response Team Leader shall undertake a postincident team debriefing to check that the scene processing has been completed and all postincident scene processing responsibilities. The attendees at the debriefing will comprise the relevant Forensic Laboratory employees (First Response Team and other specialists used—e.g., photographer, artist, etc.), the first Client employees at the scene (if available) and other stakeholders as required. This debriefing should:
   - determine what evidence was collected;
   - discuss required outcomes and how the evidence recovered will support this;
   - discuss the proposed processing to be undertaken;
   - discuss the sequence and prioritization of tasks;
   - ensure that all outstanding actions from the crime scene processing are assigned and tracked through to completion;
   - establish postscene processing responsibilities for all attendees, if appropriate.
3. Upon completion of processing, the scene can be released, after checking:
   - all areas of the scene are inspected and checked;
   - all evidence collected is accounted for and is ready and securely packed for transportation to the Forensic Laboratory;
   - all Forensic Laboratory equipment and material is packed for transportation back to the Forensic Laboratory;
   - all documentation from the scene has been completed;
   - the incident scene is released in accordance with requirements in the jurisdiction, if appropriate.
4. It is recommended the scene be released to the System Administrator or Supervisor for the area of the workstation. The scene must only be released by the Incident Manager or the First Response Team Leader.
5. A copy of the evidence/property documents listing items removed from the scene should be provided to the person who "owns" the incident scene.
6. Ensuring that all relevant evidence is identified and processed cannot be overstressed. As has been said before, it is rare that a second visit to the scene is possible and that may require a new warrant or other permission.
7. Undertake a postincident scene review to understand lessons learned and the opportunities for continuous improvement.

8.7 TRANSPORTATION TO THE FORENSIC LABORATORY

8.7.1 Minimum Handling of Exhibits

There should be a minimum number of Forensic Laboratory or other authorized personnel handling the exhibits from securing the scene until they are safely and securely locked in the Forensic Laboratory Secure Property store.

The reason for this is simple.

The fewer people handling the evidence, the fewer statements will be required, the fewer people may have to testify and the less likely mistakes will occur with handling and continuity.

8.7.2 Packing

1. Evidence to be recovered from the scene of the incident to the Forensic Laboratory must be properly packed, recorded, and labeled prior to despatch.
   - seizure records should be checked off against physical evidence bags;
   - evidence bags shall be checked to ensure that they have been properly and completely filled in;
2. Any containers used shall be appropriate for the job and be properly labeled.
3. It is extremely important that computer or other electronic equipment or media be handled gently.
4. The condition of the equipment is not known when it is seized. Any disturbance could result in connections coming loose. In addition, not all fixed magnetic media is self parking. Head parking moves the electromagnetic equipment inside a disk away from the magnetic media. The "parking" of the heads provides some protection, but should never be substituted for careful handling. It should always be assumed that the heads are not parked. Any significant trauma to the computer could result in hard drive failure.

5. The ideal packing material for a computer is the original factory container. If this cannot be located, then bubble wrap should be used if it is available; if this is not possible, the computer should be packed and carried as it was set up.
6. If possible, equipment should be packed in antistatic containers;
7. Differing jurisdictions do not always use plastic evidence bags, but prefer paper ones so that there is no risk from condensation or humidity contamination.
8. Smart phones, mobile phones, and similar devices must be packed in Faraday isolation bags or boxes, radio frequency shielded material, or aluminum foil to prevent messages being sent or received after seizure.

8.7.3 Transport

1. If the Forensic Analyst is his own Evidence Custodian, then they will hand-carry or escort the evidence back to the Forensic Laboratory. The evidence must be hand-carried/escorted and not leave the Forensic Analyst until it is signed into the Secure Property Store. This means that it must be carried on any aeroplane as hand baggage and not be put in the hold or the "Chain of Custody" is lost.
2. If evidence cannot be hand-carried, then a car or other vehicle should be used for transporting it back to the Forensic Laboratory.
3. Where possible, avoid turning the computer upside down or laying it on its side during transport.
4. When transporting a computer or other computer devices, they should not be placed in the boot (trunk) or any other area where there is the possibility of possible dramatic temperature and humidity changes.
5. In a vehicle, the ideal place for transport would be on the rear seat, placed in a manner where the computer will not fall during a sudden stop or quick maneuver.
6. All evidence must be protected from any sources of magnetism or similar sources of power that could affect the integrity of the electronic evidence.
7. Couriers should be avoided unless they can guarantee hand-to-hand contact (i.e., evidence is not left in a "hub" overnight or similar). In this case, the "Chain of Custody" must be signed by the Courier, who may need to provide a statement supporting this. This is one good reason to avoid couriers.
8. Postal services for conveying evidence are not acceptable and must not be used.

8.7.4 Movement Records

Where any exhibit is moved, the movement record form for the exhibit is updated. This shows the complete movement of any exhibit from initial receipt or seizure to final return to the Client or disposal.

The content of the Forensic Laboratory movement form is given in Appendix 17.

8.8 CRIME SCENE AND SEIZURE REPORTS

Often the Forensic Laboratory carries out a First Response action as part of overall case processing, rather than a standalone seizure operation. In this case, contemporaneous notes are used as input to the final case report and should contain:

- Client instructions;
- initial response documentation;
- entry/exit documentation;
- photographs/videos;
- crime scene sketches/diagrams and plans;
- evidence documentation;
- New Case form;
- First Responder Seizure Summary Log;
- Site Summary Form;
- seizure log;
- forensic preview forms;
- movement forms;
- other responders' documentation;
- record of consent form(s) or search warrant(s).

Where a specific report is needed for an incident scene report, it will depend on what specifically the Client requires, and this may have been agreed as part of the proposal, as defined in Chapter 6, Section 6.6. The Forensic Laboratory Incident Response Report template is given in Appendix 18.

The report is factual and does not contain any interpretations and meets the requirements of the Forensic Laboratory document control requirements, as defined in Chapter 4, Section 4.6.3, classified according to the classifications defined in Chapter 5, Appendix 16 and handled in accordance with Chapter 12, Section 12.3.14.9.

8.9 POSTINCIDENT REVIEW

One of the most important parts of the Deming Cycle is continuous improvement, and all too often this is overlooked. This should be built into the Forensic Laboratory's Integrated Management System (IMS), as defined in Chapter 4, Sections 4.3.1.5, 4.7, 4.8, and 4.9 and Chapter 6, Appendix 20.

The First Response Teams must constantly keep up with new technology, new tools and methods, and the recommendations for improvements that come from Client feedback and internal audits and reviews.

Postincident reviews should be held soon after the incident and preferably after the Incident Response Report has been completed. They should be attended by all of the First Response Team attending and any relevant Client Management staff. Depending on the incident itself; this may be a long meeting (if a major incident) or a short one for an isolated incident.

The Forensic Laboratory uses a standard agenda template for postincident reviews, and this is given in Appendix 19.

All actions raised for the Forensic Laboratory at the meeting are tracked through the CAPA database to completion. How the Client deals with them is a matter for the Client.

APPENDIX 1 - MAPPING ISO 17020 TO IMS PROCEDURES

ISO 17020 Section	Control	Procedure(s)
3	Administrative requirement	Chapter 3, Sections 3.1.2, 3.1.3, 3.1.14 Chapter 6, Section 6.2.1
4	Independence, impartiality, and integrity	Chapter 3, Section 3.1.5
4.1	General	Chapter 3, Sections 3.1.3.2, 3.1.3.16, 3.1.5, 3.1.8, Appendix 3
4.2	Independence	Chapter 3, Section 3.1.5, Appendix 3
5	Confidentiality	Chapter 6, Section 6.11
6	Organization and management	
6.1		Chapter 4, Sections 4.5.5 and 4.6.2
6.2		Chapter 3, Section 3.1.17 Chapter 18
6.3		Chapter 6, Appendix 24
6.4		Chapter 18
6.5		Chapter 18
6.6		Chapter 6, Appendix 7
7		
7.1		Chapter 3, Appendix 4 Chapter 4, Section 4.6.2 Chapter 6
7.2		Chapter 6
7.3		Chapter 6 Chapter 4
7.4		Chapter 6, Appendix 7
7.5		Chapter 4, Section 4.9
7.6		Chapter 4, Section 4.6.3
7.7		Chapter 4, Section 4.7.3 Chapter 4, Appendix 42
7.8		Chapter 4, Section 4.8, Appendix 49 Chapter 6, Sections 6.13.2, 6.13.3, Appendix 20
7.9		Chapter 4, Section 4.9, Appendix 36
8	Personnel	Chapter 18
8.1		Chapter 6, Appendix 14 Chapter 18
8.2		Chapter 4, Section 4.4.2.2 Chapter 6, Section 6.12.5, Appendices 26 and 27 This chapter, Sections 8.1.3 and 8.1.5 Chapter 18
8.3		Chapter 4, Section 4.4.2.2 Chapter 6, Section 6.12.5, Appendices 26 and 27 Chapter 18
8.4		Chapter 4, Section 4.6.2.3 Chapter 18
8.5		Chapter 18 Various policies and procedures in force in the Forensic Laboratory
8.6		Chapter 18, though the actual remuneration of employees is outside the scope of this chapter
9	Facilities and equipment	
9.1		Chapter 2 Chapter 3 Chapter 4, Sections 4.6.2.4 and 4.6.2.5 Chapter 7 This chapter, Sections 8.6.2, 8.6.3, and 8.6.4 Chapter 12, Section 12.3.8
9.2		Chapter 4, Section 4.6.2.2 Chapter 6, Section 6.12 Chapter 7, Section 7.1.1 Chapter 12, Sections 12.2.4.3, 12.4.4, and 12.6
9.3		Chapter 7, Sections 7.5.4 and 7.5.5

Continued

ISO 17020 Section	Control	Procedure(s)
9.4		Chapter 6, Section 6.12.8 Chapter 12, Sections 12.3.14.2.1.2 and 12.3.14.2.1.3
9.5		Chapter 7, Section 7.5.4
9.6		Not applicable
9.7		Chapter 7, Section 7.5.5
9.8		Not applicable
9.9		Not applicable
9.10		Not applicable
9.11		Chapter 6. Section 6.7.4 Chapter 12, Section 12.3.14, Chapter 14
9.12		Not applicable
9.13		Chapter 7, Sections 7.5.4 and 7.5.4 Chapter 12
9.14		Chapter 7, Section 7.5.5
9.15		Chapter 7, Section 7.5.4
10	Inspection methods and procedures	
10.1		Chapter 6, Sections 6.6 and 6.8 This chapter
10.2		Chapter 6, Sections 6.6 and 6.8 This chapter
10.3		Chapter 7, Section 7.5.5
10.4		Chapter 4, Section 4.6.3 Chapter 4
10.5a		Chapter 4, Section 4.6.2.2. Chapter 6, Sections 4.6 and 4.7.1, Appendix 14
10.5b		Chapter 6, Section 6.6
10.5c		Chapter 6, Sections 6.8 and 6.13.1
10.5d		Chapter 6, Sections 6.8, 6.7.1, 6.12.11, Appendix 20
10.6		Chapter 4, Section 4.6.4 Chapter 9, Sections 9.10.2.13, 9.13, and 9.15
10.7		Chapter 5, Appendix 16 Chapter 6, Sections 6.6, 6.8, and 6.11 Chapter 12, Sections 12.8.3.2 and 12.8.4

Continued

ISO 17020 Section	Control	Procedure(s)
10.8		This chapter, Section 8.6.3 Chapter 17
11	Handling inspection samples and items	
11.1		This chapter, Sections 8.6.6, 8.6.7, 8.6.10, Appendices 5 and 7
11.2		Section 8.6
11.3		Chapter 6, Section 6.6 This chapter, Section 8.6.4, 8.6.10, Appendices 5 and 7
11.4		Chapter 4, Appendix 16 Chapter 6, Section 6.6 This chapter, Sections 8.6.4, 8.6.5, 8.6.6, 8.6.7, 8.6.9, 8.6.10, 8.6.11, 8.6.15, 8.7, Appendices 5 and 7
12	Records	
12.1		Chapter 3, Section 3.1.3.17 Chapter 4, Section 4.6.4 This chapter, Section 8.6.15, Appendices 5, 7, and 15 Chapter 12, Section 12.3.13.1 Chapter 15 The Forensic Laboratory Electronic Record Management System
12.2		Chapter 4, Section 4.6.4 Chapter 9, Section 9.10.2.13
12.3		Chapter 4, Sections 4.6.4 and 4.16 Chapter 6, Section 6.11 Chapter 5, Appendix 16 Chapter 12, Sections 12.3.13.1 and 12.3.14
13	Inspection reports and inspection certificates	
13.1		Chapter 6, Section 6.12.12, Appendix 31 This chapter, Section 8.8 Chapter 9, Section 9.10.2.13
13.2		Chapter 6, Section 6.12.12, Appendix 31
13.3		Chapter 4, Section 4.6.3 Chapter 6, Appendix 31
13.4		Chapter 4, Section 4.6.3 Chapter 6, Section 6.8
14	Subcontracting	
14.1		Noted

Continued

ISO 17020 Section	Control	Procedure(s)
14.2		Chapter 6, Section 6.6 Chapter 14
14.3		Chapter 4, Section 4.7.3 Chapter 14, Sections 14.3–14.9
14.4		Chapter 14, Sections 14.5.1.3 and 14.8.2.2
15	Complaints and appeals	
15.1		Chapter 6, Section 6.14
15.2		Chapter 6, Section 6.14
15.3		Chapter 6, Section 6.14
16	Cooperation	Various job descriptions Chapter 4, Section 4.8
Annex A		
A1		Chapter 3, Sections 3.1.5 and 3.1.8
A2		Chapter 3, Sections 3.1.5 and 3.1.8, Appendix 3
A3		Chapter 3, Sections 3.1.5 and 3.1.8, Appendix 3
Annex B		
B1		Chapter 12, Section 12.3.5 and 12.3.6
B2		Chapter 3, Section 3.1.3.16 and 3.1.5 This chapter, Section 8.3, Appendix 3
B3		Noted—if applicable
Annex C		
C1		Chapter 12, Sections 12.3.5 and 12.3.6
Annex D		All of these are in the Forensic Laboratory Integrated management System

APPENDIX 2 - FIRST RESPONSE BRIEFING AGENDA

There are many different situations where a First Response presence by the Forensic Laboratory is required. It is not possible to give a detailed agenda for an initial briefing meeting, as these will vary based on who else is attending, the specifics of the incident, location, etc. However, the following is the framework that is used in the Forensic Laboratory and is amended as required for the specific circumstances of the incident where a response is required.

- status report on the incident—what is known about the situation to date;
- other parties involved—what third parties are involved (Client, Law Enforcement, others);
- roles and responsibilities—of all of those involved in the incident;
- location—of the seizure with all details relating to accessing the site;
- Health and Safety—any concerns about attending the incident scene. This will include any specific equipment Health and Safety issues known in advance, and can include any laser type equipment, dangerous emissions (e.g., microwave transmissions) or any equipment that may retain a charge after unplugging it. The First Response Team shall be advised of any equipment that poses a Health and Safety risk discovered during the First Response;
- secure areas—for temporary storage;
- smoking, eating, and refreshments facilities and locations;
- legal considerations—jurisdictional issues, Law Enforcement liaison, relevant contractual issues;
- use of other facilities on-site—e.g., toilets, phones, etc.;
- timings and mobilization—who is to go where and when and time constraints, if any;
- immediate actions—if the scene needs to be secured or if any triage needs to be undertaken on the Client's systems;
- evidence required—what is to be proved and where is may be found (if known);
- searching protocols—what can be removed and what cannot;
- business continuity—ensuring that the Client's business can continue, as far as is reasonably practicable;
- on-site forensic operations—will on-site imaging, previewing or real-time forensics be required?
- records—to be made of the Client site and identity of the evidence of the Evidence Custodian(s);
- progress meetings—if they are to take place, who will attend and when they are to be held;
- site handover—checklists for formally handing the scene back to the Client;
- postattendance meeting—details of the postincident response meeting, discussing issues, and next actions—including lessons learned for continuous improvement;
- any other issues—that are not covered in the above briefing agenda.

APPENDIX 3 - CONTENTS OF THE GRAB BAG

Different members of First Responder Teams usually tailor their grab bags for the equipment that they find most useful at an incident. Below are the Forensic Laboratory standard grab bag contents:

ESSENTIAL KIT

- consent to search forms;
- evidence seizure forms;

- business cards;
- crime scene barricade tape;
- first aid kit;
- list of contact telephone numbers for assistance;
- mobile telephones;
- PPE, as required by the briefing, however, standard equipment includes latex gloves, goggles, and electrostatic protection;
- spare batteries.

SEARCH KIT

- case-processing forms;
- A4 paper in clipboards;
- cutting instruments (knife, scissors, clippers);
- digital camera (still and video) with flash/spare memory/tripod and charger for camera battery;
- envelopes;
- evidence collection bags (various sizes);
- evidence identifier labels;
- evidence seals/tape;
- label writer;
- latex gloves;
- magnifying glass;
- measuring tape;
- evidential notebooks;
- pens and highlighters;
- permanent markers;
- photographic scale (a ruler);
- plastic bags;
- rubber bands;
- sketch paper;
- label writer spare cartridge and batteries;
- tape recorder;
- tweezers/forceps;
- small torches and extra batteries.

IMAGING KIT

> **Note**
>
> If multiple systems are to be imaged, then the items marked with asterisk will need to be increased to ensure that all systems can be imaged.

- *large hard disk for containing image of suspect device;
- assorted hard disk adaptors;
- multipoint power adaptor;
- adjustable spanner;
- antistatic wrist band;
- assorted instructions, driver CDs, etc.;
- assorted SCSI device adaptors;
- CDs—pack;
- DVDs—pack;
- forensic imaging software[b];
- clean booting floppy disk;
- clean booting CD;
- clean booting USB device;
- forensic investigation software;
- dongles (as required by the software deployed);
- ethernet card;
- extension cables;
- write blockers[c];
- various external cables (including USB, network RJ 45, FireWire, etc.);
- hard disk bay keys;
- hex-nut drivers;
- modem cable;
- mouse;
- multicard reader;
- PDA and mobile device recovery kit;
- parallel cable;
- PC internal power cables;
- Pliers, various;
- power adaptors;
- roll of labels;
- rolls of tape;
- screwdriver bits;
- screwdrivers—various heads (Phillips, flat head, posi, etc.);
- secure-bit drivers;
- portable media reader and cards;
- specialized screwdrivers (manufacturer-specific, e.g., Compaq, Macintosh);
- star-type nut drivers;
- TV connectors;
- tweezers, grabbers, etc.;
- wire strippers/cutters;
- yellow "crossover" Cat 5 cable.

PACKAGE AND TRANSPORT SUPPLIES

- antistatic bags;
- antistatic bubble wrap;
- faraday bags/boxes;
- cable ties;
- evidence bags;
- evidence tape;

b. The Forensic Laboratory will probably use a range of tools including Encase, FTK, and dd.

c. The Forensic Laboratory may use tools such as the FastBloc and Tableau write blockers.

- packing materials (avoid materials that can produce static electricity such as Styrofoam or Styrofoam peanuts);
- packing tape;
- sturdy boxes of various sizes.

APPENDIX 4 - NEW CASE FORM

Note

Depending on the case, not all of this information will be relevant.

The following details are recorded for the start of any New Case in the Forensic Laboratory:

- case name, if applicable;
- case number, generated by MARS,[d] in sequence of the form yyyy/nnnn (where yyyy is the year and nnnn is a sequential case number for the year (yyyy) starting with 0001 and going to 9999;
- Client contact details;
- Client reference;
- Client;
- Forensic Analyst(s) assigned to the case;
- jurisdiction;
- on-site contact details;
- other agencies or organizations involved;
- seizure type (overt or covert);
- details of seizure requirements, if known;
- summary of evidence requested;
- summary of the actions so far;
- incident type;
- how was the incident discovered;
- Is the incident still ongoing?
- Is there network surveillance or IDS in place?
- Has the system been taken off-line?
- If so, who authorized it?
- If not, who authorized it to remain attached to the network?
- physical security at site;
- Who has access to the system since the incident started?
- Who else knows about the incident?
- What is the logical security for the system?
- Is the source IP of the attack?
- What investigative steps have been undertaken to date?
- What are the results?

Other forms will be completed, as appropriate, during the progress of the case.

d. MARS is the Forensic Laboratory's in-house-developed case management system (Management and Reporting System).

APPENDIX 5 - FIRST RESPONDER SEIZURE SUMMARY LOG

The following are the details to be captured on the First Responder Log. Some of this will be copied onto the forms from the New Case form, as defined in Appendix 4, and the rest will be filled in as the case progresses and the facts become known.

- case no;
- case name;
- location of seizure:
  - room no;
  - building name;
  - address line 1;
  - address line 2;
  - address line 3;
  - address line 4;
  - post/zip code.
- details of incident;
- Incident Manager on-site;
- contact details;
- first on scene;
- contact details;
- is scene secured? (yes/no);
- if secured, by whom?
- contact details;
- legislative jurisdiction;
- local Client contact;
- contact details;
- overt or covert operation?
- description of incident;
- evidence required;
- Forensic Analyst(s) assigned;
- Evidence Custodian.

APPENDIX 6 - SITE SUMMARY FORM

The following are the details to be captured on the Site Summary Form. Some of this will be copied onto the forms from the New Case form, as defined in Appendix 4, and the rest will be filled in as the case progresses and the facts become known.

- case no;
- case name;
- location of seizure:
  - room no;
  - building name;
  - address line 1;
  - address line 2;
  - address line 3;
  - address line 4;
  - post/zip code.
- details of incident;

- Incident Manager on-site;
- contact details;
- first on scene;
- contact details;
- name and address details of all present at the scene and those removed from the scene;
- date and time of arrival at the scene;
- actions taken since discovery of the incident;
- assessed Health and Safety hazards and their treatments;
- records of PPE used;
- incident site boundaries;
- identified entry and exit point to the scene;
- maintain records of all actions an d observations;
- taken appropriate photographs;
- drawn appropriate plans and sketches;
- collected the relevant evidence (separate evidence logs are maintained);
- labeled all exhibits according to the naming standard in place;
- updated paper forms, notebooks, and MARS as appropriate;
- date and time of scene release;
- released to;
- released by;
- signatures.

APPENDIX 7 - SEIZURE LOG

For any item seized during an investigation, it is essential that a full Chain of Custody is maintained. To assist in this process, either a seizure log for every case can be used or the Forensic Laboratory may prefer to use specific forms relating to each item seized. The forms used should contain the following information per item seized:

CASE DETAILS

- case no;
- case name;
- location of seizure:
  - room no;
  - building name;
  - address line 1;
  - address line 2;
  - address line 3;
  - address line 4;
  - post/zip code.

DETAILS OF EVIDENCE SEIZED

- type of evidence seized (e.g., computer, disk, paper, etc.);
- location;
- make;
- model;
- serial number;
- evidence bag number;
- acquisition details of how the exhibit was seized;
- passwords recovered from the owner (Y/N)?
- if "Yes"—details;
- was the seized equipment connected to a network/internet/phone when seized (Y/N)?
- if "Yes"—details;
- was the equipment switched on at the time of seizure (Y/N)?
- if "Yes"—details;
- has the equipment been switched since seizure (Y/N)?
- if "Yes"—details;
- if yes to above, state the reason and the details of the person who switched it on (including date, time, reason competence);
- photo(s) of exhibit(s) taken (Y/N)?
- if "Yes"—attach them;
- who took them—name;
- photographer's signature;
- sketch(es) of exhibit(s) taken (Y/N)?
- if "Yes"—attach them;
- who drew them—name;
- artist's signature;
- witness signature (Forensic Analyst making seizure);
- full name;
- title;
- phone number;
- address;
- date;
- time;
- signature of person from whom seizure made;
- full name;
- title;
- phone number;
- address;
- date;
- time;
- witness signature (second one—if needed in jurisdiction);
- full name;
- title;
- phone number;
- address;
- date;
- time;
- signature of Evidence Custodian;
- full name;
- title;
- phone number;
- address;
- date;
- time.

APPENDIX 8 - EVIDENCE LOCATIONS IN DEVICES AND MEDIA

There are a variety of computers and other information storage or processing devices in use today that the Forensic Analyst may encounter. The actual information will vary from case to case as well as from device to device. Some will be general purpose devices and may contain evidence as described below and others (e.g., a dedicated computer chip such as found in a washing machine, car engine management system, or shop till) will only contain specific evidence relating to the use of the device in which they are found.

Note

It is also possible to subvert the original intended use of a device, and this should always be borne in mind when dealing with forensic case evidence recovery. The subversions will depend on the case and can vary greatly, but an example is the use of a game console or a digital video recorder (DVR) to store paedophile material.

Some of the types of potential evidence that may be recovered include:

COMPUTER FILES

User-Created Files

A user can create any number of different files and file types on a computer that contain evidence relevant to an incident or investigation.

The content of the files will depend on what the user has been doing and the case type.

The file types will typically be dependent on the software that is on the computer (or has been removed from it). User-created files can be created for one application using other software (e.g., a text editor).

Some common types of files that may be used for evidence recovery include, but are not limited to:

- address books;
- audio files;
- calendars;
- correspondence or other word-processed files;
- database files;
- documents;
- e-mail correspondence;
- images or graphics files;
- internet bookmarks;
- internet favorites;
- metadata;
- other correspondence media conversations;
- photographs;
- presentations;
- spreadsheets;
- video files.

User-Protected Files

All users have the opportunity to hide or otherwise protect evidence in a variety of different ways using a variety of different tools (some of which are freely available for download on the internet).

A user may want to protect sensitive files for perfectly valid reasons or there may be slightly more suspicious reasons for protecting files on a computer.

Typical methods of protecting files include:

- compressed files;
- encryption;
- hidden files;
- incorrectly named files (e.g., those with a bad file extension);
- password protection of files using a third party product;
- password protection of files using the file's creation software facilities;
- simple hiding of files (e.g., a jpg file embedded into a spreadsheet);
- steganography.

Computer-Created Files

In any incident or investigation, evidence can also be found in files and other data areas created as a routine function of the computer's operating system and applications and often the user is unaware of this. The sorts of information that may get written to the hard disk of a computer without the user knowing includes, but is not limited to:

- Alternate Data Streams (ADSs);
- autocomplete history files;
- backup files;
- browser histories;
- configuration files;
- cookie information;
- cookies;
- date, time, and other creation modification and deletion dates as metadata in files;
- hibernation files (showing a snapshot of RAM);
- hidden files;
- history files;
- index.dat (in windows);
- internet activity;
- location bar history;
- log files showing detailed actions undertaken by all user IDs with time and date details;
- log files;
- media player and similar file listings;
- metadata;

- open and save history files;
- other details depending on the operating system;
- passwords;
- plug-ins from downloaded files;
- printer spool files;
- recent documents;
- recycle bin;
- search history files;
- start-up menus;
- swap files;
- system files;
- temporary backup files;
- temporary files or caches;
- temporary internet files.

Other Data Areas

In addition to files created by the operating system, there are a number of other areas on a computer disk or in memory, in addition to the files above, these include, but are not limited to:

- bad clusters;
- deleted files;
- free space;
- hidden partitions;
- lost clusters;
- metadata;
- other partitions;
- reserved areas;
- reserved system areas;
- slack space;
- software registration within an application or the operating system;
- unallocated space.

OTHER DEVICES

Devices other than a computer may contain a variety of possible evidence source, and some of these include:

Device or media	Potential evidence
Cell phones	Similar to computer files above
Copiers	Similar to computer files above for copiers containing hard disks
Digital cameras	Images, metadata, audio files
DVRs	Similar to computer files above
Fax machines	Message logs, phone numbers
Firewalls	MAC address, logs, configuration information
Games consoles	Similar to computer files above
GPSs	Route information, home, and destination details
Intrusion Detection Sniffers (IDS)	Intruder detection logs
Memory Cards	Similar to computer files above
MP3 players	Files, video, and audio recordings
Network sniffers	Logs
PDAs	Similar to computer files above
Printers	Similar to computer files above for copiers containing hard disks
Routers	Logs, ACLs, routing tables
Smart cards	ID credentials
Switches	MAC address, logs

Continued

APPENDIX 9 - TYPES OF EVIDENCE TYPICALLY NEEDED FOR A CASE

While there are no hard and fast rules about what evidence is needed for a specific case, the following provide some guidance on the types of evidence that could be required for a case type. Each case should be judged on its merits and on the specific requirements of the Client, but the lists below provide a "starter for ten":

- ADSs;
- databases;
- deleted files;
- document files (e.g., word processing files or spreadsheets);
- e-mails;
- encrypted files;
- images;
- internet history;
- link files;
- metadata;
- password-protected files;
- the recycle bin;
- the registry.

APPENDIX 10 - THE ON/OFF RULE

GENERAL

During the evidential seizure process, it is usually necessary to seize some information processing equipment or forensically examine it on-site. Typically, the information processing equipment will be either:

- switched on
- switched off.

When the First Response Team arrive, decisions as to the next steps must be taken by the Team Leader to ensure that the evidence is not contaminated, based on the circumstances in which it is found, the Client's requirements and the Forensic Laboratory First Response Team's competence. The issues to be faced with possible solutions are given below with reasoning for each action. However, this should not be regarded as hard and fast rules, merely guidance that should be considered for all situations before an on-site decision is made.

THE ISSUES

The first fact to establish is whether the information processing equipment is currently powered on or powered off.

When dealing with a powered on and running information processing device,

STOP and THINK.

The necessity for considered action arises from the fact that there is no standard step-by-step procedure for maintaining the integrity of any information processing equipment that is applicable in every situation. Every situation encountered requires careful consideration of the nature of the case and the information processing equipment in question. What may be a sensible set of actions for maintaining the integrity of one piece of information processing equipment may in fact lead to loss of evidence on another.

The issues to be considered are numerous and include:

- based on the nature of the incident and the status of the information processing equipment found at the incident scene, where is crucial evidence likely to be located?
- which component or components of the information processing equipment must have their integrity maintained to ensure that the evidence is not contaminated at the scene;
- whether key evidence likely to be on the hard drive(s) or in memory?

In the past, the majority of digital forensic investigations involved the analysis of hard disk drives or solid-state memory devices that had been either separated from their host or were examined in situ (e.g., mobile phones and PDAs).

This made sense in the past as the vast majority of information contained within a computer system was usually be found on the hard drive, rather than in memory and there were few tools available to examined volatile memory (RAM or flash memory).

However, the contents of RAM and flash memory in an active information processing system undoubtedly hold some information relevant to the evidence in the case and often this can be vitally important to a case. Examples of this can include, but not be limited to:

- information that may be encrypted on disk but may be unencrypted in memory;
- processes running at the time of seizure may need to be identified or examined;
- investigation of root kits and malware (thus addressing the "malware defence");
- crash dump files;
- registry information;
- hibernation information;
- other volatile memory that has not been written to disk.

Any such information in memory will almost certainly be lost when the power supply to the information processing equipment is turned off. The standard operating procedures for the Forensic Laboratory First must have a documented and proven set of procedures to guard against the loss of this critical information that is held in memory.

IF UNABLE TO DETERMINE POWER STATE

There may be occasions when the First Responder is unable to determine the power state easily. If this is the case, then the following should be undertaken:

- check for any LEDs showing activity;
- check for disks spinning;
- check for fans running;
- other signs of activity;
- whether any connected output or input devices show any activity.

The results of the above should give an indication of power state. If still unsure, then a value judgment must be made, and the equipment is handled accordingly.

IF UNSURE OF ACTIVITY STATUS

There will be occasions when a computer is seen to be powered on, but there is nothing on the screen to indicate any activity. If this is the case, then press the "down arrow" key to redisplay the open file or the password-protected login screen, as defined in Section 8.6.6.

If the screen is displayed, the following should be checked:

- evidence of any encryption in place, which may cause potential evidence to be contaminated, if the device is powered off;
- evidence of any other type of communication between the evidence and any other device;
- evidence of any remote access being undertaken;
- signs of evidence deletion software being run.

Should any of these types of process be active, a value judgment must be made as to what to do. Typically, the power should be pulled if any processes running could be considered to interfere with the evidence.

If the screen is locked, then attempts should be made to discover the password to access it. If this is not possible, then a value judgment as to how to deal with it must be taken and then process it accordingly.

OPTIONS

Given that each forensic case is different, there may be different options to be adopted for different circumstances. Some of these are given below:

- one method is to simply to power down the information processing device using the standard operating system shutdown routine in the hope that the data in question will be written to disk. This can be an effective technique if the information in memory will indeed be written to disk, and the knowledge of whether or not this is appropriate will depend on the competence of the First Response Team Leader. However, this approach has a number of possible risks and may be subject to controversy;
  - it will change the state of the evidence (i.e., the hard drive data) and possibly lose some of the evidence held in memory by the actions of the Forensic Laboratory First Response Team and is a breach of one of the fundamental principles of digital forensic examination;
  - it may trigger a routine during the shutdown procedure (either as part of the normal shutdown process or as part of an attempt by the suspect to cover their tracks), which can be used to destroy vital information.
- another method is to carry out a live examination and attempt to analyze the state of system memory while the suspect information processing equipment is still running. This is usually considered somewhat more controversial from a forensic standpoint. As before, this is likely to alter the state of the system through the actions of the First Response Team. If this option is chosen, then all of the Team that are involved in this operation must be able to prove that they were competent to perform this action. If this option is chosen, it is necessary to:
  - ensure, as far as is reasonable practicable, that the information processing equipment has not been configured to return false information and that the results returned can be relied upon in Court and is repeatable.

As can be seen from the above, the process of recovering evidence from volatile memory for use as evidence while trying to maintain a level of integrity that allows the information to be used in court is not a trivial task. However, there are a number of occasions where it is a requirement to undertake this process.

On some occasions, it is not possible and the Forensic Analyst will only have the option of recovering the contents of the hard disk, thereby losing any evidence that may have been recovered from volatile memory.

There will be a number of occasions where it makes sense to power down an information processing device, seize it, and take it back to the Forensic Laboratory for processing. Reasons for doing this may vary and could include, but not be limited to:

- removing information processing equipment from a hostile environment;
- the need to use specialized equipment that is not available on-site but is available in the Forensic Laboratory;
- there is not enough time, within the time constraints set, to complete the required evidential recovery on-site;
- there is the need for discretion and it is not appropriate for Forensic Laboratory employees to be seen on-site.

Again, it may be necessary to examine information processing equipment on-site where:

- removal would lose evidence that may be critical to the case if the information processing equipment is powered off;
- the information processing equipment cannot, for any reason, be removed from the site.

The final decision as to what action is to be undertaken will be made by the Forensic Laboratory First Response Team Leader.

INFORMATION PROCESSING EQUIPMENT POWERED OFF ON ARRIVAL

- if information processing equipment is powered off on arrival, it should be removed from the scene for forensic examination without being powered up if at all possible;
- if information processing equipment is powered off on arrival and must be powered up and examined on-site, then this is fraught with issues, as it can claimed that the Forensic Laboratory First Response Team have altered the evidence held, which is correct. It can be further claimed that it cannot be proved what the status of the evidence was before it was powered up, which is correct. This approach should be avoided if at all possible, and if necessary must only be performed with the Client fully understanding the consequences of this action, and all actions being carried out by a fully technically competent Forensic Analyst.

INFORMATION PROCESSING EQUIPMENT POWERED ON ON ARRIVAL

There are basically two situations that can be encountered by the Forensic Laboratory First Response Team, and these are:

- powered up information processing equipment that must be examined on-site;
- powered up information processing equipment that is to be seized and taken back to the Forensic Laboratory for examination.

Where information processing equipment is to be seized and returned to the Forensic Laboratory, it will need to have the power removed from it. The correct powering down of information processing equipment is essential.

The first thing to consider is where the evidence to be recovered is likely to be located either on the disk or in memory. This will depend on the case, the Client instructions, and good practice for the situation in which the Forensic Laboratory First Response Team find themselves.

If the information processing equipment is to be examined on-site, then this is covered in Section 8.6.17.

If the information processing equipment is to be seized, then the following must be considered:

Note

There are opposing opinions regarding the "powering off" any information processing equipment that is "powered on." Basically, the two opinions are that:

- if the plug is pulled, the volatile information is lost and it may well preclude rebooting the device again;
- if a graceful shutdown is undertaken, then there may be data destruction (if the equipment has been booby trapped) or other ways that evidence may be altered during the graceful closedown process.

PULLING THE PLUG

If power is to be removed from the device by removing the power, rather than performing a graceful closedown, then the power should be literally "pulled" from the device. This entails different approaches for different information processing devices. Each is defined in the relevant section relating to different information processing devices to which they relate. No matter what device is having its "power pulled," the following guidance is relevant:

- the approach to pulling the power may depend on the operating system of the information processing device. A general guide for this is given in this Appendix, but expert advice should always be sought;
- where power is supplied through an UPS (Uninterruptible Power Supply) or similar, the power should be pulled from the device—not the UPS or wall socket;
- always pull the power from the information processing device rather than the power outlet—sometimes information processing devices have been "booby trapped" to destroy evidence;
- where a portable device is seized (i.e., a non-standard power supply)—always seize the power supply;
- where a laptop is to be seized, the battery should be removed, to prevent accidental powering up;
- with some information processing devices, it is essential to ensure that power to them is retained or they may go into "sleep" or "encrypted" mode. This may preclude access to the evidence held on the device;
- where an information processing device is shared by a number of users, and the currently logged in used is not involved in the case, a graceful closedown should be undertaken. Details of the current logged in user and programs that they are running should be recorded, along with any photographs of the screen;
- all information processing devices that are seized must be safely and securely transported to the Forensic Laboratory for examination with a full Chain of Custody documented;
- for any seized information processing device that may contain evidence it must be possible to prove that the evidence seized is that same as that which was examined in the Forensic Laboratory;
- where the legislation within the jurisdiction requires it, evidence of any alleged offence must be preserved according to the requirements of the legislation in the jurisdiction.

LIVE SYSTEMS

While historically, the "pull the plug" approach has been used, there is a move away from this for live or business critical systems and the need for live evidence collection.

APPENDIX 11 - SOME TYPES OF METADATA THAT MAY BE RECOVERABLE FROM DIGITAL IMAGES

There are a variety of standards dealing with metadata for digital images. Some cameras will allow the user to enter personal data into the camera (e.g., owner name). The majority of metadata is calculated and recorded by the camera with little input from the user, apart from taking the picture itself. Typical information recorded includes, but may vary between camera makes and models:

- compressed bits per pixel;
- current date and time;

- date and time of picture;
- Exif version;
- exposure bias;
- exposure time;
- *F* number;
- flash;
- focal length;
- GPS information (but only for some cameras);
- manufacturer;
- maximum aperture value;
- model;
- owner name and other details;
- resolution unit;
- software version;
- type of compression;
- unique number of each picture taken auto increments;
- *x*-resolution;
- YcbCr Positioning;
- *y*-resolution;

APPENDIX 12 - COUNTRIES WITH DIFFERENT FIXED LINE TELEPHONE CONNECTIONS

Below is a list of some of the countries that have different telephone connectors:

- Australia;
- Austria;
- Belgium;
- Brazil;
- The Czech Republic;
- Denmark;
- Finland and Norway;
- France;
- Germany;
- Greece;
- Holland;
- Hungary;
- India;
- Japan;
- Kuwait, Jordan, Iran, and Iraq;
- Russia and Poland;
- South Africa;
- South Korea;
- Sweden;
- Switzerland;
- Turkey;
- The United Kingdom.

Note 1

This is not a complete list, but a list of those connectors that have connection adaptor kits commercially available for them.

Note 2

Some countries may have more than one type of connector.

APPENDIX 13 - SOME INTERVIEW QUESTIONS

Note

Not all of these questions will necessarily be relevant to the case.

Below are a range of questions that can be asked from a suspect or victim at the incident scene. This is not meant to be a complete list but provides the basic set of questions that can be developed based on the specifics of the case.

THE INDIVIDUAL

The following should be ascertained:

- name;
- address;
- contact details;
- nicknames used;
- background information, including job and computing competence.

SYSTEM ADMINISTRATORS AND MANAGEMENT

- is there anything particularly sensitive about the system?
- what security mechanisms are in place?
- are there any personnel/personal issues that may affect the incident?
- have you noticed any suspicious activity recently, apart from the incident itself?
- how many people have root or administrator access?
- what remote access mechanisms exist and how are they controlled?
- what logging facilities exist and how are they managed?
- what are the current security mechanisms in place?
- how are they managed?
- what have you done since the incident was discovered?
- what were the results?

BASIC INFORMATION

- what is the computer specification?
- where was it purchased?
- when was it purchased?
- have you had it from new?

- is it always under your control?
- who else may have had access to it (full details)?
- do they have their own user accounts?
- who setup these accounts?
- details of all accounts and known passwords?
- what is the operating system?
- what applications are on it/
- what do you use it for?
- what applications do you use most?
- who loaded the applications onto it?
- where was the software purchased?
- what antivirus software do you use?
- how is it configured—scanning and updating?
- have you had any malware incidents?
- how was this handled—details, dates, type, etc.?
- who installed and configured it?
- do you have a firewall?
- how is it configured?
- who installed and configured it?
- do you use encryption?
- what type/products?
- why do you use it?
- details of all keys?
- do you use any software to cover your tracks on the internet or browse anonymously?
- what do you use?
- why?

NETWORK INFORMATION

Obviously if not networked, this section can be omitted:

- how are the different computers networked?
- do you use wireless connectivity?
- who set this up?
- how is security configured?
- what is the password and user ID for setting up the router?
- how is the router configured?
- how is remote access configured?
- who set it up?
- IP addresses in use?

STORING INFORMATION

- where do you store information?
- do you use external hard disk storage?
- do you use external USB or memory stick drives?
- do you use and other external storage devices?
- do you use any remote storage locations (e.g., on the Internet or elsewhere)?

OTHER PERIPHERALS

- what other peripherals are attached to your computer?
- what do you use them for?
- how often do you use them?
- where do you store the information recorded by the se peripherals?
- who installed them?

INTERNET ACCESS

- do you have Internet access?
- who is your supplier (ISP)?
- how do you pay for it?
- what services do you receive?
- how do you connect to the Internet?
- what do you use the Internet for?
- how often do you use it?
- what user IDs and passwords do you use for Internet access?
- what software do you use for Internet access and Web browsing?
- what search engines do you use?
- do you create favorites?
- how are favorites organized?
- were do you store favorites?
- do you use any add-ons for Internet access?
- have you created any Web sites?
- if so—details including hosters, user accounts, and passwords?
- where do you save files you download from the Internet?
- have you paid to download files from the Internet?
- if so—details?
- have you accessed and downloaded files from password-protected Web sites or those that require you to register?
- if so details?
- do you use newsgroups?
- if so, details?
- what do you use them for?
- how do you access them?
- do you use any file sharing or Peer to Peer (P2P) software?
- if so—what?
- what for?
- where do you store these files?
- what have you uploaded for sharing?
- what social network sites do you use (FaceBook, Twitter, MySpace, etc.)?
- what for?
- details of all accounts and known passwords?

E-MAIL

- do you use e-mail?
- if so—what e-mail addresses do you use and what are the passwords?
- what software do you use to access your e-mail?
- who set it up?
- does anyone else use your computer to access e-mail—if so who and user accounts and passwords?

MESSAGING AND CHATTING

- do you use chatting?
- do you use instant messaging?
- do you use any other communications services?
- details of all user accounts and passwords?
- what chat rooms do you use?
- how do you arrange off-line, private messaging or private chats?
- what nicknames or user IDs do you use?
- do you use a webcam while messaging or chatting?
- have you exchanged files with anyone while chatting, private messaging, or using other similar programs?

OTHER

Depending on the specifics of the incident and whether the interviewee is a suspect or a victim, other questions will be asked. It is the skill of the interviewer that will determine what they are.

A full keyword list should be built to assist in searching all media.

APPENDIX 14 - EVIDENCE LABELING

The following is the minimum information that shall be attached to any exhibit that is seized at an incident. The information may be integral to the evidence bag or attached as a label.

- Exhibit number;
- Case number;
- Client;
- description;
- seized from—location;
- seized from—person;
- date and time seized;
- seized by;
- signature;
- signatures of other witnesses (e.g., Evidence Custodian);
- a statement of certification of seizure.

The evidence label may also include details of Chain of Custody details attached to the evidence.

> **Note**
>
> If a new evidence bag is to be used after removing the exhibit from the original one, the original evidence bag or tag should be enclosed in the new exhibit bag or attached to the exhibit.

APPENDIX 15 - FORENSIC PREVIEW FORMS

- Case number;
- Exhibit reference number;
- reason for preview;
- location of seizure:
  - room no;
  - building name;
  - address line 1;
  - address line 2;
  - address line 3;
  - address linc 4;
  - post/zip code.
- owner;
- owner aware (Y/N);
- owner present (Y/N);
- examination details:
  - start time;
  - cnd timc;
  - BIOS keystroke(s);
  - boot sequence;
  - BIOS password (Y/N);
  - Password;
  - BIOS time;
  - BIOS date;
  - actual time;
  - actual date;
  - how connected.
- Encase boot details;
- number of hard disks;
- number of partitions:
  - total number of images identified in gallery mode;
  - approximate number of indecent child images in gallery mode;
  - approximate number of adult pornographic images in gallery mode:
  - additional Information and/or checks;
- Forensic Analyst name;
- date;
- signature.

APPENDIX 16 - A TRAVELING FORENSIC LABORATORY

The minimum specification for the Laptop PC that is the portable laboratory is:

LAPTOP

- dual boot Windows and Linux/Helix or similar;
- PCMCIA modem, network, IDE and SCSI cards;
- maximum memory available;
- maximum CPU available;
- external disk cabinet;
- Ethernet hub, cables;
- tape drive and tapes to make backups of images on-site.

SOFTWARE

- Forensic examination software;
- other software as required (preferably a full copy of a laboratory PC).

Note

The Laptop PC shall be validated before use, with records held in the Client's virtual case file.

APPENDIX 17 - MOVEMENT SHEET

The Forensic Laboratory movement form contains, for each exhibit:

- laboratory case number;
- Client/case name;
- Exhibit reference number;
- reason for movement/comment;
- Forensic Laboratory unique evidence number;
- evidence seal number;
- date;
- time;
- examiner or person receiving the exhibit;
- signature of recipient.

APPENDIX 18 - INCIDENT RESPONSE REPORT

Note 1

Not all parts of the template are used for every case, only those relevant.

Note 2

This report only covers the processing of the scene to obtain the evidence. The actual processing of the evidence is handled in Chapter 9.

If an Incident Response Report is required, then the standard Forensic Laboratory Incident Response Report template is used. If this has not been agreed by the Client in advance, then the following headings are used:

- front page;
  - Title of Report—defining the evidence examined, usually the Client's reference number (assuming it exists);
  - Client details;
  - Forensic Laboratory details;
  - Protective Marking—front page classification of report as defined in Chapter 5, Appendix 16.
- every Page;
  - Title of Report in header—typically using the unique exhibit number(s) processed;
  - Copyright notice in footer;
  - pagination in footer (page x of y) to show the report is complete;
  - version details in footer, according to the Forensic Laboratory's document control defined in Chapter 4, Section 4.6.3;
  - Protective Marking—front page classification of report as defined in Chapter 5, Appendix 16.
- Document Control Page;
  - Review History—part of the Forensic Laboratory's document control system, showing the history of the document and its updates;
  - issue status—draft or issued.
- Table of Contents;
- Client Instructions;
- details of the incident;
  - Date (incident discovered and date reported);
  - Type of incident;
  - Contact information of person detecting incident;
  - Location of incident;
  - physical security at site and how it is managed;
  - how the incident was detected;
  - other resources affected;
  - who has accessed the system since the incident was discovered?
  - who else knows about the incident?
  - what investigative steps have been taken to date?
  - what the results of the investigation produced?
  - details of First Responders (Forensic Laboratory employees and/or subcontractors).
- system(s) details;
  - make and model;

    - operating system;
    - primary user of the system;
    - systems administrator(s) if the system;
    - network/ip addresses of the system;
    - critical information on the system (with copy of risk assessment if available);
    - other relevant system information.
- seizure details;
    - details of the seizure—including all of the forms used in this chapter. This will include the details of processing the scene;
    - evidence collected;
    - Chain of Custody for all evidence seized.
- packaging;
- transportation to the Forensic Laboratory;
- incident containment;
    - whether the incident is ongoing;
    - whether network monitoring is in place;
    - whether the system is still connected to the network and who authorized it;
    - if not—who authorized it;
    - any logging in place and how the logs are being secured;
    - other steps taken to contain the incident;
- next steps recommended;
    - summary of recommendations for risk reduction;
    - timescales for actions;
- lessons learned;
    - results of the postincident review;
    - recommendations for continuous improvement.

APPENDIX 19 - POSTINCIDENT REVIEW AGENDA

- introduction to all attendees and their roles;
- a detailed timeline of the incident;
- Client instructions;
- the incident scene;
- what security was in place?
- did it work?
- did the Client employees follow their own procedures?
- First Response Team performance;
- were the First Response Team procedures followed?
- were they adequate?
- what information was needed sooner?
- were there any actions undertaken by anyone that could have prejudiced the integrity of the scene or any further evidence processing?
- what should be done differently in processing the scene for any future incidents?
- what corrective actions does the Forensic Laboratory need to undertake?
- what preventive actions does the Client need to undertake?
- what corrective actions does the Client need to undertake?
- any other lessons learned?

APPENDIX 20 - INCIDENT PROCESSING CHECKLIST

The Forensic Laboratory uses the following as a checklist for incident scene processing. It is amended as required for each case. This actually will develop into the Forensic Plan for any incident scene that needs processing.

- planning
    - initial contact and start-up.
        - intent and scope of the incident;
        - incident details;
        - does the client have its own first response capability?
        - what have they done?
        - arrangements for locating at the site including domestic and travel and other relevant arrangements;
        - sort out the initial meeting with relevant Client personnel (HR? Legal? IT, others);
- legal considerations;
    - jurisdiction;
    - overt or covert?
    - Law Enforcement involved?
    - employee privacy concerns;
    - other legal considerations Client Legal Counsel
- scope of Forensic Laboratory authority;
    - authority to seize?
    - authority to interview Client employees?
    - authority to take down production systems?
- Client requirements;
    - proposal to the Client;
    - client required outcome?
    - internal matter or criminal?
    - has a price been agreed?
    - does the client understand that scope and cost can vary?
    - reporting process;
    - escalation process;
    - access to Top management;
    - main Client contact
- resourcing
    - have the First Response Team competent employees?
    - agree First Response Team and Team Leader;
    - are outsourcing partners needed?
    - what support will Client provide;
    - timeframe required fro completion

  - is budget agreed?
  - situation report (SitRep);
  - document known facts with timeline;
  - obtain organization chart;
  - obtain all documents to date;
  - identify all people involved in the incident—including third parties, if appropriate.
- determining Approach
  - confirm facts;
    - interview schedule;
    - confirm respondent availability;
  - health and safety
    - determine health and safety risks;
    - ensure appropriate PPE available.
  - risks to investigation and mitigation;
    - can suspect(s) still access the system?
    - if so, how?
    - what sort of remote access is there?
    - how is it controlled?
    - are files likely to be protected (encryption, passwords, etc.)?
    - any suspects?
    - details of suspect(s);
    - access to passwords, encryption keys?
    - what Client security is in place?
    - does it work properly?
    - last audit report?
    - specialized equipment to evidence recovery and incident processing.
  - interviews;
    - define interview questions for respondents according to their role;
  - case processing;
    - determine evidence seizure approach;
    - location(s);
    - technology;
    - ensure that First Response Team has competences required;
    - identify workarounds if competence shortfall;
- identification and preservation of the scene;
  - locations for processing;
    - sketches;
    - photographs;
    - incident scene security and maintaining it;
    - identification of entries and exits;
    - access control methods in use and their management;
  - evidence identification;
    - is this all identified?
    - is all evidence covered by due legal process?
    - if not—what is there a legal workaround;
  - evidence seizure;
    - information processing devices to be seized;
    - information processing devices to be imaged;
    - information processing devices to undergo live acquisition;
    - information processing devices to be previewed;
    - updating of logs, notebooks and forms for all seizure activities;
  - review the site for completeness of seizure;
  - undertake secondary search;
  - release scene;
- packing and transportation;
  - appropriate packing for evidence;
  - checking out evidence from the incident site;
  - ensure appropriate transportation
- postincident review;
  - identify attendees;
  - issue agenda;
  - undertake meeting
  - produce report and recommendations;
  - raise and follow through CAPAs, as required,

Chapter 9

Case Processing

Table of Contents

9.1 INTRODUCTION TO CASE PROCESSING

Note

The Forensic Laboratory will always use tools that are validated and are in general use. This overcomes the challenge later in Court or tribunal case.

9.1.1 General

Chapter 8 dealt with evidence seizure and not evidential processing, except for forensic previewing, as defined in Chapter 8, Section 8.6.16, some on-site imaging as defined in Chapter 8, Section 8.6.17, and the need for direct data access and live acquisition as defined in Chapter 8, Section 8.6.18.

This chapter deals with the actual processing of the data captured from seized evidence as defined in Chapter 8 and the processes in the paragraph above.

The Forensic Laboratory will only undertake digital forensic case processing where it is both competent to undertake the work and it is legally permitted to do so. Therefore, it may not perform all of the actions defined in this chapter that can be performed by the Forensic Laboratory. This chapter describes all of the processes that it undertakes and each forensic laboratory should adopt them as they see fit, have the required competence, and can legally perform them.

9.1.2 Case Processing Overview

There is a well-defined four-step forensic case process that can be applied to all digital forensic cases, no matter what the evidence or circumstance, and this is defined in many text books as:

- acquire;
- analyze;
- evaluate;
- present.

Or

- collection;
- examination;
- analysis;
- reporting.

The digital evidence that is legally acceptable in the jurisdiction.

While this is the textbook definition, the Forensic Laboratory may adopt and adapt this to the following processes (Figure 9.1).

While every case that the Forensic Laboratory handle will be different, they will almost all go through some, if not all, of the stages of the model below:

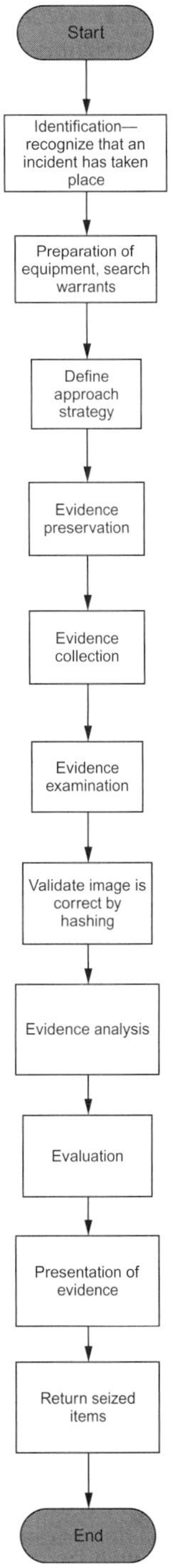

FIGURE 9.1 Case processing. (For color version of this figure, the reader is referred to the online version of this chapter.)

- *Identification*: Recognizing an incident from indicators and determining its type. This is not explicitly within the field of forensics, but significant because it impacts other steps. It is usually identified by the Client, who will engage the Forensic Laboratory after discovering an incident, as the Forensic Laboratory does not undertake proactive information-processing system management. This is the first time typically that the Client contacts the Forensic Laboratory, and the Client take-on process is defined in Chapter 6, Section 6.6.2. Depending on the case and the Client requirements, processing the case could include:
  - comparison against known data;
  - extraction of data;
  - recovery of deleted data files;
  - keyword searching;
  - password recovery;
  - decryption of encrypted material;
  - source code analysis;
  - track and observe an intruder;
  - evict an intruder and give security advice;
  - examination of storage media (many types);
  - Law Enforcement support;

- *preparation*: preparing tools, techniques, Forensic Analysts, search warrants (if needed), inclusion of other agencies (if required) and monitoring authorizations, and management support for any on-site first response as defined in Chapter 8;
- *approach strategy*: dynamically formulating an approach based on potential impact on the specific technology in question and the Client's staff or customers that may be affected by the incident. The goal of the strategy should be to maximize the collection of untainted evidence while minimizing impact to the Client or their customers as defined in Chapter 8, Sections 8.4 and 8.5.4;
- *preservation*: isolating, securing, and preserving the state of physical and digital evidence. This includes preventing people from using the digital device or allowing other electromagnetic devices to be used within the affected radius of the incident as defined in Chapter 8, Section 8.6.2;
- *collection*: on-site record the physical scene and duplicate digital evidence using standardized and accepted forensic procedures (typically done off-site but may need to be done on-site) as defined in Chapter 8, Sections 8.6.11, 8.6.16–8.6.18;
- *examination*: in-depth systematic search of evidence relating to the suspected incident. This focuses on identifying and locating potential evidence, possibly within unconventional or covert locations as defined in Section 9.10.2;
- *analysis*: determine significance, reconstruct fragments of data, and draw conclusions based on evidence found. It may take several iterations of examination and analysis to support the results as defined in Section 9.10.3;
- *evaluation*: determining the relevance of the recovered evidence, typically carried out by the lawyers. Not only will the content of the evidence be evaluated but also the chain of custody;
- *presentation*: summarize and provide explanation of conclusions. This should be written in a layman's terms using abstracted terminology. It must be noted that different requirements being met by the Forensic Laboratory will have different formats, and each will be specific to the Forensic Laboratory's processes. A standard incident response report template is given in Chapter 8, Appendix 18, and a standard case processing report is given in Chapter 6, Appendix 31. Depending on the actual work carried out by the Forensic Laboratory, the standard template for the examination of recovered evidence will be amended to cater for the case being processed;
- *returning evidence*: ensuring physical and digital property is returned to the proper owner (if the law in the jurisdiction allows) as well as determining how and what criminal evidence must be removed (if present). Again not an explicit forensics step but must be addressed. This step may require secure disposal as defined in Chapter 12, Section 12.3.14.10, and all records are kept in line with the document retention policy as given in Chapter 4, Appendix 16.

9.1.3 Contractual Requirements

The Forensic Laboratory must ensure that it meets all of the contractual requirements imposed by, and agreed with, all Clients relating to processing forensic cases. All forensic case processing, of any sort, must be subject to contract that may include a proposal or an ongoing purchase order as defined in Chapter 6, Section 6.6. A central repository of all requirements must be maintained and managed by the General Counsel in the ERMS to ensure that the Forensic Laboratory complies with all requirements.

Within each jurisdiction where the Forensic Laboratory operates, there will be different legislative requirements for the jurisdiction and Top Management must ensure that they are both aware of them and comply with them. In addition to the legislative requirements for the jurisdiction, the General Counsel must ensure that all contractual obligations are captured and applied to the relevant case or cases.

9.1.4 Work Standards

As with legislation, there are different work standards for different jurisdictions. Top Management must ensure that they are aware of them and comply with them.

Work standards may be nationally or internationally recognized good practice, or may be Client-specific requirements.

While the Forensic Laboratory has based its internal procedures on recognized good practice, or International Standards as appropriate, there is no guarantee of compliance with relevant requirements and Top Management must ensure that they are both aware of them and comply with them. Some of the sources of good practice used in developing the Forensic Laboratory's case processing procedures are given in Appendix 1.

This is in addition to ISO and National Standards, of which some are given in Appendix 2 and any number of books, journals, articles, and blogs on digital forensics, which are too numerous and rapidly changing to list.

9.1.5 Good Digital Evidence Principles

There are a number of generally accepted principles for processing a forensic case.

In the United Kingdom, the "Association of Chief Police Officers (ACPO) Good Practice Guide for Computer-Based

Electronic Evidence" describes the four key principles of handling digital evidence.

- *principle 1*: No action taken by Law Enforcement agencies or their agents should change data held on a computer or storage media which may subsequently be relied upon in Court.
- *principle 2*: In circumstances where a person finds it necessary to access original data held on a computer or on storage media, that person must be competent to do so and be able to give evidence explaining the relevance and the implications of their actions.
- *principle 3*: An audit trail or other record of all processes applied to computer-based electronic evidence should be created and preserved. An independent third party should be able to examine those processes and achieve the same result.
- *principle 4*: The person in charge of the investigation (the case officer) has overall responsibility for ensuring that the law and these principles are adhered to.

The G8 proposed principles for dealing with digital evidence are

- when dealing with digital evidence, all of the general forensic and procedural principles must be applied;
- upon seizing digital evidence, actions taken should not change that evidence;
- when it is necessary for a person to access original digital evidence, that person should be trained for the purpose;
- all activities relating to the seizure, access, storage, or transfer of digital evidence must be fully documented, preserved, and available for review;
- an individual is responsible for all actions taken with respect to digital evidence while the digital evidence is in their possession;
- any agency, which is responsible for seizing, accessing, storing, or transferring digital evidence is responsible for compliance with these principles.

The International Association of Computer Investigative Specialists (IACIS) has stated that there are three essential requirements for the conduct of a competent digital forensic examination:

- forensically sterile examination media must be used;
- the examination must maintain the integrity of the original media;
- printouts, copies of data, and exhibits resulting from the examination must be properly marked, controlled, and transmitted.

These have been synthesized into four rules for forensic case processing:

1. There should be minimal handling of any exhibit;
2. Any changes to the original media must be accounted for;
3. The rules of evidence for the jurisdiction must be met;
4. Forensic Analysts should not exceed their level of competence.

The International Organization on Computer Evidence (IOCE) has also published the "Proposed Standards for Exchange of Digital Evidence," which suggests the following principles:

1. Upon seizing digital evidence, actions taken should not change that evidence.
2. When it is necessary for a person to access the original evidence, that person must be forensically competent.
3. All activity relating to the seizure, access, storage, or transfer of digital evidence must be fully documented, preserved, and available for review.
4. An individual is responsible for all actions taken with respect to digital evidence while the digital evidence is in their possession.
5. Any agency that is responsible for seizing, accessing, storing, or transferring digital evidence is responsible for compliance with these principles.

The four different sets of principles and rules are broadly similar, and the Forensic Laboratory must ensure that it meets all of these requirements.

The U.S. National Institute of Standards and Technology (NIST) requires that disk imaging tools meet their criteria, which are

- the tool shall make a bit-stream duplicate or an image of the original disk or partition;
- the tool shall not alter the original disk;
- the tool shall be able to verify the integrity of a disk image file;
- the tool shall provide a bit-stream image or a qualified bit steam image if I/O errors are present;
- the tool shall log I/O errors;
- the tool's documentation shall be correct;
- the tool shall copy a source to a destination drive that is bigger than the source and document the parts of the disk that are not part of the copy;
- the tool shall advise the user of a source larger than the destination.

There are other good practice documents including the U.S. Secret Service "Best Practices for Seizing Electronic Evidence Pocket Guide" and the Sedona Principles for Electronic Document Production.

9.1.6 Health and Safety Issues

Health and Safety considerations are essential in all of the work carried out by the Forensic Laboratory, both inside the Forensic Laboratory's premises and on client site(s).

Full Health and Safety management considerations are covered in Chapter 18, but specific Health and Safety requirements for case processing include, but are not limited to:

- a circuit breaker should be provided above any forensic examination benches so that emergency power shutdown can be achieved in case of need;
- all Forensic Laboratory Analysts are responsible for keeping their working area in a safe, clean, and orderly manner;
- all Forensic Laboratory employees must be instructed in how to deal with an emergency (i.e., fire, bomb, etc.). These procedures, along with evacuation procedures, should be practiced on at least an annual basis;
- anti-static devices must be used not only to protect the Forensic Laboratory Analysts but also to protect any evidence that may be corrupted by electrical discharge;
- any Forensic Laboratory employees who are subject to viewing disturbing, stressful, or pedophile images must be offered counseling or psychological support from professionally qualified Counselors competent to deal with employees exposed to these issues;
- risk assessments may need to be undertaken where any equipment may be considered dangerous;
- at least one qualified First Aider should be nominated for the Forensic Laboratory. More may be needed depending on the size of the Forensic Laboratory or to comply with legislation, regulation or good practice in the jurisdiction. An alternate must be nominated in case of absence of the main First Aider. This may be another member of the Forensic Laboratory or a suitably qualified person local to the Forensic Laboratory. All qualifications and/or certificates must be maintained and it is the responsibility of the Health and Safety Manager to ensure that this happens;
- if any safety equipment has been designated or required on account of a risk assessment, it should be made available to the relevant Forensic Laboratory employee(s). It is their responsibility to use the equipment supplied;
- issues relating to electrical power supplied to the Forensic Laboratory's own equipment, to any seized equipment or Client equipment entrusted to the Forensic Laboratory;
- issues relating to the manual handling of heavy, large, or awkward equipment;
- on account of the constant adding to and removing components for the forensic PCs, special care must be taken of the risks raised by trailing cables and exposed power sources;
- the Forensic Laboratory shall be regularly checked for compliance with Health and Safety issues by the Health and Safety Manager;
- the Health and Safety Manager shall ensure that all Forensic Laboratory employees are subject to regular testing for ergonomic comfort on at least an annual basis. These may be subject to legislative or regulatory requirements in the jurisdiction. Any shortfall in legislative, regulatory, good practice, or user requirements must be addressed appropriately;
- the use of PPE, where appropriate.

There may well be other Health and Safety issues that vary from case to case and incident to incident, but these must be evaluated on a case-by-case basis and a risk assessment performed by either the Incident or Health and Safety Manager.

9.1.7 Laboratory Accreditation and Certification

Accreditation and certification of the Forensic Laboratory is a management requirement and this is covered in Chapter 19.

All relevant Accreditations and Certifications should be achieved in the relevant jurisdiction to maintain a competitive advantage. These certifications must be maintained to demonstrate to the outside world the level of skill and handling that the Forensic Laboratory has in managing forensic cases.

9.1.8 Caveat

While a forensic case may not start out as a case that is going to Court, the Forensic Laboratory makes the assumption that every case may follow that route, either due to evidence found or due to the Client's wishes. On account of this, each case shall be treated as if it were to be presented in Court.

9.2 CASE TYPES

There are a number of different case types that the Forensic Laboratory may have to investigate for a Client. The most common are

- inappropriate use of a system: using an information-processing device and either breaking the law or an acceptable use policy;
- unauthorized access: either unauthorized external or internal attackers attempting to gain access to information-processing resources;
- malware attack: of any type;
- denial of service attack: attempting to crash a system.

In all cases, the Forensic Laboratory has to be sensitive to the Client's internal processes and procedures, and especially so if a Client's systems have been used to attack or compromise another organization systems.

The Forensic Laboratory may be involved with requirements of different jurisdictions in many cases, and have to deal with a number of different agencies, all of which must be met as part of processing the case.

9.2.1 Inappropriate use

Inappropriate use can mean many things in computing, some of these include, but are not limited to:

- breach of the organization's acceptable user policy;
- committing a crime;
- leaking sensitive corporate information to external parties;
- sending inappropriate e-mail messages.

These are the typical cases where a forensic response has been required from the Forensic Laboratory.

The system or equipment that is used inappropriately can vary from a mainframe-based system to a mobile device.

Some cases of inappropriate usage will result from other case types that may have occurred.

9.2.1.1 Containment

The Forensic Laboratory is only ever called after a Client discovers a problem with their system, as it does not provide monitoring services. Therefore, it will start at the containment stage of the incident. The procedures in Chapter 8 are followed for attending the incident site.

Typically, equipment will be seized during the incident response stage and brought back to the Forensic Laboratory for imaging as defined in Section 9.9, and examination as defined in Sections 9.10, on-site imaging and remote imaging may be performed as defined in Sections 9.9.2 and 9.9.3, respectively.

There may be requirements to remove inappropriate material from a system that is not necessarily criminal (e.g., pornography in breach of the Organization's AUP) prior to returning the system to the Client. Where a criminal act has taken place, the Forensic Laboratory must advise the Client immediately, with a recommendation to advise the relevant Law Enforcement body, unless the Forensic Laboratory is legally required to immediately report the incident to Law Enforcement on discovery. If this is the case, the Client must be immediately informed. Where undertaking work for Law Enforcement, they will give directions as to the requirements of handling the equipment.

9.2.1.2 Gathering Evidence

Evidence will be gathered as part of the imaging process and then examination of the images produced. This will follow the same generic framework for all case types and for all imaged devices, but the evidence required will be stored in different locations.

9.2.1.3 Follow up

After the evidence has been produced for the Client, the following are typical options:

- Court case;
- do nothing either as no evidence of wrong doing was discovered or as the Client chooses to do nothing for some reason of their own;
- external tribunal;
- further investigation;
- improve the Client's security infrastructure to prevent recurrence of the incident;
- internal investigation and action.

9.2.1.4 Post Incident Review

A post incident review must be undertaken to learn from the incident as defined in Chapter 8, Section 8.9, and the agenda for the meeting is given in Chapter 8, Appendix 19.

9.2.2 Unauthorized Access

As there are so many possible different types of unauthorized access attacks that can take place when considering internal and external attackers, it is not possible to give procedures for handling them, but rather a series of options.

9.2.2.1 Examples

Examples of unauthorized access can be from internal or external attackers, and typical cases include, but are not limited to:

- accessing an insecure workstation in the office logged in as someone else;
- accessing and/or copying information without permission;
- accessing unsecured networks;
- attempting a root compromise;
- attempting to crack passwords by whatever means;
- running software to capture user credentials;
- theft of a laptop and using it to access the owner's account;
- undertaking a social engineering attack;
- using a script kiddie kit to attempt to access a target.

9.2.2.2 Containment

The Forensic Laboratory is only ever called after a Client discovers a problem with their system, as it does not provide monitoring services. Therefore, it will start at the containment stage of the incident. The procedures in Chapter 8 are followed for attending the incident site.

Response immediacy is essential in all unauthorized accessed incidents; this is especially true, if the access is ongoing. When dealing with unauthorized access, the immediate actions are to:

- disable the access method where the access method used by the attacker can be identified;
- disable the accounts that may have been used or compromised by the attack;
- disable the affected service where the affected service can be identified;
- for internal access attacks, ensure that physical security measures are appropriate as defined in Chapter 12, Section 12.4;
- isolate the affected systems, but this can be a problem unless up-to-date network maps are available.

9.2.2.3 *Gathering Evidence*

Depending on the specifics of the incident, it may be possible for the Forensic Laboratory First Response Team to:

- scan the attackers system to determine facts. This may be illegal within the jurisdiction and legal advice should be sought before attempting this;
- use incident databases to see if other people have suffered similar attacks and what they did;
- use open-source intelligence on the attacker. Using any facts known about the attack and using search engines to see what is known about the attacker;
- validate the attacker's IP address. Care has to be taken that the attacker is not alerted. A traceable IP address must never be used. The attacker may have used a dynamic address;
- use on-site evidence to identify the attacker (e.g., access logs and CCTV images).

9.2.2.4 *Recovery*

After an attack, the attacker usually wants to be able to return to the scene. Often an attacker will leave a backdoor access, root kit, or some other unauthorized software that may use the compromised machine as a Bot.

Depending on the level of access and how widespread the unauthorized access was will dictate the range of actions to be taken. Where it was a single workstation compromised as the user left their desk and no password enabled screensaver was implemented will have a different response than a full-scale network access with root or administrator access gained.

Recovery can include, but is not limited to:

- all passwords on the system should be changed, in case they have been compromised;
- any system that has a trust relationship with the compromised system should be inspected for signs of unauthorized access;
- any system that has a trust relationship with the compromised system should have its passwords changed if it is possible that they have been compromised as well;
- the simplest method of eradication is to do a clean installation of the system from the standard build image, as none of the installed software should be trusted;
- the method by which the system was compromised must be addressed, typically this will involve, but is not limited to:
  - configuring the network to deny all traffic unless it is expressly permitted;
  - disabling all unnecessary services and capabilities;
  - educating users on system, security, and especially social engineering attacks;
  - encrypting all laptops;
  - enforcing password screen savers;
  - enforcing strong passwords;
  - ensuring that all default passwords are changed;
  - installing system protection tools such as IDS and IPS;
  - installing centralized log consolidation;
  - implementing host-based firewalls and personal firewalls on all hosts, critical systems, and laptops;
  - patching systems;
  - placing all publicly available systems in a secure De-Militarized Zone (DMZ);
  - reviewing perimeter security and taking appropriate action to strengthen it;
  - securing all remote connection methods.
- reviewing the system for other vulnerabilities that could be exploited by an attacker and mitigate them.

9.2.2.5 *Post Incident Review*

A post incident review must be undertaken to learn from the incident as defined in Chapter 8, Section 8.9, and the agenda for the meeting is given in Chapter 8, Appendix 19.

9.2.3 Malware Attack

As there are so many possible malware attacks, it is not possible to give procedures for handling them, but rather a series of options.

9.2.3.1 *Examples*

Malware is a term that covers many different categories of attack. These include, but are not limited to:

- blended attacks;
- cookies;
- mobile code;
- pop-ups;
- Trojan hoses;

- viruses: there are a number of different types, boot sector viruses, file viruses, multipartite viruses, macro viruses, and scripting viruses;
- worms: there are two main categories of worm, network service worms, and mass mailing worms.

9.2.3.2 Containment

The Forensic Laboratory is only ever called after a Client discovers a problem with their system, as it does not provide monitoring services. Therefore, it will start at the containment stage of the incident. The procedures in Chapter 8 are followed for attending the incident site.

By their very nature, malware will spread quickly, so immediate action is mandatory on discovery of a malware attack is detected. The ideal solution is to disconnect any infected systems from the network, but this is not always possible, especially if the system performs a critical operation. If this is the case, then the Client's Top Management must make a decision based on a risk assessment whether the risk caused by taking the system down or removing it from the network outweigh the risks of leaving it connected.

Whether the system is disconnected from the network or not, there are a number of options for containing the malware outbreak and these include, but are not limited to:

- block specific hosts or services to which any infected systems are trying to communicate;
- configure e-mail servers to block suspicious content, but actively manage the quarantine area in case legitimate downloads are blocked;
- configure web browsers to block suspicious content, if available;
- consider blocking services that are used by the malware, or at least suspending them until the outbreak has been contained, and recovery to a secure state undertaken. This may have unintended consequences, as the most used propagation method for malware is e-mail. Care should be taken before closing down services as they may not only be essential but also affect other services dependent on them that may be essential;
- consider shutting down e-mail servers where there is a serious risk to the integrity of the Client's systems;
- detect non-essential programs with file transfer capabilities in accordance with the AUP;
- eliminate all open MS Windows shares;
- ensure that all open relays are closed;
- implement anti-malware software if not present and run it;
- implement spam-filtering software and run it;
- set scans and updates, as appropriate, for the Client;
- set web browsers to prevent unauthorized downloads of mobile code;
- update anti-malware software if not up-to-date and run it.

9.2.3.3 Gathering Evidence

It is unlikely in the extreme that a Client, or the Forensic Laboratory, will be able to identify the author of a piece of malware as it is either transmitted automatically or by accident from infected users.

There is only point in identifying infected systems and disinfecting them. Typically, this is carried out using anti-malware software. It is recommended that more than one tool is run to identify any infected systems, as benchmarking suggests that different tools have different success rates.

9.2.3.4 Recovery

While anti-malware software is efficient at identifying malware infections and at usually disinfecting or quarantining infected files, some files cannot be disinfected.

Recovery can include, but is not limited to:

- configuring software to quarantine suspicious files;
- consideration should be given to installing file integrity checking software to detect altered files;
- ensuring that anti-malware software is up-to-date;
- patching systems to remove exploited vulnerabilities;
- rebuilding hardware from scratch;
- recovering backups to reload the system;
- reinstallation of software;
- remove any MS Windows shares;
- run two different anti-malware products.

9.2.3.5 Post Incident Review

A post incident review must be undertaken to learn from the incident as defined in Chapter 8, Section 8.9, and the agenda for the meeting is given in Chapter 8, Appendix 19.

9.2.4 Denial of Service Attack

As there are so many possible denial of service (DoS) attacks, it is not possible to give procedures for handling them, but rather a series of options.

9.2.4.1 Examples

DoS attacks can take many forms and some include, but are not limited to:

- broadcasting on the same frequency as the wireless network and rendering it unusable;
- establish multiple login sessions so that legitimate users cannot access their systems;
- generating multiple large files to use all disk space;
- sending illegal requests to an application to crash it;
- sending malformed TCP/IP packets to crash the system;
- sending processor intensive requests to effectively fully use all CPU power;

- using bandwidth by generating large volumes of traffic. This is not usually possible from a single attacking machine as corporate bandwidth precludes this so multiple attacking machines are used to create a distributed denial of service (DDoS) attack.

9.2.4.2 Containment

The Forensic Laboratory is only ever called after a Client discovers a problem with their system, as it does not provide monitoring services. Therefore, it will start at the containment stage of the incident. The procedures in Chapter 8 are followed for attending the incident site.

Containment of a DoS or DDoS incident is usually achieved by stopping the attack.

Options for the Forensic Laboratory include, but are not limited to:

- address the vulnerability being exploited. Often this is due to having unpatched systems, so patching them should eliminate a known vulnerability;
- blocking the traffic from the source. This is not usually effective as the source address is usually spoofed or uses thousands of bots to carry out the DDoS attack. Even if blocking works, the attacker typically moves to another IP address;
- implement filtering to block the attack, however with the sophisticated hacking tools available, the attack will merely switch to another attack type. Implementing filtering can also have unintended consequences such as creating its own internal DoS in the extreme, so it should be carefully researched before being implemented;
- relocate the target is one method of overcoming the problem, but a determined attacker will find it after it has been switched to another ISP;
- remove the host from the network while remedial work is carried out, but this may have a serious business impact, but some large organizations have done this in the past to protect themselves;
- turn the attack around by using tools to switch off the attack. It must be noted that the bouncing of traffic back to source may cause an innocent party to have an attack for which legal redress may be sought;
- use the ISP to implement filtering. They will have more powerful network filtering hardware than almost all organizations and so utilize it.

9.2.4.3 Gathering Evidence

Gathering evidence on DoS and DDoS attacks is a challenging and time-consuming process.

Primary evidence will come from IP addresses; however, this is usually spoofed or uses an innocent-hijacked address. DDoS attacks may use thousands of hosts, each with multiple spoofed hosts. Usually, the IP addresses that are real and identified are intermediate systems that are generating the attack traffic and not the "master" who originated it. Tracing IP addresses through multiple ISPs is fraught with difficulty as many will not cooperate without relevant legal subpoenas (or equivalent in the jurisdiction). The time taken to obtain these is usually greater than the duration of the attack and trying to trace IP addresses after an attack has ended is well-nigh impossible in many cases.

The other main source of information will come from internal log files, but as DoS and DDoS attacks work by overwhelming the system, it follows that this will generate excessive log traffic as well. This means that there is an excessive amount to examine and this is a time-consuming process. Additionally, depending on how the logs were set up, newer log traffic may overwrite previous log traffic and therefore erase potential evidence.

9.2.4.4 Recovery

It is essential to recover systems as soon as possible in almost all cases, but they must be secured against further attacks prior to being returned to service.

Recovery can include, but is not limited to:

- denying any traffic that is not explicitly permitting, either into or out of the network;
- having the ISP implement filtering;
- moving to a different ISP;
- patching systems to remove exploited vulnerabilities;
- purchasing and installation of additional monitoring equipment, e.g., intruder detection and prevention software;
- rebuilding hardware from scratch;
- recovering backups to reload the system;
- reinstallation of software;
- tightening firewall rules.

9.2.4.5 Post Incident Review

A post incident review must be undertaken to learn from the incident as defined in Chapter 8, Section 8.9, and the agenda for the meeting is given in Chapter 8, Appendix 19.

9.2.5 Multiple Incidents

It may well be that there are multiple case types in a single incident and the processes above should be performed in parallel. A typical scenario is that:

1. a user accesses a Web site and downloads (knowingly or not) a file that is infected and the malicious code compromises a workstation;
2. the malicious code is used to infect other workstations on the system and/or other systems connected to the infected system;

3. the compromised systems are turned into a 'botnet' and are used to perform a DDoS attack on another system.

In this case, all four case types are possibly present:

- Case 1: inappropriate use, malicious code;
- Case 2: unauthorized access;
- Case 3: malicious code and unauthorized access;
- Case 4: denial of service attack and possible unauthorized access.

9.3 PRECASE PROCESSING

Having set up the Forensic Laboratory accommodation, the laboratory, and IT infrastructure, it is necessary to undertake a number of precase processing steps independent of the type of case being processed. Different types of cases to be handled are covered after this section.

9.3.1 Use of Digital Media in Forensic Cases

Types of media that this may include are

- hard disk drives;
- other disk drives;
- CDs;
- DVDs;
- backup tapes;
- USB memory sticks (aka thumb drives);
- keystroke logger media.

There may be other specialized storage media used, but these are the main types that will be used in the Forensic Laboratory.

Each of these media may play one or more essential roles in a forensic case carried out in the Forensic Laboratory, and it is essential that these media shall be properly handled, tracked, and maintained throughout their working life to eventual disposal. This type of housekeeping is essential and will also reduce the chances of challenges to the evidence itself, the Chain of Custody, or the forensic procedures followed.

All digital media to be used in Forensic Laboratory forensic cases must, wherever practicable, be purchased through existing Forensic Laboratory channels using recognized suppliers and the Forensic Laboratory process for their purchase as defined in Chapter 6, Section 6.7.4. Where this is not possible, local purchase may be authorized by the Laboratory Manager.

However they are purchased, they must be recorded in the Media Asset Register.

> **Note**
> This is different to the Forensic Laboratory Asset Register.

9.3.1.1 Hard Disks

On receipt of a new hard disk, a log for the life history of the disk shall be started. Attached to this must be the purchase order and other details to support the transaction.

Within the Forensic Laboratory, the Management and Reporting System (MARS) for Forensic Cases is used. Initial details of the hard disk shall be entered before entry into stores for use; a summary of these details is given in Appendix 3.

On receipt, each hard disk drive shall also be examined to determine that the manufacturers seal is present and unbroken. This fact shall be recorded in MARS. If it is necessary to break the seal to obtain the information above, this may be done but the seal must be resealed by applying a suitable seal that is signed and dated by a Forensic Laboratory employee who has opened the seal to examine the disk.

At this point, a new disk shall be given an unique local number of the form:

Labnnnnn

where
"Lab" is the identification of the Forensic Laboratory site of record (codes may be used to reduce the length of the label);
"nnnnn" is a sequential number starting with 0000 and going to 99999 and incremented for each disk that is introduced to the Forensic Laboratory.

This unique number will stay with this particular disk for the life cycle of the disk and if the disk has been securely destroyed or passed to another agency, then no other disk shall be given this number.

All disks must be used and stored in accordance with the manufacturer's instructions.

9.3.1.1.1 Wiping disks prior to use

Disks, once recorded and labeled, shall all be placed in a queue waiting to be low level wiped (i.e., the 7-pass process or whatever is required in the jurisdiction). This shall be carried out as an ongoing basis so that there are always "wiped" disks available for use when they are needed.

When a disk has been wiped, a new label shall be placed on the disk to show the date it was wiped, who wiped it, and with what tool. The manufacturer's bag should again be sealed with the date and the name of the person sealing it.

These details are recorded in MARS in the disk history log for the specific disk as defined in Chapter 10, Section 10.3.5.6.4. A summary of these details is given in Appendix 4.

> **Note**
> If the disk has previously been used, the disk wipe label is placed on the top of the label showing the case to which the disk was assigned.

9.3.1.1.2 Issuing a disk for use

When one or more disks are required for a case, then they are to be signed out from the secure disk store, noting the time, date, and person signing them out. This is recorded in the Hard Disk History Log in MARS as defined in Chapter 10, Section 10.3.5.6.6.

If they are not to be used on a case and returned, then this fact is noted.

9.3.1.1.3 Disk labeling

All disks will have their manufacturer's labeling and disk details on them.

The Forensic Laboratory shall add four more labels:

- wipe label: showing when the disk was last wiped, by whom, and with what tool;
- disk label: this is the locally applied unique disk label that lives with the disk for its life;
- classification label: this is the classification of the contents of the disk as given in Chapter 5, Appendix 16;
- ownership label: the details of ownership of the disk (i.e., the Forensic Laboratory), including all address and relevant contact details for the disk.

Only one of the wipe or disk labels will be visible at any one time, as disk and wipe labels will be overlaid to show the most recent action (i.e., wiping and ready for assignment or assigned to a case).

9.3.1.1.4 Disks and caddies

Hard disks should be placed in disk caddies for use to facilitate their use and to preclude possible wear and tear on the disk leads. For this reason, once a disk has been entered into Forensic Laboratory service it should be assigned to a caddy from which it is never removed. This also facilitates storage in the fire safes and reduces the risk of accidental physical damage during storage.

The outside of the caddy should have duplicates of the label placed on the actual disk so that this information can be easily seen without opening the caddy (but checks should be carried out to ensure that what is on the caddy actually is the same as on the disk inside the caddy).

9.3.1.1.5 Transfer of disks

When a disk is transferred to an outside agency or another part of the Forensic Laboratory, this fact must also be recorded in the Hard Disk History Log in MARS as defined in Chapter 10, Section 10.3.5.6.6.

Authority to transfer a disk must be obtained in writing from the Laboratory Manager and be recorded in the Hard Disk History Log.

Any disks being transferred outside the Forensic Laboratory must be labeled with the relevant classification level label as given in Chapter 5, Appendix 16.

Additionally, all disks must be clearly marked that they are the property of the Forensic Laboratory with a contact number.

9.3.1.1.6 Disk reuse

When a disk is no longer needed for its current assignment, it may be released back into the available pool of disks for use.

It is essential that the relevant Forensic Analyst ensures that any relevant backup or archival processes necessary are carried out as defined in Chapter 7, Section 7.7.4.

Once a disk is to be released back into the disk pool, it shall be wiped in accordance with current Forensic Laboratory disk wiping procedures and labeled to show when it was wiped, by whom, and with what tool as defined in Section 9.3.1.1.1.

The pool disks will then remain in the secure storage area until needed and be reissued as required in accordance with the procedures above.

All disk movements shall be recorded in the Hard Disk History Log in MARS as defined in Chapter 10, Section 10.3.5.6.

9.3.1.1.7 Forensics disk disposal

Forensic disks must be disposed of when they become unserviceable by either crashing, failing in operation, or failing regular disk checking programs (if used).

Forensic Laboratory disks must be disposed of in one of the following ways:

- use of a specialized, vetted, and approved disposal company within the jurisdiction and certificate of disposal obtained;
- be physically destroyed by Forensic Laboratory employees using a disk punch, sledge hammer, drill, or other approved method (e.g., take the disk apart and burn it to destroy the data held on the platters).

The date and method of disposal must be recorded on the Hard Disk History Log in MARS along with the person carrying out the task as defined in Chapter 10, Section 10.3.5.6.5. If the disk is sent to an outside agency for disposal, then a copy of the transfer document must be added to the relevant Hard Disk History Log. This may involve making multiple copies of the transfer note.

All Hard Disk History Logs shall be kept securely and in accordance with the Forensic Laboratory retention policy for forensic casework as given in Chapter 4, Appendix 16.

9.3.1.2 *Tapes*

Tapes will typically be used as backup and archive media, but experience indicates that these would not be used on their own for current cases, as tape is more likely to fail and is more difficult to recover than disk storage.

On receipt of a new tape, a log for the life history of the tape shall be started. Attached to this must be the purchase order and other details to support the transaction.

Within the Forensic Laboratory, the Management and Reporting System (MARS) for Forensic Cases is used. Initial details of the tape shall be entered before entry into stores for use. A summary of these details is given in Appendix 5.

At this point, a new tape shall be given an unique local number of the form:

Labnnnnn

where
"Lab" is the identification of the Forensic Laboratory site of record (codes may be used to reduce the length of the label);

"nnnnn" is a sequential number starting with 00001 and going to 99999 and incremented for each tape that is introduced to the Forensic Laboratory.

This unique number will stay with this particular tape for the life cycle of the tape and if the tape has been securely destroyed or passed to another agency, then no other tape shall be given this number.

All tapes must be used and stored in accordance with the manufacturer's instructions.

> **Note**
> These tapes are used outside the normal Forensic Laboratory IT backup cycle.

9.3.1.2.1 Wiping tapes prior to use

Tapes, once recorded and labeled, shall all be placed in a queue waiting to be low level wiped (i.e., degaussing or specialized secure wiping, whatever is required in the jurisdiction). This shall be carried out as an ongoing basis so that there are always "wiped" tapes available for use when they are needed.

When a tape has been wiped, a new label shall be placed on the tape to show the date it was wiped, who wiped it, and with what tool.

These details are recorded in MARS in the tape history log for the specific tape as defined in Chapter 10, Section 10.3.5.7.4. A summary of these details is given in Appendix 6.

> **Note**
> If the tape has previously been used, the tape wipe label is placed on the top of the label showing the case to which the tape was assigned.

9.3.1.2.2 Issuing a tape

When one or more tapes are required for case-processing operations, then they are to be signed out from the secure tape store, noting the time, date, and person signing them out. This is recorded in the Tape History Log in MARS as defined in Chapter 10, Section 10.3.5.7.6.

Tapes can be used either for general case processing backup purposes or backing up a specific set of files (e.g., a complete case to a file, a series of images for different cases to a tape, etc.).

9.3.1.2.3 Tape labeling

All tapes will have their manufacturer's labeling and some details on them.

The Forensic Laboratory shall add four more labels:

- wipe label: showing when the tape was last wiped, by whom, and what with (method or tool);
- tape label: this is the locally applied unique tape label that lives with the tape for its life;
- classification label: this is the classification of the contents of the tape as given in Chapter 5, Appendix 16;
- ownership label: the details of ownership of the tape (i.e., the Forensic Laboratory), including all address and relevant contact details for the tape.

Only one of the wipe or tape labels will be visible at any one time, as tape and wipe labels will be overlaid to show the most recent action (i.e., wiping and ready for assignment or assigned to a case).

9.3.1.2.4 Transfer of tapes

When a tape is transferred to an outside agency or another part of the Forensic Laboratory, this fact must also be recorded in the Tape History Log in MARS as defined in Chapter 10, Section 10.3.5.7.6.

Authority to transfer a tape must be obtained in writing from the Forensic Laboratory Manager and be recorded in the Tape History Log.

Any tapes being transferred outside the Forensic Laboratory must be labeled with the relevant classification level label as defined in the Forensic Laboratory IMS as given in Chapter 5, Appendix 16.

Additionally, all tapes must be clearly marked that they are the property of the Forensic Laboratory with a contact number.

9.3.1.2.5 Tape reuse

Once a tape is to be released back into the tape pool, it shall be wiped in accordance with current Forensic Laboratory tape wiping procedures and labeled to show when it was wiped, by whom, and with what tool or process as defined in Chapter 10, Section 10.3.5.7.4.

The pool tapes will then remain in the secure storage area until needed and be reissued as required in accordance with the procedures above.

All tape movements shall be recorded in the Tape History Log in MARS as defined in Chapter 10, Section 10.3.5.7.6.

9.3.1.2.6 Tape disposal

Forensic tapes must be disposed of when they become unserviceable by either crashing, failing in operation, or failing regular tape checking programs (if used).

Forensic Laboratory tapes must be disposed of in one of the following ways:

- use of a specialized, vetted, and approved disposal company within the jurisdiction and certificate of disposal obtained;
- be physically destroyed by Forensic Laboratory employees using a sledge hammer or other approved method (e.g., take the tape spool apart and burn the tape to destroy the data held on it—but beware of fumes given off and ensure that Health and Safety requirements are met).

The date and method of disposal must be recorded on the Tape History Log in MARS as defined in Chapter 10, Section 10.3.5.7.5 along with the person carrying out the task. If the tape is sent to an outside agency for disposal, then a copy of the transfer document must be added to the relevant Tape History Log. This may involve making multiple copies of the transfer note.

All Tape History Logs shall be kept securely and in accordance with the Forensic Laboratory retention policy for forensic casework given in Chapter 4, Appendix 16.

9.3.1.3 Other Digital Media

There are often other types of digital media that can be used in the Forensic Laboratory, and these will vary on the specific case or use requirements. It is not reasonable within this book to try to cover all different media types in detail, but some general guidelines are given below. Some common types of common digital media in use are

- floppy disks: boot disks for clean booting, storage of small files;
- CDs: boot disks for clean booting, copying forensic images to, or supporting a report by containing relevant files;
- DVDs: boot disks for clean booting, copying forensic images to, or supporting a report by containing relevant files;
- USB sticks (aka thumb drives): used for clean booting, copying forensic images, covert acquisitions, or supporting a report by containing relevant files;
- Key Loggers: used for covert operations.

Within the Forensic Laboratory, these media are collectively referred to as "small digital media."

Floppy disks, CDs, and DVDs are treated as stationery items within the Forensic Laboratory and are used as required and may not all have their usage monitored in a history log.

USBs and Key Loggers used in forensic cases are treated as controlled items and their usage is recorded in the same way as disks and tapes in MARS as defined in Chapter 10, Section 10.3.5.8. A summary of these details is given in Appendix 7.

> **Note**
>
> Long-term storage of important data on CDs or DVDs should be avoided if this is the only media where they are stored. Recent tests show that these media do degrade and are not suitable for this type of long-term storage (i.e., 5 years^{+}).

The following applies to these types of media.

9.3.1.3.1 Wiping small digital media prior to use

USB and Key Logger, once recorded and labeled, shall all be placed in a queue waiting to be low level wiped (i.e., specialized secure wiping or whatever is required in the jurisdiction). This shall be carried out as an ongoing basis so that there are always "wiped" USBs and Key Loggers available for use when they are needed.

When a USB or a Key Logger has been wiped, a new label shall be placed on the USB or Key Logger to show the date it was wiped, who wiped it, and with what tool.

These details are recorded in the MARS in the USB and Key Logger history log for the specific USB or Key Logger as defined in Chapter 10, Section 10.3.5.8.4. A summary of these details is given in Appendix 8.

> **Note**
>
> If the USB or Key Logger has previously been used, the USB or Key Logger wipe label is placed on the top of the label showing the case to which the USB or Key Logger was assigned.

9.3.1.3.2 Issuing small digital media

When floppy disks, CDs, or DVDs are required for case-processing operations, then they are removed from the stationery cupboard and used, as required.

USB and Key Logger issues are recorded in MARS in the small digital media log for the specific small digital media as defined in Chapter 10, Section 10.3.5.8.6.

Note 1

All USBs and Key Loggers are wiped prior to use.

Note 2

Forensic workstations that are not permitted to use these media are restricted either by removal of reading/writing devices or by software-based restriction of use.

9.3.1.3.3 Small digital media labeling

Within the Forensic Laboratory, different colored floppy disks should be used to define the use to which they are put

- red: boot disks;
- yellow: wipe disks;
- orange: tools (e.g., BIOS cracking tools).

All CDs or DVDs used actively in operational forensic work shall be clearly labeled.

Where CDs or DVDs are used as a part of a report (e.g., containing supporting materials to the case report) they should be labeled with the following:

- case number;
- date of writing data to disk or of report;
- address and contact details of laboratory from where they were issued;
- description of contents;
- contents classification;
- optionally, the Forensic Laboratory logo.

Due to size constraints, it is not always possible to affix labels to USBs and Key Loggers as if they were a disk or tape. In this case, details are affixed to a sealed envelope that contains these media.

Note

If possible, encrypted or secured USBs should be used.

9.3.1.3.4 Transfer of small digital media

When a Key Logger or a USB is transferred to an outside agency or another part of the Forensic Laboratory, this fact must also be recorded in the Small Device History Log in MARS, as defined in Chapter 10, Section 10.3.5.8.6.

Authority to transfer a Key Logger or USB must be obtained in writing from the Forensic Laboratory Manager and be recorded in the Small Digital Device Log.

Any Key Logger or USB being transferred outside the Forensic Laboratory must be labeled with the relevant classification level label as defined in the Forensic Laboratory IMS as given in Chapter 5, Appendix 16.

Additionally, all Key Loggers and USBs must be clearly marked that they are the property of the Forensic Laboratory with a contact number.

9.3.1.3.5 Small digital media reuse

Once a Key Logger or USB is to be released back into the Key Logger and USB pool, it shall be wiped in accordance with current Forensic Laboratory Key Logger or USB wiping procedures and labeled to show when it was wiped, by whom, and with what tool or process as defined in Chapter 10, Section 10.3.5.8.6.

The pool Key Loggers and USBs will then remain in the secure storage area until needed and be reissued as required in accordance with the procedures above.

All Key Logger and USB movements shall be recorded in the Small Digital Device History Log in MARS as defined in Chapter 10, Section 10.3.5.8.6.

9.3.1.3.6 Small digital media disposal

Small electronic memory devices must be disposed of in the following manner:

- CDs, DVDs, USBs, and Key Loggers can be smashed into a number of pieces using a sledge hammer, or if a local shredder can cope with it, they can be shredded;
- floppy disks can be taken apart and the Mylar disk can be either cutup or shredded;
- any small digital device can be disposed of using a specialized, vetted, and approved disposal company.

9.4 EQUIPMENT MAINTENANCE

The Forensic Laboratory must maintain all equipment that they use in a standard manner. An overview of equipment maintenance for the Forensic Laboratory is given in Chapter 7, Section 7.5.4; however, specific maintenance requirements for case processing are given below.

9.4.1 Hard Disk Drives

- hard disks shall be handled at initial receipt into the Forensic Laboratory as defined earlier regarding checking, labeling, and wiping prior to use with records maintained in MARS as defined in Chapter 10, Section 10.3.5.6.
- each time a hard drive is used, the fact will be recorded in MARS as defined in Chapter 10, Section 10.3.5.6.6.
- when not in use, hard disk drives that have been wiped shall be stored in the secure store in their disk caddy.
- any drive that becomes unserviceable shall have the fact recorded in MARS and be securely stored until secure disposal can take place. The disposal is recorded in MARS along with the disposal type. Where a certificate of disposal is obtained, this is attached to the relevant

disk record in MARS as defined in Chapter 10, Section 10.3.5.6.5.
- disk records shall be retained at least for as long as the case to which they refer is archived.

9.4.2 Tapes

- tapes shall be handled at initial receipt into the Forensic Laboratory as defined earlier regarding checking, labeling, wiping, and formatting prior to use with records maintained in MARS as defined in Chapter 10, Section 10.3.5.7.
- each time a tape is used, the fact will be recorded in MARS as defined in Chapter 10, Section 10.3.5.6.6.
- when not in use, tapes that have been wiped and formatted shall be stored in the secure store.
- any tape that becomes unserviceable shall have the fact recorded in MARS and be securely stored until secure disposal can take place. The disposal is recorded in MARS along with the disposal type. Where a certificate of disposal is obtained, this is attached to the relevant disk record in MARS as defined in Chapter 10, Section 10.3.5.6.5.
- tape records shall be retained at least for as long as the case to which they refer is archived.

9.4.3 Small Digital Media

- small digital media shall be handled at initial receipt into the Forensic Laboratory as defined earlier regarding checking, labeling, and wiping prior to use with records maintained in MARS as defined in Chapter 10, Section 10.3.5.8.
- each time any small digital media is used, the fact will be recorded in MARS as defined in Chapter 10, Section 10.3.5.8.6.
- when not in use, small digital media that have been wiped shall be stored in the secure store.
- any small digital media that becomes unserviceable shall have the fact recorded in MARS and be securely stored until secure disposal can take place. The disposal is recorded in MARS along with the disposal type. Where a certificate of disposal is obtained, this is attached to the relevant disk record in MARS as defined in Chapter 10, Section 10.3.5.8.5.
- small digital media records shall be retained at least for as long as the case to which they refer is archived.

9.4.4 Software

- a software log of all installed software shall be maintained for all forensic workstations.
- no installation shall exceed the number of permitted licenses and annual audits shall be undertaken to ensure that this is so.
- all forensic software shall be maintained at the current release level after suitable testing (if deemed necessary by the Laboratory Manager). It shall be installed after going through the Forensic Laboratory change management process as defined in Chapter 7, Section 7.4.3.
- operating system patch levels shall be monitored and applied as necessary as defined in Chapter 7, Section 7.6.3.
- any software that is installed as part of a case (i.e., recreating a suspects system) shall not be recorded. After recreation of a suspect machine, the forensic workstation used shall be wiped and reinstalled in accordance with the Forensic Laboratory's anti-contamination procedures as defined in Section 9.3.1.
- all software shall be checked to ensure that it is the correct version and that it matches any checksums or hashes, where supplied with the software.

9.4.5 Spares

The Laboratory Manager shall ensure that there are an appropriate amount of spare parts and components for maintaining the Forensic Laboratory capability.

9.4.6 Validating Forensic Tools

All systems used for forensic case processing are tested and validated to ensure that they operate correctly. The requirements for this are defined in Chapter 7, Section 7.5.5. The tests differ for various systems, but, in principle, the standard test case is used, and the achieved results of the standard tests are compared with the expected ones. If they are not the same, this suggests a fault in the system setup and must be investigated prior to using the forensic tool for case processing.

Tests are conducted on all new forensic systems and on existing systems in the following circumstances:

- installation of new operating systems;
- major hardware changes (e.g., motherboards);
- replacement of components directly involved in the imaging process (e.g., SCSI cards) with different components;
- major software upgrades or use of a new imaging software;
- use of system to image a significantly different type of media;
- doubt concerning the forensic soundness of a particular system;
- prior to the use of new device drivers (e.g., for USB, Firewire, etc.).

Tests are not conducted for:

- replacement of components not directly relevant to the imaging process;
- minor software upgrades;
- replacement of cables, monitors, etc.

9.4.7 Forensic Workstation anti-contamination Procedures

All forensic workstations shall have removable hard disks in caddies for each case. These shall be removed when not in use.

When the Forensic Analyst finishes working on a case and is going to load a new case on a forensic workstation, it is essential that this workstation is wiped and the system is reinstalled to protect against any possibility of contamination of the new case being loaded and as a defence against any possibility of tainted evidence.

After removing the working disk for the case, the Forensic Analyst shall run the anti-contamination process to wipe the system disk and reinstall the operating system and required programs on the workstation using standard image.

This process shall be recorded on the contemporaneous work record for the case in MARS. The details of the Forensic Laboratory work record are given in Appendix 9.

Note

Unless a Microsoft Site license is in use, the continuous reinstallation of the operating system may cause problems with product key usage.

9.4.8 Hash Sets

One Forensic Analyst should be nominated the Hash Set Custodian and be responsible for maintaining a current list of hash sets in the ERMS for use by all Forensic Analysts in their cases.

Forensic Analysts will use hash sets to save time during case processing to identify known files by using the MD5 hashes for files. The MD5 hash is a 128-bit fingerprint of the file that should produce a unique identity for a file (or even a disk). While there is a statistical possibility that two files can create the same hash, it is mathematically insignificant as MD 5 uses a 16 character hexadecimal value. So theoretically, there are 2^128 possible MD 5 hash values in existence, so if one had a file system with 2^128 + 1 files, it is possible to guarantee that there will be at least two different files that will generate the same hash value. As 2^128 is approximately 340 billion billion billion billion possibilities, it can be regarded as mathematically insignificant. As a matter of interest, this is a third of a Google, which is defined as 10^100. Thus, known files can be identified by their MD5 hashes.

The National Software Reference Library (NSRL) is a part of NIST and maintains a list of known hashes.

- the safe hash set is a list of known good files, such as operating systems and commercial packages. This hash set is used to filter out known good files from a case under investigation.
- the notable hash set contains hashes of known files that may be of interest to the Forensic Analyst and are worthy of further investigation. Examples of notable hash values include child pornography, malware, etc. The Forensic Analyst can also create their own hash sets if required and import them into the Forensic Laboratory's two main case processing systems (Encase and FTK). This could be used, for example, for tracing the spread of confidential corporate documents throughout the organization by creating a hash file for all relevant documents and then checking all workstations using the hash set to identify any of the documents on the workstation.
- hash categories are a method of filtering hash values into similar groupings (e.g., Hacker tools, MS office, Ignore, etc., depending on personal preference.

Using safe hash sets can greatly increase the speed of a keyword search as the search tools will ignore this, in the "Ignore" hash set. The Forensic Laboratory has a base install hash set for all of its own workstations.

Notable hash sets are used to identify files that may be of interest to the Forensic Analyst.

Where a Forensic Analyst creates their own hash sets as the inclusion of a "wrong" file included can cause a false positive and at best can be an irritant to the Forensic Analyst and at worst can cause serious embarrassment. The user of any in-house-created hash sets relies on the experience of the hash set builder. For this reason, any in-house-created hash sets are always reviewed and authorized by the Laboratory Manager. Where they are to be created, unique files must be chosen for the hash set, e.g., creatmyvirus.com is unique to the tool, but setup.dll is a part of many applications installation package. If this was included in the notable hash set as a part of the "Create My Virus" set, it would also create a false positive as setup.dll is used in many commercially available software packages such as MS Office.

Note 1

Care must be taken with using the NSRL hash sets as they contain known files that contain both notable hashes and safe hashes. Therefore, it must not be used solely as a safe hash set. Within the Forensic Laboratory, the NSRL hash set should be split into a number of subcategories and only the ones relevant to the case being processed are loaded.

While the NSRL is one of the best hash set libraries and it is free, other sources may be used, as required, by the Forensic Laboratory.

Note 2

Should the Forensic Laboratory have reservations about MD 5 hashes being challenged, there is the option of using Secure Hash Algorithm SHA–256 or SHA-512, giving 2^256 and 2^512 possibilities, as opposed to MD5's 2^128. SHA was written by the National Security Agency (NSA) in the USA.

Note 3

The Forensic Laboratory should use hashing to check the integrity of all software that they use.

9.4.9 Asset Register

- an asset register shall be maintained of all hardware and software;
- invoices for all forensic hardware, software, and other equipments shall be maintained in the accounting files for the relevant period;
- a license log of all the Forensic Laboratory licenses shall be maintained by the Forensic Laboratory;
- all forensic software must be licensed;
- regular and at least annual audits shall be undertaken to ensure that the asset register is current and correct as defined in Chapter 12, Section 12.3.14.3.4.2.

Note

This asset register may be a subset of the main Forensic Laboratory asset register or may be a separate one.

9.4.10 Previous Versions

It is essential that all previous versions of hardware and software are recreatable and so all versions of software must be retained with all versions of hardware to allow a standard build to be recreated.

This is in case any errors or queries relating to the evidence acquisition or processing arises. It must be provable that the tools in use to process the case did not cause any issues with either the imaging or analysis of the image.

9.5 MANAGEMENT PROCESSES

9.5.1 Authorities

The Forensic Laboratory must ensure that it maintains an up-to-date set of operating procedures for all digital forensic work. This must be:

- authorized by the Laboratory Manager;
- approved by the Top Management;
- reviewed on an annual basis or on influencing change, to ensure that the procedures remain suitable and effective;
- all changes are recorded in the document control section of the procedures according to the Forensic Laboratory document control procedures as defined in Chapter 4, Section 4.6.3.

9.5.2 Liaison with Law Enforcement

Appropriate liaison must be maintained with the relevant Law Enforcement agencies within the jurisdiction. A single liaison point should be nominated for general liaison, though individual Forensic Analysts will often be in regular contact with relevant Law Enforcement Officers, depending on cases being processed.

9.5.3 Other External Bodies

Appropriate liaison should be maintained with the relevant external bodies as needed within, and outside, the jurisdiction. A single liaison point should be nominated for general liaison with relevant external bodies that are either relevant to general forensic case processing or specific cases. In many cases, individual Forensic Analysts will be in regular contact with such bodies, which may also include Special Interest Groups or other professional bodies of which they are members.

9.5.4 Service Levels, Priorities, and Turn Round Times

9.5.4.1 Service Level Agreements

Unless set in the proposal or a purchase order for ongoing work as defined in Chapter 6, Section 6.6, the standard default Service Level Agreement (SLA) target for the forensic case processing is set to:

- 2 weeks from receipt to the end of initial investigation for unencrypted cases;
- 3 weeks from receipt to the end of initial investigation for encrypted cases.

Note

While these are targets, it is accepted that these are subject to variation due to a number of reasons. Specific TRTs that affect these targets may be agreed.

9.5.4.2 Priorities

Once a request for Forensic Laboratory support has been approved, the Laboratory Manager must set a priority and

TRT for the case, unless the TRT has been agreed with the Client.

This will depend on the following:

- available resources;
- possibility of destruction of property;
- potential victims;
- children at risk;
- Client or Human Resources Department deadlines;
- Court or tribunal dates;
- legal considerations;
- nature of the incident;
- possibility of death or injury based on evidence to be recovered;
- volatile nature of the evidence;
- which exhibits have the potential to provide the most relevant information for the case.

9.5.4.3 Changing Priorities and TRTs

It may well be that a case received by the Forensic Laboratory has to be completed faster than the current default SLAs. This will be agreed between the Incident Manager and the Forensic Laboratory Manager. The agreement of a higher priority or fast TRT may require the re-prioritization of case work for one or more of the Forensic Analysts.

Where this is the case, it is the responsibility of the Laboratory Manager to advise Account Managers whose Client's SLAs or TRTs may be affected. Any such changes must be recorded in the relevant case files in MARS.

9.5.5 Case Monitoring

Each week, at the Forensic Laboratory case processing meeting, a progress report on all current forensic cases shall be carried out. The update should include:

- all cases and their progress against TRTs;
- Court dates for the coming week;
- assigning any unassigned cases;
- reassigning cases, where necessary.

Where TRTs are not going to be met, the Laboratory Manager shall take appropriate action, including advising the relevant Account Manager(s).

9.5.6 Audit

In addition to the quality audits undertaken as part of the ISO 9001 process, the Laboratory Manager shall carry out regular audits of work performed by the Forensic Analysts, as follows:

- an audit of all aspects of the Forensic Analysts work (from First Responder through to Court appearances) shall be undertaken by the Laboratory Manager at least annually;
- where case files are to be audited, they should be chosen randomly to obtain a fair representation of work carried out by the Forensic Laboratory;
- records of all audits shall be retained for inspection as part of the IMS audit process as defined in Chapter 4, Section 4.7.3. The records shall also include the requirements for any corrective actions as defined in Chapter 4, Section 4.8;
- all CAPAs shall be designated to a nominated individual and shall be followed through to timely resolution by the Laboratory Manager as defined in Chapter 4, Section 4.8.2.

9.5.7 Outsourcing

There may well be times that work that would normally be carried out by the Forensic Analysts cannot be due to any number of reasons, typically:

- staff unavailability (sick, at Court, leave, etc.);
- desire to reduce any backlog;
- urgent jobs needing to be performed;
- lacking the specific skills in-house.

The choosing of an outsourcing partner is defined in Chapter 14, Section 8.2. All outsourcing must be approved by the Laboratory Manager and the Top Management, as appropriate.

9.5.8 Performance Monitoring

The Forensic Laboratory may have a number of existing SLAs as defaults, KPIs in place as part of its ISO 9001 procedures as defined in Chapter 5, Appendix 22 and Chapter 6, Appendix 9, and defined TRTs for Clients on a case-by-case basis. Case-processing KPI-reporting requirements are given in Appendix 10. These reports will all be available from MARS and should be published on a monthly basis to all relevant stakeholders, or more frequently if required.

9.5.9 Tool Selection

When the Forensic Laboratory has its chosen main case processing tools (e.g., EnCase and FTK), it may also use a number of other tools depending on the case being processed. The choice of tools to be used on a specific case will be determined by the requirements of the case, rather than slavishly following the main tools. Any new methods that are to be implemented for case processing must be validated as defined in Chapter 7, Section 7.5.5.

9.6 BOOKING EXHIBITS IN AND OUT OF THE SECURE PROPERTY STORE

The Forensic Laboratory case processing starts when the exhibit(s) first arrives at the Forensic Laboratory, unless the Forensic Laboratory was involved in a First Response incident. Incident response procedures have been covered in Chapter 8, and this chapter deals with an exhibit being processed from its arrival, through processing until either release or disposal.

These are typical processes as it is impossible, in procedures such as these, to provide specific advice for each and every situation in which the Forensic Laboratory may find itself.

Note

While the movement details are logged in MARS in the ERMS, the Forensic Laboratory also uses paper movement forms that are associated with all exhibits as given in Chapter 8, Appendix 17. In this way, a "real" signature is captured. This also allows movement to be carried out between the Forensic Laboratory and third parties.

9.6.1 Booking in Exhibits

On arrival at the Forensic Laboratory, the following must be performed (Figure 9.2).

1. Check that items are sealed and bagged and that the contents match the manifest. If they are not, then determine why this is not the case, if possible. Note the fact on the evidence movement record as given in Chapter 8, Appendix 17 and the Property Log in MARS. Consideration may be given to rejecting the exhibit should the Forensic Laboratory Manager consider this appropriate. A sample rejection of evidence letter content is given in Appendix 11.
2. Continuity labels should be completed and affixed to any exhibit, unless the continuation details are integral to the exhibit (e.g., part of the exhibit bag). Details of information to be recorded for exhibit movements are given in Appendix 12.
3. If this is not possible, then consideration may be given to rejecting the exhibit should the Forensic Laboratory Manager consider this appropriate as the "chain of custody" is incomplete. The relevant parts of MARS must be updated as defined in Chapter 10, Section 10.4.5.
4. The exhibit(s) must be booked into the Forensic Laboratory and be recorded in the Property Log and have the Movement Log updated in MARS to reflect the movement from the person delivering the exhibit to acceptance in the Forensic Laboratory. Details of information contained in the Forensic Log and exhibit movement forms are given in Appendix 13 and Chapter 8, Appendix 17, respectively.
5. A new property number must be issued to the exhibit. This will be the next sequential exhibit number available in the Property Log. This numbering system will start at 1 and go as high as necessary. This is the unique for each exhibit received from the Forensic Laboratory.

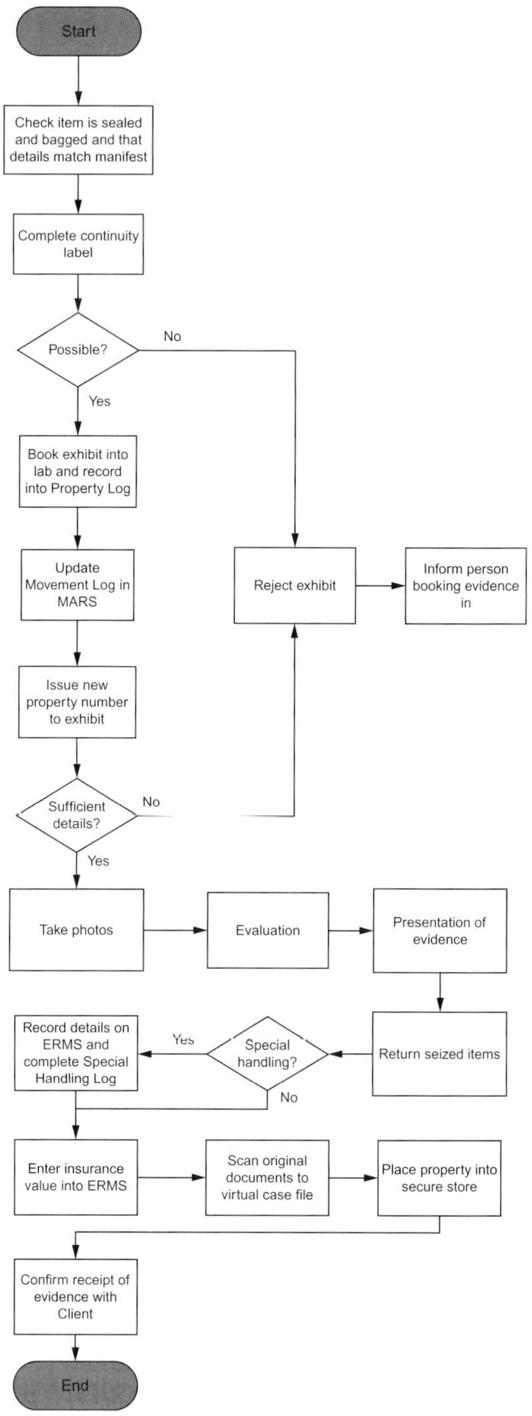

FIGURE 9.2 Booking in exhibits. (For color version of this figure, the reader is referred to the online version of this chapter.)

6. Consideration may be given to rejecting the exhibit should the Forensic Laboratory Manager consider this appropriate, if there is insufficient information available on the requirements of the case. Details of the Forensic Laboratory standard rejection letter are given in Appendix 11.

7. Digital photographs shall be taken of the property as it is signed into the Forensic Laboratory Secure Property Store. This shall show the property from all angles, specifically showing any damage to the wrapping or hardware contained in the evidence bag as well as close-up photographs of the evidence label. These photographs shall be added to the case virtual file in the ERMS.
8. Any items that require special handling shall be dealt with, this typically includes any items that need the charge maintained (e.g., mobile devices). Details of the special handling shall be recorded in the case virtual file in the ERMS. Details of any special handling procedures shall be logged in the property Special Handling Log in MARS. Details of the Forensic Laboratory Special Handling Log are given in Appendix 15.

> **Note 1**
>
> At this point, a Forensic Laboratory case number may not have been assigned to the case, so the Special Handling Log is linked to the property reference number. Once a Forensic Laboratory case number has been assigned, the property reference is linked to the case.

9. If the exhibit is to be rejected, then the Laboratory Manager must advise the person booking it in immediately and the reasons for it. It is up to the Laboratory Manager and the person booking it in to resolve the issue before the property can be accepted into the Secure Property Store.

> **Note 2**
>
> Where a property is rejected, the resolution prior to acceptance may need the involvement of other parties.

10. Insurance values are entered to the virtual case file in the ERMS for the property placed in the Secure Store to ensure that the Forensic Laboratory has sufficient insurance to cover them.
11. Any original documents are scanned prior to being added to the virtual case file in the ERMS. The originals are treated as property and stored in the Secure Property Store.
12. Once the property has been logged into the Secure Property Store, they shall be securely stored until needed for processing.
13. Confirm receipt of the exhibit(s) to the Client, a sample template confirmation letter is given in Appendix 14.

9.6.2 Booking out Exhibits

Once the Forensic Analyst is ready to start work on the case, they shall do the following:

1. Book out the exhibit(s) from the Secure Property Store and record the details in the Movement Log as given in Chapter 8, Appendix 17.
2. A copy of the Movement Log is retained in the Property Log to show that the exhibit is currently booked out to a Forensic Analyst to work on the case.

9.6.3 Returning an Exhibit

The following procedures shall be carried out for returning exhibits to the Secure Property Store:

1. The Property Log and the Movement Log shall be updated to show the return of the exhibit to the Secure Property Store as given in Appendix 13 and Chapter 8, Appendix 17, respectively.
2. The exhibits shall be resealed and the details of the exhibit be clearly visible on the Forensic Laboratory Evidence Bag. The Property Log shall be updated with the reseal number details. Details to be recorded on the Evidence Bag are given in Chapter 8, Appendix 14.
3. If the bags do not have this detail or a properly affixed seal, they should not be accepted back into the Secure Property Store, unless authorized by the Laboratory Manager, where notes covering any variation shall be entered into the Laboratory Log and also linked to the virtual case file in the ERMS.

9.7 STARTING A NEW CASE

> **Note**
>
> This is for all forensic cases processed in the Forensic Laboratory.

9.7.1 Case Numbering

Once a case has been accepted by the Forensic Laboratory, it shall be assigned a unique Forensic Laboratory case number.

This file name must be:

aaa/nnnnn/yyyy

where

- aaa is the initials that identify the Forensic Laboratory as an acronym;
- nnnnn is the case number of the year;
- yyyy is the year (taken from the system).

The case number is generated by MARS.

Every day that data are added to the case file, the file should be saved according to the naming convention as given in Chapter 4, Appendix 39.

Experience dictates that forensic software can crash and the reliance on a single backup case file created by the software is not prudent. This process allows the Forensic Laboratory to go as far back as necessary in the case file for the relevant day.

9.7.2 Assigning the Case

Once the exhibit(s) for a case have been booked into the Forensic Laboratory Secure Store, then the case shall be considered for assignment. The assignment process is:

1. On assigning the case number, the "real" case file must be started and the relevant virtual files be created by the Laboratory Manager as defined in Chapter 6, Section 6.6.2.2.
2. The Laboratory Manager shall set the priority level for the case and the Turn Round Time (TRT) and agree them with the assigned Forensic Analyst and the Client.
3. The submission forms containing the requirements of the case must be reviewed to ensure that they are clear and complete. These may have been filled in by the Client or First Responder and comprise the following forms if the exhibits were seized on-site. If the exhibit was just delivered for case processing, not all of the items below will be appropriate.
   - agreed proposal for the case processing;
   - evidence sought form, unless this is defined in the proposal as given in Appendix 16. This may be updated as the case progresses and further evidence is sought.
   - request for forensic examination (from a Client) as given in Appendix 17;
   - site summary as given in Chapter 8, Appendix 6;
   - seizure summary as given in Chapter 8, Appendix 5;
   - seizure forms as given in Chapter 8, Appendix 7;
   - movement form as given in Chapter 8, Appendix 17.
4. Once the Laboratory Manager has confirmed that all relevant paperwork is in place and correct, any issues relating to exhibits have been resolved, and any clarification of required outcomes settled, the case can be assigned. The case shall then be assigned to the appropriate Forensic Analyst. The Laboratory Manager should use Chapter 6, Appendix 14 as a checklist.
5. In this case, an appropriate Forensic Analyst is defined as one who is competent, i.e., has appropriate skills, qualifications, experience, and the workload capacity to process the case.

9.7.3 Priorities and TRTs

1. At the same time as assigning the case to the Forensic Analyst, the Laboratory Manager should set the priority of the case. Case Priorities are defined either by the Forensic Laboratory default SLAs or by the Client agreed TRTs.
2. TRTs must be set at this time so that the relevant Forensic Analyst knows the date that the job is expected to be completed.
3. The setting of new TRTs may impact current work, so this may need to be reviewed by the Laboratory Manager.
4. These instructions may be in the form of an e-mail or be verbal. They shall be added to the virtual case file in the ERMS, as appropriate.

9.7.4 Cost Revision and Confirmation

If a proposal was provided for the Client, then cost estimation is an integral part of that proposal and is given in Chapter 6, Appendix 18. Where a contract exists and a quotation is required, the costs will be given on the quotation. The cost of case processing should be checked, adjusted if necessary, and the Client advised accordingly. The need for this may be driven by additional requirements being set by the Client, additional items being seized as a part of the incident response process or any other matter that may affect the processing of the case.

The initial estimate of costs may well need to be revised, based on further requirements or on difficulties encountered (e.g., encrypted drives, etc.), and this requires a further updated estimate to be produced. This should also be produced using the Forensic Laboratory Cost Estimating spreadsheet and sent to the instructing Client with an explanation for the variation. The revised cost estimate should be saved with the date added as a part of the field name (e.g., revised cost 121231.xls—indicating a revised cost sent on December 31, 2012).

All estimates shall be stored in the virtual case file in the ERMS.

9.7.5 Creating a new Client Paper Case File

The Forensic Laboratory may have made the conscious decision to "run" a paper-based Client case file in parallel with the Client's virtual case file in the ERMS.

There are a number of items of information that can only really be captured on a paper, and a real signature is essential in a number of cases to prove the chain of custody or to demonstrate timelines.

For all of the information captured for MARS, there are hard copy forms used in the Forensic Laboratory with "real" signatures on them. The information on them is entered into MARS, and the forms are scanned and added to the Client's virtual case file, originals being stored in the secure property store.

The Client's paper case file is maintained by the Lead Forensic Analyst for the case.

9.7.6 Creating a new Client Virtual Case File

The Client's virtual case file is created at the same time as the Client's paper case file. The setting up of the Client virtual case file is covered in Chapter 6, Section 6.6.2.2 with the various storage areas defined in Chapter 6, Appendix 17. MARS will generate the Forensic Laboratory case number for the case, and all information in the paper case file is loaded into the virtual case file. The Client's virtual case file is given the name that MARS generates as the case number in the format defined in Section 9.7.1.

1. Once the relevant Forensic Analyst has been assigned to the case, they shall populate the Client's virtual case file and a Client's paper case file, unless this has already been done by the Laboratory Manager.
2. The Forensic Analyst shall ensure that all of the paperwork for the case is collated in the Client's paper case file and additionally scanned into the Client's virtual case file. Additional folders shall be added to the virtual case file as the Forensic Analyst working the case sees fit. The standard structure for a Client's virtual case file is given in Appendix 18.
3. The Forensic Analyst shall complete the following forms (if they have not already been completed):
   - new case form for cases starting at incident response as given in Chapter 8, Appendix 4;
   - evidence sought form for exhibits delivered to the Forensic Laboratory as given in Appendix 16;
   - case details as given in Appendix 17;
4. All new paperwork and correspondence shall be added to the Client's paper case file and be scanned into the Client's virtual case file.
5. The Forensic Analyst can then start to process the case.

9.8 PREPARING THE FORENSIC WORKSTATION

The procedures below are for all forensic cases whether the work is to be carried out on-site using a portable forensic workstation or using a desktop workstation in the Forensic Laboratory.

Any forensic workstation that is to be used to process a forensic case in the Forensic Laboratory must be sterile and unable to contaminate the new case from a previous case so as to avoid any suspicion of tainting. To perform this, the following is carried out:

1. The operating system disk is wiped to delete the current operating system and any files held on the disk.
2. The Forensic Laboratory standard build for the forensic workstations is loaded from the image held in the ERMS.
3. The wiping tool used is recorded on the Case Work Log. Details of the Forensic Case Work Log contents are given in Appendix 9.
4. One or more suitably sized sterile hard disks are chosen from the hard disk pool held in the Secure Property Store and are assigned to the case and loaded into the forensic workstation. The process for assigning a disk to a case is defined in Section 9.3.1.1.2.

9.9 IMAGING

9.9.1 Physical Imaging in the Forensic Laboratory

Note

This section deals specifically with cases where the Forensic Laboratory holds the actual exhibits to be imaged.

9.9.1.1 Book out the Exhibit(s)

Once the Forensic Analyst has completed the paperwork, set up the sterile forensic workstation, and set up the case, the exhibit(s) should be booked out of the Secure Property Store for examination using the exhibit booking out procedures as defined in Section 9.6.2.

9.9.1.2 External Examination of Exhibits

1. Each exhibit must then be examined by the Forensic Analyst. During this operation, the Forensic Analyst must wear latex or rubber gloves and other PPE, as appropriate (Figure 9.3).
2. The Forensic Analyst shall photograph the exhibit inside the sealed evidence bag and ensure that the seals and seal numbers are clearly visible, as is the description box on the front of the exhibit bag or the exhibit label.
3. At this point, if there are any breaks to the evidence bag or the seals have been opened this should be immediately reported to the Laboratory Manager unless this has already been recorded in the Laboratory Property Log or Movement Log as given in Appendix 13 and Chapter 8, Appendix 17, respectively.
4. It is at this point also that a visual inspection for any Health and Safety issues should be made, prior to opening the exhibit bag, and be recorded if they exist. If they exist, then the Forensic Analyst must use their judgment whether to carry on with the inspection or not. If the examination is to be stopped, then the Laboratory Manager must be informed and the fact recorded in the Case Work Log. The details of the Forensic Laboratory Case Work Log are given in Appendix 9.
5. Once the external inspection and photographs have been carried out, the equipment should be removed from the

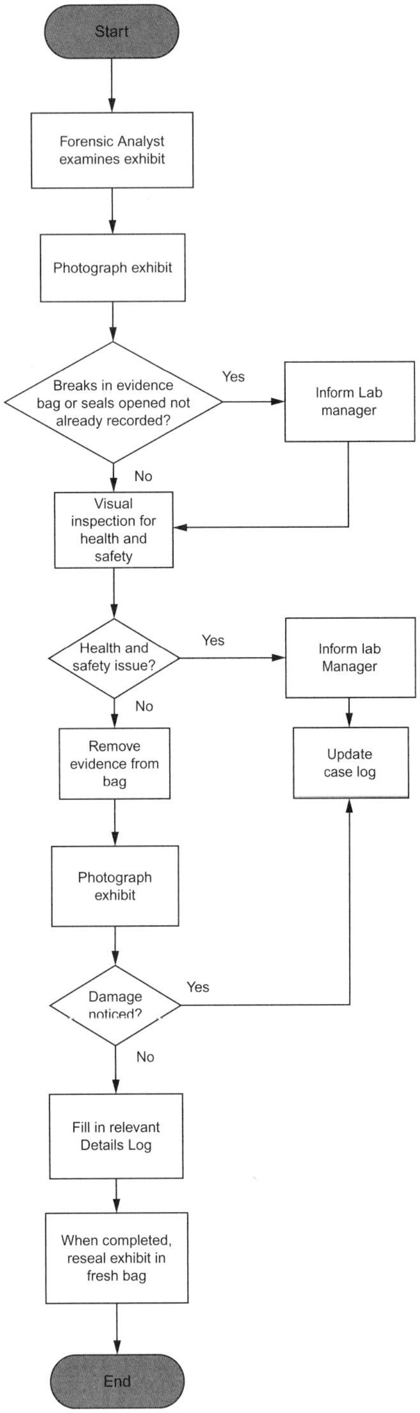

FIGURE 9.3 External examination of exhibits. (For color version of this figure, the reader is referred to the online version of this chapter.)

evidence bag, typically by slitting the bottom of the bag, leaving the seal and the exhibit details intact. The evidence bag shall be retained and used to store the exhibit in when it is returned to the Secure Property Store.

6. Once the equipment has been removed from the evidence bag, it must be photographed again. The photographs should record any damage, unusual features, serial numbers, licenses, connectors, and visible drives.
7. No physical damage should occur to any exhibit during this process, but if it does it must be recorded on the Case Work Log and photographs of the damage be taken.
8. The Computer Details Log or Other Equipment Details Log is filled in, as appropriate. The details for both of these logs are given in Appendix 19 and Appendix 20, respectively.
9. When the examination has been completed, and the original exhibit is no longer needed, it is resealed into a new exhibit bag, along with the original one (or seal, as appropriate) and resealed. The resealing is recorded in the Laboratory Log, and the details of this are given in Appendix 13.

9.9.1.3 Examination of Exhibits

1. All work on any exhibit must be carried out on anti-static mats using anti-static wrist bands to ensure that there is not tainting of the evidence by electrical discharge;
2. All forensic workbenches should have rubber antistatic matting under them to prevent accidental earthing.

9.9.1.3.1 Servers, PCs, and laptops

1. Servers, PCs, and laptops should be disassembled so that the Forensic Analyst can access any hard disk drives that are to be imaged and also investigate the interior of the exhibit (Figure 9.4).
2. Once disassembled, equipment should be photographed internally and any "strange" items photographed *in situ*, prior to removal.
3. Details of the hardware should be recorded on the Computer Details Log as given in Appendix 19.
4. Details of the hard disk must be recorded in the Hard Disk Details Log and photographs of it should be taken clearly, showing the serial number and other similar details as well as the jumper settings. Each hard disk shall have its details recorded on a separate Hard Disk Details Log, and contents are given in Appendix 21.
5. If there are more than one hard disk in the PC or laptop, then they should all be uniquely identified (e.g., using top or bottom to differential between two disks in a PC, or 1, 2, 3, etc., if multiple disks are in use. The disks must be labeled with the relevant exhibit number and also the unique identifier for the disk—e.g., labHD/00001/Top—indicating that this is the top disk from exhibit labHD/00001/1). The Case Work Log must contain details of the numbering system used and where there are multiple hard disks, multiple Hard Disk Details Log entries are created to record the details of each disk.

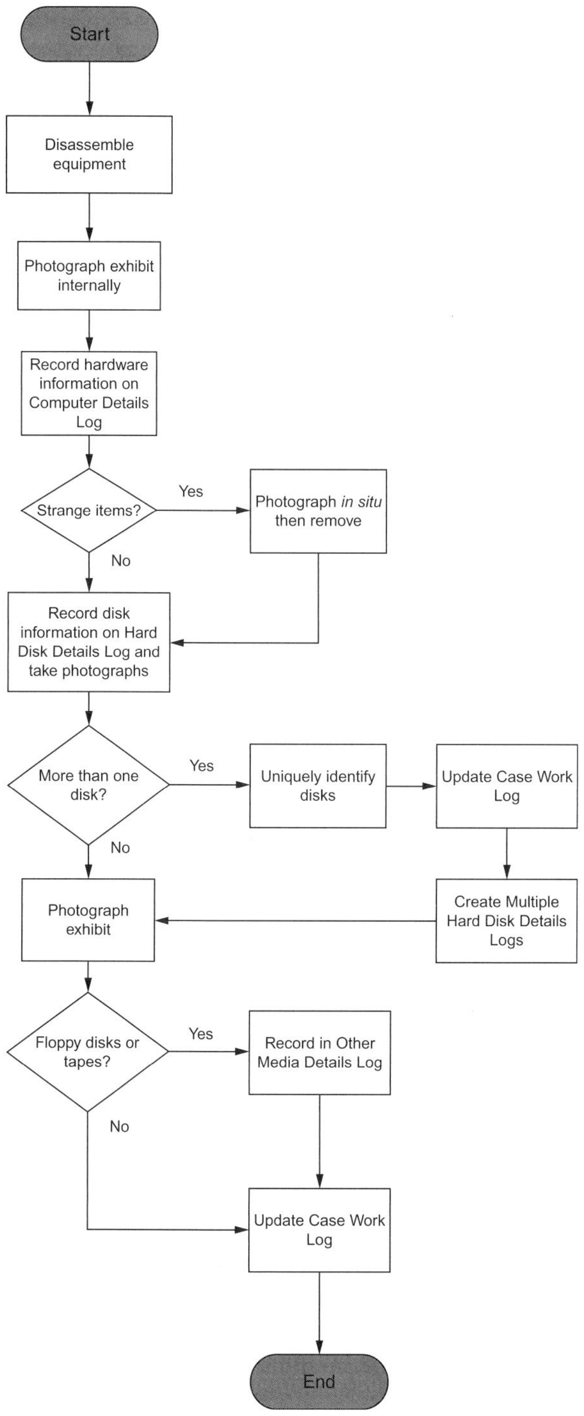

FIGURE 9.4 Examination of Servers, PCs, and Laptops. (For color version of this figure, the reader is referred to the online version of this chapter.)

Each log entry shall be clearly marked with the relevant and unique disk drive identifier.

6. If floppy disks, tape drives, or similar media are found in any PC or Laptop, they must be identified, be recorded on the Other Media Details Log with suitable annotation, and be uniquely identified as if they were additional hard disks. The Case Work Log must be updated to show that these items were found. The Other Media Details Log contents are given in Appendix 22.
7. All work carried out must be recorded in the Case Work Log as defined in Appendix 9.

9.9.1.3.2 Obtaining BIOS information

BIOS information must be obtained from Servers, PCs, and Laptops and recorded in the Forensic Laboratory Computer Details Log as given in Appendix 19. This is performed as below:

1. To perform a safe boot to obtain BIOS information, the hard disk(s) must be disconnected and a safe boot floppy diskette used to boot the PC.
2. Any hard disks inside should be removed for imaging, unless imaging is to be performed *in situ* (i.e., through the DOS, USB, or Firewire Port).
3. Once the Server, PC, or Laptop has booted, the Forensic Analyst should enter the BIOS Setup and record the following:
   - system date;
   - system time;
   - boot order.

- These details must be recorded on the Forensic Laboratory Computer Details Log.
- At the same time that the system time and date are recorded, the actual time and date must also be recorded from a known accurate time source, such as any of the atomic clocks available on the Internet. These details shall be recorded on the Forensic Laboratory Computer Details Log so that the time difference can be determined between the actual time and the system time.
- All work carried out must be recorded in the Case Work Log as defined in Appendix 9.

> **Note**
>
> Some systems may need a password to access the BIOS data, and some may require the manufacturer's boot disk to access it.

9.9.1.3.3 Tablet computers

Tablet computers refer to the range of computers that come with a touch screen and no keyboard. The tablet may have a SIM to give it access to the cellular network.

1. The tablet computer should be photographed.
2. Details of the hardware should be recorded on the Computer Details Log as given in Appendix 19.

3. All work carried out must be recorded in the Case Work Log as defined in Appendix 9.
4. Where the tablet computer has a low power level after being seized in the "on" state, connect it to a power supply so that it does not lose volatile memory until it is captured.
5. If the tablet computer was seized in the "off" state, then the Laboratory Manager shall authorize in writing a competent Forensic Analyst to undertake the examination and perform the imaging and recovery of any evidence. This authority shall be logged on the Case Work Log and countersigned by the Laboratory Manger with the time and date of the authorization. The power level shall be monitored and if the battery is low, the procedure in step 5 undertaken. This breaches the ACPO Principle 1, and so Principle 2 must be relied on. The means that the requirements for competence and being able to prove it, as required in Principle 2 are even more important, as is the requirement for the audit trail in Principle 3.
6. The tablet computer shall only be taken out of its Faraday bag in a Faraday-protected environment for examination and imaging.

9.9.1.3.4 Cell phones

1. Cell phones refer to any type of mobile device that can be used to make phone calls.
2. The cell phone should be photographed.
3. Details of the hardware should be recorded on the Cell Phone Details Log as given in Appendix 23.
4. All work carried out must be recorded in the Case Work Log as defined in Appendix 9.
5. Where the cell phone has a low power level after being seized in the "on" state, either replace the batteries and monitor it so that it does not lose volatile memory until it is captured or place it on the appropriate cradle or adaptor to charge it.
6. If the cell phone was seized in the "off" state, then the Laboratory Manager shall authorize in writing a competent Forensic Analyst to undertake the examination and perform the imaging and recovery of any evidence. This authority shall be logged on the Case Work Log and countersigned by the Laboratory Manger with the time and date of the authorization. The power level shall be monitored and if the battery is low, the procedure in step 5 undertaken. This breaches the ACPO Principle 1, and so Principle 2 must be relied on. The means that the requirements for competence and being able to prove it, as required in Principle 2 are even more important, as is the requirement for the audit trail in Principle 3.
7. The cell phone shall only be taken out of its Faraday bag in a Faraday protected environment for examination and imaging.

9.9.1.3.5 Other devices

1. "Other devices" refer to any type of device that can be connected to an information-processing device (e.g., a peripheral such as a printer, camera, MP3 player, etc.) or it may be a stand-alone device (e.g., a games console).
2. The device should be photographed.
3. Details of the device should be recorded on the Other Devices Details Log as given in Appendix 24.
4. All work carried out must be recorded in the Case Work Log as defined in Appendix 9.
5. Where the device relies on battery power and contains volatile memory and has a low power level after being seized in the "on" state, either replace the batteries and monitor it so that it does not lose volatile memory until it is captured or charge on the appropriate cradle or adaptor.
6. If the device was seized in the "off" state, then the Laboratory Manager shall authorize in writing a competent Forensic Analyst to undertake the examination and perform the imaging and recovery of any evidence. This authority shall be logged on the Case Work Log and countersigned by the Laboratory Manger with the time and date of the authorization. The power level shall be monitored and if the battery is low, the procedure in step 5 undertaken. This breaches the ACPO Principle 1, and so Principle 2 must be relied on. The means that the requirements for competence and being able to prove it, as required in Principle 2 are even more important, as is the requirement for the audit trail in Principle 3.
7. The device has radio transmission capability, and it shall only be taken out of its Faraday bag/box in a Faraday-protected environment for examination and imaging.

9.9.1.3.6 Other media

1. "Other media" refers to any type of media that is recovered and sent for forensic processing. It is similar to Section 9.3.1.3 item 6, but refers to media submitted as an exhibit rather than being located in another exhibit and discovered as part of the examination process.
2. The media should be photographed.
3. Details of the media should be recorded on the Other Media Details Log as given in Appendix 22.
4. All work carried out must be recorded in the Case Work Log as defined in Appendix 9.

9.9.1.4 General Forensic Acquisition

1. All forensic acquisition of media from exhibits must be carried out using approved write blockers wherever possible to ensure against accidental contamination or tainting of the evidence, unless the device has a write blocker built into it. Even then it is recommended that the

standard Forensic Laboratory write blocker is used, in case of the on-board device malfunctioning.

2. If a write blocker cannot be used or is unavailable for any reason, then only a suitably trained and skilled Forensic Analyst shall undertake the acquisition, using appropriate tools.
3. Consideration should be given, if a write blocker is not available to using the Linux Dynamic Dump "dd" command as this can prevent writing to the device by default.
4. Special care must be taken with mobile devices that have radio transmitters/receivers in them that can be used to change the information held on the device or, in the extreme, wipe the device. The Forensic Laboratory has a Faraday shielded area for this purpose.
5. Acquisition shall be to a wiped disk which will be dedicated to the case for the duration as defined in Section 9.8.
6. The Forensic Analyst shall check that the time and date on the acquisition PC is correct and shall annotate the Hard Disk Details Log to confirm this as given in Appendix 21.
7. The method of acquisition shall be recorded in the relevant Log with the version of the specific software used. This shall also be logged in the Case Work Log as defined in Appendix 9.
8. Once the image is created, the Forensic Analyst must be able to provide proof that it is an exact copy of the original exhibit and that this proof will be acceptable in any proceedings that the forensic case processing supports. This is carried out in the Forensic Laboratory using MD5 hashes that are normally built into digital forensic acquisition tools.

Where a disk is damaged or has multiple bad sectors, a number of acquisition tools will fail to image the disk. In this case, consideration should be given to selecting an acquisition tool such as dd_rescue or any other tool that will carry on even if it finds damaged areas. Typically, these areas are overwritten with "zeros." These are recorded in the log file so that the actual bad areas of the disk can be identified. This breaches the ACPO Principle 1, and so Principle 2 must be relied on. The means that the requirements for competence and being able to prove it, as required in Principle 2, are even more important, as is the requirement for the audit trail in Principle 3. Acquiring a damaged disk can be a very time-consuming process and a decision must be made to use this process or not.

9.9.1.4.1 Acquiring a hard disk

1. The hard disk to be imaged is connected to the acquisition machine via the write blocker to prevent evidence contamination, as appropriate. Linux tools do not need a write blocker, as the disk can be mounted as read only; Windows imaging requires a write blocker (Figure 9.5).
2. The jumper setting may have to be changed to acquire the disk, if so, record the original setting and the revised setting on the Case Work Log.

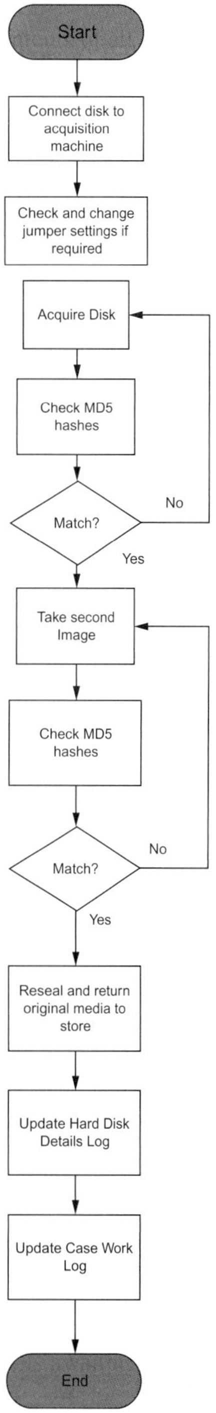

FIGURE 9.5 Acquiring a hard disk. (For color version of this figure, the reader is referred to the online version of this chapter.)

3. The acquisition software must be used according to the manufacturer's recommended procedures to acquire a forensic image of the hard disk.
4. Once the forensic acquisition has taken place using the chosen forensic imaging tool, the MD5 hashes of the acquisition and the verification should be checked to ensure that they are the same. If they are, then the bit image is exact; if they do not, then the copy is not exact and must be redone until the hashes match.
5. Experience shows that a different version of the same acquisition tool or a different acquisition tool may solve the problem.
6. Once one complete image has been taken and the hashes match a second one must be taken, this may use the same tool or use a different one. The reason for this is that if one image corrupts, there is a fall back. This process may require a second dedicated case disk for the image.
7. Once two complete and exact images have been made, the original media should be returned to the Forensic Laboratory Secure Property Store and signed back in after being resealed as defined in Section 9.9.1.7.
8. Details of the acquisition process shall be recorded on the Hard Disk Details Log as given in Appendix 21.
9. All work carried out must be recorded in the Case Work Log as defined in Appendix 9.

9.9.1.4.2 Acquiring a tablet computer

1. The tablet computer to be imaged is connected to the acquisition machine via the write blocker to prevent evidence contamination.
2. Tablet computer acquisition may require specialist software or tools and must only be undertaken by Forensic Analysts who are competent on the specialist software or tool being used.
3. The acquisition software is used, according to the manufacturer's recommended procedures to acquire a forensic image of the tablet computer. The Forensic Laboratory uses forensic software for acquiring and processing images from all tablet computers that integrate seamlessly with its main case processing software.
4. Once the forensic acquisition has taken place using the chosen forensic imaging tool, the MD5 hashes of the acquisition and the verification should be checked to ensure that they are the same. If they are, then the bit image is exact; if they do not, then the copy is not exact and must be redone until the hashes match.
5. Experience shows that a different version of the same acquisition tool or a different acquisition tool may solve the problem.
6. Once one complete image has been taken and the hashes match a second one must be taken, this may use the same tool or use a different one. The reason for this is that if one image corrupts, there is a fall back. This process may require a second dedicated case disk for the image.
7. Once two complete and exact images have been made, the original media should be returned to the Forensic Laboratory Secure Store and signed back in after being resealed as defined in Section 9.6.1.
8. Details of the acquisition process shall be recorded on the Cell Phone Details Log as given in Appendix 23.
9. All work carried out must be recorded in the Case Work Log as defined in Appendix 9.

Note 1

To examine a tablet computer, it may be necessary to turn it on and this will make changes to it as it boots up. This breaches the ACPO Principle 1, and so Principle 2 must be relied on. The means that the requirements for competence and being able to prove it, as required in Principle 2 are even more important, as is the requirement for the audit trail in Principle 3.

Note 2

Some tablet computer will implement screen locking after a set period and require entry of the pass code to access the phone. Some commercials software can bypass this, but if this is not possible, then consideration should be given to making changes to the settings on the phone to keep the pass code protection from activating. This breaches Principle 1 as in Note 1 above, so the same proviso must be made.

Note 3

The Forensic Analyst (or First Responder) should avoid touching the screen as much as possible, as this may activate the tablet computer and make changes to it.

Note 4

It may be possible to disable the account with the service provider.

Note 5

The Forensic Analyst must be aware of the possibility of the tablet computer being booby trapped or contain malware (e.g., Trojans to wipe the disk) and have a contingency plan in place if needed.

9.9.1.4.3 Acquiring cell phones

1. The cell phone to be imaged is connected to the acquisition machine via the write blocker to prevent evidence contamination.

2. Cell phone acquisition requires specialist software or tools and must only be undertaken by Forensic Analysts who are competent on the specialist software or tool being used.
3. The acquisition software is used, according to the manufacturer's recommended procedures to acquire a forensic image of the cell phone. The Forensic Laboratory uses forensic software for acquiring and processing images from all cell phones that integrates seamlessly with its main case processing software.
4. Once the forensic acquisition has taken place using the chosen forensic imaging tool, the MD5 hashes of the acquisition and the verification should be checked to ensure that they are the same. If they are, then the bit image is exact; if they do not, then the copy is not exact and must be redone until the hashes match.
5. Experience shows that a different version of the same acquisition tool or a different acquisition tool may solve the problem.
6. Once one complete image has been taken and the hashes match a second one must be taken, this may use the same tool or use a different one. The reason for this is that if one image corrupts, there is a fall back. This process may require a second dedicated case disk for the image.
7. Once two complete and exact images have been made, the original media should be returned to the Forensic Laboratory Secure Store and signed back in after being resealed as defined in Section 9.6.1.
8. Details of the acquisition process shall be recorded on the Cell Phone Details Log as given in Appendix 23.
9. All work carried out must be recorded in the Case Work Log as defined in Appendix 9.

Note 1

To examine a cell phone, it may be necessary to turn it on and this will make changes to it as it boots up. This breaches the ACPO Principle 1, and so Principle 2 must be relied on. The means that the requirements for competence and being able to prove it, as required in Principle 2 are even more important, as is the requirement for the audit trail in Principle 3.

Note 2

Some cell phones will implement screen locking after a set period and require entry of the pass code to access the phone. Some commercial software can bypass this, but if this is not possible, then consideration should be given to making changes to the settings on the phone to keep the pass code protection from activating. This breaches Principle 1 as in Note1 above, so the same proviso must be made.

Note 3

The Forensic Analyst (or First Responder) should avoid touching the screen as much as possible, as this may activate the phone and make changes to it.

Note 4

It may be necessary to put a phone in airplane mode, again this breaches principle 1 as in Note1 above, so the same proviso must be made.

Note 5

It may be possible to disable the account with the service provider.

Note 6

The Forensic Analyst must be aware of the possibility of the cell phone being booby trapped or contain malware (e.g., Trojans to wipe the disk) and have a contingency plan in place if needed.

9.9.1.4.4 Acquiring other devices

1. Depending on the device to be acquired, specialized software must be used that is dedicated to acquiring the device (Figure 9.6),
2. Where the device contains a hard disk, it should, if possible, be removed and the hard disk acquired as defined in Section 9.9.1.4.1 above.
3. With "difficult" devices, it may take considerable time to determine a way to obtain the evidence that is required. At no time should the Forensic Analyst be rushed into performing potentially unsafe forensic actions.
4. The device to be imaged is connected to the acquisition machine via the write blocker to prevent evidence contamination, if at all possible.
5. Where device acquisition requires specialist software or tools and must only be undertaken by Forensic Analysts who are competent on the specialist software or tool being used.
6. The acquisition software is used, according to the manufacturer's recommended procedures to acquire a forensic image of the hard disk.
7. Once the forensic acquisition has taken place using the chosen forensic imaging tool, the MD5 hashes of the acquisition and the verification should be checked to ensure that they are the same. If they are, then the bit image is exact; if they do not, then the copy is not exact and must be redone until the hashes match.
8. Experience shows that a different version of the same acquisition tool or a different acquisition tool may solve the problem.
9. Once one complete image has been taken and the hashes match a second one must be taken, this may use the same tool or use a different one. The reason for this is that if one image corrupts, there is a fall back.

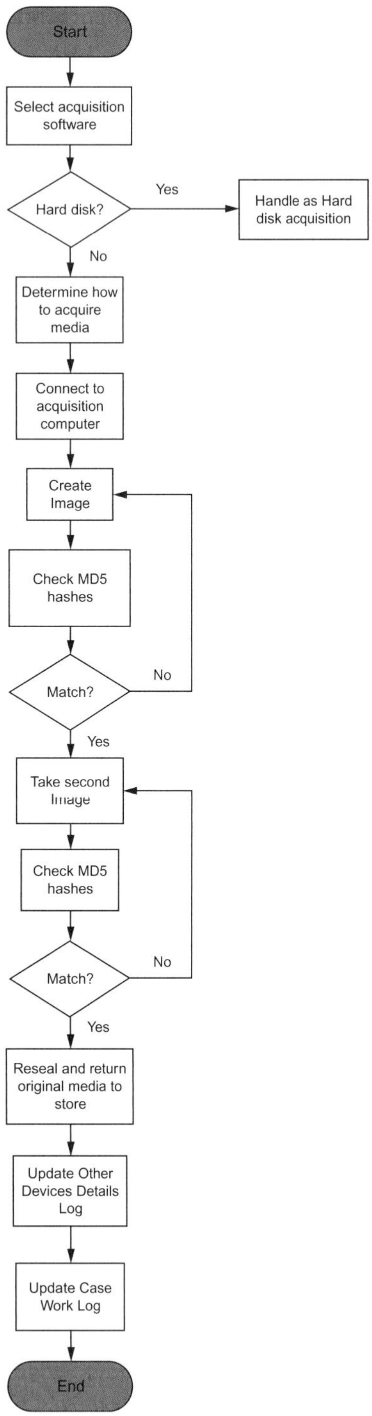

FIGURE 9.6 Acquiring other devices. (For color version of this figure, the reader is referred to the online version of this chapter.)

This process may require a second dedicated case disk for the image.

10. Once two complete and exact images have been made, the original media should be returned to the Forensic Laboratory Secure Property Store and signed back in after being resealed as defined in Section 9.6.1.
11. Details of the acquisition process shall be recorded on the Other Devices Details Log as given in Appendix 24.
12. All work carried out must be recorded in the Case Work Log as defined in Appendix 9.

Note 1

To examine a cell phone, it may be necessary to turn it on and this will make changes to it as it boots up. This breaches the ACPO Principle 1, and so Principle 2 must be relied on. The means that the requirements for competence and being able to prove it, as required in Principle 2 are even more important, as is the requirement for the audit trail in Principle 3.

Note 2

The Forensic Analyst must be aware of the possibility of the device being booby trapped or contain malware (e.g., Trojans to wipe the disk) and have a contingency plan in place if needed.

9.9.1.4.5 Acquiring other media

1. The media to be imaged is connected to the acquisition machine via the write blocker to prevent evidence contamination.
2. With "difficult" media, it may take considerable time to determine a way to obtain the evidence that is required. At no time should the Forensic Analyst be rushed into performing potentially unsafe forensic actions.
3. Some CDs and DVDs are not easy to acquire with Encase and if this is the Forensic Laboratory's primary imaging tool, other tools will have to be used to acquire them. This process may preclude them from being added to the Encase Case File for investigation so they must be examined individually (for example, the Forensic Laboratory may use a tool such as Infina-Dyne's CD/DVD Inspector).
4. There are other devices that hold electronic media that may require specialized software, tools and competence to extract and image or to be able to investigate. Circumstances will dictate the approach.
5. Where media acquisition requires specialist software or tools it must only be undertaken by Forensic Analysts who are competent on the specialist software or tool being used.
6. The acquisition software must be used in accordance with the manufacturer's recommended procedures to acquire a forensic image of the media.
7. Once the forensic acquisition has taken place using the chosen forensic imaging tool, the MD5 hashes of the acquisition and the verification should be checked to

ensure that they are the same. If they are, then the bit image is exact; if they do not, then the copy is not exact and must be redone until the hashes match.

8. Experience shows that a different version of the same acquisition tool or a different acquisition tool may solve the problem.
9. Once one complete image has been taken and the hashes match a second one must be taken, this may use the same tool or use a different one. The reason for this is that if one image corrupts, there is a fall back. This process may require a second dedicated case disk for the image.
10. Once two complete and exact images have been made, the original media should be returned to the Forensic Laboratory Secure Store and signed back in after being resealed as defined in Section 9.6.1.
11. Details of the acquisition process shall be recorded on the Other Media Details Log as given in Appendix 22.
12. All work carried out must be recorded in the Case Work Log as defined in Appendix 9.

9.9.1.4.6 Acquiring volatile memory

1. A number of devices may have volatile memory present and this is lost when it is switched off. This lends toward on-site acquisition of volatile memory. The device may be seized and returned to the Forensic Laboratory for disk imaging or the whole imaging process may be carried out on-site.
2. Hardware or software acquisition may be used depending on circumstances.
3. Volatile memory acquisition requires specialist software or tools and must only be undertaken by Forensic Analysts who are competent on the specialist software or tool being used.
4. The acquisition software or hardware is used, according to the manufacturer's recommended procedures to acquire a forensic image of the volatile memory.
5. Inspection of the device uptime since the last re-boot should be used to determine whether a full volatile memory acquisition should be undertaken. If the device has recently been rebooted, or it has been rebooted since the security incident, it may not be worth performing a full acquisition. Whatever the option chosen, the justification for it should be documented in the Case Work Log.
6. It is not possible to run an MD5 checksum on the image, as there is no original image to compare against.
7. The evidence recovered from the acquisition will depend on the device being acquired, but some volatile evidence that may be recovered is given in Appendix 25.
8. Details of the acquisition process shall be recorded on the Other Media Details Log as given in Appendix 22.
9. All work carried out must be recorded in the Case Work Log as defined in Appendix 9.

9.9.1.5 Evidence Integrity

The integrity of a digital image is of paramount importance as Courts will make decisions based on the presentation of forensic evidence and its integrity.

The integrity of the crime scene, where handled by the Forensic Laboratory as defined in Chapter 8, Section 8.6, is the first step in this process. Where the scene was not secured appropriately, it may be later found that the evidence was tainted at this stage of the incident.

When handling evidence, the rules of evidence and other legislative requirements relating to the case must be understood and implemented to ensure legislative compliance within the jurisdiction(s).

Safe and secure transportation of evidence from the incident scene must always be ensured until it is safely logged into the safe and Secure Property Store as defined in Section 9.6.1 and Chapter 8, Section 8.7, respectively.

The use of sound forensic investigative methods, including the use of write blockers to ensure that evidence is not altered during the acquisition process is mandatory within the Forensic Laboratory.

Using forensic workstation anti-contamination procedures, as defined in Section 9.4.7, ensures that there is no chance of cross contamination from another case.

Validation and testing of methods and tools as defined in Chapter 7, Section 7.5.5 is also mandatory in the Forensic Laboratory.

The use of MD5 hashing to prove that the images made are the same as the original prove that the data are unaltered, which is standard for the imaging tools used in the Forensic Laboratory as defined in Section 4.9.

The Forensic Laboratory associates all tools used in a case by placing a copy of the exact software used on the case in the virtual case file as given in Appendix 18. This ensures that the results are repeatable and ensures the integrity of the imaging or analysis phases.

The chain of custody for all exhibits and the use of the Property Log as given in Chapter 8, Appendix 17, with contemporaneous Case Work Logs as given in Appendix 9 with the other forms and checklists in use shows responsibility for all actions and full end-to-end traceability of all actions taken in a case.

9.9.1.6 Backing up the Images

Once the exhibits have been imaged as defined in Chapter 8, Section 8.6.17 and Section 9.9, they should be backed up as follows:

1. All images shall be compressed and backed up to the image drive on the Forensic Server;

2. One copy of the image shall be used as the case or working disk;
3. The second copy of the image shall be placed in the Secure Property Store in its caddy, marked with the case number, the contents, date, and who performed the image, where it will stay according to the Forensic Laboratory case retention schedule as given in Chapter 4, Appendix 16;
4. A tape copy of the Forensic Server disk containing the images shall then be run and placed in the Secure Property Store.

9.9.1.7 Reassembly and Resealing the Exhibit(s)

- once the acquisition has been successfully performed, the exhibit(s) must be returned to the exhibit store.
- in the case of large equipment, such as PCs or servers, consideration may be given to holding the media in the fire safe separate to the carcass of the server, PC, or laptop on space saving grounds; this is acceptable so long as the procedures below are followed.

9.9.1.7.1 Storing media and carcass together

Where the electronic media is to be replaced in the exhibit (or is an integral part of the exhibit) and stored in the Secure Property Store together the following procedures shall be performed:

- the exhibit shall be reassembled—BUT NOT POWERED UP;
- the exhibit shall be placed in a new evidence bag;
- the original evidence bag and seal shall be placed inside the new evidence bag;
- any additional peripherals associated with the exhibit shall be placed in the new evidence bag, if possible. If not, multiple bags shall be used;
- the evidence bag shall be sealed;
- The Forensic Laboratory Property Log shall be updated to show the new seal being applied to the exhibit as given in Appendix 13.

9.9.1.7.2 Storing media and carcass separately

It is often the case that the carcass and the electronic media have to be stored separately (typically for space considerations). Where this is the case, the following procedures shall be performed:

- the exhibit shall be reassembled but without the storage media;
- the Laboratory Manager shall agree to the separation of the exhibits, and this shall be recorded in the Forensic Laboratory Property Log;
- the carcass shall be placed in a new evidence bag;
- the original evidence bag and seal shall be placed inside the new evidence bag;
- any additional peripherals associated with the exhibit, except the electronic media, shall be placed in the new evidence bag, if possible. If not, multiple bags shall be used;
- the evidence bag shall NOT be sealed;
- the storage media shall be placed in a small evidence bag and sealed with the relevant information about the media entered onto the evidence bag;
- the Forensic Laboratory Property Log shall be updated to show the new seal being applied to the storage media only;
- the carcass shall be placed in a secure location as agreed with the Laboratory Manager;
- the relevant movement form(s) shall be updated to show the movement of the carcass to the agreed location as given in Chapter 8, Appendix 17.

9.9.2 On-Site Imaging

Where on-site imaging has to be carried out, the Forensic Analyst shall perform the task using the portable forensic workstation.

The portable forensic workstations shall have the same software tools on them as the desktop forensic workstations. In addition, dedicated imaging hardware tools are carried to facilitate on-site acquisition.

The procedures for preparing the forensic workstation as defined in Section 9.8 are carried out.

The procedures for imaging on-site are exactly the same as those above in Section 9.9.1.3.

9.9.3 Remote Imaging

The Forensic Laboratory may be able to undertake remote forensics using its chosen main case processing software. Though in practice, it will probably prefer to attend the incident scene.

It is essential that the procedures defined in Section 9.9.1.3 are applied to the process of remote forensics to ensure that full documentation exists to cover the chain of custody and proof that the integrity of the acquired image is maintained.

There are three main methods by which a Forensic Analyst can access a remote network over a network connection:

- instructing the Client's IT staff to physically attend the target device(s) and manually install a servlet application into memory to enable network access;
- preinstalling a "servlet" application on to all target devices so that it is constantly running in memory so access can be gained on authorized demand;

- using "push" technology to place a servlet application into memory on the target device(s) on demand.

While this appears to be an ideal situation, there are a number of disadvantages with the approach which is why the Forensics Laboratory may prefer to attend the incident scene. These include:

- a number of devices may not be available (e.g., failure to have laptops connected to the network). There is also the issue of not knowing all of the possible network components;
- damaged or failing source media that requires special attention to image it;
- difficulty in ensuring continuity of evidence;
- difficulty in ensuring the integrity of evidence acquired over the Internet;
- failure to access the correct network segment, even if access to the Client's network is granted;
- infected target systems;
- lack of control over the incident scene;
- lack of visibility of the incident scene;
- network bandwidth;
- network unavailability;
- no matter how good the instructions to the Client's IT staff are, they are not trained First Responders or forensic experts;
- proving access authority and limits of authority;
- stand-alone devices are not network connected.

9.10 EXAMINATION

9.10.1 Initial Examination

9.10.1.1 Loading Images into the Virtual Case File

To start processing a forensic case, the Forensic Analyst has to load the case into the relevant virtual case file held on the forensic-processing workstation.

- Depending on the size of the disk, the case may require the insertion of a larger disk than is currently in the disk caddy in the forensic workstation;
- The Forensic Analyst shall add relevant details to the virtual case file, as appropriate to the case, in the relevant case file;
- The Forensic Analyst should then load the images into the preferred forensic analysis software to create the digital case. During this process, the required information regarding the physical case shall be entered into MARS as required and prompted for.

Once the case has been set up in the relevant forensic tool, it is necessary to process it. Hard disks and other forensically acquired images are all handled in generally the same way, but items such as telephones and PDAs are handled differently and uniquely.

9.10.1.2 PDAs and Cell Phones

These should be handled in accordance with the instructions or manuals supplied with the software in use for their interrogation and investigation.

What can be recovered from these devices will vary based on such things as maintenance of charge, software in use, etc.

Typically, the following can be recovered.

9.10.1.2.1 PDAs

PDAs can run most of the software that is run on a PC or a variation of it. Typical applications that can be found include:

- word processor;
- spreadsheet;
- contacts or address books;
- to do lists and appointments;
- web browser;
- mail;
- media player;
- voice recorder;
- synchronization software;
- remote access software.

There will more than likely be other applications specific to the user found on a PDA.

9.10.1.2.2 Cell phones

The following contents of modern cell phones can be recovered and have value as evidence:

- IMEI;
- IMSI;
- short dial numbers;
- text messages;
- settings (language, date/time, tone/volume, etc.);
- stored audio recordings;
- remote access artifacts;
- stored computer files;
- logged incoming, outgoing, and missed calls;
- stored executable programs;
- stored calendar events;
- GPRS, WAP, and Internet settings;
- browser bookmarks;
- saved e-mails;
- files in folders;
- browser URLs;
- memos;
- task lists;
- key stores;

- configurations;
- alarm settings.

Note 1

The merging of technologies of the PDA, other mobile devices, and cell phones telephones means that the devices above will start to merge as will the evidence available from them.

Note 2

Cell site analysis can be undertaken, but this requires assistance from the phone's service provider. Powered-up cell phones register with the nearest base stations, and these registrations are stored by the service provider. Using this information and applying triangulation can allow a Forensic Analyst to make a reasonable estimation of the journey that the phone took for the period of the registration data.

9.10.1.3 Images Acquired to Media (e.g., Hard Disks, Floppy Disks, Thumb Drives, etc.)

While the specific software used will dictate the exact details of using the software, there are a number of procedural steps that must be gone through at the start of any case; these are below:

- check local parameters such as date and time on the system and adjust where necessary;
- set the local time zone for the media or exhibit;
- recover all possible deleted folders;
- view all pictures to see if there is any unlawful material—if there is then immediately stop any investigation, lock the workstation, and advise the Laboratory Manager who will take appropriate action including advising the appropriate Law Enforcement Agency;
- mount the image and run at least one anti-malware product against the image, recording the results of any malware recovered. It is advisable to run at least two of each tools to ensure that there was "nothing left behind." The recording of the findings is essential if there are later issues with the "Trojan Defence";
- if running Encase, run the initialize case script;
- run a signature analysis and hash all of the files;
- identify notable files from their hash values. If there are any notable files discovered, then they should be examined, and if necessary dealt with as "unlawful material" as defined in Section 9.19.2;
- identify any password protected or encrypted files or folders;
- identify any alternate data streams (ADS) that may be present. This requires specialist tools as they are invisible to the operating systems normal file listing commands;
- identify any Host-Protected Areas (HPAs) and Device Configuration Overlays (DCOs) and deal with them, as they are invisible to the operating systems and used by the manufacturer for their own purposes. However, as they are invisible to the operating system, they can be used to hide files;
- these operations shall be recorded in the Case Work Log.

9.10.2 First-Stage Examination

Having run the initial examination of the case image, it is necessary to start to recover data from the case image. Some of these can be automated and others are manual processes. The following should be carried out for all cases.

9.10.2.1 Determine Appropriate Method

Time spent in planning how to process a forensic case is time seldom wasted. The Forensic Analyst should determine the best methods and tools to obtain the required outcomes. There is no one tool that does everything in a case. A variety of methods and tools may be used to process the case.

9.10.2.2 Using Hash Sets for First-Stage Examinations

9.10.2.2.1 "Known" or "safe" files

Safe or known files (identified by their hash values) should be excluded from a case and this substantially reduces the amount of time that is taken for searching for keywords or processing other scripts or tasks.

9.10.2.2.2 "Notable" files

As part of the first-stage examination, a review of all files with notable hashes should be undertaken and if necessary dealt with as "unlawful material" as defined in Section 9.19.2. Where the Forensic Analyst has created their own hash files for a specific case as defined in Section 9.4.8, the notable files for the case using that specific set of notable files will be those relevant for the specific case.

9.10.2.3 Some File Systems Encountered

There are a number of file systems that may be encountered while processing a forensic case; these include, but are not limited to:

- BFS—BeOS;
- BREW—various cell phones;
- CDFS—CDs;
- EFS—versions of Windows;
- Ext 2—Linux, Unix, and some cell phones;

- Ext 3—Linux and some cell phones;
- Ext 4—Linux and some cell phones;
- FAT 16—MS Dos and versions of Windows;
- FAT 32—versions of Windows, some cell phones, iPods, and MP3 players;
- FATX—Games consoles;
- HFS and HFS+—MacOS and iPhones;
- HPFS—OS/2 and versions of Windows;
- Joliet—CDs;
- NTFS—versions of Windows;
- ReiserFS—Linux;
- UDF—DVDs;
- UFS—various Unix versions;
- VFS—EnCase (DCO);
- VMFS—VMWare;
- YAFFS2—various smart phones;
- ZFS—Sun systems.

A number of cell phones and mobile devices have proprietary file systems.

9.10.2.4 Automated Scripts and Tasks in Encase

If one of the main tools of the Forensics Laboratory is Encase, the following Scripts should be run (always use the most recent version and log which versions were used and place a copy in the virtual case file):

- initialize case (if not already run);
- hash all files;
- signature analysis;
- info record finder—for Windows recycle bin;
- graphics file finder;
- internet history;
- HTML parser;
- link parser;
- find unique e-mail addresses;
- registry information—for Windows.

Other scripts can and should be run depending on the exact requirements of the case, but these are the standard set that the Forensic Laboratory runs for most cases. Mobile devices have their own dedicated tools as well as Encase, and these may be used.

Additionally, the Forensic Analyst may write an Enscript for a specific task, or import one from one of the many Enscript libraries. Any new script must be validated as defined in Chapter 7, Section 7.5.5 prior to being used for case processing.

9.10.2.5 Extracting Files in File Structure

One of the initial manual processes is to extract the original file structure from the image so that it can be viewed as necessary. This can give insight into how the file structures looked in a far better manner than any tool can.

A graphical representation of the structure should be included in the Appendix for the Case Report.

9.10.2.6 Extracting Files

It is often useful to extract all of the files (by file type) as well as extracting such folders as "my documents," etc., to the case file.

- files of a single type should be grouped in the following folders:
  - archive or current;
  - deleted;
  - hidden;
  - recycled.

Specific folders should be just extracted using their own folder name.

These files should be placed on the CD or DVD that accompany the case.

9.10.2.7 Text Searches

The Client will typically give a number of search criteria that they want to have run against the image.

- these searches should be run as required.

9.10.2.8 Where to Find the "Smoking gun"

There is no definitive answer as to where to find the "smoking gun" as this will vary from case to case, but the following should provide guidance for the areas to investigate:

- access control devices;
- access records to buildings and rooms;
- address books;
- application logs;
- audit logs;
- auto-complete memory;
- backup files;
- blogs;
- cache (temporary Internet files and other files that create caches);
- cache (memory);
- calendars and appointment books;
- cell phone call records;
- chat logs;
- comments in documents that can be recovered (e.g., using "Final showing Markup" in MS Office);
- compressed files;
- configuration files;
- content addressable memory tables;
- cookies;
- crontab-type files and other scheduled tasks;
- database files;
- desktop folder;

- documents;
- e-mail files and headers, including deleted e-mails from POP, IMAP, and Web mail clients;
- event logs;
- examination of source code;
- favorites folder;
- file caches;
- files embedded in other files;
- free space—memory;
- hibernation files;
- hidden shares;
- identifying MAC address of author of a file;
- internet history files;
- images or graphics files;
- instant messaging;
- internet bookmarks or favorites;
- IP addresses;
- ISP records;
- last system shutdown time and date;
- last user shutdown time and date;
- layering of images;
- links to externally stored documents;
- listserve logs;
- location bar history;
- log files;
- media player file list;
- memory cache;
- metadata—though ensure that dates and times are properly reported. Examples of file system metadata are given in Appendix 26;
- my documents folder;
- network traffic;
- newsgroups;
- open and save history;
- packet headers;
- packet payloads;
- paper-based documents and other paper evidence;
- password-protected files;
- peer-to-peer (P2P) traffic;
- p-list files;
- previous versions of web sites (www.archive.org);
- printer spool files;
- real-time tracing and analysis;
- recent folder;
- recycle bin;
- registry contents;
- relational analysis;
- routing tables;
- send to folder;
- shadow files;
- shrunk images;
- slack space—disks;
- slack space—memory;
- sniffer program output;
- social media sites and communications (e.g., FaceBook, Twitter, MySpace, LinkedIn, etc.);
- start menu run history;
- swap files;
- syslog;
- system files;
- temporal analysis (time lining);
- temporary files;
- traffic analysis;
- trust relationships to other systems;
- unallocated clusters;
- volume slack.

9.10.2.9 Deliberately Hidden Evidence

There are a number of methods of deliberately hiding files and as computer users become more aware of technology and increasingly understand what can be recovered from a computer. Some of these methods and how they can be overcome are included below:

- $boot file—disk analysis and check contents of the attribute;
- $bad and $BadClus—examination of claimed bad clusters on the disk;
- $data attribute—check contents of the attribute;
- additional clusters added to a file—disk analysis;
- ADS—specialist tools;
- changing file attributes to make files hidden—specialist tools;
- deleted files and partitions—undelete them;
- encrypted files—attempting to find unencrypted versions of the file, overcoming weak encryption, notification of encryption software installed, acted from the suspect's computer, and if all else fails, a brute force attack;
- hidden files and directories—unhide them;
- HPA—use specialized tools;
- manually changing file system slack—disk analysis;
- manually changing volume slack—disk analysis;
- manually adding files to file slack—analysis of slack space;
- manually adding files to memory slack—analysis of slack space;
- misnamed (bad signature) files—run signature analysis;
- steganography—specialist tools and hash sets to find known steg files.

There are a number of other methods of deliberately hiding data ranging from the simple (e.g., storing data on removable media) to the very complex. For every type of data hiding, the original unencrypted file must have existed and so there may be traces of it available.

9.10.2.10 Virtualization

A virtual machine (VM) is a software implementation of a computer that executes programs like a physical computer—hence the name. A computer may run multiple VMs with the same or different operating systems.

The capability of virtualization is of great benefit to the Forensic Analyst. It allows the Forensic Analyst to set up pseudo networks on their forensic workstation, suspend, and freeze any sessions as required. VMs can be used to provide sandbox facilities to a Forensic Analyst with the facility of investing malicious or suspicious software in safety. It also allows a Forensic Analyst with access to an operating system other than the main one they are using without the need to have dual boot capability.

One of the greatest benefits of virtualization is that it allows a Forensic Analyst the ability to mount a system exactly as it was when used by the suspect. This can have a great benefit in presenting evidence to a Judge or Jury.

From a time-saving point of view, the Forensic Laboratory may use VMs as it allows a Forensic Analyst to boot an image into a virtual environment, saving a tremendous amount of time, as opposed to restoring an image to the original hardware that ran it.

From a cost perspective, VMs save money as multiple VMs can run on a single machine.

For these reasons, the Forensic Laboratory should consider implementing the use of VMs.

9.10.2.11 Investigating Peripherals and Other Devices

A number of peripherals may be included in the case to be processed. These all must be investigated for potential evidence. This may include, but not be limited to:

- access control devices;
- answering machines;
- audio recording devices;
- car engine management systems and motor vehicle event data recorders;
- CCTV;
- copiers;
- digital video recorders;
- direct attached storage;
- electronic tills;
- fax machines;
- gaming consoles;
- GPS systems;
- household and office devices containing microchips;
- IP connected devices in the home (e.g., fridges);
- MP3 and other digital music devices;
- multifunction devices;
- network attaches storage;
- network management devices;
- pagers;
- phone systems;
- photographic recording devices;
- printers and their tracking dots;
- radio frequency identification devices;
- redundant array of independent disks;
- routers;
- scanners;
- storage area networks;
- video games devices;
- VMs running multiple operating systems;
- wireless access points.

9.10.2.12 Covert and Remote Investigations

Forensic Analysts undertaking covert investigations must ensure that they are not detected by the suspect whose information-processing equipment they are investigating. Some considerations are, but are not limited to:

- break the investigation into a number of stages and spread them over a period of time so that the suspect is not alerted to unusual use patterns;
- ensure that any firewalls allow relevant traffic between the Forensic Analyst's workstation and the suspect's—failure and rejection of connections or traffic may alert the suspect;
- ensure that the investigation is strictly "need to know" and the minimum of Forensic Laboratory employees are aware of it;
- ensure that the tools used run as a system service;
- ensure that whatever tools are used leave no traces, e.g., event logs;
- ensure that resource usage is minimized—i.e., do not run multiple tasks at once, as resource usage may alert the suspect;
- only search for evidence relevant to the case, this must be seriously limited, as it is too easy to search for everything;
- use neutral naming for any remote agents or replace an innocuous name;
- ensure that the collection process does not impact normal operations or alert the suspect;
- consider the best time to carry out a covert investigation—is it in the quiet hours, when it may be noticed, or during the day so it can appear as normal traffic.

9.10.2.13 Records

The following records must be made:

- update of Case Work Log to show what has been done;
- listing of all recovered files;
- output (i.e., hard copies) of any files of note (e.g., autoexec.bat, config.sys, etc.);

- a full directory listing should be made to include folder structure, filenames, date/time stamps, logical file sizes, etc.;
- details of the installed operating systems should be noted;
- all exhibits produced are recorded as defined in Section 9.14, appropriately marked and secured as appropriate;
- the Forensic Laboratory associates all tools used in a case by placing a copy of the exact software used on the case in the virtual case file as given in Appendix 18. This ensures that the results are repeatable;
- any other items in the virtual case file or the hard copy case file that needs to be updated.

9.10.2.14 End of day Processes

At the end of the working day, the Forensic workstation and case will be in one of two states:

1. Processing instructions from the Forensic Analyst (e.g., running one or more overnight jobs);
2. Finished processing for the day.

If the forensic workstation is processing, it should be allowed to carry on running without interruption.

If the Forensic workstation has stopped processing for the day, then:

- all of the files and folders from the forensic workstation that have been created or changed shall be copied up to the virtual case file on the forensic server for backing up by the overnight server backup process as defined in Chapter 7, Section 7.7.4;
- the work disk shall be placed in the fire safe overnight until needed.

9.10.3 Second-Stage Examination

Once the initial searches and recoveries have been done, it is necessary to make detailed investigations based on either what has been recovered and is relevant to the case or to further refine what is relevant to the case.

It is at this point that the Forensic Analyst should consider the involvement of someone intimate with the detailed requirements of the case so that together they can review the case. Typically, such a process leads to:

- inclusion or exclusion of search hits found to date;
- further searches to be undertaken;
- requirements for details associated with recovered files such as metadata;
- requirements for cracking passwords or encryption;
- requirements for proving that "A" is linked to "B" and how this can be proved (e.g., that a document was created on a specific PC and the owner of the PC has been identified);
- investigation of peer-to-peer packages, Instant Messaging or similar;
- recovery of printer artifacts;
- further details from the registry being recovered;
- detailed or further requirements for files, applications, or processes identified (e.g., password breaking for files, investigation of a peer-to-peer network, further investigation of e-mail, etc.).

Note 1

It is not possible to give details of all possible outcomes as they will vary from case to case and no two cases are ever the same.

Further and better particulars of what is required at this stage are essential not only to ensure that the Forensic Analyst recovers what the Client requires but also to eliminate time wasted and to determine the type, form, and layout of any deliverables required (e.g., statements, depositions, reports, exhibits, etc.).

Note 2

When the results have been reported to the Client, this may lead to additional requirements being identified by the Client. The second-stage examination is an iterative process that carries on until the Client is satisfied with the results.

9.10.4 Best Evidence

The best evidence rule is a common law rule of evidence which can be traced back at least as far as the 18th century. In Omychund v Barker (1745), Lord Harwicke stated that no evidence was admissible unless it was "the best that the nature of the case will allow."

"Best evidence" is therefore the one that can be produced in Court. Thus, the real seized evidence is the best evidence. While in some cases, it is not possible to bring the original evidence to Court; other forms of evidence may be regarded as original evidence, but this will vary between jurisdictions. A crime scene cannot be brought into a Court room, but photographs, sketches, statements, evidence logs, etc., can be produced to illustrate the scene.

The general rule is that "secondary" evidence (i.e., a copy) will not be admissible if an original document exists, so a copy of a signed contract would not be acceptable, if the original contract exists and was available.

9.10.5 Case Progress

A record of the summary of the case progress must be held in the front of the paper case file so that it can easily be reviewed by the Laboratory Manager. The form used by the Forensic Laboratory is given in Appendix 27.

9.10.6 Choosing an Expert Witness

If the case is going to a Tribunal or Court, it will be necessary to choose an expert witness to give "expert testimony." The expert may be appointed at any stage during the case processing cycle but should have been appointed by the second-stage examination.

Advice on choosing an expert is given in Chapter 11, Appendix 2.

9.10.7 Re-Hashing the Image

At the end of processing the case and producing the case report, the image should be rehashed to show that during the investigation nothing has been changed in the image. The rehashing should be recorded on the Case Work Log and in the report to the Client. If further work is to be carried out at a later date, the image should be rehashed before any work is undertaken to show that no changes have occurred while it has been held in the Forensic Laboratory's Secure Property Store.

9.10.8 Using a Forensic Workstation for Network Investigations

When a Forensic Analyst is connected to the Internet, it must be remembered that the connection is a two-way connection. If the Forensic Analyst is using an in-house IP Address, then their origin and IP address are revealed. This leaves the Forensic Analyst open to a possible attack.

It is for this reason that:

- no Internet investigations are performed from a network-connected forensic workstation;
- an IP address not associated with the Forensic Laboratory is used for the stand-alone workstation being used;
- workstations used to access the Internet are not Windows, but Linux as there are also fewer malware exploits and Trojans on Linux than in Windows.

9.10.9 Meeting the Requirements of HB 171

HB 171 is the Australian "Guidelines for the management of IT Evidence." The Forensic Laboratory has endeavored to meet these requirements as well as all of the ISO and other national standards, and the results (and how these procedures map to HB 171) are given in Appendix 28.

9.11 DUAL TOOL VERIFICATION

In many cases that the Forensic Analysts have to deal with, there will be large amounts of evidence pointing to the guilt of the suspect.

In a number of cases, this may not be the case, and the evidence may be a single line of text, a couple of bytes, or a small file. In such cases, the Forensic Analyst shall verify the findings with a totally different tool.

The repeat of the examination and the findings with a second tool lend more reliability and credibility to the findings.

9.12 DIGITAL TIME STAMPING

Consideration should be given to Forensic Analysts to using a digital time stamping service to time stamp recovered documents and files as well as other documents produced in a case. Such a service would prove two facts:

- *existence*: that a file existed on a given date and time;
- *data integrity*: that the file was not altered since the time it was stamped.

These two facts are essential for a number of purposes, including but not limited to:

- gathering and registering binary data to be used as forensic evidence, such as computer files, memory dumps, packet recorder data, security analysis logs, etc.;
- electronically "notarizing" the date and time of the evidence recovered using a secure real-time clock held in tamper-proof hardware;
- generating secure audit logs for recovered evidence submitted and a digitally signed time certificate identifying the files submitted;
- the digitally signed time certificate provides non-repudiated evidence of existence and integrity of the files submitted.

There are a number of organizations that provide these services, and the process is:

1. The Forensic Analyst e-mails a list of MD5 hashes for evidence gathered or files recovered on a given day to the digital time stamper.
2. The service returns a PGP-signed message confirming receipt of the message and giving their reference number.

Whatever service is used, the service supplier must have their time stamp device certified by an Accredited Certification Laboratory against a known time source and provide proof of this, digitally signed by the Certification Laboratory.

9.13 PRODUCTION OF AN INTERNAL CASE REPORT

9.13.1 The Internal Report

An internal case report is a document that allows the Laboratory Manager to understand a case and determine the evidence found and how this supports, or does not support, the Client requirements.

The Forensic Analyst will be required to produce a report on the case. The report should follow the following format:

- basic case information;
- evidence sought;
- evidence found;
- attachments and appendices.

The template for a Forensic Laboratory internal report is given in Appendix 29.

9.13.2 Classification

All reports shall be released with appropriate security classifications placed on them according to either the Forensic Laboratory classification standards as given in Chapter 5, Appendix 16, or the standards of the Client, if known. If the Client's classification standards are not known, then the Forensic Laboratory Standards shall be used.

9.14 CREATING EXHIBITS

9.14.1 What is an Exhibit?

An exhibit is a real evidence that will be considered by the Court.

In forensic cases, exhibits could be:

- the seized evidence itself;
- forensically produced evidence;
- printouts of files;
- a table of file attributes (e.g., metadata);
- or anything else that is to be produced in Court or as part of the forensic investigation results.

Exhibits should be produced and referenced in statements, depositions, or reports.

A full listing of exhibit created for any case processed by the Forensic Laboratory should be entered into the Exhibits Created Log and produced as part of the case outputs. The details of the Forensic Laboratory Exhibit Log are given in Appendix 30.

Exhibit numbering is defined in Chapter 8, Section 8.6.10.

9.15 PRODUCING A CASE REPORT FOR EXTERNAL USE

9.15.1 The Report

At the end of (or even during) a case, the Forensic Analyst will be required to produce a report on the case. If the report is for internal use, as a progress report, then the Internal Case Report Template should be used as given in Appendix 29.

If the report is for an external Client, then it must follow the relevant legislative rules within the jurisdiction. Often there are differing requirements for criminal cases and civil cases in the same jurisdiction, and the Forensic Analyst must be aware of them, and comply with them for all reports produced.

9.15.2 Report Checklist

While no two reports can ever be the same, the External Case Report Template as given in Chapter 6, Appendix 31, shall serve as a checklist along with the original requirements for the contents of any report produced by any Forensic Analyst.

It is important that the Forensic Analyst remembers the following:

- the report must contain facts;
- assumptions should not be made, unless the facts back them;
- conclusions must be backed by facts;
- leads should not be identified. The report is for the Client, and it is his or her job to identify the leads. If something important is discovered during the analysis of the exhibit or processing the case, then it should be written up so that it is obvious to the Client without providing a lead;
- spell and grammar checking must be used prior to submitting the report for peer review;
- findings must all be checked and double checked;
- all findings must be repeatable by any competent Forensic Analyst and produce the same results;
- where media is provided, ensure that the media is readable and the stated fields are present and that the extraction process works.

A checklist for producing reports in the Forensic Laboratory is given in Appendix 31.

9.15.3 Peer Review

No report shall be released to a Client without it having gone through a peer review process as approved by the Laboratory Manager.

The peer review process shall not be lightly undertaken and shall be performed in a diligent manner by the reviewer(s).

There shall be a technical review that should review the validity of any findings. The review should seek answers to the following questions:

- are the conclusions reached appropriate?
- are the conclusions reached justified?
- are the notes complete for all examinations and searches?
- are the results achieved verified by dual tool verification, if required?
- are the results repeatable?

- does the deliverable cover all evidence submitted in the case (and if not, why)?
- have all appropriate examinations been carried out?
- have the relevant Forensic Laboratory procedures been followed?
- is the deliverable (report, statements, depositions, etc.) accurate;
- is the documentation relating to all examined exhibits appropriate and complete?
- were the methods used appropriate?
- were the tools used appropriate?

A record of the technical review must be associated with the case in the case files. This is performed as a case check as given in Appendix 27.

The administrative review covers meeting the Client's requirements as well as a peer reviewed by another Forensic Analyst and this shall form part of the document control process as defined in Chapter 4, Section 4.6.3 and Chapter 6, Section 6.8. This is performed as a case check as given in Appendix 27.

9.15.4 Release of a Case Report

No case report shall be released without the authority of the Laboratory Manager as defined in Chapter 6, Section 6.8.

9.15.5 Affidavits

Depending on the jurisdiction, there may be an affidavit that must be included in any deliverable. It is the responsibility of the Laboratory Manager and the Forensic Analyst to ensure that these requirements are met.

9.16 STATEMENTS, DEPOSITIONS, AND SIMILAR

Statements, depositions, and other similar documents, written by Forensic Analysts, shall be written in a consistent style in compliance with the requirements within the jurisdiction.

The specific requirements will depend on the jurisdiction, the type of document to be produced, and the requirements of the case itself. Most of these types of documents contain similar information, but the exact form and structure, as well as specific content, usually differs. The consistent information includes:

- details of the author;
- author's qualifications—may include their CV/resume as an appendix;
- author's past and current experience relevant to the case;
- background to the case;
- instructions received, including who made the request, when it was submitted and what work was requested;
- proof of continuity of evidence;
- a statement of compliance with the relevant legislation, regulation, or relevant forensic good practice;
- details of the work on the case;
- for each item investigated:
  - method—short summary of what was done with what tools;
  - results—what was found;
  - technical explanations—technical explanations of the results;
  - context and discussion—context of the findings and technical points in relation to what as requested.
- summary of the findings;
- conclusions—not always required, but may be needed. These should be strongly reinforced by the factual arguments in the document;
- appendices—as required, including:
  - list of exhibits—include summary, exhibit reference, description, and origin;
  - selected Glossary.

Some documents of this type may require a question and answer process that may require detailed answers to specific questions to be recorded.

Pages shall all be numbered (*x* of *y* pages) and be signed on every page.

The purpose of a report, statement, or deposition is to:

- accurately describe the case from start to finish;
- be able to undergo scrutiny and challenge, as appropriate;
- be created in a timely manner;
- be retained as a record of the forensic case processing undertaken;
- be understandable to the lay person;
- contain facts to support any conclusions drawn;
- contain valid conclusions, recommendations, and opinions based on the facts reported, if required;
- not be open to misinterpretation by being unambiguous.

9.17 FORENSIC SOFTWARE TOOLS

There are a number of forensic tools in use in the Forensic Laboratory. A list of tool types used is given in Chapter 7, Appendix 4.

The primary tools for forensic casework in the Forensic Laboratory are normally Encase (Guidance Software) and FTK (AccessData).

Other tools are be used as required; however, it must be assured that they have been validated for use as defined in Chapter 7, Section 7.5.5, before being used to process a case.

9.18 BACKING UP AND ARCHIVING A CASE

Full backups must be maintained for all stages of processing a forensic case.

9.18.1 Initial Forensic Case Images

- a copy of each forensic case image is compressed and placed on the "images" drive on the forensic server and this is backed up according to the Forensic Laboratory standard backup cycle as defined in Chapter 7, Section 7.7.4;
- the backup process will ensure that a complete backup of current all forensic cases is made;
- each new forensic case image added to the "images" drive and is backed up until the drive is full;
- when the "images" drive is full, a full backup of the drive is taken and the drive with the tape backup is placed in the fireproof safe.

9.18.2 Work in Progress

- the work in progress on the forensic case that has been created by the Forensic Analyst is backed up to the server on a daily basis to the relevant virtual case folder on the "cases" drive;
- on a weekly basis, the whole of the "cases" file drive from the forensic workstation is copied to the server to the "work" drive (in compressed form);
- the "cases" drive is backed up to tape every night;
- the "work" drive is backed up on a weekly basis after the compressed case files have been copied from the forensic workstation.

9.18.3 "Finished" Cases

It is not easy to determine when a case is finished as there can be further requests for information, a long period of time before the trial, tribunal, or an appeal. The process below should be undertaken when the case has been finally (as far as is known) handed over to the Client.

- when a case has been finished (as far as can be told), then the whole case virtual case file on the forensic workstation is compressed and copied to the "finished" drive;
- the forensic workstation "work disk" is removed and placed in the fireproof safe;
- a tape copy of the "finished" drive is taken and stored with the PC work disk;
- the "finished" drive is backed up on a weekly basis;
- the virtual case file on the "cases" drive remains on the drive so that rapid access to important documents and files (such as reports and statements) are possible without having to reload a tape or decompress a case.

9.18.4 Archiving a Forensic Case

- once the case has properly finished, the case should be archived and retained according to the Forensic Case Retention Schedule as given in Chapter 4, Appendix 16;
- any hard copy case papers that have not been scanned and added to virtual case file must be scanned and added to the virtual case file;
- the virtual case file from the forensic workstation should be copied to another disk of similar size and hashed to ensure that the copies are exact copies;
- the copy disk shall be suitably labeled and dated;
- the two copies of the forensic workstation virtual case file shall be sealed and placed into the fire safe;
- other tape backups of the case will exist, but there must be two copies of the final work disk as tape copies are less stable than disks;
- the hard copy case file must be held securely under control of the relevant Forensic Analyst until it is securely deposited in the Secure Property Store;
- all archiving of the hard copy case file and the virtual case file must comply with the relevant legislative, regulatory, and good practice within the jurisdiction for evidence handling.

9.18.5 Recoverability of Archives and Backups

- Every year, the Forensic Laboratory Manager shall ensure that any archived and backed up cases can be recovered from their backup media. This is performed as a task in the business continuity plan testing as defined in Chapter 13, Section 13.6.2;
- records of this testing shall be maintained and any failures shall be investigated, and procedures changed, where necessary as defined in Chapter 13, Section 13.6.4.3.

9.19 DISCLOSURE

9.19.1 The law

The Forensic Laboratory must understand and comply with the legislation relating to disclosure within the jurisdiction.

Because of the possible amount of data held on a seized device, it is possible that not all of the information held on the device has been examined by a Forensic Analyst. This can lead to issues if the requirements within the jurisdiction are to list all evidence.

If some material has not been viewed, then the Forensic Analyst will not know what it contains. In this case, an entry should be made in any report produced to that effect with the reasons why it was not viewed and confirm that "it is not known whether it contains any data that may undermine the case or assist the defence" (or similar wording as required within the jurisdiction).

Reasons for performing a limited search include, but are not limited to:

- a live examination was required;
- the equipment had to be examined on-site;
- the searching was limited by the Search Warrant or Court order;
- the size of the seized data is so large that full examination was not possible;
- the weight of evidence found is so overwhelming that further searching and investigation was not necessary.

9.19.2 "Unlawful" Material

The Forensic Laboratory must understand and comply with the legislation relating to production, possessing, or disclosing unlawful material and what constitutes unlawful material in the jurisdiction.

The production of unlawful material from original exhibits should be avoided at all costs if at all possible. In cases where production is required, the produced materials shall be closely supervised either by the Laboratory Manager or the named Forensic Analyst whose case they were produced from.

This Forensic Analyst shall have the responsibility of ensuring that the material does not leave their possession until returned to the Forensic Laboratory for destruction, unless ordered otherwise by a Court of competent jurisdiction or an Officer of the Law.

When unlawful material is to be released either to the prosecution or defence, the Forensic Laboratory must comply with the legislation within the jurisdiction. There are no universal rules for this, but the following guidelines should be used, unless there is specific legislation requiring a different course of action:

- the material should be classified as STRICTLY CONFIDENTIAL according to the Forensic Laboratory data classification standards as given in Chapter 5, Appendix 16;
- the person receiving it has a legal right to receive it;
- the person is a suitable person to receive the material;
- that the recipient receives the material personally and signs for it;
- that the requirements placed on the recipient for security and disclosure are conveyed to the recipient;
- that the person receiving the material does not relinquish the material to any other person for any reason unless ordered otherwise by a Court of competent jurisdiction or an officer of the law;
- that the material released will be suitably secured personally by the recipient;
- that the recipient undertakes not to make any copies of the material other than for production in Court;
- that the recipient undertakes either to return the material after use or to securely destroy it by appropriate means and provide evidence of such a destruction to the Laboratory Manager;
- these actions shall be recorded in the Case Work Log.

9.19.3 Viewing of Material by Defence or Prosecution

The Forensic Laboratory must understand and comply with the legislation relating to viewing material by the Defence or Prosecution within the jurisdiction.

9.19.4 Client Attorney Privileged Information

During examination of an image, it may well be that the Forensic Analyst discovers that the acquisition process has acquired Client/Attorney privileged information. If this is the case, then the Forensic Analyst is ethically and legally bound not to divulge this information. The Laboratory Manager should be informed of the discovery and the finding logged in the Case Work Log with the date and time the Laboratory Manager was advised.

9.20 DISPOSAL

1. Typically, when the need for holding any papers, files, or items for a given case has passed (i.e., the retention date has been reached), the items shall all be disposed of using secure disposal where appropriate as defined in Chapter 12, Section 12.3.14.10;
2. Records of the date and method of disposal shall be kept, as should details of who actually performed the disposal;
3. Media, if still usable, should be considered by the Laboratory Manager for reuse, as should any serviceable equipment.

APPENDIX 1 - SOME INTERNATIONAL FORENSIC GOOD PRACTICE

There are a number of good practice guides in existence in different jurisdictions. There is no guarantee that these are relevant (some are out of date compared with the rapid rate of change in digital forensics) and others may not be relevant to the jurisdiction. However, they give indications of good practice in working standards in addition to ISO standards.

Name	Publisher	Version/ date
Good Practice Guide for Computer-based Electronic Evidence	ACPO	V4/ Undated
First Responders Guide to Computer Forensics	CERT	March 2005
Guidelines for the Best Practice in Forensic Examination of Digital Technology	EFNSI	V5/July 2006
Guidelines for Best Practice in the Forensic Examination of Digital Technology	IOCE	Undated
Computer Forensics Part 2: Best Practices	ISFS	May 2004
Computer Forensics Procedures and Methods	NCFS	Undated
Forensic Examination of Digital Evidence: A Guide for Law Enforcement	NIJ	April 2004
Handbook for Computer Security Incident Response Teams (CSIRTS)	SEI	April 2003
First Responder Guide to Computer Forensics: Advanced Topics	SEI	September 2005
Best Practices for Computer Forensics	SWGDE	Version 2.1/July 2006
Best Practices for Maintaining the Integrity of Digital Images and Digital Video Scientific Working Group on Imaging Technology	SWGIT	Undated

In addition to the above, there are numerous books, journals, and articles relating to digital forensics.

APPENDIX 2 - SOME INTERNATIONAL AND NATIONAL STANDARDS RELATING TO DIGITAL FORENSICS

There are a number of International (ISO) standards that relate to digital forensics, as well as a number of national standards. The main ISO Standards are listed below and some of the better known national standards.

Standard	Name	Type	Country
HB 171-2003	Guidelines for the management of IT evidence	National	Australia and New Zealand
ISO/IEC 27037	Information technology—Security techniques—Guidelines for identification, collection, acquisition, and preservation of digital evidence	International	International
ISO/IEC 27041	Information technology—Security techniques—Guidelines for the analysis and interpretation of digital evidence	International	International
ISO/IEC 27042	Information technology—Security techniques—Guidelines for the analysis and interpretation of digital evidence	International	International
ISO/IEC 27043	Information technology—Security techniques—Digital investigation principles and processes	International	International
ISO/IEC 30121	System and software engineering—Information technology—Governance of digital forensic risk framework	International	International
SP 800-101	Guidelines on Cell Phone Forensics	National	USA
SP 800-72	Guidelines on PDA Forensics	National	USA
SP 800-86	Guide to Integrating Forensic Techniques into Incident Response	National	USA
SP 800-61	Computer Security Incident Handling	NIST	USA

Continued

Note

Some of these are published versions and some are in draft status.

APPENDIX 3 - HARD DISK LOG DETAILS

The Forensic Laboratory records the following details in MARS about all disks purchased to process forensic cases:

- make;
- model name or number;
- part number;
- serial number;
- disk type (IDE, SCSI, SATA, etc.);
- size (as recorded on disk);
- cylinders;
- heads;
- sectors;
- tracks;
- supplier;
- supplier reference number;
- purchase order number;
- date ordered;
- date received;
- sealed on arrival?
- checked by;
- resealed by;
- resealed date;
- unique Forensic Laboratory number assigned to the disk;
- action;
- notes on assignment;
- dates assigned;
- assigned by.

Note

It is recognized that not all of this information is always available, so what is available is entered.

APPENDIX 4 - DISK HISTORY LOG

The Forensic Laboratory records the following details in MARS about the history of all disks used in processing forensic cases:

- unique Forensic Laboratory number;
- action (wiped, assigned to a case (give case number), returned to store, transfer to outside agency, disposal, etc.);
- date action taken;
- action performed by;
- tool used;
- action authorized by;
- date disk resealed;
- reseal performed by.

Note

The disk history log will give a complete audit trail of all disks for their complete life cycle in the Forensic Laboratory.

APPENDIX 5 - TAPE LOG DETAILS

The Forensic Laboratory records the following details in MARS about all disks purchased to process forensic cases:

- make;
- model name or number;
- part number;
- serial number;
- disk type (DLT, AIT, LTO, etc.);
- size (as recorded on tape);
- supplier;
- supplier reference number;
- purchase order number;
- date ordered;
- date received;
- checked by;
- unique Forensic Laboratory number assigned to the tape;
- action;
- purpose used for;
- date used;
- assigned by.

Note

It is recognized that not all of this information is always available, so what is available is entered.

APPENDIX 6 - TAPE HISTORY LOG

The Forensic Laboratory records the following details in MARS about the history of all tapes used in processing forensic cases:

- unique Forensic Laboratory number;
- action (wiped, used to backup a case, used to backup a case image, returned to store, transfer to outside agency, disposal, etc.);
- date action taken;
- action performed by;
- method or tool used;
- action authorized by.

Note

The tape history log will give a complete audit trail of all tape for their complete life cycle in the Forensic Laboratory.

APPENDIX 7 - SMALL DIGITAL MEDIA LOG DETAILS

The Forensic Laboratory records the following details in MARS about USBs and Key Loggers purchased to process forensic cases:

- type (USB, Key Logger, or other);
- make;
- model name or number;
- part number;
- serial number;
- size (as recorded on device);
- supplier;
- supplier reference number;
- purchase order number;
- date ordered;
- date received;
- checked by;
- unique Forensic Laboratory number assigned to the device.

Note

It is recognized that not all of this information is always available, so what is available is entered.

APPENDIX 8 - SMALL DIGITAL MEDIA DEVICE LOG

The Forensic Laboratory records the following details in MARS about the history of all USBs and Key Loggers used in processing forensic cases:

- unique Forensic Laboratory number;
- action (wiped, used in a forensic case, returned to store, transfer to outside agency, disposal, etc.);
- date action taken;
- action performed by;
- method or tool used;
- action authorized by.

Note

The small digital media device history log will give a complete audit trail of all of these devices for their complete life cycle in the Forensic Laboratory.

APPENDIX 9 - FORENSIC CASE WORK LOG

Within the Forensic Laboratory, the following form is used. Typically, it is typed directly into MARS, but can also be used as a paper-based form and is then scanned into the virtual case file.

- case number;
- Client/case name;
- date;
- time;
- work performed;
- hours expended;
- date;
- time;
- name of Forensic Analyst;
- signature.

Each page, if using a paper copy, is to be signed and the pages numbered "*x* of *y* pages" so that completeness can be verified.

APPENDIX 10 - CASE PROCESSING KPIs

The following case performance indicators should be maintained by the Laboratory Manager on an annual basis, with reporting carried out on a monthly basis for the year:

- feedback from Clients;
- number of "assists";
- number of arrests;
- number of jobs (or cases) undertaken per year;
- number of jobs that failed their SLAs;
- number of jobs that failed their TRTs;
- number of jobs that met or bettered SLAs;
- number of jobs that met or bettered TRTs;
- number of other devices examined;
- number of PCs examined;
- number of PDAs and mobile phones examined;
- number of successful assists;
- number of terabytes of evidence imaged;
- number of years of custodial sentence;
- requests for investigation and examination;
- sentences or penalties resulting from "assists";
- sentences or penalties resulting from Forensic Laboratory-processed forensic cases;
- successful cases (as a percentage of all cases);
- training undertaken in the year for the Forensic Analysts;
- value of assets recovered/seized.

APPENDIX 11 - CONTENTS OF SAMPLE EXHIBIT REJECTION LETTER

All rejection letters follow the same format within the Forensic Laboratory and be produced on headed paper. Apart from the addressing details (Client and Forensic Laboratory) and date, the following is a recommended letter content for the rejection of any exhibit:

- addressee;
- date;
- Forensic Laboratory case number;
- description of exhibit;
- text (e.g.,

The exhibit referenced above was delivered to the Forensic Laboratory, by (name) on (date).
The exhibit referenced above was delivered to the Forensic Laboratory, by (name) on (date).
This exhibit has been examined as part of the acceptance process into the Forensic Laboratory secure property store. Based on this examination, the Forensic Laboratory is unable to accept the exhibit in its current state, because of the following reason:
Give reason(s) here. These could include, but not be limited to:

- a missing exhibit label;
- an unacceptably low level of agreement between the details on an exhibit label and those on the accompanying submission documentation;
- appropriate control samples not submitted;
- evidence of possible evidence tampering;
- illegibility in the name, identification number, or any other information on an exhibit label;
- inadequate or inappropriate packaging or sealing of an exhibit that could prejudice its integrity;
- inconsistency between the details on an exhibit label and/or accompanying submission documentation and what the exhibit actually is;
- insufficient material being available for meaningful examination or analysis (e.g., incomplete or missing labeling, no bag sealed, opened evidence bag, etc.);
- opened exhibit packaging;
- previous handling, storage or evidence of tampering with an exhibit that could prejudice its integrity;
- repeat of the same identification details on different exhibit labels;
- there being more than one label on an exhibit;
- unacceptable risk in processing the exhibit.

Please contact the writer to discuss how this may be resolved.)

- contact details.

APPENDIX 12 - SAMPLE CONTINUITY LABEL CONTENTS

Every movement of any exhibit moved from initial seizure to return of the exhibit to the Client or its originator must be documented to maintain the chain of evidence. The Forensic Laboratory records the following information:

- case number;
- Client/case name;
- exhibit reference number;
- exhibit seal number;
- date;
- time;
- name of recipient;
- signature.

APPENDIX 13 - DETAILS OF THE FORENSIC LABORATORY PROPERTY LOG

The Forensic Laboratory Property Log Book is an A3 Book, with pages numbered sequentially to counter any suggestions of page removal. It records all property (e.g., exhibits) received into and taken out of the secure property store. It also by default shows what exhibits should be currently in the secure property store, allowing exhibit audits to be carried out.

BOOKING IN PROPERTY

- property reference number;
- date booked in;
- time booked in;
- seal number;
- Client reference;
- case name;
- Client name;
- property description;
- booking in name;
- booking in signature.

ON RESEALING PROPERTY

- date resealed;
- time resealed;
- seal number;
- resealed by—name;
- resealed by—signature.

BOOKING OUT PROPERTY

- date booked out;
- time booked out;
- reason for booking out;
- booking out name;
- booking out signature.

APPENDIX 14 - EXHIBIT ACCEPTANCE LETTER TEMPLATE

All acceptance letters follow the same format within the Forensic Laboratory and are produced on headed paper. Apart from the addressing details (Client and Forensic Laboratory) and date, the following is a recommended letter content for the conformation of acceptance of one or more exhibits for forensic case processing:

- addressee;
- date;
- Forensic Laboratory case number;

- text (e.g.)
  The following exhibit(s) have been received by the Forensic Laboratory from (name) on (date).
  List the exhibit description, any of the Client's exhibit number(s), if present and the Forensic Laboratory's exhibit numbering assigned and the Property Log Book number as defined in Chapter 8, Section 8.6.10 and Section 9.6.1, respectively.
  The exhibit(s) have been logged into the Forensic Laboratory Secure Property Store on (date) for case processing.
  Please contact the writer if you have any questions relating to these exhibits.
  - contact details.

APPENDIX 15 - PROPERTY SPECIAL HANDLING LOG

Where a property booked into the Forensic Laboratory Secure Property Store needs special handling, it is recorded in MARS. Details of what is recorded is given below:

- property reference number;
- date booked in;
- time booked in;
- seal number;
- special handling processes undertaken;
- special handling processes undertaken by—name;
- special handling processes undertaken by—signature.

APPENDIX 16 - EVIDENCE SOUGHT

The requirements from a Client will vary between cases, but the Forensic Laboratory has a standard set of requirements for the evidence sought in a case. This may change from case to case, as required. The standard requirements for the Forensic Laboratory are:

- case reference number;
- Client/case name;
- details of evidence sought and/or offences suspected;
- comments or other relevant information;
- case details completed by—name;
- case details completed by—signature;
- date;
- time.

APPENDIX 17 - REQUEST FOR FORENSIC EXAMINATION

This form must be completed in all cases where computers or computer-related equipment is submitted to the Forensic Laboratory for examination. Items will not be accepted unless received in appropriate sealed bags or containers and accompanied by an exhibit label signed by the person seizing or taking possession of the equipment and the person delivering the items for examination.

The following items are recorded:

- Client reference;
- Client/case name;
- for each item submitted for examination the following must be recorded:
  - exhibit reference number;
  - description;
  - seal number;
  - insurance value.
- delivered by—name;
- delivered by—title;
- delivered by—organization;
- delivered by—signature;
- delivery date;
- delivery time;
- accepted by—name;
- accepted by—signature;
- comments (e.g., anything relevant to the exhibits being delivered);
- date entered into MARS;
- entered into MARS by—name;
- Forensic Laboratory case number (autogenerated by MARS).

APPENDIX 18 - CLIENT VIRTUAL CASE FILE STRUCTURE

If the Forensic Laboratory uses EnCase and Forensic Tool Kit (FTK) as its main forensic case processing tool, then this folder structure reflects that. Additionally, this is the base case folder structure and more folders are added as required depending on the actual case being processed.

- case files;
- compressed files for Client;
- encase images;
- files recovered in file structure;
- FTK view;
- HTML carver;
- instructions from Client;
- Internet history;
- not in report to Client;
- photos;
- recovered "Documents and Settings";
- recovered "My Documents";
- recovered attachments;
- recovered documents;
- recovered e-mail;
- recovered HTML;
- recovered images;

- recovered of note;
- recovered presentations;
- recovered recycle bin;
- recovered spreadsheets;
- report—supporting documents;
- report;
- scanned case forms;
- schedule;
- searches;
- temp;
- text search results;
- tools used in the case;
- virus scanning;
- working file.

APPENDIX 19 - COMPUTER DETAILS LOG

The following details are recorded for all exhibits that are processed in the Forensic Laboratory:

- case number;
- Client/case name;
- exhibit reference number;
- Forensic Analyst undertaking examination;
- exhibit type;
- make;
- model;
- serial number:
- date;
- time;
- identifying marks or damage;
- photographs taken (Yes/No)?
- peripherals:
  - floppy disk;
  - video card;
  - CD reader;
  - RAM strips (describe and give details);
  - CD writer;
  - SCSI card;
  - DVD reader;
  - network card;
  - DVD writer;
  - Modem;
  - ZIP disk;
  - sound card;
  - others (describe).
- BIOS settings:
  - BIOS key;
  - BIOS password;
  - boot sequence;
  - operating system;
  - system time;
  - system date;
  - actual time;
  - actual date;
- examined by:
  - full name;
  - signature
  - date;
  - time.

APPENDIX 20 - OTHER EQUIPMENT DETAILS LOG

The following details are recorded for all exhibits that are processed in the Forensic Laboratory:

- case number;
- Client/case name;
- exhibit reference number;
- equipment type;
- make;
- model;
- serial number;
- condition;
- casing type;
- identifying marks, damage, or other comments;
- photographs taken (Yes/No)?
- details of the equipment;
- examined by:
  - full name;
  - signature;
  - date;
  - time.

APPENDIX 21 - HARD DISK DETAILS LOG

The following details are recorded for all exhibits that are processed in the Forensic Laboratory:

- case number;
- Client/case name;
- exhibit reference number;
- make;
- model;
- number of partitions;
- serial number;
- size;
- cylinders;
- heads;
- sectors;
- controller details;
- jumper setting;
- time and date set correctly on the acquisition machine (Yes/No);
- Imaging:

    - tool;
    - version;
    - notes;
    - Forensic Laboratory hard disk reference for image;
    - imaged by:
        - full name;
        - signature;
        - date;
        - time.
- backup hard drive:
    - Forensic Laboratory hard disk reference;
    - serial number;
    - capacity;
    - date wiped;
    - image backup copy verified by:
        - full name;
        - signature;
        - date;
        - time.

APPENDIX 22 - OTHER MEDIA DETAILS LOG

Note

Not all of the details below are appropriate for all media (e.g., serial number on media, cylinders on flash media, etc.).

- case number;
- Client/case name;
- exhibit reference number;
- media type;
- make;
- model;
- volatile memory image taken (Yes/No)?
- number of partitions;
- serial number;
- size;
- cylinders;
- heads;
- sectors;
- photographs taken (Yes/No)?
- Imaging;
- software and version (Image 1);
- write blocker type used;
- software and version (Image 2);
- write blocker type used;
- notes;
- hashes image 1;
- hashes image 2;
- hash verification attached (Yes/No);
- if hash verification not attached, location where it can be found;
    - Forensic Laboratory hard disk reference for image;
    - imaged by:
        - full name;
        - signature;
        - date;
        - time.
- backup hard drive:
    - Forensic Laboratory Hard Disk Reference;
    - serial number;
    - capacity;
    - date wiped;
    - image backup copy verified by:
        - full name;
        - signature;
        - date;
        - time.

APPENDIX 23 - CELL PHONE DETAILS LOG

The following details are recorded for all exhibits that are processed in the Forensic Laboratory:

- case number;
- Client/case name;
- exhibit reference number;
- phone type;
- make;
- model;
- the IMEI (International Mobile Station Equipment Identity);
- the IMSI (International Mobile subscriber Identity);
- the phone's serial number;
- the SIM (Subscriber Identity Module);
- time displayed;
- date displayed;
- other information displayed on the screen;
- account holder name;
- account holder address;
- called parties;
- SMS texts;
- calling parties;
- account call records;
- account holder payment type data;
- SMS records;
- MMS records;
- services accessed;
- Internet Service Provider;
- access dates and times (if held);
- limited location-dependent information;
- downloaded files;
- e-mail;

- voicemail;
- address book/contacts;
- short dial number;
- calendar events.

APPENDIX 24 - OTHER DEVICE DETAILS LOG

The following details are recorded for all exhibits that are processed in the Forensic Laboratory:

- case number;
- Client/case name;
- exhibit reference number;
- device type;
- make;
- model;
- time displayed, if appropriate;
- date displayed, if appropriate;
- other information displayed on the screen, if appropriate.

Note

If a device contains a hard disk, it should be removed and treated as defined in Section 9.9.

APPENDIX 25 - SOME EVIDENCE FOUND IN VOLATILE MEMORY

The evidence recovered from volatile memory acquisition will vary depending on the device being acquired, but depending on the device being acquired will include, but not limited to:

- available physical memory;
- BIOS information;
- clipboard information;
- command history;
- cron jobs;
- current system uptime;
- driver information;
- hot fixes installed;
- installed applications;
- interface configurations;
- listening ports;
- local users;
- logged on users;
- malicious code that is run from memory rather than disk;
- network cards;
- network information;
- network passwords;
- network status;
- open DLL files;
- open files and registry handles;
- open files;
- open network connections;
- operating system and version;
- pagefile location;
- passwords and crypto keys;
- plaintext versions of encrypted material;
- process memory;
- process to port mapping;
- processes running;
- registered organization;
- registered owner;
- remote users;
- routing information;
- service information;
- shares;
- system installation date;
- system time;
- the memory map;
- the VAD tree;
- time zone;
- total amount of physical memory;
- unsaved files;
- user IDs and passwords.

APPENDIX 26 - SOME FILE METADATA

Typical file metadata includes, but is not limited to:

- attributes;
- author;
- category;
- character count;
- child;
- comments;
- company;
- date accessed;
- date created;
- date modified;
- date printed;
- document type;
- duplicate;
- e-mail;
- file name;
- file name and path;
- file path;
- keywords;
- last printed;
- last saved by;
- line count;
- manager;
- MD5 or SHA file hash;
- page count;
- parent;
- previous authors;

- subject;
- template used;
- title;
- total editing time;
- version;
- word count.

Note 1

In a number of packages, the user can define their own custom metadata fields.

Note 2

Some metadata is set by the organization, some is generated by the operating system, and some is entered by the Document Author.

APPENDIX 27 - CASE PROGRESS CHECKLIST

Note

Not all tasks are relevant to all cases processed by the Forensic Laboratory. Where a task is irrelevant, it shall be struck through.

The checklist used by the Forensic Laboratory for monitoring case progress contains the following tasks:

- case number;
- Client/case name;
- legal authority confirmed;
- exhibits received and accepted;
- exhibit rejection letter sent;
- photos of exhibits on arrival;
- case formally accepted;
- case assigned;
- insurance value reviewed;
- agreed TRT;
- paper case file setup;
- virtual case file setup;
- photos of exhibits on disassembly;
- imaged;
- image verified;
- BIOS data;
- recover files;
- malware scan;
- signature analysis;
- hash analysis;
- info record (o/n);
- graphics files (o/n);
- initialize case script;
- link parser link script;
- unique e-mail script;
- internet history script;
- extract documents;
- extract spreadsheets;
- extract databases;
- extract images;
- extract HTML;
- extract e-mail;
- extract files in file structure;
- "documents and settings";
- "recent files";
- "favorites";
- "my documents";
- "desktop";
- "temporary" files;
- HTML/Web carve;
- Artifacts;
- search 1;
- search 2;
- search 3;
- search 4;
- search 5;
- search 6;
- search 7;
- search 8;
- search 9;
- search 10;
- accounts;
- FTK view;
- metadata;
- write report draft;
- internal technical review of report;
- internal administrative review of report;
- agree report release;
- blow report to disk;
- sent to client;
- exhibits returned;
- backup case to disk;
- backup case to tape;
- invoiced;
- paid;
- archived.

Each item will have a date recorded when it was completed and the signature of the person performing the task.

APPENDIX 28 - MEETING THE REQUIREMENTS OF HB 171

Note

Some of these requirements are met in this Chapter at section 9.10.9. But some details are given below:

HB 171 Section	Control	Procedure(s)
3	IT Evidence Management Lifecycle	
3.1 Introduction	Introduction	Chapter 6, Section 6.6
3.2	Design for Evidence	This chapter
3.2.1	Classification and Labeling	Chapter 11 Chapter 12, Section 12.3.14.8
3.2.2	Identifying the Author of Electronic Records	Chapter 4, Section 4.6.3
3.2.3	Establishing the Authenticity of Electronic Records	Chapter 4, Section 4.6.3
3.2.3	Establishing the Authenticity of Electronic Records	Chapter 4, Section 4.6.4 Chapter 7, Section 7.4.3 This chapter
3.2.4	Establishing the Time and Date a Particular Record was Created or Altered	Signed and dated forms The audit trail in the ERMS Chapter 4, Section 4.6.4 Section 9.12
3.2.5	Establishing the Reliability of Computer Programs	Chapter 7, Section 7.5.5 Section 9.4.4 Section 9.4.6 Section 9.4.7 Section 9.4.8 Section 9.4.10
3.3	Produce Records	Signed and dated forms The audit trail in the ERMS Chapter 12
3.4	Stage 3: Collect Evidence	
3.4.1	Standards for Evidence Collection	Signed and dated forms The records in the ERMS Chapter 8 Section 9.9 Section 9.19.1
3.4.2	Contemporaneous Notes	Signed and dated forms The records in the ERMS Chapter 8, Section 8.6.15 Appendix 9
3.4.3	Relevance	Chapter 8, Section 8.6.16 Section 9.1.5

Continued

HB 171 Section	Control	Procedure(s)
3.4.4	Chain of Custody	Signed and dated forms Chapter 8, Section 8.6.4 Chapter 8, Appendix 7 Chapter 8, Appendix 17 Section 9.6 Section 9.9.1.5 Appendix 13
3.4.5	Nonreadable Electronic Records	Chapter 7, Appendix 4 Section 9.10
3.4.6	Interceptions	Chapter 8, Section 8.6.18 Section 9.9
3.4.7	Limitations	Chapter 8, Section 8.1.2 Section 9.19.1 Section 9.19.4
3.5	Stage 4: Analyze Evidence	
3.5.1	Use Evidence Copy	Chapter 8, Section 8.6.16 Chapter 8, Section 8.6.18 Section 9.1.5 Section 9.9 Section 9.10.7
3.5.2	Personnel Qualifications	Chapter 4, Section 4.4.6.2.2 Chapter 4, Section 4.6.2.3 Chapter 6, Appendix 27 Section 9.10.6 Chapter 11 Chapter 14 Chapter 18, Section 18.2
3.5.3	Completeness of Evidence	Signed and dated forms Chapter 6, Section 6.6.2.4 Section 9.10.3
3.6	Reporting and Presentation	Chapter 6, Section 6.8 Chapter 6, Appendix 31 Section 9.13 Section 9.15 Section 9.16
3.6	Determine Evidentiary Weight	Chapter 8 Section 9.1.5 Section 9.9 Section 9.10

APPENDIX 29 - INTERNAL CASE REPORT TEMPLATE

Below is a standard template for an internal forensic case report as used in the Forensic Laboratory. This is amended as required depending on the specific case requirements.

- document control;
- issue status;
- classification;
- table of contents;
- background;
- evidence required by Client;
- initial examination;
- first-stage investigation results;
- evidence found to date;
- Appendix A—Malware reporting;
- Appendix B—Encase case summary;
- Appendix C onwards—other items of note relating to the case.

APPENDIX 30 - FORENSIC LABORATORY EXHIBIT LOG

The details of what is created as an exhibit for any case will of course vary between cases. The details below are the basic template for the log, and details are added to the log as appropriate to the case:

- case number;
- Client/case name;
- exhibit reference number;
- description;
- created by:
- full name;
- signature;
- date;
- time.

APPENDIX 31 - REPORT PRODUCTION CHECKLIST

The following is a checklist for producing a forensic case report. It can be used for internal or external reports and is a check on actions being performed. The checklist can apply to the:

- hard copy case report;
- soft copy case report;
- compressed soft copy report.

The Forensic Analyst must determine which of the checklist items apply to which type of report media. The actions to be undertaken are:

- select correct file for report;
- print cover and spine;
- determine report classification;
- produce table of contents;
- background to the case;
- ensure evidence required by Client is clearly understood;
- initial examination results;
- extract files in structure;
- produce case FTK report;
- produce linkage analysis;
- produce internet history;
- produce HTML carve;
- recovered metadata;
- produce recovered files of note;
- produce recovered documents;
- produce recovered e-mail;
- produce recovered HTML;
- produce recovered images;
- produce recovered PDFs;
- produce recovered spreadsheets;
- produce recovered databases;
- produce text search results;
- produce any other recovered evidence to support the case conclusions reached;
- undergo peer review;
- produce instructions for use;
- check soft copy media works properly;
- ensure that compressed files can be decompressed;
- produce appropriate labels for each report type.

Chapter 10

Case Management

Table of Contents

10.1 OVERVIEW

There is a critical need to keep control of all cases that the Laboratory handles and this need increases with growing numbers of cases handled and more Forensic Analysts that need to be managed.

There are two different processes involved in managing cases:

- Forensic Analysts handling their own case;
- the Forensic Laboratory Manager who has oversight and manages all cases in the Forensic Laboratory.

Each Forensic Laboratory employee has different needs, and these must be met to ensure that the Forensic Laboratory delivers quality products and services.

To achieve this, the Forensic Laboratory uses a mix of hard copy forms and its own internally developed Forensic Case Management Database—MARS (Management and Reporting Tool).

To ensure that there was a complete Chain of Custody maintained and to manage and monitor Service Level Agreements (SLAs) or required Turn Round Times (TRTs), the Forensic Laboratory MARS tool has been developed.

The system was designed so that complete case management can be undertaken for all current and historic cases, as well as automated case billing and also a variety of management reports can be produced to support the management of all forensic cases in the Forensic Laboratory.

The basic system is a multi-user system for a single laboratory and handles all processes that would be performed in the laboratory.

MARS has been designed to be intuitive, easy to use, and minimize the need for typed input once the system had been properly set up.

All actions in MARS are logged to a secure audit trail, allowing interrogation of the audit log between two dates or times, for any case or for any Forensic Analyst processing a forensic case.

10.2 HARD COPY FORMS

The Forensic Laboratory can use a number of hard copy forms to support forensic case processing. These can be used in a variety of situations for all stages in the processing of a forensic case.

All hard copy forms are referred to in the rest of the book and can be used as required and are referred to in the relevant part of this book. All hard copy forms have the facility for original signatures on them and are able to be used by third parties that do not have access to MARS.

Hard copy forms, when completed, can then be scanned and added to the Client virtual case file as well as being stored in the hard copy file that is securely stored in the Secure Property Store at the end of a case.

First Responders should always carry a full set of case processing forms when they attend a Client site, and there should always be hard copy forms that can be printed from the server on an "as-required" basis.

10.3 MARS

The Management and Reporting System (MARS) has been specifically designed for handling all aspects of forensic cases in the Forensic Laboratory. It is a multiuser system, written in Microsoft Access.

Note 1

In the section, as the original Forensic Laboratory was set up in the United Kingdom, all of the setup details are relating to a UK-based company (Forensic Computing Ltd., FCL). MARS is fully configurable to any jurisdiction in the world as required.

Note 2

At the time of writing, MARS is undergoing an upgrade, so in some cases the screen shots do not completely match the text. The text contains the description of the upgraded version of MARS and is the definitive one.

10.3.1 Initial Forensic Laboratory Setup

Once MARS is started for the first time, the first task to undertake is to enter the organizational details for the Forensic Laboratory. The setup screen is shown only once, so it is essential that the information entered is correct, as it cannot be later corrected. The details entered on the screen below are used for all outputs to screen or hard copy (Figure 10.1).

Details of the contents of all of the fields in this screen are given in Appendix 1.

The user can enter details as required into all of the fields on the screen.

Finally, check that all of the information here is correct as this is the only time that this information can be set up and the only time that this screen will be viewed.

On pressing the "Continue" button, the user is asked if they are certain they want to continue with the options for "Yes" and "No."

"No" allows you to return and correct any errors and omissions, and "Yes" writes the information to file and deletes the setup program.

10.3.2 Setting up the Administrator

Once MARS is installed, it is necessary to configure it for use.

On starting MARS for the first time, one needs to setup the Administrator.

This is as shown in Figure 10.2.

Details of the contents of all of the fields in this screen are given in Appendix 2.

It is recommended that the user name identifies any Administrators as opposed to "normal" users. In the Forensic Laboratory, this is done by suffixing the User ID with the word "admin"—e.g., "dlwadmin" to indicate that this is the "dlw" user administration account as opposed to the User ID "dlw" indicating that "dlw" normal user.

MARS will assign the Administrator the relevant "Administrator" Access Rights.

Once the details are all correct, press the "Save User" button to save the Administrator.

10.3.3 MARS Users

Once setup, MARS has two categories of users:

- Administrator—typically the Laboratory Manager, who has rights to manage media, cases, suppliers, etc., and run a number of reports for all cases and infrastructure;
- Forensic Analysts—who are only able to manage their own assigned cases and run reports on them.

Once setup, users (the Administrator or Forensic Analysts) only have options in MARS that are related to their role and any cases assigned to them.

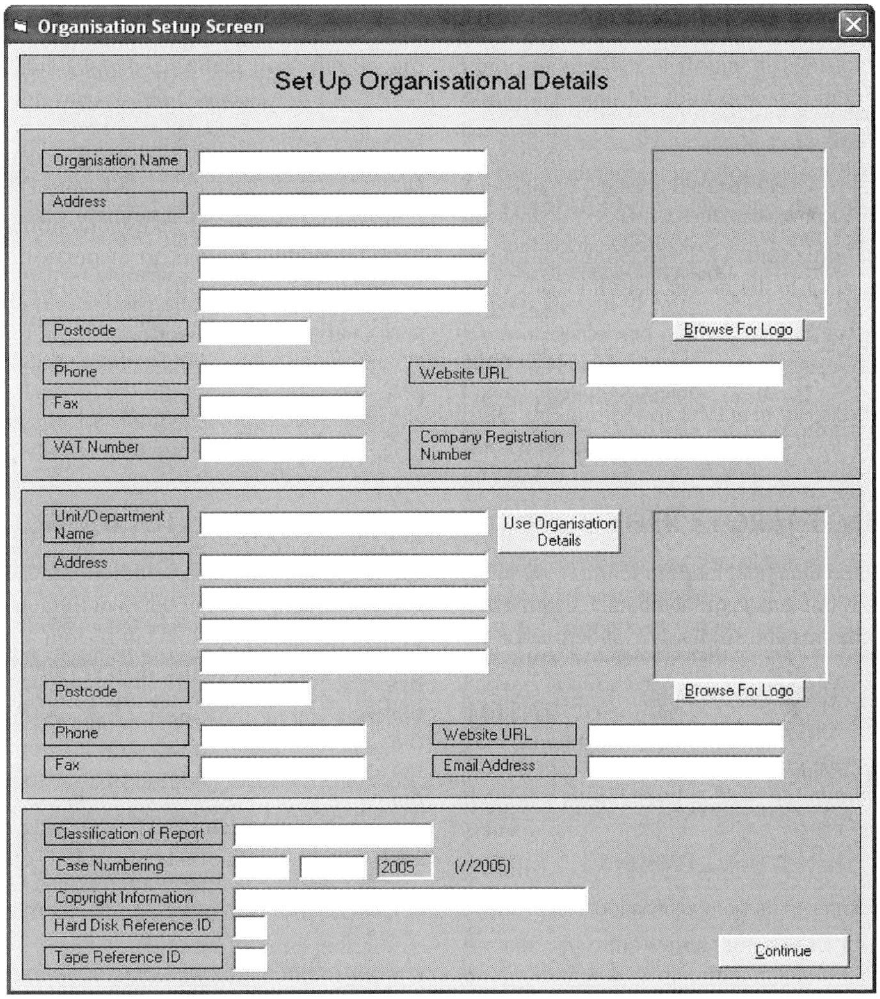

FIGURE 10.1 Initial Forensic Laboratory setup. (For color version of this figure, the reader is referred to the online version of this chapter.)

To access MARS, any user must have successfully authenticated to the network using their login credentials (User ID and biometric thumbprint scan). They must then have the MARS icon available on their desktop and Access Rights to use it to log into MARS, using their User ID and password as shown in Figure 10.3.

10.3.4 Audit Tracking

All actions taken by any user in MARS are written to the secure audit trail. These will include:

- date;
- time;
- User ID;
- action taken.

Audit reports are defined in Section 10.7.5 and output is given in Appendix 3.

10.3.5 Administrator Tasks

There are a number of tasks that the Administrator will manage and that are not accessible to "normal users." This is setting up static information relating to the operation of the Forensic Laboratory and management of forensic cases as well as some management reports.

While the term "user" is used here as a user of MARS, the person performing the forensic work is called a Forensic Analyst in the chapter elsewhere.

Note

Each of the Administrator options is similar in their operation. They allow the following operations on the data:

- entry of a new record ("save and exit" option—saves a record and returns to calling menu);

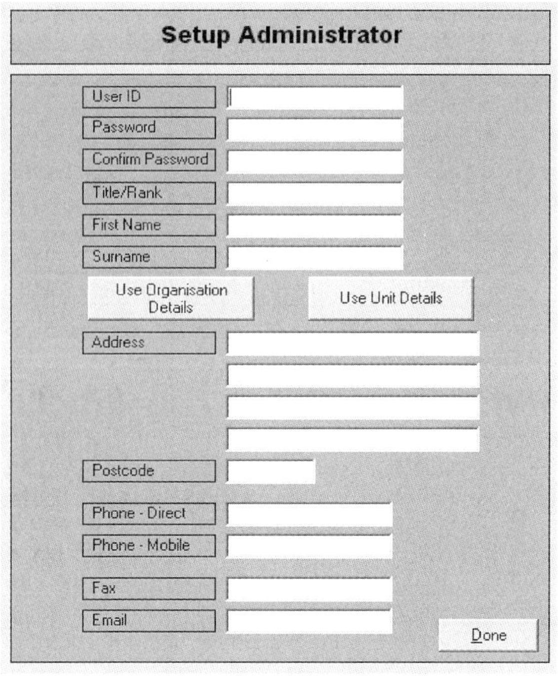

FIGURE 10.2 Setting Up the System Administrator.

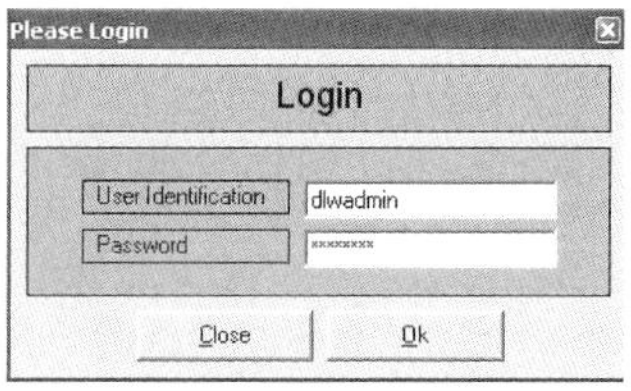

FIGURE 10.3 MARS Users. (For color version of this figure, the reader is referred to the online version of this chapter.)

- entry of a sequence of new records ("save" option—saves a record and clears screen allowing a new record to be entered);
- amendment of an existing record ("amend option"—updates record, if possible, and return to calling menu);
- exits without saving ("exit"—return to calling menu without changing or updating a record);
- delete a record ("delete and exit" option—deletes a record, if possible, and return to calling menu);
- delete a sequence of records ("delete" option—deletes a record, if possible, and clears screen allowing another record to be deleted).

Note

Where the deletion of a record could affect the referential integrity of the MARS database, the system will not permit the deletion to take place (e.g., attempted deletion of a supplier who supplied disks used in processing forensic cases, attempted deletion of a Forensic Analyst that processed a forensic case, etc.).

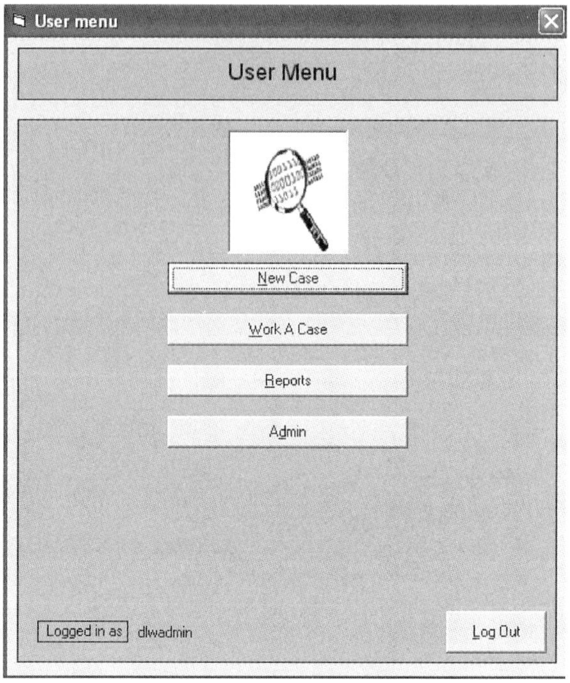

FIGURE 10.4 Administrator tasks. (For color version of this figure, the reader is referred to the online version of this chapter.)

When the Administrator logs into the system, they are presented with a main menu, as shown in Figure 10.4.

This shows that the current user is "dlwadmin" (bottom left-hand side of the screen next to "Logged in as") indicating that it is the User ID for DLW for administration purposes—not for working cases.

The logo shown is the logo entered at the start up.

10.3.5.1 Manage Users

The "Manage Users" screen is shown in Figure 10.5.

Details of the contents of all of the fields in this screen are given in Appendix 4.

10.3.5.1.1 Add a User

The blank screen is presented and the Administrator must populate all of the relevant fields and then save them to create a new user in MARS.

10.3.5.1.2 Amend a User

Typically, this is used where the Administrator needs to change a user's password or their contact details.

To amend a user, the user must already exist.

Using the drop-down box for existing users, the user to have their details amended is selected and the screen populated with their existing details from the stored record.

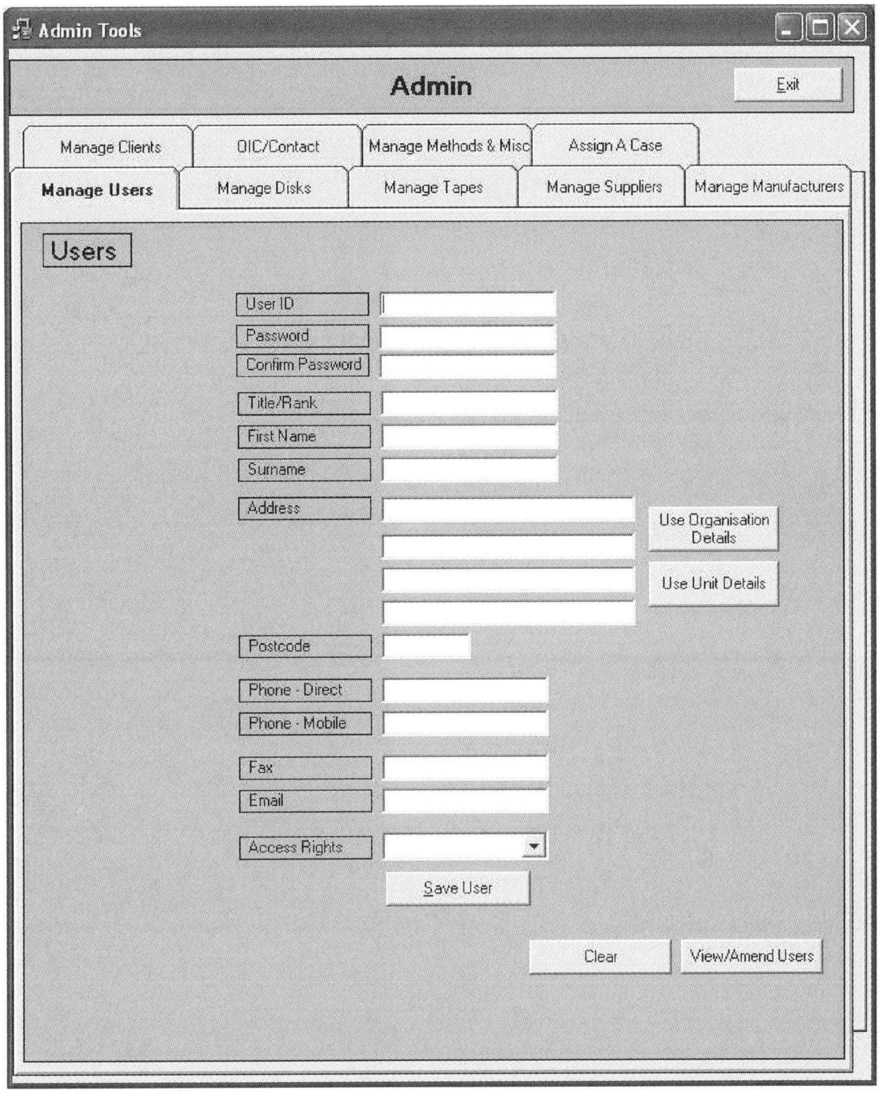

FIGURE 10.5 Manage Users. (For color version of this figure, the reader is referred to the online version of this chapter.)

The Administrator is able to update data relating to the user and save it, as appropriate. The Administrator is advised of the successful update and must acknowledge it.

10.3.5.1.3 Delete a User

To delete a user, the user must already exist.

Using the drop-down box for existing users, the user to have their details deleted is selected and the screen populated with their existing details from the stored record.

It is not possible to delete a user who has been active in the MARS system, i.e., one who has been used in the system. The Administrator will be advised that this is not possible; otherwise, the Administrator is advised of the successful deletion of the user and must acknowledge it.

10.3.5.2 Manage a Manufacturer

The "Manage Manufacturers" screen is shown in Figure 10.6.

Details of the contents of all of the fields in this screen are given in Appendix 5.

10.3.5.2.1 Add a Manufacturer

The blank screen is presented and the Administrator must populate all of the relevant fields and then save them to create a new manufacturer in MARS.

10.3.5.2.2 Amend a Manufacturer

To amend a manufacturer, the manufacturer must already exist.

Using the drop-down box for existing manufacturers, the manufacturer to have their details amended is selected and the screen populated with their existing details from the stored record.

The Administrator is able to update data relating to the manufacturer and save it, as appropriate. The

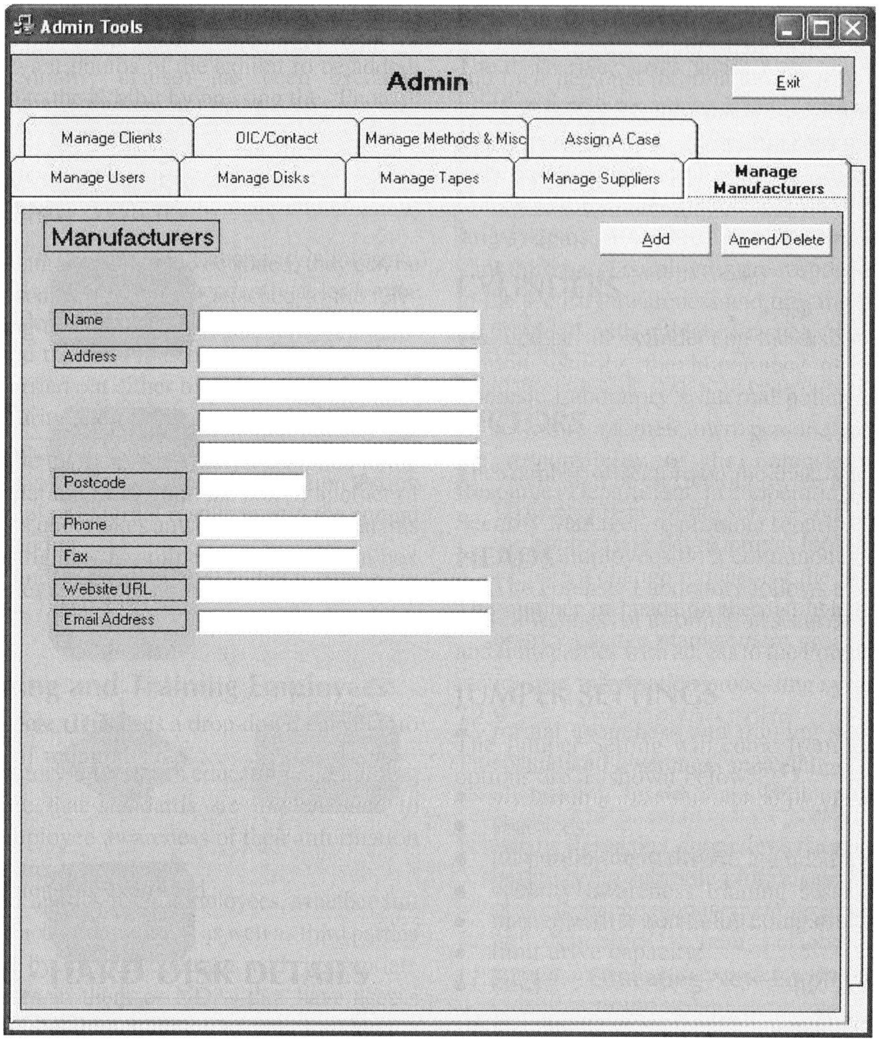

FIGURE 10.6 Manage a Manufacturer. (For color version of this figure, the reader is referred to the online version of this chapter.)

Administrator is advised of the successful update and must acknowledge it.

10.3.5.2.3 Delete a Manufacturer

To delete a manufacturer, the manufacturer must already exist.

Using the drop-down box for existing manufacturers, the manufacturer to have their details deleted is selected and the screen populated with their existing details from the stored record.

It is not possible to delete a manufacturer who has been active in the MARS system, i.e., one who has been used in the system. The Administrator will be advised that this is not possible; otherwise, the Administrator is advised of the successful deletion of the manufacturer and must acknowledge it.

10.3.5.3 Manage a Supplier

The "Manage Suppliers" screen is shown in Figure 10.7.

Details of the contents of all of the fields in this screen are given in Appendix 6.

10.3.5.3.1 Add a Supplier

The blank screen is presented and the Administrator must populate all of the relevant fields and then save them to create a new supplier in MARS.

10.3.5.3.2 Amend a Supplier

To amend a supplier, the supplier must already exist.

Using the drop-down box for existing suppliers, the supplier to have their details amended is selected and the screen populated with their existing details from the stored record.

The Administrator is able to update data relating to the supplier and save it, as appropriate. The Administrator is advised of the successful update and must acknowledge it.

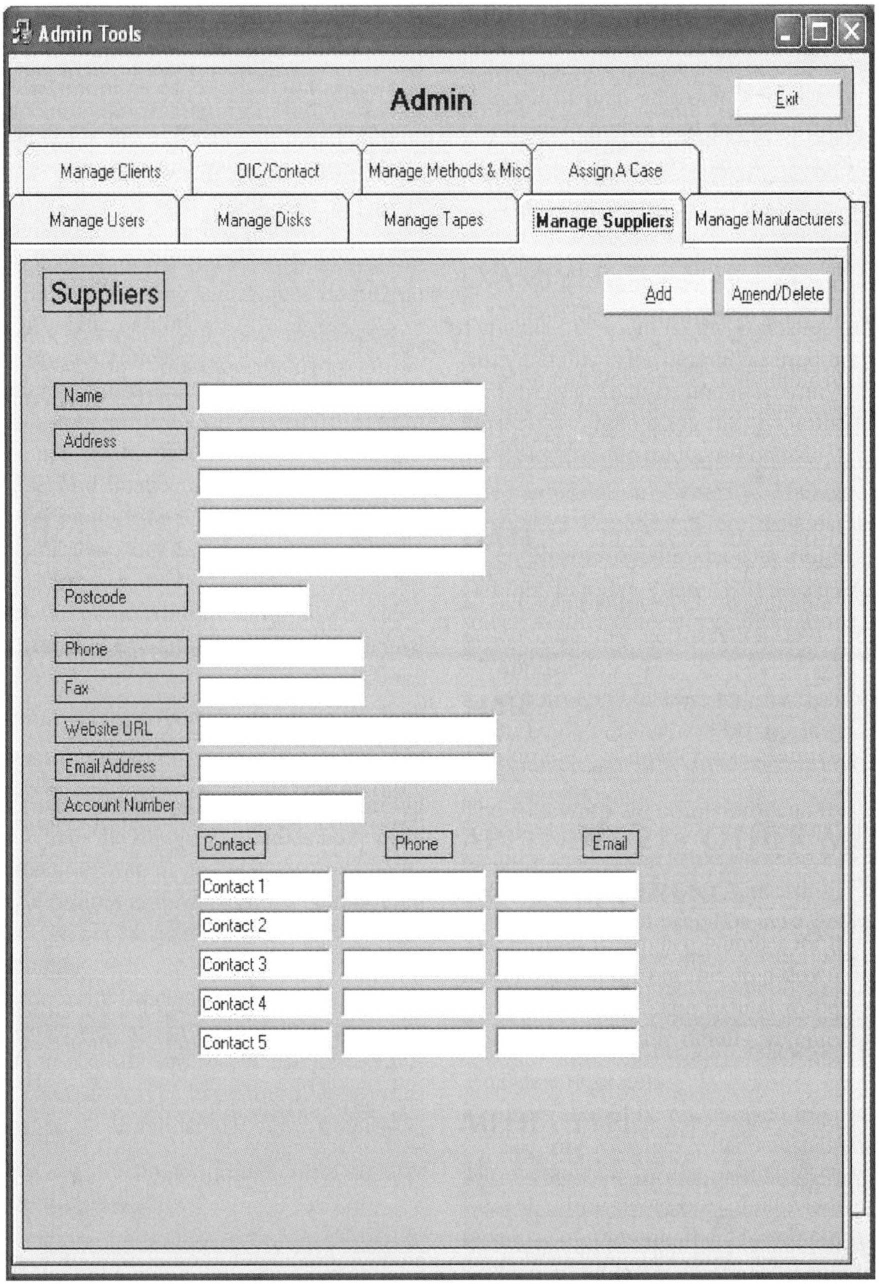

FIGURE 10.7 Manage a Supplier. (For color version of this figure, the reader is referred to the online version of this chapter.)

10.3.5.3.3 Delete a Supplier

To delete a supplier, the supplier must already exist.

Using the drop-down box for existing suppliers, the supplier to have their details deleted is selected and the screen populated with their existing details from the stored record.

It is not possible to delete a supplier who has been active in the MARS system, i.e., one who has been used in the system. The Administrator will be advised that this is not possible; otherwise, the Administrator is advised of the successful deletion of the supplier and must acknowledge it.

10.3.5.4 Manage a Client

The "Manage Clients" screen is shown in Figure 10.8.

Details of the contents of all of the fields in this screen are given in Appendix 7.

10.3.5.4.1 Add a Client

The blank screen is presented and the Administrator must populate all of the relevant fields and then save them to create a new Client in MARS.

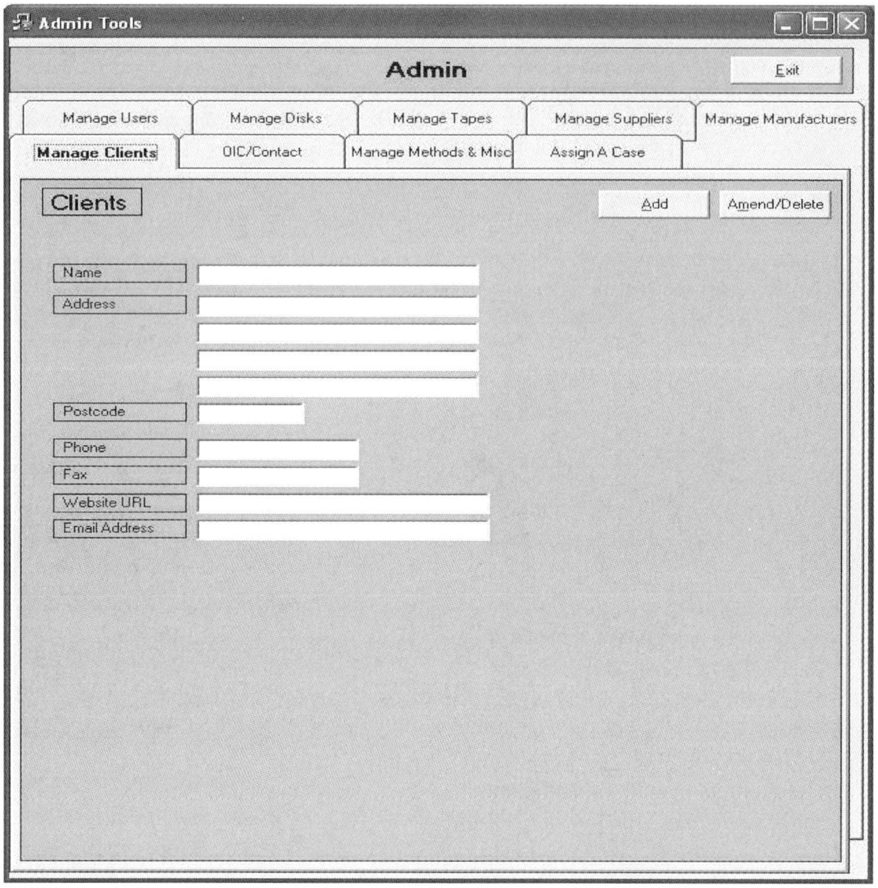

FIGURE 10.8 Manage a Client. (For color version of this figure, the reader is referred to the online version of this chapter.)

10.3.5.4.2 Amend a Client

To amend a Client, the Client must already exist.

Using the drop-down box for existing Clients, the Client to have their details amended is selected and the screen populated with their existing details from the stored record.

The Administrator is able to update data relating to the Client and save it, as appropriate. The Administrator is advised of the successful update and must acknowledge it.

10.3.5.4.3 Delete a Client

To delete a Client, the Client must already exist.

Using the drop-down box for existing Clients, the Client to have their details deleted is selected and the screen populated with their existing details from the stored record.

It is not possible to delete a Client who has been active in the MARS system, i.e., one who has had a forensic case processed in the system. The Administrator will be advised that this is not possible; otherwise, the Administrator is advised of the successful deletion of the Client and must acknowledge it.

10.3.5.5 Manage an Investigator

Note 1

In MARS parlance, an Investigator could be a corporate Investigator (or a Law Enforcement Officer) for the Client or any other investigative contact relating to a forensic case being processed by the Forensic Laboratory.

Note 2

The Client details can be used to populate the Investigator's address and contact details. If this is done, then the Administrator can still edit what is in the fields as normal—navigating by mouse or tab button. If changes to the Client details are made to tailor this for the Investigator, they are not reflected in the Client Address or contact details—only here.

The "Manage Investigators" screen is shown in Figure 10.9.

Details of the contents of all of the fields in this screen are given in Appendix 8.

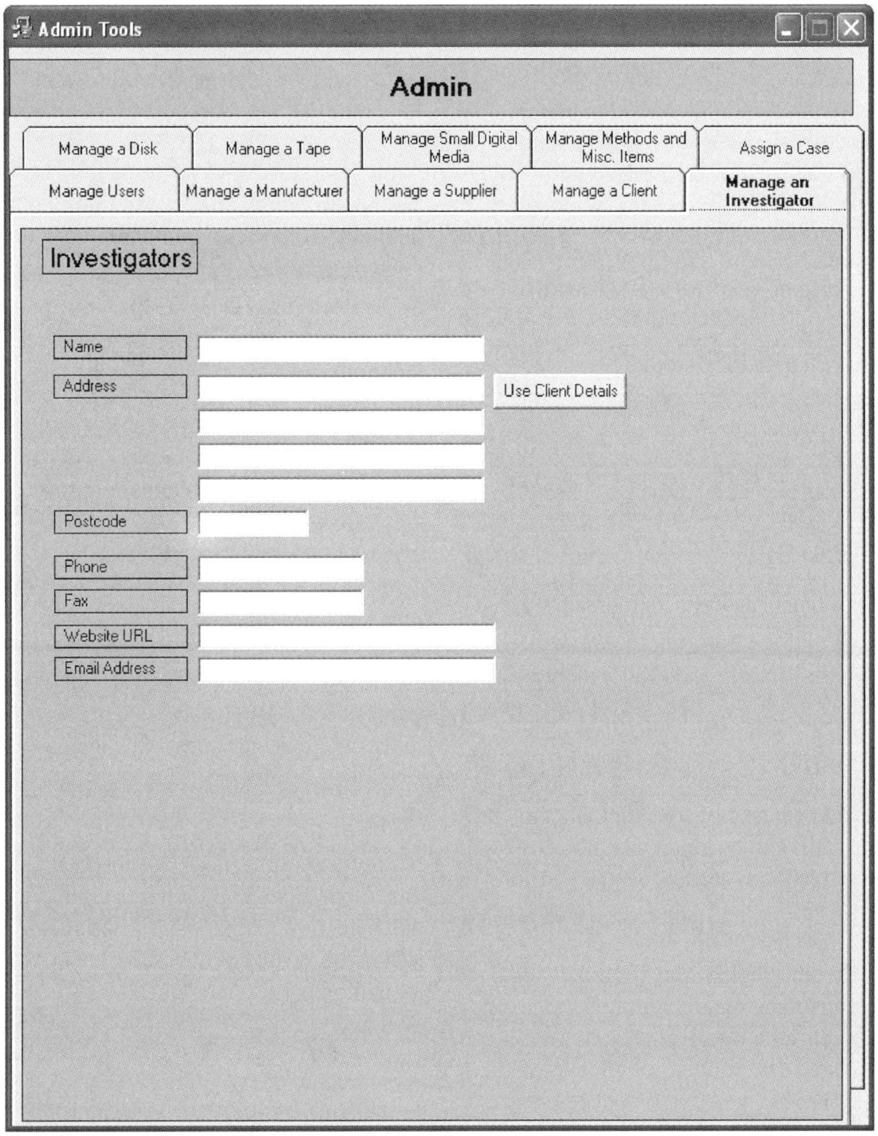

FIGURE 10.9 Manage an Investigator. (For color version of this figure, the reader is referred to the online version of this chapter.)

10.3.5.5.1 Add an Investigator

The blank screen is presented and the Administrator must populate all of the relevant fields and then save them to create a new Investigator in MARS.

10.3.5.5.2 Amend an Investigator

To amend an Investigator, the Investigator must already exist.

Using the drop-down box for existing Investigators, the Investigator to have their details amended is selected and the screen populated with their existing details from the stored record.

The Administrator is able to update data relating to the Investigator and save it, as appropriate. The Administrator is advised of the successful update and must acknowledge it.

10.3.5.5.3 Delete an Investigator

To delete an Investigator, the Investigator must already exist.

Using the drop-down box for an existing Investigator, the Investigator to have their details deleted is selected and the screen populated with their existing details from the stored record.

It is not possible to delete an Investigator who has been active in the MARS system, i.e., one who has been the Client contact used in the system. The Administrator will be advised that this is not possible; otherwise, the

Administrator is advised of the successful deletion of the Investigator and must acknowledge it.

10.3.5.6 Manage a Disk

Each disk used in the Forensic Laboratory must have its history associated with it so that a complete history of the disk can be maintained. This will contain the details entered on the screen and additionally a status flag indicating whether it can be assigned to a case or not. The status of disks in the Forensic Laboratory is as follows:

- new disks are set a status of "unassigned";
- wiped disks are set a status of "unassigned";
- disks that have been disposed of are set to "disposed";
- disks assigned to a case are set to "assigned."

Using this process, unassigned disks can be assigned to current forensics cases, as needed, without the risk of evidence contamination.

The "Manage Disks" screen is shown in Figure 10.10.

Details of the contents of all of the fields in this screen are given in Appendix 9.

10.3.5.6.1 Add a Disk

The blank screen is presented and the Administrator must populate all of the relevant fields and then save them to create a new disk in MARS.

10.3.5.6.2 Amend a Disk

To amend the details of a disk, the disk must already exist.

Using the drop-down box for existing disks, the disk to have their details amended is selected and the screen populated with their existing details from the stored record.

The Administrator is able to update data relating to the disk and save it, as appropriate. The Administrator is advised of the successful update and must acknowledge it.

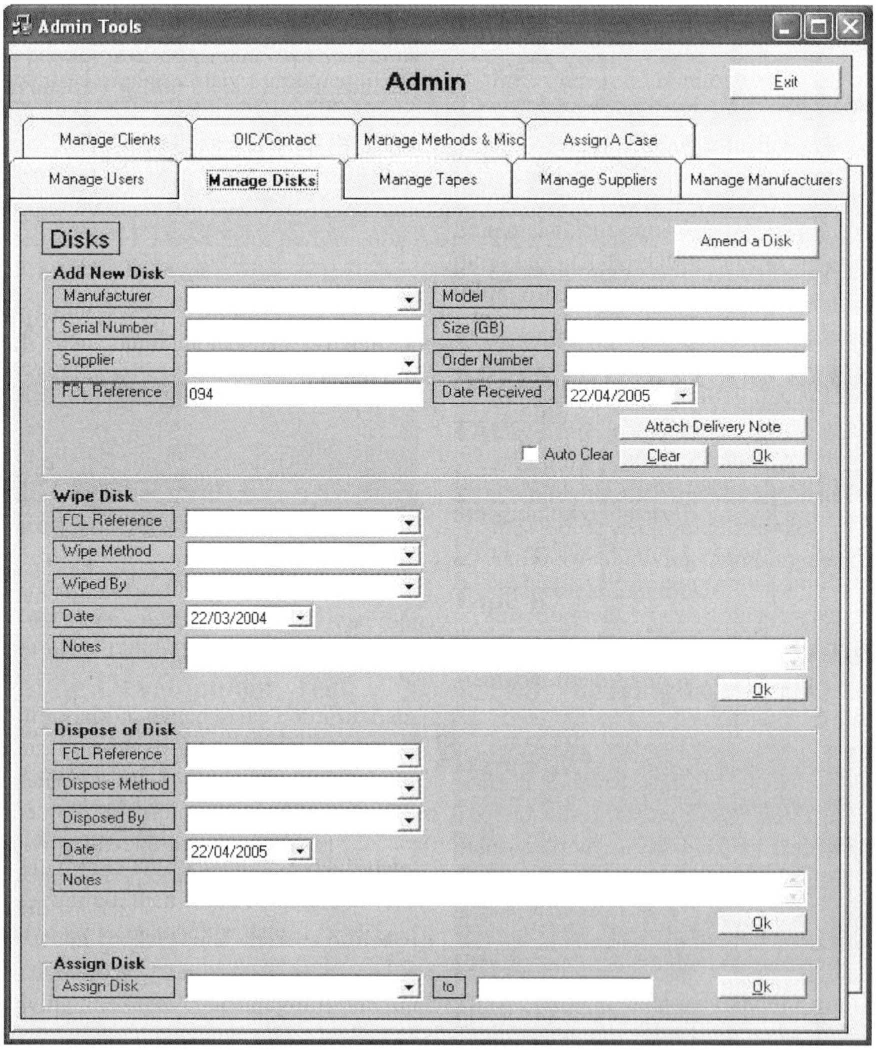

FIGURE 10.10 Manage a Disk. (For color version of this figure, the reader is referred to the online version of this chapter.)

10.3.5.6.3 Delete a Disk

To delete a disk, the disk must already exist.

Using the drop-down box for existing disks, the disk to have its details deleted is selected and the screen populated with its existing details from the stored record.

It is not possible to delete a disk that has been active in the MARS system, i.e., one that has been used in the system. The Administrator will be advised that this is not possible; otherwise, the Administrator is advised of the successful deletion of the disk and must acknowledge it.

10.3.5.6.4 Wiping a Disk

To forensically wipe a disk, the disk must already exist.

Using the drop-down box for existing disks, the disk to have its wiping details recorded in the disk's history is selected and the screen populated with its existing details from the stored record.

The Administrator is then able to enter the details of how the disk was wiped, by whom and when and add this to the disk's history log. A disk may be wiped many times during its use in the Forensic Laboratory.

10.3.5.6.5 Disposing of a Disk

To dispose of a disk, the disk must already exist.

Using the drop-down box for existing disks, the disk to have its disposal details recorded in the disk's history is selected and the screen populated with its existing details from the stored record.

The Administrator is then able to enter the details of how the disk was disposed of, by whom and when and add this to the disk's history log.

A disk cannot be disposed of unless it has been forensically wiped in the Forensic Laboratory prior to disposal unless it is a disk that has failed to operate and is being destroyed.

10.3.5.6.6 Assigning a Disk

To assign a disk to a case or a specific administrative task, the disk must already exist.

Using the drop-down box for existing disks, the disk to be assigned is selected. The disk must have a status of unassigned and have been wiped immediately prior to assignment or reassignment.

The Administrator is then able to enter the details of where the disk is to be assigned.

10.3.5.7 Manage a Tape

This process is very similar to the management of disks.

Each tape will have a history associated with it so that a complete history of the tape can be maintained. This will contain the details entered on the screen and additionally a status flag indicating whether it can be assigned or not.

The status for tapes in the Forensic Laboratory is as follows:

- new tapes are set a status of "unassigned";
- wiped tapes are set a status of "unassigned";
- tapes that have been disposed of are set to "disposed";
- tapes assigned to a case are set to "assigned."

The "Manage Tapes" screen is shown in Figure 10.11.

Details of the contents of all of the fields in this screen are given in Appendix 10.

10.3.5.7.1 Add a Tape

The blank screen is presented and the Administrator must populate all of the relevant fields and then save them to create a new tape in MARS.

10.3.5.7.2 Amend a Tape

To amend the details of a tape, the tape must already exist.

Using the drop-down box for existing tapes, the tape to have its details amended is selected and the screen populated with its existing details from the stored record.

The Administrator is able to update data relating to the tape and save it, as appropriate. The Administrator is advised of the successful update and must acknowledge it.

10.3.5.7.3 Delete a Tape

To delete a tape, the tape must already exist.

Using the drop-down box for existing tapes, the tape to have its details deleted is selected and the screen populated with its existing details from the stored record.

It is not possible to delete a tape that has been active in the MARS system, i.e., one that has been used in the system. The Administrator will be advised that this is not possible; otherwise, the Administrator is advised of the successful deletion of the tape and must acknowledge it.

10.3.5.7.4 Wiping a Tape

To forensically wipe a tape, the tape must already exist.

Using the drop-down box for existing tape, the tape to have its wiping details recorded in the tape's history is selected and the screen populated with their existing details from the stored record.

The Administrator is then able to enter the details of how the tape was wiped, by whom and when and add this to the tape's history log. A tape may be wiped many times during its use in the Forensic Laboratory.

10.3.5.7.5 Disposing of a Tape

To dispose of a tape, the tape must already exist.

Using the drop-down box for existing tape, the tape to have its disposal details recorded in the tape's history is

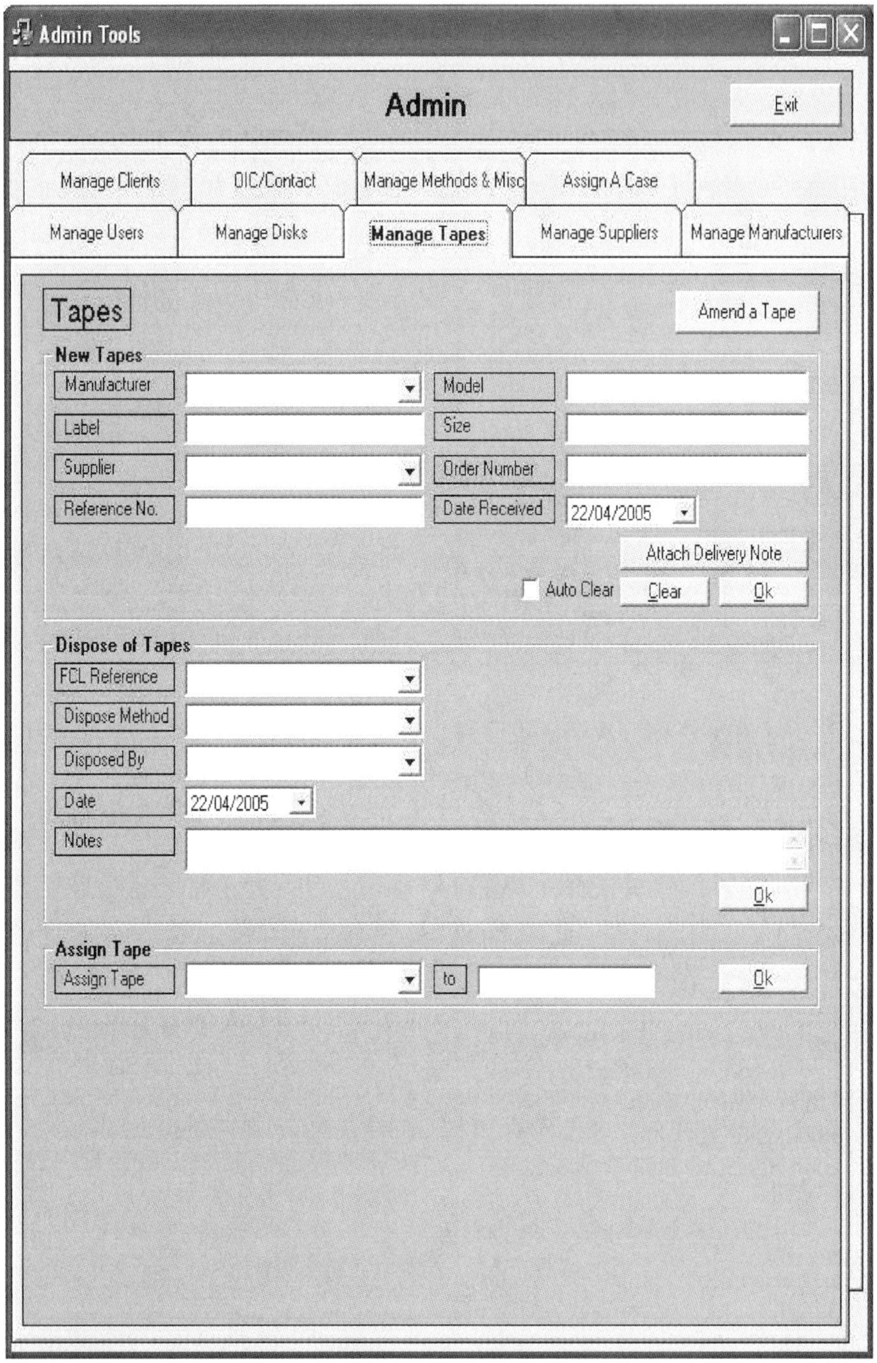

FIGURE 10.11 Manage a Tape. (For color version of this figure, the reader is referred to the online version of this chapter.)

selected and the screen populated with their existing details from the stored record.

The Administrator is then able to enter the details of how the tape was disposed of, by whom and when and add this to the tape's history log.

A tape cannot be disposed of unless it has been forensically wiped in the Forensic Laboratory prior to disposal.

10.3.5.7.6 Assigning a Tape

To assign a tape to a case or a specific administrative task, the tape must already exist.

Using the drop-down box for existing tape, the tape to be assigned is selected. The tape must have a status of unassigned and have been wiped immediately prior to assignment or reassignment.

The Administrator is then able to enter the details of where the tape is to be assigned.

10.3.5.8 Manage Small Digital Media

This process is very similar to the management of disks.

Each item of small digital media will have a history associated with it so that a complete history of the item of small digital media can be maintained. This will contain the details entered on the screen and additionally a status flag indicating whether it can be assigned or not.

The status for items of small digital media in the Forensic Laboratory is as follows:

- new items of small digital media are set a status of "unassigned";
- wiped items of small digital media are set a status of "unassigned";
- items of small digital media that have been disposed of are set to "disposed";
- items of small digital media assigned to a case are set to "assigned."

The "Manage Items of Small Digital Media" screen is shown in Figure 10.12.

Details of the contents of all of the fields in this screen are given in Appendix 11.

10.3.5.8.1 Add an Item of Small Digital Media

The blank screen is presented and the Administrator must populate all of the relevant fields and then save them to create a new item of small digital media in MARS.

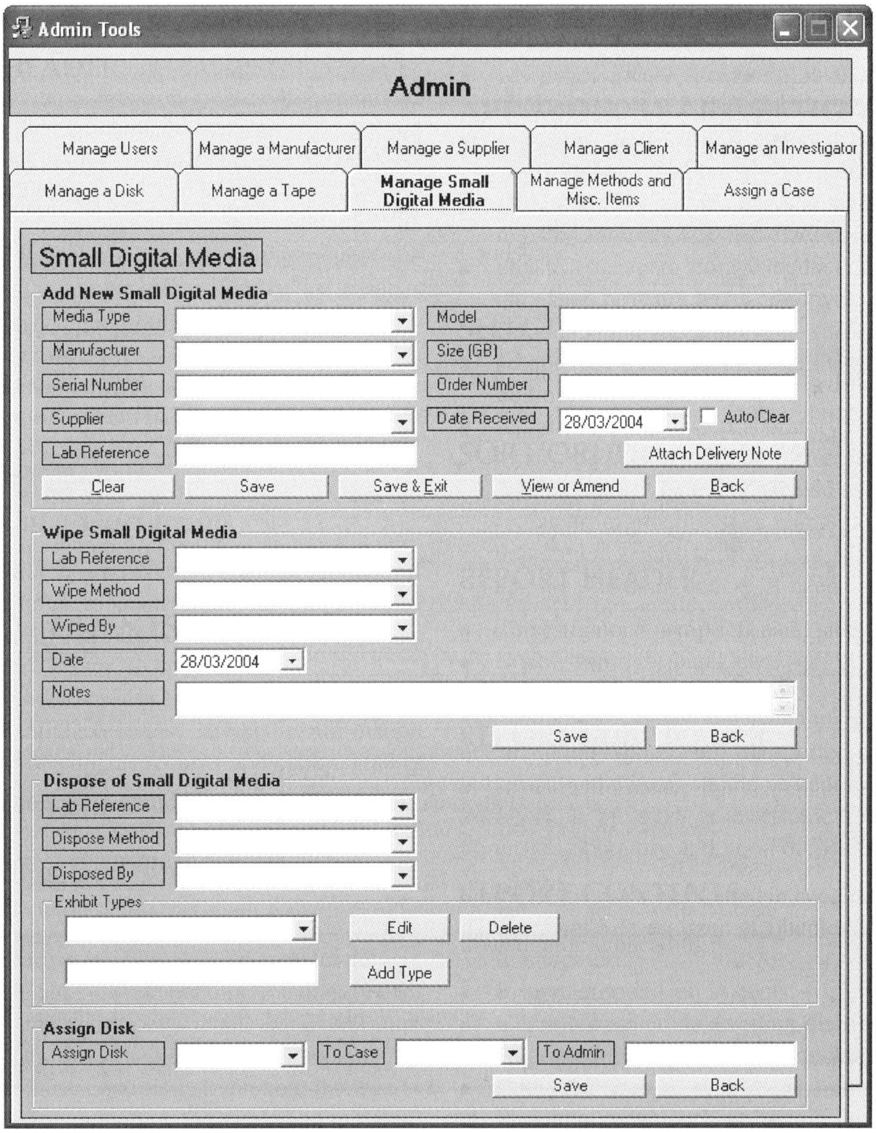

FIGURE 10.12 Manage Small Digital Media. (For color version of this figure, the reader is referred to the online version of this chapter.)

10.3.5.8.2 Amend an Item of Small Digital Media

To amend the details of item of small digital media, the item of small digital media must already exist.

Using the drop-down box for an existing item of small digital media, the item of small digital media to have their details amended is selected and the screen populated with their existing details from the stored record.

The Administrator is able to update data relating to the item of small digital media and save it, as appropriate. The administrator is advised of the successful update and must acknowledge it.

10.3.5.8.3 Delete an Item of Small Digital Media

To delete an item of small digital media, the item of small digital media must already exist.

Using the drop-down box for an existing item of small digital media, the item of small digital media to have their details deleted is selected and the screen populated with their existing details from the stored record.

It is not possible to delete an item of small digital media that has been active in the MARS system, i.e., one that has been used in the system. The Administrator will be advised that this is not possible; otherwise, the Administrator is advised of the successful deletion of the item of small digital media and must acknowledge it.

10.3.5.8.4 Wiping an Item of Small Digital Media

To forensically wipe an item of small digital media, the item of small digital media must already exist.

Using the drop-down box for existing items of small digital media, the item of small digital media to have its wiping details recorded in the item of small digital media's history is selected and the screen populated with their existing details from the stored record.

The Administrator is then able to enter the details of how the item of small digital media was wiped, by whom and when and add this to the item of small digital media's history log. An item of small digital media may be wiped many times during its use in the Forensic Laboratory.

10.3.5.8.5 Disposing of an Item of Small Digital Media

To dispose of an item of small digital media, the item of small digital media must already exist.

Using the drop-down box for existing items of small digital media, the item of small digital media to have its disposal details recorded in the item of small digital media's history is selected and the screen populated with their existing details from the stored record.

The Administrator is then able to enter the details of how the item of small digital media was disposed of, by whom and when and add this to the item of small digital media's history log.

An item of small digital media cannot be disposed of unless it has been forensically wiped in the Forensic Laboratory prior to disposal.

10.3.5.8.6 Assigning an Item of Small Digital Media

To assign an item of small digital media to a case or a specific administrative task, the item of small digital media must already exist.

Using the drop-down box for an existing item of small digital media, the item of small digital media to be assigned is selected. The item of small digital media must have a status of unassigned and have been wiped immediately prior to assignment or reassignment.

The Administrator is then able to enter the details of where the item of small digital media is to be assigned.

10.3.5.9 Manage Methods and Miscellaneous Items

This allows the user to enter manage the following:

- hard disk wiping methods;
- disk and tape disposal methods;
- imaging methods;
- operating system types;
- digital media types.

The "Manage Methods" screen is shown in Figure 10.13.

Details of the contents of all of the fields in this screen are given in Appendix 12.

10.3.5.9.1 Wipe Methods

10.3.5.9.1.1 Add a New Wipe Method A new method of wiping is entered into the lower of the box in the "Wipe Methods" section of the screen. Once the method is entered, the Administrator confirms it.

10.3.5.9.1.2 Amend a Wipe Method Using the drop-down box for existing Wipe Methods, the wipe method to be amended is displayed.

The Administrator is then able to edit the details of the wiping method.

A wiping method cannot be edited if it has been used in MARS as this may cause problems with the Chain of Custody for a given disk, as all previous occurrences of the original wipe method would have been changed.

10.3.5.9.1.3 Delete a Wipe Method Where an existing wipe method exists, it may need to be deleted if not needed or has been incorrectly entered.

A wiping method cannot be deleted if it has been used in MARS as this may cause problems with the Chain of Custody for a given disk, as all previous occurrences of the original wipe method would have been changed.

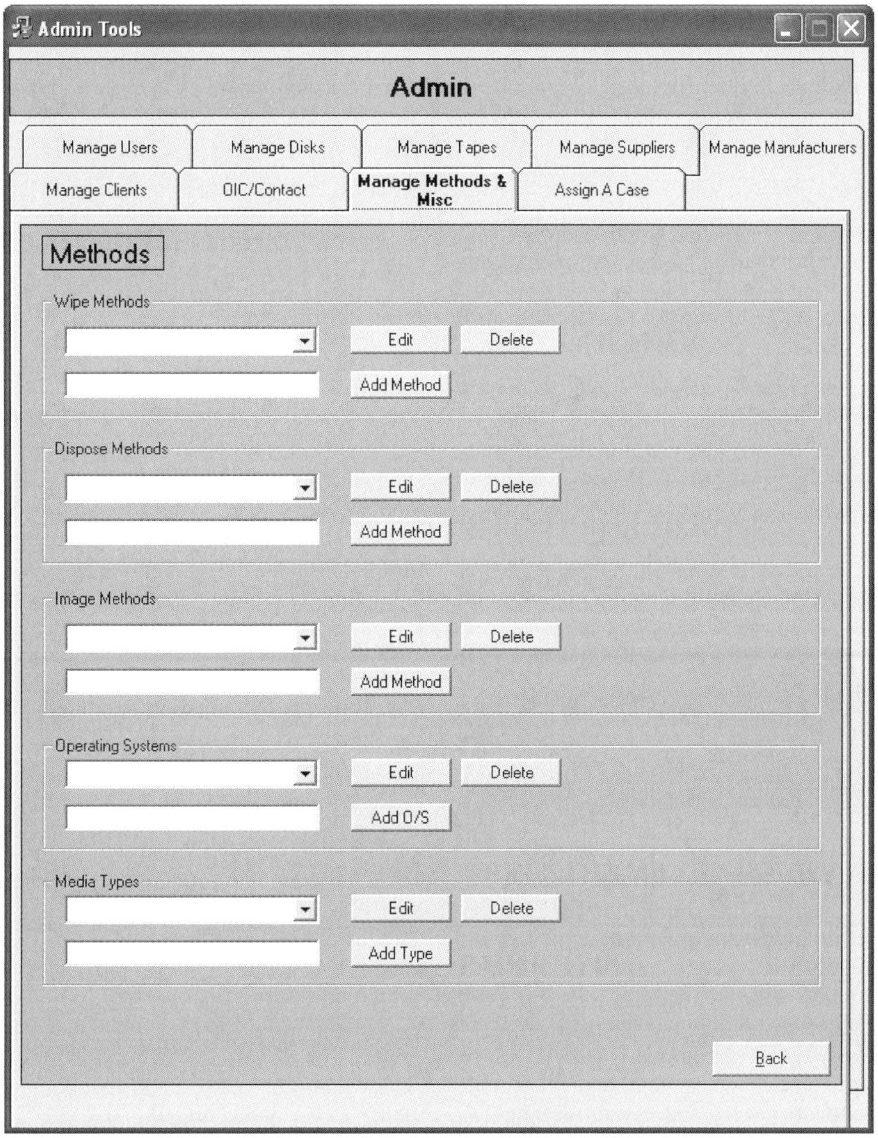

FIGURE 10.13 Manage Methods. (For color version of this figure, the reader is referred to the online version of this chapter.)

Once chosen, press the "Delete" button, as shown below.

If the Wipe Method has been previously used in MARS, deletion is prohibited.

10.3.5.9.2 Disposal Methods

10.3.5.9.2.1 Add a New Disposal Method A new method of disposing of media is entered into the lower of the box in the "Dispose Methods" section of the screen. Once the method is entered, the Administrator confirms it.

10.3.5.9.2.2 Amend a Dispose Method Using the drop-down box for existing disposal methods, the disposal method to be amended is displayed.

The Administrator is then able to edit the details of the disposal method.

A disposal method cannot be edited if it has been used in MARS as this may cause problems with the Chain of Custody for any media disposed of using the disposal method, as all previous occurrences of the original disposal method would have been changed.

10.3.5.9.2.3 Delete a Disposal Method Where an existing disposal method exists, it may need to be deleted if not needed or has been incorrectly entered.

A disposal method cannot be deleted if it has been used in MARS as this may cause problems with the Chain of Custody for media disposed of using this method, as all previous occurrences of the original disposal method would have been changed.

10.3.5.9.3 Imaging Methods

10.3.5.9.3.1 Add a New Imaging Method A new method of imaging media is entered into the lower of the box in the "Image Methods" section of the screen. Once the method is entered, the Administrator confirms it.

10.3.5.9.3.2 Amend an Imaging Method Using the drop-down box for existing imaging methods, the imaging method to be amended is displayed.

The Administrator is then able to edit the details of the imaging method.

An imaging method cannot be edited if it has been used in MARS as this may cause problems with the Chain of Custody for any media imaged using this imaging method, as all previous occurrences of the original imaging method would have been changed.

10.3.5.9.3.3 Delete an Imaging Method Where an existing imaging method exists, it may need to be deleted if not needed or has been incorrectly entered.

An imaging method cannot be deleted if it has been used in MARS as this may cause problems with the Chain of Custody for media imaged using this method, as all previous occurrences of the original imaging method would have been changed.

10.3.5.9.4 Operating Systems

10.3.5.9.4.1 Add New Operating System A new operating system to be investigated is entered into the lower of the box in the "Operating Systems" section of the screen. Once the method is entered, the Administrator confirms it.

10.3.5.9.4.2 Amend an Operating System Using the drop-down box for existing Operating Systems, the operating system to be amended is displayed.

The Administrator is then able to edit the details of the operating system.

An operating system cannot be edited if it has been used in MARS as this may cause problems with the Chain of Custody for any operating system processed in the Forensic Laboratory, as all previous occurrences of the operating system would have been changed.

10.3.5.9.4.3 Delete an Operating System Where an existing operating system exists, it may need to be deleted if not needed or has been incorrectly entered.

An operating system cannot be deleted if it has been used in MARS as this may cause problems with the Chain of Custody for any operating system processed in the Forensic Laboratory, as all previous occurrences of the operating system would have been changed.

10.3.5.9.5 Media Types

This is used where Media Types other than hard disks and tapes are to be examined or used.

10.3.5.9.5.1 Add New Media Type A new media type is to be examined other than a hard disk or tape and requires the media type to be added to MARS. The media type is entered into the lower of the box in the "Media Type" section of the screen. Once the media is entered, the Administrator confirms it.

10.3.5.9.5.2 Amend a Media Type Using the drop-down box for existing Media Types (apart from hard disks and tapes), the media type to be amended is displayed.

The Administrator is then able to edit the details of the media type.

A media type cannot be edited if it has been used in MARS as this may cause problems with the Chain of Custody for any media type processed in the Forensic Laboratory, as all previous occurrences of the media type would have been changed.

10.3.5.9.5.3 Delete a Media Type Where a media type exists, it may need to be deleted if not needed or has been incorrectly entered.

A media type cannot be deleted if it has been used in MARS as this may cause problems with the Chain of Custody for any media type processed in the Forensic Laboratory, as all previous occurrences of the media type would have been changed.

10.3.5.9.6 Exhibit Types

This is used where Exhibit Types other than computer or media are to be examined.

10.3.5.9.6.1 Add New Exhibit Type A new Exhibit Type is to be examined other than a hard disk or tape and requires the Exhibit Type to be added to MARS. The Exhibit Type is entered into the lower of the box in the "Exhibit Type" section of the screen. Once the exhibit is entered, the Administrator confirms it.

10.3.5.9.6.2 Amend a Exhibit Type Using the drop-down box for existing Exhibit Types (apart from hard disks and tapes), the Exhibit Type to be amended is displayed.

The Administrator is then able to edit the details of the Exhibit Type.

An exhibit type cannot be edited if it has been used in MARS as this may cause problems with the Chain of Custody for any Exhibit Type processed in the Forensic Laboratory, as all previous occurrences of the Exhibit Type would have been changed.

10.3.5.9.6.3 Delete a Exhibit Type Where an existing Exhibit Type exists, it may need to be deleted if not needed or has been incorrectly entered.

An Exhibit Type cannot be deleted if it has been used in MARS as this may cause problems with the Chain of Custody for any Exhibit Type processed in the Forensic Laboratory, as all previous occurrences of the Exhibit Type would have been changed.

10.3.5.10 Assign A Case

Typically, a case is assigned to a Forensic Analyst when the initial case is set up.

There are other times that a case needs to be reassigned to another Forensic Analyst and this is done here.

The "Assign A Case" screen is shown in Figure 10.14.

Using the drop-down box to select a case, the Administrator selects the case to be assigned.

Using the drop-down box to select a Forensic Analyst to assign the case to, the Administrator selects the relevant Forensic Analyst.

Once the case and the Forensic Analyst have been chosen, the Administrator confirms the assignment.

10.4 SETTING UP A NEW CASE

10.4.1 Creating a New Case

Once all of the "Static" data have been set up, it is possible to start creating forensic cases for processing. This has been

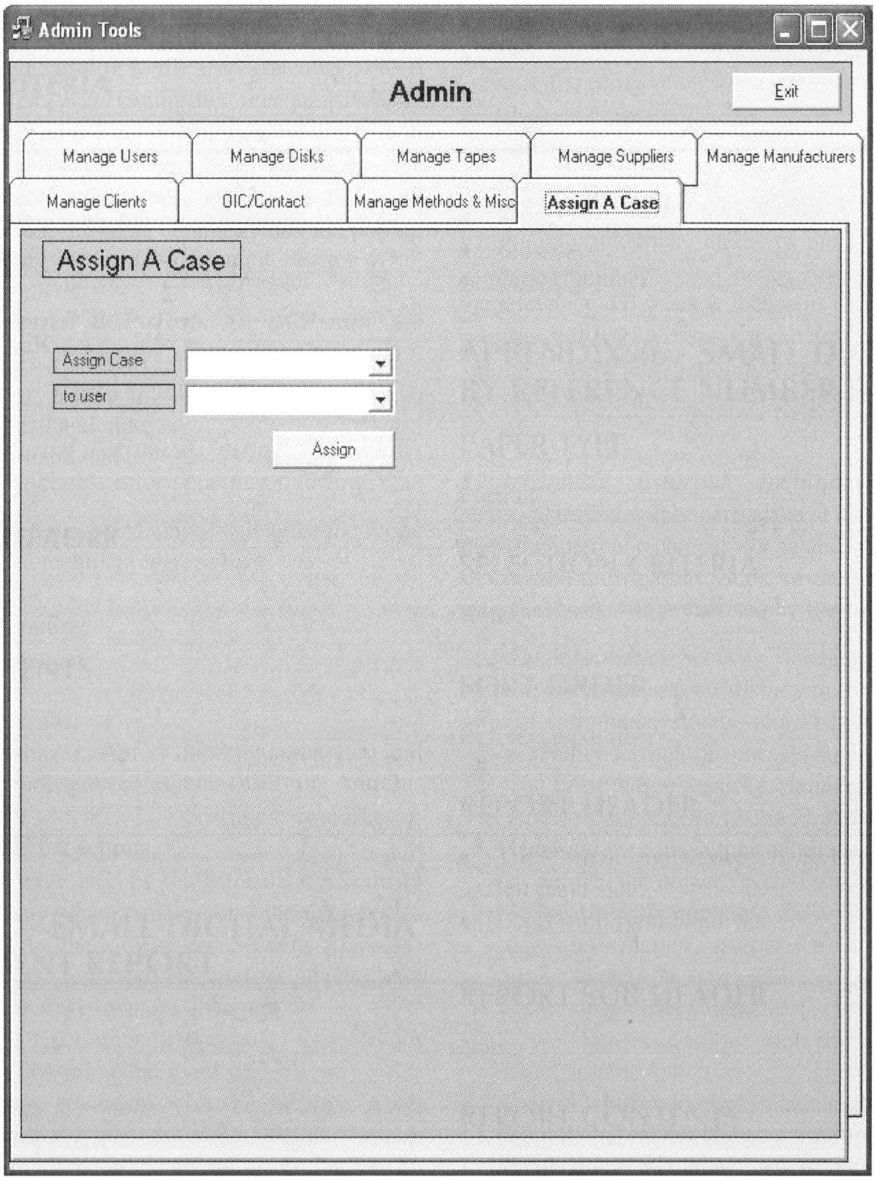

FIGURE 10.14 Assign a Case. (For color version of this figure, the reader is referred to the online version of this chapter.)

made easier by entering the static data, so it can be accessed using drop-down menus, wherever possible.

The "Add a New Case" screen is shown in Figure 10.15.

10.4.1.1 Case Number

This is automatically generated and increments by 1 for each case setup. This is based on the original numbering system setup when MARS was installed—it cannot be changed.

The case number can never be changed once assigned to a case.

10.4.1.2 Case Name

A forensic case can be called whatever is required or used to refer to the case by or what the Client has called it.

> **Note**
>
> It is possible to change the Case Name on any of the four screens in the case setup process.

10.4.1.3 Client Name

Using the drop-down box to select the Client Name for the Client instructing the work, the Administrator selects the Client.

If the Client does not already exist in the drop-down, it is possible to enter a new Client by pressing the "New" key next to the Client field.

This uses the "Manage a Client" process and screen as defined in Section 10.3.5.4.

A new Client and all their details can be input and then one can exit from the "Add Client" screen, and use the drop-down to select the newly entered Client.

> **Note**
>
> It is possible to change the Client Name on any of the four screens in the case setup process.

10.4.1.4 Investigator

Using the drop-down box to select the Investigator Name for the Client Investigator instructing the work, the Administrator selects the Investigator.

If the Investigator does not already exist in the drop-down, it is possible to enter a new Investigator by pressing the "New" key next to the Investigator field.

This uses the new Investigator process and screen as defined in Section 10.3.5.5.

A new Investigator and all their details can be input and then one can exit from the "Add Investigator" screen,

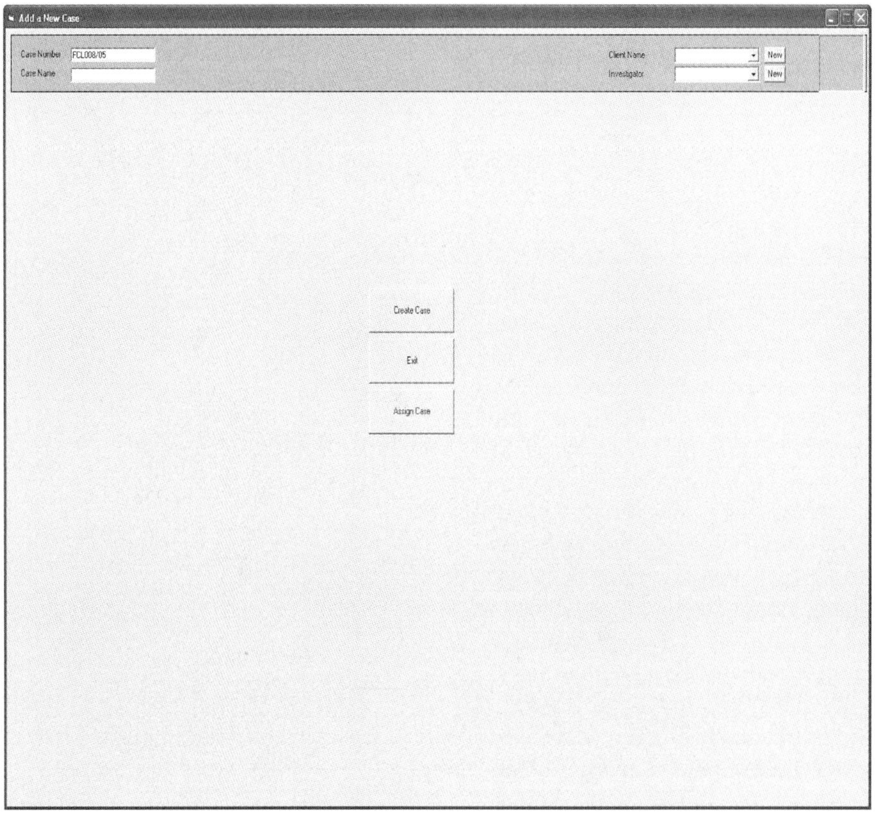

FIGURE 10.15 Create a New Case. (For color version of this figure, the reader is referred to the online version of this chapter.)

and use the drop-down to select the newly entered Investigator.

Note

It is possible to change the Investigator Name on any of the four screens in the case setup process.

10.4.1.5 Creating the Case

Once all of these details have been entered, pressing the "Create case" button creates the case in MARS and presents the "Exhibit Details Entry" screen.

10.4.2 Adding Exhibits

The "Exhibit Details" screen is shown in Figure 10.16.

Details of the contents of all of the fields in this screen are given in Appendix 12.

10.4.2.1 Add an Exhibit

The blank screen is presented and the Administrator must populate all of the relevant fields and then save them to create a new exhibit in MARS.

10.4.2.2 Entering More Exhibits

Once the first exhibit has been saved, none of the fields are blanked out so that a series of exhibits from the same place and the same person can be entered with the minimum of effort.

The fields that need to be changed are overwritten and the exhibit is saved. This process is repeated for all relevant exhibits.

If the details of the exhibits to be added are very different, then pressing the "Clear All" button clears all fields apart from the two dates that are set to the current date.

Once all of the details are added for the new exhibit, the Administrator can add the exhibit to the case in MARS.

10.4.3 Evidence Sought

The "Evidence Sought" screen is shown in Figure 10.17.

Details of the contents of all of the fields in this screen are given in Appendix 13.

10.4.3.1 Add Details to the Case

The blank screen is presented and the Administrator must populate all of the relevant fields and then press the "Add these details to the Case" button to add this information to the case in MARS.

10.4.3.2 Adding More Information

If more information becomes available during the case, it will be added in working the case part of MARS, as defined in Section 5.

10.4.4 Estimates

The "Estimates" screen is shown in Figure 10.18.

Details of the contents of all of the fields in this screen are given in Appendix 14.

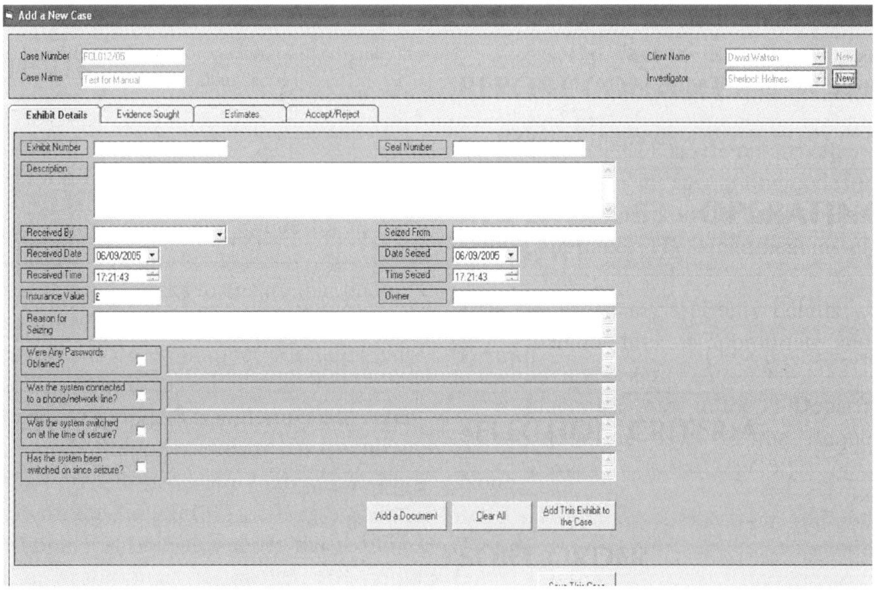

FIGURE 10.16 Exhibit Details. (For color version of this figure, the reader is referred to the online version of this chapter.)

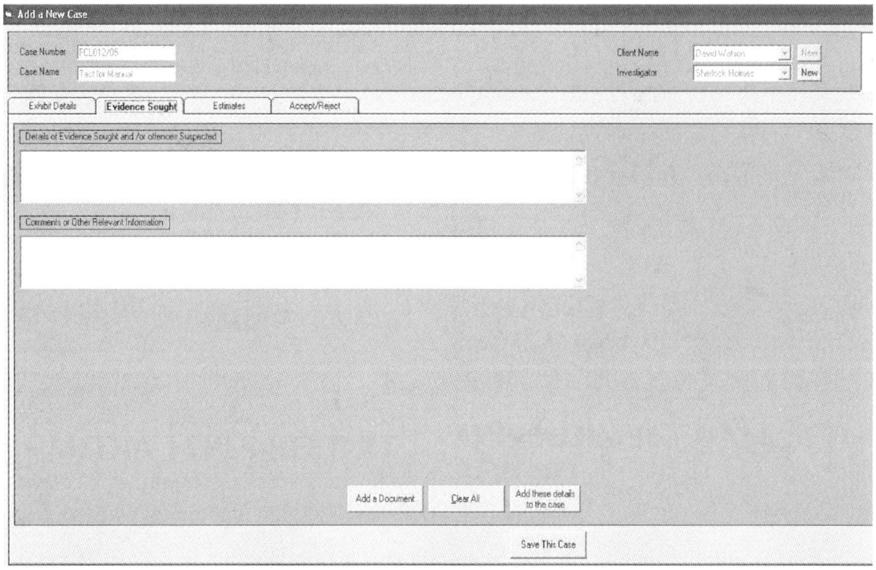

FIGURE 10.17 Evidence Sought. (For color version of this figure, the reader is referred to the online version of this chapter.)

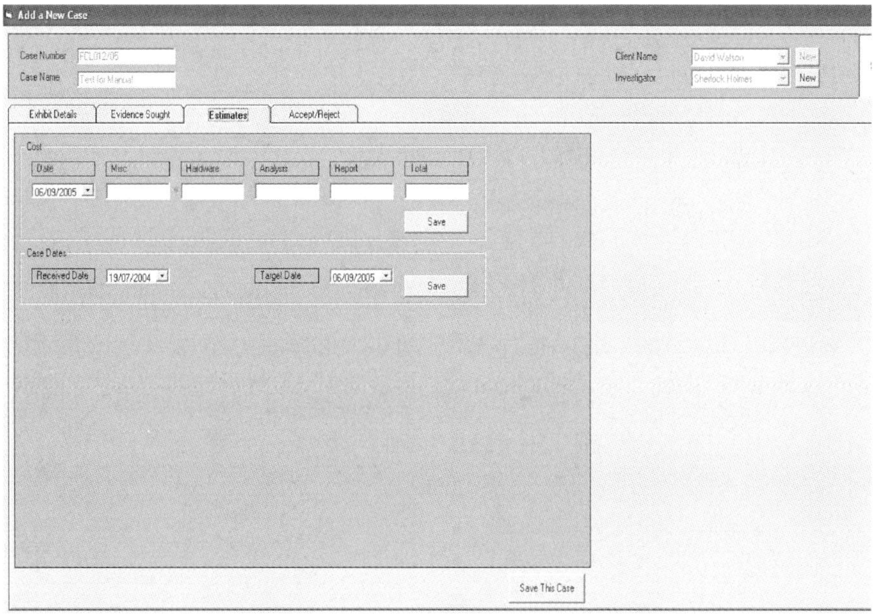

FIGURE 10.18 Estimates. (For color version of this figure, the reader is referred to the online version of this chapter.)

Estimates of cost can be entered at this stage of the case, but this can be updated as the case progresses by the Forensic Analyst, as defined in Section 10.5.9.

At this time, the Target time (or TRT) for the case can be entered, if known. This is the date that the Client wants the results by and is used to monitor case progress. If one is not known, then internally set SLAs can be used, as defined in Chapter 9, Section 9.5.4.1.

10.4.4.1 Add Estimates to the Case

The blank screen is presented and the Administrator must populate all of the relevant fields and then press the "Save" button to add this information to the case in MARS.

10.4.5 Accepted or Rejected

The "Accepted or Rejected" screen is shown in Figure 10.19:

Details of the contents of all of the fields in this screen are given in Appendix 15.

A case can be accepted or rejected using this screen. Normally jobs are accepted, but there may be reason why the job is rejected (e.g., conflict of interest, suspicion of

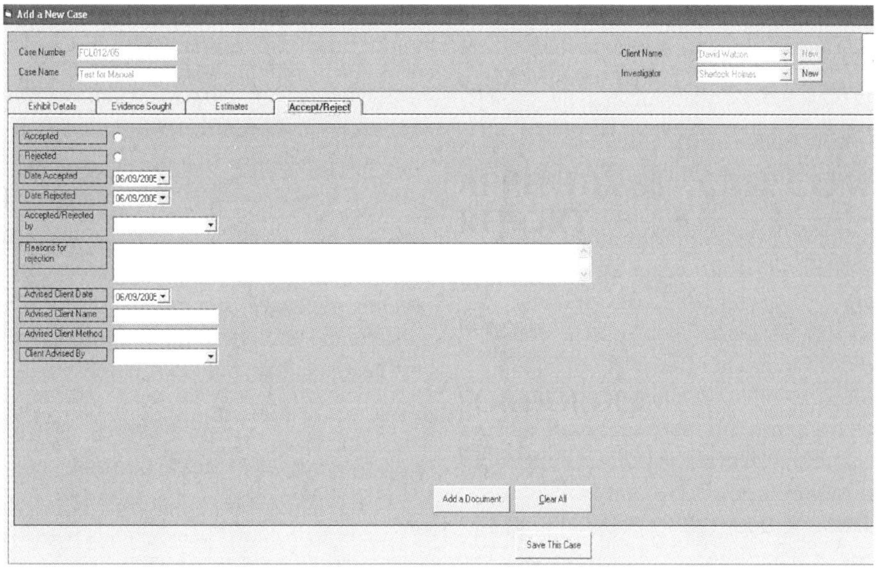

FIGURE 10.19 Accepted or Rejected Case. (For color version of this figure, the reader is referred to the online version of this chapter.)

evidence tampering, etc.), as defined in Chapter 9, Section 9.6.1.

10.4.5.1 Add Case Status

Once all information is added, press the "Save this Case" button to add the status details to the case.

10.4.6 Amend Case Details

Once the Administrator has set up a case, it may be necessary to amend some details due to errors. It is possible to amend the data setup by the Administrator.

This is done from the main menu, where the Administrator will be asked "Which case do you want to amend" and will allow selection of the case from a drop-down of all current forensic cases.

It is possible for the Administrator to amend the following:

- exhibit details;
- evidence sought;
- accept/reject case status and details.

There is no need for the Administrator to update estimates, as this will be amended by the Forensic Analyst as a part of the casework.

10.4.6.1 Amend Exhibit Details

A drop-down of exhibits for this case only will be presented so the correct one can be chosen.

Any fields can be amended except the "Exhibit Number."

More documents can be added, as required.

If the Exhibit Number is to be changed, then it must be deleted, the new one entered, and the information reentered.

10.4.6.2 Amend Evidence Sought Details

The details of the evidence being sought can be amended if required.

More documents can be added, as required.

10.4.6.3 Amend Accept or Reject Status

The accepted or rejected status of a case and any supporting details can be amended if required.

More documents can be added, as required.

10.4.7 Delete Case Details

The only part of the case that should need to be deleted would be an exhibit assigned to the wrong case or incorrectly recorded. All other changes can be undertaken by the Administrator or the Forensic Analyst working the case.

An exhibit is chosen, as in amending it, and the "Delete" button is pressed to delete it.

This will produce a confirmation box saying "Are you sure you want to delete <Exhibit No>?"

Note

Where the deletion of an exhibit is attempted that could affect the referential integrity of the MARS database, the system will not permit the deletion to take place, and a message stating "This exhibit is currently in use and cannot be deleted" is displayed.

10.5 PROCESSING A FORENSIC CASE

Once a forensic case has been assigned to a Forensic Analyst by the Administrator, the Forensic Analyst can process the case, or cases, assigned to them. When a Forensic Analyst logs into MARS, they are presented with a main menu (the User Menu), as shown in Figure 10.20.

This shows that the current user is "dlw" (bottom left-hand side of the screen next to "Logged in as") indicating that it is the User ID for "dlw" for processing cases, and not for performing administration tasks.

This is where the assigned Forensic Analyst actually processes the case. All work that they do is entered through this menu.

10.5.1 Selecting a Case

The "User Menu" screen is shown in Figure 10.21.

On taking the option to Work A case, the Forensic Analyst gets the option to choose any of the cases that are currently assigned to them.

The Case ID drop-down box provides a list of all cases that are currently assigned to the logged in Forensic Analyst. The user selects the required case number and presses the "Work Selected Case" button to work the case.

This will bring up the eight tabbed input forms as described below.

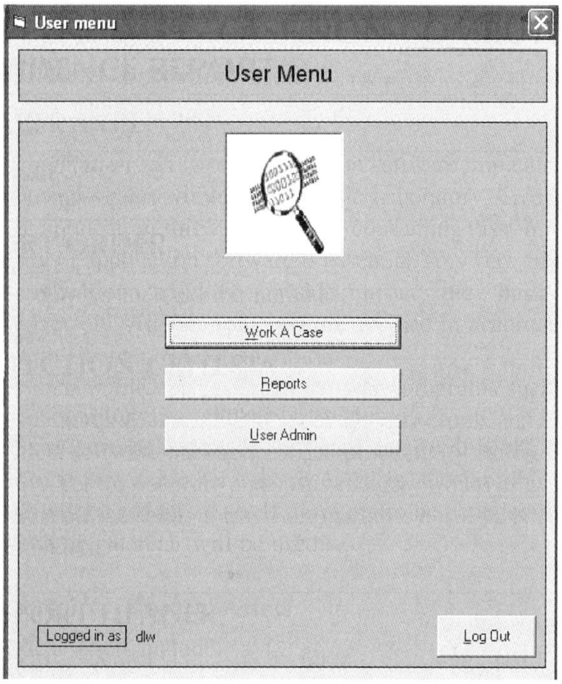

FIGURE 10.20 Processing a forensic case. (For color version of this figure, the reader is referred to the online version of this chapter.)

10.5.2 Movement Log

The "Movements" screen is shown in Figure 10.22.

Details of the contents of all of the fields in this screen are given in Appendix 16.

10.5.2.1 Add an Exhibit Movement

The blank screen is presented and the Forensic Analyst must populate all of the relevant fields and then save them to create a movement log entry for an exhibit in MARS.

10.5.2.2 Amend Movements

There is no amend process.

10.5.2.3 Delete Movements

There is no delete process as this is carried out by entering a new movement with a note that the original movement was incorrect.

10.5.3 Exhibit Examination

The "Examination" screen is shown in Figure 10.23.

Details of the contents of all of the fields in this screen are given in Appendix 17.

10.5.3.1 Add an Exhibit's Examination Record

The blank screen is presented and the Forensic Analyst must populate all of the relevant fields and then save them to create an examination record for an exhibit in MARS.

10.5.3.2 Amend an Exhibit's Details

To amend an exhibit, the exhibit must already exist.

Using the drop-down box for existing exhibits in the case, the exhibit to have its details amended is selected and the screen populated with their existing details from the stored record.

The Forensic Analyst is able to update data relating to the exhibit and save it, as appropriate. The Forensic Analyst is advised of the successful update and must acknowledge it.

10.5.3.3 Delete an Exhibit

To delete an exhibit, the exhibit has to exist.

Using the drop-down box for existing exhibits in the case, the exhibit to be deleted is selected and the screen populated with their existing details from the stored record.

It is not possible delete an exhibit that has been active in the MARS system, i.e., one that has had its details populated in MARS. The Forensic Analyst will be advised that this is not possible; otherwise, the Forensic Analyst is advised of the successful deletion of the computer and must acknowledge it.

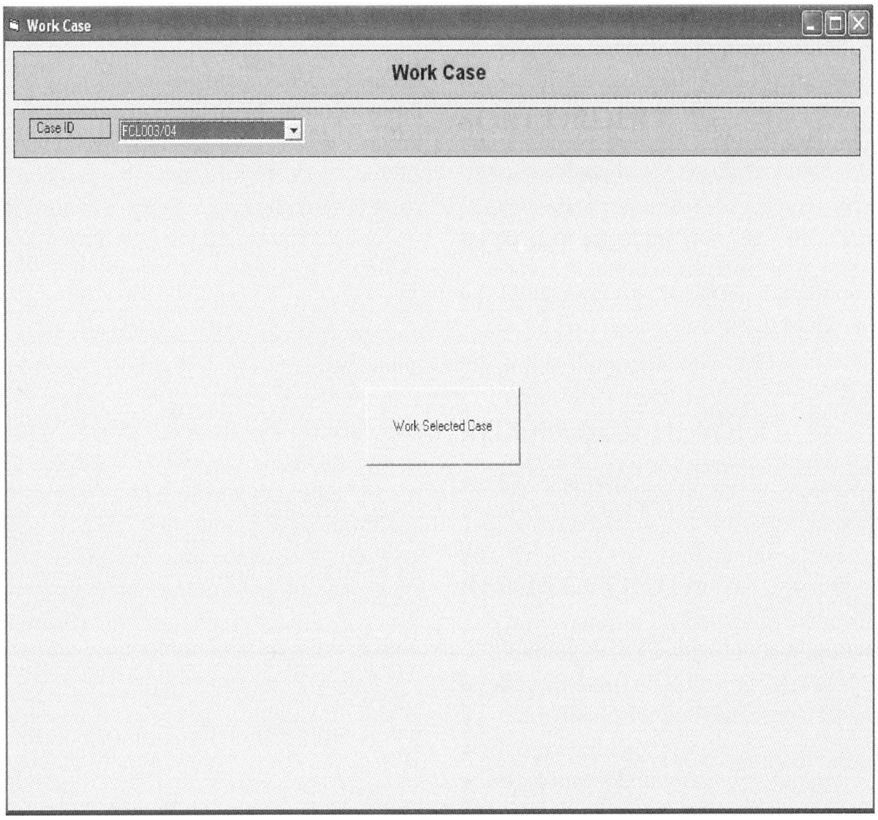

FIGURE 10.21 Selecting a Case. (For color version of this figure, the reader is referred to the online version of this chapter.)

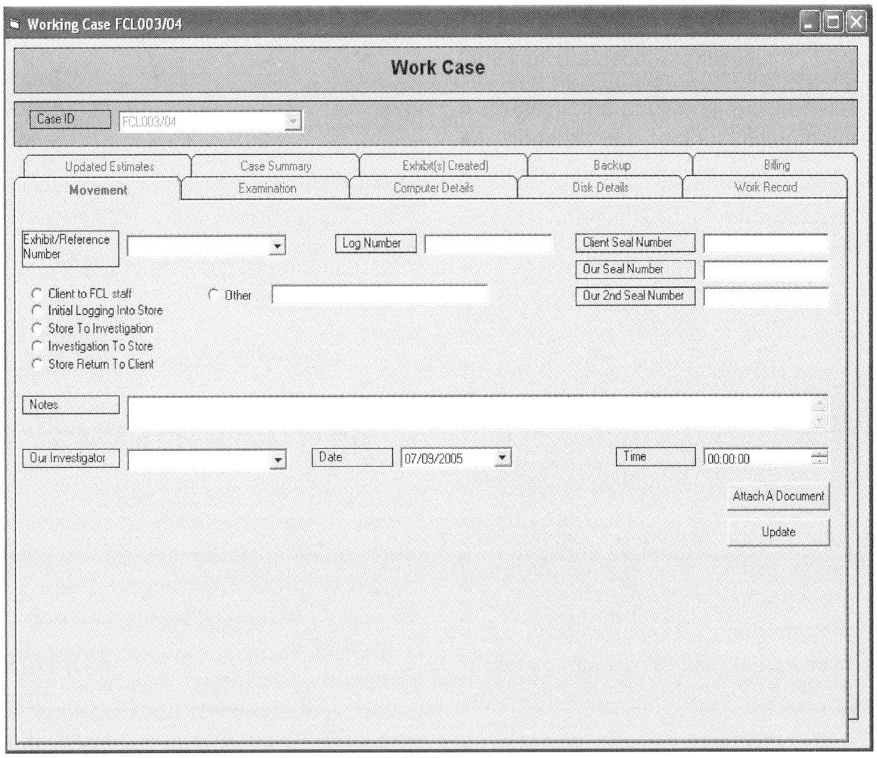

FIGURE 10.22 Movement Log. (For color version of this figure, the reader is referred to the online version of this chapter.)

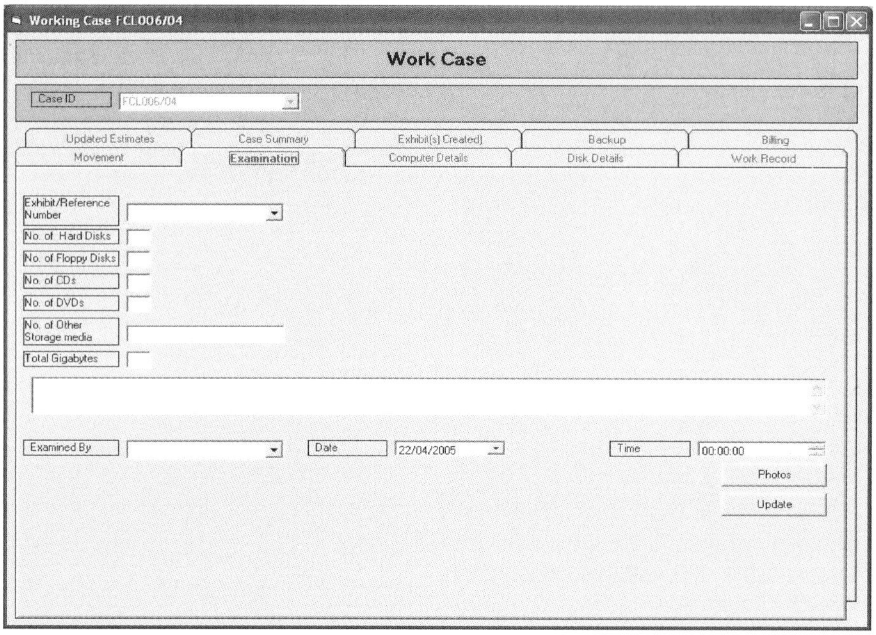

FIGURE 10.23 Exhibit Examination Log. (For color version of this figure, the reader is referred to the online version of this chapter.)

10.5.4 Computer Exhibit Details

The "Computer Details" screen is shown in Figure 10.24.

Details of the contents of all of the fields in this screen are given in Appendix 18.

10.5.4.1 Add a Computer Exhibit's Details

The blank screen is presented and the Forensic Analyst must populate all of the relevant fields and then save them to create the examination record for a computer exhibit in MARS.

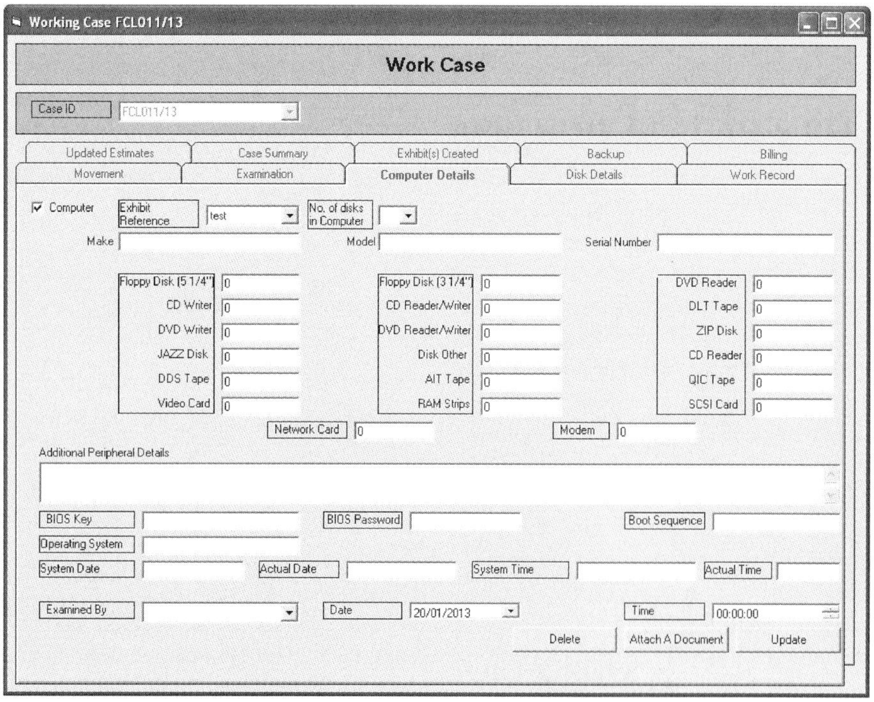

FIGURE 10.24 Computer Exhibit Details. (For color version of this figure, the reader is referred to the online version of this chapter.)

10.5.4.2 Amend a Computer's Details

To amend a computer's details, the computer must already exist.

Using the drop-down box for existing exhibits in the case, the computer to have its details amended is selected and the screen populated with their existing details from the stored record.

The Forensic Analyst is able to update data relating to the computer and save it, as appropriate. The Forensic Analyst is advised of the successful update and must acknowledge it.

10.5.4.3 Delete a Computer Exhibit

To delete a computer's details, the computer must already exist.

Using the drop-down box for existing exhibits in the case, the computer to be deleted is selected and the screen populated with their existing details from the stored record.

It is not possible delete a computer that has been active in the MARS system, i.e., one that has had its details populated in MARS. The Forensic Analyst will be advised that this is not possible; otherwise, the Forensic Analyst is advised of the successful deletion of the computer and must acknowledge it.

10.5.5 Non-Computer Exhibit Details

The "Non-Computer Details" screen is shown in Figure 10.25.

Details of the contents of all of the fields in this screen are given in Appendix 19.

10.5.5.1 Add a Non-Computer Exhibit's Details

The blank screen is presented and the Forensic Analyst must populate all of the relevant fields and then save them to create the examination record for a Non-Computer exhibit in MARS.

If the "Exhibit Type" does not already exist in the drop-down, it is possible to enter a new Exhibit Type by pressing the "New" key next to the Exhibit Type field.

This uses the new Exhibit Type process and screen as defined in Section 10.3.5.9.6.

A new Exhibit Type and all their details can be input and then one can exit from the "Add Exhibit Type" screen, and use the drop-down to select the newly entered Exhibit Type.

10.5.5.2 Amend a Non-Computer Exhibit's Details

To amend a Non-Computer exhibit's details, the Non-Computer exhibit must already exist.

Using the drop-down box for existing exhibits in the case, the Non-Computer exhibit to have its details amended is selected and the screen populated with their existing details from the stored record.

The Forensic Analyst is able to update data relating to the Non-Computer exhibit and save it, as appropriate. The Forensic Analyst is advised of the successful update and must acknowledge it.

10.5.5.3 Delete a Non-Computer Exhibit

To delete a Non-Computer exhibit's details, the Non Computer exhibit must already exist.

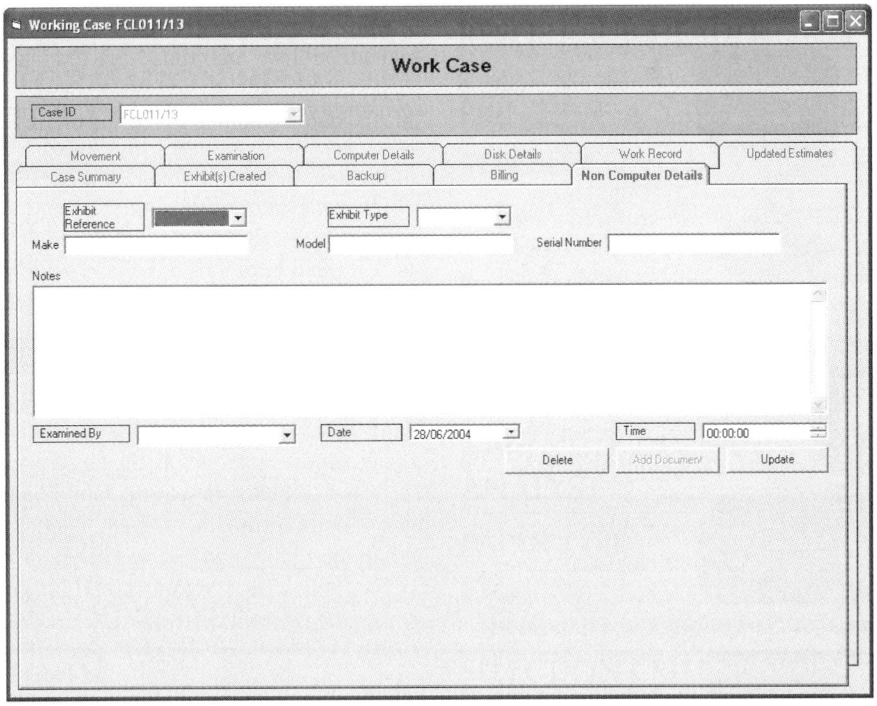

FIGURE 10.25 Non-Computer Exhibit Details. (For color version of this figure, the reader is referred to the online version of this chapter.)

Using the drop-down box for existing exhibits in the case, the Non-Computer exhibit to be deleted is selected and the screen populated with their existing details from the stored record.

It is not possible to delete a Non-Computer exhibit that has been active in the MARS system, i.e., one that has had its details populated in MARS. The Forensic Analyst will be advised that this is not possible; otherwise, the Forensic Analyst is advised of the successful deletion of the Non-Computer exhibit and must acknowledge it.

10.5.6 Hard Disk Details

The "Hard Disk Details" screen is shown in Figure 10.26.

Details of the contents of all of the fields in this screen are given in Appendix 20.

10.5.6.1 Add a Hard Disk

The blank screen is presented and the Forensic Analyst must populate all of the relevant fields and then save them to create the record for a hard disk in MARS.

10.5.6.2 Amend a Hard Disk's Details

To amend a hard disk's details, the hard disk must already exist.

Using the drop-down boxes for existing exhibits and hard disks in the case, the hard disk to have its details amended is selected and the screen populated with their existing details from the stored record.

The Forensic Analyst is able to update data relating to the hard disk and save it, as appropriate. The Forensic Analyst is advised of the successful update and must acknowledge it.

10.5.6.3 Delete a Hard Disk

To delete a hard disk, the hard disk must already exist.

Using the drop-down boxes for existing exhibits and hard disks in the case, the hard disk to be deleted is selected and the screen populated with their existing details from the stored record.

It is not possible to delete a hard disk that has been active in the MARS system, i.e., one that has had its details populated in MARS. The Forensic Analyst will be advised that this is not possible; otherwise, the Forensic Analyst is advised of the successful deletion of the hard disk and must acknowledge it.

10.5.7 Other Media Details

The "Other Media Details" are similar to a hard disk details, as shown above

Details of the contents of all of the fields in this screen are given in Appendix 21.

In this section, "Other Media" refers to any media that can store data apart from a hard disk. This includes, but is not limited to:

- CDs/DVDs;
- mobile phones;
- other types of disks (floppy, zip, jazz, etc.);

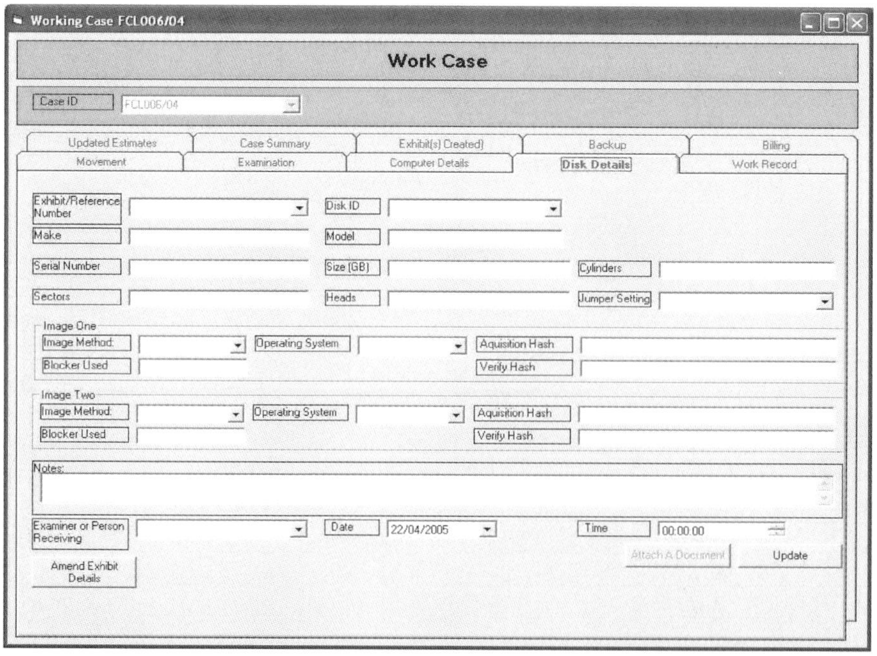

FIGURE 10.26 Hard Disk Details. (For color version of this figure, the reader is referred to the online version of this chapter.)

- mobile devices;
- tapes;
- USB drives;
- or any other data storage device.

10.5.7.1 Add an Other Media Exhibit's Details

The blank screen is presented and the Forensic Analyst must populate all of the relevant fields and then save them to create the examination record for an "other media" exhibit in MARS.

10.5.7.2 Amend an Other Media Exhibit's Details

To amend an "other media" exhibit's details, the "other media" must already exist.

Using the drop-down box for existing exhibits in the case, the "other media" exhibit to have its details amended is selected and the screen populated with their existing details from the stored record.

The Forensic Analyst is able to update data relating to the "other media" exhibit and save it, as appropriate. The Forensic Analyst is advised of the successful update and must acknowledge it.

10.5.7.3 Delete an Other Media Exhibit

To delete an "other media" exhibit's details, the "other media" exhibit must already exist.

Using the drop-down box for existing exhibits in the case, the "other media" exhibit to be deleted is selected and the screen populated with their existing details from the stored record.

It is not possible delete an "other media" exhibit that has been active in the MARS system, i.e., one that has had its details populated in MARS. The Forensic Analyst will be advised that this is not possible; otherwise, the Forensic Analyst is advised of the successful deletion of the "other media" exhibit and must acknowledge it.

10.5.8 Case Work Log

The "Work Record" screen is shown in Figure 10.27.

Details of the contents of all of the fields in this screen are given in Appendix 22.

10.5.8.1 Add a Work Record

The blank screen is presented and the Forensic Analyst must populate all of the relevant fields and then save them to create the Work Record for any actions taken by the Forensic Analyst on the case.

As the Case Work Log is to be used as evidence of actions taken by the Forensic Analyst, it is essential that the Work Record is correct before writing the record to the Case Work Log in MARS.

10.5.8.2 Amend a Work Record

There is no option to amend the Work Record for any case.

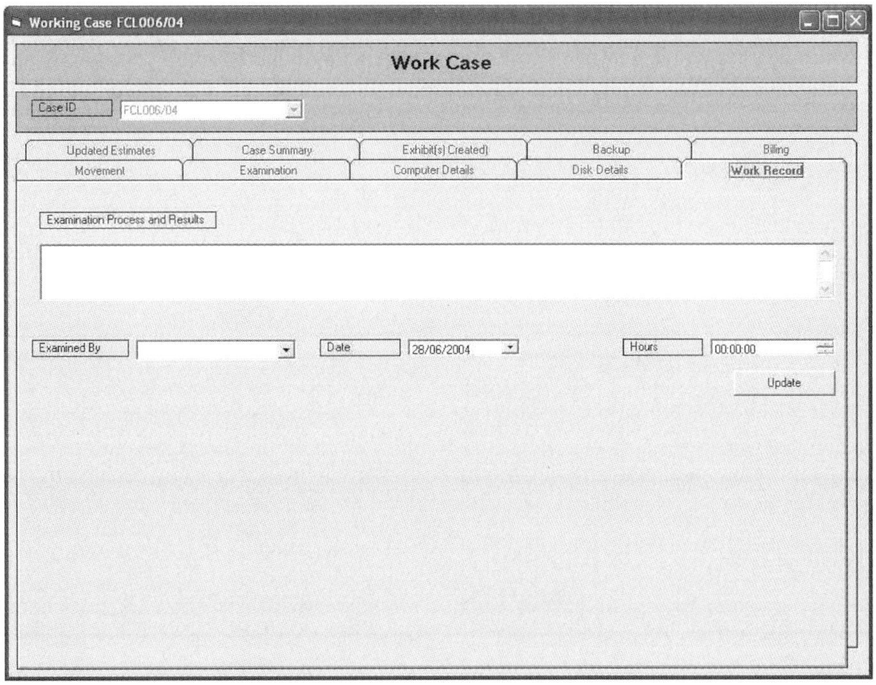

FIGURE 10.27 Case Work Log. (For color version of this figure, the reader is referred to the online version of this chapter.)

10.5.8.3 Delete a Work Record

There is no option to delete the Work Record for any case.

10.5.9 Updated Estimates

The "Updated Estimates" screen is shown in Figure 10.28.

Details of the contents of all of the fields in this screen are given in Appendix 23.

This is where revised cost or Target Dates can be entered along with the actual return date for the Case Exhibits to the Client.

10.5.9.1 Add Estimate

The blank screen is presented and the Forensic Analyst must populate all of the relevant fields and then save them to create an updated case estimate in MARS.

10.5.9.2 Amend Estimates

There is no amend process as new estimates will be entered with no amending the old ones—they are just revised and added to the case file.

10.5.9.3 Delete Estimates

There is no delete process as new estimates will be entered with no deleting of the old ones—they are just revised and added to the case file.

10.5.10 Exhibit(s) Created

The "Exhibits Created" screen is shown in Figure 10.29.

Details of the contents of all of the fields in this screen are given in Appendix 24.

This is where the Forensic Analyst or anyone involved in the case can create an exhibit. The drop-down will show only the Exhibits Created not the exhibits from the Client brought in to be examined by the Forensic Laboratory.

10.5.10.1 Add Exhibit

The blank screen is presented and the Forensic Analyst must populate all of the relevant fields and then save them to create an exhibit in MARS. The Forensic Laboratory Standard for exhibit numbering shall be used, as defined in Chapter 8, Section 8.6.10.

10.5.10.2 Amend Exhibit Created

To amend an exhibit created, the exhibit must already exist.

Using the drop-down box for created exhibits for the case, the created exhibit to have its details amended is selected and the screen populated with their existing details from the stored record.

The Forensic Analyst is able to update data relating to the exhibit created, as appropriate. The Forensic Analyst is advised of the successful update and must acknowledge it.

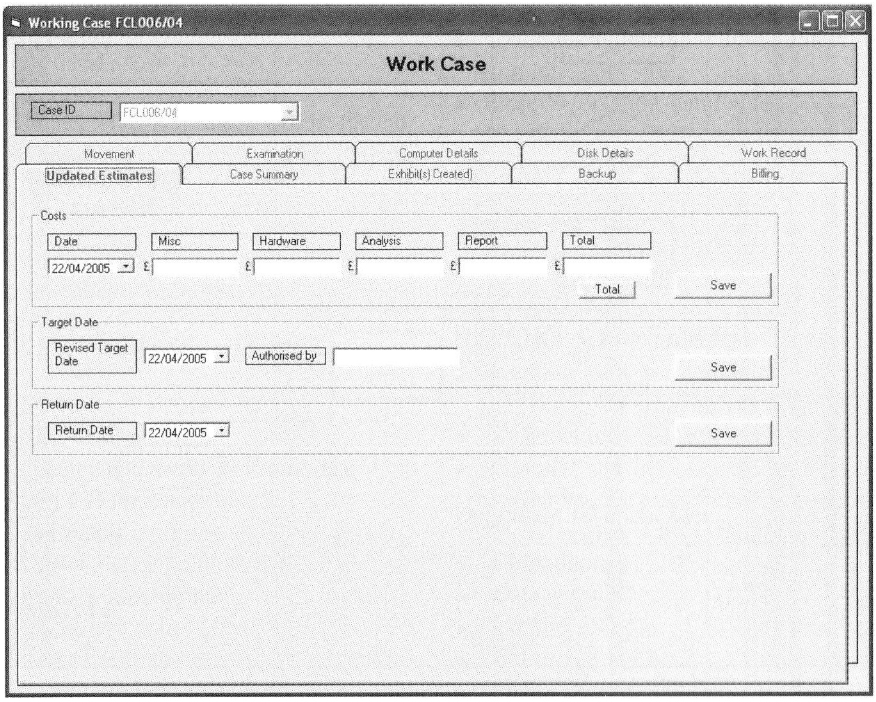

FIGURE 10.28 Updated Estimates. (For color version of this figure, the reader is referred to the online version of this chapter.)

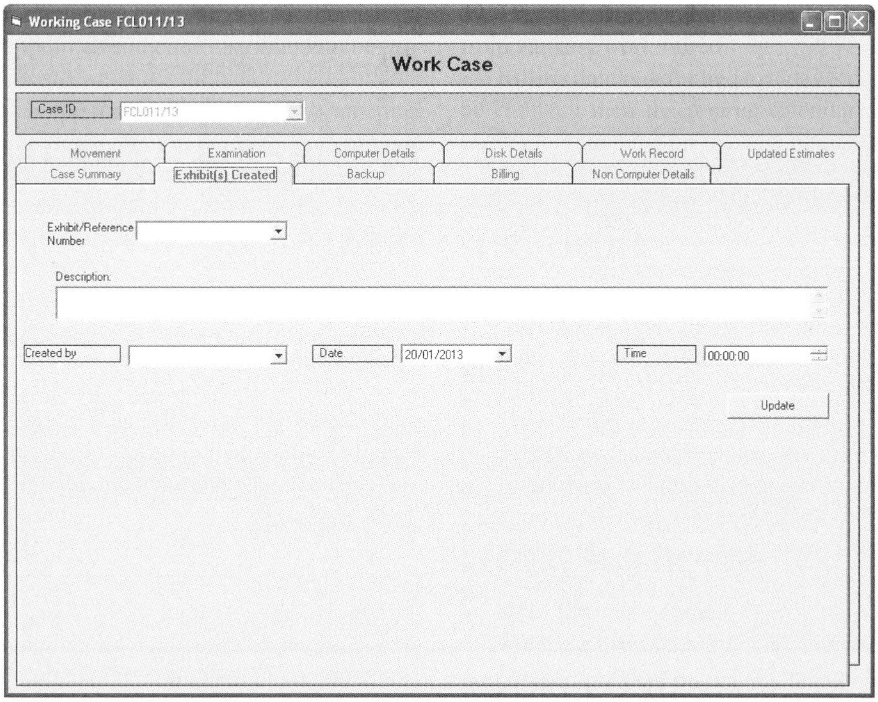

FIGURE 10.29 Exhibits Created. (For color version of this figure, the reader is referred to the online version of this chapter.)

10.5.10.3 Delete Exhibit Created

To delete an "exhibit created," the exhibit must already exist.

Using the drop-down box for existing Exhibits Created in the case, the exhibit to be deleted is selected and the screen populated with their existing details from the stored record.

It is not possible delete an exhibit that has been active in the MARS system, i.e., one that has had its details populated in MARS. The Forensic Analyst will be advised that this is not possible; otherwise, the Forensic Analyst is advised of the successful deletion of the exhibit and must acknowledge it.

10.5.11 Case Result

The "Case Result" screen is shown below.

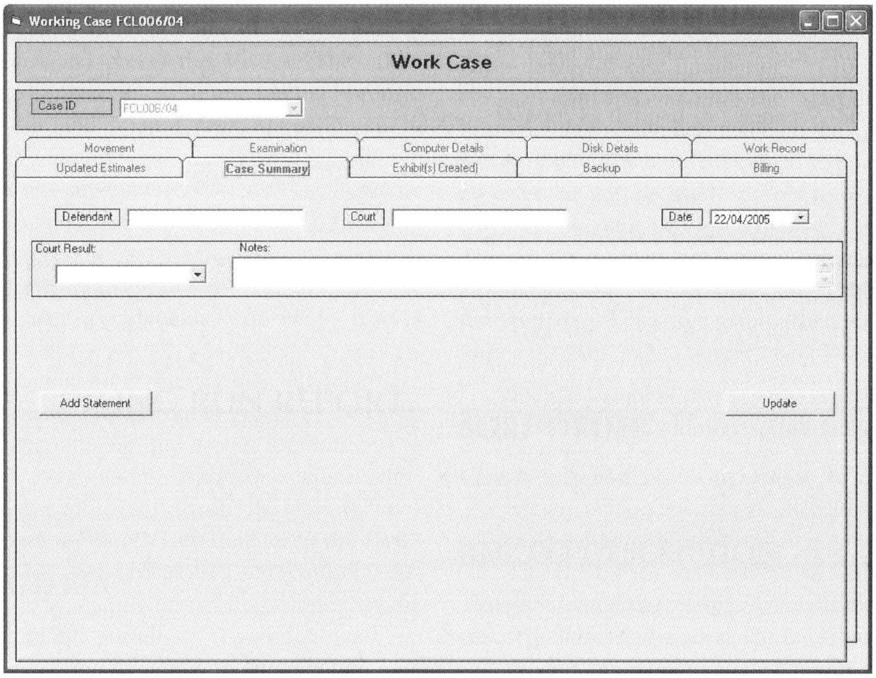

Details of the contents of all of the fields in this screen are given in Appendix 25.

One record (i.e., screen) is used for each defendant in the case.

10.5.11.1 Add Case Result

The blank screen is presented and the Forensic Analyst must populate all of the relevant fields and then save them to create the result for each defendant in the case in MARS.

10.5.11.2 Amend Case Result

There is no amend process.

10.5.11.3 Delete Case Result

There is no delete process.

10.5.12 Case Backup

The "Backup" screen is shown in Figure 10.30.

Details of the contents of all of the fields in this screen are given in Appendix 26.

10.5.12.1 Add backup

The blank screen is presented and the Forensic Analyst must populate all of the relevant fields and then save them to create an updated Case Backup record in MARS.

10.5.12.2 Amend Backups

There is no amend process as new backups will be entered with no amending the old ones.

10.5.12.3 Delete Backups

There is no delete process, as new backups will be entered with no deleting of the old ones.

10.5.13 Billing and Feedback

The "Billing and Feedback" screen is shown in Figure 10.31.

Details of the contents of all of the fields in this screen are given in Appendix 27.

10.5.13.1 Add Billing and Feedback Selection

The blank screen is presented and the Forensic Analyst must select the relevant radio buttons and then save them to select recipients for the case bill and satisfaction survey.

10.5.13.2 Amend Billing and Feedback Selection

There is no amend process as such, the Forensic Analyst will just choose a different radio button.

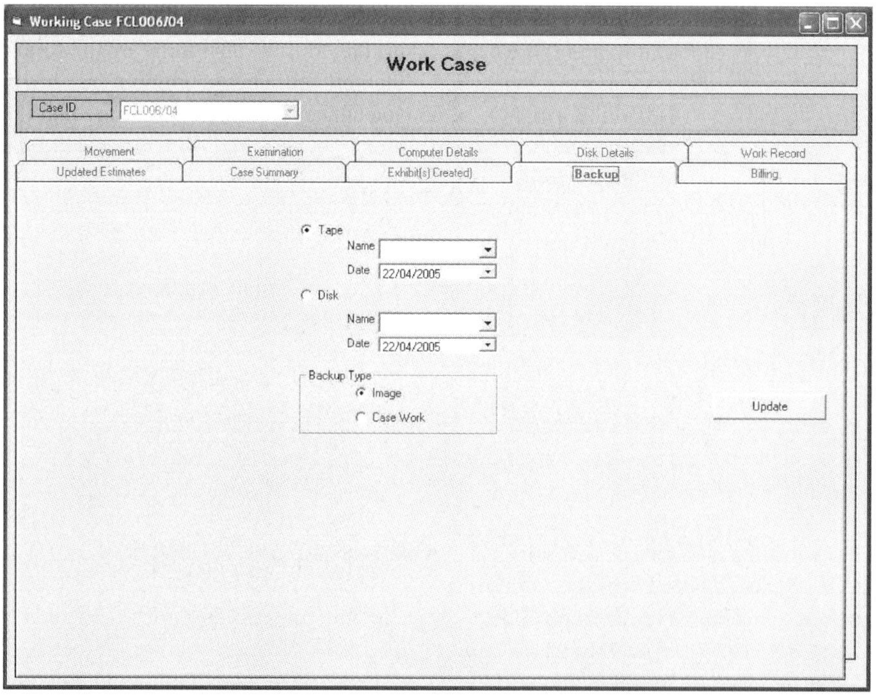

FIGURE 10.30 Case Backup. (For color version of this figure, the reader is referred to the online version of this chapter.)

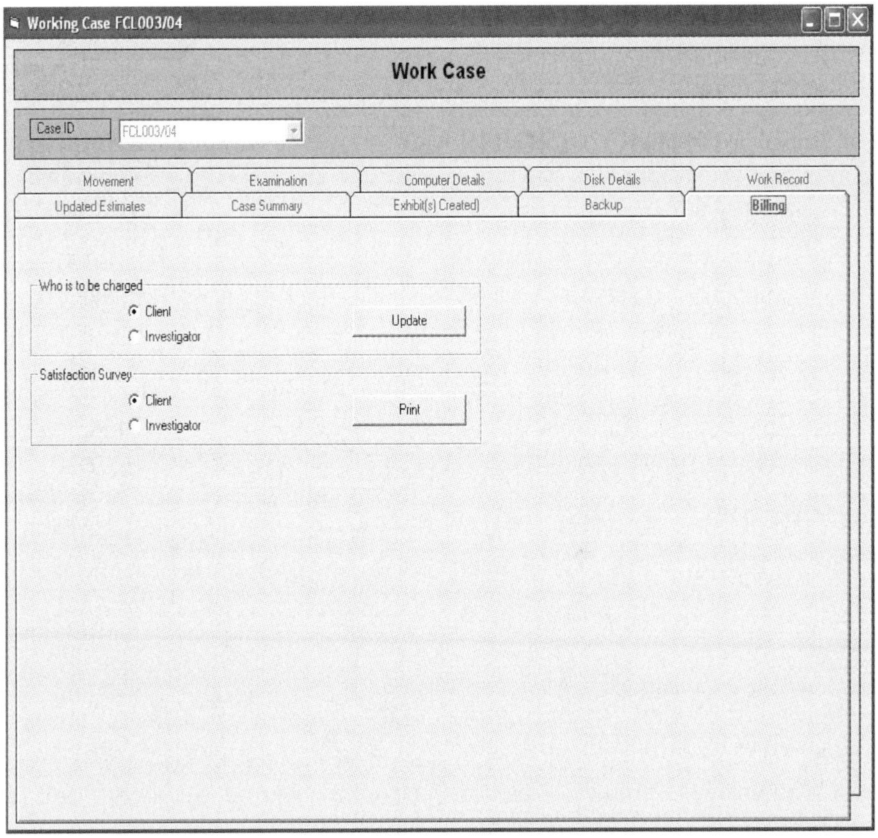

FIGURE 10.31 Billing and Feedback. (For color version of this figure, the reader is referred to the online version of this chapter.)

10.5.13.3 Delete Billing and Feedback Selection

There is no delete process. The Administrator does not have to run the billing run or the satisfaction survey run, if not required.

10.5.14 Case Feedback Received

The "Feedback Received" screen is shown in Figure 10.32.

Details of the contents of all of the fields in this screen are given in Appendix 28.

10.5.14.1 Add Case Feedback Received

The blank screen is presented and the Forensic Analyst must select the relevant ratings and comments from the Client feedback form.

10.5.14.2 Amend Case Feedback Received

To amend Case Feedback Received, the Case Feedback Received must already exist.

Using the drop-down box for Case Feedback Received for the case, the Case Feedback Received to have its details amended is selected and the screen populated with their existing details from the stored record.

The Forensic Analyst is able to update data relating to the Case Feedback Received, as appropriate. The Forensic Analyst is advised of the successful update and must acknowledge it.

10.5.14.3 Delete Billing and Feedback Selection

There is no delete process.

10.6 REPORTS GENERAL

10.6.1 Report Types

There are two types of reports that can be run from within MARS:

- Administrator reports;
- user reports.

An Administrator can print out all reports, but a user can only print out reports relevant to the cases that they are currently assigned.

10.6.2 Reporting General

For all of the reports where a selection of dates, cases, etc., can be made, the following options exist:

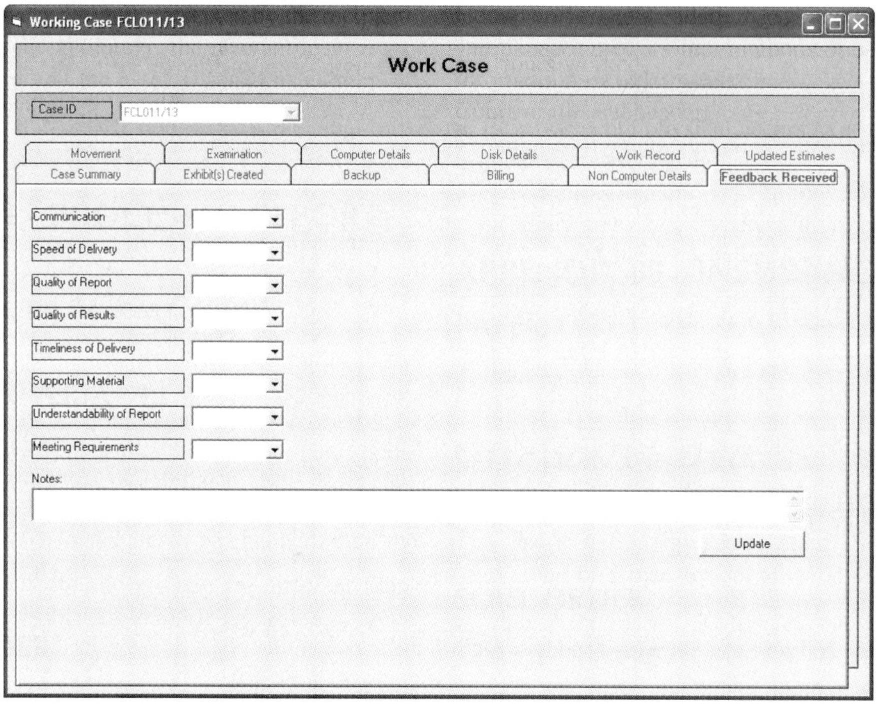

FIGURE 10.32 Case Feedback Received. (For color version of this figure, the reader is referred to the online version of this chapter.)

- case—specific case number from a drop-down box of permitted cases to print or * for all cases (either for the Administrator or all assigned to the user);
- dates—from start date to end date.

Where a large number of reports are to be printed, they will be printed in ascending order of the field searched on unless defined otherwise in the report.

If the search selection returns no "hits," the user is advised of this; otherwise, the report will be printed out using the standard attached printer.

For all (and especially) long prints, the page number being printed is displayed so that the user can see that something is actually happening.

10.6.3 General Report Layout

All reporting is set up for A4 or Letter paper.

Reports will be either Portrait or Landscape as dictated by the output produced.

All reports will have a number of standard elements in them. These are discussed below.

10.6.3.1 Report Header

These are from the information entered in Section 10.3.1 and Appendix 1.

- Title "Organisation Details"—top left-hand side;
- Logo—top right-hand side.

10.6.3.2 Report Sub-header

These are used if needed in any report.

10.6.3.3 Report Footer

These are from the information entered in Section 10.3.1 and Appendix 1.

- Copyright notice—left-hand side;
- Page *x* of *y* pages—centered;
- Date—top right-hand side.

10.7 ADMINISTRATOR'S REPORTS

The Administrator report menu is shown in Figure 10.33.

10.7.1 Static Information

10.7.1.1 Organization

This is a one page summary of the data entered when the system is first setup. The information produced in the report is given in Appendix 29.

10.7.1.2 Users

This is a listing of all users setup on the Forensic Laboratory's forensic case processing system, and so in MARS. The information produced in the report is given in Appendix 30.

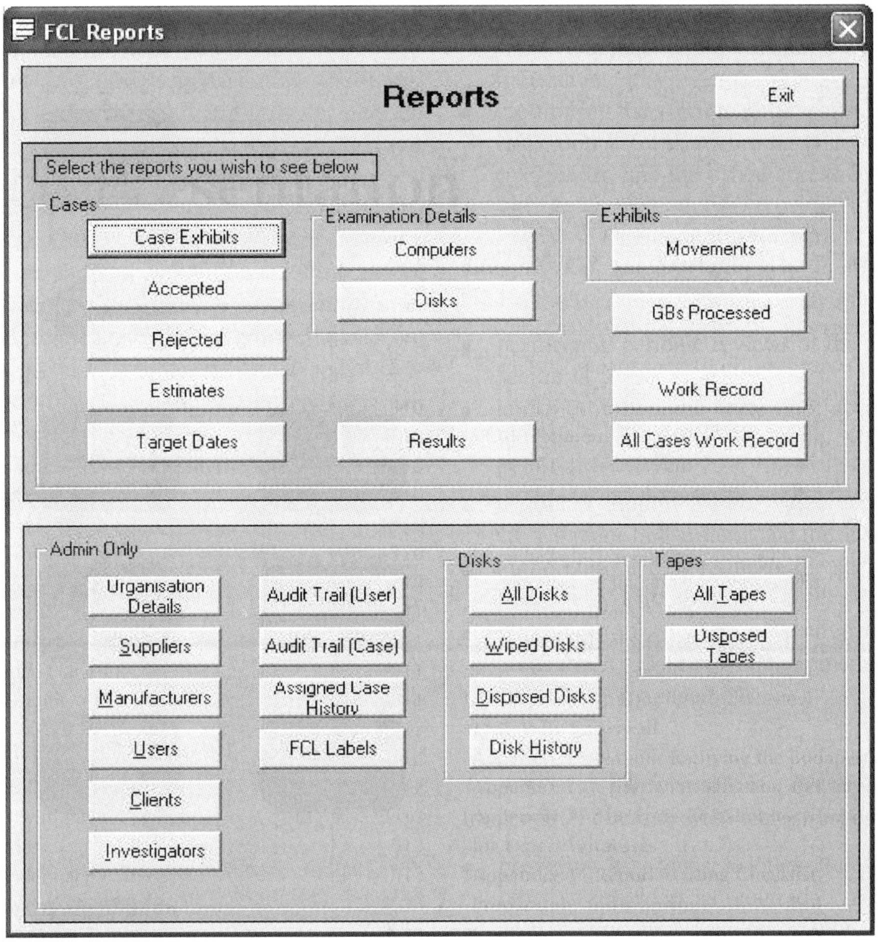

FIGURE 10.33 Administrator's Report. (For color version of this figure, the reader is referred to the online version of this chapter.)

10.7.1.3 Manufacturers

This is a report of all the Manufacturers who make the goods that are used in the Forensic Laboratory. The information produced in the report is given in Appendix 31.

10.7.1.4 Suppliers

This is a report of all the suppliers who supply goods to the Forensic Laboratory. The information produced in the report is given in Appendix 32.

10.7.1.5 Clients

This is a report of all the Forensic Laboratory's Clients, as every case that is processed will have a Client associated with it. For each Client listed all the cases for that Client shall be listed. The information produced in the report is given in Appendix 33.

10.7.1.6 Investigators

This is a very similar report to the Client report above, but it lists cases for an Investigator who is typically the Investigator in charge of the case for the Client. The information produced in the report is given in Appendix 34.

10.7.1.7 Disks

10.7.1.7.1 Disks by Assignment

This is a report showing all disks by the assignment of the case to which they are currently assigned. The information produced in the report is given in Appendix 35.

10.7.1.7.2 Disks by Reference No.

This is a report showing all disks in the Forensic Laboratory in disk Reference Number order. The information produced in the report is given in Appendix 36.

10.7.1.7.3 Wiped Disks

This is a report showing all disks in the Forensic Laboratory that have been wiped between two given dates. The information produced in the report is given in Appendix 37.

10.7.1.7.4 Disposed Disks

This is a report showing all disks in the Forensic Laboratory that have been disposed of between two given dates. The information produced in the report is given in Appendix 38.

10.7.1.7.5 Disk History

This is a report showing the actions taken on a specific disk for its life cycle in the Forensic Laboratory. The information produced in the report is given in Appendix 39.

10.7.1.8 Tapes

10.7.1.8.1 Tapes by Assignment

This is a report showing all tapes in the Forensic Laboratory in an assignment order. The information produced in the report is given in Appendix 40.

10.7.1.8.2 Tapes by Reference No.

This is a report showing all tapes in the Forensic Laboratory in tape Reference Number order. The information produced in the report is given in Appendix 41.

10.7.1.8.3 Wiped Tapes

This is a report showing all tapes in the Forensic Laboratory that have been wiped between two given dates. The information produced in the report is given in Appendix 42.

10.7.1.8.4 Disposed Tapes

This will be a report showing all tapes in the Forensic Laboratory that have been disposed of between two given dates. The information produced in the report is given in Appendix 43.

10.7.1.8.5 Tape History

This is a report showing the actions taken on a specific tape for its life cycle. The information produced in the report is given in Appendix 44.

10.7.1.9 Small Digital Media

10.7.1.9.1 Small digital media by assignment

This is a report showing all small digital media in the Forensic Laboratory in an assignment order. The information produced in the report is given in Appendix 45.

10.7.1.9.2 Small Digital Media by Reference Number

This is a report showing all small digital media in the Forensic Laboratory in small digital media Reference Number order. The information produced in the report is given in Appendix 46.

10.7.1.9.3 Wiped Small Digital Media

This is a report showing all small digital media in the Forensic Laboratory that have been wiped between two given dates. The information produced in the report is given in Appendix 47.

10.7.1.9.4 Disposed Small Digital Media

This will be a report showing all small digital media in the Forensic Laboratory that have been disposed of between two given dates. The information produced in the report is given in Appendix 48.

10.7.1.9.5 Small Digital Media History

This is a report showing the actions taken on a specific small digital media for its life cycle. The information produced in the report is given in Appendix 49.

10.7.1.10 Wipe Methods

This is a report showing all wiping methods used for wiping media used in the Forensic Laboratory. The information produced in the report is given in Appendix 50.

10.7.1.11 Disposal Methods

This is a report showing all disposal methods for disposing of media used in the Forensic Laboratory. The information produced in the report is given in Appendix 51.

10.7.1.12 Imaging Methods

This is a report showing all imaging methods for imaging media in the Forensic Laboratory. The information produced in the report is given in Appendix 52.

10.7.1.13 Operating Systems

This is a report showing all Operating Systems used in the Forensic Laboratory. The information produced in the report is given in Appendix 53.

10.7.1.14 Media Types

This is a report showing all Media Types processed by the Forensic Laboratory other than hard disks. The information produced in the report is given in Appendix 54.

10.7.1.15 Exhibit Types

This is a report showing all Exhibit Types processed by the Forensic Laboratory other than hard disks. The information produced in the report is given in Appendix 55.

10.7.2 Case setup Information

Case setup information relates to the initial setup of a case for forensic processing in the Forensic Laboratory.

10.7.2.1 Case Setup

This is a report showing all cases created in the Forensic Laboratory between two given dates or for a specific Client. The information produced in the report is given in Appendix 56.

10.7.2.2 Case Movements

This is a printout of the movements of all exhibits for a case or cases between the dates specified. The information produced in the report is given in Appendix 57.

10.7.2.3 Case Computers

This is a printout of the computers received by the Forensic Laboratory between two dates for examination. The information produced in the report is given in Appendix 58.

10.7.2.4 Case Non-Computer Evidence

This is a printout of the evidence that is not a computer received by the Forensic Laboratory between two dates for examination. The information produced in the report is given in Appendix 59.

10.7.2.5 Case Disks Received

This is a printout of the hard disks received in evidence by the Forensic Laboratory between two dates for examination. The information produced in the report is given in Appendix 60.

10.7.2.6 Case Other Media Received

This is a printout of the media that is not a hard disk received in evidence by the Forensic Laboratory between two dates for examination. The information produced in the report is given in Appendix 61.

10.7.2.7 Case Exhibits Received

This is a printout of the evidence for selected cases received by the Forensic Laboratory between two dates for examination. The information produced in the report is given in Appendix 62.

10.7.2.8 Case Work Record

This is a printout of the work performed on a given case or cases between two dates. The information produced in the report is given in Appendix 63.

10.7.2.9 Cases Rejected

This will be a showing all cases rejected by the Forensic Laboratory between two given dates or for a specific Client. The information produced in the report is given in Appendix 64.

10.7.2.10 Cases Accepted

This will be a showing all cases accepted by the Forensic Laboratory between two given dates or for a specific Client. The information produced in the report is given in Appendix 65.

10.7.2.11 Case Estimates

This is a printout of all estimates for cases between two dates. The information produced in the report is given in Appendix 66.

10.7.3 Case Processing

10.7.3.1 Cases by a Forensic Analyst

This is a printout of the cases that a Forensic Analyst has or is working between two dates. The information produced in the report is given in Appendix 67.

10.7.3.2 Cases by Client

This is a printout of the cases that a Client has in the Forensic Laboratory that are currently being processed. The information produced in the report is given in Appendix 68.

10.7.3.3 Cases by Investigator

This is a printout of the cases that an Investigator has in the Forensic Laboratory that are currently being processed. The information produced in the report is given in Appendix 69.

10.7.3.4 Case Target Dates

This is a printout of all Target Dates for cases that are being processed by the Forensic Laboratory. The information produced in the report is given in Appendix 70.

10.7.3.5 Cases within "x" days of Target Date

This is a printout of the cases within "*x*" days of the Target Date currently being processed in the Forensic Laboratory. The information produced in the report is given in Appendix 71.

10.7.3.6 Cases past their Target Date

This is a printout of the cases past Target Date that are currently being processed in the Forensic Laboratory.

The information produced in the report is given in Appendix 72.

10.7.3.7 Cases Unassigned

This is a printout of current cases in the Forensic Laboratory without a Forensic Analyst assigned to them. The information produced in the report is given in Appendix 73.

10.7.3.8 Case Exhibits Produced

This is a printout of the exhibits produced for the case between two dates. The information produced in the report is given in Appendix 74.

10.7.3.9 Case Results

This is a printout of the results of a given case or cases between two dates. The information produced in the report is given in Appendix 75.

10.7.4 Case Administration

10.7.4.1 Case Backups

This is a printout of the backups of a cases or cases between two dates. The information produced in the report is given in Appendix 76.

10.7.4.2 Billing Run

This is a printout of the work done between two dates (the last billed date and the billing date) for each case. The information produced in the report is given in Appendix 77.

10.7.4.3 Feedback Letters

This produces the letter asking for feedback on a given case or cases with the feedback form. The information produced in the report is given in Appendix 78.

10.7.4.4 Feedback Forms Printout

This is a printout of the forms scanned into the Client's virtual case file that have been received from the Client. The information produced in the report is given in Appendix 79.

10.7.4.5 Feedback Reporting Summary by Case

This is a report showing Feedback Received for cases by Case Number for all cases. The information produced in the report is given in Appendix 80.

10.7.4.6 Feedback Reporting Summary by Forensic Analyst

This will be a report showing Feedback Received for cases by Case Number for each Forensic Analyst. The information produced in the report is given in Appendix 81.

10.7.4.7 Feedback Reporting Summary by Client

This is a report showing Feedback Received for cases by Case Number for all cases. The information produced in the report is given in Appendix 82.

10.7.4.8 Complete Case Report

This is a printout of the complete case, with all information relating to a case. The information produced in the report is given in Appendix 83.

10.7.4.9 Processed Report

This is a printout of the work done in the Forensic Laboratory between two dates. The information produced in the report is given in Appendix 84.

10.7.4.10 Insurance Report

This is a printout of the evidence that is currently held by the Forensic Laboratory and lists its value for insurance purposes. The information produced in the report is given in Appendix 85.

10.7.5 Audits

10.7.5.1 Exhibit Audit Report

This is a printout of the evidence that is currently held by the Forensic Laboratory. The information produced in the report is given in Appendix 3.

10.7.5.2 Audit Trail User

This is a report showing all actions taken by a user on a case between two dates. The information produced in the report is given in Appendix 3.

10.7.5.3 Audit Trail Case

This is a report showing all actions taken by a user on a case between two dates. The information produced in the report is given in Appendix 3.

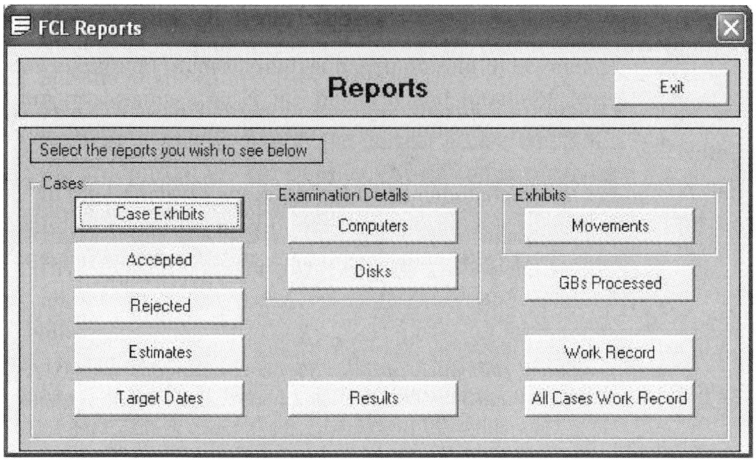

FIGURE 10.34 User Reports. (For color version of this figure, the reader is referred to the online version of this chapter.)

10.7.5.4 Assigned Case History

This is a report showing the assignments for a given case or cases. The information produced in the report is given in Appendix 3.

10.8 USER REPORTS

The user can track their own work using the same reports as the Administrator, but only for their own assigned cases.

The current user report menu is shown in Figure 10.34.

10.8.1 Case Setup Information

The following reports are available for the Forensic Analyst to view for their own cases:

- case setup;
- case movements;
- case computers;
- case non-computer evidence;
- case disks received;
- case other media received;
- case exhibits received;
- case work record;
- case estimates.

10.8.2 Case Processing

The following reports are available for the Forensic Analyst to view for their own cases:

- cases by Client;
- cases by Investigator;
- case Target Dates;
- cases within "*x*" days of Target Date;
- cases past their Target Date;
- case Exhibits produced;
- case Results.

10.8.3 Case Administration

The following reports are available for the Forensic Analyst to view for their own cases:

- case backups;
- feedback forms printout;
- feedback reporting summary by case;
- feedback reporting summary by Forensic Analyst;
- feedback reporting summary by Client;
- complete case report;
- processed report.

10.8.4 Audits

The following reports are available for the Forensic Analyst to view for their own cases:

- Exhibit audit report;
- audit trail case;
- assigned case history.

APPENDIX 1 - SETTING UP ORGANISATIONAL DETAILS

The following information is entered into setting up the Forensic Laboratory in MARS. Each field is described below:

ORGANISATION NAME

Enter the Forensic Laboratory's official name here.

ADDRESS

Enter up to four lines of the Forensic Laboratory's official registered address here.

POSTCODE

Enter the Forensic Laboratory's postcode here (note this is also called a Zip code in the USA).

PHONE NUMBER

Enter the Forensic Laboratory's main phone number, typically the main switchboard.

FAX

Enter the Forensic Laboratory's main fax number.

WEBSITE URL

Enter the Forensic Laboratory's Website URL.

VAT NUMBER

For laboratories in the United Kingdom, enter the Forensic Laboratory's VAT Number, so it can be used for billing runs (in other countries other tax references may be needed and these should be entered here).

REGISTERED COMPANY NUMBER

Enter the Forensic Laboratory's Company Number, so it can be used for corporate correspondence. The use of a registered company number will vary between jurisdictions.

LOGO

Enter the Forensic Laboratory's logo, by browsing to the relevant directory that holds it. The logo can be in BMP, JPEG, or GIF formats. It is automatically resized to be used for all output from MARS.

UNIT NAME

Enter the Forensic Laboratory's unit (or department, group, etc.) that runs the forensic service here.

UNIT ADDRESS

Where the address of the unit is the same as the Forensic Laboratory's address, press the "Use Organisation Details" button that will fill in all of the details of the Unit except the Email Address.

Any information can be over-typed as required (e.g., direct phone and fax may be different from the main Forensic Laboratory's ones).

If the unit address is different to the Forensic Laboratory's address then enter up to four lines of the address of the unit.

UNIT POSTCODE

If the unit postcode is different to the Forensic Laboratory's postcode, then enter the unit's postcode.

UNIT PHONE

If the unit phone number is different to the Forensic Laboratory's phone number, then enter the unit's phone number.

UNIT FAX

If the unit fax number is different to the Forensic Laboratory's fax number, then enter the unit's fax number.

UNIT WEBSITE URL

If the unit Website URL is different to the Forensic Laboratory's Website URL, then enter the unit's Website URL.

UNIT EMAIL ADDRESS

If the Unit has its own Email Address, then enter the Email Address here.

UNIT LOGO

If the unit has its own logo, enter it here by browsing to the relevant directory that holds it. The logo can be in BMP, JPEG, or GIF formats. It is automatically resized to be used for all output from MARS.

CLASSIFICATION OF THE REPORTS

MARS sets up the classification level for all investigation reports so that this classification appears at the top of all reports. This will indicate to any user how the information in the report has to be handled in accordance with the Forensic Laboratory's security procedures for information classification and handling, as given in Chapter 12, Section 12.3.14.6 and Section 12.3.14.9 and Chapter 5, Appendix 16.

CASE NUMBERING

This allows the Forensic Laboratory to set up its Case Numbering scheme. It must be in the format:

aaa/nnnnn/yyyy

- where aaa is the initials that identify the Forensic Laboratory as an acronym;
- nnnnn is the case number of the year;
- yyyy is the year (taken from the system).

Note 1

This should be the first case number of the Unit for the current year that will be entered into MARS.

Note 2

If historical cases are to be entered, then the oldest case number must be entered. However, all cases between the first one and the most recent one will have to be entered into MARS as MARS will automatically offer the next available number for the next case being entered.

Note 3

Once a case number has been assigned, it cannot be reassigned.

Note 4

As the first case number is entered into the entry field, it will be reflected by the details being displayed to the right of the entry box so that the display can be checked to ensure the case number is correct.

COPYRIGHT INFORMATION

The Forensic Laboratory always marks all of its output as a copyrighted document, and so the relevant copyright statement is entered here. It is used for all outputs from the MARS system.

On clicking on this field, it automatically inserts the "©" symbol followed by the Forensic Laboratory's name. This is changed as required.

HARD DISK REFERENCE ID

Any hard disk used in the Forensic Laboratory must be traceable throughout its life from purchase to disposal.

Enter here the prefix to be used for identifying hard disks.

The Forensic Laboratory uses "HD" as its Hard Disk identification prefix.

TAPE REFERENCE ID

Any tape used in the Forensic Laboratory must be traceable throughout its life from purchase to disposal.

Enter here the prefix to be used for identifying tapes.

The Forensic Laboratory uses "T" as its Tape identification prefix.

SMALL DIGITAL MEDIA ID

Any small digital media used in the Forensic Laboratory must be traceable throughout its life from purchase to disposal.

Enter here the prefix to be used for identifying small digital media.

The Forensic Laboratory uses "SDM" as its small digital media identification prefix.

APPENDIX 2 - SET UP THE ADMINISTRATOR

The following information is entered into setting up the Administrator in MARS. Each field is described below:

USER ID

Enter the User ID of the Administrator.

PASSWORD

Enter the password for the User ID.

CONFIRM PASSWORD

Reenter the password for the User ID.

TITLE/RANK

Enter the title or the rank for the Administrator.

FIRST NAME

Enter the Administrator's First Name.

SURNAME

Enter the Administrator's surname.

ADDRESS

If the Administrator is resident at the Forensic Laboratory's address, then press the "Use Organisation Details" button and this will fill in all of the relevant address details.

If the Administrator is resident at the unit address, then press the "Use Unit Details" button and this will fill in all of the relevant address details.

Otherwise, enter up to four lines of the Administrator's address.

POSTCODE

Enter the Administrator's postcode, unless it has been already entered by pressing either of the "Use Organisation Details" or "Use Unit Details" buttons.

PHONE DIRECT

Enter the Administrator's direct phone number.

PHONE MOBILE

Enter the Administrator's mobile/cell phone number.

FAX

Enter the Administrator's direct fax number.

EMAIL

Enter the Administrator's individual Email Address.

APPENDIX 3 - AUDIT REPORTS

EXHIBIT AUDIT REPORT

Paper Type

Portrait.

Selection Criteria

None.

Sort Order

Case number then exhibit.

Report Header

- Title "Insurance Listing for Exhibits"—top left-hand side;
- Logo—top right-hand side.

Report Sub-header

None.

Report Contents

- Case Name;
- Case ID;
- Exhibit Number;
- Description;
- Forensic Analyst assigned.

AUDIT TRAIL USER

Paper Type

Landscape.

Report Description

This will be a report showing all actions taken by a user on a case between a pair of dates.

Selection Criteria

Drop-down for User ID or "*" for all;

Note that if an "Administrator" is chosen, then there will be no cases available to be selected as no Administrator can "run" a case;

If all users are chosen, then list the Administrators first;

User names rather than User IDs are to be printed with the user type in brackets afterward—see examples below;

Drop-down for case number or "*" for all;

Start date and end date. The "start date" will be the earliest date any action was taken on the system, the "to date" will be today's date. If dates are to be changed, then the pop up calendar will be used.

Sort Order

Date and time order (oldest first).

Report Header

- "Audit trail for "between " <Start Date> and <End Date>"—top left-hand side;
- Logo—top right-hand side.

Report Sub-header

- User.

Report contents

- Date;
- Time;
- Case;
- Action (reporting what has been written to the audit trail).

AUDIT TRAIL CASE

Paper Type

Landscape.

Report Description

This will be a report showing all actions taken by a user on a case between a pair of dates.

Selection Criteria

Drop-down for case number or "*" for all;

Start date and end date. The "start date" will be the earliest date any action was taken on the system, the "to date" will be today's date. If dates are to be changed, then the pop up calendar will be used.

Sort Order

Case number (if appropriate) then by date and time;

New Cases to start on a new page.

Report Header

- "Audit Trail between '<Start Date>' and '<End Date>'"—top left-hand side;
- logo—top right-hand side.

Report Sub-header

- Case number.

Report Contents

- Date;
- Time;
- User—print name not User ID and user type in brackets afterward;
- Action (reporting what has been written to the audit trail).

ASSIGNED CASE HISTORY

Paper Type

Portrait.

Selection Criteria

Drop-down for case number or "*" for all;

Start date and end date. The "start date" will be the earliest date any action was taken on the system, the "to date" will be today's date. If dates are to be changed then the pop up calendar will be used.

Sort Order

Case number.

Report Description

This will be a report showing the assignments for a given case or cases.

Report Header

- Title "Case Assignment History"—top left-hand side;
- Logo—top right-hand side.

Report Sub-header

- <Case Number>—<Case Name>.

Report Contents

- Date;
- Time;
- Assigned to—print name not User ID and user type in brackets afterward;
- Assigned by—print name not User ID and user type in brackets afterward.

APPENDIX 4 - MANAGE USERS

The same screen is used for all actions relating to management of users and contains the following fields:

USER ID

The User ID of the User.

PASSWORD

The password for the User ID.

CONFIRM PASSWORD

Re-entry of the password for the User ID.

When the "Confirm" password is entered, it must be that it matches the original one entered in the field above. If it does not produce an error message "Passwords do not Match" and prompt for reentry by blanking both password fields.

TITLE OR RANK

The title or the rank for the user.

FIRST NAME

The First Name for the owner of the User ID.

SURNAME

The surname for the owner of the User ID.

ADDRESS

If the owner of the User ID is resident at the Forensic Laboratory's main address, then pressing the "Use Organisation Details" button will fill in all of the relevant address details.

If the owner of the User ID is resident at the unit's address, then pressing the "Use Unit Details" button and this will fill in all of the relevant address details.

Otherwise, enter up to four lines for the address of the owner of the User ID.

POSTCODE

The postcode of the owner of the User ID, unless it has been already entered by pressing either of the "Use Organisation Details" or "Use Unit Details" buttons.

PHONE DIRECT

The direct phone number of the owner of the User ID.

PHONE MOBILE

The mobile/cell phone number of the owner of the User ID.

FAX

The direct fax number of the owner of the User ID.

EMAIL

The individual Email Address of the owner of the User ID.

ACCESS RIGHTS

Whether this User ID is to be an "Administrator" or a "normal user."

APPENDIX 5 - MANAGE MANUFACTURERS

NAME

The Manufacturer's name.

ADDRESS

Up to four lines of the Manufacturer's address.

POSTCODE

The Manufacturer's postcode.

PHONE

The Manufacturer's phone number.

FAX

The Manufacturer's fax number.

WEBSITE URL

The Manufacturer's URL.

EMAIL

The Manufacturer's Email Address.

APPENDIX 6 - MANAGE SUPPLIERS

NAME

The Supplier's name.

ADDRESS

Up to four lines of the Supplier's address.

POSTCODE

The Supplier's postcode.

PHONE

The Supplier's phone number.

FAX

The Supplier's fax number.

WEBSITE URL

The Supplier's URL.

EMAIL

The Supplier's Email Address.

ACCOUNT NUMBER

The Account Number that the Forensic Laboratory has with the Supplier.

CONTACTS

Details of up to five contacts in the Supplier. Each can have a name, phone number, and Email Address.

APPENDIX 7 - MANAGE CLIENTS

NAME

The Client's name.

ADDRESS

Up to four lines of the Client's address.

POSTCODE

The Client's postcode.

PHONE

The Client's phone number.

FAX

The Client's fax number.

WEBSITE URL

The Client's URL.

EMAIL

The Client's Email Address.

CONTACTS

Details of up to five contacts in the Client. Each can have a name, phone number, and Email Address.

APPENDIX 8 - MANAGE INVESTIGATORS

NAME

The Investigator's name.

ADDRESS

There is a drop-down to the right of name that allows the Administrator to select a Client that the Investigator works for. Once the Client is found, their details should be displayed in fields to the right of the Investigator's input fields.

A button, next to the "Address" field is available entitled "Use Client Details." If this is pressed, then the Investigator's address details are filled in automatically with the Client details.

If these are wrong in any area, the Administrator can amend them; otherwise, all the address details on the left will have to be entered manually.

If not automatically entered, then the Administrator will be able to enter up to four lines of the Investigator's address.

POSTCODE

If not automatically entered, then this is the Investigator's postcode.

PHONE

If not automatically entered, then this is the Investigator's phone number.

FAX

If not automatically entered, then this is the Investigator's fax number.

WEBSITE URL

If not automatically entered, then this is the Investigator's URL.

EMAIL

If not automatically entered, then this is the Investigator's Email Address.

APPENDIX 9 - MANAGE DISKS

DISK DETAILS

Manufacturer

A disk manufacturer is selected from the drop-down list of manufacturers entered in Section 10.3.5.2.

Serial Number

The Serial Number of the disk.

Supplier

A supplier is selected from the drop-down list of suppliers entered in Section 10.3.5.3.

Forensic Laboratory Disk Reference

The disk Reference Number is autogenerated by MARS and cannot be changed. The numbering is based on the system that was entered in the Organisational Details when MARS was installed.

Model

The disk model name.

Size

The size of the disk in Gb.

Order Number

The Forensic Laboratory Order Number for the purchase of the disk. This number may refer to a number of different disks as a consignment.

Date Received

The date that the disk was received. This uses a drop-down calendar.

Delivery Note

The delivery note is scanned and saved to the relevant virtual file. MARS allows the Administrator to browse to the correct file and attach the scan of the delivery note to the hard disk record.

Auto Clear Entry

If a number of disks are to be entered and they are all from different sources, then the "auto clear" option should be taken. Checking this box automatically clears the screen after adding each disk, apart from the system generated disk number and today's date.

Otherwise, after entering the first disk in a series of disks from the same supplier, all of the information from the previous disk on screen (allowing bulk entry from a specific shipment of similar disks) will remain on screen.

WIPE A DISK

When a new disk arrives at the Forensic Laboratory, it must be immediately wiped forensically. Disks are also wiped forensically at a number of stages in their lifecycle in the Forensic Laboratory. This is where the details of all wiping operations are carried out, as they are all related to a specific disk.

Disk Reference

Disks to be wiped are selected from the drop-down list of disks by the Forensic Laboratory Reference Number it was assigned when introduced to the Laboratory.

Wipe Method

The Wipe Method is selected from the drop-down list that was entered in Section 10.3.5.9.1.

Wiped by

The User ID of the person performing the disk wiping is selected from the drop-down list that was entered in Section 10.3.5.1.

Date

The date that the disk was wiped. This uses a drop-down calendar.

Notes

Any notes to be associated with this process.

DISPOSE OF A DISK

When it comes time to dispose of a disk, then the fact is recorded in MARS along with the disposal method.

Disk Reference

Disks to be disposed of are selected from the drop-down list of disks by the Forensic Laboratory Reference Number it was assigned when introduced to the Laboratory.

Disposal Method

The disposal method from the drop-down list that was entered in Section 10.3.5.9.2.

Disposed by

The User ID of the person performing the disk disposal is selected from the drop-down list that was entered in Section 10.3.5.1.

Date

The date that the disk was disposed of. This uses a drop-down calendar.

Notes

Any notes to be associated with this process.

Disposal Certificate

Disposal certificates, where appropriate, are scanned in and allow the Administrator to browse to the correct file and attach the scan of the disposal certificate to the hard disk record.

ASSIGN A DISK

When a disk is to be assigned to a case or for a specific job, it is done here.

Disk Reference

Disks to be assigned to a case are selected from the drop-down list of disks by the Forensic Laboratory Reference Number it was assigned when introduced to the Laboratory.

Assign to

A disk can be assigned to either a current forensic case or to an administrative task. Assignment is carried out as below:

- forensic cases—this has a drop-down of all cases and a case can be selected to assign a disk to. The case must exist for a disk to be assigned to it and more than one disk can be assigned to a case;
- administrative purposes—allows the Administrator to enter where this disk is being assigned if not to a case. It could be for storing images, for backup, as a scratch disk, etc.

APPENDIX 10 - MANAGE TAPES

TAPE DETAILS

Manufacturer

A tape manufacturer is selected from the drop-down list of manufacturers entered in Section 10.3.5.3.

Label

The label details attached to the tape.

Supplier

A supplier is selected from the drop-down list of suppliers entered in Section 10.3.5.3.

Forensic Laboratory Tape Reference

The tape Reference Number is auto generated by MARS and cannot be changed. The numbering is based on the system that was entered in the Organisational Details when MARS was installed.

Model

The tape model name.

Size

The size of the tape in Gb.

Order Number

The Forensic Laboratory Order Number for the purchase of the tape. This number may refer to a number of different tapes as a consignment.

Date Received

The date that the tape was received. This uses a drop-down calendar.

Delivery Note

The delivery note is scanned and saved to the relevant virtual file. MARS allows the Administrator to browse to the correct file and attach the scan of the delivery note to the tape record.

Auto Clear Entry

If a number of tapes are to be entered and they are all from different sources, then the "auto clear" option should be taken. Checking this box automatically clears the screen after adding each tape, apart from the system generated tape number and today's date.

Otherwise, after entering the first tape in a series of tapes from the same supplier, all of the information from the previous tape on screen (allowing bulk entry from a specific shipment of similar tapes) will remain on screen.

WIPE A TAPE

When a new tape arrives at the Forensic Laboratory, it must be immediately wiped forensically. Tapes are also wiped forensically at a number of stages in their lifecycle in the Forensic Laboratory. This is where the details of all wiping operations are carried out, as they are all related to a specific tape.

Tape Reference

Tapes to be wiped are selected from the drop-down list of tapes by the Forensic Laboratory Reference Number it was assigned when introduced to the Laboratory.

WIPE METHOD

The Wipe Method is selected from the drop-down list that was entered in Section 10.3.5.9.1.

Wiped by

The User ID of the person performing the tape wiping is selected from the drop-down list that was entered in Section 10.3.5.1.

Date

The date that the tape was wiped. This uses a drop-down calendar.

Notes

Any notes to be associated with this process.

DISPOSE OF A TAPE

When it comes time to dispose of a tape, then the fact is recorded in MARS along with the disposal method.

Tape Reference

Tapes to be disposed of are selected from the drop-down list of tapes by the Forensic Laboratory Reference Number it was assigned when introduced to the Laboratory.

Disposal Method

The disposal method from the drop-down list that was entered in Section 10.3.5.9.2.

Disposed By

The User ID of the person performing the tape disposal is selected from the drop-down list that was entered in Section 10.3.5.1.

Date

The date that the tape was disposed of. This uses a drop-down calendar.

Notes

Any notes to be associated with this process.

Disposal Certificate

Disposal certificates, where appropriate, are scanned in and allow the Administrator to browse to the correct file and attach the scan of the disposal certificate to the tape record.

ASSIGN A TAPE

When a tape is to be assigned to a case or for a specific job, it is done here.

Tape Reference

Tapes to be assigned to a case are selected from the drop-down list of tapes by the Forensic Laboratory Reference Number it was assigned when introduced to the Laboratory.

Assign To

A tape can be assigned to either a current forensic case or to an administrative task. Assignment is carried out as below:

- forensic cases—this has a drop-down of all cases and a case can be selected to assign a tape to. The case must exist for a tape to be assigned to it and more than one tape can be assigned to a case;
- administrative purposes—allows the Administrator to enter where this tape is being assigned if not to a case. It could be for storing images, for backup, as a scratch tape, etc.

APPENDIX 11 - MANAGE SMALL DIGITAL MEDIA

SMALL DIGITAL MEDIA DETAILS

Media Type

A small digital media type is selected from the drop-down list of Small Digital Media Types entered in Section 10.3.5.8.

Manufacturer

A small digital media type manufacturer is selected from the drop-down list of Small Digital Media Types entered in Section 10.3.5.2.

Label

The label details attached to the small digital media type.

Supplier

A supplier is selected from the drop-down list of suppliers entered in Section 10.3.5.2.

Small Digital Media Reference

The small digital media type Reference Number is autogenerated by MARS and cannot be changed. The numbering is based on the system that was entered in the Organisational Details when MARS was installed.

Model

The small digital media type model name.

Size

The size of the small digital media type in Gb.

Order Number

The Forensic Laboratory Order Number for the purchase of the small digital media type. This number may refer to a number of different Small Digital Media Types as a consignment.

Date Received

The date that the small digital media type was received. This uses a drop-down calendar.

Delivery Note

The delivery note is scanned and saved to the relevant virtual file. MARS allows the Administrator to browse to the correct file and attach the scan of the delivery note to the small digital media type record.

Auto Clear Entry

If a number of Small Digital Media Types are to be entered and they are all from different sources, then the "auto clear" option should be taken. Checking this box automatically clears the screen after adding each item of small digital media, apart from the system generated small digital media number and today's date.

Otherwise, after entering the first small digital media item in a series of small digital media items from the same supplier, all of the information from the previous item of small digital media on screen (allowing bulk entry from a specific shipment of similar items of small digital media) will remain on screen.

WIPE A SMALL DIGITAL MEDIA DEVICE

When a small digital media item arrives at the Forensic Laboratory, it must be immediately wiped forensically. Small digital media are also wiped forensically at a number of stages in their lifecycle in the Forensic Laboratory. This is where the details of all wiping operations are carried out, as they are all related to a specific small digital media.

Small Digital Device Reference

Small digital media to be wiped are selected from the drop-down list of small digital media by the Forensic Laboratory Reference Number it was assigned when introduced to the Laboratory.

WIPE METHOD

The Wipe Method is selected from the drop-down list that was entered in Section 10.3.5.8.4.

Wiped by

The User ID of the person performing the tape wiping is selected from the drop-down list that was entered in Section 10.3.5.1.

Date

The date that the small digital media was wiped. This uses a drop-down calendar.

Notes

Any notes to be associated with this process.

DISPOSE OF AN ITEM OF SMALL DIGITAL MEDIA

When it comes time to dispose of an item of small digital media, then the fact is recorded in MARS along with the disposal method.

Small Digital Media Reference

Small digital media to be disposed of are selected from the drop-down list of items of small digital media by the Forensic Laboratory Reference Number it was assigned when introduced to the Laboratory.

Disposal Method

The disposal method from the drop-down list that was entered in Section 10.3.5.8.5.

Disposed by

The User ID of the person performing the small digital media disposal is selected from the drop-down list that was entered in Section 10.3.5.1.

Date

The date that the small digital media was disposed of. This uses a drop-down calendar.

Notes

Any notes to be associated with this process.

Disposal Certificate

Disposal certificates, where appropriate, are scanned in and allow the Administrator to browse to the correct file and attach the scan of the disposal certificate to the small digital media record.

ASSIGN A SMALL DIGITAL MEDIA

When an item of small digital media is to be assigned to a case or for a specific job, it is done here.

Small Digital Media Reference

Small digital media to be assigned to a case are selected from the drop-down list of small digital media by the Forensic Laboratory Reference Number it was assigned when introduced to the Laboratory.

Assign To

A small digital media device can be assigned to either a current forensic case or to an administrative task. Assignment is carried out as below:

- forensic cases—this has a drop-down of all cases and a case can be selected to assign an item of small digital media to. The case must exist for an item of small digital media to be assigned to it and more than one item of small digital media can be assigned to a case;
- administrative purposes—allows the Administrator to enter where this item of small digital media is being assigned if not to a case. It could be for storing images, for backup, as a scratch disk, etc.

APPENDIX 12 - EXHIBIT DETAILS

EXHIBIT NUMBER

The Exhibit Number of the exhibit related to the case.

SEAL NUMBER

The seal number of the exhibit.

DESCRIPTION

The description for the exhibit.

RECEIVED BY

Use the drop-down box to select the User ID for the person receiving the exhibit, as defined in Section 10.3.5.1.

SEIZED FROM

Whom the exhibit was seized from.

RECEIVED DATE

The date that the exhibit was received in the Forensic Laboratory. This uses a drop-down calendar.

SEIZED DATE

The date that the exhibit was seized. This uses a drop-down calendar.

RECEIVED TIME

The time that the exhibit was received.

TIME SEIZED

The time that the exhibit was seized.

INSURANCE VALUE

The insurance value of the exhibit. This is so that the total value of equipment held can be monitored to ensure that does not breach the value insured in the policy.

OWNER

The owner of the exhibit.

REASON FOR SEIZING

The reason for seizing.

CHECKBOXES

Password?

If any passwords were obtained from the suspect or elsewhere, the checkbox should be ticked and relevant details in the text box on the right-hand side of the checkbox.

Connected?

If the exhibit was a system and it was connected to a phone or network, the checkbox should be ticked and relevant details in the text box on the right-hand side of the checkbox.

Switched on at Seizure?

If the system was switched on at the time of seizure, the checkbox should be ticked and relevant details in the text box on the right-hand side of the checkbox.

Switched on After Seizure?

If the system has been switched on since the time of seizure, the checkbox should be ticked and relevant details in the text box on the right-hand side of the checkbox.

ADD DOCUMENT

If there are any documents relevant to the exhibit, their scanned imaged can be added by pressing on the "Add Documents" button. As many documents as required can be added.

APPENDIX 13 - EVIDENCE SOUGHT

EVIDENCE SOUGHT

The details of the Evidence Sought

COMMENTS

Any other comments or relevant information.

ADD DOCUMENT

If there are any documents relevant to the exhibit, their scanned image can be added by pressing on the "Add Documents" button. As many documents as required can be added.

APPENDIX 14 - ESTIMATES

COST

Date

The date of the estimate. This uses a drop-down calendar.

Misc

Any costs that are not covered elsewhere, e.g., travel and subsistence, meetings, etc.

Hardware

The costs estimated for any hardware required for the case. This should include disks, tapes, caddies, and additional hardware needed to image or interrogate or analyze the case.

Analysis

The estimated costs for the Forensic Analysts running the case.

Report

Cost for report production, e.g., print costs, binding, etc.

Total

This is the automatically calculated total of the other fields entered.

CASE DATES

Date Received

This defaults to the earliest date of receipt of any exhibit in the forensic case, but it can be overwritten, if required. This uses a drop-down calendar to change the date.

Target Date

The date that the Client wants the results delivered by (i.e., the TRT). This uses a drop-down calendar.

APPENDIX 15 - ACCEPT OR REJECT CASE

ACCEPTED

Check the button if the case is to be accepted. If this is selected, then the date rejected and the reason for rejection is grayed out.

REJECTED

Check the button if the case is to be rejected. If this is selected, then the date accepted is grayed out.

DATE ACCEPTED

The date the case was accepted, the date defaults to today's date. This uses a drop-down calendar.

DATE REJECTED

The date the case was rejected, the date defaults to today's date. This uses a drop-down calendar.

ACCEPTED OR REJECTED BY

Use the drop-down box to select the User ID for the person who accepted or rejected the case.

REASON FOR REJECTION

Enter the reason for rejection. This is a freeform text box.

DATE CLIENT ADVISED

The date the Client was advised of the acceptance or rejection of the forensic case, the date defaults to today's date. This uses a drop-down calendar.

ADVISED CLIENT NAME

The name of the person (in the Client's Organization) that will be advised of the acceptance or rejection of the case.

ADVISED CLIENT METHOD

The method of communication that was used to advise the Client, typically this could be phone, fax, face to face, or other. This is a free-form text box.

CLIENT ADVISED BY

Use the drop-down box to select the User ID for the person that advised the Client of the acceptance or rejection of the case.

ADD DOCUMENT

If there are any relevant documents to be added (e.g., copy of original signed fax or letter sent), they can be scanned in and the scanned image be attached to the relevant case by pressing the "Add a Document" button.

CLEAR ALL

The "clear all" button deletes all contents of all fields to allow reentry assuming that the data have not been saved.

APPENDIX 16 - MOVEMENT LOG

EXHIBIT OR REFERENCE NUMBER

The exhibit or Reference Number is selected from the drop-down box which gives the complete listing of all exhibits assigned to the forensic case. Once the exhibit has been selected, the screen is populated with all details that are listed for the exhibit. All empty fields are able to be updated as required.

LOG NUMBER

This will display the log number from the Forensic Laboratory Log Book entered when the exhibit was received into the Forensic Laboratory.

CLIENT SEAL NUMBER

This will display the Client Seal Number entered when the exhibit was received into the Forensic Laboratory.

OUR SEAL NUMBER

If the exhibit is to be sealed by the Forensic Laboratory, the Seal Number is entered here.

OUR 2ND SEAL NUMBER

If the exhibit has to be resealed for any reason, then the new Forensic Laboratory Seal Number is entered here—with a note as to why a second seal was used.

ACTION

This is the action that was taken relating to the movements of the exhibit, using the radio buttons below.

Client to the Forensic Laboratory

Indicates that the exhibit was transferred from the Client to the Forensic Laboratory.

Initial Logging into Store

Indicates that the exhibit was logged into the Secure Property Store.

Store to Investigation

Indicates that the exhibit was transferred from the Secure Property Store to a Forensic Analyst so that work could be carried out on it.

Investigation to Store

Indicates that the exhibit was transferred to the Secure Property Store from a Forensic Analyst, after work was carried out on it.

Store Return to Client

Indicates that the exhibit has been taken from the Secure Property Store and returned to the Client.

Other

Indicates that the exhibit undergoes any other movement—e.g., pass to Law Enforcement or another authorized third party. If other is chosen, a brief description of where it has gone and why it must be entered.

Notes

Any further notes to do with this exhibit movement.

OUR FORENSIC ANALYST

Typically, this will be the Forensic Analyst assigned to the case, and this is the default inserted in the box. If another of the Forensic Analysts moved the exhibit, then this must be recorded using the "Our Forensic Analyst" drop-down box and selecting the relevant Forensic Analyst.

DATE

The date the exhibit was moved, the date defaults to today's date. This uses a drop-down calendar to select another date, if required.

TIME

The time the exhibit was moved.

ADD DOCUMENT

If there are any relevant documents to be added (e.g., copy of original Movement Log with actual signatures), they can be scanned in and the scanned image be attached to the relevant case by pressing the "Add a Document" button.

APPENDIX 17 - EXAMINATION LOG

EXHIBIT REFERENCE NUMBER

The exhibit Reference Number for the exhibit to be examined is selected from the drop-down box of all exhibits in the selected case. The exhibit to be examined is selected from the list and the details are entered below.

NO. OF HARD DISKS

Enter the number of hard disks in the exhibit and on the same line enter the total disk size in Gb of hard disks in the exhibit.

NO. OF FLOPPY DISKS

Enter the number of floppy disks in the exhibit and on the same line enter the total disk size in Gb of floppy disks in the exhibit.

NO. OF CDs

Enter the number of CDs in the exhibit and on the same line enter the total disk size in Gb of CDs in the exhibit.

NO. OF DVDs

Enter the number of DVDs in the exhibit and on the same line enter the total disk size in Gb of DVDs in the exhibit.

NO. OF OTHER STORAGE MEDIA

Enter the number of other storage media in the exhibit (e.g., USB sticks, Camera Chips, etc.) and on the same line enter the total disk size in Gb of other media in the exhibit.

TOTAL

The field will automatically enter the sum of the Gb for all the items in the exhibit from the numbers entered above.

Note

The details of capacity must all be entered in Gb.

NOTES

Describe any other media and or enter any relevant details about the exhibit(s) here or any further notes to do with the examination.

EXAMINED BY

Typically, this will be the Forensic Analyst assigned to the case, and this is the default inserted in the box. If another of the Forensic Analysts undertakes any examination, then this must be recorded using the "Examined by" drop-down box and selecting the relevant Forensic Analyst.

DATE

The date the exhibit was examined, which defaults to today's date. This uses a drop-down calendar to select another date, if required.

TIME

The time the exhibit was examined.

ADD PHOTOS

If there are any relevant photos of the exhibit to be added, they can be attached to the exhibit by pressing the "Photos" button:

ADD DOCUMENT

If there are any relevant documents to be added, they can be scanned in and the scanned image be attached to the relevant case by pressing the "Add Document" button.

APPENDIX 18 - COMPUTER HARDWARE DETAILS

EXHIBIT REFERENCE

The exhibit Reference Number for the exhibit to be examined is selected from the drop-down box of all exhibits in the selected case. The exhibit to be examined is selected from the list and the details are entered below.

NO. OF DISKS IN COMPUTER

Enter the number of disks in the computer.

MAKE

Enter the computer make.

MODEL

Enter the model of the computer.

SERIAL NUMBER

Enter the computer's Serial Number.

FLOPPY DISK (5¼″)

Enter the number of 5¼″ disk drives in the computer.

FLOPPY DISK (3½″)

Enter the number of 3½″ disk drives in the computer.

DVD READER

Enter the number of DVD readers in the computer.

CD WRITER

Enter the number of CD writers in the computer.

CD READER/WRITER

Enter the number of CD reader/writers in the computer.

DLT TAPE

Enter the number of DLT tape backup devices in the computer.

DVD WRITER

Enter the number of DVD writers in the computer.

DVD READER/WRITER

Enter the number of DVD reader/writers in the computer.

ZIP DISK

Enter the number of Zip drives in the computer.

JAZZ DRIVE

Enter the number of Jazz drives in the computer.

DISK (OTHER)

Enter the number of other types of disk drive in the computer.

CD READER

Enter the number of CD readers in the computer.

DDS TAPE

Enter the number of DDS tape backup devices in the computer.

AIT TAPE

Enter the number of AIT tape backup devices in the computer.

QIC TAPE

Enter the number of QIC tape backup devices in the computer.

VIDEO CARD

Enter the number of video cards in the computer.

RAM STRIPS

Enter the number of RAM strips in the computer.

SCSI CARD

Enter the number of SCSI cards in the computer.

NETWORK CARD

Enter the number of network cards in the computer.

MODEM

Enter the number of modem cards in the computer.

ADDITIONAL PERIPHERALS DETAILS

Enter any additional details regarding any of the peripherals above for clarification or identification.

BIOS KEY

Enter the BIOS Key (i.e., the key sequence to get at the BIOS information).

BIOS PASSWORD

Enter the BIOS password.

BOOT SEQUENCE

Enter the boot sequence.

OPERATING SYSTEM

Enter the computer's operating system. If a new one is to be added, the "new" button beside it should be selected and the new operating system added. This uses the same screen as given in Section 10.3.5.9.4.

SYSTEM DATE

The system date, this defaults to today's date. This uses a drop-down calendar to select another date, if required.

ACTUAL DATE

The system date, this defaults to today's date. This uses a drop-down calendar to select another date, if required.

SYSTEM TIME

Defaults to the current time. If this needs to be changed, the up and down arrows are used.

ACTUAL TIME

Defaults to the current time. If this needs to be changed, the up and down arrows are used.

EXAMINED BY

Typically, this will be the Forensic Analyst assigned to the case, and this is the default inserted in the box. If another of the Forensic Analysts undertakes any examination, then this must be recorded using the "Examined by" drop-down box and selecting the relevant Forensic Analyst or employee.

DATE

Defaults to today's date. This uses a drop-down calendar to select another date, if required.

TIME

The time the computer was examined.

APPENDIX 19 - NON-COMPUTER EXHIBIT DETAILS

EXHIBIT REFERENCE

The Exhibit Reference Number for the exhibit to be examined is selected from the drop-down box of all exhibits in the selected case. The exhibit to be examined is selected from the list and the details are entered below.

EXHIBIT TYPE

Enter the Exhibit Type (e.g., printer, scanner, mobile phone, PDA, etc.).

MAKE

Enter the exhibit make.

MODEL

Enter the model of the exhibit.

SERIAL NUMBER

Enter the exhibit's Serial Number.

NOTES

Notes on the exhibit.

ADD PHOTOS

If there are any relevant photos of the exhibit to be added, they can be attached to the exhibit by pressing the "Photos" button.

ADD DOCUMENT

If there are any relevant documents to be added, they can be scanned in and the scanned image be attached to the relevant case by pressing the "Add Document" button.

EXAMINED BY

Typically, this will be the Forensic Analyst assigned to the case, and this is the default inserted in the box. If another of the Forensic Analysts undertakes any examination, then this must be recorded using the "Examined by" drop-down box and selecting the relevant Forensic Analyst or employee.

DATE

Defaults to today's date. This uses a drop-down calendar to select another date, if required.

TIME

The time the computer was examined.

APPENDIX 20 - HARD DISK DETAILS

EXHIBIT REFERENCE

The Exhibit Reference Number for the exhibit to be examined is selected from the drop-down box of all exhibits in the selected case. The exhibit to be examined is selected from the list and the details are entered below.

DISK ID

The hard disk in the case examined is selected from the drop-down box of all hard disks in the selected case. The hard disk to be examined is selected from the list and the details are entered below.

This will only list the disks in the case.

MAKE

The make of disk drive.

MODEL

The model of the disk drive.

SERIAL NUMBER

The disk drive Serial Number.

SIZE

The size of the disk in Gb.

CYLINDERS

The number of cylinders on the disk where possible.

SECTORS

The number of sectors on the disk where possible.

HEADS

The number of heads on the disk where possible.

JUMPER SETTINGS

The Jumper Setting will come from a drop-down and the options are as shown below:

- slave;
- master or single drive;
- cable select;
- master with a non-ATA compatible slave;
- limit drive capacity;
- other.

IMAGE 1

Details of the first image of the evidence.

> **Note**
>
> It is assumed that only two copies of the image are taken and usually this requires two tools. If only one tool is used, then just this section should be filled in.

Image Method

The imaging method will come from the drop-down where the imaging methods have been entered in the maintenance system process.

Operating System

The operating system for the acquisition box will come from the drop-down where the imaging methods have been entered in the maintenance system process.

Blocker Used

Enter the details of the write blocker used.

Acquisition Hash

The acquisition hash for the exhibit.

Verify Hash

The verification hash for the exhibit.

IMAGE 2

This is where the details of the second image of the evidence is recorded if second images are taken.

Image Method

The imaging method will come from the drop-down where the imaging methods have been entered in the maintenance system process.

Operating System

The operating system for the acquisition box will come from the drop-down where the imaging methods have been entered in the maintenance system process.

Blocker Used

Enter the details of the write blocker used.

Acquisition Hash

The acquisition hash for the exhibit.

Verify Hash

The verification hash for the exhibit.

NOTES

Any notes that the examiner needs to make or thinks appropriate are entered here.

ADD PHOTOS

If there are any relevant photographs of the disk to be added, they can be scanned or downloaded from a digital camera and then added to the case by pressing the "Add Photos" button and browsing to the selected file(s) in the folder. Click "OK" and the photographs will be attached to the case file.

ADD DOCUMENT

If there are any relevant documents to be added, they can be scanned in then added to the case by pressing the "Add Document" button and browsing to the selected file(s) in the folder. Click "OK" and the document will be attached to the case file.

EXAMINER

Typically, this will be the Forensic Analyst assigned to the case, and this is the default inserted in the box. If another of the Forensic Analysts undertakes any examination, then this must be recorded using the "Examined by" drop-down box and selecting the relevant Forensic Analyst.

DATE

Defaults to today's date. This uses a drop-down calendar to select another date, if required.

TIME

The time the computer was examined.

APPENDIX 21 - OTHER MEDIA DETAILS

EXHIBIT REFERENCE

The Exhibit Reference Number for the exhibit to be examined is selected from the drop-down box of all exhibits in the selected case. The exhibit to be examined is selected from the list and the details are entered below.

MEDIA TYPE

The media type for the exhibit to be examined is selected from the drop-down box of all Media Types. If the media type is not present, the "New" button is used to add a new media type using the screen as defined in Section 10.3.5.9.5.

MAKE

The make of the media.

MODEL

The model of the media.

SERIAL NUMBER

The media's Serial Number.

SIZE

The size of the media in Gb.

IMAGE 1

Details of the first image of the evidence.

> **Note**
> It is assumed that only two copies of the image are taken, and usually, this requires two tools. If only one tool is used, then just this section should be filled in.

Image Method

The imaging method will come from the drop-down where the imaging methods have been entered in the maintenance system process.

Operating System

The operating system for the acquisition box will come from the drop-down where the imaging methods have been entered in the maintenance system process.

Blocker Used

Enter the details of the write blocker used.

Acquisition Hash

The acquisition hash for the exhibit.

Verify Hash

The verification hash for the exhibit.

IMAGE 2

This is where the details of the second image of the evidence are recorded if second images are taken.

Image Method

The imaging method will come from the drop-down where the imaging methods have been entered in the maintenance system process.

Operating System

The operating system for the acquisition box will come from the drop-down where the imaging methods have been entered in the maintenance system process.

Blocker Used

Enter the details of the write blocker used.

Acquisition Hash

The acquisition hash for the exhibit.

Verify Hash

The verification hash for the exhibit.

NOTES

Any notes that the examiner needs to make or thinks appropriate are entered here.

ADD PHOTOS

If there are any relevant photographs of the media to be added, they can be scanned or downloaded from a digital camera and then added to the case by pressing the "Add Photos" button and browsing to the selected file(s) in the folder. Click "OK" and the photographs will be attached to the case file.

ADD DOCUMENT

If there are any relevant documents to be added, they can be scanned in then added to the case by pressing the "Add document" button and browsing to the selected file(s) in the folder. Click "OK" and the document will be attached to the case file.

EXAMINER

Typically, this will be the Forensic Analyst assigned to the case, and this is the default inserted in the box. If another of the Forensic Analysts undertakes any examination, then this must be recorded using the "Examined by" drop-down box and selecting the relevant Forensic Analyst.

DATE

Defaults to today's date. This uses a drop-down calendar to select another date, if required.

TIME

The time the media was examined.

APPENDIX 22 - WORK RECORD DETAILS

EXAMINATION PROCESS AND RESULTS

Whatever actions are taken by the Forensic Analyst on the case they must be entered here. It is probably best to enter different tasks during the day and when a break is taken to save the page and enter the remainder of the details on the screen.

ADD PHOTOS

If there are any relevant photographs of the work undertaken to be added, they can be scanned or downloaded from a digital camera and then added to the case by pressing the "Add Photos" button and browsing to the selected file(s) in the folder. Click "OK" and the photographs will be attached to the case file.

ADD DOCUMENT

If there are any relevant documents to be added, they can be scanned in then added to the case by pressing the "Add Document" button and browsing to the selected file(s) in the folder. Click "OK" and the document will be attached to the case file.

EXAMINED BY

Typically, this will be the Forensic Analyst assigned to the case, and this is the default inserted in the box. If another of the Forensic Analysts undertakes any examination, then this must be recorded using the "Examined by" drop-down box and selecting the relevant Forensic Analyst or employee.

DATE

Defaults to today's date. This uses a drop-down calendar to select another date, if required.

HOURS

This is the hours spent on the tasks being written up here. The hours spent is used for the billing process, so it needs to accurately reflect actual time spent working on the case.

APPENDIX 23 - UPDATING CASE ESTIMATES

COST

Date

The date of the estimate. This uses a drop-down calendar.

Misc

Any costs that are not covered elsewhere, e.g., travel and subsistence, meetings, etc.

Hardware

The costs estimated for any hardware required for the case. This should include disks, tapes, caddies, and additional hardware needed to image or interrogate or analyze the case.

Analysis

The estimated costs for the Forensic Analysts running the case.

Report

Cost for report production, e.g., Print costs, binding, postage and packaging etc.

Total

This is the automatically calculated total of the other fields entered.

CASE DATES

Target Date

The date that the Client wants the results delivered by (i.e., the TRT). This uses a drop-down calendar.

Revised Target Date

Defaults to the existing Target Date (or today's date if there is no date yet entered), but if another date is required, then it can be inserted. This uses a drop-down calendar to change the date.

Authorized By

Typically, this will be the Forensic Laboratory Manager, and this must be recorded using the "Examined by" drop-down box and selecting the Laboratory Manager or whoever authorized the revised Target Date.

Return Date

This is the date that the evidence is actually returned to the Client.

ADD PHOTOS

If there are any relevant photographs of the exhibit being returned to be added, they can be scanned or downloaded from a digital camera and then added to the case by pressing the "Add Photos" button and browsing to the selected file(s) in the folder. Click "OK" and the photographs will be attached to the case file.

ADD DOCUMENT

If there are any relevant documents to be added, they can be scanned in then added to the case by pressing the "Add Document" button and browsing to the selected file(s) in the folder. Click "OK" and the document will be attached to the case file.

APPENDIX 24 - CREATE EXHIBIT

EXHIBIT REFERENCE

The drop-down will be used to determine the existing exhibits, and when a new one is to be entered, it will be typed into the box and added to the case.

DESCRIPTION

The description of the exhibit.

CREATED BY

Typically, this will be the Forensic Analyst assigned to the case, and this is the default entered into the box. If another of the Forensic Analysts has created an exhibit, this must be recorded using the "Created by" drop-down box and selecting the relevant Forensic Analyst from the list.

DATE

This defaults to today's date, but if another date is required, then it can be inserted. This uses a drop-down calendar to change the date.

APPENDIX 25 - CASE RESULT

DEFENDANT

The name of the defendant.

COURT

The name of the Court where they are to appear.

DATE

The date that they are in Court. This defaults to today's date, but if another date is required, then it can be inserted. This uses a drop-down calendar to change the date.

COURT RESULT

The result from the Court from the drop-down—either "guilty" or "not guilty."

Custodial Sentence

The jail term in years, months, and days.

Suspended Sentence

The suspended term in years, months, and days.

Community Service

The community service in years, months, and days.

Fine

The fine in the form of the relevant local currency for the Forensic Laboratory (i.e., any values converted to the currency for the Forensic Laboratory's jurisdiction).

NOTES

Any notes to do with the defendant should be entered here.

ADD STATEMENT

If there are any relevant statements to be added, they can be scanned in then added to the case by pressing the "Add Statement" button and browsing to the selected file(s) in the folder. Click "OK" and the statement will be attached to the case file.

APPENDIX 26 - CASE BACKUP

TAPE

If a tape backup of the case is to be made, then the tape button should be checked.

Tape ID

The tape should be selected from the drop-down list of tapes available for backup next to "name."

Date

This defaults to today's date, but if another date is required, then it can be inserted. This uses a drop-down calendar to change the date.

DISK

Disk ID

The disk should be selected from the drop-down of disks available for backup next to "name."

Date

This defaults to today's date, but if another date is required then it can be inserted. This uses a drop-down calendar to change the date.

BACKUP TYPE

The backup type should be chosen using the relevant radio button. This will either be a backup of the:

- case image;
- worked case.

APPENDIX 27 - BILLING AND FEEDBACK

CHARGED

This defines who is to be billed for the case by using the radio button choice.

SATISFACTION

This defines who is to be sent the satisfaction survey for the case by using the radio button choice.

PRINT

This button actually prints the hard copy bill and satisfaction survey for the identified recipient(s). This can be canceled using the print facility in MS Word, if required.

APPENDIX 28 - FEEDBACK RECEIVED

COMMUNICATION

The Feedback Received from the Client about the case (marked 1-5 using the radio buttons).

SPEED OF DELIVERY

The Feedback Received from the Client about the case (marked 1-5 using the radio buttons).

QUALITY OF REPORT

The Feedback Received from the Client about the case (marked 1-5 using the radio buttons).

QUALITY OF RESULTS

The Feedback Received from the Client about the case (marked 1-5 using the radio buttons).

TIMELINESS OF DELIVERY

The Feedback Received from the Client about the case (marked 1-5 using the radio buttons).

SUPPORTING MATERIAL

The Feedback Received from the Client about the case (marked 1-5 using the radio buttons).

UNDERSTANDABILITY OF REPORT

The Feedback Received from the Client about the case (marked 1-5 using the radio buttons).

MEETING REQUIREMENTS

The Feedback Received from the Client about the case (marked 1-5 using the radio buttons).

NOTES

Any notes or comments from the Client to be associated with this feedback form.

APPENDIX 29 - ORGANIZATION REPORT

PAPER TYPE

Portrait.

SELECTION CRITERIA

None.

SORT ORDER

None.

REPORT HEADER

- Title "Organization Details"—top left-hand side;
- Logo—top right-hand side.

REPORT SUB-HEADER

Here, will be three subheaders as defined below and in the contents

- Organization;
- Unit or Department;
- Miscellaneous.

REPORT CONTENTS

Subheader—"Organization"

- Organization Name
- Address
- Postcode
- Phone
- Fax
- URL
- Vat Number
- Company registration
- Organization logo.

Subheader—"Unit or Department"

- Unit or Department name;
- Address;
- Postcode;
- Phone;
- Fax;
- Email Address;
- URL;
- Unit or Department Logo.

Subheader—"Miscellaneous"

- Report classification;
- Case Numbering information (start number);
- Copyright notice;
- Hard disk numbering start;
- Tape numbering start;
- Other media numbering start.

APPENDIX 30 - USERS REPORT

PAPER TYPE

Portrait.

SELECTION CRITERIA

Drop-down for user or "*" for all.

SORT ORDER

User name.

REPORT HEADER

- Title "Users"—top left-hand side;
- Logo—top right-hand side.

REPORT SUB-HEADER

User name (repeated for each different user).

REPORT CONTENTS

- User ID;
- Title;
- First Name;
- Surname;
- Address;
- Postcode;
- Phone;
- Mobile;
- Fax;
- Email;
- Access Rights (user or Administrator).

APPENDIX 31 - MANUFACTURERS REPORT

PAPER TYPE

Landscape.

SELECTION CRITERIA

Drop-down for manufacturer or "*" for all.

SORT ORDER

Manufacturer name.

REPORT HEADER

- "Manufacturers"—top left-hand side;
- Logo—top right-hand side.

REPORT SUB-HEADER

Manufacturer name (repeated for each different manufacturer).

REPORT CONTENTS

Multiple manufacturers on a page,

- Manufacturer name;
- Address;
- Postcode;
- Phone;
- Fax;
- URL;
- Email Address.

APPENDIX 32 - SUPPLIER REPORT

PAPER TYPE

Landscape.

SELECTION CRITERIA

Drop-down for supplier or "*" for all.

SORT ORDER

Supplier name.

REPORT HEADER

- "Suppliers"—top left-hand side;
- Logo—top right-hand side.

REPORT SUB-HEADER

Supplier name (repeated for each different supplier).

REPORT CONTENTS

Multiple suppliers on a page:

- Supplier name;
- Account Number;
- Address;
- Postcode;
- Phone;
- Fax;
- URL;
- Email Address;
- Contacts 1-5 (If no details in all—leave blank).

APPENDIX 33 - CLIENTS REPORT

PAPER TYPE

Landscape.

SELECTION CRITERIA

Drop-down for Clients or "*" for all.

SORT ORDER

Client Name.

REPORT HEADER

- "Clients"—top left-hand side;
- Logo—top right-hand side.

REPORT SUB-HEADER

- Client;
- Cases.

REPORT CONTENTS

Client subheading

- Client Name;
- Address;
- Postcode;
- Phone;
- Fax;
- URL;
- Email Address.

Cases subheading

- Case number(s);
- Case Name(s).

APPENDIX 34 - INVESTIGATOR'S REPORT

PAPER TYPE

Landscape.

SELECTION CRITERIA

Drop-down for investigators or "*" for all.

SORT ORDER

Investigator then case.

REPORT HEADER

- "Investigators"—top left-hand side;
- Logo—top right-hand side.

REPORT SUB-HEADER

- Investigator name;
- Cases.

REPORT CONTENTS

Investigator subheading

- Investigator;
- Client Name;
- Address;
- Postcode;
- Phone;
- Fax;

- URL;
- Email Address;
- Case Number(s);
- Case Name(s).

Cases subheading

- Case Number(s);
- Case Name(s).

APPENDIX 35 - DISKS BY ASSIGNMENT REPORT

PAPER TYPE

Portrait.

SELECTION CRITERIA

None.

SORT ORDER

Assignment order.

REPORT HEADER

- "Disks (By Assignment)"—top left-hand side;
- Logo—top right-hand side.

REPORT SUB-HEADER

None.

REPORT CONTENTS

- Assigned To;
- Date Assigned;
- Serial Number;
- Size (Gb);
- Supplier;
- Manufacturer;
- Model;
- Disk Label;
- Order Number.

APPENDIX 36 - DISKS BY REFERENCE NUMBER REPORT

PAPER TYPE

Portrait.

SELECTION CRITERIA

None.

SORT ORDER

Disk Reference Number.

REPORT HEADER

- "Disks (by reference)"—top left-hand side;
- Logo—top right-hand side.

REPORT SUB-HEADER

None.

REPORT CONTENTS

- Disk label;
- Date assigned;
- Assigned to;
- Serial Number;
- Size (Gb);
- Supplier;
- Manufacturer;
- Model;
- Order Number.

APPENDIX 37 - WIPED DISKS REPORT

PAPER TYPE

Landscape.

SELECTION CRITERIA

Start date and end date. The "start date" will be the earliest date any action was taken on the system, the "to date" will be today's date. If dates are to be changed then the pop up calendar will be used.

SORT ORDER

Date order and then disk reference.

REPORT HEADER

- "Disks wiped between '<Start Date>' and '<End Date>'"—top left-hand side;
- Logo—top right-hand side.

REPORT SUB-HEADER

None.

REPORT CONTENTS

- Date wiped;
- Disk label;
- Wiping method;

- Serial Number;
- Size (Gb);
- Supplier;
- Manufacturer;
- Model;
- Order Number.

APPENDIX 38 - DISPOSED DISKS REPORT

PAPER TYPE

Landscape.

SELECTION CRITERIA

Start date and end date. The "start date" will be the earliest date any action was taken on the system, the "to date" will be today's date. If dates are to be changed then the pop up calendar will be used.

SORT ORDER

Date order and then disk reference.

REPORT HEADER

- "Disks disposed of between " <Start Date> "and" <End Date>"—top left-hand side;
- Logo—top right-hand side.

REPORT SUB-HEADER

None.

REPORT CONTENTS

- Date disposed of;
- Disk label;
- Disposal method;
- Serial Number;
- Size (Gb);
- Supplier;
- Manufacturer;
- Model;
- Order Number.

APPENDIX 39 - DISK HISTORY REPORT

PAPER TYPE

Landscape.

SELECTION CRITERIA

Drop-down for disk number or "*" for all.

Start date and end date. The "start date" will be the earliest date any action was taken on the disk the "to date" will be today's date. If dates are to be changed then the pop up calendar will be used.

SORT ORDER

Disk number then date order if multiple disks chosen. If a single disk, then in date order.

REPORT HEADER

- "Disk history between " <Start Date> "and" <End Date>"—top left-hand side;
- Logo—top right-hand side.

REPORT SUB-HEADER

Disk reference.

REPORT CONTENTS

- Date of action;
- Assignment;
- Action by (including user status—user or Administrator);
- Tools or methods for action.

APPENDIX 40 - TAPES BY ASSIGNMENT REPORT

PAPER TYPE

Portrait.

SELECTION CRITERIA

None.

SORT ORDER

Assignment order.

REPORT HEADER

- Title "Tapes by Assignment"—top left-hand side;
- Logo—top right-hand side.

REPORT SUB-HEADER

None.

REPORT CONTENTS

- Assigned to;
- Date assigned;

- Serial Number;
- Size;
- Supplier;
- Manufacturer;
- Model;
- Reference;
- Order Number.

APPENDIX 41 - TAPES BY REFERENCE NUMBER REPORT

PAPER TYPE

Portrait.

SELECTION CRITERIA

None.

SORT ORDER

Reference Number

REPORT HEADER

- Title “Tapes by Reference Number” top left-hand side;
- Logo—top right-hand side.

REPORT SUB-HEADER

None.

REPORT CONTENTS

- Tape Reference Number;
- Date assigned;
- Assigned to;
- Size;
- Supplier;
- Manufacturer;
- Model;
- Reference;
- Supplier;
- Order Number.

APPENDIX 42 - WIPED TAPES REPORT

PAPER TYPE

Landscape.

SELECTION CRITERIA

Start date and end date. The “start date” will be the earliest date any action was taken on the system, the “to date” will be today’s date. If dates are to be changed then the pop up calendar will be used.

SORT ORDER

Date order and then tape reference.

REPORT HEADER

- “Tapes wiped between “<Start Date> “and” <End Date>”—top left-hand side;
- Logo—top right-hand side.

REPORT SUB-HEADER

None.

REPORT CONTENTS

- Date wiped;
- Tape label;
- Wiping method;
- Size (Gb);
- Supplier;
- Manufacturer;
- Model;
- Order Number.

APPENDIX 43 - DISPOSED TAPES REPORT

PAPER TYPE

Landscape.

SELECTION CRITERIA

Start date and end date. The “start date” will be the earliest date any action was taken on the system, the “to date” will be today’s date. If dates are to be changed then the pop up calendar will be used.

SORT ORDER

Date order and then tape order.

REPORT HEADER

- Title “Tapes Disposed of Between ‘ <Start Date>’ and ‘<End Date>’”—top left-hand side;
- Logo—top right-hand side.

REPORT SUB-HEADER

None.

REPORT CONTENTS

- Date disposed of;
- Tape reference;
- Disposal method;
- Disposed by;
- Notes.

APPENDIX 44 - TAPE HISTORY REPORT

PAPER TYPE

Landscape.

SELECTION CRITERIA

Drop-down for tape number or "*" for all.

Start date and end date. The "start date" will be the earliest date any action was taken on the disk the "to date" will be today's date. If dates are to be changed, then the pop up calendar will be used.

REPORT HEADER

- Title "Tape History Between '<From Date>' and '<To Date>'"—top left-hand side;
- Logo—top right-hand side.

REPORT SUB-HEADER

Tape Reference.

REPORT CONTENTS

- Date of action;
- Assignment;
- Action by (including user status—user or Administrator);
- Tools or methods for action.

APPENDIX 45 - SMALL DIGITAL MEDIA BY ASSIGNMENT REPORT

PAPER TYPE

Portrait.

SELECTION CRITERIA

None.

SORT ORDER

Assignment order.

REPORT HEADER

- Title "Small Digital Media by Assignment"—top left-hand side;
- Logo—top right-hand side.

REPORT SUB-HEADER

None.

REPORT CONTENTS

- Assigned to;
- Date assigned;
- Media type;
- Serial Number;
- Size;
- Supplier;
- Manufacturer;
- Model;
- Reference;
- Order Number.

APPENDIX 46 - SMALL DIGITAL MEDIA BY REFERENCE NUMBER REPORT

PAPER TYPE

Portrait.

SELECTION CRITERIA

None.

SORT ORDER

Reference Number

REPORT HEADER

- Title "Small Digital Media by Reference Number"—top left-hand side;
- Logo—top right-hand side.

REPORT SUB-HEADER

None.

REPORT CONTENTS

- Small digital media Reference Number;
- Date assigned;

- Assigned to;
- Size;
- Supplier;
- Manufacturer;
- Model;
- Reference;
- Supplier;
- Order Number.

APPENDIX 47 - WIPED SMALL DIGITAL MEDIA REPORT

PAPER TYPE

Landscape.

SELECTION CRITERIA

Start date and end date. The "start date" will be the earliest date any action was taken on the system, the "to date" will be today's date. If dates are to be changed, then the pop up calendar will be used.

SORT ORDER

Date order and then tape reference.

REPORT HEADER

- "Small Digital Media wiped between " <Start Date> "and" <End Date>"—top left-hand side;
- Logo—top right-hand side.

REPORT SUB-HEADER

None.

REPORT CONTENTS

- Date wiped;
- Media type;
- Small digital media label;
- Wiping method;
- Size (Gb);
- Supplier;
- Manufacturer;
- Model;
- Order Number.

APPENDIX 48 - DISPOSED SMALL DIGITAL MEDIA REPORT

PAPER TYPE

Landscape.

SELECTION CRITERIA

Start date and end date. The "start date" will be the earliest date any action was taken on the system, the "to date" will be today's date. If dates are to be changed, then the pop-up calendar will be used.

SORT ORDER

Date order and then small digital media order.

REPORT HEADER

- Title "Small Digital Media Disposed of between '<Start Date>' and '<End Date>'"—top left-hand side;
- Logo—top right-hand side.

REPORT SUB-HEADER

None.

REPORT CONTENTS

- Date disposed of;
- Small digital media reference;
- Disposal method;
- Disposed by;
- Notes.

APPENDIX 49 - SMALL DIGITAL MEDIA HISTORY REPORT

PAPER TYPE

Landscape.

SELECTION CRITERIA

Drop-down for small digital media number or "*" for all.

Start date and end date. The "start date" will be the earliest date any action was taken on the disk the "to date" will be today's date. If dates are to be changed, then the pop-up calendar will be used.

REPORT HEADER

- Title "Small Digital Media History between '<From Date>' and '<To Date>'"—top left-hand side;
- Logo—top right-hand side.

REPORT SUB-HEADER

Small digital media reference.

REPORT CONTENTS

- Date of action;
- Assignment;
- Action by (including user status—user or Administrator);
- Tools or methods for action.

APPENDIX 50 - WIPE METHODS REPORT

PAPER TYPE

Portrait.

SELECTION CRITERIA

None.

SORT ORDER

Wipe Method (alphabetical).

REPORT HEADER

- Title "Media Wiping Methods"—top left-hand side;
- Logo—top right-hand side.

REPORT SUB-HEADER

None.

REPORT CONTENTS

- Wiping method.

APPENDIX 51 - DISPOSAL METHODS REPORT

PAPER TYPE

Portrait.

SELECTION CRITERIA

None.

SORT ORDER

Disposal method (alphabetical).

REPORT HEADER

- Title "Disk Disposal Methods"—top left-hand side;
- Logo—top right-hand side.

REPORT SUB-HEADER

None.

REPORT CONTENTS

- Disposal method.

APPENDIX 52 - IMAGING METHODS REPORT

PAPER TYPE

Portrait.

SELECTION CRITERIA

None.

SORT ORDER

Imaging method (alphabetical).

REPORT HEADER

- Title "imaging methods"—top left-hand side;
- Logo—top right-hand side.

REPORT SUB-HEADER

None.

REPORT CONTENTS

- Imaging method.

APPENDIX 53 - OPERATING SYSTEMS REPORT

PAPER TYPE

Portrait.

SELECTION CRITERIA

None.

SORT ORDER

Operating system (alphabetical).

REPORT HEADER

- Title "Operating Systems"—top left-hand side;
- Logo—top right-hand side.

REPORT SUB-HEADER

None.

REPORT CONTENTS

Operating Systems.

APPENDIX 54 - MEDIA TYPES REPORT

PAPER TYPE

Portrait.

SELECTION CRITERIA

None.

SORT ORDER

Media Types (alphabetical).

REPORT HEADER

- Title "Media Types Processed"—top left-hand side;
- Logo—top right-hand side.

REPORT SUB-HEADER

None.

REPORT CONTENTS

- Media Types.

APPENDIX 55 - EXHIBIT TYPE REPORT

PAPER TYPE

Portrait.

SELECTION CRITERIA

None.

SORT ORDER

Exhibit Types (alphabetical).

REPORT HEADER

- Title "Exhibit Types Produced"—top left-hand side;
- Logo—top right-hand side.

REPORT SUB-HEADER

None.

REPORT CONTENTS

- Exhibit Types.

APPENDIX 56 - CASE SETUP DETAILS REPORT

PAPER TYPE

Portrait.

SELECTION CRITERIA

Drop-down for case number or "*" for all.

SORT ORDER

Case number.

REPORT HEADER

- Title "Case Setup Details"—top left-hand side;
- Logo—top right-hand side.

REPORT SUB-HEADER

- Case Number;
- Requirements;
- Exhibits.

REPORT CONTENTS

Case number subheading (from case setup menu):

- Case name (left-hand side);
- Case number (right-hand side);
- Client and address details (left-hand side);
- Investigator and address details (right-hand side);
- Any documents scanned in.

Requirements subheading (from Case Requirements Tab):

- Evidence Sought;
- Comments case (one under another);
- Any documents scanned in.

Exhibits subheading (from Exhibits tab):

For each Exhibit—it has the Exhibit Number as a sub-subheading then followed by the details about the exhibits in exhibit order (alphabetical). This will include:

- Exhibit Number;
- Seal Number;
- Description;
- Received By;
- Seized From;
- Received Date;
- Seized Date;
- Received Time;
- Time Seized;
- Insurance Value;
- Owner;
- Reason for Seizing;
- Password(s) Recovered—give them or "None";
- Connected—give details or "No";
- Switched on at seizure—give details or "No";
- Switched on after seizure—give details or "No";
- Any documents scanned in.

APPENDIX 57 - CASE MOVEMENT REPORT

PAPER TYPE

Landscape.

SELECTION CRITERIA

Drop-down for case number or "*" for all.

Start date and end date. The "start date" will be the earliest date any action was taken on the system, the "to date" will be today's date. If dates are to be changed then the pop up calendar will be used.

SORT ORDER

Case order then date (and time if used) within case.

REPORT HEADER

- Title "Exhibit Movements Between '<From date>' to '<To Date>'"—top left-hand side;
- Logo—top right-hand side.

REPORT SUB-HEADER

- Case number (case name).

REPORT CONTENTS

- Date of action;
- Exhibit ID;
- Laboratory Log ID number;
- Seal number;
- Movement type;
- User who moved the exhibit.

APPENDIX 58 - CASE COMPUTERS REPORT

PAPER TYPE

Portrait.

SORT ORDER

Case Number then Exhibit Number.

SELECTION CRITERIA

Drop-down for case number or "*" for all.

Start date and end date. The "start date" will be the earliest date any computer was received by the lab, the "to date" will be today's date. If dates are to be changed, then the pop up calendar will be used.

REPORT HEADER

- Title "Computer Exhibits Received Between '<From date>' to '<To Date>'"—top left-hand side;
- Logo—top right-hand side.

REPORT SUB-HEADER

- Case Details;
- Computer Details;
- BIOS Details.

REPORT CONTENTS

Each computer is printed on a separate page.

Case details subheader

- Case Name;
- Exhibit Number;
- Examined By;
- Examination Date.

Computer Details subheader

- Make;
- Model;
- Serial Number;
- 3½ drives;
- 5¼ drives;
- Zip drives;
- DVD readers;
- DVD rewriters;

- DVD readers;
- CD reads;
- CD rewriters;
- CD writers;
- RAM strips;
- Jazz drives;
- Graphics cards;
- AIT drives;
- DLT drives;
- QIC drives;
- SCSI cards;
- Other disk drives;
- Modem cards;
- Network cards;
- Other peripherals that exist if they are relevant;
- Notes.

BIOS details subheader

- BIOS key;
- BIOS password;
- System time;
- System date;
- Actual time;
- Actual date;
- Date difference;
- Time difference;
- Boot sequence;
- Operating system;
- Any photographs attached;
- Any documents scanned in.

APPENDIX 59 - CASE NON-COMPUTER EVIDENCE REPORT

PAPER TYPE

Portrait.

SORT ORDER

Case number then exhibit number.

SELECTION CRITERIA

Drop-down for case number or "*" for all.

Start date and end date. The "start date" will be the earliest date any computer was received by the lab, the "to date" will be today's date. If dates are to be changed then the pop up calendar will be used.

REPORT HEADER

- Title "Non-Computer Exhibits Received Between '<From date>' to '<To Date>'"—top left-hand side;
- Logo—top right-hand side.

REPORT SUB-HEADER

- Case details;
- <Exhibit Type>

REPORT CONTENTS

Each Non-Computer exhibit starts on a separate page.

Case details subheader

- Case name;
- Exhibit Number;
- Examined by;
- Examination Date.

<Exhibit Type> Subheader

- Make;
- Model;
- Serial Number;
- Notes;
- Any photographs attached;
- Any documents scanned in.

APPENDIX 60 - CASE DISKS RECEIVED REPORT

PAPER TYPE

Portrait.

SELECTION CRITERIA

Drop-down for case number or "*" for all.

Start date and end date. The "start date" will be the earliest date any computer was received by the lab, the "to date" will be today's date. If dates are to be changed then the pop up calendar will be used.

SORT ORDER

Case Number then Exhibit Number.

REPORT HEADER

- Title "Details for Disks Received Between '<From date>' to '<To Date>'"—top left-hand side;
- Logo—top right-hand side.

REPORT SUB-HEADER

- Case number;
- Computer details;
- Disk Exhibit Number.

REPORT CONTENTS

Case details subheader

- Case name;
- Case ID;
- Examined by;
- Examination date.

Computer Details subheader

- Make;
- Model;
- Serial Number;

Hard disk details subheader

- Make;
- Model;
- Serial Number;
- Heads;
- Cylinders;
- Sectors;
- Size;
- Jumper setting.

Image 1 sub-subheader—with Image 1 in Big Print

- Imaging method used;
- Blocker used;
- Operating system;
- Acquisition hash;
- Verification hash.

Image 2 sub-subheader

- Imaging method used;
- Blocker used;
- Operating system;
- Acquisition hash;
- Verification hash.

If there is no second imaging method used, then the fields will be blank.

- Any photographs attached;
- Any documents scanned in.

APPENDIX 61 - CASE OTHER MEDIA RECEIVED

PAPER TYPE

Portrait.

SELECTION CRITERIA

Drop-down for case number or "*" for all.

Start date and end date. The "start date" will be the earliest date any computer was received by the lab, the "to date" will be today's date. If dates are to be changed, then the pop up calendar will be used.

SORT ORDER

Case Number then Exhibit Number.

REPORT HEADER

- Title "Other Media Received Between '<From date>' to '<To Date>'"—top left-hand side;
- Logo—top right-hand side.

REPORT SUB-HEADER

- Case number;
- Disk Exhibit Number.

REPORT CONTENTS

Case details subheader

- Case name;
- Case ID;
- Examined by;
- Examination date.

Other media details subheader

- Make;
- Model;
- Serial Number

Other media details subheader

- Make;
- Model;
- Serial Number

Image 1 sub-subheader—with Image 1 in Big Print

- Imaging method used;
- Blocker used;
- Operating system;
- Acquisition hash;
- Verification hash.

Image 2 sub-subheader

- Imaging method used;
- Blocker used;
- Operating system;
- Acquisition hash;
- Verification Hash.

If there is no second imaging method used, then the fields will be blank.

- Any photographs attached;
- Any documents scanned in.

APPENDIX 62 - CASE EXHIBITS RECEIVED REPORT

PAPER TYPE

Portrait.

SELECTION CRITERIA

Drop-down for case number or "*" for all.

Start date and end date. The "start date" will be the earliest date any computer was received by the lab, the "to date" will be today's date. If dates are to be changed, then the pop-up calendar will be used.

SORT ORDER

Case number then exhibit order.

REPORT DESCRIPTION

This is a printout of the evidence received for selected cases received by the lab between two dates for examination.

REPORT HEADER

- Title "Exhibits Received Between '<From date>' to '<To Date>'"—top left-hand side;
- Logo—top right-hand side.

REPORT SUB-HEADER

None.

REPORT CONTENTS

- Case ID;
- Case name;
- Exhibit Number;
- Description;
- Any photographs attached;
- Any documents scanned in.

APPENDIX 63 - CASE WORK RECORD

PAPER TYPE

Portrait.

SELECTION CRITERIA

Drop-down for case number or "*" for all.

Start date and end date. The "start date" will be the earliest date any exhibit was produced in the lab, the "to date" will be today's date. If dates are to be changed, then the pop-up calendar will be used.

SORT ORDER

Case number then date.

REPORT DESCRIPTION

This is a printout of the work performed on a given case or cases between two dates.

REPORT HEADER

- Title "Work Performed Between '<From date>' to '<To Date>'"—top left-hand side;
- Logo—top right-hand side.

REPORT SUB-HEADER

- Case ID.

REPORT CONTENTS

- Case ID;
- Case name;
- Date;
- Work performed;
- User name;
- Hours.

APPENDIX 64 - CASES REJECTED REPORT

PAPER TYPE

Portrait.

SELECTION CRITERIA

All cases where the case was rejected—i.e., where the "Rejected" box is ticked.

Start date and end date. The "start date" will be the earliest date any case was rejected and the "to date" will be today's date. If dates are to be changed, then the pop-up calendar will be used.

SORT ORDER

Case Number order.

REPORT HEADER

- Title "Cases Rejected Between '<From Date>' and '<To Date>'"—top left-hand side;
- Logo—top right-hand side.

REPORT SUB-HEADER

None.

REPORT CONTENTS

- Case Number;
- Date rejected;
- Rejected by;
- Date Client advised;
- Who was advised;
- How they were advised;
- Reasons for rejection—if this goes over a line on the report then the output should go into multiple lines left aligned for the field;
- Copy of any documents scanned in.

APPENDIX 65 - CASES ACCEPTED

PAPER TYPE

Portrait.

SELECTION CRITERIA

All cases where the case was accepted—i.e., where the "Accepted" box is ticked.

Start date and end date. The "start date" will be the earliest date any case was rejected and the "to date" will be today's date. If dates are to be changed, then the pop-up calendar will be used.

SORT ORDER

Case Number order.

REPORT HEADER

- Title "Cases Accepted Between '<From Date>' and '<To Date>'"—top left-hand side;
- Logo—top right-hand side.

REPORT SUB-HEADER

None.

REPORT CONTENTS

- Case Number;
- Date accepted;
- Accepted by;
- Date Client advised;
- Who was advised;
- How they were advised;
- Copy of any documents scanned in.

APPENDIX 66 - CASE ESTIMATES REPORT

PAPER TYPE

Portrait.

SELECTION CRITERIA

Drop-down for case number or "*" for all.

Start date and end date. The "start date" will be the earliest date any action was taken on the system, the "to date" will be today's date. If dates are to be changed, then the pop-up calendar will be used.

SORT ORDER

By case then by date.

REPORT HEADER

- Title "Case Estimates"—top left-hand side;
- Logo—top right-hand side.

REPORT SUB-HEADER

- Case Number.

REPORT CONTENTS

- Date;
- Misc;
- Hardware;
- Analysis;
- Report;
- Total.

APPENDIX 67 - CASES BY FORENSIC ANALYST

PAPER TYPE

Portrait.

SELECTION CRITERIA

Drop-down for Forensic Analyst or "*" for all.

Start date and end date. The "start date" will be the earliest date any exhibit was produced in the lab, the "to date" will be today's date. If dates are to be changed then the pop up calendar will be used.

SORT ORDER

Forensic Analyst then date.

REPORT HEADER

- Title "Case Assignments Between '<From date>' to '<To Date>'"—top left-hand side;
- Logo—top right-hand side.

REPORT SUB-HEADER

- <Forensic Analyst>.

REPORT CONTENTS

- Case name;
- Case ID;
- Date started;
- Target Date;
- Days to Target Date (if past then printed in red);
- Status.

APPENDIX 68 - CASES BY CLIENT REPORT

PAPER TYPE

Portrait.

SELECTION CRITERIA

Drop-down for Client or "*" for all.

Start date and end date. The "start date" will be the earliest date any exhibit was produced in the lab, the "to date" will be today's date. If dates are to be changed, then the pop up calendar will be used.

SORT ORDER

Client then date.

REPORT HEADER

- Title "Case Assignments Between '<From date>' to '<To Date>'"—top left-hand side;
- Logo—top right-hand side.

REPORT SUB-HEADER

- Client.

REPORT CONTENTS

- Case name;
- Case ID;
- Date started;
- Target Date;
- Days to Target Date (if past then printed in red);
- Status.

APPENDIX 69 - CASES BY INVESTIGATOR REPORT

PAPER TYPE

Portrait.

SELECTION CRITERIA

Drop-down for Investigator or "*" for all.

Start date and end date. The "start date" will be the earliest date any exhibit was produced in the lab, the "to date" will be today's date. If dates are to be changed, then the pop-up calendar will be used.

SORT ORDER

Investigator then date.

REPORT DESCRIPTION

This is a printout of the cases that an Investigator has or is working between two dates.

REPORT HEADER

- Title "Case Assignments Between '<From date> to '<To Date>'"—top left-hand side;
- Logo—top right-hand side.

REPORT SUB-HEADER

- Investigator.

REPORT CONTENTS

- Case name;
- Case ID;
- Date started;
- Target Date;
- Days to Target Date (date if past then printed in red);
- Status.

APPENDIX 70 - CASE TARGET DATES REPORT

PAPER TYPE

Portrait.

SELECTION CRITERIA

Drop-down for case number or "*" for all.

This is only for cases currently open.

SORT ORDER

Case Number.

REPORT HEADER

- Title "Case Target Dates"—top left-hand side;
- Logo—top right-hand side.

REPORT SUB-HEADER

None.

REPORT CONTENTS

- Case Number;
- User assigned;
- Date Received;
- Target Date;
- Days remaining (if past then printed in red).

APPENDIX 71 - CASES WITHIN *"X"* DAYS OF TARGET DATE REPORT

PAPER TYPE

Portrait.

SELECTION CRITERIA

Entry field for number of days prior to Target Date for report.

This is only for cases currently open.

SORT ORDER

By days closest to Target Date.

REPORT HEADER

- Title "Case Target Dates with '<*x*>' 'Days or less to Target Date'"—top left-hand side;
- Logo—top right-hand side.

REPORT SUB-HEADER

None.

REPORT CONTENTS

- Case Number;
- User assigned;
- Date Received;
- Target Date;
- Days remaining (if past then printed in red).

APPENDIX 72 - CASES PAST TARGET DATE REPORT

PAPER TYPE

Portrait.

SELECTION CRITERIA

This is only for cases currently open.

SORT ORDER

By days past Target Date.

REPORT DESCRIPTION

This is a printout of the cases past Target Date.

REPORT HEADER

- Title "Cases Past Target Date"—top left-hand side;
- Logo—top right-hand side.

REPORT SUB-HEADER

None.

REPORT CONTENTS

- Case Number;
- User assigned;
- Date Received;
- Target Date;
- Days past Target Date.

APPENDIX 73 - CASES UNASSIGNED REPORT

PAPER TYPE

Portrait.

SELECTION CRITERIA

Any case that has not got a currently assigned Forensic Analyst.

SORT ORDER

Case number.

REPORT HEADER

- Title "Cases Currently Unassigned"—top left-hand side;
- Logo—top right-hand side.

REPORT SUB-HEADER

None.

REPORT CONTENTS

- Case name;
- Case ID;
- Date started;
- Target Date;
- Days to Target Date (if past then printed in red).

APPENDIX 74 - CASE EXHIBITS PRODUCED REPORT

PAPER TYPE

Portrait.

SELECTION CRITERIA

Drop-down for case number or "*" for all.

Start date and end date. The "start date" will be the earliest date any exhibit was produced in the lab, the "to date" will be today's date. If dates are to be changed, then the pop-up calendar will be used.

SORT ORDER

Case number then exhibits produced.

REPORT HEADER

- Title "Exhibits Created Between '<From date>' to '<To Date>'"—top left-hand side;
- Logo—top right-hand side.

REPORT SUB-HEADER

- Case details;
- Exhibit Details.

REPORT CONTENTS

Case details subheader

- Case name;
- Case ID;

Exhibit Details subheader

- Exhibit Number;
- Description;
- Created by;
- Any photographs attached;
- Any documents scanned in.

APPENDIX 75 - CASE RESULTS REPORT

PAPER TYPE

Portrait.

SELECTION CRITERIA

Drop-down for case number or "*" for all.

Start date and end date. The "start date" will be the earliest date any exhibit was produced in the lab, the "to date" will be today's date. If dates are to be changed, then the pop-up calendar will be used.

SORT ORDER

Case then Date.

REPORT HEADER

- Title "Case Results '<From date>' to '<To Date>'"—top left-hand side;
- Logo—top right-hand side.

REPORT SUB-HEADER

- Case ID;
- Defendant(s).

REPORT CONTENTS

Case ID subheader

- Case name;
- Case ID.

Defendant ID subheader

- Defendant;
- Date;
- Court;
- Jail;
- Suspended;

- Community Service;
- Fine;
- Notes.

APPENDIX 76 - CASE BACKUPS REPORT

PAPER TYPE

Portrait.

SELECTION CRITERIA

Drop-down for Case ID or "*" for all.

Start date and end date. The "start date" will be the earliest date any exhibit was produced in the lab, the "to date" will be today's date. If dates are to be changed, then the pop-up calendar will be used.

SORT ORDER

Case number order.

REPORT HEADER

- Title "Case Backups Between '<From date>' to '<To Date>'"—top left-hand side;
- Logo—top right-hand side.

REPORT SUB-HEADER

- Case ID;
- Backups.

REPORT CONTENTS

Case ID subheader

- Case name;
- Case ID.

Backups subheader

- Date;
- Backup media type (disk or tape);
- Media name (disk or type ID);
- Backup Type (Image or Case).

APPENDIX 77 - BILLING RUN REPORT

PAPER TYPE

Portrait.

SELECTION CRITERIA

Drop-down for case or "*" for all.

The details recorded for the billing run will be those from the last work billed.

Billing date is defaulted to today's date but if dates are to be changed then the pop up calendar shall be used. This means that the bills produced will cover from last unbilled information to the billing date.

SORT ORDER

None.

REPORT HEADER

- Title "Work Performed Between '<From date>' and '<To Date>'"—top left-hand side;
- Logo—top right-hand side.

REPORT SUB-HEADER

- Case ID—case name.

REPORT CONTENTS

- Date;
- Work performed;
- User name;
- Hours.

APPENDIX 78 - FEEDBACK LETTERS

PAPER TYPE

Portrait.

SELECTION CRITERIA

Drop-down for case number or "*" for all.

Start date and end date. The "start date" will be the earliest date any action was taken on the system, the "to date" will be today's date. If dates are to be changed, then the pop-up calendar will be used.

The case must be closed to have a feedback letter sent. This is determined by having something in the "Court Result" filed in the "Results" tab. If there are no letters to send out, then a message to this effect is displayed on screen rather than the page counter.

SORT ORDER

Case Number order.

REPORT DESCRIPTION

This will be a letter asking for feedback on a given case or cases.

REPORT HEADER

- Title "Case Feedback Form";
- Logo—top right-hand side.

REPORT SUB-HEADER

None.

REPORT CONTENTS

- The Letter (template attached);
- The Form;
- The letter will contain input from the following fields:
  - Forensic Laboratory Address;
  - System Date;
  - Investigator Name;
  - Investigator Address;
  - Case name;
  - Forensic Laboratory Reference Number.

APPENDIX 79 - FEEDBACK FORMS PRINTOUT

PAPER TYPE

Portrait.

SELECTION CRITERIA

Drop-down for case number or "*" for all.

Start date and end date. The "start date" will be the earliest date any action was taken on the system, the "to date" will be today's date. If dates are to be changed, then the pop-up calendar will be used.

REPORT CONTENTS

- The two pages of scanned feedback form.

REPORT HEADER

- N/A.

REPORT FOOTER

- N/A.

REPORT ORDER

Case order.

APPENDIX 80 - FEEDBACK REPORTING SUMMARY BY CASE

PAPER TYPE

Landscape.

SELECTION CRITERIA

Drop-down for case number or "*" for all.

Start date and end date. The "start date" will be the earliest date any action was taken on the system, the "to date" will be today's date. If dates are to be changed, then the pop-up calendar will be used.

SORT ORDER

Case Number.

REPORT HEADER

- Title "Case Feedback Summary";
- Logo—top right-hand side.

REPORT SUB-HEADER

None.

REPORT CONTENTS

- Case Number;
- User that the case is assigned to currently;
- Client;
- Communication Score;
- Speed Score;
- Quality Score;
- Timeliness Score;
- Accompanying Material Score;
- Understandability Score;
- Meeting Requirements Score.

APPENDIX 81 - FEEDBACK REPORTING SUMMARY BY FORENSIC ANALYST

PAPER TYPE

Landscape.

SELECTION CRITERIA

Drop-down for user or "*" for all.

Start date and end date. The "start date" will be the earliest date any action was taken on the system, the "to date" will be today's date. If dates are to be changed, then the pop-up calendar will be used.

SORT ORDER

User then Case Number.

REPORT DESCRIPTION

This will be a report showing Feedback Received for cases by Case Number for each Forensic Analyst between two dates.

REPORT HEADER

- Title "Case Feedback Summary by Forensic Analyst";
- Logo—top right-hand side.

REPORT SUB-HEADER

Forensic Analysts name (converted from User ID).

REPORT CONTENTS

- Case Number;
- Client;
- Communication Score;
- Speed Score;
- Quality Score;
- Timeliness Score;
- Accompanying Material Score;
- Understandability Score;
- Meeting Requirements Score.

APPENDIX 82 - FEEDBACK REPORTING SUMMARY BY CLIENT

PAPER TYPE

Landscape.

SELECTION CRITERIA

Drop-down for a Client or "*" for all.

Start date and end date. The "start date" will be the earliest date any action was taken on the system, the "to date" will be today's date. If dates are to be changed, then the pop-up calendar will be used.

SORT ORDER

Client then Case Number.

REPORT HEADER

- Title "Case Feedback Summary";
- Logo—top right-hand side.

REPORT SUB-HEADER

- Client Name.

REPORT CONTENTS

- Case Number;
- User case is assigned to currently;
- Communication Score;
- Speed Score;
- Quality Score;
- Timeliness Score;
- Accompanying Material Score;
- Understandability Score;
- Meeting Requirements Score.

APPENDIX 83 - COMPLETE CASE REPORT

PAPER TYPE

Portrait and portrait where appropriate.

SELECTION CRITERIA

Drop-down for Case ID or "*" for all.

REPORT DESCRIPTION

This is a printout of the complete case.

It will be made up of previous reports that are defined above.

REPORT HEADER

- Title "Complete Case Report for '<Case ID>'"—top left-hand side;
- Logo—top right-hand side.

REPORT SUB-HEADER

- Each of the titles of the previous reports with their sub-headers included.

REPORT CONTENTS

The contents of the following reports (already defined in the text):

- Case requirements;
- Case movements;
- Computer Details;
- Other media details;
- Disk details;
- Other media details;

- Work Record;
- Exhibits produced;
- Case Results;
- Case feedback;
- Case Backups.

APPENDIX 84 - PROCESSED REPORT

PAPER TYPE

Portrait.

SELECTION CRITERIA

Drop-down for examiner or "*" for all.

Start date and end date. The "start date" will be the earliest date for the media processed in the lab, the "to date" will be today's date. If dates are to be changed, then the pop-up calendar will be used.

REPORT HEADER

- Title "Work Performed Between '<From date>' to '<To Date>'"—top left-hand side;
- Logo—top right-hand side.

REPORT SUB-HEADER

- Exhibits processed;
- Media processed;
- Hours worked;
- Court results.

REPORT CONTENTS

Exhibits processed subheader

- List of exhibits.

Media processed subheader

- Disks;
- Other media.

Hours worked subheader

- Hours worked.

Court results subheader

- Court results.

APPENDIX 85 - INSURANCE REPORT

PAPER TYPE

Portrait.

SELECTION CRITERIA

None.

SORT ORDER

Case number then evidence number.

REPORT HEADER

- Title "Insurance Listing for Exhibits" top left-hand side;
- Logo—top right-hand side.

REPORT CONTENTS

- Case name;
- Case ID;
- Exhibit Number;
- Description;
- Value;
- Automatic total of values.

REPORT ORDER

Exhibit order within cases.

Chapter 11

Evidence Presentation

Table of Contents

11.1 OVERVIEW

Note

This is not an attempt at providing legal guidance, but the experiences that the authors have had in testimony in Courts and tribunals. This is purely as seen from the authors' view of presentation of evidence, reports, and testimony and studiously attempts to avoid any legal issues as these are left to the Lawyers in the Legal Team on the case.

After completing the processing of a forensic case, the Forensic Analyst will have to present their findings to the Client. This is usually in the form of a report but can require Court attendance.

The Forensic Analyst may, depending on jurisdiction, be regarded as an "Expert Witness."

Other Forensic Laboratory employees may have to give evidence if they have been involved in the case (e.g., the First Responder, the imager, and the Forensic Analyst undertaking the analysis of the evidence if they are different people, and possibly the Laboratory Manger to testify about tool validation).

It is essential that the forensic processing of a case is not let down by the evidence presentation.

Whatever presentation is required by the Client, it must be based on sound (and best) evidence, as defined in Chapter 8, Section 8.2, Chapter 9 Section 9.1.5, and Chapter 9, Section 9.10.4. This is why it is essential to ensure that all actions regarding the evidence are recorded and the Forensic Analysts are competent.

All Forensic Analysts must be taught to believe that credibility is believability and that the reputation of the Forensic Laboratory depends on this, so they must all be competent in presenting their testimony.

11.2 NOTES

During forensic case processing, all those involved in the processing the case will make a number of notes, these can include, but not be limited to:

- drawings;
- filling in Forensic Laboratory checklists;
- filling in Forensic Laboratory forms;
- personal notebooks;
- photographs;
- sketches.

Notes are made for a variety of different reasons. Some examples of the different types of notes and their selected audiences are given below.

11.2.1 Notes for the Forensic Analyst

These are typically notes made by a Forensic Analyst that record their own actions during processing a forensic case. These are made contemporaneously and are used to provide records of actions, as defined in Chapter 4, Section 4.6.4. These are primarily used by the Forensic Analyst as the basis for writing reports, statements, and depositions, as they record actions taken at the time. They are also used for refreshing memory, where permitted, when giving testimony or at meetings with other forensic experts as part of the case.

11.2.2 Notes for Colleagues

These are the same as those for the Forensic Analyst, but their purpose is different. These notes are there so that any report produced by the Forensic Analyst can be peer reviewed by other Forensic Laboratory employees to ensure that the opinions given or conclusions reached are sound and based on the processing of the case. These are also used if a new Forensic Analyst needs to take over processing a case where the original Forensic Analyst is not available for any reason.

11.2.3 Notes for the Case

These are the same as those for the Forensic Analyst, but their purpose is different. These are to record the actions taken by the Forensic Analyst so that the "other side" can see what actions were taken and be able to repeat the actions and produce the same results. It is also necessary for all involved in the case to understand why any opinions are formed or conclusions were reached. It also allows anyone involved in the case to see exactly what actions were taken and also what actions were omitted.

11.2.4 Note Taking

The taking of notes in forensic case processing in the Forensic Laboratory is a personal matter for the Forensic Analyst, but within the structure set by the procedures set by the Forensic Laboratory. Within the Forensic Laboratory, notes must:

- be available to back up any reports, statements, or depositions made as well as opinions made or conclusions reached;
- be made contemporaneously;
- be signed and dated by the Forensic Laboratory employee making them;
- be readable.

These notes are there so that any report produced by the Forensic Laboratory can be backed up by contemporaneous notes.

11.3 EVIDENCE

The rules for admissibility of evidence are governed by the laws of the jurisdiction of the Court or tribunal where the evidence is to be introduced. For this reason, among others, it is essential that all Forensic Laboratory employees connected to a case are fully familiar with these requirements and comply with them.

The rules are typically defined as "the Rules of Evidence" for the jurisdiction. These vary between jurisdictions and types of Court or tribunal.

11.3.1 Rules of Evidence

The Rules of Evidence will vary with the jurisdiction and as such, only generic advice can be given here. There are, however, some widely accepted standards and norms that are used, for example, the Daubert standard which is a rule of evidence regarding the admissibility of an Expert Witnesses' testimony during U.S. federal legal proceedings, as defined in Chapter 1, Section 1.1.6. The Daubert standard looks at the scientific "soundness" of the processes and procedures that have been used in the case to determine whether they are acceptable.

Some different Rules of Evidence include:

- Australia—Federal Court Rules;
- UK—Criminal Procedure Rules (2012)—specifically Parts 27-36;
- UK Civil Procedure Rules—specifically Part 35;
- the USA—Federal Rules of Evidence (FRE)—specifically Article V11, Sections 701-706.

It is of note that in the United states there are the FRE, but many states have adopted their own sets of rules, some of which differ from, and some of which are identical to, the FRE.

The Rules of Evidence cover such matters as:

- basis of opinion testimony;
- contents of reports;
- Court powers over Experts;
- different types of Expert and their duties;
- disclosure;
- discussion between Experts;
- qualifications of Experts;
- testimony.

The exact details of the contents of the Rules of Evidence will vary between the different jurisdictions, but the above are some of the common areas covered.

11.3.2 Authenticity of Evidence

In general terms, all evidence presented for a case must be authenticated, which typically means that a Witness testifies to its authenticity either in the form or a statement or deposition and/or by giving oral testimony. This could be from:

- the First Responder, who seized it;
- the Evidence Custodian, who logged it in and out;
- the Forensic Analyst that imaged it;
- the Forensic Analyst that analyzed it;
- anyone else that was involved in the Chain of Custody or processing the case, including the owner of the seized equipment or data.

In some cases, it is not necessary to authenticate evidence as it is accepted as being authentic according to the Rules of Evidence in force for the jurisdiction or both sides agree to accept it as authentic. It will vary between jurisdictions as to what is accepted without the need for authentication through testimony.

It is essential when preparing for any Court or tribunal hearing that the Forensic Laboratory ensures that the relevant Witnesses are able to testify to the existence and validity of the evidence produced, describe how it was discovered, maintain its Chain of Custody, and verify that it has not been tampered with.

11.3.3 Evidence Handling

Different jurisdictions have different requirements for digital evidence handling procedures; some of these are defined in Chapter 1, Section 1.1.6. This is not a definitive list. In Europe, the Budapest Convention on Cybercrime was the first international treaty seeking to address computer crime and Internet crimes by harmonizing national laws, improving investigative techniques, and increasing cooperation among nations. This has met with success, and while it is an European initiative, a number of other nations have ratified it, and as at the time of writing, these are given in Appendix 1.

11.3.4 Admissibility of Evidence

Again this will depend on the jurisdiction and the Court or tribunal and so it is essential that Forensic Laboratory understands these requirements and complies with them.

They generally include the requirements for the evidence to be:

- credible: believable within the confines of the case;
- material: it substantiates an issue that may be in question relating to the case;
- obtained legally: the issue of fruits of the poisonous tree is defined in Chapter 8, Section 8.1.2.
- relevant: proving a point in the case;
- reliable: showing that the source of the evidence makes it reliable, including ensuring the Chain of Custody.

While the Rules of Evidence vary in different jurisdictions, the Forensic Laboratory must always strive to, not only meet the requirements but, exceed them. This approach reduces the chance of any evidence being ruled as "inadmissible" and also demonstrates professional competence. As defined in Chapter 9, Section 9.1.5, the Forensic Laboratory should meet the requirements of ACPO, IASIS, G8, and IOCE.

Evidence derived from the original evidence seized or supplied (e.g., a printout, display, or product of the imaging and analysis) that becomes an exhibit, as defined in Chapter 9, Section 9.14, must also have a Chain of Custody associated with it. The Forensic Analyst that produced it in the Court or tribunal must formally produce the exhibit and give testimony to support its admissibility.

Depending on the jurisdiction, "hearsay" evidence may be admitted, but care must be taken with this.

11.3.5 Types of Evidence

There are a number of different types of evidence that can be produced at a Court or tribunal and the Rules of Evidence apply to them all. The Forensic Laboratory must ensure that it knows the Rules of Evidence for them all and complies with them for the jurisdiction. Types of evidence from processing a digital forensic case can include but are not be limited to:

- *derived*: a representation of "Best Evidence" that can be used to illustrate how opinions may be derived and conclusions drawn. This can use number of different media and must meet the Rules of Evidence in the jurisdiction. Some examples are defined in Section 11.3.1;
- *documents*: a business record that can be authenticated and produced in admissible evidence;
- *evidentiary*: statements of fact from a Forensic Laboratory employee who has been involved in a case but is not an Expert Witness;
- *expert*: opinions and conclusions of an Expert Witness;
- *real*: an actual physical piece of evidence that can be produced and examined in the Court or tribunal, typically "Best Evidence";
- *testimony*: the contemporaneous recollections of a Witness to some action that is relevant to the case.

11.3.6 Weight of Evidence

Once the admissibility of evidence has been addressed, its weight can be considered. Weight of evidence relates to the value that the evidence brings to the case, and it is accepted that this is a subjective measure, especially when dealing with a Jury.

The relevant attributes of evidence include, but are not limited to:

- *accurate*: based on facts that are demonstrable, including Forensic Laboratory procedures that are explainable by a Forensic Laboratory employee. This may also require details of the validation of the methods or tools used, as defined in Chapter 7, Section 7.5.5;
- *authenticity*: specifically linked to the case;
- *complete*: in as much as it tells the complete "history" of an item of evidence.

11.3.7 Evidential Continuity

This is also known as the Chain of Custody and has been defined in Chapter 8, Section 8.6.4. It is essential that the Forensic Laboratory is able to accurately state everything that has happened to the exhibit from its original acquisition to it being exhibited in the Court or tribunal, and who was accountable and responsible for it during that time. Typically, this will entail statements, checklists, pocket books, photographs, etc., from, as appropriate:

- the First Responder seizing it;
- the First Responder taking pictures of, and sketching, the incident scene;
- the on site Exhibit Custodian;
- the First Responder transporting it back to the Forensic Laboratory Secure Property Store;
- the Evidence Custodian at the Secure Property Store signing the exhibit(s) in and out;
- the Forensic Analyst(s) carrying out the initial examination;
- the Forensic Analyst(s) performing the imaging;
- the Forensic Analyst(s) undertaking the first-stage examination;
- the Forensic Analyst(s) undertaking the second-stage and subsequent examinations;
- the Forensic Analyst(s) conveying the exhibit(s) to the Court or tribunal;
- the Evidence Custodian at the Court or tribunal who safely stores it;
- the Forensic Analyst(s) who create exhibits derived from the original evidence, as defined in Chapter 9, Section 9.14;
- any other person who has had custody of the exhibit or handled it for any reason or even the Forensic Analyst who validated the tool or method as defined in Chapter 7, Section 7.5.5.

The whole Chain of Custody process is designed to ensure the integrity of the evidence and reduce the opportunity of contamination.

11.3.8 Issues with Digital Evidence

There are different issues with digital evidence to other types of physical evidence that are encountered by the Forensic Laboratory when processing a digital forensic case. Issues relating to evidence volatility have been covered in Chapter 8, Section 8.6.18.2. Other challenges facing the Forensic Laboratory and the Forensic Analysts processing cases for their Clients are defined in Chapter 20.

11.4 TYPES OF WITNESS

However, the Forensic Analyst has to present the evidence from processing a case; the physical and intangible evidence must be supported by some testimony, whether it is written or oral.

In the Forensic Laboratory all cases handled are always regarded as a possible criminal case and the relevant rules for criminal evidence production must be followed.

Note

A Forensic Laboratory Analyst may be an Evidentiary Witness or an Expert Witness, depending on the Client's requirements and the Court or tribunal's acceptance of the evidence.

11.4.1 An Evidentiary Witness

An "Evidentiary Witness" (depending on the jurisdiction) is someone who has direct knowledge of a forensic case processed by the Forensic Laboratory. Evidentiary Witnesses can only report on, or testify, to what they saw, heard, or did (i.e., facts). They are often referred to as Witnesses of Fact. They cannot give authoritative opinions or draw conclusions from what they observed or did (e.g., a Forensic Analyst who only imaged a disk cannot give an opinion on the evidence contained on it, only how the imaging was done and the image was verified).

In some jurisdictions, this is called a "Non-testifying Expert Consultant," but advice must be taken to ascertain the status of all claimed Experts within the jurisdiction.

11.4.2 An Expert Witness

An "Expert Witness" is different from an Evidentiary Witness in that they can give opinions or draw conclusions about a forensic case processed by the Forensic Laboratory. The interesting thing about an Expert Witness is that they may have had no involvement in the processing of the forensic case but they have a special technical expertise or knowledge that qualifies them to draw conclusions or give opinions on technical matters. Often, an Expert Witness can prepare a report on their opinions and conclusions, giving reasons for those opinions and conclusions.

An Expert Witness can be a Forensic Laboratory employee (typically the Forensic Analyst processing the case) or may be an external Expert Witness chosen specifically for the case, as defined in Chapter 9, Section 9.10.6.

Where an external Expert Witness is to be selected, careful consideration of their suitability must be undertaken, and some guidance is given in Appendix 2 for the selection of an external Expert Witness. Obviously, the same standards will apply, as appropriate, to Forensic Laboratory employees that perform an Expert Witness role.

Within the Forensic Laboratory, a code of conduct for employees acting as Expert Witnesses has been developed and should be implemented and this is given in Appendix 3.

Note

Within some jurisdictions, an Expert Witness can act as an Advocate, and in others, this is not permitted. A thorough understanding of the legislative and procedural requirements of the jurisdiction is essential and must be complied with.

11.4.3 Single Joint Expert Witnesses

In some cases, a Single Joint Expert Witness may be appointed. A Single Joint Expert Witness represents both parties, rather than each party having their own appointed Expert Witness(es). A Single Joint Expert Witness must show transparency and fairness to both, or all, parties that they represent.

11.4.4 Court-Appointed Expert Witnesses

In some cases, a Judge will direct an Expert Witness to act for the parties. Typically, the Expert Witness will be drawn from a list of suitable candidates. The reasons for this vary but may include situations where the party's Expert Witnesses are in dispute and a single authoritative view is required of the interpretation of the evidence.

11.4.5 Experts not Acting as Expert Witnesses

There are times that a Forensic Analyst, or other Forensic Laboratory employee, may be required to act as an Expert, but not act as an Expert or Evidentiary Witness. In these cases, they are asked to perform tasks such as explaining technical aspects of a case in layman's terms, reviewing statements and evidence presented to identify any anomalies and suggest questions relating to them. In situations like this, the Expert is used more as a Consultant and, as they never provide sworn evidence, is generally unknown to a Court or tribunal.

In other cases, the Expert may be present in a Court or tribunal and provide information on the evidence that a Witness provides as part of their testimony or suggest questions that may be asked as part of the cross-examination process, but not give formal testimony.

11.4.6 Overriding Duty

The overriding duty of an Expert Witness is to assist the Court in the interpretation of the evidence and not the party that pays or instructs them.

11.4.7 Codes of Conduct for Expert Witnesses

Different jurisdictions will have different requirements for their Expert Witnesses, and typically professional bodies for Expert Witnesses will have their own Codes of Conduct. However, these are not always consistent and not directly relevant to the presentation of digital evidence. The Code of Conduct that has been developed and should be applied to any employee giving evidence, in any form, is given in Appendix 3.

11.4.8 Code of Conduct for Evidentiary Witnesses

The Code of Practice for Expert Witnesses, referred to above, is also applied to Evidentiary Witnesses apart from those parts not relevant (i.e., giving opinions and drawing conclusions).

11.4.9 Different Jurisdictions

Different jurisdictions will treat Witnesses in accordance with their own Rules of Evidence and procedures and any Witness must be aware of these requirements before giving evidence.

11.5 REPORTS

11.5.1 General

The writing of the report is one of the most important tasks that is undertaken in the Forensic Laboratory. This may seem a strong statement to make, but in reality, the quality of the reports that are produced by the Forensic Laboratory is not only the "shop window" to the work that is done but is also fundamental in representing all of the forensic processing that has taken place in the case. The report represents a written statement of the findings of the Forensic Analyst(s) processing the case.

The process for producing a report is defined Chapter 4, Section 4.6.3 and for external reports is defined in Chapter 9, Section 9.15 with a standard template for report production given in Chapter 6, Appendix 31. Different jurisdictions will have specific requirements for report production and these must be understood and met.

Whatever the specific requirements for report production, a good report will be clear, well organized, concise, and accurate; it must be:

- *admissible*: the report should be written in the format that may be prescribed within the jurisdiction or should follow good practice;
- *concise*: the report must tell the complete story in as few words as possible. After preparing the first draft of the report, it will be revised, probably a number of times, to eliminate redundant or unnecessary material and add additional findings. This process is defined in Chapter 4, Section 4.6.3.4.3;
- *accurate*: the report must clearly record or reference all of the relevant findings and observations. Information obtained during case processing should be validated through the use of as many sources as are necessary. All of the material presented in the report should be able to be substantiated from the evidence available. The report should not contain any opinions or views of the Forensic Analyst, unless they are acting as Expert Witnesses for the case and recognized as such by the Court or tribunal;
- *understandable*: the report must be understandable to decision-makers and as far as possible, written in terms that are easily understood;
- *complete*: the report must contain all of the information required to explain any opinions given or conclusions reached, as appropriate. This means that it should include exculpatory material as well as the inculpatory;
- *believable*: the report must be believable to the intended audience. This means that not only does it have to written in language that can be understood by the audience, but also that there should be an adequate level of explanation and detail for the audience to be able to believe the material presented.

The Forensic Laboratory should produce reports that meet the requirements of ISO 17025, as given in Chapter 6, Appendix 31, though it should be able to meet any report production requirements for the jurisdiction as required by the Court or tribunal and the relevant Rules of Evidence.

The main purpose of a report is to assist the Court or tribunal in evaluating the admissibility, and weight, of any evidence found on the digital devices and media that were examined for the case by the Forensic Laboratory.

11.5.2 Audience Identification

> **Note**
>
> A report should "stand on its own" in as much as it contains all the relevant information regarding the subject so that no external resources need to be referenced.

Fundamental to the production of any report is an understanding of the purpose for which it is to be written and the audience for whom it is intended. For a Forensic Analyst, it is very easy to produce a technically detailed and very complete report that will be totally unusable for the audience for whom it is intended. This is not advocating that the technical detail should not be included, but it may well be that the most suitable place for this is in the Appendices with the main body of the report being in plain language that the layperson can understand it. Reports that are to be viewed by a Jury must be "Jury friendly" and not open to misinterpretation.

By identifying the intended audience from the start, the report can be written and structured in the most suitable manner.

The Forensic Laboratory document review process defined in Chapter 4, Section 4.6.3.4.3, Chapter 6, Section 6.8, and Chapter 9, Section 9.15 for all reports ensures a proper peer review process has taken place and this should ensure that the report is "fit for purpose."

11.5.3 Types of Report

There are five main types of report that are likely to be produced by a Forensic Analyst in the Forensic Laboratory. Three of these report types are similar in the processes that are involved but differ in the legal restrictions, the type of digital evidence, and the structure of the report. The main types of report are given in the following sections.

11.5.3.1 Forensic Reports for Criminal Cases

This is probably the oldest and best known of the reports and comes under the remit of law enforcement (or agents and agencies working on their behalf). Forensic reports for criminal cases are normally intended to facilitate an investigation and to be entered as evidence before the Court. It is important that these reports use simple terms that the layman will be able to understand. Either the relevant Rules of Evidence or the Client will define the specific reporting requirements.

11.5.3.2 Electronic Discovery or eDiscovery

This type of report is similar to the forensic report for a criminal case but relates to civil litigation. The processes are exactly the same as for criminal cases, but there are legal limitations and restrictions such as the scope of the investigation, human rights, and privacy, that relate to eDiscovery. Either the relevant Rules of Evidence or the Client will define the specific reporting requirements.

11.5.3.3 Industrial Disciplinary Tribunals

This type of report is again similar to the forensic report for a criminal case but relates to the relevant rules, policies, and procedures within an organization. This type of report is produced for internal disciplinary proceedings to deal with inappropriate activity by members of staff. While they do not normally require the same level of detail as a criminal report, it should be borne in mind that an investigation that has started off as a computer misuse may discover evidence of criminal activity, so the same duty of care should be taken in the handling of the evidence and preparation of the report. As has been stated in Section 11.4, the Forensic Laboratory always adopts this approach. Either the relevant Rules of Evidence or the Client will define the specific reporting requirements.

11.5.3.4 Intrusion Investigations

This type of report is different from the previous three. An intrusion investigation report is produced as a result of a network intrusion which may have been a hacker trying to steal corporate information or access corporate resources. The aim of this report is to identify the entry point of the attack, the degree of and scope of the penetration and to highlight the measures that can be taken to mitigate the effects of the attack. Again, this could result in a criminal trial, if the perpetrator can be identified, so the same duty of care should be taken in the handling of the evidence and preparation of the report, as if it were a criminal case at the outset. Either the relevant Rules of Evidence or the Client will define the specific reporting requirements.

11.5.3.5 Intelligence Gathering

This type of report is produced to provide intelligence to help track, stop, or identify illegal activity. This activity may be criminal in nature or nation-sponsored espionage. This type of report does not require that the evidence has been collected in a forensically sound manner as it will normally not be taken to the Court. The aim of this report is to understand what has happened, what tools and techniques were used, and who was responsible.

11.5.3.6 Statements and Depositions

Statements and depositions have been covered in Chapter 9, Section 9.16.

11.5.3.7 Report Checklists

While there is a report production checklist given in Chapter 9, Appendix 31, and the procedures within the Forensic Laboratory for document production defined in Chapter 4, Section 4.6.3. However, the checklist that is used for all reports produced by the Forensic Laboratory is given in Appendix 4 and for statements in Appendix 5.

11.5.4 Level of Detail in Reports

The level of detail that is included in the report will depend on the type of report and the intended audience. There are increasing constraints on the level of effort that can be invested in any case, although of course this will vary with the importance and priority of the case. With the increasing size of the storage media that is in use and the potential volume of information that is available, the report must be written in a way that provides a complete picture of the evidence, but which provides detail on the relevant areas, otherwise reports will become larger and the relevant evidence will become obscured in irrelevant detail.

11.5.5 Duty of Care

One of the issues that is often overlooked is that of ensuring the quality of the report itself. The report represents the efforts that the Forensic Laboratory have been made in all of the previous phases of processing the case, and no matter how well they have been carried out, a poorly presented report may cause the case to fail. The use of the report checklist, as defined in Chapter 9, Appendix 31, and the review of deliverables as defined in Chapter 6, Section 6.8, all go to improving the quality of reports produced by the Forensic Laboratory. Underlying this, reports must meet the criteria defined in Section 11.5.1.

The process of continuous improvement, as defined in Chapter 4, Section 4.8, eliciting feedback from Clients as given in Chapter 6, Appendix 20, and the handling of complaints as defined in Chapter 6, Section 6.14 ensures the quality of product realization in the Forensic Laboratory (i.e., the results of forensic case processing).

11.5.6 Duty to the Client

The Forensic Analyst who produces the report must fulfill their commitment to the duty of care by ensuring that the report meets the criteria defined by the Client in the agreed proposal or other instruction documents as well as those defined in the relevant Rules of Evidence or similar.

The report must meet the requirement that was specified in the tasking from the Client.

11.5.7 Duty to the Court

The Forensic Analyst who produces the report has an overriding duty to assist the Court in the discovery of fact. This will be interpreted differently from jurisdiction to jurisdiction and will also depend on the legal system in place, but the duty to the court is perhaps well summed up in the preamble to the Code of Ethics of the California Association of Criminalists which states that:

It is the duty of any person practicing the profession of criminalistics to serve the interests of justice to the best of his ability at all times. In fulfilling this duty, he will use all of the scientific means at his command to ascertain all of the significant physical facts relative to the matters under investigation. Having made factual determinations, the criminalist must then interpret and evaluate his findings. In this he will be guided by experience and knowledge which, coupled with a serious consideration of his analytical findings and the application of sound judgment, may enable him to arrive at opinions and conclusions pertaining to the matters under study. These findings of fact and his conclusions and opinions should then be reported, with all the accuracy and skill of which the criminalist is capable, to the end that all may fully understand and be able to place the findings in their proper relationship to the problem at issue. In carrying out these functions, the criminalist will be guided by those practices and procedures which are generally recognized within the profession to be consistent with a high level of professional ethics. The motives, methods, and actions of the criminalist shall at all times be above reproach, in good taste and consistent with proper moral conduct.

11.6 TESTIMONY IN COURT

Experience has shown that the majority of digital forensic cases are resolved prior to trial; however, a number of them require Forensic Analysts to testify in Court or at a tribunal. Presentation of case evidence can be an unnerving prospect and experience, and so the Forensic Laboratory must ensure that all of its employees that may be required to give evidence are appropriately trained.

11.6.1 Team Work

When being presented in a Court, it is important that the evidence presented is able to withstand cross-examination. In order for this to happen, the report has to meet the conditions given above, but also the person presenting it must be experienced and fully aware of the contents of the report and the collection and analysis processes that were used to extract the facts. This requires the Forensic Analyst(s) that processed the case and the Client's Legal Team to work as a team so that poor presentation or understanding of the case by the Legal Team does not undermine the work carried out by the Forensic Laboratory and the Forensic Analyst(s) that processed the case. If the Legal Team are not able to "speak the same language" relating to the case, it is essential that the Forensic Analyst(s) "educate" the Legal Team so that they have a full understanding of all aspects of the case, the evidence processed, the exhibits produced, the opinions given, and the conclusions drawn as well as the reasons for them. The other side of this coin is that the Forensic Analyst(s) must also understand how best to present their findings in the correct form of testimony in the Court or tribunal.

For these reasons, the Forensic Laboratory must try to ensure that the Client's Legal Team and the Forensic Analyst(s) who processed the case undertake joint training so that the outcome of this is that they can work as an effective and efficient team.

11.6.2 Pretrial Meetings

It is essential that prior to the trial itself, the Client's Legal Team and the Forensic Analyst(s) have met an appropriate number of times to ensure that they both understand the requirements for presenting the case effectively and undergoing cross-examination. The scope and limitations of the evidence produced must also be clearly understood by the Legal Team as well as the Forensic Analyst(s).

Pretrial meetings must also try to determine how the "other side" will present their case and to have answers to questions that they are likely to raise. A good example of this is a child pornography case where the defence often used is that "someone else put a Trojan Horse on my computer, and it downloaded these pictures." The Forensic Analyst can state that their standard operating procedures ensure that two different malware products are run on acquired images to determine if any malware, including Trojan Horses, was found, as defined in Chapter 9, Section 9.10.1.3.

11.6.3 Reviewing Case, Notes, and Reports

It is essential that the Forensic Analyst(s) going to testify in a Court or tribunal fully refresh their memory of all aspects of the case, the evidence processed, the exhibits produced, the opinions given, and the conclusions drawn as well as the reasons for them. A Forensic Analyst who has not done this can find themselves and the case seriously disadvantaged.

11.6.4 First Impressions Count

To paraphrase Samuel Johnson, "you never get a second chance to make a first impression." While this has little to do with the processing of a case, the first impression that a Witness makes will affect their credibility. Unfair as this may seem, it is a part of human nature and so must be understood and addressed.

First impressions to consider include, but are not limited to:

- *attitude*: a confident attitude is essential;
- *body language*: non-verbal communication can give a different impression to the actual words spoken;
- *clothing*: conservative dress is essential as it portrays confidence and trustworthiness, even if every day dress in the Forensic Laboratory is jeans and a tee shirt;
- *entry*: entry into the Witness Box or stand should be confident without swaggering;
- *eye contact*: with the Judge and individual members of the Jury is essential. Looking someone in the eye portrays non-verbal communication which has been shown to indicate that the speaker is trustworthy, honest, and sincere. Those unable to look someone in the eye are often thought of as shifty and untrustworthy, Eye contact, or rather lack of it can also undermine the credibility of a Witness;
- *grooming*: is as important as clothing. A disheveled Witness trying to claim that they processed the case responsibly and followed the required procedures may be undermined by appearances;
- *spoken language*: testimony must be in terms the Judge and Jury can understand without using complex technical jargon, multiple, or repeated disfluencies or filler words;
- *stance*: when giving testimony stood up, stance is important, especially if the testimony is to be "given" to the Judge. Training in presentation is essential in Court or tribunal etiquette.

The Witness giving testimony is trying to impress on the Judge and the Jury that they are responsible and credible, and the way in which they present themselves will say a lot about these qualities.

There are a number of nervous habits, gestures, and other non-verbal communications that can undermine the credibility of a Witness and distract the audience. Some of these, to be avoided at all costs, are given in Appendix 6.

While etiquette is often overlooked, and may these days be largely unwritten, there are often definite expected rules of etiquette in a Court or tribunal. Some of the most important points are given in Appendix 7.

11.6.5 Being an Effective Witness

One of the most challenging aspects of presenting the report in a Court or tribunal is that the technical complexity of the material that is being presented will often far exceed the knowledge of the Judge or the Jury. Consideration will have to given to how complex computer terms can be explained in terms that can be understood. The Forensic Analyst presenting the report should never forget that it is not unknown for the defence, if they cannot undermine the confidence of the court in the report itself and the processes used to produce it, to attempt to undermine the credibility of the Witness presenting it.

There is no substitute for being well prepared for giving testimony in a Court or tribunal. Time spent in effective preparation is never wasted. Within the Forensic Laboratory, the Laboratory Manager must ensure that all Forensic Analysts who are going to give testimony are properly prepared and will often attend pretrial meetings to review progress. Being unprepared will usually be seen as being unprofessional and can seriously undermine the credibility of the testimony and the Witness.

The Forensic Analyst(s) giving testimony will be required to provide details of their:

- educational qualifications;
- forensic certifications;
- training received that is relevant to the case;
- details of experience in similar cases;
- details of previous testimony given.

One of the basic rules of testifying is to listen to the question carefully and give consideration to the response and then answer the question as fully as possible. A rushed answer can cause problems.

Another basic rule is to only answer the question asked and not volunteer any information that was not asked. This may seem obvious, but the more that is given to "the other side" affords the possibility of more questions to be asked.

While it can be frustrating when testifying and the "other side" are able to make the Forensic Analyst lose their temper or become overly sarcastic, the Forensic Analyst's credibility can be seriously damaged.

Any testimony given must be unbiased, independent, based on facts and clearly presented. The weight of the testimony given depends on the credibility of the Witness.

11.6.6 Using Visual Aids

The old adage of "a picture is worth a thousand words" really is true. Where necessary, and permitted by the Court or tribunal, consideration should be given to using visual aids to clarify and points that may be difficult for the Judge and/or Jury to understand.

Some visual aids that can be used include, but are not limited to:

- animation;
- charts;
- diagrams;
- photographs;
- sketches.

Linking testimony to a visual aid can create a lasting image of understanding the point being explained.

Live on line demonstrations can be very effective so long as they work. It cannot be over-stressed that these must be rehearsed so that any possible "glitches" are overcome and there is a plan in place if any of the live demonstration does not work properly, as this can seriously undermine the credibility of the testimony.

As well as rehearsing any live demonstrations, ensure that there is adequate setup time in the court, this can include power, internet connections, and other relevant issues relating to the demonstration. Ensure that there is a sanitized forensic workstation being used and that the Judge, Jury, or others cannot see details of any other case. As this is an exhibit, it must be treated as such and have a full Chain of Custody available.

The Witness will need to determine from the Legal Team whether any visual aids need to be disclosed pretrial.

11.6.7 Using Feedback

During and after giving testimony, the Forensic Analysts will receive feedback as follows:

11.6.7.1 During Testimony

While giving evidence, it is essential to be able to look the Judge and Jury in the eye and hold eye contact (but do not stare or glower), as it is possible to determine how testimony is being received by the audience. They will be making non-verbal responses about how the testimony is received. By understanding this feedback and reacting to it, the Witness can keep their audience engaged and not send them to sleep.

11.6.7.2 Posttrial Review

After a trial, all Forensic Laboratory employees who gave testimony will have their performance assessed as part of the Forensic Laboratory's continuous improvement process. The Laboratory Manager will detail an experienced Expert Witness to examine the presentation and provide feedback, as well as requesting feedback from the Client on the Forensic Analyst's presentation of testimony. The form used for this is given in Appendix 8.

11.7 WHY CASES FAIL

Cases may fail at any point in the process and for a whole range of reasons, but the most common causes are:

- *Chain of Custody issues*: This is one of the easiest avenues for a defence to attack and a significant number of cases have now failed as a result of the Chain of Custody not being maintained. This is addressed by the Forensic Laboratory by use of the movement log, as given in Chapter 8, Appendix 17, with contemporaneous case work logs, as given in Chapter 9, Appendix 9 with the other forms and checklists in use shows responsibility for all actions and full end-to-end traceability of all actions taken in a case;
- *Legality of the seizure of the evidence*: Cases may fail because of a challenge to the legality of the way in which the evidence was seized. This is addressed by the Forensic Laboratory by ensuring all legislative requirements are met for the case, as defined in Chapter 9, Section 9.1.2;
- the scope of the investigation was too narrow and as a result the evidence presented was not complete. This is addressed by the Forensic Laboratory by ensuring the Client's required outcomes are properly defined and agreed by reviewing and agreeing the proposal as given in Chapter 6, Section 6.6.2.4;
- failure to convince the Judge or Jury of what took place. This is most common in complex cases such as fraud but can affect any case where the evidence is very technical or in a specialist area that the Jury may not have a good knowledge of the subject. This is addressed by the Forensic Laboratory by ensuring that reports are

properly reviewed for completeness and understanding in layman's terms as defined in Section 11.5.1;

- disputable interpretation of the evidence. The meaning of the evidence that is presented can be interpreted in more than one way. This is addressed by the Forensic Laboratory by the peer review process to determine that opinions given and conclusions drawn are based on sound scientific principles and are complete, as defined in Chapter 9, Section 9.15.3.

APPENDIX 1 - NATIONS RATIFYING THE BUDAPEST CONVENTION[a]

Nation	Signed	Ratified	Entry into force
Albania	23/11/2001	20/06/2002	01/07/2004
Armenia	23/11/2001	12/10/2006	01/02/2007
Australia		30/11/2012	01/03/2013
Austria	23/11/2001	13/06/2012	01/10/2012
Azerbaijan	30/06/2008	15/03/2010	01/07/2010
Belgium	23/11/2001	20/08/2012	01/12/2012
Bosnia and Herzegovina	09/02/2005	19/05/2006	01/09/2006
Bulgaria	23/11/2001	07/04/2005	01/08/2005
Canada	23/11/2001		
Croatia	23/11/2001	17/10/2002	01/07/2004
Cyprus	23/11/2001	19/01/2005	01/05/2005
Czech Republic	09/02/2005		
Denmark	22/04/2003	21/06/2005	01/10/2005
Dominican Republic		07/02/2013	01/06/2013
Estonia	23/11/2001	12/05/2003	01/07/2004
Finland	23/11/2001	24/05/2007	01/09/2007
France	23/11/2001	10/01/2006	01/05/2006
Georgia	01/04/2008	06/06/2012	01/10/2012
Germany	23/11/2001	09/03/2009	01/07/2009
Greece	23/11/2001		
Hungary	23/11/2001	04/12/2003	01/07/2004
Iceland	30/11/2001	29/01/2007	01/05/2007
Ireland	28/02/2002		
Italy	23/11/2001	05/06/2008	01/10/2008
Japan	23/11/2001	03/07/2012	01/11/2012
Latvia	05/05/2004	14/02/2007	01/06/2007
Liechtenstein	17/11/2008		
Lithuania	23/06/2003	18/03/2004	01/07/2004
Luxembourg	28/01/2003		
Malta	17/01/2002	12/04/2012	01/08/2012
Moldova	23/11/2001	12/05/2009	01/09/2009
Montenegro	07/04/2005	03/03/2010	01/07/2010
The Netherlands	23/11/2001	16/11/2006	01/03/2007
Norway	23/11/2001	30/06/2006	01/10/2006
Poland	23/11/2001		
Portugal	23/11/2001	24/03/2010	01/07/2010
Romania	23/11/2001	12/05/2004	01/09/2004
Serbia	07/04/2005	14/04/2009	01/08/2009
Slovakia	04/02/2005	08/01/2008	01/05/2008
Slovenia	24/07/2002	08/09/2004	01/01/2005
South Africa	23/11/2001		
Spain	23/11/2001	03/06/2010	01/10/2010
Sweden	23/11/2001		
Switzerland	23/11/2001	21/09/2011	01/01/2012
The former Yugoslav Republic of Macedonia	23/11/2001	15/09/2004	01/01/2005
Turkey	10/11/2010		
Ukraine	23/11/2001	10/03/2006	01/07/2006
The United Kingdom	23/11/2001	25/05/2011	01/09/2011
The United States	23/11/2001	29/09/2006	

Continued

a. http://conventions.coe.int/Treaty/Commun/ChercheSig.asp?NT=185&CM=8&DF=&CL=ENG.

APPENDIX 2 - CRITERIA FOR SELECTION AN EXPERT WITNESS

There are few qualifications available for any Expert Witness in digital forensics today, but this will change. Anyone can put "Digital Forensic Expert Witness" on their business card, but choosing the "right" one is a matter that is of utmost importance, as it could win or lose the case, no matter how good the Forensic Analyst's examination and analysis has been.

The Forensic Laboratory has identified a number of criteria that should be used in selecting an Expert Witness (and the same generally applies to outsourcing suppliers, as covered in Chapter 14).

The criteria used are subjective, but the criteria and the reasons shall be documented and form a record on the Client's virtual case file stored in the ERMS.

For any Expert Witness to be considered, The Forensic Laboratory considers, but is not limited to, the following criteria:

- have any credentials from a Law Enforcement organization?
- have any Law Enforcement organization or investigations experience?
- have formal ongoing and recorded training (CPD/CPE)?
- have past performance in the field required?
- have recommendations from recognized professional digital forensic bodies?
- understand the process not the tool?
- does their CV and references supplied pass scrutiny?
- have they published articles in journals or books?
- have they experience in the hardware in the case?
- have they experience in the operating system in the case?
- have they experience in the tools used in the case?
- how long have they been actually performing forensic examination/when did they start their forensic career?
- how long will it take to process the case?
- is their cost acceptable?
- is there a confidentiality agreement in place?
- what level of security vetting do they hold for the jurisdiction?
- what professional qualifications have they got relating to forensics?
- what tools will they use and are they appropriately trained in their use?
- who trained them?
- will the Forensic Laboratory's case be one of many handled by the Expert Witness or will the Forensic Laboratory get personal attention from the Expert Witness, portrayed as carrying out the work?

APPENDIX 3 - THE FORENSIC LABORATORY CODE OF CONDUCT FOR EXPERT WITNESSES

While the Forensic Laboratory will need to develop its own Code of Conduct for Expert Witnesses, it should be recognized that legislation, procedures, and accepted practices may, in some jurisdictions, conflict with this Code of Conduct. In cases such as this, the legislation, procedures, and accepted practices must be followed. The Expert Witness:

- must tell the truth under oath and not commit perjury;
- has a duty to impartially serve the Court or tribunal;
- has a secondary duty to serve the best interests of the instructing party;
- depending on the jurisdiction, may or may not be able to act as an Advocate;
- ensure the Client's requirements are clearly understood and clarify any areas of uncertainty;
- shall not be paid, depending on the outcome of a case (as this may affect the Expert Witness' objectivity);
- shall ensure that their terms of engagement are clearly stated, including their limit of liability in their engagement letter;
- must be able to display competence in their technical duties;
- must continually maintain and update their skills and provide proof of this through Continuing Professional Development (CPD) or Continual Professional Education (CPE) submitted and audited by the relevant professional bodies to which the belong;
- must gain qualifications and certifications relevant to their work that are generally accepted as appropriate and good practice for their work;
- must be able to demonstrate the required duty of care for the case;
- must avoid conflicts of interest, as given in the Forensic Laboratory's Conflict of Interest Policy Chapter 3, Appendix 3;
- must immediately report to the Laboratory Manager if they feel that their work is being compromised by undue influence or by not being permitted to perform tests or investigations that they feel are appropriate to the case;
- must be scrupulously honest and forthright in their dealings with all involved in a case;
- must be honest about their limitations and not accept instructions outside their limitations;
- must not discriminate against anyone based on any grounds, whatsoever;
- shall maintain Client confidentiality;
- ensure safe custody of all exhibits and other materials relating to the case while in their custody;
- ensure, through the Laboratory Manager, that appropriate insurance is in place to protect both themselves and the Forensic Laboratory;
- use necessary visual aids and explanations, as permitted in the Court or tribunal to help explain complex of technical matters;
- shall obtain Best Evidence, where available, relating to the case so that reliance on assumptions is minimized and opinions and conclusions are based on verifiable fact;
- must clearly state any assumptions and the reasons for them;
- must consider all possible options, opinions, and theories relating to the case, before forming their own opinions and conclusions;
- produce reports and testimony as required for the relevant legislation, procedures or accepted practices for the Court or tribunal;

- must bring to the immediate attention of the Laboratory Manager, and the Client, any change to any opinion given or conclusion drawn during the case after submitting their report. This may involve production of a supplemental report that also clearly states the reasons for the revised opinion given and/or conclusion drawn;
- must endeavor to reach agreement with other Expert Witnesses on material facts in the case;
- must, where appropriate, provide a list of matters that are agreed between the Expert Witnesses, and those not agreed with the reason for them. This is usually a joint report form the Expert Witnesses involved;
- must comply with all directions from the Court or tribunal.

APPENDIX 4 - REPORT WRITING CHECKLIST

PREPARATION AND PLANNING

- addresses intended audience (who)?
- clearly identifies requirements and research (how)?
- identifies where the report refers to (where)?
- the purpose of the report is clearly defined and met (why)?
- the relevant facts are present (what)?
- times and dates are clearly stated (when)?

CONTENT AND STRUCTURE

- answers the key questions?
- contains an opinion or range of opinions or conclusions—as appropriate?
- correct use of appendices?
- does the report "stand alone"?
- ensures Chain of Custody throughout?
- ensures that facts are clearly separated from opinions and conclusions?
- glossary of terms and acronyms used is included?
- identifies all of the facts relevant to the case?
- identifies further information—if required?
- identifies the issues clearly and identifies them based on the Client's required outcomes?
- identifies the key questions to be answered?
- includes facts to support the opinions given and conclusions drawn?
- meets the requirements of ISO 17025 as given in Chapter 6, Appendix 31.
- use of key checklists and internal forms?

LAYOUT

- classification of report appropriate?
- consistent use of language?
- correct font (the Forensic Laboratory will use a standard font (Ariel 12)?
- correct use of headers and footers?
- correct use of headings and subheadings?
- diagrams used appropriately?
- pagination correct?
- paragraph numbering correct (and line numbering—if required)?
- photographs used appropriately?
- sketches used appropriately?
- "white space" present?

LANGUAGE USED

- first person—if appropriate?
- accurate?
- clear and understandable?
- concise?
- grammatically correct?
- logical structure?
- short sentences and accurate?

PRESENTATION AND LANGUAGE

- binding?
- grammar checked?
- layout?
- look and feel?
- overall view?
- paper—appropriate paper weight
- readability?
- structure?

FINAL PRESENTATION

- passed peer review?

APPENDIX 5 - STATEMENT AND DEPOSITION WRITING CHECKLIST

The requirements of statements and depositions do vary between jurisdictions and the generic checklist below is that which is used in the Forensic Laboratory:

AUTHOR'S DETAILS

- name;
- address—Forensic Laboratory or personal—as required;
- occupation.

LAYOUT AND LANGUAGE

- as per requirement in the jurisdiction;
- classification as used for the jurisdiction;

- concise language;
- grammar correct;
- manually checked for mistakes—not just computer checked;
- margins;
- meets requirements of in-house reports;
- figures and diagrams numbered;
- page numbered "*x* of *y*," in appropriate place;
- peer reviewed;
- punctuation correct;
- short sentences;
- spelling correct;
- structure tells a story;
- tone appropriate;
- white space.

CONTENT

- consistent with other case documents;
- consistent with proposed oral testimony;
- consistent with the exhibits;
- contents logically sequenced;
- dealt with any weaknesses in the case;
- exhibits kept separate;
- exhibits properly labeled;
- facts separated from assumptions, opinions, beliefs, and conclusions;
- glossary of terms;
- identifies the facts to support the issues;
- identifies the issues;
- include all strengths of case;
- introduction;
- list of documents referenced;
- list of exhibits referenced;
- professional opinion based on fact;
- signed and dated;
- statement of truth, if required in jurisdiction;
- structure;
- where possible, do not make assumptions or inferences.

APPENDIX 6 - NON-VERBAL COMMUNICATION TO AVOID

There are a number of non-verbal communications that should be avoided as can undermine the credibility of a Witness by distracting the Judge and/or Jury from the testimony being given. These include, but are not limited to:

- allowing a pager or cell phone to ring;
- arrogant or condescending tone;
- being late;
- biting the lip or nails;
- clicking the top of a pen;
- cracking knuckles;
- drumming fingers;
- fidgeting;
- folding arms across the body;
- inappropriate communication that the Judge/Jury does not understand;
- jingling keys or change in pockets;
- leaning on hands and rocking backward and forward;
- overuse of "fillers";
- picking at the body, especially the nose;
- poor posture;
- playing with items of clothing;
- pointing at the Judge or Jury;
- rolling the eyes;
- rubbing the eyes;
- scratching any part of the body;
- slouching, if sitting;
- twiddling thumbs.

APPENDIX 7 - ETIQUETTE IN COURT

This section could be called "No—No's."

Different Courts and tribunal in different Jurisdictions will have different expected levels of etiquette; however, the following should generally be accepted by the Forensic laboratory as a minimum level of acceptable standards of etiquette in any Court or tribunal, anywhere;

- answer questions asked fully and honestly but do not volunteer too much information;
- avoid "taboo" subjects;
- be on time;
- be respectful, polite, and courteous to everyone, from the front desk staff to the Judge and Jury, and the "other side";
- be well prepared;
- do not upset the Judge;
- it is acceptable to say, "I do not understand the question" and ask for a rephrasing;
- no matter what—a Witness of any type must not lose their temper with anyone questioning them;
- remain focused;
- be respectful and sincere;
- the Witness must be aware of questions that may leave them in a disadvantaged position (e.g., questions that are like "is it possible that..." often it is possible, but no answer should be given that detracts from the evidence presented, the opinions given, and the conclusions drawn);
- turn your cell phone and pager off (in some jurisdictions, this is regarded as "contempt of Court" and in an offence.

APPENDIX 8 - TESTIMONY FEEDBACK FORM

CASE DETAILS

- case number;
- Client/case name;
- defendant;
- court location;
- court type;
- Forensic Analyst giving testimony;
- date(s) of testimony.

FEEDBACK

The Forensic Laboratory requires feed back on the following aspects of the testimony:

Personal Impressions

- ability to respond to feedback;
- attitude;
- dress;
- entry to the Witness Box;
- eye contact;
- non-verbal communication;
- personal appearance;
- understanding of Court Etiquette;
- voice (volume, tone, and understandability).

Delivery of Testimony

- ability to explain complex issues;
- ability to use appropriate language;
- clarity of delivery;
- conciseness of delivery;
- confidence level;
- decline to answer questions that required knowledge outside their experience and competence;
- knowledge level relating to the case and the case processing tools and methods used;
- level of preparation;
- remain within the scope of their experience and competence;
- response to questions;
- use of visual aids.

The above all are marked as follows:

1—very poor;
2—poor;
3—good;
4—very good;
5—excellent;
N/A—not applicable.

LENGTH OF TESTIMONY

- evidence in chief;
- cross-examination.

CASE RESULT

What was the result of the case/investigation that this testimony was used to support (Did the testimony play a pivotal role)?

CORRECTIVE ACTIONS RECOMMENDED

Any corrective actions needed to improve the Forensic Analyst's testimony presentation.

SIGN OFF

- signed;
- date;
- name.

Chapter 12

Secure Working Practices

Table of Contents

12.1 INTRODUCTION

Information is now globally accepted as being a vital asset for most, if not all, organizations and businesses and the Forensic Laboratory is no exception. Information may be printed or written on paper, stored electronically, transmitted by post or e-mail, shown on films, or spoken in conversation. Whatever the form that information takes, organizations like the Forensic Laboratory need to have processes and procedures to protect it.

Information security can be characterized as the preservation of:

- confidentiality—ensuring that access to information is appropriately authorized;
- integrity—safeguarding the accuracy and completeness of information and processing methods;
- availability—ensuring that authorized users have access to information when they need it.

ISO 27001 is a specification for the management of information security (ISO 27001 is the specification and ISO 27002 is the Code of Practice). It is applicable to all sectors of industry and commerce and not confined to information held on computers. It addresses the security of information in whatever form it is held, and this is applicable throughout the Forensic Laboratory.

As such, the confidentiality, integrity, and availability of the Forensic Laboratory information are essential to maintain competitive edge, deliverability to Clients, legal compliance, and commercial image. ISO 27001 supports this. It is easy to imagine the consequences for the Forensic Laboratory if its information was lost, destroyed, corrupted, or misused.

In adopting ISO 27001, the Forensic Laboratory is not immune from security breaches but will make these breaches less likely and reduce the consequential cost and disruption if they do occur. It also demonstrates that:

- the Forensic Laboratory has addressed, implemented, and controlled the security of its information and Client information entrusted to it;
- it provides reassurance to Clients, employees, trading partners, and stakeholders that the Forensic Laboratory has implemented secure systems based on perceived risk;
- it demonstrates credibility and trust;

- it confirms that relevant legislation and regulations within the jurisdiction are being met;
- it ensures that a commitment to information security exists at all levels throughout the Forensic Laboratory.

The Forensic Laboratory Information Security Policy is given in Chapter 4, Appendix 10.

The Forensic Laboratory should aim to achieve certification to ISO 27001 by an Accredited Certification Body and meet the requirements of ISO 27001 using the Statement of Applicability (SoA) as given in Appendix 1. While it must choose its controls from ISO 27001, Annex A, it is free to choose other controls if they are indicated by the risk assessment undertaken on the assets in the scope of certification. It has used ISO 27001 as a baseline and selected other controls as required for other sources or the risk assessment output.

12.2 PRINCIPLES OF INFORMATION SECURITY WITHIN THE FORENSIC LABORATORY

There are nine Generally Accepted Information Security Principles (GAISP—Version 3.0) that provide guidance in the security of information. While the Forensic Laboratory should aim to achieve ISO 27001 certification, these principles are adjudged to be appropriate as well. How they are met is given in Appendix 2.

These are:

12.2.1 Accountability Principle

Information security accountability and responsibility must be clearly defined and acknowledged.

12.2.2 Awareness Principle

All parties, including but not limited to the Information Owners and information security practitioners, with a need to know, should have access to applied or available principles, standards, conventions, or mechanisms for the security of information and information systems, and should be informed of applicable threats to the security of information.

12.2.3 Ethics Principle

Information should be used, and the administration of information security should be executed, in an ethical manner.

12.2.4 Multidisciplinary Principle

Principles, standards, conventions, and mechanisms for the security of information and information systems should address the considerations and viewpoints of all interested parties.

12.2.5 Proportionality Principle

Information security controls should be proportionate to the risks of modification, denial of use, or disclosure of the information.

12.2.6 Integration Principle

Principles, standards, conventions, and mechanisms for the security of information should be co-ordinated and integrated with each other and with the organization's policies and procedures to create and maintain security throughout an information system.

12.2.7 Timeliness Principle

All accountable parties should act in a timely, co-ordinated manner to prevent or respond to breaches of, and threats to, the security of information and information systems.

12.2.8 Assessment Principle

The risks to information and information systems should be assessed periodically.

12.2.9 Equity Principle

Management shall respect the rights and dignity of individuals when setting policy and when selecting, implementing, and enforcing security measures.

12.3 MANAGING INFORMATION SECURITY IN THE FORENSIC LABORATORY

While GAISP defines principles for information security and there are a number of national and international standards for information security, the Forensic Laboratory should aim to adopt ISO 27001 and the supporting standards within the ISO 270xx series of standards, and it is to ISO 27001 that the Forensic Laboratory should aim to be certified.

12.3.1 Managing Organizational Security

The Forensic Laboratory should encourage a multidisciplinary approach to information security that involves the cooperation and collaboration of managers, users, administration staff, auditors, security staff, and specialist skills in areas such as insurance and risk management. External third parties are also involved.

The Forensic Laboratory will manage the implementation of information security through:

- an Information Security Committee;
- allocation of information security responsibilities;
- authorization for new information processing facilities;
- provision for specialist information security advice;
- independent reviews of the information security systems implemented in the Forensic Laboratory.

12.3.1.1 The Forensic Laboratory Information Security Committee

Information security is a business responsibility shared by all Forensic Laboratory employees. To ensure that information security is properly incorporated into the Forensic Laboratory business activities, a management board should be created to promote security and this is called the Information Security Committee. Its terms of reference are given in Chapter 4, Appendix 31. There are a number of other management committees set up to manage various other aspects of the Forensic Laboratory, and these are all listed in Chapter 4, Appendices 27–34.

12.3.1.2 Allocation of Information Security Responsibilities

The Forensic Laboratory must ensure that the responsibilities for the protection of individual assets and for carrying out specific information security processes are clearly defined.

Responsibilities are:

- The Information Security Policy, as given in Chapter 4, Appendix 10, provides general guidance on the allocation of security roles and responsibilities within the Forensic Laboratory;
- the Information Security Manager has overall responsibility for the development and implementation of security, and to support the identification of controls. The Information Security Manager's job description is given in Appendix 4;
- generic responsibilities are defined in the scope statement for the Forensic Laboratory's Integrated Management System (IMS), as given in Chapter 5, Appendix 11;
- defined responsibilities for all other aspects of information security are contained within the documents of this Information Security Management System (ISMS) or in their specific job descriptions;
- all employees have specific job descriptions that include the requirements for information security.

12.3.1.3 Authorization for New Information Processing Facilities

The Forensic Laboratory must ensure that all new information processing facilities are authorized before implementation is allowed. This authorization is detailed within the relevant documents of this ISMS and includes:

- business approval via the Business Owner and the Business Risk Owner (if different people);
- Information Security Manager approval to ensure that all relevant security policies and requirements are met and that all relevant risks have been identified and treated as appropriate;
- hardware and software testing to ensure that new information processing facilities are compatible with other system components;
- information protection approval for processing personal information.

All new IT facilities are only allowed into the live environment via the change management process, as defined in Chapter 7, Section 7.4.3.

12.3.1.4 Provision for Specialist Security Advice

Initial specialist information security advice is in the first instance provided by the relevant Forensic Laboratory employee. Where additional or specialized advice is required, it is sought from:

- the Information Security Manager;
- vendors;
- other security professionals;
- Special Interest Groups and specialist professional bodies;
- local or national authorities.

The Information Security Manager shall co-ordinate the use of these sources of advice.

The Information Security Manager shall provide access to external specialist security advice on an 'as needed' basis. The assessment of security threats and the level of internal knowledge provide indicators for whether external security advice is required.

> **Note**
> All use of external advisers is governed by the controls for employing third parties as defined in Chapter 14.

The Information Security Manager and other relevant Forensic Laboratory employees are encouraged to join/attend appropriate information security bodies and maintain contacts with Law Enforcement authorities, Regulatory bodies, information service providers, and telecommunication operators. All Forensic Laboratory employees are reminded to be discrete when discussing the Forensic Laboratory issues with non-Forensic Laboratory employees and must never divulge confidential information to Forensic Laboratory employees who are not authorized to have access to that information. Non-Disclosure Agreements

(NDAs) must be used where Forensic Laboratory information is passed to a third party, unless a contract (with an appropriate confidentiality clause) has been executed between the Forensic Laboratory and the third party.

12.3.1.5 Independent Review of the Information Security System

The implementation of the Forensic Laboratory's information security system is reviewed independently at least once each year to provide assurance that practices properly reflect the policy and that it is feasible and effective.

This review is carried out either by independent internal staff trained in a security audit function or (at the discretion of the Information Security Manager) carried out by a third party company. This is in addition to any penetration testing undertaken by internal or external resources and the annual Certification Body audits.

The process for undertaking internal audits is defined in Chapter 4, Section 4.7.3.

12.3.2 Educating and Training Employees in Information Security

The Forensic Laboratory undertakes educating and training employees to ensure that standards are implemented to ensure continued employee awareness of their information security responsibilities.

This requirement applies to all employees, whether full time, part time, contract, or temporary, as well as third parties not already covered by explicit contracts with appropriate confidentiality clauses in them or NDAs that have access to Forensic Laboratory information or information processing systems.

This includes:

- security awareness:
  - educating new employees (induction training);
  - guidelines for educating new employees;
  - maintaining employee awareness.
- specialized ongoing security training (e.g., mobile device security training, annual refresher training, etc.).

12.3.2.1 Security Awareness

Awareness of securing information requirements is an important responsibility of every Forensic Laboratory employee on a daily basis. Loss of information could result in a loss of work hours spent creating information as well as several more work hours trying to recover. Information lost outside the work environment could result in the violation of customer confidentiality, a contractual or legislative breach.

It is ultimately the responsibility of the Forensic Laboratory Top Management to ensure business managers, IT users, and others with access to the Forensic Laboratory information and information processing systems understand the key elements of information security, why it is needed, and their personal information security responsibilities.

Awareness of information security is maintained via effective awareness and training programs at the Forensic Laboratory for all employees and third parties with access to Forensic Laboratory information or information processing systems. All Forensic Laboratory employees and relevant third party employees are responsible for participating in the security awareness and training program. They must be provided with guidance to help them understand information security, the importance of complying with the Forensic Laboratory's internal policies and standards, and to be aware of their own personal responsibilities. It is the responsibility of the Forensic Laboratory Human Resources Department, in cooperation with the Information Security Manager, to promote security awareness and training to all employees on a continuous basis.

The Forensic Laboratory follows these guidelines to promote awareness of information security among all employees and third parties with access to the Forensic Laboratory information and information processing systems to ensure that:

- formal awareness and training sessions are run using specialized awareness material;
- all training sessions are kept up-to-date with current practices;
- all training sessions are attended by all employees;
- security awareness training sessions are reviewed at least annually by the Information Security Manager.

12.3.2.1.1 Educating New Employees

Upon permanent or contract employment at the Forensic Laboratory:

1. All employees must be briefed, as part of their induction, on the application of information system security policies and standards within the Forensic Laboratory, as given in Chapter 6, Appendix 11.
2. A written summary of the basic information security measures must be available in the Forensic Laboratory Information Security Policy, which is supplied to all employees at induction. A signed copy is to be kept in the employee's personnel file.
3. New employees must have access to the IMS and supporting policies and procedures.
4. New employees must be able to:
   - understand their responsibilities as a user of Forensic Laboratory and Client information and Forensic Laboratory resources and information processing systems;
   - be able to identify information security resources;
   - be able to identify examples of sensitive and/or confidential information in their department;
   - understand the impact of security violations and other security incidents.

12.3.2.1.2 Guidelines for Educating New Employees

The following aspects of information security are included when educating all new employees:

- user ID and password requirements;
- computer security, including malware protection, malware reporting, and malware elimination;
- the appropriate handling (and destruction) of information of different classifications;
- awareness of social engineering techniques employed by hackers;
- information backup guidelines;
- business continuity and disaster recovery;
- the Forensic Laboratory information security program;
- internet access;
- e-mail use;
- information security monitoring processes that are in use;
- use of the Forensic Laboratory equipment and information outside the office;
- incident reporting;
- whom to contact for additional information.

12.3.2.1.3 Maintaining Employee Awareness

The Forensic Laboratory recognizes that retention and applicable knowledge of employees increases considerably when the matter is subject to revision and refreshment. To assist with this:

- all the Forensic Laboratory employees must be rebriefed on information security at least annually by the Information Security Manager;
- the Information Security Manager shall develop and implement a security awareness program, which addresses periodic information security awareness update requirements. A written summary of the basic information security measures must be made available for each employee.

Some of the issues covered by the periodic security updates may include, but are not limited to:

- how the Forensic Laboratory deals with users who do not comply with security policies;
- success of security policies;
- problems or difficulties experienced by employees;
- changes to security policies;
- incident reporting;
- security metrics;
- learning from incidents and issues affecting the Forensic Laboratory;
- malicious software discovered.

12.3.2.2 Security Training

Education and training must be provided to all Forensic Laboratory employees who are involved in controlling, using, running, developing, and securing information and information processing systems.

Security training shall provide all employees with the knowledge they require to assess security requirements, propose security controls, and to ensure that controls function effectively.

The objective of security training at the Forensic Laboratory is to ensure that:

- security controls are applied correctly to the Forensic Laboratory information and information processing systems;
- all employees understand their responsibilities;
- the IT Department develops systems in a disciplined manner.

The Information Security Manager and the Human Resources Department are responsible for ensuring that all employees obtain adequate training via:

- advising employees of available courses;
- encouraging certification and qualifications, where applicable;
- ensuring knowledge transfer from relevant third parties to employees, where appropriate;
- maintenance of individual employee's training records.

The following are points of focus for security training:

- all users will be forced to choose quality passwords following the password standard;
- passwords and user IDs must be kept confidential and changed on a regular basis, unless strong passwords have been approved as defined in Section 12.6;
- access cards or other security mechanisms may not be shared by anyone and should immediately be reported if lost or stolen;
- users should be encouraged to contact the Information Security Manager when unusual situations occur;
- building security should be alerted whenever a user's access card or key has been compromised;
- users should protect mobile computing devices by using physical locks to lock away sensitive media and documentation and to log off if leaving them unattended;
- users should be trained not to provide information to anyone representing himself or herself as a member of the IT Department (i.e., social engineering) that could allow that person to gain access to classified or Client information;
- all documents received regarding security issues should be read carefully.

12.3.3 Managing Information Security for Employees

It is essential that good information security practices are implemented in the Forensic Laboratory and that all employees understand these from their initial employment. This includes:

- a policy for screening applicants during recruitment, as defined in Chapter 18, Section 18.1.3.7 and Appendix 20;
- policies for promoting information security for employees—which covers:
  - job descriptions;
  - confidentiality agreements;
  - terms and conditions of employment.

The implementation and maintenance of information security policies and procedures with respect to employees are the responsibility of the Forensic Laboratory Human Resources Department, based on recommendations provided by the Information Security Manager.

12.3.3.1 Promoting Information Security in Employees

The Forensic Laboratory must pursue an active policy of encouraging and promoting awareness of information security issues in all employees.

To assist with information security awareness, the Forensic Laboratory will implement the following:

- defining security roles in job descriptions;
- issuing confidentiality agreements;
- issuing terms and conditions of employment.

12.3.3.2 Defining Security Roles in Job Descriptions

The Forensic Laboratory policy for defining security roles in job definitions is:

- all new job applicants must be provided with a job description when applying for employment;
- job descriptions for all existing employees should be available on request by the Human Resources Department;
- all job descriptions must include a responsibility for handling Forensic Laboratory and Client information in accordance with the Forensic Laboratory's ISMS, and a reference to the Information Security Policy;
- employment roles with specific information security tasks or activities must be listed in the relevant job description.

12.3.3.3 Issuing Confidentiality Agreements

Confidentiality agreements help reinforce the Forensic Laboratory's commitment to information security by reinforcing employee attitudes that all Forensic Laboratory and Client information which they handle during the course of their work shall be treated on a confidential basis.

Responsibility for maintaining the confidentiality agreement lies with the Human Resources Department in association with the General Counsel.

The Forensic Laboratory policy for issuing confidentiality agreements shall be that:

1. All Forensic Laboratory employees must be issued with, and sign, a confidentiality agreement (agreements are normally issued at time of recruitment and form a part of the contract of employment).
2. No employee shall be allowed access to Forensic Laboratory and Client information or information processing systems without signing the agreement.
3. The Forensic Laboratory confidentiality agreement must define the undertakings to which an employee agrees with respect to maintenance of confidentiality and information security.

The confidentiality agreement is subject to periodic reviews by the Human Resources Department as follows:

- reviews must be conducted following changes to:
  - job roles;
  - legislation;
  - the Forensic Laboratory policy on Information Security.
- any changes to the confidentiality agreement must be implemented by the Human Resources Department with suitable input from the General Counsel or specialized external legal sources.

12.3.3.4 Issuing Terms and Conditions of Employment

Terms and conditions of employment are stated in an employee contract that is issued to each employee and specifies the particulars of the employment relationship between the Forensic Laboratory and the employee. The issue of information security must be expressly addressed.

Responsibility for maintaining the employee contract lies with the Human Resources Department with suitable input from the General Counsel or specialized external legal sources.

The Forensic Laboratory policy for issuing terms and conditions of employment is:

- all the Forensic Laboratory employees must be issued with terms and conditions of employment;
- no employee must be allowed access to Forensic Laboratory or Client information or information processing facilities systems without signing the terms and conditions.

The Forensic Laboratory terms and conditions shall outline:

- the need of employees to comply with current statutory legislation and regulations;
- the security responsibilities of employees outside the workplace and while working away (e.g., on business trips or working away from the office);
- the disciplinary procedures that would be applied if information security policies are breached;

- confirmation that it is the Forensic Laboratory's responsibility to provide appropriate training and education in the subject of information security.

> **Note**
>
> The Human Resources Department is responsible for taking disciplinary action against employees who breach the terms and conditions of their employment.

12.3.4 Termination or Change of Employment

The Forensic Laboratory must ensure that all employees who change employment or leave the Forensic Laboratory for any reason are appropriately processed. This is to ensure that there is a clean break and that all such employees are reminded of their contractual responsibilities in their post-employment phase.

To assist in the process, the Forensic Laboratory must ensure that the following areas are covered with the relevant staff:

- termination responsibilities;
- return of assets;
- removal of access rights.

These are covered in Chapter 18, Section 18.1.

12.3.5 Segregation of IT Duties

The Forensic Laboratory has implemented a number of controls for maintaining and enforcing segregation of IT duties to:

- reduce security risks via accidental or deliberate misuse of the Forensic Laboratory or Clients information or information processing systems;
- reduce opportunities for unauthorized access or modification of services or information.

Segregation of duties within the IT Department helps ensure that the Forensic Laboratory's information assets are safeguarded by segregating duties. This ensures that access to computers, production information, software, documentation, and operating systems and utilities is limited (and potential damage from the actions of one person is reduced). All Forensic Laboratory employees are organized to achieve adequate segregation of duties, to the greatest extent possible.

> **Note**
>
> Where the Forensic laboratory is a relatively small organization and where segregation of duties is not achievable, compensatory controls are used, for example, audit trails and management supervision.

Daily management of the policy of IT duty segregation is the responsibility of all Line Managers in the Forensic Laboratory. Formal maintenance of these guidelines is the responsibility of the Information Security Manager (in association with other key IT management staff).

Where possible, the following IT duties are performed by separate groups/employees:

- IT management;
- software development;
- program migration;
- systems operations/daily administration;
- Service Desk;
- network management.

Account creation and maintenance ensures that elements of segregation are automatically performed via a user's 'acco-settings' unit.

User profiles are developed taking into consideration segregation of duties. These user profiles shall be reviewed periodically, and it is the responsibility of the Line Managers to report any changes to the Service Desk and the Information Security Manager to record any changes.

12.3.6 Segregation of Other Duties

The Forensic Laboratory must not only implement segregation for IT duties but also ensure that no one person is able to control a whole process and that there is always external oversight.

Risk assessments have been carried out to ensure that the risks of segregation failures are understood and appropriate controls implemented to reduce the risks as far as practical.

The following processes also have segregation enforced in addition to IT access segregation:

- raising payment requests and paying them;
- acquiring and disposing of assets;
- managing the employee database and paying salaries.

12.3.7 Electronic Mail

The Forensic Laboratory should adopt a number of security measures for e-mail users that cover:

- e-mail accounts;
- protection of e-mail;
- acceptable use of e-mail;
- unacceptable use of e-mail.

12.3.7.1 E-mail Accounts

E-mail accounts should be provided to Forensic Laboratory employees following completion of an official account request from the employee's Line Manager.

An e-mail account is strictly confidential and is exclusively for the use of the employee for whom it has been created. In addition, e-mail passwords must not be shared under any circumstances between employees.

The size of each e-mail user's mailbox is limited according to the standard currently defined by the Forensic Laboratory IT Department.

No e-mail accounts are deleted when an employee is terminated, they are archived in case of future need.

12.3.7.2 Protection of E-mail

Measures include:

- e-mail messages containing confidential information shall only be sent to recipients who have the right to know the confidential information;
- e-mail messages containing confidential information shall have suitable controls implemented to protect against unauthorized access, modification, or disclosure during transmission;
- sending options, privacy markings, and expiry options shall be set (if available) within e-mail Client application "Microsoft Outlook" or other mail Client, as appropriate within the Forensic Laboratory. The use of internal settings is not as strong as using a dedicated encryption solution.

12.3.7.3 Acceptable Use of E-mail

Note

Acceptable use of the Forensic Laboratory's information processing resources is fully covered in the Acceptable Use Policy in Chapter 4, Appendix 26.

Acceptable use of the Forensic Laboratory e-mail system is:

- communication between employees and external parties of the Forensic Laboratory for business purposes only;
- transmission of information related to the Forensic Laboratory operations (financial information, statistical information, newsletters, reports) that are essential for the accomplishment of an employee's daily job;
- sending and receiving official internal memos;
- to inform employees of new policies and procedures that have been adopted;
- to inform employees of products and services provided by the Forensic Laboratory;
- sending and receiving messages containing information in relation to recent developments in a particular area of business, which assist with knowledge improvement.

12.3.7.4 Unacceptable Use of E-mail

The following activities are considered unacceptable use of the Forensic Laboratory e-mail system:

- transmission of confidential information either belonging to the Forensic Laboratory or a Client without prior authorization/approval;
- copying, transmission, or acceptance of material that is copyright protected;
- transmission or acceptance of any material that may be reasonably considered offensive, disruptive, defamatory or derogatory, including but not limited to sexual comments or images, racial slurs or other comments or images that would offend someone on the basis of his/her race, national origin, gender, sexual orientation, religious or political beliefs, disability, or on any other basis;
- transmission or acceptance of any information that may lead to any illegal or criminal activity, or breach of local, national, or international laws;
- transmission or acceptance of any marketing material that has no relationship with products and services of the Forensic Laboratory;
- sending of messages to external "newsgroups" or bulletin boards without it being expressly defined in the employee's job responsibilities;
- deliberate transmission or acceptance of malicious code such as viruses, Trojan Horses into the network;
- subscription to Internet mailing lists is prohibited without prior approval from the employee's Line Manager;
- attempts to gain unauthorized access to e-mail accounts;
- unauthorized cracking or decryption attempts in relation to passwords or encrypted files;
- disclosure of the personal user passwords to unauthorized third parties;
- attempts to alter the sender's identity during the transmission of electronic messages;
- activities involving gambling, speculative, illegal, or other such activities.

12.3.8 Leaving Equipment Unattended

Note

Chapter 7, Section 7.3.4 gives details of the controls that the Forensic Laboratory uses to control the business and security risks associated with the physical location of electronic office systems (photo copiers, fax machines, printers, scanners, projectors, and video machines).

The Forensic Laboratory should implement a number of controls to ensure that information processing and communication systems are adequately protected if users need to leave equipment such as computer workstations or laptops unattended;

- employees must always protect easily mobile computing devices and components against theft by locking items in secure areas when they are unattended;
- sensitive media and documentation must always be securely stored when not in use;
- computers that are left temporarily unattended must have access temporarily blocked using either of the following:
  - a manual password protected keyboard lock facility initiated by a user before leaving the computer;
  - an automatic password protected screen saver that is activated after 15 min of inactivity.
- terminate active sessions when finished, unless the device is secured using an appropriate locking mechanism, e.g., a password protected screen saver;
- protect removable storage media (CDs, disks, flash memory, and tapes) against theft or copying, by complying with the Forensic Laboratory Clear Screen and Clear Desk Policy, as given in Chapter 4, Appendix 13.

12.3.9 Mobile Computing

Note

In the Forensic Laboratory, mobile computing includes all mobile computing devices that can be used independently of the Forensic Laboratory network but can establish a connection to the network.

The Forensic Laboratory will need to implement a number of policies and procedures to protect their mobile computing facilities. These include:

- general policy on mobile computing;
- responsibilities of users;
- responsibilities of the Forensic Laboratory IT Department;
- using mobile computing devices.

12.3.9.1 General Policy on Mobile Computing

A Forensic Laboratory policy on mobile computing is given in Chapter 4, Appendix 18.

12.3.9.2 User's Responsibilities

It is the responsibility of users to:

1. Accept the conditions of use contained within the mobile computing policy and all other the Forensic Laboratory IT Department policies.
2. Not to attach unauthorized equipment to the Forensic Laboratory computer network.
3. Ensure that they have specific authorization from the Forensic Laboratory IT Department before they can connect to the network using a mobile computing device.
4. Not to explicitly set up a mobile computing device to be a specific function server (e.g., file server or e-mail server).
5. Not to transfer network settings or host identities from one machine to another (whether already registered or not).
6. Ensure that any equipment connected to the system is in good working condition.
7. Back up any business information held locally on a mobile computing device.

12.3.9.3 Responsibilities of the Forensic Laboratory IT Department

It is the responsibility of the Forensic Laboratory IT Department to:

1. Develop, maintain, and update the mobile computing policy and security standards in conjunction with the Information Security Manager.
2. Maintain details of all networks and access points.
3. Resolve mobile communication problems.
4. Authorize mobile connections to the network following a request from a Line Manager for one of their employees.
5. Monitor performance and security where necessary.
6. Monitor the development of new mobile computing technology and evaluate network technology enhancements.
7. Provide support to mobile computing device users.
8. Safeguard the security of the Forensic Laboratory information and information processing resources.
9. Ensure that systems administrators and users understand the security implications and performance limitations of mobile computing device technology.

12.3.9.4 Using Mobile Computing Devices

The Forensic Laboratory mobile computing device users must follow these guidelines:

1. All users must exercise particular care when using mobile computing devices in public places to:
   - avoid unauthorized access to the Forensic Laboratory network;
   - avoid disclosure or information stored locally on a computing device, or which may be accessed via the Forensic Laboratory network;
   - avoid overlooking by unauthorized persons;
   - ensure the physical protection of mobile computing device (including risks from theft and leaving equipment unattended).

2. No business-critical information is only stored locally on a mobile computing device.
3. Ensure that the access control mechanisms (which are maintained by the Forensic Laboratory IT Department) only allow a mobile computing device to access the Forensic Laboratory computer network following successful identification and authentication.

12.3.10 Securing IT Assets Off-Site

The Forensic Laboratory must implement a number of policies and procedures to control the security of IT assets and information in terms of off-site use in order to minimize loss and damage to the business. It covers:

- general guidelines for securing IT assets off-site;
- securing mobile computing devices off-site;
- securing mobile phones off-site;
- securing IT assets for maintenance off-site.

All IT assets that are used outside the Forensic Laboratory premises must be subject to rigorous controls to accommodate the security risks of working outside the Forensic Laboratory premises.

12.3.10.1 General Guidelines for Securing IT Assets Off-Site

The following guidelines govern securing of IT assets off-site:

- computers and other information processing systems is only supplied to Forensic Laboratory employees based on a justified business need;
- employees must obtain the approval of their Line Manager before the Forensic Laboratory IT Department can grant a request for off-site equipment;
- employees who are approved for off-site working must attend specialized training from the Information Security Manager relating to the risks of off-site working and controls required to be implemented;
- employees who are approved to telework must have received a risk assessment of their home prior to being granted approval for teleworking, if appropriate in the jurisdiction;
- teleworking or mobile computing devices must be returned to the IT Department when a business justification is no longer valid;
- all employees must abide by hardware and software license agreements and acknowledge that software programs are subject to copyright and patent laws as defined in the license agreements;
- all employees must make every effort to secure Forensic Laboratory and Client information and information processing systems when out of the office and in their own homes.

12.3.10.2 Securing Mobile Computing Devices Off-Site

The following guidelines govern the use of mobile computing devices off-site:

- only the Forensic Laboratory authorized mobile computing devices using standard hardened build configurations can be used;
- enable the security features in all mobile computing devices, where available, as part of the secure hardened build;
- personally owned mobile computing devices shall not be connected to any Forensic Laboratory network. The Forensic Laboratory does not subscribe to the BYOD culture;
- mission critical information shall never be permanently stored on a mobile computing device. All Forensic Laboratory and Client information must be uploaded regularly into the ERMS;
- proprietary information may only be loaded onto a mobile computing device following appropriate authorization;
- strong authentication devices shall be used to protect mobile computing devices, where appropriate and possible. If this is not possible, the strongest possible authentication process shall be used. If this is not acceptable for the business risk involved, the device shall not be used;
- connection of a mobile computing device to the Forensic Laboratory network, or any other Forensic Laboratory equipment, must be authorized by the Forensic Laboratory IT Department;
- unauthorized software must not be loaded onto a mobile computing device. This includes software downloaded from the Internet;
- mobile computing devices must be locked away at all times, when not in use, and should never be left on view in a motor vehicle or left in hotel rooms.

12.3.10.3 Securing Mobile Phones Off-Site

As mobile phones become increasingly powerful and are used to connect to corporate networks, they pose an increasing risk if they are compromised in any way.

The following guidelines govern the use of mobile phones:

- Forensic Laboratory employees must report any loss or damage to a Forensic Laboratory mobile phone to the Service Desk and the service provider as soon as possible;
- any loss to a Forensic Laboratory mobile phone must be reported to the Information Security Manager immediately after the service provider has been notified, so that a risk assessment of the loss may be undertaken;

- the Service Desk must ensure that the service provider has blocked the line of a lost mobile phone as soon as possible and also record the loss in the Asset Register;
- where possible, remote "kill switches" and mobile phone tracking applications should be utilized;
- PIN codes shall be used to protect all Forensic Laboratory mobile phones;
- only Forensic Laboratory issued mobile phones shall be used for Forensic Laboratory business. No personal mobile shall be used for any Forensic Laboratory business;
- mobile phones should never be used as a means to connect a networked PC directly to the Internet unless the use of the device to provide VPN access is more secure than other means of access.

12.3.10.4 Securing IT Assets Sent for Maintenance Off-Site

In the case of IT assets that are sent off-site for maintenance:

- Forensic Laboratory assets may only be sent for off-site maintenance to an approved and authorized third party;
- where possible, all maintenance should be carried out on-site;
- any information held in any IT asset that is sent off-site must be removed or made inaccessible. This includes removing hard disks, encrypting information, securely erasing it, or other measures;
- all maintenance must be carried out under contract, with an approved third party who has suitable confidentiality clauses in place, as defined in Chapter 14, Section 14.3.3.

12.3.11 Retaining Documents

The Forensic Laboratory must implement a number of policies and procedures to control the record retention and disposition process. The Forensic Laboratory Retention Schedule is given in Chapter 4, Appendix 16.

To prevent unauthorized or accidental disclosure of the information, it is essential to exercise care in the information disposal, including protecting its security and confidentiality during storage, transportation, handling, and destruction.

12.3.12 Handling and Securing Storage Media

The Forensic Laboratory must implement a number of policies and procedures to manage how the Forensic Laboratory controls and physically protects its storage media that covers computer media (e.g., tapes, disks) and system documentation.

The objective of these controls is to prevent damage to the Forensic Laboratory assets or interruption to the Forensic Laboratory business activities.

It covers:

- guidelines for handling the Forensic Laboratory media;
- securing media in transit;
- managing removable computer media.

12.3.12.1 Guidelines for Handling the Forensic Laboratory Media

The following guidelines govern handling of media at the Forensic Laboratory:

- Forensic Laboratory information must only be generated in hard copy or stored on computer media to the extent necessary to complete normal business operations or forensic case processing;
- copies of information must be kept to a minimum to better facilitate control and distribution. All records, and especially vital records, must be managed and controlled by the ERMS;
- when not in use, confidential and forensic case file information must be stored in locked drawers, cabinets, or rooms specifically designated for the purpose (and which are accessible only by authorized individuals). Original paper records must be stored in the document registry and only scanned electronic copies be used;
- physical access to storage media and the document registry shall be restricted to employees who require access for authorized job purposes;
- authorization lists are all regarded as confidential information;
- recipients of Forensic Laboratory or Client information or any media sent via inter-office mail, courier, or other means, must be clearly labeled with the appropriate recipient information, i.e., name, position, company or department name, address, etc. A return address must also be provided, in case of need.

12.3.12.2 Securing Media in Transit

Media items are vulnerable to unauthorized access, misuse, or corruption while being transported and therefore distribution of media items should be kept to a minimum. When transporting physical or electronic records between the Forensic Laboratory and non-Forensic Laboratory sites:

- all media must be secured in accordance with its classification level, as given in Chapter 5, Appendix 16, and this includes:
  - printer spools on systems;
  - printed materials awaiting distribution;
  - printed materials awaiting pickup for external delivery services;
  - media items, such as backup tapes awaiting pickup for off-site storage.

- only authorized courier and delivery service companies must be used;
- Information Owners must maintain a formal record within the ERMS, which provides evidence of removals and recipients of documents or computer media (to provide an audit trail should retrieval of such information be required);
- any information sent by postal service or courier must be protected from unauthorized access, misuse, or corruption. Forensic Laboratory employees must ensure packaging for information, and the media it is stored on, is sufficient to protect contents from physical damage or tampering and, where applicable, in accordance with the manufacturers specifications and its classification;
- for confidential information, consider using:
  - locked containers;
  - tamper-resistant packaging;
  - delivery by hand;
  - delivery upon signature.

Minimum requirements for handling all assets of any classification are defined in Section 12.3.14.9.

- where computer media is provided to/from third parties, provisions must be made for computer malicious software checks of information media both at the time of receipt and before dispatching.

12.3.12.3 Management of Removable Media

The following controls should be in place:

- no information processing systems in the Forensic Laboratory shall contain removable hard disks (unless specifically authorized, this includes servers with removable disks and tapes under the control of the IT Department and forensic case processing equipment, where each forensic case is held on its own removable hard disk);
- a register of all requests and installations of removable storage devices should be maintained by the Service Desk;
- all employees should be aware of the Forensic Laboratory's protection measures in relation to removable storage media, such as disks, CDs, and tapes, through induction and appropriate awareness and training programs. This includes physical security to prevent theft and environmental controls to prevent media degradation;
- employees should limit the use of removable computer media such as floppy disks, CDs, and tapes to store sensitive information files (every effort shall be made to store all electronic records and documents in the Forensic Laboratory ERMS);
- manufacturing specifications must be met when storing any electronic records and documents on media items such as tapes, floppy disks, hard drives, or optical media;
- if the contents of reusable media are no longer required, it should be erased;
- all disposition records shall be authorized as defined in Section 12.3.14.10.3.2.

> **Note**
>
> If the Forensic Laboratory servers use removable media for backup, the policies and procedures for backing up servers is defined in Chapter 7, Section 7.7.4.

12.3.13 Managing Compliance

The Forensic Laboratory should implement a number of policies and procedures to ensure that the Forensic Laboratory complies with all legal and system technical requirements. It covers:

- complying with legal and regulatory requirements within the jurisdiction;
- reviewing the information security system;
- reviewing system technical compliance.

12.3.13.1 Complying with Legal Requirements

The Forensic Laboratory information systems must comply with all required legal and regulatory requirements by implementing the following processes and procedures:

- identifying applicable legislation and regulation within the jurisdiction;
- protecting intellectual property rights within the jurisdiction;
- safeguarding the Forensic Laboratory forensic case processing and general business records;
- information protection and privacy of personal information;
- preventing misuse of information systems;
- collecting evidence for compliance;
- regulation of cryptographic controls within the jurisdiction.

12.3.13.1.1 Identifying Applicable Legislation

All relevant statutory, regulatory, and contractual requirements are defined in various Forensic Laboratory documentation in the IMS including policies, standards, procedures, contracts, and project documentation.

A list of these is maintained by the Information Security Manager in the SoA document, as given in Appendix 1 and by the General Counsel for all contractual obligations that need to be met, specifically in the areas of information security and Service Level Agreements (SLAs).

Changes to this list are maintained by the Information Security Committee, where the General Counsel is a member.

12.3.13.1.2 Protecting Intellectual Property Rights

The Forensic Laboratory must ensure that it meets all legislative and licensing requirements for all intellectual property rights for any third party suppliers (e.g., Software Developers as well as publishers of printed or electronic documents). In this context, "Software" means computer instructions or information that is stored electronically. The Forensic Laboratory will have contracts and licenses with software vendors, which enable the use of their software by specific groups of computer users or for specified applications. These contracts acknowledge the ownership of the copyright in the software. The use of such software outside the terms of the contracts is prohibited.

As well as respecting the rights of third parties whose copyright material the Forensic Laboratory uses, it must ensure that any third party that uses its copyright material also respects those rights.

The following controls shall be in place for the Forensic Laboratory using third-party copyright material:

- all software and other intellectual products are only purchased from reputable sources;
- unless authorized by the Copyright Owner, software cannot be copied to another location;
- software cannot be loaned for use outside the department for which it is licensed, where appropriate;
- software manuals and other documentation may only be copied in accordance with the provisions of the license agreement;
- books and journals are usually subject to copyright legislation and this must also be met. The requirements vary from jurisdiction, and the Forensic Laboratory must ensure that it meets the relevant requirements;
- Forensic Laboratory funds cannot be used to purchase software that has been copied without approval of the Copyright Owner (i.e., pirated software);
- illegally copied software from any source cannot be run on the Forensic Laboratory computers;
- "shareware" must also be used only in compliance with the shareware agreement accompanying the software.

A software register shall be maintained by the Forensic Laboratory IT Department to ensure that the Forensic Laboratory complies with their legal requirements in relationship to its Intellectual Property Rights obligations. The register should include details of site-licensed software, Original Equipment Manufacturer software, and software acquired from authorized sources. Software license management software shall also be used to audit software installation throughout the Forensic Laboratory.

The minimum level of information required for each software application is given in Appendix 3.

The Forensic Laboratory must regularly perform audits on software to ensure that no unauthorized software is installed and used on its information processing systems. The process for this is:

1. Each year the IT Manager authorizes a software audit on a randomly selected sample of information processing devices or all devices, as appropriate.
2. The Information Security Manager performs the audit and compares the results with the asset register.
3. The IT Manager and the Information Security Manager investigate any discrepancies.
4. Discrepancies are raised as incidents.
5. Where discrepancies are found, discussion with the relevant individuals and/or Line Managers is undertaken; where a justifiable business requirement is identified, the Finance Department is authorized to purchase additional licenses to ensure compliance.
6. If there is no business justification identified, disciplinary action may be considered against the employee who has installed the software.
7. Software found on information processing equipment for which no evidence of purchase can be found must be removed immediately, unless it is validated through purchase of new license(s).

12.3.13.1.3 Safeguarding the Forensic Laboratory Records

The Forensic Laboratory will need a number of controls and processes in place to protect physical and electronic records loss, destruction, and falsification.

The following controls should be considered:

- record retention periods are determined by the legislative, regulatory, and contractual requirements;
- all Forensic Laboratory records are categorized into specific record types, with each type having its own retention period;
- storage and handling procedures are managed using the ERMS;
- original physical records are all stored in the document registry, with scanned copies being placed in the relevant virtual case or business file held in the ERMS. The ERMS is regularly backed up to prevent information loss;
- all electronic records are subject to the in-house file naming convention implemented in the Forensic Laboratory, as given in Chapter 4, Appendix 39;
- record disposition should take place according to the procedures in Section 12.3.14.10.3.2.

12.3.13.1.4 Data Protection and Privacy of Personal Data

The Forensic Laboratory must ensure compliance to all legislative, regulatory, and contractual requirements relating to information protection and the privacy of personal information.

Personal information is any kind of information that can be used to identify a specific individual. Personal information includes information such as Client contact details, forensic case records, and employment records—in fact, all types of personal information that needs to be collected, processed, and retained during the normal course of the Forensic Laboratory business.

Personal information can be found in electronic format, such as voice and number information stored on a phone or information on mobile computing devices and desktop computers (including e-mail). It may also be retained in physical records, such as filing systems, diaries, card indexes, and even photographs.

Different jurisdictions have different requirements for information protection and the privacy of personal information, and the Forensic Laboratory must ensure that these are met.

12.3.13.1.5 Preventing Misuse of Information Systems

The Forensic Laboratory's information processing facilities are for business use only. Limited personal use of Internet facilities may be permitted, but not from forensic case processing equipment. The use of any Forensic Laboratory information processing systems for non-business purposes is minimal. Excessive activity and specific activity are regularly monitored to detect and prevent abuse of the privilege. The following controls shall be in place:

- all Forensic Laboratory employees are provided with business specific accounts related solely to their role in the Forensic Laboratory;
- when an employee logs in, a message is displayed on the screen, stating that this is the Forensic Laboratory owned system and unauthorized access is not permitted—the employee must accept the message on the screen in order to continue with the log-on process. The Forensic Laboratory log-on banner is given in Appendix 5;
- usage monitoring is performed on all the Forensic Laboratory information processing systems, including Internet and e-mail facilities.

12.3.13.1.6 Collecting Evidence for Compliance

The Forensic Laboratory has a number of controls in place for collecting evidence of compliance if a problem arises with legal implications. Evidence is collected to ensure that any action taken against a Forensic Laboratory employee or any third party follows the appropriate procedures.

Note

The responsibility for defining the evidence gathering processes lies with the following:

- Information Security Manager;
- Human Resources Manager;
- General Counsel;
- IT Manager;
- Other Managers whose operations may be affected by the evidence collection process.

The Human Resources Department will be the lead department for employee disciplinary matters.

In general terms, the incident response procedures used by the Forensic Laboratory should be followed, as defined in Chapter 7, Section 7.4.1, and Chapter 8.

The following controls are in place:

- all evidence collection must conform to the rules for evidence laid down in the relevant law or in the rules of the specific court in the jurisdiction;
- all evidence collected must comply with the following rules:
  - admissibility of evidence—the Forensic Laboratory information processing systems must comply with all published standards and codes of practice for the production of admissible evidence so that it can be used in Court;
  - weight of evidence—the Forensic Laboratory information processing systems will be designed so that a trail of evidence can be followed for both physical and electronic records independent of the media on which it is held;
  - adequate evidence—the Forensic Laboratory information processing systems must have controls so that storage and processing of information is consistent throughout the period that evidence can be recovered.

12.3.13.1.7 Regulation of Cryptographic Controls

The Forensic Laboratory must ensure that the use of cryptographic controls complies with all legal requirements for the jurisdiction. All cryptographic controls must be purchased and licensed from reputable sources.

12.3.13.2 Reviewing the Information Security System Compliance

The Forensic Laboratory must undertake a program of security reviews of their information security system to ensure compliance with security policies and standards to:

- validate that all employees are conforming to documented requirements;
- determine if security activities are performing as expected;

- determine, using agreed metrics, that the agreed security objectives have been met, as given in Appendix 6;
- determine actions that need to be taken to resolve any non-conformances identified, using the Forensic Laboratory CAPA process.

12.3.13.2.1 Responsibilities

Forensic Laboratory Line Managers shall ensure that all security procedures within their area of responsibility are carried out correctly to achieve compliance with security policies and standards.

The Information Security Manager is responsible for planning and commissioning all forms of information security compliance checking.

12.3.13.2.2 Review Framework

All reviews of information security system compliance must be carried out according to the IMS Calendar agreed by the Information Security Committee and approved by the Management Review. The Forensic Laboratory IMS Calendar is given in Chapter 4, Appendix 42.

12.3.13.2.2.1 Internal Audits Internal audits are carried out using the procedures defined in Chapter 4, Section 4.7.3.

12.3.13.2.2.2 Internal BCP Tests All BCP tests are carried out using the procedures defined in Chapter 13, Section 13.6.

12.3.13.2.2.3 Internal Technical Testing The following procedures are undertaken for penetration testing:

1. The Information Security Manager will agree the scope and frequency of technical testing for:
   - firewall audits;
   - open port scanning;
   - account reviews;
   - patch testing;
   - workstation scans.

   With the IT Manager. This is done by automated and non-invasive specialized tools.
2. The IT Manager provides IT Department resources to produce the relevant reports.
3. The results are examined by the Information Security Manager and any discrepancies or other anomalies are investigated by the Information Security Manager.
4. Firewall audits are reviewed for appropriateness, and where needed, permissions are changed.
5. Any open ports (incoming or outgoing) that are not authorized shall be immediately closed.
6. Access rights are reviewed with the relevant Asset Owner for continued business need. Where there is no justified need, the rights are removed by the IT Department immediately.
7. Where missing patches are identified, they shall be reviewed for appropriateness and risk to the Forensic Laboratory by the Information Security Manager and the IT Manager.
8. If any workstation scan shows unauthorized activity, it shall be investigated and appropriate action taken, including disciplinary action if required.
9. Where appropriate, remedial action is taken and tracked through the CAPA process, as defined in Chapter 4, Section 4.8.
10. All changes to the IT infrastructure are addressed through the Forensic Laboratory change management process, as defined in Chapter 7, Section 7.4.3.

> **Note**
> All system access to review compliance must be monitored and logged to ensure that an adequate audit trail is created. Any tools used during the audit must be protected from unauthorized use.

12.3.13.2.2.4 External Audits A number of third parties may undertake audits of the Forensic Laboratory. These typically include Clients, Insurers, Regulators, and the relevant CAB. Each will have its own specific audit procedures, but they will have a consistent theme that will be similar to the internal audit process in the Forensic Laboratory, as defined in Chapter 4, Section 4.7.3.

12.3.13.2.2.5 External Technical Testing External technical testing will be carried out at least once a year to validate the internal technical testing and will be carried out by specialized third parties. Some of the testing may be invasive, and so it will be handled by the following process:

1. The Information Security Manager identifies an area of the information security system that requires a technical compliance review (e.g., penetration testing, vulnerability testing, or other technical test).
2. The Information Security Manager appoints a suitably qualified supplier to plan and perform the review.
3. The Reviewer plans the compliance review as follows:
   - defines the objectives and scope of the review;
   - identifies the inputs to the review:
     - information systems (hardware and software) in scope;
     - system documentation;
     - Owners of information and information assets;
     - users;
     - identifies a suitable date and time for the review.
4. The Reviewer prepares a brief outline review plan describing the above details. The plan is issued to all Forensic Laboratory employees involved in the review

(who may comment on the plan) and suitable arrangements are then made to conduct the review.

5. Any contractual matters are agreed, including any "hold harmless agreements".
6. The Reviewer undertakes the review.
7. The IT Manager, the Information Security Manager and relevant Forensic Laboratory employees review the technical compliance of the information systems reviewed in the scope.
8. Non-conformance with information security standards is identified.
9. CAPAs are raised as appropriate using the Forensic Laboratory CAPA process, as defined in Chapter 4, Section 4.8.
10. All changes required are managed through the Forensic Laboratory change management process, as defined in Chapter 7, Section 7.4.3.

Note

All system access to review compliance must be monitored and logged to ensure that an adequate audit trail is created. Any tools used during the audit must be protected from unauthorized use.

12.3.14 Managing Assets in the Forensic Laboratory

All assets within the Forensic Laboratory must be handled in a standard, consistent, and appropriate manner according to their classification. This is a specific requirement for information assets, but other assets must also be managed appropriately (e.g., fixed assets).

During their life cycle in the Forensic Laboratory, physical assets will go through a number of phases before eventual disposal. These phases typically may include:

- a new asset is purchased and added to the asset database in the Finance Department with Ownership details;
- an asset is re-assigned to a new Asset Owner and the asset information database updated with the new Asset Owner details. This may be to an individual being an Asset Owner or an interdepartmental transfer, so the asset is owned by the Departmental Asset Owner;
- an asset is upgraded or updated, where the asset register is updated with the relevant details and Ownership details remain unchanged, unless a transfer is also part of the upgrade process;
- disposal of an asset.

12.3.14.1 Establishing Accountability of Assets

The Forensic Laboratory has established accountability of assets in terms of the fixed assets register, the IT Service Desk Asset Register, and Ownership for tangible as well as intangible assets (e.g., electronic files and reputation).

The following controls are implemented:

- an asset is defined as an element or component of a system. It could be hardware or software, information files, transaction profiles, terminals, terminal input/output, disk/tape volumes, business information, etc.;
- an Owner is the Forensic Laboratory employee who has responsibility for a pre-determined set of assets and who is therefore accountable for the integrity, availability, and confidentiality of the asset. An Owner is also accountable for the consequences of the actions of users of these assets;
- all assets must have an agreed Owner. Normally business information will be owned by the business user at Top Management level;
- Owners may delegate all or part of their administrative responsibilities and authority to a Custodian. However, irrespective of any such delegation, overall accountability is retained by the Owner;
- a Custodian will normally be at middle management level within the Forensic Laboratory IT Department.

12.3.14.2 Purchasing Assets

All capital and IT assets must be purchased through official procedures to ensure accountability of the purchaser and the asset itself, as defined in Chapter 6, Section 6.7.4.

A simplified flowchart of the purchase process is shown in Figure 12.1:

12.3.14.2.1 Roles and Responsibilities

12.3.14.2.1.1 Individual departments

1. A Forensic Laboratory employee identifies a need for an asset that they do not have and discusses the requirement with their Line Manager.
2. The purchase may be for a specific case, a specific project, or an upgrade to existing services.
3. The Line Manager discusses this with the employee and either agrees to attempt the purchase or rejects it.
4. Assuming that the Line Manager agrees the purchase, they check for budgetary approval and obtain any necessary approvals for the purchase.
5. The Line Manager (now the Requestor) will then raise a purchase order in association with the Finance Department.
6. If the required asset has not been received by the contracted or agreed time, the Finance Department is advised.
7. When the asset is delivered to the Forensic Laboratory, the Requestor checks the delivery for completeness and that it is fit for purpose.
8. The Requestor advises the Finance Department accordingly.

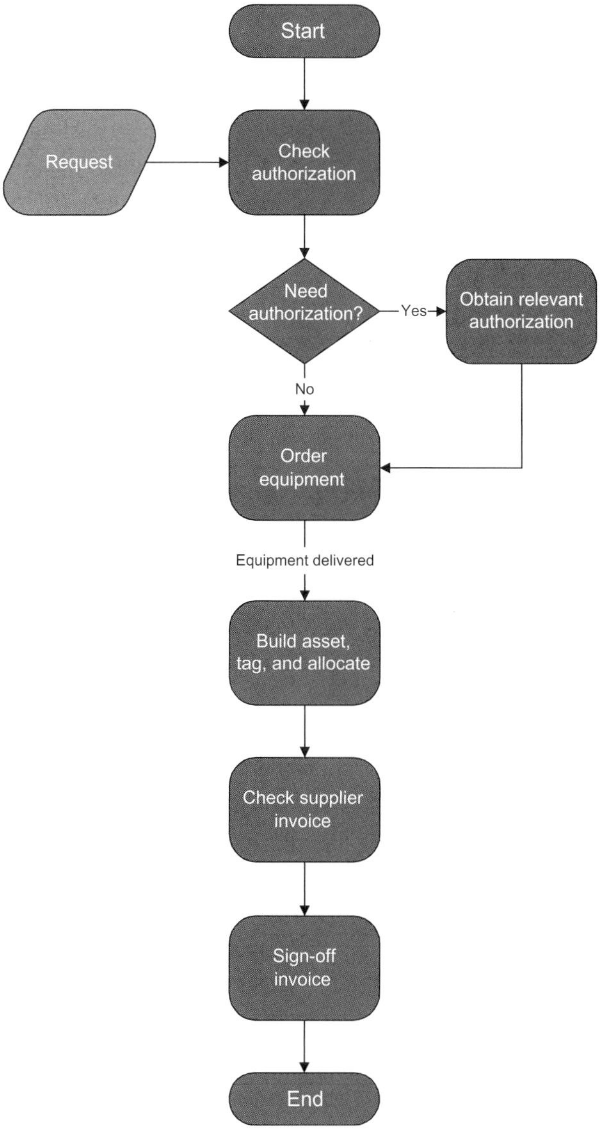

FIGURE 12.1 Purchasing process. (For color version of this figure, the reader is referred to the online version of this chapter.)

12.3.14.2.1.2 Finance Department

1. The Finance Department assists the Requestor in raising a purchase order.
2. The Finance Department checks to ensure that budgetary approval is in place.
3. A Finance Department order number for large purchases or projects is obtained.
4. A check on the current suppliers is undertaken to determine whether a suitable supplier already has a contract in place with the Forensic Laboratory. If so, the purchase is placed with the supplier.
5. If no existing supplier is able to supply the required asset, an alternate supplier must be sourced. This could be a recommendation from the Requestor or a supplier agreed after a search of the market for the required asset.
6. Once the supplier is identified, the Finance Department places the order with the supplier.
7. If the required asset has not been received from the supplier in the specified time, they will contact the supplier to expedite delivery.
8. When the Finance Department has been advised of the delivery of the asset; they:
   - contact the supplier if the asset is damaged, not fit for purpose, or is rejected for some other reason. They will either request a replacement or cancel the order;
   - implement the payment process, if the asset has been accepted by the Requestor.
9. Add the asset to the Finance Department asset register and add an asset tag, if appropriate.
10. Register any warranty details with the supplier or manufacturer, if appropriate and add these to the Finance Department Asset Register.

12.3.14.2.1.3 IT Department

1. The IT Department will check to see if there is a suitable asset that meets the Requestor's needs held in stock in the IT Department store;
2. If there is, the asset is issued to the Requestor and:
   - the IT Department Service Desk database is updated with the issue details;
   - the Finance Department is advised, if appropriate;
   - the IT Department implements the assets for the Requestor, using the change management process, if required;
   - any required training is given to the Requestor on the new asset.
3. If not, the IT Department:
   - assists the Requestor in selection of an appropriate asset to meet the Requestor's needs;
   - assists the Requestor in the selection of a suitable supplier;
   - checks all IT assets on arrival;
   - reconciles all accounting codes to relevant projects;
   - adds the asset to the Service Desk application;
   - undertakes IT Department asset tagging, if applicable;
   - registers any warranty details with the supplier or manufacturer, if appropriate and adds these to the asset register;
   - places the asset in the IT Department Stores;
   - issues the asset to the Requestor as described above.

Note

For all assets in the Service Desk Asset Register, the minimum information to be recorded is given in Appendix 7.

12.3.14.3 *Physical Asset Transfer*

There are a number of times where a physical asset may be transferred in the Forensic Laboratory, each is dealt with below:

12.3.14.3.1 Asset Transfer between Individuals

Note

This is not applicable to IT assets (see below).

1. The Forensic Laboratory employee who wants to transfer a physical asset to another employee fills in an asset transfer form.
2. The Forensic Laboratory employee to receive the asset and become the new Asset Owner countersigns the asset transfer form, accepting the transfer of the asset and the responsibilities and accountabilities for that asset.
3. The asset transfer form is sent to the Finance Department, so that the asset register can be updated with the new Asset Owner details.

12.3.14.3.2 Asset Transfer from Storage to an Individual

Note

This is not applicable to IT assets (see below).

1. Where an asset is to be issued to a Forensic Laboratory employee from the store, it will be issued from the store. The store asset transfer form is filled in to transfer the asset from the store.
2. The Forensic Laboratory employee to receive the Asset and become the new Asset Owner countersigns the asset transfer form, accepting the transfer of the asset and the responsibilities and accountabilities for that asset.
3. The asset transfer form is sent to the Finance Department, so that the asset register can be updated with the new Asset Owner details.

12.3.14.3.3 Asset Transfer between Departments

Note

This is not applicable to IT assets (see below)

1. The Forensic Laboratory Departmental Asset Owner who wants to transfer a physical asset to another department fills in an asset transfer form.
2. The Forensic Laboratory Departmental Asset Owner to receive the asset and become the new Asset Owner countersigns the asset transfer form, accepting the transfer of the asset and the responsibilities and accountabilities for that asset.
3. The asset transfer form is sent to the Finance Department, so that the asset register can be updated with the new Asset Owner details.

12.3.14.3.4 Issue of an IT Asset

Note

All IT Assets must be issued via the IT Department and cannot be transferred directly between individual Forensic Laboratory employees. This allows the IT Department to check them prior to issue or re-issue. All IT assets are issued from the IT Department Store and are:

- placed there on purchase, prior to initial issue.
- recovered there on employee termination.
- recovered there when no longer needed by their current Owner.

12.3.14.3.4.1 New IT Assets

1. A new asset is received into the Forensic Laboratory, as described above.
2. The asset is built to the relevant standard hardened build waiting issue.
3. The asset is tested to ensure that it meets its defined need, including testing all applications and connections.
4. The IT Department stores fill in their part of the asset transfer form.
5. The asset transfer form is countersigned by the new Asset Owner and the asset issued to them. Appropriate training may be undertaken at this stage, as defined in Section 12.3.2.2, for security training and as defined in Chapter 18, Section 18.2.1, for general usage training.
6. The Service Desk asset register is updated with the new Asset Owner details.

12.3.14.3.4.2 Reissued IT Assets

1. When an IT asset is received back into the IT Stores, it is checked to ensure that it is still fit for purpose.
2. If the asset is capable of processing and storing information, it is ensured that the information on it has been backed up either to the ERMS or main backup (e.g., case file information from forensic case processing, business information from business area workstations, or configuration information from network components).
3. Once the backups have been carried out, and verified, all information is then securely erased.
4. A new build is carried out using the relevant standard hardened build.
5. Issue is then carried out as for new assets above.

All physical and IT assets are audited on an annual basis to ensure that they are still accounted for. If a discrepancy is encountered, it is investigated and, where appropriate, an incident must be raised. These audits are carried out by the Information Security Manager using the internal auditing process defined in Chapter 4, Section 4.7.3.

Note

If an asset is lost or stolen, an incident is raised and the relevant asset register updated to reflect the asset's status.

12.3.14.4 Removing Assets from the Forensic Laboratory Premises

The Forensic Laboratory must implement controls for the removal of assets to reduce security risks by loss of material and to secure the Forensic Laboratory business equipment and information:

- Forensic Laboratory employees must never remove assets from the Forensic Laboratory premises without prior authorization of an appropriate Manager, unless personally issued to them (e.g., a mobile computing device such as a laptop) and recorded on the asset register; this includes:
  - computer hardware and software;
  - electronic office hardware and equipment (e.g., audio visual equipment, fax machines, etc.,);
  - information on any medium.
- all authorized assets that are removed from the Forensic Laboratory business premises that are not personally issued to the employee must be logged out and logged back in, when returned;
- all employees are made aware during induction that spot checks may be made by the Forensic Laboratory security staff.

12.3.14.4.1 Asset Removals Procedure

The procedure by which the Forensic Laboratory authorizes and tracks all assets that are removed from the Forensic Laboratory premises should be as below. This ensures that asset removals obtain adequate removal justification prior approval, and that continual controls are exercised over asset location and movement.

If a need is identified to remove an asset from the Forensic Laboratory premises, for example:

- a temporary off-site loan for project work;
- loan of equipment between the Forensic Laboratory premises;
- teleworking needs.

The procedure for removing and returning assets is:

1. The Forensic Laboratory employee seeks authorization from the Asset Owner to remove the asset. Information that should be included in the request is given in Appendix 8.
2. The Asset Owner considers the request including:
   - the impact on the business;
   - the risk to the business;
   - the physical security of the asset during transit and while out of the Forensic Laboratory;
   - the issues concerning the security of the Forensic Laboratory information that may be held on the asset (and actions that may need to be taken to safeguard or remove that information prior to the removal of the asset).
3. If the request is rejected, the Asset Owner provides the Requestor with formal notification (e.g., via an e-mail) and no further action is taken.
4. If the request is approved, the Asset Owner provides the Requestor with formal authorization (e.g., via an e-mail) and any terms under which the asset is to be removed, for example:
   - the dates and limiting timescales;
   - the issues concerning physical security when out of the Forensic Laboratory;
   - the actions concerning the safeguarding of the asset and the Forensic Laboratory information (e.g., transport arrangements, removal of information, etc.).
5. The Requestor submits a request form to the Service Desk. This forms the basis of an asset control list and acts as an audit trail for all authorized asset removals from the Forensic Laboratory premises.
6. The Service Desk raises a ticket to track the asset removal, and details of the request are updated in the asset register in accordance with the procedures for Managing the Asset Register, as defined in Section 12.3.14.
7. The asset is removed from the Forensic Laboratory premises in accordance with the agreed terms.
8. On return of the asset to the Forensic Laboratory premises, the Requestor who required the asset:
   - arranges for inspection of the asset by the Asset Owner, who authorizes any appropriate action in the event that there is a problem;
   - notifies the Service Desk that the asset has been returned.

Note

In the event that an asset is not returned on the due date, the Service Desk escalates the matter in accordance with the process for Managing Incidents, as defined in Chapter 7, Section 7.4.1.

9. The Service Desk updates the asset register and closes the asset removal notification ticket in the Service Desk system.

12.3.14.5 Managing Information Assets

Information assets are the lifeblood of the Forensic Laboratory, and they must be protected according to relevant legislative and regulatory requirements in the jurisdiction as well as recognized good practice and contractual requirements. Once all of the information assets within the Forensic Laboratory have been identified, they can be classified and appropriate decisions regarding the level of security to be applied to them can be identified to protect them.

Additionally, the Forensic Laboratory can also decide about the level of information redundancy that is necessary (e.g., keeping an extra copy of information on an extra hot standby server).

The Forensic Laboratory may choose to classify information into four categories as follows:

12.3.14.5.1 Information Assets

This is Forensic Laboratory information. This information has been collected, classified, organized, and stored in the ERMS. It includes:

- *databases:* Information about customers, personnel, production, sales, marketing, finances held in the ERMS. This information is critical for the business. Its confidentiality, integrity, and availability is of utmost importance.
- *information files:* Transactional information giving up-to-date information about each event, also typically held in the ERMS, but may be held elsewhere.
- *operational and support procedures:* These have been developed over the years and provide detailed instructions on how the Forensic Laboratory performs various activities and are held in the IMS (and also backed up into the ERMS).
- *archived* information: Old records that may be required to be maintained by legislation, regulation, good practice, or contractual requirements. Typically, these are held in the ERMS.
- *continuity plans, fallback arrangements:* These are developed to overcome any disaster and maintain the continuity of business. Absence of these will lead to *ad hoc* decisions in a crisis, and they are held in the ERMS as well as on the secure corporate Web site.

12.3.14.5.2 Software Assets

Software assets include:

- *application software*: Application software implements business rules within the Forensic Laboratory. Creation of application software is a time-consuming task; Integrity of application software is essential. Any flaw in the application software could impact the business adversely. All forensic tools are verified in accordance with Chapter 7, Section 7.5.5;
- *system software*: Packaged software programs such as operating systems, DBMS, development tools and utilities, software packages, office productivity suites, etc. Most of the software under this category would be available off the shelf, unless the software is obsolete or non-standard.

12.3.14.5.3 Physical Assets

Physical assets include:

- *computer equipment:* Mainframe computers, servers, desktops, and laptop computers;
- *communication equipment*: Modems, routers, switches, PABXs, and fax machines;
- *Storage media*: Magnetic tapes, disks, CDs, USBs, removable drives, DLTs, and DATs;
- *technical equipment*: Power supplies, air conditioners, UPS, generators.

12.3.14.5.4 Services

These are information processing services that the Forensic Laboratory has outsourced, and include, but are not limited to:

- *communication services*—voice communication, information communication, value added services, wide area network, etc.;
- *environmental conditioning services*—heating, lighting, air conditioning, and power.

12.3.14.6 Classification of Assets

Note

Asset classification typically refers to information, but can also refer to the infrastructure on which the information is actually stored and processed. Examples of this include:

- PCs and laptops holding sensitive forensic case files;
- systems containing information that may need to be physically and logically isolated to implement appropriate information security;
- other situations where classified information (either classified by the Forensic Laboratory or a Client) must be handled according to its classification;
- assets can include paper, recordings, magnetic or paper tapes, disks/diskettes, and microfilms;
- data held in other forms such as shorthand notebooks are also classified. This classification process also includes information from any third party that has been entrusted to the Forensic Laboratory in the course of normal business dealings.

The following is a typical classification schema:

- *confidentiality*—whether the information could be freely distributed or must it be restricted to certain identified individuals;
- *value*—the asset value, whether it is a high-value item, costly to replace, or a low-value item;
- *time*—whether the information is time sensitive and if its confidentiality status may change after some time.

Within the Forensic Laboratory, the following may be adopted as the schema with the reasons given for the adoption. Should the reasoning or types of information held change, the schema will need to be reviewed, and the schema is given in Chapter 5, Appendix 16.

- *confidentiality*—this is applicable to the Forensic Laboratory as all forensic case files are confidential as is most internally produced information and records. Access rights to all information is based on justified business need and reflected in the Forensic Laboratory's Access Control Policy, as given in Chapter 4, Appendix 11. Access rights may be granted to named Forensic Laboratory employees or defined groups of Forensic Laboratory employees.

Not included are:

- *value*—as the Forensic Laboratory does not process any payments that are of high value (i.e., it is not a financial institution);
- *time*—timeliness is not an issue within the Forensic Laboratory (e.g., release of company financial results prior to official release). All information held in the ERMS is subject to regular review and this, combined with legislative, regulatory, and contractual requirements is seen as appropriate without additional levels of information classification.

Confidentiality classifications in use in the Forensic Laboratory are:

- Public;
- Internal Use Only;
- Confidential;
- Strictly Confidential.

The definitions of the classifications are given in Chapter 5, Appendix 16.

Note

Other classifications from Clients may differ from these classifications and they must either be assigned to the required Forensic Laboratory classification or a specific set of handling procedures be defined according to the Client's requirements produced.

12.3.14.7 Duties of Information Owners and Custodians

Information Owners, and Custodians on their behalf, are responsible for:

1. Classifying information, functions, and systems according to the classifications in use in the Forensic Laboratory, as given in Chapter 5, Section 5.5.6.6;
2. Ensuring that risk management is applied to the processes carried out on their information, as defined in Chapter 5.
3. Ensuring that adequate and cost-effective measures are employed to minimize the risks to the integrity, availability, and confidentiality of their information.
4. Agreeing the level of security to be applied to the creation, reading, updating, execution, and deleting of information, and authorizing any changes to these levels.
5. Ensuring that the level of auditing available is in line with these standards.
6. Ensuring that adequate recovery procedures are in place for all situations for their information and that these meet the requirements of Client SLAs, if appropriate.
7. Regularly testing recovery procedures to ensure that recovery processes do work and meet SLAs.
8. Agreeing access levels for all Forensic Laboratory employees (and authorized third parties) to their information.
9. Reviewing, on a regular basis, with the Information Security Manager, all access to their information is based on justified business needs.
10. Establishing a local security administration function that has responsibility for the access control and monitoring procedures to be applied to the resources. The responsibilities of this function will consist of coordinating, monitoring, and administration, and these responsibilities should be performed by different people in order to provide segregation of duties. In all cases, the monitoring and administration functions must be separate.
11. The IT Department, as custodian, has the responsibility to ensure that production information files under their control are only updated, deleted, or otherwise changed by authorized programs operating within the change control procedures.
12. Ensuring that all operations involving personal information comply with any relevant personal privacy legislation.
13. Defining the backup requirements for their information. The IT Department must ensure that this is performed according to the Owner's requirements and that it is restorable.

12.3.14.8 Labeling Assets

Note

While the Asset Owner is responsible for classification of all of their assets, usually this is performed by the Custodian.

The Forensic Laboratory Asset Owner must ensure that all assets are classified and labeled according to the classification scheme in place. Output from systems containing classified information must also be classified to the same level as the system processing the information.

Items for consideration include, but are not limited to:

- information processing systems;
- printed reports;

- screen displays;
- recorded media (e.g., tapes, disks, CDs, DVDs);
- electronic messages (before, during, and after transmission);
- file transfers (before, during, and after transmission);
- system output (while in the system as well as having been output from the system).

For each classification level, handling procedures including the secure processing, storage, transmission, declassification, and destruction have been defined in Section 12.3.14.

Labeling and secure handling of classified information is a key requirement for information sharing arrangements. Physical labels are a common form of labeling. However, some information assets, such as documents in electronic form, cannot be physically labeled and electronic means of labeling must be used.

12.3.14.8.1 Documents

All documents shall be marked with their classification in the footer on every page, according to the document control requirements defined in Chapter 4, Section 4.6.3 and appropriate appendices.

12.3.14.8.2 Physical Assets

All physical assets shall have a self-adhesive sticker showing the asset number and the asset's classification securely attached to it.

12.3.14.8.3 Information Assets

Where labeling is not feasible, other means of designating the asset number of information may be applied, e.g., via procedures or metadata.

12.3.14.9 Handling Classified Assets

All classified assets in the Forensic Laboratory must be handled according to their classification. A definition of the classifications is given in Chapter 5, Appendix 16.

Assets may only be handled by those who have a justified business need to access them according to the Forensic Laboratory Access Control Policy.

Where a Client entrusts its classified information to the Forensic Laboratory, it shall be handled in line with the most appropriate Forensic Laboratory information classification. Ideally, this shall be agreed in writing with the Client so that there is no misunderstanding.

It should also be noted that the Forensic Laboratory requires that the:

- storage of any media is in accordance with manufacturers' specifications;
- the distribution of classified material is kept to a minimum.

These procedures apply to information in documents, information processing systems, networks, mobile computing devices, mobile communications, mail, voice mail, voice communications, in general, multimedia, postal services/facilities, use of facsimile machines, and any other sensitive items, e.g., blank cheques and invoices.

The current handling procedures used in the Forensic Laboratory are the default ones, unless overridden by the Client and are given in Appendix 9.

12.3.14.10 Disposing of Assets

There are two types of asset in the Forensic Laboratory that may need to be disposed of; these are in addition to electronic and physical record disposition. Assets can be disposed of by Forensic Laboratory employees or an outsourcing provider can be used. Generic requirements for outsourcing providers are given in Chapter 14, Section 14.8, but specific requirements for outsourcing providers for IT asset disposal are given below.

12.3.14.10.1 Asset Disposal by Outsourcers

Asset disposal of physical assets that contain no sensitive material (e.g., furniture) can be carried out by any service provider or even a charity if appropriate. However, when disposing of IT assets, extreme caution must be undertaken. The procedures for preparation for disposal are the same as those for maintenance, as defined in Chapter 7, Section 7.5.1.1. If the Forensic Laboratory is going to ship media that has not been wiped to an outsource disposal service provider, then additional safeguards must be in place. The procedures for using an outsource disposal service provider are:

1. A need is identified for the disposal of one or more IT Assets. The IT Manager selects an approved outsource provider from the list of approved providers and contacts them to arrange collection of the asset(s).
2. The asset(s) are stored in the secure holding area to await disposal.
3. The asset register is updated to show the disposal and the details required for this are given in Appendix 10.
4. The outsource provider will arrive to collect the asset(s) for disposal. Destruction may be performed at their location or on-site at the Forensic Laboratory premises. It is essential that the vehicle used to either perform the destruction or to convey the asset(s) to their premises must be fit for purpose and able to provide appropriate levels of security.
5. The method of disposal and/or destruction shall be agreed with the IT manager, based on the classification or sensitivity of the data held on the asset(s).
6. The outsource provider shall supply a destruction certificate, as appropriate, to the IT Manager, who will scan it

and associate it with the asset's records in the Service Desk Asset Register.

7. Where appropriate, the IT Manager shall advise the Finance Department.

Note 1

The loading and unloading area should be covered by CCTV.

Note 2

Where practical, all assets should be appropriately recycled as part of the Forensic Laboratory's commitment to the environment.

Note 3

The Security Manager shall undertake random checks of the disposal process.

12.3.14.10.2 Physical Assets

These procedures apply to any non-IT capital asset to be disposed of within the Forensic Laboratory and would typically involve fixtures and fittings. The Asset Owner determines, in association with the Finance Department, that an asset is to be disposed of. The details needed for disposal of a physical asset are given in Appendix 10.

12.3.14.10.3 IT Assets

The following controls should be in place to prevent careless disposal of IT assets and unauthorized disclosure of sensitive information:

- all media items are disposed of in a manner commensurate with the classification of information stored within them and using one of the acceptable methods of disposal;
- waste or recycling bins are not appropriate means of disposal for media items containing sensitive information; it is the responsibility of all Information Owners, Custodians, or holders of classified information to ensure that appropriate disposal occurs;
- The following are acceptable methods of disposal:
  - crosscut shredders—these are available throughout the Forensic Laboratory's premises and they must be used to dispose of all documents, floppy disks, and similar media that can be shredded;
  - wiping of computer media—all information stored on hard disks shall be removed by secure wiping that securely erases all data from the hard disks;

Note

Normal formatting does not securely erase information on media.

  - hard disk destroyers—hard disks that cannot be wiped successfully shall be physically destroyed using a hard disk destroyer under the control of the Laboratory Manager;
  - other methods of disposal may be used with the authorization of the Information Security Manager.

Note

Only the IT Manager is authorized to dispose of IT assets.

A simplified flowchart of the disposal process is shown in Figure 12.2:

12.3.14.10.3.1 IT Department Roles and Responsibilities The IT Manager is the central authority for all IT asset disposals.

The IT Department, via the Service Desk, is the first point of contact for all Forensic Laboratory employees who want to dispose of an IT asset. The responsibilities of this role include:

- maintaining IT stores;
- reallocating IT equipment;

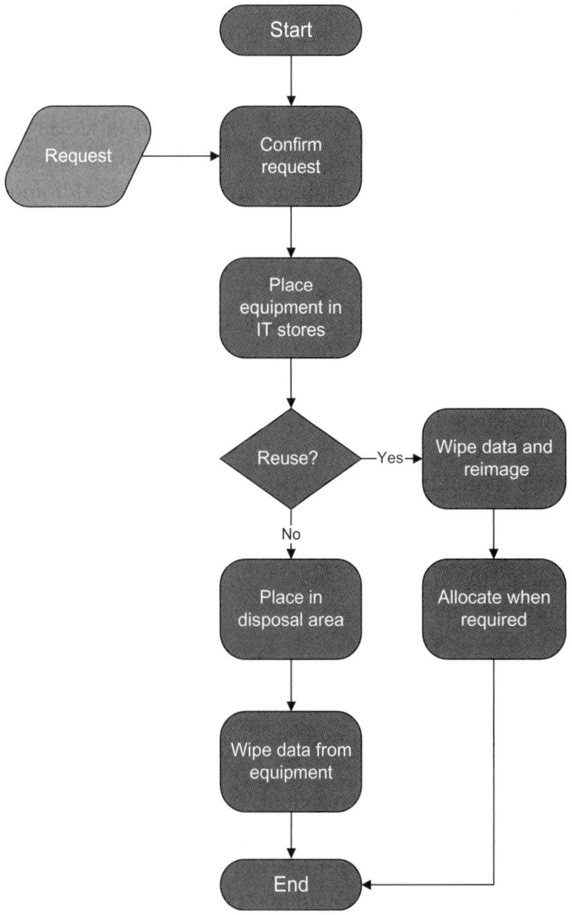

FIGURE 12.2 Disposal of IT assets. (For color version of this figure, the reader is referred to the online version of this chapter.)

- erasing information from equipment;
- logging disposal certificates;
- updating the asset register.

12.3.14.10.3.2 Disposing of an IT Asset Procedure

1. A Forensic Laboratory employee e-mails the IT Department and requests a change to their IT equipment, which causes a piece of equipment to be removed or reports a fault to the Service Desk that will result in an IT asset disposal.

Note 1

The Forensic Laboratory employee must have discussed the proposed disposal with the registered Owner of the IT asset before contacting the Service Desk, where appropriate.

Note 2

Only equipment that requires replacement based on a business need/justification or is confirmed to be faulty is replaced.

2. The Service Desk logs the request and the IT Department performs a brief investigation into whether the equipment needs replacing or is faulty. If the equipment needs replacing or is faulty, the IT Department confirms this and arranges for delivery/collection of the redundant equipment.

If the equipment is to be replaced, it is delivered to/collected by the IT Department and then placed into the IT Department stores. When a request for new equipment is made at the Service Desk, the IT Department store is checked to see whether equipment can be re-used. If it can be re-used, it is assigned to the relevant user and the Asset Register is updated. All PCs and storage (disks, etc.) are securely erased and then re-imaged before use.

Note

All unallocated equipment details are changed in the Asset Register to "IT spares."

If the equipment cannot be re-used due to a fault or the equipment is too outdated to be of any use, it is disposed.

3. The IT Department places the equipment for disposal into the disposal area.
4. An authorized member of the IT Department performs the disposal of the equipment.
5. The Service Desk and the Finance Department records the disposal details against the asset.

12.4 PHYSICAL SECURITY IN THE FORENSIC LABORATORY

The first layer of security in the Forensic Laboratory is physical security. These are general controls that are reinforced for secure areas within the Forensic Laboratory and for IT areas.

All physical security measures are managed by the Facilities Department and are in place to help prevent unauthorized access, damage, and interference to the Forensic Laboratory's business operations.

There are five different areas for increased physical security over and above the standard office security in place in the Forensic Laboratory:

- secure IT areas, which include:
  - the server rooms (the data center);
  - wiring closets;
  - the IT store (for incoming stores and those waiting disposal).
- secure delivery area;
- the Forensic Laboratory itself where forensic case processing is performed;
- the document registry.
- the Secure Evidence Store.

Similar processes are in place for all of these areas, but typically the authorizer(s) for the area are (or at least maybe) different Forensic Laboratory Managers.

Secure area access is defined in Section 12.4.4 and is given in the Physical Security Policy in Chapter 2, Appendix 2.

12.4.1 General Forensic Laboratory Physical Controls

The following physical security controls are typical of those that may be in place in the Forensic Laboratory:

1. The Forensic Laboratory does not have signage stating what activities are carried out on the site.
2. Access to the Forensic Laboratory is passed a manned reception area. All Visitors and service engineers are required to report to this reception area before being granted access, as defined in Section 12.4.2.
3. The only access point to the Forensic Laboratory is through the manned reception, which is manned 24/7. During the working day, two Forensic Laboratory employees man the reception desk, so that they can manage the switchboard, Visitors, and deliveries.
4. All emergency exits are only operable from inside using break glass locks and are alarmed.
5. CCTV covers the entrance and all exits, as well as all secure areas (as defined above). The use of CCTV in the Forensic Laboratory is defined in Section 12.4.5 and how it is managed is defined in Chapter 7, Section 7.5.3.
6. All access to the Forensic Laboratory is via access control cards with associated PIN numbers. This is for employees as well as Visitors and service engineers.

7. Access to secure areas within the Forensic Laboratory is as above but reinforced with biometric fingerprint readers.
8. Full burglar alarms are in place throughout the Forensic Laboratory for both perimeter and internal detection. The alarm system is connected to a 24/7 manned site.
9. Full fire detection and quenching is in place throughout the Forensic Laboratory. The alarm system is connected to a 24/7 manned site. Fire quenching is provided using a variety of quenching mechanisms, from fire blankets in the kitchens to FM 200 in the Data Center.
10. Where a secure area has been defined, it is secured from real floor to real ceiling, rather than just using internal partition walling.

Specific procedures to support physical security access control are given in the following sections:

12.4.2 Hosting Visitors

Note

The Forensic Laboratory defines anyone not under a contract of employment to them as a "Visitor."

The Forensic Laboratory is likely to experience a large number of Visitors for a number of reasons, and this includes, but is not limited to:

- interviews;
- forensic case viewing;
- meetings;
- equipment maintenance;
- equipment or service support.

Visitors to the Forensic Laboratory, unless properly managed and controlled, can pose great risks to the Forensic Laboratory, its information or information processing systems.

12.4.2.1 Definitions

The following definitions are in use in the Forensic Laboratory:

Term	Meaning
Visitor	An individual, not an employee, who visits the Forensic Laboratory premises for any reason (this includes Visitors who attend for: training; interviews, maintenance visits, meetings, etc.) Visitors may also visit the Data Center or the Disaster Recovery (DR) site, but they are subject to additional requirements for these locations in addition to those for "normal" Visitors to the office
Host	A Forensic Laboratory employee who sponsors a Visitor
Escort	A Forensic Laboratory employee who accompanies a Visitor during their time on Forensic Laboratory premises

12.4.2.2 General

This procedure applies to all Visitors to the Forensic Laboratory, the Host and Escort for those Visitors.

The Forensic Laboratory takes seriously the security of its Visitors, its own assets, and those entrusted to them by Clients and ensures that all are appropriately protected.

These procedures are implemented to prevent unauthorized access, damage, and interference to critical or sensitive business information as well as provide appropriate protection to Forensic Laboratory's employees and visitors.

12.4.2.3 Levels of Access

There are four levels of access granted to all Forensic Laboratory facilities, including the Data Center and the Disaster Recovery (DR) site. These are defined below:

12.4.2.3.1 Normal Access

This is access granted to Forensic Laboratory employees who, as part of their job role, have a business need to access a specific area of the Forensic Laboratory. Their access cards or other access credentials enable the permitted access.

12.4.2.3.2 Access Authorizer

This is access granted to specific Forensic Laboratory employees who, as part of their job role, are permitted to authorize other Forensic Laboratory employees or Visitors to temporarily or permanently access specific areas of Forensic Laboratory (e.g., Human Resources Manager for Forensic Laboratory employee's access to the office, IT Manager for access to the Data Center, etc.).

12.4.2.3.3 Escorted Access

This is the standard access level granted to Visitors to the Forensic Laboratory. They are continuously monitored by their Escort during their time on Forensic Laboratory premises. All Visitors shall have a current Forensic Laboratory Visitor and Visit Checklist filled in for them. The contents of the Forensic Laboratory Visitor and Visit Checklist are given in Appendix 11.

12.4.2.3.4 Unescorted Access

This is access granted to maintenance engineers and others who work for third parties that have a business need to visit Forensic Laboratory and are covered by existing NDAs or contracts containing a confidentiality agreement and who have had a current Forensic Laboratory Visitor and Visit Checklist filled in for them.

Unescorted Access Visitors will still have to sign into, and out of, the Data Center and are subject to the Rules of the Data Center. The Rules of the Data Center are given in Appendix 12.

12.4.2.4 *The Visit Life Cycle*

The swim lane diagram in Figure 12.3 outlines the life cycle of a visit to the Forensic Laboratory.

12.4.2.4.1 Prior to the Visit

All visits to the Forensic Laboratory must be scheduled in advance, preferably with at least 24 hours notice, and the following must be undertaken before the visit:

1. A requirement for a visit is identified.
2. The Forensic Laboratory employee who is hosting the visit (the Host) is identified.
3. The Host obtains from the Visitor the information required to facilitate the visit and fills in the relevant parts of the Forensic Laboratory Visitor and Visit Checklist, as given in Appendix 11.
4. The Host obtains relevant authorities, as required.
5. The Host checks to determine if an existing NDA or contract is in place to cover the visit.
6. The Host confirms the visit details with the Visitor and advises them to report to Reception.
7. The Host advises the Facilities Manager of visit.
8. The Facilities Manager advises the Receptionists of the visit.

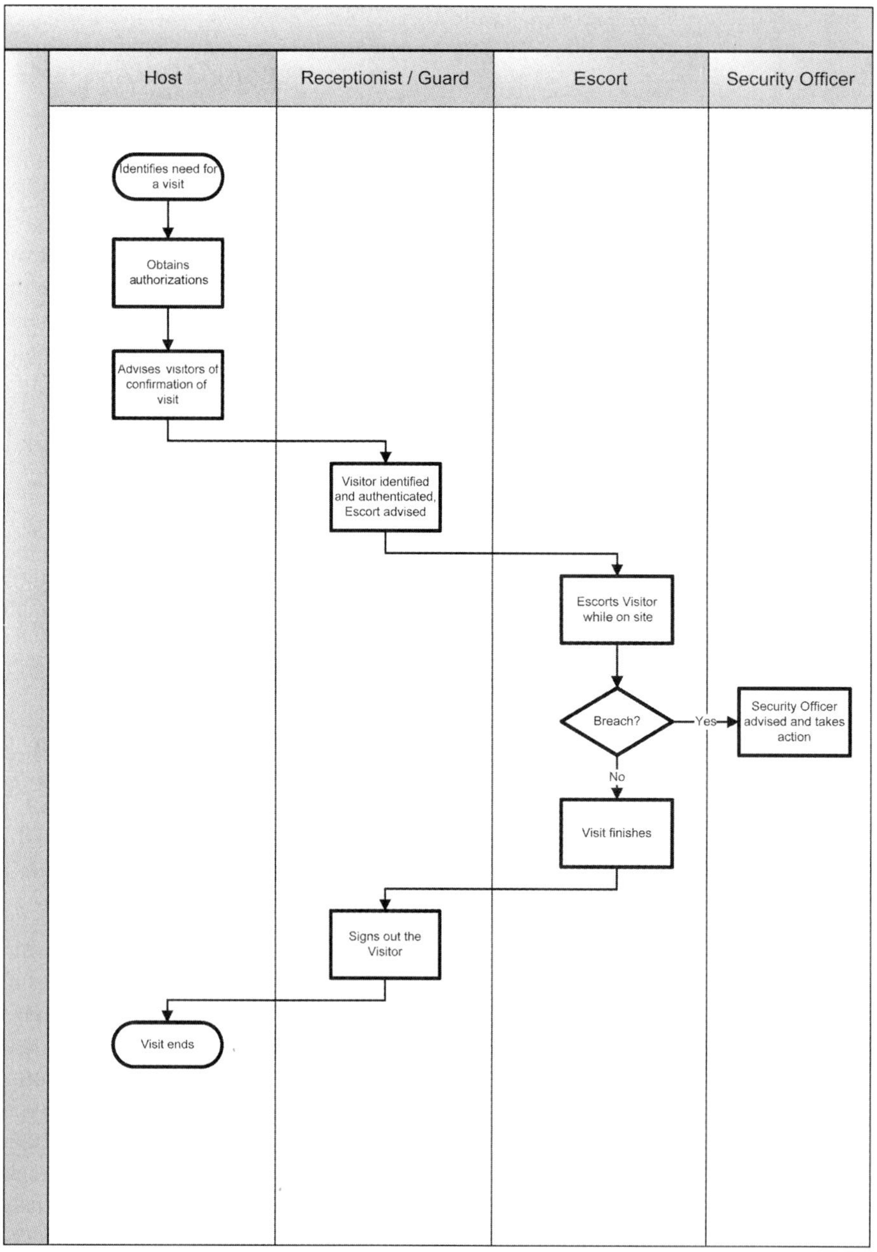

FIGURE 12.3 Visit life cycle. (For color version of this figure, the reader is referred to the online version of this chapter.)

9. The Host ensures that they are available for the visit, or that they have appointed someone else who will be present, to be the Host/Escort for the visit.
10. Where the visit is for training purposes or a meeting, rather than an individual Visitor, the Host shall provide a roster of expected attendees to the Receptionists. The Host will have been expected to set up the facilities for training (e.g., classroom, equipment, etc.) or a meeting (meeting room, etc.).
11. Typically, Visitors will arrive during the working day, but if an emergency call out is required (e.g., hardware or maintenance engineers), then these shall be handled by the night security guards.
12. Personal visits are not permitted except in an emergency. In this case, the procedure below is followed, but the Host is the subject of the emergency visit.

12.4.2.4.2 On Arrival

Note

The Host and the Escort may be the same person or may be different people. For simplicity, the term "Escort" has been used in this section to identify the Forensic Laboratory employee escorting the Visitor.

When the Visitor arrives at the Forensic Laboratory offices:

1. They report to Reception, who checks their offered ID, if appropriate, and issues them their personal Forensic Laboratory Visitor pass.
2. The Forensic Laboratory Receptionist contacts the Escort, their nominated deputy, or someone in the same business area if neither are available, and advises them of the Visitor's arrival and places the Visitor into the reception area.
3. The Escort arrives and greets the Visitor. They then undertake the Visitor briefing as defined in the Forensic Laboratory Visitor and Visit Checklist, as given in Appendix 11.
4. All relevant actions are undertaken and the Forensic Laboratory Visitor and Visit Checklist is retained by the Escort (or their nominated deputy) as a record when completed, with associated signed forms, and given to the Information Security Manager who keeps it as a record for later audit.
5. The Escort ensures that the Visitor swipes into the office and wears their visitor badge.
6. The Escort then accompanies the Visitor for their visit to the Forensic Laboratory and is responsible and accountable for their Visitor while they are on site. This includes ensuring that they wear their Visitor badge, comply with local Forensic Laboratory procedures and requirements, and return their badges at the end of the visit and swipe out when leaving.

12.4.2.4.3 During the Visit

Note

The Host and the Escort may be the same person or may be different people. For simplicity, the term "Escort" has been used in this section to identify the person escorting the Visitor.

1. The Escort escorts the Visitor into the appropriate area(s).
2. During the visit, the Visitor must be monitored at all times, where practical. Visitors should never be left unattended, as far as is practical for Office visits. Where a visit is to a secure area, they must be accompanied at all times.
3. Where the Visitor is a "known" contractor (i.e., one that is subject to relevant non-disclosure or contractual agreements that are current and in force), this requirement is not necessary (e.g., plant watering, maintenance engineers, etc.). These Visitors shall wear Visitor passes and optionally their own company ones at all times while they are on site.
4. During a visit, if the Escort notices that the Visitor is in breach of any security or safety requirements mandated by the Forensic Laboratory or any other inappropriate activity, they should advise the Visitor. If the Visitor does not amend their behavior, the Escort shall immediately raise an incident and advise the Information Security Manager, by appropriate means, for action, as defined in Chapter 7, Section 7.4.1.
5. Should the Visitor be required to leave the office at the Forensic Laboratory's request, the Escort shall ensure that this is done immediately.
6. The only exception to these requirements is where emergency access is required for emergency service or emergency building work access. This shall be treated as an incident and an incident Report raised. Appropriate retrospective authorities shall be recorded on the Incident Report, as defined in Chapter 7, Section 7.4.1.

12.4.2.4.4 Accessing Secure Areas

Within the Forensic Laboratory, there are five secure areas that are identified in Section 12.4. These areas have a higher requirement for security in place than the rest of the Forensic Laboratory office on account of the information, assets, or the resources they contain.

Where a Visitor is also going to access one of these secure areas, the following additional procedures should be followed:

1. Any Visitor requiring access to a secure area must declare this in advance of their visit, otherwise access may not be permitted.
2. The Host shall ensure that the Visitor swipes into the secure area after the Host has authenticated themselves with their access card and their biometrics.

3. The Host shall advise the Visitor of any relevant rules for the secure area and this briefing shall be recorded on the Forensic Laboratory Visitor and Visit Checklist.
4. The Visitor shall only be permitted to those secure areas authorized on the Forensic Laboratory Visitor and Visit Checklist.
5. Should the Visitor be required to leave a secure area at Forensic Laboratory's request, the Host shall ensure that this is done immediately (and also the building if required).
6. Where the Visitor is a maintenance engineer or similar, the supplier shall, where practicable, provide a list of authorized engineers to the Forensic Laboratory so that these may be recorded on the "known" access list for the secure area.
7. Where an arriving engineer, or similar, is not on the "known" list, their credentials must be checked, according to the Forensic Laboratory Visitor and Visit Checklist, prior to permitting access.
8. No unauthorized Visitor or Forensic Laboratory employee shall be permitted access to any secure area.
9. The relevant authorizing Manager shall have the right to refuse admission to anyone or to terminate a visit should they feel it appropriate. In this case, an incident report shall be raised.
10. The only exception to these requirements is where emergency access is required for emergency service or emergency building work access. This shall be treated as an incident and an incident Report raised. Appropriate retrospective authorities shall be recorded on the Incident Report, as defined in Chapter 7, Section 7.4.1.

12.4.2.4.5 Ending the Visit

12.4.2.4.5.1 Forensic Laboratory Office

1. When the visit is complete, the Escort escorts the Visitor to the reception desk.
2. The Visitor swipes out and returns their Visitor card.
3. The Visitor leaves.

12.4.2.4.5.2 Secure Areas In addition to the above, the Escort shall ensure that the Visitor swipes out of any secure area to which they were authorized access.

12.4.2.5 End of Day Procedures

At the end of the day, the Receptionists shall:

1. Reconcile the Visitor passes to ensure that they have all been returned.
2. Ensure that they hold no ID for any Visitors.
3. Ensure that the Visitor Log is properly completed and sign it off as a true and accurate record.
4. Alert the Information Security Manager of any issues during the day, including Visitor passes not returned.

12.4.2.6 Unwanted Visitors

The following actions are performed to handle unwanted Visitors:

1. If it is a simple situation, the Receptionists refuse entry to the Forensic Laboratory premises or calls for assistance, as appropriate.
2. If the Visitor is already inside Forensic Laboratory premises, then appropriate action should be taken, including calling the security guards, if necessary. Decisions to call local law enforcement must be authorized by Top Management.

12.4.3 Managing Deliveries

The Forensic Laboratory will normally have a number of deliveries and collections during the day. All deliveries are made to the Receptionists at the front desk who have access to the incoming Secure Delivery Store. The following controls are in place to protect deliveries from unauthorized access, removal, destruction, or loss:

- all deliveries to the Forensic Laboratory are held in the designated and Secure Delivery Store at reception;
- only designated Forensic Laboratory employees have access to the Secure Delivery Store;
- all incoming deliveries must be registered before being moved to the Secure Delivery Store or directly to the intended recipient;
- all deliveries must be inspected, prior to acceptance for potential hazards;
- removal from the Secure Delivery Store can only be undertaken by designated Forensic Laboratory employees and the removal documented and added to the ERMS.

12.4.3.1 Procedure for Receiving Deliveries

The Forensic Laboratory follows this procedure to receive deliveries and therefore maintain isolation of environments between the Forensic Laboratory's delivery reception facilities and information processing areas (Figure 12.4).

1. A Forensic Laboratory employee (usually the one mentioned in the delivery note) receives notification of a delivery. They advise the Facilities Manager to:
   - make the Receptionists aware of the delivery so that they can be advised of the arrival or to handle it if they are not available and place it in the Secure Delivery Store;
   - request that the Receptionists advise them on arrival so that they can personally receive the delivery on behalf of the Forensic Laboratory.
2. Often deliveries are attempted without prior notification. In this case, the Receptionists will attempt to contact the intended recipient so they can collect in person. If they are not available, the Receptionists will receive

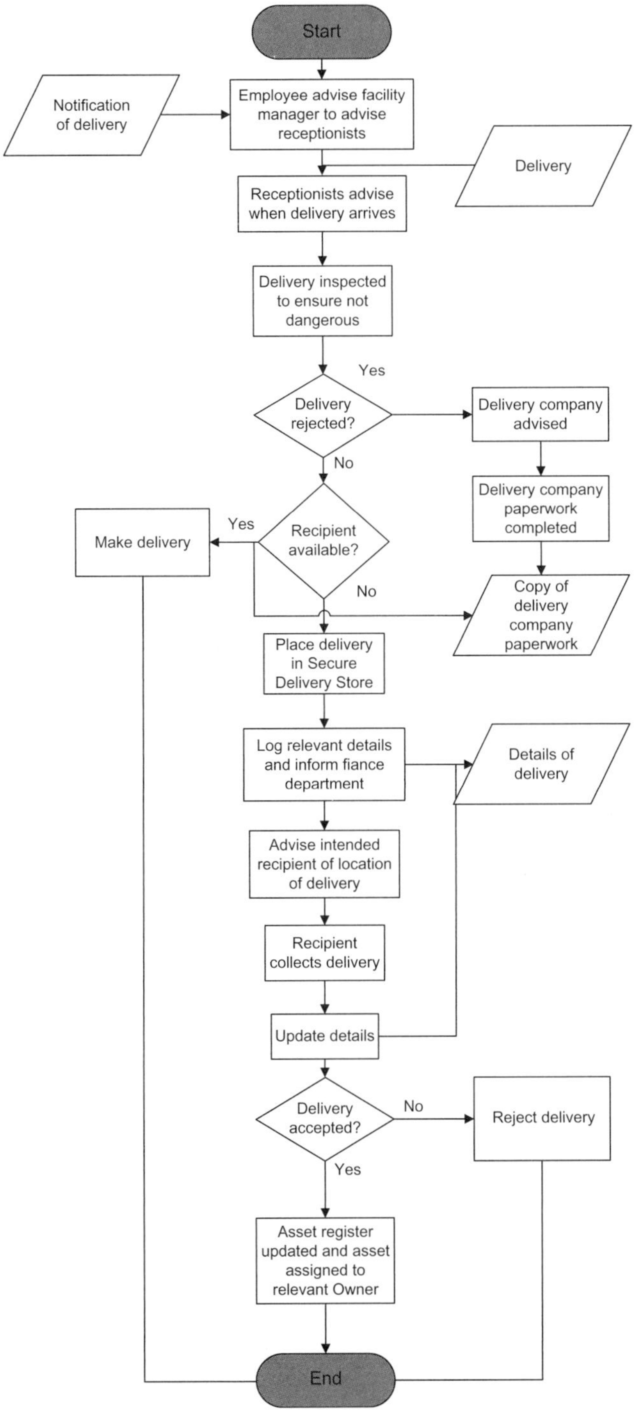

FIGURE 12.4 Procedure for receiving deliveries. (For color version of this figure, the reader is referred to the online version of this chapter.)

the delivery on their behalf and place it into the Secure Delivery Store.

3. Whether the delivery is to be received by the intended recipient or the Receptionists, it must be subject to a routine initial inspection to ensure that no dangerous items are brought onto the premises.
4. If the delivery is rejected for any reason, the delivery company is advised of the reason and the delivery not accepted. The paperwork from the delivery company is completed and a copy of it retained by the Forensic Laboratory and added to the ERMS and the Finance Department advised.
5. After the initial inspection is carried out and the delivery accepted, it is either taken by the intended recipient or placed in the Secure Delivery Store by the Receptionists. The paperwork from the delivery company is completed and a copy of it retained by the Forensic Laboratory and added to the ERMS and the Finance Department advised.
6. If the delivery has to go into the Secure Delivery Store or is collected by the intended recipient, the following information is logged and the Finance Department advised:
   - date and time of delivery;
   - delivery by (courier or other details);
   - item description;
   - delivery inspection results;
   - received by;
   - date and time of transfer into the secure holding area, if applicable;
   - name of the person who transferred it to the Secure Delivery Store;
   - location of the items in the Secure Delivery Store, if required;
   - intended recipient, if known;
   - date and time of transfer from the Secure Delivery Store, if applicable;
   - name of the person who transferred it from the Secure Delivery Store;
   - any other relevant information (as required).
7. If the delivery goes into the Secure Delivery Store, the Receptionists will advise the intended recipient and arrange a suitable time for its collection.
8. When the delivery is collected by the intended recipient, the details above are updated accordingly.
9. When the delivery is finally received by the intended recipient (either on delivery or via the Secure Delivery Store) and the following checks undertaken on unpacking:
   - the delivery is validated as being the correct/expected item(s);
   - the delivery is validated as complete;
   - an inspection is made for any potential hazards.

In the event that after unpacking, an item is not acceptable for any reason, it should be rejected by the supplier's delivery rejection process and the Finance Department advised accordingly.

> **Note**
>
> Care must be taken to ensure that any rejection of a delivery takes place within the period defined for this process by the supplier.

10. Where the delivery is finally accepted by the recipient, and the Forensic Laboratory, the relevant asset registers are updated and the asset assigned to its relevant Owner.

Note

The loading and unloading area should be covered by CCTV.

12.4.4 Managing Access Control

Physical access control is the first layer of security in the defence-in-depth model employed within a Forensic Laboratory. This is implemented throughout the Forensic Laboratory to differing levels depending on whether they are the general office or secure areas as defined in Section 12.4.

12.4.4.1 Authorizations

Within the Forensic Laboratory, there are different Managers who are responsible for authorizing access to areas. These are:

Area	Relevant Authorizing Manager
Forensic Laboratory office[a]	Human Resources Manager Information Security Manager
Secure IT areas	IT Manager Information Security Manager
Secure Delivery Store	Facilities Manager Information Security Manager
Forensic case processing area	Laboratory Manager Information Security Manager
Secure Evidence Store	Laboratory Manager Information Security Manager

[a]This is the basic entry level to the Forensic Laboratory and all additional accesses to "secure areas" require this basic access authority.

Note 1

The Information Security Manager is a co-signature to the authorizations to ensure that there is no one person that authorizes access.

Note 2

Where the term "Relevant Manager" is used below, it refers to those defined in the table above.

12.4.4.2 Working in Secure Areas

All areas must be secured within the Forensic Laboratory, not only those areas defined as "secure areas." These controls are implemented throughout the Forensic Laboratory to help prevent unauthorized access to, modification of, erasure, loss, abuse, or other methods of deletion of classified information or other assets:

- always secure physical access to a secure area on entry and when leaving the area;
- never allow unauthorized employees or Visitors entry to a secure area except where authorized access is required (e.g., by a service engineer, or by third party support staff, Clients);
- always obtain permission from the Relevant Managers when entry to a secure area is required;
- never leave a Visitor or Service Engineer unattended or unsupervised in a secure area;
- other guidelines that should be considered for access to secure areas include:
  - photographic or audio recording equipment is not permitted in any secure area;
  - food or drinks are not allowed in the Data Center.

12.4.4.3 Managing Access to Secure Areas

Access control to the secure areas must be implemented to help prevent unauthorized access, damage to, and interference with any Forensic Laboratory or Client assets in secure areas.

Access to secure areas is restricted to authorized Forensic Laboratory employees. It is the policy of the Forensic Laboratory to periodically review access rights with the Relevant Managers and to update those access rights where necessary:

- access requirements to secure areas should be changed regularly (e.g., periodic changes of PIN codes) and, in particular, when a Forensic Laboratory employee is terminated, for those areas where they had authorized access;
- all access requirements and rights to secure areas must be regularly reviewed and updated (as appropriate) by the Relevant Managers, especially in the event of a security breach or other influencing change.

The process by which the Forensic Laboratory manages access to secure areas is shown in Figure 12.5:

12.4.4.3.1 Roles and Responsibilities

The following roles and responsibilities are defined for controlling access to secure areas within the Forensic Laboratory:

12.4.4.3.1.1 Facilities Manager The Facilities Manager is responsible for the following processes in all Forensic Laboratory sites:

- applying authorized access requests to the physical access controls and ensuring that access is granted;

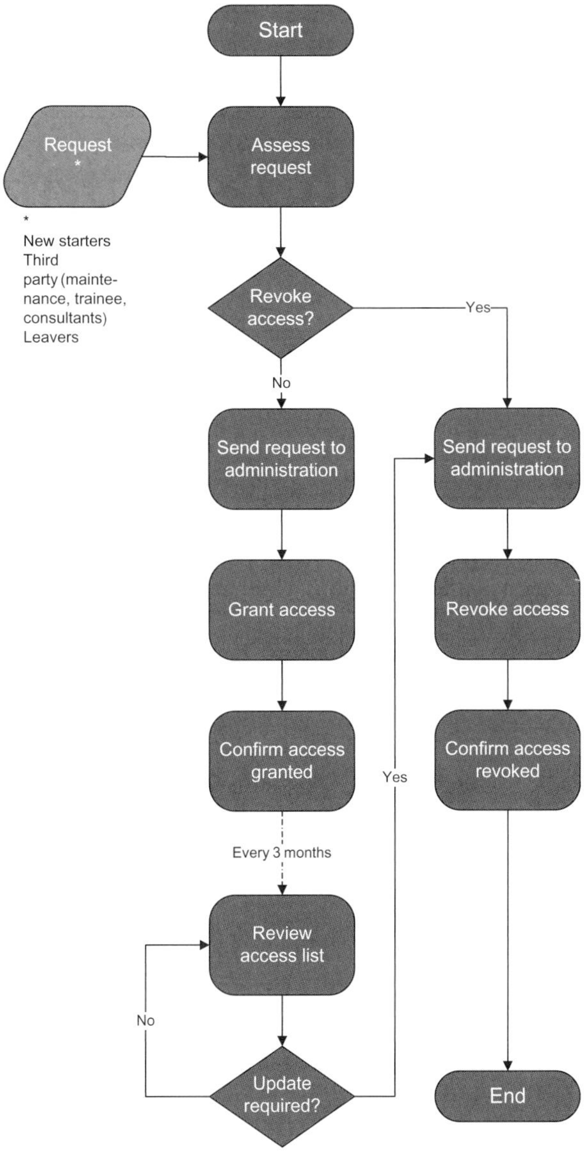

FIGURE 12.5 Security process. (For color version of this figure, the reader is referred to the online version of this chapter.)

- managing the Receptionists and the Secure Delivery Store;
- applying authorized access revocations from the physical access controls and ensuring access is removed;
- maintaining a secure physical environment in accordance with agreements with the Forensic Laboratory management;
- performing periodic reviews of the Secure Delivery Store access rights and physical security controls with other Relevant Managers;
- assessing requests for access to secure areas with the Relevant Managers;
- confirming that access to a secure areas is granted or revoked in accordance with a specific business-justified request;
- monitoring the voice recording system, the close circuit television (CCTV) recording system, the manned security guards, and the office access control system.

12.4.4.3.1.2 IT Manager The IT Manager is responsible for:

- performing periodic reviews of the physical controls to secure IT areas;
- performing periodic reviews of access rights to secure IT areas with other Relevant Managers and Asset Owners;
- technical support for the voice recording system, the CCTV recording system, and the access control system;
- authorizing access requests for access to the Forensic Laboratory Data Center;
- maintaining a secure physical environment for secure IT areas in accordance with agreements with the Forensic Laboratory management.

12.4.4.3.1.3 Information Security Manager The Information Security Manager is responsible for:

- providing assistance to other Relevant Managers and other stakeholders as required;
- undertaking audits, as appropriate.

12.4.4.3.2 Granting Access to Secure Areas The Forensic Laboratory policy is to grant access to secure areas on a temporary basis only to authorized employees and all access rights are reviewed every 3 months.

This means that access to secure areas is under continuous review.

The following actions are performed to grant access:

1. The Requester sends the Access Request Form to the Service Desk, who logs the request in the Service Desk System.
2. The Relevant Manager(s) validate the request and determine whether access to a secure area is required by the employee, according to their job role. For example:
   - some IT Department employees may require access to certain secure areas for server or network management and cabling (e.g., Data Center and Wiring Closets);
   - some third parties working for the Forensic Laboratory (or for their Clients) may require access for specific purposes (e.g., third party support engineers for server management in the Data Center);

- Service Desk employees may require access to particular area for access to IT equipment (e.g., Secure Delivery Store);
- Client's employees may require access to view forensic case material.

Note

Some IT Department employees may not be granted access to a secure areas, and may instead be hosted by another Forensic Laboratory employee, who has authorized access.

3. The Facilities Manager ensures that a pass with the required access rights is available, as required.

12.4.4.3.3 Revoking Access Rights to Secure Areas

Where access to secure areas within the Forensic Laboratory is to be revoked, for whatever reason, the following actions must be performed to revoke access:

1. The Relevant Manager determines that access to a secure area is no longer required by the Forensic Laboratory employee. Typically, this is when:
   - the employee is terminated;
   - a project requiring the employee to use the area has finished;
   - the employee is subject to disciplinary measures involving a secure area;
   - an access rights review has determined that access is no longer justified.
2. The Relevant Manager sends a request to the Service Desk to create a Service Desk case for revoking the access. The request should contain the following details:
   - access removal authorization;
   - name of the employee for which access is to be removed;
   - date on which access is to be removed.
3. The Facilities Manager is advised of the details of the revocation requirement.
4. The Facilities Manager confirms that access to the secure area is removed on the day required, advises relevant stakeholders, and then confirms this with the Service Desk to close the Service Desk case.

Note

No prior warning is needed for access rights revocation to be performed immediately by the Facilities Manager on request.

12.4.4.3.4 Reviewing Access to Secure Areas

Access to all secure areas must be regularly reviewed to ensure that all access to them is based on a current justified business need.

The following actions are performed to review access:

1. Every 3 months the Information Security Manager should obtain a list from the Facilities Manager of all employees who have access to the various secure areas.
2. The Information Security Manager meets with Relevant Managers and works through the lists to determine if there is a justified and continued business need for the access to continue.
3. If access is still required to a secure area, no further action is taken and the employee remains on the access list.
4. If access is no longer required, the procedure to revoke access to a secure area is followed.
5. Records of all access rights reviews are added to the ERMS.

12.4.5 CCTV in the Forensic Laboratory

Where allowed within the jurisdiction, a CCTV system shall be installed in the Forensic laboratory to cover, at least:

- all entrances;
- all exits;
- secure areas in the office;
- the area immediately outside the office;
- the delivery and collection area;
- the perimeter of the office;
- the reception area.

The exact legislative requirements in the jurisdiction for using CCTV must be understood, as defined in Section 12.3.13.1.1. These requirements must be met.

Roles and responsibilities for managing the CCTV system have been defined in Chapter 7, Section 7.5.3.1.

CCTV is used within the Forensic Laboratory primarily to record events but also as a deterrent.

Professional installers must be used to plan, install, and service the CCTV system and provide training to the IT Department who maintain it internally.

If the CCTV system is not connected to the network, the system time must be regularly reviewed and updated. This may be done manually against a known time source and a log retained of the date of the check and any time drift since the last check. If it is network connected, then it should be possible to automatically perform this task, as defined in Chapter 7, Section 7.7.5. If this is not possible, the manual approach must be undertaken.

Where CCTV evidence is required for retrieval, the procedures for this are defined in Chapter 7, Section 7.5.3.3. If this is to be used as evidence, then the rules of evidence for the jurisdiction must be followed to produce it as an exhibit and the chain of custody maintained as defined in Chapter 8, Section 8.6.4.

12.4.6 Reviewing Physical Access Controls

All physical access controls to the Forensic Laboratory must be reviewed to ensure that they remain appropriate and fit for purpose. These are reviewed at least annually, after any major incident or any influencing control by the Information Security Manager, the IT Manager, Health and Safety Manager, and the Facilities Manager, with input from Top Management, if appropriate.

Items discussed include:

- adequacy of existing physical access controls to all Forensic Laboratory areas and specifically those defined as secure areas;
- new access controls that may be required;
- changes required to existing physical controls and supporting systems;
- adequacy of existing procedures relating to physical security;
- updates of risk assessments;
- any incidents relating to physical security breaches;
- any CAPAs raised after reviews, audits, or tests that relate to physical security.

Any changes agreed to be implemented shall be managed through the CAPA process and the change management process, if applicable. There will be different responsibilities for these changes, depending on where they are to be implemented.

12.5 MANAGING SERVICE DELIVERY

IT operations are essential to the deliverability of Forensic Laboratory products and services to internal and external Clients. Operational procedures are detailed below.

Service delivery to either internal departments or from any third party supplier shall include the agreed security arrangements, service definitions, and aspects of service management. In the case of outsourcing arrangements, the Forensic Laboratory should plan the necessary transitions (of information, information processing facilities, and anything else that needs to be moved) and should ensure that security is maintained throughout the transition period. This process must be overseen by the Information Security Manager, the Service Delivery Manager, and the IT Manager. This applies to transfers from, and to, the Forensic Laboratory.

The Forensic Laboratory must ensure that the third party maintains sufficient service capability together with workable plans designed to ensure that agreed service continuity levels are maintained following major service failures or disaster that requires invocation of the Business Continuity Plan.

SLAs must be agreed with all suppliers and Clients so that the Forensic Laboratory can measure deliverability of third party suppliers as well as the services they deliver to their internal and external Clients.

The Forensic Laboratory monitors and reviews third party services, it ensures that the information security terms and conditions of the agreements are being adhered to, and that information security incidents and problems are managed properly. Regular second party audits are undertaken as given in Chapter 4, Appendix 42.

This shall involve a service management relationship and process between the Forensic Laboratory and relevant third party suppliers. It must cover:

1. Monitoring service performance levels to check adherence to the agreements.
2. Reviewing service reports produced by the third party and arrange regular progress meetings, as required, by the agreements.
3. Providing information about information security incidents and review of this information by the third party and the Forensic Laboratory, as required by the agreements and any supporting guidelines and procedures.
4. Reviewing third party audit trails and records of security events, operational problems, failures, tracing of faults and disruptions related to the product(s) and service(s) delivered.
5. Resolving and managing any identified problems.

The responsibility for managing the relationship with any third party shall be assigned to the Forensic Laboratory Finance Department. The Forensic Laboratory Information Security Manager shall be responsible for any auditing or compliance requirements for the services.

The Forensic Laboratory must ensure that they take appropriate action when deficiencies in the service delivery are observed.

The Forensic Laboratory must, through the Information Security Manager, ensure that they maintain sufficient overall control and visibility into all security aspects for sensitive or critical information or information processing systems accessed, processed, or managed by a third party.

The Forensic Laboratory must, through the Information Security Manager, ensure that they control all security activities including, but not limited to:

- change management;
- identification of vulnerabilities;
- information security incident reporting/response through a clearly defined reporting process, format, and structure;
- access control and review;
- risk management.

In all cases of outsourcing, the Forensic Laboratory must be aware that the ultimate responsibility for information processed by an outsourcing service provider remains with the Forensic Laboratory and is owned by the relevant Forensic Laboratory Information Owner.

Full details of outsourcing requirements in the Forensic Laboratory are given in Chapter 14, Section 14.8.

12.6 MANAGING SYSTEM ACCESS

In order to enforce the Access Control Policy, as given in Chapter 4, Appendix 11, it is essential that the Forensic Laboratory manages access to systems for which they have responsibility.

The high level process for managing access to Forensic Laboratory systems is the Forensic Laboratory Access Control Policy that is supported by a number of different procedures.

This policy defines the principles, standards, guidelines, and responsibilities related to accessing the Forensic Laboratory information and information processing systems. This policy is intended to support information security by preventing unauthorized access to information and information processing systems.

New technologies and more automation are increasing opportunities for information sharing. Therefore, the Forensic Laboratory must seek a balance between the need to protect information resources and allowing greater access to information and applications. Several factors affect how the Forensic Laboratory controls access to its information and information processing systems—this includes a calculation of risk and consequences of unauthorized access.

While the Access Control Policy forces regular password changes, experience shows that this often leads to weaker passwords being chosen as users run out of new ideas.

Within the Forensic Laboratory, a conscious decision may be made to have long passwords that are strong and do not expire, where the risk is acceptable. For these systems, the Information Security Manager must regularly run password-cracking software to identify weak passwords. When found, the Owner of the password is advised of procedures for strong passwords.

> **Note**
> This is instead of the traditional "passwords should expire on a time-prescribed basis, at least every 60 days" approach with all of the inherent weaknesses of password cycling and increased Service Desk calls on password changeover.

12.6.1 Access Control Rules for Users and User Groups

All users and user groups that need to access the Forensic Laboratory information and information processing systems have specific, pre-determined access rights to information, operating systems, and applications that conform to, and are restricted by, the Access Control Policy as given in Chapter 4, Appendix 11.

12.6.1.1 Introduction to User Groups

User groups are used in the Forensic Laboratory on all platforms and in all applications, where possible. Good security practice is not to assign permissions of any kind to an individual user, but rather assigning all permissions on a group basis, and then assigning a user to a user group:

- user groups provide access to shared resources;
- user groups defined by respective team or function;
- each Departmental Manager has authority over access to their department's shared folder.

12.6.1.2 Roles and Responsibilities

12.6.1.2.1 IT Manager

The IT Manager is responsible for:

- creating, documenting, and maintaining user group profiles that meet the requirements of the Access Control Policy, as given in Chapter 4, Appendix 11;
- ensuring that adequate user group controls are in place.

12.6.1.2.2 Information Security Manager

The Information Security Manager is responsible for reviewing user group profiles and user group membership.

12.6.1.2.3 Departmental Managers

Each Departmental Manager is the central authority for the department's user groups. The responsibilities of this role include liaising with the Resource Owner about changes to critical servers or changes that have a major impact on product(s) and service(s).

12.6.1.2.4 Service Desk

The Service Desk acts as first-linc support for user group maintenance. The responsibilities of this role include:

- logging the requests for adding or removing users within user groups in the Service Desk ticketing system;
- assigning users to, or removing them from, user groups via the Service Desk ticketing system;
- creating new user groups via the Service Desk ticketing system.

12.6.1.2.5 Application Administrators

Application administrators are responsible for:

- requesting the Service Desk to create, maintain, or delete user groups;
- adding and removing users within user groups.

12.6.1.3 Reviewing User Groups

1. At least each year, or at any time when required for operational reasons, the IT Manager and the Information Security Manager list out all user groups, their access rights with their members.

2. The Information Security Manager meets with each of the User Group Owners and reviews the access rights and the membership of the groups.
3. Where a group has inappropriate rights, the Information Security Manager obtains the correct access rights for the group from the User Group Owner and they advise the Service Desk of the required changes.
4. If a user group is now redundant, the Information Security Manager confirms this with the User Group Owner and they advise the Service Desk of the required changes.
5. The Service Desk advises the Information Security Manager and the User Group Owner of the completion of the changes and the new rights assigned.

12.6.2 Managing Privileges for User Accounts

The use of special privileged user access accounts is tightly restricted by the Forensic Laboratory IT Department so that special privileged user access is granted on a need-to-have basis. Such privileges are usually only assigned to specific system administrators.

The Forensic Laboratory standards on user registration and de-registration also apply to management of privileged users' access.

However, additional measures may be applied to system-wide privileges (such as the administrator account in Windows and root in Unix-type systems) that enable the user to access powerful utilities and bypass system or application controls.

Third parties are not allowed to use privileged accounts. Instead, emergency user IDs and passwords are used. For maintenance purposes, third parties needing privileged access will be assigned privileged maintenance user ID, which will be activated upon commencement of maintenance work. Upon completion of the maintenance work, the third party user ID is deactivated. All actions performed by third parties are logged from activation to deactivation.

12.6.3 Maintaining Server Passwords

The relevant members of the IT Department that provide server support all know their own passwords and users IDs and these will permit access to the Forensic Laboratory servers. The exception to this is any server that is classed as secure, for whatever reason (e.g., Client requirement, Information classification, or need to know principle). Procedures for accessing secure servers are given below.

12.6.3.1 Guidelines for Securing Server Passwords

1. Passwords for "standard" servers that provide day-to-day services for the Forensic Laboratory users are provided via a normal user login with IT Department employees placed in the administrator user group.
2. Passwords for secure servers are generated, recorded and then stored in the IT Manager's safe.
3. A password for an individual secure server is written on paper and placed in a sealed envelope clearly marked with the relevant server name. It is signed across the back of the envelope, which is secured across the signature with clear adhesive tape.
4. Secure server passwords can only be removed from the safe by the following:
   - IT Manager;
   - Information Security Manager;
   - Top Management.
5. A note is made in the password log each time a password is retrieved from the safe.
6. All secure server passwords are changed when a member of the Forensic Laboratory IT Department with server administration rights is terminated for whatever reason.

12.6.3.2 IT Manager Role and Responsibilities

The IT Manager is the central authority for server password changes. The responsibilities of this role include:

- ensuring that adequate server password controls are in place;
- passwords for secure servers are changed;
- recording changed passwords and storing them in their safe;
- retrieving passwords from the safe.

12.6.3.3 Retrieving a Secure Server Password

1. An authorized member of the IT Department requests access to a secure server for operational purposes.
2. The IT Manager confirms that access is required and retrieves the required password from the safe. The IT Manager records the retrieval in the password log book that is also kept in the safe.
3. The envelope for the relevant server is passed to the IT Department member requesting it, who opens it and uses it to access the server.
4. The envelope and the password are securely disposed of by immediate shredding.
5. After the work is completed, the process for changing a secure server password is followed.

6. The new password is placed in a sealed envelope as above.
7. The IT Manager places the envelope back in the safe and records its return in the log book.

12.6.3.4 Changing a Secure Server Password

Note

All secure server passwords MUST be changed when a member of the IT Department with administrator rights leaves the Forensic Laboratory, for whatever reason. For operational reasons, these changes may not be performed immediately.

1. The IT Manager retrieves the relevant secure server password(s) from their safe. The IT Manager records the retrieval in the password log book that is also kept in the safe.
2. The IT Manager generates new password(s) for the secure server(s) using the Forensic Laboratory password standard.
3. The IT Manager changes the password(s) on the relevant secure servers and then places the written copy of the password(s) back in the relevant envelopes.
4. The IT Manager places the envelope(s) back in the safe and records the return of the envelope in the log book. The previous passwords are securely destroyed by shredding.

12.6.4 Maintaining User Accounts

Every day use of the Forensic Laboratory information processing systems is achieved using user IDs and passwords, with additional biometric scanners for some users.

Note

Third parties working for the Forensic that require access to information and information processing systems are treated in the same manner as Forensic Laboratory employees for this process, but the responsibility for them lies with their Line Manager.

12.6.4.1 An Overview of User Accounts

All Forensic Laboratory employees, and authorized third parties working for the Forensic Laboratory, are provided with user accounts to enable them to access their workstation and network resources, and with application accounts to enable them to access specific Forensic Laboratory applications.

1. User accounts can only be created and maintained by the Service Desk on receipt of appropriately authorized requests.
2. The Service Desk has permission to unlock locked accounts and reset passwords on receipt of an authorized and verified request.
3. All requests for new user accounts must be provided to the Service Desk by the user's authorized Line Manager and where necessary countersigned by the relevant Information Owner (ideally, requests should be made at least 2 days before the account is required). A sample set of requirements for a user account maintenance form is given in Appendix 13.
4. All requests for user account amendments must be provided to the Service Desk by the user's authorized Line Manager and where necessary countersigned by the relevant Information Owner.
5. Requests for user account deletions are sent from the Human Resources Department to the Service Desk.

12.6.4.2 Roles and Responsibilities

12.6.4.2.1 Service Desk

The Service Desk acts as a first point of contact for all account management facilities. The responsibilities of this role include:

- recording and tracking all requests via the Service Desk system;
- acting as the first point of contact for the creation, maintenance, and deletion of all user accounts;
- ensuring all requests for account maintenance are only accepted from appropriate Forensic Laboratory authorizing Line Managers.

12.6.4.2.2 Forensic Laboratory Line Management

Only appropriate Forensic Laboratory Line Managers can request new accounts and changes to existing accounts. The responsibilities of this role include:

- properly authorize the creation or amendment of a user account;
- submit a request for the creation or amendment of an account to the Service Desk using the user account maintenance form;
- supply the Service Desk with all the necessary information that they require for administering an user account;

12.6.4.2.3 Human Resources Department

The Human Resources Department co-ordinates leavers and starters within the Forensic Laboratory. The responsibilities of this role include:

- notifying the Information Security Manager, the Service Desk, and the employees' Line Manager of starters and leavers on a regular basis;

- notifying the relevant Line Manager and the IT Manager in the event of an urgent requirement for account modification or deletion;
- advising the IT Department of any account management issues.

12.6.4.3 Creating a New User Account

New user accounts are created for the Forensic Laboratory users to provide them with access to their workstation and network resources.

A simplified flowchart of the account creation process is shown in Figure 12.6:

The process to create a new account is as follows.

1. The Line Manager of the new Forensic Laboratory employee completes an user account maintenance form.
2. This will set up an account and other requirements for the user, as required by their job function.

> **Note**
>
> If a request for a new account is received directly from a user and is not properly authorized, the Service Desk responds to indicate that the request is invalid and must come from the user's Line Manager with the appropriate authorization.

3. The Service Desk logs the request in the Service Desk system and checks that the authorization is correct using the Outlook address book to confirm management responsibility.

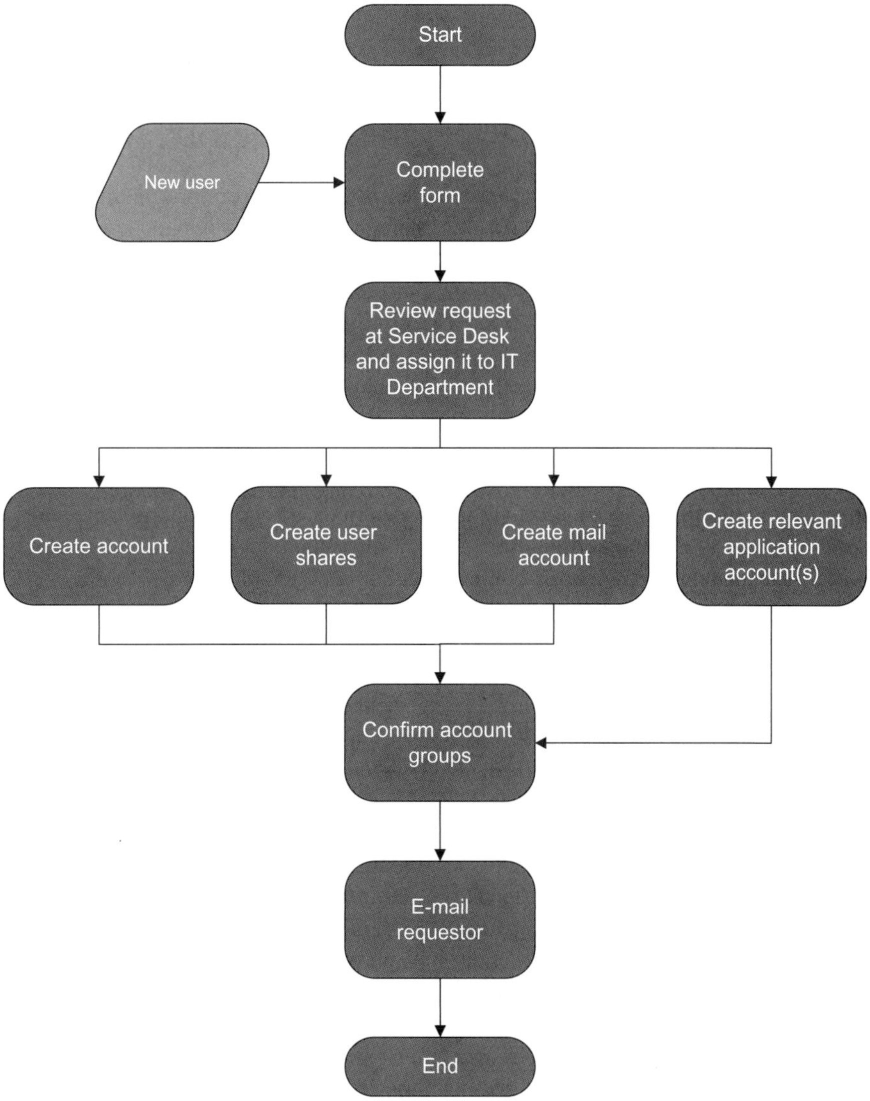

FIGURE 12.6 Creating a new user account.

4. The Service Desk checks that the user account management form has been correctly completed and authorized as follows:
   - checks the requested user details;
   - checks the services required.

   If all the details required are present, the Service Desk assigns the case to the member of the Service Desk acting as the account administrator, and the relevant application administrator(s) to create or manage the account. If some details are missing, the Service Desk contacts the Requestor to obtain the missing details.
5. The administrator creates the user's account. This can include:
   - user group settings;
   - full user details as required by the account setup process;
   - entering an initial password to be changed on access;
   - other details as required by the operating system, applications requested, or other details on the account setup form.
6. The Service Desk advises the Requestor of successful setup.

12.6.4.4 Creating a New Application User Account

New application user accounts are created for Forensic Laboratory employees and third party employees working for the Forensic Laboratory to provide them with access to specific applications that run on any operating system that require an additional login account.

A simplified flowchart of the account creation process is shown in Figure 12.7:

The process to create a new account is as follows.

1. The Forensic Laboratory employee's Line Manager completes an user account maintenance form.
2. This will set up an application account and other requirements for the user, as required by their job function.

> **Note**
>
> If a request for a new account is received directly from a user and is not properly authorized, the Service Desk responds to indicate that the request is invalid and must come from the user's Line Manager with the appropriate authorization.

3. The Service Desk logs the request in the Service Desk system and checks that the authorization is correct using the Outlook address book to confirm management responsibility.
4. The Service Desk checks that the user account management form has been correctly completed and authorized as follows:

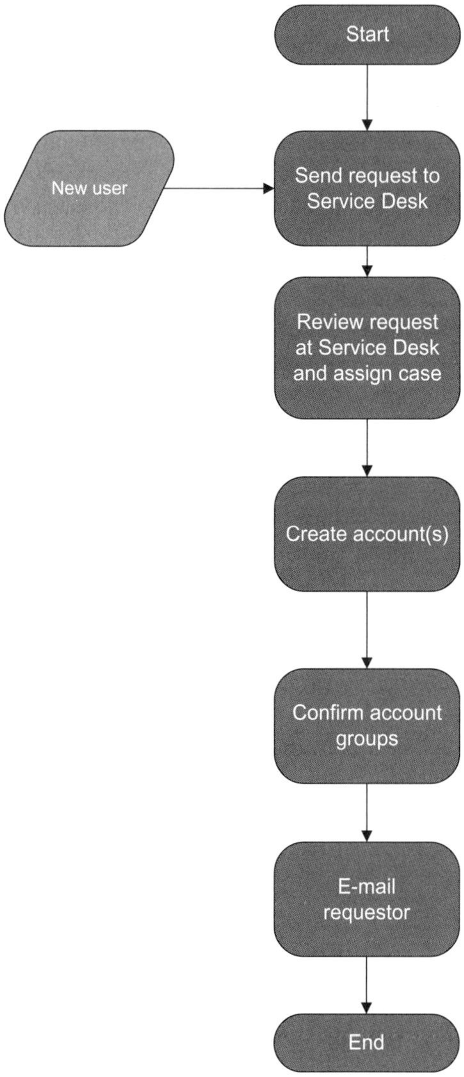

FIGURE 12.7 Creating a new application user account. (For color version of this figure, the reader is referred to the online version of this chapter.)

   - checks the requested user details;
   - checks the services required.

   If all the details required are present, the Service Desk assigns the case to the member of the Service Desk, acting as the account administrator, or the relevant application administrator(s) to create or manage the account. If some details are missing, the Service Desk contacts the Requestor to obtain the missing details.
5. The relevant administrator sets up the new application account with the default password, to be changed on access, if possible and appropriate.
6. The Service Desk confirms that the new user's details have been created by sending the logon details and initial password to the account holder.
7. The Service Desk advises the Requestor of the successful setup.

12.6.4.5 *Amending an Existing User Account*

The process to amend an existing user account is as follows.

1. The Forensic Laboratory employee's Line Manager contacts the Service Desk with details of the change required, for example, requesting Internet or Skype access or additional functions within an application.

Note

If a request for a change is received directly from a user, the Service Desk responds to indicate that the request is invalid and must come from the user's Line Manager with the appropriate authorization.

2. The Service Desk logs the request in the Service Desk system and checks that the authorization is correct using the Outlook address book to confirm management responsibility.
3. The Service Desk creates a case and assigns it to the relevant administrator(s).
4. The relevant amendments are made.
5. The administrator(s) confirms that the user's details have been amended by e-mailing the summary to the Requestor and the account holder.

12.6.4.6 *Suspending an Existing User Account*

Accounts are suspended when a user is temporarily away from the Forensic Laboratory, for example, on maternity leave or on secondment.

The process to suspend an existing user account operating systems and applications is as follows.

1. The Human Resources Department contacts the Service Desk with details of the suspension.

Note

If a request for a suspension is received directly from a user, the Service Desk responds to indicate that the request is invalid and must come from the Human Resources Department with the appropriate authorization.

2. The Service Desk logs the request in the Service Desk system and checks that the authorization is correct using the Outlook address book to confirm management responsibility.
3. The Service Desk creates a case and assigns it to the relevant administrator(s).
4. The Service Desk confirms that the user's account has been suspended by e-mailing the confirmation to the Requestor.

Note

Accounts suspended in the production environment must also be suspended in the following environments, where appropriate:

- development;
- test;
- DR site.

12.6.4.7 *Deleting an Existing User Account*

Accounts are deleted when a user leaves the Forensic Laboratory.

Note 1

When a user's Windows account is deleted, all their information on shared drives is also deleted. If some of the information is important, the user's Line Manager must ensure that it has been safely backed up or stored elsewhere before the account is deleted.

Note 2

User accounts may also be deleted during periodic reviews of access rights.

Note 3

There are some applications, particularly financial, that require full transaction histories. For these applications, a user is not deleted but is suspended permanently. The Service Desk does not delete accounts in these circumstances.

The process to delete an existing user account is as follows.

1. The Service Desk receives notification of a requirement for deletion of a user account, either from:
   - the Human Resources Department informing them of the "leavers list";

Note 4

In urgent cases, the Human Resources Department may immediately e-mail the Service Desk to inform them of the requirement of an immediate deletion because an employee is leaving, and that the account requires immediate deletion.

2. In the case of the regular "leavers list" notifications provided by the Human Resources Department, it contains the list of leavers and their departure dates, so these accounts are marked for deletion on the required date.
3. In the case of an immediate deletion, this will contain the account(s) for immediate deletion.

4. The Service Desk logs the request in the Service Desk system and checks that the authorization is correct using the Outlook address book to confirm management responsibility.
5. The Service Desk creates a case and assigns it to the relevant administrator(s) to disable the account for 3 months and schedules it for deletion, if appropriate.

Note 5

Accounts deleted in the production environment must also be deleted in the following environments, where appropriate:

- development;
- test;
- DR site.

12.6.5 Managing Application Access Control

Any software that is not an operating system is defined within the Forensic Laboratory as an "Application." The Forensic Laboratory prevents unauthorized access to information in applications, which is held in the Forensic Laboratory information processing systems.

The Forensic Laboratory's Access Control Policy restricts access to the capabilities of the Forensic Laboratory applications and associated information only to authorized users, and to enforce strict user access controls. Application access privileges are restricted to privileges required by each user to perform their job. User access privileges shall be granted in accordance with user account registration and approved by the relevant application or information Owners.

For applications that are developed in-house, specific access control mechanisms must be incorporated in the design, as defined in Section 12.9.6, and in the Forensic Laboratory Access Control Policy, as given in Chapter 4, Appendix 11.

Note

User profiles and roles are maintained to help define access rights.

12.6.5.1 Restricting Access to Information

The following controls and guidelines are in place to restrict access to information via applications:

1. User profiles must be used to define specific access rights to programs and files (e.g., read, write, delete, run, etc.).
2. All access is restricted unless explicitly permitted.
3. Menus shall be used to restrict access to application capabilities, where appropriate.
4. Restrictive application menus shall be used to stop users gaining access to system prompts or command lines.
5. Knowledge and information shall be restricted on a "need to know" basis, and publication of application content and functionality (e.g., through editing of user documentation).
6. All access shall must comply with the Forensic Laboratory user ID and password standards.
7. The need for special access privileges shall be minimized.
8. Outputs from applications handling sensitive information shall be controlled to ensure that:
   - only relevant information is released;
   - information is only released to authorized users and/or locations.

12.6.6 Managing Operating System Access Control

Restricting access to information and information processing systems is easiest at the operating system level. The Forensic Laboratory ensures that operating system access control is implemented by implementing the following controls, where applicable.

12.6.6.1 Automatic Terminal Identification

Terminal or workstation identification may be used to automatically authenticate connections initiated from a specific location or computer equipment, where technically feasible. An identifier in, or attached to, the workstation is checked by the system to indicate whether the session request should be allowed. Users can therefore be restricted to a set of specific terminals for logging into a specific system, e.g., only terminals in the Human Resources Department can access the personnel or payroll application. To ensure the effectiveness of this control, it may be necessary to also physically protect the terminal or workstation in order to maintain the security of the terminal identifier.

12.6.6.2 Managing Login

Access to information and information processing systems should be through a secure login procedure to minimize the risk of unauthorized access. The approval of the IT Manager and Information Security Manager must be obtained before any important features of the login process are bypassed, disabled, or changed.

The following guidelines should be considered for the Forensic Laboratory IT:

1. Where technically feasible, identification of the Forensic Laboratory, the network, the location, or any details of the host must not appear prior to a successful login.
2. Before being given the opportunity to log into any Forensic Laboratory information processing system, users must be presented with a login banner which:

- provides users with a chance to terminate the login before accessing a computer that they are not authorized;
- provides the Forensic Laboratory with legal grounds to prosecute unauthorized access. The Forensic Laboratory log-on banner is given in Appendix 3, but this may have to be changed depending on legislative requirements in the jurisdiction.

3. Where possible, login banners on the Forensic Laboratory computers should include a special notice, which indicates:
   - that the system is to be used only by authorized users;
   - by continuing to use the system, a user represents that he/she is an authorized user;
   - use of the system is for business purposes only and constitutes consent to monitoring.
4. No Forensic Laboratory system should facilitate a login procedure via help messages, which could aid an unauthorized user.
5. There should be maximum and minimum time restrictions for the login process (if login time is exceeded, the system should terminate the login where possible).
6. Three consecutive authentication failures shall lock users out of the resource to which they are attempting to gain access (in which case they will have to have their account manually reset) after being authenticated by the Service Desk.
7. Systems must be configured not to provide any information following an unsuccessful login (this includes identifying which portion of login sequence (user ID or password) was incorrect).
8. Login mechanisms must not store authentication details in clear text, such as in scripts, macros, or cache memory.
9. Login screens for production systems or applications must be different to login screen for systems or applications in the development environment (e.g., include a notification that the application is in the development environment), if possible.

12.6.6.3 User Identification and Authorization

In the production environment, all Forensic Laboratory information processing system users must have a unique user ID.

In the development environment, a user can be assigned more than one user ID, provided that it is done so in a controlled and authorized manner.

12.6.6.4 Managing User Passwords

Prior to being granted access to any Forensic Laboratory information processing systems, users are required to enter a valid user ID and password. This is the minimum acceptable level of authentication, which is applicable to all Forensic Laboratory information systems and users, including the IT Department (except in the case of privileged users and those processing forensic cases, where a higher level of authentication method is required).

To ensure passwords are properly controlled, these minimum standards have been developed for the Forensic Laboratory (which must be applied and enforced on all systems):

- minimum password length of eight characters;
- alphanumeric, special, and upper and lower case characters are mandated;
- passwords must be changed every 60 days or alternatively:
  - passwords shall remain confidential to the user and at least 12 alphanumeric characters long. Passwords are not a single dictionary word, repeating character strings, or identifying information that is linked to the user. For those that are permitted unexpiring passwords, where the risk is acceptable, the Information Security Manager must regularly run password cracking software to identify weak passwords. When a weak password is found, the Owner of the password is advised of procedures for strong passwords.
- a password history is maintained so that previous passwords cannot be used after being changed;
- the maximum password history is three generations;
- maximum log on attempts before lockout is three;
- users must log on in order to change their password;
- no passwords should be displayed on log on screens.

12.6.6.5 Use of System Utilities

Operating systems have utilities that can circumvent system and application controls. It is the policy of the Forensic Laboratory that use of these utilities is restricted and controlled so that:

1. Only authorized employees (system administrators, IT operations employees, etc.) have access to such utilities (i.e., those with a justified business need to access and use them).
2. Use of system utilities is granted in accordance with the Forensic Laboratory's privileged user registration standards.
3. Use of system utilities is monitored and logged.
4. Utilities should be removed from the system when not required.

12.6.6.6 Terminal Time-Outs

Use of time-out facilities in operating systems can be used to clear the terminal screen, and either close down or not close down application and network sessions after a terminal has been inactive for a specified period of time. This automatic facility prevents access by unauthorized persons to, in particular, inactive terminals in sensitive areas or those operating high-risk systems.

The following standards should be employed in the Forensic Laboratory:

1. Any sessions that are not active for 15 min must be automatically terminated (except if justifiable by business case, e.g., for performing end-of-day activities).
2. Systems that cannot automatically terminate connections must have password-protected screen savers or terminal locks that must be activated in accordance with the Forensic Laboratory Clear Screen Policy, as given in Chapter 4, Appendix 13.
3. Users must not attempt to circumvent the use of these controls.
4. PCs, mobile computing devices, and servers (when applicable) must be configured with a password-protected screen-saver (the screen-saver must require the entry of a password after a PC, mobile computing devices, or server console has been left idle for 15 minutes).
5. Where possible, in addition to password-protected screen savers, systems shall force users off after a predetermined period of inactivity (except if justifiable by business case, e.g., for performing end-of-day activities). The user should have to log back into the system.

12.6.6.7 Limiting Connection Times

Limiting connection times allows the Forensic Laboratory to provide additional security for systems that are considered high risk. Time restrictions shall be imposed for particular processes such as batch processing, file transmissions, and for sensitive computer applications, particularly those with terminals installed in high-risk locations. Limiting the time for user access narrows the window of opportunity for unauthorized access.

12.6.7 Monitoring and Reviewing System Access and Use

To ensure individual accountability and to enable incidents such as access violations to be investigated and resolved, access and use of information and information processing systems is logged. Access events that are logged (including login and files accessed) and the review process that is followed (including frequency and responsibility) are determined between the Information Security Manager and relevant System and Information Owners. While physical access to areas is covered in Section 12.4.4.3.4, a similar process is carried out for logical access control, with the frequencies of reviews stated in the IMS Calendar, which is given in Chapter 4, Appendix 42.

To assist with monitoring access to the Forensic Laboratory computer network, the Forensic Laboratory uses automated event logging for purposes of recording exceptions and other security-related events.

To undertake a system access review, the Information Security Manager follows the procedure below:

1. The Information Security Manager checks the IMS Calendar to determine when the next review is to take place.
2. Consideration is given to the planned review cycle and if there are any areas suffering unauthorized access incidents.
3. At every review, all of the administrator accounts are checked, along with any high-risk applications.
4. The Information Security Manager specifies the requirements for the review and has the relevant reports run. These will include:
   - group membership;
   - access rights for the group;
   - any members of the group with rights in addition to the standard group rights;
   - any account not used for 30 days;
   - review of disabled accounts;
   - any directly assigned rights that the user has;
   - any accounts that are locked out;
   - any accounts that do not meet the Forensic Laboratory account policy.
5. All rights are reviewed by the Information Security Manager with the relevant System or Information Owner, who has to formally approve that the rights assigned are correct and appropriate for the user.
6. Any anomalies found are investigated by the Information Security Manager, the IT Manager, and the relevant Information or System Owner.
7. The outcome of the investigation may lead to:
   - removal of currents rights granted;
   - revision of current rights granted;
   - revision of rights to be assigned.
8. Any changes are raised as a CAPA and managed through the CAPA process.

12.6.8 Implementing Enforced Paths

The Forensic Laboratory prevents users from selecting routes outside the approved routes between their user workstation and the services that they are authorized to access (i.e., user roaming).

At the Forensic Laboratory, enforced paths of access are implemented via:

1. Allocation of dedicated lines or telephone numbers.
2. Separation of networks, depending on the information system's criticality, to increase the level of security provided during information transport/storage.

3. Use of security gateways or proxy servers to control allowed access to communications.
4. Configuration of network devices.
5. Implementation of traffic-filtering controls.

12.6.9 Enabling Teleworking for Users

The Forensic Laboratory may choose to implement a number of controls for teleworking for employees and third party employees who work remotely from a fixed location outside the Forensic Laboratory business premises (these guidelines apply to employees or authorized third party employees who may be, or plan to be, working from home).

12.6.9.1 Obtaining Approval for Teleworking

A formal request must be submitted to the Forensic Laboratory Service Desk by an authorized Line Manager for approval if a teleworking environment involves remote access to the Forensic Laboratory information processing systems:

1. An authorized Line Manager (the Requestor) submits a formal request to the Forensic Laboratory Service Desk for teleworking approval and opens a ticket with the Service Desk. The Forensic Laboratory Teleworking Request Form contents are given in Appendix 14. Details must include:
   - name of user;
   - description of the business need;
   - location and description of teleworking environment;
   - equipment to be used;
   - access required to information and information processing systems.
2. The request is reviewed by the IT Manager, the Information Security Manager, and the relevant Information and Application Owners. In cases that are considered high risk, a detailed risk assessment must be undertaken by the Information Security Manager. The following risks are considered when reviewing a teleworking request:
   - physical security of the proposed teleworking site;
   - security requirements for communications with the Forensic Laboratory networks and access to the Forensic Laboratory information processing systems;
   - potential threats from unauthorized access to information and information processing systems.
3. The site is visited by the IT Manager and the Information Security Manager who undertakes a risk assessment and audit of the site, using the procedures defined in Chapter 4, Section 4.7.3.
4. The IT Manager provides the Requestor with approval (or in the event that the request is considered high risk, alternative arrangements may be put to the relevant Line Manager for further discussion).
5. Any appropriate corrective action is undertaken at the proposed location, and the Teleworker undertakes relevant training.
6. After approval is issued, the IT Department performs the following:
   - issue the user with details of the work permitted, the remote connection(s) permitted, the Forensic Laboratory systems that the user is allowed to access remotely, and levels of access that are permitted;
   - enable the required connections.

12.6.10 Guidelines for Securing Teleworking Environments

The following guidelines must be followed for securing teleworking environments where remote access is required to the Forensic Laboratory information processing systems:

1. All users must abide by these teleworking guidelines.
2. All users must abide by the Forensic Laboratory IT Department guidelines on Mobile and Teleworking computing when working remotely from the Forensic Laboratory.
3. Users are responsible for backing up any business information that may be stored locally (generally business information should not be stored locally on mobile or teleworking computers).
4. Users are responsible for the physical security of the teleworking site and should exercise particular care to:
   - avoid unauthorized access to the Forensic Laboratory network;
   - avoid disclosure or information;
   - avoid overlooking by unauthorized persons, including family and Visitors;
   - ensure the physical protection of Forensic Laboratory equipment (including risks from theft and leaving equipment unattended).
5. The Forensic Laboratory IT Department is responsible for providing support services for teleworking issues associated with remote access to the Forensic Laboratory information processing systems.
6. Remote connections to the Forensic Laboratory information processing systems shall be monitored for security and audit purposes.
7. The Forensic Laboratory IT Department will revoke rights of remote access to information processing systems when:
   - an user fails to comply with any Forensic Laboratory information security guideline, policy, or procedure;
   - teleworking activities cease to exist;
   - the Human Resources Department or relevant Line Manager indicates that Teleworking is no longer appropriate for the user.

12.7 MANAGING INFORMATION ON PUBLIC SYSTEMS

The Forensic Laboratory has a formal approval process before information is made publicly available. This process is owned by the Chief Operating Officer.

The Forensic Laboratory manages publicly accessed Web server hardware and software in order to minimize risks that may arise as a result of information being made generally available through Web technologies.

> **Note**
>
> A lot of potential problems that are associated with Web servers can be mitigated by either completely separating the Web server from the private networks via a strong DMZ, or having it completely off-site, and managed by a third party under contract. (i.e., a Web hosting service).

In general, the Forensic Laboratory must ensure that:

1. Security risks to the Forensic Laboratory caused by poorly managed and maintained Web servers are mitigated.
2. Web servers connected to the Forensic Laboratory network shall be managed in such a way that the Forensic Laboratory presents an image of reliability.
3. Web facilities handled and managed by third parties comply with the Forensic Laboratory information security requirements, including change and incident management.
4. Material related to the Forensic Laboratory must only be published on the formal Forensic Laboratory Web server(s).
5. the production process for any externally published documents is defined in Chapter 4, Section 4.6.3.
6. Any of the Forensic Laboratory published material must be formally approved by the "business" prior to publication on any Web sites, using the Forensic Laboratory change management process, as defined in Chapter 7, Section 7.4.3.
7. Records of the review and approval process must be stored in the ERMS.

12.7.1 Hardware and Software Standards

The following guidelines apply to ensure that configuration standards are maintained for systems containing publicly available information:

1. Web servers shall conform to standards for configuration that represent current good practice. Specifics of configuration for hardware, server operating systems, Web server software, and any other relevant software are reviewed and updated on regular basis.
2. All systems are patched to manufacturer recommended levels at all times.
3. All server applications are patched to manufacturer recommended levels at all times.
4. The control of technical vulnerabilities and patching are defined in Chapter 7, Sections 7.6.2 and 7.6.3, respectively.

12.7.2 Information Security Standards

The following guidelines apply to ensure that information security standards are maintained for systems containing publicly available information:

1. The requirements of the Forensic Laboratory Information Security Policy must be met at all times.
2. Industry good practices for information security applied to Web server configuration and management shall be implemented and followed at all times.
3. Information security requirements are reviewed regularly.

12.7.3 Published Information Guidelines

The following guidelines apply to ensure that material published on publicly available systems is suitable for release:

1. The Forensic Laboratory document management process is responsible for checking information before publication to a Web server.
2. Once internally checked, it may be submitted to the CAB, as defined in Chapter 7, Section 7.4.3, for document change control approval. Attendance at that CAB is mandatory for all stakeholders that may be affected by any published information.
3. The Forensic Laboratory IT Department provides tools to enable the authorized departments to publish information to the Web server, but only after formal approval for publishing is granted.
4. The Forensic Laboratory IT Department enables designated and authorized Forensic Laboratory departmental employees to access Web servers based on business need only.

12.7.4 Server Management Guidelines

The following guidelines apply to ensure that servers containing publicly available information are managed appropriately:

1. Web servers are only accessed by designated IT Department employees.
2. Web servers are managed in order to assure maximum availability, balanced with appropriate security for the content, based on a risk assessment undertaken by the

Information Security Manager and the relevant content Owner(s).
3. Downtime is scheduled well in advance to ensure that viewers have advance notice of the work and is timed to coincide with periods of minimum usage.
4. The IT Department regularly checks Web servers to determine that all hardware and software is correct including versions and patches installed.
5. The IT Department regularly reviews server and other logs for publicly available systems to determine, and then suggest appropriate action for the following:
   - the number of times that security on the Forensic Laboratory Web servers is compromised or there are compromise attempts detected.
   - the total time a registered Web server is not available to respond to http requests.
   - the number of instances of information published without the correct approvals.
6. Where Web servers are managed or hosted by third parties, the above applies and formal reports of monitoring must be submitted to the IT Manager and the Information Security Manager on a regular basis.

12.7.5 Reviewing Security for Public Systems

The process by which the Forensic Laboratory manages and reviews information on public systems is as follows:

1. The Forensic Laboratory IT Department is responsible for Web servers security review. The assessment covers the following areas:
   - hardware and software standards;
   - information security standards;
   - published information;
   - server management.
2. The Forensic Laboratory IT Department assesses the requirements from a security perspective, taking particular notice of changes in configuration settings, access by employees and external partners.
3. The Forensic Laboratory IT Department sends an e-mail outlining their findings to the IT Manager and the Information Security Manager together with any recommendations as appropriate.
4. The IT Manager checks the findings and determines whether the recommendations can be approved. Additional discussions are held with the Information Security Manager and any other stakeholders to clarify any of the findings or recommendations.
5. The IT Manager confirms the decisions as follows:
   - if approved, the IT Manager sends an e-mail to the IT Department Team and the Information Security Manager confirming that the recommendations can be implemented.

Note

The request is not granted on a permanent basis. A review of the request must be scheduled by the IT Manager and the Information Security Manager within 12 months to ensure that the request remains valid.

   - if rejected, the IT Manager sends an e-mail to the IT Department and the Information Security Manager outlining the reasons for rejection.
6. The IT Department implements the changes to the public servers system.
7. At the appointed time according to the review schedule, the public servers are assessed again to check whether the changes remain valid using the above procedure.

12.8 SECURELY MANAGING IT SYSTEMS

As well as managing the IT infrastructure, the Forensic Laboratory IT Department must securely manage IT operations on behalf of their internal and external Clients. These are typically day-to-day operational issues.

12.8.1 Accepting New Systems

When the Forensic Laboratory accepts a new system, it must ensure that all changes to the Forensic Laboratory information processing systems have been subjected to rigorous testing and checking prior to their implementation in the live environment.

All changes to the Forensic Laboratory information systems must be undertaken in accordance with the Forensic Laboratory change management procedures, as defined in Chapter 7, Section 7.4.3.

12.8.1.1 Guidelines for System Acceptance

Acceptance criteria for new systems are:

- all security assessments must have been performed, and security controls developed, tested, documented, and signed off by the Information Security Manager;
- all performance and capacity requirements must be fulfilled;
- all development problems must be successfully resolved;
- testing proves there will be no adverse effect on existing live systems;
- all specifications have been met;
- the system can be supported by the Forensic Laboratory IT on a continuing basis (for example, via the Service Desk);
- roll-back arrangements are in place in the event of the changes failing to function as intended (all roll-backs

must be performed in accordance with the Forensic Laboratory change management procedures);
- sign-off has been obtained from the key stakeholders (for example, the business unit, System Administrator(s), Application Owner, etc.);
- error recovery and restart procedures are established, and contingency plans have been developed or updated;
- system operating procedures have been tested;
- users are educated in the use of the system, and the IT Department are trained to run the system correctly.

In addition, the following checks should be observed when accepting a new system:

- old software, procedures, and documentation must be discontinued;
- acceptance checks, release and configuration management processes, as defined in Chapter 7, Sections 7.4.4 and 7.4.5, respectively, must ensure that only tested and approved versions of software are accepted into the live environment;
- responsibility must be transferred to system operators after installation is complete.

12.8.1.2 Procedures for Assessing and Accepting a New System

The process by which the Forensic Laboratory accepts new systems is as follows:

1. Appropriate members of the IT Department, under the supervision of the IT Manager, assesses the system and sends the assessment reports to the Information Security Manager to determine whether any changes and enhancements are required to meet the security standards of the Forensic Laboratory. A report is produced outlining the changes.
2. The IT Manager and the Information Security Manager review the report and then send it to relevant stakeholders for comment. Follow-up discussions can be held with the developers to clarify any areas of concern or other relevant issues raised.
3. Appropriate members of the IT Department, with input from the Information Security Manager, develop security, test, and acceptance procedures that act as the basis for testing a beta version of the system, where it is developed in-house or a trial version if it is a COTS product.
4. Later in the development cycle, the developers release a beta version of the system for testing purposes.
5. The test team installs the beta or trial version of the system and performs security checks on it according to test and acceptance procedures.
6. For Forensic Tools, Validation Testing is carried out, as defined in Chapter 7, Section 7.5.5.
7. The results of the testing and all security recommendations are documented in a report and sent to the Information Security Manager.
8. The Information Security Manager checks the results and security recommendations and passes on those that require action to the development team or the supplier. The development team or the supplier, as appropriate, implements the security recommendations and signs off the work with the Information Security Manager and other relevant stakeholders through additional testing and formal approval at the CAB, as defined in Chapter 7, Section 7.4.3.

12.8.2 Securing Business Information Systems

The following security standards are in place at the Forensic Laboratory to control the business and security risks associated with business information systems such as accounting systems, voice recording systems, photo copiers, fax machines, printers, scanners, projectors, and video machines.

12.8.2.1 Roles and Responsibilities

12.8.2.1.1 Information Security Manager

The Information Security Manager is responsible for risk assessments.

12.8.2.1.2 IT Manager

The IT Manager is responsible for configuration and management of the information processing systems.

12.8.2.1.3 Information System Owners

The Owner of the information system has specific responsibilities for classification of assets, as defined in Section 12.3.14.6. In addition to those responsibilities, they are responsible for:

- undertaking a risk assessment, with the Information Security Manager, to take into account all known vulnerabilities in all the administrative and forensic case processing systems in the Forensic Laboratory and particularly in terms of physical access and connection with due regard for the access control, as defined in Chapter 5;
- any special considerations to known vulnerabilities in the administrative and forensic case processing systems where information is shared between different users or departments/units within the Forensic Laboratory;
- full consideration of the vulnerabilities of information in business communication systems, e.g., recording phone calls or conference calls, confidentiality of calls, storage of facsimiles, opening mail, distribution of mail etc.
- policy and appropriate controls to manage information sharing;

- information processing systems (especially printers, faxes, and photocopiers) must only be installed in areas that are not freely accessible;
- where possible, information processing systems handling classified or sensitive information should only be installed in rooms or areas that are constantly occupied or are otherwise secured;
- where possible, entry to areas containing information processing systems should be controlled, and usage of those systems and all peripherals connected to them restricted to appropriate and authorized business users;
- controls must be implemented to prevent incoming fax messages from being viewed or removed by unauthorized employees or Visitors;
- printers must be sited in accordance to the classification of information that is being printed;
- processing output that is spooled must be controlled via proper configuration of print servers to prevent reports from being accidentally selected from different print spool queues and/or directed to a different printer;
- printers and copiers must not be left unattended by Forensic Laboratory employees if Confidential or Strictly Confidential information is being printed or copied;
- fax machines must not be left unattended if Confidential or Strictly Confidential information is being faxed;
- all waste generated in the course of copying, printing, and faxing Confidential or Strictly Confidential information must be destroyed in accordance with the procedure for disposal of media, as defined in Section 12.3.14.10;
- information sent via a fax must include a Forensic Laboratory cover page with a disclaimer that the information sent is for the use of the intended recipient only;
- excluding categories of sensitive business information and classified documents if any system does not provide an appropriate level of protection for that information;
- restricting access to diary information relating to selected individuals, e.g., personnel working on sensitive projects or cases;
- ensuring that the Access Control Policy of the information processing system is appropriate for its intended and authorized business use, including users allowed to use the system and the locations from which it may be accessed;
- restricting selected system and administrative facilities to specific categories of user;
- identifying the status of information processing system users, e.g., Forensic Laboratory employees and any third party employees in directories and by user-naming convention of all accounts for the benefit of other users;
- retention and backup of information held on the system, as given in Chapter 4, Appendix 16, and defined in Chapter 7, Section 7.7.4, respectively;
- business continuity arrangements, as defined in Chapter 13.

12.8.3 Ensuring Correct Data Processing

It is the Forensic Laboratory's policy to ensure that all information input, processing, and output are validated to ensure that the output from the information processing system meets the expectations defined. All validation tests must be recorded and securely maintained, forensic tool validation is defined in Chapter 7, Section 7.5.5, but normal validation is covered below.

To do this, the Forensic Laboratory checks that information has not been modified by any unauthorized process during its life cycle. Testing is carried out at the following stages:

- data input;
- data processing;
- data output.

12.8.3.1 Security During Data Input

The Forensic Laboratory should consider implementing the following controls during information input to ensure that information is validated as correct and appropriate:

- data input requirements are fully validated during system development, testing, and user acceptance;
- data input is subject to full validation checks such as out-of-range values, invalid characters, and missing or incomplete information;
- users regularly check information input into systems.

12.8.3.2 Security During Data Processing

The Forensic Laboratory should consider implementing the following controls during information processing to ensure that information is not corrupted:

- data processing requirements are validated during system development, testing, and user acceptance;
- programs and batch systems are run in the correct order;
- users regularly check processing systems to ensure that operations are running properly;
- message authentication is performed on systems where integrity of the message is paramount, such as systems with credit card information and sensitive e-mails.

12.8.3.3 Security during data output

The Forensic Laboratory should consider implementing the following controls during information output to ensure that information is validated as correct and appropriate:

- data output requirements are validated during system development, testing, and user acceptance;
- data output is subject to validation checks such as out-of-range values, invalid characters, and missing or incomplete information;
- users regularly check information output from systems;

- input is followed through the processing life cycle to ensure that the actual output produced is as expected from the text packs and test cases.

12.8.3.4 *Types of Testing*

The Forensic Laboratory should implement the following types of testing prior to submission of any system upgrade or before a new system is submitted to the CAB:

- integration testing;
- link testing;
- performance testing;
- regression testing to ensure that no new change corrupts a previous working change;
- unit testing;
- User Acceptance Testing (UAT);
- validation for Forensic Tools is defined in Chapter 7, Section 7.5.5.

Within the Forensic Laboratory, standard test cases and test packs are used with automated testing tools to ensure completeness and consistency of testing, rather than relying on any human bias.

12.8.3.5 *Test Records*

The Forensic Laboratory maintains full records of all testing for later audits. These test packs, with the results, shall be submitted to the change management process.

12.8.4 Information Exchange

The Forensic Laboratory ensures that formal exchange policies, procedures, and controls are in place to protect the exchange of any information through the use of all types of communication facilities.

Information exchange occurs through the use of a number of different types of communication facilities, including electronic mail, voice, facsimile, video, and other forms of electronic media.

Software exchange occurs through a number of different mediums, including downloading from the Internet and acquired from vendors selling COTS products.

The business, legal, and security implications associated with electronic information interchange, electronic communications, and the requirements for controls must be considered and their risks assessed and appropriately treated before information exchange is undertaken.

Information could be compromised due to lack of awareness, policy, or procedures on the use of information exchange facilities, e.g., being overheard on a mobile phone in a public place, mis-direction of an electronic mail message, answering machines being overheard, unauthorized access to dial-in voice-mail systems, or accidentally sending facsimiles to the wrong facsimile equipment.

Business operations could be disrupted and information could be compromised if communications facilities fail, are overloaded, or interrupted.

Information could be compromised if accessed by unauthorized users.

12.8.4.1 *Information Exchange Procedures and Controls*

The procedures and controls to be followed when using electronic communication facilities for information exchange should consider the following items:

1. There shall be procedures designed to protect exchanged information from interception, copying, modification, mis-routing, and destruction.
2. There shall be procedures for the detection of, and protection against, malicious code that may be transmitted through the use of electronic communications, as defined in Chapter 7, Section 7.6.1.
3. Procedures for protecting communicated sensitive electronic information that is in the form of an e-mail attachment.
4. Policy and guidelines outlining acceptable use of electronic communication facilities.
5. Forensic Laboratory employees and any authorized third party's responsibilities not to compromise the Forensic Laboratory, e.g., through defamation, harassment, impersonation, forwarding of chain letters, unauthorized purchasing, entering unauthorized contracts, etc.
6. Use of cryptographic techniques to protect the confidentiality, integrity, and authenticity of information and provide nonrepudiation services.
7. Retention and disposal guidelines for all business correspondence including messages, in accordance with relevant national and local legislation and regulations as given in Chapter 4, Appendix 16, and defined in Chapter 7, Section 7.7.4, respectively.
8. Not leaving sensitive or critical information on printing facilities, e.g., copiers, printers, and facsimile machines, as these may be accessed by unauthorized personnel.
9. Controls and restrictions associated with the forwarding of communication facilities, e.g., automatic forwarding of electronic mail to external mail addresses.
10. Reminding all Forensic Laboratory employees and any third parties working for the Forensic Laboratory that they should take appropriate precautions, e.g., not to reveal sensitive information, to avoid being overheard when using a mobile phone, etc. by.
    - Being aware of people in their immediate vicinity particularly when using mobile phones.

- Being aware of wiretapping, and other forms of eavesdropping through physical access to the phone handset or the phone line, or using scanning receivers, or people at the recipient's end.
- Not leaving messages containing sensitive information on answering machines since these may be replayed by unauthorized persons, stored on communal systems, or stored incorrectly as a result of mis-dialing.

11. Reminding all Forensic Laboratory employees and any third parties working for the Forensic Laboratory about the problems of using facsimile machines, namely:
    - unauthorized access to built-in message stores to retrieve messages;
    - deliberate or accidental programming of machines to send messages to specific numbers;
    - sending documents and messages to the wrong number either by mis-dialing or using the wrong stored number.
12. Reminding all Forensic Laboratory employees and any third parties working for the Forensic Laboratory not to register demographic information, such as their e-mail address or other personal information, in any software to avoid collection for unauthorized use.
13. Reminding all Forensic Laboratory employees and any third parties working for the Forensic Laboratory that modern facsimile machines and photocopiers have page caches and store pages in case of a paper or transmission fault, which will be printed once the fault is cleared.
14. Reminding all Forensic Laboratory employees and any third parties working for the Forensic Laboratory that many modern photocopiers and printers have hard disks that can store spooled or printed images.

In addition, all Forensic Laboratory employees and any third parties working for the Forensic Laboratory should be reminded that they should not have confidential conversations in public places or open offices and meeting places with walls that are not sound proofed.

12.8.4.2 Exchange Agreements

The Forensic Laboratory must ensure that formal and legally binding exchange agreements are established, where appropriate, for the exchange of information and software between themselves and any external parties.

Exchange agreements should consider the following security conditions:

- management responsibilities for controlling and notifying transmission and receipt;
- procedures for notifying sender of transmission and receipt;
- procedures to ensure traceability and non-repudiation;
- minimum technical standards for packaging and transmission;
- courier identification standards, if appropriate;
- responsibilities and liabilities in the event of information security incidents, such as loss of information;
- use of an agreed labeling system for sensitive or critical information, ensuring that the meaning of the labels is immediately understood and that the information is appropriately protected, as defined in Sections 12.3.14.8 and 12.3.14.9;
- ownership and responsibilities for information protection, copyright, software license compliance, and similar considerations;
- technical standards for recording and reading information and software;
- any special controls that may be required to protect sensitive items, such as cryptographic keys.

Policies, procedures, and standards must be established and maintained to protect information and physical media in transit, and should be referenced in such exchange agreements.

The security content of any agreement should reflect the sensitivity and classification of the business information involved.

12.8.5 Cryptographic Controls

For secure communication, digital certificates are required for some systems within the Forensic Laboratory, depending on the information classification and Client requirements.

The Forensic Laboratory Policy for Cryptographic Controls is given in Chapter 4, Appendix 15.

12.8.5.1 Guidelines for Key Management

The Network Administration Team is responsible for the management of cryptographic keys. The tasks that are performed are:

1. Cryptographic keys are generated directly by a member of the Network Administration Team—no copy of the key is taken for storage.
2. Cryptographic keys become part of the device configuration and are subsequently backed up when the configuration is saved.
3. If any compromise of a cryptographic key is detected, the Network Administration Team changes the cryptographic key directly on the device. This may require the requesting of a new cryptographic key and distributing it to all relevant users.
4. If any compromise occurs, the Information Security Manager is alerted and an incident is raised at the Service Desk, as defined in Chapter 7, Section 7.4.1.

5. All changes to keys are noted within the Service Desk system against the asset record.

> **Note**
>
> Some one-time key pads may need to be generated and written down for devices such as routers. If this is the case, then the key shall be stored securely with server passwords as defined in Section 12.6.3.1.

12.8.5.2 Managing Keys Procedures

The process by which the Forensic Laboratory manages device keys is as follows:

1. The Network Administration Team assess the requirements for a new key:
   - when the existing key is suspected to be compromised;
   - when a new device is installed;
   - when devices are relocated.
2. The Network Administration Team opens a ticket within the Service Desk.
3. The Network Administration Team accesses the device and generates the key. A note is made of the key details.
4. The Network Administration Team records the details of the key against the device information.
5. The ticket is closed.

12.9 INFORMATION PROCESSING SYSTEMS DEVELOPMENT AND MAINTENANCE

Information processing systems include operating systems, infrastructure, business applications, off-the-shelf products, services, and user-developed applications.

12.9.1 System Development Life Cycle

The following policies apply to the system development life cycle:

1. All projects must have security considered at every point in the development life cycle. This means adopting an appropriate secure software/system development life cycle.
2. The Information Security Manager has the power to halt the implementation or commissioning of any project that has insufficient security controls built into it.
3. The Information Security Manager shall be one of the mandatory signatures at all "gate" reviews.
4. No project must be implemented that may prejudice the Forensic Laboratory information and information processing systems on account of security failures (if the system were installed).

12.9.2 Program Specification

All projects must have the requirements for security considered and specified from the start of the project. The requirements for controls depend on the classification of the information handled or accessed by the system, Client requirements, and the appropriate risk assessment.

All new programs, projects, or upgrades to existing programs and projects must formally have their security measures approved and their residual risks knowingly accepted by the information Owner and the Information Security Manager. This must be formally recorded and be available for audit, forming part of the project documentation, and be available for the CAB to consider, as defined in Chapter 7, Section 7.4.3.

12.9.3 Security of System Files

12.9.3.1 Control of Operational Software

The following procedures apply to control operational software:

1. All operational software (whether live or still in development) must be fully controlled.
2. Only executable code must be held on operational systems (source code must be retained securely in appropriate system areas).
3. All access to program source code and associated files must be audited, and access regularly reviewed by the Information Security Manager.
4. Updated or new source code cannot be released into the live environment without first undergoing and passing appropriate tests and being approved by the CAB, as defined in Chapter 7, Section 7.4.3.

12.9.3.2 Protection of System Test Data

The following procedures apply to protection of system test information:

1. All test information must be protected against unauthorized access, erasure, modification, and disclosure.
2. There shall be a separate authorization each time operational information is copied to a test system.
3. Where test information contains personal information, the requirements of the relevant information protection legislation within the jurisdiction must be met.
4. Ideally, personal information should be sanitized to prevent real names being divulged.
5. After use, the test information must be securely stored so that it can be re-used for regression testing, if required, or securely deleted.
6. Any hard copy output from the testing process must be securely disposed of, preferably by shredding, but according to the procedure defined in Section 12.3.14.10.

12.9.3.3 *Access to Program Source Library*

The following procedures apply to access to program source libraries:

1. Access to program source libraries must be fully controlled.
2. Program source libraries must not be held in operational systems.
3. Old versions of code must be archived.

12.9.4 Security in Development and Support Processes

12.9.4.1 *Packaged Solution Use*

Where the Forensic Laboratory uses a packaged (or COTS) solution, it shall be maintained at a level supported by the manufacturer. Any changes to a packaged solution shall be submitted to the Forensic Laboratory IT Department change management process after full testing, before promotion to the live environment, as defined in Chapter 7, Section 7.4.3.

12.9.4.2 *Fixes and Service Packs*

The Information Security Manager and the IT Manager shall subscribe to all relevant sources of information to ensure that all patches required to address published vulnerabilities are implemented. Vendor issued amendments to software must be fully tested and passed by the Forensic Laboratory change management process before being applied to existing software in the production environment. This process is fully defined in Chapter 7, Sections 7.6.2 and 7.6.3.

12.9.4.2.1 Change Control Procedures

All changes to live system must be controlled via the Forensic Laboratory change management process, as defined in Chapter 7, Section 7.4.3.

12.9.4.2.2 Technical Review of Operating System Changes

Application systems are reviewed and tested when changes occur, as defined in Chapter 7, Section 7.6.2.

12.9.4.2.3 Restrictions on Changes to Software Packages

Modifications to software packages are discouraged and essential changes strictly controlled. All changes must be controlled via the Forensic Laboratory change management process, as defined in Chapter 7, Section 7.4.3.

12.9.4.2.4 Covert Channels and Trojan Code

The purchase, use, and modification of software is controlled and checked to protect against possible covert channels and Trojan code.

12.9.4.2.5 Outsourced Software Development

Where software is developed by a third party, it must be subject to contractual terms that ensure that the development meets all requirements, is of appropriate quality, and is fully tested prior to submission to the Forensic Laboratory.

All software developed by third parties shall be fully tested by the Forensic Laboratory before acceptance and shall only be implemented in the live environment via the Forensic Laboratory change management process, as defined in Chapter 7, Section 7.4.3.

Where this involves a forensic tool, it shall be subject either to external validation testing by a competent laboratory or internal validation as defined in Chapter 7, Section 7.5.5.

12.9.5 Developing Software Applications

The process that controls how code is accessed and worked with is the same for all applications developed within the Forensic Laboratory.

All access to source code is controlled at the file level by the use of user groups for the relevant developers group. Forensic Laboratory employees who are employed to develop or maintain software are automatically included in the group as part of the user account creation process.

> **Note**
> No development can be performed on source code unless the development or changes required have been approved by the Forensic Laboratory management.

A simplified flowchart of the software development process is shown in Figure 12.8:

12.9.5.1 *Roles and Responsibilities*

12.9.5.1.1 Software Developer

The Software Developer is the person who creates and maintains software application(s) within the Forensic Laboratory IT Department. The responsibilities of this role include:

1. Checking development requirements.
2. Developing the code.
3. Pre-testing code prior to formal testing.
4. Preparing the code for formal testing.
5. Submitting the RfC to the CAB for release of the code to the production environment.

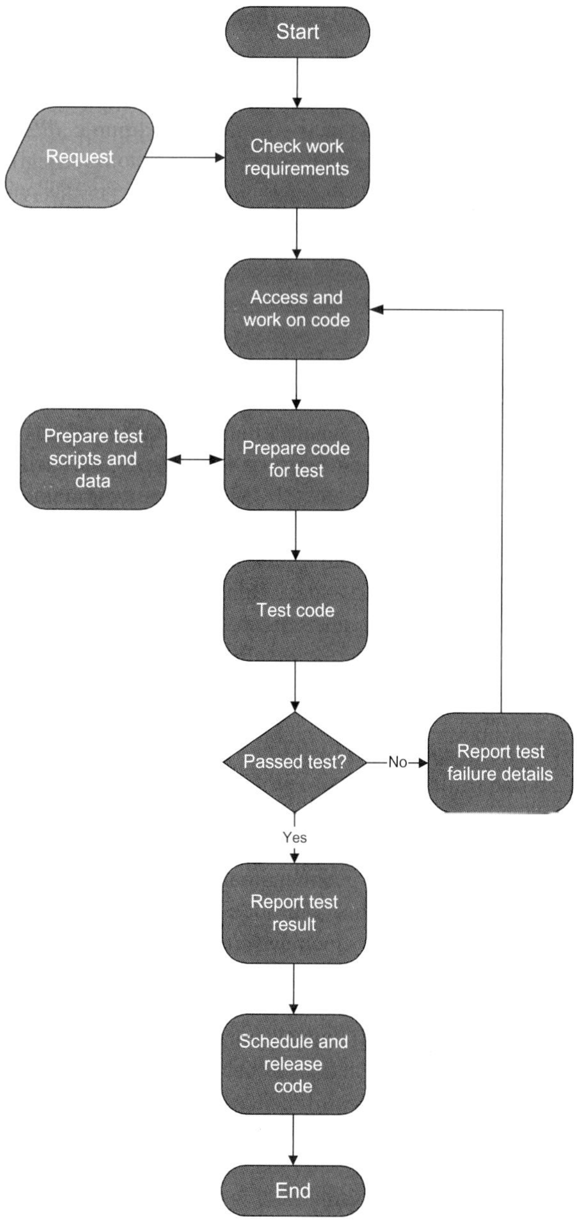

FIGURE 12.8 Developing software applications. (For color version of this figure, the reader is referred to the online version of this chapter.)

12.9.5.1.2 Quality Assurance

The Quality Assurance function tests any in-house developed software (as well as any externally sourced software). The responsibilities of this role include:

1. Checking the test criteria.
2. Performing a test against the agreed test criteria.
3. Reporting the results of a test to the Software Developer.

12.9.5.1.3 IT Manager

The IT Manager is the central authority for system development. The responsibilities of this role include ensuring that adequate system development controls are in place.

12.9.5.2 Developing the code

To develop the code, a Software Developer performs the following tasks:

1. Check the requirements for the work. This is normally on a development specification or a change request, but can also be on an e-mail.
2. Access a copy of the live source code using the appropriate development tools.

Warning

No development work shall be performed on the live source code.

3. Work shall be carried out by the relevant member of the IT Department on the source code as appropriate using the appropriate development tools and standards.
4. Prepare a change request for the implementation of the software and put this request through the Forensic Laboratory change management process.

12.9.5.3 Testing the code

The Forensic Laboratory applies the following policies to code testing:

1. All the Forensic Laboratory systems must be fully tested before being submitted for release via the Forensic Laboratory change management process. Full testing means unit, functional, system, performance and integration testing, as well as user acceptance and regression testing (where appropriate).
2. All test results must be recorded and securely maintained for later audit. To test the code, the testers perform the following tasks:
3. Confirm the test criteria and prepare any test packs and information that are required for the test.
4. Send an e-mail to the assigned testers and confirm the test requirements.
5. The tester(s) performs the tests against the specified criteria using any supplied test scripts and information. The results are recorded in an e-mail that is sent back to the relevant Software Developer(s) and the Information Security Manager.
6. If any changes are required to code following testing, the relevant Software Developer(s) implements them and then generates a further set of tests as above.
7. If no changes are required to the code, it is released to the change management process.

12.9.5.4 Releasing the code

To release the code to the production environment, a Software Developer performs the following tasks:

1. Confirms that the testing has been successfully completed against the test criteria and that it has been approved by the CAB.
2. Files all of the documentation relating to the release in the ERMS.
3. Makes a live version of the source code.
4. Advises the Release Manager of the proposed release so that it can be scheduled.

The Release Manager shall:

- Schedule the update to the live software application.
- Confirm the release of the software application through the Forensic Laboratory users and the timetable for release.

Note

The job description for the Release Manager is given in Chapter 7, Appendix 20.

12.9.6 Security Standards for Systems Development

These standards should be used within the context of the Forensic Laboratory's Secure System Development Life Cycle. They are designed as a checklist to ensure that proper attention is given to all aspects relevant to the secure implementation of developed software.

A secure system development life cycle methodology should be implemented to consider security issues in all phases so that:

1. All security concerns are addressed.
2. Test criteria are met prior to implementation of operational software.
3. Change management procedures for operational software are implemented.
4. Discrepancies for all information and software are reported, monitored, and resolved.

Note

The Forensic Laboratory does not perform development or modification on purchased software packages.

12.9.6.1 Standards for Systems Development Projects

The Forensic Laboratory Software Developers shall consider the following aspects of information security on system development projects:

1. A security specialist shall be appointed to provide security advice for the project—this is usually the Information Security Manager.
2. Any Forensic Laboratory employee that is involved in software development shall have the appropriate training, experience, and qualifications for the required development work.
3. The IT Manager, and other stakeholders as appropriate, shall review the completion of major phases of the system and provide formal sign-offs that make them personally liable and accountable for the development. These shall be recorded in the ERMS.
4. Software Developers should be restricted when amending information and software in live areas.
5. Audits shall be performed internally within IT to monitor development progress.
6. Project management methods shall be used to control the development process.

12.9.6.2 Standards for Systems Development Methods

The Forensic Laboratory IT Department shall follow these standards for system development methods:

1. All system development shall be planned and approved.
2. All systems shall be documented to a formal standard.
3. Users shall be consulted in all stages of system development.
4. The security issues for a development must be identified by a formal risk analysis.
5. The Information Security Manager must ensure that the required security features are included in the system.
6. A configuration management system shall be implemented during development and implementation. The Forensic Laboratory configuration management process is defined in Chapter 7, Section 7.4.5.

12.9.6.3 Standards for System Design

The Forensic Laboratory shall follow these information security standards during system design:

1. All changes to a system must be formally controlled via the Forensic Laboratory change control process, as defined in Chapter 7, Section 7.4.3.
2. All change requests must be authorized before they take place.
3. Techniques for error prevention, error detection, and system recovery shall be part of design standards.
4. Testing standards shall be developed and implemented including:
    - user acceptance testing;
    - parallel and/or pilot running of systems;
    - independent testing of software changes prior to implementation.
5. Security mechanisms shall be independently tested and proved to work as claimed in system documentation.

6. All system design must be reviewed and signed off.
7. A full test strategy must be agreed and documented.
8. The use of live data for testing is defined in Section 12.9.3.2, note that the relevant Business Owner should approve this and care may need to be taken in handling output if the information includes sensitive financial or other information.
9. All errors shall be tested after correction to ensure that they have been eliminated as part of the regression testing process and that no new ones have been introduced.

12.9.6.4 Standards for the Development Environment

The Forensic Laboratory IT Department shall follow these standards during the preparation of the systems development environment:

1. Effective control mechanisms shall be implemented to control multiple versions of software.
2. There must be adequate backup procedures.
3. There shall be adequate procedures to govern "emergency fixes" (but, in general, this must only be used for EMERGENCIES).
4. No utilities shall be used that could bypass control measures.

12.9.6.5 Standards for Software Testing

The Forensic Laboratory IT Department shall follow these standards for software testing:

1. Results of software testing must be documented and approved by the IT Manager and the System Owner.
2. Those who undertake testing should be made aware of the need to observe confidentiality of the information used in the testing process.
3. Software testing must take place in a specialized testing environment and should test the full functionality of the system (the test environment).
4. Only authorized Forensic Laboratory employees shall perform software tests.
5. Output of software tests must be considered as confidential information.
6. Security of the existing system must not be decreased while system testing is taking place.
7. Tests should prove that the system complies with all design specifications and any required security measures.

12.9.7 Standards for System Implementation

During the process of bringing developed software into operational use (the implementation process), many activities will be performed, which can have influence on the security of information processing systems. These standards provide help to ensure that during the process of bringing the software into operational use, the security of the information system will comply with the defined security requirements.

The Forensic Laboratory follows these standards during the implementation process:

1. The Information Security Manager must be involved in all system developments and implementations, and be a signatory at all review stages for system approval.
2. New system working procedures must fulfill the required security levels.
3. System authorizations given to users must not exceed the required system authorization to compete their tasks.
4. There shall be control facilities to check that no user can exceed their given system access authorizations.
5. Security measures implemented for a system shall be part of the user training.
6. Only authorized Forensic Laboratory employees can change and modify information on any information processing system.
7. System end users must be trained on how to use all systems and their security features.
8. The security of existing systems must not be endangered during the training of the end users.
9. Transfer of software and information from the test area into the live environment must be controlled in an appropriate manner, using the Forensic Laboratory change management process, as defined in Chapter 7, Section 7.4.3.
10. Transfer of information and software between the live and test areas must be undertaken securely (tests should be undertaken to make sure this has been done correctly), as defined in Chapter 7, Section 7.4.4.
11. During the period of transfer, information and software must not be made available to unauthorized users.

12.9.8 Security Standards for Third Party Systems Development

These standards shall be used within the context of the project management framework which the Forensic Laboratory adopts for systems development by third parties. They are designed as a checklist to ensure that proper attention is given to all aspects that are relevant to the secure implementation of software, which is developed on behalf of the Forensic Laboratory by a third party.

All project work for third party system development must be conducted in accordance with the Forensic Laboratory's policies and procedures on systems development projects.

12.9.8.1 Developing System Specifications/Requirements

The Forensic Laboratory IT Department shall consider the following aspects of information security when developing a specification or requirements for a system that is to be developed by a third party:

1. The Forensic Laboratory IT Department must appoint a security specialist to provide information security advice and be responsible for all aspects of information security throughout the development project (this is usually the Forensic Laboratory Information Security Manager).
2. All information security requirements must be formally documented in a system specification or requirements document.
3. Specific information security requirements that must be addressed in a system specification or requirements document are:
   - information security requirements for each phase of the development life cycle, including development, testing, and implementation;
   - information security requirements/considerations for the third party that is to develop the system;
   - licensing arrangements, code ownership, escrow, and copyright issues (where applicable);
   - methods by which the Forensic Laboratory IT Department will certify the quality and accuracy of the work that is performed.
4. Rights of access for the Forensic Laboratory IT Department and the Information Security Manager to audit the quality and accuracy of the work done.
5. Contractual requirements for quality of code.

12.9.8.2 Requests for Proposals and Quotations

The Forensic Laboratory IT Department should consider the following aspects of information security during requests for proposals and quotations for a system that is to be developed by a third party:

1. All information security issues that are outlined in the system specification or requirements document must be addressed and formally agreed.
2. Issues of code ownership and copyright throughout the development life cycle must be formally agreed by the Forensic Laboratory and the third party.

12.9.8.3 System Development

The Forensic Laboratory IT Department shall consider the following aspects of information security during development of a system by a third party:

1. Any systems development work that is carried out for the Forensic Laboratory must be performed in accordance with the Forensic Laboratory IT Department's policies on systems development design, methods, and environment.
2. Periodic reviews shall be conducted to ensure that third parties meet contractual requirements for quality of code, and quality and accuracy of work performed.

12.9.8.4 System Testing

The Forensic Laboratory IT Department must consider the following aspects of information security during the testing of systems that are developed by a third party:

1. Testing must be carried out in accordance with the Forensic Laboratory's systems testing procedures, as defined in Sections 12.9.5.3, 12.9.6.5, and 12.9.8.4.
2. Testing must be carried out according to an agreed testing plan.
3. Testing must provide a certification of the quality and accuracy of the work carried out to the satisfaction of the security specialist appointed to the project.
4. Testing must be performed for the detection of malicious and Trojan code and to detect known vulnerabilities, especially for Web-based applications.
5. Testing must prove that the system complies with any required security measures.

12.9.8.5 System Implementation and Sign-Off

The Forensic Laboratory IT Department must consider the following aspects of information security when implementing systems that are developed by a third party:

1. Implementation must be carried out in accordance with the Forensic Laboratory IT Department's policies and procedures on systems implementation through the change management and release processes as defined in Chapter 7, Sections 7.4.3 and 7.4.4.
2. Implementation must comply with the defined security requirements.
3. The security specialist appointed to the project must be involved in system implementation at each stage and be a sign-off at each stage.
4. Sign-off with the third party must only take place following completed and successful system testing and implementation.

12.9.9 Reviewing Application Systems

The Forensic Laboratory performs a technical review of application systems when changes occur to ensure that there is no adverse impact on operational security. Typical changes are installing a newly supplied software releases or patches.

This framework by which the Forensic Laboratory Information Security Manager performs a technical review is:

1. A member of the IT Department identifies an update or change to an application system and contacts the IT Manager to discuss details.
2. The IT Manager and the Information Security Manager identify and assign a suitably qualified member of the IT Department to perform a technical review and schedule it.

Note

The Forensic Laboratory ensures that any relevant specialist technical expertise is used during technical review including the appropriate software tools that generate technical reports for subsequent interpretation by a technical specialist.

3. The appointed member of the IT Department performs a full technical review including:
   - assessing the changes to the application system;
   - checking the application control and integrity procedures to ensure that they will not be compromised by the operating system changes.
4. The appointed member of the IT Department discusses the findings with the IT Manager and the Information Security Manager. The IT Manager determines whether a rollout of the application is feasible. If so, the appointed member of the IT Department performs further investigation work as follows:
   - designing an annual support plan and budget to cover future reviews and system testing resulting from operating system changes;
   - highlighting changes required to IT business continuity plans.
5. The appointed member of the IT Department discusses the additional details with the IT Manager. The IT Manager and the Information Security Manager confirm whether the application will be rolled out. If rollout is approved, the work is scheduled.

12.9.10 Separating Development, Test, and Operational Environments

The development, test, and operational facilities are separated in the Forensic Laboratory to reduce the risk of unauthorized access or change to the operational environment.

There are a number of procedures that are in place in the Forensic Laboratory IT Department for controlling the segregation of the IT environments used for the Forensic Laboratory operations, test, and development.

Formal maintenance of these standards is the responsibility of the IT Manager, in association with other key stakeholders.

12.9.10.1 Development, Test, and Operational Environments Separation Standards

The following standards shall be implemented in the Forensic Laboratory:

1. Separate controlled environments exist for:
   - development, test, and production of source and executable code;
   - operation of executable code, applications, and IT systems.
2. Only the relevant IT Department employees shall have authorized access to the development environment (developers for development purposes plus library management, other employees, where necessary, for administrative purposes).
3. Compilers or other system development tools are never installed on production machines.
4. All code must be compiled into an executable format before being moved into the production environment.
5. Software is only transferred from the test environment to the operational environment after completion of the system testing required by the Forensic Laboratory change management process, as defined in Chapter 7, Section 7.4.3. All changes to the Forensic Laboratory information systems must be undertaken in accordance with the Forensic Laboratory change management procedures.
6. Sensitive information must not be copied into the test environment.
7. The test environment must mirror the operational environment.
8. Where possible, different log-on screens should be displayed to indicate the environment in which an application is running—for example, the login screen for a production system or application must include a notification that it is a production environment.

APPENDIX 1 - THE FORENSIC LABORATORY SOA

MANDATORY CONTROLS (SECTION 4-8)

Control Section	Management Components	
4.1	**General Requirements**	
	The organization shall develop, implement, maintain, and continually improve a documented ISMS within the context of the organization's overall business activities and risk. For the purpose of this standard, the process used is based on the PDCA model.	
4.2	**Establishing and managing the ISMS Requirement**	**Forensic Laboratory Procedures**
4.2.1	**Establish the ISMS**	
4.2.1. a)	Define the scope of the ISMS in terms of the characteristics of the business, the organization, its location, assets, and technology.	Chapter 5, Appendix 11
4.2.1. b)	Define an ISMS policy in terms of the characteristics of the business, the organization, its location assets, and technology that: 1. includes a framework for setting its objectives and establishes an overall sense of direction and principles for action with regard to information security. 2. takes into account business and legal or regulatory requirements, and contractual security obligations. 3. establishes the strategic organizational and risk management context in which the establishment and maintenance of the ISMS will take place. 4. establishes criteria against which risk will be evaluated and the structure of the risk assessment will be defined. 5. has been approved by management.	Chapter 4, Appendix 10 Chapter 5, Appendix 11 This chapter, Appendix 5, Section 12.3.13.1.1
4.2.1. c)	**Define a systematic approach to risk assessment** Identify a risk assessment methodology that is suited to the ISMS, and the identified business information security, legal and regulatory requirements. Set policy and objectives for the ISMS to reduce risks to acceptable levels. Determine criteria for accepting the risks and identify the acceptable levels of risk.	Chapter 5, Sections 5.6 and 5.9.1
4.2.1. d)	**Identify the risks** 1. Identify the assets within the scope of the ISMS and the Owners of these assets. 2. Identify the threats to those assets. 3. Identify the vulnerabilities that might be exploited by the threats. 4. Identify the impacts that losses of confidentiality, integrity, and availability may have on these assets.	Chapter 5, Section 5.7.1, Appendices 6, 8, 9, and 12
4.2.1. e)	**Assess and evaluate the risks** 1. Assess the business impacts upon the organization that might result from security failures, taking into account the consequences of a loss of confidentiality, integrity, or availability of the assets. 2. Assess the realistic likelihood of security failures occurring in the light of prevailing threats and vulnerabilities, and impacts associated with these assets, and the controls currently implemented. 3. Estimate the levels of risks. 4. Determine whether the risks are acceptable or require treatment using the criteria for accepting risks established in 4.2.1 c) 2).	Chapter 5, Sections 5.7.4 and 5.9.1, Appendices 13 and 14
4.2.1. f)	**Identify and evaluate options for the treatment of risks** Possible actions include:	Chapter 5, Section 5.7.4, Appendix 15

Continued

Control Section	Management Components	
	1. applying appropriate controls. 2. knowingly and objectively accepting risks, providing they clearly satisfy the organization's policies and the criteria for accepting risks (see 4.2.1. c) 2)). 3. avoiding risks; and 4. transferring the associated business risks to other parties, e.g., insurers, suppliers.	
4.2.1. g)	**Select control objectives and controls for the treatment of risks** Select control objectives and controls for the treatment of risks. Control objectives and controls shall be selected and implemented to meet the requirements identified by the risk assessment and risk treatment process. This selection shall take account of the criteria for accepting risks (see 4.2.1. c) 2)) as well as legal, regulatory, and contractual requirements. The control objectives and controls from Annex A shall be selected as part of this process as suitable to cover the identified requirements. The control objectives and controls listed in Annex A are not exhaustive and additional control objectives and controls may also be selected.	Chapter 5, Section 5.9, Appendix 15 ISO 27001 Annex A
4.2.1. h)	Obtain management approval of the proposed residual risks.	Chapter 5, Section 5.11 This chapter, Section 12.10
4.2.1. i)	Obtain management authorization to implement and operate the ISMS.	This chapter, Section 12.10
4.2.1. j)	**Prepare a SoA** A SoA shall be prepared that includes the following: 1. the control objectives and controls selected in 4.2.1. g) and the reasons for their selection. 2. the control objectives and controls currently implemented (see 4.2.1 e) 2)); and 3. the exclusion of any control objectives and controls in Annex A and the justification for their exclusion.	Chapter 5, Section 5.10 This chapter, Appendix 1
4.2.2	**Implement and operate the ISMS** The organization shall do the following. a. Formulate a risk treatment plan that identifies the appropriate management action, resources, responsibilities, and priorities for managing information security risks (see 5). b. Implement the risk treatment plan in order to achieve the identified control objectives, which includes consideration of funding and allocation of roles and responsibilities. c. Implement controls selected in 4.2.1. g) to meet the control objectives. d. Define how to measure the effectiveness of the selected controls or groups of controls and specify how these measurements are to be used to assess control effectiveness to produce comparable and reproducible results (see 4.2.3 c)). e. Implement training and awareness programs (see 5.2.2). f. Manage operation of the ISMS. g. Manage resources for the ISMS (see 5.2). h. Implement procedures and other controls capable of enabling prompt detection of security events and response to security incidents (see 4.2.3. a)).	Chapter 5, Sections 5.6, 5.9, 5.6.1, 5.6.2, and 5.6.3, Appendices 14, 17, 15, and 22 Chapter 4, Section 4.6.2 Chapter 7, Section 7.4.1
4.2.3	**Monitor and review the ISMS** The organization shall do the following. a. Execute monitoring and reviewing procedures and other controls to: 1. promptly detect errors in the results of processing. 2. promptly identify attempted and successful security breaches and incidents. 3. enable management to determine whether the security activities delegated to people or implemented by information technology are performing as expected. 4. help detect security events and thereby prevent security incidents by the use of indicators; and 5. determine whether the actions taken to resolve a breach of security were effective. b. Undertake regular reviews of the effectiveness of the ISMS (including meeting ISMS policy and objectives, and review of security controls) taking into account results of security audits, incidents, results from effectiveness measurements, suggestions, and feedback from all interested parties. c. Measure the effectiveness of controls to verify that security requirements have been met.	Chapter 7, Section 7.4.1 Chapter 6, Section 6.7.3 Chapter 5, Appendix 17 Chapter 4, Sections 4.7.2, 4.9, and 4.8 Chapter 7, Section 7.4.1

Continued

Control Section	Management Components	
	d. Review risk assessments at planned intervals and review the residual risks and the identified acceptable levels of risks, taking into account changes to: 1. the organization; 2. technology; 3. business objectives and processes; 4. identified threats; 5. effectiveness of the implemented controls; and 6. external events, such as changes to the legal or regulatory environment, changed contractual obligations, and changes in social climate. e. Conduct internal ISMS audits at planned intervals (see 6). f. Undertake a management review of the ISMS on a regular basis to ensure that the scope remains adequate and improvements in the ISMS process are identified (see 7.1). g. Update security plans to take into account the findings of monitoring and reviewing activities. h. Record actions and events that could have an impact on the effectiveness or performance of the ISMS (see 4.3.3).	
4.2.4	**Maintain and improve the ISMS** The organization shall do the following. a. Implement the identified improvements in the ISMS. b. Take appropriate corrective and preventive actions in accordance with 8.2 and 8.3. Apply the lessons learnt from the security experiences of other organizations and those of the organization itself. c. Communicate the actions and improvements to all interested parties with a level of detail appropriate to the circumstances and, as relevant, agree on how to proceed. d. Ensure that the improvements achieve their intended objectives.	Chapter 4, Sections 4.8 and 4.6.5
4.3	**Documentation Requirements**	
4.3.1	**General** The ISMS documentation shall include the following: a. documented statements of the ISMS policy (see 4.2.1. b)) and objectives. b. the scope of the ISMS (see 4.2.1. a)). c. procedures and controls in support of the ISMS. d. a description of the risk assessment methodology (see 4.2.1. c)). e. the risk assessment report (see 4.2.1. c) to 4.2.1. g)). f. the risk treatment plan (see 4.2.2. b)). g. documented procedures needed by the organization to ensure the effective planning, operation and control of its information security processes, and describe how to measure the effectiveness of controls (see 4.2.3 c)). h. records required by this International Standard (see 4.3.3); and i. the SoA. All documentation shall be made available as required by the ISMS policy.	Chapter 4, Appendix 10 Chapter 5, Appendix 11, Sections 5.6, 5.8.2, and 5.6.1 Chapter 5, Appendix 11 This chapter, Appendix 1
4.3.2	**Control of Documents** Documents required by the ISMS shall be protected and controlled. A documented procedure shall be established to define the management actions needed to: a. approve documents for adequacy prior to issue. b. review and update documents as necessary and reapprove documents. c. ensure that changes and the current revision status of documents are identified. d. ensure that relevant versions of applicable documents are available at points of use. e. ensure that documents remain legible and readily identifiable. f. ensure that documents are available to those who need them, and are transferred, stored, and ultimately disposed of in accordance with the procedures applicable to their classification. g. ensure that documents of external origin are identified. h. ensure that the distribution of documents is controlled. i. prevent the unintended use of obsolete documents; and j. apply suitable identification to them, if they are retained for any purpose.	Chapter 4, Section 4.6.3

Continued

Control Section	Management Components	
4.3.3	**Control of records** Records shall be established and maintained to provide evidence of conformity to requirements and the effective operation of the ISMS. They shall be protected and controlled. The ISMS shall take account of any relevant legal or regulatory requirements and contractual obligations. Records shall remain legible, readily identifiable, and retrievable. The controls needed for the identification, storage, protection, retrieval, retention time, and disposition of records shall be documented and implemented. Records shall be kept of the performance of the process as outlined in 4.2 and of all occurrences of significant security incidents related to the ISMS.	Chapter 4, Section 4.6.4
5	**Management Responsibility**	
5.1	**Management Commitment** Management shall provide evidence of its commitment to the establishment, implementation, operation, monitoring, review, maintenance, and improvement of the ISMS by: a. establishing an ISMS policy. b. ensuring that ISMS objectives and plans are established. c. establishing roles and responsibilities for information security. d. communicating to the organization the importance of meeting information security objectives and conforming to the Information Security Policy, its responsibilities under the law, and the need for continual improvement. e. providing sufficient resources to establish, implement, operate, monitor, review, maintain, and improve the ISMS (see 5.2.1). f. deciding the criteria for accepting risks and the acceptable levels of risk. g. ensuring that internal ISMS audits are conducted (see 6); and h. conducting management reviews of the ISMS (see 7).	Chapter 4, Appendix 10, Sections 4.6.5, 4.6.2, 4.7.3, and 4.9 This chapter, Appendix 5 Chapter 6, Section 6.2.1.4 Chapter 5, Section 5.9.1
5.2	**Resource Management**	
5.2.1	**Provision of resources** The organization shall determine and provide the resources needed to: a. establish, implement, operate, monitor, review, maintain, and improve an ISMS. b. ensure that information security procedures support the business requirements. c. identify and address legal and regulatory requirements and contractual security obligations. d. maintain adequate security by correct application of all implemented controls. e. carry out reviews when necessary and to react appropriately to the results of these reviews; and f. where required, improve the effectiveness of the ISMS.	Chapter 4, Sections 4.6.2.1, 4.6.3, 4.7, 4.9, and 4.8 Chapter 3, Section 3.13.1.1.1 Chapter 5, Section 5.22.3
5.2.2	**Training, awareness, and competency** The organization shall ensure that all personnel who are assigned responsibilities defined in the ISMS are competent to perform the required tasks by: a. determining the necessary competencies for personnel performing work effecting the ISMS. b. providing training or taking other actions (e.g., employing competent personnel) to satisfy these needs. c. evaluating the effectiveness of the actions taken; and d. maintaining records of education, training, skills, experience, and qualifications (see 4.3.3). The organization shall also ensure that all relevant personnel are aware of the relevance and importance of their information security activities and how they contribute to the achievement of the ISMS objectives.	Chapter 18, Section 18.2, 18.2.2 and 18.2.5 Chapter 4, Sections 4.6.2.2 and 4.6.2.3 This chapter, Section 12.3.2
6	**Internal ISMS audits** The organization shall conduct internal ISMS audits at planned intervals to determine whether the control objectives, controls, processes, and procedures of its ISMS: a. conform to the requirements of this International Standard and relevant legislation or regulations. b. conform to the identified information security requirements. c. are effectively implemented and maintained; and d. perform as expected.	Chapter 4, Section 4.7.3 This chapter, Appendix 6

Continued

Control Section	Management Components	
	An audit program shall be planned, taking into consideration the status and importance of the processes and areas to be audited, as well as the results of previous audits. The audit criteria, scope, frequency, and methods shall be defined. The selection of auditors and conduct of audits shall ensure objectivity and impartiality of the audit process. Auditors shall not audit their own work. The responsibilities and requirements for planning and conducting audits, and for reporting results and maintaining records (see 4.3.3) shall be defined in a documented procedure. The management responsible for the area being audited shall ensure that actions are taken without undue delay to eliminate detected nonconformities and their causes. Follow-up activities shall include the verification of the actions taken and the reporting of verification results (see 8).	
7	**Management review of the ISMS**	
7.1	**General** Management shall review the organization's ISMS at planned intervals (at least once a year) to ensure its continuing suitability, adequacy, and effectiveness. This review shall include assessing opportunities for improvement and the need for changes to the ISMS, including the Information Security Policy and information security objectives. The results of the reviews shall be clearly documented and records shall be maintained (see 4.3.3).	Chapter 4, Section 4.9
7.2	**Review input** The input to a management review shall include: a. results of ISMS audits and reviews. b. feedback from interested parties. c. techniques, products, or procedures, which could be used in the organization to improve the ISMS performance and effectiveness. d. status of preventive and corrective actions. e. vulnerabilities or threats not adequately addressed in the previous risk assessment. f. results from effectiveness measurements. g. follow-up actions from previous management reviews. h. any changes that could affect the ISMS; and i. recommendations for improvement.	Chapter 4, Section 4.9.2, Appendix 36
7.3	**Review output** The output from the management review shall include any decisions and actions related to the following. a. Improvement of the effectiveness of the ISMS. b. Update of the risk assessment and risk treatment plan. c. Modification of procedures and controls that effect information security, as necessary, to respond to internal or external events that may impact on the ISMS, including changes to: 1. business requirements. 2. security requirements. 3. business processes effecting the existing business requirements. 4. regulatory or legal requirements. 5. contractual obligations; and 6. levels of risk and/or criteria for accepting risks. d. Resource needs. e. Improvement to how the effectiveness of controls is being measured.	Minutes and actions (CAPAs) from 7.2 above Chapter 4, Appendix 36, Section 4.9.3
8	**ISMS improvement**	
8.1	**Continual improvement** The organization shall continually improve the effectiveness of the ISMS through the use of the Information Security Policy, information security objectives, audit results, analysis of monitored events, corrective and preventive actions, and management review (see 7).	Chapter 4, Appendix 14, Section 4.8

Continued

Control Section	Management Components	
8.2	**Corrective action** The organization shall take action to eliminate the cause of nonconformities with the ISMS requirements in order to prevent recurrence. The documented procedure for corrective action shall define requirements for: a. identifying nonconformities. b. determining the causes of nonconformities. c. evaluating the need for actions to ensure that nonconformities do not recur. d. determining and implementing the corrective action needed. e. recording results of action taken (see 4.3.3); and f. reviewing of corrective action taken.	Chapter 4, Sections 4.8.2, 4.7.3.9, 4.8.2, and 4.8.4, Appendix 49 Chapter 6, Section 6.13.2
8.3	**Preventive action** The organization shall determine action to eliminate the cause of potential nonconformities with the ISMS requirements in order to prevent their occurrence. Preventive actions taken shall be appropriate to the impact of the potential problems. The documented procedure for preventive action shall define requirements for: a. identifying potential nonconformities and their causes. b. evaluating the need for action to prevent occurrence of nonconformities. c. determining and implementing preventive action needed. d. recording results of action taken (see 4.3.3); and e. reviewing of preventive action taken. The organization shall identify changed risks and identify preventive action requirements focusing attention on significantly changed risks. The priority of preventive actions shall be determined based on the results of the risk assessment.	Chapter 4, Sections 4.8.3, 4.8.2, and 4.8.4

STATEMENT OF APPLICABILITY (CONTROLS IN ISO 27001—SECTION A5-A15)

Control	Include	Exclude	Risk Assessment Method 1	Risk Assessment Method 2	Risk Assessment Method 3	The Forensic Laboratory Corporate Risk Register	Notes
A.5.1.1 Information Security Policy document	√		√	√	√	√	Chapter 4, Appendix 10
A.5.1.2 Review and evaluation	√		√	√	√	√	Chapter 4, Appendix 10
A.6.1.1 Management commitment to information security	√			√	√	√	Chapter 4, Section 4.6.2 This chapter, Section 12.3.3
A.6.1.2 Information security coordination	√		√	√	√	√	Chapter 4, Appendices 27, 28, and 31
A.6.1.3 Allocation of information security responsibilities	√		√	√	√	√	Chapter 18 Various job descriptions in the chapters
A.6.1.4 Authorization process for IT facilities	√		√	√	√	√	Chapter 7, Section 7.4.3 This chapter, Section 12.3.1.3

Continued

Control	Include	Exclude	Risk Assessment Method 1	Risk Assessment Method 2	Risk Assessment Method 3	The Forensic Laboratory Corporate Risk Register	Notes
A.6.1.5 Confidentiality agreement	√		√	√	√	√	This chapter, Section 12.3.1.4 Chapter 18, Section 18.1.4
A.6.1.6 Contact with authorities	√		√	√	√	√	Various job descriptions This chapter, Section 12.3.1.4
A.6.1.7 Contact with Special Interest Groups	√		√	√	√	√	This chapter, Section 12.3.1.4
A.6.1.8 Independent review of information security	√		√	√	√	√	This chapter, Sections 12.3.1.5 and 12.3.13.2 Certification Body Audits Second party Audits on the Forensic Laboratory by Clients
A.6.2.1 Identification of risks related to third parties	√		√	√	√	√	Chapter 5 Chapter 14, Section 14.3.2
A.6.2.2 Addressing security when dealing with Clients	√		√	√	√	√	Chapter 14, Section 14.2.1
A.6.2.3 Addressing security in third-party agreements	√		√	√	√	√	Chapter 14, Section 14.3.3
A.7.1.1 Inventory of assets	√		√	√	√	√	This chapter, Section 12.3.14
A.7.1.2 Ownership of assets	√		√	√	√	√	This chapter, Section 12.3.14.7
A.7.1.3 Acceptable use of assets	√		√		√	√	Chapter 4, Appendix 26
A.7.2.1 Classification guidelines	√		√	√	√	√	Chapter 5, Appendix 16 This chapter, Section 12.3.14.6
A.7.2.2 Information labeling and handling	√		√	√	√	√	This chapter, Sections 12.3.12, 12.3.14.8, and 12.3.14.9, Appendix 8
A.8.1.1 Roles and responsibilities	√		√	√	√	√	Various job descriptions Chapter 18, Section 18.1.2.1
A.8.1.2 Screening	√		√	√	√	√	Chapter 4, Appendix 20 This chapter, Section 12.3.3 Chapter 18, Section 18.1.3
A.8.1.3 Terms and conditions of employment	√		√	√	√	√	Chapter 18, Section 18.1.2.4
A.8.2.1 Management responsibilities	√			√	√	√	Various job descriptions Chapter 4, Section 4.6.2
A.8.2.2 Information security education and training	√		√	√	√	√	Chapter 4, Section 6.2 This chapter, Section 12.3.2

Continued

Control	Include	Exclude	Risk Assessment Method 1	Risk Assessment Method 2	Risk Assessment Method 3	The Forensic Laboratory Corporate Risk Register	Notes
A.8.2.3 Disciplinary process	√		√		√	√	Part of the Human Resources function and not information security issue, so not covered
A.8.3.1 Termination responsibilities	√		√	√	√		Chapter 4, Appendix 12 This chapter, Section 12.3.4
A.8.3.2 Return of assets	√		√		√		This chapter, Section 12.3.4
A.8.3.3 Removal of access rights	√		√	√	√		This chapter, Section 12.3.4
A.9.1.1 Physical security perimeter	√		√	√	√	√	Chapter 2, Section 2.4
A.9.1.2 Physical entry controls	√		√	√	√	√	Chapter 2, Sections 2.4.3, 2.4.1, 2.4.4, and 2.4.5 This chapter, Sections 12.4.1 and 12.4.4
A.9.1.3 Securing offices, rooms, and facilities	√		√	√	√	√	
A.9.1.4 Protecting against external and environmental threats	√		√	√	√	√	Chapter 2, Sections 2.3, 2.4.1, and 2.4.2
A.9.1.5 Working in secure areas	√		√	√	√	√	This chapter, Section 12.4.1
A.9.1.6 Public access, delivery, and loading areas	√		√	√	√	√	This chapter, Section 12.4.3
A.9.2.1 Equipment siting and protection	√		√	√	√	√	Chapter 2, Sections 2.4 and 2.5 Chapter 7, Section 7.3.4, Appendix 6
A.9.2.2 Supporting utilities	√		√	√	√	√	Chapter 2, Section 2.3
A.9.2.3 Cabling security	√		√	√	√	√	Chapter 2, Section 2.3.2 Chapter 7, Section 7.3.2.1 This chapter, Section 12.4.4.3.2
A.9.2.4 Equipment maintenance	√		√	√	√	√	Chapter 7, Section 7.5.4
A.9.2.5 Security of equipment off premises	√		√	√	√	√	Chapter 4, Appendix 18 This chapter, Section 12.3.10
A.9.2.6 Secure disposal or reuse of equipment	√		√	√	√	√	This chapter, Section 12.3.14.10
A.9.2.7 Removal of property	√		√	√	√	√	This chapter, Section 12.3.14.10, Appendix 7

Continued

Control	Include	Exclude	Risk Assessment Method 1	Risk Assessment Method 2	Risk Assessment Method 3	The Forensic Laboratory Corporate Risk Register	Notes
A.10.1.1 Documented operating procedures	√		√	√	√	√	The IMS
A.10.1.2 Change management	√		√	√	√	√	Chapter 7, Section 7.4.3
A.10.1.3 Segregation of duties	√		√	√	√	√	This chapter, Sections 12.3.5 and 12.3.6
A.10.1.4 Separation of development, test, and operational facilities	√		√		√	√	This chapter, Section 12.9.10
A.10.2.1 Service delivery	√			√	√	√	This chapter, Section 12.5 Chapter 14, Section 14.8.2
A.10.2.2 Monitoring and review of third-party services	√		√	√	√	√	Chapter 14, Section 14.2.2
A.10.2.3 Managing changes to third-party services	√			√	√	√	Chapter 7, Section 7.4.3
A.10.3.1 Capacity planning	√			√	√	√	Chapter 7, Section 7.4.6
A.10.3.2 System acceptance	√		√	√	√	√	Chapter 7, Section 7.4.3
A.10.4.1 Controls against malicious code	√		√	√	√	√	Chapter 7, Section 7.6.1
A.10.4.2 Controls against mobile code	√		√	√	√	√	Chapter 7, Section 6.1
A.10.5.1 Information backup	√		√	√	√	√	Chapter 7, Section 7.41
A.10.6.1 Network controls	√		√	√	√	√	Chapter 7, Section 7.7
A.10.6.2 Security of network services	√		√	√	√	√	Chapter 7, Section 7.7
A.10.7.1 Management of removable computer media	√		√	√	√	√	Chapter 7, Section 7.7
A.10.7.2 Disposal of media	√		√	√	√	√	This chapter, Section 12.3.14.10
A.10.7.3 Information handling procedures	√		√	√	√	√	This chapter, Section 12.3.14.9
A.10.7.4 Security of system documentation	√		√	√	√	√	Access control within the IMS
A.10.8.1 Information and software exchange agreements	√		√	√	√	√	This chapter, Sections 12.7 and 12.8.4
A.10.8.2 Exchange agreements	√		√	√	√		This chapter, Sections 12.7 and 12.8.4 Chapter 14, Section 14.2

Continued

Control	Include	Exclude	Risk Assessment Method 1	Risk Assessment Method 2	Risk Assessment Method 3	The Forensic Laboratory Corporate Risk Register	Notes
A.10.8.3 Physical media in transit	√		√	√	√	√	This chapter, Section 12.3.12.2
A.10.8.4 Electronic messaging	√			√	√	√	Chapter 4, Appendix 26 This chapter, Section 12.3.7
A.10.8.5 Business information systems	√		√	√	√	√	The IMS This chapter, Section 12.8.2
A.10.9.1 Electronic commerce security							Not applicable to the Forensic Laboratory
A.10.9.2 Online transactions							Not applicable to the Forensic Laboratory
A.10.9.3 Publicly available systems	√			√	√	√	This chapter, Section 12.7
A.10.10.1 Audit logging	√		√	√	√	√	Chapter 7, Section 7.4.10
A.10.10.2 Monitoring system use	√		√	√	√	√	Chapter 7, Sections 7.3.5, 7.4.6, 7.4.7, and 7.1.8 This chapter, Section 12.6.7
A.10.10.3 Protection of log information	√			√	√		Chapter 7, Section 7.4.10
A.10.10.4 Administrator and operator logs	√		√	√	√	√	Chapter 7, Section 7.4.10
A.10.10.5 Fault logging	√		√	√		√	Chapter 7, Section 7.4.10
A.10.10.6 Clock synchronization	√			√	√	√	Chapter 7, Section 7.5
A.11.1.1 Access Control Policy	√		√	√	√	√	Chapter 4, Appendix 11
A.11.2.1 User registration	√		√	√	√	√	This chapter, Section 12.6.4
A.11.2.2. Privilege management	√		√	√	√	√	This chapter, Sections 12.6.2, 12.6.4, and 12.6.5
A.11.2.3 User password management	√		√	√	√	√	This chapter, Sections 12.6.3 and 12.6.6
A.11.2.4 Review of user access rights	√		√	√	√	√	This chapter, Sections 12.3.1.5, 12.4.6, 12.6.1.3, and 12.6.7
A.11.3.1 Password use	√		√	√	√	√	This chapter, Sections 12.6.3 and 12.6.6
A.11.3.2 Unattended user equipment	√			√	√	√	Chapter 4, Appendix 13 This chapter, Section 12.3.8

Continued

Control	Include	Exclude	Risk Assessment Method 1	Risk Assessment Method 2	Risk Assessment Method 3	The Forensic Laboratory Corporate Risk Register	Notes
A.11.3.3 Clear Desk and Clear Screen Policy	√		√	√	√	√	Chapter 4, Appendix 13
A.11.4.1 Policy on use of networked services	√		√	√	√	√	Chapter 4, Appendix 19
A.11.4.2 User authentication for external connections	√		√	√	√	√	Chapter 7, Section 7.3
A.11.4.3 Equipment identification in networks	√		√	√	√	√	This chapter, Section 12.6.6
A.11.4.4 Remote diagnostic and configuration port protection	√		√	√	√	√	Chapter 7, Section 7.3
A.11.4.5 Segregation in networks	√		√	√	√	√	Chapter 7, Section 7.3 This chapter, Section 12.3.5 and 12.3.6
A.11.4.6 Network connection control	√		√	√	√	√	Chapter 7, Section 7.3 This chapter, Section 12.6
A.11.4.7 Network routing control	√		√	√	√	√	Chapter 7, Section 7.3 This chapter, Section 12.6
A.11.5.1 Secure log-on procedures	√		√	√	√	√	This chapter, Section 12.6.6.2
A.11.5.2 User identification and authentication	√		√	√	√	√	This chapter, Section 12.6
A.11.5.3 Password management system	√		√	√	√	√	This chapter, Section 12.6
A.11.5.4 Use of system utilities	√		√	√	√	√	This chapter, Section 12.6.6.5
A.11.5.5 Session time-out	√		√	√	√	√	This chapter, Section 12.6.6.6
A.11.5.6 Limitation of connection time	√		√	√	√	√	This chapter, Section 12.6.6.7
A.11.6.1 Information access restriction	√		√	√	√	√	This chapter, Section 12.6
A.11.6.2 Sensitive system isolation	√		√	√	√	√	Chapter 7, Section 7.3.4.1
A.11.7.1 Mobile computing and communications	√		√	√	√	√	Chapter 4, Appendix 18
A.11.7.2 Teleworking	√		√		√	√	This chapter, Section 12.6.9
A.12.1.1 Security requirements analysis and specification	√		√	√	√	√	This chapter, Section 12.9.6

Continued

Control	Include	Exclude	Risk Assessment Method 1	Risk Assessment Method 2	Risk Assessment Method 3	The Forensic Laboratory Corporate Risk Register	Notes
A.12.2.1 Input data validation	√		√	√	√	√	This chapter, Section 12.9.5.3
A.12.2.2 Control of internal processing	√		√	√	√	√	This chapter, Section 12.9.5.3
A.12.2.3 Message authentication		√	√			√	This chapter, Section 12.3.7
A.12.2.4 Output data validation	√		√	√	√	√	This chapter, Section 12.9.5.3
A.12.3.1 Policy on the use of cryptographic control	√		√	√			Chapter 4, Appendix 15
A.12.3.2 Key management	√		√				Chapter 4, Appendix 15 This chapter, Section 12.8.5
A.12.4.1 Control of operation software	√		√	√		√	Chapter 7, Section 7.6
A.12.4.2 Protection of system test data	√		√	√	√	√	This chapter, Section 12.9
A.12.4.3 Access control to program source code		√		√	√	√	This chapter, Section 12.9
A.12.5.1 Change control procedures	√		√	√	√	√	Chapter 7, Section 7.4.3
A.12.5.2 Technical review of operating system changes	√			√	√	√	Chapter 7, Section 7.4.3 This chapter, Section 12.3.13.2.2
A.12.5.3 Restrictions on changes to software packages	√			√	√	√	This chapter, Section 12.3.13.2.2
A.12.5.4 Information leakage	√		√	√	√	√	This chapter, Section 12.3.13.2.2
A.12.5.5 Outsourced software development		√	√		√	√	This chapter, Section 12.9.8
A.12.6.1 Control of technical vulnerabilities	√				√	√	Chapter 7, Section 7.6.2
A.13.1.1 Reporting of security incidents	√		√	√	√	√	Chapter 7, Section 7.4.1.4
A.13.1.2 Reporting of security weaknesses	√		√	√	√	√	Chapter 7, Section 7.4.1.4
A.13.2.1 Responsibilities and procedures	√		√	√	√	√	Chapter 7, Section 7.4.1.3
A.13.2.2 Learning from incidents	√		√	√	√	√	Chapter 8, Appendix 18 Chapter 7, Section 7.4.1.6

Continued

Control	Include	Exclude	Risk Assessment Method 1	Risk Assessment Method 2	Risk Assessment Method 3	The Forensic Laboratory Corporate Risk Register	Notes
A.13.2.3 Collection of evidence	√		√		√	√	Chapter 7, Section 7.4.1.7 Chapter 8 This chapter, Section 12.3.13.1.6
A.14.1.1 Business continuity management process	√		√	√	√	√	Chapter 13, Section 13.5
A.14.1.2 Business continuity and impact analysis	√		√	√	√	√	Chapter 13, Section 13.5
A.14.1.3 Writing and implementing continuity plans	√		√	√	√	√	Chapter 13, Section 13.5
A.14.1.4 Business continuity planning framework	√		√	√	√	√	Chapter 13, Section 13.5
A.14.1.5 Testing, maintaining, and reassessing business continuity plans	√		√	√	√	√	Chapter 13, Section 13.6
A.15.1.1 Identification of applicable legislation	√			√	√	√	This chapter, Section 12.3.13.1.1
A.15.1.2 Intellectual Property Rights (IPR)	√			√		√	This chapter, Section 12.3.13.1.2
A.15.1.3 Protection of organizational records	√		√	√	√	√	This chapter, Section 12.3.13.1.3
A.15.1.4 Data protection and privacy of personal information	√			√	√	√	This chapter, Section 12.3.13.1.4
A.15.1.5 Prevention of misuse of information processing facilities	√		√	√	√	√	This chapter, Section 12.3.13.1.5
A.15.1.6 Regulation of cryptographic controls		√					Chapter 4, Appendix 15 This chapter, Section 12.3.13.1.7
A.15.2.1 Compliance with security policies and standards	√		√	√	√	√	Chapter 4, Section 4.7.3 This chapter, Section 12.3.13
A.15.2.2 Technical compliance checking	√		√	√	√	√	Chapter 4, Section 4.7.3 This chapter, Section 12.3.13.2.2.5
A.15.3.1 Information System audit controls	√		√	√		√	Chapter 4, Section 4.7.3
A.15.3.2 Protection of system audit tools	√		√	√		√	Chapter 4, Section 4.7.3 This chapter, Section 12.6

STATEMENT OF APPLICABILITY (CONTROLS NOT IN ISO 27001)

Control	Include	Exclude	Cobra IT Risk Assessment	COBRA Op. Risk Assessment	From SPRINT	The Forensic Laboratory Corporate Risk Register	Notes
Copyright notices to be put in source code	√		√				To be addressed as appropriate
Structured design methodology (e.g., SDLC) should be used	√		√				To be addressed as appropriate
All staff should be forced to take their annual holiday entitlement	√		√	√			To be addressed as appropriate
A review of the company's internal communications with staff should be considered. The emphasis should be placed on the techniques of improving staff morale	√		√				To be addressed as appropriate
Dependence upon individuals for significant or critical functions should be avoided wherever possible. To achieve this, consider a program of cross training, periodic job rotation/transfer and other measures		√	√	√			To be addressed as appropriate
Every Project should have a business case and/or legal, or regulatory, reason for its inception	√		√	√			To be addressed as appropriate
Ensure a service level agreement is in place to obtain replacement components and/or service within an acceptable time		√	√	√			To be addressed as appropriate
Operator errors		√			√		To be addressed as appropriate
Redundancy and resilience	√				√		To be addressed as appropriate
Spares	√				√		To be addressed as appropriate

APPENDIX 2 - MEETING THE REQUIREMENTS OF GAISP

Principle	How Met?
Accountability Principle	This chapter, Section 12.3.14.7
Awareness Principle	The IMS and the ISMS Chapter 4, Section 4.6.2.2 This chapter, Section 12.3.2
Ethics Principle	Chapter 11, Appendix 3 The whole ethos of the Forensic Laboratory
Multidisciplinary Principle	The IMS and ISMS, based on the principles of risk management
Proportionality Principle	Chapter 5
Integration Principle	The IMS and ISMS, based on the principles of risk management
Timeliness Principle	Chapter 7, Section 7.4.1 Chapter 8
Assessment Principle	Chapter 4, Section 4.7.3 Chapter 5
Equity Principle	Legislation within the jurisdiction and the implementation of IMS and ISMS, based on the principles of risk management

APPENDIX 3 - SOFTWARE LICENSE DATABASE INFORMATION HELD

The following details are held of all software installations in the Forensic Laboratory software license database:

- product name;
- product version;
- vendor;
- manufacturer;
- number of licenses purchased;
- date purchased;
- locations where installed (i.e., user and computer details);
- number of licenses in use;
- patches installed;
- updates installed;
- license type;
- license renewal date;
- proof of license;
- software key(s);
- registration details;
- date retired.

APPENDIX 4 - INFORMATION SECURITY MANAGER, JOB DESCRIPTION

OBJECTIVE AND ROLE

The Information Security Manager (ISM) is responsible for establishing and monitoring adherence to ISO 27001 information security standards in the Forensic Laboratory. Information security covers information on any media that is owned by the Forensic Laboratory or is entrusted to their care.

Typically information security is defined as having the following aspects:

- Confidentiality;
- Integrity;
- Availability;
- Accountability;
- Auditability;
- Nonrepudiation;
- Authenticity.

PROBLEMS AND CHALLENGES

The primary challenge for the ISM is establishing a good working relationship with all Forensic Laboratory employees that encourage cooperation and teamwork to ensure that effective information security is in place. The ISM needs to balance the needs of providing appropriate information security countermeasures against the problems of possibly stifling innovation and implementing draconian countermeasures that Forensic Laboratory employees resent and try to circumvent.

PRINCIPAL ACCOUNTABILITIES

The ISM:

- develops and maintains the Forensic Laboratory information security policy;
- develops and maintains all relevant information security procedures in the Forensic Laboratory;
- assists the Human Resources Manager in development and maintenance of the Forensic Laboratory Handbook of Employment and associated Human Resources procedures;
- undertakes appropriate training for Forensic Laboratory employees, Clients and Visitors, as appropriate. This includes induction training, ongoing awareness training and specialized training;
- chairs the Forensic Laboratory Information Security Committee in its policy development effort to maintain the security and integrity of the Forensic Laboratory's information assets in compliance with legislation, regulation, and certification standards;

- provides project management and operational responsibility for the administration, coordination, and implementation of information security policies and procedures across all information processing systems throughout the Forensic Laboratory;
- performs periodic information security risk assessments including disaster recovery and business contingency planning, and coordinates internal audits to ensure that appropriate access to all Forensic Laboratory information assets is maintained;
- identifies and implements information security controls, based on risk assessments, as appropriate;
- serves as a central repository for information security-related issues and performance indicators;
- assesses changes submitted to the Change Advisory Board (CAB) for information security issues;
- attends the CAB, as appropriate;
- develops, implements, and administers a coordinated process for response to such issues;
- functions, when necessary, as an approval authority for platform and/or application security and coordinates efforts to educate Forensic Laboratory employees in good information security practices;
- maintains a broad understanding of laws relating to information security and privacy, security policies, industry best practices, exposures, and their application to the Forensic Laboratory's information processing environment;
- makes recommendations for short- and long-range security planning in response to future systems, new technology, and new organizational challenges;
- undertakes a rolling program of information security audits and tests, as defined in the IMS Calendar;
- ensures that all access to Forensic Laboratory information, or information held by the Forensic Laboratory for its Clients, is subject to agreed access levels, contractual agreements, and relevant legislation;
- acts as an advocate for security and privacy on internal and external committees as necessary;
- develops, maintains, and administers the security budget required to fulfil the Forensic Laboratory's information security expectations.
- gains and maintains ISO 27001 certification;
- assists the Business Continuity Manager in gaining and maintaining the ISO 22301 certification;
- develops plans for migration of information security policies and procedures to support the Forensic Laboratory's future directions;
- develops the Forensic Laboratory's long range information security strategy;
- participates in international, national, and local SIG presentations, and publishes articles describing the Forensic Laboratory's information security initiatives and how they relate to the business;
- develops and manages effective working relationships with all appropriate internal and external stakeholders;
- maintains external links to other companies in the industry to gain competitive assessments and share information, where appropriate;
- identifies the emerging information technologies to be assimilated, integrated and introduced within the Forensic Laboratory, which could significantly impact the Forensic Laboratory's ability to maintain a secure working environment;
- interfaces with external industrial and academic organizations to maintain state-of-the-art knowledge in emerging information security issues and to enhance the Forensic Laboratory's image as a first-class solution provider utilizing the latest thinking in this field;
- adheres to established Forensic Laboratory policies, standards, and procedures;
- performs all responsibilities in accordance with, or in excess of, the requirements of the Forensic Laboratory's Integrated Management System.

AUTHORITY

The ISM has the authority to:

- set the Forensic Laboratory's information security requirements;
- monitor production service offerings for adherence to the Forensic Laboratory's information security standards;
- monitor the Forensic Laboratory's internal processes and procedures for adherence to the Forensic Laboratory's information security standards;
- identify and implement appropriate controls, based on business risk assessments to protect the Forensic Laboratory's product and service offerings;
- enforce the Forensic Laboratory's information security requirements.

CONTACTS

Internal

Contacts within the Forensic Laboratory are throughout the whole business. Reporting will be outside the line management areas that are being reported on, so the ISM will report directly to Top Management.

External

Those external to Forensic Laboratory will be with appropriate Special Interest Groups (SIGs), other Information Security professionals, and organisations. These will vary between different jurisdictions.

REPORTS TO

The ISM reports to:

- Top Management.

APPENDIX 5 - LOGON BANNER

The following banner is used on all Forensic Laboratory information processing equipment, where possible:

> This is a private information processing system for authorized users performing authorized functions only. Unauthorized use is prohibited and may constitute a criminal offense under the <state legislation>.
> Unauthorized use by authorized users shall result in disciplinary action to the full extent permitted.
> Press OK below to accept these terms of use.

Note

The relevant legislation for the jurisdiction should be stated above. Specific legal advice should be sought for the relevant jurisdiction, as this book does not claim to provide legal advice.

APPENDIX 6 - THE FORENSIC LABORATORY'S SECURITY OBJECTIVES

ISO 27001 requires the Forensic Laboratory to set security objectives (0.1, 0.2, 4.2.3, 4.2.4, 4.3.1, 5.1, 7.1, and 8.1 refer) for the ISMS. These are business-driven objectives that the ISMS are to achieve.

Security objectives are driven by legislative, regulatory, Client, and internal requirements.

The Forensic Laboratory has agreed that the security objectives below are meeting its current requirements and these are to be regularly reviewed at each Management Review meeting or on any influencing change that may affect them.

ISO 27001 requires that employees understand the Security Objectives, why they are important, and what they can do to help the Forensic Laboratory achieve them.

The following are the business driven security objectives of the ISMS in the Forensic Laboratory, agreed by Top Management:

1. Increase client base because of ISO 27001 Accredited Certification;
2. Increase Client satisfaction with improved information security requirements, independently verified;
3. Commit sufficient resources to information security within the Forensic Laboratory to maintain appropriate information security and retain ISO 27001 Accredited Certification;
4. Continuously review and improve the Forensic Laboratory's information security implementation;
5. Ensure that all Forensic Laboratory employees know their security roles and responsibilities;
6. Ensure that all Forensic Laboratory assets, and assets held by the Forensic Laboratory on behalf of any third party, are appropriately protected against loss, disclosure, unauthorized modification, or deletion;
7. Ensure that the Forensic Laboratory is appropriately protected through contractual means when dealing with any third party, including measurement of services delivered against SLAs;
8. Ensure the physical security of the Forensic Laboratory's offices against unauthorized access;
9. Ensure that the Forensic Laboratory's IT Department securely delivers the services required by internal and external Clients;
10. Ensure that the Forensic Laboratory's IT services are continuously monitored and corrective and/or preventive action is taken, if needed;
11. Ensure that all access to information is based on a documented business need, and that this is regularly reviewed;
12. Ensure that any development undertaken, or products purchased by the Forensic Laboratory, have appropriate information security in place, based on perceived risk and/or Client requirements. This includes complete testing against predefined criteria prior to purchase or implementation;
13. Minimize the number of security incidents that may affect delivery of the Forensic Laboratory's services, and learn from any incident to prevent recurrence;
14. Ensure that in case of any incident that requires invocation of business continuity plans there is minimal impact on the delivery of the Forensic Laboratory's services to Clients;
15. Meet all legislative and contractual requirements for information security.

These are derived from existing documentation within the Forensic Laboratory, implied contractual terms and good information security practice.

The Information Security Manager shall produce quarterly reports showing how these security objectives are met by use of the defined metrics, as given in Chapter 5, Appendix 22. A report, showing year on year trending shall be presented to the annual Management Review by the Information Security Manager.

APPENDIX 7 - ASSET DETAILS TO BE RECORDED IN THE ASSET REGISTER

The following are the minimum details to be recorded for any asset in the IT Department Asset Register, in addition to the disposal details given in Appendix 10:

ASSET DETAILS

- asset description;
- barcode;
- asset number;

- manufacturer;
- asset type;
- model number;
- serial number;
- date last audited.

CURRENT OWNER DETAILS

- name;
- location;
- phone;
- e-mail;
- classification, if appropriate;
- date assigned.

VALIDATION AND MAINTENANCE DETAILS

- date last validated;
- validation interval;
- warranty details;
- date of warranty expiry;
- maintenance details;
- date of last maintenance visit;
- date of next planned maintenance visit;
- manufacturer's documentation location;
- results of last validation test;
- reference of validation testing identifier.

UPDATED BY

- asset register updated by, name;
- asset register updated, date;
- ERMS updated by, name;
- ERMS updated, date.

APPENDIX 8 - DETAILS REQUIRED FOR REMOVAL OF AN ASSET

The following details are required for removal of an asset from the Forensic Laboratory's premises:

- name of Requestor;
- Requestor's contact details;
- date of request;
- item to be removed;
- asset number;
- purpose/justification of the asset removal;
- intended location of asset;
- intended removal date;
- transportation details, if appropriate;
- intended return date;
- Asset Owner's name;
- Asset Owner's contact details;
- authorization signature;
- date asset register updated;
- asset register updated by;
- date asset returned;
- date asset register updated;
- asset register updated by.

APPENDIX 9 - HANDLING CLASSIFIED ASSETS

The table below shows the minimum requirements for how assets are to be handled in the Forensic Laboratory. These procedures are mandatory for all classified assets and are summarized below:

Requirement	Public	Internal Use	Confidential	Strictly Confidential
Page numbering "*x* of *y* pages"			√	√
Numbered copies			√	√
Classification in footer of each page	√	√	√	√
Strict access control lists applied for assets			√	√
Standard Forensic Laboratory document control table required	√	√	√	√
Movement of document to be held in a register				√
Permission to copy required and to be recorded			√	√
To be held in secure containers when not in use			√	√
Allowed to be sent by normal fax to open office	√	√		

Continued

Requirement	Public	Internal Use	Confidential	Strictly Confidential
Allowed to be sent by normal fax if recipient confirms they are stood by receiving fax			√	√
Can be sent by unencrypted e-mail	√	√		
Only to be sent by encrypted e-mail			√	√
Disposal to be by crosscut shredder[a]			√	√
Disposal shall be recorded in the register			√	√
Can be carried and handed over by hand[b]	√	√	√	√
Can be sent in a sealed single envelope internally or externally	√	√		
Can be sent internally or externally in a tamper proof envelope or container			√	√
Delivery receipt required				√

[a]If a crosscut shredder is not appropriate (e.g., for a hard disk or non-paper asset), then a suitable alternative should be used. Advice on alternate methods of disposal can be obtained from the Information Security Manager.
[b]By a known and trusted Forensic Laboratory employee or a trusted and bonded courier service who has a suitable contract in place.

APPENDIX 10 - ASSET DISPOSAL FORM

The contents of the Forensic Laboratory Asset Disposal form are given below:

FORM

- asset description;
- barcode;
- asset number;
- location;
- condition;
- reason for disposal;
- method of disposal;
- age of asset;
- expected date of disposal;
- written down value, if appropriate;
- sold to, if appropriate;
- sale price, if appropriate;
- donated to, if appropriate;
- Asset Owner name;
- Asset Owner signature;
- Finance Department authorizer name;
- Finance Department authorizer signature;
- date of authorization;
- asset register updated by, name;
- asset register updated, date;
- ERMS updated by, name;
- ERMS updated, date.

Within the form, the following codes are used:

CONDITION CODES

The following condition codes are used in the asset disposal process:

- P—poor;
- F—fair;
- G—good;
- E—excellent.

REASON FOR DISPOSAL

- B—beyond economic repair;
- D—damaged and no longer fit for purpose;
- O—obsolete;
- R—replaced by upgrade;
- S—surplus to requirements;
- T—theft or loss.

METHOD OF DISPOSAL

- C—computer recycle scheme;
- D—donated;
- I—already scrapped without approval;
- P—used for parts;
- S—scrapped;
- So—sold;
- TI—traded in.

APPENDIX 11 - VISITOR CHECKLIST

The Forensic Laboratory captures the following information for all Visitors to any site:

VISITOR DETAILS

- name;
- employer;
- mobile no;
- office no;
- reason for visit:
  - meeting;
  - service visit;
  - case progress review;
  - other (describe);
- describe visit details and justification if Data Center or DR site visit.

HOST DETAILS

- name;
- mobile no;
- office no.

ESCORT DETAILS

- name;
- mobile no;
- office no;
- alternate contact details:
  - name;
  - mobile no;
  - office no.

VISIT DETAILS

- date;
- time;
- access authority to the following needed:
  - office;
  - Data Center;
  - Forensic Laboratory;
  - DR site;
  - other (describe).
- authorizer name(s);
- signature(s);
- date(s).

CHECKLIST

- subject to existing contract with confidentiality clause (Date);
- subject to existing NDA (Date);
- new NDA signed (Date);
- Information Security Policy received;
- Visitor briefing received (including emergency procedures);
- rules of the Data Center received.

For each of the above, the date they were actioned and the signature of the Forensic Laboratory employee performing the action are recorded.

SIGNATURES

Signatures to confirm the above details and to comply with their requirements are required from the Visitor and the Host/Escort.

NEW NDAS

If a new NDA is executed, a copy is given to the Visitor and one retained by the Information Security Manager.

APPENDIX 12 - RULES OF THE DATA CENTER

- all Visitors must be pre-approved by the IT Manager, or his nominee, and escorted at all times;
- the IT Manager's word is final on all authorizations for access to the Data Center;
- all Visitors to the Data Center must register their access and egress using their Visitor badge;
- the Data Center main door must be kept closed and locked all the times;
- all Data Center hardware changes including additions, removals, and/or re-configurations must follow the Forensic Laboratory change management procedures, and must be co-ordinated with, and approved by, the IT Manager;
- all cables connected to any device in the Data Center must be maintained in a safe, orderly, and documented fashion;
- no material is to be stored on top of any server rack and a minimum of 18″ clearance between racks and the ceiling must be maintained;
- all packing materials, cardboard, boxes, plastic, etc., must be removed from the premises (including the Tape Vault) when work is complete;
- any non-essential or personal item left in the Data Center may be confiscated;
- all cabinet doors must be closed, or locked if appropriate, after work completion;
- all Forensic Laboratory employees with access to the Data Center must acquire familiarity with the installed fire-quenching system;
- the following items are prohibited in the Data Center:
  - explosives;
  - weapons;
  - hazardous materials;
  - alcohol, illegal drugs, or other toxicants;
  - electromagnetic devices that may interfere with any Forensic Laboratory information processing systems;
  - radioactive materials;
  - photographic or recording equipment (other than authorized media backup devices);
  - Visitor's mobile phones;
  - food;
  - drink.

Any violations of the above rules must be reported to the IT Manager as an information security incident, as defined in Chapter 7, Section 7.4.1.

APPENDIX 13 - USER ACCOUNT MANAGEMENT FORM CONTENTS

One form is used in the Forensic Laboratory for all management of user accounts. The form below covers account:

- creation;
- modification;
- deletion.

ACCOUNT OWNER DETAILS

- name;
- forename;
- employer;
- position;
- room number;
- phone;
- e-mail address;
- start date;
- status (permanent, part time, direct contractor, third party, other);
- end date (for fixed-term contracts and known end dates only).

AUTHORIZED REQUESTOR DETAILS

- name;
- forename;
- position;
- room number;
- phone;
- e-mail address;
- signature.

REQUEST TYPE

- new user;
- account modification;
- account deletion.

HARDWARE REQUIRED

- desktop;
- forensic workstation (Windows);
- forensic workstation (Unix and variants);
- Apple Mac;
- laptop;
- desk phone—define type;
- other specialized forensic case processing hardware;
- secureID.

MOBILE DEVICES REQUIRED

- Blackberry;
- iPhone;
- other mobile device—define.

COMMUNICATIONS ACCOUNTS

- corporate e-mail;
- e-mail distribution lists—define;
- outlook calendars—define;
- groups to be a member of—define;
- internet access;
- Skype;
- Lync;
- other.

DRIVE ACCESS

- standard Forensic Laboratory shared drive;
- standard department shared drive;
- personal home drive;
- others—define.

SOFTWARE REQUIRED

- Forensic Laboratory standard desktop;
- Forensic Laboratory standard forensic toolkit;
- other—define.

INFORMATION ACCESS

- ERMS;
- finance system;
- human resources system;
- forensic case processing;
- others—define.

> **Note**
> For each application or information to be accessed, each application or information database must be authorized by the Application or Information Owner. This authorization can be by signature on the form or by e-mail associated to the application.

FORENSIC CASE PROCESSING

For each forensic case, specific access rights are assigned so that only named Forensic Laboratory employees can have access to the case:

- define case number.

SETUP DETAILS

- name;
- forename;
- position;
- room number;
- phone;
- e-mail address;
- date actions completed;
- date user advised (e-mail);
- signature.

APPENDIX 14 - TELEWORKING REQUEST FORM CONTENTS

A form to authorize teleworking is used in the Forensic Laboratory in conjunction with the Account Management Form, as given in Appendix 13, for managing Teleworkers.

PROPOSED TELEWORKER DETAILS

- name;
- forename;
- employer;
- position;
- phone;
- e-mail address;
- status (permanent, part time, direct contractor, third party, other).

PROPOSED TELEWORKER LOCATION

- address;
- description of the site;
- details of security controls currently in place;
- other people having access to the site.

AUTHORIZED REQUESTOR DETAILS

- name;
- forename;
- position;
- room number;
- phone;
- e-mail address;
- signature.

BUSINESS JUSTIFICATION

- details of the business justification.

DURATION OF TELEWORKING

- proposed start date;
- frequency of review for continued business need;
- proposed end date (if known).

COMMUNICATION METHOD

- define secure communications method;
- defined strong authentication to be used;
- risk assessment carried out by;
- risk assessment carried out on;
- frequency of risk assessment update;
- approved by the Information Security Manager on.

TELEWORKING ADDITIONAL MEASURES REQUIRED

- define any teleworking equipment needed for a secure home office—e.g., secure storage, shredder, etc.;
- additional controls required by the risk assessment and agreed by the Information Security Manager;
- frequency of teleworking site to be audited and added to the IMS Calendar, as given in Chapter 4, Appendix 42.

LEGISLATIVE REQUIREMENTS

- have all relevant legislative requirements been identified (e.g., Health and Safety, personal data, and privacy requirements);
- have all relevant legislative requirements been met?
- is appropriate insurance cover in place?
- has the teleworking site been audited prior to operations commencing?
- Auditor name;
- audit date;
- non-conformances raised are on the relevant audit report, as defined in Chapter 4, Section 4.7.2, and are dealt with through the CAPA process.

TRAINING

- date teleworking training undertaken;
- teleworking training undertaken by;
- frequency of training update.

AUTHORITY AND APPROVAL

- formal approval signed by;
- formal approval signed on;
- terms and conditions accepted by the Teleworker on;
- copy lodged with Human Resources department on.

Note

Authority for teleworking is not permitted until all CAPAs are cleared.

Chapter 13

Ensuring Continuity of Operations

Table of Contents

13.1 BUSINESS JUSTIFICATION FOR ENSURING CONTINUITY OF OPERATIONS

13.1.1 General

Business continuity is essential to all businesses, and the Forensic Laboratory is no exception. The Forensic Laboratory has a number of Service Level Agreements (SLAs) and Turn Round Times (TRTs) in place for Clients. The Forensic Laboratory will typically be contractually obliged to meet these requirements, as well as court dates, and any incident that affects case processing in the Laboratory must have one or more Business Continuity Plans in place to ensure continuity of operations.

The Forensic Laboratory will need to put in place the processes and procedures to protect against, reduce the likelihood of occurrence of, prepare for, respond to, and recover from any incidents that may occur that affect forensic case processing.

IS 22301: 2012 Societal security—Business continuity management systems—Requirements provides the method of certification of the Forensic Laboratory's Business Continuity Management System (BCMS). This is supported by ISO 22313: 2012 Societal security—Business continuity management systems—Guidance.

As is common with ISO Standards, ISO 22301 is based on the Plan-Do-Check-Act or Deming cycle, as defined in Chapter 4, Section 4.3.

Note

Clause 14 of ISO 27001 and ISO 27002 also provides guidance on business continuity as do a number of other ISO[a] and national standards. This section of the book is based on ISO 22301.

13.1.2 PDCA Applied to the BCMS

Applying PDCA to the BCMS gives the following stages:

- Plan—establishing the Business Continuity Policy, as given in Chapter 4, Appendix 9, setting objectives, and defining targets processes and procedures to continuously improve the Forensic Laboratory's business continuity capability;
- Do—implement and operate the processes and procedures defined at the Plan stage;
- Check—monitoring the implementation of the processes and procedures and review performance against targets and objectives defined at the Plan stage and reporting the results of these reviews to management for preventive or corrective action, as appropriate;
- Act—undertaking the corrective and preventive actions based on the performance review at the Check stage, using the Forensic Laboratory's CAPA process, as defined in Chapter 4, Section 4.8.

13.1.3 BCMS Scope and Purpose

The scope of the BCMS that will be implemented in the Forensic Laboratory is to provide resilience for its critical business activities through the implementation of controls that minimize the impact of a disruption on its business products, services, employees, and infrastructure located in the Forensic Laboratory.

- The scope of the IMS and so the BCMS is given in Chapter 5, Appendix 11;

[a] These include ISO 24762—Information technology—Security techniques—Guidelines for information and communications disaster recovery services, ISO 27031 Information technology—Security techniques—Guidelines for communication technology readiness for business continuity, ISO 22399 Societal security—Guidelines for incident preparedness and operational continuity management, HB 292: A practitioner's guide to business continuity management (Australia), CSA Z1600: Standard on emergency management and business continuity (Canada), SI 24001: Security and Continuity Management Systems (Israel), and TR19: BCM Framework and technical reference (Singapore), and NFPA 1600 Standard on disaster recovery management systems (USA).

- risk reduction will be implemented by the implementation of controls identified in the ISO 27001 Statement of Applicability and is defined in Chapter 5. The Forensic Laboratory's risk appetite has been defined in Chapter 5, Appendix 14;
- generic outsourcing and supplier agreements relating to premises and IT operations are defined in the IMS scope (e.g., gas, water, electricity, telephone, internet, other services, and suppliers). Specific forensic outsourcing and supplier agreements are all subject to individual contracts with SLAs and are regularly subject to second party audits by the Forensic Laboratory;
- products and services within the Forensic Laboratory are defined simply as forensic case processing, and this includes all of the activities outlined in this book;
- it is acknowledged that the Forensic Laboratory is likely to be highly dependent on its supply chain for delivery of its products and services; however, there is little ability to manage some of these (e.g., electricity, water, internet access, etc.). These risks must be recorded in the risk register and are managed as appropriate;
- security objectives have been defined in Chapter 12, Appendix 5, and business continuity objectives have been defined in Section 13.1.5;
- suppliers are approved from a financial probity perspective as well as from a security perspective including the supply chain risk and their own contingency arrangement. Details held about suppliers are given in Appendix 1. The headings of the financial and security questionnaire are given in Appendix 2. The key suppliers are all regularly subject to second party audits, as defined in the IMS Calendar in Chapter 4, Appendix 42;
- Client details are all maintained in MARS in the ERMS;
- the BCMS is owned by the Business Continuity Manager in the Forensic Laboratory, whose job description is given in Appendix 3.

13.1.4 Requirements

The Forensic Laboratory identifies its own requirements based on legislative, regulatory, and contractual duties, as defined in Chapter 12, Section 12.3.13.1 as well as Section 13.1.7.

- Business continuity arrangements are required to support the Forensic Laboratory's key business operations and ensure that these operations continue to operate in the event of a disruption.
- the high-level Forensic Laboratory business activities that are covered by these arrangements are:
  - Client contracts and Client management activities;
  - specifications, development, and management activities;
  - case processing activities;
  - case testing and reviewing activities;
  - case delivery activities;
  - financial management activities;
  - supporting infrastructure activities including:
    - IT systems;
    - employees;
    - building facilities;
    - contracted third parties.

13.1.5 Organizational BCP Objectives

The objectives of business continuity at the Forensic Laboratory are to:

- identify business activities that are critical to the Forensic Laboratory's operations;
- reduce risk to an acceptable level in line with the Forensic Laboratory's risk appetite, as defined in Chapter 5, Section 5.5.9.1;
- ensure that all Forensic Laboratory employees know their responsibilities;
- provide a planned and tested response to business disruptions;
- successfully manage disruptions to business operations;
- be measurable, in line with the security objectives defined in Chapter 5, Appendix 22, using ISO 27001 Clause 14. Other specific measurable objectives can be developed as needed based on legislative, regulatory, and Client requirements;
- regularly test plans to ensure that they are effective;
- provide regular training to ensure that employees are competent in business continuity matters;
- continuously improve response to incidents and learn from them.

13.1.6 Acceptable Level of Risk

The Forensic Laboratory must recognize that not all risks can be mitigated fully and that a level of residual risk remains and that this has to be knowingly accepted and regularly monitored using the risk register, as given in Chapter 5, Appendix 17.

The Forensic Laboratory BCMS has been designed to support the critical business activities of the Forensic Laboratory, once assessed through risk management and business impact assessment exercises. Details of the Forensic Laboratory Business Impact Analysis (BIA) forms are given in Appendix 4.

The main processes that support the business have been identified in the business risk assessment process, as defined in Chapter 5. Risk treatment has been implemented by the implementation of controls identified in the ISO 27001 Statement of Applicability as given in Chapter 12, Appendix 1.

The Forensic Laboratory has identified its acceptable levels of risk and how to evaluate this in Chapter 5, with the Forensic Laboratory risk appetite being given in Chapter 5, Appendix 14.

The Forensic Laboratory has accepted the residual risk and actively manages the risks through its risk register and risk processes. The Forensic Laboratory Management should regularly review the risks to company activities and agree to the appropriate treatment of risks.

Note

Often it is wrongly thought that risk is always a negative outcome, but this is not always true. The positive side of risk is called an opportunity, and opportunities also require a business continuity response if adopted by the Forensic Laboratory.

As part of the Forensic Laboratory's risk management process, a business risk workshop must always be undertaken, usually driven by the BIA that will identify the relevant business processes to be evaluated. The process is as follows:

- after undertaking the BIA, a clear picture of business processes in the Forensic Laboratory will be presented with all internal and external linkages, this includes any outsourcing risks, which are covered in Chapter 14, Section 14.8.1.2;
- once these processes and their linkages have been agreed by the relevant business Owner, a business risk assessment can be carried out on the processes identified. While this is part of the risk assessment process, as defined in Chapter 5, within the Forensic Laboratory it is an outcome of the BIA process but it will also be used to populate the Statement of Applicability, as given in Chapter 12, Appendix 1 and the Corporate Risk Register, as given in Chapter 5, Appendix 17;
- the advantage of this approach is that all relevant business Owners are present with Top Management. Where individual interviews on a "one-on-one" basis usually provide a biased and skewed perception based on the respondent's views, a workshop allows all views to be challenged and have Top Management make objective decisions, rather than respondent's subjective ones;
- based on the results of the BIA from all relevant business Owners, the top-level business processes can be identified within the Forensic Laboratory with internal and external linkages and also they can be agreed, which is not the case with the BIA process;
- once agreed, the risks can be documented. This is always undertaken in business terms facilitated by the Information Security Manager and the Business Continuity Manager, who can then turn business-driven results into terms of information security controls;
- using the risk process in Chapter 5, the risks identified in this process can be evaluated and added to the SoA and the Corporate Risk Register, as appropriate, after consensual agreement between the relevant business Owners and Top Management.

13.1.7 Statutory, Regulatory, and Contractual Duties

The Forensic Laboratory ensures that all applicable statutory, regulatory, and contractual requirements are included in the BCMS as appropriate.

There will be different legislative and regulatory requirements in different jurisdictions and these must be identified, both as part of the ISO 27001 and OSI 22301 implementation process, as defined in Chapter 12, Section 12.3.13.1, and as part of the requirements for operating the Forensic Laboratory.

Contracts with Clients and suppliers identify any business continuity-related contractual requirements.

13.1.8 Interests of Key Stakeholders

The Forensic Laboratory BCMS ensures that the interests of key stakeholders are identified and incorporated into the BCMS. The typical key stakeholders are as follows:

- employees—people who work on the Forensic Laboratory products and services;
- Clients—organizations that use or purchase the Forensic Laboratory products and services;
- suppliers—organizations or third-party consultants who provide services or products to the Forensic Laboratory;
- investors—organizations and people who provide finance and support to the Forensic Laboratory business activities.

13.2 MANAGEMENT COMMITMENT

Top Management commitment to the BCMS must be demonstrable in the Forensic Laboratory by all management and employees.

Within the Forensic Laboratory, Top Management will need to demonstrate this level of commitment and leadership by:

- establishing, approving, and communicating the Forensic Laboratory Business Continuity Policy, as given in Chapter 4, Appendix 9 to all employees and relevant third parties;
- identifying the Forensic Laboratory's objectives for its BCMS and business continuity response capability, as defined in Section 13.1.5;
- embedding business continuity and the BCMS into the IMS, which is used as the main business tool by all employees and relevant third parties, as defined in Section 13.8;

- providing appropriate resources for operating and continuous improvement of the Forensic Laboratory's business continuity capability, as defined in Section 13.2.1;
- ensuring that induction and information security training cover the requirements of business continuity and the importance of each employee's input to the process, as defined in Section 13.3;
- developing a range of scenarios appropriate to the Forensic Laboratory and identifying Business Continuity Strategies that address them, as defined in Section 13.4;
- developing an appropriate business continuity response appropriate for the Forensic Laboratory, as defined in Section 13.5;
- undertaking regular testing of Business Continuity Plans, as defined in Section 13.6;
- continuously improving the IMS, as defined in Chapter 4, Section 4.8, and the BCMS in particular, as defined in Section 13.7.

13.2.1 Provision of Resources

The Forensic Laboratory is committed to ensuring that appropriate resources have been assigned to the business continuity process and the IMS generally, as defined in Chapter 4, Section 4.6.2 and for the BCMS specifically in this section.

The Forensic Laboratory should appoint a Business Continuity Manager to oversee the business continuity process; their job description is given in Appendix 3.

When setting up the BCMS in the Forensic Laboratory, manpower resources must be ring-fenced for the project to ensure that implementation occurred and certification was achieved. The high-level project plan for this is given in Appendix 5.

Ongoing manpower resources must also be made available for ongoing development, testing, and continuously improving the Forensic Laboratory's business continuity response.

Information, data, and communication channels must be available as required as soon as possible after the invocation of any BCP to relevant employees.

An alternate working environment, in case the Forensic Laboratory is unavailable, must be available. This may be a dedicated hot work site owned by the Forensic Laboratory, through a commercially available warm site to home and Client site working. Whatever is required must be available to ensure ongoing case processing. Wherever forensic case processing is to be carried out in a business continuity environment, the Forensic Analysts and other Forensic Laboratory employees must have the relevant facilities, equipment, consumables, etc., to undertake forensic case processing as defined by the BIA for reduced working.

Additional to case processing requirements are peripheral services that support case processing and these include human resources, finance, facilities, physical security, etc. Peripheral resources also include those resources outside the direct control of the Forensic Laboratory (e.g., suppliers, outsourcing partners, service providers, etc.).

As an output of the risk management process undertaken, as defined in Chapter 5, relevant controls were identified, sourced, and implemented to treat risk by ensuring that all Forensic Laboratory employees and relevant third parties undergo appropriate training for their role in the business continuity response capability, as defined in Section 13.3.

Undertaking internal audits of the business continuity capability as well as second party audits of key suppliers, as defined in Chapter 4, Section 4.7.3.

The BCMS and other management systems implemented in the Forensic Laboratory are subject to regular Management Reviews, as defined in Chapter 4, Section 4.9, with corrective and preventive actions being tracked through the CAPA system to completion.

13.3 TRAINING AND COMPETENCE

The Forensic Laboratory has policies and procedures for recruiting employees, to ensure that:

- all employees have the necessary technical and interpersonal skills that are required for attaining the Forensic Laboratory's management system objectives;
- employees have the necessary training, skills, and personal development to fully contribute to the design, development, production, and support of the Forensic Laboratory products and services on recruitment, as defined in Chapter 4, Section 4.6.2.2;
- those employees who need additional training have identified this as part of their annual appraisal process using the Training Needs Analysis process, as defined in Chapter 18, Section 18.2.2;
- ongoing training and awareness updates are a critical part of employee development and must be completed, as planned.

The Forensic Laboratory has policies for promoting business continuity awareness and training for employees to ensure that business continuity forms part of the core values of the Forensic Laboratory, that business continuity is effectively managed throughout the Forensic Laboratory, and that all employees are aware of, and are adequately trained to fulfill their business continuity responsibilities. This specifically covers:

- roles and responsibilities;
- recruitment;
- introducing new employees;
- managing business continuity awareness and education;
- managing skills training for business continuity response;

- training records;
- performing employee appraisals.

13.3.1 Roles and Responsibilities

13.3.1.1 Business Continuity Manager

The Business Continuity Manager is responsible and accountable for all aspects of developing, implementing, maintaining, and testing the Forensic Laboratory's BCPs. Their job description is given in Appendix 3.

13.3.1.2 Forensic Laboratory Top Management

The Forensic Laboratory Top Management constitute executives or other management level employees who are responsible for the following with regard to business continuity aspects of employee recruitment and training. The Top Management are responsible for:

- recruiting employees in accordance with the relevant Forensic Laboratory recruitment procedures;
- defining requirement specifications for new employees, especially those with a business continuity element in their job role;
- ensuring that all employees have the necessary skill sets and personal qualities to perform their role in attainment of the Forensic Laboratory's objectives, and specifically the business continuity objectives;
- assigning appropriate team mentors to new employees;
- ensuring that employees observe the appropriate Forensic Laboratory policies and procedures as defined in the IMS and specifically the BCMS;
- performing employee appraisals, and determining/initiating action based on the findings of appraisals;
- identifying opportunities for employee business continuity training, and determining requirements for the ongoing employee development;
- providing authorization for employee business continuity training.

Specific Forensic Laboratory Managers have individual job descriptions for their delegated roles, and these are given in various chapters throughout this book and are centrally defined in Chapter 18, Section 18.1.5.

13.3.1.3 Forensic Laboratory Employees

Employees are responsible and accountable for complying with all of the Forensic Laboratory's policies, standards, and procedures in the IMS and specifically the BCMS.

Some employees will be part of the various recovery teams supporting BCPs and will have to perform the defined role, as appropriate.

Employees must understand their contribution to the business continuity process.

13.3.2 Managing Business Continuity Awareness and Education

Note

This section is in addition to the general promotion of awareness of management systems that is given to new employees at induction as defined in Chapter 4, Section 4.6.2.2 and given in Chapter 6, Appendix 11.

13.3.2.1 Overview

Awareness of business continuity is an essential aspect of business continuity management in the Forensic Laboratory. Employees need to be aware and understand that business continuity is an ongoing commitment that has the full and demonstrable support of Top Management, and which provides a framework for ensuring the resilience of critical activities in the event of a disruption to the Forensic Laboratory.

It is ultimately the responsibility of the Forensic Laboratory Top Management to ensure that all employees and relevant third party employees understand the key elements of business continuity in the Forensic Laboratory, the approach, why it is needed, and their personal business continuity responsibilities. It is the responsibility of the Business Continuity Manager to promote business continuity awareness to all employees on a continuous basis.

Awareness of business continuity is typically delivered in the Forensic Laboratory via an ongoing business continuity education and information program where employees are provided with information and guidance to help them understand business continuity and its importance to the business.

The Forensic Laboratory should follow these guidelines to promote awareness of business continuity:

1. A business continuity management education and training program is run on a regular basis to promote and enhance business continuity management awareness.
2. All employees are kept up-to-date with current business continuity management activities via information updates from the Business Continuity Manager (e.g., e-mail updates following a business continuity management exercise).
3. Business continuity management awareness needs are reviewed on an ongoing basis to identify new awareness requirements, evaluate the effectiveness of their delivery, and identify improvements to the awareness program.

13.3.2.2 Guidelines for Educating New Employees in Business Continuity

1. In addition to the "normal" induction training, when joining the Forensic Laboratory, all employees:

- must be briefed, as part of their induction, on the culture of business continuity within the Forensic Laboratory, and as a minimum include the following:
  - the importance of business continuity in the Forensic Laboratory;
  - business continuity and recovery objectives;
  - the Forensic Laboratory's business continuity management education and information program;
  - who to contact for additional information.
- must be directed to the Business Continuity Management System element of the IMS;
- must be able to:
  - understand that they have responsibilities with regard to business continuity;
  - identify business continuity resources (the BCMS part of the IMS and any plans that they are involved with);
  - understand that they have a role to play in helping the Forensic Laboratory successfully operate and improve business continuity.

2. As part of the induction process, new employees are made aware of the Forensic Laboratory's IMS with supporting management system policies and objectives, with the following points of focus:
   - the IMS exists to ensure promotion of quality, information security, resilience, and Corporate Social Responsibility (CSR) throughout the design, development, production, and support of the Forensic Laboratory products and services;
   - the Forensic Laboratory has specific measurable objectives with regard to obtaining quality in the design, development, production, and support of their products and services;
   - all employees are responsible for applying IMS procedures and policies within the Forensic Laboratory, and play a key role in the attainment of quality, information security, resilience, and CSR objectives;
   - all the Forensic Laboratory products and services must be developed in accordance with the requirements of the IMS;
   - the IMS includes the BCMS that describes policies and procedures by which the Forensic Laboratory ensures that critical business activities are resumed in the event of a disruption to the Forensic Laboratory;
   - the IMS includes a number of separate management systems that have been integrated, which describe policies, procedures, and controls that the Forensic Laboratory employs for the promotion of quality, information security, resilience, and CSR throughout the design, development, production, and support of the Forensic Laboratory products and services;
   - a variety of System Management Owners are responsible for their management systems and will outline their contribution to the Forensic Laboratory and the employee's role and responsibilities. Their job descriptions are defined in Chapter 18, Section 18.1.5.

13.3.2.3 Business Continuity Management Education and Information Program

1. The Forensic Laboratory must implement a business continuity education and information program, the purpose of which is to:
   - build a culture of business continuity within the Forensic Laboratory;
   - embed business continuity management in all Forensic Laboratory products and services;
   - enhance awareness and understanding of business continuity among all employees;
   - communicate business continuity objectives to employees;
   - instill confidence in the Forensic Laboratory's ability to deal with disruptions to the business;
   - ensure that all the Forensic Laboratory employees are aware of their individual importance and contribution to the Forensic Laboratory's business continuity objectives, and in maintaining the delivery of company products and services.
2. The business continuity education and information program is the responsibility of the Business Continuity Manager with the support of the Forensic Laboratory Top Management, and is delivered on a regular basis (at least once a year), and additionally, on an as-needed basis as determined by the Business Continuity Manager (e.g., following a business continuity management exercise, an audit non-conformance being raised, or any other influencing change).
3. The business continuity management education and information program is normally delivered by the Business Continuity Manager in a workshop format, and is attended by *all* Forensic Laboratory employees, as well as relevant third party employees. If considered appropriate, the Business Continuity Manager may invite representatives from suppliers (with the approval of Top Management).
4. Issues covered during a business continuity education and information program workshop vary, but typically include:
   - the status of business continuity within the Forensic Laboratory;
   - planned developments for business continuity within the Forensic Laboratory (improvements, emerging/changing business activities and their likely impact, etc.);
   - changes to company business continuity processes, Business Continuity Plans, etc.;
   - problems or difficulties experienced by employees;

- employee's training requirements for business continuity;
- employees feedback on all aspects of business continuity management at the Forensic Laboratory (including learning from incidents);
- internal and external BCMS audits.

13.3.2.4 Reviewing and Improving Business Continuity Awareness

1. The review, evaluation, and improvement of business continuity awareness at the Forensic Laboratory is an ongoing, internal process that aims to:
   - identify new requirements for business continuity management awareness among employees;
   - provide a means for delivering awareness requirements;
   - confirm that objectives for business continuity management awareness among employees are being met;
   - improve business continuity management awareness and its delivery throughout the Forensic Laboratory.
2. These reviews are the responsibility of the Business Continuity Manager and are typically performed:
   - on an ongoing basis (as part of the Business Continuity Manager role);
   - following a full-scale business continuity management exercise or an invocation of a Business Continuity Plan in the event of a disruption;
   - during internal audits of the BCMS to examine compliance with the ISO 22301 standard;
   - following a business continuity management education and information program session.
3. The process by which the Forensic Laboratory reviews and improves business continuity awareness is:
   - the Business Continuity Manager identifies areas of business continuity awareness that require review based on:
     - lack of employees understanding or performance with regard to business continuity;
     - issues identified at business continuity management education and information sessions;
     - operational, performance, or understanding issues arising from a Business Continuity Plan exercise or invocation;
     - audits performed on the BCMS to confirm its compliance with the ISO 22301 standard.
   - the Business Continuity Manager performs a review and:
     - determines the current level of awareness;
     - confirms the desired level of awareness;
     - identifies gaps in employees awareness;
     - evaluates how business continuity awareness activities are performing (e.g., the business continuity management education and information sessions and in particular whether any activities are not performing as expected);
     - identifies possible improvements to business continuity awareness delivery.
   - the Business Continuity Manager produces a brief report that documents the findings of the review. The report typically covers:
     - objectives and scope of the review;
     - recommendations for improvements to business continuity awareness (if any improvements are identified);
     - recommendations on how improvements are to be implemented (if any improvements are identified).
4. The report is distributed to the Forensic Laboratory Top Management.
5. The Business Continuity Manager and the Forensic Laboratory Top Management review the identified improvements and:
   - agree the proposed improvements;
   - obtain approval for implementing improvements;
   - seek consultation with other employees, as necessary, on how improvements can be delivered;
   - agree on how to deliver the necessary improvements.
6. The agreed improvements are implemented as corrective or preventive actions using the Forensic Laboratory CAPA process, as defined in Chapter 4, Section 4.8 through the Forensic Laboratory Change Management process.

13.3.3 Managing Skills Training for Business Continuity Management

13.3.3.1 Overview for Managing Skills Training for Business Continuity Management

1. Appropriate education and skills training must be provided to all the Forensic Laboratory employees who are involved in planning, implementing, exercising, maintaining, and improving business continuity.
2. Training should be provided for Top Management and Line Managers so that they have the knowledge and skills that they require to manage the business continuity management program, perform risk and threat assessments, perform a BIA, develop and implement BCPs, and run business continuity tests and exercises.
3. Training shall be provided for all Forensic Laboratory employees and any relevant third party employees so that they have the knowledge and skills that they require to undertake their nominated roles during incident response or business recovery.
4. The Business Continuity Manager and the Human Resources Department are responsible for ensuring that employees obtain adequate training to perform their business continuity roles via:
   - identification of employees skills and competences for business continuity management;

- advising employees of available courses as part of the Training Needs Analysis process, as defined in Chapter 18, Section 18.2.2., and encouraging certification where applicable;
- ensuring knowledge transfer between employees and third parties, as appropriate;
- maintenance of individual personnel training records, as defined in Section 18.2.1.8 and Chapter 4, Section 4.6.2.3;
- active participation in business continuity management planning, implementation, exercising, maintenance, and improvement.

13.3.3.2 Identifying Employees Skills and Competences for Business Continuity

1. The Forensic Laboratory ensures that all employees, including appropriate third party employees, are adequately trained to perform their assigned business continuity management tasks, to enhance the professional and personal development of individuals, and to ensure that all employees can fully contribute toward achievement of business continuity objectives.
2. Training and development needs for all employees are identified at the Forensic Laboratory using these methods:
   - at least once a year Managers or Team Leaders meet with their team members to perform appraisals aimed at evaluating the skill set of their employees, and determining whether additional training may be required to:
     - enhance the skills of the employee;
     - aid personal development.
3. After the appraisal is performed, employee's records are updated with the date and outcome of the review:
   - at the planning stage of a new project or case, employees may identify specific training that is required to enable them to be assigned to a particular project, or aspect of a project;
   - an employee identifies the training that they would like to receive and seeks approval from their Line Manager to attend a course;
   - the Business Continuity Manager, or an employee, identifies a gap in the skills or competencies that is required to enable them to perform a particular business continuity role;
   - the Business Continuity Manager, or an employee, identifies a gap in the skills or competencies that are required to enable them to perform a particular business continuity role.

13.3.3.3 Reviewing Training Outcomes

1. All employees training, which is performed to improve the skills and competences of employees for business continuity purposes, is reviewed to:
   - evaluate the effectiveness of the training;
   - determine if the training was adequate.

The process for evaluation of training is given in Chapter 18, Section 18.2.2.7.

13.3.4 Training Records

The Forensic Laboratory maintains training records for all employees undertaking business continuity management and disaster recovery training, as defined in Section 18.2.1.8 and Chapter 4, Section 4.6.2.3.

13.4 DETERMINING THE BUSINESS CONTINUITY STRATEGY

In order to determine the correct strategy(ies) for business continuity within the Forensic Laboratory, it is necessary to ensure that all of the Forensic Laboratory requirements are captured, including legislative and regulatory requirements within the jurisdiction as well as Client requirements.

> **Note**
> This also includes any outsourcing that is undertaken by the Forensic Laboratory.

To determine the Forensic Laboratory Business Continuity Strategy, a number of issues need to be examined before an appropriate strategy (or set of strategies) is defined and agreed.

13.4.1 Overall Activity Strategy

This is a review of the overall strategy for the business continuity response activity within the Forensic Laboratory; issues considered in the review include:

- maximum tolerable period of disruption to the affected business activity;
- costs of implementing a Business Continuity Strategy for the business activity to address disruptions in a timely manner according to contractual or other business drivers;
- consequences of failing to implement a Business Continuity Strategy for the business activity.

The outcomes are documented by the Business Continuity Manager and sent to Top Management for review and action.

13.4.2 Key Products and Services

The Forensic Laboratory will have a list of the following high-level key company products and services that support the Forensic Laboratory's objectives. It is the job of the Business Continuity Manager to either agree with these products and services or amend the list to accurately reflect the requirements of the Forensic Laboratory. It is these products and services that are included within the BCMS:

- acquire Clients;
- maintain Clients;
- process invoices;
- supplier process;
- process cases;
- internal procedures (non-IT);
- deliver Client's requirements;
- internal IT Management.

The key Forensic Laboratory processes will have had their risks assessed in the BIA, as given in Appendix 4, and in the Business Risk Workshops, as defined in Section 13.1.6.

13.4.3 Business Continuity Policy

The Forensic Laboratory will have developed and implemented a Business Continuity Policy that sets the high-level requirements for business continuity within the business. This is approved by Top Management and is given in Chapter 4, Appendix 9.

13.4.4 The Approach

The approach to determining a Business Continuity Strategy for the Forensic Laboratory is:

- identifying critical business activities using the BIA process, as defined in Section 13.1.6;
- performing the risk assessments on critical activities, as defined in Chapter 5 and Section 13.1.6;
- implementing appropriate controls as defined in the ISO 27001 Statement of Applicability, as given in Chapter 12, Appendix 1;
- determining residual risk and how to treat it, as defined in Chapter 5, Section 5.5.8 and Chapter 5, Section 5.6;
- determining the approach to business continuity, based on the findings.

Once the approach to business continuity is determined, the appropriate strategies are selected for development into a Business Continuity Strategy and the relevant plans for the Forensic Laboratory.

1. The basis for the Forensic Laboratory's business continuity response is determined by a regular review of business activities in a BIA, which is normally performed by the Business Continuity Manager at least once each year and also when new business systems, products, or services are introduced. Risk assessments are performed on those activities identified as critical.
2. In addition to this, business-driven risk workshops and infrastructure risk assessments are performed in conjunction with the BIA, as required.
3. This enables the Forensic Laboratory to identify their critical activities, and the resources needed to support them, their dependencies and to understand the threats to them.
4. The implementation of controls identified by the risk assessment and treatment process reduces the likelihood, but not necessarily the severity of any threat that may exploit a vulnerability to become and incident and need to be treated as such.
5. Residual risks must be accepted by the Risk Owner or as a blanket acceptance by Top Management as acceptable after risk treatment. This is subject to regular review at the Management Review and formally approved with records retained if this is according to the requirements of ISO 27001, Clause 4.2.1 h.
6. The criticalities are included in the BCP with the Recovery Time Objectives (RTOs). From this, the Forensic Laboratory chooses appropriate risk treatments and determines an appropriate Business Continuity Strategy or strategies that ensures that:
   - RTOs are met;
   - appropriate resources are available for resumption of critical and key activities;
   - suppliers are not single points of failure for resumption purposes;
   - all dependencies have been identified for key business processes and activities;
   - recovery has been prioritized according to business need;
   - minimum levels of service that can be tolerated.

13.4.4.1 Reviewing Employee Resource Options

This is a review and identification of strategies to ensure that core skills and knowledge are maintained by the Forensic Laboratory employees so that the Forensic Laboratory is protected against the loss or absence of key employees. Strategies considered in the review can include:

- development of process documentation that allows employees to undertake roles with which they are unfamiliar;
- multiskill training and cross-training of employees to spread skills across a number of people;
- succession planning to develop employees' skills and knowledge;
- use of permanent or occasional third-party support supported by contractual agreements;
- knowledge management programs supported by off-site storage for protection of data.

The selected strategies for each critical business activity are documented by the Business Continuity Manager.

13.4.4.2 Reviewing Work Location and Buildings Options

This is a review and identification of strategies to reduce the impact of the unavailability of the Forensic Laboratory office building—or parts of it—so that the Forensic Laboratory employees can relocate to continue working.

> **Note**
> The review must make estimates on the timescale for unavailability—the RTO. An RTO of less than a day may mean no action is required, whereas an RTO of a few days or several months means that employees must relocate to continue work.

Strategies considered in the review include:

- increase in office density to accommodate more employees in specific areas of the building;
- displacement of employees performing less urgent business processes (to enable employees performing a higher priority activity to continue work);
- remote working from alternative sites (such as home, Client, or other non-Forensic Laboratory locations);
- reciprocal arrangements with other organizations. These need to be approached with extreme care and the Forensic Laboratory has to determine whether it is prepared to accept the risk of reciprocal arrangements;
- third-party alternative sites from a commercial or service company, including dedicated or syndicated space and mobile facilities;
- resilient operations to provide a continuously available solution.

The selected strategies for each critical business activity are documented by the Business Continuity Manager.

13.4.5 Reviewing Supporting Technology Options

This is a review and identification of strategies to reduce the impact of the unavailability of supporting technology that underpins a critical business activity.

> **Note**
> Supporting technology covers any provision from within the Forensic Laboratory and services or products contracted by the Forensic Laboratory from third parties.

Strategies considered in the review review include, but are not limited to:

- storage of older or unused equipment for spares or emergency use;
- provision of duplicate technology at an alternative site in advance or post-disruption (for example, failover or dark site);
- provision of ship-in contracts to include equipment in the event of a disruption;
- planned temporary re-direction of telecommunications services;
- provision of remote working.

The selected strategies for each critical business activity are documented by the Business Continuity Manager.

13.4.6 Reviewing Information and Other Data Options

This is a review and identification of strategies to ensure that information and data required by the Forensic Laboratory in both hard-copy and electronic formats are protected and recoverable within the required timescale.

Strategies considered in the review can include:

- provision for confidentiality of information so that the required level of confidentiality is maintained during a disruption;
- provision for integrity of information so that information restored is accurate;
- provision for availability of information is available at the time needed;
- provision for currency of information for replication across systems without hampering the Forensic Laboratory employees' ability to resume operations;
- remote storage of records including off-site managed document stores and optical copies for hardcopy records and data vaulting for electronic records.

The selected strategies for each critical business activity are documented by the Business Continuity Manager.

13.4.7 Reviewing Supplies and Equipment Options

This is a review and identification of strategies to ensure that the business supplies required by the Forensic Laboratory are available to support its critical business activities.

1. Strategies considered in the review can include:
    - storage of supplies at an alternative location;
    - arrangements with third parties for delivery of supplies or stock at short notice;
    - transfer of some operations to an alternate location either in-house, a third party or a Client site;
    - storage of older or unused equipment for spares or emergency use;
    - risk mitigation for unique or long lead-time equipment through a planned program of replacement.

2. The selected strategies for each critical business activity are documented by the Business Continuity Manager.

> **Note**
>
> Where the Forensic Laboratory has a single source of supply that relates to a critical business activity, potential alternative supplies must be identified to ensure continuity of supply.

13.4.8 Reviewing Third Parties and Other Stakeholders Options

This is a review and identification of strategies to ensure that the requirements of third parties and other stakeholders are understood and managed during response actions by the Forensic Laboratory.

1. Strategies considered in the review can include, but is not limited to:
   - provision of requirements for individual third parties as part of overall response actions;
   - protection of third party and the Forensic Laboratory interests;
   - understanding of arrangements with civil emergency responders.
2. The selected strategies for each critical business activity are documented in a report by the Business Continuity Manager.
3. The Business Continuity Manager documents the selected strategies and circulates them to the Top Management for comment.

> **Note**
>
> For some strategies, it may be appropriate to use the services of a third party. The arrangements to obtain information from a third party about a service or to contract business continuity services to a third party are performed by the Business Continuity Manager in consultation with other relevant Forensic Laboratory Managers. Agreements with third parties are governed by strict rules to ensure confidentiality and assurance.

4. The Forensic Laboratory Top Management meet with the Business Continuity Manager to review the report, to confirm that the continuity strategies have been properly undertaken, and to address the likely causes and effects of disruption to the Forensic Laboratory critical business activities. The Forensic Laboratory Top Manager signs off the continuity strategies.

13.4.9 Reviewing Business Continuity Strategy

The Forensic Laboratory must select the appropriate strategies to meet its business continuity objectives for critical business activities identified in the BIA and the business driven workshops. This allows the Forensic Laboratory to provide a level of confidence that critical business activities will remain operational in the event of a disruption to the business.

1. Through the selection of appropriate strategies, the Forensic Laboratory ensures that it:
   - has a fit-for-purpose, pre-defined and documented incident response structure to provide effective response and recovery from disruptions (including Business Continuity Plans);
   - understands how it recovers each critical business activity within the agreed time-frame;
   - understands the relationships between key employees and third parties, and how these relationships are managed during recovery activities.

> **Note**
>
> For those critical business activities that have not been added to the Business Continuity Strategy (i.e., business activities for which risks have been accepted), no further assessment is performed.

2. For each critical business activity identified during a BIA and which has been added to the Business Continuity Strategy, a review of the appropriate strategies covers the following:
   - implementation of the appropriate measures to reduce the likelihood of incidents occurring and/or reduce the potential effects of those incidents;
   - resilience and mitigation measures;
   - continuity for critical activities during and following an incident;
   - accounting for those activities that have not been identified as critical.

> **Note**
>
> For some strategies, it may be appropriate to use the services of a third party. The arrangements to obtain information from a third party about a service or to contract business continuity services to a third party are performed by the Business Continuity Manager in consultation with other relevant Forensic Laboratory Managers. Agreements with third parties are governed by strict rules to ensure confidentiality and assurance.
>
> The selected Business Continuity Strategies are documented and then signed-off by Top Management.

3. The process by which the Forensic Laboratory select appropriate Business Continuity Strategies is:
   - the Business Continuity Manager, together with the appropriate Forensic Laboratory employees, meets to review the signed-off approach to business continuity.

13.4.10 Agreeing to a Strategy

Once a strategy has been developed, it shall be reviewed, amended as necessary and:

- the strategy is agreed to;
- the strategy is formally approved by Top Management;
- the strategy is used as the basis for developing a business continuity management response appropriate for the Forensic Laboratory.

13.5 DEVELOPING AND IMPLEMENTING A BUSINESS CONTINUITY MANAGEMENT RESPONSE

13.5.1 BCMS Structure

The BCMS structure used in the Forensic Laboratory is as below:

1. The BCMS development and ongoing management shall be performed by the Business Continuity Manager.
2. The development of the BCMS must be performed inhouse. A project timeline for the development of a BCMS for the Forensic Laboratory is given in Appendix 5.
3. A set of BCMS documentation will be developed that encompasses:
   - an overview of the BCMS;
   - incident scenarios, as given in Appendix 6
   - BIAs for all business areas, as given in Appendix 4;
   - BCP Strategy options, as defined in Section 13.4 and as given in Appendix 7;
   - BCPs for each business area, as defined in Section 13.5.4;
   - BCP testing scenarios, as defined in Section 13.6 and as given in Appendix 11;
   - BCP test results and any corrective action;
   - supporting material (e.g., forms, templates, and checklists).
4. Responsibility for the maintenance of specific sections within the BCMS is allocated to key Forensic Laboratory employees, typically the Business Continuity Manager, but some areas will be assigned or delegated to other employees.
5. The Forensic Laboratory BCMS is produced as a series of FrontPage, Excel, PowerPoint, Access, Word, or PDF documents accessed via an HTML front end for viewing using an HTML browser. All Forensic Laboratory computers should have an Internet browser installed, apart from dedicated forensic workstations on the segregated laboratory network.
6. All BCMS documents shall follow the requirements of document control, as defined in Chapter 4, Section 4.6.3.
7. All BCMS documents produced by the Forensic Laboratory will be retained in accordance with the Forensic Laboratory document retention policy and schedule, as given in Chapter 4, Appendix 16.
8. Responding to and resolving, hardware, software, and service interruptions is crucial for the provision of information processing systems and services for the Forensic Laboratory's internal and external business Clients. If problems cannot be resolved quickly and efficiently with minimum disruption by the Forensic Laboratory, their business Clients cannot perform their assigned tasks, which can, in turn, potentially impact delivery of products and services, for Clients, partners and the ability of the Forensic Laboratory to conduct their normal business operations. Timely recovery of critical business activities is essential.
9. The initial response is critical, and the Forensic Laboratory has three discrete processes that interlink to address this issue:
   - incident management;
   - business continuity management response;
   - reviewing and continuously improving the Business Continuity Plans implemented in the Forensic Laboratory.

13.5.2 Incident Management

This is a well-tried and trusted process in the Forensic Laboratory and is part of the ISO 27001 process, and is defined in Chapter 7, Section 7.4.1.

This process covers internal incidents reported to the Service Desk as well as any international or national incidents that may occur that are advised through national or international reporting channels.

13.5.3 Forensic Laboratory Business Continuity Response

There are many different types of plans that can be developed but typically they fall into one of two groups:

- Incident Management Plan (IMP)—describes the key management tasks required during the initial stages of a disruption to business operations. This plan is typically followed while the Forensic Laboratory Top Management obtain an understanding of the incident and then organize full response actions;
- Business Continuity Plan (BCP)—describes all the planned activities to enable the Forensic Laboratory to recover or maintain its critical business activities in the event of a disruption to normal business operations. This type of plan is invoked in whole or part and at any stage of the response to a disruption.

IMPs and BCPs are produced to ensure that all the critical business activities identified in the Business Continuity Strategy have an appropriate managed response to a disruption. A specific plan does not have to contain the same headings or items, but all the plans must collectively address the full requirements defined for business continuity within the Forensic Laboratory.

Note 1

Depending on the size of the forensic laboratory, response actions to a disruption may be contained within one BCP. As the forensic laboratory, expands, additional requirements for business continuity may mean the division of activities into several specific BCPs.

Note 2

For simplicity, all plans below have been referred to as BCPs as that is what is implemented in the Forensic Laboratory.

13.5.4 Developing a Business Continuity Plan

Production of a BCP is a key stage in the development of an appropriate response to the threats identified by the Forensic Laboratory to its critical business activities.

The main purposes of a BCP is to document the activities that are required to respond to a disruption to normal business operations, the recovery activities that are required to resume operations, the ways in which these activities are managed to restore operations within the required time frame and the roles and responsibilities involved in the process.

Note 1

BCPs are developed to be "living" documents and must be maintained so that they reflect the current circumstances of the Forensic Laboratory.

Note 2

This process applies to any BCP developed at the Forensic Laboratory including IMPs.

The process by which the Forensic Laboratory develops a BCP is given in Figure 13.1.

1. The Business Continuity Manager, together with the appropriate Forensic Laboratory Managers and employees, meets to review the signed-off approach to business continuity, the identified threats to the Forensic Laboratory critical business activities, and to obtain a clear understanding of the requirements for the BCP.
2. Any existing BCPs must be reviewed to determine the level of integration with the new BCP. If an update to an existing BCP is required instead of a new BCP, then it must follow the BCP updating and approval process.
3. A clear communication plan is agreed for pre- and post-invocation of the BCP. This must be regularly tested and maintained to ensure that it remains current.
4. The Business Continuity Manager produces a draft of the BCP. The minimum requirements for the contents of a BCP within the Forensic Laboratory are given in Appendix 8.
5. Where a third party is involved in response activities, details of the activities performed by the third party must be obtained and incorporated into the BCP. The Business Continuity Manager must make arrangements for this material to be obtained from the third party.
6. The Business Continuity Manager produces the BCP according to the Forensic Laboratory procedures for document production, as defined in Chapter 4, Section 4.6.3.
7. Once agreed, each BCP is then:
   - classified as a confidential document and subject to full document handling protection and control;
   - stored both on-site and off-site in hardcopy and electronic formats ready for use during a disruption;
   - issued to the relevant third parties in reduced form subject to confidentiality agreements (for example, removing the elements not performed by the third party but retaining key communications and reporting information).

13.5.5 Updating and Approving a BCP

As the Forensic Laboratory and its business expands, its requirements for business continuity change, which affects the existing BCPs for responding to a business disruption.

When changes are identified to the agreed critical business activities, all BCPs must be reviewed and updated to reflect the current requirements of the Forensic Laboratory.

The process by which the Forensic Laboratory updates a BCP is given in Figure 13.2.

1. The Business Continuity Manager, together with the appropriate Forensic Laboratory employees, meets to review the changed business requirements of the Forensic Laboratory as identified in a revised approach to business continuity, the updated threats to the Forensic Laboratory's critical business activities, and to obtain a clear understanding of the revised requirements.

Note

Any changes to the Forensic Laboratory business mean that revised risk assessments and BIA are required before a BCP can be updated.

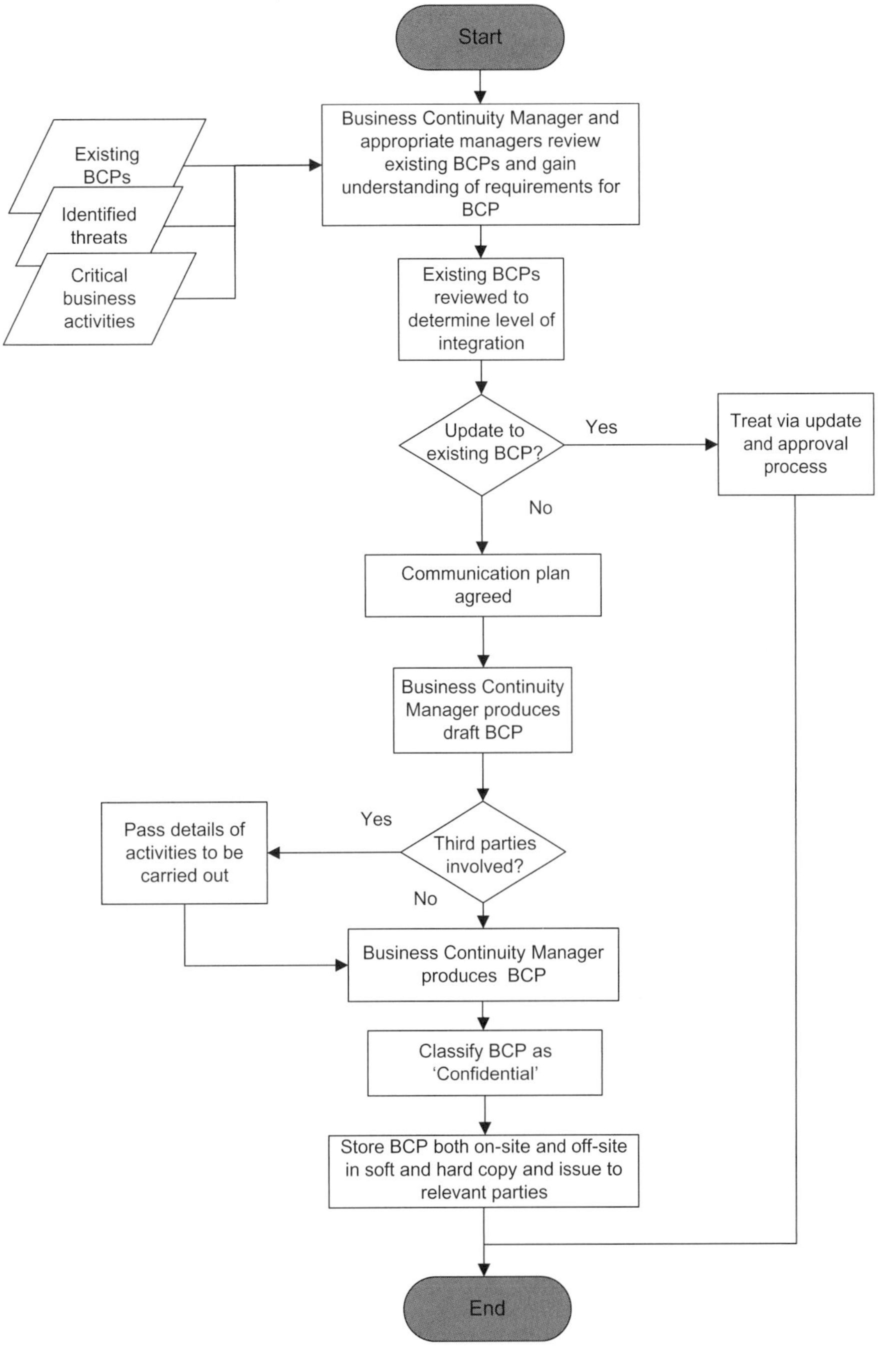

FIGURE 13.1 Developing a Business Continuity Plan. (For color version of this figure, the reader is referred to the online version of this chapter.)

2. Minor changes to a BCP, such as changes to employee's contact details can normally be updated directly by the Business Continuity Manager without peer review and approval. Typically, the volatile information will be contained in the Appendix to the BCP. The table of contents for the Appendix to the Forensic Laboratory BCP is given in Appendix 9.
3. The outcome of the meeting is a detailed list of the required changes to existing BCPs and potential new BCPs. This is passed to the Forensic Laboratory Top Management for review and the list of details for changes is given in Appendix 10.
4. The Change Advisory Board (CAB) reviews the list of changes required to the BCP and confirms:
   - changes that are acceptable and can be implemented; or
   - changes that are not acceptable and that need to be further discussed.

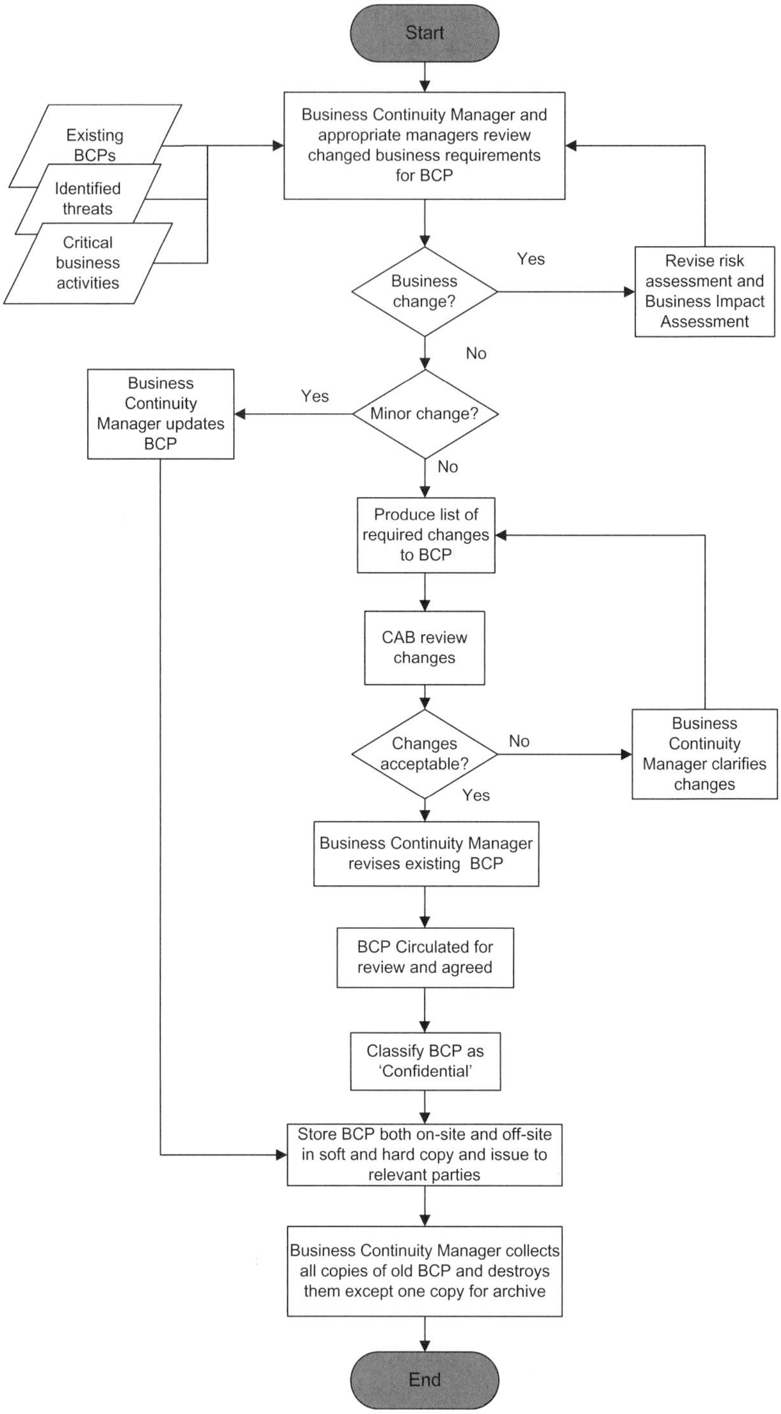

FIGURE 13.2 Updating and approving a BCP. (For color version of this figure, the reader is referred to the online version of this chapter.)

If the changes are not accepted, the Business Continuity Manager clarifies the changes that have not been approved and re-submits information as required. The change management process is defined in Chapter 7, Section 7.4.3.

5. The Business Continuity Manager revises the existing BCP (and drafts a new BCP if one needs to be developed), according to the document control procedures defined in Chapter 4, Section 4.6.3.
6. The amended, or new, BCP is reviewed according to the Forensic Laboratory document control standards.
7. Once agreed, each new or revised BCP is then:
   - classified as a confidential document and subject to full document handling protection and control, as defined in Chapter 12, Section 12.3.14.9;
   - stored both on-site and off-site in hardcopy and electronic formats ready for use during a disruption;

- issued to the relevant third parties in reduced form, subject to confidentiality agreements (for example, removing the elements not performed by the third party but retaining key communications and reporting information).

> **Note**
>
> Minor changes to a BCP do not normally need a major release update and can be issued as an incremental release, e.g., 1.1, 1.2, etc.

8. The Business Continuity Manager ensures that all issued hardcopies and electronic copies of the previous version of the BCP are collected and securely destroyed. At least one copy must be retained for archive purposes.

13.5.6 Reviewing and Improving the BCP Development Process

Review and continual improvement of the Forensic Laboratory process to create and update business continuity BCPs is an ongoing, internal process, which seeks to confirm that the correct objectives are being met. The purpose of a review is to:

- determine whether the BCP development activities (people and methods) are occurring as expected;
- examine the process with a view to improvement of work methods;
- identify improvements to the process.

Reviews are the responsibility of the Business Continuity Manager and are typically performed:

- on an ongoing basis (as part of the Business Continuity Manager role);
- following a full-scale BCP exercise or an invocation of a BCP in the event of a disruption;
- during internal audits of the BCMS to examine compliance with the ISO 22301 management system.

The process by which the Forensic Laboratory reviews and improves the BCP development process is:

1. The Business Continuity Manager identifies areas of the BCP development process that require review based on:
   - aspects of the process that are not performing as expected;
   - matters arising from BCP exercises or invocations;
   - audits performed on the process to confirm compliance with the ISO 22301 management system.
2. The Business Continuity Manager reviews the process, and determines:
   - how BCP development activities are performing (in particular whether any activities are not performing as expected);
   - the effectiveness of the process;
   - the effectiveness of any previous improvements to the process;
   - possible new improvements to the process and methodology.
3. The Business Continuity Manager produces a brief report that documents the findings of the review. The report typically covers:
   - objectives and scope of the review;
   - recommendations for new improvements to the process and methodology (if any improvements are identified);
   - recommendations on how improvements are to be implemented (if any improvements are identified).

   The report is distributed to the relevant stakeholders, including Top Management, for review.
4. The Business Continuity Manager reviews the identified improvements with the Forensic Laboratory Top Management and:
   - outlines the proposed improvements;
   - obtains approval for implementing improvements;
   - seeks consultation with other employees as necessary on how improvements to the process can be implemented;
   - agrees on how to implement the necessary improvements.
5. The agreed process and methodology improvements are implemented. The Business Continuity Manager manages the implementation, as required.

13.5.7 Reviewing and Improving BCP Implementation

Review and continual improvement of the Forensic Laboratory process to assess the business continuity requirements and then selection of appropriate continuity strategies is an ongoing, internal process that seeks to confirm that the correct objectives are being met. The purpose of a review is to:

- determine whether assessment activities (people, technology, and/or methodology) are occurring as expected;
- examine the process with a view to improvement of work methods, the assessment and selection methodologies used;
- identify improvements to the business continuity implementation process and methodology.

Reviews are the responsibility of the Business Continuity Manager and are typically performed:

- on an ongoing basis (as part of the Business Continuity Manager role);
- following a full-scale BCP exercise or an invocation of a BCP in the event of a disruption;

- during internal audits of the business continuity management system to examine compliance with the ISO 22301 management system.

The process by which the Forensic Laboratory reviews and improves the business continuity implementation process is:

1. The Business Continuity Manager identifies areas of the business continuity implementation process that require review based on:
   - aspects of the process that are not performing as expected;
   - matters arising from BCP exercises or invocations;
   - audits performed on the process to confirm compliance with the ISO 22301 management system.
2. The Business Continuity Manager reviews the process and determines:
   - how business continuity implementation activities are performing (in particular whether any activities are not performing as expected);
   - the effectiveness of the risk assessment and BIA methodologies;
   - the effectiveness of the risk requirements process;
   - the effectiveness of any previous improvements to the process and methodology;
   - possible new improvements to the process and methodology.
3. The Business Continuity Manager produces a brief report that documents the findings of the review. The report typically covers:
   - objectives and scope of the review;
   - recommendations for new improvements to the process and methodology (if any improvements are identified);
   - recommendations on how improvements are to be implemented (if any improvements are identified).

   The Forensic Laboratory's plan for table of contents for the review is given in Appendix 12.
4. The report is distributed to the Forensic Laboratory Top Management for review.
5. The Business Continuity Manager reviews the identified improvements with the Forensic Laboratory Top Management and:
   - outlines the proposed improvements;
   - obtains approval for implementing improvements;
   - seeks consultation with other employees as necessary on how improvements to the process can be implemented;
   - agrees on how to implement the necessary improvements.
6. The agreed process and methodology improvements are implemented. The Business Continuity Manager manages the implementation, as required.

13.6 EXERCISING, MAINTAINING, AND REVIEWING BUSINESS CONTINUITY ARRANGEMENTS

The Forensic Laboratory must plan and implement business continuity exercising to verify the effectiveness of the business continuity arrangements and to identify areas of BCPs that require amendment.

13.6.1 Roles and Responsibilities

13.6.1.1 Business Continuity Manager

The Business Continuity Manager is the person who has responsibility for the management of the business continuity exercising at the Forensic Laboratory. In addition to the job responsibilities for the role, as given in Appendix 3, the Business Continuity Manager is specifically responsible for:

- maintaining the business continuity exercise and test program;
- planning business continuity exercises and tests;
- drafting business continuity exercise and test plans;
- taking part in business continuity exercises and tests;
- appointing facilitators and/or observers for the business continuity exercises and tests;
- collating information from completed business continuity exercises and tests;
- generating reports on the outcome of a business continuity exercise and/or test;
- analyzing completed business continuity exercises and tests;
- identifying and agreeing on action points and improvements arising from business continuity exercise and test reviews;
- implementing improvements arising from business continuity exercise and test reviews, if required.

13.6.1.2 Forensic Laboratory Top Management Responsibilities

The Forensic Laboratory Top Management is responsible for providing management support to the Business Continuity Manager during BCP testing and exercising. In addition to the job responsibilities for their specific role, they are responsible for:

- supporting the Business Continuity Manager in all aspects of business continuity exercise and test management as required;
- ensuring that appropriate resources are made available for the exercise or test;
- taking part in the exercise or test, as appropriate;

- providing input to the revision and approval of the business continuity exercise and test program;
- providing sign-off for business continuity exercise and test plans;
- agreeing action points and improvements to business continuity arrangements following an analysis of a business continuity exercise or test.

13.6.2 Business Continuity Exercise and Test Exercises

Business continuity exercises and tests validate the effectiveness of the Forensic Laboratory business continuity arrangements by testing the Business Continuity Plans, procedures, and employees in a controlled manner.

The purpose of performing business continuity exercises and tests is to:

- test the effectiveness of the Forensic Laboratory's business continuity arrangements;
- validate the technical, logistical, and administrative aspects of BCPs;
- validate the recovery infrastructure;
- practise the Forensic Laboratory's ability to recover from a disruption;
- evaluate the Forensic Laboratory's current business continuity competence;
- develop team work and raise awareness of business continuity throughout the Forensic Laboratory;
- identify shortcomings and implement improvements to the Forensic Laboratory's business continuity readiness.

Business continuity exercises and tests are governed by an exercise or a scenario plan. While each individual exercise may test a specific plan or element of a plan, the range of exercises performed over a year validates the overall the business continuity arrangements. The template for the scenario plan that might be used in the Forensic Laboratory is given in Appendix 11.

Business continuity exercises and tests are typically performed on one of three levels:

- simple—typically a short and uncomplicated exercise—typically a desk check;
- medium—typically a walk-through of a plan or a part of a plan, a simulation, or an exercise of critical activities only, such as a server rebuild from backup tapes;
- full—typically a complex exercise that is a full test run of a plan.

Each business continuity exercise and/or test has three phases:

- preparing a plan to cover the exercise to ensure that all resources are available, the level of exercise is valid, and the objectives of the exercise are clear;
- performing the exercise in a controlled manner to check the validity of the BCP that is being tested;
- reviewing the exercise to analyze the actions and outcomes and determine whether the exercise objectives were achieved and adopt the lessons learned.

13.6.3 Maintaining the Business Continuity Exercise and Test Program

Exercising the BCPs is a key business continuity activity that allows the Forensic Laboratory to validate the effectiveness of its business continuity arrangements by testing BCPs, supporting procedures, and employee's understanding of them.

To ensure that all aspects of business continuity exercises and tests are fully considered, the Forensic Laboratory must maintain a program that covers the frequency and type of exercises. This ensures that the business continuity arrangements as a whole are validated at least once each year, as in the IMS Calendar, given in Chapter 4, Appendix 42.

The exercise program is assessed and updated at least once every 6 months and is the responsibility of the Business Continuity Manager. The program is approved by Top Management.

The process by which the Forensic Laboratory maintains the business continuity exercise and test program is:

1. The Business Continuity Manager assesses the business continuity exercise and test requirements for the next 6-month period and determines whether any changes are required to suit business needs. Generally:
   - business continuity exercises and tests are prioritized to meet business continuity needs and recovery objectives;
   - an exercise or test of the Forensic Laboratory's overall business continuity capability should be programmed to take place at least once every 12 months;
   - the exercises and tests added to the program should be appropriate to the Forensic Laboratory's recovery objectives.

> **Note**
> Where third parties have activities within a plan, suitable arrangements must be made to test these activities as part of the program by either involving the third party in a Forensic Laboratory exercise or test or enabling the activities of the third party to be performed separately.

A review can also take place on an *ad hoc* basis if events trigger a revision of the program (e.g., a significant change in the external business environment or an internal change to processes, employees, technology, or business activities).

2. The Business Continuity Manager meets with the Forensic Laboratory Top Management to discuss the program with a view to its revision and covers the following key aspects:
   - the current program;
   - requirements and priorities for business continuity validation and exercising;
   - outcomes from previous business continuity exercises and tests (e.g., a need to re-run an exercise or any relevant corrective and preventive actions);
   - timescales and resource availability;
   - the levels of exercising required (these may vary in complexity from a simple desk exercise or walk-through of options, to a selected set of recovery activities or a full test of a BCP).
3. The Forensic Laboratory Top Management approve the revised program including:
   - a list of business continuity exercises and tests required;
   - scheduling of each business continuity exercise and test;
   - levels of testing required for each exercise.
4. The approved program in the IMS Calendar is updated by the Business Continuity Manager and is issued to all relevant the Forensic Laboratory employees.
5. The issue of the program may lead to a revision of the business continuity awareness program to ensure that all employees are aware of when exercises will be held.

13.6.4 Performing Business Continuity Exercises and Tests

All business continuity exercises are designed to test the Forensic Laboratory's BCPs, and the Forensic Laboratory must adopt a positive attitude toward this exercising to ensure that business continuity competence strengths are acknowledged within the Forensic Laboratory, and to allow weaknesses to be seen as opportunities for improvement rather than criticism.

Business continuity exercises and tests are an ongoing process at the Forensic Laboratory that are conducted in accordance with the business continuity exercise and test program (which is maintained by the Business Continuity Manager). There are three key phases to complete a business continuity exercise and/or test, as defined above.

13.6.4.1 Planning a Business Continuity Exercise or Test

All business continuity exercises and tests must be fully planned to ensure that specific objectives for an exercise are agreed. The level of detail in an exercise plan varies depending on the scope and level of the exercise selected.

The Business Continuity Manager ensures that business continuity exercise plans contain enough detail to allow the employees who are responsible for conducting, monitoring, and reviewing a business continuity exercise or test to fully assess requirements from a business continuity perspective, and to conduct and review an exercise.

The process by which the Forensic Laboratory plans a business continuity exercise or test is:

1. The Business Continuity Manager, together with appropriate Forensic Laboratory employees, meets to plan a business continuity exercise or test. This discussion may be spread over several sessions and can include requirement-gathering sessions with key stakeholders, other Forensic Laboratory personnel, and others who may need to be involved in the exercise (e.g., partners or suppliers), or who need to develop information that is required for the exercise (e.g., scenarios).
   Items for consideration include:
   - reports/outcomes/reviews from previous business continuity exercises and tests;
   - current business activities and the effect the exercise may have on those activities (e.g., inter-dependencies of business activities and technologies);
   - exercise scope (what is included, what is not included);
   - aims and objectives;
   - exercise level;
   - development of scenarios and sets of assumptions to put the exercise in context (which should be suitably realistic and detailed);
   - roles and responsibilities;
   - timings, duration, and resources;
   - reporting requirements.

Note

Exercises should be planned so as to minimize risks from incidents occurring as a result of the exercise. In the event that a business continuity exercise or test is considered to pose a risk to business activities, the Business Continuity Manager may conduct a risk assessment of the exercise (if a risk assessment is deemed appropriate) to assess the risk consequences of the exercise on business operations.

2. The Business Continuity Manager drafts an exercise plan. The plan should include the following:
   - exercise overview, aims, and objectives;
   - scope of the exercise (what is included and what is not included);
   - exercise level (simple, medium, or complex)—and details of how the exercise is to be conducted;

- exercise scenario and assumptions—date, time, current business workloads, political and economic conditions, seasonal issues, etc., as required;
- timescales;
- relevant BCPs (or sections of BCPs);
- required exercise participants (this may include representatives from third parties, suppliers, or partners if relevant);
- roles and responsibilities for employees involved in the exercise;
- notification and awareness requirements to the Forensic Laboratory and third parties (where required);
- post-exercise review and reporting arrangements.

Additionally, a business continuity exercise plan may detail:

- any risks identified (and how these risks are to be mitigated);
- budget requirements (if appropriate).

The draft exercise plan is circulated for review to the Forensic Laboratory Top Management and other stakeholders, including third parties, where required.

3. The Forensic Laboratory Top Management reviews the exercise plan and provides suitable feedback.
4. The Business Continuity Manager implements changes to the draft exercise plan, as required.
   Where changes are implemented, the exercise plan may be re-issued for additional review and feedback. Where no further changes are required, the revised exercise plan is issued as version 1.0, as defined in Chapter 4, Section 4.6.3. This is the version of the exercise plan that is used to prepare for, and run, the exercise.
5. The Forensic Laboratory Top Management sign-off the exercise plan.
6. The Business Continuity Manager distributes the signed-off exercise plan ready for the exercise.

> **Note**
> Where appropriate, a business continuity education and information session may be convened to make employees aware of the forthcoming exercise.
> The business continuity exercise or test is then conducted in accordance with the plan, and the results/outcomes are recorded.

13.6.4.2 *Performing a Business Continuity Exercise or Test Exercise*

Business continuity exercises or tests are performed according to the signed-off exercise plan and are managed by the Business Continuity Manager using the procedures for exercising BCPs.

Before the exercise or test begins, the Business Continuity Manager ensures that:

- all equipment, employees and other required resources are available (including any third parties as required);
- copies and the business continuity exercises or tests plan and the appropriate BCP are available;
- Forensic Laboratory employees are aware that a business continuity exercise or test is to be performed.

> **Note**
> There may be occasions where an exercise or test with no warning given to employees may be considered by the Forensic Laboratory Top Management. This should be carried out at a time where there is little operational impact on account of the test being performed.

The process by which the Forensic Laboratory performs a business continuity exercise or test is:

1. The Business Continuity Manager starts the exercise.
2. The relevant Forensic Laboratory employees (and third parties as required) complete their activities according to the BCP specified in the exercise and the exercise plan.
3. The Business Continuity Manager (and additional Facilitators, if required) facilitates the exercise.
4. The Business Continuity Manager (and additional Observers, if required) monitors the exercise through observations and progress reports provided by employees.
   Where issues arise that may affect the conduct of the exercise, these are escalated to the Business Continuity Manager for determination.

> **Note**
> The Business Continuity Manager may also have activities to perform during the exercise.

5. When the exercise finishes, the Business Continuity Manager declares that the exercise is over.

13.6.4.3 *Reviewing a Business Continuity Exercise or Test*

Reviews of business continuity exercises or tests are performed as soon as possible after an exercise or test is completed to analyze the exercise or test outcome, and to determine if exercise or test objectives were achieved and identify lessons learned.

A report of the business continuity exercise or test results is produced by the Business Continuity Manager as part of the review and sent to Top Management for comment.

Note

The review of a business continuity exercise or test must also include a review of the business continuity exercise or test processes to determine whether the business continuity exercise or test activities (people and methods) are occurring as expected. Updates to the processes should be considered.

The process by which the Forensic Laboratory reviews a business continuity exercise or test is as follows:

1. The Business Continuity Manager reviews the evidence from the exercise or test and generates a report on its outcome.

   This evidence includes the results of exercise and/or test activities, feedback from participants and observers, and also questionnaire results from selected participants to capture any lessons they may have learned, if appropriate.

   The report template used in the Forensic Laboratory is given in Appendix 12.
2. The report is circulated to the Forensic Laboratory Top Management, key employees, and other third parties, as required.
3. The Business Continuity Manager and the Forensic Laboratory Top Management meet to discuss the report, analyze the exercise or test, and identify and agree action points and improvements.

   Possible action points or improvements identified may include:
   - updates to BCPs, for example, a revision of a plan's approach to recovery or updates to details of specific tasks, actions, responsibilities, etc.;
   - changes to the Forensic Laboratory's overall Business Continuity Strategy;
   - changes to business continuity operating procedures;
   - a re-run of an exercise that has shown serious deficiencies;
   - changes to the business continuity exercise or test program;
   - feedback to participants on the outcome of an exercise or test, and the lessons learned (e.g., via a business continuity education and information session);
   - recommendations for improvements to the process and methodology.
4. Action points and improvements are agreed at the meeting, noted in the minutes, actioned through the Forensic Laboratory's CAPA process.
5. The Business Continuity Manager manages the implementation of the agreed action points through the Forensic Laboratory's CAPA process.

13.7 MAINTAINING AND IMPROVING THE BCMS

The Forensic Laboratory must be committed to a program of continuous improvement of their IMS and other management subsystems, including the BCMS. This process is defined for the IMS in Chapter 4, Section 4.8. The Forensic Laboratory Top Management should perform regular audits and reviews of the management system, as defined in Chapter 4, Section 4.7.3, with a view to continuous improvement, and focus on:

- how business activities are performing (in particular, whether any activities are not performing as expected);
- the effectiveness of system controls and policies;
- the level of risk to the Forensic Laboratory, based on changes to technology, business objectives, and processes;
- the scope of the BCMS, and whether it requires changing;
- potential improvements to processes and procedures in the BCMS.

For reviews of business continuity management arrangements, this review additionally focuses on include:

- ensuring that all key company products and services are included in the Business Continuity Strategy;
- ensuring that all policies and strategies, plans, etc., reflect the Forensic Laboratory's priorities and requirements;
- confirming that the Forensic Laboratory's competence and business continuity capability is effective, fit-for-purpose, and appropriate to the level of risk;
- considering the effectiveness and outcomes from ongoing business continuity capability maintenance, exercising, and testing programs;
- evaluating business continuity training, awareness, and communication among employees, as appropriate.

The outcome of this review process can include:

- corrective action;
- preventive action.

13.8 EMBEDDING BUSINESS CONTINUITY FORENSIC LABORATORY PROCESSES

To ensure that business continuity is implemented, managed, and embedded effectively within the Forensic Laboratory, a business continuity awareness program is maintained to define and manage this.

The business continuity program is the responsibility of the Business Continuity Manager, with assistance provided by the Forensic Laboratory Top Management.

The program covers the following items:

- a high-level plan that describes the design, build, and implementation of the program which is defined in the business justification for implementing business continuity in the Forensic Laboratory;
- assigning the responsibilities for business continuity at a Top Management level, these responsibilities are documented in the BCMS and are reviewed each year during an audit and also as part of the annual appraisal process, as defined in Chapter 18, Section 18.2.4;
- reviewing employee skills and training requirements to meet the Forensic Laboratory's objectives for business continuity as part of the annual appraisal process, as defined in Chapter 18, Section 18.2.4;
- raising the awareness of business continuity within the Forensic Laboratory as a whole—to provide for greater levels of understanding by employees about how they contribute to business continuity through workshops, training, and documentation such as quick reference material and presentations, as defined in Section 13.3;
- developing and maintaining the relevant BCPs and IMPs to manage and resolve business disruptions, as defined in Section 13.5.4;
- performing exercises on the business continuity capability to ensure that it remains effective and fit-for-purpose, as defined in Section 13.6;
- reviewing and updating the BCMS documentation to ensure that it remains effective and reflects the processes in place at the Forensic Laboratory;
- reviewing and updating the risk assessments and the BIA to ensure that the objectives for business continuity remain current, as defined in Chapter 5;
- reviewing and updating the Forensic Laboratory's business continuity arrangements through a self-assessment of the BCMS to ensure that these arrangements remain suitable, adequate, and effective.

The Forensic Laboratory should implement ISO 22301, which was released on May 15, 2012, and obtain certification to it by an accredited CAB to replace its existing BS 25999 certification. The transition period for this conversion of BS 25999 Certifications to ISO 22301 is by May 2014, BS 25999 having been withdrawn in November 2012. The mapping between the BCMS and the relevant ISO 22301 clauses is given in Appendix 13.

The differences between ISO 22301 and BS 25999:2 are given in Appendix 14. A number of new terms have been included in ISO 22301 and these are given in the Glossary. While this gives detailed differences between the content of the two standards, ISO 22301 is officially recognized worldwide, while BS 25999 was primarily recognized in the United Kingdom but had a number of certificated sites worldwide.

13.9 BCMS DOCUMENTATION AND RECORDS—GENERAL

The Forensic Laboratory must produce a document set to support the BCMS in operation. This includes documentation and records as below:

13.9.1 Documentation

The following documentation will need to be created:

- scope and objectives, as given in Chapter 5, Appendix 11 and defined in Section 13.1.2;
- the business continuity management policy, as given in Chapter 4, Appendix 9;
- provision of resources, as defined in Chapter 4, Section 4.6.2 and Section 13.2;
- competency of the Forensic Laboratory employees, as defined in Section 13.3, Chapter 4, Section 4.6.2.2. and Chapter 18, Section 18.2.1;
- risk assessment, management, and treatment process, as defined in Chapter 5;
- Business Continuity Strategy, as defined in Section 13.4;
- incident response plans, as defined in Chapter 7, Section 7.4.1 and Chapter 8;
- testing procedures, as defined in Section 13.6;
- internal auditing procedures, as defined in Chapter 4, Section 4.7.3;
- Management Review procedures, as defined in Chapter 4, Section 4.9;
- continuous improvement procedures, as defined in Chapter 4, Section 4.8.

13.9.2 Records

The following records should exist, as a minimum:

- training records, as defined in Chapter 4, Section 4.6.2.3 and Chapter 18, Section 18.2.1.8;
- results of business impact analyses and risk assessments, as defined in Chapter 5;
- BCPs as defined in Section 13.5.4 and Section 13.5.5;
- IMP(s), as defined in Chapter 7, Section 7.4.1;
- results of business continuity exercises, as defined in Section 13.6;
- internal audit results and responses, as defined in Chapter 4, Section 4.7.3;
- Management Review results, as defined in Chapter 4, Section 4.9;
- corrective and preventive actions, as defined in Chapter 4, Section 4.8.

13.9.3 Control of Documents and Records

Documents and records must be managed according to the Forensic Laboratory document and record management procedures, as defined in Chapter 4, Section 4.6.3 and Chapter 4, Section 4.6.4, respectively.

APPENDIX 1 - SUPPLIER DETAILS HELD

The Forensic Laboratory holds the following information on its suppliers, apart from transaction, correspondence, and payment details:

- supplier name;
- key supplier (Y/N)?
- financial status—credited rating;
- supplier address;
- supplier phone;
- supplier fax;
- supplier URL;
- supplier legal status and business registration details;
- supplier account number of the Forensic Laboratory;
- date supplier returned financial and security checklist;
- approved as a supplier on date;
- approved by;
- last audit date;
- last audit result;
- next audit date;
- products and/or services provided;
- SLA in force;
- date of last SLA review;
- results of last SLA review;
- date of next SLA review;
- supplier risk category;
- supplier contacts:
  - name;
  - e-mail;
  - phone;
  - cell phone;
  - fax.

APPENDIX 2 - HEADINGS FOR FINANCIAL AND SECURITY QUESTIONNAIRE

While this is a standard form, some details may be left out, as appropriate. It is probably not appropriate for detailed financial information to be obtained for the company watering the plants, but certainly parts of the information security section will be required as their staff will have access to the Forensic Laboratory premises. Likewise, an outsourcing partner or hosting service will need to have all details used as financial stability is critical and they will have access to Forensic Laboratory information and information processing systems. The Finance Department and the Information Security Manager determine the sections to be used and may add additional questions, as needed.

Finance

- financial status.

Management Systems

- Management Systems implemented;
- Certifications and Accreditations held, including copies of certificates;
- management responsibility for Management Systems.

Information Security

- information security policy;
- organizational setup;
- organizational assets;
- human resources security;
- physical and environmental security;
- operational security;
- identity, authentication, and system access;
- system acquisition, development, and maintenance;
- information security incident handling;
- business continuity;
- compliance and governance.

Quality

- the quality system.

APPENDIX 3 - BUSINESS CONTINUITY MANAGER, JOB DESCRIPTION

OBJECTIVE AND ROLE

The Business Continuity Manager (BCM) is responsible for managing the business continuity process, developing the Business Continuity Plans (BCPs) to support the process, testing the BCPs, maintaining them, and continuously improving them.

In addition, during a disaster, the BCM is responsible for the continued operation of the business' infrastructure. The BCM is also responsible for long-range disaster recovery planning to provide the highest level of protection possible for the Forensic Laboratory's Clients.

The scope of responsibility includes both the internal and outsourced business/IT functions.

The main objective is to ensure that the Forensic Laboratory's products and services to their Clients are resumed within required, and agreed, timescales.

PROBLEMS AND CHALLENGES

Business Continuity is an absolutely critical function of the Forensic Laboratory's everyday business operations. For this responsibility, there is no substitute for advanced planning.

The BCM faces the challenge of developing ever-current BCPs and managing recovery in an efficient and effective manner.

The BCPs plan must be reviewed, tested, and updated on a regular basis, in association with Clients, external service providers, and other relevant stakeholders.

PRINCIPAL ACCOUNTABILITIES

The BCM:

- plans and charts the direction for the BCP process;
- establishes procedures and priorities for the business continuity process;
- performs or facilitates BIA for all the Forensic Laboratory products and services and systems;
- ensures the development and maintenance of all BCPs needed by the business for their Clients;
- performs risk assessments and implements risk management to reduce risk to an acceptable level to reduce the likelihood of service interruptions, where practical and cost justifiable;
- maintains a comprehensive testing schedule for all BCPs, in line with business requirements and after every significant change in products and services offered to the Forensic Laboratory's Clients. The testing process must cover not only the Forensic Laboratory's BCPs but also communication with all relevant stakeholders, not matter what the actual disruption is;
- undertakes regular reviews, at least annually or on influencing change, with the relevant process or system Owner, to ensure that the BCPs accurately reflect business need;
- undertakes regular reviews of training and awareness materials used in the Forensic Laboratory to ensure that they are still appropriate and fit-for-purpose;
- provides regular reports to Top Management on all business continuity management activities in the Forensic Laboratory;
- monitoring national and international threat advisory systems incorporating them into current BCPs within the Forensic Laboratory;
- ensures that an appropriate communication plan is in place for Forensic Laboratory employees and third-party employees as appropriate, relating to all matters relating to business continuity response and planning within the Forensic Laboratory. Communication covers training, awareness sessions, meetings, and formal communication plans as given in Chapter 5, Appendix 1;
- assesses changes submitted to the CAB for impact on the BCP plans and recovery processes;
- attends the CAB, as appropriate;
- reviews all insurance coverage in the event of a disaster to ensure that they are appropriate. A review of relevant coverage amounts should be performed at 3-month intervals to ensure optimal coverage in the event of a disaster and amendments to cover made as needed;
- secures the scene of a disaster and ensures that all movement of equipment into and out of the scene is authorized and recorded;
- co-ordinates and manages all recovery activities during the business continuity process;
- co-ordinates and supervises all special projects relating to business continuity and capacity;
- develops plans for migration of BCPs, the business continuity and recovery process policies and procedures to support the Forensic Laboratory's future directions;
- maintains the Forensic Laboratory's BCMS certification;
- develops the Forensic Laboratory's long-range business continuity and business recovery strategy;
- defines direction of in-house technical training seminars to improve overall employee awareness, response time, and ability to look into the Forensic Laboratory's future business continuity and business recovery requirements;
- participates in international, national, and local SIG presentations, and publishes articles describing the Forensic Laboratory's activities and assessments of business continuity and business recovery and how they relate to the business;
- develops and manages effective working relationships with all appropriate internal and external stakeholders;
- maintains external links to other companies in the industry to gain competitive assessments and share information, where appropriate;
- identifies the emerging information technologies to be assimilated, integrated, and introduced within the Forensic Laboratory, which could significantly impact the Forensic Laboratory's business continuity and business recovery ability;
- interfaces with external industrial and academic organizations in order to maintain state-of-the-art knowledge in emerging business continuity and business recovery issues and to enhance the Forensic Laboratory's image as a first-class solution provider utilizing the latest thinking in this field;
- adheres to established Forensic Laboratory policies, standards, and procedures;

- performs all responsibilities in accordance with, or in excess of, the requirements of the Forensic Laboratory Integrated Management System (IMS).

AUTHORITY

The BCM has the authority to:

- attend the CAB and comment on proposed changes;
- develop, maintain, and implement, where necessary, the BCPs;
- supervise the entire recovery process during a disaster or a test.

CONTACTS

Internal

This position requires contact with all levels of the Forensic Laboratory employees to determine recovery requirements, perform Business Impact Assessments (BIAs), perform risk assessments, and maintain and test BCPs.

External

Externally, the Forensic Laboratory will maintain contacts with Suppliers and Vendors, as required. Additionally, contact will be maintained with the Forensic Laboratory's Clients to determine their requirements as well as the Forensic Laboratory insurers to ensure that insurance coverage is appropriate.

REPORTS TO

The BCM reports to:

- Top Management.

APPENDIX 4 - CONTENTS OF THE FORENSIC LABORATORY BIA FORM

The following is captured during the BIA process in the Forensic Laboratory:

- date of BIA;
- name of respondent;
- respondent contact details;
- respondent title;
- number of staff reporting to respondent;
- respondent responsibilities;
- key functions and tasks undertaken;
- definition and quantification of risks to these functions and tasks;
- criticality of failure to provide these functions and tasks over a range of times (typically 2 hours, 4 hours, 1 day, 2 days, 1 week, 2 weeks, 1 month, more than 3 months);
- financial loss of failure to provide these functions and tasks over a range of times (typically 2 hours, 4 hours, 1 day, 2 days, 1 week, 2 weeks, 1 month, more than 3 months);
- maximum outage for these functions and tasks sustainable;
- RTOs for each function;
- impact of disruptions to these functions and tasks in terms of Strategy, Finance, Customer Relationship, Supplier Relationship, Legal or Regulatory, Personnel, Operations, etc.;
- input and outputs for each of these functions and tasks;
- minimum numbers of staff to perform each of these functions and tasks;
- minimum equipment to perform each of these functions and tasks;
- how functions and tasks would be performed in case of unavailability of the main Forensic Laboratory;
- any other relevant comments.

Typically, where quantifications are needed, the following is used:

0—no impact/not applicable,
1—little impact,
2—some impact,
3—significant impact,
4—severe impact,
5—catastrophic impact.

The Consequences table given in Chapter 5, Appendix 5 is used to assist with the quantification process in the Forensic Laboratory.

APPENDIX 5 - PROPOSED BCMS DEVELOPMENT AND CERTIFICATION TIMESCALES

Initial BCMS development and certification targets are as follows:

- task 1: Business continuity process lifecycle development, scope confirmation, and required documents identified:
  - duration 2 weeks.
- task 2: Management systems production, including BIAs and development of BCPs:
  - duration: 24 weeks.
- task 3: Stage 1 Audit by Certification Body:
  - duration: 1-2 days, depending on size of the Forensic Laboratory.
- task 4: Management systems training:
  - duration: 1 week.

- task 5: Testing BCPs, updating where necessary and undertaking the Management Review:
  - duration: 8 weeks.
- task 6: Stage 1 Audit by Certification Body:
  - duration: 1-2 days, depending on size of the Forensic Laboratory.

APPENDIX 6 - INCIDENT SCENARIOS

Any number of scenarios can be developed based on the perceived risks that the Forensic Laboratory faces and management opinions. These may include, but not be limited to:

- partial interruption of computer services (e.g., Critical server, multiple hard disk failure, with no available mirrored drives. The impact obviously will depend on the number of disks affected, the number of mirrored disks, the level of RAID and the type of server, and spares held);
- telecommunications failure (e.g., Failure of the communications switch during the working day. This affects all communications that are serviced through it);
- e-mail failure (e.g., loss of either the mail server, ISP or a service provider failure);
- power or other utility failure (e.g., loss of electricity, water, etc., for a varying period);
- temporary interruption of office occupation (e.g., bomb or fire in the vicinity precludes access to the Forensic Laboratory's office for a period of up to 1 week, occurrence outside office hours. There is no damage to any Forensic Laboratory equipment or office);
- short to medium interruption of office occupation (e.g., bomb or fire in the vicinity precludes access to the Forensic Laboratory's office for a period of a month while rebuilding and refurbishing takes place. Minimal damage to office and contents, occurrence outside office hours. Time period—up to a month);
- office destroyed or very seriously damaged (e.g., bomb explosion or fire in the close vicinity that structurally affects the Forensic Laboratory's office and destroys most of the contents. The off-site store is not affected. The damage precludes access to the office for salvage for a considerable time, and the building needs rebuilding and complete renovation, occurrence outside office hours);
- loss of key employees (e.g., one or more key employees is either seriously injured or killed in the scenarios above, or leaves the Forensic Laboratory for whatever reason. This would obviously depend on who the "key employee" actually was).

In each scenario above, or any others that are developed by the Forensic Laboratory, the following must be considered as essential high-level phases of the recovery process:

- initial response;
- communications (internal to employees and external to Clients, other stakeholders, suppliers, the press, etc.);
- implementing the relevant BCP;
- relocating staff;
- setting up alternate premises as the office for case processing;
- working at the alternate premises;
- final recovery either back to the original Forensic Laboratory office or a new one—depending on the damage.

The point of these scenarios is to try, based on the BIA results, to determine the possible scenarios that the Forensic Laboratory consider as appropriate. The high-level stages of the response and recovery process are considered with possible elapsed time and impact on the delivery of the Forensic Laboratory's products and services to Clients.

APPENDIX 7 - STRATEGY OPTIONS

There are a number of strategic options that must be considered based on the risks that the Forensic Laboratory faces and the relevant scenarios that it has developed. Options include, at a high level, the following:

- hot standby;
- cold standby;
- reciprocal arrangements;
- using another Forensic Laboratory site;
- finding an office to rent;
- home working and Client site working;
- a hybrid solution;
- do nothing.

Each option will have pros and cons associated with it, and these must be considered in line with the Forensic Laboratory's legislative, regulatory, and contractual commitments to determine an appropriate strategy for a given scenario. The choice of strategy will also depend on the expected duration of the outage and the Forensic Laboratory should consider the following timescales in Business Continuity Planning:

- short term (less than 1 day);
- short to medium term (2-5 days);
- medium term (5-10 days);
- medium to long term (more than 10 days).

APPENDIX 8 - STANDARD FORENSIC LABORATORY BCP CONTENTS

The BCPs at the Forensic Laboratory must contain the following items:

- a purpose and scope;
- recovery objectives and timescales;
- a named the Forensic Laboratory Owner.

The following items do not need to be in each and every BCP, but all of the BCPs combined must collectively contain:

- lines of communications;
- key tasks and reference information;
- roles and responsibilities for people and teams having authority during and following an incident;
- guidelines and criteria regarding which individuals have the authority to invoke each BCP and under what circumstances;
- method by which the BCP is invoked and implemented;
- meeting locations with alternatives, and up-to-date contact and mobilization details for any relevant third parties and resources that might be required to support the response;
- internal and external communications processes;
- resource requirements for all stages of the recovery process;
- process for standing down once the incident is over;
- reference to the essential contact details for all key stakeholders;
- details to manage the immediate consequences of a business disruption giving due regard to:
  - welfare of Forensic Laboratory employees;
  - strategic and operational options for responding to the disruption;
  - prevention of further loss or unavailability of critical activities.
- details for managing an incident including:
  - provision for managing issues during an incident;
  - processes to enable continuity and recovery of critical activities.
- details on how, and under what circumstances, the Forensic Laboratory will communicate with employees and their relatives, key stakeholders, and emergency contacts;
- details of the Forensic Laboratory's media response following an incident:
  - the incident communications strategy;
  - preferred interface with the media;
  - guideline or template for drafting a statement for the media;
  - appropriate spokespeople.
- method for recording key information about the incident, actions taken, and decisions made;
- details of actions and tasks that need to be performed;
- details of the resources required for business continuity business recovery at different points in time;
- prioritized objectives in terms of the critical activities to be recovered, the timescales in which they are to be recovered, and the recovery levels needed for each critical activity.

APPENDIX 9 - TABLE OF CONTENTS TO THE APPENDIX TO A BCP

Each site will have different details and requirements for recovery operations, but this checklist will form a basis of what is needed. However, each site will have its own specific requirements:

- alternate premises details;
- alternate premises requirements;
- backup and recovery overview;
- building contacts;
- emergency notification list;
- employee contact details;
- employees to travel to the recovery site;
- equipment needed for inspection of incident scene;
- equipment to be brought from the off-site store;
- equipment to be brought to the recovery site;
- evacuation assembly points;
- fire wardens;
- first aiders;
- hardware failure details;
- health and Safety regulations;
- identified services and applications to be recovered;
- identified services and applications;
- impact of disruption to key tasks and functions;
- information to obtain from a caller;
- insurance policy details;
- key task and function criticality;
- key tasks and functions identified;
- management succession list;
- materials source;
- membership of the Readiness Team;
- minimum staff required for recovery operations;
- off-site recovery procedures;
- off-site store details;
- office key holders;
- organogram;
- overview of business processes;
- press release recipients;
- recovery site details;
- recovery team details;
- recovery team responsibilities;
- sample press release;
- software failure details;
- sources of government advice;
- sources of industry advice;
- supplier details;
- telecoms failure details;
- tell-tale signs of a letter bomb;
- top Management permitted to talk to the press;
- training.

APPENDIX 10 - BCP CHANGE LIST CONTENTS

The following are the minimum contents in the formal BCP change list:

- Date;
- Summary of review;
  - required change;
  - reason for change;
  - accept/reject?
  - by;
  - date.

Each change should be put through the Change Management process, so it can be reviewed by all stakeholders prior to implementation.

APPENDIX 11 - BCP SCENARIO PLAN CONTENTS

The following are the minimum contents in the BCP Scenario Plan:

- scenario rules;
- scenario objectives;
- the Event:
  - issues;
  - objective;
  - scope;
  - roles and responsibilities;
  - actions;
  - timings, duration, and resources.
- reporting requirements.

APPENDIX 12 - BCP REVIEW REPORT TEMPLATE CONTENTS

The template for a BCP review plan used in the Forensic Laboratory is:

- management summary;
- re-assertion of the exercise or test aims, objectives, and scope;
- results and outcomes;
- exercise or test highlights and successes;
- shortcomings and lessons learned;
- issues for further investigation and action;
- recommendations for action and improvement (if any action points and improvements have been identified);
- process of implementation of changes:
  - timeline;
  - resources;
  - integration to current systems;
  - related CAPAs;
  - related requests for change.

APPENDIX 13 - MAPPING IMS PROCEDURES TO ISO 22301

This appendix contains the mapping of ISO 22301 to the procedures developed to implement the standard.

ISO 22301 Clause	Control	Procedure
4	Context of the organization	
4.1	Understanding of the organization and its context	Chapter 5, Appendix 11 Chapter 5, Section 5.5.9.1 Chapter 5, Appendix 14 This chapter, Section 13.1 This chapter, Section 13.4.2
4.2	Understanding the needs and expectations of interested parties	This chapter, Section 13.1.7 This chapter, Section 13.1.8
4.3	Determining the scope of the business continuity management system	Chapter 5, Appendix 11 This chapter, Section 13.1.3 This chapter, Section 13.1.5 This chapter, Section 13.1.8
4.4	Business continuity management system	Chapter 4
5	Leadership	
5.1	Leadership and commitment	This chapter, Section 13.2 This chapter, Appendix 3
5.2	Management commitment	Chapter 4, Section 4.6.2 Chapter 4, Section 4.7.3 Chapter 4, Section 4.8 Chapter 4, Section 4.9 Chapter 4,

Continued

ISO 22301 Clause	Control	Procedure
		Appendix 9 This chapter, Section 13.1.6 This chapter, Section 13.2 This chapter, Section 13.3.1 This chapter, Section 13.6 This chapter, Section 13.7 This chapter, Appendix 3
5.3	Policy	Chapter 4, Appendix 9
5.4	Organizational roles, responsibilities, and authorities	This chapter, Section 13.3.1 Chapter 18, Section 18.1.5
6	Planning	
6.1	Actions to address risks and opportunities	Chapter 5 This chapter, Section 13.1.6
6.2	Business continuity objectives and plans to achieve them	Chapter 4, Section 4.8 Chapter 5, Appendix 22 This chapter, Section 13.1.5 This chapter, Appendix 5
7	Support	
7.1	Resources	Chapter 4, Section 4.6.2 This chapter, Section 13.2.1
7.2	Competence	Chapter 4, Section 4.6.2.2 This chapter, Section 13.3
7.3	Awareness	Chapter 6, Appendix 11 This chapter, Section 13.3.2
7.4	Communication	Chapter 4, Section 4.6.5 This chapter, Appendix 8

Continued

ISO 22301 Clause	Control	Procedure
		Chapter 5, Appendix 1
7.5	Documented information	Chapter 4, Section 4.6.3 Chapter 4, Appendix 9 Chapter 4
8	Operation	
8.1	Operational planning and control	This chapter, Section 13.4 Chapter 14
8.2	Business Impact Analysis and risk assessment	Chapter 5 Chapter 12, Section 12.3.13.1.1 This chapter, Section 13.1.6 This chapter, Section 13.1.7 This chapter, Appendix 4
8.3	Business Continuity Strategy	Chapter 5 This chapter, Section 13.2.1 This chapter, Section 13.4
8.4	Establish and implement business continuity procedures	Chapter 7, Section 7.4.1 This chapter, Section 13.5 This chapter, Appendix 8
8.5	Exercising and testing	This chapter, Section 13.6
9	Performance evaluation	
9.1	Monitoring, measurement, analysis, and evaluation	Chapter 4, Section 4.7.3 Chapter 4, Section 4.9
9.2	Internal audit	Chapter 4, Section 4.7.3
9.3	Management Review	Chapter 4, Section 4.9
10	Improvement	
10.1	Nonconformity and corrective action	Chapter 4, Section 4.8
10.2	Continual improvement	Chapter 4, Section 4.8

APPENDIX 14 - DIFFERENCES BETWEEN ISO 22301 AND BS 25999

This appendix contains the detailed mapping of ISO 22301 to BS 25999.

ISO 22301 Clause	Clause	BS 25999 Clause	Clause (where exists)
0.1	General		General
0.2	PDCA model		PDCA cycle
0.3	Components of PDCA in this International Standard		
1	Scope	1	Scope
2	Normative references		
3	Terms and definitions	2	Terms and definitions
4	Context of the organization		
4.1	Understanding of the organization and its context	4.1	Understanding of the organization
4.2	Understanding the needs and expectations of interested parties		
4.3	Determining the scope of the business continuity management system	3.2.1	Scope and objectives of the BCMS
4.4	Business continuity management system		
5	Leadership		
5.1	Leadership and commitment		
5.2	Management commitment		
5.3	Policy	3.2.2	BCM Policy
5.4	Organizational roles, responsibilities, and authorities		
6	Planning		
6.1	Actions to address risks and opportunities	6.1.1 6.1.2	General Preventive action

Continued

ISO 22301 Clause	Clause	BS 25999 Clause	Clause (where exists)
6.2	Business continuity objectives and plans to achieve them	3.2.1.1	Scope and objectives of the BCMS
7	Support		
7.1	Resources	3.2.3	Provision of resources
7.2	Competence	3.2.4	Competency of BCM personnel
7.3	Awareness	3.3	Embedding BCM in the organization's culture
7.4	Communication	4.3.2 4.3.3	Incident response structure Business Continuity Plans and Incident Management Plans
7.5	Documented information	3.4	BCMS documentation and records
8	Operation		
8.1	Operational planning and control		
8.2	Business Impact Analysis and risk assessment	4.1.1 4.1.2 4.1.3	Business Impact Analysis Risk assessment Determining choices
8.3	Business Continuity Strategy	4.2 3.2.3 4.3.2	Determining Business Continuity Strategy Provision of resources Incident response structure
8.4	Establish and implement business continuity procedures	4.3.2 4.3.3	Incident response structure Business Continuity Plans and Incident Management Plans
8.5	Exercising and testing	4.4.2	BCM exercising
9	Performance evaluation		

Continued

ISO 22301 Clause	Clause	BS 25999 Clause	Clause (where exists)
9.1	Monitoring, measurement, analysis, and evaluation	4.4.3	Maintaining and reviewing BCM arrangements
9.2	Internal audit	5.1	Internal audit
9.3	Management Review	5.2	Management Review of the BCMS

Continued

ISO 22301 Clause	Clause	BS 25999 Clause	Clause (where exists)
10	Improvement		
10.1	Nonconformity and corrective action	6.1.1 6.1.3	General Corrective action
10.2	Continual improvement	6.2	Continual improvement

Chapter 14

Managing Business Relationships

14.1 THE NEED FOR THIRD PARTIES

All organizations need to have Clients and suppliers of some type, and the Forensic Laboratory is no exception. It considers the following category of business relationships as being relevant to the Forensic Laboratory, either now or in the future:

- Clients, for whom they undertake forensic case processing;
- suppliers of office and IT equipment (e.g., IT suppliers, office furniture, etc.);
- suppliers of IT services (e.g., ISPs, hardware maintenance, etc.);
- suppliers of office services (e.g., cleaners, plant watering, service engineers);
- utility service providers (e.g., ISPs, water, electricity, gas, etc.);
- individual consultants engaged on case processing (e.g., Expert Witnesses or experts in an area of forensic case processing that is not available, for any reason, in the Forensic Laboratory);
- outsourcing providers for IT services (e.g., outsourcing of e-mail, telephony services up to full-scale data center outsourcing).

Note 1

Some IT suppliers are responsible for providing warranty cover or maintenance contracts for the products they supply.

Note 2

Each category has its own issues and risks relating to the services they provide and how their disruption can affect the Forensic Laboratory.

Note 3

Suppliers of equipment and services to the Forensic Laboratory are defined throughout in this chapter.

Note 4

This chapter is not intended as legal advice but just how the Forensic Laboratory manages their business relationships. It is recommended that any legal issues are taken up with legal experts in the relevant jurisdiction.

Note 5

This chapter is not intended to be a treatise on Client, supplier, or outsourcing management, merely the processes and procedures that are implemented in the Forensic Laboratory to meet relevant Management System and other requirements. They must be adapted to specific circumstances.

Note 6

The Forensic Laboratory has a relationship management policy in force for Clients and all types of suppliers, as given in Chapter 4, Appendix 21.

Note 7

This chapter does not relate to provision of IT services to Forensic Laboratory employees, merely support for forensic case processing. In this case, the IT Department is viewed as a supplier to the Forensic Laboratory for case processing.

Note 8

The Forensic Laboratory may employ temporary workers or students on placement. In these cases, they are either treated as employees if they are not involved in any forensic case processing or if they are, they are considered as individual consultants providing case processing expertise.

It is essential that the Forensic Laboratory manages these risks from the very outset, during the service or product provision, and as long as required after the termination of business relationships between the parties.

14.2 CLIENTS

The Forensic Laboratory ensures that management of Client relations is implemented across the whole organization by following approved processes and guidelines.

First class Client relationships are at the heart of the Forensic Laboratory's business, and management of relationships is a strategy that the Forensic Laboratory will need to adopt to understand more about their Clients' needs and behavior, to develop stronger working relationships, and to enhance the products and services that are provided.

14.2.1 Forensic Laboratory Mechanisms for Managing Customer Relations

The following mechanisms are implemented to ensure that management of Client relations complies with the Forensic Laboratory relationship management policy, as given in Chapter 4, Appendix 21.

14.2.1.1 Identification of Clients, Products, Services, and Stakeholders

Forensic Laboratory Clients, products, services, and stakeholders are identified via Service Level Agreements (SLAs) or Turn Round Times (TRTs), as follows:

- all Clients of the Forensic Laboratory services are identified in SLAs or TRTs, as defined in the proposal of call-off contract in Chapter 6, Section 6.6.2.3, and its review in Chapter 6, Section 6.6.2.4;
- each SLA or TRT describes a product or service that is provided by the Forensic Laboratory to particular business Client for forensic case processing;
- one SLA or TRT is in place for each Client or specific case;
- each SLA identifies:
  - the product or service provided by the Forensic Laboratory;
  - the Client;
  - all service stakeholders.

> **Note**
> Where SLAs do not exist for a Client or a supplier, they are developed, as defined in Section 14.4.

14.2.1.2 Client Service Monitoring and Review

The following mechanisms are implemented to ensure that Client services are continually monitored and reviewed by the Forensic Laboratory (Figure 14.1):

1. A formal review of all the Forensic Laboratory products and services is performed at least once each year, as agreed between the parties or after any incident or influencing change.
2. Any changes arising from the annual service review are performed in accordance with the Forensic Laboratory change management procedures as defined in Chapter 7, Section 7.4.3, and tracked through the CAPA process, as defined in Chapter 4, Section 4.8.
3. Interim monitoring and review of Client services is performed via the Account Manager for the Client and the formal meetings that they have with the Client.
4. These meetings review products and services provided by the Forensic Laboratory to each Client and:
   - focus on the business aspects of products and services delivered;
   - act as the Forensic Laboratory contact point for regular monitoring and review of the operational aspect of their products and services;
   - act as the Forensic Laboratory forum for monitoring SLAs and TRTs for Clients.
5. After meeting a Client, the Account Manager schedules a meeting with the Laboratory Manager to review performance for the Client, and this will cover, but not be limited to:
   - performance and achievements against SLAs and/or TRTs;
   - Client and service requirements;
   - service changes and action plans;
   - awareness of business needs.

   Inputs include, but are not limited to:
   - Client complaints, if any, as defined in Chapter 6, Section 6.14;
   - Client feedback forms returned for each case processed, as given in Chapter 6, Appendix 20;
   - Client calls to the Service Desk indicating support levels needed and provided;
   - any incidents involving the Client;
   - production schedules;
   - system change schedules;
   - operational statistics from MARS reports, as defined in Chapter 10, Section 10.7.3 and 10.7.4;
   - for internal Clients other operational statistics will be covered, as appropriate.
6. All meetings between the Account Manager and the Laboratory Manager, with other Forensic Laboratory employees as needed, are minuted and added to the relevant virtual case file.
7. All recommendations for improvement are included in the continuous improvement process, as defined in Chapter 4, Section 4.8, and followed through to completion using the CAPA process.
8. All changes are managed through the Forensic laboratory change management process, as defined in Chapter 7, Section 7.4.3.
9. Where appropriate, they will be recorded in the Service Improvement Plan (SIP), as given in Chapter 7, Appendix 14.

14.2.1.3 Client Complaints

The Client complaint process has been defined in Chapter 6, Section 6.14.

14.2.1.4 Client Feedback

The Client feedback forms are given in Chapter 6, Appendix 20, and are used as input into the review process defined in Section 14.2.1.2.

14.2.1.5 Service Desk

The Service Desk provides monthly and "on demand" reports, relating to Client contact with the Service Desk; again, this is used as input into the review process defined in Section 14.2.1.2.

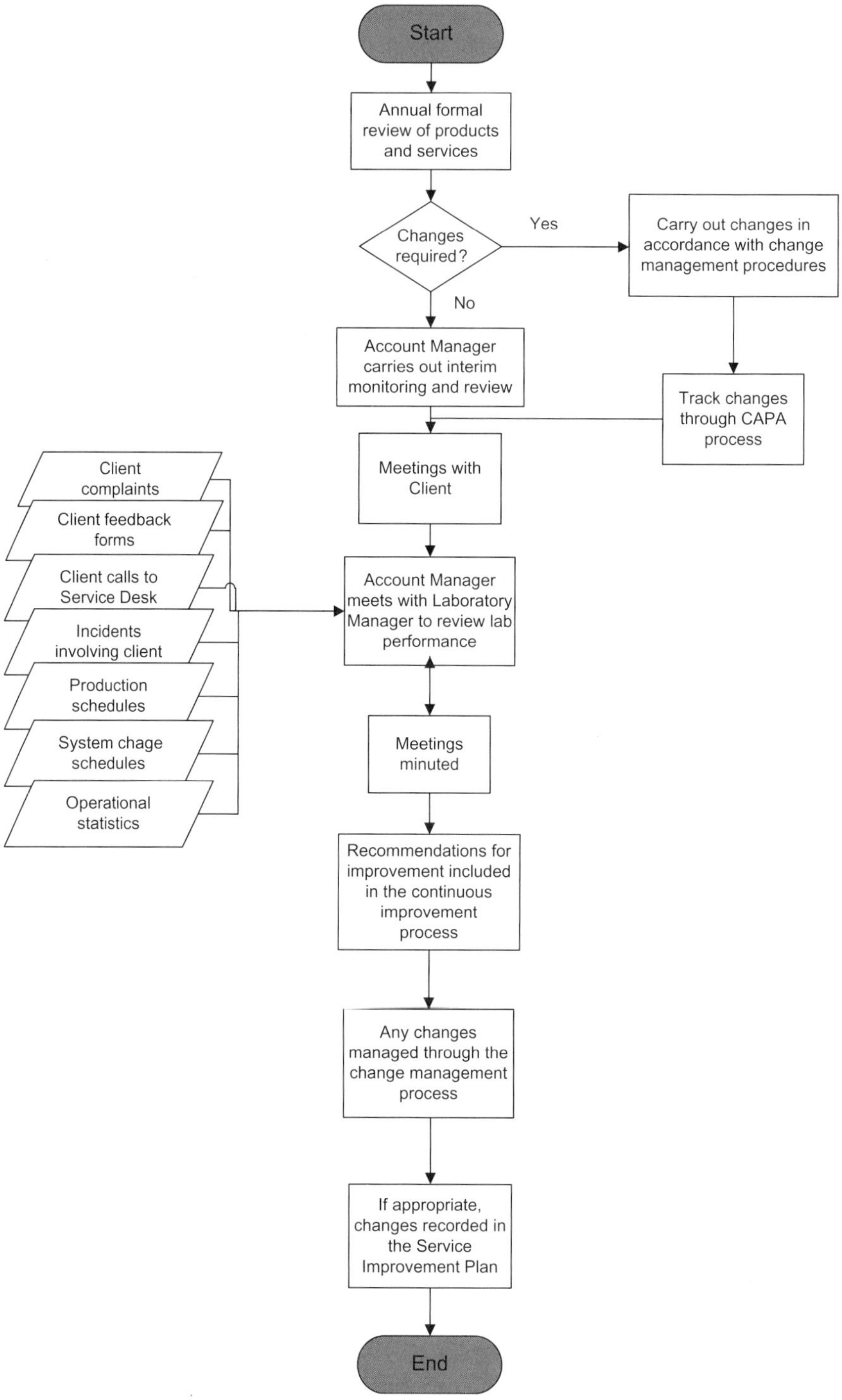

FIGURE 14.1 Client service monitoring and review. (For color version of this figure, the reader is referred to the online version of this chapter.)

14.2.2 Managing Products and Services

The Forensic Laboratory must change with the times and changes in technology as required by their Clients, and so products and services must be updated to reflect changes in these requirements. This covers:

- creating a new product or service;
- implementing a new product or service;
- changing an existing product or service;
- closing an existing product or service.

14.2.2.1 Creating a Product or Service

To ensure that products and services are planned and implemented effectively within the Forensic Laboratory, the Forensic Laboratory Manager, with other employees as required, defines and produces one or more service plans. These plans cover all the required aspects of implementing a new service within the Forensic Laboratory (Figure 14.2).

1. A business Client identifies a new service that they would like to be implemented by the Forensic Laboratory.

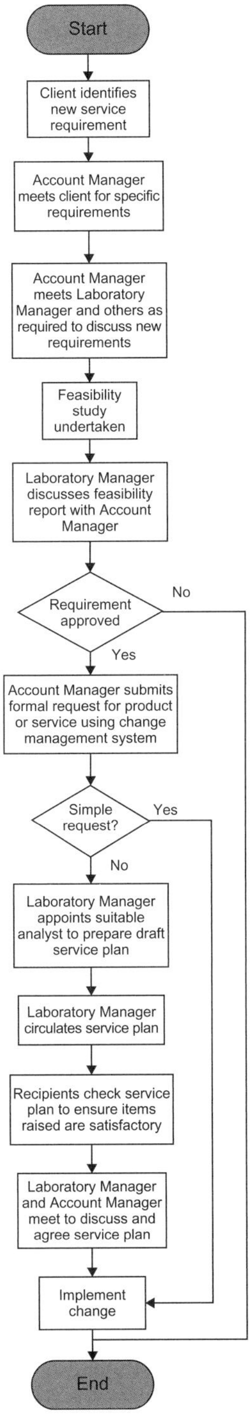

FIGURE 14.2 Creating a product or service. (For color version of this figure, the reader is referred to the online version of this chapter.)

2. The Account Manager meets the Client to ascertain the specific requirements of a new service required.
3. The Account Manager meets with the Laboratory Manager, and other digital forensic experts as required, to discuss the new requirements.
4. An initial feasibility study is carried out by the Laboratory Manager and any required Forensic Laboratory employees, and an initial report produced as to:
   - whether the product or service is one that can potentially be provided by the Forensic Laboratory;
   - whether there are competent Forensic Analysts available or they require training;
   - whether the required tools are available, or if not, the implications of their acquisition;
   - whether the Client can make any funds available for putting the product or service in place.
5. The Laboratory Manager discusses the initial feasibility report with the Account Manager.
6. Assuming it is approved, the Account Manager submits a formal request for the product or service to be implemented, using the Forensic Laboratory change management process, as defined in Chapter 7, Section 7.4.3. This must cover:
   - product or service requirements and service levels;
   - budgets;
   - staff resources;
   - SLAs and other targets or service commitments;
   - service management processes, procedures, and documentation.
7. If the request for a product or service is very simple to implement, the Laboratory Manager just confirms to the Account Manager that they will provide it. If the requested service is not simple or is potentially costly, the further investigation process is undertaken, as defined in step 8 below.
8. The Laboratory Manager appoints a suitable Forensic Analyst to prepare a draft service plan. This plan reflects the Client requirements and also the capability of the Forensic Laboratory to provide the required product or services as set out in step 6 above. The service plan template used in the Forensic Laboratory is given in Appendix 1. This is used as a base and adapted as needed.
9. The Laboratory Manager circulates the service plan to the Account Manager and other relevant Forensic Laboratory employees for comment.
10. The recipients review the service plan and ensure that all items raised are satisfactory from the Forensic Laboratory's perspective. All comments are passed back to the Laboratory Manager, who reviews them and implements appropriate changes, as defined in Chapter 4, Section 4.6.3. A copy of the finalized plan is sent to the Account Manager.
11. The Laboratory manager and the Account Manager meet to discuss the service plan. They negotiate to

determine the final service based upon the details within the plan. At the end of these negotiations, the service plan is agreed in principle subject to confirmation in a SLA.

12. Once agreed, the product or service must be implemented.

14.2.2.2 Implementing a Service

Once a service plan has been agreed, the next stage is to implement the provisions of the service plan within the Forensic Laboratory to provide the product or service to the Client.

1. The Laboratory Manager arranges a meeting with all affected Forensic Laboratory employees and requests that they review the service plan and prepare further details for input to the meeting.
2. The Laboratory Manager and the affected Forensic Laboratory employees meet to discuss the implementation of the product or service. The following details must be confirmed during the discussion:
   - the allocation of funds and budgets for each aspect of the plan;
   - the allocation of roles and responsibilities for the implementation of the product or service;
   - provision for documenting and maintaining the policies, plans, and procedures that are affected by the product or service;
   - the identification and management of risks to the product or service defined in the service plan;
   - the identification of the managing teams for the product or service, including the possible need of recruitment of new employees;
   - the management of the teams supporting the product or service including the Service Desk;
   - training relating to the new product or service, where required (e.g., new tools or methods);
   - communicating details about the new product or service to the Forensic Laboratory's Clients and any suitable prospective Clients.
3. The Laboratory Manager is responsible for implementing the new product or service and implements it according to the agreed service plan. The product or service must be implemented in accordance with the Forensic Laboratory change management process as defined in Chapter 7, Section 7.4.3.
4. The Laboratory Manager regularly produces updates of the implementation progress of the new product or service to interested parties and stakeholders.
5. When implementation is complete, and the product or service available for Clients, the Laboratory manager advises all Account Managers that the product or service is now successfully running.
6. The Laboratory Manager updates the Service Catalogue with details of the new product or service and ensures that product or service metrics information is being collected.
7. The review and improvement of the product or service can now be performed within the framework of service management, as defined in Chapter 7, Section 7.4.7 to review the outcome of implementing the service against the service implementation plan.

14.2.2.3 Changing an Existing Product or Service

A product or service can be changed at the request of either a Client or from within the Forensic Laboratory itself as part of its continuous improvement process, as defined in Chapter 4, Section 4.8. The process to change a product or service is generally the same as the process for creating a new product service (although not all steps may need be followed depending upon the change required). As a minimum, the process for changing a service involves:

- identifying and agreeing the details of the change with the Client;
- ensuring that all resources are available;
- planning the implementation of the change;
- implementing the change and confirming its success.

Note

A formal change to a product or service is not the same as improving a product or service through the continuous improvement process.

14.2.2.4 Closing a Product or Service

A product or service can be closed if there is no longer any demand for it.

1. The Laboratory Manager and relevant Account Managers meet to discuss the requirement for closing a product or service. The Account Managers must confirm that the product or service is no longer required and when it is to be withdrawn.
   If a similar product or service is required, this must be treated as a request for a new product or service and the procedure for creating a product or service, as defined in Section 14.2.2.1, is followed.
2. The Laboratory Manager and relevant Account Managers meet to discuss the withdrawal of a product or service. The following details must be confirmed during the discussion:
   - confirmation of the closure of the product and service due to lack of demand from Clients;

- the reallocation of roles and responsibilities away from the product or service;
- the impact of the withdrawal of the product or service on existing employees and operations generally;
- impact upon the service management system and any associated SLAs;
- provision for updating policies, plans, and procedures that are affected by the withdrawal of the product or service, including the Service Catalogue;
- the identification and management of risks to the Forensic Laboratory on withdrawal of the product or service;
- communicating details about the withdrawal of the product or service to the Forensic Laboratory and Clients.

Note

The withdrawal of a product or service should be processed through the change management process, as defined in Chapter 7, Section 7.4.3.

3. The Laboratory Manager draws up a withdrawal plan which is reviewed by the Account Managers and any other affected parties.
4. The Forensic Laboratory withdraws the product or service at the scheduled time. All documents associated with the product or service must be withdrawn by the Laboratory Manager and archived in the ERMS, as appropriate.
5. The Laboratory Manager updates the Service Catalogue and removes the product or service from it. No further metrics information is collected.
6. The Laboratory Manager conducts a review of the product or service withdrawal and reviews the outcome against the withdrawal plan.

14.3 THIRD PARTIES ACCESSING THE FORENSIC LABORATORY

14.3.1 General

While the Forensic Laboratory has internal processes and procedures for handling Client information entrusted to it, based on agreements in force, internal handling procedures, or the classification of the information, a similar process must be put in place for third parties (e.g., suppliers, consultants under contact to the Forensic Laboratory, or outsourcing partners). The levels of security of any Forensic Laboratory or Client information shall not be reduced by the introduction of third party products or services.

Where any third party of the type defined in Section 14.1 has access to Forensic Laboratory information (including Client information held for Clients by the Forensic Laboratory) and information processing systems, a risk assessment must be undertaken, as defined in Chapter 5. This must determine the risks associated with the product or service being provided, and controls needed to reduce the risk to an acceptable level, as given in Chapter 5, Appendix 14, and be subject to regular risk reviews using the corporate risk register, as given in Chapter 5, Appendix 17.

Any control requirements identified must be agreed between the parties, made part of the contract and the key suppliers subject to second party audits as defined in Chapter 4, Section 4.7.3, and given in the IMS Calendar, as given in Chapter 4, Appendix 42.

14.3.2 Identification of Third Party Risks

Where there is any need for any third party to have access to Forensic Laboratory information or information processing systems, a risk assessment must be carried out, as defined in Chapter 5 to identify and quantify risks, as well as define controls to be implemented to reduce these risks to an acceptable level.

Some of the issues to be considered for third party risk assessments are given in Appendix 2.

Once the risk assessment has been undertaken, it is subject to a formal report to the Risk Committee, as given in Chapter 4, Appendix 33, if the risk level, information classification, or the level of access to Forensic Laboratory and Client information warrants it. The Risk Committee will consider the report, the risks to be managed, and the recommended controls, and take a final decision on the third party having access to Forensic Laboratory information processing systems, on what basis any additional controls are to be put in place to reduce the risks identified to an acceptable level.

No access by a third party to any Forensic Laboratory information processing systems shall be permitted until appropriate controls are in place. Depending on access types and levels, this can include:

- signing confidentiality agreements or Non Disclosure Agreements (NDA), as given in Chapter 12, Section 12.3.3.3;
- signed contracts specifying the required information security controls and service levels to be provided, as defined in Section 14.3.3, 14.5.2 and 14.8.2.1;
- implementation of any required additional security controls indicated by the risk assessment and agreed by the Risk Committee;
- appropriate training for any third party employees relating to induction training, specialized security or project training, and other training as appropriate.

14.3.3 Third Party Contractual Terms Relating to Information Security

Note

This does not constitute legal advice, but is a checklist that the Forensic Laboratory uses with its General Counsel for agreements covering third party access to the Forensic Laboratory information and information processing systems.

Whether a confidentiality agreement, NDA, or full contract is executed between the parties, it must clearly define both party's obligations, responsibilities, and liabilities involved in accessing, processing, communicating, or managing the Forensic Laboratory's offices, information, and information processing systems. The execution of the relevant agreement signifies acceptance of these obligations, responsibilities, and liabilities.

While confidentiality agreements and NDAs are typically standard, contracts can vary greatly depending on the specific circumstances and level of access required by the third party and will depend on information and information processing systems accessed. The Forensic Laboratory must ensure that all relevant clauses are in place to protect their information and information processing systems against unauthorized access, erasure, modification, or disclosure of information.

For information security issues only, the Forensic Laboratory has produced the checklist provided in Appendix 3 for discussion with the Legal Counsel in drafting appropriate contractual terms for any third party, as defined in Section 14.1.

The agreement should ensure that there is no misunderstanding between the Forensic Laboratory and the third party and that if issues do arise, they are contractually covered.

Wherever possible, the Forensic Laboratory should use its own agreements with all third parties, but recognize that there are occasions when the third party's agreement must be used. In cases such as this, careful consideration should be given to the contract terms to ensure that the Forensic Laboratory information security is not prejudiced and that it can meet the requirements in the contract. The Forensic Laboratory has to make a decision, based on a risk assessment whether to undertake any forensic case processing or supply of products and services if the contract terms do not exactly match the Forensic Laboratory's requirement.

14.4 MANAGING SERVICE LEVEL AGREEMENTS

At the heart of service delivery are SLAs. These agreements document the full details for a product or service to be provided together with the corresponding service level targets and workload characteristics.

14.4.1 Creating an SLA

SLAs are created in conjunction with Account Managers for a specific product or service (Figure 14.3).

1. A Client identifies a new product or service that they would like to be implemented by the Forensic

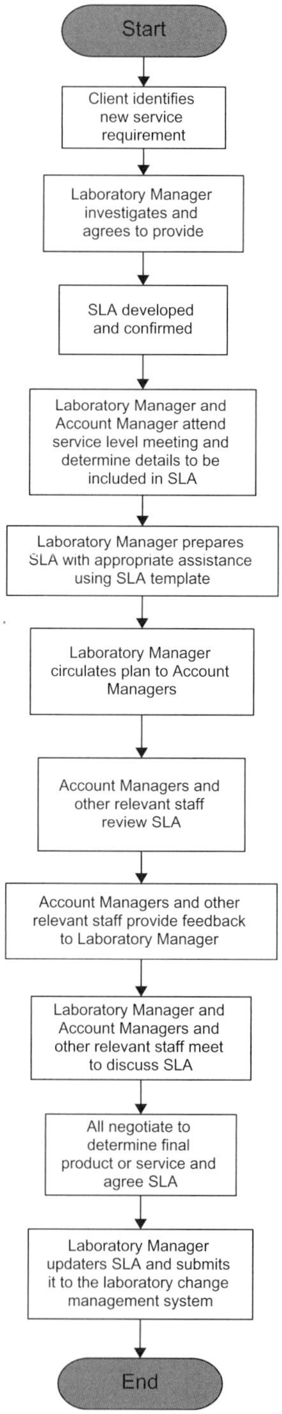

FIGURE 14.3 Create an SLA. (For color version of this figure, the reader is referred to the online version of this chapter.)

Laboratory. The Laboratory Manager investigates the feasibility of the product or service and then agrees to provide it as defined in Section 14.2.2.1.
In order to confirm the product or service details and have measurable targets, an SLA must be confirmed between the Forensic Laboratory and the Client.

2. The Laboratory Manager and the relevant Account Manager (and optionally a Client representative) attend a service level meeting, which outlines the details to be included in the SLA for the required product or service. The minutes of the meeting form the Terms of Reference for the proposed SLA.
The Client's business needs and budget must be basis for the content, structure, and targets of the SLA. The targets, against which the delivered product or service are to be measured, must be clearly stated and match the Client's needs.

Note

Only the key targets are included in the SLA to ensure that the correct business focus is identified for the service.

3. The Laboratory Manager prepares an SLA with the assistance of the relevant Account Manager(s), other Forensic Laboratory employees and, optionally, the relevant Client(s). The SLA template that the Forensic Laboratory uses is given in Appendix 4. This is amended as appropriate for the product or service being provided.
4. The Laboratory Manager circulates the plan to the relevant Account Managers and/or Forensic Laboratory employees for comment.
5. The relevant Account Managers, and other relevant Forensic Laboratory employees, review the SLA and ensure that all items raised are satisfactory from the product or service delivery perspective. All comments are passed back to the Laboratory Manager. The document is updated in accordance with the procedures defined in Chapter 4, Section 4.6.3. A copy of the finalized SLA is sent to the relevant Account Managers.
6. The Laboratory Manager meets with the Account Managers, and optionally the relevant Client(s) representatives, to discuss the SLA.
7. All relevant parties negotiate to determine the final product or service SLA based upon the details within the plan. At the end of these negotiations, the SLA is agreed.
8. The Laboratory Manager updates the SLA with the agreed details and then submits it to the Forensic Laboratory change management process, as defined in Chapter 7, Section 7.4.3, for approval and implementation. The SLA is now a working document.

14.4.2 Monitoring and Reviewing an SLA

The monitoring and reviewing of SLAs is performed on a regular basis to ensure that the targets are being met.

A formal review is performed at least each year or when a significant change is required to the SLA. The review determines whether the SLA remains effective.

1. On a regular basis, normally monthly, the Laboratory Manager collects performance information for product and service delivery. This information comes from a variety of sources:
   - internal reporting from MARS;
   - Service Desk calls relating to the product or service;
   - Client complaints;
   - Client feedback forms on case processing;
   - feedback from meetings with the Account Managers;
   - other input, as appropriate.
2. The Laboratory Manager prepares a service report that documents the current service levels and sends this to the relevant Account Managers. The report details:
   - current service levels against targets;
   - trends in service levels;
   - explanations to support problem areas;
   - identification of improvements, where required.
3. If any clarification on the report is required by an Account Manager, this is provided by the Laboratory Manager.
4. If any improvements to the product or service are identified, these are processed as appropriate.

Note

Any changes to an SLA must be processed through the Forensic Laboratory change management system, as defined in Chapter 7, Section 7.4.3.

14.5 SUPPLIERS OF OFFICE AND IT PRODUCTS AND SERVICES

The Forensic Laboratory ensures that management of Office and IT supplier relations is implemented across the whole of the organization by following the processes and guidelines that comply with the Forensic Laboratory policy for relationship management, as given in Chapter 4, Appendix 21.

Managing relations with office and IT suppliers allows the Forensic Laboratory to manage its interactions with the organizations that supply Forensic Laboratory with Office and IT products and services. Within Forensic Laboratory, the goal of office and IT supplier relationship management is to streamline and make more effective the processes between Forensic Laboratory and its office and IT product and service suppliers (in the same way that the Client relationship management strategy attempts to streamline and make more effective the processes between Forensic Laboratory and its Clients).

By implementing a series of guidelines and processes for managing their office and IT suppliers (and making them aware of these), the Forensic Laboratory can create a common frame of reference that enables effective communication with office and IT suppliers who use different business practices and terminology. To this end, the Forensic Laboratory office and IT supplier management strategy increases the efficiency of processes associated with managing office and IT suppliers.

The generic high-level process for purchasing is defined in Chapter 6, Section 6.7.4, with handling of purchased assets in Chapter 12, Section 12.3.14.

14.5.1 Selecting a New Supplier of Office and IT Equipment

An approved supplier list is maintained by the Finance Department in the Forensic Laboratory. Any purchases for the office should use this list of approved and vetted suppliers, wherever possible, as defined in Chapter 12, Section 12.3.14.2.1.2. The details of suppliers on the approved supplier list are given in Chapter 13, Appendix 1.

Where a product or service is not available for any reason from the approved supplier list, authority may be given by the Finance Department for a local purchase if the need is urgent.

If the need is not urgent, then the Forensic Laboratory will identify a suitable supplier with the Requestor and undergo the supplier approval process as defined in Chapter 13, Section 13.1.3, and the checklist given in Chapter 13, Appendix 2.

The process for selecting a new supplier and placing him on the approved supplier list in the Forensic Laboratory is shown below (Figure 14.4):

1. A need is identified to add a supplier of a product or service to the approved supplier list;
2. The Requestor and the Finance Department agree on the specific products(s) or service(s) required;
3. The Finance Department contacts the supplier to determine whether they can supply the product or service and the terms and conditions for it. This may take the form of a simple purchase order process or be a full Request for Information (RFI), Request for Quotation (RFQ), or a Request for Proposal (RFP) depending on what product or service is to be supplied. There are a number of other "Request for…" (RFx) procurement processes. A description of these is given in Appendix 5. The Forensic Laboratory template for the preparation of all RFx documents is given in Appendix 6.

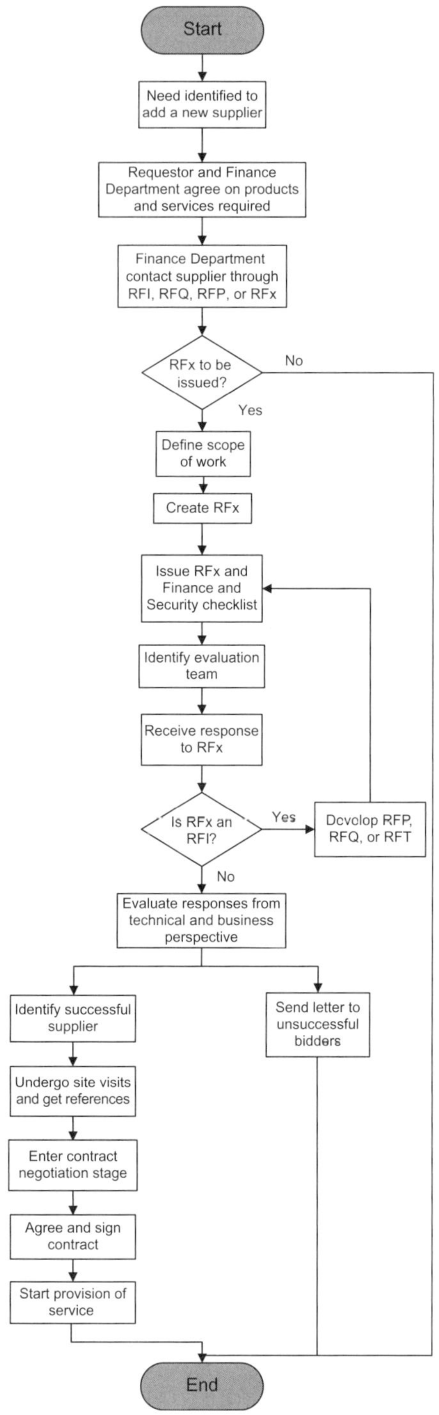

FIGURE 14.4 Selecting a new supplier of office and IT equipment. (For color version of this figure, the reader is referred to the online version of this chapter.)

4. If an RFx document is to be issued, then undertake the following:
   - define scope of work;
   - create evaluation criteria;
   - create RFx document using the template given in Appendix 6.

5. Issue the RFx document and the financial and security checklist, as given in Chapter 13, Appendix 2, to selected potential suppliers with the anticipated time-frame for the evaluation and selection process. The steps in this process used in the Forensic Laboratory are given in Appendix 7.
6. Identify the evaluation team and train them if required.
7. Receive back results of the RFx submissions.
8. If the RFx was an RFI, then develop the RFP, RFQ, or RFT and repeat steps 5-7 above for the RFx.
9. Evaluate the responses from a technical and business perspective using the defined evaluation criteria.
10. Identify the successful supplier.
11. Send appropriate unsuccessful bidder letters, as appropriate.
12. Undergo site visits and take up references.
13. Enter contract negotiation stage.
14. Agree and sign contract.
15. Start provision of product(s) or service(s).

14.5.2 Requirements for Office and IT Supplier Contracts

All new contracts that are established between the Forensic Laboratory and any supplier of office and IT products and services require that appropriate contracts are in place and executed between the parties prior to starting the service or allowing access to any Forensic Laboratory premises (unless as a hosted visitor, as defined in Chapter 12, Section 12.4.2), information of information processing systems.

Where appropriate, SLAs are set up with suppliers of office and IT products and services, these SLAs must include details as given in Appendix 4.

14.5.3 Monitoring Supplier Service Performance

The Forensic Laboratory does continuous monitoring of products and services provided by suppliers in order to:

- monitor products and services provided by suppliers;
- measure service performance against agreed SLAs;
- help identify and correct potential problems with suppliers and/or their products and/or services;
- develop actions for service improvement, as defined in Chapter 7, Section 7.4.8.

The monitoring process is:

1. Performance and operational statistics for a supplier service are obtained from the supplier in accordance with:
   - agreements reached regarding the provision of service statistics during contract negotiation;
   - supplier commitments for statistics provision (as documented in the SLA);
   - performance statistics for supplier services are provided to the Service Level Manager.
2. The statistics are collated by the Service Level Manager (additional performance information available from Forensic Laboratory sources should be included, as appropriate).
3. The performance of the service is reviewed between the Service Level Manager, the Finance Department, key users of the product or service, and the supplier. Additional items which may be discussed include:
   - changes to the service scope;
   - changes to the service and business requirements.
4. Any agreed actions concerning the possible improvement of the service are agreed and documented.
5. If the performance of the service is business critical, the issue is escalated, as defined in Section 14.5.5.
6. Corrective actions are determined and agreed between the Forensic Laboratory and the supplier using the process defined in Chapter 4, Section 4.8, and the supplier's own processes, as appropriate. They are tracked to satisfactory resolution using the Forensic Laboratory's CAPA process and a PIR is carried out to determine that the corrective action is completed.
7. Any other suggested actions for service improvement are incorporated into the Forensic Laboratory SIP, as given in Chapter 7, Appendix 14, and for discussion during the annual review of supplier contracts as defined in Section 14.5.4.

14.5.4 Reviewing Supplier Contracts

The Forensic Laboratory undertakes a formal review of all contracts with suppliers of products and services to the Forensic Laboratory. This review is performed on an annual basis and is the responsibility of the Finance Manager. The review meeting comprises the Finance Manager, the Service Level Manager, the Laboratory Manager, and other Managers affected by the provision of products and services. There may be a number of meetings undertaken for different products and services.

The process is:

1. The Finance Manager gathers information on each supplier contract requiring review. Inputs include:
   - existing contracts;
   - SLAs for supplier products and services;
   - the SIP;
   - feedback from service level reporting;
   - feedback from the complaints process;
   - feedback from the Service Desk;
   - any other relevant feedback for the supplier(s) under discussion.

2. The performance and requirements of each supplier contract is evaluated, with assistance from relevant Forensic Laboratory Managers, as required. Items for consideration include:
   - validation of supplier's contractual obligations;
   - affirmation of the service adequacy for the Forensic Laboratory's business requirements;
   - product availability and performance;
   - service availability and performance;
   - supplier availability and performance;
   - Forensic Laboratory funds and budgets;
   - contract disputes;
   - planned changes to the scope of required products and/or services;
   - future Forensic Laboratory business requirements;
   - planned changes to the Forensic Laboratory infrastructure;
   - the overall Forensic Laboratory strategy for provision of services in the SIP, as given in Chapter 7, Appendix 14.
3. The Finance Manager, in association with relevant Forensic Laboratory Managers, drafts a supplier contract improvement plan that covers the resources, communications, and documentation needed to implement the required improvements.
   New targets for improvements in quality, costs, and resource utilization should be included, in addition to details on the predicted improvement measures to assess the effectiveness of the change (if required).
4. The contract improvement plan and the SIP are circulated to relevant Forensic Laboratory Managers for comment, as appropriate. Any comments from within Forensic Laboratory are incorporated into the contract improvement plan and the SIP.
5. The Forensic Laboratory performs the relevant actions detailed in the contract improvement plan and the SIP. Where necessary, the Finance Manager may renegotiate the contract terms with a supplier.
6. Outcomes are reported to the relevant Forensic Laboratory Managers, as required.

14.5.5 Resolving Contractual Disputes with Suppliers

The Forensic Laboratory follows this process in the event that a contractual dispute arises between the Forensic Laboratory and a supplier of products and/or services with which the Forensic Laboratory has contracted.

Complaints and disputes may originate for a wide variety of reasons, real or perceived, and they reflect negatively on the integrity of a product or service. In such circumstances, the Forensic Laboratory needs to work vigorously to identify causes and implement solutions. Ideally, this should be accomplished through a collaborative, interest-based process that seeks mutual gain by establishing a solution, building trust, and promoting open and clear communications with a supplier.

The Forensic Laboratory makes every effort to prevent disputes from arising with a supplier by being as clear as possible when communicating its needs and requirements during contract negotiation and SLA determination. It is Forensic Laboratory policy to:

- adopt a non-confrontational approach to enhance or preserve good supplier relationships;
- resolve concerns in a manner that is timely and that provides options and satisfactory results to both the Forensic Laboratory and the supplier.

The process is:

1. A contractual dispute or issue with the provision of a product or services from a supplier is identified.
2. The relevant Forensic Laboratory Manager(s) and the Finance Manager discuss the dispute internally to determine an initial action plan.
3. The Finance Manager discusses the dispute informally with the supplier contact (to attempt to reach a resolution before escalating the matter to higher management). During this stage, Forensic Laboratory should provide written concerns to the supplier (and vice versa).

If the dispute is successfully resolved, the resolution is documented and relevant Forensic Laboratory Managers are informed of the outcome. Changes may be fed back into the SIP and also Forensic Laboratory policies and procedures for management of services suppliers.

If the process is not successful, the dispute is escalated to Top Management.

Note

Only the Chief Financial Officer is permitted to discuss a contract dispute with a supplier after a dispute has been escalated to Top Management.

4. If escalated, the dispute is discussed by the Forensic Laboratory Top Management fora; this may include:
   - Risk Committee meetings, as given in Chapter 4, Appendix 33;
   - Service Delivery Committee meetings, as given in Chapter 4, Appendix 34;
   - special meetings convened by Top Management to discuss the dispute.
5. Action is determined and agreed between the attendees at the relevant meeting, the minutes of which are documented and retained as records, as defined in Chapter 4,

Section 4.6.4, and stored in the ERMS. Outputs must include:
- a formal action plan;
- roles and responsibilities;
- timescales.

6. The Chief Financial Officer negotiates with the supplier to resolve the dispute. Options may include:
   - re-negotiation of contract terms;
   - re-definition of SLAs;
   - termination of contract in line with the guidelines for managing termination of a supplier service, as defined in Section 14.5.6.

If the dispute is successfully resolved, the resolution is documented and relevant Forensic Laboratory Managers are informed of the outcome. Changes may be fed back into the SIP and also Forensic Laboratory policies and procedures for management of services and suppliers.

If the process is not successful, the dispute is escalated.

7. If the dispute is escalated, options may include external resolution processes:
   - mediation by a neutral third party to reach a mutually agreeable resolution;
   - arbitration by a neutral arbitrator (selected by the parties) in a more formalized proceeding where evidence and arguments for each side is presented to the arbitrator to reach a final determination imposed on the parties;
   - litigation—where a settlement cannot be agreed.

Note

The dispute resolution process, including Alternate Dispute Resolution (ADR), and the jurisdiction should have been agreed in the contract.

When the dispute is successfully resolved, the resolution is documented and relevant Forensic Laboratory Managers are informed of the outcome. Changes may be fed back into the SIP and also Forensic Laboratory policies and procedures for management of services and suppliers.

14.5.6 Managing Termination of Supplier Services

All contracts or SLAs between suppliers and the Forensic Laboratory for products and/or services to Forensic Laboratory must include details of:

- expected end of product or service provision;
- outline arrangements or responsibilities in the event of an early end to product or service provision;
- outline arrangements or responsibilities for transfer of service (if appropriate).

When supplier services are terminated, the Forensic Laboratory must always consider:

- the impact on the provision of services to Forensic Laboratory and its Clients;
- alternative arrangements for service provision to Forensic Laboratory and their Clients.

14.6 UTILITY SERVICE PROVIDERS

In a number of jurisdictions, the Forensic Laboratory has no choice on the selection of utility service providers as they are the national suppliers. Situations such as this are the provision of:

- electricity;
- gas;
- local infrastructure services;
- water.

In cases such as this where there is a monopoly, the Forensic Laboratory has little option but to accept the terms and conditions and the supply of those services. However, alternate support or sourcing must be considered as part of the risk assessment process as defined in Chapter 5.

Where a monopoly does not exist, utility service providers should be treated as suppliers of office and IT products and services as defined in Section 14.5.

14.7 CONTRACTED FORENSIC CONSULTANTS AND EXPERT WITNESSES

Within the Forensic Laboratory, there are occasions when external resources are needed in forensic case processing, these are typically:

- the need for an Expert Witness;
- covering a shortfall in staffing for any reason;
- the need for a specific skill not present in the Forensic Laboratory.

As the digital forensic world is rather small, it is likely that any required Expert Witness or Forensic Analyst is known to the Forensic Laboratory; however, a selection process that stands up to due diligence must be followed in all cases.

Note 1

Consultants such as these are regarded as "sub-contractors" within the ISO Management System process and other Accreditation processes (e.g., ASCLD).

> **Note 2**
>
> In some jurisdictions, some forensic case processing is preferred to be carried out by Law Enforcement primarily, their appointed suppliers secondarily, and not by sub-sub-contractors. The Forensic Laboratory must be aware of these constraints and any legal ramifications of the use of sub-contractors in these types of cases.

The criteria for selecting an Expert Witness are given in Chapter 11, Appendix 2. The same criteria apply for Forensic Consultants apart from the fact that their experience is primarily in case processing with specific tools and methods, but may also require Expert Witness work (Figure 14.5).

1. The Forensic Laboratory identifies a need for a Forensic Consultant that has skills not currently available.
2. The requirements for the role are identified.
3. A search of "known" Forensic Consultants is undertaken. If there is already one under contract to the Forensic Laboratory, they are approached for the task.
4. If there is no "known" availability, then a search must be undertaken, using appropriate resources, for a competent Forensic Consultant to meet the requirement.
5. The role of the digital Forensic Consultant will typically include:
   - providing the Forensic Laboratory with the skills, knowledge, and/or equipment that is required to undertake the task;
   - communicating with all relevant Forensic Laboratory employees, at all levels, who are involved with the task;
   - assisting the Forensic Laboratory in the effective planning, operation, control, and delivery of the task.
6. The Forensic Consultant, as well as demonstrating competence, must be able to demonstrate ethical behavior, compliance with the rules of evidence in the jurisdiction, and appropriate personal attributes, as given in Appendix 8.
7. The employment of a Forensic Consultant must be approved by the Laboratory Manager, and where appropriate, by Top Management.
8. The Laboratory Manager verbally offers the Forensic Consultant the work when terms are agreed.
9. The Laboratory Manager, with input from General Counsel, drafts a letter that offers the Consultant the work within the terms verbally agreed. The letter must contain at least the following information:
   - brief summary of the case or project;
   - charges and invoicing arrangements for the work;
   - period of the work;
   - start date of the work;

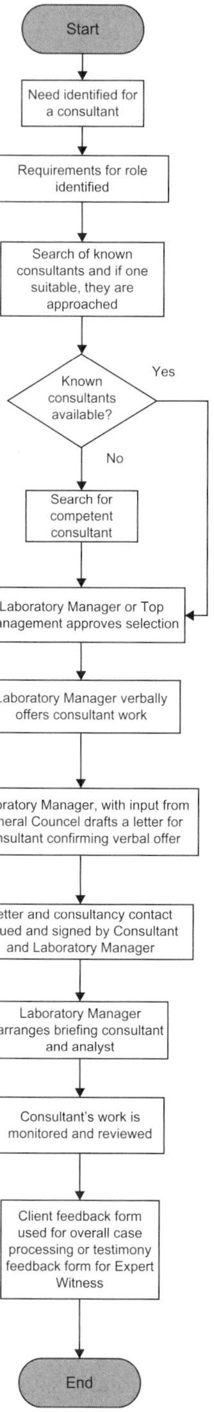

FIGURE 14.5 Contracted Forensic Consultants and Expert Witnesses. (For color version of this figure, the reader is referred to the online version of this chapter.)

   - estimated end date of the work;
   - roles and responsibilities;
   - contractual obligations;
   - request to confirm acceptance of the offer in writing.
10. The letter is sent with a copy of a Consultancy Contract that the Laboratory Manager and Forensic Consultant

must sign before the Forensic Consultant can start work. Terms may be sent via an e-mail. The exact contents of the Consultancy Contract will depend on custom, practice, and legislative requirements for the jurisdiction as well as the following, where appropriate:
- agreed contract objectives that are SMART, as defined in Chapter 3, Section 3.1.17;
- a defined contract plan with milestones and deliverables defined;
- defining a process to confirm that the contract terms have been met.

11. Under no circumstances can a contract Forensic Consultant start work on processing a forensic case if a signed contract has not been received. It is the responsibility of the Laboratory Manager to ensure that a signed contract is received within a reasonable timescale to enable work to commence promptly.
12. The Laboratory Manager arranges a briefing between the contract Forensic Consultant and the relevant Forensic Laboratory Forensic Analysts for the specific case.
13. Once employed, their work is monitored and reviewed in the same way as a supplier, as defined in Sections 14.5.3–14.5.6.

The Client sign-off and feedback form, as given in Chapter 6, Appendix 20, is used for overall case processing, while the testimony feedback forms are used for Expert Witnesses, as given in Chapter 11, Appendix 8.

Note

The Forensic Consultant may have to be security cleared according to the requirements of the jurisdiction to undertake some forensic case processing.

14.8 OUTSOURCING

Note 1

In this context, within the Forensic Laboratory, outsourcing refers to the outsourcing of IT services. Forensic case processing may have contract Forensic Consultants working on a case, as defined in Section 14.7.

Note 2

The Forensic Laboratory may manage all of its IT capability in-house, but should this change, the following processes and procedures shall be used.

A quote from BS 7799—the precursor to ISO 270xx:

"The use of an external contractor to manage computer or network facilities may introduce a number of potential security exposures, such as the possibility of compromise, damage, or loss of data at the contractor's site. These risks should be identified in advance, and appropriate security measures agreed with the contractor, and incorporated into the contract."

If any aspect of the Forensic Laboratory's IT service provision is outsourced, the agreements should address how the third party will guarantee that adequate security, as defined by the risk assessment, will be maintained, and how security will be adapted to identify and deal with changes to risks.

Some of the differences between outsourcing and the other forms of third party service provision include the question of liability, planning the transition period and potential disruption of operations during this period, contingency planning arrangements and due diligence reviews, and collection and management of information on security incidents. Therefore, it is essential that the Forensic Laboratory plans and manages the transition to an outsourced arrangement and has suitable processes in place to manage changes and the renegotiation/termination of agreements.

Note

This book is not about the technical side of IT outsourcing, it is only focusing on the security of forensic case processing if outsourcing of IT operations is implemented for some or all of the IT operations undertaken in the Forensic Laboratory.

Where outsourcing takes place, the Forensic Laboratory must ensure that it maintains control over the provision of any outsourced services through the following requirements:

- a continuous process of feedback for these services, including complaints and service level failures;
- a process of continuous improvement, as defined in Chapter 4, Section 4.8;
- a process of ongoing internal audits (also of the outsource provider itself—i.e., second party audits), as defined in Chapter 4, Section 4.7.3;
- addressing security and control in dealings with third parties, as defined by the risk assessment and treatment process defined in Chapter 5;
- addressing security and control in third party contracts, as given in Appendix 3.

14.8.1 Determining Objectives of Outsourcing

The first step in the outsourcing process is to determine the objective of outsourcing some or all of the Forensic Laboratory's IT operations and the required outcomes. Without this essential step, any outsourcing will not deliver the required or expected benefits and outcomes.

14.8.1.1 Benefits of Outsourcing

Marketing material is full of the benefits of outsourcing IT operations, but the Forensic Laboratory must have defined its own benefits and required outcomes, rather than rely on marketing material. Some of the claimed benefits include:

- ability of the organization to concentrate on core functions, rather than IT (Peter Drucker—"Do what you do best—and outsource the rest");
- acquire innovative ideas from the outsource provider;
- control expenses;
- delegation of responsibilities of difficult-to-manage functions to an outsource provider, while still reaping the benefits of the functions;
- faster setup of a new function or service;
- freeing up internal resources to concentrate on core processes;
- gain access to skills and competencies not available in-house;
- gain high-quality IT staff;
- gain market access and business opportunities through the outsource provider's network;
- gain the benefits of reengineering;
- generate cash by transferring assets to the outsource provider;
- greater ability to control delivery dates (e.g., via penalty clauses);
- greater flexibility and ability to define the requisite service;
- higher quality service due to focus of the outsource provider;
- improve credibility and image by associating with superior outsource provider;
- increase commitment and energy in non-core areas;
- increase flexibility to meet changing business conditions;
- less dependency upon internal resources;
- lower costs due to economies of scale;
- lower ongoing investment required for internal infrastructure;
- minimize technology risk;
- purchase of industry good practice;
- specific outsource provider benefits, depending on the specific outsource provider's skills;
- turn fixed costs into variable costs.

14.8.1.2 Risks of Outsourcing

The flipside of the claimed benefits of outsourcing is the risks that outsourcing can introduce to the Forensic Laboratory. As has been said before, the Forensic Laboratory would never outsource its forensic case processing, but may use contract Forensic Consultants, so these risks are for mainstream IT operations outsourcing.

- availability of resources when needed (e.g., BCP invocation);
- being "locked in" to a specific outsource provider and their preferred technology;
- different approaches and commitments to information security relating to Forensic Laboratory and Client information and information processing systems;
- different outcome requirements. The Forensic Laboratory can define its required outcomes, but at the end of the day, the outsource provider is only really interested in making a profit from the relationship;
- difficulty of undertaking forensic incident response;
- even if the IPR is covered in the outsourcing contract, there is nothing to stop an unscrupulous outsourcer, or a member of their staff, in IPR theft for later reuse;
- failure to "go the extra mile" as employees would;
- hidden costs, where anything outside strict contractual terms will require an additional fee—which may not have been agreed in advance;
- impact on Forensic Laboratory employee morale;
- inappropriate contract terms;
- IPR ownership may be an issue, where the outsourcing provider develops processes, procedures, methods, or tools during the duration of the contract unless clearly resolved in the contract;
- lack of control over security of Forensic Laboratory and Client information, including access to it;
- lack of organizational culture and commitment;
- legislative differences relating to IPR and privacy, if offshoring;
- legislative issues relating to where data may be stored for privacy concerns, especially if using the "cloud";
- liability issues so that in the case of an information security breach, the Client(s) whose information has been compromised will have to take legal action against the Forensic Laboratory as they are the contracting party, then the Forensic Laboratory will have to take action against the outsourcing service provider;
- linguistic issues if outsourcing is really off-shoring;
- loss of management control over operational issues;
- loss of the team spirit or personal touch within the Forensic Laboratory between the outsource provider's employees and Forensic Laboratory employees;
- not complying with intangible aspects of the contract (e.g., Forensic Laboratory culture, ethos, and ethics);
- physical and logical security processes and procedures, especially if off-shoring, are not necessarily to the same level as those required by the Forensic Laboratory;
- problems with auditing the outsource provider, especially if off-shoring;
- problems with terminating the outsourcing contract if documentation is not accurate and current;
- problems with terminating the outsourcing contract if proprietary systems are used;

- proprietary systems are used that are not understood in-house or by the next outsourcing provider;
- reliance on an unrelated third party is an often overlooked issue in outsourcing. The outsourcing provider may go bankrupt, merge, or be taken over, and the Forensic Laboratory has no control over these processes;
- sacrifice of quality is a strong possibility as the outsource service provider is motivated by profit. As the price in the contract is fixed, the only way of increasing profit is to reduce costs. In effect, this means, from experience, that the outsource service provider will do the minimum to meet contractual requirements and charge for anything not covered by the contract and this will almost certainly affect the quality of deliverables to the Forensic Laboratory and so to the Client;
- some IT functions are not easy to outsource;
- unequal contracting parties—outsourcing service providers are experts at outsourcing contracts whereas the Forensic Laboratory has never undertaken an outsourcing contact;
- unknown contingency capabilities.

14.8.2 Selecting an Outsourcing Service Provider

Should the Forensic Laboratory ever consider outsourcing some parts of its IT operations, then it is necessary to select an appropriate outsourcing service provider. If there is no list of outsource service providers on the approved suppliers list maintained by the Finance Department, then an outsourcing service provider will have to be selected.

The process for selecting an outsourcing service provider is similar to that for selecting a supplier, as defined in Section 14.5.1, but with a number of significant differences, and is shown below:

1. The Forensic Laboratory makes a Top Management decision to outsource some or all of its IT operations. The areas to be outsourced are defined and the objectives of outsourcing are agreed. A business case for this is produced.
2. The IT Manager and the Finance Manager meet to discuss requirements, plan a budget, and determine the new structure after outsourcing is implemented.
3. The IT Manager researches the market for possible outsource service providers that may meet the Forensic Laboratory's agreed requirements. The building of this list can come from a variety of sources, including:
   - experiences of colleagues;
   - professional and trade bodies or shows;
   - Internet searches;
   - advertising and marketing material, etc.
4. The profile of a potential outsource service provider is defined and agreed internally.
5. Once a list of possible outsource providers has been produced, a full RFI is used to obtain detailed information about outsource service providers and their service offerings. The Forensic Laboratory template for the preparation of an RFI is given in Appendix 6.
6. Create the RFI specifically tailored to the selection of an outsourcing service provider for all or part of the Forensic Laboratory IT systems. This will include:
   - define scope of work;
   - create evaluation criteria;
   - process for completing the RFI.
7. The RFI is issued to all outsource service providers on the list, identifying key issues that the Forensic Laboratory requires information on. These should be prioritized and weighted for the evaluation criteria.
8. Identify the RFI evaluation team and train them if required.
9. Receive back results of the RFI submissions and evaluate the responses, based on the specific requirements stated. This should produce a clear picture of the market and its trends, and where various outsource provider offering fit into the marketplace. After evaluation, there should be clear information to be able to:
   - draft a comprehensive RFP to meet the Forensic Laboratory's stated objectives;
   - produce a list of no more than three to five possible candidates to receive the RFP.
10. Issue the RFP and the financial and security checklist, as given in Chapter 13, Appendix 2, to selected potential outsource service providers with the anticipated timeframe for the evaluation and selection process. The steps in this process used in the Forensic Laboratory are given in Appendix 7.
11. Identify the RFP evaluation team and train them if required.
12. Receive back results of the RFP submissions.
13. Evaluate the responses from a technical and business perspective using the defined evaluation criteria. Some other tips for selecting an appropriate outsourcing service provider are given in Appendix 9.
14. Identify the successful outsource service provider.
15. Send appropriate unsuccessful bidder letters, as appropriate.
16. Undergo site visits and take up references.
17. Enter contract negotiation stage.
18. Agree best and final offer (BAFO).
19. Agree and sign contract.
20. Start outsource service provision transition process.

14.8.2.1 Requirements for Outsourcing Contracts

Outsourcing contracts are not like any other supplier contract, and it is likely, if not certain, that the outsourcing service provider will have more experience than the Forensic Laboratory in outsourcing contracts, so expert advice will be needed. An experienced outsourcing expert Lawyer is needed for this as it is outside the competence of in-house Legal Counsel. While not competent to provide legal advice, the Forensic Laboratory has defined a number of areas that must be addressed in any outsourcing contract; these are given in Appendix 10.

14.8.2.2 Monitoring Outsourcing Service Supplier Performance

The Forensic Laboratory shall operate continuous monitoring of outsourced products and services provided by the outsource service provider in order to:

- monitor products and services provided by outsource service provider;
- measure service performance against agreed SLAs;
- help identify and correct potential problems with the outsource service provider and/or their products and/ or services;
- develop actions for service improvement, as defined in Chapter 7, Section 7.4.8.

The monitoring process is:

1. Performance and operational statistics for any outsourced service are obtained from the outsource service provider in accordance with:
   - agreements reached regarding the provision of service statistics during contract negotiation;
   - supplier commitments for statistics provision (as documented in the SLA);
   - performance statistics for supplier services are provided to the Service Level Manager.
2. The statistics are collated by the Service Level Manager (additional performance information available from Forensic Laboratory sources should be included, as appropriate).
3. The outsource service provider's performance is reviewed between the Service Level Manager, the Finance Department, key users of the product or service, and the outsource service provider on a regular basis (at least monthly), with formal reporting in place. Additional items that may be discussed include:
   - changes to the outsource service scope;
   - changes to the service and business requirements.
4. Any agreed actions concerning the possible improvement of the outsource service are agreed and documented.
5. If the performance of the outsource service is business critical, the issue is escalated, as defined in Section 14.8.2.4.
6. Corrective actions are determined and agreed between the Forensic Laboratory and the outsource service provider using the process defined in Chapter 4, Section 4.8, and the outsource service provider's own processes, as appropriate. They are tracked to satisfactory resolution using the Forensic Laboratory's CAPA process and a PIR is carried out to determine that the corrective action is completed.
7. Any other suggested actions for outsourced service improvement are incorporated into the Forensic Laboratory SIP, as given in Chapter 7, Appendix 14, and for discussion during the review of the outsource service provider's contract as defined in Section 14.8.2.3.

14.8.2.3 Reviewing the Outsourcing Contract

The Forensic Laboratory shall undertake a formal review of the outsourcing contract on the terms agreed in the contract, which should be typically yearly. Performance will be reviewed on an ongoing basis, that is, every month (or more frequently, if needed) with formal records of the meetings and actions being tracked through the Forensic Laboratory CAPA process.

The review is the responsibility of the Chief Financial Officer. The review meeting comprises the Chief Financial Officer, the Service Level Manager, the Laboratory Manager, and other relevant Managers with the outsource service provider's management team.

The process is:

1. The Chief Financial Officer gathers information on the provision of the services provided by the outsourcer service provider. Inputs include:
   - the existing contract;
   - the SLA for the provision of the outsourcing services;
   - the SIP;
   - feedback from service level reporting;
   - feedback from the complaints process;
   - feedback from the Service Desk;
   - any other relevant feedback relating to the outsourced service provision.
2. The performance requirements of the outsource service provider are evaluated, with assistance from relevant Forensic Laboratory Managers, as required. Items for consideration include:
   - validation of outsource service provider's contractual obligations;
   - affirmation of the service adequacy for the Forensic Laboratory's business requirements;
   - service availability and performance;
   - Forensic Laboratory funds and budgets;
   - contract disputes;
   - planned changes to the scope of required outsource service;
   - future Forensic Laboratory business requirements;

- planned changes to the Forensic Laboratory infrastructure;
- the overall Forensic Laboratory strategy for provision of services in the SIP, as given in Chapter 7, Appendix 14.

3. The Chief Financial Officer, in association with relevant Forensic Laboratory Managers, drafts a contract improvement plan which covers the resources, communications, and documentation needed to implement the required improvements.
4. The contract improvement plan and the SIP are circulated to relevant Forensic Laboratory Managers for comment, as appropriate. Any relevant and accepted comments from within Forensic Laboratory are incorporated into the contract improvement plan and the SIP.
5. The Forensic Laboratory performs the relevant actions detailed in the contract improvement plan and the SIP. Where necessary, the Chief Financial Officer may re-negotiate the contract terms with the outsource service provider.
6. The outsource service provider implements any relevant changes through the Forensic Laboratory change management process, as defined in Chapter 7, Section 7.4.3.
7. Outcomes are reported to the relevant Forensic Laboratory Managers, as required.

14.8.2.4 Resolving Contractual Disputes with an Outsource Service Provider

The Forensic Laboratory should follow this process in the event that a contractual dispute arises between the Forensic Laboratory and the outsource service provider.

Complaints and disputes may originate for a wide variety of reasons, real or perceived, and they reflect negatively on the integrity of either the delivery of services by the outsource service provider to the Forensic Laboratory or the delivery of products and services to a Client by the Forensic Laboratory.

In such circumstances, the Forensic Laboratory needs to work vigorously to identify causes and implement solutions. Ideally, this should be accomplished through a collaborative, interest-based process that seeks mutual gain by establishing a solution, building trust, and promoting open and clear communications with the outsource service provider.

The Forensic Laboratory makes every effort to prevent disputes from arising with the outsource service provider by being as clear as possible when communicating its needs and requirements during contract negotiation and SLA determination. It should be the Forensic Laboratory policy to:

- adopt a non-confrontational approach to enhance or preserve good relationships with the outsource service provider;
- resolve concerns in a manner that is timely and that provides options and satisfactory results to both the Forensic Laboratory and the outsource service provider.

The process is:

1. A contractual dispute or issue with the provision of service from the outsource service provider is identified.
2. The Chief Financial Officer and relevant Forensic Laboratory Manager(s) discuss the dispute internally to determine an initial action plan.
3. The Chief Financial Officer discusses the dispute informally with the outsource service provider contact (to attempt to reach a resolution before escalating the matter to higher management). During this stage, Forensic Laboratory should provide written concerns to the outsource service provider (and vice versa).

If the dispute is successfully resolved, the resolution is documented and relevant Forensic Laboratory Managers are informed of the outcome. Changes may be fed back into the SIP and also Forensic Laboratory policies and procedures for management of services suppliers.

If the process is not successful, the dispute is escalated to Top Management.

> **Note**
>
> Only the Chief Financial Officer is permitted to discuss a contract dispute with the outsource service provider.

4. If escalated, the dispute is taken by the Chief Financial Officer to the rest of the Forensic Laboratory Top Management; this may include:
   - Risk Committee meetings, as given in Chapter 4, Appendix 33;
   - Service Delivery Committee meetings, as given in Chapter 4, Section 4.6.4;
   - special meetings convened by Top Management to discuss the dispute.
5. Action is determined and agreed between the attendees at the relevant meeting, the minutes of which are documented and retained as records, as defined in Chapter 4, Section 4.6.4 and stored in the ERMS. Outputs must include:
   - a formal action plan;
   - roles and responsibilities;
   - timescales.
6. The Chief Financial Officer negotiates with the outsource service provider to resolve the dispute. Options may include:
   - renegotiation of contract terms;
   - redefinition of SLAs;
   - termination of contract in line with the guidelines for managing termination of a supplier service, as defined in Section 14.5.6.

If the dispute is successfully resolved, the resolution is documented and relevant Forensic Laboratory Managers are informed of the outcome. Changes may be fed back into the SIP and also Forensic Laboratory policies and procedures for management of services and suppliers.

If the process is not successful, the dispute is escalated.

7. If the dispute is escalated, options may include external resolution processes:
   - mediation by a neutral third party to reach a mutually agreeable resolution;
   - arbitration by a neutral arbitrator (selected by the parties) in a more formalized proceeding where evidence and arguments for each side are presented to the arbitrator to reach a final determination imposed on the parties;
   - litigation—where a settlement cannot be agreed.

> **Note**
>
> The dispute resolution process, including ADR, and the jurisdiction should have been agreed in the contract.

When the dispute is successfully resolved, the resolution is documented and relevant Forensic Laboratory Managers are informed of the outcome. Changes may be fed back into the SIP and also Forensic Laboratory policies and procedures for management of services and suppliers.

14.8.2.5 Managing Termination of an Outsourcing Contract

Any outsourcing agreement must include details of:

- expected end-to-service provision;
- outline arrangements or responsibilities in the event of an early end-to-service provision;
- outline arrangements or responsibilities for transfer of service and IPR back to the Forensic Laboratory or another outsource service provider.

When outsourcing services are terminated, the Forensic Laboratory must always consider:

- the impact on the provision of the outsourced services to Forensic Laboratory and its Clients;
- alternative arrangements for outsourced service provision to Forensic Laboratory and their Clients.

14.9 USE OF SUB-CONTRACTORS

14.9.1 By the Forensic Laboratory

The Forensic Laboratory uses Forensic Consultants on contract as sub-contractors on occasion for a specific purpose. Purposes range from:

- requirement of a specific tool for a case where there is no in-house expertise;
- covering for unexpected demand on case load;
- clearing any backlog of cases;
- covering for staff shortages—e.g., illness and holiday issues;
- the need for an Expert Witness.

In every case where a sub-contractor is to be used, the Client will be advised of the identity and qualifications of the Forensic Consultant to be used. The Client is requested to confirm that they accept the Forensic Consultant to work on processing their case.

All forensic cases to be processed that may involve sensitive or classified information should be processed by the Forensic Laboratory's employees and not a contracted Forensic Consultant.

The Forensic Laboratory maintains a list of "known and trusted" Forensic Consultants. This includes qualification, certifications, and areas of expertise to assist in selection of a Forensic Consultant for a specific requirement. In some cases, it will be necessary for the Forensic Consultant to have an ISO 17025 Accredited Forensic Laboratory with a suitable scope of accreditation.

Only the Laboratory Manager can authorize the use of a Forensic Consultant. In some sensitive cases, it may be necessary to obtain Top Management approval as well.

The Forensic Laboratory is accountable and responsible to the Client for the delivery and quality of any sub-contracted forensic case processing. The exception to this rule is where a Client requests a specific sub-contractor to work on their case.

When the case has been processed by the Forensic Consultant, all exhibits relating to the case and any work product must be returned to the Forensic Laboratory for storage in the Secure Property Store and in the ERMS in the Client virtual file as appropriate. Movement forms, as given in Chapter 8, Appendix 17, shall be used to maintain the Chain of Custody.

14.9.2 By Suppliers or Outsourcing Service Providers

The Forensic Laboratory does not permit this, unless agreed to at the contract negotiation stage. Due diligence must be undertaken relating to the use of any sub-contractor and they will be required to complete the financial and security questionnaire, as given in Chapter 13, Appendix 2.

The supplier or outsource provider shall be accountable for the work of any subcontactors they engage. The Forensic Laboratory shall have the right to perform second party audits, as defined in Chapter 4, Section 4.7.3, on any subcontractors engaged, their suppliers, or outsource service provider, and the right to demand termination of their use, if appropriate (e.g., Client complaints, substandard work, conflict of interest, etc.).

14.10 MANAGING COMPLAINTS

The receipt of a complaint is a serious issue within the Forensic Laboratory.

The Forensic Laboratory process and procedures for managing Client complaints are defined in Chapter 6, Section 6.14.

Complaints that the Forensic Laboratory may have with its suppliers are given in Section 14.5.5 and 14.8.2.4.

14.11 REASONS FOR OUTSOURCING FAILURE

There are a wide range of causes for the failure of outsourcing arrangements. Detailed below are some of the potential failure points that may arise during an outsourcing process:

- *failure to define requirements*—too often requirements are poorly defined and when the outsourcer meets them, they are not what is required, even if it is what was requested;
- *failure to understand and comply with the SLA*—Even if well structured, it is not uncommon for SLAs to be mis-understood or not complied with. It is important to monitor the performance of the conduct of the outsourced task to ensure that both the Forensic Laboratory and the outsource provider understand and follow the terms of the SLA;
- *failure to understand the potential costs and savings*—If cost is one of the factors in the outsourcing decision, both the Forensic Laboratory and the outsourcing organization must have a clear understanding about the financial aims of the outsourced function. The aims should be stated and the way in which they will be monitored should be clearly stated. The SLA must define and report on what is expected to be delivered by both the Forensic Laboratory and the outsourcing party;
- *ineffective contract management*—If the contract management process is not efficient or not efficiently implemented, there is an increasing risk that if the outsourcing arrangement is not well designed, managed, and executed there will be a failure in the contract;
- *outsourcer attitudes*—experience dictates there is the possibility of an "us" and "them" approach. The Client wants lots of work, often in addition to the contract, carried out as part of the work to be performed. The outsource provider will stick to the contract, unlike the situation where the Client's employees were carrying out the work;
- *outsourcing for the wrong reason*—often an organization sees that the solution to a problem is to outsource the problem. This gives the illusion of a "fix" but often ends up with a worse situation as the organization now has less control over the problem. The other main reason for outsourcing is financial. While this brings short-term benefits in many cases, the organization loses in-house skills that are essential, especially when the outsourcing contract is terminated for any reason. The outsource provider may not adopt and adapt the same cultural values and dedication that permanent employees have;
- *poor contract drafting*—in general, Lawyers are not expert IT specialists and IT specialists are not Lawyers. Unless the two parties work together, there can be problems with contract drafting relating to required outcomes and how to measure them;
- *poor SLAs defined*—if the SLAs defined are inappropriate, then there is little chance of continuous improvement being achieved;
- *risk assessment is not carried out*—If the risks relating to the outsourcing of the task are not clearly researched and understood before the outsourcing process in initiated, then poor decisions may be made;
- *the outsourcing of a function or process or function that is not efficient*—If a process or function does not work well within the digital Forensic Laboratory, it may be tempting to outsource it to another organization—to outsource the problem. This should be avoided because if the business requirements cannot be adequately communicated and managed within the Forensic Laboratory, it is unlikely to be successfully outsourced. The process or function should be fixed before it can be outsourced.

There are numerous other reasons for failure and many books have been written about this.

APPENDIX 1 - CONTENTS OF A SERVICE PLAN

An example service plan template that can be used in the Forensic Laboratory contains:

- the roles and responsibilities for implementing, operating, and maintaining the product or service;
- activities to be performed by Clients and third party suppliers (where required);
- changes to the existing service management framework, products, and services (where required);
- communication plan for all relevant parties;
- contracts and agreements to align with the changes in business need;
- manpower and recruitment requirements;
- skills and training requirements, e.g., end users, technical support;
- processes, measures, methods, and tools to be used in connection with the service;
- budgets and timescales;
- service acceptance criteria;
- the expected outcomes from operating the service expressed in measurable terms.

APPENDIX 2 - RISKS TO CONSIDER WITH THIRD PARTIES

While different third parties will have different risks associated with the products and services they provide to the Forensic Laboratory, the following template is used, as appropriate, for consideration of risks:

- the Forensic Laboratory information and information processing systems that the third party will be able to access;
- the Client information that is located on those information processing systems;
- the type of access the third party will have to the Forensic Laboratory's information and information processing systems, and this includes:
  - physical access (e.g., to offices, data centers, wiring closets, other areas of risk);
  - logical access (e.g., what access, and level of access they have to information processing systems holding Forensic Laboratory or Client information);
  - network connectivity between the Forensic Laboratory and the third party, including identification and authentication mechanisms and protection of transmitted data;
  - methods of access in place (e.g., dedicated line, remote roving access on mobile devices, etc.);
  - type of access (e.g., on site or remote to the Forensic Laboratory office).
- existing controls in place;
- additional controls required by the risk assessment to adequately protect the Forensic Laboratory's information and information processing systems;
- the criticality of the information processing systems that the third party can access;
- the level of vetting and screening of the third party employees who can access the Forensic Laboratory information and information processing systems;
- contractual and insurance measures in place against unauthorized access, modification, disclosure, or reassure of information by a third party employee;
- how identification authorization is achieved, especially for remote connections by third parties;
- how frequently remote access needs to be re-confirmed, both during a session and on an ongoing basis;
- the controls that the third party has in place to assure the Forensic Laboratory that they are appropriate to store Forensic Laboratory and Client information and guard against unauthorized access, modification, disclosure, or erasure;
- the controls that the third party has in place to assure the Forensic Laboratory that they are appropriate for transmission or exchange of Forensic Laboratory and Client guard against unauthorized access, modification, disclosure, or erasure;
- how effectively these controls are implemented, with regular metrics reporting and second party audits;
- impact of data corruption of data during transmission and controls to mitigate this risk;
- certifications and accreditations held and their value;
- the impact of the third party not being able to access Forensic Laboratory information processing systems for a variety of times, using the scenarios given in Chapter 13, Appendix 6;
- status of the third party's business continuity response and its effectiveness;
- impact of the third party being unavailable to undertake their contracted role for a variety of times, using the scenarios given in Chapter 13, Appendix 6;
- how information security incidents are handled by the third party and the process for reporting them to the Forensic Laboratory;
- how conflicts of interest are handled by the third party;
- identification of any possible conflicts of interest;
- legal, regulatory, and Client requirements.

> **Note**
>
> This is not a complete list; the Information Security Manager will amend it as appropriate for any third party to be assessed.

APPENDIX 3 - CONTRACT CHECKLIST FOR INFORMATION SECURITY ISSUES

All identified security requirements shall be addressed before giving any third party access to the Forensic Laboratory's premises, assets, information, or information processing systems.

The following checklist should be used to address security and information security specifically, in any contractual terms. Not all items are relevant to all contracts, and this will depend on the type and extent of access given, the information classification, the information processing systems to be used:

PRODUCT OR SERVICE DESCRIPTION

- scope of service provided (and if necessary what is NOT covered);
- description of the product or service to be provided;
- a description of the information to be accessed in the product or service and its classification, as given in Chapter 5, Appendix 16, or the third party's classification and definition so it can be mapped to the Forensic Laboratory classification system;
- the target level of service and unacceptable levels of service, as defined in the SLA, the Forensic Laboratory template for SLAs is given in Appendix 4;
- the definition of verifiable performance criteria (i.e., metrics against the SLA);

- a formal, documented procedure by which the supplier manages the product or service to Forensic Laboratory;
- maintenance arrangements (if relevant);
- expected end of service.

ROLES AND RESPONSIBILITIES

- roles and responsibilities for:
  - the Forensic Laboratory;
  - the third party;
  - responsibilities regarding hardware and software installation and maintenance;
  - commitment for provision of statistics to/from the third party for service level reporting about the product or service provided, as defined in Chapter 7, Section 7.4.9.

COMMUNICATIONS AND REPORTING BETWEEN THE PARTIES

- a clear reporting structure and agreed reporting formats, including:
  - contact points;
  - Account Manager responsible for the contract for the product or service provided;
  - mechanisms of interaction (including procedures/methods for review of services and escalation of service issues);
  - formats and requirements for service level reporting.
- arrangements for reporting, notification, and investigation of information security incidents and security breaches, as well as violations of the requirements stated in the agreement.

INFORMATION SECURITY CONTROLS REQUIRED

- information security requirements for each element of a product or service provided before access to Forensic Laboratory premises, information, or information processing systems;
- commitment to information security to protect all information and information processing systems against unauthorized access, modification, erasure, or disclosure of information and information processing systems;
- the Forensic Laboratory information security policy, as given in Chapter 4, Appendix 10;
- the risk management process in place;
- asset protection, including:
  - physical and logical processes and procedures to protect the Forensic Laboratory's assets, including premises, information, information processing systems, and software, including management of known vulnerabilities, as defined in Chapter 7, Section 7.6;
  - integrity requirements;
  - confidentiality requirements;
  - availability requirements;
  - authenticity requirements;
  - auditability requirements;
  - accountability requirements;
  - restrictions on copying and disclosing information;
  - controls to ensure the return, or destruction, of information and assets at the end of, or at an agreed point in time during, the agreement.
- processes and procedures for ensuring human resources security, including screening of employees and the right to review screening of employees who can access premises, information, and information processing systems with the right to refuse access, if appropriate;
- access control policy, covering:
  - a process for revoking access rights or interrupting the connection between systems;
  - a requirement to maintain a list of individuals authorized to use the product or service being made available, what their rights and privileges are with respect to such use, and a commitment to provide timely updates to the access list;
  - a statement that all access that is not explicitly authorized is forbidden;
  - an authorization process for user access and privileges;
  - permitted access methods, and the control and use of unique identifiers such as user IDs and passwords;
  - the different reasons, requirements, and benefits that make the access by the third party necessary;
  - the right to monitor, and revoke, any activity related to the Forensic Laboratory's information or information processing systems.
- user and administrator training in methods, procedures, and security;
- ensuring user awareness for information security responsibilities and issues;
- a clear and specified process of incident management, as defined in Chapter 7, Section 7.4.1;
- a clear and specified process of problem management, as defined in Chapter 7, Section 7.4.2;
- a clear and specified process of change management, as defined in Chapter 7, Section 7.4.3;
- a clear and specified process of release management, as defined in Chapter 7, Section 7.4.4;
- a clear and specified process of configuration management, as defined in Chapter 7, Section 7.4.5;
- a clear and specified process of capacity management, as defined in Chapter 7, Section 7.4.6;
- a clear and specified process of service management, as defined in Chapter 7, Section 7.4.7;
- a clear and specified process of service improvement, as defined in Chapter 7, Section 7.4.8;

- a clear and specified process of service reporting, as defined in Chapter 7, Section 7.4.9;
- the establishment of an escalation process for any process;
- the right to audit responsibilities defined in the agreement, to have those audits carried out by a third party, and to enumerate the statutory rights of auditors;
- business continuity processes in place with results of tests being provided, as appropriate, on a timely basis.

LEGAL MATTERS

- the respective liabilities and responsibilities with respect to legal matters and how it is ensured that the legal requirements are met (e.g., privacy legislation, computer-related legislation, etc.);
- intellectual property rights, licensing and copyright assignment, and protection of any collaborative or outsourced work;
- escrow arrangements in the event of failure of the third party.

MISCELLANEOUS

- provision for the transfer of personnel, where appropriate;
- involvement of the Forensic Laboratory or the third party with sub-contractors and the security controls these sub-contractors must implement and the process for advising of, and receiving authorization for, the use of sub-contractors.

CONTRACT TERMINATION AND RE-NEGOTIATION

- conditions for re-negotiation/termination of agreements:
  - a contingency plan should be in place in case either party wishes to terminate the relationship before the end of the agreement;
  - re-negotiation of the agreement if the risk profile or security requirements of either party change.

Note 1

This can be used for Clients and suppliers.

Note 2

This is not a complete checklist and other items should be added as required.

APPENDIX 4 - SLA TEMPLATE FOR PRODUCTS AND SERVICES FOR CLIENTS

As a minimum, the SLA must have the following information included or directly referenced (in other documents):

- brief product or service description;
- validity period and/or SLA change control mechanism;
- product or service authorization details;
- brief description of communications relating to the product or services, including reporting mechanisms and frequencies;
- contact details for Forensic Laboratory employees (and Client employees, if appropriate) authorized to act in emergencies, to participate in incident and problem management, recovery, or workaround, as defined in Chapter 7, Section 7.4.1;
- the service hours (e.g., 09:00 to 17:00, date exceptions (e.g., weekends, public holidays), critical business periods, and out of hours cover, etc.);
- scheduled and agreed interruptions, including notice to be given, number per period;
- Client responsibilities (e.g., security, reporting, instructions, etc.);
- service provider liability and obligations (e.g., security, reporting, instructions, etc.);
- impact and priority guidelines;
- escalation and notification process;
- complaints procedure, as defined in Chapter 6, Section 6.14;
- service targets;
- upper and lower workload limits (e.g., the ability of the product or service to support the expected volume of work or system throughput);
- high-level financial management details relating to the product or service;
- action to be taken in the event of a product or service interruption, based in the incident management procedures, but specifically for the product or service, as defined in Chapter 7, Section 7.4.1;
- housekeeping procedures;
- glossary of terms relating to the product or service, as required;
- supporting and/or related products and services;
- any exceptions to the terms given in the SLA.

APPENDIX 5 - RFX DESCRIPTIONS

There are a number of different documents in the RFx family and a number of others that are used in the Contract Management Process. Though there are a number of textbooks that describe the process in detail, given below is the summary of the RFx documents used in the Forensic Laboratory, their use in the Forensic Laboratory, and the template used as the basis of any of the documents.

REQUEST FOR INFORMATION

RFIs are primarily used as a planning tool to gather information to be used as input to a detailed procurement document (e.g., an RFP). They are typically used where the Forensic Laboratory does not have adequate information about a product or service to be sourced to create a meaningful and detailed procurement document. A large number of possible suppliers (more than 10 perhaps) are identified and sent RFIs. This is a coarse filter to reduce the number of potential suppliers to fewer than five who receive the detailed procurement document. This process will produce information about:

- suppliers and their details (finance, location, capacity, etc.);
- state of the market;
- market trends;
- contact details;
- delivery criteria;
- pricing information;
- product and service offerings;
- product and service plans;
- supplier competition;
- supplier focus (current and future).

> **Note**
> More details may well be collected than the above, but this is a minimum set.

RFQ—REQUEST FOR QUOTATION

RFQs (quotations) are used where it is possible to tightly define the product or service required. There may be the requirement for a fixed price, a range of prices based on quantity, or some other agreed pricing structure.

REQUEST FOR QUALIFICATION

Requests for Qualifications are typically used for obtaining professional service consultancy and evaluation is solely based on the supplier's qualification and price is not considered until after selection. This is a "get the best and worry about price afterwards" approach that may occasionally be appropriate where competency of the supplier is paramount.

REQUEST FOR PROPOSAL

RFPs are used where a solution is needed, but it cannot be clearly and concisely defined, so there are few objective criteria for evaluation available or there are criteria other than price to be considered. These are often based on the results of an RFI response. The supplier is expected to use its best efforts to state how the requirement will be met and use their competence and innovation to propose a solution. Different suppliers will propose different approaches, tools, and methods to be evaluated. The RFP usually results in a creative or collaborative partnership being formed between the supplier and the Forensic Laboratory. It is essential that the RFP is a quality document that captures all requirements and outcomes in as much detail as possible, as this will clearly define the required deliverables. A poorly defined RFP will result in a poorly performing deliverable, if it meets the requirements at all.

REQUEST FOR TENDER

Requests for Tender (RFTs) are used where there is a strict requirement for quality, quantity, and delivery schedules, as opposed to a request being sent to potential suppliers. These are often based on feedback from an RFI and typically ask for a fixed price. RFTs must be tightly defined and where it is possible, be concise and explicit on the product or service definition.

APPENDIX 6 - THE FORENSIC LABORATORY RFX TEMPLATE CHECKLIST

The following template is used, as appropriate, for all RFxs produced in the Forensic Laboratory by choosing the appropriate clauses from the list or adding specific ones relating to the product or service being sourced. It is of no particular order:

- RFx title;
- RFx reference number;
- RFx date;
- Forensic Laboratory details;
- Forensic Laboratory overview;
- addressee;
- applicable Forensic Laboratory policies and procedures—which have to be accepted as part of the contract;
- bankruptcy information (corporate and Top Management);
- business continuity capability;
- business requirements;
- communication processes;

- confidentiality agreement/NDA;
- conflict of interest declaration;
- contact details for any queries;
- contract management process including service reporting;
- contract monitoring, including second party audits;
- contract period;
- contract variance;
- cost/pricing structure;
- delivery criteria;
- delivery schedule;
- description of solutions including appropriate supporting material;
- detailed information on the product or service required;
- draft contract;
- due date;
- evaluation criteria;
- implementation schedule;
- incident management processes;
- information;
- innovative ideas;
- inspection of products and acceptance/rejection process;
- instructions on how to reply to the RFx;
- insurance coverage;
- legal status;
- legislative, regulatory, or other requirements;
- maintenance-related issues;
- outstanding complaints, litigation relating to the supplier and/or the products or services to be supplied;
- past performance;
- performance measures;
- pre-submission conference, if applicable;
- privacy and security measures in place;
- procurement process schedule;
- quality requirements;
- quantities or volumes;
- references;
- relationship with any partners or sub-contractors in the response for provision of products or services;
- relevant experience;
- relevant qualifications (certifications, accreditations, and personal qualifications), including copies where appropriate;
- response format;
- RFx timeline;
- scope of work;
- solutions;
- staffing and competencies;
- supplier's corporate information and profile;
- support available;
- technical proposal evaluation process;
- terms and conditions;
- the supplier selection process;
- training required.

APPENDIX 7 - RFX TIMELINE FOR RESPONSE, EVALUATION, AND SELECTION

The following template is used for defining the timeline for the submission, evaluation, and selection of an RFx document:

Stage	Due Date
Issue RFI	⟨Date⟩
Questions for RFI due by	⟨Date⟩
Responses for RFIs due	⟨Date⟩
Supplier demonstrations	⟨Date⟩
Shortlist defined for receipt of RFP	⟨Date⟩
Issue RFP	⟨Date⟩
Questions for RFP due by	⟨Date⟩
Responses for RFPs due	⟨Date⟩
Supplier demonstrations	⟨Date⟩
Shortlist defined	⟨Date⟩
Site visits and reference taken	⟨Date⟩
Contract negotiations	⟨Date⟩
Contract signed	⟨Date⟩
Service commences	⟨Date⟩

APPENDIX 8 - FORENSIC CONSULTANT'S PERSONAL ATTRIBUTES

Personal attributes for any Forensic Consultant are essential. The Forensic Laboratory recruits Forensic Consultants who have the following personal attributes, as well as other criteria:

- accountable—able to take responsibility for his/her own actions;
- communicative—able to listen to, and effectively interface with, all levels of both Forensic Laboratory and the Client's employees, confidently and with sensitivity relating to the forensic case being processed and any other relevant matters;
- decisive—capable of reaching timely conclusions and opinions based on logical reasoning and analysis of evidence recovered;
- discrete—ensuring that confidentiality of any forensic case processing and any other Forensic Laboratory matters are kept confidential, as defined in Chapter 12, Section 12.3.3.3 or their contract of employment, as applicable;
- ethical—agree to ethical practices and follow relevant codes of conduct and codes of ethics;

- fair—in all dealings giving a balanced view;
- meticulous—in record keeping and report production;
- observant—constantly and actively aware of the Forensic Laboratory's culture and values;
- perceptive—aware of, and able to understand, the need for excellence in forensic case processing and the need for continuous improvement;
- practical—realistic and flexible with good time management;
- self-reliant—able to act and function independently while interacting effectively with others within the Forensic Laboratory;
- tenacious—persistent, focused on achieving objectives;
- truthful—in all aspects of forensic case processing;
- versatile—able to adapt to different situations in forensic cases and provide alternative and creative solutions to forensic case processing situations.

APPENDIX 9 - SOME TIPS FOR SELECTING AN OUTSOURCING SERVICE PROVIDER

This is to find out more about the potential outsource service provider's culture, business model, employees, management, technology, solutions, success, and security. The Forensic Laboratory must determine at the outset whether any proposed outsource service provider is right for their needs. While the evaluation criteria will provide quantitative and repeatable scores for the selection process, some qualitative criteria that should be considered include:

- a commitment to retaining control of operations and services with the Forensic Laboratory;
- a guarantee of not being locked into either particular hardware or proprietary software;
- a proven track record in the operations and services required by the Forensic Laboratory;
- a sustainable business model;
- agreements relating to any IPR created in the outsourcing relationship;
- an appropriate technology refresh cycle;
- appropriate management systems and experience that match the Forensic Laboratory's requirements;
- appropriate references relating to similar outsourcing being provided to the Forensic Laboratory and not just proposed products and services—but mature ones;
- assured continuity of the outsourcing team so that the initial team in the transfer process is the team for the duration of the outsourcing contract;
- broad experience of the required operations and service;
- business profile being appropriate for the Forensic Laboratory's needs;
- details of undertaking the knowledge transfer process;
- declaration of the use of sub-contractors;
- demonstrable and appropriate information security in place to protect the Forensic Laboratory's information and information processing systems against unauthorized access, modification, erasure, or disclosure;
- details of the last technology upgrade undertaken;
- escalation procedures that meet the requirements defined in the Forensic Laboratory's IMS;
- evidence of a quality management system in place, preferably certification to ISO 9001;
- experience in effective handling of human resource issues relating to the transition;
- good, if not outstanding, reference for the provision of the operations and services to be provided across a range of industry sectors;
- guaranteed quantifiable cost savings;
- guarantees that there are no conflicts of interest with any of their, or the Forensic Laboratory's, Clients;
- other recognized international or national accreditations and/or certifications (e.g., ISO 27001, ISO 22301, or relevant national ones according to the jurisdiction);
- project management processes that match the ones in use in the Forensic Laboratory;
- proof of the current and ongoing competence of the outsource service provider's employees (including CPE/CPD).

APPENDIX 10 - AREAS TO CONSIDER FOR OUTSOURCING CONTRACTS

The following do not constitute legal advice, but are the areas where the Forensic Laboratory must ensure that appropriate terms are in an outsourcing contract from an information security viewpoint, not the whole legal contract—which is the domain of Lawyers:

- agree ownership of physical assets;
- agree ownership of software assets;
- define change management process;
- define information security (and other) incident process;
- define SLAs and SLA reporting process;
- determine review dates and checkpoints;
- determine, if appropriate, a pilot with stop/go clauses;
- explicitly define monitoring and reporting processes;
- explicitly define responsibilities;
- explicitly define staffing requirements;
- explicitly define the IPR terms;
- explicitly define the outsourcing requirement scope;
- explicitly define the re-negotiation process;
- explicitly define the termination process;
- explicitly define the transition process;
- explicitly define what is outside the outsourcing scope;
- penalties for non-conformance;
- understand completely the terms of the contract offered. This is even more important if offshoring.

Chapter 15

Effective Records Management

15.1 INTRODUCTION

Every organization has the ability to improve its efficiency and the services it delivers to its Clients, and the Forensic Laboratory is no exception. As the Forensic Laboratory creates documents and records for the majority of its products and services, it is essential that these are suitably protected throughout their life cycle.

The proper management of records is essential for upholding the Forensic Laboratory's reputation as a provider of forensic case processing and digital evidence. It ensures that the Forensic Laboratory can satisfy the scrutiny of other digital forensic experts, as well as the relevant legislative and regulatory processes. Records held by the Forensic Laboratory will be needed as evidence to support the conclusions that the Forensic Analysts make in processing all cases.

An inability to provide records, of known provenance, will be a major failure in the accountability and transparency of the decision-making process, supporting the digital evidence provided and the conclusions drawn from it.

The systematic creation and capture of records in its record keeping systems, supporting activity on any case processed by the Forensic Laboratory, is fundamental to the efficient and effective management of all cases.

The systematic management of records ensures that the Forensic Laboratory is able to:

- conduct all of its business in a structured, orderly, efficient, accountable, and transparent manner, especially forensic case processing;
- meet identified legislative and regulatory requirements in the jurisdiction as well as relevant codes of practice and contractual requirements;
- protect Client and other stakeholder's interests;
- provide continuity of operations in case of any incident that could affect normal business operations;
- support and document all decision making, conclusions reached, and opinions given.

All records must be kept for varying periods of time according to legislation within the jurisdiction, contractual requirements, established good practice, and internal business requirements. The default retention periods for the Forensic Laboratory are given in Chapter 4, Appendix 16. Records must be disposed only in accordance with officially approved disposal procedures and records made of all disposals, as defined in Chapter 12, Section 12.3.14.10.

There are a number of schemes that describe the requirements of storage and management of records, and these include:

- ISO 15489—Information and documentation—Records Management;
- Model Requirements for the Management of Electronic Records Version 2 (MoReq2). Details of functional requirements for MoReq2 are given in Appendix 1;
- Open Archival Information and Systems Reference Model (OAIS). This has been ratified now as ISO 14721;
- Designing and Implementing Record Keeping Systems (DIRKS);
- International Standard Archival Authority Record for Corporate Bodies, Persons, and Families, ISAAR (CPF);
- Electronic Records Management Software Applications Design Criteria Standard—US DoD 5015.02-STD.

The Forensic Laboratory may choose to adopt ISO 15489 as its preferred Records Management standard and implement this as part of its Integrated Management System (IMS). Few Certification Bodies offer certification to ISO 15489, and the Forensic Laboratory should pursue this when it becomes widely available. Mapping of ISO 15489 Part 1 to Forensic Laboratory procedures in the IMS is given in Appendix 2.

In order to understand the concept of "Records Management," some basic definitions and concepts need to be understood.

15.1.1 What is a Record?

ISO 15489 defines a record as "recorded information in any form, including data in computer systems, created or received and maintained by an organization or person in the transaction of business, and kept as evidence of such activity."

Records consist of information recorded in any medium or form, including hardcopy correspondence, spreadsheets, e-mail, databases, content appearing on Web sites, plans, publications, photographs, registers, diaries, film, handwritten notes, and maps. Records are maintained as evidence of any activity relating to a case being processed by the Forensic Laboratory.

Examples of records within the Forensic Laboratory include:

- case instructions;
- case notes;
- complaints;
- computer-generated evidence (e.g., as audit logs);
- evidence recovered;
- exhibits;
- filled in case forms;
- forensic images;
- meeting minutes;
- policies;
- procedures;
- recovery scene documentation, including photographs, drawings, and handwritten notes;
- reports;
- statements or depositions;
- etc.

Records of all types within the Forensic Laboratory are regarded as "assets" within the Forensic Laboratory, as defined in Chapter 12, Section 12.3.14, throughout their life cycle.

When evaluating records, the Forensic Laboratory must determine what physical records must be converted into electronic records, with appropriate linkages. Scanned images must ensure that records are complete, with all linkages correctly in place after migration to the Electronic Records Management System (ERMS).

After scanning of physical record, the Forensic Laboratory must determine what must happen to the original source records. This must be based on Client contracts, legislative and regulatory requirements, and other relevant drivers.

15.1.2 What is a Vital Record?

The Forensic Laboratory defines "Vital Records" as those records without which the Forensic Laboratory could not continue to operate. These records are those, which in the event of a disaster, that are essential for the continued operation of the Forensic Laboratory.

While all records within the Forensic Laboratory have some importance, all of the forensic case records and some general business records are defined as "Vital Records."

Vital Records are those that contain the information needed to re-establish the Forensic Laboratory in case of a disaster that destroys the laboratory. These are the records that protect the Forensic Laboratory's interests and those assets and interests of all other stakeholders, including Clients.

Vital Records are always identified as such. With physical records, they are physically marked on every page or any appropriate place. The marking must not affect the admissibility of hard copy evidence, so in the case of photographs or other similar physical records they are housed in plastic see-through housings that are marked appropriately. Electronic records are marked with their embedded metadata annotated appropriately. All records in the ERMS are marked as appropriately classified, as defined in Chapter 5, Section 5.5.6.6 and given in Chapter 5, Appendix 16.

15.1.3 What is a Document?

While a record is evidence of an activity, a document is formatted information that can be used by any Forensic Laboratory employee, typically in electronic, digital, or paper format. They serve to convey information to other recipients of the documents, both inside the Forensic Laboratory or outside it. Examples of documents within the Forensic Laboratory include:

- agendas;
- blank forms waiting to be filled in;
- books or instruction manuals for equipment;
- checklists.

> **Note 1**
> Agendas are not records, they are the intention of the meeting, and the minutes produced are the records.

> **Note 2**
> Blank forms become records when they are filled in (e.g., an exhibit movement form, as given in Chapter 8, Appendix 17).

15.1.4 What is Records Management?

Records Management is a logical and organized approach to the creation, maintenance, use, and disposition of records, as given in Section 15.6, Chapter 4, Appendix 16; Chapter 12, Section 12.3.14.10. Records Management ensures that the Forensic Laboratory can control the quality and quantity of information that it creates and receives, and ensures that it is able to meet the requirements of its stakeholders and meets its legislative, regulatory, and other business requirements.

15.1.5 What is a Record Keeping System?

A record keeping system is "an information system that captures, maintains, and provides access to records over time." This can be a manual system that will typically store paper records (e.g., filing cabinets and files and the contents of the Secure Property Store for paper records) or an electronic system (e.g., a database or an ERMS).

15.1.6 Records Life Cycle

Records all go through a common life cycle, and this is:

- creation;
- use;
- retention;
- disposal.

Between the creation and use stages, records are defined as being "current," i.e., they are used to carry out day-to-day work (Figure 15.1).

Between the use and retention stages, the records are defined as "semi-current," i.e., they only need to be referred to occasionally or have to be retained for legal, regulatory, contractual, or other business reasons.

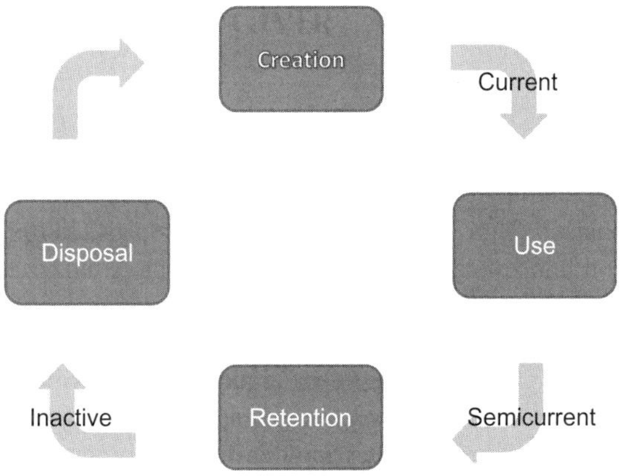

FIGURE 15.1 Record life cycle. (For color version of this figure, the reader is referred to the online version of this chapter.)

Between the retention and disposal stages, the records are defined as "inactive," i.e., a decision has to be made whether to keep them or dispose of them.

15.1.7 Why Records Must be Managed

Correct Record Management in the Forensic Laboratory underpins the whole of the forensic case processing and associated administrative processes. It is essential that if the Forensic Laboratory is to uphold its reputation as a transparent, competent, and accountable forensic service provider. The need to properly manage records is evidenced by the crucial role that they play in all aspects of a forensic case. Only too often are cases lost as the evidence is tainted due to failures in Record Management, typically, evidence movement.

15.1.8 Benefits of Effective Records Management

There are numerous benefits to be gained by the Forensic Laboratory embracing good practice for Records Management. These include:

- allowing rapid identification and recovery of records;
- conducting the Forensic Laboratory's business in an orderly, efficient, and accountable manner;
- defining authorities and responsibilities, as given in Appendix 15, and various job descriptions, as defined in Chapter 18, Section 18.1.5;
- defining consistent procedures for managing records throughout the Forensic Laboratory;
- delivering the Forensic Laboratory's products and services in a consistent and equitable manner;
- ensuring continuity whenever Forensic Laboratory employees move employment;
- facilitating finding records requested through legal processes, e.g., discovery orders, or similar;
- improving quality of information by providing Forensic Laboratory employees with reliable and up-to-date records;
- increasing efficiency by ensuring records are readily identifiable and available;
- maintaining corporate, personal, and collective memory;
- meeting legislative and regulatory requirements including archival, audit, and oversight activities;
- preventing the illegal, arbitrary, and premature destruction of records, thereby protecting the Forensic Laboratory's corporate memory and ensuring that it is kept available for future reference;
- promoting administrative efficiencies by ensuring that Forensic Laboratory employees, and third parties acting on their behalf, have timely access to relevant and complete records;

- promoting informed decision making;
- protecting the interests of the organization and the rights of employees, Clients, and present and future stakeholders;
- providing consistency, continuity, and productivity in management and administration;
- provide continuity in the event of a disaster;
- providing evidence of business and personal decisions and actions on forensic cases processed by the Forensic Laboratory;
- providing protection and support in defending decisions made by the Forensic Laboratory in all forensic case processing;
- saving space by preventing records from being held longer than necessary;
- underpinning the Forensic Laboratory's accountability and transparency by ensuring that its case processing processes can stand up to external scrutiny, if required.

15.1.9 Stakeholders in the Forensic Laboratory's Record Keeping Process

The Forensic Laboratory is accountable to a number of stakeholders who all have an interest in the Forensic Laboratory's effective and efficient management of its records. These include, but are not limited to:

- Forensic Laboratory management;
- Forensic Laboratory employees;
- Clients;
- Courts;
- law enforcement;
- lawyers;
- other digital forensic experts;
- Regulators, where appropriate;
- Auditors.

15.2 LEGISLATIVE, REGULATORY, AND OTHER REQUIREMENTS

15.2.1 Legislative, Regulatory Requirements, and Codes of Practice

The Forensic Laboratory, depending on its location and relevant jurisdiction, is subject to a number of legislative, regulatory, and other requirements that affect digital forensic case processing operations and also the requirements to undertake Record Management. It is essential that the Forensic Laboratory understands these requirements in its Records Management policies and procedures and is able to evidence this.

These include:

- legislation;
- regulation;
- contractual requirements;
- mandatory standards of practice;
- voluntary codes of conduct and ethics—both organizationally and individually.

While there are a number of pieces of legislation that specifically cover record keeping, the majority of them have some implications of record keeping within the Forensic Laboratory. While these will vary between jurisdictions, a generic set of legislation and regulation that can affect the Forensic Laboratory has been identified, and is given in Appendix 3.

Typically, these will have requirements in them for:

- definitions of a "record" and record types;
- requirements for a record keeping plan defined;
- how records are handled during the record life cycle;
- security of data, especially personal data;
- retention periods;
- disposal methods;
- responsibilities and accountabilities;
- requirements for training;
- requirements for auditing and other monitoring activities;
- offences and penalties for compliance failure.

15.2.2 Principles of Record Management Within the Forensic Laboratory

Records, within the Forensic Laboratory, are created or received, accessed, and stored during processing of forensic cases as well as day-to-day business activities.

In order to comply with the relevant legislative, contractual, and business requirements, as well as providing appropriate traceability, accountability, and transparency, the Forensic Laboratory should implement a record keeping process. This has been developed and implemented to create and maintain authentic, reliable and useable records, and protect the integrity of those records, for as long as required.

In order to implement the record keeping system, the Forensic Laboratory needs to undertake a process that determines what records should be created, managed, and retained in each process relating to either forensic case processing or normal business activities. This includes:

- assessing the risks of failure to have authentic and reliable records, as defined in Chapter 5;
- complying with relevant legislative, contractual, and business requirements, as well as internal Forensic Laboratory processes, procedures and work instructions, as defined in Chapter 12, Section 12.3.13.1;
- deciding how to organize records so as to support requirements for use;

- determining requirements for retrieving, using, and transmitting records between business processes and other users;
- ensuring that all records are secured according to their classification and any other relevant requirements, specifically legislative ones, as given in Chapter 5, Appendix 16;
- ensuring that records are retained according to the Forensic Laboratory Record Retention schedule, as given in Chapter 4, Appendix 16;
- deciding how that metadata will be persistently linked and managed;
- identifying the metadata that should be created with the record and through record processing;
- identifying and evaluating opportunities for continued improvement of the effectiveness, efficiency, or quality of the record keeping processes;
- preserving records and making them available to authorized Forensic Laboratory employees according to legitimate business needs;
- deciding the form and structure of records that should be created and managed.

15.3 RECORD CHARACTERISTICS

Records, within the Forensic Laboratory, must have the following characteristics.

15.3.1 General Requirements

Within the Forensic Laboratory, all records must be able to show that they accurately reflect the message of the record, be that actions taken, decisions made, or instructions or material communicated. All records within the Forensic Laboratory have to be able to support the business in its defined needs for those records and provide a transparent, accountable audit trail for the record's life cycle.

As well as the record itself, the integral metadata (for electronic records having such a facility) or the associated metadata (for paper records and electronic records that do not have appropriate integral metadata) must be permanently and irrevocably linked to the record by the appropriate means to fully document any business transaction involving the record.

In the Forensic Laboratory, the metadata used must define the following functions:

- the business context in which the record was created, received, and used should be apparent in the record, whether it be for a forensic case or in general business transactions;
- the links between any documents that may be combined to either form a whole or part of a record (e.g., manuals or checklists used to create a specific piece of evidence);
- the links between the record and other records that may combine to create a whole forensic case;
- the structure of the record (i.e., record structure and relationships between the elements that make up the record itself, to ensure that the record remains intact and of known integrity).

The Records Management processes and procedures used within the Forensic Laboratory must be used to produce records with the following attributes, where much of this is achieved using the procedures shown in Chapter 4, Section 4.6.4.

15.3.1.1 Record Authenticity

Record authenticity is essential in the Forensic Laboratory, as the records created and used by the Forensic Laboratory employees are used in forensic cases.

The Forensic Laboratory defines an authentic record as one where it can be proved that it:

- has been created or sent at the time purported (i.e., nonrepudiation of time, typically by digital time stamping);
- has been created or sent by the person who claims to have created or sent it (i.e., nonrepudiation or origin);
- is what it claims to be.

The Forensic Laboratory must implement procedures for information handling and information security that ensure that all Forensic Laboratory users:

- are not permitted to use accounts that do not provide accountability (e.g., Administrator, root, etc.), unless appropriate compensating controls are in place, as defined Chapter 12, Section 12.6;
- are uniquely identified, as defined Chapter 12, Section 12.6.6.3;
- have a full user account registration history available, as defined Chapter 12, Section 12.6.4;
- have their access rights regularly reviewed for continued business need, as defined Chapter 12, Section 12.6.7;
- have their access rights set by the relevant information, system, process, or business owners, as defined Chapter 12, Section 12.6.

In addition to the management of all user accounts, the Forensic Laboratory uses a mixture of organizational and technical controls to ensure that records are protected against:

- unauthorized access;
- unauthorized disclosure;
- unauthorized destruction;
- unauthorized modification;
- unauthorized use.

and that during a record's life cycle, using organizational or technical measures, the following processes are controlled:

- record creation;
- record disposition;
- record maintenance;
- record receipt;
- record transfer;
- record use.

15.3.1.2 Record Reliability

Record reliability is essential in the Forensic Laboratory, as the records created and used by the Forensic Laboratory employees are used in forensic cases.

All records must be able to stand internal and external scrutiny and be depended on as a full and accurate representation of the transaction(s), activity(ies), or fact(s) to which they provide evidence.

In most cases, records within the Forensic Laboratory are created contemporaneously by the person undertaking the transaction or activity to which the record relates. If not contemporaneous, procedures must mandate the creation of records immediately afterward, as soon as is reasonable practicable.

Where records are received from a third party, the Forensic Laboratory has no direct control over their reliability. However, they should:

- be logged into the Forensic Laboratory record keeping system on receipt;
- be handled in accordance with contractual requirements, information security classifications, or other instructions accompanying them, as given in Chapter 12, Section 12.3.14.9;
- be securely stored in the Secure Property Store, if appropriate;
- ensure that all movements of the record are tracked, as appropriate, for internal movement or disposition, using the movement sheet, as given in Chapter 8, Appendix 17;
- have a full evidence trail for the complete time while in the possession of the Forensic Laboratory.

15.3.1.3 Record Integrity

Record integrity is essential in the Forensic Laboratory, as the records created and used by the Forensic Laboratory employees are used in forensic cases at various Courts and Tribunals.

Integrity, when dealing with any records, refers to the record being complete and unaltered by any unauthorized process. Authorized processes and procedures can be used for either updating or annotating an existing record, but these will all have an audit trail associated with them.

Record updating or annotation can only be undertaken by Forensic Laboratory employees who are specifically authorized to perform these tasks in accordance with their user access rights to the record, as defined in Chapter 12, Section 12.6.5.1.

The audit trail of any record in the Forensic Laboratory should show, as a minimum, the following:

- the identity of person (or process) making the update or annotation;
- the date of update or annotation;
- the time of annotation;
- the update or annotation made.

Depending on the system in use, the following may also be recorded:

- IP address of machine used;
- machine identity of machine used.

15.3.1.4 Record Usability

There is no point in the Forensic Laboratory having records that are not fit for purpose and use.

The Forensic Laboratory defines a usable record as one that can be:

- assured to be reliable;
- easily and fully retrieved from the Forensic Laboratory record keeping system;
- easily located in the Forensic Laboratory record keeping system;
- interpreted by both Forensic Laboratory employees and any relevant external parties (e.g., other forensic experts, lawyers, law enforcement, or a Court of competent jurisdiction);
- of assured integrity;
- only created by an authorized user;
- presented in a meaningful manner to its intended audience or recipients;
- securely stored in the Forensic Laboratory record keeping system;
- shown to be directly related to the transaction(s), activity(ies), or fact(s) to which it provides evidence;
- shown to have all appropriate linkages to other related documents, records, or sequence steps;
- shown to identify the processes and procedures that created it;
- shown to identify the relevant context (business or forensic case), with appropriate details.

15.4 A RECORDS MANAGEMENT POLICY

15.4.1 Why a Record Keeping Policy?

The Forensic Laboratory is accountable for all of its actions relating to the forensic cases it processes and this is typically evidenced through the existence and maintenance of good record keeping allowing traceable fact-based decision taking to be demonstrated.

A policy is the key component of any "leg" of good corporate governance, including management standards, and it sets the scene for an appropriate direction and cultural requirement within the Forensic Laboratory.

ISO 15489 also asserts the importance of corporate control structures by stipulating the policy as a requirement for compliance to the standard. "An organization seeking to conform to this part of ISO 15489 should establish, document, maintain, and promulgate policies, procedures, and practices for Records Management to ensure that its business need for evidence, accountability, and information about its activities is met."

Within the Forensic Laboratory, it should be used to demonstrate its commitment to undertake record keeping in an effective, efficient, diligent, and accountable manner. It is also used to:

- show that it applies to all relevant records regardless of format, including electronic records;
- communicate this commitment clearly and effectively to all employees;
- define the record keeping responsibilities of all Forensic Laboratory employees;
- demonstrate commitment to comply with record keeping standards and guidelines;
- demonstrate Top Management commitment through the authorization of the policy;
- identify any legislation that affects the Forensic Laboratory's record keeping requirements within the jurisdiction;
- promote good record keeping practices.

15.4.2 Key Components of a Record Keeping Policy

In keeping with other policies, a record keeping policy should be a brief set of statements that provides a broad picture of how the Forensic Laboratory should create and manage its records to satisfy legislative, regulatory, business, and relevant stakeholder expectations.

Typically, the following headings are used:

- purpose;
- policy statement;
- scope;
- policy context;
- legislation, regulation, and standards;
- record keeping systems;
- responsibilities;
- monitoring and review;
- authorization;
- policy review.

The Forensic Laboratory Record Keeping Policy is given in Appendix 4.

15.5 DEFINING THE REQUIREMENTS FOR RECORDS MANAGEMENT IN THE FORENSIC LABORATORY

15.5.1 General

Note

The requirements defined below are applicable to both paper and digital records, but the implementation and benefits may only be applicable to digital records in some cases (e.g., metadata). No distinction is made below between each type of record; it is up to the reader to determine what is applicable to which type of record.

In defining an appropriate Record Management System within the Forensic Laboratory, a project should be set up to identify the optimum system to be implemented for the way that the Forensic Laboratory actually works. It showed how the Forensic Laboratory will define the systems it requires for the way it works and for the requirements of the jurisdictions within which it operates. This can be used as a template to implement a Record Management System or as a template to determine a tailored solution that meets specific needs.

15.5.2 Objectives

Prior to starting to define requirements for Records Management in the Forensic Laboratory, Top Management has to identify and agree the objectives to be met by the new system. After a number of workshops, Top Management must agree to the objectives that are given in Appendix 5.

15.5.3 Choosing a Design and Implementation Methodology

The Forensic Laboratory may choose to use the standard System Development Life Cycle process to manage the design and implementation of its Records Management System. This has the traditional eight steps:

- initiation;
- feasibility;
- analysis;
- design;
- development;
- testing;
- implementation;
- postimplementation review.

The Forensic Laboratory should adapt these to suit its requirements as below:

15.5.3.1 Initiation

Top Management must support the project and become the project sponsors appointing an experienced project manager to oversee the project. A team of subject matter experts will be assembled to evaluate the feasibility of the project.

Resources throughout the Forensic Laboratory for undertaking the project will be identified and protected to ensure that they are available for the project. This can be assisted by using a "responsibilities chart" clearly showing roles, boundaries, timescales, budgets, and targets.

15.5.3.2 Feasibility Study

The team carries out preliminary investigations to produce a business case for the implementation of an appropriate Records Management System. Information is collected using the following methods:

- competitive evaluation;
- examination of documentation;
- interviews;
- observation;
- sampling;
- workshops.

In order to determine the Forensic Laboratory's:

- business drivers;
- contractual drivers;
- critical success factors;
- legislative drivers;
- political drivers;
- regulatory drivers;
- requirements to meet good practice;
- specific roles and functions.

and define the ideal requirements for a Record Management System suitable for the Forensic Laboratory, this is then compared and contrasted against the existing Records Management System and the gaps and weaknesses are identified. The business case is based on these findings, resource requirements, and associated costings.

The business case is then presented to the Forensic Laboratory Top Management, who approves the project based on the business case. The outline of a business case is given in Appendix 6. The outline of the ERMS project is given in Appendix 7.

15.5.3.3 Business Analysis

Once approval for the project to start has been given, it is essential to determine the detailed requirements for each business process or function in the Forensic Laboratory to determine the information flows within and between different business functions. It is seen as essential that the whole of the Forensic Laboratory is evaluated rather than on a department-by-department basis. Often a departmental strategy will be ideal for that department alone and not fit into an organization-wide strategy.

The method of collection of this information is the same as the initial feasibility, but using specialized questionnaires and forms for the workshops.

It is essential to determine what records are kept and why and how they fit into the overall record retention schedule. Only too often, it is discovered that records are held "just in case" and this is wasteful of resources and in some cases is actually illegal. Retention limits, as well as, archiving requirements and purging functions all were included in defining what records should be retained, and what should be destroyed.

For each business activity, whether part of forensic case processing or the general business of the Forensic Laboratory, each business function, activity, and transaction must be examined to establish a hierarchy of them, their interactions, and document the flow of business processes and the transactions that comprise them. This leads to the risk of not having appropriate records in place or the risk of failing to have an appropriate Record Management System in place based on the drivers established in the Feasibility Stage. This may identify that there are some records that could be created and stored totally in electronic media, while there may still be a need for non-electronic records (e.g., bench journals, notebooks, paper forms, etc.). This may lead to the development of a hybrid Record Management System that best satisfies the needs of the Forensic Laboratory.

It is essential that the Forensic Laboratory defines its true requirements for Records Management. Simply finding a better method of managing the current volume of records in the Forensic Laboratory is not the desired outcome of the project.

15.5.3.4 Existing Records Management System Evaluation

Once the ideal Record Management System for the Forensic Laboratory had been defined using the results of the stages above, it will be necessary to determine how well the existing systems meet these requirements. This is carried out by evaluating all of the specific requirements of the ideal system against the existing system and producing a "Gap Analysis." The Gap Analysis also evaluates the risks of failure of compliance with the ideal requirements.

15.5.3.5 Resolution Strategies

Having evaluated the gaps between the existing Records Management System and the ideal Records Management System, a number of strategies can be developed to address the gap.

A variety of strategies that can be considered include:

- do nothing;
- change existing policies and procedures;
- apply different strategies to physical records and electronic records;
- amend the existing ERMS to cover new requirements;
- convert all physical records to electronic records and purchase a new ERMS;
- convert all physical records to electronic records and amend the existing ERMS to cover new requirements;
- purchase a new ERMS that handles electronic records as required but allows registration of physical records as well and allows all records in the Forensic Laboratory to be handled in a consistent manner. This may mean that two systems will have to be run in parallel, the ERMS as well as the physical record registry.

Each of the strategies should be evaluated, and during this, some changes may be suggested to them as part of the evaluation process. Consideration of the risk, costs, feasibility of implementation in a timely manner, user acceptance, and other criteria must be undertaken, and eventually a strategy is to be chosen.

15.5.3.6 Selection of an ERMS

Once the decision as to which strategy has been taken, products in the market place can be evaluated for those that meet the specific requirements stated by the Forensic Laboratory.

This should be carried out by the traditional Request for Information (RFI) and Request for Proposal (RFP) process against a large number of suppliers. The criteria used for selecting products are given in Appendix 8.

A short list is then produced and Requests for Proposal (RFPs) sent to them. These can then be evaluated, and a selection is made.

15.5.3.7 Pilot Implementation and Testing

The implementation stage is carried out with assistance from the Supplier and performed as a "Pilot Exercise" to see how the system will work, and check that the Supplier's claims were valid.

A variety of different records in both physical and electronic format can then be loaded into the ERMS for testing purposes. At the same time, a new Document Registry can be built for the pilot and the physical records housed in the Secure Property Store. As the ERMS is being implemented, a variety of documentation will need to be produced. This includes:

- policies;
- procedures;
- work instructions;
- forms;
- checklists;
- test packs and expected test results;
- training.

Once the proof of concept has been satisfactorily demonstrated, agreement can be given to migrate all of the records to the new ERMS.

All stakeholders are signatories at all gates in the project so collective responsibility is assured and any risks are knowingly accepted. This will be formally approved at the CAB, using the Forensic Laboratory's change management system defined in Chapter 7, Section 7.4.3.

The project, including the pilot, can be run using standard project management processes from the Project Management Institute.

15.5.3.8 Full Implementation and Record Migration

The full implementation is a phased process, migrating function by function within the Forensic Laboratory. As a fallback, it may be decided to run the new and old system in parallel for a number of months, where possible. This will identify any variations with the full migration to the new system. Full testing is carried out, as defined in Chapter 12, Section 12.8.3.

Once full migration has been achieved, it may be decided that all electronic records from the old system should be retained as an archive and still retain their authenticity, reliability, integrity, and usability, in case of need. The choice will be made as to whether the archive is to be indefinite, with relevant hardware, operating system software, and application software retained in case of the need to fallback.

As part of the implementation process, all users of the ERMS should be given appropriate training, as defined in Section 15.8.1.1, which is to be recorded on all personnel files, as defined in Chapter 4, Section 4.6.2.3 and Chapter 18.2.1.8. Specific and detailed training must be given to the Forensic Laboratory Service Desk as they are providing first and second line support.

15.5.3.9 Decommissioning an old ERMS

Where an old ERMS is to be decommissioned, no more records shall be added to it, even though they should be accessible. During parallel running, they will be online, but once the new ERMS is fully accepted, the old ERMS can be archived, including all relevant hardware and software, so that it can be decommissioned if needed. The decision to perform disposal and disposition on the archived system will depend on legislative requirements.

The archived system must still be able to prove that all records held in it have retained their authenticity, reliability, integrity, and usability, as defined in Section 15.3.1.

15.5.3.10 Post Implementation Review

A post implementation review (PIR) must be carried out as a multiple phase PIR for the ERMS, as it is so critical to the services and products provided by the Forensic Laboratory. The initial PIR will be carried out after a month and can consist of a questionnaire to all users to obtain subjective qualitative and quantitative feedback about the system.

Details of a user questionnaire are given in Appendix 9.

After 3 months, a full system PIR was undertaken as there should be enough system records available (including the Service Desk) as well as user familiarity with the system. The PIR is evaluated against the criteria defined in the RFI.

After the PIR has been completed, regular reviews of the ERMS are undertaken and reported on at the Management Reviews, as defined in Chapter 4, Section 4.9, with trending information. Any shortfall or non-conformance identified is then raised and tracked through the CAPA system, as defined in Chapter 4, Section 4.8.

15.6 DETERMINING FORENSIC LABORATORY RECORDS TO BE MANAGED BY THE ERMS

15.6.1 General

One of the most important decisions in Records Management is to ensure that the correct records are retained in the Forensic Laboratory. There are two types of records held in the Forensic Laboratory:

- forensic case records;
- general business records.

As has been noted earlier, some records fall into both categories (e.g., financial records relating to case billing).

15.6.2 General Business Records

The Forensic Laboratory approach to physical records may be to scan all physical records, retaining originals where necessary in the secure property store. Scanned records are then registered in the ERMS and copies associated in the relevant case file or general business file.

Having scanned and digitized all physical records, linked them to the ERMS, they can be easily located and accessed.

General business records to be retained will depend on a variety of factors and these will depend on how the Forensic Laboratory is structured and how it operates. As this book is about digital forensics, these records have been ignored, and what is included in the Forensic Laboratory will be a matter of choice for the Top Management. However, they will be subject to many of the requirements and controls below for forensic case processing records.

15.6.3 Forensic Case Records

Forensic case records to be managed by the Forensic Laboratory can be identified by:

- legislative and regulatory requirements;
- accountability requirements for case processing within the jurisdiction;
- good practice;
- existing procedures in place for case processing;
- the risk of not being able to produce records as part of a forensic case during its life cycle.

In practical terms, this actually means that for any case, including quotations and estimates for cases not processed by the Forensic Laboratory, all records from initial contact to case disposition must be retained in the ERMS. Case disposition can be either transferred from the Forensic Laboratory to a third party authorized to receive them or destruction at the end of the relevant retention time period for the case type by Forensic Laboratory employees.

Forensic case records that are stored on digital media will usually have metadata that can be attached to the record. A list of metadata in use in the Forensic Laboratory for MicroSoft Office Documents and E-mail is given in Appendices 10 and 11, respectively.

There are other packages that can also store metadata and these should be used as required. One example of metadata in another program is the use of Exchangeable Image File (Exif) format. Exif is a standard that specifies the formats for images, sound, and ancillary tags used by digital cameras (including smart phones), scanners, and other hardware handling recorded image and sound files.

The metadata tags defined in the Exif standard cover a broad spectrum of information such as:

- artist (camera owner)*;
- camera settings (e.g., the camera model and make, and information that varies with each image such as orientation (rotation), aperture, shutter speed, focal length, metering mode, and ISO speed information);
- copyright information;
- date and time a picture was taken*;
- descriptions (of the image);

- thumbnail preview of the image on the camera's LCD screen, in file managers, or in photo manipulation software.

Note 1

The list above is not complete, for a full description of Exif data in use look in the current standard V2.3 CIPA DC—008 Translation 2010, Exchangeable image file format for digital still cameras.

Note 2

Those items marked with an "*" are only accurate if the camera has had these details set, otherwise their default is "null."

Note 3

There are also specifications for .jpeg files and .wav files.

Note 4

Another common form of metadata is XMP in Adobe products.

Care must be exercised when using Exif data or relying on it for the following reasons:

- Exif does not store time zone-related information with the image, resulting in time recorded for the image being made of dubious provenance;
- Exif is not a maintained standard;
- Exif is very often used in images created by scanners, but the standard makes no provisions for any scanner-specific information;
- Exif only specifies a format for .tiff and .jpeg files;
- Exif standard has no provision for video files;
- Exif uses file offset pointers that can become easily corrupted;
- some manufacturers use camera settings not defined in the Exif standard.

It is for the reasons above that the Forensic Laboratory enters manual metadata with such images or audio files, treating them as paper records in the ERMS.

Paper records have their metadata entered with an image of the record into the ERMS, the original record being deposited in the Document Registry in the Secure Property Store.

A list of some of the forensic case records stored by the Forensic Laboratory is given in Appendix 12.

15.6.4 Document Retention

Business records and forensic case records managed by the Forensic Laboratory are retained for set periods of time according to the requirements defined a variety of sources. Record retention within the Forensic Laboratory must:

- meet current legislative and regulatory requirements, though consideration of changes to legislation and regulation that may become effective needs to be considered during the life cycle of a forensic case;
- meet current and future needs of all stakeholders for all forensic cases. This will include all of the interests of stakeholders that have an interest in a forensic case. This can include law enforcement, lawyers, the Courts, other forensic experts, etc.;
- meet current and future internal business needs for forensic case processing within the Forensic Laboratory. This includes decisions and activities relating to forensic case processing as part of the Forensic Laboratory's corporate memory in case of future need. As well as maintaining the Forensic Laboratory's corporate memory it also allows traceability, transparency, and accountability to be assured, while disposing of records when they are no longer required through an authorized process, as defined in Chapter 12, Section 12.3.14.10.3. This process also ensures that the record's reliability and authenticity can be assured by future users, even on changes of technology, so long as the record transfer has been carried out according to the Forensic Laboratory record transfer procedures;
- consider the risk of not being able to produce records as part of a forensic case during its life cycle.

In practical terms, this actually means that for any forensic case, including quotations and estimates for cases not processed by the Forensic Laboratory, all records from initial contact to case disposition are retained in the ERMS. Case disposition can be either transfer from the Forensic Laboratory to a third party authorized to receive them or destruction at the end of the relevant retention time period for the case type. The record of Forensic Laboratory's retention policy is given in Chapter 4, Appendix 16.

15.7 USING METADATA IN THE FORENSIC LABORATORY

Record keeping metadata may be defined as data describing the context, content, and structure of records and their management over their complete life cycle. In essence, metadata facilitates the Record Management process by giving context to the content of the record and facilitates Record Management according to the Forensic Laboratory's record keeping principles.

Depending on the record type and the jurisdiction, there may be legislative or other requirements for the application and use of metadata.

Using metadata considerably facilitates the accessibility to, and management of, records in the Forensic Laboratory. It enables records to be found whenever they are needed by providing different search methods for the efficient location of relevant records, and it allows tight control to be exercised over access to confidential and sensitive information.

The use of metadata to control access to information is extremely important, especially where there are confidentiality or privacy implications. This includes all forensic case records as well as internal administrative records such as Human Resources records.

The audit trail provided by metadata can be crucial in giving assurances about a record's authenticity by authoritatively demonstrating who created the record, when it was accessed, modified, and destroyed. The use of metadata also plays an important role in helping to ensure that records are retained for their appropriate retention period before any disposition action can be undertaken.

The systematic and consistent application of metadata is used in the Forensic Laboratory to assist in the record keeping process and to ensure that the Forensic Laboratory's records can be relied upon to support all of their operations relating to forensic case processing and internal operations.

15.7.1 The Benefits of Creating and Using Metadata

It is essential that records that have been captured into the Forensic Laboratory's ERMS can be efficiently retrieved whenever needed. Furthermore, records require sufficient contextual and descriptive metadata to ensure that they are meaningful and can be properly managed over time.

Accordingly, the creation and use of metadata provides the following benefits:

- enabling access to confidential records, or those subject to privacy requirements, to be effectively controlled by assigning relevant access/security levels at the time of creation and/or registration into the Forensic Laboratory's ERMS;
- enabling records required for a specific forensic case or investigation to be readily identified;
- enabling the efficient searching for records by utilizing various search criteria including search by title, keywords, dates, location;
- ensuring that records are retained for their minimum retention period;
- facilitating compliance with legislative, regulatory, contractual, business, and good practice requirements;
- facilitating efficient and timely disposition of records;
- facilitating the migration of records through successive upgrades of hardware and software and providing evidence of these activities;
- providing audit trails that show evidence of who has accessed a record and when;
- providing evidence of disposition actions;
- supporting accountability, auditing processes, and transparency of processes relating to record use within the Forensic Laboratory.

From the benefits above, it is easy to see why metadata for record keeping purposes is an integral component of Records Management within the Forensic Laboratory.

There are two main standards for metadata, these are:

- Dublin Core Data Initiative (DCMI), since adopted by ISO as ISO 15386. Information and documentation—The Dublin Core Metadata Element Set. There are 15 core elements of the Dublin Core Metadata Standard, and these are given in Appendix 13;
- National Archives of Australia Metadata Standard, which captures up to 25 different elements, and these are given in Appendix 14.

The Forensic Laboratory uses a mixture of both standards.

15.7.2 Responsibilities

The general roles and responsibilities for record keeping in the Forensic Laboratory are given in the Records Management Policy, as given in Appendix 4.

Generic requirements are given in Appendix 15 with specific requirements being given in Chapter 18 in specific job descriptions.

15.7.3 Record Keeping Metadata Needed

In order to manage records appropriately within the Forensic Laboratory, it is necessary to use metadata within the ERMS as well as metadata within each record where metadata can be stored. In the case of the Forensic Laboratory, this is entering metadata for records into the Microsoft Office Suite.

15.7.3.1 In the ERMS

There are a number of metadata fields that are needed for the management of records within the Forensic Laboratory, and the ones used are listed in Appendix 10 for Office documents and Appendix 11 for e-mail.

15.7.3.2 Microsoft Office Suite

All of the Forensic Laboratory case processing and business processes are underpinned by the Microsoft Office Suite. The use of the Microsoft Office Suite requires the input of metadata in the following packages, at least:

- Access;
- Excel;

- PowerPoint;
- Word.

Outlook (e-mail) has a different set of rules and the relevant metadata for e-mail must be used.

It is therefore essential that all Forensic Laboratory employees comply with the requirement to create minimum metadata for the records they create using Microsoft Office applications, as given in Appendix 10.

The automatically entered metadata, which is shown under "Properties" in each of the Microsoft Office application suite, includes, but is not limited to:

- author;
- date document created;
- date last accessed;
- date last printed;
- date modified;
- location of the document.

While documents are created in Microsoft Office, some of the metadata is automatically created; however, this must be checked to ensure that it is correct, it will also need input for fields such as "keywords," etc.

Other metadata must be manually entered under "Properties." This includes the:

- comments;
- document subject;
- document title;
- keywords.

15.7.3.3 E-Mail

E-mail transmissions are official Forensic Laboratory records within the meaning of the law and are therefore subject to the same record keeping requirements as records created or registered as part of forensic case processing or everyday business operations.

As with any record, all e-mail messages, together with any attachments, must be included in the Forensic Laboratory ERMS system, and securely retained according to relevant legislative, regulatory, contractual, and business requirements. Without record keeping metadata, e-mail messages cannot be accepted as authentic and reliable evidence of the business activity it purports to support.

It is essential that associated metadata is captured and stored with each e-mail record. Without this metadata, the meaning and value of the e-mail as an authentic record is considerably de-valued.

In many Court cases, email evidence, and its authenticity, is frequently challenged. In the Forensic Laboratory, using the ERMS, it shall be possible to prove that:

- an e-mail message was sent through a certain server(s);
- the date and time it was delivered to the recipient;
- the date and time it was read by the recipient;
- the date and time it was sent to the recipient.

Automatically generated metadata such as the sender, recipient, date and time is tagged to e-mail transmissions. To facilitate the correct classification of the e-mail record, the Forensic Laboratory employees must always include a title in the subject heading.

Sample e-mail metadata to be captured and managed for all e-mail messages (based on Microsoft Outlook) is given in Appendix 11.

15.7.3.4 Hard Copy Records On-Site

There are a number of occasions when hard copy records are either created in the Forensic Laboratory or received by it. These need to be tracked in the same way as on-site electronic records. Within the Forensic Laboratory, all hard copy records are assigned a record number (typically a bar code).

Metadata is then recorded in the record in the ERMS against the record number, as given in Appendix 10.

15.7.3.5 Hard Copy Records Sent Off-Site

Records of hard copy records that are sent off-site must also be maintained (e.g., off-site secure archive stores). While it is not possible to attach metadata to hard copy records in the same way as it is with electronic records, it is possible to assign them in the Forensic Laboratory ERMS.

The data used in the ERMS within the Forensic Laboratory are given in Appendix 16.

15.7.3.6 Retaining Metadata

Record keeping metadata is essentially a record in itself and, as such, should be treated as a record. Where electronic records are created (e.g., Microsoft Word), then the record's metadata is integral to the record itself and both are treated as one record. In some cases, however, the metadata for a record is retained separately from the record (e.g., a paper record where the record keeping metadata has been entered into the Forensic Laboratory's ERMS).

In general, most record keeping metadata associated with a record must be retained for at least as long as the retention period of the record to which it relates. In some cases, the record keeping metadata must be retained for a longer period.

Retaining some record keeping metadata elements past the life of a record to which they are linked is an integral part of demonstrating accountability and transparency. It provides, for example, auditable evidence of the Forensic Laboratory's record disposition authority and actions.

The Forensic Laboratory should consider retaining the following in the ERMS after disposition of any record:

- record number;
- record title;
- date created;
- date of disposal;
- method of disposal;
- disposal authority;
- event log of the record.

The retention of this metadata provides evidence about how records have been used in the Forensic Laboratory and managed over time by providing an audit trail of all actions undertaken on the records and their associated metadata.

15.8 RECORD MANAGEMENT PROCEDURES

Within the Forensic Laboratory, the ERMS manages general business records as well as dictating how a forensic case progresses. As the ERMS will be built to ensure that forensic cases are properly managed, as well as manage business records, this must be the case. Within the life cycle of a record, there are a number of phases, and each is covered below.

15.8.1 Common Processes

There are a number of common processes and procedures for general business records and forensic case processing, and these are covered below.

15.8.1.1 Training

All Forensic Laboratory employees, and relevant third parties acting on their behalf, must undergo appropriate training for their job role, including the use of the ERMS.

Training records are maintained in individual personnel files, as defined in Chapter 4, Section 4.6.2.3 and Chapter 18, Section 18.2.1.8.

All training is carried out in accordance with the procedures in Chapter 4, Section 4.6.2.2.

Needs for training are identified during the training needs analysis process at the annual appraisal process, as defined in Chapter 18, Section 18.2.2.

All Forensic Laboratory employees must be trained to understand their roles and responsibilities for Records Management within the Forensic Laboratory. Generic responsibilities for Records Management within the Forensic Laboratory are defined in Section 15.7.2 and given in Appendix 4.

15.8.1.2 General

When records are stored in the ERMS, they are always stored on media where their reliability, usability, authenticity, and preservation for the duration of the forensic case life cycle are assured. Once they have been archived, they will still need to retain these properties.

All electronic records should be backed up within the Forensic Laboratory according to the backup procedures in place, as defined in Chapter 7, Section 7.7.4. This includes long-term archiving. Physical records are always retained in fireproof safes and never removed after they have been scanned, unless for a specific reason, otherwise electronic scanned images are used.

Where electronic records are to be migrated from one ERMS to another, the process described in Section 15.5.3.8 must be followed to ensure that the migration is complete and of assured integrity. As a backup, the Forensic Laboratory must always retain the hardware, software, manuals, data, backups, and other components of the old ERMS so that it can be accessed if needed. As part of this process, a regular schedule of testing the past ERMSs can actually be restored with their records accessed must be undertaken.

Where physical and electronic records are transferred to an authorized third party, they must be subject to the checking of the authorization and a full log of records transferred on the appropriate movement sheet, as defined in Chapter 8, Appendix 17 and the Forensic Laboratory Property Log, as defined in Chapter 9, Appendix 13. Physical records will be transferred in their "native" format and electronic records in whatever format that the third party requires, assuming that the Forensic Laboratory has the technology to provide the required format. If the required format is not currently possible, either the Forensic Laboratory will need to obtain the necessary technology to produce the required format or agree to an alternative format that they can produce.

15.8.1.3 Record Capture

Record capture is the process of entering records into the Forensic Laboratory ERMS to establish the relationship between the record and its constituent parts (i.e., its context, the record creator) and any linkages to other records and/or documents.

This process typically will use metadata either embedded into the record itself, or metadata added into the ERMS, and permanently associated with the record. Examples of some metadata in use in the Forensic Laboratory for forensic cases are given in Appendices 10 and 11.

All forensic case processing records in the ERMS are linked by the common Forensic Laboratory Case number that is uniquely assigned to each case, whether it is completed or not. Details of a forensic case numbering system that can be used in the Forensic Laboratory are given in Chapter 9, Section 9.7.1. Exhibit numbering is given in Chapter 8, Section 8.6.10.

Access rights and security settings for forensic cases are set on a per case basis and are set up at the point of record capture in the ERMS. General business record access control is dependent on job roles.

At the same time, as the record capture process is undertaken, default values or settings are entered (e.g., disposition, retention periods, etc.).

General business records can come in many forms, physical and electronic. Where information to comprise a record is captured (or copied, converted, or moved) from an external source to the ERMS, there is the potential of information loss. Information loss refers to the record in the ERMS not exactly matching the original source document. This can be due to a number of reasons, including but not limited to:

- human error in the scanning or copying processing that results in information loss;
- loss of metadata on conversion between different application formats;
- physical destruction of the original physical record, which may be of critical importance (e.g., latent prints, paper type, type impressions from a typewriter, etc.);
- resolution loss on scanning where legibility may be lost.

Careful consideration must be made of the possible loss of information, especially in forensic case processing, which is why original physical records are all stored for the duration of the forensic case life cycle in the Document Registry in the Secure Property Store. The decision to retain original business records is a matter for the relevant business manager who owns them to determine typically based on experience and consideration of the cost of storage matched against the cost of failure to have the original document. In some cases, originals must be retained no matter what (e.g., legal contracts).

When creating or importing documents into the ERMS, their authenticity, integrity, and reliability for later scrutiny are of paramount importance as is their usability, as defined in Section 15.3.1. While this is under the Forensic Laboratory's control for records it creates, it has little control over those that are produced by a third party, so it is essential that checks are carried out to ensure that it has not been tampered with and that the originator is verifiable. The level of checking for documents from third parties will depend on their business criticality. In the case of exhibits, these must all be accompanied by a movement sheet to demonstrate the chain of custody, as given in Chapter 8, Appendix 17.

Where documents are converted from one format to another, it is essential to ensure that all metadata is also captured; so, the context of the captured record is properly understood.

Where records are scanned, appropriate detailed work instructions are in place to handle the preparation of documents for scanning. These cover such issues as:

- physical examination of documents prior to scanning and undertaking any necessary risk assessment and evaluation of possible scanning problems;
- outsize documents that may need to be photo-reduced or have multiple copies made of parts of them and then scan the constituent composite parts;
- removal of binding mechanisms (e.g., comb binding, staples, etc.);
- procedures for dealing with attachments (e.g., post it notes) affixed to the document;
- dealing with photocopies, rather than original documents, including their marking as such;
- integrity of multipage documents to overcome possible human error in the scanning process (e.g., missing a page due to paper misfeed that is not immediately noticed);
- checking the integrity of the output against the original source document;
- dealing with faint or low-resolution source material;
- dealing with delicate documents (e.g., the need to photocopy first, in case of damage by the scanning process, use of document wallets, etc.);
- the scanner type to be used (e.g., single sheet, batch, color, or black and white);
- output format (e.g., single or double sided and paper size). The Forensic Laboratory will scan all forensic case processing notes for use in the Client virtual case file as single sided. This allows the "back of the previous page" to be used for notes directly related to the right-hand page. This facilitates the "page turning" syndrome where information may be missed or it causes difficulty in page turning;
- the use of photographic capture as opposed to scanning;
- requirements for scanning resolution for different types of document;
- post scanning image enhancement, in case it affects the original document in which case the original must be retained);
- protection of source documents (e.g., the content of some fax paper may deteriorate over time);
- regular validation of the scanning process (a test pack of documents of different types is used, and the validation process is carried out with records of the results retained in the similar way that forensic tools are validated, as defined in Chapter 7, Section 7.5.5. This is the responsibility of the Records Manager);
- data extraction from documents using processes such as optical character recognition, intelligent character recognition, optical mark reading, bar codes, or direct manual keyboard entry, and the quality of the results. Extreme care must be exercised if used for forensic case processing, as manipulation may be regarded as "tampering" with the evidence.

In the Forensic Laboratory ERMS, record registration is carried out at the same time as record capture. Registration is the formal recognition of record capture in the Forensic Laboratory ERMS. At the point of registration, the Forensic Laboratory uses a known trusted time source for recording the identity of a document, using its hash value to prove that:

- a file existed on a given date and time;
- the file was not altered since the time it was stamped.

The procedures for this are defined in Chapter 9, Section 9.12.

15.8.1.4 Indexing

Indexing is a vital part of Record Management as it allows for easy retrieval of a record or series of records. If indexing information is corrupted or unavailable for any reason, the record may also be unavailable or only be found after additional manual searching.

Business records are automatically indexed, whereas all forensic case file information is manually indexed by the relevant Forensic Analyst(s) processing the case. As the records for a forensic case are all held in the Client virtual case file, the use of manual indexing is not an overly onerous task.

All changes to the indexes are subject to audit for their lifetime clearly showing a "before and after image." Index databases often require the index to be rebuilt to improve performance, as is common with all database systems, and the manufacturer's recommendations must be followed.

15.8.1.5 Records Stored in the Forensic Laboratory

The Forensic Laboratory stores two general types of records relating to forensic case work. Each is handled differently, but both are captured and registered in the Forensic Laboratory ERMS. The two types are:

- physical records;
- electronic records.

15.8.1.5.1 Physical Records

A number of records relating to forensic cases within the Forensic Laboratory are created or received as physical records. These may be:

- audio or video recordings (e.g., Dictaphone records, cassettes, answer phone tapes, non-digital video);
- microfiche;
- paper records;
- photographs.

The Forensic Laboratory w[illegible] physical records are to be conve[illegible] for entry into the ERMS, if possible, w[illegible] ical records being placed into the Forensic [illegible] ument Registry and retained in the Secure Prop[illegible]

Once a physical record has been converted into a[illegible] tronic one, the appropriate metadata is associated with [illegible] when it is captured into the Forensic Laboratory ERMS.

Only electronic copies of the records shall be used in any forensic case, unless there is a need to revert to original source material. In any case, the Forensic Laboratory will have a record of all accesses to any original physical record and a movement form will have been filled in for any movements to or from the secure property store, as given in Chapter 8, Appendix 17.

15.8.1.5.2 Electronic Records

Electronic records often have the ability to have metadata associated with them within the record. Where this is not possible, the relevant metadata is associated with the record in the ERMS, as defined in Section 15.7.

15.8.1.6 Record Classification

For all forensic cases, the records may be classified as "Vital Records." General business records are normally classified according to the classification system in Appendix 17.

The classification of all forensic case records as "Vital Records" will be a conscious decision as all forensic cases are of a similar type.

All records entered into the Forensic ERMS should have a consistent naming standard, as given in Chapter 4, Appendix 39, and all completed forms and records contain a unique Forensic Laboratory Case Reference Number, as defined in Chapter 9, Section 9.7.1.

However, records for a case will be classified for sensitivity and confidentiality requirements, as defined in Chapter 5, Section 5.5.6.6. This classification process sets the requirements for information security for the case.

15.8.1.7 Document Control

As well as using the Forensic Laboratory naming conventions, as given in Chapter 4, Appendix 39, all records created by the Forensic Laboratory shall be subject to document and version control. Using a rigid document and version control process allows recovery to any version of a document on a given day by using the Forensic Laboratory version control procedures, as defined in Chapter 4, Section 4.6.3.

...electronic

...tory are stored in ...perty Store in the ...e ERMS with asso- ...aged by the Record ...sponsible for the safe- ...se records.

...sible for ensuring that all physical r... d registered into the ERMS against the app... ic case virtual case file, as defined in Chapter 9, ... on 9.7.6. Once captured, the physical record is copied into appropriate electronic format and transferred to the appropriate Forensic Analyst for the case. The transfer is recorded in the ERMS, and the original record is securely stored.

Any transfer of the original physical record must be authorized, and the transfer is recorded in the ERMS according to the Forensic Laboratory records transfer procedure using the movement form, as given in Chapter 8, Appendix 17.

15.8.1.8.2 Electronic Record Storage

All electronic records will be stored in the ERMS with associated metadata. Where these have been received from a third party, they will typically require metadata to be associated with them prior to storage in the ERMS.

Where electronic records are created in the Forensic Laboratory, they will all have metadata added to them, where possible, so that it is embedded in the document. If this is not possible, then appropriate metadata will be associated with the record in the ERMS.

Any transfer of the electronic record will be authorized, and the transfer is recorded in the ERMS according to the Forensic Laboratory records transfer procedure.

Note 1

The server(s) and media—including archival and backup drives—also need to be physically secured to the appropriate level as defined by the Forensic Laboratory risk management process, as defined in Chapter 5. It would make no sense to keep the paper records in a safe or a secure locker if someone can walk off with the server or drives.

Note 2

Electronic records may be compressed to save space, either for storage or for transmission.

Note 3

Encryption is used in the Forensic Laboratory for confidentiality, integrity, and non-repudiation purposes.

15.8.1.9 Access to Records

Access to all records will be according to the Access Control Policy in force in the Forensic Laboratory, as given in Chapter 4, Appendix 11. This gives group access rights as well as specific access rights per forensic case. In some cases, these will also be confirmed in the metadata of the records in the ERMS.

In general terms, the only Forensic Laboratory employees allowed to access a forensic case are as follows:

- write access—the Forensic Analyst(s) actively working on the case;
- read access—the Forensic Analyst(s) who have oversight of the case (e.g., Case Managers) or those that need read access for quality assurance purposes (e.g., Quality Assurance Manager, Audit Manager. Where a Client requires access to a live case, that is, in the ERMS, they may be granted temporary "read-only" access under controlled conditions. Clients visiting the Forensic Laboratory shall have their access controlled and monitored according to the procedures, as defined in Chapter 12, Section 12.4.2. All access rights are regularly reviewed to ensure that authorization is appropriate according to business need, as defined in Chapter 12, Section 12.4.6 for physical security and Chapter 12, Section 12.6.2 for logical access. Records of all authorities for access are recorded in the Service Desk system as defined in Chapter 12, Section 12.6.1 and Section 15.6.2.

All output (e.g., printouts or output on magnetic or digital media) shall be securely disposed of according to the classification of the record, as defined in Chapter 12, Section 12.3.14.10.

15.8.1.10 Output

Output from the ERMS must meet the requirements for authenticity, integrity, reliability, and usability, as defined in Section 15.3.1. In addition to this, the Forensic Laboratory should use a known trusted time source for recording the identity of a document, using its hash value to prove that:

- a file existed on a given date and time;
- the file was not altered since the time it was stamped.

The procedures for this are defined in Chapter 9, Section 9.12.

The procedures for ensuring that all clocks in information processing equipment are synchronized are given in Chapter 7, Section 7.7.5.

Output must also meet the rules of evidence for the jurisdiction.

Output formats will vary. Obviously, scanned images should be reproduced as a facsimile image, supported by the original, where appropriate. The output from MARS may be defined by the Forensic Laboratory to suit its purposes for reporting, as defined in Chapter 10, Sections 10.6–10.8.

15.8.1.11 *Transmission*

Records, and any documents transmitted to and from the Forensic Laboratory, are subject to the data handling rules depending on the classification of the record or document, as defined in Chapter 12, Sections 12.3.12 and 12.3.14.9.

Digital signatures should be used by all Forensic Analysts.

E-mail must be prohibited from use for certain classification as there is no guarantee of timeliness of delivery. For forensic case processing, secure transmission methods are agreed as part of the proposal process, as defined in Chapter 6, Sections 6.6.2.3 and 6.6.2.4. Remote secure connections to and from the Forensic Laboratory are covered in Chapter 7, Section 7.7.3.

Where a physical exhibit is being transmitted, it is the Forensic Laboratory's standard process to maintain the chain of custody using the exhibit movement forms, as given in Chapter 8, Appendix 17.

15.8.1.12 *Retention*

Record and document retention is defined by legislative, regulatory, good practice, and Client contractual requirements. A document retention schedule for the Forensic Laboratory is given in Chapter 4, Appendix 16.

15.8.1.13 *Record Review*

On an annual basis, or on influencing change, the Forensic Laboratory Records Manager must review all records in the ERMS with their owners (typically the relevant Forensic Analyst for a forensic case and relevant business unit managers) to determine whether the records should be considered for disposition.

Record reviews are undertaken to ensure that records in primary storage are not held there for longer than necessary. Primary storage is an expensive medium to manage, both in terms of space requirements and dedicated Forensic Laboratory employees to manage both physical and electronic records.

Where appropriate, records that do not need to remain in primary storage will be considered for transfer to archive storage.

Where transfer to archive storage is authorized, transfer shall be undertaken using the Forensic Laboratory procedures for transfer of records.

15.8.1.14 *Disposal an[illegible]*

Record disposition, whether for [illegible] records, can only be carried out as a con[illegible] rized process in the Forensic Laboratory, bu[illegible] dictated by the Client's policies and procedures. [illegible] tion requests must be carefully evaluated prior to autho[illegible] being granted for one of the following disposition actions within the Forensic Laboratory:

- immediate physical destruction of the record (this may include electronic destruction processes such as secure overwriting and deletion of a record), as defined in Chapter 12, Section 12.3.14.10;
- migration from one internal system to another;
- transfer of records to another Forensic Laboratory employee;
- transfer of records to an authorized third party.

The record disposition authorization form for use in the Forensic Laboratory is given in Appendix 18.

> **Note**
>
> Record disposition (typically disposal or transfer) may also be the result of an annual review of records held by the Forensic Laboratory.

15.8.1.15 *Audit Trails and Tracking*

All actions taken on any forensic case must have an audit trail associated with the action, clearly showing:

- Who did what?
- When?
- Where it was carried out?
- Why?
- How it was done?

These processes are defined in Section 15.3.1.3.

The audit trail can be either a secure audit trail within the Forensic Laboratory computer system (e.g., operating system audit trails, application system audit trails, the ERMS audit trail, specialized tool audit trails) or it can be the use of the physical movement forms, as given in Chapter 8, Appendix 17, and the Property Log, as given in Chapter 9, Appendix 13.

Where a record is booked out to an authorized recipient, it can have actions associated with it for completion recorded in the ERMS as a form of workflow. This facilitates the Forensic Laboratory in ensuring that required actions are carried out in the time-scale defined in the ERMS by the Forensic Laboratory employee to whom the record is assigned. Reporting can be carried out for all actions past their "due by date" as well as providing reporting on the efficiency of actions and meeting turn

ıned in
and in
ted.
cord move-
nsic Labora-
Party) audits,
ugh the regular
vide independent
ation and effective
ory's management

er satisfaction surveys
orensic case. An example
custom... is given in Chapter 6, Appendix 2...

Any complaint... against the Forensic Laboratory for its forensic case proce... ng must be investigated. Procedures for this are defined in Chapter 6, Section 6.14.

Any complaints and all feedback received are reviewed at the regular Management Review meetings, as defined in Chapter 4, Section 4.9.

The process for internal auditing is given in Chapter 4, Section 4.7.3. For auditing the Forensic Laboratory Record Management System, the following areas of internal audit should be undertaken:

- records inventory;
- creation and receipt of records;
- storage of records;
- disposition of records;
- electronic records;
- security and confidentiality of records;
- reliability of records;
- Records Management Policy;
- Records Management Training.

15.8.1.16 Backup

Backup of the ERMS is covered in Chapter 7, Section 7.7.4.

15.8.1.17 Business Continuity

Business continuity in the Forensic Laboratory is covered in Chapter 13.

15.8.1.18 ERMS Maintenance

Maintenance of all Forensic Laboratory hardware and software is covered in Chapter 7, Section 7.5.4.

15.8.1.19 Change Management

Change management procedures for managing changes to the ERMS and documents are given in Chapter 7, Section 7.4.3.

15.8.1.20 Securely Managing the ERMS

The risks to the ERMS, and the Forensic Laboratory as a whole, are defined in Chapter 5.

Managing the IT infrastructure that underpins the ERMS is given in Chapter 7.

Secure working procedures for the Forensic Laboratory are given in Chapter 12.

15.8.1.21 Third Parties

The use of third parties for any part of processing any document or record (business or forensic case file) in the Forensic Laboratory is defined in Chapter 14.

15.8.2 Forensic Case Processing

As well as meeting the general requirements identified in Section 15.8.1, the creation of a Client virtual case file is different from normal business records as it has its own creation and naming processes, as defined below.

15.8.2.1 Case Creation

The first step in Records Management is the creation of a record within the ERMS (Figure 15.2). This process is as follows:

1. A requirement for a new case is identified. This could be the result of any communication from a prospective Client to the Forensic Laboratory.
2. The recipient of the communication contacts the Records Manager with details of the communication.
3. If the communication has any hard copy records associated with it (e.g., a letter), they are sent to the Records Manager, who will scan them and add to the virtual case file, as defined in Chapter 9, Section 9.7.6, and the structure is given in Chapter 9, Appendix 18. The original physical record is added to the case file in the Document Registry.
4. The Records Manager assigns a case number to the incoming communication and advises the Requestor of the Case Number.
5. All relevant metadata must be added, whether by the Records Manager or the Forensic Analyst.
6. The Records Manager assigns access rights to the virtual case file to the Requestor as read/write and their Line Manager as read-only. Other Forensic Laboratory employees shall be granted access to the virtual case file according to the Forensic Case Laboratory Access Control Policy, as given in Chapter 4, Appendix 11.
7. The new case will be automatically backed up as part of the overnight backup process, as defined in Chapter 7, Section 7.7.4.

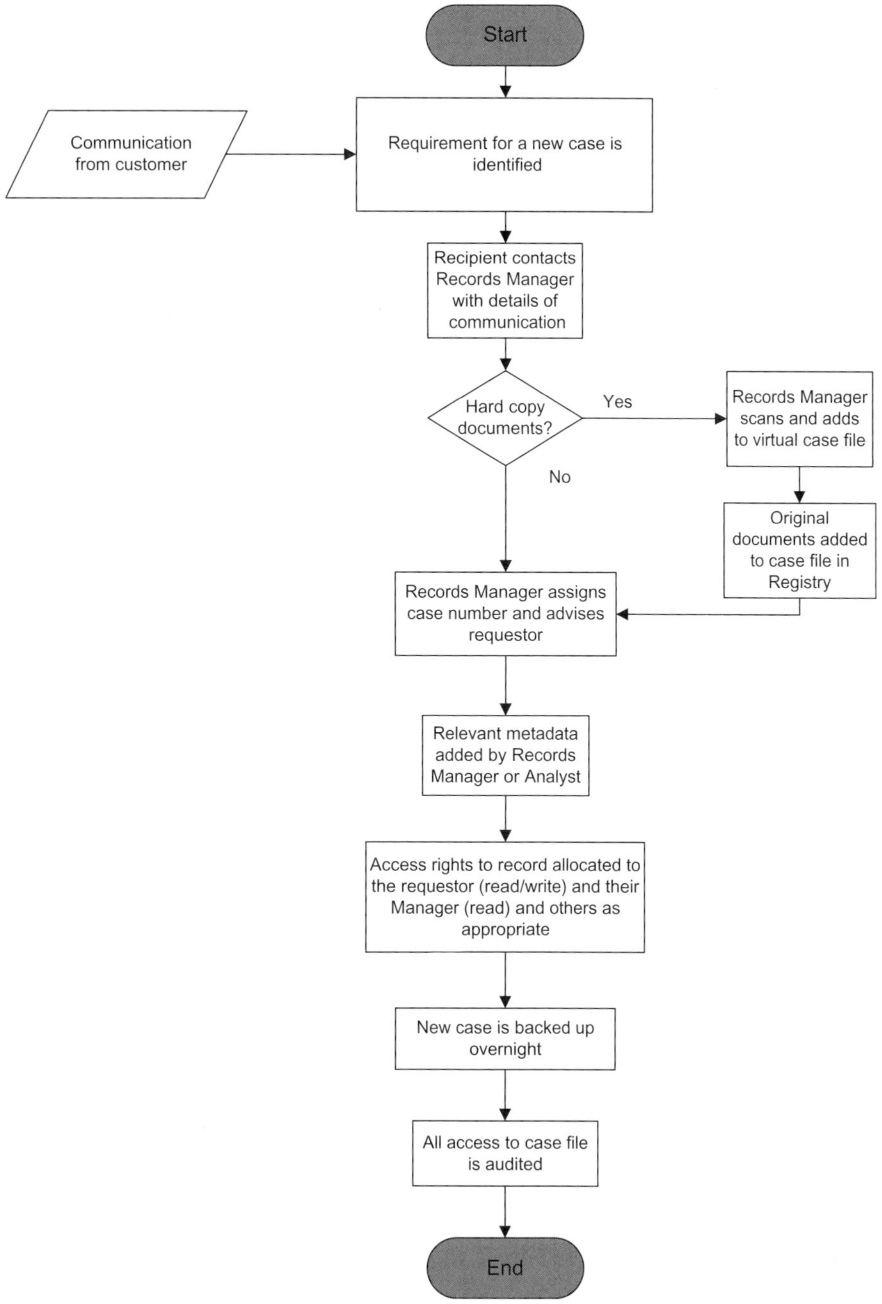

FIGURE 15.2 Case creation. (For color version of this figure, the reader is referred to the online version of this chapter.)

8. All access to the virtual case file will be written to the audit trail. The new case form used for setting up a new virtual case file is given in Chapter 8, Appendix 4.

15.8.2.2 Adding Records to the Virtual Case File

Once the virtual case file has been set up, the relevant Forensic Analyst(s) will add records to the case for the duration of the case life cycle.

1. If the communication has any hard copy records associated with it (e.g., a letter, filled in form, pocket book records, etc.), they are sent to the Records Manager, who will scan them and add to the virtual case file. The original physical record is added to the case file in the Document Registry held in the Secure Property Store.
2. If electronic records are created, then these are automatically added to the relevant virtual case file. The ERMS ensures that all documents created have appropriate metadata added to them as part of the record creation.

3. All document naming is as defined in the records control procedure, as defined in Chapter 4, Appendix 39. This ensures that for any document the previous version is available.
4. All access to the virtual case file will be written to the audit trail.

15.8.3 Record Disposition

This is covered in Section 15.8.1.14.

15.9 BUSINESS CONTINUITY

The Forensic Laboratory has a business continuity plan in place that also addresses the requirements of record keeping. This is defined in Chapter 13.

The Forensic Laboratory must undertake a specific risk assessment to determine the effects of the loss of the ERMS. How to undertake a risk assessment is defined in Chapter 5.

A Business Impact Analysis is undertaken to determine the Recovery Time Objectives and Maximum Tolerable Periods of Disruption, as defined in Chapter 13, Section 13.4.1 and given in Chapter 13, Appendix 4.

The results of the risk assessment in the Forensic Laboratory are used to create a Statement of Applicability for ISO 27001, as given in Chapter 12, Appendix 1. This indicates the controls to be implemented to reduce the risk of a disaster happening. Additionally, the incident management process, as defined in Chapter 7, Section 7.4.1 ensures that timely action is taken on discovery of any incident, actions which may require the invocation of the BCP.

There may be a number of specific facilities needed over and above the standard BCP for Records Management. These include the requirements for physical record recovery, as given in Appendix 19 and Appendix 20.

APPENDIX 1 - MoReq2 FUNCTIONAL REQUIREMENTS

MoReq2 defines the following functional requirements:

- create new files;
- maintain classification schemes and files;
- capture records;
- delete files and records;
- search for and read records;
- change the contents of records;
- capture and change metadata about records;
- manage retention and disposal transactions;
- export and import files and records;
- view audit trail data;
- provide access to authorized users.

APPENDIX 2 - MAPPING OF ISO 15489 PART 1 TO FORENSIC LABORATORY PROCEDURES

ISO 15489: 1 Clause	Control	IMS procedure
4	Benefits of Records Management	Section 15.1.8
5	Regulatory environment	Chapter 12, Section 12.3.13.1 Section 15.2 Appendix 3
6	Policy and responsibilities	
6.1	General	The Forensic Laboratory IMS and the ERMS
6.2	Policy	Section 15.4 Appendix 4
6.3	Responsibilities	Section 15.8 Appendix 15 Appendix 18 Various job descriptions in Chapter 18
7	Records Management requirements	
7.1	Principles of Records Management Program	Chapter 13 Section 15.2.2 Section 15.7 Section 15.8
7.2	Characteristics of a record	
7.2.1	General	Section 15.3.1 Section 15.7
7.2.2	Authenticity	Section 15.3.1.1 Section 15.8
7.2.3	Reliability	Section 15.3.1.2
7.2.4	Integrity	Section 15.3.1.3 Section 15.8.1.7 Section 15.8.1.10
7.2.5	Usability	Section 15.3.1.4 Section 15.7 Section 15.8.1.4 Section 15.8.1.9
8	Design and implementation of a records system	
8.1	General	Section 15.5.2
8.2	Records systems characteristics	

Continued

ISO 15489: 1 Clause	Control	IMS procedure
8.2.1	Introduction	
8.2.2	Reliability	Section 15.3.1.2
8.2.3	Integrity	Chapter 12 Section 15.3.1.3 Section 15.8.1.7 Section 15.8.1.10
8.2.4	Compliance	Chapter 12, Section 12.3.13
8.2.5	Comprehensiveness	Appendix 15
8.2.6	Systematic	Section 15.8
8.3	Designing and implementing records systems	
8.3.1	General	Section 15.5 Appendix 5
8.3.2	Documenting records transactions	Chapter 4, Section 4.7.3 Section 15.7 Section 15.8.1.14 Section 15.8.1.15
8.3.3	Physical storage medium and protection	Chapter 2, Section 2.4 Chapter 4, Appendix 16 Chapter 5, Appendix 16 Chapter 12, Section 12.3.12 Chapter 12, Section 12.3.14 Chapter 12, Section 12.4 Section 15.8.1.8 Chapter 13
8.3.4	Distributed management	Appendix 8
8.3.5	Conversion and migration	Section 15.5.3.8
8.3.6	Access, retrieval, and use	Section 15.8.1.4 Appendix 8
8.3.7	Retention and disposition	Chapter 4, Appendix 16 Section 15.6.4 Section 15.8.1.2 Section 15.8.1.4
8.4	Design and implementation methodology	Chapter 12, Section 12.3.13.1 Section 15.2.1 Section 15.5.3
8.5	Discontinuing records systems	Section 15.5.3.9
9	Records Management processes and controls	

Continued

ISO 15489: 1 Clause	Control	IMS procedure
9.1	Determining documents to be captured into a records system	Section 15.6 Section 15.7
9.2	Determining how long to retain records	Chapter 4, Appendix 16 Chapter 12, Section 12.3.13.1 Section 15.2 Section 15.6.4 Section 15.8.1.2 Appendix 3
9.3	Records capture	Chapter 9, Section 9.7.6 Chapter 9, Appendix 18 Section 15.7 Section 15.8.1.3 Section 15.8.1.4 Section 15.8.1.15
9.4	Registration	Section 15.8.1.3
9.5	Classification	
9.5.1	Classification of business activities	Chapter 5, Appendix 16 Chapter 12, Section 12.3.14.6 Section 15.8.1.6
9.5.2	Classification systems	Chapter 5, Appendix 16 Chapter 12, Section 12.3.14.6 Section 15.6 Section 15.8.1.6
9.5.3	Vocabulary controls	Section 15.6
9.5.4	Indexing	Section 15.8.1.4
9.5.5	Allocation of numbers and codes	Chapter 4, Appendix 39 Chapter 8, Section 8.6.10 Chapter 10, Section 10.4.1.1
9.6	Storage and handling	Chapter 12, Section 12.3.14
9.7	Access	Section 15.8.1.9
9.8	Tracking	
9.8.1	General	Chapter 12, Section 12.6.7 Section 15.7 Section 15.8.1.4
9.8.2	Action tracking	Section 15.8.1.15
9.8.3	Location tracking	Section 15.8.1.4 Chapter 8, Section 8.7.4 Chapter 8, Appendix 17
9.9	Implementing disposition	Chapter 12, Section 12.3.14.10 Section 15.8.1.14 Appendix 18

Continued

ISO 15489: 1 Clause	Control	IMS procedure
9.10	Documenting Records Management processes	The Forensic Laboratory Integrated Management System (IMS) and the Electronic Records Management System (ERMS) Chapter 4, Appendix 16 Chapter 12, Section 12.3.13.1 Section 15.8.1.14 Appendix 18
10	Monitoring and auditing	Chapter 4, Section 4.7.3 Chapter 12, Section 12.3.1.5 Chapter 12, Section 12.3.13.2 Chapter 12, Section 12.4.4.3.4 Chapter 12, Section 12.6.1.3 Chapter 12, Section 12.6.7 Chapter 12, Section 12.9.9 Section 15.8.1.15
11	Training	Chapter 4, Section 4.6.2.2 Chapter 4, Section 4.6.2.3 Section 15.8.1.1

APPENDIX 3 - TYPES OF LEGISLATION AND REGULATION THAT WILL AFFECT RECORD KEEPING

The list below gives subject areas and is offered as a checklist to identify specific legislation or regulation in the jurisdiction that may affect record keeping in the Forensic Laboratory. It is not meant to be a complete list.

- access to information;
- business focused legislation;
- computer use and misuse;
- copyright, designs, and patents;
- criminal;
- data protection;
- defence and homeland security;
- emergency planning and business resumption;
- evidence;
- financial information;
- health and medical information;
- health and safety;
- human resources;
- human rights;
- identity theft and identity protection;
- information management;
- information security;
- insurance;
- privacy;
- workplace and workforce.

APPENDIX 4 - FORENSIC LABORATORY RECORD KEEPING POLICY

The Forensic Laboratory record keeping policy is reproduced below.

PURPOSE

The purpose of this policy is to establish a framework for the creation and management of records within the Forensic Laboratory. The Forensic Laboratory is committed to establishing and maintaining record keeping processes and supporting procedures that meet, or exceed, its business needs, accountability requirements, and relevant stakeholder expectations.

POLICY STATEMENT

The Forensic Laboratory's records are its "corporate memory," and as such are a vital asset for ongoing operations, providing valuable evidence of forensic case processing and business transactions.

The Forensic Laboratory recognizes its legislative, regulatory, contractual, and internal business requirements and is committed to the principles and practices set out in the ISO 15489 (Information and documentation—Records Management). It is also committed to implementing the best available record keeping processes and procedures, with supporting systems, to ensure the creation, maintenance, and protection of accurate and reliable records. All record keeping activities within the Forensic Laboratory shall comply with this policy and its supporting procedures.

SCOPE

This policy applies to all Forensic Laboratory employees and any third parties working on its behalf.

This policy applies to:

- all aspects of the Forensic Laboratory's operations;
- all records created during forensic case processing and any business transactions. This includes any computer applications and operating systems used to create records including, but not limited to:
  - database applications;
  - e-mail;

- internet access;
- operating system and application audit logs;
- specialized software.

This policy provides the overarching framework for any other Forensic Laboratory record keeping policies, procedures, or work instructions.

POLICY CONTEXT

The Forensic Laboratory's record keeping policies, procedures, and work instructions are tightly integrated with other policies, procedures, and work instructions in the Forensic Laboratory's IMS.

The Records Manager is responsible for developing, implementing, and maintaining all record keeping strategies with supporting policies, procedures, and work instructions.

LEGISLATION, REGULATION, AND STANDARDS

The Forensic Laboratory has identified the following legislation that applies to records and information processed as part of ongoing operations:

- <relevant legislation defined here>

The Forensic Laboratory has identified the following regulations that apply to records and information processed as part of ongoing operations:

- <relevant regulations defined here>

The Forensic Laboratory has developed record keeping systems that capture and maintain records with appropriate evidential characteristics in accordance with its obligations under the legislation and regulations identified above.

The Forensic Laboratory is committed to current good practice in record keeping, and has developed record keeping policies, procedures, systems, and work instructions consistent with ISO 15489.

RECORD KEEPING SYSTEMS

The Forensic Laboratory's record keeping system is a hybrid ERMS and paper records. While copies of paper records may be scanned into the ERMS, the originals shall be securely retained, even if captured in accordance with the admissibility of electronic evidence within the jurisdiction.

The Forensic Laboratory's record keeping systems are dedicated to the creation and maintenance of authentic, reliable, and usable records for as long as they are required to effectively and efficiently support forensic case processing or any business activities.

The record keeping systems shall manage the following processes:

- the creation or capture of records within the record keeping system;
- the storage of records;
- the protection of record integrity and authenticity;
- the security of records;
- access to, and accessibility of, records;
- the disposal of records according to relevant legislative, regulatory, contractual, or business requirements.

RESPONSIBILITIES

This policy has been authorized by Top Management.

Line Managers are responsible for the implementation of this policy through resource allocation, demonstrable commitment, and other management support.

The Records Manager is responsible for overseeing the design, implementation, and maintenance of this record keeping policy, as well as monitoring compliance.

System administrators are responsible for maintaining the technology for all record keeping systems, including responsibility for maintaining the integrity and authenticity of records and audit trails.

System designers are responsible for designing IT and other systems that comply with the requirements of this policy.

The Information Security Manager is responsible for ensuring that appropriate information security has been implemented and managed to ensure security of records during their life cycle. Typically, this will be confirmed by internal audit.

All Forensic Laboratory employees are responsible for the creation of accurate and reliable records of their activities as defined by this policy and complying with its requirements.

> **Note**
> Employees include any third party working on the Forensic Laboratory's behalf.

All responsibilities for record keeping are defined in the relevant job descriptions.

MONITOR AND REVIEW

This policy is scheduled for review at least on an annual basis, unless an incident or other influencing change necessitates review.

APPENDIX 5 - RECORD MANAGEMENT SYSTEM OBJECTIVES

Top Management defined the following objectives for the Records Management System to be implemented in the Forensic Laboratory.

- to continuously improve the Records Management processes in the Forensic Laboratory by an ongoing process of performance assessment and corrective or preventive action where needed;
- to develop a formal training program, with supporting processes and procedures, on Records Management that is appropriate to all Forensic Laboratory employees and third parties working on their behalf;
- to ensure that full and accurate records are made, captured into, maintained by and accessible in the ERMS;
- to ensure that records within the ERMS are retained, managed, and disposed of in accordance with relevant legislation, regulation, good practice within the jurisdiction, as well as Client's contractual requirements;
- to exploit current and emerging technology to assist in the management of case processing and general business records within the Forensic Laboratory;
- to have demonstrable Top Management Support to implement an appropriate ERMS, with appropriate resources to support its ongoing operations;
- to have an ERMS that can record and monitor the various stages of action of all types of correspondence (including forensic case processing) from receipt to closure;
- to have an ERMS that will capture, store, index, and make available to all authorized users details of forensic case processing and general business records;
- to have an ERMS that will provide efficient tracking and retrieval of logical and physical records using metadata and other keyword searches.

APPENDIX 6 - BUSINESS CASE CONTENTS

The business case for the implementation of the Forensic Laboratory's ERMS contains the following sections:

- synopsis of the current situation and how the project will improve management of records and information in the Forensic Laboratory;
- business benefits of implementing an ERMS, including the impact and effect the system will have on the business immediately after implementation and beyond;
- business options and recommendations;
- objectives and business drivers;
- key performance indicators;
- project budget;
- plans for stakeholder involvement;
- implementation plan;
- risk mitigation strategies;
- change management initiatives.

APPENDIX 7 - OUTLINE OF THE ERMS PROJECT

The ERMS project had three main phases with a number of subphases as shown below:

INITIATION PHASE

- initial analysis;
- develop the business case;
- seek and gain approval from project sponsor;
- draft technical and functional requirements.

IMPLEMENTATION PHASE

- analyze business needs and processes;
- work with stakeholders to identify process improvements, including use of workflow;
- develop a communications strategy for implementation;
- develop training material;
- analyze impact of new ERMS on existing IT infrastructure and need for changes;
- ensure IT infrastructure ready for deployment;
- develop records migration strategy for existing records;
- develop administration model to manage ERMS;
- develop and gain approval from all stakeholders for records security model;
- develop and gain approval for business rules relating to Record Management for the ERMS and Document Registry;
- develop, or update, the record classification scheme;
- review and update the technical and functional requirements to incorporate any changes identified to date;
- procurement phase (to include RFI, RFP, evaluation of proposals, and entry into contract with chosen service provider);
- develop implementation and rollout strategy and plan;
- implement the pilot and configure it for the Forensic Laboratory needs;
- review pilot and make adjustments as needed until the ERMS meets the complete Forensic Laboratory needs;
- develop a full rollout and implementation plan;
- develop a support model for the implementation and rollout;
- operate phased implementation and rollout by departments;
- collect feedback as rollout and implementation progresses and make adjustments as needed;
- train all ERMS users according to their roles and responsibilities;
- act on feedback as feedback is obtained.

POST IMPLEMENTATION PHASE

- develop PIR plan;
- undertake PIR;
- raise appropriate CAPAs based on PIR;
- implement required changes through change control;
- ensure continuous improvement through ongoing auditing after the PIR.

APPENDIX 8 - SELECTION CRITERIA FOR AN ERMS

As part of the ERMS package evaluation process from the RFI exercise, all packages were compared against a set of criteria. These are reproduced low:

Criteria	Requirement
Authenticity	As defined in Section 15.3.1.1 This may have an additional login to the ERMS with access rights definable and must have a fully secure audit trail
Reliability	As defined in Section 15.3.1.2 Additionally: • the ERMS should be able to capture all records in the scope of the business activities it covers in the Forensic Laboratory; • organize captured records in a logical and understandable manner that reflects the business structures within the Forensic Laboratory; • be capable of being used as the prime record repository within the Forensic Laboratory with no issues about the reliability of the records produced; • provide easy and intuitive access to records, as defined by the user's access rights, as well as any associated metadata or linked records and documents.
Integrity	As defined in Section 15.3.1.3 Additionally: • maintain record integrity during any transfer into or out of the ERMS; • provide processes for user account monitoring down to individual users; • provide user Identification and Access management processes, including two factor authentication (various technologies); • provide appropriate security based on the perceived risks to the system, as defined in Chapter 5; • permit authorized actions only (specifically destruction or transfer), based on authorized access rights, as defined in Chapter 12, Section 12.6.5.1; • provide full audit trail facilities with configurable reporting capabilities. **Note** These will be in addition to those facilities provided by the operating system as it cannot provide this level of granularity.
Usability	As defined in Section 15.3.1.4
Compliance	The ERMS must be compliant with all legislation, regulation, codes of practice and good practice within the jurisdiction where it is operated Where appropriate, certification should be provided
Completeness	The ERMS must capture and securely store all records in complete form (including linkages, related documents, other records, and all other elements that comprise the record) within the defined scope for the Forensic Laboratory
Retention periods	The ERMS must be able to set different retention periods for different records or record types, as given in Chapter 4, Appendix 16
Distributed management	While the Forensic Laboratory will initially be located in one location, this may change with other offices opening in different jurisdictions. The ERMS must be able to support distributed management of records between multiple offices, in different jurisdictions. There will be one office nominated as the main data center, but others will be nominated as fallback sites in case of disaster. Different offices will retain ownership of their own records, even if stored at another site, and this must be facilitated through the ERMS. The main data center will be responsible for all issues relating to day-to-day operations, including backups
User interface	A GUI should be provided and this may be a Web interface
Transfers and migrations	Where transfers or migrations are undertaken, the ERMS must ensure the authenticity, integrity, reliability, usability, and security of all existing records for their entire life cycle. A full audit trail must show all actions taken on all records, including transfers and migrations
Accessibility	The ERMS must provide a timely, intuitive, and efficient process for locating, retrieving, and using records according to business need and access rights for the user

Continued

Criteria	Requirement
	Audit trails of all access attempts (successful or not) must be maintained securely and must provide configurable reports of audit activity as required, as defined in Section 15.3.1.3
Disposition	As defined in retention periods, the ERMS must be able to implement appropriate record disposition according to the retention schedule, with an appropriate secure audit trail Disposition must only be possible by authorized users, as defined in Chapter 12, Section 12.6.5.1

APPENDIX 9 - INITIAL ERMS FEEDBACK QUESTIONNAIRE

The following subjective questions can be asked and the user is asked to score them as below using the Forensic Laboratory standard feedback scoring process:

- overall experience;
- new ERMS overall;
- creating new records;
- registering records;
- locating records;
- retrieving records;
- record linkage to documents or other records;
- metadata use for searching;
- printing and scanning;
- audit trail use;
- documentation supplied was of great assistance;
- training received was of great assistance;
- Service Desk support was of great assistance;
- I felt involved in the process and listened to;
- implementation was well handled;
- my expectations were met.

The following rankings were used:

1. totally dissatisfied.
2. somewhat dissatisfied.
3. neither satisfied or dissatisfied.
4. somewhat satisfied.
5. very satisfied.

In addition to these qualitative questions, the following four qualitative questions can also be asked:

what I like most about the new ERMS? (Please explain);

what I like least about the new ERMS? (Please explain);

what can the Forensic Laboratory do to improve its ERMS? (Please explain);

any other comments or clarifications of answers above? (Please enter below).

APPENDIX 10 - METADATA REQUIRED IN THE ERMS

The following metadata is used in the Forensic Laboratory:

Note

"M/O" refers to whether the entry of the field is mandatory or optional

Field	M/O?	Purpose	Comments
Record number	M	Allocates a unique number to identify any record in the ERMS	All record numbers must be entered in accordance with the numbering system in the ERMS. No records can be entered into the ERMS without a valid record number
Title	M	The text used to name the subject of each record	Facilitates searching and retrieval of records by searching on a record's official title or words contained in the title
Creator (also sometimes called Author)	M	The unique identity of the creator of the record	This may be a Forensic Laboratory employee or an external creator
Date created	M	The date the record was created	Dates may be automatically generated by the ERMS or manually input (over-riding automatically created ones)
Date registered	M	The date and time a record is captured into the ERMS	Automatically set by the ERMS as opposed to the date of creation
Date Closed	M	The date the record was closed	Automatically generated by the ERMS when a file is closed
Notes	O	Allows for additional descriptive information to be associated with a record	The notes field should be used if the record title does not provide sufficient information to permit effective searching

Continued

Field	M/O?	Purpose	Comments
Retention Period	M	The period for which the record must be retained for legislative, regulatory, contractual, or business reasons	This should define the period and the reason
Disposition method	M	The method of disposition required	How the record is to be dispositioned
Disposition date	M	The date of disposition	A trigger for starting the relevant disposition process
Audit trail	M	An audit trail of all actions taken on the record from creation/ registration, to disposition	This will show a complete history of all actions on the record, including sign in and out and changes made
Access rights	M	Access rights for the record	Defining who can have access to the record—linked to Active Directory for Microsoft systems
Movements	M	Recording the actions taken on the record	This is a record, like the audit trail, that records all other Forensic Laboratory employees' activity relating to the record. This specifically applies to the signing in and out of the record
Location	M	Where the record is located	This may be an electronic or hard copy record location. Where an electronic record in the ERMS, this is automatically generated by the ERMS
Record type	M	Defining the type of record to which the metadata refers	A number of pre-defined records are used in the Forensic Laboratory to identify record types
Related records	M	Identifies links between different records and identifies the linkages between them	This should be automatically generated by the ERMS for some records, but may need manual input to the "Notes" field
Keywords	M	The key words relating to the record	These are typically free text entries and are usually left to the creator to define

APPENDIX 11 - SAMPLE E-MAIL METADATA

Note
"M/O" refers to whether the entry of the field is mandatory or optional

Field	M/O?	Purpose	Comments
Bcc	M	Recipients of the e-mail message but whose names are not visible to other recipients of the e-mail	Manually entered
Cc	M	Recipients other than the primary recipient of the e-mail message	Manually entered
Date received	M	Shows the time when a message was received by the intended recipient	Autogenerated
Date sent	M	Date and time message sent	Autogenerated
From	M	Sender's identity	Autogenerated
Message ID	M	A unique identification code assigned by the e-mail Client to each message. This may be important when authenticating e-mail	System generated
Message options	O	These permit the sender to attach importance and sensitivity levels to messages	When these options are selected, the importance and sensitivity level will be displayed in both electronic and hardcopy

Continued

Field	M/O?	Purpose	Comments
Security settings	O	The contents and attachments of confidential messages can be encrypted (scrambled) by using the security settings The option of adding a digital signature to an e-mail is also available	
Subject	M	The subject/title of the e-mail message	Entered manually
To	M	The recipient(s) of the e-mail transmission	Manually entered

APPENDIX 12 - FORENSIC CASE RECORDS STORED IN THE ERMS

The following are some of the records or record types that the Forensic Laboratory will normally keep for a Windows PC forensic case.

Where an estimate or quotation is produced and the case does not proceed, the records to the point of abandonment are entered into the ERMS.

The Forensic Laboratory will probably use Encase and FTK as its main forensic tools, but a variety of other specialized tools will also be used.

Where the evidence is hardware or media other than a PC, appropriate records relating to the exhibit are taken. Those given below are intended to be representative of a case.

WHERE RECEIVED IN THE FORENSIC LABORATORY

- initial contact details (fax, letter, e-mail, or records of visit or phone call);
- instructions from the Client;
- case summary from the Client;
- supplementary information from the Client;
- any correspondence between the Client and the Forensic Laboratory;
- initial quotation/estimate to Client;
- Client contact details (phone, fax, mobile, e-mail, address);
- Client case reference;
- Forensic Laboratory case reference number assigned;
- internal Forensic Laboratory forms used during forensic case processing;
- exhibits received and accepted;
- movement records;
- rejection notice (if applicable);
- updated insurance schedule;
- case acceptance letter;
- case assignment details;
- agreed turn round times (TRTs);
- case file;
- virtual case file;
- notes on exhibits;
- photographs of exhibits;
- image(s) created;
- evidence of verification of imaging process;
- details of initial examination of exhibits;
- details of the BIOS and time offset;
- details of any relevant metadata, if present;
- work instructions made contemporaneously by the assigned Forensic Laboratory Analyst;
- details of files recovered from the image;
- a copy of the file structure of the exhibits;
- results of malware scanning (the Forensic Laboratory should use at least two tools to ensure that a complete scan is undertaken);
- results of any signature analysis for the image;
- results of the analysis of the image;
- the extracted information record;
- results of recovery of all graphics files;
- the "initialise Case" report from Encase;
- the link parser report;
- extracts of all unique e-mail addresses;
- Internet history report;
- extracted documents;
- extracted spreadsheets;
- extracted databases;
- extracted images;
- extracted html files;
- extracted e-mail;
- extracted "Favorites";
- extracted "My Documents";
- extracted "Recent";
- extracted "Documents and Settings";
- extracted "Desktop";
- extracted temporary files;
- internet file carve from Encase;
- other artifacts;
- the FTK view of the case;
- results of all searches;
- statements or reports as required;
- authority for release of statements or reports;
- iterations of statements or reports between the Client and the Forensic Laboratory;
- handover of final report and any supporting exhibits to the Client;
- records backup of case to disk and tape;
- case archived.

Note

Some of these records may require iterated discussion with the Client (also entered into the ERMS) based on the results found (e.g., search results indicate the need for additional searches).

WHERE AN ON-SITE SEIZURE IS UNDERTAKEN

Where the Forensic Laboratory has to actually seize evidence on-site, as defined in Chapter 8, whether a "friendly" seizure or not, the following additional records are entered into the ERMS:

- health and safety briefing notes;
- briefing notes for the location of seizure;
- details of others to be present;
- details of what is to be seized;
- evidence log;
- details of evidence bags used;
- identity of the exhibit custodian;
- photos of the seizure site;
- diagrams of the seizure site;
- handover paperwork, if appropriate;
- photos of the equipment to be seized, including the labeled leads;
- notebooks and other contemporaneous notes;
- details of how the exhibits were transported to the Secure Property Store;
- movement forms.

GENERAL

In addition to the records above, all records of any actions taken by anyone to do with the case will be treated as a record and entered into the ERMS, whether it is an electronic or paper record.

Where different exhibits are to be examined, the records above will be amended, or added to, in order to accommodate the exhibits being seized or examined.

APPENDIX 13 - DUBLIN CORE METADATA ELEMENTS

Number	Element
1	Contributor—an entity responsible for making contributions to the content of the resource
2	Coverage—the extent or scope of the content of the resource
3	Creator—an entity primarily responsible for making the content of the resource
4	Date—date of an event in the life cycle of the resource
5	Description—an account of the content of the resource
6	Format—the physical or logical manifestation of the resource
7	Identifier—an unambiguous reference to the resource within a given context
8	Language—the language of the intellectual content of the resource
9	Publisher—the entity responsible for making the resource available
10	Relation—a reference to a related resource
11	Rights—details of the rights held in and over the resource
12	Source—a reference to the resource from which the present resource is derived
13	Subject—the topic of the content of the resource
14	Title—a name given to the resource
15	Type—the nature or genre of the content of the resource

APPENDIX 14 - NATIONAL ARCHIVES OF AUSTRALIA METADATA STANDARD

Number	Element
1	Category—the category of the entity being described (such as series for records or work group for agents)
2	Identifier—an unique identification number or name
3	Name—the name or title of the entity
4	Date—start and end dates of the entity
5	Description—a narrative description of the entity
6	Related entity—identification of any related entities
7	Change history—changes to an entity's metadata values
8	Jurisdiction—the jurisdiction within which the entity operates
9	Security classification—the security status or sensitivity of the entity
10	Security caveat—additional warning or guidance about security or confidentiality issues
11	Permissions—identification of security requirements or permissions for access
12	Rights—other access or rights requirements

Continued

Number	Element
13	Contact—information about how to contact an agent
14	Position—the name of the current position held by an agent
15	Language—language of the record
16	Coverage—the jurisdiction, time, or geographic space covered by the entity
17	Keyword—the subject(s) documented by the record
18	Disposal—current disposal authorities and actions for the record
19	Format—information about the actual format of the record
20	Extent—physical dimensions, size, or duration of the record
21	Medium—physical carrier of the record, particularly manual records
22	Integrity check—a method for determining whether the record has changed in transmission or storage
23	Location—current location of the record, physically or in a computer system
24	Document form—the recognized form of the record, such as agenda, diary, form, or memorandum
25	Precedence—the current time sensitiveness of a record, such as how quickly it needs to be acknowledged

APPENDIX 15 - RESPONSIBILITIES FOR RECORDS MANAGEMENT IN THE FORENSIC LABORATORY

Specific roles and responsibilities for all Forensic Laboratory employees are defined in their detailed job descriptions. However, some high level and general roles and responsibilities are given below:

TOP MANAGEMENT

- recognize the importance of a robust Records Management System in the Forensic Laboratory;
- demonstrate commitment to the Records Management process in the Forensic Laboratory;
- provide appropriate resources (tools, training, and ring-fenced employees) to manage the Records Management System;
- support and endorse the Records Management Policy;
- ensure that a robust and effective Records Management Program is established and maintained;
- ensure that all types of records are managed by the Records Management Program (i.e., physical and electronic records);
- ensure that regular auditing of the Records Management System is undertaken and corrective or preventive action is undertaken, where appropriate;
- include the Forensic Laboratory Record Management System in the Management Review.

LINE MANAGERS

- familiarize themselves with and follow the Forensic Laboratory's Records Management procedures;
- ensure that they understand and follow the procedures for their reports;
- identify records, and specifically Vital Records, within their areas of responsibility for capture in the ERMS;
- ensure that there is an up-to-date inventory maintained of all records that they own;
- review, on an ongoing basis, the records that they own for completeness, reliability, and relevance within the ERMS;
- ensure that, where necessary, Forensic Laboratory employees have appropriate security clearances to undertake their work;
- undertake annual appraisals, with assistance from the Human Resources Department, and identify any training needs for their reports;
- provide input to the disposition requirements of all records within their area of responsibility;
- undertake peer reviews of their report's work.

EMPLOYEES

- ensure that records are properly created and managed. This includes the responsibility to ensure that appropriate metadata is manually included with the records they create or receive, where possible. This shall include ensuring that:
  - all mandatory record keeping metadata is systematically and consistently applied to all records created, or registered, as part of all forensic case processing as well as everyday business activities;
  - all records are entered into the Forensic Laboratory ERMS on creation or registration;
  - mandatory record keeping metadata is systematically and consistently applied to all records created, where the software permits this. The main application suite for business applications is Microsoft Office;
  - mandatory record keeping metadata is systematically and consistently applied to all hardcopy records;
  - record keeping metadata is securely retained for as long as required by legislative, regulatory, contractual, or preservation requirements;

- the integrity and authenticity of records is assured by ensuring that the Forensic Laboratory record keeping system guarantees against any unauthorized modification of a records metadata and that a full audit trail of record access and movement is maintained.
- follow the Forensic Laboratory's Records Management procedures;
- ensure that they dispose of hard copy output appropriately;
- report any suspicious activity or faults according to the Forensic Laboratory Incident Management procedures and not try to "prove" a weakness in the Forensic Laboratory's systems or procedures.

RECORDS MANAGEMENT TEAM

- establish and lead the Forensic Laboratory Records Management Team;
- establish the Forensic Laboratory Records Management Policy and procedures;
- update the Forensic Laboratory Records Management Policy and procedures, as needed;
- support the Forensic Laboratory's Record Management System users;
- issue Records Management guidance;
- develop and undertake training to all users, as appropriate;
- ensure that the ERMS is functioning correctly;
- create and maintain access rights for all records according to authorized business needs;
- administer the ERMS and Registry as required.

AUDIT MANAGER

- undertake audits of the ERMS according to the IMS calendar or on an as-required basis according to the internal audit procedures, as defined in Section 8.1.15.

QUALITY MANAGER

- undertake quality audits and reviews of all samples of work products and services relating to forensic case work as well as general business operations;
- provide regular management reports relating to ISO 9001 procedures and agreed quality objectives.

APPENDIX 16 - METADATA FOR RECORDS STORED OFF-SITE

Note

"M/O" refers to whether the entry of the field is mandatory or optional

Field	M/O?	Purpose	Comments
Borrowed date	M	The date the file/ carton was signed out	
Borrower	M	Identity of anyone "borrowing the carton"—for whatever reason	
Box number	M	The unique ID of the box containing the record	
Date sent off-site	M	The date when a carton is collected and taken to the off-site storage facility	
Destroy year	M	The date when records in a specific carton are to be destroyed in accordance with the Forensic Laboratory retention schedule	
Destroyed	M	The "marker" to show when written authorization has been provided to the off-site storage provider confirming the destruction of cartons listed in the periodic disposal report	
Recall barcode number	M	The unique barcode number provided by the off-site storage provider that is provided to each of the Forensic Laboratory's cartons that they are managing	
Record number	M	Allocates a unique number to identify any record in the ERMS	All record numbers must be entered in accordance with the numbering system in the ERMS. No records can be entered into the ERMS without a valid record number
Returned date	M	The date the file/ carton was returned	
Returner	M	Identity of person returning the carton or file	

APPENDIX 17 - RECORDS CLASSIFICATION SYSTEM

The Forensic Laboratory uses a four-level classification system for records within the ERMS. These are as follows:

Classification	Description	Some examples
Business critical	Records without which the Forensic Laboratory could not continue to operate. Records that give evidence of status and protect the Forensic Laboratory and its Clients Irreplaceable	• Legal documents; • Contracts; • Accounts; • All forensic case records.
Important	Important to the continued operation of the Forensic Laboratory. Could be reproduced from a variety of source documents, from Clients/suppliers, or backups. Replaceable	• Procedures; • Nonessential business records.
Useful	Loss would cause temporary inconvenience to the Forensic Laboratory Replaceable	• Most regular business correspondence
Nonessential	No value to the Forensic Laboratory beyond either the time limits of the life cycle of the record or records/ documents for public consumption Replaceable	• Advertising material; • Published articles.

APPENDIX 18 - DISPOSITION AUTHORIZATION

The same form is used for requesting authority for disposition, authorizing disposition, and recording disposition method. It contains:

- date;
- requestor;
- address;
- office phone;
- mobile phone;
- e-mail;
- description of record(s) for which disposition is required;
- location of record(s);
- forensic case file number, if appropriate;
- retention expiry date;
- signature and name of requestor;
- disposition authorized;
- disposition method agreed:
  - physical or logical destruction;
  - retain for a further period;
  - archive and retain for a further period;
  - transfer to a named third party.
- authorized by and date;
- date of disposition;
- disposition effected by name and signature;
- destruction method, if appropriate;
- certificate of destruction, if appropriate;
- confirmation of retention for a further period;
- confirmation of archival in-house and retention for a further period;
- details of third party to receive it;
- movement sheet completed, if appropriate;
- property log updated, if appropriate.

APPENDIX 19 - ADDITIONAL REQUIREMENTS FOR PHYSICAL RECORD RECOVERY

While the standard BCP allows recovery of IT systems and electronic records as well as specific business functions, the requirements for physical record (e.g., paper documents, photographs, etc.) are not covered. Some of the specific requirements for the BCP are given below for Record Management recovery:

- has consideration of fire pre-planning been undertaken specifically for physical records with the local fire service?
- are the physical records covered by non-water fire quenching systems (e.g., Halon or FM 200)?
- are specialized document recovery specialists identified in the BCP?
- if records are wet as part of fire quenching, where can they be laid out to dry and sort?
- while wet records can be recovered and burned records not, has it been ensured that space will always be available for records to be dried and sorted?
- if the original Forensic Laboratory accommodation is unavailable for any reason, where will the refurbished records be located?

- while records recovery specialists may advise that movement of physical records after a fire, with ensuing water damage, may cause irreparable damage, immediate action may be required.
- have the Records Management Team been trained in how to safely and securely undertake immediate actions that will not overly damage the physical records?
- is there someone who can undertake a risk assessment of the area for records recovery and make recommendations according to local health and safety requirements?
- is there a process for handling burnt records?
- is there a process for "hoovering up" material relating to physical records?
- how will microfilms be recovered?
- have specialist equipment suppliers for Records Management been identified and documented?
- have specialists for Records Management been identified and documented?
- have specialist checklists been created for records recovery?
- are appropriate forms in use for record recovery?

APPENDIX 20 - SPECIALIZED EQUIPMENT NEEDED FOR INSPECTION AND RECOVERY OF DAMAGED RECORDS

EQUIPMENT

The following equipment should be stored off-site and be used if inspection and recovery of the damaged physical records is required:

- adhesive tape (clear);
- blotting paper (archival);
- brooms;
- building plans;
- camera (Digital or Polaroid) and films (or video camera);
- cling film;
- clipboards;
- crates;
- dehumidifiers to prevent the onset of mold;
- dictaphones;
- dry wipe boards;
- entry signs (prohibiting entry, smoking, etc.);
- first aid kit;
- flip charts;
- hazard tape;
- medical supplies;
- mops and buckets;
- newsprint (plain);
- packing materials and crates for record recovery (these may be water-draining packing crates, but these also have a downside);
- paper clips;
- pens (multicolored);
- plastic sheeting to protect the damaged area;
- plastic sheeting;
- plastic wallets (A4 and larger);
- polythene freezer bags;
- record register;
- rubbish bags;
- scissors;
- sponges;
- squeegees;
- string;
- tape for securing a variety of items;
- tie on labels;
- torches and batteries;
- ventilators to draw spores away from the Records Management Team—the area must be well ventilated;
- wax crayons (water resistant);
- wrapping paper;
- writing pads.

CLOTHING

Before touching any physical records, personal protective equipment (PPE) should be issued to the Records Management Team. The team must have received training how to use any PPE issued.

The following should be used, as a minimum:

- stout shoes or boots;
- hard hats;
- protective eye wear;
- protective gloves;
- coveralls or overalls;
- respirators.

Chapter 16

Performance Assessment

16.1 OVERVIEW

Every organization has the ability to improve its efficiency and the services it delivers to its Clients, and the Forensic Laboratory is no exception.

To ensure that the Forensic Laboratory is able to continuously improve its management systems, associated procedures, and products and services that it delivers to its Clients, it is necessary to monitor and measure how well the applicable requirements from those systems are being met. This is carried out using the following processes:

- monitoring and measurement;
- SLAs and TRTs;
- evaluation of compliance;
- security metrics;
- internal audit;
- Client feedback;
- Complaints management;
- handling of non-conformities;
- Management Review.

Each of these processes is covered in different parts of this book, but are summarized below for ease of reference.

16.2 PERFORMANCE ASSESSMENT

16.2.1 Monitoring and Measurement

The Forensic Laboratory shall carry out monitoring and measurement of its management systems and other internal processes to determine the extent to which their requirements are met. This shall be carried out using a mix of the following:

- trend analysis, as defined in Chapter 6, Section 6.13.4; Chapter 7, Sections 7.4.1.3.3, 7.4.1.6, 7.4.6.4, 7.4.8.1, and 7.4.10.4; and Chapter 14, Section 14.4.2;
- internal audits, as defined in Chapter 4, Section 4.7.3 and Chapter 15, Section 15.8.1.15;
- external audits, as defined in Chapter 12, Section 12.3.13.2;
- Management Review, as defined in Chapter 4, Section 4.9;
- BCP exercise feedback, as defined in Chapter 13, Sections 13.6.4 and 13.7;
- penetration testing, as defined in Chapter 12, Section 12.3.13.2.2;
- self assessments, as defined in Chapter 13, Section 13.8;
- examination of Complaints, as defined in Chapter 6, Section 6.14;
- examination of incident reports, as defined in Chapter 7, Section 7.4.1;
- examination of fault logs, as defined in Chapter 7, Section 7.4.10.6;
- examination of problem reports, as defined in Chapter 7, Section 7.4.2;
- such other processes as management sees fit.

The scope, frequency, aims and objectives of these tests, and reviews shall be defined and be agreed with the Audit Committee. Records of these monitoring and measurement processes shall be maintained with associated corrective and/or preventive action requests. The Terms of Reference for the Audit Committee is given in Chapter 4, Appendix 27.

The results of these tests and any associated corrective and/or preventive action requests shall be communicated to relevant stakeholders, as appropriate.

16.2.2 SLAs and TRTs

The TRTs required by a Client and the SLAs defined by the Laboratory Manager and agreed with the Client, are defined in Chapter 6, Section 6.6, must be under constant review. These include:

- requests for investigation and examination;
- number of jobs (or cases) undertaken per year;
- number of Terabytes of evidence imaged;
- number of PCs examined;
- number of mobile devices examined;
- number of other devices examined;
- training undertaken in the year for all Forensic Analysts;
- successful cases (as a percentage of all cases);
- sentences or penalties resulting from forensic cases;
- number of "assists";
- number of successful "assists";
- sentences or penalties resulting from "assists";
- numbers of jobs that met or bettered TRTs;
- number of jobs that failed their TRTs;
- numbers of jobs that met or bettered SLAs;
- number of jobs that failed their SLAs;
- feedback from Clients (using the Client Feedback Forms).

16.2.3 Evaluation of Conformance

The results of the monitoring and measurement processes above shall be used to evaluate the level of compliance that the Forensic Laboratory has for the aims and objectives of its management systems, other governing processes, and legislative requirements.

A formal report of these evaluations shall be maintained and presented, with their supporting records, to the relevant oversight committees:

- ISO 9001—Quality Committee, as defined in Chapter 4, Appendix 32;
- OHSAS 18001—Health and Safety Committee, as defined in Chapter 4, Appendix 30;
- ISO 22301—Business Continuity Committee as defined in Chapter 4, Appendix 28;
- ISO 27001—Information Security Committee, as defined in Chapter 4, Appendix 31;
- Audit Committee, as defined in Chapter 4, Appendix 27;
- Risk Committee, as defined in Chapter 4, Appendix 33.

At a high level, metrics are quantifiable measurements of some aspects of a management system. There are some identifiable attributes that collectively characterize the level of compliance of the management system. This is a quantitative measure of how much of that attribute the management system has, and can be built from lower level physical measures that are the outcome of monitoring and measurement.

Typically, the following types of metrics should be identified and studied:

- process metrics—specific metrics that could serve as quantitative or qualitative evidence of the level of maturity for a particular management system that could serve as a binary indication of the presence or absence of a mature process;
- management system metrics—a measurable attribute of the result of a capability maturity process that could serve as evidence of its effectiveness. A metric may be objective or subjective, and quantitative or qualitative.

The first type of metric provides information about the processes themselves. The second type of metric provides information on the results of those processes and what they can tell the stakeholders about how effective the use of the processes has been in achieving an acceptable security outcome. These metrics categories tailor their own metrics program to measure their progress against security objectives.

There are a number of capability maturity models that can be used to evaluate compliance levels and that are recognized worldwide. They include:

- Capability Maturity Model for quality;
- Capability Maturity Model for health and safety;
- Capability Maturity Model for business continuity;
- Capability Maturity Model for System Security Engineering (this has since become ISO/IEC 21827:2008);
- Capability Maturity Model for Information Security;
- Building in Security Maturity Model;
- Capability Maturity Model for people;
- Capability Maturity Model for portfolio, program, and project management.

While these are specific maturity models for aspects of the Forensic Laboratory's management systems, there is no specific Capability Maturity Mode for the operation of forensic laboratories at the time of writing.

Note

The Forensic Laboratory should adopt and adapt a number of these for its own use and develop a Forensic Capability Maturity Mode.

16.2.4 Security Metrics

Security metrics are measured on a regular basis, as defined in Chapter 5, Appendix 22.

16.2.5 Internal Audit

The internal audit process is defined in Chapter 4, Section 4.7.3.

16.2.6 Client Feedback

Client feedback is essential to the Forensic Laboratory as it allows Clients to provide comments on the products and services they receive from the Forensic Laboratory. It is closely linked to "Complaints" but allows any feedback to be provided in a structured manner rather than a complaint being some dissatisfaction with the products and services provided.

Client feedback can be:

- in person;
- by telephone;
- in writing by letter;
- online by completing the Complaints form or the feedback form.

Unstructured feedback that provides qualitative feedback will be provided by the following feedback processes:

- in person;
- by telephone;
- in writing by letter;
- online by completing the complaints form.

These forms of feedback allow free form communication, whereas a feedback form "scores" the Forensic Laboratory product or service offering and allows quantitative measurements to be made.

The Forensic Laboratory Client forensic case processing feedback process is defined in Chapter 14, Section 14.2.1.2 with the form and is given in Chapter 6, Appendix 20.

The Forensic Laboratory testimony feedback form is given in Chapter 11, Appendix 8.

16.2.7 Managing Client complaints

The procedures for managing Client complaints are defined in Chapter 6, Section 6.14.

16.2.8 Handling of Non-conformities

Where non-conformities have been identified either from:

- *internal audit finding*—any discrepancy in the management system found and reported by Internal Auditors;
- *external audit finding*—any discrepancy in the management system found and reported by External Auditors;
- *management review finding*—any discrepancy in the management system found and reported by a Management Review of the Management System;
- *system certification body audit finding*—any discrepancy in the management system found and reported during the Certification Audit cycle by the relevant Certification Body;
- *incident*—any incident identified and reported that affects the expected outcome of the management system and may lead to corrective or preventive action;
- *preventive action*—the processing of ideas or suggestions for process and product improvement within the management systems.

They shall be reviewed to determine action to be taken, as defined in Chapter 4, Section 4.8.

The review shall be in the form of a formal response to the audit report or incident.

The Forensic Laboratory should also use trend analysis for identification of persistent non-conformance or incidents or faults.

In some cases, the response to the audit report will suffice, but if action is needed it shall be raised as a Corrective Action Request (CAR), and communicated to all relevant stakeholders as appropriate.

Corrective action is often derived from the above and agreed with the person raising it. The raising and agreeing of a Corrective Action Plan (CAP) will derive the required agreed corrective action.

Depending on the nature and severity of the non-conformance, it will be discussed at the next relevant management system meeting. In exceptional circumstances, an emergency meeting can be, and may be, called. It is essential to:

- determine the root cause of the non-conformity;
- evaluate the corrective action needed to be taken to ensure that the non-conformity does not recur.

Corrective action is the result of something going wrong (e.g., an incident or accident). Preventive action seeks to identify potential issues before they become faults, failures, incidents, or accidents. The implementation of preventive action often costs less than corrective action and is typically easier to implement.

Preventive action is usually more difficult to identify, but the Forensic Laboratory regularly assesses its products and services and infrastructure to help identify trends:

- ongoing staff awareness is essential so that employees and third parties spot things that appear wrong or "not quite right" and they are encouraged to report them through the normal fault or incident reporting process—or where warranted to the relevant management system Owner or Line Manager. The Forensic Laboratory has a "no blame culture";
- the Forensic Laboratory analyzes trends to see if there are specific incidents that occur more frequently than others;
- the Forensic Laboratory maintains a corporate risk register as well as risk registers for specific projects. These, with the results from the Business Impact Analysis, shall be used to determine high-level risks that should be addressed and so controls are defined to treat these risks.

When a potential preventive action is identified, it is assessed and processed as a corrective action, where the Auditee is the relevant Owner for the operational area.

16.2.9 Management Reviews

Management Reviews are defined in Chapter 4, Section 4.9.

Chapter 17

Health and Safety Procedures

Table of Contents

17.1 GENERAL

17.1.1 The Importance of People and a Safe Workplace

No organization can function without people, an organization's most important asset. Work can make a positive or negative impact on an individual employee's mental and physical health in the Forensic Laboratory. They can be affected if they are exposed to harm as part of their everyday duties (e.g., an unsafe work environment, violence in the workplace, or unsafe working practices). However, with a safe and secure workplacc, where employees are interested in their job, feel safe, and know they are using safe working practices, job satisfaction can increase and improvements in the employee's personal health and well-being can result.

Organizations that successfully manage health and safety in the workplace recognize the relationship between risk management and employee health and its relationship with the business itself. A good Health and Safety Policy is aligned with all other Human Resources type policies and other corporate policies designed to demonstrate Top Management commitment to ensuring a safe and secure working environment for all the Forensic Laboratory employees and third parties working on their behalf. Increasingly, employees are undertaking mobile and teleworking, and these risks must also be managed.

The aim of implementing appropriate Health and Safety Policies in the Forensic Laboratory is to improve the health and safety performance within all operational areas so that accidents and ill-health are substantially reduced, if not totally eliminated, and that work is a satisfying experience for all employees to the benefit of the employee as well as the Forensic Laboratory.

The Forensic Laboratory must recognize the relationship between the health and safety of its employees, the Human Resources Department, and the very core of its business as they recognize that its employees are the key resource. Like other ethical and responsible organizations, the Forensic Laboratory:

- recognizes the benefits of a fit, healthy, enthusiastic, competent, and committed workforce;
- realizes that good human resources policies within the Forensic Laboratory can be undermined by poor or weak Health and Safety Policies and procedures;
- visibly demonstrates that they are not concerned with "paying lip service" to health and safety issues, relevant legislation and regulation within the jurisdiction but are genuinely committed to continuously improving the workplace for their employees;
- promotes a positive healthy and safe workplace for all its employees and third parties working on their bchalf.

Accidents, ill-health, and safety-related incidents are seldom random events but are usually due to some failure in control or process and often involve multiple contributory factors and events. The immediate cause may well be a human one, but the root cause is more often a management failure. This is why, for each incident or accident, the Forensic Laboratory must establish the root cause and continuously improve its health and safety performance. Health and safety in the Forensic Laboratory starts with visible and demonstrable commitment from Top Management, without this, the implementation will fail.

The ultimate goal of the Forensic Laboratory is to improve its health and safety performance so that accidents, injuries, work-related health issues and "near misses" are either eliminated or reduced to an acceptable level. The Forensic Laboratory's risk appetite is defined in Chapter 5, Section 5.5.9.1 and given in Chapter 5, Appendix 14. Work should be part of a satisfying lifestyle for all employees and be a benefit to both them and the Forensic Laboratory.

The Forensic Laboratory must adopt a total loss approach concentrating on effective prevention of operational health and safety (OH&S) incidents, identifying and eliminating (where possible) root causes of incidents, as given in Chapter 4, Appendix 49. The traditional organizational approach has been to manage issues at the end of the process or when an incident occurs. This is costly, inefficient, and ineffective in all areas. The Forensic Laboratory will need to build OH&S into the IMS and embedded from the start, just like quality, information security, etc. The Forensic Laboratory should adopt a process-based approach where excellent business processes are designed "in" rather than having management system failures detected by inspection, auditing, or other means and then addressed after an OH&S failure.

17.1.2 Management Requirements

The Forensic Laboratory is committed to the provision of a safe working environment as a key element of their goal of achieving quality in every aspect of its operations. In addition, around the world, there are a number of different legislative and regulatory requirements that the Forensic Laboratory has to address and prove demonstrable compliance.

The Occupational Health and Safety Management Systems (OHSAS) 18001/2 standards for occupational health and safety have a common management system that will need to be integrated into the Forensic Laboratory's Integrated Management System (IMS). The management system follows the traditional Plan-Do-Check-Act process, as defined in Chapter 4, Section 4.3.1. Specifically, in terms of OH&S, this means:

- *Plan*—establish the objectives and processes necessary to deliver results in accordance with the Forensic Laboratory's Occupational Health and Safety Policy;
- *Do*—implement the processes and procedures to support the policy;
- *Check*—monitor and measure the processes against the OH&S Policy, objectives, legal, and other relevant requirements within the jurisdiction;
- *Act*—undertake necessary corrective or preventive actions to continuously improve performance in the areas of OH&S, as defined in Chapter 4, Section 4.8.

Within the Forensic Laboratory, there are three main areas where OH&S is applicable. These are:

1. The working environment (in the office, laboratory, teleworking, or mobile working).
2. On undertaking first responder or similar duties at a location remote to the normal work place and collecting evidence for return to the working environment.
3. Processing evidence as part of normal duties in the working environment.

To achieve the above, the Forensic Laboratory has established, documented, implemented, maintained, monitored, and continuously improved its OH&S Management System for the defined scope, as given in Chapter 5, Appendix 11. This has been integrated into the Forensic Laboratory's IMS so that economies of scale and management system integration can be implemented, reducing duplication of effort across the different implemented management systems.

17.1.3 The Forensic Laboratory OH&S Policy

The Forensic Laboratory OH&S Policy should be defined to be appropriate to the requirements of the specific laboratory setup, its operation, and the legislative requirements in the jurisdiction(s) where it is in operation. This may cause different policies to be adopted for different laboratories in different jurisdictions.

It will need to ensure that it gives a commitment to prevention of accidents, ill-health due to work, safety incidents, and that all relevant legislation and regulations within the jurisdiction are at least met, or preferably exceeded.

As with other management frameworks in the Forensic Laboratory's IMS, the OH&S framework should be populated with appropriate documents, be implemented, maintained, monitored, and continuously improved. Education and awareness must be undertaken from induction time and refresher training undertaken, especially if an accident or incident occurs, as defined in Chapter 4, Section 4.6.2.2 and the checklist given in Chapter 6, Appendix 11.

Top Management must enforce the OH&S Policy, as with all other Forensic Laboratory policies, starting at the top and reaching every Forensic Laboratory employee and third-party employees working on their behalf, as well as ensuring that the OH&S Policy is regularly reviewed. This should happen at least annually at the Management Review, as defined in Chapter 4, Section 4.9, after an incident or accident or any other influencing change.

The checklist for developing an OH&S Policy is given in Appendix 1.

The Forensic Laboratory OH&S Policy is also given in Appendix 2.

17.1.4 Responsibilities

Within the Forensic Laboratory, OH&S process, there are a number of responsibilities at every level in the organization. The following responsibilities may be present in the Forensic Laboratory.

17.1.4.1 Top Management

Top Management's responsibilities include, but are not limited to:

- agreeing and authorizing the OH&S Policy;
- reviewing OH&S performance;
- setting direction for OH&S within the Forensic Laboratory;
- ensuring that appropriate resources are available to support the Forensic Laboratory OH&S Policy;
- ensuring that there is demonstrable Top Management support for the OH&S Policy;

- keeping up with relevant legislation and regulation within the jurisdiction;
- planning for OH&S issues.

17.1.4.2 Health and Safety Manager

The Health and Safety Manager's responsibilities include, but are not limited to:

- developing and maintaining a suitable and relevant Health and Safety Policy, processes, and procedures;
- undertaking risk assessments, as appropriate, for the Forensic Laboratory working environment;
- being a competent person to provide advice and guidance on all OH&S issues;
- ensuring that appropriate controls are in place to reduce OH&S risks to acceptable levels;
- undertaking training, as required, for all the Forensic Laboratory employees in OH&S;
- undertaking auditing and monitoring activities for the Forensic Laboratory OH&S system, including any remediation required, on behalf of Top Management;
- keeping up-to-date with legislative and regulatory changes in OH&S within their jurisdiction.

The Forensic Laboratory's Health and Safety Manager's job description is given in Appendix 3.

17.1.4.3 Line Managers

Line Manager's responsibilities include, but are not limited to:

- complying with all OH&S Policy requirements, including supporting procedures;
- taking care of their own OH&S and that of others who may be affected by their work;
- implementing the Forensic Laboratory OH&S Policy in their areas of responsibility;
- ensuring that the appropriate controls are in place in their area of responsibility;
- liaising with the Health and Safety Manager, including advising of any change in working procedures that may require risks to be re-assessed;
- communicating the requirements of the IMS, and specifically the OH&S Management System, to their reports;
- monitoring the effectiveness of controls in their area of responsibility;
- setting an example for their reports in the area of OH&S.

17.1.4.4 The Forensic Laboratory, Generally

The Forensic Laboratory has a duty of care to their employees, and any third parties working on their behalf, to provide a safe working environment, as far as is reasonably practicable. This includes, but is not limited to the provision and maintenance of:

- safe access and egress to the Forensic Laboratory premises;
- safe systems of work;
- safe plant and equipment for use anywhere in the Forensic Laboratory;
- information, instructions, procedures, and training for all Forensic Laboratory employees relating to OH&S;
- a safe location where any Forensic Laboratory employees may work, including teleworking, mobile working, and on-site working.

17.1.4.5 Employees

All the Forensic Laboratory employees responsibilities include, but are not limited to:

- comply with all OH&S Policy requirements, including supporting procedures;
- take reasonable care of their own OH&S and that of others who may be affected by their work;
- maintain clean and tidy individual work areas;
- co-operate with Line Managers in all OH&S matters;
- not to intentionally, or recklessly, interfere with any plant, equipment, or material relating to the provision of OH&S in the Forensic Laboratory or in any location where the Forensic Laboratory employees may be working;
- correctly use any OH&S equipment or personal protective equipment (PPE) that they are required to use as part of their job role;
- know where to find, and use, any safe system of working procedures;
- inform their Line Manager of any change of condition that may affect their work performance (e.g., pregnancy) that may affect existing risk assessments or working practices and procedures;
- report any OH&S incidents, accidents, or health issues to their Line Managers.

17.1.5 Benefits

17.1.5.1 Direct Benefits

The direct benefits of an effective OH&S Management System to the Forensic Laboratory include, but are not limited to:

- an OH&S system that is specifically tailored to the Forensic Laboratory, as it is risk driven;
- less money spent for overtime benefits;
- less time lost due to OH&S incidents;
- lower costs for job accommodations for injured employees;
- lower employee's compensation insurance costs;

- lower expenditures for return-to-work programs;
- lower medical expenditures;
- legislative compliance is easier to attain and prove with appropriate records;
- provides a manageable method for continuous improvement of OH&S within the Forensic Laboratory;
- demonstrates visible Top Management commitment;
- is a part of corporate governance;
- demonstrates corporate social responsibility;
- provides re-assurance to enforcement authorities;
- provides an emergency preparedness capability;
- has a process-based systematic risk management process.

17.1.5.2 Indirect Benefits

OH&S can also make big reductions in indirect costs, due to:

- better employee relations;
- better use of human resources;
- higher quality work products;
- increased morale;
- increased productivity;
- reduced employee turnover.

17.1.5.3 Family Benefits

Employees and their families can also benefit from safety and health because:

- their incomes are protected;
- their family lives are not hindered by injury;
- their stress is not increased.

Simply put, protecting employees in the Forensic Laboratory's best interest. OH&S adds value to the business, workplaces, and the lives of their employees.

17.2 PLANNING FOR OH&S

17.2.1 General

This is the first stage in the PDCA cycle for implementing a robust OH&S Management System.

The reduction of, and response to, OH&S incidents is part of the OH&S Management System, which is part of the Forensic Laboratory IMS. The OH&S Management System addresses the types of incidents, accidents, and health hazards that could happen in the Forensic Laboratory.

17.2.2 Legal, Regulatory, and Other Requirements

It is essential that the Forensic Laboratory identifies all relevant legal and regulatory requirements for OH&S within the jurisdiction and that these are all taken into consideration when the OH&S Management System is being implemented and operated. This is defined in Chapter 12, Section 12.3.13.1. The Forensic Laboratory ensures that they at least meet the minimum requirements and they aim to exceed them wherever possible and continuously improve their OH&S Management System.

Within many jurisdictions there are different legislative and regulatory OH&S requirements that may affect the Forensic Laboratory. They may have different requirements in performing tasks such as risk assessments or to provide protection for different people (e.g., employees, members of the public, etc.). Top Management must ensure that they are aware of such differences, and it is imperative that a competent external resource is used to provide specialist advice.

Top Management must also ensure that they maintain the list of applicable legislation and regulations and that their OH&S Management System is updated to ensure compliance with any relevant changes, as defined in Chapter 12, Section 12.3.13.1.

Some examples of drivers for OH&S are given in Appendix 4.

All the Forensic Laboratory employees must be made aware of these requirements, as must anyone else who may be affected by the work that the Forensic Laboratory carries out.

17.2.3 Objectives

The Forensic Laboratory must identify and document OH&S objectives within the IMS for the whole of the Forensic Laboratory's business. These objectives have been defined and are relevant to operations carried out in the workplace and it is recommended that the Forensic Laboratory adopt the SMART approach used to evaluate OH&S objectives, as defined in as defined in Chapter 3, Section 3.1.17.

The Forensic Laboratory objectives are given in the Appendix 5. Actual objectives for each Forensic Laboratory site will vary and must be defined and reported back to the Management Review as defined in Chapter 4, Section 4.9.

The Forensic Laboratory must establish, implement, monitor, and maintain an OH&S Management System with supporting framework to achieve these objectives.

Within the Forensic Laboratory, responsibilities of OH&S must be established and communicated at all levels of employees. This is reinforced at induction and refresher training, as given in Chapter 6, Appendix 11. Where additional training is required for those with specific responsibilities (e.g., OH&S Manager, Display Screen Equipment (DSE) Assessor, etc.), it shall be incorporated into training plans after being identified by relevant TNA reviews, as defined in Chapter 18, Section 18.2.2.

The Management Review will ensure that at least annually the OH&S objectives are reviewed, adjusted as necessary, and ensure to continuously improve the OH&S Management System, as defined in Chapter 4, Section 4.9.

17.2.4 Planning for Hazard Identification

It is essential that Top Management ensures that appropriate plans are put in place to develop and implement the OH&S Management System. Plans should cover all the Forensic Laboratory operations whether in the laboratory itself or at any location remote to it.

17.2.4.1 General Workplace Hazard Identification

It is the responsibility of the Forensic Laboratory Top Management to identify hazards that may affect their employees or third parties working on their behalf. A hazard is defined as:

- the potential for harm to an employee.

These can happen in everyday tasks in the Forensic Laboratory or be related to an occasional specific task (e.g., forensic evidence seizure or a visitor to the Forensic Laboratory).

A list of common hazards that may be found in the Forensic Laboratory is given in Appendix 6.

Inspection of the workplace should be carried out to identify hazards present, or likely to be present, by Top Management and/or the Health and Safety Manager. This is one of the major components of the Forensic Laboratory OH&S Management System and demonstrates management commitment. This process will identify existing and potential hazards in the workplace, wherever it happens to be. While hazard identification is the first step in the process, the likelihood of the risk happening must also be calculated and controls put in place to reduce the risk to an acceptable level. If hazards are identified and not treated, then the OH&S Management System and Top Management's commitment to it will lose credibility with the employees.

While there are a number of hazards that can be identified in the workplace and employees work, jobs for hazard identification should be prioritized as follows:

- jobs with highest incident or "near miss" rate;
- jobs with the potential to cause serious incidents, even if there is no previous history of incidents;
- jobs that are new in the Forensic Laboratory or have recently changed;
- all other jobs.

Hazard identification should also be reviewed on a regular basis, at least annually, after any incident, "near miss," or on influencing change to the jobs undertaken by employees.

17.2.4.2 Performing the Hazard Analysis

The first task that the Forensic Laboratory must undertake was a review of the OH&S incident history. Obviously, there would be no incident history if it were to be a newly commissioned site. This process also assists in prioritization of the jobs to be examined for hazards.

When undertaking workplace hazard identification, it is essential to involve all the Forensic Laboratory employees in the process. They have a unique understanding of how they perform their job, and this is invaluable for identification of hazards. Involving all employees will help to minimize any omissions and demonstrates management commitment to the employees as well as obtaining their "buy in" to the process. They will also feel involved in the process and will "own" the results for their own specific workplace.

As part of the process, all Forensic Laboratory employees should be involved in discussions as to what they perceive as hazards in their job. They may also have ideas for likelihood of occurrence and methods for reducing them to acceptable levels. If there are any hazards identified that pose an immediate danger, they must be immediately treated to reduce the risk to an acceptable level, as defined by the Forensic Laboratory's risk appetite given in Chapter 5, Section 5.5.9.1 and Chapter 5, Appendix 14.

Once all of the jobs have been identified in the Forensic Laboratory, they should be prioritized for inspection and hazard analysis. Part of the inspection process will be to break jobs down into component tasks or steps, where appropriate, to facilitate the hazard analysis process. All employees must also be involved in this process to ensure that the work breakdown is correct.

The goal of the inspection of the employee's workplace and discussions is to identify:

- what can go wrong (i.e., the hazard);
- the consequences for the employee as well as the Forensic Laboratory;
- who else may be affected (e.g., third parties working on behalf of the Forensic Laboratory, members of the public, visitors to the Forensic Laboratory, etc.);
- whether a specific class of employees are at risk (e.g., pregnant employees, disabled employees, first responders, etc.);
- circumstances in which the hazard can occur;
- any other factors that may contribute to the hazard occurring.

A consistent approach to documenting the findings should be adopted in the Forensic Laboratory using Hazard Identification Forms. The contents of the Forensic Laboratory Hazard Identification Form are given in Appendix 7.

Rarely will a hazard have a single root cause and a single effect, more likely it will be the result of a number of factors happening together. This is where the employee's knowledge about their job is invaluable.

Some areas of the Forensic Laboratory's operations that should be examined are given in Appendix 8.

17.2.5 Risk Assessment

Once all of the possible hazards have been identified for each job and tasks in the Forensic Laboratory, the level of risk attached to each must be determined. OH&S risk assessments are simply a careful examination of the likelihood of the hazard occurring and its potential impact. The risk assessment process that can be used in the Forensic Laboratory is defined in Chapter 5. It is recommended that these are placed in the Corporate Risk Register, as given in Chapter 5, Appendix 17.

Again, much of the input to this process will come from discussion with the employees themselves and inspection of past accidents or near misses, if available. Some inputs to the risk assessment processes used in the Forensic Laboratory are given in Appendix 9.

The purpose of risk assessment is to rate the hazards or risks in terms of harm they can cause. Ideally, all hazards should be eliminated, but often this is not possible and they have to be reduced to an acceptable level. Different levels of health and safety consequences are given in Appendix 10 and these should be used in combination with the consequences table given in Chapter 5, Appendix 5, specifically the following columns:

- value;
- embarrassment level;
- published outside organization;
- financial cost of disruption to activities.

Note

The "value" value in Appendix 10 and Chapter 5, Appendix 5 are mapped directly to each other.

There are a number of different approaches to reducing, or eliminating, OH&S risks. These include the following approaches:

- using a less risky option of working;
- preventing access to the hazard source;
- organizing work in the Forensic Laboratory to reduce the exposure to the hazard;
- ensuring that all the Forensic employees have appropriate PPE to reduce the risk of the hazard occurring;
- ensuring that there are recovery facilities available in case the risk crystallizes (e.g., first-aid facilities).

The controls chosen need not have a major financial impact, and ideally they should be low-cost solutions.

Risk assessments must be regularly reviewed at least annually, after any incident and on any influencing change (e.g., legislative change or change in personal medical circumstances for an employee such as a disability, injury, or pregnancy).

Any change in working practices shall have an OH&S risk assessment carried out on the change (or new process, as applicable) and all OH&S issues shall be considered and addressed prior to the implementation of the change. Any changes shall use the Forensic Laboratory's change management process, as defined in Chapter 7, Section 7.4.3, and ensure that the risks are all identified, recorded, and managed to either eliminate the risk or reduce it to an acceptable level using the Forensic Laboratory's continuous improvement process, as defined in Chapter 4, Section 4.8.

17.2.6 Control Selection

After carrying out the risk assessment and hazard identification, the risks should be prioritized and treated appropriately using a variety of controls. These can be additional to existing controls or totally new ones. The hierarchy for implementing controls to reduce the risks is as follows:

- elimination of the risk;
- reduction to within the Forensic Laboratory's risk appetite;
- implementation of engineering controls;
- administrative or procedural controls including signage;
- using PPE.

There are a number of basic OH&S precautions that have been taken as a basic set of controls for employees working in the Forensic Laboratory. These include specific situations as well as generic laboratory controls, and these include:

17.2.6.1 General Controls

17.2.6.1.1 Electrical Hazards

- all electrical equipment used in the Forensic Laboratory must be maintained in accordance with the manufacturers' recommendations;
- all electrical equipment used in the Forensic Laboratory must be regularly inspected to ensure that it has no defects. If defects are found, they must be immediately dealt with and unsafe electrical equipment must be taken out of service until they are made safe. Hazards to check for include, but are not limited to:
  - damaged electrical outlets or plugs;
  - equipment that is overheating (e.g., feels hot), smells (e.g., sparking, smoke, or electrical smell);
  - frayed power leads;
  - gives off electrical shocks;

  - has loose connections and is sparking or arcing;
  - other tell-tale signs of defective electrical equipment that is not maintained in accordance with the manufacturers' recommendations.
- ensure that any employees who use personally owned equipment in the Forensic Laboratory have it tested in accordance with jurisdictional requirements and that it is regularly tested, just like Forensic Laboratory-owned equipment;
- ensure that all electric leads are routed to reduce the likelihood of them causing any hazard. Ideally, specifically designed trunking should be used;
- ensure that power sockets are not overloaded or that employees have "daisy-chained" numerous extension leads, specifically multi-socket extensions;
- where floor sockets are in use, ensure that appropriate covers are used to ensure that they do not become a hazard and that walkways are routed to avoid them (or they are not used if in a walkway);
- ensure that all the Forensic Laboratory employees know what types of fire extinguisher are to be used on electrical fires (i.e., carbon dioxide and powder), how to recognize them and ensure that they are clearly marked;
- ensure that where an employee identifies a possible electrical defect they immediately report it and await instructions rather than attempt to rectify it themselves.

17.2.6.1.2 Falls

- ensure that all equipment or other materials used in the Forensic Laboratory are stored properly to prevent falls;
- ensure that all Forensic Laboratory employees are trained appropriately so that the risk of falls is minimized in their work;
- employees must know how to stack materials and equipment to minimize the risk of falls;
- steps and dedicated stepping devices must be used to reach high shelves and not use inappropriate devices (e.g., a chair);
- ensure that all employees using stepping devices (e.g., step ladders) know how to use them properly, including having assistance to secure it and hold it firmly;
- promptly report any storage materials that appear damaged or broken;
- ensure that employees know that heavier items should be stored closer to floor level, rather than on higher shelves.

17.2.6.1.3 Fire and Other Emergencies

- detailed emergency procedures must be developed for the Forensic Laboratory to cover fire and other emergencies, including evacuation plans and assembly points;
- evacuation drills must be practiced at least once a year for all employees;
- an appropriate number of Fire Wardens must be appointed and trained in their duties;
- ensure that all employees know the location of emergency equipment (e.g., first-aid kits, etc.) and how to use them;
- ensure that all employees know the location of all fire call points, fire extinguishers, and fire blankets and how to use them;
- ensure that all employees know escape routes and assembly point(s);
- ensure that all employees know the sound(s) and the meaning of any alarms.

17.2.6.1.4 First Aid and Accident Reporting

- ensure that all Forensic Laboratory employees know how to report any accident or "near miss," even if they do not result in an incident relating to an employee or visitor to the Forensic Laboratory premises;
- ensure that all accidents and near misses are reported via Line Managers;
- ensure that there is a process for anonymous reporting of incidents (or suspected incidents) and that it is available to all the Forensic Laboratory employees;
- ensure that trained First Aiders are available, as per legislative requirements, and the that their qualifications/certifications are maintained;
- ensure that first-aid equipment, as appropriate to the Forensic Laboratory, is available as required, throughout the Forensic Laboratory;
- ensure that first-aid provision is adequate and appropriate for the requirements of the Forensic Laboratory;
- where appropriate, all relevant legislation and regulations within the jurisdiction of the Forensic Laboratory must be met, and that it is aware of its legal liability in the provision of first aid and that all employees are aware of this and do not prejudice the Forensic Laboratory in this area, as defined in Chapter 12, Section 12.3.13.1;
- ensure that there are sufficient "First Aiders" available for the Forensic Laboratory, as required either by internal procedures or the legislation within the jurisdiction;
- ensure that first aid is applied wherever a person is subject to an incident, where life needs to be preserved or the consequences of the incident are minimized or controlled until appropriate professional help is available. First aid should also be administered where injuries are minor and need no external medical health (e.g., treatment does not need to be administered by a healthcare professional);
- ensure that all employees know both who their "First Aiders" are and how to contact them, as well as the location of any first-aid facilities within the Forensic Laboratory;
- while the Forensic Laboratory employees may not be required by legislation or regulation within the jurisdiction to treat members of the public (or even visitors to

the Forensic Laboratory), this is an individual choice that must be made by the employee;

- the level of first-aid provision within the Forensic Laboratory should be determined by risk assessment, which will in turn be determined by such factors as:
  - workplace hazards and risks;
  - the size of the Forensic Laboratory;
  - incident history within the Forensic Laboratory;
  - the work and disposition of the Forensic Laboratory employees;
  - needs of lone workers;
  - needs of Teleworkers;
  - needs of mobile workers;
  - needs of employees of other organizations that are working with the Forensic Laboratory employees;
  - annual leave and other absences of First Aiders.
- ensure that only competent First Aiders undertake First-Aider tasks and that their competence is maintained;
- appropriate first-aid equipment must be held by relevant Forensic Laboratory employees. Within the Forensic Laboratory itself, equipment must be identified by signage appropriate to the requirements of the legislation and regulation within the jurisdiction. For individual employees, they shall hold either the minimum required first-aid equipment defined by the legislation and regulation within the jurisdiction or agreed internal requirements based on relevant risk assessments;
- ensure that all employees know what incidents need to be reported according to the legislation and regulations within the jurisdiction and how to report them, as defined in Chapter 7, Section 7.4.1;
- ensure that employees, when assisting an injured colleague, do not place themselves in danger. They should also protect the injured colleague from further harm from source of the danger, assuming it is safe so to do.

17.2.6.1.5 Hand Tools—Powered

- there will be occasions where the Forensic Laboratory employees will need to use powered hand tools (e.g., electric screwdrivers or other small tools in the laboratory necessary for performing their job). All employees must be trained in their safe use, prior to being allowed to operate them. In some jurisdictions, it may be necessary to undertake certificated training as a prerequisite;
- where appropriate, PPE shall be used;
- ensure that employees actually use the correct tool for the job.

17.2.6.1.6 Housekeeping

- all the Forensic Laboratory employees must ensure that they maintain a tidy work place and eliminate any hazards due to untidy or unsafe working practices;
- ensure that all walkways and corridors are kept clear of obstructions;
- ensure all that rubbish (whether confidential or not) is disposed of in the proper bins, including recycling for environmental or other purposes, as appropriate. All bins must be regularly emptied to prevent risks of either overflow or information leakage;
- all sharp edges on equipment, furniture, buildings, or even sharp items of equipment themselves (e.g., knives) are appropriately protected to prevent employees injuring themselves;
- ensure that any equipment used in a case that is being used at the employee's desk is securely stored.

17.2.6.1.7 Lone Working

Lone working occurs when a Forensic Laboratory employee is engaging any work-related activity where there is no other employee present to take any action needed to assist in case of need.

- while the Forensic Laboratory does not preclude lone working (especially for those involved in teleworking or mobile working), the situation must be properly managed and monitored;
- within the laboratory or offices, lone working should be avoided as far as possible;
- any employee who is required to perform lone working must be provided with the facility to summon emergency or other assistance if it is required (e.g., medical emergency, intruders, etc.);
- employees must minimize the risk to their well-being while lone working;
- consideration should be given to the provision of personal alarms to a manned station;
- some tasks may be prohibited while lone working is being undertaken;
- separate risk assessments should be undertaken for individuals undertaking lone working, especially for anyone who may have health-related issues.

17.2.6.1.8 Manual Handling

- all the Forensic Laboratory employees who may be involved in manual handling must be appropriately trained before performing such operations. Refresher training must also be undertaken in accordance with the Training Needs Assessment requirements, as defined in Chapter 18, Section 18.2.2. Failure to provide appropriate training may leave employees open to injury and possible claims against the Forensic Laboratory;
- appropriate aids must be provided to facilitate handling large, heavy, or awkward equipment. These will include trolleys and other wheeled equipment;
- where aids to manual handling are to be used within the Forensic Laboratory, risk assessments must be undertaken to ensure that these aids do not themselves introduce new hazards;

- all Forensic Laboratory employees should avoid attempting to lift or move equipment or other items that they cannot easily manage on their own. Assistance should always be sought, if required, and no employee should attempt operations beyond their own capability;
- all employees should be taught good manual handling techniques if they are likely to be handling loads that are bulky, heavy, awkward, have sharp edges, or any other relevant hazards. Records of all training undertaken must be maintained by the Human Resources Department, as defined in Chapter 4, Section 4.6.2.3 and Chapter 18, Section 18.2.1.8.
- where heavy, large, or awkward loads are to be moved, the journey should be planned. All possible hazards that may affect the journey should be removed or the hazard minimized. This includes being able to see any hazards as they occur on the journey;
- any employee identifying a hazardous situation relating to manual handling must report this to their Line Manager or the Forensic Laboratory Health and Safety Manager;
- all employees must ensure that their actions in manual handling do not put other employees at risk and follow appropriate procedures or work instructions related to manual handling as part of their work.

17.2.6.1.9 Personal Protective Equipment—General

- there will be some occasions where routine laboratory tasks may require the use of PPE. Where this is a requirement, all employees must undergo appropriate training and use the PPE provided in the correct manner to reduce the risk of injury, with records of the training maintained as defined in Chapter 4, Section 4.6.2.3;
- employees must be educated to safely store their PPE and replace it if it becomes damaged.

17.2.6.1.10 Safety Signage

- depending on the OH&S legislation in the jurisdiction for the Forensic Laboratory, appropriate safety signage must be displayed. There may be a variety of different sign types (e.g., color, shape, and meanings), and employees must understand the difference between them. Some are advisory (e.g., Fire Exit), others provide warnings for risks that are present (e.g., slippery floors), others are prohibitory (e.g., No Smoking), others are related to first aid or fire fighting (e.g., location of a first-aid kit or fire extinguisher).

17.2.6.1.11 Slips and Trips

- ensure that all areas have appropriate lighting so that employees can see the floor space and steps;
- ensure that there are no areas that become wet or slippery;
- ensure that appropriate footwear is worn, where appropriate;
- ensure that there are no holes or worn areas in carpets or floors that could contribute to a fall or slip;
- ensure that employees do not run or move too fast inside the Forensic Laboratory, while teleworking, or when on site;
- ensure that employees are familiar with manual handling techniques, including the safe carrying of loads, to ensure that vision is not impaired leading to a slip or trip;
- ensure that drawers are not opened so that a risk occurs either from an employee walking into an unexpected hazard or that a chest of drawers or a cabinet overbalances.

17.2.6.1.12 Smoking, Alcohol, and Drug Use

- the Forensic Laboratory should have a smoking policy in place that defines where and when smoking is permitted. Typically, this will depend on the legislation within the jurisdiction;
- where smoking is permitted, all employees must be trained to ensure that they dispose of cigarette ends and other smoking materials responsibly and minimize the risk of fire;
- the Forensic Laboratory should have an alcohol policy in place that defines where and if alcohol consumption is permitted in the office (e.g., a formal office function). In general terms, alcohol consumption should be strictly prohibited in the laboratory itself. Rules for employees who appear under the influence of alcohol in the workplace must be defined as part of the Human Resources Department;
- the Forensic Laboratory should have a drug use/abuse policy in place that defines what action an employee is to take is they are taking prescription medication that may affect their work. Illegal drugs shall be strictly prohibited. Rules for employees who appear under the influence of drugs in the workplace must be defined as part of the Human Resources Department.

17.2.6.1.13 Stress

- the Forensic Laboratory recognizes that stress in the workplace can be of major concern to employees. Stress can be due to a number of reasons (e.g., work pressure, workplace bullying, cases being worked—e.g., pedophilia, etc.);
- during times of increased work pressure (e.g., tight Turn Round Times), the Forensic Laboratory must ensure that the OH&S of all employees is not put at increased risk;
- risk assessments must identify all work-related stressors and appropriate action be taken to reduce them. Where

appropriate, close monitoring of the situation shall be undertaken;

- the Forensic Laboratory shall provide a confidential counseling service for any employee suffering stress that is related to their role, or from external factors that affects their work;
- Line Managers shall monitor workloads to ensure that no employee is subject to work overload. This will also include monitoring of working hours and overtime worked;
- eliminate, as far as reasonably practicable, any workplace harassment or bullying of any type;
- the Human Resources Department should regularly monitor absence statistics to identify any significant trends;
- preventive action to reduce stress is more effective that trying to find a cure and all employees should be encouraged to advise the Human Resources Department, the OH&S Manager, or their Line Manager(s) on any concerns at the earliest opportunity. Any identified preventive action agreed to be implemented, must be implemented using the procedures defined in Chapter 4, Section 4.8.

17.2.6.1.14 Waste Disposal (General)

- the principles of good waste management are:
  - reduction;
  - recycling;
  - recovery;
  - responsible safe disposal.
- all the Forensic Laboratory employees have a duty of care to ensure that they only purchase minimum quantities of materials through the approved purchasing process, as defined in Chapter 6, Section 6.7.4 and Chapter 14, Section 14.5;
- all materials are recycled wherever possible in line with local recycling schemes. However, care must be taken to ensure that confidential material (paper, storage media, etc.) is not subject to unauthorized access, modification, or disclosure;
- specific procedures must be put in place for handling and disposing of confidential materials of all types, as defined in Chapter 12, Section 12.3.14.10;
- only authorized waste disposal consultants shall be used. There shall be traceability of all material being disposed of and the Information Security Manager shall retain all disposal certificates.

17.2.6.2 Incident Response Controls

While the controls above are relevant for the office or laboratory, a number of them will be relevant for incident response situations where the Forensic Laboratory employees are required to attend a client site to recover forensic evidence, provide first responder services or other services as required, as defined in Chapter 8. While all incident response situations may be different, the controls above should form the basis of good OH&S practices for incident response. Part of the planning process for any incident response activities shall include a health and safety briefing, either carried out by the First Response Team Leader (or their designate) or the instructing Client, as defined in Chapter 8, Sections 8.1.4 and 8.6.3. The First Response Team Leader is responsible for ensuring that all health and safety issues at the incident are identified, documented, and treated accordingly.

- the prime task of the First Response Team Leader is to ensure the health and safety of all persons at the incident site;
- if possible, a health and safety briefing shall be carried out prior to any move to the incident site;
- consideration should be given to unfamiliar equipment that may pose an electrical hazard to the First Response Team;
- some electrical equipment may hold an electric charge after unplugging;
- consideration should be given to unfamiliar equipment that may pose a manual handling hazard or have sharp edges that may cause any other injury;
- if imaging on site, consideration must be given to the safe handling of all equipment and ensure that the Forensic Analyst does not void manufacturer's warranties;
- some equipment may give out radio waves that may be dangerous (e.g., microwave transmissions);
- some equipment may have lasers attached that may damage eyesight;
- travel and subsistence issues should be dealt with for any Forensic Laboratory employee traveling to, and from, an incident scene, as appropriate;
- any controls put in place must not affect the evidence or its secure recovery;
- unfamiliar chemicals and liquids may be present at the incident site;
- on arrival at the incident site, the First Response Team Leader should scan the incident site for sounds, smells, sounds, or anything else that does not "seem right." This may require the incident risk assessment to be revised with appropriate additional risk treatment put in place.

17.2.6.3 Work Controls for Forensic Case Processing

Most OH&S hazards and risks are the same for forensic case processing as those in the office environment but with some additional ones. Within the laboratory, the following additional risks apply:

- a large percentage of forensic cases today deal with pedophile material. Mandatory counseling for all those involved in pedophile cases should be undertaken on a regular basis;
- counseling and evaluation must take place for all new employees prior to them working on any pedophile or other possibly distressing cases;
- when an employee stops working for the Forensic Laboratory or is deployed on other duties, a final counseling session should take place;
- records of counseling must be maintained on the employee's Human Resources records;
- Line Managers should be trained to detect any possible signs of distress among their employees relating to any case work (or other external factors). If detected, the Line manager should consult with the Human Resources Department to determine treatment to reduce the effect of the hazard;
- all workstations in the laboratory should have rubber mats located under and around the workbenches to prevent earthing;
- no employee should be unnecessarily exposed to disturbing images of any type;
- circuit breakers must be provided to cut power to all equipment locally and for the whole laboratory in case of accident;
- antistatic flooring and wristbands must be provided to protect employees, as well as volatile evidence.

17.2.6.4 Teleworking Controls

- teleworking is defined as an employee who spends a significant amount of their work time working from their home or some other fixed location. It is different from mobile working as it is from a fixed location remote from the Forensic Laboratory premises;
- depending on the legislation within the jurisdiction, the Forensic Laboratory may have a legal requirement to provide a safe and secure working environment for Teleworkers in their own home or other remote site and be legally liable for its provision and maintenance. They may also be liable for any equipment they provide to the Teleworker but usually not for equipment and facilities provided by the Teleworker;
- all Teleworkers shall have risk assessments carried out on their working environments, wherever they are, and not be permitted to undertake any teleworking until the risk assessment has been carried out and appropriate risk treatment is put in place;
- for those teleworking from home, the risks are not only to the employee, but also to their families, visitors to their home, etc., and these cannot be overstated, especially if there are young children present;
- all Forensic Laboratory-supplied equipment that a teleworking employee uses should be regularly checked to ensure that it is properly maintained in accordance with manufacturer's recommendations and is not in any condition that may cause harm to the employee or their family;
- anyone providing training for safe working to a Teleworker must, themselves, be competent to provide such training. All records of such training must be recorded in line with the procedures defined in Chapter 4, Section 4.6.2.3 and Chapter 18, Section 18.2.1.8;
- in general terms, the teleworking employee's home should be regarded as an extension of the office and all OH&S risks treated as if they were in the office.

17.2.6.5 Mobile Working Controls

Mobile working is where any Forensic Laboratory employee uses an information processing device of any type while traveling outside the office. This is different from teleworking, which is from a fixed remote location, as it can be from any location anywhere in the world.

- all mobile workers shall be trained in issues relating to mobile working, both from a security and health and safety viewpoint. All records of such training must be recorded in line with the procedures defined in Chapter 4, Section 4.6.2.3;
- all the Forensic Laboratory-supplied equipment that a mobile employee uses should be regularly checked to ensure that it is properly maintained in accordance with manufacturer's recommendations and is not in any condition that may cause harm to the employee;
- in general terms, any mobile working location should be regarded as an extension of the office and all OH&S risks treated as if they were in the office.

17.2.6.6 Display Screen Equipment

DSE refers to any equipment that is used to present information to a user from an information processing device. These include visual display units, visual display terminals, cathode ray tubes, liquid display crystal screens, or any other similar technology. These can be attached to servers, desktop computers, laptops, notebooks, or any form of mobile information processing device. Health problems can be caused by poor design of the employee's workspace, and careful design can substantially reduce or even eliminate the risk of any DSE-related health risks.

- all the Forensic Laboratory employees will use computers and so will use some form of DSE and this will also include Teleworkers. It is essential that the Forensic Laboratory complies with any relevant DSE legislation or regulation within the relevant jurisdiction, this may

include a definition as to whom the legislation or regulation applies;
- most issues related to DSE, health, and safety have little to do with the DSE itself, but its use, and so the Forensic Laboratory must ensure that any DSE is used appropriately and does not negatively impact the health and safety of its employees;
- typical issues relating to DSE use are upper limb disorders (ULDs). These are typified by pains in the hands, wrists, neck, shoulders, or back. Other issues can be stress and temporary eye strain (but not eye damage). Many issues can be avoided by simple measures that the Forensic Laboratory should adopt. Additionally, prolonged use of DSE can lead to tired eyes and may affect eyesight;
- all the Forensic Laboratory employees shall be protected from issues relating to DSE hazards according to the legislation and regulations within the jurisdiction;
- the initial stage of assessment of any hazards within the employee's workplace is for the employee to fill in an initial DSE Assessment checklist. This primarily relates to desktop and laptop computers in the office or laboratory. The DSE Assessment checklist used by the Forensic Laboratory is given in Appendix 11;
- all the Forensic Laboratory employees shall undertake eyesight tests on at least an annual basis and obtain suitable glasses for DSE work. The Forensic Laboratory shall contribute to those according to legislation within the jurisdiction or as defined by local working practices;
- DSE use can induce stress in employees, but this is usually due to work pressure and not the physical use of DSE. The Forensic Laboratory risk assessments must ensure that when DSE risk is evaluated, the level of work and work pressure is included;
- all DSE must be ergonomically situated to ensure that the hazardous effect of its use is minimized and that they meet the legislation or regulations in the jurisdiction;
- workplace lighting must be appropriate for prolonged DSE use;
- employees should be educated that prolonged and uninterrupted DSE use may be harmful and that regular breaks should be taken. In some jurisdictions, this is recommended or mandated. The training syllabus used by the Forensic Laboratory for training employees about risks from DSE is given in Appendix 12;
- where a DSE user is pregnant, has just given birth, or is breastfeeding, a regular risk assessment must be undertaken to ensure that any risks of hazards are minimized or avoided. The same applies for any employee with any other disabilities or medical issues;
- where mobile computing devices are used, they may have smaller screens or keyboards and employees should be advised that these may not be appropriate for prolonged use. Alternative communication devices, or devices like docking stations, should be used wherever possible, especially if the employee has raised an issue with the use of a small screen or keyboard;
- wherever possible, aids to assist mouse or pointing devices should be used. These include mouse pads with wrist rests, dedicated wrist rests, other types of pointing devices such as tracker balls, etc.;
- one of the most important factors to reduce, if not eliminate, ULD is the proper evaluation of the workplace (whether in the office or for Teleworkers and others) from an optimum ergonomic viewpoint. These should be regularly carried out with their results documented and retained with the employee's personnel records held by the Human Resources Department. This is more important if the employee is pregnant, just given birth, breast feeding, or has some medical complaint that affects their work;
- appropriate furniture must be supplied to all employees to reduce the likelihood of ULD. This includes adjustable seating, appropriate lighting, alternative input devices, document holders, footrests, glare avoidance measures (e.g., location away from windows or blinds), etc.;
- when using DSE, employees should understand the requirements to have a clean screen, have fonts that are "easy on the eyes," ensure that text is large enough to read, that the screen does not flicker, etc.;
- where issues (incidents) have been reported relating to DSE, the Forensic Laboratory must address the most serious risks first and prioritize all other issues;
- all DSE assessors (and others involved in determining controls) must be aware of possible claims of exaggeration that may be made and take appropriate action;
- all employees shall fill in a DSE Assessment checklist themselves for each DSE that they use. The DSE Assessment checklist used by the Forensic Laboratory is given in Appendix 11;
- DSE Assessor shall evaluate the filled-in DSE Assessment checklists and consider further controls for treating the risks and hazards identified. The forms for this are given in Appendix 13;
- all employees must be educated to ensure that they report any persistent pain/discomfort that they experience from DSE use within the Forensic Laboratory. This shall be formally reported in the mandatory "Accident Book" where required by the legislation or regulation within the jurisdiction. Where this is not mandated, it should be reported to the Health and Safety Manager, their Line Manager, or the Service Desk. It shall be treated as an incident as defined in Chapter 7, Section 7.4.1;
- the Forensic Laboratory shall comply with any legislative or regulatory requirements for eye tests relating to DSE use within the jurisdiction. This may include regular eye tests for employees while employed by the Forensic Laboratory;

- where any change of equipment, working practice, or employee tasking occurs, consideration of a revised risk assessment must be undertaken;
- ensure that all employees are aware of the measures taken to protect them and their own personal responsibilities to report any influencing changes or incident.

Note

The Forensic Laboratory must undertake baseline assessments for each employee and an additional one for those deemed specifically at risk (e.g., pregnancy, disability, etc.), rather than an individual risk assessment for each employee.

17.2.6.7 Pregnancy Controls

- females who are pregnant, just given birth, or breastfeeding have additional OH&S needs above other employees, and these may be covered by specific legislation within the jurisdiction of the Forensic Laboratory. They must have additional risk assessments performed for them, as soon as they advise the Human Resources Department that they are pregnant. Depending on the legislation in the jurisdiction, this may have to be done irrespective of the Human Resources Department being advised on the pregnancy or it may be that the trigger to perform risk assessments is the formal notification of the pregnancy;
- as with normal risk assessments, any hazards should be identified that are specific to the situation (i.e., pregnancy), their possible harm should be calculated, the hazard treated by application of one or more controls, and the situation monitored regularly. This will be relative to unborn children, newly born children, or breastfed children;
- regular risk assessments must be undertaken during the pregnancy, after birth, and during breastfeeding as this is a dynamic process not a static one. Different risks may be present at different times during the pregnancy, immediately after birth and during breastfeeding;
- where this process does not reduce the hazard risk to an acceptable level, the Forensic Laboratory should consider adjustment of working patterns or conditions of work for relevant employees. This situation may be covered in legislation within the jurisdiction (e.g., prolonged maternity leave);
- where working at night is undertaken by an employee who is pregnant, just given birth, or breastfeeding, this may require an additional risk assessment to consider these specific risks;
- if the risk assessment identifies additional risks to any employee who is pregnant, just given birth, or breastfeeding, they shall be advised of it and also any measures that the Forensic Laboratory is taking to reduce or avoid the risks. This process involves a consultation process between the employee and the Forensic Laboratory;
- employees who are pregnant, just given birth, or breastfeeding also have a duty of care to themselves to protect themselves as well as any controls that the Forensic Laboratory may put in place;
- while pregnant, just given birth, or breastfeeding, some substances that would not normally be hazardous (e.g., chemical cleaning materials) may well prove to be. These should be risk assessed for the specific situation. Many chemical products already carry identification and warning labels relating to toxicity, though these may vary between different jurisdictions;
- while there is not a great deal of reliable empirical evidence linking chemicals with genetic disorders, the Forensic Laboratory should adopt a precautionary stance with regard to dealing with any chemicals that could be linked to possible reproductive disorders. This approach should also be adopted for Teleworkers who are pregnant, just given birth, or breastfeeding;
- during pregnancy, the body changes shape and this will affect body posture and can often affect working practices. Ongoing risk assessments must be undertaken and steps taken to reduce any effects that the pregnancy may bring. This will be especially relevant in seating, manual handling, use of PPE, and use of information processing devices of all types;
- while an employee is pregnant, just given birth, or is breastfeeding, the Forensic Laboratory should consider provision of a safe and secure location for resting and breastfeeding to take place, as well as easy access to toilet (and associated hygiene) facilities;
- where emergency evacuation is needed (e.g., a fire alarm), the Forensic Laboratory shall ensure that any employee who is pregnant, just given birth, or breastfeeding shall have an appointed "buddy" to assist them in the evacuation process;
- disclosure to the Human Resources Department of a pregnancy, or any information relating to it, must be treated in the strictest confidence and not divulged if the mother to be does not wish the fact to be known;
- the Forensic Laboratory shall comply with all legislation within the jurisdiction relating to pregnancy and maternity/paternity rights.

17.2.7 Creating the Risk Register

Once the risk assessment has been carried out, the results must be documented and managed using the Corporate Risk Register.

The contents of the Forensic Laboratory Corporate Risk Register are given in Chapter 5, Appendix 17.

17.3 IMPLEMENTATION AND OPERATION OF THE OH&S MANAGEMENT SYSTEM

Once all of the planning for the Forensic Laboratory OH&S Management System has been completed and the risk treatment agreed, the relevant controls must be implemented and maintained. To ensure that the controls are properly implemented, the following must happen:

17.3.1 Resource Provision

- Top Management must take visible and demonstrable ownership and final accountability for the OH&S Management System;
- a Health and Safety Manager shall be specifically appointed by Top Management to specifically manage the OH&S Management System on a day-to-day basis (i.e., be the Custodian). This may be one of a number of roles that the employee fulfills or may be a dedicated role as the Forensic Laboratory grows;
- Top Management must ensure that there are sufficient competent resources appointed and in place to effectively implement, manage, monitor, and continuously improve the OH&S Management System, as defined in Chapter 4, Section 4.6.2.1;
- Top Management must ensure that there is sufficient budget allocated to implement, manage, monitor, and continuously improve the OH&S Management System, as defined in Chapter 4, Section 4.6.2.1;
- Top Management must ensure that there is sufficient technology to implement, manage, monitor, and continuously improve the OH&S Management System, as defined in Chapter 4, Section 4.6.2.1. This includes office and laboratory equipment as well as PPE;
- the OH&S Management system policies, procedures, and supporting infrastructure must be fully documented and made available to all the Forensic Laboratory employees within the IMS;
- regular reports relating to the operation of the OH&S Management System must be produced for the Management Review and continuous improvement, as defined in Chapter 4, Sections 4.8 and 4.9, respectively;
- health and safety posters must be clearly displayed, as required by the legislation and regulation within the jurisdiction. This shall include the location and identity of key OH&S appointed employees within the Forensic Laboratory.

17.3.2 Some Operational Responsibilities and Accountabilities

Specific OH&S responsibilities will be contained in individual job descriptions and agreed between the employee, their Line Manager, and the Human Resources Department. However, an overview of generic operational responsibilities, in addition to those defined in Section 17.1.4, is given below:

17.3.2.1 Top Management

Note

This is a role for a nominated member of Top Management, rather than a collective responsibility for day-to-day operations.

- Top Management owns OH&S within the Forensic Laboratory;
- Top Management ensures that appropriate resources are present to effectively develop, implement, manage, monitor, and continuously improve the OH&S Management System, as defined in Chapter 4, Section 4.6.2.1;
- Top Management approves the Forensic Laboratory Health and Safety Policy, as given in Appendix 2;
- Top Management shall appoint an employee (the Health and Safety Manager), with appropriate authority, to develop, implement, manage, monitor, and continuously improve the OH&S Management System;
- Top Management shall attend the Management Review and approve the changes necessary, as decided at the review.

17.3.2.2 Health and Safety Manager

A full job description for the Health and Safety Manager is given in Appendix 3.

17.3.2.3 Forensic Laboratory Line Management

In addition to the responsibilities above, the Forensic Laboratory Line Management will have the following responsibilities:

- make an official record of risk assessment findings;
- address the risks found in the office, laboratory, or on site to eliminate them or reduce them to an acceptable level, as defined in Chapter 5, Appendix 14;
- provide training and awareness to all employees, appropriate with their job roles;
- provide a safe and secure workplace for all employees (wherever that is);
- ensure that all equipment (including any plant and machinery) is safe to use, that safe working practices are set up and followed, and that employees receive appropriate training to use it;

- provide adequate first-aid facilities, including trained First Aiders;
- set up emergency response plans, maintain them, and ensure that they are regularly tested, as defined in Chapter 13;
- advise all the Forensic Laboratory employees of any potential hazards in any of the work that they undertake as part of their role. This can include hazards from working in the laboratory, office, or on site as well as any hazards present in any equipment or materials in use in any location;
- ensure that all the Forensic Laboratory premises meet requirements in the jurisdiction for ventilation, temperature, lighting, washing, and resting facilities, as appropriate;
- ensure that the correct equipment is used for all tasks and that it is properly maintained according to the manufacturer's specifications, as defined in Chapter 7, Section 7.5.4;
- prevent or control exposure to any hazards that may affect an employee's health and welfare;
- provide appropriate PPE for all employees, as needed;
- ensure that appropriate signage is located throughout the Forensic Laboratory premises to advise on health and safety issues, as required in the jurisdiction;
- maintain records of any OH&S incidents or "near misses," and report them to appropriate authorities as required in the jurisdiction.

17.3.2.4 Employees

As well as the Forensic Laboratory Management responsibilities for OH&S, each employee has responsibilities as well as rights, and these include:

- take reasonable care of their own health and safety while at work, wherever that may be;
- take reasonable care not to put fellow employees, visitors to the Forensic Laboratory premises, third-party employees, or members of the public at risk during the performance of their role;
- co-operate with the Forensic Laboratory management in all OH&S matters, including reporting incidents, "near misses," using PPE when required and undertaking training as required;
- advise the Forensic Laboratory management, as appropriate, on any health issues that may affect their work or require a risk assessment to be revised (e.g., becoming pregnant, are taking any medication, or have any disability or injury that may affect their work, etc.);
- advise the Forensic Laboratory management of any OH&S concerns that they may have;
- use all equipment in the correct manner.

17.3.3 Competence, Training, and Awareness

All the Forensic Laboratory employees shall be deemed competent in the area of OH&S by ensuring that they undertake appropriate training and attend mandatory awareness sessions with records of training and awareness maintained on their Human Resources file, as defined in Chapter 4, Section 4.6.2.3 and Chapter 18, Section 18.2.1.8.

All training needs in the area of OH&S shall be identified in the Training Needs Analysis (TNA) process undertaken at least on an annual basis as part of the employee's performance assessment, as defined in Chapter 18, Section 18.2.2.

As in common with other management systems implemented in the Forensic Laboratory (e.g., ISO 9001, ISO 27001, etc.), all employees shall be made aware of their contribution to the continuous improvement of the OH&S Management System as well as the possible consequences of failure to comply with the requirements of the OH&S Management System.

Levels of training required shall depend on the specific responsibilities and accountabilities of the employee and the risk that they face in their specific role within the Forensic Laboratory, as defined in Chapter 4, Section 4.6.2.2.

17.3.4 Communications

Within the Forensic Laboratory, Top Management shall establish an appropriate process for communication of the OH&S Policy and supporting procedures to all employees or visitors to their premises.

Effective communication of the OH&S message relies on information that:

- comes into the Forensic Laboratory;
- flows within the Forensic Laboratory;
- is transmitted from the Forensic Laboratory.

Incoming information will consist of legislative or regulatory requirements as well as developments within OH&S management practice and risk control.

Information flow within the Forensic Laboratory will include the whole range of OH&S information from the OH&S Policy through to lessons learned and incident reporting and corrective action as part of the Management Review process. The Communications Plan used in the Forensic Laboratory is given in Chapter 5, Appendix 1.

For employees, this shall consist of the online OH&S Management System and regular awareness and training sessions as well as regular practice of relevant procedures (e.g., evacuation). Employees shall also be encouraged to be involved in the identification and reporting of hazards and the selection of appropriate controls to treat the risk to an acceptable level. This shall apply to current as well as planned working practices in the Forensic Laboratory.

Where appropriate, they shall be involved in the investigation of any incident or "near miss" that affects them.

For visitors, they shall all be given an OH&S briefing and records of this shall be held in the visitor's book.

Where an external organization requests information about the Forensic Laboratory's OH&S Policy and procedures, records of this shall be maintained by the Health and Safety Manager.

17.3.5 OH&S Documentation

Within the IMS, the OH&S documentation shall include the following:

- the Forensic Laboratory OH&S Policy and its scope;
- the measurable OH&S objectives (or KPIs) set by the Forensic Laboratory Top Management;
- procedures, work instructions, and forms used to support the Forensic Laboratory's OH&S Policy;
- relevant records to provide objective evidence of the Forensic Laboratory's conformance to the requirements of the OH&S Management System and relevant standards that have been used to develop it.

All documents and records shall be controlled in accordance with the Forensic Laboratory document and record control procedures, as defined in Chapter 4, Sections 4.6.3 and 4.6.4, respectively.

17.3.6 Hierarchy of OH&S Controls

Once the hazard and risk analysis of the Forensic Laboratory has been undertaken, it is necessary to implement a number of controls to treat the risk or reduce its impact to an acceptable level.

The order of precedence and effectiveness of control implementation is:

- engineering controls;
- administrative controls;
- PPE.

In an ideal world, all controls would be engineering ones, but the Forensic Laboratory has to be realistic and understand that a totally engineering control approach is impractical. Therefore, a mix of all three types of control will be used.

17.3.6.1 Engineering Controls

These are controls that treat the hazard or reduce it to an acceptable level, including but not limited to:

- designing the premises, process, or operation to treat the hazard or reduce it to an acceptable level;
- enclosing the hazard by use of appropriate controls;
- isolating the hazard by using appropriate controls;
- removal or re-direction of the hazard.

17.3.6.2 Administrative Controls

These are controls that treat the hazard or reduce it to an acceptable level, including but not limited to:

- developing and implementing administrative procedures, work instructions, and safe working practices for all locations where the Forensic Laboratory employees may work;
- monitoring and controlling exposure to hazardous situations or materials;
- use of alarms, signs, and warning notices;
- training, awareness, and developing competencies appropriate to job roles.

17.3.6.3 Personal Protective Equipment

These are controls that treat the hazard or reduce it to an acceptable level, including but not limited to the following situations:

- where engineering or administrative controls either do not treat the hazard or reduce it to an acceptable level;
- while engineering or administrative controls are being developed or are not fully implemented;
- where implemented engineering or administrative controls do not provide sufficient protection against the identified hazards or risks;
- during situations where engineering or administrative controls are not feasible or appropriate (e.g., incident response off-site).

17.3.6.4 Implementing Controls

Each of the above categories of controls has its place in the Forensic Laboratory, however, the most effective controls to implement are engineering controls. If this is not possible, then administrative or PPE controls should be considered.

17.3.7 Some Generic Controls

There are a number of generic controls that can be implemented in the Forensic Laboratory's office and laboratory environments. Different locations may have specific requirements, but this is a generic list.

All the Forensic Laboratory employees must:

- ensure that their actions do not cause a hazard, accident, or injury to fellow employees or visitors to the office or laboratory by following stated working practices and procedures;
- maintain a clean and tidy workspace;
- replace all material (equipment, evidence, and files) in their correct location after use and not leave them out in the incorrect storage area;

- return all equipment in a condition fit for the next user, reporting any identified defects to the appropriate reporting point and labeling the equipment appropriately;
- never block or obstruct a fire escape route;
- never allow combustible materials to build up and cause a possible fire hazard;
- ensure that when any chemical (including cleaning materials, correction fluids, or other chemicals that may pose a hazard if used incorrectly) is used that it is used in accordance with manufacturer's instructions;
- where there are options available for cleaning equipment or offices, that the safer option is used (e.g., wipes rather than sprays, etc.);
- where chemicals have been used, that hands are washed;
- not to take exhibits into the office area but only allow them to be located in the secure property store or laboratory;
- not to eat in the laboratory;
- report any potential hazard that they identify to their Line Manager or Health and Safety Manager;
- wear appropriate PPE, as required;
- know where first-aid kits are located and the identity of First Aiders;
- know and regularly practice the emergency evacuation procedure;
- ensure that all waste from the laboratory and office is disposed of appropriately, as defined in Chapter 12, Section 12.3.14.10. This includes recycling, if appropriate, and secure disposal of confidential material as well as anything else that may cause a hazard;
- ensure that anti-static devices are used in the Laboratory.

Where changes or new processes and procedures are made in working processes, a risk assessment of the process must be undertaken. Where the change is to be implemented, the Forensic Laboratory change management process must be followed, as defined in Chapter 7, Section 7.4.3. All existing and new operations procedures and work instructions relating to operations in the Forensic Laboratory must be integrated into the IMS. This will include:

- operational procedures;
- work instructions;
- records, as appropriate.

17.3.8 Emergency Preparedness and Response

The Forensic Laboratory shall establish procedures and maintain them for incident response. These will be for a variety of different reasons including OH&S ones as well as other possible incidents that require an emergency response, as defined in Chapter 8.

The Forensic Laboratory shall maintain emergency response equipment in line with any legislative or regulatory requirements and good practice for the jurisdiction.

Every incident shall be reported and handled according to the Forensic Laboratory Incident Management procedures, as defined in Chapter 7, Section 7.4.1.

Each situation shall be judged on its merits and the risks it poses to the Forensic Laboratory.

The Forensic Laboratory shall regularly test its Emergency and Business Continuity Plans, as defined in Chapter 13, Section 13.6.4.

17.4 CHECKING COMPLIANCE WITH OH&S REQUIREMENTS

17.4.1 Monitoring and Measurement of Compliance

The Forensic Laboratory must establish, implement, and maintain one or more procedures to monitor and measure OH&S performance within the organization. This shall be consistent with the processes of the other management systems implemented within the Forensic Laboratory and the Forensic Laboratory uses the SMART process, as defined in Chapter 3, Section 3.1.17.

- this process, for OH&S, must ensure that the measurements are appropriate for the Forensic Laboratory;
- the measurement and monitoring process is in line with, and reports against, the Forensic Laboratory's quality objectives (KPIs);
- measures the effectiveness of the controls implemented in the Forensic Laboratory for health as well as safety;
- ensures that any issues identified within the OH&S Management System are completely resolved using the Forensic Laboratory's continuous improvement process, as defined in Chapter 4, Section 4.8;
- ensure that appropriate records are available for all internal audits, self-assessments, external audits, or other assessments as appropriate within the jurisdiction, as given in Chapter 4, Section 4.6.4.

Monitoring and measurement of compliance shall include legislative, regulatory, and Management System requirements. The reporting of monitoring and measurement of compliance shall depend on the requirements of legislative, regulatory, and Management System requirements depending on the jurisdiction.

The Forensic Laboratory must be able to answer the following questions:

- are controls in place to minimize the hazard or to eliminate it?

- do these controls comply with at least the minimum legislation within the jurisdiction?
- do they operate effectively?

Measurement is a key step in any management process and with the Forensic Laboratory CAPA process forms the basis of continuous improvement within the Forensic Laboratory, as defined in Chapter 4, Section 4.8 and Chapter 16. If measurement is not carried out correctly, the effectiveness of the OH&S system cannot be validated, which in turn undermines the effective control of health and safety risks. Typically, health and safety statistics rely on the reporting of injuries or incidents, or lack of them. This is a measure of failure and the Forensic Laboratory shall not use this as a single measure of health and safety effectiveness, it shall use a basket of positive and negative measures to show effectiveness of its controls.

The reasons for this are that the reporting of injury or incident rates alone has a number of inherent problems:

- a low injury rate can lead to complacency;
- an organization can have what appears to be a low injury rate on account of low numbers of employees exposed to the hazard or sheer luck;
- employees may stay off work for reasons that are not directly linked with the severity of their injury or the incident;
- injury or incident rates do not measure the severity of the incident or injury;
- injury or incident rates reflect outcomes, not the root cause of the incident or injury;
- just using incident or injury rates can lead to under reporting in order to maintain a "good" result, especially if linked to a reward system;
- to have a statistic, it requires a control to fail for the incident or injury to take place;
- when an incident or injury occurs, it is as a consequence of the hazard not being under control and the risk crystallizing rather than an indication that the hazard was properly controlled.

What is needed is a systematic approach for deriving meaningful measures of the effectiveness of the health and safety measures in place and how this links to the risk control process for treating them to an acceptable level.

The reason for measuring health and safety performance is to provide information on the effectiveness of the Forensic Laboratory's controls to control risks to employees' health and safety. It does this by:

- providing information on how the OH&S Management System works in practice;
- identifying areas of the Forensic Laboratory where preventive or remedial action is required;
- providing a basis for continuous improvement;
- providing feedback on remedial action taken.

If the measurement process cannot be used for these purposes, it is of little practical use. Health and safety performance measurement within the Forensic Laboratory should answer such questions as:

- what is the status of the current implemented health and safety controls relative to the stated objectives?
- how does the Forensic Laboratory compare with other similar organizations?
- is health and safety performance getting better or worse over time?
- is the OH&S process effective?
- is the OH&S process reliable?
- is the OH&S process efficient?
- is the OH&S process proportionate to the hazards and risks identified?
- is the OH&S process in place for all areas of the Forensic Laboratory's operations?
- does the Forensic Laboratory have an effective OH&S culture embedded in all of their business processes and operations?

As has been said above, the pre-requisite for effective health and safety plans and objectives is that they should be SMART. This should provide the basis of fact-based management decisions to control OH&S within the Forensic Laboratory.

The measurement of OH&S success used in the Forensic Laboratory is given in Appendix 14.

17.4.1.1 Active Monitoring Systems

An active monitoring system shall be embedded in the Forensic Laboratory so that it has feedback on OH&S issues *before* an incident occurs. It shall include monitoring and management, through the OH&S Management System, of specific OH&S objectives as well as meeting relevant legislative and regulatory requirements. This can then provide a solid basis for factual-based decision making by Top Management. The main advantages of active monitoring is that it is in "real time" and can reinforce positive achievement in OH&S within the Forensic Laboratory by publicizing and rewarding "good" OH&S work rather than penalizing failures after the event (i.e., an OH&S incident). This can have a serious impact on employee motivation within the Forensic Laboratory.

Active Monitoring Systems should seek to:

- undertake routine monitoring against defined OH&S objectives;
- check that the OH&S system is operating effectively and efficiently;

- ensure that all employees have appropriate job descriptions, including OH&S responsibilities;
- undertake systematic inspection of the Forensic Laboratory premises for all OH&S risks;
- ongoing monitoring and management of OH&S to ensure the effectiveness within the Forensic Laboratory;
- ongoing audit (and other similar processes, e.g., self-assessments, tests, etc.) to ensure continuous improvement;
- ensure that Top Management continuously improves the OH&S Management System;
- ensure that preventive and corrective action is taken, as needed;
- ensure remedial action is taken in a timely manner;
- ensure that effective OH&S controls are implemented and managed according to risk exposure;
- regular monitoring must be carried out according to the published IMS Calendar, after an incident or after an influencing change.

17.4.1.2 Reactive Monitoring Systems

A reactive OH&S monitoring system should be implemented that seeks to answer the following questions relating to injuries, ill-health related to work, losses, or near misses:

- arc thcy occurring?
- how serious are they?
- is OH&S performance getting better or worse?
- what are the costs (not just financial)?
- what are the potential consequences?
- what controls were in place?
- what is the nature of the root cause?
- what remedial (corrective or preventive) action is needed?
- where are they occurring?

Performance measurement should be carried out by appropriate means and this can include:

- audits;
- direct observation;
- examination of monitoring devices;
- examination of records;
- self-assessments;
- talking to employees.

These can be used individually or in combination, as appropriate.

17.4.2 Audits

The Forensic Laboratory shall undertake regular OH&S audits according to their annual IMS Calendar, as given in Chapter 4, Appendix 42. This shall include the following types of audits:

- Certification Body (third party) audits;
- external (third party) audits;
- internal (first party) audits;
- self-assessments (first party audits);
- supplier (second party) audits.

The purpose of the audits is to evaluate and continuously improve the OH&S Management System implemented within the Forensic Laboratory and ensure that the Management System:

- implementation conforms to the requirements of the OH&S Management System;
- has been properly implemented and maintained;
- is effective in meeting the defined OH&S objectives;
- is monitored appropriately;
- produces timely and useful management reports for Top Management action;
- has any corrective and preventive OH&S action effectively implemented and either eliminates the hazard or reduces the risk to an acceptable level;
- Auditors are independent of the area being audited.

All first and second party audits performed by the Forensic Laboratory shall be conducted in line with the Forensic Laboratory Internal Audit procedures, as defined in Chapter 4, Section 4.7.3.

17.4.3 Incident Reporting, Investigation, and Management

The immediate purpose of incident (including "near misses") is to identify immediate and underlying causes so that the reoccurrence of the incident is minimized if not eliminated. All the Forensic Laboratory employees and visitors to the Forensic Laboratory are required to report any incidents, injuries, or near misses so that appropriate preventive or corrective action may be taken. While individual employees may be occasionally reluctant to report an incident, injury, or "near miss," Line Managers must be encouraged to generate a positive OH&S culture where the emphasis is on continuous improvement and not a "blame" culture.

The process for reporting information security incidents is followed, as defined in Chapter 7, Section 7.4.1, but for OH&S incidents rather than information security incidents. This has the advantage of using a common incident-reporting process and a single incident database held by the Service Desk.

Details of what should be recorded on an incident report are the main information defined in Chapter 7, Section 7.4.1.4 relating the identity and details of the employee reporting the incident. Additionally, there is some OH&S specific information required and this is given in Appendix 15.

Wherever there is an incident, including any injury or near miss, it must be investigated. The Forensic Laboratory must ensure that is develops, implements, and maintains a procedure to investigate the incident in a timely manner. This must include:

- identifying the underlying failure of either implemented controls, or lack of controls, that caused or contributed to the incident;
- analyzing the incident to determine the root cause, as given in Chapter 4, Appendix 49;
- updating any relevant risk assessments, if appropriate;
- identifying any appropriate corrective action;
- identifying any preventive action;
- identifying any other opportunities for continual improvement;
- implementing relevant action through the Forensic Laboratory's continuous improvement process, as defined in Chapter 4, Section 4.8;
- updating any relevant procedures;
- communicating the results of the investigation and any updated procedures and/or work instructions;
- undertaking a PIR to ensure that the controls implemented have treated the hazard, or at least reduced it to an acceptable level or risk, as defined in the Continuous Improvement Policy given in Chapter 4, Appendix 14;
- creating a record of the investigation and all actions taken.

The implementation of the Forensic Laboratory incident management process is essential to ensure that all OH&S (and any other incidents) are managed in a consistent and effective manner. The Forensic Laboratory OH&S Incident Investigation checklist and form is given in Appendix 16.

While the OH&S Incident Investigation checklist and form may be filled in by the Health and Safety Manager, it may be carried out by another Forensic Laboratory employee. The completed forms are reviewed by the Health and Safety Manager, and Top Management, if appropriate (e.g., member of public involved, serious injury or death). The Incident Review form contents are given in Appendix 17.

Note

There may be specific reporting requirements specified within legislation and/or regulations within the jurisdiction of the Forensic Laboratory operations for the reporting of incidents (e.g., types, reporting formats, reporting timescales, etc.).

17.5 IMPROVING THE OH&S MANAGEMENT SYSTEM

17.5.1 Management Review

Within the Forensic Laboratory, the Top Management shall review the OH&S Management System at regular intervals, at least annually, on influencing change or after any incident. As the Forensic Laboratory has an IMS, OH&S issues will be dealt with at the common Management Review process, as defined in Chapter 4, Section 4.9 unless a specific alternative requirement is identified.

The agenda for the inclusion of OH&S matters is given in Chapter 4, Appendix 36.

Records of all decisions made at Management Reviews must be documented and retained as records, as defined in Chapter 4, Section 4.6.4. This is the main review point of all OH&S objectives and performance review and is the primary point for reviewing and adjusting the objectives or deciding any corrective or preventive action. The Management Review may use the inputs from any other OH&S meetings or incident reports, or action may be taken after these without the need to call for a Management Review. Records of any such actions must be taken and managed through the Forensic Laboratory CAPA process.

The mapping between the IMS and OHSAS is given in Appendix 18.

APPENDIX 1 - OH&S POLICY CHECKLIST

The Forensic Laboratory's Top Management has defined and authorized the Forensic Laboratory's OH&S Policy and ensures that its OH&S Management System, within the defined scope:

- has demonstrable Top Management commitment;
- has appropriate financial and physical resources committed to maintain and improve OH&S, as defined in Chapter 4, Section 4.6.2;
- includes the commitment to at least comply with applicable legislative and regulatory requirement within the jurisdiction of operations for the Forensic Laboratory, as defined in Section 17.3.1; Chapter 12, Section 12.3.13.1;
- is appropriate to the nature and scale of the risks faced by the Forensic Laboratory in all of its operations, as defined in Chapter 5 and this chapter, Section 17.2.5;
- appoints competent Forensic Laboratory employees to assist in the implementation of the Forensic Laboratory OH&S Policy, as defined in Chapter 4, Section 4.6.2.1 and elsewhere for specific management systems and job descriptions;
- ensures that a proper and effective risk assessment system identifies hazards, as defined in Section 17.2.5 and Chapter 5;
- assesses the risks and implements measures to remove, reduce, or control the risks so far as is reasonably practicable; as defined in Section 17.3.6 and Chapter 5;
- re-assesses risks where new processes are implemented within the Forensic Laboratory and that employee

training is undertaken on these changes, as defined in Chapter 4, Section 4.6.2.2 and this chapter, Section 17.3.3;
- includes a commitment to prevention of any OH&S incident, accident, or illness;
- has a framework that establishes the overall direction and realistic and achievable objectives for OH&S within the Forensic Laboratory, as defined in the IMS;
- has the OH&S framework implemented within the Forensic Laboratory's IMS, which is consistent with all other Forensic Laboratory policies, processes, and procedures;
- is documented, implemented, and maintained;
- has its OH&S performance measured and monitored;
- ensures that all equipment used by the Forensic Laboratory is suitable for its intended purpose and that it is maintained in a safe condition;
- establishes arrangements for use, handling, transportation, and storage of any items that are used as part of the employee's duties in the Forensic Laboratory;
- has any accident, illness, and safety incident fully investigated to determine its root cause, as given in Chapter 4, Appendix 49;
- is committed to continuous improvement of its OH&S Management System, as defined in Chapter 4, Section 4.8;
- is communicated to all the Forensic Laboratory employees, ensuring that they all are made aware of their personal accountabilities and responsibilities;
- is regularly reviewed, at least annually, after any incident or accident or on influencing change to ensure that is remains appropriate.

APPENDIX 2 - THE FORENSIC LABORATORY OH&S POLICY

It is the Forensic Laboratory's intention to provide a safe and healthy working environment in accordance with the Occupational Health and Safety legislation and regulations in force in the jurisdiction.

The responsibility for health, safety, and welfare within the Forensic Laboratory is placed with Top Management. At the heart of this commitment to health and safety are the seven core safety principles that all the Forensic Laboratory employees are required to embrace and which facilitate this commitment to continual improvement of health and safety performance. These are:

1. All injuries can be prevented.
2. For the Forensic Laboratory employees, and third parities working on their behalf, involvement is essential.
3. Top and Line Management is responsible for preventing injuries.
4. Working safely and contributing to safety improvements is a condition of employment.
5. All operating exposures can be safeguarded.
6. Training Forensic Laboratory employees to work safely is essential.
7. Prevention of personal injury makes good business sense.

Top Management, through the various management system committees and line management, ensures that all employees on the Forensic Laboratory premises fulfill these commitments by:

- pursuing the deployment of the Forensic Laboratory safety strategy and the goal of zero injuries, accidents, or health and safety incidents;
- ensuring that arrangements and resources exist to support this policy;
- effective management of occupational health and safety;
- recognizing the risks inherent in a consultancy and service management organization;
- conducting and maintaining risk assessments and safe systems of work;
- working toward meeting the requirements of OHSAS 18001, the Health and Safety Management specification[1];
- the Forensic Laboratory shall continue to invest in health and safety improvements on a progressive basis, setting objectives and targets in its annual health and safety programs;
- the Forensic Laboratory shall seek to engage and involve all employees, and third parties working on their behalf, in creating and maintaining a safe working environment.

This policy is issued and maintained by the Health and Safety Manager, who also provides advice and guidance on its implementation and ensures compliance.

All the Forensic Laboratory employees shall comply with this policy.

APPENDIX 3 - HEALTH AND SAFETY MANAGER JOB DESCRIPTION

OBJECTIVE AND ROLE

The Health and Safety Manager is responsible for initiating, developing, and maintaining the culture of health and safety management within the Forensic Laboratory.

PROBLEMS AND CHALLENGES

The Health and Safety Manager is challenged with balancing the health and safety requirements for providing a safe

1. OHSAS has been chosen as an international standard. However, any national standard can be substituted.

and secure working environment for the Forensic Laboratory employees with stifling innovation and development of the Forensic Laboratory's product and service offerings.

PRINCIPAL ACCOUNTABILITIES

The Health and Safety Manager:

- develops and maintains a suitable and relevant Health and Safety Policy for the Forensic Laboratory;
- provides the Forensic Laboratory employees with a safe workplace without risk to health;
- provides the Forensic Laboratory employees with a workplace that satisfies health, safety, and welfare requirements for ventilation, temperature, lighting, sanitary, washing, and rest facilities, as defined within the jurisdiction;
- provides the Forensic Laboratory employees with safe plant and machinery, and safe movement, storage, and use of articles and substances;
- provides the Forensic Laboratory employees with adequate provision of first aid and welfare facilities and support;
- provides the Forensic Laboratory employees and visitors to the Forensic Laboratory premises with suitable and current information and supervision concerning Health and Safety Policies and practices;
- undertakes proper and timely assessment of risks to health and safety, and implementation of measures and arrangements identified, as necessary, from the assessments;
- provides the Forensic Laboratory employees with emergency procedures, first-aid facilities, safety signs, relevant protective clothing and equipment, and incident reporting to the relevant authorities;
- liaises, as necessary, with other organizations and relevant authorities, and provides assistance and co-operation concerning audits and remedial actions;
- prevents exposure to, or adequate protection from, hazardous substances, and danger from flammable, explosive, electrical, noise, radiation, and manual handling risks;
- reports on health and safety practices and systems;
- develops the Forensic Laboratory's health and safety strategy;
- defines the direction of in-house technical training seminars to improve overall employee awareness of health and safety issues;
- participates in international, national, and local Special Interest Groups (SIGs) presentations, and publishes articles describing the Forensic Laboratory's health and safety systems and how they relate to the business;
- develops and manages effective working relationships with all appropriate internal and external stakeholders;
- maintains external links to other companies in the industry to gain competitive assessments and share information, where appropriate;
- identifies the emerging information technologies to be assimilated, integrated, and introduced within the Forensic Laboratory, which could significantly impact the Forensic Laboratory's health and safety compliance;
- interfaces with external industrial and academic organizations in order to maintain state-of-the-art knowledge in emerging health and safety issues and to enhance the Forensic Laboratory's image as a responsible employer;
- adheres to established Forensic Laboratory policies, standards, and procedures;
- performs all responsibilities in accordance with, or in excess of, the requirements of the Forensic Laboratory IMS.

AUTHORITY

The Health and Safety Manager has the authority to:

- develop long-range budget estimation for health and safety issues;
- input to acquisition and use of facilities and resources throughout the Forensic Laboratory;
- perform risk assessments for health and safety in the Forensic Laboratory, as required;
- audit the implementation of health and safety within the Forensic Laboratory;
- establish and make decisions about health and safety reporting methods and outputs;
- determine preventive and corrective action to ensure that the Forensic Laboratory retains a safe and legally compliant working environment.

CONTACTS

Internal

Contacts within the Forensic Laboratory are throughout the whole business.

External

Those external to the Forensic Laboratory will be with appropriate SIGs, other health and safety professionals and organizations, as appropriate.

REPORTS TO

The Health and Safety Manager reports to:

- Top Management.

APPENDIX 4 - SOME EXAMPLES OF OH&S DRIVERS

There are a number of legislative, regulatory, or other drivers that affect the Forensic Laboratory's OH&S Management System and its supporting procedures. These include, but are not limited to:

- agreements with employees, including employment contracts;
- agreements with local or national authorities;
- agreements with trade or similar unions, if appropriate;
- codes of practice or conduct;
- contractual conditions from Clients;
- corporate governance requirements;
- corporate social responsibility;
- good practice;
- judgements or rulings affecting the Forensic Laboratory;
- legislation within the jurisdiction;
- permits, licenses, or any forms of authorization to operate the Forensic Laboratory;
- regulations within the jurisdiction.

APPENDIX 5 - THE FORENSIC LABORATORY OH&S OBJECTIVES

There is no such thing as a definitive list of OH&S objectives, below are some that can be used as a baseline by the Forensic Laboratory for inclusion in its OH&S Management System:

- reduce the number of OH&S incidents by x% by the end of the year (or define a number rather than percentage);
- identify any trends in incidents and implement corrective or preventive action as appropriate;
- ensure that 100% of the Forensic Laboratory employees (and third-party employees working on their behalf) have received OH&S Management System training on an annual basis (either induction or refresher training);
- review all risk assessments during the year to ensure that they are still effective and appropriate;
- encourage all employees to report all OH&S incidents and "near misses";
- ensure that 100% of reported OH&S incidents and "near misses" are investigated to determine their root cause and implement corrective or preventive action as appropriate;
- where OH&S audits indicate a shortfall in implemented processes and procedures, to implement corrective or preventive action as appropriate;
- ensure that all employees who are working on "stressful" cases or situations have access, as required, to appropriate forms of counseling;
- comply with 100% of legislative and regulatory requirements applicable in the jurisdiction to the Forensic Laboratory;
- undertake risk assessments for 100% of cases where Forensic Laboratory employees have to act as first responders on a Client site;
- ensure that all First Responders are equipped with appropriate PPE for the duties that they are required to undertake;
- undertake 100% maintenance of all the Forensic Laboratory equipment in accordance with the manufacturers' recommendations;
- review the whole OH&S Management System on at least an annual basis at the Management Review, after an OH&S incident or on influencing change.

APPENDIX 6 - SAMPLE HAZARDS IN THE FORENSIC LABORATORY

The following is the standard list of possible hazards that may be found in the Forensic Laboratory. It is not meant to be a complete list, as each location may have its own specific hazards.

Hazard	Description
Bullying	Possible intimidation of the Forensic Laboratory employees, whether in the laboratory or out on site (e.g., working with a third party or recovering evidence)
Chemical (corrosive)	A chemical that, when it comes into contact with metal, an employee's skin or other materials will cause damage to the material it contacts
Chemical (flammable)	A chemical that, when exposed to a heat ignition source, results in combustion
Chemical (toxic)	A chemical that may be encountered by an employee typically by absorption through the skin or inhalation. The amount of chemical involved is critical in the determination of its effect
Electrical (fire)	Where an electrical power source causes a fire due to overheating, arcing, or similar
Electrical (loss of power)	Where the electrical power supply fails and thereby causes equipment failure or data loss
Electrical (shock)	Where an employee is exposed to an electrical current that may cause injury or death to the employee
Electrical (static damage)	Where volatile memory or media is damaged by a static electrical discharge
Ergonomics	Employee injury due to incorrect working environment or repetitive strain (e.g., incorrect positioning of workplace environment while using computers)

Continued

Hazard	Description
Fire	Where the workplace is susceptible to a fire
Health	Where an employee suffers from some health issue that may affect the performance of their duties (e.g., a permanent physical or mental disability or a temporary one such as pregnancy or injury)
Mechanical failure	Where equipment used in the Forensic Laboratory can fail due to poor maintenance or where the equipment is used contrary to the manufacturer's recommended limits
Noise	Where the workplace is subject to noise levels in excess of the permitted limits
Trip or stumble	Where an employee has a fall while walking on normal surfaces. This could be due to a slippery surface or a hazard placed on a floor (e.g., a trailing cable)
Visibility	Where the workplace is insufficiently lit and this impacts the employee's sight and ability to perform their duties safely
Weather	Where inclement weather, of any type, can affect operations in the Forensic Laboratory
Workload	Where the employee has an excessive workload or is subject to disturbing images in a forensic case
Workplace specific	Where the employee is working in a specific workplace that has its own specific hazards (e.g., mobile working, teleworking, or attending the scene of an incident)
Workplace violence	Possible violence in the Forensic Laboratory premises or out on site (e.g., working with a third party or recovering evidence)

APPENDIX 7 - HAZARD IDENTIFICATION FORM

The following details are recorded on the Forensic Laboratory Hazard Analysis forms for each hazard identified:

- job title;
- job location;
- Hazard Analyst;
- date;
- risk level (1-25), as given in Chapter 5, Appendix 14;
- task description;
- hazard description;
- any past incidents relating to the hazard identified;
- persons at risk (e.g., employees, members of the public, etc.);
- consequence;
- current controls implemented;
- effectiveness of current controls implemented;
- controls recommended;
- comments;
- additional controls implemented;
- date of proposed implementation;
- owner of the implementation;
- CAPA number;
- date PIR carried out;
- PIR carried out by;
- signature of employee carrying out PIR.

APPENDIX 8 - SOME AREAS FOR INSPECTION FOR HAZARDS

Some areas for inspection for OH&S hazards in the Forensic Laboratory include, but are not limited to:

- *buildings*—floors, walls, ceilings, entrances, exits, stairs, laboratories, viewing areas, areas surrounding the laboratory, loading bays;
- *electricity supply*—equipment, switches, breakers, cabling, insulation, extensions, cables, electrically powered tools, electrical grounding, national electric code compliance;
- *evacuation plan*—established procedures for an emergency evacuation, last test results, as defined in Chapter 13;
- *fire prevention*—extinguishers, alarms, sprinklers, smoking rules, fire exits, employees assigned as Fire Wardens, separation of flammable materials and dangerous operations, employee training;
- *first-aid system*—medical care facilities, accessible first-aid kits, first-aid-trained employees;
- *hand and power tools*—inspection prior to use, storage, repair, maintenance, grounding, training, use, and handling;
- *heating and ventilation*—type, effectiveness, temperature, humidity, controls, natural and artificial ventilation, national lighting code compliance;
- *laboratory housekeeping*—confidential waste disposal, tools used in the forensic process, cleaning methods, local work areas, remote work areas, storage areas;
- *lighting*—type, intensity, controls, conditions, diffusion, location, glare, and shadow control;
- *maintenance*—providing regular and preventive maintenance on all equipment used in the Forensic Laboratory, maintaining records of all maintenance undertaken, and training personnel on the correct use and servicing of equipment for which they are responsible;
- *personnel*—training, including hazard identification training, experience, PPE for use in incident response and in the workplace;
- *PPE*—type, size, maintenance, repair, age, storage, training, care and use, rules of use, especially when working off-site;

- *processing a case*—specific problems with any equipment, finding unexpected items in seized material, manual handling;
- *shipping seized material*—manual handling, training;
- *storage of seized material*—manual handling, safe storage heights, packaging;
- *transportation*—motor vehicle safety, seat belts, vehicle maintenance, safe driver programs, recovery of evidence from site.

Note

Remember that this is just a checklist and not a definitive statement of what is mandatory for the Forensic Laboratory.

APPENDIX 9 - INPUTS TO THE RISK ASSESSMENT PROCESS

Inputs to the risk assessment can include, but are not limited to:

- any emergency procedures in place;
- any environmental conditions that may affect the task being undertaken;
- details of any PPE in place;
- details of any specific manufacturers' instructions for operating any equipment;
- details of non-employees that may be affected by the work the Forensic Laboratory undertakes;
- employee competences;
- incident and near miss data;
- legislative and regulatory requirements within the jurisdiction;
- levels of employee training (work specific as well as OH&S specific) using training records as defined in Chapter 4, Section 4.6.2.3 and Chapter 18, Section 18.2.1.8;
- location details where the task is performed;
- OH&S statistics;
- results of any OH&S monitoring activities;
- results of any past risk assessments;
- safety arrangements and controls in place;
- security arrangements in place;
- skill and experience of the person undertaking the risk assessment and hazard analysis;
- the effect of "knock on" failures;
- the impact of any disruption to services or utilities in the Forensic Laboratory;
- the impact of any equipment failure in the Forensic Laboratory;
- work instructions;
- work procedures.

APPENDIX 10 - OH&S RISK RATING

Value	Type of Effect Level of Effect	Personal Safety Implication
1	Insignificant	Minor injury to individual
2	Minor	Minor injury to several people
3	Significant	Major injury to individual
4	Major	Major injury to several people or death of individual
5	Acute	Death of several people

APPENDIX 11 - DSE INITIAL WORKSTATION SELF-ASSESSMENT CHECKLIST

This checklist provides a generic aid to risk assessment for DSE use, but may need to be adjusted to meet the specific requirements of legislation or regulation within a specific jurisdiction. Local advice must be sought to ensure that it is correct and comprehensive; however, some thoughts for a self-assessment checklist to be filled in by the employee include, but are not limited to:

- name of assessor;
- job title;
- workstation location (one form shall be used for each information processing device where the user has more than one);
- asset number;
- employee being assessed;
- date of assessment;
- further action required? (Yes/No).[2]

CHAIR

- is the chair comfortable?
- is the chair adjustable (height, tilt, etc.)?
- does the employee know how to adjust their chair?
- do the employee's feet fit flat on the floor without effort when working?

DESK AND WORKPLACE

- is there enough room for all of the employee's equipment to be close at hand (i.e., on the desk or other furniture around the desk)?

2. This should be raised as a CAPA and followed through using the Forensic Laboratory continuous improvement process, as defined in Chapter 4, Section 4.8.

- is there enough room to change position when using DSE?
- is all equipment and other essential job items within easy reach?
- is there sufficient storage space available for secure storage, if needed, as well as for normal storage?
- is there enough space to allow wrists and hands to rest for easy use of the keyboard, mouse, or any other devices?
- does the employee have a wrist rest?

DISPLAY SCREENS

- are the characters clear and readable?
- is the screen clean and are cleaning materials made available to the employee?
- do the text and background colors work well together?[3]
- is the text size comfortable to read?
- is the image stable? (i.e., free of flicker or other movement);
- is the screen's specification suitable for its intended use?
- is brightness and/or contrast adjustable?
- can the screen swivel and tilt?
- is the screen free from glare and reflections?[4]
- where there is a risk of glare from external sources, are adjustable window coverings provided and in adequate condition?

KEYBOARDS

- is the keyboard separate from the screen?
- does the keyboard tilt?
- is it possible to find a comfortable keying position?
- does the employee have a wrist wrest or mouse mat with a wrist rest?
- do the employees have good keyboard techniques?
- are the characters on the keys easily readable?[5]

POINTING DEVICES

- is the device suitable for the tasks it is used for?
- is the device close enough to the employee to facilitate easy use?
- is there support for the employee's wrist and forearm?
- does the device work smoothly at a speed that suits the employee?
- does the employee know how to maintain the device (e.g., cleaning)?

3. Consider the W3 requirements (http://www.w3.org/) or others as appropriate.
4. This may vary between different times of day, locations (if a Teleworker or mobile worker) or other situations and these must be taken into account.
5. Some mobile computing devices have very small screens and keys that are difficult to use for employees with large fingers.

- is the surface that the employee is using the device on appropriate?
- has the employee been trained in how to adjust the setting on their screens, pointing devices, and furniture to minimize the hazards present?

SOFTWARE

- is the software suitable for the task that the employee is performing?
- have there been any usability issues with the software?

FURNITURE

- is the working environment appropriate for the tasks carried out by the employee (e.g., work surface large enough to perform expected tasks)?
- can the employee comfortably reach all the equipment and papers they need to use in the execution of their job role?
- are surfaces free from glare and reflection, either from external or internal sources?
- is the employee's chair suitable for their job roles? (This may include back rests, arm rests, or even foot stools.)

GENERAL WORKING ENVIRONMENT

- is there enough room to change position and vary movement?
- does the employee take regular breaks from using their computer (give approximate length and frequency of breaks)?
- is the lighting suitable, e.g., not too bright or too dim to work comfortably?
- does the environment (heat, airflow, etc.) feel comfortable?
- are temperature and humidity levels comfortable?
- are levels of noise comfortable?
- has the employee been trained in using DSE equipment so that they are aware of the risks and can adjust their general working environment?
- does the employee have to work to tight deadlines and TRTs?

HEALTH CONCERNS

- does the employee suffer from any discomfort or other symptoms when using DSE?
- specify if appropriate
  - hands;
  - arms;
  - shoulders;
  - neck;
  - lower back;

- other part of the body;
- tired or sore eyes after using any DSE?

Note

Remember that this assessment is completed by the employee (the DSE user) and is used to evaluate risks by a DSE Assessor. It is their perception of how they are exposed to any hazards as part of their work with DSE only and not their larger working environment.

APPENDIX 12 - DSE TRAINING SYLLABUS

This is the training syllabus used for educating the Forensic Laboratory employees about the risks of, and controls to be implemented for, DSE use. Other requirements may be mandated depending on the legislation and/or regulations in the jurisdiction: The list below is for DSE users:

- the risks from using DSE;
- the importance of good posture, changing position, and regular breaks;
- how to adjust furniture (chairs, keyboards, mice or other pointing devices, desks, lights, etc.) to help avoid risks. This should also include space under the desk as well as equipment on the desktop and the local environment;
- organizing the workplace to avoid awkward or frequently repeated stretching movements;
- avoiding reflections and glare on or around the screen;
- the importance of adjusting and cleaning the screen;
- who to contact for help and to report problems or symptoms of DSE health issues;
- understanding and carrying out the DSE risk self-assessment process.

Additional training for DSE Assessors includes:

- how to undertake risk assessments for DSE;
- how to review the DSE self-assessment checklists that employees have filled in;
- identification of obvious (and less obvious) hazards;
- identification of hazards in specific situations (e.g., pregnancy);
- understanding where additional information and help is needed, and knowing sources of such guidance within the jurisdiction;
- understanding filled-in risk assessment and self-assessment questionnaires and being able to identify controls to reduce the risk to an acceptable level;
- how to maintain appropriate records for the life cycle of a risk according to the requirements of the legislation or regulation within the jurisdiction;
- how to advise employees at risk as to controls that need to be put in place to reduce the risk to an acceptable level;
- being able to communicate the risk level of DSE use to all levels of employee within the Forensic Laboratory;
- the need for appropriate resources to ensure that appropriate controls are implemented within the Forensic Laboratory to reduce the risks relating to DSE to an acceptable level.

Types of training that are used include, but are not limited to:

- videos;
- computer-based training;
- wall charts;
- seminars (internal or external led);
- professionally arranged external courses.

Note 1

A number of organizations produce DSE training materials.

Note 2

A mixture of the above is used in the Forensic Laboratory, as appropriate.

APPENDIX 13 - DSE ASSESSORS CHECKLIST

This checklist provides a detailed DSE checklist for a competent DSE Assessor and should be used to obtain further and better details where the initial self-assessment performed by a Forensic Laboratory employee may indicate a possible risk. It also includes items to consider and actions to be taken. It is generic and may need to be adjusted to meet the specific requirements of legislation or regulation within a specific jurisdiction. Local advice must be sought to ensure that it is correct and comprehensive; however, some thoughts for a DSE Assessment checklist to be filled in by the DSE Assessor include, but are not limited to:

- name of assessor;
- job title;
- employee being assessed (the DSE User);
- employee's signature;
- job title;
- workstation location (one form shall be used for each information processing device where the user has more than one);
- asset number;
- date of assessment;
- date of review to be undertaken;

- action required[6];
- CAPA number;
- date action completed.

CHAIR

Risk Factor	Things to Consider
Is the chair comfortable?	Consider replacing the chair or using a support.
Is the chair adjustable (height, tilt, etc.)?	If it is not, consider replacing it or using a support, if appropriate Ensure that the lower back is properly supported.
Does the employee know how to adjust their chair?	If not—train them how to adjust it for optimum comfort. Ensure that the chair is adjusted to suit the employee. Train the employee in how to adjust their posture. Consider using chairs that are fully adjustable and that have arm rests Ensure that the employee's back is supported with relaxed shoulders. Ensure the armrests are also properly adjusted. **Note** Adjustment may also include adjustments to the DSE itself.
Do the employee's feet fit flat on the floor without effort when working?	If not, consider adjusting the chair or providing a footrest of appropriate height.

DESK AND WORKPLACE

Risk Factor	Things to Consider
Is there enough room for all of the employee's equipment to be close at hand (i.e., on the desk or other furniture around the desk)?	Consider a larger desk or other working surface if there is not enough space. Create more room by removing printers and/or scanners from the employee's desk. Create more room by removing infrequently used materials (e.g., reference material) from the desk and storing it elsewhere. Consideration of additional power sockets may be needed to relocate equipment. There should be the ability to have flexibility in the employee's workspace to permit optimal comfort and usability.
Is there enough room to change position when using DSE?	Space is needed by all employees to stretch and fidget. Consider re-arranging the employee's workplace to permit optimum movement. Remove any obstructions and any materials or equipment stored under the desk, wherever possible. Ensure all cables are tidily stored so they do not present a trip or snag hazard.
Are all equipment and other essential job items within easy reach?	Consider rearranging all DSE equipment, materials, etc., to bring frequently used items in easy reach. Consider using document holders to minimize uncomfortable head or eye movements.
Is there sufficient storage space available for secure storage if needed, as well as for normal storage?	Ensure that secure storage is provided. Ensure that other storage facilities are available as close as possible to the employee, but not so close that it restricts their ability to move freely.
Is there enough space to allow wrists and hands to rest for easy use of the keyboard, mouse, or any other devices?	Consider rearranging the desk to ensure that this is possible.
Does the employee have a wrist rest?	Consider providing wrist rests.

Continued

6. This should be raised as a CAPA and followed through using the Forensic Laboratory continuous improvement process, as defined in Chapter 4, Section 4.8.

DISPLAY SCREENS

Risk Factor	Things to Consider
Are the characters clear and readable?	Ensure that the screen is clean and cleaning materials are available. Check that the text and background colors work well together, and if not adjust them for optimum use, if possible. Consider implementing the W3 requirements—undertake a Bobby Test.
Is the screen clean and are cleaning materials made available to the employee?	Ensure that the screen is clean and cleaning materials are available.
Do the text and background colors work well together?	Check that the text and background colors work well together, and if not adjust them for optimum use, if possible. Consider implementing the W3 requirements—undertake a Bobby Test.

Continued

Risk Factor	Things to Consider
Is the text size comfortable to read?	Software or hardware settings may need to be adjusted to change text size, if possible. Consider implementing the W3 requirements—undertake a Bobby Test.
Is the image stable (i.e., free of flicker or other movement)?	Consider using different screen colors to reduce flicker. Consider altering the screen refresh rate. Consider the power supply and whether it is stable. Consider replacing the screen.
Is the screen's specification suitable for its intended use?	Ensure that the screen type suits the applications in use (e.g., intensive graphic work may require attention to detail that requires a large screen with high resolution and definition). Consider all the Forensic Laboratory employees for having multiple screens off their main workstation.
Are brightness and/or contrast adjustable?	Separate controls should be available for all screens. However, so long as the employee can read the screen easily at all times, they are not really necessary.
Can the screen swivel and tilt?	Not all screens can swivel and tilt. However, consideration of purchasing a separate swivel and tilt mechanism should be undertaken. Replacement of the screen should be considered if: The existing swivel and/or tilt mechanism is inappropriate or does not function properly or the employee has problems getting the screen into a comfortable working position. Consideration may also be given to a monitor stand if the screen height is uncomfortable for the employee.
Is the screen free from glare and reflections?	Identify any source of reflections that affect the employee. Reduce the effect of any reflections by moving the screen or even the employee's desk. Consideration may be given to providing a suitable screen to stop the reflection or glare. Consideration may be given to changing the font and background colors. Dark backgrounds and light fonts are less prone to glare and reflections. A number of controls may be needed to reduce the effect of glare and reflections.
Where there is a risk of glare from external sources, are adjustable window coverings provided and in adequate condition?	Check that all blinds and curtains are in good working order and if not repair or replace them. If this does not fix the problem, consider anti-glare screen filters.

Continued

KEYBOARDS

Risk Factor	Things to Consider
Is the keyboard separate from the screen?	This is a requirement for being able to adjust the working environment, but in some cases may not be possible (e.g., a laptop). Where this is not possible, an external keyboard should be considered.
Does the keyboard tilt?	A keyboard stand should be considered.
Is it possible to find a comfortable keying position?	Consider pushing the screen further back on the desk to gain more space for wrists and hands. Try a mixture of all of the "things to consider" given in this appendix to provide a comfortable position.
Does the employee have a wrist wrest or mouse mat with a wrist rest?	Consider provision of wrist rests or mouse pads with wrist rests.
Does the employee have good keyboard techniques?	Consider training the employee in good keyboard techniques, these include, but are not limited to: ● setting up the workspace properly (screen keyboard, desk, chair, etc.); ● not overstretching; ● not hitting the keys too hard; ● ensuring that the wrist is comfortable; ● etc.
Are the characters on the keys easily readable?	Keyboards should be kept clean If the keys cannot be read, after cleaning, consider replacing the keyboard. Always ensure that keyboards are matt to reduce the chance of glare or reflection.

POINTING DEVICES

Risk Factor	Things to Consider
Is the device suitable for the tasks it is used for?	Ensure that the device being used is appropriate for the task. Ensure that the device has been properly set up for the user. This may require resetting some of the user settings. If the employee has a problem with one type of device, consider trying another (e.g., tracker ball instead of a mouse).
Is the device close enough to the employee to facilitate easy use?	Most devices are best located as close to the user, screen and keyboard as possible. Ensure that this is the case. Consider training for the employee specifically for their pointing device including all of the items considered in this appendix to ensure maximum comfort.
Is there support for the employee's wrist and forearm?	Support may be gained from the desktop itself. If this is not appropriate for the employee then a specific wrist or arm support should be considered. Typically, these are foam or gel filled. Gel-filled ones mold themselves to the employee's wrist or arm.
Does the device work smoothly at a speed that suits the user?	All pointing devices with moving parts should be regularly cleaned (e.g., tracker ball in a mouse). Cleaning materials should be made available for all employees. Ensure that the surface on which the pointing device is used is appropriate for the device. Consideration should be given to providing appropriate mouse mats or similar. Ensure that the employee is aware how to change the setting on their pointing device and clean it.
Does the employee know how to maintain the device (e.g., cleaning)?	All pointing devices with moving parts should be regularly cleaned (e.g., tracker ball in a mouse). Cleaning materials should be made available for all employees.
Is the surface that the employee is using the device on appropriate?	Ensure that the surface on which the pointing device is used is appropriate for the device. Consideration should be given to providing appropriate mouse mats or similar.
Have employees been trained in how to adjust the setting on their screens, pointing devices, and furniture to minimize the hazards present?	Ensure all employees have been trained in all aspects of their information processing equipment that they use to the required levels and in line with the manufacturer's recommendations.

SOFTWARE

Risk Factor	Things to Consider
Is the software suitable for the task that the employee is performing?	Software should assist the employee to do their job, minimize stress and make them more effective and productive. Ensure that all employees have been given appropriate training in any software that they use in the Forensic Laboratory and that their records of training are maintained by the Human Resources Department.
Have there been any usability issues with the software?	Review fault and incident logs and take appropriate action.

FURNITURE

Risk Factor	Things to Consider
Is the working environment appropriate for the tasks carried out by the employee (e.g., work surface large enough to perform expected tasks)?	Consider a larger desk or other working surface if there is not enough space. Create more room by removing printers and/or scanners from the main desk. Create more room by removing infrequently used materials (e.g., reference material) from the desk and storing it elsewhere. Consideration of additional power sockets may be needed to relocate equipment. There should be the ability to have flexibility in the employee's workspace to permit optimal comfort and usability.
Can the employee comfortably reach all the equipment and papers they need to use in the execution of their job role?	Consider re-arranging all equipment, materials, etc., to bring frequently used items in easy reach. Consider using document holders to minimize uncomfortable head or eye movements.
Are surfaces free from glare and reflection, either from external or internal sources?	Identify any source of reflections that affect the employee. Reduce the effect of any reflections by moving the screen and other equipment or even the employee's desk. Consideration may be given to providing a suitable screen to stop the reflection or glare. Consideration may be given to changing the font and background colors. Dark backgrounds and light fonts are less prone to glare and reflections. A number of controls may be needed to reduce the effect of glare and reflections.
Is the employee's chair suitable for their job roles? (This may include backrests, armrests or even footstools.)	See section of chairs above.

GENERAL WORKING ENVIRONMENT

Risk Factor	Things to Consider
Is there enough room to change position and vary movement?	Space is needed by all employees to stretch and fidget. Consider rearranging the employee's workspace to permit optimum movement. Remove any obstructions and any materials or equipment stored under the desk, wherever possible. Ensure all cables are tidily stored so they do not present a trip or snag hazard.
Does the employee take regular breaks from using your computer (give approximate length and frequency of breaks)?	Determine breaks taken and advise on optimizing this.
Is the lighting suitable, e.g., not too bright or too dim to work comfortably?	Employees should be able to control their own lighting levels, whether it is from overhead lights, desk lamps, or natural light from windows. Ensure that the employee can control their own lighting environment. Consider using shades or other local light sources if needed—but ensure that the light sources provided do not themselves cause glare and reflection.
Does the environment (heat, airflow, etc.) feel comfortable?	Information processing equipment may affect the environment. Consider circulation of fresh air. Consider green plants as they increase moisture in the air. Consider humidifiers, if appropriate. Consider how the office/laboratory environment controls work and are set.
Are temperature and humidity levels comfortable?	Information processing equipment may affect the environment. Consider circulation of fresh air. Consider green plants as they increase moisture in the air. Consider humidifiers, if appropriate. Consider how the office/laboratory environment controls work and are set.
Are levels of noise comfortable?	Consider the source of the level of noise and consider moving it away from the employee (e.g., printers). If this does not work to reduce to an acceptable level consider putting equipment in a soundproof environment (e.g., box, container, or room).

Continued

Risk Factor	Things to Consider
Has the employee been trained in using DSE equipment so that you are aware of the risks and can adjust your general working environment?	Ensure all employees have been trained to the level that their job roles requires and that records of such training are maintained by the Human Resources Department.
Does the employee have to work to tight deadlines and TRTs?	Consider the effect of tight deadlines on the employee's environment.

HEALTH CONCERNS

Risk Factor	Things to Consider
Discomfort—hands	Specific issues relating to DSE use and hands
Discomfort—arms	Specific issues relating to DSE use and arms
Discomfort—shoulders	Specific issues relating to DSE use and shoulders
Discomfort—neck	Specific issues relating to DSE use and the neck
Discomfort—lower back	Specific issues relating to DSE use and the lower back
Discomfort—other parts of the body	Specific issues relating to DSE use and other parts of the body
Discomfort—eyes	Specific issues relating to DSE use and eyes

APPENDIX 14 - MEASUREMENT OF OH&S SUCCESS

The checklist below identifies the main areas of the Forensic Laboratory that should be reviewed and measured where possible. The checklist can be used for measurement purposes as well as an input to operational internal audits.

MANAGEMENT COMMITMENT

- do all levels of management demonstrate that OH&S is an embedded part of their job?
- does Top Management demonstrably show that they visibly support the OH&S Management System?
- does Top Management ensure that OH&S is not compromised in pursuit of other corporate goals?
- does Top Management ensure that regular reviews and audits of OH&S are undertaken?
- does Top Management provide appropriate resources to effectively implement, maintain, measure, and monitor the OH&S Management System?

- does Top Management receive regular reports on OH&S status within the Forensic Laboratory?
- does Top Management regularly review OH&S performance within the Forensic Laboratory against other similar organizations?
- does Top Management take appropriate remedial action when it is identified?
- has Top Management endorsed the OH&S Policy?
- is the OH&S Policy prominently displayed in all working locations?
- is the OH&S Policy regularly reviewed?

ORGANIZATIONAL AND OPERATIONAL REQUIREMENTS

- are there clear OH&S objectives set with realistic targets?
- do all employees understand that they are clearly personally accountable for OH&S issues within their areas of control?
- do job descriptions for all employees specify OH&S responsibilities?
- does the Health and Safety Manager have direct access to Top Management on OH&S issues?
- is there an effective OH&S Management System in place?
- is there an incident and injury reporting system in place (including near misses)?

COMPETENCE, AWARENESS, AND TRAINING

- are OH&S training records maintained by the Human Resources Department?
- do all employees receive annual OH&S awareness sessions?
- do all employees receive appropriate OH&S training when they start work or change jobs?
- is competent OH&S advice available to Top Management either from internal or external sources?
- is OH&S covered at induction for all employees and third-party employees working on the Forensic Laboratory's behalf?
- is there a process for defining competencies for all roles within the Forensic Laboratory?
- is there a process for measuring the effectiveness of any OH&S training that employees undertake?
- is there a TNA process in place for all employees following changes to equipment, standards, processes, or procedures to ensure that effective training is implemented in a timely manner?
- is there a follow-up process for new employees to ensure that they have received appropriate OH&S training?
- where "on-the-job-training" is carried out, that it is carried out in a consistent, reliable, and measurable manner?

OPERATIONAL PROCESSES

- are operational procedures and work instructions available to all employees in a clear and easily readable format?
- are PPE requirements rigorously enforced?
- are procedures and work instructions regularly reviewed and updated as needed?
- are there clearly documented procedures and work instructions for all work undertaken by the Forensic Laboratory employees?
- is conformance to operational procedures regularly monitored and measured?
- is the management system effective?
- is there a consistent process in place to identifying hazards and measuring OH&S risks?
- is there a procedure in place to ensure that safe working practices are defined, documented, followed, and updated as appropriate?
- is there an effective Quality Management System in place?
- are PPE requirements identified for all employees in all locations where they work?

EMERGENCY AND INCIDENT RESPONSE

- are lessons learned from an invocation of the plans and procedures or tests used for updating the plans and procedures?
- are post-implementation reviews undertaken to ensure that the hazard has been treated?
- are the procedures and plans easily understandable?
- are the procedures and plans well communicated and understood by all employees?
- are there effective emergency and incident response plans?
- do all employees understand their own responsibilities?
- how frequently are they tested?
- are they regularly reviewed, and updated as required?
- is remedial action implemented using the Forensic Laboratory's CAPA process?
- is root cause analysis undertaken?
- is there a documented emergency response procedure?
- is there a formal incident or injury investigation process in place?

AUDIT

- are the auditors independent of the areas that they are auditing?
- how are audit recommendations followed up?
- how do the auditors demonstrate that they are competent?
- is the IMS Calendar followed?
- is the audit work program comprehensive?
- is there an annual IMS Calendar published that covers all operations in the Forensic Laboratory?

COMMUNICATING THE OH&S MESSAGE

- are there regular OH&S meetings, with records, involving relevant stakeholders?
- are there regular updates of the OH&S message to all employees?
- do all employees, including Top Management, attend OH&S awareness training sessions?
- is a frank two-way communication possible on OH&S issues?
- is OH&S covered at induction for all employees, including third-party employees working on behalf of the Forensic Laboratory?
- is there a clearly defined process for communicating the OH&S message within the Forensic Laboratory?
- is there an easy-to-use and effective system for reporting hazards, including feedback to the repartee?
- is there an easy-to-use system in place to elicit OH&S suggestions and ideas?
- is there clear communication of organizational as well as individual conformance with the OH&S Management System?
- is there communication and consultation on OH&S objectives and measurable targets?

APPENDIX 15 - SPECIFIC OH&S INCIDENT REPORTING REQUIREMENTS

While there may be legislative or regulatory requirements in the specific jurisdiction where the Forensic Laboratory is located, the following is a generic list of details to be recorded on an incident report that covers actual accidents, injuries, ill-health that is due to a work-related cause or a "near miss." This should be filled in as soon as possible after the incident and no later than 7 days after its occurrence unless the injured employee is not well enough/incapable of doing it. In this case, a witness should fill it in if possible. Completed forms should be sent securely to the Health and Safety Manager, the Service Desk for recording the incident, and the Forensic Laboratory employee with supervisory responsibility for the area where the incident occurred:

- name of person(s)[7] involved in the incident;
- address of person(s) involved in the incident (including phone numbers and e-mail address);
- date(s) of birth;
- sex(es);
- job title(s), if a Forensic Laboratory employee;
- experience in their role, if a Forensic Laboratory employee;
- status of each person involved in the incident (employee, visitor to the Forensic Laboratory, member of the public, etc.)
- location of incident;
- date of incident;
- time of incident;
- nature of incident (define fully—even if a "near miss");
- other relevant information as deemed appropriate;
- date of incident report.

Note

Where an accident is "serious" (e.g., loss of life, injury requiring medical care rather than on-site first aid, etc.), a telephonic report of the incident should be made immediately to the Health and Safety Manager and the formal report submitted as above.

APPENDIX 16 - OH&S INVESTIGATION CHECKLIST AND FORM CONTENTS

While there may be legislative or regulatory requirements in the specific jurisdiction where the Forensic Laboratory is located, the following is a generic list of details to be recorded on an OH&S incident investigation report that covers actual accidents, injuries, ill-health that is due to a work-related cause or a "near miss." This should be filled in as soon as possible after the incident report is received and no later than 7 days after its occurrence, by the Forensic Laboratory employee with supervisory responsibility for the area where the incident occurred. Completed forms should be sent securely to the Forensic Laboratory Health and Safety Manager and the Service Desk for incident record updating:

- incident number;
- name of person(s)[7] involved in the incident;

7. The person(s) involved in the incident may not be a Forensic Laboratory employee.

- address of person(s) involved in the incident (including phone numbers and email address);
- date(s) of birth;
- sex(es);
- job title(s), if a Forensic Laboratory employee;
- experience in their role, if a Forensic Laboratory employee;
- status of each person involved in the incident (employee, visitor to the Forensic Laboratory, member of the public, etc.);
- location of incident;
- date of incident;
- time of incident;
- nature of incident (define fully—even if a "near miss");
- other relevant information as deemed appropriate;
- worst consequences of incident;
- what stopped incident reaching worst case scenario?
- whether first aid was administered, and if so what?
- whether an ambulance attended or not?
- ambulance incident log number;
- were any of the people involved in the incident hospitalized for more than 24 hours?
- weather conditions;
- type of lighting in place and effectiveness of it;
- floor or ground conditions;
- were the person(s) involved in the incident under supervision, and is so whose (name, title);
- details of any PPE being worn or that should have been worn that was not being worn;
- details of any procedures that should have been followed for the task being carried out or the area where the incident took place;
- whether a risk assessment had been undertaken for the task being carried out or the area where the incident took place;
- the date of the last review of the risk assessment;
- whether any similar incidents had occurred in the same task or area where the incident took place, and if appropriate, their incident reference numbers;
- controls that were in place or should have been in place to either treat the risk and reduce it to an acceptable level;
- number of days absent from work (for employees) or incapacitated and unable to fully follow their normal lives (non-employees);
- immediate cause (e.g., unsafe working conditions, unfamiliar equipment being examined, etc.);
- root cause (e.g., no risk assessment undertaken or reviewed, lack of training, etc.);
- immediate action taken;
- further corrective action or preventive action taken to prevent recurrence of the incident;
- CAPA number;
- target date for completion of CAPA;
- name of any witnesses to the incident;
- address of any witnesses to the incident (including phone numbers and e-mail address);
- name of employee having supervisory control where the incident took place;
- job title of the employee having supervisory control where the incident took place;
- contact details of the employee having supervisory control where the incident took place;
- signature of the employee having supervisory control where the incident took place;
- date of investigation report;
- name of investigating employee;
- title of investigating employee;
- signature of investigating employee.

Note

Not all items above will be relevant to an incident, and if not they should be marked as "Not Applicable."

APPENDIX 17 - OH&S INCIDENT REVIEW

While there may be legislative or regulatory requirements in the specific jurisdiction where the Forensic Laboratory is located, the following is a generic list of details to be recorded on an incident review report that covers actual accidents, injuries, ill-health that is due to a work-related cause or a "near miss." The results of the review must be discussed and agreed with the appropriate level of Forensic Laboratory management to agree actions to be taken. The results of this meeting shall be formally recorded in the OH&S Incident Log and reviewed at the Management Review meeting.

- incident number;
- name of person(s) involved in the incident;
- comments on the investigation report;
- comments on proposed CAPA;
- confirmation that the PIR shows that the risk has been treated and reduced to an acceptable level;
- details of the revised risk assessment carried out;
- other relevant information as deemed appropriate;
- date of investigation review;
- name of Health and Safety Manager;
- signature of Health and Safety Manager;
- name of Top Management representative, if appropriate;
- counter-signature of Top Management representative, if appropriate.

APPENDIX 18 - OHSAS 18001 MAPPING TO IMS PROCEDURES

OHSAS 18001 Clause	Control	IMS Procedure
4	OH&S Management System elements	
4.1	General requirements	Chapter 4 Chapter 5, Appendix 11
4.2	OH&S Policy	Chapter 4, Section 4.4.2, Appendix 7
4.3	Planning	
4.3.1	Hazard identification, risk assessment, and determining controls	Chapter 5, Appendix 17 This chapter, Sections 17.2.4–17.3.6
4.3.2	Legal and other requirements	Chapter 12, Section 12.3.13 This chapter, Section 17.2.2
4.3.3	Objectives and program(s)	Chapter 3, Section 3.1.17 This chapter, Sections 17.1.4, 17.2.3, and 17.3.2, Appendix 4
4.4	Implementation and operation	
4.4.1	Resources, roles, responsibility, accountability, and authority	Chapter 4, Section 4.6.2.1 This chapter, Sections 17.1.4, 17.3.1, and 17.3.2, Appendix 3
4.4.2	Competence, training, and awareness	Chapter 4, Sections 4.6.2.2 and 4.6.2.3 This chapter, Sections 17.1.4, 17.3.1, and 17.3.3 Chapter 18, Section 18.2
4.4.3	Communication, participation, and consultation	Chapter 5, Appendix 1 Chapter 12, Section 12.4.2 This chapter, Sections 17.3.4 and 17.4.3
4.4.4	Documentation	Chapter 4 This chapter, Section 17.3.5

Continued

OHSAS 18001 Clause	Control	IMS Procedure
4.4.5	Control of documents	Chapter 4, Section 4.6.3
4.4.6	Operational control	Chapter 4 Chapter 7, Section 7.4.3 Chapter 12, Section 12.4.2 Chapter 14, Sections 14.3 and 14.5 This chapter, Sections 17.2.4, 17.2.6, and 17.3.7
4.4.7	Emergency preparedness and response	Chapter 13 This chapter, Section 17.3.8
4.5	Checking	
4.5.1	Performance measurement and monitoring	Chapter 16 This chapter, Section 17.2.3
4.5.2	Evaluation of compliance	Chapter 4, Sections 4.6.4, 4.7.3, and 4.9 This chapter, Section 17.4, Appendix 14
4.5.3	Incident investigation, non-conformity, corrective action, and preventive action	
4.5.3.1	Incident investigation	Chapter 4, Section 4.8 Chapter 7, Section 7.4.1 This chapter, Section 17.4.3, Appendices 15, 16, and 17
4.5.3.2	Non-conformity, corrective and preventive action	Chapter 4, Sections 4.6.3, 4.6.4, 4.7.3, and 4.8, Appendix 49 Chapter 5 Chapter 6, Sections 6.8 and 6.14
4.5.4	Control of records	Chapter 4, Section 4.6.4
4.5.5	Internal audit	Chapter 4, Section 4.7.3 This chapter, Section 17.4.2
4.6	Management Review	Chapter 4, Section 4.9, Appendix 36 This chapter, Section 17.5.1

Chapter 18

Human Resources

Table of Contents

18.1 EMPLOYEE DEVELOPMENT

Note

This chapter is not intended to be an Human Resources manual, but to merely identify areas of information security that are required by the relevant standard that must be considered if Certification is sought. These are also regarded as good practice and should be present in some form or other in any forensic laboratory.

18.1.1 Overview of Employee Development

In order for the Forensic Laboratory to succeed, it needs competent employees and third parties that can use appropriate tools to acquire, preserve, analyze, and present the evidence recovered for a specific case as well as other duties as required.

In line with the Deming Cycle, as defined in Chapter 4, Section 4.3, the Forensic Laboratory must be continuously improving its employee's competence and, by the same token, improving its own deliverability skills for its Clients.

The Forensic Laboratory should integrate its Human Resources processes into its Integrated Management System (IMS) so that they can be managed in line with the requirements of the relevant management standards that have been implemented in the Forensic Laboratory.

The Forensic Laboratory will need to recognize that properly developed and managed employees are critical for ongoing business development and continuous improvement, as defined in Chapter 4, Section 4.8.

Human Resources management is integrated into the PDCA cycle as shown in the four principles below:

- *commitment*—making a commitment to develop all employees to help them achieve the business objectives of the Forensic Laboratory, as defined in Chapter 3, Section 3.1.17, Chapter 6, Section 6.2.2.1 and given in Chapter 6, Appendix 9;
- *planning*—regularly review the needs and plans for the training and development of employees in the Forensic Laboratory;
- *action*—take action to train and develop Forensic Laboratory employees to enable them to competently perform their roles;
- *evaluation*—evaluate the investment in employee training and to assess achievement and improve its effectiveness through a process of continuous improvement.

The Forensic Laboratory will need to fully integrate its Human Resources processes and procedures into the IMS and have demonstrable commitment from Top Management to support these principles.

While these four principles remain the guiding processes for HR within the Forensic Laboratory, it is readily accepted that there are numerous HR processes for generic HR requirements within the various jurisdictions within which a forensic laboratory may reside and operate, as well as other appropriate international or national standards.

Each of the principles is expanded below:

18.1.1.1 Commitment

The Forensic Laboratory must show its commitment to these principles by integrating them into their IMS.

Top Management must also demonstrably recognize that properly developed and managed employees are critical for ongoing business development and continuous improvement. They must also ensure that there are appropriate competent resources to perform the tasks that the Forensic Laboratory has committed to deliver. The use of the IMS for all employees, and relevant third-party employees, where appropriate policies, procedures, forms, and checklists can be referenced should be introduced as part of induction training as given in Chapter 6, Appendix 11.

All employees must be committed to personal development plans to improve their competence.

Job descriptions, with well-defined roles and responsibilities, must be agreed between all employees and Top Management.

18.1.1.2 Planning

The Forensic Laboratory must ensure that there is a continuous program of training and awareness for its employees. This is essential to develop the full potential of those employees and further the Forensic Laboratory's business objectives.

Combining this with an appropriate process of controlled business planning, it will pay dividends for the Forensic Laboratory.

18.1.1.3 Action

The Forensic Laboratory must take action to ensure that it appropriately develops and trains its employees. It does this by:

- identifying forthcoming business requirements, as defined in Chapter 3, Section 3.1.13;
- performing a training needs analysis (TNA), as defined in Section 18.2.2;
- undertaking training, awareness, and development for relevant employees, as defined in Chapter 4, Section 4.6.2.2 and Section 18.2.1;
- creating and maintaining records of training undertaken, as defined in Section 18.2.1.8 and Chapter 4, Section 4.6.2.3;

- recording continuous professional development and continuous professional education credits as defined in Section 18.2.1.8 and Chapter 4, Section 4.6.2.3;
- "bringing employees on" from the moment that they join the Forensic Laboratory.

18.1.1.4 Evaluation

The Forensic Laboratory must ensure that any investment in its employees is evaluated to ensure that it:

- is appropriate;
- is effective;
- provides value for money;
- supports personal objectives;
- supports the Forensic Laboratory's business objectives.

This is carried out by:

- reviewing staff performance as defined in Section 18.2.4;
- reviewing training, awareness, and competence as defined in Section 18.2.5 and given in Appendix 1.

18.1.2 Recruitment Overview

The Forensic Laboratory needs to attract and recruit employees with the necessary skills and experience that will help them to improve the quality of the products and services which it provides to its Clients. This process is applied to all Forensic Laboratory employees, including third-party employees working for the Forensic Laboratory (Figure 18.1).

1. A Manager (at any level from Top Management downwards) identifies a possible requirement for a new employee to:
   - fill a vacancy, for example, when an employee leaves the company;
   - address employee shortages, skills gaps, and new competency requirements.
2. When identifying a requirement for a new employee, the Manager considers:
   - reasons for recruiting;
   - possible alternatives to recruitment;
   - competence profile required by the role;
   - timescales—when does the Forensic Laboratory require the employee with the competence profile to start work;
   - implications and possible options if the Forensic Laboratory are not able to recruit appropriate employees.
3. The Manager develops a requirement specification which includes details on:
   - skill sets and competence profile required of the new employee;
   - how the recruitment is to be performed/managed (e.g., by the Forensic Laboratory itself, referrals from existing employees, a recruitment agency, etc.);
   - outline of costs of employment.

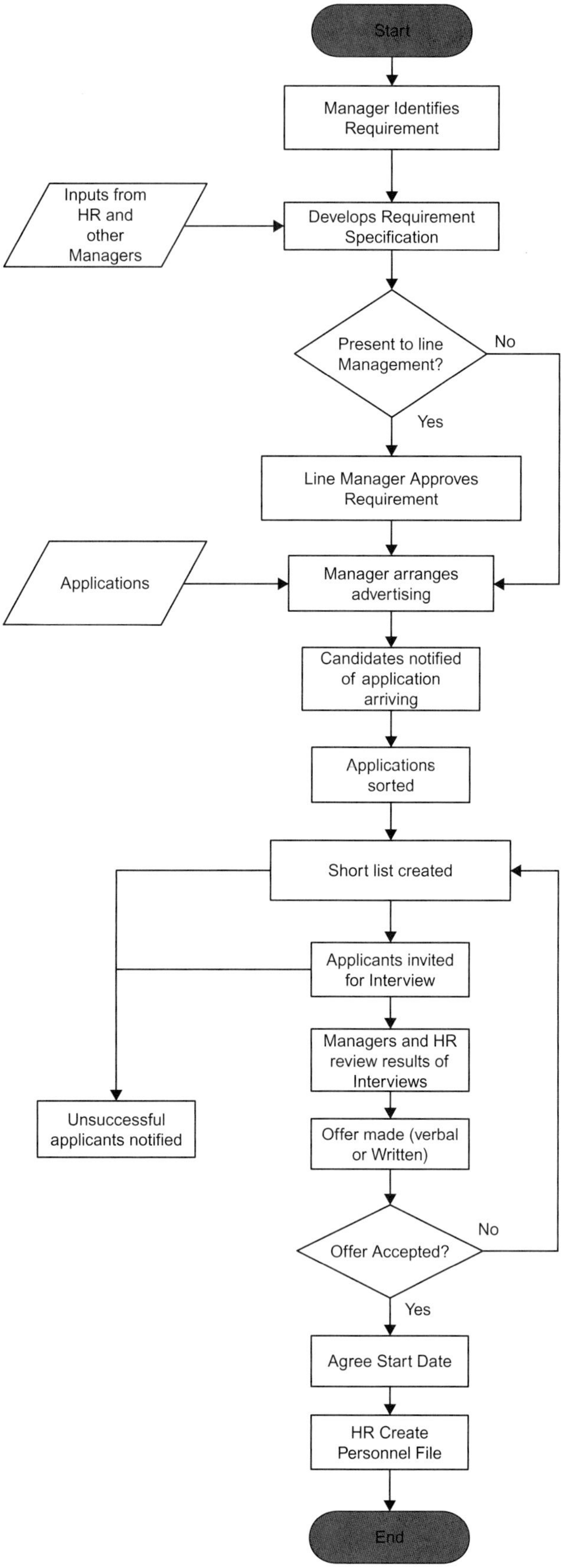

FIGURE 18.1 Recruitment Overview. (For color version of this figure, the reader is referred to the online version of this chapter.)

4. Requirements specifications are developed in consultation with other Managers and the HR Department, as required. The Manager then presents the requirement specification to their line management, if appropriate.
   - if a requirement specification is approved, authorization to proceed with the recruitment process is given;
   - if a requirement specification is rejected, it may be amended and re-presented, or the recruitment process terminated;
   - if changes and updates are required to the recruitment profile, the requirement specification is amended (and then reissued for review as required).
5. The Manager arranges the appropriate recruitment advertising via the HR Department or directly, for example, by:
   - placement of advertisements by the Forensic Laboratory;
   - advertisement internally to current employees;
   - engagement of an appropriate recruitment agency.
6. The recruiting Manager receives applications from candidates, either directly or via the Department, who may do an initial "sift" of candidates. Where the Forensic Laboratory is managing the advertising, the recruiting Manager notifies all candidates of receipt of their application. Different recruitment agencies will have their own internal procedures.
7. The recruiting Manager presents suitable applications to their management, if appropriate, with a view to selection of candidates for interview based upon matching of available competencies to the requirement specification.
8. The recruiting Manager or the HR Department contacts candidates or the recruitment agency, if used, to either:
   - arrange an interview for successful candidates, or
   - notify unsuccessful candidates that their application is not being progressed further.
9. Interviews are often conducted using the "grandfather" principle where:
   - the recruiting Manager or HR Department conducts interviews with each candidate to obtain a view on their competence and suitability—in some cases, a standard interview test may be conducted as part of this interview to help assess candidate suitability;
   - the Line Manager of the recruiting Manager interviews candidates who are selected and approved by the recruiting Manager.
10. The interviewer(s) meet to review the candidates and:
    - a candidate may be invited back for a further interview, if required and where appropriate, either with the same or a different interviewer;
    - a candidate is recommended for employment (and a salary offer decision made), subject to successful employee screening as defined in Section 18.1.3 and other checks, as appropriate;
    - unsuitable candidates are rejected.
11. If a candidate accepts the offer (in writing or verbally), a start date is agreed and confirmed in writing, together with a draft contract and job description for the new employee.
12. The HR Department creates a personnel folder for the employee and files all documentation relating to the employee's recruitment, where appropriate.

> **Note**
>
> Consistent recruitment processes, including employee screening, must be undertaken for all Forensic Laboratory employees—regardless of seniority of the position or employment type. This may have serious consequences if the employee is not subject to the appropriate employee screening process.

18.1.2.1 Employees Roles and Responsibilities

18.1.2.1.1 Roles and Responsibility Definitions for Job Applicants

- where the Forensic Laboratory is recruiting employees, a clear statement of the security roles and responsibilities for that role must be included as part of the job advertisement.
- during the interview process for all candidates, the interviewer must assure themselves that the potential recruit understands these responsibilities clearly.

18.1.2.1.2 General Roles and Responsibilities

General roles and responsibilities for all Forensic Laboratory employees are given in documents such as the Forensic Laboratory's:

- Scope Statement for the IMS;
- Information Security, Acceptable Use, and other relevant Policies;
- Employment Handbook.

18.1.2.1.3 Specific Roles and Responsibilities

Specific roles and responsibilities for jobs and tasks are given in documents such as:

- duties of Owners and Custodians;
- specific job descriptions as defined in Section 18.1.5.

18.1.2.1.4 Roles and Responsibilities for Third Parties Employed in the Forensic Laboratory

Where third parties (e.g., contractors and Consultants) are employed by the Forensic Laboratory to perform specific tasks, they will be advised of their specific responsibilities by the same sorts of documents as earlier and also their contracts of employment.

18.1.2.2 Management Responsibilities

There are a number of management responsibilities for the Forensic Laboratory's Managers to ensure that all employees are aware of their responsibilities in information security and the requirements of the IMS. This covers ensuring that all Forensic Laboratory employees must have ongoing updating of their specific responsibilities, including information security and legislative requirements, throughout their employment lifecycle with the Forensic Laboratory. This is achieved at a number of stages in the employment cycle and uses a variety of different media and methods.

> **Note**
>
> This includes any third-party employees working for the Forensic Laboratory.

18.1.2.2.1 Prior to Employment

Prior to employment, at the recruitment stage, all prospective employees shall be advised of the roles and responsibilities with regard to information security and legislative requirements for the post for which they are applying.

This shall be agreed between the HR Department and the Manager to whom they will report. This information shall be available at the pre-employment stage to the applicant.

The applicant shall be made aware of these responsibilities, and the interviewer must satisfy themselves that the applicant understands them.

18.1.2.2.2 New Employees

When a new employee starts employment in the Forensic Laboratory, they must undergo the standard induction process, which will cover, but not be limited to, the following:

- the Forensic Laboratory Handbook of Employment;
- various Forensic Laboratory Policies as defined in Section 18.1.8.

As well as the induction process covering the policies above, the employee shall be handed the job description for their role, as defined in Section 18.1.5. Each job description contains specific details for the information security responsibilities for their role.

The new employee should be encouraged to ask any questions relating to his/her job and information security responsibilities in the Forensic Laboratory generally.

An induction checklist is given in Chapter 6, Appendix 11.

18.1.2.2.3 During Employment

Annually, there is mandatory refresher training for all Forensic Laboratory employees. This is general information security refresher training, and records of the training are retained in personnel files, as defined in Section 18.2.1.8 and Chapter 4, Section 4.6.2.3.

Additional training may be undertaken after an incident for either specific employees or all employees if the incident warrants it.

For employees being issued with specific information processing equipment (e.g., laptops) or undertaking a new process (e.g., mobile working or teleworking), specific training is undertaken.

18.1.3 Employee Screening

18.1.3.1 Definitions

There are a number of definitions that need to be clearly understood, their specific use in the Forensic Laboratory, and these are defined here. These are:

- *ancillary employees*—employees involved in ancillary activities such as administration, personnel, building maintenance, and cleaning;
- *provisional employment*—the initial period of employment for a new employee during which security screening is continuing, if the Forensic Laboratory chooses to employ the individual prior to the completion of screening;
- *confirmed employment*—employment (beyond the period of provisional employment, if any) granted upon successful completion of security screening and any additional criteria applied by the Forensic Laboratory;
- *relevant employment*—employment which involves, or may involve, the acquisition of, or access to, information or equipment, the improper use of which could involve the Forensic Laboratory, any of their Clients, in a security incident or other risk that may negatively impact the Forensic Laboratory;
- *Screening Controller*—the individual in the Forensic Laboratory responsible for security screening;
- *security screening period*—the period of years immediately prior to the commencement of relevant employment or transfer to relevant employment, or back to the school leaving age, if deemed appropriate.

18.1.3.2 Overview

Different levels of screening may need to be carried out in the Forensic Laboratory in different jurisdictions, where there are different requirements. The level of screening will vary for different roles based on their access to information and its sensitivity. The guidance below is that which is proposed for use in the Forensic Laboratory, but other forensic laboratories may vary this on their own specific requirements or the requirements of the jurisdiction.

In the Forensic Laboratory, this brings together the requirements for verifying:

- identity;
- residential addresss(es);
- the right to work in the jurisdiction;
- employment history;
- qualifications;
- criminal records;
- financial status.

Additionally, the following may need to be obtained:

- personal character reference(s);
- other references for applicants in specific situations.

While some of the above requirements may be internal to the Forensic Laboratory, some (e.g., right to work in a given jurisdiction) are usually legal requirements, as defined in Chapter 12, Section 12.3.13.1.1. Breaches of these may be criminal offences in the jurisdiction with a variety of penalties applicable.

18.1.3.3 General Requirements

The Forensic Laboratory shall:

- not offer employment to any applicant whose career or history indicates that they would be unlikely to resist the opportunities for illicit personal gain, the possibilities of being compromised, or the opportunities for creating any other breach of security, which such employment might offer;
- not offer employment to any potential recruit who, where required, cannot produce a valid work permit, visa, or worker registration card within the timescales required by law in the relevant jurisdiction;
- make clear to all employees employed in employee security screening, and to those with authority to offer provisional or confirmed employment, that the Forensic Laboratory requires that the highest standards of honesty and integrity should be maintained in view of the special circumstances of the environment in which they are employed;
- carry out employee security screening prior to any engagement for relevant employment or to employees being transferred to relevant employment from other duties for which they have not previously been subjected to employee security screening. However, provisional employment may be offered in some cases, based on a risk assessment on current employee screening status;
- ensure that employee security screening has been carried out on all individuals, at every level in the Forensic Laboratory, already employed;
- inform applicants and employees being screened that their personal data will be used for the purposes of employee security screening and that any documents presented to establish identity and proof of residence may be checked using an ultra violet scanner or other method to deter identity theft and fraud. The Forensic Laboratory shall also inform the applicant or employee that any original identity documents that appear to be forgeries will be reported to the relevant authority;
- create an employee screening policy and procedures and embed them into the recruitment process. A checklist for an employment screening policy is given in Appendix 2;
- ensure that employee security screening is applied to all levels of new employees in the Forensic Laboratory, including Top Management.

Successful completion of employee security screening is one criterion upon which the decision to grant confirmed employment may be based.

18.1.3.4 Involvement in the Employee Screening Process

The size and structure of the Forensic Laboratory and the level and role of the applicant's position are used to determine which departments should be involved in the employee security screening process. In the Forensic Laboratory, this includes, but may but be limited to:

- *Human Resources*—The HR Department is used to conduct or commission employee security screening. It is essential that the HR Department has a thorough understanding of the screening process and the applicable legislation within the employment jurisdiction;
- *Information and Physical Security*—The Information Security Manager is responsible for assisting the HR Department in the employee security screening process. The Information Security Manager is responsible for dealing with security concerns that emerge from the screening checks, as well as advising on the levels of checks that are required for required for different posts within the Forensic Laboratory;
- *Management*—In the Forensic Laboratory, Managers play a significant role in recruitment. They must be involved in the recruitment and interview process, and they should look for information which may influence the direction of the employee security screening process;
- *Legal Counsel*—Employee security screening processes must comply with the relevant legislation in the jurisdiction. The Legal Counsel, whether internal or external to the Forensic Laboratory, plays a critical role in the development of the employee security screening processes. They must be consulted in the production of all documents or forms that are to be used for the employee security screening process;

- *others*—Other functions within the Forensic Laboratory that may be involved include procurement, and audit—those responsible for confirming that any contractors are adequately screening their employees.

Within the Forensic Laboratory, there is only one single Owner of the employee security screening process (the Screening Controller) who is accountable and responsible for it. The Screening Controller must ensure that the screening process is robust and is consistently applied across the whole Forensic Laboratory and to all prospective employees. If the screening process is to be performed internally, then the Screening Controller must ensure that there are an appropriate number of properly trained employees to undertake employee security screening.

Third Parties—The Forensic Laboratory may choose to use an external employee security screening agency or a recruitment agency. If it does, the Security Controller must ensure that the third party understands how their products and services fit into the recruitment and screening process. The Security Controller must ensure that roles and responsibilities of both parties are both understood and communicated to all relevant parties. Additionally, where a third party is responsible for making employee security screening decisions that affect the applicant, that they follow a documented and repeatable decision-making process. By repeatable, it means that any competent person having the same information would come to the same conclusions if they followed the agreed employee security screening procedures.

Even if the decision-making process is outsourced, the Forensic Laboratory still remains responsible and accountable for the effective implementation of the employee security screening process. This is especially true where contractors and Consultants are recruited, as they sometimes do not go through the same screening processes as other employees (e.g., full time or part timers).

18.1.3.5 Application Forms

Using an appropriate application form is considered to be good practice as the applicant receives a standardized application form that will define the information that is required for any specific post. The use of an application form also ensures that the applicant confirms the information by signature that the information supplied is correct.

The application form that can be used by the Forensic Laboratory provides the majority, if not all, of the information required for the employee screening process. The Forensic Laboratory employee application form is given in Appendix 3, with the supporting notes for completion of the form given in Appendix 4.

It may be necessary to customize the application form depending on the post the application form is being used for. For example, educational qualifications may not be required for a semi-skilled staff role (e.g., drivers or cleaners), but additional information may be required for senior or specialized posts. Applicants should be clear what information is required, and the Forensic Laboratory shall not request information which is irrelevant to the post.

The form highlights the fact that employee security screening will take place and that the applicant must provide their consent for checks to be undertaken. It also includes a clear statement that lies or omissions are grounds to terminate the recruitment process or employment, no matter when they are discovered. This is important legally but anecdotal reporting suggests that it can also have significant deterrent value. The actual wording of the application form, the consents, the information required, and the screening process have been checked by Legal Counsel to ensure that they meet all of the relevant legal requirements in the jurisdiction where it is used.

Note

Depending on the jurisdiction, there may be specific requirements for explicit consent to process some personal data. In all cases, Legal Counsel shall be involved to ensure that all legislative requirements relating to the recruitment and employee security screening process are met. Where consent forms are used, in addition to the Reference Authorization given in Appendix 9, they shall be associated with the applicant's or employees file as appropriate (e.g., Medical Consent forms, processing sensitive personal data, etc.). These documents shall be held securely by the HR Department and their disposition is defined in the Document Retention Schedule, as given in Chapter 4, Appendix 16. Appropriate disposal methods are defined in Chapter 12, Section 12.3.14.10.

18.1.3.6 Employment Screening Levels

One of the most important aspects of any screening strategy is deciding what pre-employment checks to perform for each post advertised. The Forensic Laboratory does not perform the same employee security screening checks for all applicants, regardless of the post, as this can add unnecessary cost and delays to the recruitment process and may not be the most efficient employee security screening strategy. Within the Forensic Laboratory, the employee security screening process is tailored according to the post advertised and the risks to the Forensic Laboratory that the post presents. In all cases, full employee security screening is carried out.

The opportunity to cause harm or damage is a key consideration in any employee security risk assessment and an important factor in determining the level of employee security screening checks that are required.

> **Note**
> The Forensic Laboratory will normally have three general levels of employee security screening, as shown below, but a specific level may be introduced for a specific post, based on the levels shown below.

18.1.3.6.1 Minimum Level of Employee Security Screening

As a minimum, all new employees shall:

- verify identity (normally by a birth certificate);
- verify address (the investigator should actually visit the address), if possible and practical;
- confirm right to work in the country;
- complete self-declaration criminal record form.

The Forensic Laboratory must be satisfied about a prospective employee's identity (because of the risks of identity fraud), their address, that the applicant has a right to work in the country. Failure to do so may lead to subsequent civil and criminal liabilities. On account of the work that the Forensic Laboratory carries out, the applicant should declare any criminal record that they have according to the relevant criminal record declaration legislation for the jurisdiction.

18.1.3.6.2 Medium Level of Employee Security Screening

The medium level of screening shall cover the minimum requirements above and

- most recent academic qualifications;
- relevant professional qualifications;
- most recent employment references (at least 3 years, preferably 5 years);
- basic confirmation with the past employer's HR Department of the applicant's employment history (e.g., dates, post, and reason for leaving).

18.1.3.6.3 High Level of Employee Security Screening

The high level of screening shall cover the requirements above and

- all academic qualifications;
- all professional qualifications;
- employment references to cover at least 5 years (preferably 10-15 years);
- basic confirmation with the past employer's HR Department of the applicant's employment history (e.g., dates, post, and reason for leaving) and preferably past Line Manager's references, if possible;
- financial status;
- interviews with references;
- interviews with residential neighbors, if appropriate.

18.1.3.7 Security Screening Procedures

18.1.3.7.1 The Employment Screening Plan and Records

The Forensic Laboratory will need to develop an employee security screening plan that meets its requirements with clear steps and time constraints for the process.

It is also essential that the Forensic Laboratory ensures that there is a screening file for each applicant that contains all of the information for each applicant so that there is an audit trail, records, and that any gaps and omissions are identified. The process for maintaining records within the Forensic Laboratory is defined in Chapter 4, Section 4.6.4.

18.1.3.7.2 Verifying Identity

Identity is the most fundamental employee security screening check. It should therefore be the first part of the employee security screening process, and no other checks should be carried out until the applicant's identity has been established and satisfactorily proved.

There are three elements to an identity:

- *biometric identity*—the attributes that are biologically determined and unique to an individual (e.g., fingerprints, voice, retina, facial structure, DNA profile);
- *attributed identity*—the components of an applicant's identity that they are given at their birth, including their name, place of birth, parents' names, and addresses;
- biographical identity—an individual's personal history, including, but not limited to:
  - registration of birth;
  - education and qualifications;
  - details of taxes and benefits paid by, or to, the individual;
  - employment history;
  - registration of marriage/civil partnership;
  - mortgage account details;
  - insurance policies;
  - interactions with banks, utilities, etc.

The objectives of verifying identity are to relate the applicant to the information they have given about themselves by:

- determining that the claimed identity is genuine and relates to the applicant or employee;
- establishing that the applicant or employee owns and is rightfully using that identity.

The traditional method of determining an identity is to have the applicant present documents to the corroboration of the applicant's or employee's:

- full name—forenames and last names;
- signature;
- date of birth.

Applicants should be required to provide, with their application form, the following:

- a document containing the individual's photograph, such as a passport, government identity document, or photographic driving license.

The level of assurance about the applicant's identity will increase with the number and quality of the documents received. It is important to stress that documents do not have equal value. The ideal document:

- is issued by a trustworthy and reliable source;
- is difficult to forge;
- is dated and current;
- contains the applicant or employee's name, photograph, and signature;
- requires evidence of identity before being issued.

Copies may be submitted with an application, but unless they are certified by a Notary Public or similar, the originals should be produced at the interview stage. Some document types that may be considered for verifying identity are given in Appendix 5.

Government documents may have a number of characteristics that make them difficult to forge. These will vary from document to document and from issuing body to issuing body in different jurisdictions, but some of the checks that may be considered are given in Appendix 6.

18.1.3.7.3 Verifying Address

This check confirms that the address actually exists, relates to a real property, and establishes that the applicant or employee either permanently resides there or has previously resided at the address.

Verifying the address given by the applicant or employee is important because it affirms that some other information provided is correct (e.g., an address on a driving license or official correspondence). An applicant or employee may wish to omit their current or a former address to conceal adverse information, such as a poor credit rating or criminal convictions. The Security Controller, in association with other stakeholders in the employee security screening process, must determine the level of address confirmation that is required. The requirement for address verification for a cleaner or driver will be less than that for a Finance Director. In the latter case, a full disclosure of all addresses may be judged necessary.

The applicant or employee should provide documentation to prove residence at the address(es) they have provided. Providing documentation for previous addresses may be difficult for the applicant or employee if the verification checking covers a long time period. Where this is the case, the applicant or employee may have gaps in proving residency for which they are unable to account. While there may be perfectly plausible explanations for these gaps (e.g., foreign residence, travel, loss of documentation, etc.), there may also be an attempt to conceal information that may be prejudicial to their application (e.g., criminal conviction, etc.).

If there are gaps in the applicant's address verification, the following process is undertaken:

1. Request further documentation to cover the gap(s);
2. Consider the length of the gap(s). If it is less than say 3 months and the level of employee screening is low or medium, the Security Controller may consider that the effort to confirm the gap(s) based on the risk. This is part of the agreed procedures for employee security screening in the Forensic Laboratory;
3. Where the gap(s) are discovered while using a third-party employee security screening service provider, a process for handling this is also part of the agreed employee screening procedures. How the third party handles this should be well understood prior to their engagement and subject to second-party audits;
4. Where the gap(s) are for claimed foreign travel, then a cross reference to the applicant's or employee's passport may indicate entry and exit stamps for the claimed period. However, this is not always the case as travel between some countries, depending on nationality, may not require the passport to be stamped. In this case, alternative proof should be sought to cover the period of foreign travel claimed;
5. If the applicant was actually working abroad, they may have other documentation to prove their foreign residence (e.g., contract of employment, rental agreement for living accommodation, bank statements, etc.).

If the Forensic Laboratory is unable to obtain satisfactory explanations for gaps and/or inconsistencies in the addresses the applicant or employee provides, the decision may be made to not to employ the applicant.

Some document types that may be considered for verifying address(es) are given in Appendix 7.

18.1.3.7.4 Verifying the Right to Work

The Forensic Laboratory must ensure that its employees have the right to work in the jurisdiction where the Forensic Laboratory is located. In some jurisdictions, an employer who is negligent or not sufficiently diligent in establishing the applicant's, or employee's, right to work in the jurisdiction may be liable for criminal and/or civil action. In some jurisdictions, an employer who knowingly employs an illegal worker will face more severe penalties. Additionally, some jurisdictions have penalties per illegal worker.

Once the applicant has been employed, the Forensic Laboratory has an ongoing duty in most jurisdictions, to ensure that the employee has the right to remain employed (i.e., work permits, visas, etc.).

In some jurisdictions, it is possible to have a "statutory defence" so long as the Forensic Laboratory has undertaken appropriate employee security screening and aftercare. It will be usually necessary for the Forensic Laboratory to provide records to prove that this process has been diligently carried out.

Different jurisdictions will have different requirements for proving the right to work, and the Forensic Laboratory must understand these, as defined in Chapter 12, Section 12.3.13.1.1, and use them in their employee security screening checks for confirming the right to work.

The standard questions used by the Forensic Laboratory to ask for verifying right to work are given in Appendix 8.

The Forensic Laboratory shall ensure that

- the applicant produces the relevant documents to prove the right to work in the jurisdiction;
- the applicant is the rightful owner of the documents produced;
- the documents produced permit the work the applicant will be performing;
- they check, as far as they are able, that the documentation produced is consistent with the claims made and with each other (e.g., validity, dates, other details match, etc.);
- they check, as far as they are able that the documentation produced has not been tampered with in any way;
- where inconsistent documentation is produced, the applicant is requested to provide further documentation to support their application for employment with the Forensic Laboratory;
- they retain copies (photocopies or digital scans, as acceptable within the jurisdiction) for all documentation supplied in the employee security screening process. For passports and similar, only relevant pages should be copied (e.g., front cover, data page, and pages with relevant visas, permits, etc.)[1];
- they retain documents securely according to legislative requirements for the jurisdiction, including document retention and data privacy requirements.

18.1.3.7.5 Verifying Employment History

Employment history checks involve verifying an applicant's employment history as stated on their application form, in terms of:

- dates of employment;
- position;
- duties and responsibilities;
- salary;
- reason for leaving.

The applicant's current employer should not normally be contacted without prior written permission from the applicant. The form used by the Forensic Laboratory for authorization for seeking references is given in Appendix 9.

The length of the period of previous employer's checks will depend on the role for which the applicant is being considered and the level of employee security screening applied to the post. Obviously, the more of the applicant's employment history that is checked the better so a complete picture is built about the applicant's past employment history.

A Line Manager's reference is not, strictly speaking, part of the employee security screening process as it does not verify factual information but is opinion evidence. It is also open to abuse by exaggerating claims about the applicant, either positively or detrimentally. However, it can help the Forensic Laboratory to make an assessment of the applicant's personality, etc.

Some jurisdictions have privacy laws that may restrict the information that can be supplied as a past employer's reference and some employers do not allow references to come from anyone other than the HR Department. Additionally there is an increasing reluctance on the part of many employers to provide frank and timely comments on an individual's character because they are concerned about claims for defamation. On account of this, an employer's reference may add little more than confirmation of employment, dates employed, and position held.

The Forensic Laboratory should use a standardized reference form for all written employer references. This has the advantage of identification of relevant information required about the applicant and is presented in such a way that it makes it reasonably easy for the employer to respond. The Employer Reference Form used for this in the Forensic Laboratory is given in Appendix 11.

Where an oral reference has been taken from an employer, this must also be verified. The form used for this is given in Appendix 12 and is filled in by the Reference Taker who takes the oral reference. Once the oral reference has been taken, a letter of confirmation is sent to the Reference Giver to confirm what was recorded as the oral reference. The letter for this is given in Appendix 13 and a copy of the oral reference record (i.e., the filled in Oral Reference Form as given in Appendix 12) and the Reference Authorization (as given in Appendix 9) is enclosed with the letter.

18.1.3.7.6 Verifying Qualifications

Qualification checks involve verifying an applicant's claimed qualifications as stated on their application form

1. In some jurisdictions, government documents are copyrighted, so care must be made to fully comply with this legislative requirement, where it exists.

or curriculum vitae (resume) for educational or professional qualifications, in terms of:

- educational establishment attended;
- course dates (from and to);
- title of the course;
- grade/mark awarded;
- qualification achieved (educational or professional);
- being in good standing (professional qualifications).

As part of the profile for each post, the educational and professional qualifications required for it are defined as part of the job advertising process. For some posts (e.g., cleaners, etc.) it may not be necessary to request qualifications; however, all technical and management posts will be required to provide claimed qualifications.

Original copies of qualifications should be requested, but certified copies are acceptable if certified by a Notary or Lawyer permitted to certify documents within the jurisdiction. If a plain photocopy is provided, it must be verified with the issuing organization.

The applicant's supplied qualifications shall be checked to ensure that they are genuine and that the claimed qualifications match the application form and the applicant's curriculum vitae (resume). A standard checklist that can be used by the Forensic Laboratory for this is given in Appendix 14.

18.1.3.7.7 Verifying Criminal Records

For all posts in the Forensic Laboratory, any prior criminal convictions, or similar may preclude any applicant from employment, bearing in mind the work that the Forensic Laboratory performs. As this is the case, it is essential that the Forensic Laboratory obtains details of any applicant's criminal record. In many jurisdictions, "spent" convictions do not have to be declared, but the law relating to this will vary between jurisdictions, and the Forensic Laboratory must be aware of, and understand, the implications of the relevant legislation. Professional legal advice must be sought. There are usually exemptions from not disclosing spent convictions for certain categories of jobs and it is almost certain that the Forensic Laboratory will be covered by the exemption to uphold and support law and order, but this is not certain for all jurisdictions.

There are a number of ways of obtaining and verifying any criminal activity associated with an applicant and these are discussed in subsequent sections.

18.1.3.7.7.1 A Criminal Record Declaration The Forensic Laboratory uses a Criminal Record Declaration Form that the applicant fills in and submits with their application form. A form that can be used by the Forensic Laboratory is given in Appendix 15.

The declaration requires the applicant to give details of any criminal convictions or Courts Martial. This relies on the honesty of the individual and any declaration shall be verified to ensure that it is complete and correct. The form states that verification will take place.

The criteria for determining whether a conviction, whether spent or unspent, is a bar to employment should be clearly defined in the Forensic Laboratory's employee security screening policy and supporting procedures. In general terms, the following guidance should be considered:

- the age of the applicant when the offence was committed;
- the length of time since the offence was committed;
- the nature and the background of the offence;
- the seriousness of the offence;
- whether there were a number of offences or just a single offence;
- whether the offence casts doubt on the applicant's integrity;
- whether the offence could cast doubt on the Forensic Laboratory's reputation, especially as employees may well have to give testimony in court;
- whether the offence is relevant to the post for which the applicant is applying (e.g., a fraud conviction would affect the decision to appoint the applicant to a Finance Department post, but it may not be relevant to a post where there is no interaction with money);
- whether the offence would affect the applicant's ability to fulfill the requirements of their role.

18.1.3.7.7.2 Verifying the Criminal Record Declaration How the verification process is performed through the relevant government agencies will vary from jurisdiction to jurisdiction, but in most jurisdictions, it is possible to verify the declaration.

It may also be possible to use a specialized third-party screening service provider to perform this verification process that is familiar with the requirements of the jurisdiction. This will apply to both "home" declarations as well as those from overseas.

18.1.3.7.8 Verifying Financial Status

Financial status checks involve verifying an applicant's financial status and may well be seen by the Forensic Laboratory as essential in some roles within the organization. Interpretation of the results of financial status checks is not a straightforward matter and, like personal references, is not necessarily seen as a core aspect of employee security screening.

Financial checks can provide details about many different aspects of an applicant's financial background. Types of checks can include, depending on the jurisdiction:

- credit information—listed at the applicant's current and previous addresses. This sort of information can include court matters, bankruptcies, etc.;
- credit history—a report from a local or international credit reference agency;
- Company Officer's search—using the national company register or other organizations that maintain such information, to ascertain whether the applicant has been or currently is, an Officer or Director of a company, or equivalent in the jurisdiction and whether they have ever been disqualified from being a Company Officer.

For sensitive positions, and particularly those that involve handling money, additional questions regarding previous handling of money and related issues are usually asked by the Forensic Laboratory.

Financial enquiries can be conducted in a number of ways including:

- as part of online searches, the Forensic Laboratory can use specialized databases, and it is possible to undertake a number of different searches. These can be cross referenced against paper evidence provided by the applicant;
- various national and international credit reference agencies can provide financial details on individuals. Again, these can be cross referenced against paper evidence provided by the applicant;
- specialist, third-party employee security screening service providers can usually offer financial reporting services. In these cases, the Forensic Laboratory evaluates their service offering to ensure it meets their specific requirements.

The Forensic Laboratory then evaluates the reports it receives about the applicant, from whatever source, assuming that a financial employee security screening report is required for the post. This requires judgment calls to be made as the reports may not provide clear cut answers to the financial health of the applicant. Guidance on how to interpret the results forms part of the Forensic Laboratory's screening process and procedures. The procedures must be clear and unambiguous to allow the process to be repeatable and consistent, if challenged.

18.1.3.7.9 Personal Character Reference(s)

A personal character reference is similar to a Line Manager's reference in that it is not, strictly speaking, part of the employee security screening process as it does not verify factual information but is opinion evidence. It is also open to abuse by exaggerating claims about the applicant, either positively or detrimentally. No applicant will knowingly choose a referee that will give them a bad reference.

When considering the value of the reference, consideration should be given to the credibility of the Reference Giver. Given the above, the personal character reference can also help the Forensic Laboratory to make a further assessment of the applicant's personality, etc., from a different viewpoint than the Line Manager's, assuming one was submitted.

The Personal Reference Form which can be used for this in the Forensic Laboratory is given in Appendix 16.

Where an oral reference has been taken for a personal reference, just as with oral references from an employer, this must also be verified. The form used for this is given in Appendix 17 and is filled in by the Reference Taker who takes the oral reference. Once the oral reference has been taken, a letter of confirmation is sent to the Reference Giver to confirm what was recorded as the oral reference. The letter for this is given in Appendix 13 and a copy of the oral reference record (i.e., the filled in Oral Reference Form as given in Appendix 17) and the Reference Authorization (as given in Appendix 9) is enclosed with the letter.

18.1.3.7.10 Other Reference(s)

The applicant may present pre-prepared references, either from an employer or a personal character reference. Where this is the case, the Forensic Laboratory must satisfy itself that the reference is genuine, or disregard it and request a replacement reference directly from the Reference Giver.

If the reference is to be accepted, an audit trail of the steps taken to ensure the reference(s) are genuine should be retained on the screening file. Such checks include:

- telephonic verification of the reference from the Reference Giver, as given in Appendix 13, the relevant oral reference record and the Reference Authorization, as given in Appendix 9, though a supplied phone number from the applicant should not be relied upon;
- checking that the employer actually exists by reference to paper or electronic records (e.g., National Company Register, business directories, Chamber of Commerce, etc.).

Where a reference for a period of self employment is claimed it should come from a relevant government department (e.g., Tax Office), a professional adviser to the business (e.g., a banker, accountant or solicitor) to confirm that the applicant's business was properly conducted and was terminated in a satisfactory manner.

Depending on the applicant's individual circumstances, other or additional references may also be required. If, for example:

- the applicant claims to have been working overseas for a period of three or more months consecutively, every effort should be made to obtain a reference from the employer;
- an employer's reference is not available (e.g., the employer has ceased trading), a reference should be attempted to be obtained from an Officer or Line Manager from the employer's staff;

- the applicant claims to have been in full time education, a reference from the academic institute should be obtained in lieu of an employer's reference;
- the applicant claims military service, an reference should be obtained from the relevant unit Commanding Officer.

The Other Reference Form used for this in the Forensic Laboratory is given in Appendix 18.

Where an oral reference has been taken for a personal reference, just as with oral references from an employer, this must also be verified. The form used for this is given in Appendix 19 and is filled in by the Reference Taker who takes the oral reference. Once the oral reference has been taken, a letter of confirmation is sent to the Reference Giver to confirm what was recorded as the oral reference. The letter for this is given in Appendix 13 and a copy of the oral reference record (i.e., the filled in Oral Reference Form as given in Appendix 19) and the Reference Authorization (as given in Appendix 9 is enclosed with the letter.

18.1.3.7.11 Interviews

Interviews provide a unique opportunity to evaluate the applicant using two way dialogue and observation. In addition to this, the interviewer can request additional or missing information, as well as attempt to resolve any apparent inconsistencies in the information provided or when combined with the results of online searches of the reports from specialized third-party screening service providers or other sources. If an applicant knows that they will be subject of one or more interviews, it has been suggested that this encourages them to be honest in the whole application process.

The interview also allows the applicant and the interviewer to assess each other first hand, and the feedback from the applicant can also give pointers toward the applicant's integrity and reliability.

The Forensic Laboratory should issue clear guidelines for interviewers for dealing with situations where either the evidence supplied by the applicant, or discovered as part of associated checks, reveals inconsistencies or raises concerns. This may not automatically indicate some level of attempting to subvert information and there may well be a perfectly reasonable explanation for it. Situations such as these must be carefully and sensitively handled during the interview, though clear guidance must be provided to the interviewer for determining when the authorities or police should be involved (e.g., suspected forged documents).

Within the Forensic Laboratory, all employment interviews are undertaken by the HR Department in association with the relevant Line Managers. The interview and onboarding process follows their internal procedures.

18.1.3.7.12 The Employment Decision

The Forensic Laboratory's employee security screening strategy clearly sets out how to deal with the results of all checks carried out, particularly where the results produce potentially adverse or conflicting information. It is not necessary to complete the screening process, if initial checks indicate that an applicant has provided inaccurate information or that there are significant doubts raised initially about an applicant's honesty, integrity of reliability that could harm the Forensic Laboratory.

Most of the screening checks do not require interpretation, the information provided is either true or false. However, where checks requiring a judgment call to be made are performed, the Forensic Laboratory has clear guidelines for interpretation of the results and determining what is acceptable and what is not. The Forensic Laboratory's method of determining what is acceptable, or not, is by setting thresholds for specific roles for the different areas of the employee security screening process.

At the Forensic Laboratory's discretion, employment may commence after completion of limited security screening by this stage. Such employment is deemed to be provisional employment, and the Forensic Laboratory should have carried out limited security screening. This should, as a minimum, include the following for each applicant undergoing the employee security screening process.

- establishment of a screening file, as given in Appendix 20;
- a signed application form declaration;
- all the information requested to have been supplied (e.g., through a fully completed application form) and a full review of the information provided to confirm that there is nothing to suggest that the individual will not be likely to complete security screening satisfactorily.

Under no circumstances should provisional employment commence until the limited security screening, as identified above, has been completed. During the period of provisional employment, the individual should be classed as employed, subject to satisfactory completion of security screening.

> **Note**
>
> Where it is imperative that an applicant starts employment with the Forensic Laboratory prior to the completion of the employee security screening process, this may be done after the risk has been assessed and knowingly accepted by Top Management using the Top Management Acceptance of Employment Risk Form, as given in Appendix 21.

18.1.3.7.13 Electronically Cross-Checking Information Provided

The traditional, paper-based approach is cheaper than the electronic approach. Also, it allows original documentation to be closely examined by the Forensic Laboratory. If necessary, this can include the use of an ultra-violet (UV) light source and magnifying glass to increase the prospect of identifying any basic forgeries, a checklist for some methods of detecting forged documents is given in Appendix 6. However, just relying on a paper-based approach has a number of disadvantages, some of which include:

- documents can easily be forged;
- false or stolen documents can easily be purchased;
- starting with one key forged document can allow other genuine documents to be procured from the production of the original forged or purchased document;
- with good forgeries or stolen/purchased documents, only an expert may be able to identify them;
- document verification can be labor intensive and time-consuming process.

One method that the Forensic Laboratory can use to undertake the employee security screening process is to combine the traditional paper-based approach with online checks against the paper documents held. There are a number of online databases that can be searched; some are free, while others require a payment for their use. Using online searching capabilities can build a "picture" of the applicant and corroborate the paper base evidence provided or the applicant's claims.

By searching relevant databases for records associated with the name, date of birth and address(es) provided by an individual, it is possible to build a picture of that individual's past and current life. A long history of varied transactions and events indicates that the identity is more likely to be genuine. A history that lacks detail and/or depth may indicate that the identity is false.

There is a problem in as much as online checks only confirm what is present, they do not necessarily confirm that the applicant is the rightful owner of the identity that they claim. The interview process is used to assure the interviewer that the applicant is providing appropriate documentation.

Note 1

One of the issues that must be understood is that the quality and accuracy of the data in the online databases or other online sources may be questionable.

Note 2

The quality and quantity of information on online databases varies between different jurisdictions, and total reliance on online databases in some jurisdictions is not recommended.

18.1.3.8 Using a Third-Party Screening Service Provider

There are occasions when the Forensic Laboratory may choose to use a third-party screening service provider. This may be a specialist company or a service provided by a recruitment agency. If this option is chosen, the Forensic Laboratory must ensure that they understand the range of services being offered. There are a number of advantages of this approach, and these include:

- compliance with government, regulatory and legislative requirements;
- cutting edge technology;
- flexibility in services used;
- global reach, with the larger service providers;
- reduced setup and training costs;
- typically, faster results as they service providers are specialists.

Where a third-party service provider is used, the Forensic Laboratory must ensure that the security of the applicant's data is assured. A checklist for selecting a third-party screening service provider is given in Appendix 22.

18.1.3.9 Employing Third Parties

The Forensic Laboratory employs third parties from time to time, these may be individuals on a contract or a service provider providing a variety of essential services to the Forensic Laboratory. Whichever the case, any third party employed by the Forensic Laboratory, or permitted access to Forensic Laboratory information and information processing resources, must have these screening procedures successfully applied to them prior to employment. However, as has been stated in Section 18.1.3.7.12, Top Management may choose to knowingly accept the risk of incomplete employee security screening.

The level of screening required will depend on the third party's levels of access to information and information processing resources. All third parties employed by the Forensic Laboratory must have a nominated and accountable owner of the relationship to ensure that the correct level of employment security screening is undertaken. Ideally, this will be the Screening Controller, but all Forensic Laboratory employees wanting to employ a third party must ensure that the Screening Controller is made aware of the employment of all third parties.

Where a recruitment consultancy is engaged to supply applicants for a specific role in the Forensic Laboratory, the contracts between the parties must clearly define the responsibilities for security screening of applicants. A checklist for this is given in Appendix 23.

The Forensic Laboratory may accept the fact that a third party has undertaken appropriate employment screening that meets the requirements of those set by the Forensic

Laboratory. If they cannot demonstrate this, the Forensic Laboratory shall undertake the screening process themselves or engage an appropriate specialist employee security screening service provider. Proof that any third party who has been subject of the relevant employee security screening process should be placed on the applicant (or employee's) screening file with the results of the screening process. A sample of these records shall be independently audited under the direction of the Screening Controller, as given in Appendix 20.

18.1.3.10 Individuals Employed in the Screening Process

The Screening Controller and all of those Forensic Laboratory employees carrying out the employee security screening process will, themselves, be subject to employee security screening in accordance with these procedures. However, the process of segregation of duties must be adhered to so that no-one is charge of their own employee security screening process.

The Screening Controller and all of those Forensic Laboratory employees carrying out the employee security screening process shall individually sign a confidentiality agreement relating to the disclosure of the Forensic Laboratory's confidential information and/or material with respect to an applicant or employee's past, present, and future.

Where the tasks of interviewing, employee security screening, and deciding whether to employ or to terminate employment are carried out, attention must be given to the division of functions and authority for internal control purposes. Again this reinforces the principle of segregation of duties, as defined in Chapter 12, Section 12.3.5 and Chapter 12, Section 12.3.6.

For example, where an employee has been engaged on a provisional basis, any subsequent offer of confirmed employment should be authorized only by someone other than the individual who authorized the provisional employment, and the individual authorizing confirmed employment should see and review the employee's file in each case.

18.1.3.11 Employee Security Screening Training

The Screening Controller and all of those Forensic Laboratory employees carrying out the employee security screening process of applicants or employees shall be fully trained to perform their duties. This training shall be regularly reviewed and updated as required (e.g., on a time elapsed process or changes of legislation, regulation or standards relating to the employee security screening process within the jurisdiction.

The relevant employee's HR training record should be updated, as defined in Section 18.2.1.8 and Chapter 4, Section 4.6.2.3, and the contents used for input to their TNA.

18.1.3.12 Employee Screening Records

All employee screening records shall be maintained and stored securely in the relevant screening file and measures shall be put in place to prevent unauthorized access, disclosure modification, or erasure. These requirements should be met by the implementation of ISO 27001 within the Forensic Laboratory.

The Forensic Laboratory shall maintain the following concerning employee security screening procedures:

- a separate file for each applicant to undergo employee security screening must be maintained. This includes every employee from Top Management down to the newest recruit. The files of all employees currently employed on a provisional basis shall be identified separately from other Forensic Laboratory employee files;
- details of all occasions where Top Management (or other management) discretion has been used to accept any risks for gaps or inconsistencies in the employee screening file for an applicant or employee and offer employment must be documented and placed in the relevant screening file using the Top Management Acceptance of Employment Risk Form, as given in Appendix 21;
- updated Employee Security Screening files, as given in Appendix 20, for all applicants and employees.

All screening files shall clearly indicate, where applicable, that an applicant is employed on a provisional basis, showing prominently the dates on which provisional employment commenced and is to cease; the latter should be not later than n^2 weeks after the date of commencement of provisional employment.

The full screening file should be retained during the applicant's employment in the Forensic Laboratory by the Screening Controller, with a copy held on the applicant's personnel file held by the HR department.

Where employment is ceased for whatever reason, the full screening file should be retained according to the Forensic Laboratory's document retention schedule, as defined in Chapter 4, Appendix 16. In jurisdictions where there is privacy legislation for personal data, the legislation should define handling, retention, and security requirements. The Forensic Laboratory must ensure that they comply with these requirements and ensure that they protect the contents of the screening file (and other personal data) against unauthorized access, disclosure, modification, or erasure.

2. The period of provisional employment without finishing the employee screening process will vary between posts.

18.1.4 Contracts, Confidentiality, and Non-Disclosure Agreements

In order to address the need to protect the Forensic Laboratory's confidential information, all employees shall be subject to a confidentiality agreement or clause in their employment contracts. Additionally, any third party that may have access for legitimate reasons to the Forensic Laboratory's confidential data must be subject to execution of a non-disclosure agreements (NDAs) prior to having access to that data, as defined in Chapter 14, Section 14.3.3. Confidentiality clauses must be constructed with appropriate legal advice and be legally enforceable within the relevant jurisdiction(s). It is also necessary for the Forensic Laboratory to determine their specific business requirements for such agreements, and this will include consideration of at least the following:

- a legal definition of the information to be protected (i.e., what constitutes the confidential information to be protected);
- the expected duration of the agreement, and this may be a period of time or may need to be indefinitely;
- action to be taken at the termination of the agreement (employment contract, confidentiality agreement or NDA);
- the responsibilities of the parties to the agreement during the term of the agreement;
- ownership of information created as part of employment, where appropriate;
- permitted uses of any confidential information covered by the agreement;
- right to audit or monitor any activities that involve the use or processing of confidential information covered by the agreement;
- the process for advising the owner of the confidential information in the case of any incident, unauthorized disclosure, or security breach relating to the confidential information;
- process for return, or disposal, of any confidential information covered by the agreement at the termination of the agreement, including proof of secure disposal;
- action expected to be taken, and possible penalties, in the case of a breach of the agreement.

The Forensic Laboratory will have a number of different standard forms and types of contract for different situations or jurisdictions. These are in addition to specific contracts that are created for non-standard situations. All agreements in use by the Forensic Laboratory shall be subject to regular review.

Requirements for confidentiality clauses in employment contracts, confidentiality agreements, and NDAs shall be regularly reviewed for continued business need or when business, regulatory, or legislative changes occur that may affect the requirements for protecting confidential information.

All employment contracts shall be held centrally by the HR Department. Confidentiality agreements and NDAs shall also be centrally held by a nominated Forensic Laboratory employee and a register of them be maintained; this is a duty that is normally carried out by the Legal Counsel. They shall be regularly audited to ensure that they are all present and that the Forensic Laboratory is compliant with them.

Forensic Laboratory employees are advised that they shall not to sign any confidentiality agreement or NDA that may legally bind the Forensic Laboratory without the authority of the Legal Counsel.

18.1.5 Job Descriptions

All Forensic Laboratory employees must have up to date job descriptions relevant to their role(s). In the Forensic Laboratory, there are a number of employees that will have a number of different roles and so a number of different job descriptions relevant to them.

In the Forensic Laboratory, the job description has four main uses:

- *organizational position*—it defines where the job is positioned in the Forensic Laboratory's organization structure and shows reporting lines;
- *recruitment*—it provides essential information to applicants, so they can see if they meet the requirements of the role. At the same time, it provides information to the recruiter for evaluation of the applicants and to determine an applicant's suitability and competence for a job;
- *legal*—a job description forms part of the legally binding contract of employment. Other elements include the contract of employment itself as well as the Forensic Laboratory's Employee Handbook and other documents depending on legal requirements within the jurisdiction;
- *performance appraisal*—individual objectives can be set based on the job description for use at the appraisal process.

Job descriptions within the Forensic Laboratory should all follow the same format, as a minimum:

- job title;
- objective and role;
- problems and challenges;
- principal accountabilities;
- authority;
- contacts (internal and external);
- reports to.

All job descriptions contain a requirement to comply with all legislation and Forensic Laboratory policies and procedures.

Job descriptions shall be used as the basis of the employee's appraisal and need to be regularly reviewed to ensure that they remain appropriate.

While not all job descriptions in the Forensic Laboratory are shown below, those with specific information security requirements are shown:

- Information Security Manager, as given in Chapter 12, Appendix 4;
- Quality Manager, as given in Chapter 6, Appendix 7;
- Forensic Laboratory Manager, as given in Chapter 6, Appendix 24;
- Forensic Analyst, as given in Chapter 6, Appendix 25;
- Service Desk Manager, as given in Chapter 7, Appendix 8;
- Incident Manager, as given in Chapter 7, Appendix 9;
- Problem Manager, as given in Chapter 7, Appendix 13;
- Change Manager, as given in Chapter 7, Appendix 16;
- Release Manager, as given in Chapter 7, Appendix 20;
- Configuration Manager, as given in Chapter 7, Appendix 23;
- Capacity Manager, as given in Chapter 7, Appendix 25;
- Service Level Manager, as given in Chapter 7, Appendix 28;
- Business Continuity Manager, as given in Chapter 13, Appendix 3;
- Health and Safety Manager, as given in Chapter 17, Appendix 3;
- Investigation Manager, as given in Appendix 24;
- Forensic Laboratory System Administrator, as given in Appendix 25;
- Employees, as given in Appendix 26.

18.1.6 Competence on Arrival

All new Forensic Laboratory employees shall have their competence evaluated during the recruitment process and so most should be competent to perform their role from initial employment. However, there will be times that an employee (e.g., a new entrant or an employee on transfer or promotion) may not have all of the competences required for their role and part of their job will include initial training. During the recruitment process, a competence assessment shall be carried out, matching the applicant against the requirements of the job description. The results of this evaluation can be used as input to the TNA process, as defined in Section 18.2.2.

The Forensic Laboratory may use psychometric testing as part of the recruitment process. There are a number of different tests that be used, and these fall generally into two broad categories:

- interest and personality tests;
- aptitude and ability tests.

These are administered only by competent testers who can interpret the results correctly. Results of psychometric testing are added to the employee's personnel file.

18.1.7 Induction

All new employees who join the Forensic Laboratory shall be assigned a "mentor" who is personally responsible for:

- inducting the new employee to Forensic Laboratory working methods, practices, and the Forensic Laboratory work environment;
- induction of the new employee into their team;
- acting as a focal point for any issues;
- ensuring that the new employee's details are passed to the Finance Manager;
- ensuring that an appropriate work place is available to the employee when they start work (work station, keys, security codes, access to IT facilities, etc.);
  The procedure for this is that:

  1. The HR Department performs the first part of the induction process which ensures that all personal information is collated and that generic documentation is both issued and received. The induction checklist used is given in Chapter 6, Appendix 11.
  2. The relevant Line Manager introduces the new employee to the existing team members (and other employees, as appropriate) and then performs the second part of the induction that describes the Forensic Laboratory (this task may be delegated to another employee, as necessary).
  3. The employee's Line Manager continues with the induction program and describes the new employee's role within the Forensic Laboratory, their area of work, and introduces them to their assigned mentor.
  4. The employee's Line Manager continues and describes the Forensic Laboratory's site facilities, and ensures that the new employee is provided with the relevant building keys, security access codes, and alarm codes as appropriate.
  5. Any equipment necessary for performing their role is issued to the new employee.
  6. Each of the Management System Owners outlines their part of the IMS, as appropriate. This focuses on:
     - that the IMS exists to ensure promotion of quality, security, continuity, environmental responsibility, health and safety, and legislative compliance throughout the design, development, production, and support of the Forensic Laboratory products and services. Specific information security requirements are defined in Chapter 12, Section 12.2.3;
     - the Forensic Laboratory has specific measurable objectives with regard to obtaining quality in the design, development, production, and support of the Forensic Laboratory products and services;
     - all Forensic Laboratory employees are responsible for applying the IMS procedures and policies

within the Forensic Laboratory, and play a key role in the attainment of the IMS objectives;
- all Forensic Laboratory products and services must be developed in accordance with the requirements of the IMS;
- all new Forensic Laboratory employees understand their responsibilities with regard to attainment of IMS objectives and how their contribution affects this, positively or negatively;
- new employees understand the impact of violating the IMS procedures and policies.

The employee's induction form, as given in Chapter 6, Appendix 11, is completed and then filed with the employee's other HR records. The employee's training record is updated to show that they have undertaken Induction Training.

18.1.8 Policies and Procedures

The Forensic Laboratory has a number of policies and procedures in place in the IMS, and these include, but are not limited to:

- acceptable use policy, as given in Chapter 4, Appendix 26;
- access control policy, as given in Chapter 4, Appendix 11;
- business continuity policy, as given in Chapter 4, Appendix 9;
- change or termination policy, as given in Chapter 4, Appendix 12;
- clear desk and clear screen policy, as given in Chapter 4, Appendix 13;
- conflict of interest policy, as given in Chapter 3, Appendix 3;
- continuous improvement policy, as given in Chapter 4, Appendix 14;
- document retention policy, as given in Chapter 4, Appendix 16;
- employment screening policy, as given in Chapter 4, Appendix 20;
- environment policy, as given in Chapter 4, Appendix 6;
- health and safety policy, as given in Chapter 4, Appendix 7;
- information security policy, as given in Chapter 4, Appendix 10;
- mobile computing policy, as given in Chapter 4, Appendix 18;
- network services policy, as given in Chapter 4, Appendix 19;
- quality policy, as given in Chapter 3, Appendix 4.

Supporting procedures for all of these policies, along with relevant forms and checklists, are located in the Forensic Laboratory IMS.

18.2 DEVELOPMENT

18.2.1 Ongoing Training

After induction training has been undertaken, as defined in Section 18.1.7, all employees will embark on a schedule of specific forensic training as well as ongoing organization-based training. Generic training requirements are defined in Chapter 4, Section 4.6.2.2. Ongoing organization training for the Forensic Laboratory includes annual updates for the IMS system and training for specific issues as required.

Note

The specific requirements for information security awareness training are defined in Chapter 12, Section 12.3.2.

18.2.1.1 Promotion of IMS Awareness

Awareness of IMS objectives is an important responsibility of every Forensic Laboratory employee on a daily basis. The objective of IMS awareness at the Forensic Laboratory is to:

- ensure that all Forensic Laboratory employees are aware of the IMS in operation in the Forensic Laboratory, their importance to the Forensic Laboratory in the attainment of the IMS objectives for the design, development, and production of the Forensic Laboratory's products and services;
- explain why the management systems are needed for the different standards implemented in the Forensic Laboratory and why a top level IMS has been implemented to incorporate all of the common requirements of the different standards in integrated system rather than replicating them for each standard implemented;
- ensure that all Forensic Laboratory employees are aware of their personal responsibilities and follow correct policies, procedures, and work instructions to ensure attainment of the objectives of the relevant management system;
- ensure that all Forensic Laboratory employees design, develop, and produce products and services, as well as manage and maintain them, in an appropriate and disciplined manner, in accordance with the requirements of the Forensic Laboratory management systems.

The relevant Forensic Laboratory Management System Owner is responsible for promoting awareness of their management among employees, including:

- awareness sessions are performed by the relevant Management Systems Owners when a new employee joins the Forensic Laboratory to ensure they are aware of the management systems, and their contribution toward the successful attainment of company management system objectives;

- all employees are kept up to date with changing and current management system practices and objectives;
- the management system awareness program and its effectiveness is reviewed at least annually by the Management System Owner as part of the relevant management system audit and management review process, using the Training Feedback Form given in Appendix 1. Where improvements to the program are proposed to the Forensic Laboratory Top Management that they are agreed and implemented using the continuous improvement process, as defined in Chapter 4, Section 4.8.

To promote ongoing awareness, the relevant Management System Owner should periodically re-brief all the Forensic Laboratory employees on their management system and the attainment of current management system objectives (for example, following successful re-certification of the relevant management system by the Certification Body, prior to an internal audit of the management system, or following improvements to the management system). Some of the issues covered by periodic updates include:

- the Forensic Laboratory internal audit program, as defined in the IMS Calendar, given in Chapter 4, Appendix 42;
- the ongoing success of the management system, e.g., recertification by the relevant Certification Body, Accreditation by the relevant Accreditation Service, or demonstrable improvements in KPI results;
- improvements to the relevant management system and attainment of those management system objectives;
- how improvements to the relevant management system affect working practices within the Forensic Laboratory;
- making changes to the relevant management system policies, procedures, and work instructions;
- understanding problems or difficulties experienced by Forensic Laboratory employees while using the IMS;
- how the Forensic Laboratory deals with employees who do not comply with management system policies, procedures, and work instructions.

18.2.1.2 Maintaining Employee IMS Awareness

The Forensic Laboratory recognizes that retention and applicable knowledge of employees increases considerably when the matter is subject to revision. To assist with this:

- all Forensic Laboratory employees must be re-briefed on all parts of the IMS annually, or on influencing change by the relevant Management System Owner;
- the relevant Management System Owner shall develop and implement an awareness program for their management system, which addresses periodic management system awareness update requirements;
- some of the issues covered by the periodic management system updates include:
  - how the Forensic Laboratory deals with employees who do not comply with the requirements of the IMS, its policies, procedures, and work instructions;
  - success of implementation and use of the IMS, its policies, procedures, and work instructions;
  - problems or difficulties experienced with the IMS, its policies, procedures, and work instructions;
  - any changes to the IMS, its policies, procedures, and work instructions;
  - breaches and incidents relating to the IMS;
  - etc.

18.2.1.3 Other Business-Related Training

There are a variety of business type training sessions for a range of specific subjects that are applicable to Forensic Laboratory employees. Some will be applicable to all employees, others will be applicable to specific employees doing a specific task (e.g., Laptop Security), and others will be indicated by the annual appraisal process and the employee's TNA, as defined in Section 18.2.2. Generic requirements for all types of training are defined in Chapter 4, Section 4.6.2.2.

18.2.1.4 Information Security Training

Awareness of information security requirements relating to information held by the Forensic Laboratory is an essential responsibility of every Forensic Laboratory employee on a daily basis. Unauthorized access, disclosure, modification, or erasure of Forensic Laboratory information could result in a loss of work hours spent creating information, as well as more work hours trying to recover it and possible severe reputational loss or financial penalties. Information compromise inside or outside the work environment could result in the violation of Client confidentiality or relevant privacy legislation in the jurisdiction. This could lead to criminal charges or civil litigation.

It is ultimately the responsibility of the Forensic Laboratory Top Management to ensure that all employees with access to Forensic Laboratory information and information processing resources understand the key elements of information security, why it is needed, and their personal information security responsibilities.

All employees shall participate in the security awareness and training program, as defined in Chapter 12, Section 12.3.2.

All Forensic Laboratory employees must be provided with guidance to help them understand information security, the importance of complying with the relevant policies, procedures, and work instructions relating to information security within the Forensic Laboratory and to be aware of their own personal responsibilities. It is the responsibility of the Forensic Laboratory Line Managers, in cooperation with the Information Security Manager, to promote security awareness and training to all employees on a continuous basis.

The Forensic Laboratory shall follow these guidelines to promote awareness of information security among all employees with access to the Forensic Laboratory information and information processing resources:

- formal awareness and training sessions are run using specialized awareness material;
- all training sessions are kept up to date with current practices;
- training sessions must be attended by all Forensic Laboratory employees, including Top Management;
- information security awareness training sessions are regularly reviewed by the Information Security Manager;
- feedback from the information security awareness training sessions is regularly reviewed by the Information Security Manager to ensure continuous improvement is in place.

The objective of security training at the Forensic Laboratory is to ensure that:

- the Forensic Laboratory uses appropriate risk management techniques and tools to choose appropriate security controls;
- information security controls are applied correctly to the Forensic Laboratory information and information processing resources;
- the Forensic Laboratory develops products and services, and process cases, in a disciplined and secure manner.

The HR Manager and relevant Management System Owners are responsible for ensuring that the Forensic Laboratory employees obtain adequate training via:

- advising employees of available courses and seminars that are appropriate to their needs;
- encouraging membership of suitable professional bodies;
- encouraging personal certification, where applicable;
- ensuring knowledge transfer from third parties to Forensic Laboratory employees;
- identifying on-line training resources and encouraging employees to use them;
- implementing a learning management system with learning re-inforcement that is part of the annual awareness update process. Those employees that do not pass the marking threshold shall have to retake the training until they do pass.

18.2.1.5 Technical Training for Forensic Laboratory Employees

All Forensic Laboratory employees involved in case processing have to be technically trained in a number of different areas of digital forensics. A list of areas of required knowledge is given in Appendix 27.

18.2.1.6 Training Development Within the Forensic Laboratory

It is essential that all Forensic Laboratory employees who handle forensic cases are properly trained, but because this is a relatively new field, few competency frameworks currently exist that can be relied upon to authenticate training.

Often it is tempting to send employees who handle forensic cases for product-specific training before a clear understanding of the underlying principles of computer operations and general forensic procedures are clearly understood, in order to make Forensic Laboratory employees who handle cases productive employees as soon as possible. However, without basic understanding of the hardware and general forensic procedures, employees who handle cases and have only product specific knowledge will produce work that may be of little use as any evidence found cannot be supported by the knowledge of how it got there. A possible framework for initial development for overcoming this issue is given in Chapter 6, Appendix 26.

18.2.1.7 Individual Certification or Not?

As well as undertaking general training and role-specific training, the Forensic Laboratory encourages its employees to enhance their professional and personal development. Individual certification lends gravitas to Forensic Laboratory employees when they are giving evidence either orally or in writing. As part of the certification process, individual employees usually have to undertake reporting requirements for Continuing Professional Development (CPD) or Continuing Professional Education (CPE), and these records shall be associated with the employees training records, as defined in Section 18.2.1.8 and Chapter 4, Section 4.6.2.3.

While individual certification is not a pre-requisite, it is a matter for the employee and the Forensic Laboratory to determine whether certification should be sought or not, and if so what certifications should be pursued.

A list of some existing security and forensic certifications that should be considered is given in Chapter 6, Appendix 27.

> **Note**
> This list is expanding rapidly and current certifications should be researched to determine the optimum ones for an employee.

As well as certifications, membership of professional bodies should also be considered. There are a variety of national and international professional bodies that can be considered. Some of the better known ones are listed in Appendix 28.

18.2.1.8 Training Records

All Forensic Laboratory employees must have full training records maintained as part of their HR file, as defined in Section 18.2.1.8 and Chapter 4, Section 4.6.2.3. This will also contain the training and development plan.

Copies of the following training records or certificates are retained on an employees personnel file:

- academic qualifications;
- awareness sessions attended;
- certifications gained;
- continual professional development (CPD) logs;
- continual professional education (CPE) logs;
- external courses attended;
- internal course attended;
- other accolades or commendations achieved as part of the training process;
- professional qualifications;
- relevant training or re-training undertaken whilst employed by the Forensic Laboratory;
- remedial action as part of the TNA process.

After training or gaining a new or updated qualification all Forensic Laboratory employees must send in a training evaluation form, as given in Appendix 1, to the Human Resources Department to both provide feedback and allow their training records to be updated.

18.2.2 Training Needs Analysis

The Forensic Laboratory will use TNA for all employees as part of the annual appraisal process, as defined in Section 18.2.4, for the employee and also the annual review of business strategy. TNA uses the "training wheel" approach, which is a variation on Dr. W. Edwards Deming's "Plan-Do-Check-Act" (PDCA) cycle, as used by the Forensic Laboratory and defined in Chapter 4, Section 4.3.1. It goes through the following stages.

18.2.2.1 Identifying Business Needs

The whole process of TNA starts off with identifying the needs of the business. After all, if there is no justifiable business need for undertaking some specific training why should it be undertaken?

There are two specific types of business needs:

Planned—this is where there are either environmental needs to be met (e.g., planned legislative changes) or business needs to be met that align with the business strategy and objectives. The Forensic Laboratory must ensure that it is constantly aware of environmental changes on the horizon that may affect it, as well as evaluating (and constantly reevaluating) its business strategy and objectives and managing the business to meet them;

Unplanned—this occurs when some event that was not planned for by the Forensic Laboratory occurs (e.g., a flurry of complaints from Clients, a major case collapsing on account of a failure in the Forensic Laboratory's processes, etc.) that needs to be urgently fixed and where training appears to be the solution. However, care should be taken not to rush into this solution as it can be costly and not always be effective in solving the underlying root cause of the problem.

18.2.2.2 Identifying Training Needs

Having identified the business needs, whether they are planned or unplanned, they must be turned into training needs. There are three different levels of training needs that the Forensic Laboratory considers:

- *organizational*—this is where a training need is identified for all of the Forensic Laboratory employees and is typically a new initiative or a legislative change;
- *group*—this is where a specific group, or groups, of Forensic Laboratory employees have a specific training need identified that relates only to them (e.g., a new tool or process to be used in their specific work area);
- *individual*—this will typically be derived from the employee appraisal process, as defined in Section 18.2.4, and will include any remediation training, training according to the employee's training plan or could be an unplanned event (e.g., a promotion requiring management training).

The Forensic Laboratory may use any or all of five tools below to assist in this process and these are:

- *human resource planning*—which includes how to resource the Forensic Laboratory according to the business strategy and objectives as well as employee appraisals;
- *succession planning*—which is a subset of HR planning but aims to ensure that there is cover for any specific role. While this typically refers planning for management succession, it can also refer to a specialist role and often covers issues like cross training employees, so there are always at least two employees with a specific skill;
- *critical incidents*—which are typically "one off" incidents that can affect the Forensic Laboratory's credibility or reputation in the marketplace (e.g., a loss of a major Client, audit failure, etc.). The root cause of any such incident must be determined, as defined in Chapter 4, Section 4.8.1 and given in Chapter 4, Appendix 49, and then consideration given as to whether training is actually the correct solution;
- *management information systems*—which uses monitoring and analysis of a variety of key performance indicators or quality objectives to determine areas of the Forensic Laboratory's performance that may need improvement. This is a performance management process and may also indicate a need for additional training;

- *performance appraisals*—which is the individual employee's annual appraisal, as defined in Section 18.2.4, that identifies weaknesses in the employee's performance that can be resolved by training or as part of the employee's training plan.

While training may be a solution to an identified problem, careful determination of the root cause of the problem may indicate other solutions that are more effective. These could include:

- better use of technology;
- improving procedures;
- employee rotation or changes;
- re-design of job roles.

18.2.2.3 Specifying Training Needs

Having identified that a training need exists, it is necessary to specify the requirement precisely. The Forensic Laboratory will use a gap analysis approach identifying the key tasks, deliverables and competencies for a specific role, and the employee's performance, whether this is for an individual employee or a group of them. The gap analysis is carried out using a combination of data gathering approaches within the Forensic Laboratory and may include, but not be limited to:

- critical incident reviews;
- desk research or competitor analysis;
- direct observation of the employee's performance;
- interviews;
- psychometric assessments;
- self-assessment questionnaires.

18.2.2.4 Turning Training Needs into Action

Once the decision that a training solution is appropriate has been agreed, then the type of training to be used must be determined. Within the Forensic Laboratory, training is divided into formal and informal training as defined below.

18.2.2.4.1 Formal Training

In the Forensic Laboratory, this is defined as classroom training with the tutor "teaching" the participants. Heavy trainer input is usually required for knowledge transfer, with less being required for skill and attitude training where the trainer becomes more of a "facilitator." However, there are a number of alternatives to classroom training, and they can use a number of different training media. The choice of these will depend on training material availability, budget, cultural fit, etc.

Some options include:

18.2.2.4.1.1 Out of Doors Training For management, leadership, and team building training, this is often used and usually comprises a number of practical tasks to be performed, either on an individual basis or as teams. This may include competitions to build bridges or overcome obstacles, assault courses, paintball competitions, or confidence exercises such as zip lines and high-level bridges.

18.2.2.4.1.2 Computer-Based Training This type of training is typically used for knowledge-based competencies. The advent of multimedia training and virtual online classrooms has made this form of training both affordable and a real contender to replace formal classroom training in a number of areas for the Forensic Laboratory, including internal training and awareness courses. Though it does have the disadvantage that face-to-face interaction is limited, so a mix of traditional classroom and virtual online training may be needed.

18.2.2.4.1.3 Distance Learning There are a wide range of distance learning programs available for a variety of training. Often they include tutor and classroom sessions as part of the training and typically will have assessments and/or examination(s). Distance learning can deliver very straightforward and highly focused training to a full degree or beyond.

18.2.2.4.1.4 Job Rotation This is a formal process where a pre-planned sequence of different role experiences is undertaken by an employee. Within the Forensic Laboratory, it is used at the start of employment for employees to gain a full understanding of different processes that make up the whole organizational structure, as appropriate to their role. This option is used for a graduate or school leaver to understand the whole process of digital forensics in the Forensic Laboratory or for management training for a new promotee.

18.2.2.4.1.5 Job Shadowing This is another formal process, often used with other types of training, which involves the employee observing or working alongside relevant post holders to gain experience a particular task or skill.

18.2.2.4.2 Informal Training

While there are a number of formal training methods used in the Forensic Laboratory, as defined earlier, there are a number of very useful informal ones that the Forensic Laboratory may use.

These are often seen as a cheap option when compared against formal training, but the Forensic Laboratory can use this type of training when:

- it is being used for developing a skill (rather than learning a new one);
- there is need for specific training tailored to the specific work environment in the Forensic Laboratory;

- an individual employee responds better to this type of training than any other;
- there are no formal training courses available;
- there is a limited training budget;
- there is a time constraint in that there is no formal training available within the required time frame.

18.2.2.4.2.1 ***Coaching*** Coaching within the Forensic Laboratory can be undertaken by either a Line Manager or an external consultant while the employee being coached can be anyone who wants to get better at their work. Coaching can be carried out in a series of coaching sessions, but the Forensic Laboratory has found that it is often best used informally through discussions between Line Managers and other employees as part of their daily tasks.

Coaching is a collaborative process to manage the employee to deliver better results in their role. In the process, the Coach is responsible for keeping the coaching focused on a clearly defined goal and the employee being coached to generate ideas, options, and methods for achieving a goal, taking action to achieve it and reporting the progress toward the goal. One of the most common reasons for coaching to fail is to get these roles confused and the Forensic Laboratory is very careful to ensure that this does not occur.

The process that the Forensic Laboratory uses is the "GROW" model:

- *goal*—defining the required outcome;
- *reality*—identifying the current situation and future trends;
- *options*—identifying new ideas for achieving the goal;
- *what/who/when*—deciding on the plan of action to achieve this.

As can be seen, again this is a variation of W. Edwards Deming's PDCA cycle, as defined in Chapter 4, Section 4.3.1.

Note

Coaching can be very time consuming for the Coach and the Forensic Laboratory must ensure that coaching does not affect a Line Manager's ability to manage effectively.

18.2.2.4.2.2 ***Mentoring*** Mentoring is similar to coaching, and the Mentor can be part of a formal or informal training process. A Mentor can play a number of roles in the Forensic Laboratory; these can range from:

- acting as the "buddy" for new employee to assist them settle into their role;
- a "listening ear" to any level of employee in the Forensic Laboratory, and they do not even have to be other employees but may be outsiders. If they are external to the Forensic Laboratory, care must be taken to ensure that there is no leakage of confidential information or that if confidential information may be discussed that appropriate Confidentiality Agreements or NDAs are in place;
- acting as a "sounding board" for new ideas, again care must be taken about disclosure of confidential information;
- taking a proactive role in another employee's development.

18.2.2.5 The Training Specification

The training specification is a blueprint for the training to be undertaken to meet the gap in performance identified and to measure its effectiveness. The exact form of a training specification will vary between different types of training that the Forensic Laboratory may want to undertake, and the Training Specification used by the Forensic Laboratory is given in Appendix 29.

It is essential that any training that the Forensic Laboratory undertakes meets the stated training objectives (often referred to as "learning" objectives). These are descriptions of the performance and/or behaviors that the employees are expected to exhibit at the end of the training. It is essential that these are clearly and precisely defined as they will be the basis of the evaluation of the effectiveness of the training. The Forensic Laboratory may choose to adopt the SMARTER approach for the evaluation of training, and this is used to evaluate training objectives:

- *Specific*—avoiding poorly defined training objectives;
- *Measurable*—ensuring that it is possible to measure the training objective when complete and to know if it was achieved;
- *Attainable*—not using a training objective that can never be achieved;
- *Realistic*—ensuring that the employee is capable of achieving the objective;
- *Timelines*—ensuring each objective has written within it a timeline (date) for completion;
- *Extending*—the task should stretch the employee's capabilities;
- *Rewarding*—ensuring that the employee is rewarded for delivery in an appropriate manner.

Note

This is a variation on the SMART approach used in the Forensic Laboratory for measurements of objective, as defined in Chapter 3, Section 3.1.17.

While it may appear an onerous task to create a training specification for each training course for each employee, sometimes a shorter specification can be used. Where the course is for only one or two employees, it may be that this is not required, but for some specialized or management positions, it is essential.

The creation of the training specification ensures that the requirements are clearly thought through, allow commercial offerings to be compared against them in detail, and provide the basis for the all important step of evaluation of the training.

18.2.2.5.1 Develop or Purchase?

Having developed the training specification, The Forensic Laboratory has to either develop a course to meet the training objectives or find a commercial offering that meets them.

> **Note**
> There may be other options available such as amending an existing course or reusing modules from other courses.

The "develop or buy?" decision for the Forensic Laboratory is influenced by five main factors:

- *number of employees to be trained*—it is cheaper to develop a course if there are a large number of employees to be trained;
- *the competencies to be trained*—if the competencies are Forensic Laboratory specific, it is better to develop a course;
- *the time constraints*—if a course is not needed immediately, it may be better to develop a course;
- *the skills required for the trainer*—if the required skills of the trainer do not exist outside the Forensic Laboratory, then they may have no choice but to develop a course;
- *the learning experience required*—if there is a need to train employees together, then it may be better to develop a course.

Another solution that the Forensic Laboratory may consider is to "buy in" a course with a trainer and run it on site. Different situations within the Forensic Laboratory will require different solutions, and this is a judgment call that Forensic Laboratory Top Management must make.

18.2.2.5.2 Choosing a Supplier

If developing or purchasing a course, it is essential that the supplier meets the training objectives set by the Forensic Laboratory for their training: The process used by the Forensic Laboratory is similar to that of the tendering process that exists for any service, as defined in Chapter 14, Section 14.5, and follows the specific steps below for choosing a training supplier, as opposed to any other office product or service:

- research the market to find suitable Suppliers;
- create a shortlist of five or six that seem to be the closest match to the training requirements;
- ask the shortlist to submit a training RFP based on the agreed training specification. A checklist for evaluation training proposals is given in Appendix 30;
- evaluate the proposals against the training specification, and based on the responses, select two or three;
- invite them for an interview. A checklist for evaluation at the interview is given in Appendix 31;
- follow up with the supplier's Client references, if required;
- based on the responses to all of the above, select a supplier.

If purchasing an existing course, then the following should be considered:

- create a shortlist of five or six that seem to be the closest match to the training requirements and then determine:
  - how well the course content and learning objectives meets the Forensic Laboratory's training objectives;
  - the quality of the course based on feedback;
  - the costs of the course;
  - the timing of the course;
  - the location of the course, which can have a cost implication and also a staff unavailability issue if the course is held at a distant location.
- based on the responses to all of the above, select a supplier.

18.2.2.6 Planning the Training

Having determined the training needs from a number of sources, the Forensic Laboratory plans the training to be delivered in terms of:

- what training should be included based on a variety of constraints;
- the order for carrying out training on an organizational, group, and employee level;
- what training can be postponed without impacting the Forensic Laboratory's ability to deliver quality products and services;
- fallback plans in case of changing requirements or supplier failure.

While it is possible to plan for most training, often training needs are unplanned and so there must be a great degree of flexibility in the Forensic Laboratory's training plans.

18.2.2.7 Training Evaluation

Training evaluation is carried out for three main reasons:

- to continuously improve training content and delivery quality;

- to assess the effectiveness of the course in meeting the Forensic Laboratory's training objectives;
- to justify the course by proving the benefits outweigh the costs.

For each of these reasons, hard empirical data must be collected.

The evaluation is at four different levels:

- reaction level—what the employee thought of the training;
- immediate level—what the employee learned from the training;
- intermediate level—the effect the training had on the employee's job performance;
- ultimate level—the effect the training had on the Forensic Laboratory's performance.

These levels are further defined below.

The main methods of collecting data are:

- questionnaires, as given in Appendix 1;
- interviews;
- observation;
- desk research.

A mixture of all of these methods can be used, as appropriate, in the Forensic Laboratory, as each has its advantages and disadvantages.

18.2.2.7.1 Reaction Level Evaluation

This form of evaluation is usually undertaken using forms that the employee has filled in either at the end of the course or on their return to the Forensic Laboratory with the Human Resources Department or the employee's Line Manager using the Form given in Appendix 32. These evaluation forms are used to evaluate the training and are stored with the employee's personnel records, as defined in Section 18.2.1.8 and Chapter 4, Section 4.6.2.3.

18.2.2.7.2 Immediate Level Evaluation

This form of evaluation is aimed and determining how much the employee has actually learned on the course. Typically, this is done using quizzes and/or exam at the end of the course that is based specifically on the content of the course. There are three main methods of obtaining immediate level evaluation:

- simple "Yes"/"No"/"Don't Know" or "True"/"False"/"Don't Know" type answers to multiple questions covering the course content;
- multiple choice questions where the employee is offered a number of possible answers and has to choose the correct answer(s);
- open-ended questions which require free form essay style answers to the question asked.

The first two are useful for testing simple knowledge retention, and the last one is mainly used for determining the employees understanding and application of the concepts learned and applying them to real situations. The Forensic Laboratory should use the form given in Appendix 1 for all course feedback with other forms, as appropriate.

18.2.2.7.3 Intermediate Level Evaluation

Intermediate level evaluation determines how well the employee has assimilated the knowledge or skills learned to improve their job performance. This is the most important level of evaluation, and if the TNA has been properly carried out, the training undertaken should close any employee's performance gap. When combined with the immediate level evaluation, this can be a clear indicator of how good the training actually was for the employee(s). If the results for both are poor for one or two employees, where many are attending, this can indicate a specific issue with the specific employee(s) performing poorly. Multiple poor results can indicate that the training was possibly inappropriate for the employees or that the training and the way the material was delivered were poor. These two evaluation levels shall be carefully examined to determine the effectiveness of the training being undertaken. Wherever results are poor for one or more employee, the reason for the poor results must be determined and appropriate action taken to address the root cause.

A range of tools can be used to evaluate intermediate level evaluation; these include:

- independent assessment;
- management review;
- observation;
- peer review;
- self-assessment questionnaires.

The Forensic Laboratory uses the appropriate "mix and match" of the tools above to evaluate the effectiveness of all employee training undertaken.

18.2.2.7.4 Ultimate Level Evaluation

In some ways, this is the most difficult level to evaluate as the method of measuring performance may not be easy to implement or measure. There are a number of reasons for this:

- there are often no direct or obvious performance measures (e.g., management or leadership training);
- many factors apart from the training undertaken can affect performance (e.g., economic conditions can affect sales even if a sales training course was world class);
- often performance measures are measured for a whole department, and it is not possible to identify the effects of the training unless all members of the department attended the training.

The optimum measurement process uses the SMARTER approach, as defined in Section 18.2.2.5, and has a six stage approach:

1. identify the key performance indicators that are to be used for performance measurement.
2. ensure that the performance figures are available in the right form prior to the training being undertaken.
3. determine how long it will be before the training has made the optimum impact on operations within the Forensic Laboratory.
4. determine the new performance figures from the period immediately after training was undertaken to the point determined earlier.
5. identify an other factors that may affect performance on operations within the Forensic Laboratory.
6. compare the results of the "before" and "after" training.

The Forensic Laboratory must determine appropriate key performance indicators (or quality objectives in ISO 9001 terms) for measuring the effectiveness of training. Examples will vary between different departments within the Forensic Laboratory and the Business Owners must be accountable and responsible for determining them. Some examples that are easy to measure include:

- absenteeism levels;
- level of orders or sales;
- meeting case turn round times (TRTs);
- number of successful case outcomes;
- reduction in customer complaints;
- increasing referrals from existing customers;
- etc.

18.2.3 Monitoring and Reviewing

The Forensic Laboratory must implement suitable monitoring systems to evaluate performance of products and services, this is in addition to technical IT performance monitoring and review. Examples of this in the Forensic Laboratory are defined in Chapter 4, Section 4.7.1; Chapter 5, Section 5.7.1.5; Chapter 6, Section 6.13.1; Chapter 9, Section 9.5.5; Chapter 9, Section 9.5.8; Chapter 14, Section 14.2.1.2; Chapter 14, Section 14.4.2; Chapter 14, Section 14.5.3; Chapter 14, Section 14.8.2.2; Chapter 16; and Chapter 17, Section 17.4.1 in addition to Continuous improvement and Management Review, defined in Chapter 4, Sections 4.8 and 4.9, respectively.

This will include reviewing employee performance and development requirements. Generally, monitoring will be an ongoing process and reviewing is also performed at the end of a project or case, during a project or case review.

Monitoring systems in the Forensic Laboratory will capture performance measures on an ongoing basis, using computer as well as manual systems. System use is also monitored to ensure that they are used in accordance with the acceptable use and other policies in force in the Forensic Laboratory.

Reviews are performed by Top Management, Line Managers, or Account Managers, as appropriate, on a particular process, project, or case. In the Forensic Laboratory, reviews can be formal or informal and can cover the following:

- Client and employee liaison;
- compliance with Forensic Laboratory procedures and suggestions for procedures improvement;
- identification of training gaps;
- innovation and ideas generation;
- problems resolved;
- research and information gathering techniques;
- review of a process, project, or case;
- suggestions for personal improvement and setting of objectives;
- writing and editing performance and Client feedback.

The review is documented in the form of a report and is filed in the Client's virtual case file in the ERMS and the relevant Forensic Laboratory employee's personnel file as appropriate, as defined in Chapter 4, Section 4.6.4. Following a review, notes and revisions may be required in the following areas:

- First Responder procedures;
- Forensic Laboratory quality procedures;
- Forensic Laboratory security procedures;
- other Forensic Laboratory procedures;
- employee training and development plans.

18.2.4 Employee Appraisals

All Forensic Laboratory employees must undergo annual appraisals where training needs and performance are analyzed. The appraisal process shall be carried out in line with the Human Resources good practice for the jurisdiction.

> **Note**
> This is not intended to replace the standard HR approach but ensures that TNA, continuous improvement, and all IMS issues are covered at appraisal time.

To ensure the ongoing and continuing development of all employees, the Forensic Laboratory undertakes periodic appraisals of all employees to:

- evaluate the competence of employees;
- determine if training is required;
- assess the need for any personal development;
- determine any other requirements for the ongoing development of employees.

Appraisals are performed for all Forensic Laboratory employees at least once a year, or more if deemed necessary, and are the responsibility of Line Managers at all levels in association with the Human Resources Department.

The Forensic Laboratory employee appraisal process is:

1. A Line Manager arranges an appraisal with a member of their team at the appropriate time with the Human Resources Department.
2. The Line Manager and the Human Resources employee conducting the appraisal review the employee's training records contained in their personnel file.
3. The Line Manager and the Human Resources employee conduct the appraisal with the employee. Activities may include:
   - assessment of the performance of the employee with regard to their work competences; evaluation of qualifications and skill sets;
   - review of project and case processing work completed;
   - identification of key competences and skills for future development;
   - identification of requirements for training or personal development;
   - review and evaluation of any training and personal development which has been undertaken since the last appraisal;
   - review and evaluation of any training undertaken to carry out system management and business process—at which point the relevant business process or Management System Owner should be present.

   For appraisals of Line Managers, appraisal activities may additionally cover:
   - review and evaluation of employee management skills;
   - review and evaluation of project management skills (task management, schedule management, risk management, etc.);
   - evaluation of team leadership qualities;
   - identification of requirements for management skills development and/or training.
4. The Line Manager and the Human Resources employee conducting the appraisal agree any further action which is required with the employee.

If training is required, this may be performed by internal or external resources and as formal or informal training as defined in Section 18.2.2.4. Management approval is required for all types of training and may be arranged by either an employee (with the authorization of their Line Manager) or a Line Manager on behalf of the employee via the Human Resources Department.

The relevant Management System Owner must approve specific management system training.

18.2.5 Competence

Competence is checking that the individual Forensic Laboratory employee is able to conduct a specific task.

While Forensic Laboratory employees have a planned schedule of training and awareness according to internal procedures and the results of the employee's appraisals and resulting TNA, this does not guarantee competence, so the Forensic Laboratory ensures that all employees are competent on a regular basis. Where competence is found to be not present, corrective action is taken as defined in Chapter 4, Section 4.8 and Section 18.2.2.3.

The Forensic Laboratory has a performance assessment process in place, as defined in Chapter 16; however, this is, aimed at the performance of the Forensic Laboratory as a whole, rather than individual employees.

Individual employees' competence is evaluated using the following techniques and these are used as input to the appraisal process defined in Section 18.2.4. If a serious concern is raised, a meeting with the employee, the Human Resources Manager, and relevant Line Managers is called when needed. The techniques include:

- *formal observation*—Line Managers and the Laboratory Manager will observe the progress made by the employee and make recommendations to improve performance, where appropriate;
- *case reviews*—at the end of a forensic case, the case and its processing is always reviewed and any lessons learned are used as part of the continuous improvement process, as defined in Chapter 4, Section 4.8;
- *Client feedback*—as given in Chapter 6, Appendix 20;
- *Client complaints*—as defined in Chapter 6, Section 6.14;
- *Testimony feedback*—as given in Chapter 11, Appendix 8;
- gaining of additional qualifications;
- other forms of observation.

Note

A number of forensic organizations have their own requirements for competency testing. Where appropriate, these would be used either in association with the Forensic Laboratory's procedures or in addition to them.

18.2.6 Proficiency

Proficiency is where a Forensic Laboratory employee has attained a series of competences that demonstrate proficiency in a specific discipline, as opposed to competence in a specific task.

Annual proficiency testing should be undertaken in the Forensic Laboratory and is used to confirm that Forensic Analysts are qualified to continue performing their role, irrespective of specific competencies, qualifications, or certifications (Figure 18.2).

Where proficiency is found to be not present, corrective action is taken as defined in Chapter 4, Section 4.8 and Section 18.2.2.3.

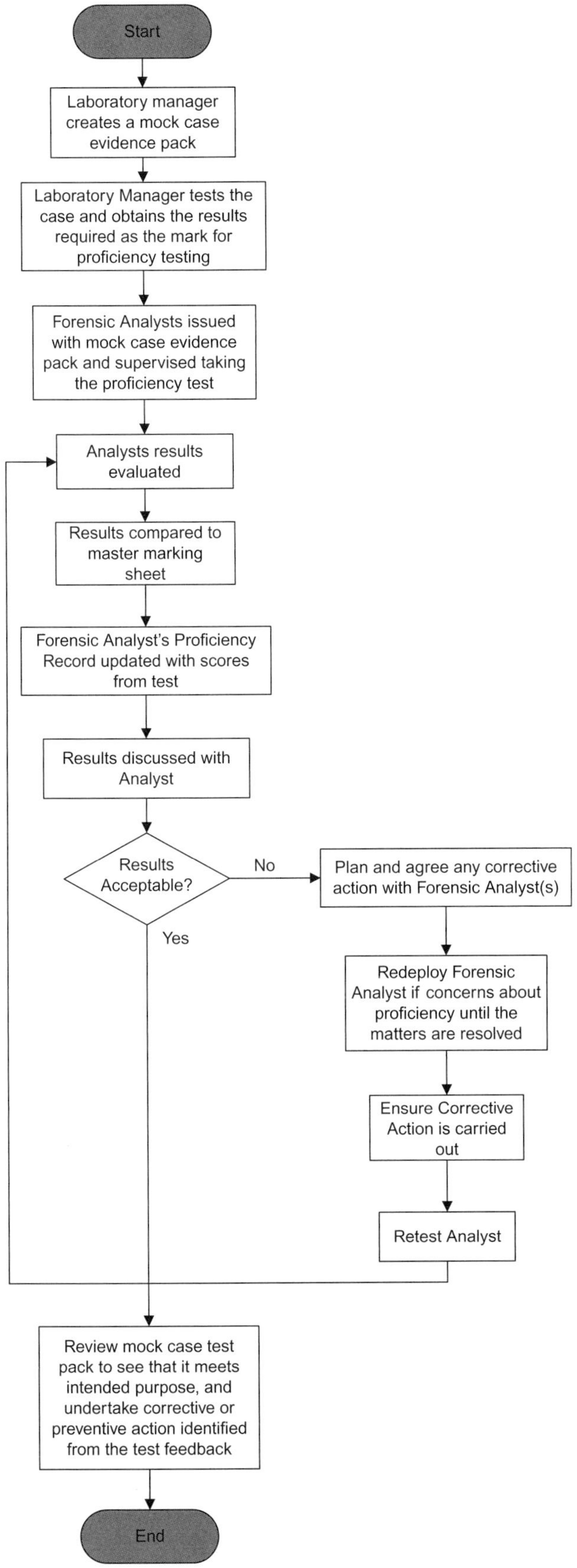

FIGURE 18.2 Proficiency. (For color version of this figure, the reader is referred to the online version of this chapter.)

Within the Forensic Laboratory, the following procedures are used to test an individual Forensic Analyst's proficiency:

1. The Laboratory Manager will create a mock case evidence pack, containing the evidence to be recovered, processed, and presented that are to be used to test the Forensic Analysts proficiency.
2. The Laboratory Manager will test the case and obtain the results required as the mark for the proficiency testing.
3. Relevant Forensic Analysts are issued the mock case evidence pack and are supervised undertaking the proficiency test.
4. Evaluating the results obtained by the Forensic Analysts undertaking the test.
5. Comparing the results obtained with the master marking sheet.
6. Update the Forensic Analyst's Proficiency Record with the scores from the test.
7. Discuss the results with the relevant Forensic Analysts.
8. Plan and agree any corrective action with the relevant Forensic Analyst(s), if appropriate.
9. Re-deploy the Forensic Analyst if there are concerns about proficiency until the matters are resolved.
10. Ensure that the corrective action is carried out, if appropriate.
11. Re-test the Forensic Analyst after corrective action, if appropriate.
12. Review the mock case test pack to see that it meets its intended purpose and undertake any corrective or preventive action identified from the test feedback.

Note

There are a number of different mock case scenario packs in use in the Forensic Laboratory, used to test different proficiencies.

18.2.7 Code of Ethics

The Code of Ethics for the Forensic Laboratory for processing all forensic cases given in Appendix 33.

This is in addition to any personal Codes of Ethics that Forensic Laboratory employees may have due to their professional organization memberships or personally held certifications.

The Forensic Laboratory Code of Ethics has been created so that there is no conflict of interest between the varying Codes of Ethics in place.

18.3 TERMINATION

When an employee changes employment or is terminated for any reason, it is essential that the appropriate process for ensuring a clean break is undertaken, to do this the following parties in the Forensic Laboratory must define responsibilities that must be carried out and documented, with records available for audit:

- all responsibilities in the termination process shall be explicitly defined;
- all termination procedures shall be documented and comply with current legislation.

> **Note**
>
> Special care must be taken if the termination concerns a possible disgruntled (or soon to be disgruntled) employee.

18.3.1 Permanent Employee Terminations

Where permanent employees are terminated, the following responsibilities exist.

18.3.1.1 Human Resources Department

The Human Resources Department procedure is:

1. To ensure that the employee is reminded of their obligations under their confidentiality agreement.
2. To ensure that all termination paperwork is finalized and correct and that Human Resources records are updated to reflect the termination and its associated procedures.
3. To obtain a list of all the Forensic Laboratory assets held by the employee from the Finance Department and/or the IT Department.
4. To ensure that all the Forensic Laboratory assets held by the employee are returned to the Forensic Laboratory.
5. Where the Forensic Laboratory assets (e.g., information) are held on the employees own personal equipment, procedures shall in place to ensure that this information is returned to the Forensic Laboratory and is securely erased from the employee's hardware.
6. Where the Forensic Laboratory assets (e.g., information) are held by the employee and not held by the Forensic Laboratory in a documented form, procedures shall be in place to ensure that this information is transferred to the Forensic Laboratory in an appropriate form (e.g., readable form or knowledge transfer).
7. To ensure that the IT Department is advised of the forthcoming termination and the date of it. It may be necessary to ensure that this information is kept confidential if the employee does not know of the termination.
8. To ensure that the employee termination checklist, as given in Appendix 34, is completed and countersigned by the terminated employee.

> **Note**
>
> It may be that the Information Security Manager is required to perform any security debriefing, including reminders about confidential information, where the risk assessment warrants it.

18.3.1.2 Finance Department

The Finance department has the responsibility:

- to provide a list of all assets held by the employee when asked by the Human Resources Department in a timely manner.
- to recover the assets from the Human Resources Department and update the current status of the assets recovered in the Asset Register.

18.3.1.3 IT Department

The IT department has the responsibility:

- to provide a list of all assets held by the employee when asked by the Human Resources Department in a timely manner;
- to recover the assets from the Human Resources Department and update the current status of the assets recovered in the IT Asset Database;
- to disable the employee's account(s), but not to delete them, as given in the Termination Checklist in Appendix 34;
- to change all passwords that the employee may have known if the accounts or services still exist after the employee has been terminated. A risk assessment of this may need to be undertaken. This should be done in association with the relevant Resource or Asset Owner and the Information Security Manager.

18.3.1.4 Employee's Line Manger

The Line Manager has the responsibility to assist the Human Resources and IT Departments where appropriate to facilitate the termination process.

The Line Manager is responsible for informing relevant Clients, contractors, or third-party users of changes in responsibilities and of employee changes and new operating arrangements.

18.3.1.5 Employee

The employee has the responsibility:

- to return all assets held when asked by the Human Resources Department on a timely basis;
- to return all documents and other the Forensic Laboratory assets whether they are recorded in the Asset Register or the IT Asset Database or not, in a timely manner;
- to comply with the terms and conditions of employment for the period after termination;
- to confirm compliance with the termination procedures and the requirements within them in writing so that a record can be made available for later auditing, as given in the Termination Checklist in Appendix 34.

18.3.2 Other Employee Terminations

This covers temporary or contract employees and employees of authorized third-party service providers who are terminated, and the following responsibilities exist.

The same process as that defined in Section 18.3.1 is followed, with the addition of the requirements below:

18.3.2.1 Agency or Outsourcing Partner

The agency or outsourcing partner has the responsibility:

1. To ensure that the temporary, contract, or third-party employee complies with all the Forensic Laboratory requirements.
2. To ensure that any Forensic Laboratory information or documentation is either returned, or disposed of, in accordance with contractual requirements.
3. To delete all information belonging to the Forensic Laboratory, or their Clients, from their information processing systems and warrant that this has taken place.

18.3.3 Change of Employee Responsibilities

Change of employment will use the same procedures as those defined in Section 3.1, where applicable. Changes of responsibility or employment should be managed as the termination of the respective responsibility or employment, and the new responsibility or employment should be controlled as if the employee was a new hire.

Note

It is essential that access rights are updated immediately on change of employment so that the employee does not continue to amass inappropriate access rights.

18.3.4 Removal of Access Rights

On termination or change of employment, all of the employee's access rights must be reviewed.

18.3.4.1 Termination

Where employees are terminated, all access rights that they had must be removed and all access rights that they had access to as part of their duties that are grouped or shared must be immediately changed. Where the termination is planned, consideration should be given to whether or not the employee should still have any access to the Forensic Laboratory information processing systems during the notice period. It may be that restricted access is considered but a risk assessment of the risks posed by the employee still having access presents to the Forensic Laboratory. The following should be considered in making this decision:

- who initiated the termination;
- the reason for the termination;
- the employee's role and current access rights;
- any relevant Human Resources or disciplinary issues that are currently in progress;
- the value of the assets the employee can access;
- the possible reputational risk to the Forensic Laboratory that the employee could inflict;
- the employee's technical competence;
- consideration of disgruntled employee's (or soon to be ex-employees) is a major risk factor that must be carefully considered. Emergency access right removal must be undertaken, if needed;
- in the Forensic Laboratory, employee activity is monitored, as theft of corporate information is a simple matter with the current media capacity available at the desktop.

18.3.4.2 Employment Change

Where an employee changes roles within the Forensic Laboratory, the Human Resources Department and the relevant Line Managers must ensure that all of the employee's access rights are changed when they change jobs or roles to reflect their new responsibilities.

It is essential that employees that move jobs or roles do not keep accumulating access rights. Access rights of this type include, but are not limited to:

- physical and logical access;
- keys;
- identification cards;
- information processing resource access;
- subscriptions;
- corporate memberships;
- corporate schemes;
- representation as a member of the Forensic Laboratory on any committee, etc.

18.3.5 Return of Assets

When an employee leaves the Forensic Laboratory, it is essential that they return all assets that they have been issued during their employment which are owned by the Forensic Laboratory. A checklist of items to be returned is given in the Termination Checklist in Appendix 34.

Where an employee has used their own computer equipment for the Forensic Laboratory purposes, this shall be recorded on the authorization for use. These employees will be required to bring any equipment used into the Forensic Laboratory offices so that the Information Security Manager can ascertain that there is no Forensic Laboratory information still remaining on it.

Where necessary, an appropriate secure wiping process shall be used for computers and mobile devices.

Consideration shall be given to the swapping of an employee's storage media on a "like-for-like" basis rather than performing a secure erasure. Assets of this type include, but are not limited to:

- hard disks;
- floppy disks;
- other disk drives;
- CDs;
- DVDs;
- backup tape;
- USB/Firewire type storage devices.

Note

These media may not be recorded on the asset register.

Where an employee has essential or critical knowledge for a project or the Forensic Laboratory generally, a process of knowledge transfer to at least one other employee must be undertaken unless this has already been documented and a formal handover taken place.

Should any assets not be handed back at this point, their contract of employment, the associated Forensic Laboratory Handbook of Employment, and the issuing paperwork for the asset all require that the asset shall be returned on demand and specifically at termination of employment with the Forensic Laboratory. If this is the case, appropriate action shall be taken against the employee in consultation with the Forensic Laboratory's legal advisors.

APPENDIX 1 - TRAINING FEEDBACK FORM

The form below can be used to collect feedback from all Forensic Laboratory employees for all internal and external training undertaken. It provides qualitative as well as quantitative feedback.

- name;
- course title;
- training provider;
- date of the course;
- instructor name (mandatory if internal training);
- training feedback:
  - the objectives of the training were clearly defined;
  - participation and interaction were encouraged;
  - the topics covered were relevant to me;
  - I can use the product(s) more effectively than I could before I attended the training;
  - the content was organized and easy to follow;
  - the materials distributed were helpful;
  - this training experience will be useful in my work;
  - the trainer was knowledgeable about the training topics;
  - the trainer was well prepared;
  - the instructor answered questions effectively;
  - my training objectives were met;
  - the time allotted for the training was sufficient;
  - if trained via the internet, the interface technology was easy to use and an effective way for me to receive training;
  - the accommodation and facilities were adequate and comfortable.
- each of the points above is graded or scored as follows:
  - 0—Not applicable;
  - 1—Strongly Disagree;
  - 2—Disagree;
  - 3—Neutral;
  - 4—Agree;
  - 5—Strongly Agree.
- additionally:
  - what did you like most about this training?
  - what did you like least about this training?
  - what aspects of the training could be improved?
  - how do you hope to change your working practices in the Forensic Laboratory practice as a result of this training?
  - would you recommend this training to other Forensic Laboratory employees and if not explain why?
- any other comments;
- date;
- signature.

APPENDIX 2 - EMPLOYEE SECURITY SCREENING POLICY CHECKLIST

The following should be considered for including in an employee security screening policy:

- acknowledgement by the applicant that misrepresentation, or failure to disclose material facts, either during application or throughout employment may constitute grounds for immediate dismissal and/or legal action;
- define criteria for failing/rejecting an applicant;
- embed the employee security screening process into the recruitment process;
- ensure that the applicant gives consent for the employee security screening process to meet legal requirements in the jurisdiction for the whole process, including further checks;
- ensure the whole recruitment process, including the employee security screening process and supporting forms, are legally compliant for the jurisdiction;
- ensure those performing employee security screening have appropriate resources, including training and budget;
- have a process for dealing with fakes or forged supporting documentation;
- identify the Security Controller;

- inform applicants that confirmed employment is conditional on satisfactory completion of the employee security screening process, even if provisional employment is offered;
- involve all relevant stakeholders in the employee security screening process and ensure that they all communicate effectively for the employee security screening process;
- maintain a list of employee security screening service providers for specialist tasks;
- undertake employee security screening for all employees.

Maintain a screening file as part of the Human Resources file for the applicant or employee.

APPENDIX 3 - EMPLOYMENT APPLICATION FORM

The following are included in the Forensic Laboratory employment application form:

- post applied for;
- surname;
- other surnames if the applicant has changed their surname for any reason (e.g., marriage or other legitimate reasons for changing their surname;
- alias—if appropriate (e.g., stage name);
- forenames;
- address(es) for last *n*[3] years;
- contact details;
- date of birth;
- place of birth;
- nationality;
- whether a work permit is required or not;
- current employer and current role information;
- cast employment for last *n*[4] years;
- education history and qualifications;
- professional qualifications and certifications;
- training courses undertaken with results;
- reasons for applying for the post;
- other information that may relevant (e.g., details of disabilities, driving license holder);
- personal and employer reference details;
- a declaration of completeness and truth that is signed and dated.

The form contains a clear statement that employee security screening will take place. Applicants must provide their consent to undergo employment security screening. This may be via the Forensic Laboratory or a third-party screening service provider, as appropriate.

Applicants should also affirm whether their current employer can be contacted for a reference. If not agreed at the point of a conditional job offer for temporary employment, then an agreement that permanent employment is conditional (or not) on a satisfactory reference from the immediate past employer.

In addition to this form, there will be additional forms to cover:

- criminal history;
- consent for employee security screening;
- other requirements, as appropriate for the post applied for.

There may be additional information required for specific roles, which will be defined by the role.

APPENDIX 4 - EMPLOYMENT APPLICATION FORM NOTES

THE APPLICATION FORM

The application form plays an important part in the selection process, decisions to shortlist candidates for interview are based solely upon the information you supply on your form and the form provides a basis for the interview itself.

Curriculum Vitaes (CVs) or resumes alone will not be accepted. However, CVs will be accepted *in addition* to a fully completed application form.

You may complete the form on a word-processor but please use the appropriate headings and format.

SECTION 1: PERSONAL DETAILS

Please give your surname and initials. You are not, however, required to provide your preferred title and/or your forenames. If you have a title or other name you would like to be called (should you be called for an interview), you may at your discretion enter those details.

SECTION 2: EDUCATION AND PROFESSIONAL QUALIFICATIONS

List membership of professional institutes, in-house courses, and professional qualifications if applicable. Essential qualifications will be checked on appointment to a post.

SECTION 3: PRESENT POST

Please provide brief information in respect of responsibilities including reporting and management duties. This section should not be left blank unless the position you are applying for is your first job;

3. The period of addresses to be disclosed will vary between posts.
4. The period of past employment to be disclosed will vary between posts.

Should you be selected for the role "your reason for leaving or wishing to leave" may be verified if we take references per Section 7.

SECTION 4: PREVIOUS EMPLOYMENT

Do not simply list the duties of your jobs. Please give a brief explanation of the main duties of your previous jobs;

While you are not required to provide dates in relation to previous jobs, it is important you confirm whether or not you have had material gaps in your employment. If you have, it would be helpful if you could provide relevant details.

SECTION 5: RELEVANT SKILLS, ABILITIES, KNOWLEDGE, AND EXPERIENCE

This section is vital;

Think about what evidence you can provide to demonstrate you have the necessary skills, ability, knowledge, experience, and competence required;

You may have acquired these in a variety of ways, e.g., through work, running a home, voluntary work, hobbies, etc.;

Address each of the criteria separately and briefly outline how you meet each one, providing specific examples.

SECTION 6: OTHER INFORMATION

A simple list will suffice unless positions held and the skills/experience attained are directly relevant to the position for which you are applying.

SECTION 7: REFERENCES

Should you be selected for the role we will want to take up referees as outlined below. However, if possible we would like to do this earlier in the process;

Employment references—please provide referee details to cover recent relevant employment;

Academic references—if you are a school leaver or graduate entrant and do not have any previous employment history, please supply the details of a school/college tutor;

Personal references—if you have no previous employment, please give details of someone who can provide a character reference;

We reserve the right to take up references from any previous employer.

SECTION 8: DECLARATION

This section must be signed by the applicant. It is a declaration of the validity of the information in the application and confirms that misleading information would be sufficient grounds for terminating of employment.

APPENDIX 5 - SOME DOCUMENTS THAT CAN VERIFY IDENTITY

The following document types may be considered for verifying an identity:

- adoption certificate;
- Armed Forces identity card;
- current photo card driving license;
- current signed full passport;
- full birth certificate;
- marriage/civil partnership certificate;
- National Identity Card;
- other valid documentation relating to immigration status or permits to work;
- Police registration document.

Note

It must be understood that a government cannot give an individual an identity that is only something the individual can do. Of the examples above, the only one that really proves identity is a birth certificate, but it is difficult to link a paper birth certificate to an individual applicant. A passport is only a travel document, a driving license is only a permit to drive, etc.

Multiple copies of the above all verifying the claimed identity do strengthen the verification process.

APPENDIX 6 - DOCUMENT AUTHENTICITY CHECKLIST

Some items to be checked on officially issued documents include, but are not limited to:

- font used;
- Holograms;
- lamination of photographs;
- number of pages, if applicable (e.g., a passport);
- numbering sequence;
- paper type;
- perforations, if applicable;
- size;
- stamps applied;
- UV reaction;
- validity;
- Watermarks.

APPENDIX 7 - VERIFYING ADDRESSES

The following document types may be considered for verifying an address:

- a utility bill;
- a bank statement;
- a rental or tenancy agreement;
- a letter from a recognized government department;
- a mortgage statement from a recognized lender.

Where such documentation is provided, it should relate to the period claimed.

APPENDIX 8 - RIGHT TO WORK CHECKLIST

Note

This requirement is applicable to employees, as well, to ensure that they have a continued right to work in the Forensic Laboratory. This is only applicable to certain classes of employee.

The following are used in the Forensic Laboratory for making a declaration relating to nationality and immigration status declaration for the right to work in the jurisdiction:

- advice that if the applicant is employed, corroboration of answers given on the form will be sought to confirm answers given;
- Surname/Family Name;
- full Forenames;
- any aliases/other names used;
- sex (Male/Female);
- full current address;
- date of birth;
- nationality at birth;
- nationality now (if different);
- Whether the applicant has held any other nationality. If so, give details;
- whether the applicant is subject to immigration control.[5] If so, give details;
- whether the applicant is lawfully resident in the country;
- whether there are any restrictions on the applicant's continued residence in the country. If so, give details;
- whether there are any restrictions on the applicant's ability to take up the type of work the Forensic Laboratory is offering the applicant. If so, give details;
- a declaration that the information on the form is true, accurate, and complete to the best of the applicant's knowledge and that if they have made a false declaration it may prejudice their hiring or continued employment;
- a declaration that should the information contained on the form at the start of employment change during the applicant's employment by the Forensic Laboratory that the applicant will advise either the Human Resources function or the Screening Controller;
- signature;
- date;
- a declaration that the Forensic Laboratory will hold this information in the strictest confidence and that all relevant privacy legislation covering the information and documents supplied will be met;
- the declaration should ensure that the applicant is giving explicit (and not implicit) consent for holding and processing this data in line with the employee security screening process.

5. Immigration Control is where the applicant requires permission (or "leave") to enter or remain in a country but do not have it or where the applicant has leave to enter or remain but is subject to a formal undertaking. A formal undertaking is typically where the applicant's sponsor makes a formal legal undertaking that they will support the applicant during their period of residence in the country.

APPENDIX 9 - REFERENCE AUTHORIZATION

Note

The wording used for the reference authorization must be checked to ensure that it is appropriate for the jurisdiction and meets the requirements of the relevant legislation.

PLEASE READ THIS CAREFULLY BEFORE SIGNING THE DECLARATION

Note

This requirement is applicable to employees, as well, to ensure that they have a continued right to work in the Forensic Laboratory. This is only applicable to certain classes of employee.

I understand that employment with the Forensic Laboratory is subject to satisfactory references and employee security screening in accordance with good practice within the jurisdiction.

I undertake to cooperate with the Forensic Laboratory in providing any additional information required to meet these criteria.

I authorize the Forensic Laboratory and/or its nominated agent to approach previous employers, schools/colleges, character referees, or Government Agencies to verity that the information I have provided is correct.

I authorize the Forensic Laboratory to make a consumer information search with a credit reference agency, which will keep a record of that search and may share that information with other credit reference agencies.

I understand that some of the information I have provided in this application will be held on a computer and some or all will be held in manual records.

I consent to the Forensic Laboratory's reasonable processing of any sensitive personal information obtained for the purposes of establishing my medical condition and future fitness to perform my duties. I accept that I may be required to undergo a medical examination where requested by the Forensic Laboratory.

Subject to the legislation relating to medical records in the jurisdiction, I consent to the results of such examinations to be given to the Forensic Laboratory.

I understand and agree that if so required I will make a Statutory Declaration in accordance with the provisions of the relevant legislation relating to Statutory Declarations (or equivalent), in confirmation of previous employment or unemployment. A copy of the Statutory Declaration used by the Forensic Laboratory is given in Appendix 10.

I hereby certify that, to the best of my knowledge, the details I have given in this application form are complete and correct.

I understand that any false statement or omission to the Forensic Laboratory and/or its representatives may render me liable to dismissal without notice.

Signature

Printed Name

Witness signature

Witness printed name (this is usually a Forensic Laboratory employee)

Date.

APPENDIX 10 - STATUTORY DECLARATION

Note

The use of Statutory Declarations is not universal, and the form of the Declaration may well vary between jurisdictions, so Legal Advice must be taken to ensure that the declaration, if used, is appropriate to the relevant legislation.

I [full name] of [address]

DO SOLEMNLY AND SINCERELY DECLARE as follows:

[See below for matter to declare]

and I make this solemn declaration conscientiously believing the same to be true and by virtue of the provisions of the [state the relevant legislation]

SIGNED [ ]

DECLARED at [ ]

in the County of [ ]

on this [ ] day, the [ ] of [ ] 20[ ]

Before me [ ]

Lawyer/Solicitor/Commissioner for Oaths/Judge.

MATTER TO DECLARE (EXAMPLES):

- that I was self-employed as a [job title] for the period(s) from [date] to [date];
- that I was registered as unemployed for the period(s) from [date] to [date];
- that I was employed as a [job title] for the period(s) from [date] to [date] by [name of employer] of [address];
- that I was not employed from [date] to [date] because [state reason];
- that I was known as [state previous name] for the period from [date] to [date].

APPENDIX 11 - EMPLOYER REFERENCE FORM

The form used for employer references in the Forensic Laboratory is given below:

EMPLOYEE OR APPLICANT

- full name of the subject of the reference.

PREVIOUS EMPLOYER

- name;
- location;
- contact;
- phone;
- e-mail.

EMPLOYMENT DETAILS

- dates of employment—confirmed by employer;
- what was their title?
- what did their duties involve?

MISCELLANEOUS

- are you related to the subject?—if so, please state your relationship;
- do you consider the subject to be strictly honest, conscientious, reliable, and discreet?
- are you aware of any factor(s) concerning the subject that may affect their fitness to be employed by the Forensic Laboratory?—if so please explain;
- would you be content to employ the individual again?

DECLARATION

- a declaration that the information on the form is true, accurate, and complete to the best of the Reference Giver's knowledge and belief;
- name;
- signature;
- position in the organization;
- date;

- phone number;
- e-mail address;
- company detail and company stamp (if applicable);
- a declaration that the Forensic Laboratory will hold this information in the strictest confidence and that all relevant privacy legislation covering the information and documents supplied will be met.

APPENDIX 12 - EMPLOYER'S ORAL REFERENCE FORM

The following information is transcribed onto an Oral Reference Form by the Reference Taker with input from the Reference Giver:

The form used for employer references in the Forensic Laboratory is given below:

EMPLOYEE OR APPLICANT

- Full name of the subject of the reference.

PREVIOUS EMPLOYER

- name;
- location;
- contact;
- phone;
- e-mail.

EMPLOYMENT DETAILS

- dates of employment—claimed by employee or applicant;
- dates of employment—confirmed by employer;
- what was their title?
- what did their duties involve?

MISCELLANEOUS

- are you related to the subject?—if so, please state your relationship;
- do you consider the subject to be strictly honest, conscientious, reliable, and discreet?
- are you aware of any factor(s) concerning the subject that may affect their fitness to be employed by the Forensic Laboratory?—if so, please explain;
- would you be content to employ the individual again?

DECLARATION

- name of Reference Taker;
- signature;
- position in the Forensic Laboratory (or third-party specialized employee security screening organization);
- date;
- phone number;
- e-mail address;
- Security Controller's name;
- countersigned by the Security Controller;
- a declaration that the Forensic Laboratory will hold this information in the strictest confidence and that all relevant privacy legislation covering the information and documents supplied will be met.

> **Note**
>
> If response indicates that applicant is NOT suitable for proposed employment, bring to the immediate attention of Screening Controller.

APPENDIX 13 - CONFIRMATION OF AN ORAL REFERENCE LETTER

> **Note**
>
> This letter is sent on headed Forensic Laboratory stationery (paper or e-mailed as a secured PDF) to the Reference Giver to confirm his/her information. It is signed by the Screening Controller.

[Name]

[Address]

[Date]

We refer to our conversation with you on [date] about [title and name] in connection with the application made to us by the above-named for employment as [specify].

Details of the information which you supplied to us orally are enclosed, and we would be obliged if you would kindly confirm these details fairly reflect the information you supplied.

Due to the nature of our business, it is vitally important that we employ only individuals of integrity who are likely to be able to resist the opportunities for improper personal gain or other information security breaches which such employment might offer and who are responsible and conscientious.

Our internal procedures based on our ISO 9001 and ISO 27001 certifications require us to obtain written confirmation of all references we receive in connection with applicants for employment.

A copy of a Form of Authority signed by the applicant is enclosed and also a stamped, addressed envelope for the favor of your reply.

Yours Faithfully

[Name]

[Title]

[Specify Enclosures]

APPENDIX 14 - QUALIFICATION VERIFICATION CHECKLIST

The following are considered for checking paper certificates of educational and professional qualifications:

- matching names on all documents or explanation for change (marriage, etc.);
- matching dates from documents to application forms;
- logo is correct;
- no evidence of tampering;
- quality of the paper;
- Watermarks (if present);
- embossing (if present).

Each establishment that has issued the certificate presented should be contacted to ascertain the validity of the document produced, if possible and practical.

APPENDIX 15 - CRIMINAL RECORD DECLARATION CHECKLIST

Note

Depending on the jurisdiction, the terminology may need to be changed to reflect the requirements of the legislation within the jurisdiction.

The following is used in the Forensic Laboratory for making a declaration relating to a criminal record declaration:

- advice that if the applicant is employed, corroboration of answers given on the form will be sought to confirm answers given;
- Surname/Family Name;
- full Forenames;
- full current address;
- date of birth;
- a declaration whether the applicant has ever been convicted or found guilty by a Court of Competent Jurisdiction of any offence in any country (excluding parking but including all motoring offences even where a spot fine has been administered by the Police) or absolutely/conditionally discharged or whether there is there any current action pending;
- a declaration whether the applicant has ever been convicted by a Court Martial, sentenced to detention, or dismissed from service in any county's armed services;
- a declaration whether the applicant is aware of any other matters in their background that may affect their suitability or reliability for the post for which they are applying;
- a note to say that "Spent" convictions, according to the legislation in the jurisdiction, need not be declared;
- for each of the three questions above, a "Yes"/"No" reply box is used for this, and if the answer is "Yes," the applicant is required to give further details;
- a declaration that the information on the form is true, accurate, and complete to the best of the applicant's knowledge and that if they have made a false declaration it may prejudice their hiring or continued employment;
- signature;
- date;
- a declaration that the Forensic Laboratory will hold this information in the strictest confidence and that all relevant privacy legislation covering the information and documents supplied will be met;
- the declaration should ensure that the applicant is giving explicit (and not implicit) consent for holding and processing these data in line with the employee security screening process.

APPENDIX 16 - PERSONAL REFERENCE FORM

The form used for personal references in the Forensic Laboratory is given below.

EMPLOYEE OR APPLICANT

- full name of the subject of the reference.

THE REFERENCE GIVER

- name;
- location;
- contact;
- phone;
- e-mail.

RELATIONSHIP DETAILS

- over what period have you known [name]?
- how would you define your relationship with [name]?
- are you related to [name]?—if so, please state your relationship.

MISCELLANEOUS

- do you consider the subject to be strictly honest, conscientious, reliable, and discreet?
- are you aware of any factor(s) concerning the subject that may affect their fitness to be employed by the Forensic Laboratory?—if so, please explain.

DECLARATION

- a declaration that the information on the form is true, accurate, and complete to the best of the Reference Giver's knowledge and belief;
- name;
- signature;
- date;
- phone number;
- e-mail address;
- a declaration that the Forensic Laboratory will hold this information in the strictest confidence and that all

relevant privacy legislation covering the information and documents supplied will be met.

APPENDIX 17 - PERSONAL ORAL REFERENCE FORM

The following information is transcribed onto an Oral Reference Form by the Reference Taker with input from the Reference Giver:

The form used for personal references in the Forensic Laboratory is given below.

EMPLOYEE OR APPLICANT

- full name of the subject of the reference.

THE REFERENCE GIVER

- name;
- location;
- contact;
- phone;
- e-mail.

RELATIONSHIP DETAILS

- over what period have you known [name]?
- how would you define your relationship with [name]?
- are you related to [name]?—if so, please state your relationship.

MISCELLANEOUS

- do you consider the subject to be strictly honest, conscientious, reliable, and discreet?
- are you aware of any factor(s) concerning the subject that may affect their fitness to be employed by the Forensic Laboratory?—if so, please explain.

DECLARATION

- name of Reference Taker;
- signature;
- position in the Forensic Laboratory (or third-party specialized employee security screening organization);
- date;
- phone number;
- e-mail address;
- Security Controller's name;
- countersigned by the Security Controller;
- a declaration that the Forensic Laboratory will hold this information in the strictest confidence and that all relevant privacy legislation covering the information and documents supplied will be met.

Note

If response indicates that applicant is NOT suitable for proposed employment, bring to immediate attention of Screening Controller.

APPENDIX 18 - OTHER REFERENCE FORM

Note

This form is used where it is inappropriate to use either the Employer Reference Form or the Personal Reference Form. Situations where this is relevant can include, but are not limited to.

- living abroad;
- periods of unemployment;
- a trade; reference;
- education conformation;
- Military service conformation;
- where an employer no longer exists and a past employee provides a reference.

The form used for other references in the Forensic Laboratory is given below.

EMPLOYEE OR APPLICANT

- full name of the subject of the reference.

THE REFERENCE GIVER

- name;
- location;
- contact;
- phone;
- e-mail.

DETAILS REQUIRED

- [Define exactly what is required];
- over what period have you known [name]?
- how would you define your relationship with [name]?
- are you related to [name]?—if so, please state your relationship.

MISCELLANEOUS

- do you consider the subject to be strictly honest, conscientious, reliable, and discreet?

- are you aware of any factor(s) concerning the subject that may affect their fitness to be employed by the Forensic Laboratory?—if so, please explain.

DECLARATION

- a declaration that the information on the form is true, accurate, and complete to the best of the Reference Giver's knowledge and belief;
- name;
- signature;
- date;
- phone number;
- e-mail address;
- a declaration that the Forensic Laboratory will hold this information in the strictest confidence and that all relevant privacy legislation covering the information and documents supplied will be met.

APPENDIX 19 - OTHER REFERENCE FORM

> **Note**
> This is the oral version of the Other Reference Form and is used for the reasons given in Appendix 18.

The following information is transcribed onto an other Reference Form by the Reference Taker with input from the Reference Giver:

The form used for other references in the Forensic Laboratory is given below.

EMPLOYEE OR APPLICANT

Full name of the subject of the reference.

THE REFERENCE GIVER

- name;
- location;
- contact;
- phone;
- e-mail.

DETAILS

- [Define exactly what is required];
- over what period have you known [name]?
- how would you define your relationship with [name]?
- are you related to [name]?—if so, please state your relationship.

MISCELLANEOUS

- do you consider the subject to be strictly honest, conscientious, reliable, and discreet?
- are you aware of any factor(s) concerning the subject that may affect their fitness to be employed by the Forensic Laboratory?—if so, please explain.

DECLARATION

- name of Reference Taker;
- signature;
- position in the Forensic Laboratory (or third-party specialized employee security screening organization);
- date;
- phone number;
- e-mail address;
- Security Controller's name;
- countersigned by the Security Controller;
- a declaration that the Forensic Laboratory will hold this information in the strictest confidence and that all relevant privacy legislation covering the information and documents supplied will be met.

> **Note**
> If response indicates that applicant is NOT suitable for proposed employment, bring to immediate attention of Screening Controller.

APPENDIX 20 - EMPLOYEE SECURITY SCREENING FILE

Any job applicant in the Forensic Laboratory will have their own employee security screening file. In some cases, this will be updated during employment (e.g., an internal move to a post with a higher security clearance requirement). The contents of the employee security screening file are given below.

APPLICANT DETAILS

- Surname;
- Forenames;
- Address;
- phone;
- date of birth;
- place of birth;
- nationality;
- former or dual nationality: (with dates if applicable);
- employee ID Number (if applicable);
- Tax ID or other government ID (if applicable);
- date employment commenced;

- date employment terminated;
- screening period.

INFORMATION GIVEN BY THE APPLICANT

- dates (from and to);
- employer;
- other information;
- code (see below);
- request sent;
- confirmation of facts;
- audited by.

CODES IN USE

- AR—Accountant's Reference;
- CL—Chaser Letter;
- CR—Character Reference;
- DR—Documentation Request;
- ER—Education Reference;
- FI—Further Information Request;
- GR—Government Department Request;
- LR—Lawyer's Reference;
- OR—Other Request (Define);
- SDR—Statutory Declaration Request;
- TR—Trade Reference;
- WR—Work (Employer) Reference.

DOCUMENTS SEEN

Note

These are just tick boxes with comments if appropriate, and a copy is retained on the applicant's file. Ideally, original documents are presented but if a copy, comments must be made on it.

- the following are inspected:
  - work registration card;
  - Birth certificate;
  - current passport;
  - Military or Service Discharge Certificate;
  - photo Driving License;
  - Marriage Certificate;
  - proof of address;
  - work permit;
  - Visa;
  - educational qualifications.
- there is a note to check whether the documents seen are originals or copies or not available. Where copies are provided or they are not available, comment must be made on this.
- the documents seen are also subject to audit.

PROCESSES UNDERTAKEN

Note 1

A number of processes are undertaken, and these are tracked through to completion:

- Financial checks;
- Reference requests;
- Follow ups after oral references;
- Other processes as required.

Note 2

The dates of requests and receipt are recorded for each processes with notes as appropriate. The processes are subject to audit.

CERTIFICATION OF IDENTITY

For each document listed, its date of issue should also be recorded, if there is one present.

- document 1;
- document 2;
- document 3;
- document 4;
- document 5.

REFERENCES

At least one work reference is required and at least on personal one.

For each Referee, the following should be listed:

- Surname;
- Forenames;
- address;
- phone;
- relationship;
- length of association.

AUTHORIZATION

Note

This section of the file records the authorization employment (or not) and contains:

- authorization of acceptance of employment risk by Top Management, as given in Appendix 21;
- authorizer name, signature, and date;
- authorization date for provisional employment;
- authorizer name, signature, and date;
- authorization date for conformed employment;
- authorization for employment declined;
- decliner name, signature, and date.

CERTIFICATION

The file shall contain a statement from the Screening Controller or the employee that carried out the verification checks, for each time something new is added to the file, to state that they have verified the documents presented and updated the file.

- name;
- appointment/post;
- signature;
- date.

Each file should contain the documents that have been referred to in the summary sheet above.

APPENDIX 21 - TOP MANAGEMENT ACCEPTANCE OF EMPLOYMENT RISK

Note 1

Risks identified during the employee security screening process may be signed off by Top Management, as acceptable, if the applicant is to be employed in the new post where the employee security screening process has not been completed, but the risks are deemed acceptable.

- Surname;
- Forenames;
- date commenced provisional employment;
- items requiring acceptance of risk (define);
- Screening Controller Name;
- signature;
- date;
- Top Management Declaration.

The above named applicant's employee security screening file has been reviewed, and I have accepted this applicant as being appropriate for offering provisional employment and accept the risk of incomplete employee security screening.

- name;
- signature;
- position;
- date.

Note 2

The Top Management providing sign-off must be independent of operations and the screening process.

Note 3

If the risks are not accepted, then the form is not signed by Top Management as they do not accept the risks.

APPENDIX 22 - THIRD-PARTY EMPLOYEE SECURITY SCREENING PROVIDER CHECKLIST

The following issues should be considered when selecting a third-party screening service provider:

- are their screening processes totally transparent?
- are they as good as they claim?—obtain references from existing Clients;
- are they subject to any current litigation?
- can they meet all of the needs of the Forensic Laboratory?
- does their contract with the Forensic Laboratory give the right to audit the employee security screening process?
- how do their costs and service levels compare with other employee security screening service providers?
- how do they deal with incomplete or conflicting information?
- how many complaints have they had in the last year?
- how will personal data, and specifically the Forensic Laboratory's employee's personal data, be secured against unauthorized access, modification, disclosure, or erasure?
- is their work repeatable by a competent alternative?
- what access to overseas information do they have?
- what information can they access?
- what is their continuous improvement process?
- what is typical TRTs for a full screening report in jurisdictions of interest to the Forensic Laboratory?
- what level of reporting do they provide?
- what level of employee security screening do the screening service provider's employees undergo?
- what quality processes do they have in place?
- what certifications do they hold relevant to their products and services?
- what services do they provide?
- will they make employment recommendations based on the results of the screening process or leave it to the Forensic Laboratory to make the final decision based on their findings?

APPENDIX 23 - RECRUITMENT AGENCY CONTRACT CHECKLIST

The following items should be considered for inclusion in any contract with a recruitment consultancy for all types of employee to be engaged by the Forensic Laboratory:

- details of the employee security screening requirements for different posts;
- a statement that the Forensic Laboratory retains the right to audit the recruitment agency's employee security screening process and details of applicants at any time;

- a statement that the recruitment agency must inform the Forensic Laboratory if any applicant supplied by the recruitment agency is undergoing any disciplinary procedures, has been arrested or similar;
- a statement that the recruitment agency will be liable for financial penalties if they have not performed the level of employee security screening required according to contractual requirements;
- a statement to the effect that the recruitment agency will not be paid for any applicant that has not undergone security screening according to contractual requirements.

Note

There may be issues that arise if the applicant does not tell the truth or omits prejudicial information on their application forms, and this is not picked up by the recruitment agency.

APPENDIX 24 - INVESTIGATION MANAGER, JOB DESCRIPTION

OBJECTIVE AND ROLE

The Investigation Manager is responsible for all aspects of investigations carried out in the Forensic Laboratory. This covers the long- and medium-term planning as well as the day-to-day conduct of investigations.

The main objectives are to ensure that investigations are conducted in a manner that is compliant with relevant legislation, regulations, and standards within the jurisdiction and that products and services offered to Clients are available, when required, at an acceptable cost and of superior quality.

PROBLEMS AND CHALLENGES

The efficient conduct of an investigation is only achieved by ensuring that all aspects of the investigation are planned and managed well. The Investigation Manager faces the challenge of ensuring the development, maintenance, and implementation of all relevant policies and procedures.

The Investigation Manager must ensure that the required resources are available and working efficiently and that all tasks are carried out to meet the quality standards defined by the Forensic Laboratory. The Investigation Manager needs to liaise with the Laboratory Manager to manage resources.

PRINCIPAL ACCOUNTABILITIES

The Investigation Manager:

- has an in depth understanding of data collection and preservation principles;
- has an in depth understanding of investigative procedures;
- has an in depth understanding of investigative legislation, regulation, standards, and good practice within the jurisdiction;
- has a good understanding of the Client's needs in digital forensic investigation management;
- conducts and leads digital forensic investigation tasks from beginning to end, including task acceptance, the processing of digital media through to report production, and billing;
- leads the Request for Proposal (RFP) process or quotation process for Client engagements, including the production of budget estimates, in association with the Laboratory Manager and the relevant Account Manager;
- maintains regular contact, through the relevant Account Manager with Clients to help ensure Client satisfaction and that their expectations are properly managed. This will include progress reports, both internally and externally, where required;
- conducts Client and internal team meetings to document Client requirements, with the relevant Account Manager, while making recommendations and determining the best solutions;
- ensures that the Forensic Laboratory Quality procedures are followed for all investigations carried out;
- ensures work quality is of a consistently high standard;
- manages a range of priorities and tasks on a daily basis;
- manages employee development by conducting annual employee appraisals and TNA in association with the Human Resources Department;
- briefs the Laboratory Manager on the progress of investigations;
- maintains investigation training and awareness throughout the Forensic Laboratory and third parties acting on their behalf, on the importance, and impact of maintaining stringent controls;
- manages the case Post Implementation Review (PIR) process;
- participates in international, national, and local SIG presentations, and publishes articles describing the Forensic Laboratory's investigation management system how it relates to the business;
- develops and manages effective working relationships with all appropriate internal and external stakeholders;
- maintains external links to other companies in the industry to gain competitive assessments and share information, where appropriate;
- identifies the emerging information technologies to be assimilated, integrated, and introduced within the Forensic Laboratory, which could significantly impact the Forensic Laboratory's investigation management processes;

- interfaces with external industrial and academic organizations in order to maintain state-of-the-art knowledge in emerging investigation management issues and to enhance the Forensic Laboratory's image as a first-class solution provider utilizing the latest thinking in this field;
- adheres to establish the Forensic Laboratory policies, standards, and procedures;
- performs all responsibilities in accordance with, or in excess of, the requirements of the Forensic Laboratory IMS.

AUTHORITY

The Investigation Manger has the authority to:

- plan and implement investigations;
- supervising the conduct of digital forensic investigations.

CONTACTS

Internal

This position requires contact with all levels of Forensic Laboratory employees, and specifically the Laboratory Manager, for the day-to-day conduct of investigations, to ensure the maintenance and implementation of procedures.

External

Externally, the Investigation Manager will maintain contacts with Suppliers and Vendors, as required. Additionally, contact will be maintained with the Forensic Laboratory's Clients to determine their requirements in association with the relevant Account Manager.

REPORTS TO

The Investigation Manager reports to:

- Top Management.

APPENDIX 25 - FORENSIC LABORATORY SYSTEM ADMINISTRATOR, JOB DESCRIPTION

> **Note**
>
> The System Administrator for the Forensic Laboratory is a different role to the System Administrator for the remainder of the Forensic Laboratory's IT systems, who reports to the IT Manager.

OBJECTIVE AND ROLE

The System Administrator is responsible for the effective provisioning, installation/configuration, operation, and maintenance of system hardware and software and related infrastructure within the Forensic Laboratory's laboratory.

The System Administrator will also undertake technical research and development to enable continuing innovation within the Forensic Laboratory's laboratory infrastructure. This individual ensures that system hardware, operating systems, and software systems adhere to the relevant Forensic Laboratory procedures.

PROBLEMS AND CHALLENGES

Efficiency in the Forensics Laboratory is only achieved by ensuring that all aspects of the information systems that are used within the laboratory operate efficiently and are managed in a professional manner, following the laid down procedures and to an acceptable quality standard. The System Administrator must ensure that all IT work in the laboratory adheres to all of the relevant policies and procedures in the IMS.

PRINCIPAL ACCOUNTABILITIES

The System Administrator/Operator:

- installs new and or rebuilds existing systems and configures hardware, peripherals, services, settings, directories, and storage in accordance with Forensic Laboratory standards and procedures;
- develops and maintains installation and configuration procedures and records;
- contributes to, and maintains, system standards;
- researches and recommends innovative and, where possible, automated approaches for system administration tasks;
- performs regular system monitoring to verify the integrity and availability of all hardware, systems, and key processes, monitor system and application logs, and control regular scheduled tasks such as backups;
- performs regular security monitoring to identify possible misuse of the Forensic Laboratory's information processing resources;
- performs regular file archiving and purging as required;
- creates, modifies, and deletes user accounts as required;
- investigates and troubleshoots faults, incidents, problems, and other issues that may affect the delivery of the Forensic Laboratory's products and services to Clients that are reliant on the laboratory's IT services;
- restores and recovers systems after hardware or software failures. Coordinates and communicates with departments that have been affected;
- applies system patches and upgrades on a regular basis;

- upgrades administrative tools and utilities and configure/add new services as necessary;
- produces periodic performance reports to Top Management on IT performance in the laboratory;
- carry out ongoing performance tuning, hardware upgrades, and resource optimization as required;
- manages employee development by conducting annual employee appraisals and TNA in association with the Human Resources Department;
- maintains IT training and awareness throughout the Forensic Laboratory and third parties acting on their behalf, on the importance, and impact of maintaining stringent controls, in association with the Information Security Manager;
- manages the information security incident PIR process;
- participates in international, national, and local SIG presentations, and publishes articles describing the Forensic Laboratory's IT systems and how they relates to the business;
- develops and manages effective working relationships with all appropriate internal and external stakeholders;
- maintains external links to other companies in the industry to gain competitive assessments and share information, where appropriate;
- identifies the emerging information technologies to be assimilated, integrated, and introduced within the Forensic Laboratory, which could significantly impact the Forensic Laboratory's IT and forensic case processing;
- interfaces with external industrial and academic organizations in order to maintain state-of-the-art knowledge in emerging IT and forensic case processing management issues and to enhance the Forensic Laboratory's image as a first-class solution provider utilizing the latest thinking in this field;
- adheres to established the Forensic Laboratory policies, standards, and procedures;
- performs all responsibilities in accordance with, or in excess of, the requirements of the Forensic Laboratory IMS.

AUTHORITY

The System Administrator/Operator has the authority to:

- manage and maintain the Forensic Laboratory's laboratory information systems.

CONTACTS

Internal

The Systems Administrator is required to maintain contact with all levels of Forensic Laboratory employees, and specifically the Laboratory Manager, for the day-to-day operation of the information systems to support forensic case processing.

External

Externally, the Systems Administrator will maintain contacts with Suppliers and Vendors, as required.

REPORTS TO

The System Administrator reports to:

- the Laboratory Manager.

APPENDIX 26 - EMPLOYEE, JOB DESCRIPTION

OBJECTIVE AND ROLE

Employees are responsible for delivering products and services to the Forensic Laboratory's Clients.

PROBLEMS AND CHALLENGES

Day-to-day issues, as met, during working with Clients and internal processes within the Forensic Laboratory.

PRINCIPAL ACCOUNTABILITIES

Employees:

- understand their responsibilities as a Forensic Laboratory employee with regard to attainment of management system objectives in the design, development, production, and support of the Forensic Laboratory's products and services;
- deliver quality solutions to internal and external Clients on time and on budget;
- Identify opportunities for further training and personal development (and seeking appropriate authorization from a Manager or Team Leader);
- cooperate with the Managers and Team Leaders when an appraisal is performed to ensure that the appraisal conducted effectively;
- develop and manages effective working relationships with all appropriate internal and external stakeholders;
- adhere to established the Forensic Laboratory policies, standards, and procedures;
- perform all responsibilities in accordance with, or in excess of, the requirements of the Forensic Laboratory IMS.

REPORTS TO

Employees report to:

- relevant Line Managers.

APPENDIX 27 - AREAS OF TECHNICAL COMPETENCE

Within the Forensic Laboratory, all Forensic Analysts need to know the following:

- the Law:
  - know specific legal system and relevant legislation;
  - what is permissible and what is not in all aspects of forensic case processing.
- basic computer knowledge:
  - data interface technology;
  - diagnosing and troubleshooting systems;
  - different types of storage and their characteristics;
  - dynamic/static IP—addressing;
  - e-commerce, digital signatures;
  - encryption/compressed files;
  - file sharing and peer to peer concepts;
  - file systems and logical/physical—slack space, etc.;
  - hardware and peripherals;
  - hidden files/flags/rename/steganography;
  - image capturing devices, including write blockers;
  - installing, configuring, and maintaining computer systems;
  - internet protocols (TCP, IP);
  - internet services: web, www, chat, file transfer protocol (FTP), Internet Relay Chat (IRC), newsgroups;
  - network operating systems;
  - network protocols;
  - network-specific devices (e.g., switches, firewalls, routers, etc.);
  - network topologies;
  - operating systems (i.e., Windows, Novell, Unix, and variants as well as PDAs, etc.);
  - software—forensic as well as non-forensic software;
  - system time and file time stamps;
  - time critical/perishable data, i.e., log files, e-mail on servers, memory dumps.
- identification and preservation of digital evidence at the scene:
  - computer/digital devices;
  - equipment/systems/software/infrastructure;
  - evidence handling;
  - first response requirements;
  - investigative techniques.
- collecting digital evidence:
  - First Responder procedures;
  - ability to recognize potential sources of evidence;
  - Chain of Custody (evidence);
  - computer hardware;
  - network infrastructure;
  - operating systems;
  - packaging and transport evidence;
  - types of storage media;
  - volatile data;
  - image capture;
  - image storage;
  - image transfer.
- image processing:
  - anti-contamination procedures;
  - setting up a Client virtual case file;
  - processing a case using in-house agreed procedures and tools;
  - need for contemporaneous notes.
- product-based training:
  - there are a number of tools that will be in use in the Forensic Laboratory and all Forensic Analysts must be qualified to use them by attending the manufacturer's own (or authorized) training courses. These may include:
    - Guidance Software;
    - AccessData;
    - Paraben.
  - These are the main Suppliers of tools that are in common use in the Forensic Laboratory. A list of tool categories in use in forensic laboratories is given in Chapter 7, Appendix 4, and many of these either do not need or have certified training programs.
  - The following Vendors of tools that are commonly used by Forensic Laboratories have product certification programs, and these include, but are not limited to:
    - AccessData;
    - CheckPoint;
    - Cisco;
    - Guidance Software;
    - MicroSoft;
    - Paraben.
- forensic skills required:
  - adhere to back-up, archiving and retention policy;
  - adhere to the continuity of Chain of Custody procedures;
  - advise relevant stakeholders as to the evidential weight of recovered data;
  - assist in interviews of suspects, where relevant;
  - comply with the relevant Forensic Laboratory policies and procedures for forensic case processing;
  - documentation of case notes on contemporaneous basis;
  - engage in peer-review to ensure quality, impartiality, and good practice;
  - ensure currency of knowledge of relevant legislation and case law for the relevant jurisdiction(s);
  - ensure intelligence is correctly recorded within appropriate systems;
  - ensure that all equipment is maintained/replaced/updated to ensure optimum efficiency;

  - ensure the security and continuity of exhibits within the Forensic Laboratory;
  - keep up-to-date with current forensic computing techniques and tools;
  - keep up-to-date with the advances in computer technology;
  - keep up-to-date with the technology of digital media and its use;
  - liaise with Prosecution and Defence representatives in an impartial manner;
  - maintain a full contemporaneous work log for each forensic examination;
  - prepare reports and briefings on relevant new legislation and its effect in the area of forensic case processing;
  - produce and present training and awareness lectures/talk within the Forensic Laboratory and for external bodies.
- report writing and testifying:
  - description of evidentiary procedures for digital capture;
  - mock court role playing;
  - presentation of credentials;
  - rehearsals and preparation;
  - writing expert reports;
  - writing statements according to legislative requirements in the jurisdiction.

APPENDIX 28 - SOME PROFESSIONAL FORENSIC AND SECURITY ORGANIZATIONS

Note 1

Each jurisdiction will have its own specific organizations or Chapters of an international organization.

Note 2

Some of these organizations offer certifications, others do not.

Note 3

It is impossible to list these all, so a selection of better known international ones has been given, and these are ones that the Forensic Laboratory employees are members of, are aware of, or hold certifications from.

SPECIFIC FORENSIC ORGANIZATIONS

- AAFS—American Academy of Forensic Sciences—http://www.aafs.org/;
- ADFSL—The Association of Digital Forensics, Security and Law—http://www.adfsl.org/;
- CDFS—Consortium of Digital Forensic Specialists—http://www.cdfs.org/index.php;
- DFA—Digital Forensics Association—http://www.digitalforensicsassociation.org/;
- F3—First Forensic Forum www.f3.org.uk/;
- FSS—Forensic Science Society—http://www.forensic-science-society.org.uk/home;
- HTCI—High Tech Crime Institute Group—http://www.gohtci.com/;
- HTCIA—High Technology Crime Investigation Association—www.htcia.org;
- HTCN—High Tech Crime Network—www.htcn.org;
- IACIS—International Association of Computer Investigative Specialists—www.iacis.com;
- IISFA—International Information Systems Forensics Association—http://www.iisfa-network.org/;
- IOCE—International Organization on Computer Evidence—http://www.ioce.org/fileadmin/user_upload/2002/ioce_bp_exam_digit_tech.html;
- ISFCE—International Society of Forensic Computer Examiners—www.isfce.com.

INFORMATION SECURITY ORGANIZATIONS

- ACFE—Association of Certified Fraud Examiners—www.acfe.com;
- APWG—Anti-Phishing Working Group—www.anti-phishing.org;
- ASIS—American Society for Industrial Security—www.asisonline.org;
- BCS—British Computer Society—www.bcs.org/;
- CSI—Computer Security Institute—www.gocsi.com;
- FBI Infragard— www.infragard.org;
- IEEE—Institute of Electrical and Electronic Engineers—www.ieee-security.org;
- IIA—Institute of Internal Auditors—www.theiia.org;
- ISACA—Information Systems Audit and Control Association—www.isaca.org;
- ISC2—International Information Systems Security Certification Consortium—www.isc.org;
- ISSA—Information Systems Security Association—www.issa.org;
- SANS—System Administration, Networking, and Security Institute—www.sans.org.

APPENDIX 29 - TRAINING SPECIFICATION TEMPLATE

The following template should be used for the development of a training specification for use in the Forensic Laboratory:

- background to the business need that has given rise to the training need;

- identification of the employee(s) that require the training;
- overall aim of the training and details how the business need has been met;
- the objective(s) of the training;
- training methods and style to be used;
- the required skills of the trainer;
- the method of evaluation of the training. An evaluation form, as given in Appendix 1, must be filled in by all employees attending the training but this should also include a link back to meeting the business need, but this may take some time to evaluate;
- timescale for delivery of the training;
- the proposed venue (in house or external);
- any other relevant details.

APPENDIX 30 - TRAINING PROPOSAL EVALUATION CHECKLIST

The following is used in the Forensic Laboratory for evaluating a training proposal based on a supplied training specification RFP:

- a well written and concise response to the training specification RFP;
- a clear description of how the supplier will meet the defined training objectives;
- ensuring that the training methods are appropriate to the Forensic Laboratory's needs;
- full details of the proposed trainers, including their qualifications, relevant experience, experience of training similar or the same courses, or even past experience in the Forensic Laboratory as a training service provider;
- experience of the supplier providing the same or similar courses;
- a realistic timetable for delivery;
- a full breakdown of costs;
- sample Client references;
- any other material that may be considered relevant.

APPENDIX 31 - TRAINING SUPPLIER INTERVIEW AND PRESENTATION CHECKLIST

The following are used in the Forensic Laboratory for evaluating a training supplier's interview performance and presentation based on a supplied training specification RFP.

INTERVIEWS

The interview gives the Forensic Laboratory an opportunity to probe or clarify any of the answers given in the formal training RFP response submitted. Some issues to consider are:

- what is the structure of the training?
- how will it meet the training objectives?
- how will the training methods assist in meeting the training objectives;
- who will actually deliver the training?
- what are their qualifications and competencies of the trainer for the subject matter of the training course;
- what are the qualifications and competencies of anyone involved in developing a new course (if appropriate);
- what is their professional reputation, based on feedback, for the subject matter they are going to develop/teach?
- what complaints for training have they received in the past year?
- have they received any training awards that are nationally, industry wide, or internationally recognized?
- how will they evaluate their success for the delivery?
- confirmation that they will be able to meet both the required timescales and volume of employees;
- confirmation of costs;
- confirmation of any other contractual details;
- any other information that may be relevant.

PRESENTATION

The following is considered by the Forensic Laboratory in evaluating the prospective supplier's presentation:

- a good opening—if they cannot manage that, how will they hold the attention of the Forensic Laboratory employees attending their training courses?
- good presentation and communication style;
- a clear structure, with all relevant areas covered in a logical and concise manner—again a possible indicator of how they run their courses;
- good timekeeping for the stated length on the interview;
- a good close with a concise summary and conclusions;
- professional handling of any questions raised.

APPENDIX 32 - TRAINING REACTION LEVEL QUESTIONNAIRE

The following form can be used in the Forensic Laboratory as its training reaction level questionnaire.

Note

For each section the markings in the 'Marking Scheme' are used, giving quantitative feedback.

GENERAL

- course title;
- course date;
- course supplier;
- name of employee;
- job title.

PRECOURSE BRIEFING

- whether a precourse briefing was given and if it was:
  - were the learning objectives of the course explained;
  - why the course was appropriate to the employee;
  - understanding how the course related to the employee's job role.

TRAINING OBJECTIVES

- define up to five of the employee's training objectives that were met by the course and their level of relevance;
- how relevant did the employee think the course was to their job role (scale of 1-5).

TRAINING METHODS

- for each of the training methods used in the course, evaluate their usefulness to the employee (scale of 1-5 or not applicable);
- methods of training could include, but not be limited to:
  - breakout sessions;
  - case studies;
  - classroom training;
  - extra sessions with the tutor/coaching;
  - group discussion;
  - handouts;
  - practicals;
  - quizzes;
  - role play;
  - syndicate work;
  - videos.

TRAINERS

For each trainer, rate their performance (scale of 1-5):

- ability to relate the subject to the employees;
- appropriate course pace;
- engaging with the class;
- knowledge;
- practical experience.

FACILITIES AND ADMINISTRATION

- for item below, evaluate the quality facilities and administration for the course (scale of 1-5 or not applicable):
  - audio visual equipment;
  - breakout rooms;
  - catering;
  - clarity of joining instructions;
  - convenience of location;
  - handling of queries;
  - timeliness of joining instructions;
  - training room(s).

OTHER COMMENTS

Allow any other comments that the employee wants to put in.

MARKING SCHEME

The marking scheme to be used is:

- 0—Not applicable;
- 1—Very Poor;
- 2—Poor;
- 3—Neutral;
- 4—Good;
- 5—Very Good.

APPENDIX 33 - THE FORENSIC LABORATORY CODE OF ETHICS

This is the Forensic Laboratory's own Code of Ethics. It has been designed to meet not only the Forensic Laboratory's own requirements but also to incorporate other known Codes of Ethics from other forensic and security organizations that publish them.

Where an inconsistency is discovered between the Forensic Laboratory's Code of Ethics and other published ones, the discrepancy shall be investigated and the Forensic Laboratory's Code of Ethics be amended, if appropriate.

- act in all dealings with honesty, objectivity, and impartiality;
- admit to mistakes and errors and continuously improve;
- be able to demonstrate due care;
- be able to report a possible miscarriage of justice to an appropriate person without fear of recrimination;
- be able to terminate their engagement if they feel undue pressure is being applied to them;
- be honest about skills and limitations and rely on other qualified experts when needed;
- be honest and forthright in dealing with others;
- be open minded and not discriminatory on any grounds;
- be paid for their work and not a desired outcome that may influence their objectivity;
- be prepared to re-visit forensic casework if any new evidence is discovered that may impact findings to date;
- be professional and perform all work in a competent, accurate, timely, and cost-effective manner;
- be respectful of intellectual property rights;

- charge reasonable fees and expenses as agreed between the parties and in line with good practice;
- credit other people's work;
- declare any conflicts of interest as soon as they are identified;
- ensure security of all case processing exhibits at all times while in their possession;
- establish the integrity and continuity of any exhibits as soon as they are received and maintain the chain of custody while in the Forensic Analyst's possession;
- have open communications with the Client and keep the Client informed of any major developments;
- maintain and update technical and other relevant skills;
- maintain professional competence;
- maintain the highest standards of professionalism and ethical conduct;
- only use validated methods, unless preparing a new method for validation. Even then, the method shall not be used until validated;
- only work and provide evidence within the limits of professional competence;
- preserve confidentiality unless otherwise ordered by a court of competent jurisdiction or explicitly by the instructing Client;
- remember that their overriding duty to serve the Court or tribunal, and that that their secondary duty is to the Client instructing them, as appropriate in the jurisdiction;
- report any reportable offence to the proper legal authorities as required by the legislation in the jurisdiction;
- respect confidentiality relating to all matters relating to forensic case work and Forensic Laboratory operations generally;
- strive to ensure the integrity and repeatability of the work carried out.

APPENDIX 34 - TERMINATION CHECKLIST

The following checklist is used in the Forensic Laboratory for employee terminations. Where the employee is undertaking an internal move or promotion, those parts of the form that are irrelevant are omitted.

EMPLOYEE DETAILS

- employee name;
- employee ID number;
- employee position;
- period of service (from and to dates).

GENERAL QUESTIONS

1. Please identify the reason(s) for initially seeking and accepting a position with the Forensic Laboratory:
   - compensation;
   - fringe benefits;
   - location;
   - reputation of the Forensic Laboratory;
   - career change;
   - job responsibilities;
   - technical challenges;
   - other.

> **Note 1**
> These are tick boxes and allow comments to be added.

2. Have your feelings changed?

> **Note 2**
> This is a "Yes/No" question and allows comments to be added.

3. Did you understand the job expectations when you were hired?

> **Note 3**
> This is a "Yes/No" question and allows comments to be added.

4. Did you receive sufficient training to meet those expectations?

> **Note 4**
> This is a "Yes/No" question and allows comments to be added.

5. Did you know how or where to get information you needed to succeed in your job?

> **Note 5**
> This is a "Yes/No" question and allows comments to be added.

6. What did you find to be the most satisfying and enjoyable about your experience with the Forensic Laboratory?

> **Note 6**
> This is a free form answer and allows comments to be added.

7. What did you find to be least satisfying and enjoyable about your experience with the Forensic Laboratory?

Note 7

This is a free form answer and allows comments to be added.

JOB SPECIFIC QUESTIONS

This section attempts to rate aspects of the employee's "employment experience" using quantitative and qualitative feedback. The following scoring is used for aspects of employment:

- 1—Very Poor;
- 2—Poor;
- 3—Neutral;
- 4—Good;
- 5—Very Good.

The aspects to be evaluated are:

1. Opportunity for advancement.
2. Performance appraisals.
3. Physical working conditions.
4. Technical challenges.
5. Your salary.
6. Vacation/holidays.
7. Other company benefits.
8. Feeling of belonging.
9. Work/home life balance.
10. Internal communications.
11. Access to appropriate resources.
12. Please provide any constructive feedback you feel would be beneficial toward improving the effectiveness of the Forensic Laboratory as an employer.

Note 8

This is a free form answer and allows comments to be added.

13. What would make you interested in returning to work at the Forensic Laboratory?

Note 9

This is a free form answer and allows comments to be added.

14. Do you feel that your particular job was important to the overall operational success of the Forensic Laboratory?

Note 10

This is a "Yes/No" question and allows comments to be added.

EVALUATION OF MANAGEMENT

This section attempts to rate aspects of the employee's "perception of their Line Manager" using quantitative and qualitative feedback.

The following scoring is used for aspects of employment:

- 1—Very Poor;
- 2—Poor;
- 3—Neutral;
- 4—Good;
- 5—Very Good.

The aspects to be evaluated are:

1. Demonstrates fair and equal treatment.
2. Provides appropriate recognition.
3. Resolves complaints/difficulties in timely fashion.
4. Follows Forensic Laboratory policy and procedures.
5. Informs employee of matters relating to work in a timely manner.
6. Encourages feedback.
7. Is knowledgeable in own job.
8. Expresses instructions clearly.
9. Develops cooperation.
10. Provides assistance, training, and mentoring as needed.
11. If you came back to work for the Company, would you work for the same Line Manager?

Note 11

This is a "Yes/No" question and allows comments to be added.

12. How would you rate your own performance on the job?

Note 12

This question uses the rankings above and allows comments to be added.

NEW ROLE

This section attempts to determine details of reasons for leaving and the new role to which the employee is moving:

1. Which of the following methods did you use to search for a new position?

- advertisements;
- Recruitment Consultants;
- personal contacts;
- client contact;
- other.

Note 13
This is a tick box answer and allows comments to be added.

2. Are you leaving for a similar job?

Note 14
This is a "Yes/No" question and allows comments to be added.

3. How is your new job different from your old one?

Note 15
This is a free form text answer.

4. Are you staying in the same industry?

Note 16
This is a "Yes/No" question and allows comments to be added.

5. What part does salary play in your decision to leave?

Note 17
This is a free form text answer.

6. What made you begin looking for another position, or if appropriate what made you listen to the offer to interview for another position?

Note 18
This is a free form text answer.

7. What is your primary reason for leaving?
   - compensation;
   - fringe benefits;
   - location;
   - supervision;
   - career change;
   - job fit;
   - other.

Note 19
This is a tick box answer and allows comments to be added.

8. If you used Recruitment Consultants, which ones did you find the most useful?

Note 20
This is a free form text answer.

9. What could the Forensic Laboratory have done to prevent you from leaving?

Note 21
This is a free form text answer.

10. What does the job you are going to offer you that your job here did not?

Note 22
This is a free form text answer.

11. Any Other Feedback/Comments/Suggestions?

Note 23
This is a free form text answer.

The form is then signed and dated by the employee and the Human Resources employee conducting the exit interview.

RETURN OF ASSETS

This section is a checklist of items that have been issued to the employee as part of their job role that are to be returned on termination. The list comes from the Finance or IT asset register listing and anything that the employee hands over at the exit interview:

- laptop;
- credit card;

- access card;
- other IT equipment;
- media returned;
- all Forensic Laboratory (or Forensic Laboratory Client's) information—on any media;
- car and keys;
- office keys;
- other (Define).

Note 24

The form is then signed and dated by the employee and the Human Resources employee conduction the exit interview.

IT DEPARTMENT ACTIONS

This section is a checklist of tasks to be performed by the IT Department as part of the termination process.

Each item has a date, the name and signature of the person carrying out each task.

Not all tasks will be relevant to each employee being terminated, so they are stated as "Not done" dated and signed. The tasks are:

- all employee accounts disabled;
- administration/root passwords changed (define);
- other "shared" passwords changed (define);
- removed from access list (physical);
- removed from access list (logical);
- e-mail archived;
- pin numbers and access codes changed (define);
- voicemail diverted to Line Manager;
- voicemail access code changed;
- mobile phone either reassigned or terminated;
- check all IT equipment returned via Human Resources Department;
- other tasks required (Define).

Chapter 19

Accreditation and Certification for a Forensic Laboratory

Table of Contents

19.1 ACCREDITATION AND CERTIFICATION

19.1.1 Definitions

The terms "Accreditation" and "Certification" are often used interchangeably by those who do not understand what they mean. They have different meanings and should be used correctly. Their definitions are given below:

ISO 17011 defines Accreditation as:

"Third-party attestation related to a Conformity Assessment Body conveying formal demonstration of its competence to carry out specific conformity assessment tasks."

Accreditation is a formal, third-party recognition of competence to perform specific tasks. It provides a means to identify a proved, competent evaluator so that the selection of a Conformity Assessment Body (CAB) (Laboratory, inspection, or Certification Body) is an informed choice.

ISO 17011 defines Certification as:

"Third-party attestation related to products, processes, systems, or persons."

Certification is a formal procedure by which an accredited or authorized person or agency assesses and verifies (and attests in writing by issuing a Certificate) the attributes, characteristics, quality, qualification, or status of individuals or organizations, goods or services, procedures or processes, or events or situations, conforms with established requirements or standards.

Note

Certification of a Management System is sometimes called Registration.

19.1.2 The International Accreditation Forum

Accreditation Bodies (ABs) can apply to join the International Accreditation Forum (IAF). When they have been evaluated by their peers as competent, they sign arrangements that enhance the acceptance of products and services across national borders.

The purpose of the arrangement, the IAF Multilateral Recognition Arrangement (MLA), is to ensure mutual recognition of Accredited Certification between signatories to the MLA, and subsequently acceptance of Accredited Certification in many markets based on one Accreditation.

Accreditations granted by IAF MLA signatories are recognized worldwide, based on their equivalent Accreditation programs, therefore reducing costs and adding value to business and consumers. This creates a framework to support international trade through the removal of technical barriers.

AB members of the IAF are admitted to the MLA only after stringent evaluation of their operations by a peer evaluation team.

These arrangements are managed by the IAF, in the fields of Management Systems, products, services, personnel, and other similar programs of Conformity Assessment, and the International Laboratory Accreditation Cooperation (ILAC), in the field of laboratory and inspection Accreditation. Both organizations, ILAC and IAF, work together and co-ordinate their efforts to enhance the Accreditation and the Conformity Assessment processes worldwide.

19.1.3 The Hierarchy of ISO Standards for Accreditation and Certification

There is a distinct hierarchy for Accreditation and Certification within ISO Standards.

At the top level is the AB that will accredit CABs, who in turn will certify or register Clients.

19.1.3.1 Accreditation Bodies

The following ISO Standards are applicable to ABs:

- ISO/IEC 17011:2004 Conformity Assessment—General requirements for ABs accrediting CABs.

ABs are recognized/peer evaluated by the IAF.

ABs are established in many countries with the primary purpose of ensuring that CABs in their country are subject to oversight by an authoritative body.

19.1.3.2 Conformance Assessment Bodies

The following ISO Standards are applicable to CABs:

- ISO/IEC 17020:2012 Conformity Assessment—Requirements for the operation of various types of bodies performing inspection (This relates to Inspection Bodies.);
- ISO/IEC 17021:2011 Conformity Assessment—Requirements for bodies providing audit and Certification of Management Systems (This relates to Certification Bodies and typically relates to Management Systems.). This replaced ISO/IEC Guide 62:1996 General requirements for bodies operating assessment and Certification/Registration of quality systems, and ISO/IEC Guide 66:1999 General requirements for bodies operating assessment and Certification/Registration of Environmental Management Systems;
- ISO/IEC TS 17022:2012 Conformity Assessment—Requirements and recommendations for content of a third-party audit report on Management Systems;
- ISO/IEC 17024:2003 Conformity Assessment—General requirements for bodies operating Certification of persons (This relates to individuals.);
- ISO/IEC 17025:2005 General requirements for the competence of testing and calibration laboratories (This relates to testing and calibration laboratories—i.e., The Forensic Laboratory.);
- ISO/IEC 17043:2010 Conformity Assessment—General requirements for proficiency testing (This replaced ISO Guide 43 ISO/IEC Guide 43-1:1997 Proficiency testing by inter-laboratory comparisons—Part 1: Development and operation of proficiency testing schemes and Part 2: Selection and use of proficiency testing schemes by Laboratory ABs.);
- ISO/IEC 17065 Conformity Assessment—Requirements for bodies certifying products, processes, and services (This replaced ISO/IEC Guide 65:1996 General requirements for bodies operating product Certification systems.).

CABs are assessed and Accredited by the relevant AB.

While these are the ISO Standards relevant to Accreditation and Certification, a number of organizations throughout the world have adopted and adapted them to suit their own specific requirements.

A number of these relate to forensic laboratories, two of the main ABs offering ISO 17025 "plus" are the American Society of Crime Laboratory Directors/Laboratory Accreditation Board (ASCLD/LAB)—http://www.ascld-lab.org/ and The American Association for Laboratory Accreditation (A2LA)—http://www.a2la.org/index.cfm.

19.1.4 Standards and Regulations Applicable to the Forensic Laboratory

To gain either Accredited or Certified status, a forensic laboratory can choose the standards it wishes to meet and demonstrate to a third party that it meets those requirements.

These are typically:

- international standards;
- national standards.

This book has applied the requirements of the following standards to a forensic laboratory.

19.1.4.1 Accreditation

The following Accreditations are addressed with the procedures in this book:

- ISO/IEC 17025:2005 General requirements for the competence of testing and calibration laboratories.

Note 1

It is not possible to list all of the specific variations on ISO 17025 Accreditation, so the generic ISO 17025 Management System has been chosen as a "vanilla" Accreditation. The different variations of ISO 17025 are always based on ISO 17025 with extra requirements over and above the "vanilla" ISO 17025.

Note 2

The Forensic Laboratory is regarded as a "Testing" Laboratory in ISO 17025 terms, rather than a "Calibration Laboratory."

19.1.4.2 Certifications

The following Certifications are addressed with the procedures in this book:

- ISO 22301 Societal Security—Business Continuity Management Systems;
- BS OHSAS 18001 Occupational Health and Safety;
- ISO 9001:2008 Quality Management Systems—Requirements;
- ISO/IEC 27001:2005 Information Technology—Security techniques—Information Security Management Systems—Requirements.

19.1.4.3 Compliance

The following standards are used in this book and procedures implemented are compliant with them as there are no processes for Certification or Accreditation for them:

- BS 7858:2006+A2:2009 Security screening of Individuals employed in a security environment. Code of practice;
- ISO 10002:2004 Quality management—Customer satisfaction—Guidelines for complaints handling in organizations;
- ISO 10003:2007 Quality management—Customer satisfaction—Guidelines for dispute resolution external to organizations;
- ISO/IEC 17020:1998 General criteria for the operation of various types of bodies performing inspection;
- PAS 99:2006 Specification of common Management System requirements as a framework for integration.

19.1.4.4 Regulations and Legislation

In a number of jurisdictions, there are emerging a number of Forensic Regulators, who are implementing Forensic Regulations within their jurisdiction.

In the United Kingdom, the function of the Forensic Science Regulator is to ensure that the provision of forensic science services across the criminal justice system is subject to an appropriate regime of scientific quality standards.

In the United States, a number of States have mandated that Crime Laboratories are Accredited.

Similar requirements may exist, or be planned, for other countries.

19.1.4.5 ISO 9001 and ISO 17025

ISO 17025 covers a number of technical competence requirements that are not covered in ISO 9001.

Certification against ISO 9001 does not, in itself, demonstrate the competence of a forensic laboratory to produce technically valid data and results.

In effect, a forensic laboratory must decide whether it requires being Accredited to ISO 17025, Certified to ISO 9001, or both. Accreditation and Certification are two separate processes. No Laboratory that claims ISO 17025 Accreditation can also automatically claim ISO 9001 Certification and likewise ISO 9001 Certification does not provide ISO 17025 Accreditation status.

19.1.5 Benefits of Accreditation and Certification for the Forensic Laboratory

19.1.5.1 Accreditation

Formal recognition of competence of a forensic laboratory by an AB in accordance with international criteria has many advantages:

- a competent workforce performing tasks within the Forensic Laboratory;
- a positive reputation for the Forensic Laboratory for having achieved ISO 17025 Accreditation;
- a public statement that the Forensic Laboratory has met the highest operational requirements;
- assurance of the accuracy and integrity of the Forensic Laboratory's processes and outputs;
- demonstrable compliance verified by a third-party AB;
- increased confidence in reports issued by the Forensic Laboratory;
- international recognition for the Forensic Laboratory;
- marketing advantage;
- potential increase in business due to enhanced customer confidence and satisfaction;
- processes and procedures for the operation of the Forensic Laboratory are documented and tested;
- quality assurance of test and calibration data;
- rigorous quality processes that equate to fewer failures and errors;
- savings in terms of time and money due to reduction or elimination of the need for rework;
- suitability, calibration, and maintenance of test equipment;

- the Forensic Laboratory has better control of operations and feedback to ascertain whether they have a sound quality assurance system and are assessed as technically competent;
- traceability of measurements and calibrations to International Standards.

19.1.5.2 Certification

If the Forensic Laboratory gains Certification (where applicable) and conformance to the standards referred to in this chapter, then it will have the following advantages:

- allows the Forensic Laboratory to seek new markets where they may have been precluded, if they had not gained the relevant Certification;
- assures management and customers of the Forensic Laboratory's information security, quality, business continuity, and health and safety measures in place;
- builds team spirit as the Integrated Management System (IMS) requires a team, not an individual, approach;
- creates an organizational structure to ensure that roles and responsibilities are clearly defined;
- demonstrates conformance with the relevant standards verified by a third-party CAB, where a Certification process exists;
- demonstrates legal and regulatory compliance;
- demonstrates that the Forensic Laboratory is continually improving and refining its Management Systems by achieving and maintaining its Certification(s);
- demonstrates to relevant stakeholders, through a third party, that the Forensic Laboratory uses industry-respected best practices;
- demonstrates to stakeholders that the Forensic Laboratory is run effectively and continuously improves its processes;
- detects defects that do occur earlier and they are corrected at a lower cost;
- develops a Statement of Applicability that identifies controls to be implemented to address the risks relating to information security identified in the Forensic Laboratory;
- ensures that corrective action is taken whenever defects in products and services occur;
- ensures that a commitment to the components in the IMS (e.g., ISMS, BCMS, QMS, etc.) exists at all levels throughout the Forensic Laboratory;
- ensures that an appropriate incident management process is in place;
- ensures that there is an ongoing compliance and monitoring mechanism in place;
- identifies, evaluates, and treats risks in the Forensic Laboratory, in a timely manner, in line with their risk appetite;
- improves the Forensic Laboratory's image and builds a better reputation;
- improves management control and reporting, ensuring improved and fact-based decision making;
- improves staff responsibility, commitment, and motivation through ongoing Assessment;
- increases customer confidence in the Forensic Laboratory's products and services;
- integrates information security, quality, business continuity, and health and safety into a common IMS to exploit synchronicity between standards with similar management requirements;
- makes a public statement that the Forensic Laboratory has addressed its own information security needs, as well as those of Clients who entrust their information to them;
- makes it easier for new employees "get up to speed" by following documented procedures;
- potentially reduced insurance premiums;
- provides a positive health and safety track record;
- reduces the risk of accidents and therefore lower employee absence;
- reduces operational costs.

19.1.6 Establishing the Need for Accreditation and/or Certification

The common requirements for the Forensic Laboratory for Accreditation and/or Certification include:

- improving the quality of products and services provided to its Clients;
- adopting, developing, and maintaining processes and procedures which may be used to assess its level of conformance to relevant standards;
- providing an independent, impartial, and objective process of Accreditation and Certification by which it benefits from a total operational review on a regular basis;
- offering to the general public and to its Clients a means of identifying that it has demonstrated conformance with established standards and allow possible Clients to make informed choices;
- in some cases, Accreditation is mandated for specific standards.

19.1.7 Requirements for Accreditation and/or Certification

In order to achieve Accreditation or Certification, the Forensic Laboratory must demonstrate to a competent third party that it meets the requirements of the standard(s) against which it is being assessed.

Once the need for an Accreditation or Certification has been agreed and identified, it is necessary to determine which ABs or CABs can offer the services required. This may involve an AB or CAB from within the jurisdiction or may require a specific service to be procured from outside the jurisdiction.

19.2 ACCREDITATION FOR A FORENSIC LABORATORY

Note 1

In this book, "audit" refers to first- and second-party audits undertaken by the Forensic Laboratory and "assessment" is used for third-party audits.

Note 2

In the Forensic Laboratory, all policies, procedure, forms, checklists and work instructions for both Accreditation and Certification are implemented in the IMS. References are made to the IMS in this Chapter as it is assumed that all forensic laboratories will adopt this approach.

The process for gaining Accreditation is broadly similar for any standard throughout the world. However, different ABs may have different requirements based on their scopes or on the jurisdiction within which they operate.

The generic approach is shown below, but when Accreditation is sought, the specific AB requirements must be met.

Whichever process for Accreditation is taken, the Forensic Laboratory will undergo similar processes as defined below.

19.2.1 Self-evaluation Prior to Application

While it may not be a mandatory requirement for Accreditation, it is a sensible approach to perform a self-assessment as preparation for the Accreditation process. This should determine whether the Forensic Laboratory's processes, procedures, and records meet the requirements of the Accreditation sought.

This may require the:

- purchase of a number of standards;
- completion of self-assessment forms for use prior to seeking Accreditation and undertake any identified Corrective Actions or Preventive Actions (CAPAs) arising from the self-evaluation process.

The Forensic Laboratory may choose to undertake the self-assessment in-house or contract a third-party service provider to perform the task on their behalf.

19.2.2 Selecting an AB

Once the required Accreditation has been agreed, the Forensic Laboratory should:

1. Research the market to see what ABs provide the required Accreditation services.
2. Obtain marketing materials from each of the possible ABs to determine the range of services that they provide.
3. Research other forensic laboratories to determine the ABs that they have used and their opinion of the services provided.
4. Create a shortlist of three possible ABs from whom to obtain quotations for the Accreditation required, if possible. It may well be that there is only one AB operating in the jurisdiction or that the use of the national AB is mandated.

Note

Where a Forensic Laboratory already has a relationship with an AB, the first approach should be made to that AB for additional services, if they can provide them. This will have the benefit of reduced costs for integrated audits and the fact that the AB already "knows" their Client's business.

19.2.3 Accreditation Information to be Made Available

In order to assist in selection of an AB, all ABs shall make publicly available, and update at adequate intervals, the following:

- detailed information about the AB's Assessment and Accreditation processes, including arrangements for granting, maintaining, extending, reducing, suspending, and withdrawing Accreditation;
- documentation containing the requirements for Accreditation, including technical requirements specific to each field of Accreditation, that the AB offers;
- general information about the fees relating to the Accreditation;
- a description of the rights and obligations of CABs;
- information on the CABs that the AB has accredited in a publicly available register;
- information on procedures for lodging and handling complaints and appeals;
- information about the authority under which the Accreditation program operates;
- a description of its rights and duties;
- general information about the means by which it obtains financial support;
- information about its activities and stated limitations under which it operates.

From this information, an informed choice of AB can be made by the Forensic Laboratory.

19.2.4 Selection of an AB

Once the quotation(s) from the shortlist of ABs for the provision of Accreditation services have been received by the Forensic Laboratory with the range of services offered, the Forensic Laboratory is in the position to make an informed choice about the selection of an appropriate AB.

19.2.5 Application

Once the ABs have been selected for the provision of Accreditation, the Forensic Laboratory should initiate the Accreditation process. In order to initiate the Accreditation process, the Forensic Laboratory shall:

1. Obtain the relevant application forms from the selected ABs (often called the "Application Pack").
2. Fill in relevant application forms and return them to the relevant AB.
3. Provide a copy of the Forensic Laboratory Quality Manual.
4. Pay the relevant fees.
5. Execute the relevant contracts.

While application forms will vary between ABs, the application process should require the Forensic Laboratory to typically provide the following information on the application forms:

- the legal name and full address of the Forensic Laboratory;
- the ownership and legal status of the Forensic Laboratory;
- the Forensic Laboratory's Authorized Representative's name and contact information;
- an organizational chart defining relationships that are relevant to performing testing and calibrations covered in the Accreditation request;
- a general description of the Forensic Laboratory, including its facilities and scope of operation;
- declarations relevant to the application;
- the requested Scope of Accreditation.

By signing the application, the Forensic Laboratory's Authorized Representative commits the Forensic Laboratory to fulfill the conditions for Accreditation. While these will vary between ABs, a typical set of conditions for Accreditation is given in Appendix 1.

The Forensic Laboratory's Authorized Representative must review all documents provided with the application package and become familiar with the requirements and how the Forensic Laboratory meets them, before signing the application.

19.2.6 Scope of Accreditation

The form and definition of the Scope of Accreditation will depend on the Accreditation sought by the Forensic Laboratory.

ABs will have forms and guidance to assist the Forensic Laboratory in defining their scope for Accreditation.

Typically, the AB works closely with the Forensic Laboratory to define the Scope of Accreditation to ensure that the Forensic Laboratory's Clients are provided with an accurate and unambiguous description of the range of calibration/tests covered by the Forensic Laboratory's Accreditation.

This is the reason that the Forensic Laboratory is required to list, in its Application Form, the standard specifications or other methods or procedures relevant to the calibration or tests for which Accreditation is sought, and the major items of laboratory equipment used to conduct those calibrations/tests.

In some cases, as the Assessment proceeds, it may become clear that the Forensic Laboratory is not in a position to achieve Accreditation for certain areas within the proposed scope. In cases such as this, the Lead Assessor may be able to recommend Accreditation for a suitably reduced or re-defined schedule.

The Scope of Accreditation for the Forensic Laboratory is regarded as being in the public domain, as ABs are required to maintain a public register of organizations that they have Accredited.

19.2.7 Fees for Accreditation

Fees will vary for each specific part of the Assessment between ABs in different jurisdictions and may even be for different standards.

Additionally, fees will normally change over time.

For this reason, no details of fees are given.

19.2.8 Processing Applications

Upon receipt of the Forensic Laboratory's application for Accreditation, the AB will:

- log the application;
- acknowledge the receipt of the application in writing (typically e-mail these days) to the Forensic Laboratory;
- confirm payment of fees;
- review the Forensic Laboratory's application, to ensure that:
  - the application is complete;
  - correct fees are paid.

> **Note**
> Where the application is unclear or incomplete, the AB shall request further clarification or documents until they are satisfied that the application is complete.

Additionally, the AB will check to see that they:

- have fully understood the Forensic Laboratory's requirements;

- can arrange Assessment Teams with all the necessary expertise and competence;
- can make realistic estimates of the timescales and costs involved.

The AB will review the Quality Manual and any supporting documentation supplied by the Forensic Laboratory and determine the apparent conformance of the documents submitted for the relevant standard. The AB can then recommend whether:

- a pre-assessment visit should take place;
- exceptionally, plans for the Forensic Laboratory's Assessment to the relevant standard can proceed without any pre-assessment visit (This would typically be following discussions between the Forensic Laboratory and the AB.);
- the Forensic Laboratory is not in a position to proceed to pre-assessment.

Proper completion and submission of records and documents are required before the Assessment process can start.

19.2.9 Assigning the Lead Assessor

After reviewing the Forensic Laboratory's application and determining that it is complete, the AB will assign a Lead Assessor to manage the application. (This is often also referred to as the Assessment Manager.) The Lead Assessor will typically have an understanding of the area of calibration, testing, or sampling concerned and will be able to discuss with the Forensic Laboratory's Authorized Representative any matters that may arise during the processing of the application, as far as possible.

Most ABs try to ensure that the Lead Assessor is responsible for processing the Forensic Laboratory's application through the Accreditation life cycle for at least the first full three-year cycle.

The Lead Assessor will perform the Contract Review and is responsible for selecting and appointing the Assessment Team.

19.2.10 Appointing the Assessment Team

The Assessment Team comprises a Lead Assessor and as many Technical Assessors or Experts as are necessary to provide the technical expertise to adequately assess the Forensic Laboratory's competence.

Technical Assessors and Experts are selected on the basis of their professional and academic achievements, experience in the field of testing or calibration, management experience, training, technical knowledge, and communications skills. They evaluate all information collected from the Forensic Laboratory and to conduct the Assessment at the Forensic Laboratory and any other sites where activities to be covered by the Accreditation are performed.

Assessors are assigned to conduct an on-site Assessment of the Forensic Laboratory on the basis of how well their experience matches the type of testing or calibration to be assessed, as well as the absence of conflicts of interest.

The Forensic Laboratory has the right to object to the appointment of any Technical Assessor(s) or Expert(s) and, in such cases, the AB will endeavor to offer an alternative. In the event that a suitable alternative cannot be identified, or the grounds for objection are considered to be unreasonable, the AB will typically reserve the right to appoint the original Technical Assessor(s) and Expert(s) to the Assessment Team.

19.2.11 Document Review

The Lead Assessor assigned to assess the Forensic Laboratory's application reviews the quality manual and related Management System documentation submitted with the application to ensure that they cover all aspects of the Management System related to the requirements of the Accreditation sought.

The Lead Assessor may ask for additional Management System documents and/or records in order to facilitate the Document Review.

The Lead Assessor may identify non-conformances in the documentation during the Document Review.

Any non-conformance identified during the Document Review will be discussed with the Authorized Representative, and the Forensic Laboratory is given the opportunity to address them prior to progressing to the next stage in the Accreditation process.

Based on the Document Review, the AB may require the Forensic Laboratory to address any identified non-conformances before any on-site Assessment is scheduled.

In these cases, the Lead Assessor will provide a list of the non-conformances to the Forensic Laboratory in writing. If the Management System documentation requires significant revision, the AB may require the Forensic Laboratory to improve its documentation and resubmit it for further review prior to proceeding with the Accreditation process.

If the non-conformances are serious enough, the Lead Assessor can "suspend" the Accreditation process until the gaps have been satisfactorily been addressed.

If a non-conformance is found, it will be marked as to its severity, and the Forensic Laboratory is advised of it.

Different ABs different terminologies for assessing conformance to the requirements of the Management Systems, and a standard one is defined in Chapter 4, Section 4.7.3.5.

If any non-conformances are identified, the Forensic Laboratory will be required to formally respond to the audit report and state how they are going to address any non-conformances raised. In the Forensic Laboratory, this is performed by the raising of a CAPA, though some organizations call them as CARs (Corrective Action Requests).

A typical response for an audit report is given in Appendix 2.

The Document Review is usually carried out on-site, but may be performed off-site, if required.

19.2.12 Pre-assessment Visit

Note 1

Some ABs may require pre-assessment visits and others leave them as optional. The Forensic Laboratory should always take advantage of a pre-assessment visit for Accreditation or Certification, if offered.

Note 2

The Forensic Laboratory may, if the ABs permits it, request a longer pre-assessment visit.

The pre-assessment visit is usually carried out by the Lead Assessor (accompanied by a Technical Assessor where appropriate) and is usually completed in 1 day.

The pre-assessment visit allows discussion with the Forensic Laboratory's Top Management on the extent to which the Forensic Laboratory's Management System, Quality Manual, and operating procedures appear to fulfill the requirements for Accreditation to the relevant standard.

The pre-assessment visit is structured so that the Assessment Team can ascertain that the essential components of the Forensic Laboratory's Management System for quality, administrative, and technical operation of the Laboratory are present. The Assessment Team needs to establish whether the Forensic Laboratory has defined responsibilities and the means of meeting each of the requirements of the relevant standard.

As well as examining the documented Management System prepared by the Forensic Laboratory, the Assessment Team will usually take the opportunity to discuss the proposed Scope of Accreditation and to carry out a brief examination of the forensic laboratory's facilities.

As part of the examination, the Assessment Team may discuss any documented in-house methods used for activities that form part of the Scope of Accreditation and any in-house calibrations and/or tests used in support of accredited measurement activities.

This should provide evidence to the Assessment Team that such methods have been validated, as defined in Chapter 7, Section 7.5.5, and to allow any changes necessary to be made to the systems or procedures prior to the Initial Assessment. Also covered during the pre-assessment visit will be the Forensic Laboratory's policy and procedures for estimating uncertainty of measurement, as given in Chapter 7, Appendix 31.

During the Pre-assessment visit, the Assessment Team may raise non-conformances where they identify any areas that appear to require attention in order to fulfill the requirements for Accreditation.

The Forensic Laboratory will be reminded that the pre-assessment visit is not a full Assessment and will be advised of the structure and scope of the full assessment visit.

At the end of the pre-assessment visit, the Assessment Team will make a report of their visit and its findings, including any non-conformances, to the AB. The report should indicate:

- whether a further pre-assessment visit is recommended;
- whether plans for Initial Assessment of the Forensic Laboratory can proceed;
- specific reasons why plans cannot proceed;
- whether an inter-laboratory comparison (e.g., measurement audit) is needed.

A copy of the report of the pre-assessment visit will be passed on to the Forensic Laboratory. At the same time, the Assessment Team will discuss timescales for the full Assessment visit and may provisionally agree dates for it.

After the pre-assessment visit, the Lead Assessor will determine:

- the composition of the full Assessment Team;
- the effort (in man days) required for the Initial Assessment visit including time for preparation and standard post-visit activities.

This will take into account all factors necessary to enable a reliable assessment of the Forensic Laboratory's competence to perform the full range of activities proposed for inclusion in its Scope of Accreditation, including:

- whether it is necessary to assess all activities, or if a representative sample can be selected;
- the need to assess all key activities;
- handling of multi-site locations, where necessary, to ensure that all key activities are assessed.

This forms part of the ABs Contract Review procedure and is agreed and approved by an independent decision maker.

Pre-assessment visits are strictly prohibited from performing any consultancy services. This includes giving any advice on selecting any CAPAs but can include discussing the appropriateness and sufficiency of a proposed CAPA.

19.2.13 Scheduling the Initial On-Site Assessment

Once any outstanding CAPAs from the Pre-assessment visit have been closed out, the Forensic Laboratory is ready, and able, to proceed to the Initial Assessment.

If a date has been provisionally agreed and it is still feasible, then this date will be confirmed, if it is not, another mutually agreed date will be confirmed. If the scheduled date needs to be changed for any reason by the Forensic Laboratory, then it shall contact the AB and request an alternate date. The Forensic Laboratory is responsible for any costs associated with the date change.

An assessment usually takes between 1 and 5 days, depending on the size of the Forensic Laboratory being assessed and its Scope of Accreditation. Every effort is made to conduct all assessments with as little disruption as possible to the Forensic Laboratory's normal operations.

A detailed visit plan will be prepared indicating the section/activities/location(s) to be assessed by each Assessor and specify the calibrations/testing/sampling that each Assessor must witness during the visit, including any on-site activities and in-house calibrations, as necessary.

Copies of the visit plan to the Forensic Laboratory will be distributed to the Forensic Laboratory and to all of the Assessment Team, allowing all parties to raise any issues with the visit plan.

The Assessment Visit will not be scheduled until all outstanding non-conformances have been addressed.

19.2.14 Logistics of the Initial On-Site Assessment

Once the Assessment Team has been appointed and the date of the Assessment visit agreed, the logistics of planning the visit are undertaken.

Typically, an AB makes its own travel and accommodation arrangements, but assistance from the Forensic Laboratory may be required.

In addition to having the operations defined in the Scope of Accreditation ready for the assessment, the Forensic Laboratory will have to arrange:

- a secure room or a working area for the Assessment Team;
- all employees on the agenda for assessment to be available, or their alternates;
- refreshments, including lunch;
- one or more "Guides" appointed to ensure that the Assessment Team can get to the right places in the Forensic Laboratory at the right time and facilitate any requests for information.

Prior to arrival on-site, any other specific needs will be advised to the Forensic Laboratory.

19.2.15 Opening Meeting

At the beginning of the all Assessments, an Opening Meeting is conducted. This is attended by the Assessment Team and relevant Top Management from the Forensic Laboratory.

This meeting is held at the start of the Assessment to:

- enable the Assessment Team and the Forensic Laboratory's Top Management and nominated representatives to become acquainted;
- to confirm the purpose of the Assessment;
- to remind the Forensic Laboratory of what is expected during the assessment;
- confirm Guides for the duration of the visit;
- allow for any last minute changes to the schedule (e.g., unavailability of an Auditee and replacement, security briefing—if not already carried out, health and safety briefing—if not already carried out, etc.).

It sets the scene for the Assessment and is chaired by the Lead Assessor and any questions about what is to occur during the on-site Assessment should be resolved at this meeting.

The Forensic Laboratory should ensure that the Assessment Team are taken on a brief tour of the Forensic Laboratory in order to familiarize the Assessment Team with the facility and to introduce them to the relevant employees in their work environment, if appropriate.

A typical Opening Meeting Agenda is given in Chapter 4, Appendix 46.

19.2.16 Other Meetings

When appropriate, or when requested by the Forensic Laboratory or the Assessment Team, a meeting can be set up between the Assessment Team and the Forensic Laboratory nominated employee(s).

19.2.17 The Assessment

Following the Opening Meeting and tour, the Assessment Team will start the Assessment of the Forensic Laboratory.

The on-site Assessment is conducted at all Forensic Laboratory location(s) where work and testing is performed that is in scope, or if not, a representative sample of them.

Witnessing of the testing and sampling activities carried out by the Forensic Laboratory form the most important part of the Assessment. Although the Assessment should, as far as possible, make use of current work being performed, the AB may request the Forensic Laboratory to provide a demonstration of some activities that are not currently being performed, in order to cover the range of tests for which Accreditation is sought.

The Assessment Team will use checklists provided by the AB to ensure that there are consistent assessments across all forensic laboratories being assessed.

Typically, the Lead Assessor will examine the Forensic Laboratory's Management System and quality documentation with the Forensic Laboratory Quality Manager and any other appropriate employees, to verify that it meets the requirements of the Standard.

The Technical Assessors will proceed according to the agreed agenda and examine the Forensic Laboratory's

Management System in operation and the competence of the employees to perform specific activities. All components of the Management System involved will be assessed. This will typically involve the following:

- examination of the Management System in action;
- reviews of quality and technical records;
- examination of equipment and facilities;
- interviews with employees;
- observing demonstrations of testing and work performed;
- examination of tests and work performed.

They will determine whether the treatment of measurement uncertainty is in accordance with international criteria and the specific requirements of the AB. It may not always be necessary to examine every procedure in operation in the Forensic Laboratory because of the similarities between some activities; however, the Technical Assessors will verify the implementation of the working procedures listed in the Assessment Agenda.

They will typically ask to see the equipment involved, the manufacturer's manuals, validation of testing and establish the state of calibration of the equipment, where appropriate. They will examine documentation concerning working procedures and testing in progress and will review associated records and reports/Certificates.

During the Assessment of the Forensic Laboratory, the Technical Assessors will examine the processes for establishing traceability of measurements including any in-house calibrations and the results from participation in appropriate proficiency testing schemes and other quality control and quality assessment procedures. They will also assess procedures used to establish the validity of methods used, as defined in Chapter 7, Section 7.5.5.

As well as examining equipment and processes, the Technical Assessors will also assess the competence of the Forensic Laboratory employees performing the processes. The Technical Assessors will require access to Human Resources records for relevant Forensic Laboratory employees who routinely perform or affect the quality of the testing or calibration for which Accreditation is sought. This will typically include:

- resumes/CVs;
- job descriptions of key personnel;
- training plans and records;
- competency evaluations;
- proficiency evaluations.

The Forensic Laboratory must ensure that it only provides information relevant to the Scope of Accreditation and does not divulge information that may violate the individual employee's rights to privacy.

The objective of on-site Assessment is to establish, by observation and examination, whether the Forensic Laboratory's products and services meets the requirements of ISO 17025. Observations made will be based on objective evidence and will be recorded and verified with the relevant Forensic Laboratory employee.

19.2.18 Recording Assessment Findings

As the Assessment progresses, each Assessor will record their findings; these records provide objective evidence on which the Lead Assessor will base the recommendations for Accreditation to the AB. All AB's have forms for handwritten or electronically produced findings. Nonconformances are recorded on a Non-conformance Report or a CAR, and the contents of a typical CAR are given in Chapter 4, Appendix 45.

After the Assessment Team have completed their individual assignments, they meet to produce a coordinated view of the Forensic Laboratory's work. The Lead Assessor then compiles the Assessment Report form based on the findings recorded by the individual Assessors. All nonconformances will be graded and have objective evidence to support the finding. Different ABs use varying terms for grading of non-conformances and an example is defined in Chapter 4, Section 4.7.3.5, though different ABs may use different terminology.[1] Examples for each category are given in Appendix 3.

All Assessments will have a formal Assessment Report produced before the Closing Meeting, or a short while after the end of the Assessment if agreed with the Forensic Laboratory. The Assessment Report:

- will summarize the Assessors' findings;
- indicates key areas needing corrective or improvement action;
- contains the Lead Assessor's recommendations about Accreditation.

Typically, the recommendation may be for:

- an unconditional offer of Accreditation;
- a conditional offer (e.g., subject to the satisfactory clearance of non-conformances);
- a refusal for Accreditation.

In some cases, it may be appropriate to recommend that an offer of Accreditation be made for a reduced scope.

Report formats will vary between ABs, but a typical Assessment Report content is given in Chapter 4, Appendix 48.

The Assessment Report may be left with the Forensic Laboratory at the Closing Meeting or may be produced within a fixed time period after the end of the Assessment. This process varies between ABs and is often subject to

1. ILAC-G20:2002, Guidelines on Grading of Nonconformities gives details of the grading process.

agreement between the parties. In some cases, a provisional report is produced, and a final report is produced after closing out all of the non-conformances raised.

19.2.19 Factors Affecting the Recommendation

In deciding the recommendation for Accreditation, the Lead Assessor must take into account the extent of competence and conformance within the Forensic Laboratory to ISO 17025 found during the assessment.

If there are no non-conformances found, the Lead Assessor normally recommends that Accreditation be offered immediately to the Forensic Laboratory.

If there are some non-conformances found, the Lead Assessor normally recommends that Accreditation is offered subject to satisfactory action being taken by the Forensic Laboratory to address the non-conformances raised.

If there are one or more areas in which the extent of competence or conformance is not acceptable, but there are no overall major systems failures, the Lead Assessor may recommend Accreditation for an appropriately reduced Scope for the Forensic Laboratory.

If the number and seriousness of the non-conformances are such that the Forensic Laboratory's Management System and organization fail to demonstrate competence or conformance with the requirements of ISO 17025, the Lead Assessor's recommendation will be that Accreditation is refused and that the Forensic Laboratory would be advised to discuss future actions with the AB.

19.2.20 Closing Meeting

The Accreditation Assessment concludes with a Closing Meeting held by the Lead Assessor and the Assessment Team and relevant Forensic Laboratory employees.

The purpose of the Closing Meeting is to formally present the Assessment conclusions, including any documented non-conformities.

The Lead Assessor presents a summary of the results of the Assessment and informs the Forensic Laboratory Top Management of the recommendation that will be made to the AB regarding the granting of Accreditation.

The Lead Assessor chairs the Closing Meeting.

Depending on the ABs, an Assessment Report may be left with the Forensic Laboratory, otherwise the report will be sent within an agreed timescale to the Forensic Laboratory.

Whatever report is produced, it will list any non-conformances identified.

A typical Closing Meeting Agenda is given in Chapter 4, Appendix 47.

On return to their office, the Lead Assessor will submit the Assessment Report, with the recommendation for Accreditation to the AB.

19.2.21 Quality Assurance of the Assessment Report

The AB will undertake a quality review of the Assessment Report, including any non-conformities or comments documented by the Assessment Team.

The quality review of the Assessment Team's findings is an important element of the AB's internal quality control.

The purposes of the quality review include considering consistency of interpretations, appropriate relationships between the non-conformance(s) raised and the clause(s) to which the non-conformance is assigned, and to consider the recommended level assigned to each non-conformance raised by the Assessment Team.

If there are any changes to the Lead Auditor's recommendation already provided to the Forensic Laboratory, this is then notified to them with the justification for the revision.

19.2.22 Addressing Non-conformances

The Forensic Laboratory is informed of any non-conformances raised by the Assessment Team during the on-site Assessment, and these non-conformities are documented in the on-site Assessment Report.

The Forensic Laboratory must respond in writing to the AB within the specified period after the date of the on-site Assessment Report, addressing all documented non-conformances. A Corrective Action Plan must include a list of actions, target completion dates, and names of persons responsible for discharging those actions.

When creating the Corrective Action Plan, a forensic laboratory shall reference each non-conformance by the item number shown on the on-site Assessment Report. There is no set standard form for a Corrective Action Plan; in the Forensic Laboratory, Corrective Action Plans are derived from the formal audit response, as given in Appendix 2, and then have appropriate CAPAs raised as defined in Chapter 4, Section 4.8.

The Forensic Laboratory may ask for clarification of a non-conformance from either the Assessor (who raised it) at the Closing Meeting or that AB at any time after the Closing Meeting.

The Forensic Laboratory may also challenge the validity of a non-conformance by writing to the Lead Assessor at the AB.

Where non-conformities have been raised, they shall be satisfactorily resolved before Accreditation can be granted.

Should closeout take longer than the agreed time, the Forensic Laboratory may submit a revised Corrective Action Plan, providing evidence of resolved actions and a revised timescale for planned actions, if accepted by the AB. This process will be at the AB's discretion. Typical closeout periods are given in Appendix 4.

Where there are a substantial number of non-conformances raised, the AB may require an additional on-site Assessment, at additional cost to the Forensic Laboratory, prior to granting Accreditation.

19.2.23 The Accreditation Decision

Contrary to popular opinion, it is not the Lead Assessor that grants Accreditation status, but the AB, based on the recommendation of the Lead Assessor. The AB's Top Management are responsible for all Accreditation actions, including granting, renewing, suspending, and revoking any AB Accreditation.

The Accreditation decision is based on their review of information gathered during the Accreditation Assessment and a determination by the Lead Assessor as to whether, or not, all requirements for Accreditation have been fulfilled.

The evaluation process considers the Forensic Laboratory's record as a whole, including:

- information provided on the application;
- results of Management System documentation review;
- on-site Assessment Reports;
- actions taken by the Forensic Laboratory to correct non-conformances;
- results of proficiency testing, if required.

Based on this evaluation, the AB will determine whether or not the Forensic Laboratory should be Accredited. If the evaluation reveals non-conformances beyond those identified in the Assessment process, the AB shall inform the Forensic Laboratory in writing of the non-conformances. In this case, the Forensic Laboratory shall respond to the AB as if it were the outcome of the Assessment Report.

All non-conformances must be resolved to the AB's satisfaction before Accreditation can be granted.

Once the decision to grant Accreditation has been taken (whether in full or in reduced scope), the AB will advise the Forensic Laboratory in writing with the proposed Accreditation details. This will include the Scope of Accreditation and the Schedule. The Forensic Laboratory must formally agree, in writing, to this prior to the granting of Accreditation. Some ABs will use a "real" date for Accreditation renewal, and others may use a specified renewal date.

19.2.24 Accreditation Certificate

Once the Forensic Laboratory has been approved for Accreditation, it will typically receive a letter of granting of Accreditation and the Accreditation Certificate.

The Certificate will typically include:

- bear a unique Certificate number;
- identify the Forensic Laboratory and the address(es) to which the Scope of Accreditation refers;
- date when the Accreditation was granted;
- the date of expiration of Accreditation.

In addition to a Certificate of Accreditation, the Forensic Laboratory will receive a corresponding Scope of Accreditation document. The scope document will specify the discipline(s) and each category in which the Forensic Laboratory is accredited.

During the Assessment process, the assigned Lead Assessor will work with the Forensic Laboratory to appropriately identify the Scope of the Accreditation. Accreditation will be limited in each discipline to the categories of testing in which the Forensic Laboratory is working at the time of Assessment. Each category will be identified by the Forensic Laboratory, agreed to by the Lead Assessor, and agreed by the AB.

Although presented to the Forensic Laboratory, each Accreditation Certificate and Scope of Accreditation document remains the property of the AB. Failure to remain compliant with Accreditation standards could result in the revocation of Accreditation and the return of the Certificate to the AB.

Some ABs encourage the publicizing of Accreditations gained and actively supports a presentation ceremony with attendant media interest.

19.2.25 The Accreditation Cycle

To maintain ISO 17025 Accreditation, the Forensic Laboratory must comply with the AB's requirements for maintaining Accreditation, and this may vary between ABs.

Typically, Accreditation is granted for a renewable period defined by the AB provided that the Forensic Laboratory:

- continues to meet all applicable Management System standards;
- continues to meet all applicable AB requirements;
- submits to scheduled on-site Surveillance Assessments.

Once the Forensic Laboratory has achieved Accreditation, it is necessary for it to continue to meet the requirement of the standard(s) under which it was accredited for the duration of the Accreditation Cycle.

The Forensic Laboratory will be advised by its AB of the dates for planned Surveillance or Re-assessment Assessments. However, the AB will normally reserve the right to make an unannounced visit at any time.

19.2.26 Surveillance Visits

The AB will have an established and documented program for carrying out periodic surveillance activities and Surveillance Visits at sufficiently close intervals to ensure that the

Forensic Laboratory continues to comply with all Accreditation criteria.

The Forensic Laboratory will be subject to a cycle of Surveillance Visits, typically at yearly intervals, though the first one after initial Accreditation normally has a shorter interval, typically 6 months: this interval is shorter than other surveillance intervals to avoid a commonly occurring problem that, after the Initial Assessment, there is a decrease in quality awareness in the Forensic Laboratory. The second and subsequent Surveillance Visits will typically be on a 12-month cycle and certainly no longer than 18 months.

In deciding on the interval of the Surveillance Visits and related activities for the Forensic Laboratory, the AB may take into account the Forensic Laboratory's performance at previous Surveillance Visits. A minimum of three consecutive visits with good performance may lead to fewer Surveillance Visits in the future. Conversely, if the Forensic Laboratory's performance deteriorates, the frequency of surveillance activities (and visits) may be increased.

An AB may decide to conduct the Surveillance Visits without prior notice or with short notice only (less than 2 weeks) as a mechanism to lower the frequency of visits.

Surveillance Visits will include such activities as:

- enquiries from the AB to the Forensic Laboratory on aspects concerning its Accreditation;
- declarations by the Forensic Laboratory with respect to their operations;
- requests to the Forensic Laboratory to provide documents and records, including updates from quality manuals;
- assessing the Forensic Laboratory's performance;
- other means of monitoring the Forensic Laboratory's performance.

The purpose of a surveillance visit is to determine whether or not the Forensic Laboratory is continuing to fulfill the requirements for Accreditation.

At the Opening Meeting, the Lead Assessor will establish whether all significant changes in the Forensic Laboratory's status or operations have been notified to the AB and will confirm that there are no outstanding CAPAs from the previous visit.

If the surveillance visit reveals that there have been significant changes in the Forensic Laboratory's operations, e.g., to employees, equipment, or the range of services available, these matters shall be recorded by the Lead Assessor. Assessors shall check that the changes have not lessened the Forensic Laboratory's capabilities and that they have already been fully notified to the AB.

During a Surveillance Visit, the Assessors will not check the whole operational system, as they did on the Initial Assessment, but a representative sample so that the entire Forensic Laboratory is covered during the Accreditation Cycle. The scope of Surveillance Visits is planned based on the outcome of previous visits. The Lead Assessor will normally include an assessment of Management Review, Audits, and Complaint Records at each Surveillance Visit.

At the conclusion of a Surveillance Visit, the Lead Assessor will produce an Assessment Report and make a recommendation to the AB on the Forensic Laboratory's continuing Accreditation. Where a number of non-conformances are found and that the Forensic Laboratory is not able to demonstrate that it is conforming with the requirements of ISO 17025, then sanctions will be recommended.

19.2.27 Re-assessments

Unlike a Surveillance Visit, a re-assessment visit will involve a comprehensive re-examination of the Forensic Laboratory's Management System and testing activities and will be similar in format and detail to the Initial Assessment.

The AB will have a documented process for performing re-assessments, including the time interval between the Initial Assessment and Re-assessment and between Re-assessments.

This time period should not exceed 5 years, but different ABs may use shorter time periods. Shorter time periods are typically used if the AB does not perform Surveillance Visits, but just performs Re-assessments.

The process for undertaking the Initial Assessment is followed for Re-assessments.

At the end of the Re-assessment visit, the Lead Assessor (as with an Initial Assessment) will make a recommendation to the AB on the continuing Accreditation of the Forensic Laboratory.

Sanctions will be recommended where the number and seriousness of the non-conformances identified in the Forensic Laboratory's Management System indicate that it is not able to demonstrate that the requirements of ISO 17025 continue to be met.

19.2.28 Proficiency Testing

There are a number of different proficiency testing programs in place throughout the world. Some are Accredited and some are not, and each will have its own rules and specific requirements.

Proficiency testing is a component of the Surveillance process, but it cannot replace Surveillance Visits as it usually only covers a small part of the scope for which the Forensic Laboratory is Accredited, and therefore cannot reflect the overall performance of the Forensic Laboratory and its quality system.

As part of ISO 17025 Accreditation, the Forensic Laboratory is expected to select appropriate schemes and implement them.

In addition to this, inter-laboratory comparisons should be carried out, where appropriate. However, the Forensic Laboratory must ensure that they do not breach any Client Confidentiality agreements in this process.

19.2.29 Changes to the Scope

The Forensic Laboratory can request a change to its Scope of Accreditation. This can be to increase or decrease scope or temporarily suspend some part of the Accreditation.

Especially in the case of extensions of scope, the Forensic Laboratory should give advance warning to the AB of the intention to increase the scope. It is recommended that, on-cost grounds and minimizing business interruption, extension to the scope is assessed as part of the ongoing Surveillance or Re-assessment Visits.

The AB will have forms for this and will require specific documentation to be produced for extensions of scope.

Any extension to the Scope of Accreditation may require the AB to check to determine any additional technical expertise required for the visit that handles the scope extension.

If the change of scope is urgent, then the AB can arrange a special interim visit to address this issue.

All requests for changing scope must be made in writing to the AB.

19.2.30 Special Interim Assessments

If the AB receives any written claims or complaints creating doubts concerning the Forensic Laboratory's conformance with ISO 17025, then it will carry out surveillance activities (inquiries) or even a Special Interim Assessment as soon as possible after it becomes aware of the complaint. The required action, in this case, will be decided by the AB.

Where a Special Interim Assessment is undertaken, the scope of the Assessment will be determined by the AB, based on the nature of the concerns brought to their attention.

The Forensic Laboratory may be required to provide relevant documentation to the AB prior to their visit to the forensic laboratory. The findings of the Assessment Team will be reported to the Forensic Laboratory's Top Management, as normal and also to the AB for consideration.

The Forensic Laboratory Top Management shall be notified of any sanctions under consideration for the non-conformance and shall have the right to make representations in person at any subsequent meeting in which the Forensic Laboratory's alleged non-conformance is considered. The AB will decide what, if any, sanction will be imposed. Sanctions are defined in Section 19.2.33.

There may be some occasions when the Forensic Laboratory itself requests a Special Interim Assessment, reasons for this could include:

- extensions of scope not carried out at Surveillance Visit time;
- relocation to a new site;
- other management needs.

19.2.31 Conformance Records

The Forensic Laboratory must generate and maintain appropriate records of conformance with all applicable requirements of the Accreditation program throughout each Accreditation Cycle.

Once the Forensic Laboratory becomes Accredited, it must maintain records to demonstrate conformance with ISO 17025 requirements, as defined in Chapter 4, Section 4.6.4.

Record retention requirements are defined by the AB and ISO 17025 that ensure availability of records for Assessment purposes and the ability to dispose of out-of-date records. Legislative requirements of record retention must be met, as given in Chapter 4, Appendix 16.

19.2.32 Disclosure of Non-conformance

Once the Forensic Laboratory becomes Accredited, it is required to remain conformant to the requirements of the Accreditation program through each Accreditation Cycle.

The Forensic Laboratory is required to disclose to the AB all substantive occurrences of non-conformance within a defined period after determining that the non-conformance has occurred.

Disclosure of such occurrences must be in writing to the AB and must include a summary of the occurrence(s) and a statement of actions taken or being taken by the Forensic Laboratory to:

- determine the root cause of the non-conformance;
- determine who may have been impacted by the occurrence(s);
- notify those who are potentially impacted by the occurrence(s);
- appropriately correct and/or eliminate the cause of the occurrence(s).

Where a non-conformance occurs, it shall be handled using the Forensic Laboratory's Incident management procedures, as defined in Chapter 7, Section 7.4.1.

The AB may undertake a Special Interim Assessment to further investigate the non-conformances and/or impose sanctions as appropriate to the non-conformance.

19.2.33 Sanctions

Once Accreditation has been granted to the Forensic Laboratory, it is expected that it will consistently remain in conformance with the requirements under which it was

Accredited. The AB recognizes that unforeseen circumstances may cause the Forensic Laboratory to experience temporary non-conformance with some of the requirements.

When it is recognized that the Forensic Laboratory is experiencing, or has experienced, a period of non-conformance, it must take appropriate corrective action(s) to return to conformance.

Failure to take timely, appropriate and required corrective actions regarding non-conformance may result in any of the following sanctions:

- *probation* for a specified time during which the Forensic Laboratory must comply with specified requirements and/or conditions;
- *suspension* for a specified time during which the Forensic Laboratory must demonstrate that the problem has been remedied;
- *revocation* (*also called Withdrawal in some cases*) for a specified time during which the Forensic Laboratory must address any non-conformances and after which it must pass an Assessment prior to being reinstated.

If any of these sanctions are applied by the AB, the Forensic Laboratory will be advised as to their practical implications. This may include the prohibiting of displaying or advertising the AB's Logo or Accreditations Marks.

The AB will typically not require the Forensic Laboratory to return of its Accreditation Certificate or Scope of Accreditation/Schedule documents at this stage.

19.2.33.1 Appeal of Sanction

If the Forensic Laboratory's Accreditation status is classified by the AB as probationary, suspended, or revoked, they may appeal against the sanction imposed. Typically, this would be done by the Forensic Laboratory Top Management.

Written reasons for appeal must be filed with the AB within a set period of the decision to apply a sanction. Usually, the Forensic Laboratory Top Management will have the right to appear in person before the AB to make representations.

19.2.33.2 Removal of Sanction

Probation and suspension sanctions will be removed when the Forensic Laboratory can demonstrate to the satisfaction of the AB that the non-conformances which resulted in probation or suspension have been corrected.

This may require a Special Interim Assessment or other measures defined by the AB.

If the Forensic Laboratory has had its Accreditation revoked, it may need to reapply for Accreditation and resubmit to the entire Assessment and Accreditation process.

19.2.34 Voluntary Termination of Accreditation

The Forensic Laboratory may at any time terminate its ISO 17025 Accredited status by advising the AB in writing of their desire to do so.

When the AB receives the Forensic Laboratory's request for termination, it will:

- terminate their Accreditation;
- formally notify the Forensic Laboratory that its Accreditation has been terminated;
- instruct the Forensic Laboratory to return its Certificate and Scope of Accreditation;
- instruct the Forensic Laboratory to remove any related Accreditation logos or marks from any Forensic Laboratory material;
- remove the Forensic Laboratory from its register of Accredited Laboratories and address other tasks it is required to undertake to terminate the Accreditation.

If the Forensic Laboratory wishes to reapply for Accreditation, it will reapply as above.

19.2.35 Appeals

The Forensic Laboratory has the right to appeal at any time during any Assessment process. An appeal process is present in all ABs, and this process must be followed. This will vary between ABs.

19.2.36 Obligations of Accredited Laboratories

As a condition of Accreditation, the Forensic Laboratory shall inform the AB within a defined period of any significant changes relevant to the Forensic Laboratory's Accreditation, in any aspect of its status or operation relating to:

- its legal, commercial, ownership, or organizational status;
- the organization, top management, and key personnel;
- main policies;
- resources and premises;
- Scope of Accreditation;
- other such matters that may affect the ability of the Forensic Laboratory to fulfill requirements for Accreditation.

The Forensic Laboratory's obligations may also, depending on the AB, include:

- a commitment to continually fulfill the requirements for Accreditation within the Forensic Laboratory's Scope of Accreditation, including an agreement to adapt to changes in the requirements in accordance with schedules adopted by the AB;

- affording such accommodation and cooperation as necessary to enable the AB to verify fulfillment of requirements for Accreditation;
- providing access to information, documents, and records as necessary for inspections or Assessments and maintenance of Accreditation;
- where applicable, providing access to documents or other information that provides insight into the level of independence and impartiality of the Forensic Laboratory from any related body;
- arranging the witnessing of the Forensic Laboratory services when requested by the AB;
- claiming Accreditation only with respect to the scope for which the Forensic Laboratory has been granted Accreditation;
- not using its Accreditation in such a manner as to bring the AB into disrepute.

19.2.37 Obligations of the AB

The AB shall make publicly available information about the current status of the Accreditations that it has granted. This shall be maintained to ensure that it is correct and current. The following information shall be published:

- name and address of each Accredited organization;
- dates of granting Accreditation and expiry dates, as applicable;
- Scope of Accreditation.

The AB shall:

- provide the Accredited organizations with information about suitable ways to obtain traceability of measurement results in relation to the scope for which Accreditation is provided;
- provide information about international arrangements in which it is involved, where applicable;
- give due notice of any changes to its requirements for Accreditation. It shall take account of views expressed by interested parties before deciding on the precise form and effective date of the changes. Following a decision on, and publication of, the changed requirements, it shall verify that each of their Accredited organizations carry out any necessary adjustments.

19.2.38 Use of the AB's Logos and Marks

Every AB, as the owner of the Accreditation logos and marks that are intended for use by the AB's Accredited organizations, will have rules for their use. These will typically vary between different ABs, and compliance with the rules for use of the logos and marks is a requirement for the Forensic Laboratory's continued Accreditation. Failure to comply with these conditions may result in suspension or revocation of their Accreditation. These will typically include requirements such as:

- the ability to use the AB's logos and marks is granted to the Forensic Laboratory for the limited purpose of announcing their Accredited status, and for use on reports that describe only activities within the scope of their Accreditation;
- when the Forensic Laboratory has applied for Accreditation, but not yet achieved, it may make reference to its applicant status. At this time, the Forensic Laboratory shall not use the AB's logos or marks in a manner that implies Accreditation;
- the Forensic Laboratory shall have a policy and procedure for controlling the use of the AB's Logos and Marks, based on the requirements of the AB;
- the AB's logos and marks shall not be used in a manner that brings the AB into disrepute or misrepresents the Forensic Laboratory's Scope of Accreditation or Accredited status;
- when the AB's logos and marks are used to reference the Forensic Laboratory's Accredited status, they shall be used only in accordance with the AB's rules governing the use of their logo and mark, including and associated captions;
- the terms *certified* or *registered* shall not be used when referencing their AB Accreditation or conformance to ISO/IEC 17025 requirements. The correct term is *Accredited*;
- the Forensic Laboratory shall not use the AB's logo or mark in any way that the AB may consider misleading or unauthorized;
- the Forensic Laboratory must cease to use the AB's logo mark if they are under a sanction or have withdrawn from the AB's Accreditation scheme.

19.2.39 Misuse of the AB's Logo and Mark

19.2.39.1 By an Accredited Laboratory

Misuse of marks and logos may be identified when the Assessment Team performs one of the Assessments in the Accreditation Cycle.

If this is the case, then the circumstance of the misuse will be recorded in the Assessment Report, and the Lead Assessor shall advise the Forensic Laboratory of the misuse at the time of the Assessment, and this will be raised as a non-conformance, requiring corrective action to be taken.

Alternatively, the AB may receive correspondence about alleged logo or mark misuse. In this case, the AB shall investigate the allegation. If the AB determines that the Forensic Laboratory is misusing its logo or mark, it will take such action as it considers appropriate. This may include:

- requests for corrective action;
- suspension of Accreditation;
- revocation of Accreditation;
- legal action.

Continued or persistent mark or logo misuse may lead to permanent revocation of the Certificate.

19.2.39.2 By Non-clients

Alternatively, the AB may receive correspondence about alleged logo or mark misuse by a non-client. The AB shall investigate and take appropriate action; however, this will not include the sanctions possible if the alleged offender was one of their Accredited laboratories. Typical recourse will include direct resolution with the alleged offender.

If that fails, recourse to the appropriate bodies shall be undertaken (e.g., Legal action, etc.).

19.2.40 Other ABs

There are a number of other ABs that deal with Forensic Laboratory Accreditations, and these include:

- A2LA;
- ASCLD;
- Laboratory Accreditation Bureau (LAB).

All ABs will either adopt ISO 17025 as it stands or use it with their own local jurisdictional and other amendments. Specific requirements from these types of ABs must be sought for achieving the relevant Accreditation status.

19.3 CERTIFICATION FOR A FORENSIC LABORATORY

Note

In the Forensic Laboratory, all policies, procedure, forms, checklists and work instructions for both Accreditation and Certification are implemented in the IMS.

References are made to the IMS in this Chapter as it is assumed that all forensic laboratories will adopt this approach.

There are a number of different ISO Standards Certifications that the Forensic Laboratory can achieve, and the ones addressed in this book are those defined in Section 19.1.4.2.

Like Accreditation, the process of gaining Certification for any of these standards is broadly similar for any standard using any CAB throughout the world. However, different CABs may have different requirements based on their scopes or on the jurisdiction within which they operate.

This is a generic approach below.

19.3.1 Self-evaluation Prior to Application

While it may not be a mandatory requirement for Certification, it is a sensible approach to perform a self-assessment as preparation for the Certification process. This should determine whether the Forensic Laboratory's processes, procedures, and records meet the requirements of the Certification sought.

This may require the:

- purchase of a number of standards;
- completion of self-assessment forms for use prior to seeking Certification and undertake any identified CAPAs arising from the self-evaluation process.

The Forensic Laboratory may choose to undertake the self-assessment in-house or contract a third-party service provider to perform the task on their behalf.

19.3.2 Selecting a CAB

Once the required Certification(s) have been agreed, the Forensic Laboratory should:

1. research the market to see what CABs provide the required Certification services.
2. obtain marketing materials from each of the possible CABs to determine the range of services that they provide.
3. research other forensic laboratories and other organizations to determine the CABs that they have used and their opinion of the services provided.
4. create a shortlist of three possible CABs from whom to obtain quotations for the Certification(s) required.
5. if possible, a CAB that provides all of the required Certification Services required should be chosen. This will allow integrated Certification Audits to be carried out, with associated cost savings and a CAB who knows all aspects of the Forensic Laboratory's business.

Note

Where the Forensic Laboratory already has a relationship with a CAB, the first approach should be made to that CAB for additional services, if they can provide them. This will have the benefit of reduced costs for integrated audits and the fact that the CAB already "knows" their Client's business.

19.3.3 Certification Information to be Made Available

In order to assist in selection of a CAB, all CABs shall make publicly available, and update at adequate intervals, the following:

- a detailed description of the initial and continuing Certification activity, including the application, Initial

Audits, surveillance audits, and the process for granting, maintaining, reducing, extending, suspending, withdrawing Certification, and Recertification;
- the normative requirements for Certification;
- information about the fees for application, initial Certification, and continuing Certification;
- the CAB's requirements for prospective Clients:
  - to comply with Certification requirements;
  - to make all necessary arrangements for the conduct of the audits, including provision for examining documentation and the access to all processes and areas, records, and personnel for the purposes of initial Certification, surveillance, recertification, and resolution of complaints;
  - to make provisions, where applicable, to accommodate the presence of observers (e.g., Certification Auditors, Accreditation Service Observers, or Trainee Auditors).
- documents describing the rights and duties of Certified Clients, including requirements, when making reference to its Certification in communication of any kind in line with the CAB's Rules and Regulations for Logo and Mark Usage;
- information on procedures for handling complaints and appeals;
- a description of the rights and obligations of a CAB's Clients;
- information on the Clients that the CAB has accredited in a publicly available register.

From this information, an informed choice of CAB can be made by the Forensic Laboratory.

19.3.4 Appointing a CAB

Once the quotation(s) from the shortlist of CABs for the provision of Certification services have been received by the Forensic Laboratory with the range of services offered, the Forensic Laboratory is in the position to make an informed choice about the selection of an appropriate CAB.

19.3.5 Scope of Certification

The form and definition of the Scope of Certification will depend on the Certification sought by the Forensic Laboratory.

For ISO 27001, the scope must be defined as a minimum in terms of the following:

- assets in scope;
- organization;
- location(s);
- technology.

Other ISO Standards require the scope to be defined as a "boundary," but do not specifically set headings or requirements. They are more to define the boundary of the scope and it is up to the applicant (i.e., the Forensic Laboratory) to define the scope on their own words.

19.3.6 Application

The CAB requires the Forensic Laboratory's Authorized Representative to provide the necessary information to enable it to establish the following:

- the desired Scope of Certification;
- the Forensic Laboratory's general features, including:
  - its legal name;
  - the address(es) of its physical location(s) in the scope;
  - significant aspects of its process and operations;
  - any relevant legal obligations.
- general information, about the Forensic Laboratory relevant to its scope for Certification(s) being sought, including:
  - description of activities;
  - human resources;
  - technical resources;
  - information concerning all outsourced processes used by the Forensic Laboratory that may affect conformance to requirements of relevant standards.
- the standard(s) for which the Forensic Laboratory is seeking Certification;
- information concerning the use of consultancy relating to the Management System.

19.3.7 Fees for Certification

Fees will vary for each specific part of the Assessment between CABs in different jurisdictions and may even be for different standards.

Additionally, fees will normally change over time.

For this reason, no details of fees are given.

19.3.8 Processing Applications

Upon receipt of the Forensic Laboratory's application for Certification, the CAB will:

- log the application;
- acknowledge the receipt of the application in writing (typically e-mail these days) to the Forensic Laboratory;
- confirm payment of fees;
- review the Forensic Laboratory's application, to ensure that:
  - the application is complete;
  - correct fees are paid.

Note

Where the application is unclear or incomplete, the CAB shall request further clarification or documents until they are satisfied that the application is complete.

Additionally, the CAB will check to see that they have fully understood the Forensic Laboratory's requirements.

19.3.9 Assigning the Lead Assessor

Note

For all Management System Assessments, the application of ISO 19011—Guidelines for auditing Management Systems is used.

After reviewing the Forensic Laboratory's application and determining that it is complete, the CAB will assign a Lead Assessor to manage the application. (This is often also referred to as the Assessment Manager.) The Lead Assessor will typically have an understanding of forensic laboratories and their operations and will be able to discuss with the Forensic Laboratory's Authorized Representative any matters that may arise during the processing of the application.

Most CABs try to ensure that the Lead Assessor is responsible for processing the Forensic Laboratory's application through the Certification life cycle for at least the first full cycle.

The Lead Assessor will perform the Contract Review and is responsible for selecting and appointing the Assessment Team.

19.3.10 Review of the Application

Before proceeding with the Assessment, the Lead Assessor will review the application. This will check that the information supplied by the Forensic Laboratory and its Management System is sufficient for the conduct of the Assessment and that:

- the requirements for the Forensic Laboratory's Certification(s) are clearly defined and documented;
- any known difference in understanding between the CAB and the Forensic Laboratory is resolved;
- the CAB has the competence and ability to perform the required Certification activities;
- the Scope of Certification(s) sought, the location(s) of the applicant organization's operations, time required to complete Assessments, and any other issues influencing the Certification activities are taken into account (language, safety conditions, threats to impartiality, etc.);
- records of the justification for the decision to undertake the Assessment are maintained.

Based on this review, the CAB shall determine the competences it needs to include in its Assessment Team and for the Certification decision.

19.3.11 Appointing the Assessment Team

The Assessment Team comprises a Lead Assessor and as many Assessors or Experts as are necessary to provide the technical expertise adequately to assess the Forensic Laboratory's competence.

Technical Assessors and Experts are selected on the basis of their professional and academic achievements, experience in digital forensics, experience in the relevant standards and communications skills. They evaluate all information collected from the Forensic Laboratory and to conduct the Assessment at the Forensic Laboratory and any other sites where activities to be covered by the Scope of Certification are performed.

Assessors are assigned to conduct an on-site Assessment of the Forensic Laboratory on the basis of how well their experience matches requirements of the standards for which Certification is sought.

The Forensic Laboratory has the right to object to the appointment of any Assessor(s) or Expert(s) and, in such cases, the CAB will endeavor to offer an alternative. In the event that a suitable alternative cannot be identified, or the grounds for objection are considered to be unreasonable, the CAB will typically reserve the right to appoint the original Assessor(s) and Expert(s) to the Assessment Team.

19.3.12 Assessment Duration

As part of the Assessment Plan that the CAB sends to the Forensic Laboratory, the CAB will have to determine the time needed to complete the Forensic Laboratory's Assessment cycle. This is derived from consideration of:

- the requirements of the relevant Management System standard;
- the Forensic Laboratory's size and complexity;
- the technological and regulatory context in which the Forensic Laboratory operates;
- any outsourcing of any activities included in the scope of the Forensic Laboratory's Management System(s);
- the results of any prior assessments;
- number of sites and multi-site considerations, assuming that the Forensic Laboratory has more than one site in Scope of Certification.

In the case of ISO 27001, guidance is given in ISO 27006: Information technology—Security techniques—Requirements for bodies providing audit and Certification of Information Security Management Systems. ISO 27006 Annex C gives details of these time requirements that may be used.

Once the Assessment Plan has been defined, it must be sent to the Forensic Laboratory in advance of any Assessment so that the Forensic Laboratory can meet the requirements of the plan.

19.3.13 Optional Pre-assessment Visits

Note 1

While not a part of the formal assessment, the Forensic Laboratory can request a short pre-assessment visit if they choose. These visits are usually to review and discuss any specific concerns that the applicant may have. They are also called "Gap Analysis Assessments" by some CABs.

The pre-assessment visit is usually carried out by the Lead Assessor (accompanied by one or more Assessors where appropriate) and is usually completed in 1 day.

The pre-assessment visit allows discussion with the Forensic Laboratory's Top Management on the extent to which the Forensic Laboratory's Management Systems appear to fulfill the requirements for Certification to the relevant standard(s).

In ISO 27001, it could be used for ensuring that the ISMS is appropriate, prior to undertaking a full Document Review. (Stage 1 audit). ISO management standards can also use pre-assessment visits as a "gap analysis" of their current processes.

As well as examining the documented Management System(s) prepared by the Forensic Laboratory, the Assessment Team will usually take the opportunity to discuss the proposed Scope of Certification and to carry out a brief examination of the Forensic Laboratory's facilities.

During the pre-assessment visit, the Assessment Team may raise non-conformances where they any areas that appear to require attention in order to fulfill the requirements for Certification.

The Forensic Laboratory will be reminded that the pre-assessment visit is not a full Assessment and will be advised of the structure and scope of the Stage 1 Assessment visit.

At the end of the pre-assessment visit, the Assessment Team will make a report of their visit and its findings, including any non-conformances, to the CAB. The report should indicate:

- whether a further pre-assessment visit is recommended;
- whether plans for the Stage 1 Assessment for the Forensic Laboratory can proceed;
- specific reasons why plans cannot proceed.

A copy of the report of the pre-assessment visit will be passed on to the Forensic Laboratory, and this is usually in the standard form for Stage 1 and Stage 2 Audits, as given in Chapter 4, Appendix 48. At the same time, the Assessment Team will discuss timescales for the Stage 1 Assessment visit and may provisionally agree dates for it.

Typically, just after the pre-assessment visit, the Lead Assessor will determine:

- the composition of the full Assessment Team;
- the effort (in man days) required for the Stage 1 Assessment visit including time for preparation and standard post-visit activities.

This will take into account all factors necessary to enable a reliable Assessment of the Forensic Laboratory's competence to perform the full range of activities proposed for inclusion in its Scope of Certification, including:

- whether it is necessary to assess all activities, or if a representative sample can be selected;
- the need to assess all key activities;
- handling of multi-site locations, where necessary, to ensure that all key activities are assessed.

Pre-assessment visits are strictly prohibited from performing any consultancy services. This includes giving any advice on selecting any CAPAs but can include discussing the appropriateness and sufficiency of a proposed CAPA.

19.3.14 Scheduling the Stage 1 Assessment

Once any outstanding CAPAs from the pre-assessment visit (if raised and the visit has taken place) have been closed out, the Forensic Laboratory is ready, and able, to proceed to the Stage 1 Assessment.

If a date has been provisionally agreed and it is still feasible, then this date will be confirmed, if it is not, another mutually agreed date will be confirmed. If the scheduled date needs to be changed for any reason by the Forensic Laboratory, then it shall contact the CAB and request an alternate date. The Forensic Laboratory is responsible for any costs associated with the date change.

The Stage 1 Assessment can take place off-site or on-site.

A Stage 1 Assessment usually takes between 1 and 5 days, and this will depend on the:

- size of the Forensic Laboratory being assessed;
- Scope of Certification;
- number of standards against which Certification is sought.

Every effort is made to conduct all Assessments with as little disruption as possible to the Forensic Laboratory's normal operations.

A detailed visit plan will be prepared indicating the section/activities/location(s) to be assessed by each Assessor, and specify the activities that each Assessor must witness during the visit.

Copies of the visit plan to the Forensic Laboratory will be distributed to the Forensic Laboratory and to all of the Assessment Team, allowing all parties to raise any issues with the visit plan.

The Stage 1 Assessment visit will not be scheduled until all outstanding non-conformances have been addressed.

19.3.15 Logistics of the Stage 1 Assessment

Once the Assessment Team has been appointed and the date of the Assessment visit agreed, the logistics of planning the visit must be undertaken.

Typically, a CAB makes its own travel and accommodation arrangements, but assistance from the Forensic Laboratory may be required.

In addition to having the operations defined in the Scope of Certification ready for the Assessment, the Forensic Laboratory will have to arrange:

- a secure room or working area for the Assessment Team;
- all employees on the agenda for assessment to be available, or their alternates;
- refreshments, including lunch;
- one or more "Guides" appointed to ensure that the Assessment Team can get to the right places in the Forensic Laboratory at the right time and facilitate any requests for information.

Prior to arrival on-site, any other specific needs will be advised to the Forensic Laboratory.

Where the Stage 1 Assessment is to be carried out at the CAB's offices, the logistics will be much simpler.

19.3.16 Opening Meeting

At the beginning of all Assessments, an Opening Meeting is conducted. This is attended by the Assessment Team and relevant Top Management from the Forensic Laboratory.

This meeting is held at the start of the Assessment to:

- enable the Assessment Team and the Forensic Laboratory's Top Management and nominated representatives to become acquainted;
- to confirm the purpose of the Assessment;
- to remind the Forensic Laboratory of what is expected during the assessment;
- confirm Guides for the duration of the visit;
- allow for any last minute changes to the schedule (e.g., unavailability of an Auditee and replacement, security briefing—if not already carried out, health and safety briefing—if not already carried out, etc.).

It sets the scene for the Assessment and is chaired by the Lead Assessor and any questions about what is to occur during the on-site Assessment should be resolved at this meeting.

The Forensic Laboratory should ensure that the Assessment Team are taken on a brief tour of the forensic-laboratory in order to familiarize the Assessment Team with the facility and to introduce them to the Forensic Laboratory employees.

A typical Opening Meeting Agenda is given in Chapter 4, Appendix 46.

19.3.17 Other Meetings

When appropriate, or when requested by the Forensic Laboratory, a meeting can be set up between the Assessment Team and the Forensic Laboratory nominated employees.

19.3.18 Stage 1 Assessment

Note

These are often referred to as Documentation or Initial Audits.

The process for carrying out a Stage 1 Assessment should be consistent across all CABs. Its purpose is to:

- assess the Forensic Laboratory's IMS documentation;
- evaluate the Forensic Laboratory's location and site-specific conditions and to undertake discussions with their authorized employees to determine their preparedness for the Stage 2 Assessment;
- review the Forensic Laboratory's status and understanding regarding requirements of the standard(s) for which Certification is sought, in particular, with respect to the identification of key performance or significant aspects, processes, objectives, and operation of the Forensic Laboratory's IMS;
- collect necessary information regarding the Forensic Laboratory's Scope of the IMS, processes, and location(s), with related statutory and regulatory aspects and compliance requirements (e.g., quality, environmental, legal, associated risks, etc.);
- review the allocation of resources for the Stage 2 Assessment and agree with the Forensic Laboratory about the details of the Stage 2 Assessment;
- provide a focus for planning the Stage 2 Assessment by gaining a sufficient understanding of the Forensic Laboratory's IMS and on-site operations in the context of possible significant aspects;
- evaluate whether the Internal Audits and Management Review are being planned and performed, and that the level of implementation of the IMS substantiates that the Forensic Laboratory is ready for the Stage 2 Assessment.

19.3.19 Recording Stage 1 Assessment Findings

As the Assessment progresses, each Assessor, assuming that there are more than one for the Stage 1 Assessment, will record their findings, and these records provide objective evidence on which the Lead Assessor will base the recommendations for Certification to the CAB. Report formats will vary between CABs, but a typical Assessment Report content is given in Chapter 4, Appendix 48.

After the Assessment Team has completed their individual assignments, they meet to produce a coordinated view of the Forensic Laboratory's work. The Lead Assessor then compiles the Assessment Report form based on the findings recorded by the individual Assessors. All non-conformances will be graded and have objective evidence to support the finding. Different CABs use varying terms for grading of non-conformances and an example is defined in Chapter 4, Section 4.7.3.5, though different CABs may use different terminology. Examples for each category are given in Appendix 3.

All Assessments will have a formal Assessment Report produced before the Closing Meeting or a short while after the end of the Assessment if agreed with the Forensic Laboratory. The Assessment Report:

- will summarize the Assessors' findings;
- indicate key areas needing corrective or improvement action;
- contain the Lead Assessor's recommendations about Certification.

The Assessment Report may be left with the Forensic Laboratory at the Closing Meeting or may be produced within a fixed time period after the end of the Assessment. This process varies between CABs and is often subject to agreement between the parties. In some cases, a provisional report is produced, and a final report is produced after closing out all of the non-conformances raised.

19.3.20 Joint Assessments

Where the Forensic Laboratory is seeking more than one Certification or wishes to add an additional one to those that they already have, they can, if the CAB agrees, combine Assessments for more than one Management System.

Where more than one Management System is to undergo Certification, it may be that the Stage 1 and Stage 2 Assessments can be combined as well as for the Surveillance or Triennial Review Assessments.

Joint Assessments will require more planning and logistical support unless a single Assessor is carrying out the Joint Assessment.

19.3.21 Factors Affecting the Recommendation for a Stage 2 Assessment

In deciding the recommendation for progressing to Stage 2 Assessment, the Lead Assessor must take into account the extent of competence and conformance within the Forensic Laboratory to the standard(s) against which they are seeking Certification.

Where there are some Major non-conformances found, the Lead Assessor normally recommends that progress to a Stage 2 Assessment is delayed until the Major non-conformances are addressed. Any agreed CAPAs to address any non-conformances raised at the Stage 1 Assessment will be automatically reviewed and checked during the Stage 2 Assessment.

19.3.22 Closing Meeting

The Stage 1 Assessment concludes with a Closing Meeting held by the Lead Assessor and the Assessment Team and relevant Forensic Laboratory Top Management and employees.

The purpose of the Closing Meeting is to formally present the assessment conclusions, including any documented non-conformities.

The Lead Assessor presents a summary of the results of the Assessment and informs the Forensic Laboratory Top Management of the recommendation that will be made to the CAB.

Depending on the CABs, an Assessment Report may be left with the Forensic Laboratory, otherwise, the report will be sent within an agreed timescale to the Forensic Laboratory.

Whatever report is produced, it will list any nonconformances identified.

A typical Closing Meeting Agenda is given in Chapter 4, Appendix 47.

Immediately after the Closing Meeting, the Lead Assessor will submit the Assessment Report to the CAB, with the recommendation for either progressing to a Stage 2 Assessment or delaying it until all outstanding non-conformances are closed out.

19.3.23 Quality Assurance of the Assessment Report

The CAB will undertake a quality review of all Assessment Reports, including any non-conformities or comments documented by the Assessment Team.

The quality review of the Assessment Team's findings is an important element of the CAB's internal quality control.

The purposes of the quality review include considering consistency of interpretations, appropriate relationships between the non-conformance(s) raised and the clause(s) to which the non-conformance is assigned, and to consider the recommended level assigned to each non-conformance raised by the Assessment Team.

If there are any changes to the Lead Auditor's recommendation already provided to the Forensic Laboratory, this is then notified to the forensic laboratory along with the justification for the revision.

19.3.24 Addressing Non-conformances

The Forensic Laboratory is informed of any non-conformities raised by the Assessment Team during the Stage 1 Assessment, and these non-conformances are documented in the Stage 1 Assessment Report.

The Forensic Laboratory must respond in writing to the CAB within the specified period after the date of the Stage 1 Assessment Report, addressing all documented non-conformances. A Corrective Action Plan must include a list of actions, target completion dates, and names of persons responsible for discharging those actions.

A typical response for an Assessment Report is given in Appendix 2.

When creating the Corrective Action Plan, the forensic laboratory shall reference each non-conformance by the item number shown on the on-site Stage 1 Assessment Report. There is no set standard form for a Corrective Action Plan; in the Forensic Laboratory, Corrective Action Plans are derived from the formal audit response, as given in Appendix 2, and then have appropriate CAPAs raised as defined in Chapter 4, Section 4.8.

The Forensic Laboratory may ask for clarification of a non-conformance from either the Assessor (who raised it) at the Closing Meeting or the CAB at any time after the Closing Meeting.

The Forensic Laboratory may also challenge the validity of a non-conformance by writing to the Lead Assessor at the CAB.

The Forensic Laboratory must analyze the cause of the non-conformances and describe the specific correction and corrective actions taken, or planned to be taken, to eliminate detected non-conformities, within a defined time.

The Forensic Laboratory must submit their corrections and corrective actions to the CAB for review and to determine if they are acceptable.

Should closeout take longer than the agreed time, the Forensic Laboratory may submit a revised Corrective Action Plan, providing evidence of resolved actions and a revised timescale for planned actions, if accepted by the CAB. This process will be at the CAB's discretion. Typical closeout periods are given in Appendix 4.

Depending on the number and seriousness of the non-conformances raised, the CAB may require them to:

- undergo an additional full Assessment;
- undergo an additional limited Assessment;
- provide documented evidence (to be confirmed during future surveillance audits).

To verify effective correction and corrective actions.

19.3.25 Scheduling the Stage 2 Assessment

Once any outstanding CAPAs from the Stage 1 Assessment visit have been closed out, the Forensic Laboratory is ready, and able, to proceed to the Stage 2 Assessment.

If a date has been provisionally agreed and it is still feasible, then this date will be confirmed, if it is not, another mutually agreed date will be confirmed. If the scheduled date needs to be changed for any reason by the Forensic Laboratory, then it shall contact the CAB and request an alternate date. The Forensic Laboratory is responsible for any costs associated with the date change.

The Stage 2 must take place on-site.

A Stage 2 Assessment usually takes between 1 and 5 days, and this will depend on the:

- size of the Forensic Laboratory being assessed;
- Scope of Certification;
- number of standards against which Certification is sought.

Every effort is made to conduct all Assessments with as little disruption as possible to the Forensic Laboratory's normal operations.

A detailed visit plan will be prepared indicating the section/activities/location(s) to be assessed by each Assessor and specify the activities that each Assessor must witness during the visit.

Copies of the visit plan to the Forensic Laboratory will be distributed to the Forensic Laboratory and to all of the Assessment Team, allowing all parties to raise any issues with the visit plan.

The Stage 2 Assessment Visit will not be scheduled until all outstanding non-conformances have been addressed from the Stage 1 Assessment.

19.3.26 Logistics of the Stage 2 Assessment

These will be similar to those from the Stage 1 Assessment.

19.3.27 Opening Meeting

The Opening Meeting will be similar to that from the Stage 1 Assessment.

19.3.28 Stage 2 Assessment

> **Note**
>
> These are often referred to as Certification or Registration Assessments.

The purpose of a Stage 2 Assessment is to evaluate the implementation, including effectiveness, of the Forensic Laboratory's IMS and the relevant Management System(s) for which Certification is being sought.

While the Stage 1 Assessment may take place at the Forensic Laboratory, or remotely, the Stage 2 Assessment must take place at the Forensic Laboratory. The Stage 2

Assessment will include, but not be limited to, the following:

- information and evidence about conformance to all requirements of the applicable Management System Standard or other normative document;
- performance monitoring, measuring, reporting, and reviewing against key performance objectives and targets (consistent with the expectations in the applicable Management System Standard or other normative document);
- the Forensic Laboratory's Management System(s) and performance as regard legal compliance;
- operational control of the Forensic Laboratory's processes;
- internal audits undertaken, their results, and how any non-conformances raised were addressed;
- the results of the Management Review(s) of the Management Systems implemented;
- management responsibility for the Forensic Laboratory's implemented policies;
- the links between the normative requirements, policy, performance objectives and targets (consistent with the expectations in the applicable Management System Standard or other normative document), any applicable legislative requirements, responsibilities, competence of personnel, operations, procedures.

19.3.29 Recording Stage 2 Assessment Findings

These will be similar to those from the Stage 1 Assessment.

19.3.30 Factors Affecting the Recommendation

In deciding the recommendation for Certification, the Lead Assessor must take into account the extent of competence and conformance within the Forensic Laboratory of the implementation of the Management System(s) to the standards to which Certification is sought. This will involve:

- analysis of all information and objective evidence gathered during the Stage 1 and Stage 2 Assessments;
- reviewing of all of the findings;
- agreeing on the audit conclusions.

If there are no non-conformances found, the Lead Assessor normally recommends that Certification is offered immediately.

If there are Major non-conformances found, the Lead Assessor normally recommends that Certification is delayed until all non-conformances are addressed.

If a small number of Minor non-conformances are found, the Lead Assessor may recommend Certification after the Corrective Action Plan has been agreed.

19.3.31 Closing Meeting

The Closing Meeting will be similar to that from the Stage 1 Assessment; however, the conclusion will be about the recommendation for Certification, rather than proceeding to the Stage 2 Assessment.

19.3.32 Quality Assurance of the Assessment Report

The quality assurance process for a Stage 2 Assessment report is the same as the Stage 1 process.

19.3.33 Addressing Non-conformances

Non-conformances raised at the Stage 2 Assessment shall be dealt with in the same way as those raised at the Stage 1 Assessment.

However, failure to close them out may affect the granting of Certification for the relevant Management System Standard.

19.3.34 Granting Initial Certification

When the Lead Assessor makes a recommendation for Certification for a Management System Standard, the following information, as a minimum, must be sent to the CAB to enable the Certification decision to be made:

- the Assessment Reports;
- comments on the non-conformances raised and, where applicable, the correction and corrective actions taken by the Forensic Laboratory;
- confirmation of the information provided by the Forensic Laboratory to the CAB in support of its application for Certification;
- a recommendation whether or not to grant Certification, together with any conditions or Observations.

The CAB shall make the Certification decision on the basis of an evaluation of the Assessment findings and conclusions and any other relevant information that is appropriate.

19.3.35 Confidentiality of the Assessment Process

CABs require all participants in the Assessment and Certification process to recognize and respect the confidentiality of information relating to the Forensic Laboratory.

CABs use non-disclosure agreements or confidentiality agreements, either stand-alone or as part of the engagement contract, to ensure confidentiality of the Forensic Laboratory's information. Assessors do not take documentation belonging to the Forensic Laboratory off-site, unless they are performing an off-site Document Review.

19.3.36 Certification Certificates

Once the CAB has granted Certification status, the Forensic Laboratory will be issued with the Certificate for the appropriate Certifications.

The Certificate shows the Standard to which it applies, the name of the applicant, the defined Scope of Certification, the issue, and the expiry dates.

The defined Scope Statement is usually agreed between the Lead Assessor and the applicant as part of the Assessment process.

19.3.37 Obligations of Certified Organizations

While the obligations differ between CABs, they may have slightly differing obligations. A typical set of these is:

- a duty to inform the CAB of changes in circumstances—the Forensic Laboratory must inform the CAB immediately in writing of any changes that may occur to the Forensic Laboratory's circumstances that are reasonably likely to affect the compliance of the Forensic Laboratory's Management System to the standard used for their Certification;
- to make no misleading statements—the Forensic Laboratory's may not make any misleading statement concerning their application for, or achievement of, Certification to anyone. This will include the statements that they make in their advertising brochures (whether used for internal or external use);
- to ensure that no harm is caused to the CAB's name—the Forensic Laboratory may not say or do anything that could be reasonably believed to have the effect of harming the CAB's name or putting them into ill repute. This includes anything that may cause any person to question the authenticity or merit of the Forensic Laboratory's Certification;
- to fulfill all of the obligations for gaining and maintaining Certified status;
- to assist in the assessment process by providing the appropriate resources (i.e., all records, documentation, work areas, and personnel relevant to the Scope of Certification). The information provided must be in sufficient detail to enable the Lead Assessor to draw reasonable conclusions from it;
- the Certification Certificate and the relevant Certification Mark(s) may be displayed, but this must be done in compliance with the contractual terms agreed;
- to promptly pay fees due.

19.3.38 Postassessment Evaluation

All CABs seek feedback from those undergoing Assessment for Certification as to the effectiveness and performance of their staff during the Assessment process.

Evaluations can be formal and completed on-line or on paper, or informally as an unsolicited e-mail or other communication.

These are important Quality Objectives or Key Performance Indicators and provide invaluable feedback on services offered and possible problem areas or opportunities for improvement.

19.3.39 Certification Cycle

Management System Certification is granted for a period of 3 years provided that the Forensic Laboratory:

- continues to meet all applicable Management System standards;
- continues to meet all applicable CAB requirements;
- submits to scheduled on-site Surveillance Assessments and Triennial Assessments.

Note

The Forensic Laboratory does not need to submit a new application for Certification, and the Triennial Assessment is a continuation of the surveillance cycle. The dates and timing of the Triennial Assessment will be agreed with the Forensic Laboratory at the Surveillance Assessment immediately prior to the Triennial Assessment.

19.3.40 Extending the Scope of Certification

Where the Forensic Laboratory wants to extend the scope of its Management System Certification, it will discuss this with its CAB.

The scope extension may be incorporated into the next Surveillance Assessment if the scope extension has a minor impact on the current Certification. If the change has a significant impact, then a visit with an additional Surveillance Assessment may be required. This will depend on the CAB's specific requirements.

19.3.41 Surveillance Activities

There are two main Assessment processes for monitoring conformance in Management Systems. These are:

- Surveillance Assessments;
- Triennial Assessments.

19.3.41.1 Surveillance Assessments

Details and dates for Surveillance Assessments are agreed at the Assessment prior to the Surveillance Assessment itself. An agenda is sent to the Forensic Laboratory prior to the Assessment and agreed.

Surveillance Assessments can be regarded as Interim Assessments and are part of the required Certification cycle and are typically carried out during:

- year 1—Surveillance Assessment;
- year 2—Surveillance Assessment;
- year 3—Re-certification—called the Triennial Assessment (on or about the third anniversary of the granting of the first Certificate).

However, different CABs may use different time periods between successive Assessments, but they are conducted at least once a year.

It may also be that the first Assessment is closer to the Stage 2 Assessment than a year. This typically happens if the Forensic Laboratory was regarded as a high-risk applicant or had a number of Minor Non-conformances that needed proof of being satisfactorily closed out. Surveillance Assessments are on-site Assessments, but not necessarily full assessments of the Forensic Laboratory's Scope of Certification.

During a Surveillance Assessment, the following, as a minimum, are evaluated:

- continued conformance with the mandatory controls in the relevant standard;
- results of internal audits and the Management Review;
- a review of actions taken on non-conformances identified during any previous audits or assessments;
- the treatment of complaints;
- the effectiveness of the Management System(s) with regard to achieving the Forensic Laboratory's objectives;
- the progress of planned activities aimed at continual improvement;
- continuing operational control;
- the use of marks, logos, and/or any other reference to Certification;
- a selection of other controls in the relevant standard;
- any changes in the Forensic Laboratory's organizational infrastructure or working practices;
- where the Forensic Laboratory has more than one site, ensure that all sites are visited at least once in the Assessment cycle, if possible.

As with Stage 1 and Stage 2 Assessments, each assessment will have an agenda prepared and agreed prior to the Assessment.

The Assessment, reporting and raising of non-conformances is carried out in the same manner as a Stage 2 Assessment.

19.3.41.2 Triennial Assessment

The Triennial Assessment is a full Conformance Assessment performed at the end of the 3-year Assessment Cycle. The duration is typically shorter than the Stage 2 Assessment as there should be fewer non-conformances found as the Forensic Laboratory has been subjected to the previous 3 years worth of Assessments in the Assessment Cycle and the Certification Body has now "known" the Forensic Laboratory for 3 years.

The Triennial Assessment shall cover the following:

- changes in working practice or technology since the last audit (to determine whether relevant controls are in place and effective);
- the effectiveness of the Management System(s) in its entirety in the light of internal and external changes and its continued relevance and applicability to the Scope of Certification;
- the demonstrated Top Management commitment to maintain the effectiveness and improvement of the Management System(s) in order to enhance overall performance;
- whether the operation of the Certified Management System(s) contributes to the achievement of the Forensic Laboratory's policy and objectives;
- any outstanding CAPAs;
- all mandatory controls;
- any controls in the standard that have not yet been covered in the 3-year Assessment cycle;
- any sites in the Scope of Certification that have not been covered within the 3-year Assessment cycle, if appropriate and practical.

As with Stage 1 and Stage 2 Assessments, each assessment will have an agenda prepared and agreed prior to the Assessment.

Additionally at the Triennial Assessment, the Lead Assessor shall consider the following in determining the outcome of the Triennial Assessment:

- number of non-conformances over the last 3 years;
- repeated occurrences of non-conformances against the same controls in the relevant standard;
- failures to implement adequate and effective countermeasures against any non-conformance(s) raised in a timely manner.

The Assessment, reporting and raising of nonconformances is carried out in the same manner as a Stage 2 Assessment.

19.3.42 Maintaining Certification

The CAB shall maintain the Forensic Laboratory's Certification based on demonstration that it continues to satisfy the requirements of the relevant Management System standards. It will maintain the Forensic Laboratory's Certification(s) based on a positive conclusion by the Lead Assessor following assessment.

19.3.43 Joint Assessments

It is possible to undertake joint assessments, where more than one standard is assessed at either the Surveillance Assessment or the Triennial Audit in the same manner as a joint Assessment for Stage 1 or Stage 2 Assessment.

19.3.44 Other Means of Monitoring Performance

A CAB retains the right to monitor the Forensic Laboratory's ongoing performance through all other reasonable means available to them. In addition to on-site Assessments, the following surveillance activities may include:

- enquiries from the CAB to the Forensic Laboratory on any aspects of Certification;
- reviewing any of the Forensic Laboratory's statements with respect to its operations (e.g., promotional material, Web site);
- requests to the Forensic Laboratory to provide documents and records (on paper or electronic media);
- investigation of any complaints received;
- other means of monitoring the Forensic Laboratory's performance.

19.3.45 Sanctions

Where the Forensic Laboratory fails to meet the requirements of ongoing Certification, the CAB will require corrective action to be taken to address the non-conformance. Where the Forensic Laboratory does not take appropriate timely action or fails to take appropriate action to meet their Certification obligations, a number of sanctions can be imposed, these include:

19.3.45.1 Suspension of a Certificate

The Forensic Laboratory's Certificate should be suspended if they:

- advise the CAB of significant changes to the organization that render the existing Certificate invalid;
- fail to take corrective action in a specific period;
- if the Certificate, the CAB trade mark, or Certification mark is misused;
- do not meet its obligations to the Certification Body.

The reasons for suspending the Certificate must be recorded, advised to the Forensic Laboratory in writing.

The Forensic Laboratory's name must be removed from any lists of Certified organizations that the CAB holds or lists maintained by a third party based on the granting of a Certificate.

The CAB must be satisfied that the Forensic Laboratory is complying with all the requirements of Certification prior to re-awarding (or un-suspending) the Certificate.

When the Forensic Laboratory has complied with the requirements of the Certification process and the Certificate is re-awarded, the re-awarding of the Certificate must be transmitted to all relevant stakeholders.

19.3.45.2 Withdrawal of Certificates

The Forensic Laboratory's Certificate should be withdrawn if:

- they, after suspension, have taken no, or insufficient, corrective action within the required period;
- persistent misuse of the Certification or Registration Mark(s);
- breach of the CAB's Regulations (e.g., refusal to permit the CAB to perform its duties);
- breach of other CAB requirements.

The reasons for withdrawing the Certificate must be recorded and advised to the Forensic Laboratory in writing.

The Forensic Laboratory's name must be removed from any lists of Certified organizations that the CAB holds or lists maintained by a third party based on the granting of a Certificate.

The CAB must be satisfied that the Forensic Laboratory is complying with all the requirements of Certification prior to re-awarding (or unsuspending) the Certificate.

When the Forensic Laboratory has complied with the requirements of the Certification process and the Certificate is re-awarded, the re-awarding of the Certificate must be transmitted to all relevant stakeholders.

19.3.45.3 Canceling the Certificate

The Forensic Laboratory's Certificate should be canceled if they:

- terminate their business arrangement with the CAB.

The reasons for canceling the Certificate must be recorded and advised to the Forensic Laboratory in writing.

The Forensic Laboratory's name must be removed from any lists of Certified organizations that the CAB holds or lists maintained by a third party based on the granting of a Certificate.

19.3.46 Appeals and Complaints

Differing CABs will all have slightly different appeals and complaints processes, but the generic process is that:

- appeals and complaints are usually made to the normal contact (e.g., the Certification Manager). Once an appeal or a complaint is received, the internal procedures for the CAB are used.

19.3.47 Obligations of the CAB

The CAB shall maintain and make publicly accessible, or provide upon request, information describing its audit processes and Certification processes for granting, maintaining, extending, renewing, reducing, suspending, or withdrawing Certification, and about the Certification activities, types of Management Systems, and geographical areas in which it operates. This information must be accurate and not misleading.

In addition, it shall make publicly accessible information about suspended, withdrawn, or canceled Certificates, as well as validating any Certificate, on request.

Where there is a change in the requirement for Certification, the CAB shall advise the Forensic Laboratory of the change and verify that the Forensic Laboratory complies with any new requirements.

19.3.48 The Forensic Laboratory's Obligations

The Forensic Laboratory will have a contractually enforceable arrangement to ensure that it advises the CAB of any matters that may affect its capability to fulfill the requirements of any standards to which it is Certified. This may include, but not be limited to, changes in:

- the legal, commercial, organizational status, or ownership;
- organization and management (e.g., key managerial, decision making, or technical staff);
- contact address and sites;
- scope of operations under the certified Management System;
- major changes to the Management System and processes.

19.3.49 Use of the CAB's Logos and Marks

The rules governing the use of a CAB's logos and marks are similar to those of an AB, which are covered earlier.

APPENDIX 1 - TYPICAL CONDITIONS OF ACCREDITATION

To gain and maintain Accreditation, the Forensic Laboratory shall agree in writing to comply with the ABs conditions for Accreditation.

The Forensic Laboratory's Authorized Representative, when signing the application forms, will attest that the information in the application is correct and to commit the Forensic Laboratory to fulfill the conditions for gaining and maintaining Accreditation, which will typically include:

- complying at all times with the AB's requirements for Accreditation as defined in the relevant technical documents, terms and conditions, and contractual requirements for Accreditation;
- fulfilling the Accreditation procedure, especially to:
  - receiving and assisting the Assessment Team in their duty;
  - paying the fees due to the AB whatever the result of the Assessment may be, and to accept and pay the charges relating to the process of maintaining the Forensic Laboratory's Accreditation;
  - participating in proficiency testing, as required;
  - following the Rules and Regulations for AB logo use and for referencing Accreditation status;
  - resolving all non-conformances in a timely manner.
- reporting to the AB within the specified time period of any major changes that affect the Forensic Laboratory's:
  - legal, commercial, organizational, or ownership status;
  - organization and management; e.g., key managerial staff;
  - policies or procedures, where appropriate;
  - location;
  - personnel, equipment, facilities, working environment, or other resources, where significant;
  - Authorized Representative or Approved Signatories;
  - other such matters that may affect the Forensic Laboratory's capability, scope of Accredited activities, or compliance with the AB's requirements for Accreditation.

APPENDIX 2 - CONTENTS OF AN AUDIT RESPONSE

The Forensic Laboratory audit response will include the following:

- details of the audit report being responded to;
- reference;
- non-conformance details;
- non-conformance type;
- corrective action required;
- comments on finding;
- proposed CAPA response.

APPENDIX 3 - MANAGEMENT SYSTEM ASSESSMENT NON-CONFORMANCE EXAMPLES

A non-conformance must be recorded whenever the Assessor discovers that the documented procedures are inadequate to prevent breaches of the system requirements, or they are adequate but are not being followed correctly, or there are no documented procedures in place. Some examples to illustrate the definitions given in Chapter 4, Section 4.7.3.5 are given below:

Major Non-conformance

Examples

Some examples could include:

- after previous warnings, the Forensic Laboratory is still using the AB or CAB's logo and/or marks in contravention of the AB or CAB's Rules and Regulations for their use;
- ongoing and systematic breaches of the requirements have been found;
- some of the procedures for document control and record control are not incomplete or are not being followed;
- the Forensic Laboratory has lost its key technical manager(s) for particular work and no longer has competent employees doing that work. They continue to perform work that needs competent employees and did not advise the AB or CAB of this;
- the Forensic Laboratory has no records of the training plans for the past year, any evidence of appraisals and Training Needs Analysis being undertaken;
- the Management Review for the current year has not been done;
- there a number of outstanding CAPAs and no evidence of them having been closed out;
- there is no procedure for control of non-conforming work (or recall of incorrect reports);
- there is significant evidence that the Quality Management System is seriously failing and there are no records of any internal audits being carried out.

Obviously, Major Non-conformances will depend on the Assessment Team's findings and the Lead Assessor's evaluation of the finding.

Minor Non-conformance

Examples

Some examples could include:

- a hard copy of an obsolete procedure was found;
- one customer complaint had been acted upon but not been closed out;
- one employee had not got an up-to-date job description;
- the document control procedure requires specific reviewers to review all procedures before implementation. Records show that a document has not gone through this process but has been released;
- the Forensic Laboratory Exhibits Log has one or two incomplete entries.

Obviously, Minor Non-conformances will depend on the Assessment Team's findings and the Lead Assessor's evaluation of the finding.

It should be noted, however, that a number of Minor Non-conformances in the same area can be symptomatic of a system breakdown and could therefore be compounded into a Major Non-conformance.

Observation

In situations where the Assessor considers that potential non-conformant situations may arise, an Observation may be issued. Organizations are free to identify corrective and preventive actions to Observations as they wish, but Auditors should take note of previous Observations raised when performing their audits and look for signs of improvement.

Opportunity for Improvement

Additionally, while not a non-conformance marking an Assessor may identify an area of the Management System that could be improved but still is conformant. The Assessor has to ensure that this is an objective comment and does not constitute consulting.

APPENDIX 4 - TYPICAL CLOSEOUT PERIODS

Different ABs and CABs may have different periods permissible for closeout of non-conformances, and in some cases, these will be agreed with a Client on a case-by-case basis. However, the ones listed below are typical closeout periods.

Assessment type	Period allowed for providing evidence of closeout after a Corrective Action Plan is agreed
Initial	Normally, no more than 3 months
Surveillance	Normally, 1 month, exceptionally 3 months
Re-assessment	Normally, 1 month, exceptionally 3 months
Extension to scope	Normally, no more than 3 months

Chapter 20

Emerging Issues

Table of Contents

20.1 INTRODUCTION

Digital forensics is a relatively new discipline in forensic science, the first case being in the late 1970s and early 1980s. In those days, there were no established procedures and no specialized tools, just hex editors.

As has been stated in Chapter 1, Section 1.1.6, there is a need to have appropriate, scientifically robust, and repeatable procedures that meet the legislative requirements for the jurisdiction.

With the rapid changes in technology available, and its use, digital forensics will always be playing catch-up as new technology appears and the ways it is used for both legal and illegal purposes.

The processing of a forensic case in the Forensic laboratory follows the following steps, as defined in Chapter 1, Section 1.1.1:

- preserving the evidence;
- identifying the evidence;
- extracting the evidence;
- documenting the evidence recovered and how it was recovered;
- interpreting the evidence;
- presenting the evidence (either to the Client or a Court).

Some of the problems with digital evidence generally were outlined in Chapter 1, Section 1.1.7.

This chapter looks at the specific current and future challenges that the Forensic Team faces when processing forensic cases.

20.2 SPECIFIC CHALLENGES

20.2.1 Legislative Issues

20.2.1.1 Changing Laws

Laws are constantly being changed to keep pace with developments in technology and the potential sources of evidence that this creates and also the way in which the new technologies are exploited by criminals.

20.2.1.2 Time to Enact Legislation

New legislation needs to be carefully crafted to address issues of digital evidence and computer crime and this takes time. Rushed or "knee jerk" legislation can cause legislative nightmares unless it is appropriate for the task in hand. This often means that the technology has moved on since the legislative drafting process started and means that the legislation may be inappropriate, flawed, or need major revision to make it effective.

20.2.1.3 Following Legislative Procedures

It is essential that the legislative procedures for seizing evidence are followed exactly in the jurisdiction to ensure that any seizure is legal. This also means that the exact scope of what is to be seized has to be clearly and properly defined. The tools and techniques also have to meet the requirements of the legislation and be validated.

20.2.1.4 Evidence in Different Jurisdictions

Given the Internet and global connectivity, it is often the case that evidence can be located in more than one jurisdiction for the same case, or even that the actual location of the evidence is not known (e.g., cloud computing). This can cause a logistical nightmare for seizure as well as knowing the relevant legislation for the final jurisdiction where the case will be heard and how this will interact with the other jurisdictions. As has been found in the past, what is illegal in one jurisdiction may be legal (or not illegal) in another jurisdiction for any number of reasons. This does not always mean that the different jurisdictions are different countries, but where different states have different legislations in the same country.

20.2.1.5 Spoliation

Spoliation can be the result of a deliberate act or negligence. Claims of spoliation may be made if appropriate and the Forensic Laboratory must be able to respond to any challenge of spoliation. This will depend on fully documented cases and having repeatable processes undertaken by competent Forensic Analysts. Depending on the jurisdiction, this may be a criminal offence where the act is intentional. Again the importance of having appropriately validated tools, techniques, and procedures in place, that these are followed and that there are contemporaneous records to support all stages of the processing of the case is essential.

20.2.1.6 Privacy Issues

Individual privacy and the needs of the Forensic Analyst will frequently be in conflict.

20.2.1.7 Judicial Decisions

In a Court of law, of any type, the Judge is rarely a digital forensic expert, a Judge is an expert in the law and its interpretation. The digital forensic evidence provided is normally only part of the evidence produced to the Judge for decision making. The Judge is there to come to a conclusion based on the relevant tests applicable to the Court when compared with the law in the jurisdiction.

Ensuring that the Judge understands the evidence presented is therefore essential.

20.2.1.8 Common Language

There is no common language in use that is accepted in digital forensic cases across multiple jurisdictions. Many different universities have "jumped on the bandwagon" and provide digital forensic courses, but they do not have a common and universally accepted level of academic standards. This leads to a number of "qualified" experts throughout the world, all having differing levels of competence.

20.2.2 Technology Issues

20.2.2.1 Rapid Changes in Technology

Rapid changes in technology are driving the need for the development of new tools, techniques, and procedures to process forensic cases that use the new technologies deployed. This is a classic case of digital forensics having to play "catch-up."

New tools, techniques, and procedures all need to be validated prior to use, as defined in Chapter 7, Section 7.5.5 and see Section 20.2.12.2.

20.2.2.2 Wireless Connectivity

The problem of the ever wider use of wireless connectivity, coupled with the increasing ranges for connectivity that are being achieved will inevitably cause increasing problems in the future for the Investigator. The initial problem at the crime scene will be to determine what devices are relevant to the investigation. At any location, there are likely to be a number of access points and the density of these is likely to increase, as there is a greater take-up of wireless connectivity. The next problem is that if the suspect is skilled they may be using a wireless channel that is not in the standard range and which could easily be overlooked. Another problem will be keeping the device isolated during the collection and analysis phases.

20.2.2.3 Cloud Computing

While there is nothing new in the elements that make up what is now called cloud computing (Software as a Service, Platform as a Service, Infrastructure as a Service), the developing implementations of cloud-based systems for document storage and data management, such as Google Docs, Microsoft 365, and others are being increasingly used by a large number of organizations. With this move to cloud computing, there is an increasing need for a wide range of digital forensics from criminal investigation to e-discovery. One of the issues that will continue to develop as a result of this will be the requirement to effectively deal with large volumes of cloud-based data.

The problem with cloud computing and forensics is that the organization's information is no longer under their control, breaking all of the rules of information security and personal ownership.

A clear contract with the cloud supplier is needed to ensure that appropriate legislative and business requirements are met, and in the future, consideration will have to be given to ensure that services are "forensically ready."

20.2.2.4 Mobile Devices

The digital forensics of mobile devices is already a significant problem for many digital forensic laboratories. The type of device will dictate the procedures that need to be followed during a forensic investigation. Mobile phones can be divided into a number of categories which are:

- standard mass market phones (Nokia, Motorola, Samsung, LG, etc.);
- Blackberry devices;
- Android devices;
- iPads;
- other tablets;
- Chinese mobile phones.

20.2.2.4.1 Standard Mass Market Phones

The forensics of standard phones has well-established processes and procedures. The main problem that will be encountered in the future is the number of new models and the increasing number of data cable and power cables that the Forensic Laboratory will need to maintain in order to deal with them. A secondary issue will be with the isolation of these devices. There is currently increasing evidence that Faraday bags may not be as effective as previously thought and additional effort and testing will be required to prove their efficacy. Future issues will include the increasing availability of functionality for encryption and remote wiping. On the positive side, there is an increasing use of the Joint Test Action Group (JTAG) interface on mobile phones. The JTAG interface was originally designed to test circuit boards in processors and memory chips. The use of the JTAG interface could provide direct access to the processors and memory. This means that the use of the operating system is avoided. This approach is still developing as it relies on knowledge of the architecture of the device.

20.2.2.4.2 Blackberry Devices

The Blackberry is in a permanent state of "push messaging," and for this reason, they need to be contained in a shielded container until they can be taken to a safe-shielded location where they can be examined. The encryption of Blackberry devices will continue to be an issue for Forensic Analysts and Investigators, and the remote wipe functionality will be a problem if the device is not isolated.

20.2.2.4.3 Android Devices

The rapid evolution of Android-based devices, currently both phones and tablets and in the future net books and laptops, will cause a range of new problems. The development has already seen the use of two different file systems and four major releases of the software in a relatively short period. There is also a lack of experience to date on the processing of these devices and the processes and procedures are still developing, which causes problems with validation of tools, techniques, and procedures.

20.2.2.4.4 iPads

The iPad is currently on version three and there have been large number of software versions released. There are currently no solutions for the physical extraction of the iPad2 unless the device is jail-broken. The rapid pace of releases for the iPad will mean that there is a constant battle to update knowledge and tools to be able to image these devices.

20.2.2.4.5 Other Tablets

The advent of the Tablet has been widely adopted, and most of the major manufacturers and the Chinese are all producing their own versions. There are a wide range of operating systems being used for Tablet computers including Windows™, Android, OSX, and Blackberry OS 2. Data and power connectors will continue to be an issue, and Tablets will also be affected by many of the issues that are found in mobile phones.

20.2.2.4.6 Chinese Mobile Phones

Chinese mobile phones are a major challenge for Forensic Analysts as the manufacturers of these devices do not follow standards and as a result, the way in which the device operates cannot be predicted. Other issues with these devices will continue to be the non-standard operating systems, data cables, and power cables. The issue with data cables may lead to the battery becoming depleted with a resultant loss of volatile data.

20.2.2.5 Large Disks

Larger and larger electro-mechanical hard drives will continue to be an issue in static digital forensics. This is because there is a physical limitation to the speed that data can be transferred. The time taken to image a disk will continue to increase as the size of disks increases. The volume of data that the disks will potentially contain will also mean that additional time will be required to index and analyze the massive volumes of data. Three terabyte disks are already in common use even in the home environment and the speed of increase in storage volumes are not likely to reduce at any time in the near future.

20.2.2.6 Alternative Technologies

There is an increasing diversity of computer processors in use in all aspects of our lives. Cars have engine management systems, and satellite navigation systems and household devices such as refrigerators and washing machines now increasingly have network connectivity and computer processors to enable them to be remotely operated. The extraction of potential evidence from these devices means that there is a requirement for new tools and techniques and knowledge of the architecture of the processor and any digital storage media in the device.

20.2.2.7 Game Consoles

The increasing number of consoles for gaming that are in use and their increasing storage and processing capability mean that they are a current and future digital forensic problem. These devices are similar in most aspects to computers and can be used for internet browsing and also e-mail. Recently, game consoles have been used for storing pedophile material, and standard forensic tools are not currently able to process them.

20.2.2.8 Proprietary Operating Systems

The development of new proprietary operating systems for both alternative and conventional technologies will continue to cause digital forensic issues. With each new operating system, there is a need for new tools, techniques, and procedures. There is also a need for the acquisition of skills by the Forensic Analyst on new operating systems. This causes an issue of a diversification of the range of skills that are required within the Forensic Laboratory.

20.2.2.9 Non-compliant Hardware

The proliferation of non-compliant hardware means that there is a need for device-specific data and/or power connectors and the development of new tools, techniques, and procedures for the examination of these devices.

20.2.2.10 Solid-State Devices

One of the problems that will cause Forensic Analysts more problems in the future is the use of solid-state storage. These devices use a system for wear leveling, which is used to maximize the lifetime of the flash memory in a mobile phone or disk as flash memory can only be written and erased a certain number of times. Wear leveling utilizes both software and hardware means to ensure that all areas of the memory are used an equal number of times. Solid-state devices have a purge routine that functions after a device has been "quick formatted." This is a function that is required before new data can be written to the storage; however, there is a problem that once the storage media is connected to a power supply, even if it has been interrupted, this process will resume as the device can initiate the routine independent of a computer.

20.2.2.11 Detective Tools and Fitness for Forensic Purpose

There are a number of detective tools in place in the IT Infrastructure (e.g., monitoring systems, Intruder Detection Systems, etc.) that can identify incidents and breaches. While these have been designed to perform these tasks, few have been designed with the identification and preservation of digital evidence for later analysis.

20.2.2.12 Network Forensic Issues

While early digital forensic cases dealt with a single computer, a large number of today's cases will involve network forensics. Network forensics is not as mature as forensic analysis of a single stand-alone computer. Some of the challenges faced in network forensics include, but are not limited to:

- analyzing encrypted network traffic;
- consistent analysis of network traffic and protocols;
- handling different devices (types and makes) of network devices;
- preservation of large volumes of network traffic;
- proving integrity of network traffic;
- secured networked applications (e.g., Skype);
- the accurate capture of real-time traffic in high-speed networks;
- time issues across different networks;
- visual display of network traffic;
- volatile nature of network traffic.

20.2.3 Human Issues

20.2.3.1 Training

As technology changes rapidly, there is a need to undertake training on new tools, techniques, and procedures. This has an impact on the cost of training and the time that the Forensic Analyst has to spend away from case processing. It also means that Forensic Analysts have to be familiar with more and more different tools, techniques, and procedures. This also causes an issue of a diversification of the range of skills that are required within the Forensic Laboratory.

20.2.3.2 Competence and Proficiency

Forensic Analysts have to prove their competence and proficiency regularly as defined in Chapter 18, Section 18.2.5 and 18.2.6, respectively. Should they fail any competence or proficiency testing, they will be unable to undertake relevant parts of forensic case processing until they have proved their competence and/or proficiency.

20.2.3.3 Maintaining Records

Records ideally should be contemporaneous to reflect what was happening at the time or what actions were carried out at the time. Unless the Forensic Analyst or First Responder is always diligent in this task, it is too easy to "leave it till later" and documentation and record failures occur. This can become a real problem later in the case where critical records have been overlooked (e.g., breaking the chain of custody).

20.2.3.4 Complying with Procedures

The Forensic Laboratory has defined procedures for all stages of case processing, and all Forensic Analysts and First Responders are mandated to follow these. If it can be proved that they did not follow in-house procedures, then this is open to challenge. This is why it is essential that all Forensic Analysts and First Responders follow the relevant procedures for the jurisdiction.

20.2.3.5 Going Beyond the Safety Zone

There are occasions where a Forensic Analyst starts a case that they are competent to process and that as the case progresses they are no longer competent or proficient to proceed with new requirements. It is at this point that the Forensic Analyst should declare the problem to their Line Manager or the Laboratory Manager, but sadly sometimes they struggle on. When challenged on their evidence, their lacking of competence or proficiency can then have a detrimental effect on the outcome of the case. The worst possible case is where a Forensic Analyst starts a case knowing that they are neither competent nor proficient to process the case.

20.2.3.6 Standard Procedures

There is a lack of standard procedures for forensic case processing throughout a jurisdiction as different Forensic Analysts may follow different internal procedures.

20.2.4 Preserving the Evidence

20.2.4.1 Volume of Data

The volume of data to be captured is growing rapidly based on the rapidly increasing sizes of hard disks. If on-site imaging is to be carried out, this can create a problem not only of size of data to be captured and the time capturing the image can take. It is essential for First Responders that they have suitable media for capturing possibly huge amounts of data and also tools to do this accurately and with optimum speed.

20.2.4.2 Challenging the Chain of Custody

The chain of custody is often attacked at this stage and, sadly, this is often successful, especially where a number of different people have been involved in a major case. The more people seizing the evidence and handling it till it is received in the secure property store the more likely it is that failures occur at this stage. This is often compounded by having members of the seizure teams working for different organizations that have different procedures.

20.2.4.3 Changes Made During Preservation

During the preservation stage, it may be that the original evidence may be changed by the process, though the ideal situation is that the copy of the evidence worked on during the case processing is an exact copy of the original. If unavoidable changes have been made (e.g., live capture), then unless the Forensic Analyst is competent and can accurately and convincingly explain the changes to the evidence and why they were unavoidable, then the evidence may be challenged. This is enshrined in the ACPO Guidelines as principle 2, as defined in Chapter 1, Section 1.1.8.

20.2.5 Identifying the Evidence

20.2.5.1 Numbers of Systems

As computing has become more pervasive, the potential evidence that is sought is no longer found on a single PC or server but can be spread across multiple systems. This means that multiple systems need to be imaged and investigated. Combined with the increasing volume of data issues, as defined in Section 20.2.2.5 and Section 20.2.7.1, the possible multiple jurisdictional issues, as defined in Section 20.2.1.4, this will increase the cost of case processing, as defined in Section 20.2.12.4. An additional dimension to this is that different computers can often be under the control of a number of different organizations.

20.2.5.2 At the Scene

Where a seizure is undertaken, it must be legal for any evidence seized. This can cause problems if the scope of the potential evidence is not known and "seizure creep" occurs making some of the evidence seized an illegal seizure. There is rarely a second chance to return to the scene to undertake a second seizure, so it is essential that the seizure paperwork is correct and covers all relevant and required evidence. This can cause problems in defining in the actual scope for seizure.

20.2.5.3 During Processing

The identification phase can be attacked by obscuring the connection between the evidence obtained and the incident to which it refers. Any evidence found must be able to link the evidence to the incident, to enable conclusions and opinions that are repeatable, to be drawn. If this is not provable, then it is possibly subject to challenge. It must be remembered the evidence that is collected must not only include evidence that can prove the suspect's actions (inculpatory) but also evidence that could prove their innocence (exculpatory).

20.2.6 Collecting the Evidence

20.2.6.1 Completeness of Evidence Seized

The collection phase can be attacked by either limiting the completeness of the data that is being collected or causing the tools, techniques, procedures, and competence of the Forensic Analyst processing the case, to be called into question.

20.2.6.2 Transporting the Evidence

Where evidence is to be seized at the scene and transferred to another location for examination and analysis, the issue of its transportation from the site of seizure to the Forensic Laboratory can cause issues. The methods of transportation should be safe and secure and protect the evidence from any unauthorized modification or tampering. If this cannot be proven, then it is possible to challenge the transportation process. This is especially the case with mobile devices that may have a remote wipe capability or batteries that can become exhausted and lose volatile memory.

20.2.7 Extracting the Evidence

20.2.7.1 Volume of Data

The volume of data to be searched is growing rapidly and the time taken to undertake comprehensive searching is a factor of the number, type, and complexity of searches to be undertaken. The use of specialist tools is essential to recover all of the evidence relevant to the case, and this is a time-consuming process, which also affects the costs of processing the case. All tools, techniques, and procedures for extracting the evidence must be validated and in some cases will require dual tool verification and if this is not the case, the evidence may be challenged.

20.2.7.2 Speed of Searching

With increasing volumes of data to be searched and the number, type, and complexity of searches to be undertaken, the speed of searching can be seriously impacted, which also affects the costs of processing the case.

Depending on the timetable for the case to be processed (either for Client or Court requirements), full extraction of all evidence may not be possible. Either the delivery date (TRT or Court date) may have to be amended, if possible, or incomplete extraction may occur. In the latter case, a challenge may well be made to the recovered evidence and its completeness of producing inculpatory evidence as well as exculpatory evidence.

20.2.7.3 Completeness of Extracting

It is infeasible that every case has been thorough and completely finished as a case could actually be investigated for years to exhaust every possible avenue of enquiry. There comes a point where the investigation of a forensic case must come to an end and it is usually a function of cost of case processing, time constraints, or the Officer in the Case deciding that "enough is enough."

At this point, there may still be inculpatory evidence as well as exculpatory evidence that has not been discovered, and this may leave the case processing open to challenge.

20.2.8 Documenting How It Was Recovered

20.2.8.1 Chain of Custody

Only too often is the chain of custody broken and doubt cast on the authenticity and legal acceptance. This is one of the most common methods of undermining a case, and in theory the creation and maintenance of the chain of custody should be a simple process to maintain.

20.2.9 Interpreting the Evidence

20.2.9.1 Difference of Interpretation Opinions

The interpretation of the evidence can be attacked by calling into question the interpretation of the evidence as there are always multiple ways of interpreting evidence that is recovered during case processing. The "other side" will always put their interpretation on the evidence recovered and this leads to challenges of interpretation of the evidence by either side in a forensic case.

20.2.9.2 Time Issues

When trying to determine the time line of a forensic case, this can prove problematic as time can be a major issue if clocks are amended or different correlating logs are using different times or are in different jurisdictions.

While timestamps that are generated are usually reliable, the sources that they come from, unless proven to be accurate, can themselves be unreliable and therefore pass on an unreliable time. There are also differences between operating systems where universal time is used as opposed to the government-mandated time (i.e., including daylight saving hours).

It is also possible for a user to tamper with the time on a PC and change it forward or backward as required and create transactions or documents on the new (amended and tampered with time).

This can affect trying to reverse time lines as well as taking them forward and is a common area of challenge.

20.2.9.3 Consistency

Given a forensic image, it is possible that a number of Forensic Analysts will interpret the evidence available differently. There are no international standards for interpretation of evidence and all Forensic Analysts will interpret evidence according to their own competencies.

20.2.10 Presenting the Evidence (Either to the Client or a Court)

20.2.10.1 Lack of Visibility

Digital evidence cannot be seen and is volatile, unlike some other forms of evidence. On account of this, it is often a major challenge to explain digital evidence and digital case processing of the evidence to a non-technologist and link produced results to the original evidence in a form that they can readily comprehend. This problem is applicable to the judiciary that are involved in prosecuting, defending, or judging a case as well as the general public who may serve on juries or a Client.

20.2.10.2 Method of Presentation

The method of presentation must be appropriate to the audience (either the Client or a Court) so that the audiences understand the evidence being presented and that this links the evidence to the incident and allows repeatable and justifiable conclusions to be drawn or opinions presented. The evidence and conclusions drawn from it must be convincing to the intended audience. The wrong method of presentation, actions supporting it, or failure to convince the intended audience can seriously affect the intended outcome of the evidence presentation and so affect the outcome of the case.

Some methods of presentation may require the Forensic Analyst to obtain outside assistance for creating convincing presentations.

20.2.10.3 Completeness of the Presentation

The presentation phase can be attacked by attacking the reliability and completeness of reports that the Forensic Analyst has produced. This is why it is essential that all work products in the case are peer reviewed by a competent reviewer to ensure their completeness, that the results are repeatable, and that they are fit for purpose. If this is not the case, then they will be subject to challenge, which in turn can lead to challenges relating to the Forensic Analyst's competence and proficiency.

20.2.11 Anti-forensics and Counter-Forensics

Anti-forensics are the measures that are taken to prevent digital forensic case processing from being carried out while counter-forensics measures are those taken to inhibit or undermine a digital forensic investigation.

The term anti-forensics was originally used by the hacking community and was first used in around 2006. Dr. Marc Rogers from Purdue University has defined anti-forensics as "Attempts to negatively affect the existence, amount and/or quality of evidence from a crime scene, or make the analysis and examination of evidence difficult or impossible to conduct." However, this description encompasses both antiforensics and counter-forensics and the terms are often used interchangeably. The methods described below encompass both antiforensics and counter-forensics.

Antiforensic and counter-forensic methods include:

20.2.11.1 Encryption

The use of encryption does not necessarily mean that it is for the purpose of antiforensics although in some ways, it is the perfect antiforensics tool. In the majority of cases that encryption is used, it will be for the purpose of ensuring privacy and confidentiality. The use of encryption is one of the most difficult for the Forensic Analyst to overcome unless they gain an insight into the encryption keys that have been used. The probability of cracking even a medium grade of encryption is extremely remote with the level of resources that are available to the average digital forensics laboratory. The use of encryption is becoming increasingly common and the number of freely available and easy-to-use encryption tools is becoming more widespread. New operating systems such as Windows Vista and Windows 7 have the BitLocker Drive Encryption feature included and there are other disks and file encryption tools such as Pretty Good Privacy and Truecrypt. Applications such as WinZip, Microsoft Office, and Adobe Acrobat provide the ability for the password protection of individual files and groups of files. At the network level, the Secure Sockets Layer and the use of Virtual Private Networks make the collection of network traffic extremely difficult.

20.2.11.2 Data Hiding

There are a number of ways to hide data, at least from cursory searches. Data can be hidden in the slack and unallocated spaces on computer hard drives and in the metadata of many types of files. Data can also be hidden in closed sessions on compact discs or on other peoples' systems that have been hijacked. Some of the main methods used for hiding data include Steganography, Covert Channels, and trail obfuscation.

20.2.11.2.1 Steganography

Steganography has been around for more than two millennia and early examples include the tattooing of messages on the courier's scalp and hiding it by letting the hair grow. Modern Steganography is the hiding of information within digital files. Data may be hidden in most types of files including image, audio, video, and executable files and given the wide range of tools and methods that can be used to hide data within files its use is very difficult to detect. While encryption protects the contents of a communication but does not hide the path taken (who was the sender and who was the recipient), Steganography can be used to hide not only the data but also the recipient (if it is posted in an image on a Web site, it could be accessed by a large number of people, but only the person it was intended for would know that it was there).

20.2.11.2.2 Covert Channels

A covert data channel is a communication channel that is hidden inside a legitimate communication channel. An example of this is the Transmission Control Protocol/Internet Protocol (TCP/IP) suite, which has a number of weaknesses that can be exploited to enable covert communications. An example of this is the covert channels that are based on modification of network protocol header values. In a 1985 U.S. Department of Defense publication "Trusted Computer System Evaluation" defined a covert channel as: "Any communication channel that can be exploited by a process to transfer information in a manner that violates the system's security policy." This chapter goes on to describe two separate categories of covert channels: storage channels and timing channels. It defines them as "Covert storage channels include all vehicles that would allow the direct or indirect writing of a storage location by one process and the direct or indirect reading of it by another. Covert timing channels include all vehicles that would allow one process to signal information to another process by modulating its own use of system resources in such a way that the change in response time observed by the second process would provide information."

20.2.11.2.3 Trail Obfuscation

Trail obfuscation has been an issue for almost as long as there have been publically accessible computers. It can be achieved by logon spoofing, IP spoofing (often used for Distributed Denial of Service attacks), and Medium Access Control address spoofing. Other methods of trail obfuscation such as e-mail and Web anonymizers that provide privacy services or the wiping or modification of server log files or the changing of file dates.

20.2.11.2.4 Disk and File Wiping

There are a number of tools available that can wipe either whole disk drives or files. Commonly available tools including programs such as Blancco, BC Wipe, and Eraser can erase either the whole contents of a disk or individual data files. This is normally achieved by overwriting the target a number of times with random data strings. Other tools such as Evidence Eraser can be used to remove temporary files, Internet history, cache files, and wipe both slack and unallocated spaces.

20.2.11.2.5 Physical Destruction

The physical destruction of the media is an extremely effective method of preventing any evidence that the media contained from being recovered and has the advantage of being visible and checkable. However, while disk and file wiping tools are freely available and either freeware or very cost-effective, the physical destruction of the media requires either specific tools or the application of considerable force and may not be achievable at short notice.

20.2.11.2.6 Attacks on Digital Forensics Tools

Direct attacks on the digital forensics process are the latest form of anti-forensics. While all other antiforensic techniques are passive, the direct attack on the process is an active measure. All six of the phases of the digital forensic process, Identification, Preservation, Collection, Examination, Analysis, and Presentation are potentially liable to attack, as shown above.

There have already been a number of attacks on several of the main digital forensics tools, including Computer Online Forensic Evidence Extractor (COFEE), EnCase, FTK, and SleuthKit. An example of this is the application called DECAF that was released by hackers to undermine the Microsoft forensic toolkit, COFEE, which is only available to law enforcement agencies.

20.2.12 Miscellaneous

20.2.12.1 Accreditation and Certification

There is a growing demand for the certification of both individual digital forensics practitioners and laboratories to be certified and accredited. This is in part driven by the growing maturity of the science of digital forensics and in part as a result of the growing understanding of the range of skills and knowledge that are needed to conduct effective digital forensic investigations. In the United Kingdom, the quality standard required by the Home Office Forensic Regulator of all digital forensic laboratories is ISO 17025. In the United States, there has been an ongoing discussion as to whether Digital Forensic Investigators should be required to carry a Private Investigator's license and in addition there are the U.S. Department of Justice regulations that govern computer forensics, and the best practices employed by the International Association of Computer Investigative Specialists.

20.2.12.2 Testing and Validation

The testing and validation of tools will be an increasing problem in the future with the increasing diversity of tools that will be required. With the increasing diversity of hardware and operating systems as well as the new technologies that are coming into use there is a requirement for more tools. The life cycle of software and many of the technologies is short, but the testing and validation of the tools required to carry out a forensic investigation of the tools is lengthy.

No tool, process, or procedure should ever be used that has not been validated.

20.2.12.3 Key Dependence of Digital Evidence

Frequently, digital evidence is vital to the success of any case.

20.2.12.4 Growth in the Need for Digital Forensics

Increasingly, what was seen as traditional crime now has some element of information processing systems associated with it (e.g., mobile devices) and these devices must be processed in the prosecution of the crime. This has an impact on the cost of processing a forensic case, as well as the time to prepare the evidence needed to prosecute the case. This leads to the situation where a decision may be made that the costs of the prosecution of the case mean that it is not followed up, as the overhead of forensic case processing makes it impractical to pursue.

20.2.12.5 Training

As has been stated above, there are a variety of academic (or other) courses available. Many of these courses are taught by academics (or others) who have never actually processed a forensic case and so are totally unaware of what this entails. Many academic institutes and commercial training providers seem to have seen this subject as a "cash cow" and are not particularly worried about the outcome so long as they have fee paying students to fill the course. This problem is exacerbated by the lack of standard processes and procedures for many aspects of the digital forensic process.

20.2.13 Focus

Typically, digital forensic tools have been created to solve issues where evidence is on a computer. They were not developed to detect and resolve crimes against an information processing system.

Appendix

Acronyms

The following Acronyms are used in this book or are standard Digital Forensic Acronyms.

A&K Afhankelijkheids-en kwetsbaarheidsanalyse
A2LA American Association for Laboratory Accreditation
AAFS American Academy of Forensic Sciences
AB Accreditation Body
ACFE Association of Certified Fraud Examiners
ACL Access Control List
ACPO Association of Chief Police Officers (UK)
ADFSL Association of Digital Forensics, Security and Law
ADR Alternate Dispute Resolution
AIO All in One Devices
AIRMIC Association of Insurance and Risk Managers in Industry and Commerce
AIT Advanced Intelligent Tape
ALE Annual Loss Expectancy
ANSI American National Standards Institute
APWG Anti-Phishing Working Group
ARO Annual Rate of Occurrence
ARP Address Resolution Protocol
ASCLD/LAB The American Society of Crime Laboratory Directors/Laboratory Accreditation Board
ASIS American Society for Industrial Security
AT Advanced Technology (IBM PC Term)
ATA Advanced Technology Attachment
AUP Acceptable Use Policy
AV Asset Value
BAFO Best and Final Offer
BCM Business Continuity Management
BCM Business Continuity Manager
BCMS Business Continuity Management System
BCP Business Continuity Plan
BCS British Computer Society
BFS BeOS File System
BIA Business Impact Analysis
BICSI Building Industry Consulting Service International
BIOS Basic Input/Output System
BREW Binary Runtime Environment for Wireless
BS British Standard
BSI British Standards Institute
BYOD Bring Your Own Device
CAB Change Advisory Board
CAB Conformance Assessment Body
CAD Computer-Aided Diagram
CaM Capacity Manager
CAPA Corrective Action and Preventive Action
CAR Corrective Action Request
CBA Cost–Benefit Analysis
CCTA Central Computer and Telecommunications Agency
CCTV Close Circuit Television
CD Compact Disk
CDFS Compact Disk File System
CDFS Consortium of Digital Forensic Specialists
CENELEC Comité Européen de Normalisation Électrotechnique—the European Committee for Electrotechnical Standardization
CERT Computer Emergency Response Team
CfM Configuration Manager
CFTT Computer Forensics Tool Testing (program)
CI Configuration Item
CM Change Manager
CM Configuration Management
CMA Computer Misuse Act (UK Legislation)
CMDB Configuration Management Data Base
CMM Capability Maturity Model
CMS Capacity Management System
CMS Code Management System
CMS Configuration Management System
CMT Crisis Management Team
COTS Commercial off the Shelf
CPD Continuing Professional Development
CPE Continuing Professional Education
CPU Central Processing Unit
CRAMM CCTA Risk Analysis and Management Method
CRM Certified Reference Material
CRT Cathode Ray Tube
CSF Critical Success Factor
CSI Computer Security Institute
CSIRTS Computer Security Incident Response Team

CSR Corporate Social Responsibility
CTOSE Cyber Tools On-Line Search for Evidence
CV Curriculum Vitae (Resume)
DAS Direct Attached Storage
DAT Digital Audio Tape
DCMI Dublin Core Data Initiative
DCO Device Configuration Overlay
DDoS Distributed Denial of Service
DFA Digital Forensics Association
DFRWS Digital Forensic Research Workshop
DHL Definitive Hardware Library
DIRKS Designing and Implementing Recordkeeping Systems
DLT Digital Linear Tape
DMZ De-Militarized Zone
DNS Domain Name Server
DoD Department of Defence (USA)
DOJ Department of Justice (USA)
DoS Denial of Service
DR Disaster Recovery
DRP Disaster Recovery Plan
DRT Disaster Recovery Team
DSE Display Screen Equipment
DSL Definitive Software Library
DVD Digital Video Disk
DVR Digital Video Recorder
EA European Cooperation for Accreditation
EBIOS Expression des Besoins et Identification des Objectifs de Sécurité
ECAB Emergency Change Advisory Board
ECPA Electronic Communications Privacy Act
EFS (Windows) Encrypting File System
EMEA Europe, Middle East, and Africa
ENFSI European Network of Forensic Science Institutes
EPTIS European Proficiency Testing Information System
ERMS Electronic Record Management System
EU European Union
EU27 The current 27 Member States that make up the EU
Ext2 Second Extended File System
Ext3 Third Extended File System
F3 First Forensic Forum
FAQ Frequently Asked Questions
FAT File Allocation Table
FBI Federal Bureau of Investigation (USA)
FRE Federal Rules of Evidence (USA)
FSC Forward Schedule of Changes
FSR Forensic Science Regulator (UK)
FSS Forensic Science Society
FTP File Transfer Protocol
G20 Group of 20 (20 economies that represent over 80% of the GWP (Gross World Product) and two-thirds of the world's population)
G8 The governments of eight of the world's largest economies; it includes Canada, France, Germany, Italy, Japan, Russia, the United Kingdom, and the United States
GAISP Generally Accepted Information Security Principles
GDP Gross Domestic Product
GLP Good Laboratory Practice
GPS Global Positioning System
GWP Gross World Product (the total world GDP)
HFS Hierarchical File System
HPA Host Protected Area
HPFS High-Performance File System
HTCI High Tech Crime Institute
HTCIA High Technology Crime Investigation Association
HTCN High Tech Crime Network
HTML HyperText Markup Language
HTTP HyperText Transfer Protocol
HTTPS HyperText Transfer Protocol Secure
HVAC Heating, Ventilation, and Air Conditioning
IACIS International Association of Computer Investigative Specialists
IAF International Accreditation Forum
IBM International Business Machines
ICR Intelligent Character Recognition
IDS Intruder Detection System
IEC International Electrotechnical Commission
IED Intelligent Electronic Device
IEEE Institute of Electrical and Electronic Engineers
IETF Internet Engineering Task Force
IIA Institute of Internal Auditors
IISFA International Information Systems Forensics Association
ILAC International Laboratory Accreditation Cooperation
IM Incident Manager
IMAP Internet Message Access Protocol
IMP Implementation Management Team
IMP Incident Management Plan
IMS Integrated Management System
IOCE International Organization on Computer Evidence
IP Internet Protocol
IRC Internet Relay Chat
IPS Intruder Prevention System
ISAAR (CPF): International Standard Archival Authority Record for Corporate Bodies, Persons and Families,
ISACA Information Systems Audit and Control Association
ISC2 International Information Systems Security Certification Consortium
ISFCE International Society of Forensic Computer Examiners
ISFS Information Security and Forensics Society

ISMS Information Security Management System
ISO International Standards Organization
ISP Internet Service Provider
ISSA Information Systems Security Association
IT Information Technology
ITIL IT Infrastructure Library
ITT Invitation to Tender
JD Job Description
JTAG Joint Test Action Group
Kb Kilo byte
KEDB Known Error Data Base
KFF Known File Filter
KPI Key Performance Indicator
L-A-B Laboratory Accreditation Bureau
LAN Local Area Network
LCD Liquid Display Crystal
LE Law Enforcement (Typically, a government employee responsible for enforcing some aspect of the law.)
LED Light Emitting Diode
LMS Learning Management System
LTO Linear Tape Open
MAC Media Access Control
MARIỌN Méthodologie d'Analyse des Risques Informatiques et d'Optimisation par Niveau
Mb Mega byte
MD5 Message Digest 5
MEHARI Method for Harmonized Analysis of Risk
MFP Multi-Function Peripherals
MLA Multilateral Agreement
MMS Multimedia Messaging Service
MoReq2 Model Requirements for the Management of Electronic Records Version 2
MTPD Maximum Tolerable Period of Disruption
MVEDR Motor Vehicle Event Data Recorder
NAS Network Attaches Storage
NCR Non-Conformance Report
NDA Non-Disclosure Agreement
NEC National Electrical Code
NFPA National Fire Protection Association
NIJ National Institute of Justice (USA)
NIST National Institute of Standards and Technology (USA)
NSA National Security Agency—some times referred to as No Such Agency (USA)
NSRL National Software Reference Library
NT New Technology
NTFS NT File System
NTP Network Time Protocol
OAIS Open Archival Information and Systems Reference Model
OCR Optical Character Recognition
OCTAVE Operationally Critical Threat, Asset, and Vulnerability Evaluation
OEM Original Equipment Manufacturer
OH&S Operational Health and Safety
OHSAS Occupational Health and Safety Management Systems
OLA Operation Level Agreements
OMR Optical Mark Reading
OOV Order of Volatility
OS Operating System
P2P Peer to Peer
PABX Private Automatic Branch Exchange
PACE Police and Criminal Evidence Act (UK legislation)
PAR Preventive Action Request
PARC Pao Alto Research Centre (Xerox)
PC Personal Computer (used by IBM but originally from PARC)
PDA Personal Digital Assistant
PDCA Plan-Do-Check-Act
PDEA Philippine Drug Enforcement Agency
PDF Portable Document Format
PIR Post Implementation Review
PM Problem Manager
PMI Project Management Institute
POP Post Office Protocol
PPE Personal Protective Equipment
PS/2 Personal System/2 (IBM PC Term)
QIC Quarter Inch Cartridge (tape)
QMS Quality Management System
RAM Random Access Memory
RBOP Release Back-Out Plan
RfC Request for Change
RFC Request for Comment
RFI Request for Information
RFID Radio Frequency Identification
RFP Request for Proposal
RFO Request for Offer
RFQ Request for Qualification
RFQ Request for Quotation
RFT Request for Tender
RFx The collective term for "Request for . . .." documents
RIPA Regulation of Investigatory Powers Act (UK legislation)
RM Release Manager
ROSI Return on Security Investment
RSA Rivest-Sharmir-Adelman
RTO Recovery Time Objective
SAN Storage-Attached Network
SANS System Administration, Networking, and Security Institute
SATA Serial ATA
SEI Software Engineering Institute (Part of Carnegie Mellon University)
SF Success Factor
SHA Secure Hash Algorithm

SI International System of Units (System International D'Unites)
SIG Special Interest Group
SIM Subscriber Identity Module (of a cell phone)
SIO Senior Investigating Officer
SIP Service Improvement Plan
SLA Service Level Agreement
SLE Single Loss Expectancy
SLM Service Level Management or Service Level Manager
SMS Short Message Service
SoA Statement of Applicability
SPOF Single Point of Failure
SRO Senior Responsible Owner
SSDLC Secure Software/System Development Life Cycle
SWGDE Scientific Working Group on Digital Evidence
SWOT Strengths, Weaknesses, Opportunities, and Threats
TCP Transmission Control Protocol
TIA Telecommunications Industry Association
TNA Training Needs Analysis
ToR Terms of Reference
TRT Turn Round Time
UCs Underpinning Contract
UDF Universal Disk Format
UFS Unix File System
ULD Upper Limb Disorder
UPS Uninterruptible Power Supply
URL Uniform Resource Locator
USP Unique Selling Point
VDT Visual Display Terminal
VDU Visual Display Unit
VFS Virtual File System
VM Virtual Machine
VMFS Virtual Machine File System
WAN Wide Area Network
XT Xtended technology (IBM PC Term)
YAFFS2 Yet Another Flash File System v2
ZFS Zettabyte File System

Bibliography

The contents of this book have been developed over a number of years since the author's first forensic case in the early 1980s and reflect 40 plus years of changing technology experience.

During this time, there have been dramatic changes in the law, tools, training, and technology and many books, journals, and other sources of good practice have been used to develop the procedures contained in this book to their current state, and of course, they will keep evolving as digital forensics and technology does, but always having to play "catch up."

On account of this, only the following has been used in this bibliography:

- Specific standards used;
- Sources of multiple procedural advice.

The authors freely admit using many books written by excellent authors as input to this book, and their contribution is gratefully acknowledged—some going back to the 1980s; however, it is impossible to list them all—so the decision has been made to list none of them. The list would be both impossible to create to ensure that everyone that has contributed was included and the bibliography would probably constitute the largest chapter of the book.

INTERNATIONAL STANDARDS

Note 1

Formal and correct titles from the ISO Web site are used, rather than the short form versions used, or referred to, in the book.

Note 2

These titles were correct at the time of writing (i.e., some are CD or FDIS status and will be issued in due course.

- IEC 31010:2009 Risk management—Risk assessment techniques;
- ISO 10002:2004 Quality management—Customer satisfaction—Guidelines for complaints handling in organizations;
- ISO 10003:2007 Quality management—Customer satisfaction—Guidelines for dispute resolution external to organizations;
- ISO 14001:2004 Environmental management systems—Requirements with guidance for use;
- ISO 14644-5:2004 Cleanrooms and associated controlled environments—Part 5: Operations;
- ISO 14721:2012 Space data and information transfer systems—Open archival information system (OAIS)—Reference model;
- ISO 15489-1:2001 Information and documentation—Records management—Part 1: General;
- ISO 15836:2009 Information and documentation—The Dublin Core metadata element set;
- ISO 19011:2011 Guidelines for auditing management systems;
- ISO 22301:2012 Societal security—Business continuity management systems—Requirements;
- ISO 22399 Societal security—Guideline for incident preparedness and operational continuity management;
- ISO 31000:2009 Risk management—Principles and guidelines;
- ISO 9000:2005 Quality management systems—Fundamentals and vocabulary;
- ISO 9001:2008 Quality management systems—Requirements;
- ISO Guide 35:2006 Reference materials—General and statistical principles for certification;
- ISO Guide 73:2009 Risk management—Vocabulary;
- ISO/IEC 17011:2004 Conformity assessment—General requirements for Accreditation bodies accrediting conformity assessment bodies;
- ISO/IEC 17020:2012 Conformity assessment—Requirements for the operation of various types of bodies performing inspection;
- ISO/IEC 17021:2011 Conformity assessment—Requirements for bodies providing audit and Certification of management systems;
- ISO/IEC 17024:2003 Conformity assessment—General requirements for bodies operating certification of persons;
- ISO/IEC 17025:2005 General requirements for the competence of testing and calibration laboratories;
- ISO/IEC 17043:2010 Conformity assessment—General requirements for proficiency testing;

- ISO/IEC 17065:2012 Conformity assessment—Requirements for bodies certifying products, processes, and services;
- ISO/IEC 21827:2008 Information technology—Security techniques—Systems Security Engineering—Capability Maturity Model® (SSE-CMM®);
- ISO/IEC 24762:2008 Information technology—Security techniques—Guidelines for information and communications technology disaster recovery services;
- ISO/IEC 24764:2010 Information technology—Generic cabling systems for data centres;
- ISO/IEC 27000:2012 Information technology—Security techniques—Information security management systems—Overview and vocabulary;
- ISO/IEC 27001:2005 Information technology—Security techniques—Information security management systems—Requirements;
- ISO/IEC 27002:2005 Information technology—Security techniques—Code of practice for information security management;
- ISO/IEC 27003:2010 Information technology—Security techniques—Information security management system implementation guidance;
- ISO/IEC 27004:2009 Information technology—Security techniques—Information security management—Measurement;
- ISO/IEC 27005:2011 Information technology—Security techniques—Information security risk management;
- ISO/IEC 27031:2011 Information technology—Security techniques—Guidelines for information and communication technology readiness for business continuity;
- ISO/IEC 27035:2011 Information technology—Security techniques—Information security incident management;
- ISO/IEC 27037:2012 Information technology—Security techniques—Guidelines for identification, collection, acquisition, and preservation of digital evidence;
- ISO/IEC CD 27041 Guidance on assuring suitability and adequacy of investigation methods;
- ISO/IEC CD 27042 Guidelines for the analysis and interpretation of digital evidence;
- ISO/IEC CD 27043 Incident investigation principles and processes;
- ISO/IEC DIS 30121 System and software engineering—Information technology—Governance of digital forensic risk framework;
- ISO/IEC Guide 51:1999 Safety aspects—Guidelines for their inclusion in standards;
- ISO/IEC TS 17022:2012 Conformity assessment—Requirements and recommendations for content of a third-party audit report on management systems;
- ISO/PAS 22399:2007 Societal security—Guideline for incident preparedness and operational continuity management;
- ISO/TR 10013:2001 Guidelines for quality management system documentation;
- ISO/TR 15489-2:2001 Information and documentation—Records management—Part 2: Guidelines.

NATIONAL STANDARDS

Various different countries national standards have been used as reference materials, these include:

- American National Standards Institute (ANSI) (USA);
- Australian Standards/New Zealand Standards (AS/NZS and HB series);
- British Standards (BS series—UK);
- Canada (CSA series);
- National Institute of Standards and Technology (NIST SP 800 series and others—USA).

GUIDANCE FROM AUTHORITATIVE SOURCES

Documents from the following Organizations, including, but not limited to:

- American Association for Laboratory Accreditation (A2LA);
- American Society of Crime Laboratory Directors (ASCLD);
- Association of Chief Police Officers (UK);
- Association of Insurance and Risk Managers in Industry and Commerce (AIRMIC) (UK);
- Cyber Tools On-Line Search for Evidence (CTOSE) (EU);
- Department of Justice (DOJ) (USA);
- European Cooperation for Accreditation (EA) (EU);
- European Network of Forensic Science Institutes (ENFSI) (EU);
- Federal Bureau of Investigation (FBI) (USA);
- Forensic Science Regulator (UK);
- Forensic Science Service (FSS) (UK);
- Information Systems Audit and Control Association (ISACA) (USA);
- International Accreditation Forum (IAF);
- International Laboratory Accreditation Cooperation (ILAC);
- International Organisation on Computer Evidence (IOCE);
- Internet Engineering Task Force (RFCs);
- Laboratory Accreditation Bureau (L-A-B).
- National Institute of Justice (USA);
- Scientific Working Group on Digital Evidence (SWGDE) (USA);
- Scientific Working Group, Imaging Technology (SWGIT) (USA);
- Software Engineering Institute (Carnegie Mellon University—USA);
- United Kingdom Accreditation Service (UKAS) (UK);
- U.S. Secret Service (USSS) (USA).

Index

Note: Page numbers followed by *f* indicate figures and *b* indicate boxes.

B

D

G

H

I

S